p 22-34 Tues

35-48 Thurs

-58 Tues

-66 Thurs

-75 Tues

-90 Thurs

-108 Tues

-115.
133 Tues 23

-152 Thurs
too cases

-215 Thurs 10/9

571-589

UNIVERSITY CASEBOOK SERIES

CASES AND MATERIALS

TORT LAW AND ALTERNATIVES

SIXTH EDITION

by

MARC A. FRANKLIN
Frederick I. Richman Professor of Law
Stanford University

ROBERT L. RABIN
A. Calder Mackay Professor of Law
Stanford University

WESTBURY, NEW YORK
THE FOUNDATION PRESS, INC.
1996

Library of Congress Cataloging-in-Publication Data
Franklin, Marc A.
    Cases and materials on tort law and alternatives / by Marc A.
Franklin and Robert L. Rabin. — 6th ed.
      p.   cm. — (University casebook series)
    Includes index.
    ISBN 1–56662–342–1 (hc)
    1. Torts—United States—Cases. I. Rabin, Robert L. II. Title.
III. Series.
KF1249.F7 1996
346.7303—dc20
[347.3063]   96–12256

 *TEXT IS PRINTED ON 10% POST CONSUMER RECYCLED PAPER*

1st Reprint–1996

PREFACE TO THE SIXTH EDITION

Tort law remains such a dynamic area that we find ourselves continuing to question basic assumptions about the organization of the book and the interplay of doctrinal issues from the outset of our preparation of each new edition. As a consequence we have added a considerable amount of new material, in some instances because it reflects recent developments, but in other instances simply because we thought that the new material offered better pedagogical approaches for reflecting our understanding of the current state of tort law and alternative systems. The upshot is that of the 106 cases in the new edition, 30 are new and almost all of these are from the last five years. Of these 106 cases, 40 were decided within the past ten years.

In particular, we have updated the principal case coverage in the products liability area to focus on new developments in design defect and duty to warn case law. In addition, we provide comprehensive treatment of recent innovations in causation with particular emphasis on toxic harms and medical malpractice. We have also taken note of the continuing legislative and judicial attention to the remedial and process dimensions of the tort system by revising the coverage of damages, insurance and no-fault alternatives.

As in the last edition, we have continued to revise and expand the intentional tort chapter. In addition, we have thoroughly revised the coverage of defamation, and updated the privacy and intentional economic harm materials.

We hope you will find that our efforts to revise and reshape the book capture the continuing intellectual vitality of tort law.

MARC A. FRANKLIN
ROBERT L. RABIN

Stanford, California
March 1996

*

ACKNOWLEDGMENTS

This revision has been substantially aided by the assistance of Colin T. Moran and Jay D. Wexler, students at the Stanford Law School. Our colleagues, William Cohen and Thomas C. Grey, have made helpful comments at various points during the revision. Technical assistance in preparing the manuscript was provided by Joy Nabi. The revision received support from the Dorothy Redwine Estate, and from the Stanford Legal Research Fund, made possible by a bequest from Ira S. Lillick and by gifts from other friends of the Stanford Law School.

We would also like to thank the authors and copyright holders of the following works, who permitted their inclusion in this book:

American Law Institute. Restatement of Torts, Restatement (Second) of Torts, copyright © 1938, 1965, 1977, 1979 by the American Law Institute. Reprinted with the permission of the American Law Institute;

American Law Institute. Report to the American Law Institute, Enterprise Responsibility for Personal Injury, Volume II, pp. 187–92, 232–36, copyright © 1991 by the American Law Institute. Reprinted with the permission of the American Law Institute;

Calabresi, Guido, The Costs of Accidents (New Haven, Yale University Press, 1970) copyright © 1970 by Yale University;

Calabresi, Guido and Jon Hirschoff, Toward a Test for Strict Liability in Torts, reprinted by permission of The Yale Law Journal Company and Fred B. Rothman & Company from The Yale Law Journal, Vol. 81, pp. 1055, 1062–63, 1071;

Fleming, John, The Collateral Source Rule and Loss Allocation in Tort Law, 54 California Law Review, 1478, 1546–49 (1966) copyright © 1966, California Law Review, Inc. Reprinted by permission;

Harper, Fowler, Fleming James, Jr., and Oscar Gray, The Law of Torts, 2d ed. 1986, reprinted by permission of Little, Brown & Co. (Inc.);

Kramer, Orin and Briffault, Richard, Workers Compensation: Strengthening the Social Compact, pp. 13–27, 73–75 (1991), reprinted by permission of Insurance Information Institute;

Michelman, Frank I., Book Review of "The Costs of Accidents," reprinted by permission of The Yale Law Journal Company and Fred B. Rothman & Company from The Yale Law Journal, Vol. 80, pp. 647, 648–59;

Morris, Clarence and C. Robert Morris, Jr., Morris on Torts (2d ed. 1980) copyright © 1980 The Foundation Press, Inc.;

National Conference of Commissioners on Uniform State Laws, Uniform Correction or Clarification of Defamation Act. Reprinted by permission;

Posner, Richard A., Economic Analysis of Law, 4th ed. 1992, reprinted by permission of Little, Brown & Co., Inc.;

Posner, Richard A., A Theory of Negligence, Journal of Legal Studies, Vol. 1, pp. 29, 32–33 (1972), reprinted with the permission of the University of Chicago Press;

Rabin, Robert L., Some Thoughts on the Efficacy of a Mass Toxics Administrative Compensation Scheme, 52 Maryland L.Rev. 951, 955–62 (1993);

Rabin, Robert L., Environmental Liability and the Tort System, 24 Houston L.Rev. 27, 28–32 (1987);

Rabin, Robert L., The Historical Development of the Fault Principle: A Reinterpretation, 15 Ga.L.Rev. 925, 950 (1981);

Ross, H. Laurence, Settled Out of Court (1980 ed.), reprinted with permission, Aldine de Gruyter, New York, copyright © 1980 by H. Laurence Ross;

Schwartz, Gary, Tort Law and the Economy in Nineteenth Century America: A Reinterpretation, reprinted by permission of The Yale Law Journal Company and Fred B. Rothman & Company from The Yale Law Journal, Vol. 90, pp. 1717–27.

SUMMARY OF CONTENTS

*

TABLE OF CONTENTS

*

TABLE OF CASES

Principal cases are in bold type. Non-principal cases are in roman type. References are to Pages.

CHAPTER I

INTRODUCTION TO TORT LIABILITY

A. PROLOGUE

This book is concerned with the array of injuries that are by-products of a complex society, and with how the legal system responds to the diverse problems raised by such injuries. We will consider a broad range of situations including automobile collisions, airplane crashes, medical mishaps, consumer product injuries, industrial accidents, toxic exposures, fist fights, false accusations of misconduct, invasions of privacy, and false statements to competitors' prospective customers. In each situation, someone claims that another has caused harm and looks to the law for relief. We will not consider how the criminal law might react, but deal only with civil redress. Among civil harms our focus will be on those that do not arise out of disputes over contractual interpretation. The primary concern of tort law has been whether one whose actions harm another should be required to pay compensation for the harm done.

For several centuries tort law was the one outlet through which the legal system did provide such redress. In recent years, other sources of compensation have grown dramatically; indeed, a study by the Institute for Civil Justice finds that tort liability payments comprise only 7 percent of the total compensation for economic loss in nonfatal accidents in the United States—11 percent when tort payments for intangible loss are added in. (The figures rise to 22 percent and 33 percent, respectively, in the category of motor vehicle accident victims.) See D. Hensler, et al., Compensation for Accidental Injuries in the United States, pp. 107–08 (1991). Nonetheless, as another study of the tort system has underscored, the role of tort as a compensation scheme remains pivotal:

> . . . the situation in this country leaves many Americans at risk of suffering sizable uninsured medical expenses and income loss as a result of illness or injury. Perhaps one-fourth of the non-elderly population has no medical insurance and must depend on savings or charity if they need expensive care. A significant percentage of workers have little or no protection against short-term, non-employment-related disability. Again, only savings, charity, or, for some, a state welfare payment will be available if they are unable to work for a period up to six months. For long-term disability Social Security offers protection, but only if the inability to work meets a stringent standard of *totality,* and only for a portion of the disabled person's lost wages. The majority of workers have no

insurance for long-term disability except for the partial coverage supplied through the Social Security system or, if the disability is employment-related, the workers' compensation system.

Currently the tort system partially fills some of these gaps by compensating many persons who would not otherwise receive reimbursement for the medical expenses and wage losses occasioned by an illness or injury. Without tort damages many of these accident victims would be uncompensated or undercompensated for their out-of-pocket losses.

Report to the American Law Institute, Enterprise Responsibility for Personal Injury, Vol. II, pp. 555–56 (1991).

We will first consider physical harm to one's person—commonly called the "personal injury"—because it presents serious legal, economic, social, and political problems. Although we will discuss intentional physical harm, we will stress unintentional physical (and emotional) harm, which is far more common and presents great analytical and philosophical dilemmas. The last part of the book will introduce other interests the law seeks to protect, such as reputation and privacy.

B.   WHEN SHOULD UNINTENDED INJURY RESULT IN LIABILITY?

The fundamental issue addressed by a system of tort liability for unintended injury is when losses should be shifted from an injury victim to an injurer or some other source of compensation. Of course, no tort system would be required in the first place if losses were simply allowed to remain where they fall. (Is it clear that such a "no-liability" system would be objectionable?) On the other hand, a system of social insurance could be established that provided full compensation in every instance of harm to the individual. Again, choosing this option would obviate the need for judicial fashioning and administration of a body of tort principles.

Because considerations of injury prevention and fairness have been thought to dictate rejection of the no-liability option, and limited resources (and perhaps fairness, as well?) have been thought to preclude the social insurance approach, the courts have developed a complex network of liability rules for determining the allocation of losses in cases of unintended harm. These rules, located in an intermediate zone between no-liability and universal compensation, reflect not only the influence of those polar positions, but perhaps even more importantly, a tension between two court-fashioned liability principles—strict liability and negligence—that will be a pervasive concern of ours in the portion of this course devoted to unintentional harm. The following case provides an opportunity for a first look at the issue. We will also use it as a means of introducing the basic procedural aspects of tort litigation.

Hammontree v. Jenner*

Court of Appeal of California, 1971.
20 Cal.App.3d 528, 97 Cal.Rptr. 739.

■ LILLIE, J. Plaintiffs Maxine Hammontree and her husband sued defendant for personal injuries and property damage arising out of an automobile accident. The cause was tried to a jury. Plaintiffs appeal from judgment entered on a jury verdict returned against them and in favor of defendant.

The evidence shows that on the afternoon of April 25, 1967, defendant was driving his 1959 Chevrolet home from work; at the same time plaintiff Maxine Hammontree was working in a bicycle shop owned and operated by her and her husband; without warning defendant's car crashed through the wall of the shop, struck Maxine and caused personal injuries and damage to the shop.

Defendant claimed he became unconscious during an epileptic seizure losing control of his car. He did not recall the accident but his last recollection before it, was leaving a stop light after his last stop, and his first recollection after the accident was being taken out of his car in plaintiffs' shop. Defendant testified he has a medical history of epilepsy and knows of no other reason for his loss of consciousness except an epileptic seizure; prior to 1952 he had been examined by several neurologists whose conclusion was that the condition could be controlled and who placed him on medication; in 1952 he suffered a seizure while fishing; several days later he went to Dr. Benson Hyatt who diagnosed his condition as petit mal seizure and kept him on the same medication; thereafter he saw Dr. Hyatt every six months and then on a yearly basis several years prior to 1967; in 1953 he had another seizure, was told he was an epileptic and continued his medication; in 1954 Dr. Kershner prescribed dilantin and in 1955 Dr. Hyatt prescribed phelantin; from 1955 until the accident occurred (1967) defendant had used phelantin on a regular basis which controlled his condition; defendant has continued to take medication as prescribed by his physician and has done everything his doctors told him to do to avoid a seizure; he had no inkling or warning that he was about to have a seizure prior to the occurrence of the accident.

In 1955 or 1956 the Department of Motor Vehicles was advised that defendant was an epileptic and placed him on probation under which every six months he had to report to the doctor who was required to advise it in writing of defendant's condition. In 1960 his probation was changed to a once-a-year report.

Dr. Hyatt testified that during the times he saw defendant, and according to his history, defendant "was doing normally" and that he continued to take phelantin; that "[t]he purpose of the [phelantin] would be to react on the nervous system in such a way that where, without the

---

* Text omissions are indicated by three dots. Omitted citations are indicated by [   ]. There is no indication when footnotes are omitted. When they do appear, footnotes are numbered as in the material quoted.—Eds.

medication, I would say to raise the threshold so that he would not be as subject to these episodes without the medication, so as not to have the seizures. He would not be having the seizures with the medication as he would without the medication compared to taking medication''; in a seizure it would be impossible for a person to drive and control an automobile; he believed it was safe for defendant to drive.

Appellants' contentions that the trial court erred in refusing to grant their motion for summary judgment on the issue of liability and their motion for directed verdict on the pleadings and counsel's opening argument are answered by the disposition of their third claim that the trial court committed prejudicial error in refusing to give their jury instruction on absolute liability.[1]

Under the present state of the law found in appellate authorities beginning with Waters v. Pacific Coast Dairy, Inc., 55 Cal.App.2d 789, 791–793 [131 P.2d 588] (driver rendered unconscious from sharp pain in left arm and shoulder) through Ford v. Carew & English, 89 Cal.App.2d 199, 203–204 [200 P.2d 828] (fainting spells from strained heart muscles), Zabunoff v. Walker, 192 Cal.App.2d 8, 11 [13 Cal.Rptr. 463] (sudden sneeze), and Tannyhill v. Pacific Motor Trans. Co., 227 Cal.App.2d 512, 520 [38 Cal.Rptr. 774] (heart attack), the trial judge properly refused the instruction. The foregoing cases generally hold that liability of a driver, suddenly stricken by an illness rendering him unconscious, for injury resulting from an accident occurring during that time rests on principles of negligence. However, herein during the trial plaintiffs withdrew their claim of negligence and, after both parties rested and before jury argument, objected to the giving of any instructions on negligence electing to stand solely on the theory of absolute liability. The objection was overruled and the court refused plaintiffs' requested instruction after which plaintiffs waived both opening and closing jury arguments. Defendant argued the cause to the jury after which the judge read a series of negligence instructions and, on his own motion, BAJI 4.02 (res ipsa loquitur).

Appellants seek to have this court override the established law of this state which is dispositive of the issue before us as outmoded in today's social and economic structure, particularly in the light of the now recognized principles imposing liability upon the manufacturer, retailer and all distributive and vending elements and activities which bring a product to the consumer to his injury, on the basis of strict liability in tort expressed first in Justice Traynor's concurring opinion in Escola v. Coca Cola Bottling Co., 24 Cal.2d 453, 461–468 [150 P.2d 436]; and then in Greenman v. Yuba Power Products, Inc., 59 Cal.2d 57 [27 Cal.Rptr. 697, 377 P.2d 897, 13

---

1. "When the evidence shows that a driver of a motor vehicle on a public street or highway loses his ability to safely operate and control such vehicle because of some seizure or health failure, that driver is nevertheless legally liable for all injuries and property damage which an innocent person may suffer as a proximate result of the defendant's inability to so control or operate his motor vehicle.

"This is true even if you find the defendant driver had no warning of any such impending seizure or health failure." [This is the instruction plaintiffs requested.—Eds.]

A.L.R.3d 1049]; Vandermark v. Ford Motor Co., 61 Cal.2d 256 [37 Cal. Rptr. 896, 391 P.2d 168]; and Elmore v. American Motors Corp., 70 Cal.2d 578 [75 Cal.Rptr. 652, 451 P.2d 84]. These authorities hold that "A manufacturer [or retailer] is strictly liable in tort when an article he places on the market, knowing that it is to be used without inspection for defects, proves to have a defect that causes injury to a human being." (Greenman v. Yuba Power Products, Inc., supra, 59 Cal.2d 57, 62; Vandermark v. Ford Motor Co., supra, 61 Cal.2d 256, 260–261.) Drawing a parallel with these products liability cases, appellants argue, with some degree of logic, that only the driver affected by a physical condition which could suddenly render him unconscious and who is aware of that condition can anticipate the hazards and foresee the dangers involved in his operation of a motor vehicle, and that the liability of those who by reason of seizure or heart failure or some other physical condition lose the ability to safely operate and control a motor vehicle resulting in injury to an innocent person should be predicated on strict liability.

We decline to superimpose the absolute liability of products liability cases upon drivers under the circumstances here. The theory on which those cases are predicated is that manufacturers, retailers and distributors of products are engaged in the business of distributing goods to the public and are an integral part of the over-all producing and marketing enterprise that should bear the cost of injuries from defective parts. [*Vandermark* and *Greenman*]. This policy hardly applies here and it is not enough to simply say, as do appellants, that the insurance carriers should be the ones to bear the cost of injuries to innocent victims on a strict liability basis. In Maloney v. Rath, 69 Cal.2d 442 [71 Cal.Rptr. 897, 445 P.2d 513], followed by Clark v. Dziabas, 69 Cal.2d 449 [71 Cal.Rptr. 901, 445 P.2d 517], appellant urged that defendant's violation of a safety provision (defective brakes) of the Vehicle Code makes the violator strictly liable for damages caused by the violation. While reversing the judgment for defendant upon another ground, the California Supreme Court refused to apply the doctrine of strict liability to automobile drivers. The situation involved two users of the highway but the problems of fixing responsibility under a system of strict liability are as complicated in the instant case as those in Maloney v. Rath (p. 447), and could only create uncertainty in the area of its concern. As stated in *Maloney*, at page 446: "To invoke a rule of strict liability on users of the streets and highways, however, without also establishing in substantial detail how the new rule should operate would only contribute confusion to the automobile accident problem. Settlement and claims adjustment procedures would become chaotic until the new rules were worked out on a case-by-case basis, and the hardships of delayed compensation would be seriously intensified. Only the Legislature, if it deems it wise to do so, can avoid such difficulties by enacting a comprehensive plan for the compensation of automobile accident victims in place of or in addition to the law of negligence."

The instruction tendered by appellants was properly refused for still another reason. Even assuming the merit of appellants' position under the facts of this case in which defendant knew he had a history of epilepsy, previously had suffered seizures and at the time of the accident was attempting to control the condition by medication, the instruction does not except from its ambit the driver who suddenly is stricken by an illness or physical condition which he had no reason whatever to anticipate and of which he had no prior knowledge.

The judgment is affirmed.

■ WOOD, P.J., and THOMPSON, J., concurred.

Appellants' petition for a hearing by the Supreme Court of California was denied December 16, 1971.

NOTES AND QUESTIONS

1. In *Hammontree,* there is no indication that plaintiff was in any way to blame for her injuries. Defendant's loss of control of his automobile appears to have been the precipitating event that caused the harm to her. Why should it make any difference whether he had reason to believe that he might suffer a seizure? Why shouldn't it suffice that he caused the harm? Consider the following criticism of strict liability from O. W. Holmes, The Common Law, pp. 94–96 (1881):

> The general principle of our law is that loss from accident must lie where it falls, and this principle is not affected by the fact that a human being is the instrument of misfortune. . . . If this were not so, any act would be sufficient, however remote, which set in motion or opened the door for a series of physical sequences ending in damage; such as riding the horse, in the case of the runaway, or even coming to a place where one is seized with a fit and strikes the plaintiff in an unconscious spasm. Nay, why need the defendant have acted at all, and why is it not enough that his existence has been at the expense of the plaintiff? The requirement of an act is the requirement that the defendant should have made a choice. But the only possible purpose of introducing this moral element is to make the power of avoiding the evil complained of a condition of liability. There is no such power where the evil cannot be foreseen. . . .

> A man need not, it is true, do this or that act,—the term *act* implies a choice,—but he must act somehow. Furthermore, the public generally profits by individual activity. As action cannot be avoided, and tends to the public good, there is obviously no policy in throwing the hazard of what is at once desirable and inevitable upon the actor.

> The state might conceivably make itself a mutual insurance company against accidents, and distribute the burden of its citizens' mishaps among all its members. There might be a pension for paralytics, and state aid for those who suffered in person or estate from tempest or wild beasts. As between individuals it might adopt the mutual insurance principle *pro tanto,* and divide damages when both were in fault, as in the *rusticum judicium* of the admiralty, or it might throw all loss upon the actor irrespective of fault. The state does none

of these things, however, and the prevailing view is that its cumbrous and expensive machinery ought not to be set in motion unless some clear benefit is to be derived from disturbing the *status quo*. State interference is an evil, where it cannot be shown to be a good. Universal insurance, if desired, can be better and more cheaply accomplished by private enterprise. The undertaking to redistribute losses simply on the ground that they resulted from the defendant's act would not only be open to these objections, but, as it is hoped the preceding discussion has shown, to the still graver one of offending the sense of justice. Unless my act is of a nature to threaten others, unless under the circumstances a prudent man would have foreseen the possibility of harm, it is no more justifiable to make me indemnify my neighbor against the consequences, than to make me do the same thing if I had fallen upon him in a fit, or to compel me to insure him against lightning.

Is Holmes persuasive?

2. Suppose that defendant made his living as a driver and argued that the social benefits derived from his engaging in the activity outweighed the very small likelihood of injury. Would that be a reason to reject strict liability in favor of holding defendant liable only for negligent acts? Consider the following economic perspective on the issue in Posner, A Theory of Negligence, 1 J.Legal Studies 29, 33 (1972):

Perhaps, then, the dominant function of the fault system is to generate rules of liability that if followed will bring about, at least approximately, the efficient—the cost-justified—level of accidents and safety. Under this view, damages are assessed against the defendant as a way of measuring the costs of accidents, and the damages so assessed are paid over to the plaintiff (to be divided with his lawyer) as the price of enlisting their participation in the operation of the system. Because we do not like to see resources squandered, a judgment of negligence has inescapable overtones of moral disapproval, for it implies that there was a cheaper alternative to the accident. Conversely, there is no moral indignation in the case in which the cost of prevention would have exceeded the cost of the accident. Where the measures necessary to avert the accident would have consumed excessive resources, there is no occasion to condemn the defendant for not having taken them.

3. The grounds for rejecting strict liability in favor of negligence referred to in the two preceding notes, as well as the counter-arguments, will be explored in much greater detail throughout this book. Why does the court refuse to adopt a strict liability approach in *Hammontree*?

4. Is there a distinctive argument for strict liability here because plaintiff was on her own property when the accident occurred? In Louisville Ry. Co. v. Sweeney, 157 Ky. 620, 163 S.W. 739 (1914), plaintiff was struck by a gate that had been rammed by a telephone pole knocked over by the defendant's runaway trolley car. Plaintiff was standing in her front yard. Arguably, there had been no negligence in the loss of control of the trolley.   Upholding a judgment for plaintiff, the court approved a jury instruction based on a strict liability theory:

> The plaintiff as the owner of her property was entitled to the undisputed possession of it.   The entry of the defendant upon it, either by its street car or by the pole which it set in motion was a trespass. One who trespasses upon another and inflicts injury, is liable for the injury unless caused by the act of God or produced by causes beyond his control.

Do you find the reasoning in *Sweeney* persuasive?   *Sweeney* was overruled in Randall v. Shelton, 293 S.W.2d 559 (Ky.1956).   Commentators seem to agree that in most cases a trespass is not established where the harm is unintended and non-negligently caused.   See Restatement (Second) of Torts § 166.   Nevertheless, as we shall see, a party's status as land occupier has strongly influenced the character of tort liability rules.

5.   As the court indicates, strict liability in tort is now recognized for some aspects of defective product injuries.   We will examine the products liability area in great detail in Chapter VIII.   For now, however, consider briefly the analogy to auto accidents.   On initial consideration, do you find the court's distinction between liability of an enterprise for its product-related injuries and liability of drivers for auto accidents convincing? Would you be more disposed to hold defendant strictly liable if he had been a taxi driver engaged in his business?

6.   Why is it "not enough to simply say . . .   that the insurance carriers should be the ones to bear the cost of injuries to innocent victims on a strict liability basis"?   The influence of insurance on tort liability will be another recurrent theme in this course.   The institutional aspects of insurance are covered in Chapter X.

7.   Consider the prospect of establishing strict liability against defendant on the basis of a statutory violation of the Vehicle Code.   In the cited case of Maloney v. Rath, the court refused to hold defendant strictly liable for her non-negligent violation of the traffic law (brake failure due to her garage mechanic's negligence), stating that:

> In few cases, however, are the facts likely to be as simple as they are here.   In the next case an accident might be caused by the combination of a brake failure and a stoplight failure under circumstances that would have permitted effective use of an emergency handbrake had the following motorist been properly alerted by the stoplight required by the Vehicle Code.   (Veh.Code § 24603.)   In another case, a pedestrian might stumble and fall on a dangerous and defective pavement causing a motorist having the right of way to drive across the center line of the highway and strike a speeding oncoming car.   Who is to be strictly liable to whom in such cases?   However imperfectly it operates, the law of negligence allocates the risks and determines who shall or shall not be compensated when persons simultaneously engaged in the common enterprise of using the streets and highways have accidents.

Would the determination of who was to be held strictly liable in such cases be markedly more difficult than deciding who would be liable for negligence?

Assume that, irrespective of negligence, the defendant in *Maloney* would be *criminally* liable for violation of Vehicle Code § 24603 (note that defendant in *Hammontree* had complied with a reporting requirement to the Department of Motor Vehicles). Should that affect liability in tort? Again, this issue will be explored in greater depth later, see p. 63, infra, as will the potential legislative solutions to the accident problem referred to toward the end of the *Hammontree* opinion, see Chapter XI.

8. The court uses the terms "strict liability" and "absolute liability" interchangeably in the course of its opinion. Treating the two terms as synonymous is likely to cause confusion. As we will see, the various forms of strict liability that have been recognized are virtually never "absolute." Consider a single example. In no case of product-related injuries, is liability "absolute" in the sense that plaintiff need only establish that defendant's product "caused" the injury. Typically, plaintiff must also establish a defect in the product, and under certain conditions, plaintiff's own conduct will bar recovery. We will explore a number of other limitations on the "absolute" character of strict liability. For present purposes, we simply note that strict liability should be kept distinct, in your mind, from absolute liability.

C. THE LITIGATION PROCESS

1. *Procedure.* In personal injury cases and in litigation generally the aggrieved party must initiate the claim and pursue it until she gains redress or has exhausted her legal remedies. Why should she bear this burden? What are the alternatives? In this case, Maxine Hammontree and her husband's first step would be to consult and then retain an attorney, whose first step would be to try to obtain a settlement from those charged with causing her harm. If that fails, the claimant becomes a plaintiff before the courts by filing a complaint stating what occurred and the relief sought. The "complaint" will allege "facts" that plaintiff contends justify granting relief. The legal theory under which the plaintiff is proceeding will usually be apparent from the nature of the facts that the plaintiff contends to be material to her case.

The person sued, the defendant, will retain an attorney who will consider several options available at this early stage of the proceedings. If the plaintiff has sued the defendant on what the attorney believes to be a novel—and unsound—legal theory, the defendant may make a motion to dismiss the complaint—also called a demurrer—on the ground that even if the allegations of fact in the complaint are true, there is no sound legal theory upon which plaintiff is entitled to relief. The defendant will support this motion with legal arguments. When the plaintiff's attorney responds by arguing that the legal theory is sound, the issue will be posed for the judge. For example, assume a complaint that alleged that the defendant failed to invite the plaintiff to a social event, knowing that such a snub would hurt the plaintiff, and that plaintiff suffered emotional distress. The defendant might move to dismiss that complaint on the ground that even if all the facts are true, there is no valid legal reason for the defendant to pay for the plaintiff's distress. This raises a legal question for the judge to decide—under the relevant law.

If the judge decides for the defendant, the plaintiff's case will be dismissed and the litigation will be at an end unless the plaintiff decides to appeal. (Sometimes the judge will grant the plaintiff permission to amend the allegations to add essential facts to invoke a sound theory where one was lacking before. A defendant who still believes the complaint to be inadequate will make another motion and the case will proceed as before.)

If the judge denies the defendant's motion to dismiss the complaint, the judge will be saying in effect that the plaintiff's complaint states a good legal theory and the plaintiff will be entitled to recover damages from the defendant if the plaintiff can prove that the essential facts alleged in the complaint are true. At this stage procedures diverge. In some states a defendant may appeal the judge's ruling immediately; in other states the defendant must usually wait until the trial is completed before appealing from unfavorable rulings. Under the latter view the defendant must now contest the plaintiff's allegations of fact or admit them and be held legally liable.

The defendant may meet the plaintiff's fact allegations in a pleading called an "answer" in which the defendant denies some or all of the plaintiff's allegations of fact and perhaps adds some new ones of his own that will destroy the plaintiff's case. Although we traditionally resolve fact disputes at a trial, that process is used only for genuine disputes of fact. Some apparent disputes can be decided without a trial because one of the parties has conclusive evidence that it is telling the truth. Thus, for example, if a merchant sues a customer for not paying a bill and the customer asserts payment we have an apparent dispute of fact. If, in addition, the customer can present a cancelled check and the merchant does not claim that the check was forged or in some other way irrelevant to this transaction, we will not need a trial because the dispute is so one-sided that reasonable jurors could resolve it only in favor of the customer. There is no need to hold a trial because the conclusion is foreordained. The customer would make a motion for "summary judgment" and attach a sworn statement and copies of the check and bill of sale. If the plaintiff does not respond with evidence that restores a genuine fact dispute, the judge will grant buyer's motion for summary judgment and enter an order dismissing the case—not on the grounds that the plaintiff's legal theory was inadequate but rather on the grounds that the plaintiff's facts cannot possibly be proven to be true and that a trial would be unnecessary.

It is no coincidence that the foregoing example involved contracts, in which documentary evidence is usually available. In tort cases, on the other hand, the situation is usually quite different because many of the episodes that concern us happen suddenly and rarely lend themselves to documentation. We are more likely to encounter disputes between eyewitnesses as to whether the defendant went through the intersection on a green light or on a red light, or whether a particular product was being used properly at the time plaintiff was hurt. We will often be at the mercy of recollection without being able to reconstruct or to document. The question of which witnesses are telling the truth is classically reserved for trial and for the decision of the trier of fact, usually a jury of six to twelve persons chosen from the community. Occasionally, we shall see cases in which the facts are determined by the trial judge who, in addition to deciding legal questions, doubles as fact finder as well.

At the trial the plaintiff has the burden of proving the essential facts of her case. That is to say, she must persuade the jury that her version of the facts is "more likely than not" what occurred. In other states, she must persuade the jury of her version by a "preponderance of the evidence." However formulated, plaintiff's burden in a civil case is less onerous than the requirement in criminal trials that the state must prove its case "beyond a reasonable doubt." Why? The jury will also be told that if after all of their deliberations they are in equipoise—they cannot decide which side presented the stronger case—they are to return a verdict against the party who had the burden of proof, generally the plaintiff.

Sometimes, however, the trial may not reach the jury stage. If, after plaintiff has presented her evidence, the defendant believes that an essential fact has not been proven, the defendant may make a motion for a "directed verdict," sometimes called "judgment as a matter of law." This, in effect, asks the judge to rule that the plaintiff's evidence is so lacking on at least one essential fact that no jury could reasonably find in the plaintiff's favor and thus it is pointless to continue the trial. The plaintiff will argue against the motion by trying to show that she has presented enough evidence on each essential point so that a jury could find that her version is more likely than not to have occurred. The judge again will be called upon to rule. A judge who rules in favor of the defendant will dismiss the case and the litigation will be over unless the plaintiff appeals successfully. A judge who denies the motion is essentially saying that the plaintiff has presented sufficient facts from which a jury could reasonably find in the plaintiff's favor at this stage of the case—and the trial will continue.

If the defendant should rest without presenting any evidence, the case then proceeds to the closing arguments. Each attorney will summarize the case and will try to persuade the jury to accept a favorable version of the facts. The jury will then be "charged" by the judge. The charge will tell the jurors about burdens of proof and the legal rules they should apply to the facts they find. After deliberation, the jury reports its "verdict" to the judge.

If the defendant does present evidence, he will proceed much as did the plaintiff by calling witnesses and introducing documents to bolster the defendant's contentions about what happened in the case. At the end of the defendant's evidence, defendant may again move for a directed verdict on the ground that his presentation has been such a powerful refutation of the plaintiff's claims that no jury could reasonably decide for the plaintiff.* Again, the judge will grant or deny the motion. Or, the judge may "reserve decision"—delay deciding it until learning how the jury has reacted to the case. If the jury decides the same way the judge would have, the result is clear. If the jury decides for the plaintiff, but the judge thinks the defendant should have received a directed verdict, the judge may now dismiss the case. The advantage of waiting for the jury is that if an appellate court thinks the jury verdict should stand, it can reverse the trial judge's decision and reinstate the jury's verdict. If the judge had granted the directed verdict without waiting for the jury's verdict, and the appellate court disagreed, the only recourse would be to order a complete new trial.

After a verdict for the plaintiff, an unresigned defendant has several choices. He may move for judgment notwithstanding the verdict (judgment n.o.v.—non obstante veredicto) on essentially those grounds involved in seeking a directed verdict: that the jury has reached a verdict that no jury could reasonably have reached on the evidence in this case.

In some cases, the plaintiff's case is so lacking that no jury could reasonably find in plaintiff's favor; in other cases the plaintiff has presented evidence that would justify a jury believing her side but the defendant has presented an overwhelming amount of conflicting evidence. In the first situation, the judge will properly grant a directed verdict (or judgment n.o.v.) since there is nothing to support the plaintiff's case. In the second situation, however, some evidence supports the plaintiff's contention. This might arise, for example, when the issue is whether the defendant drove through a red light. The plaintiff and an admittedly intoxicated bystander swear that the light was red but ten sober disinterested bystanders swear that it was green. If the jury believes the plaintiff and her witness it could reasonably find that the light was red. This would mean that the judge could not properly grant a directed verdict for the defendant because there is evidence that a jury could reasonably believe to support the plaintiff's case. On the other hand, what about the ten disinterested bystanders who swear that the light was green? If the jury finds that the light was green that verdict would also be supported by the evidence.

Although we have said the judge could not grant a directed verdict when there is a conflict between sets of witnesses, the judge may have an abiding sense that the party who prevailed before the jury did not have the preponderant case, and that the jury may have been swayed by some other factor such as the severity of the plaintiff's injury. This may lead the judge to order a new trial to see whether a second jury will respond to this evidence as did the first jury.

---

* After all evidence is in, the plaintiff may also move for a directed verdict if the evidence will permit only that outcome. Similarly, plaintiffs may move for summary judgment on the question of the defendant's liability if no triable question of fact appears to remain in the case.

A good example of this situation occurred in Markus v. City of New York, 42 A.D.2d 527, 344 N.Y.S.2d 761 (1973), in which the critical question was whether a curve in the road was marked with a warning sign. Plaintiff testified that there were no signs warning of the curve. "On the other hand, several patrolmen and two employees of the Department of Parks testified that there were such signs. The alleged failure on the part of the City to give adequate warnings is a question for the triers of the fact." The jury found for the plaintiff. The quoted passage indicates that it would have been error for the trial judge to have granted a directed verdict against the plaintiff. Here, however, the appellate court concluded that the verdict was "against the weight of the credible evidence" and directed a new trial. If the second jury reaches the same result as the first, the judges may conclude that the jurors are correct in accepting the plaintiff's view of the facts rather than those of the several defense witnesses. (Note that here the trial judge, playing the role of "thirteenth juror," thought the dispute one for the jury. The appellate court, though not seeing the witnesses, thought that plaintiff's testimony alone was overwhelmed by the contrary testimony and wanted to have the reactions of another jury.)

On occasion the jury can persuade the court. In one case a jury awarded $25,000 for the pain and suffering of a 70–year–old man for 29 days before he died. The appellate court ordered a new trial unless plaintiff agreed to a reduced award of $5,000. Plaintiff refused and the case was tried a second time. The second jury awarded $20,000 for the same item and the trial judge refused to reduce it. This time, the appellate court upheld the award even though it had previously said that $5,000 was appropriate. "In doing so, we are influenced by the fact that a second jury has indicated its belief that such an amount is not excessive." Tucker v. City of New York, 54 A.D.2d 930, 388 N.Y.S.2d 133 (1976).

Both of these motions are used largely by the defense, but they are also available to the plaintiff if the jury returns a verdict for the defendant. The plaintiff's likeliest recourse, however, is to try to obtain a new trial by asserting that the trial judge committed errors in the admission or exclusion of evidence or the charge to the jury, and that these errors were "prejudicial."

After reaching a conclusive disposition of the case, the judge will enter judgment in favor of the successful party. As we have seen, this may occur at any of several stages. It may be at the outset, if the judge grants defendant's motion to dismiss the plaintiff's complaint on the ground that it asks for relief in a situation in which the law does not provide relief. It may happen on a directed verdict at the end of the plaintiff's case or following all the evidence. It may happen after the verdict, when the trial judge accepts what the jury has done, rejects the defense motions, and enters a judgment for the plaintiff for the amount awarded by the jury.

These motions all occur at the trial court level, but virtually all the cases in this book are appellate cases and we now turn to the issues presented by an appeal. In general, "the trial judge tries the case and the appellate court tries the trial judge." The party against whom judgment has been entered will seek to persuade the appellate court that the trial judge committed prejudicial error in making rulings in the case. Note that the plaintiffs in *Hammontree* did not challenge the sufficiency of the evidence on appeal; they conceded that there was enough evidence from which the jury could reasonably have accepted defendant's version, and did not contend that the trial judge should have found the defendant's evidence absolutely or relatively insufficient.

They did, however, claim that the judge committed a specific legal error in failing to charge that the jury could find defendant liable irrespective of negligence on his part. This is a question of law and the appellate court will decide whether the ruling was erroneous and, if so, whether the error was prejudicial to appellants' case.

2. *Hammontree Reconsidered.* In view of this brief look at the procedural aspects of tort litigation, consider the following questions about *Hammontree:*

a. How do you think the jury instruction on liability tendered by the judge differed from the plaintiffs' rejected instruction? A version of the charge frequently used by California judges may be found at p. 34, infra.

b. According to the court, plaintiffs withdrew their claim of negligence during the trial, and apparently sought to proceed exclusively on a strict liability theory. Why might plaintiffs have adopted this strategy?

c. If plaintiffs' theory of the case had been adopted, would they have been entitled to summary judgment on liability, as they requested? Summary judgments and directed verdicts in favor of plaintiffs are rare as compared to successful motions by defendants on these grounds. Why do you think this is the case?

d. In view of the trial court's rejection of plaintiffs' theory, might defendant have been entitled to a directed verdict? At what stage in the trial might defendant have tendered the motion? Might summary judgment in his favor have been warranted?

3. *Damages.* Once a plaintiff has brought herself within the rules allowing recovery for personal injury, the traditional goal of tort law has been to restore her to the equivalent of her condition prior to the harm. Most plaintiffs seek money damages, though other remedies exist: sometimes a plaintiff would prefer an injunction to prevent conduct that threatens harm, and in a defamation case the plaintiff may prefer a retraction. In personal injury cases, money damages are viewed as the best solution. Can you think of anything better?

The categories of personal injury damage available to a plaintiff are meant to compensate for both tangible and intangible loss. Tangible losses may already have been incurred or be predictable. The former include such easily proven items as doctors' bills, hospital bills, and other actual medical expenses. Loss of income is proven almost as easily, especially if the plaintiff is salaried. The projection of such loss, especially for self-employed victims, is speculative, but may be facilitated by effective use of expert testimony. Experts also assist in the projection of medical costs.

The common law provides that plaintiff sue only once for the harm she has suffered, and statutes of limitations establish time limits within which she must do so. Plaintiff has no further legal recourse after she recovers a judgment, even if she sustains unanticipated harm that is related to the defendant's tortious conduct. Might this explain why plaintiffs who suffer potentially serious harm may wait a long time before suing? What should the law do if the plaintiff makes an unexpected recovery shortly after winning an award that anticipated a continuing disability? Instead of accepting projections and predictions, the law might have required plaintiff to sue at regular intervals for damages incurred since the last suit. Might the opportunity for recurring access to the court delay plaintiff's recuperation? What other arguments would support a single lump sum judgment? What arguments would weigh against it?

The intangible element of pain and suffering, which plays a central role in most cases of serious personal injury, presents problems of valuation as to both past and future. Through this item the law recognizes that the impact of the injury is more than financial. Suppose Maxine Hammontree had suffered serious injuries that left her crippled and disfigured. It is difficult to put price tags on such consequences, but if the law seeks to restore the plaintiff to her prior condition or its equivalent, the continuing pain and embarrassment she suffers must be assessed and translated into monetary terms.

Note that plaintiffs in *Hammontree* also sued for property loss because of the damage to the shop caused by defendant's loss of control of his auto. This is another common category of damage in personal injury cases, particularly in auto accident situations. (The subject of damages is discussed in detail in Chapter X.)

4. *Attorneys and Fees.* The attorney's fee presents two questions: who pays and how much. In Great Britain the losing litigant pays the attorney's fees and other litigation costs of the prevailing party as well as her own. In the United States it was feared that such a rule would deny persons of limited means access to the courts in close cases. When the courts were used mainly to settle vast estates or large commercial disputes and poor people had few claims, it may have been appropriate for a losing party to pay for both attorneys, but with the industrial revolution, the railroad, and later the automobile, wider access to the courts was essential. Requiring a party to pay even her own attorney presents serious problems for the poor, and tort litigation in this country has come to be handled by what is called the contingent fee system: the injured person pays a fee only if her case is concluded successfully—and the fee is a previously set percentage of the amount recovered. In many other legal systems throughout the world the contingent fee is unethical and in some it is illegal. What might cause this view of the contingent fee? What may be said in its defense? What are the alternatives?

Most personal injury cases in this country are handled for the plaintiff's side by a specialized group of lawyers who accept cases on a contingent fee basis. Lawyers for the defense are also specialized and represent either insurance companies or large commercial and industrial enterprises. Some are permanent employees of their client; others work in independent law firms that are compensated according to the time devoted to a particular case.

5. *Plaintiffs.* The Hammontree case involved an adult plaintiff. Her age, physical condition, and occupation would have been relevant to her damage recovery. In other situations it may be more difficult to find the proper plaintiff and to measure the recoverable loss. If a minor is hurt, suit generally will be brought on her behalf by her parent or guardian, and a damage award will be divided so that the minor will recover for any permanent physical harm (though the money will be placed in trust for her) and her parent will recover medical expenses borne on the child's behalf. It is now generally held that an infant who is born alive may sue through a legal guardian for harm suffered before birth. This problem is well discussed in Woods v. Lancet, 303 N.Y. 349, 102 N.E.2d 691 (1951).

Recoveries in cases of death are regulated by statute because under early common law the death of either the plaintiff or the defendant terminated the lawsuit. The death of the defendant now rarely causes the abatement of otherwise valid lawsuits. As for a deceased victim, two separate interests are involved: the victim's interest in her own bodily security and her dependents' interest in continued economic support and in other factors we shall consider later. The first is protected by "survival" statutes that allow the estate of the deceased to bring suit for any harm for which the deceased could have sued had she survived. This would include such items as medical expenses, lost wages, and pain and suffering up to her death. The second interest is generally recognized through "wrongful death" statutes. One common pattern provides that an action may be brought by and on behalf of legally designated beneficiaries, usually close family members or next of kin, to recover for the pecuniary loss that the death has caused. Generically these statutes are called Lord Campbell's Acts, after the first such statute adopted in 1846 in England. The survival and wrongful death interests may be vindicated in a single action.

In a lawsuit on behalf of a dead victim the actual plaintiff is usually an administrator (administratrix) or executor (executrix). An administrator is named by the court to handle the affairs of one who died intestate (with no will). If the deceased has left a will, it usually names an executor to handle the settling of estate matters, including bringing and defending lawsuits. In these cases the deceased may be referred to as the decedent, as plaintiff's intestate, or as plaintiff's testator.

Why is Maxine Hammontree's husband a co-plaintiff? Although the property damage to their jointly-owned business is one reason, it may be that his principal claim is for loss of consortium—loss of his wife's companionship—due to the injuries she suffered. The various aspects of "relational harm" in cases of death and injury are discussed in Chapter IV.

6. *Defendants.* Few tort suits are brought solely on principle; only a recovery of damages can restore the injured plaintiff. Thus the plaintiff's lawyer must find a defendant who, if found liable, will have the money, whether from his or her own funds or through insurance, to respond to a judgment. This search for the solvent party explains why in many cases the most obvious tortfeasor is not sued. If the obvious defendant cannot be found or has limited resources, suit usually will be brought against a solvent defendant who, though having a more tenuous relationship to the occurrence, may also be liable for plaintiff's harm.

Employees in the scope of their employment. Suppose that defendant in *Hammontree* had been driving a delivery truck for his corporate employer when the accident occurred. Plaintiffs would have been certain to sue the employer and no one would question the responsibility of the corporate defendant for the misconduct of its driver. (The driver himself may also be a defendant, though it is less likely that he can respond in damages.) For centuries the rule of respondeat superior has rendered masters liable to third parties for misconduct of their servants—at least while the servant is acting in the scope of employment. This responsibility is defined broadly: the master cannot escape liability for the servant's failure to obey traffic rules by claiming that the servant was acting outside the scope of employment when violating traffic rules that he or she had been told to obey. Is it reasonable to hold the master liable for the servant's torts? Does it affect your opinion that the master is legally entitled to be indemnified by the servant for any money that the master has had to pay the injured victim on account of the servant's conduct?

The 1977 Report of the California Citizens' Commission on Tort Reform, "Righting the Liability Balance," reviewed the origins of vicarious liability. It noted that as England emerged from the Middle Ages, the "growth of commerce carried on over longer and longer distances by ever larger firms, multiplied the number of situations in which injury could occur and decreased the probability that the parties would know each other" and could settle their disputes through some informal or communal mechanism. The report continued (27–28):

> The system struggled in a number of ways to accommodate these sweeping changes in economic organization. Probably the most important was incorporation into the Common Law of the principle that an employer is liable for the acts of his employees as though they were his own acts, if the actions are taken in connection with the worker's employment, and if negligence on the part of the employee can be shown. This doctrine, which came to be known as the rule of "vicarious liability," was adapted from the long-standing practice of the specialized merchants' Court system, now largely defunct, and from a similar policy of the Court of Admiralty. The transplantation, which occurred in the Seventeenth Century, was sometimes stated in language that suggested the Courts' awareness that the rule was an expression of a particular social and economic theory. With respect to social

philosophy, the doctrine was a striking departure from the older principle that a master should be responsible for only those particular actions which he directly commands, because they are immediate extensions of his will.

Whether or not intentionally applied, the economic thesis underlying the rule was more complicated, and in some ways extraordinarily modern. In effect, the Courts held that it was not only just but efficient to visit the costs of liability upon productive enterprises as one of the accepted prices of doing business and earning a profit. Put another way, by implication they ruled that it would be inefficient either to allow liability to rest solely with individual employees (many of whom did not have the money to pay judgments), or to levy the costs of employment-related injury on the society as a whole by treating them as frictional costs associated with the totality of economic activity and, therefore, as a public responsibility. (Obviously, the Courts could not have directed the government to take on this expensive function, but if they had refused to find liability in employees or employers, they could have exerted pressure in that direction.) In the jargon of modern economists, the Courts chose the point of profit-making as the point at which the costs of injury should be "internalized," or made part of the calculation by which each participant in the market determined the price he would accept for the goods or services he had to sell. The employee, said the Courts, was not required to add into the price of his labor the funds required to build a reserve against a possible tort judgment, except to the degree that he expected the employer to utilize his right to sue the employee for indemnification after damages had been paid. The employer, on the other hand, was required to set his prices in the knowledge that he was liable for payment of damages whether or not he could later collect reimbursement from the employee.

To the limited degree that this rationale was consciously followed, it doubtless reflected a keen appreciation of contemporary economic reality, in which, for example, the actual freedom of most employees to manipulate the prices of their labor was very limited. But there was also a broader sweep to the effect. Vicarious liability was consistent with the older objectives of the tort system, but it helped further to redefine the concept of deterrence, and it added two important new and partially conflicting principles. With regard to deterrence, it suggested that the effective point to create sources of discipline against injurious behavior was, again, at the point where profit was realized. Thus, the employer, concerned about his liability, might be expected to police the behavioral rules and to make compliance by his employees a condition of employment. In addition, by placing the liability burden upon an economic actor who actually enjoyed sufficient freedom in the market to adjust the price of his wares to take into account the losses he might incur, the rule served the newer objective of *spreading the risk* among all of his customers. Also, although most opinions of the Courts of the period scrupulously avoided explicit reference to it, vicarious liability imposed the burden of payment on the actor most likely to have the financial capacity to compensate, and thereby helped to establish the principle that *liability should be at least partially a function of the ability to pay. . . .*

Is "spreading" the loss a self-justifying principle? Under the "deep pocket" theory, masters bear the loss because they are better able to pay; under a loss-spreading theory, masters bear the loss initially on the assumption that they will be able and willing to pass the ultimate costs on to a number of others, including their customers. Is it "appropriate" for customers and others to bear the cost? If so, is it because the loss hurts less when shared by a large number, or because it is "desirable" that the price of an activity reflect the social costs associated with it? Is it clear what the Commission means when it says that vicarious liability was perceived to be "not only just but efficient"? We reconsider many of these questions in other contexts shortly. The classic treatment of vicarious liability is T. Baty, Vicarious Liability (1916). A good treatment that reflects more recent economic thinking is P. Atiyah, Vicarious Liability (1967).

Employees out of the scope of their employment. The foregoing discussion explored reasons for holding employers liable for harm done by their employees in the scope of their employment. The implication that this liability does not extend to torts committed by employees outside the scope of their employment is generally correct, but there is a growing exception— liability on the employer for negligently hiring the employee in the first place or for retaining the employee after one or more incidents that should have warned the employer of the dangerous propensities of the employee.

In Foster v. The Loft, Inc., 26 Mass.App.Ct. 289, 526 N.E.2d 1309 (1988), plaintiff customer at defendant's bar was punched by a bartender in a melee that broke out after the customer's friend complained that his drink had been improperly mixed. We explore claims for intentional harm in Chapter XII. The claim against the defendant bar owner was not that the bartender was functioning within the scope of his employment, but that the owner had hired someone to deal with the public in a hectic environment (a large complex of five bars) who had previously pleaded guilty to assault and battery with a knife and to related charges. Although refusing to hold that an employer can never hire a person with a criminal record, the court did conclude that the jury could reasonably find that the owner failed to take reasonable steps to screen the employees who would be dealing most closely with the public in an atmosphere that was "volatile" and in which "there was a high potential for violence."

How does this analysis differ from that of respondeat superior?

Independent contractors. As we have seen, the master's liability for the servant's negligence has an extensive common law history. But the law developed quite differently when the defendant employed an independent contractor rather than a servant. Briefly, the difference between the two relationships was that the employer had no control over the way the independent contractor chose to perform the tasks for which he had been employed. The major consequence of that difference was that until late in the 19th century those who hired independent contractors were not held liable for the negligence of those contractors. Since then, a growing list of exceptions has developed by which these employers have been held liable—especially when they employ the contractor to perform inherently dangerous tasks. The complex nature of this subject may be seen in the Restatement (Second) of Torts, which devotes 19 sections to developing exceptions to the general rule of non-liability. §§ 409–429.

In the *Maloney* case, involving the brake failure, the court concluded that the owner of the car should be held liable for the negligence of the garage mechanic who negligently worked on the brakes, even though the owner had chosen a reputable mechanic and had no reason to suspect that the job was badly done. The court stressed two statutory requirements that car brakes be in working order. These were said to show that the legislature recognized that improperly maintained motor vehicles threaten "a grave risk of serious bodily harm or death." Responsibility for proper maintenance of such potentially dangerous property "properly rests with the person who owns and operates the vehicle." That person "selects the contractor and is free to insist upon one who is financially responsible and to demand indemnity from him."

The *Maloney* result was rejected in Hackett v. Perron, 119 N.H. 419, 402 A.2d 193 (1979):

> Garage mechanics are not employees or agents of their customers. To charge owners with their negligence would be tantamount to imposing absolute liability. . . . It is true that plaintiff may have been faultless, but defendant also was without fault. We do not live in a riskless society and it is no part of the judicial function to fashion the law so that every injured person can find someone to hold liable. We refuse to decide which of two innocent co-users of our highways should be held liable. The fault system provides a fair method of apportioning the risk of co-users of our highways and we will not depart from it.

7. During much of this course we will read and discuss appellate opinions. You should know from the outset that these opinions are only a fraction of the yield of the legal process; in personal injury law, for example, perhaps only three percent of all claims actually go to trial and far fewer are appealed. The few appellate decisions, of course, shape the evolution of the law; cases are dropped and settlements are made on the basis of predictions of how the trial and appellate courts will view the controversy. Thus our appellate focus means that instead of seeing a cross-section of typical personal injury cases, we shall consider a small group of particularly significant cases.

Notice that tort problems are likelier to reach litigation than are contract problems. Parties to a contract are seeking an agreement that

will provide specific foreseeable benefits.   Even if a dispute arises, they
have strong incentives to reach an accord that will preserve their mutually
advantageous relationship.   In tort situations, however, most claims arise
from unintended harms.   Prior legal counseling is rare.   The attorney
usually enters after the harm has occurred, and with litigation in mind if
settlement negotiations fail.   Often, the parties initially become aware of
one another when at least one of them is hurt—and probably angry.   There
is no continuing relationship between the parties encouraging them to
settle, and tort suits are hotly disputed because the critical events—as in a
car crash—may have taken place within a few seconds.

Court structure.   The California court system is fairly typical of state
judicial organization—with its trial court of general jurisdiction (the superi-
or court), a group of regional intermediate appellate courts (the court of
appeal) and a single highest court (the supreme court).   The major aberration in naming courts is the important state of New York.   There the trial
level court is called, "the supreme court," the regional intermediate appellate court is the "appellate division of the supreme court," and the state's
highest court is called the "court of appeals."

8.   Suggestions for further reading appear throughout this book.   Two
general books on tort law will be helpful on the doctrinal issues discussed.
F. Harper, F. James, Jr. and O. Gray, The Law of Torts (2d ed. 1986)(6
vols.) and Prosser and Keeton on Torts (5th ed. 1984).   Throughout the
book, cases and notes will refer to relevant sections of the Restatement of
the Law of Torts (4 vols. 1934–39) and the Second Restatement (4 vols.
1965–79).   The Restatement is an unofficial effort to summarize the
decisional law on a subject.   It is prepared by the American Law Institute,
a group of lawyers, judges, and scholars.   The intellectual foundations of
tort law are explored in R. Rabin, Perspectives on Tort Law (4th ed. 1995)
and S. Levmore, Foundations of Tort Law (1994).   The litigation process is
explored in M. Franklin, The Biography of a Legal Dispute (1968).

CHAPTER II

THE NEGLIGENCE PRINCIPLE

A. HISTORICAL DEVELOPMENT OF FAULT LIABILITY

The law of negligence is of relatively recent origin. As late as 1850, one finds only a handful of isolated cases that refer to liability based on negligence. In A History of American Law (2d ed. 1985), Lawrence Friedman observes (at p. 467) that prior to the nineteenth century:

> The common law had little to say about personal injuries brought about by carelessness—the area of life and law that underwent most rapid growth in the [nineteenth] century. The modern law of torts must be laid at the door of the industrial revolution, whose machines had a marvelous capacity for smashing the human body.

Was the pre-industrial era characterized by strict liability? Some commentators have thought so. Others have argued that fault considerations always tempered the strictness of tort doctrine in cases of unintended harm. The debate is complicated by the fact that tort law, as Friedman points out, only ripened into a field during the latter part of the nineteenth century. Before the industrial revolution, the infrequent cases of accidental harm that occurred were filtered through the Anglo–American writ system—a procedural system requiring that tort-like wrongs be pleaded as actions in "trespass" or "trespass on the case," rather than the substantive categories we now employ. The flavor of the writ system is well captured in the classic distinction put forward by Fortescue, J., in Reynolds v. Clarke, 1 Strange 634, 92 Eng.Rep. 410 (1726):

> [I]f a man throws a log into the highway, and in that act it hits me; I may maintain trespass, because it is an immediate wrong; but if as it lies there I tumble over it, and receive an injury, I must bring an action upon the case; because it is only prejudicial in consequence, for which originally I could have no action at all.

We begin our consideration of negligence with a closer look at the English common law approach that laid the foundations for the American treatment of unintended harm. In the following excerpt, Gary Schwartz draws upon the leading historical accounts in addressing the question of whether pre-industrial injury law was dominated by a strict liability approach.

22

Tort Law and the Economy in Nineteenth Century America: a Reinterpretation

Gary T. Schwartz.
90 Yale Law Journal 1717, 1722–27 (1981).

Research into pre–1800 English tort doctrine is fraught with hazards. One can look at judges' remarks ventured in the course of what amounted to oral argument. But as has been observed, "[t]o ransack the Year Books for large statements of doctrine made in irrelevant circumstances by judges barely conscious of their significance is neither a pleasing nor a profitable task." One can also study the pleadings and trial verdicts available in the mostly unpublished plea rolls and rely on them in attempting to infer the pertinent liability standards. But the process of drawing "believable inferences" from raw documents of this sort is frequently "perilous." And whether one turns to the Year Books or the plea rolls, questions of substantive law frequently are obscured or confounded by the demands of the English writ system.

Despite these inadequacies of evidence,[35] many scholars have confidently found huge portions of strict liability in traditional English law. Professor Gregory finds strict liability inherent in the English writ of trespass.[36] But this alignment of English trespass with strict liability is misleading. As developed in the late twelfth century, the early writ of trespass—far from entailing strict liability—seems to have been primarily addressed to intentional harm-causing conduct, conduct that would now be identified as basically criminal. To be sure, by a process we now may be barely able to reconstruct, trespass began to extend to conduct that involved *"vi et armis"* (the trespass formula) only in the loose sense of harm that was forcibly, even if accidentally, inflicted. The propriety of this extension was confirmed, and the standard of liability in trespass explicitly—though ambiguously—discussed, in Weaver v. Ward,[41] a 1616 case concerning the accidental discharge of firearms. Although *Weaver* did suggest that the trespass-plaintiff's proof of immediately caused harm established a prima facie case, it also indicated that the defendant could refute liability by showing that what happened had been an "inevitable accident"—that the defendant had been "utterly without fault" or had "committed no negligence." While these various formulations clearly rule out the idea of unqualified strict liability, their precise meaning is far from clear.[42]

---

35. Even if medieval law *had* been subject to a significant strict liability rule, that rule would require interpretation. Perhaps medieval thinking imputed a motive (whether conscious or unconscious) to every action in a way that just about eliminated the concept of unintended harm. See A. Ehrenzweig, Psychoanalytic Jurisprudence 244 (1971). Perhaps in a simple medieval world, almost every serious injury was the result of intentional or at least negligent conduct.

See J. Fleming, An Introduction to the Law of Torts 3 (3d ed. 1967); [ ].

36. . . . A semantic point: "strict liability" was not a phrase that courts employed during the periods under review. On those occasions when strict liability was considered, the idea was conveyed in a variety of indirect ways.

41. Hobart 134, 80 Eng.Rep. 284 (1616). . . .

42. . . .

The question of the liability standard in trespass was further complicated by what was then routine trespass procedure. A trespass writ generally took the form of a "stark uninformative declaration." In answering the writ the defendant could offer a "blank plea of Not Guilty," and then present to the jury whatever extenuating evidence he thought relevant. The standard of liability in trespass thus was left to the effective discretion of the individual jury, and we simply lack information as to how juries exercised this discretion; jury verdicts of guilty and not guilty remain largely "inscrutable."

Professor Malone emphasizes the strict liability he finds in the English fire cases. Though the judicial statements in question contain certain strict liability phrases, they also avail themselves of the language of negligence. Whether these negligence references were mere rhetorical flourishes or were instead intended to posit an actual liability standard is a question that has provoked disagreement. No one contends, however, that a strict liability rule applied to fires that were accidentally set. Rather, the rule is said to have covered deliberately started fires that accidentally spread to a neighbor's property. Even these fires were subject to strict liability only to the extent that they remained "within the control" of the defendant. And since, for example, an unexpectedly strong wind tended to negate control, the control requirement can easily be regarded as a correlate or proxy for fault.

The fire cases were pleaded in trespass on the case. As a general matter, the case variation on the trespass writ provided a remedy for English victims who could not make any plausible claim of forcible injury. In the absence of such a claim, however, the case plaintiff needed to explain in his writ why the imposition of liability was appropriate in his situation. Since it appears that a number of situations were found sufficient in this respect, case possessed from the start a catch-all or "miscellaneous" quality that makes it difficult to generalize about its standard of liability. Traditionally, however, case has been affiliated with negligence, and overall this affiliation seems fair. The earliest instances of case involved suits against professionals like blacksmiths, physicians, and veterinarians who were held liable for negligence in their undertakings. In the fifteenth and sixteenth centuries, a limited number of claims were litigated in case between parties not in any preexisting contractual relation; for these claims, a liability standard approaching negligence was applied. By the late seventeenth century, collision suits began to come before the courts—collisions of vessels at sea, of horse-drawn carriages on highways, and of carriages with pedestrians. Since these collisions involved forceful contacts, they raised a clear trespass possibility. Yet, for several possible reasons,[61] these suits were frequently pleaded in case, with liability depending on proof of the

---

Related to the "inevitable accident" defense was the idea that trespass would not lie if the object immediately causing the injury—a ship or a horse, for example—had escaped the defendant's control. . . .

61. One reason was loss of control. See note 42 supra. Another reason was vicarious liability. [ ].

defendant's negligence. Even when the facts of a particular collision led to its being presented in trespass, it appears that negligence was recognized as the liability pivot. Of course, collisions of one sort or another—often involving railroads—came to typify tort litigation in the nineteenth century.

One early fire opinion, in vacillating between strict liability and negligence, indicates that an employer could be held strictly liable for the within-the-employment negligence of his employee in allowing a fire to spread. In general, any claim of vicarious liability relegated a plaintiff to case, and as late as 1685 the law was willing—the fire cases apart—to hold employers liable only for torts they had actually commanded. In its sixteenth-century form, moreover, the command rule evidently required the employer to have "commanded the very act in which the wrong consisted (unless the command had been to do a thing in itself unlawful)." Gradually, however, in eighteenth-century England the modern notion developed that the employer could be held liable for any of his employee's scope-of-employment torts;[68] but in personal injury cases this notion seems to have been associated with the assumption of some negligent conduct on the employee's part.

Therefore, whatever the strict liability possibilities that may have harbored in the writ of trespass, these possibilities evidently were connected to or at least contained by a narrow rule of employer vicarious liability, a rule that, as it eventually expanded, acquired a noticeable negligence orientation. Negligence, moreover, was all along the accepted standard of liability in the malpractice and the collision cases. Indeed, if one searches traditional English tort law for clear instances of strict liability, one winds up mainly with the animal cases. Even these cases reveal an uncertain prior history. Cattle owners originally were held liable for those cattle trespasses that their owners deliberately incited; and the early suits over animals attacking humans may well have involved plain negligence on the part of the animals' custodians. To be sure, over time each of these animal doctrines inclined in the direction of strict liability. But the explanations for these evolutions remain very much in doubt; and in any event the modest animal rules posed no particular threat to nineteenth-century industrialization.

To sum up, then, the strict liability strands in traditional English law seem ambivalent and confused; the negligence strands, both more distinct and more capable of extended application.

NOTES AND QUESTIONS

1. The leading historical sources analyzed by Schwartz are J. Baker, An Introduction to English Legal History (1979); C. Fifoot, History and Sources of the Common Law (1949); A. Harari, The Place of Negligence in the Law of Torts (1962); S. Milsom, Historical Foundations of the Common

---

68. The account afforded here is in opposition to the common assumption that the scope-of-employment test is of "ancient" origin. [ ]

Law (2d ed. 1981); T. Plucknett, A Concise History of the Common Law (1956); M. Pritchard, Scott v. Shepherd (1773) and the Emergence of the Tort of Negligence (1976); Arnold, Accident, Mistake and the Rules of Liability in the Fourteenth Century Law of Torts, 128 U.Pa.L.Rev. 361 (1979); Gregory, Trespass to Negligence to Absolute Liability, 37 Va.L.Rev. 359 (1951); and Malone, Ruminations on the Role of Fault in the History of the Common Law of Torts, 31 La.L.Rev. 1 (1970).

2. Virtually all of these sources take as their starting point the question of whether strict liability was dominant at early common law, or whether it was tempered to some extent by fault considerations. As we trace the modern development of negligence and strict liability in the materials that follow, keep in mind the possibility of another perspective: that the pre-industrial era was in fact substantially committed to a "no-liability" approach based on court-imposed immunities, limited duties and restrictive notions of what constituted an actionable claim in the first instance. This thesis is developed in Rabin, The Historical Development of the Fault Principle: A Reinterpretation, 15 Ga.L.Rev. 925 (1981), arguing that "no-liability" thinking continued to influence tort law well into the negligence era.

See also Gilles, Inevitable Accident in Classical English Tort Law, 43 Emory L.J. 575 (1994), arguing that English precedents in the pre-industrial era established a liability regime falling between strict causal-based liability and negligence—one in which "the question was not whether actors had behaved unreasonably—whether they *should* have avoided the accident—but whether they *could* have avoided it by greater practical care."

3. Undoubtedly, the leading English precedents played a role in shaping early American tort law. In the early nineteenth century, however, the states began to develop their own accident law. Again, there is scholarly disagreement over the role of strict liability in the early post-Revolutionary period. Compare M. Horwitz, The Transformation of American Law, 1780–1860 (1977), pp. 67–108, and Gregory, cited in note 1 supra, with Schwartz at pp. 1727–34, and Schwartz, The Character of Early American Tort Law, 36 UCLA L.Rev. 641 (1989). Whatever the situation might have been before 1850, the universality of the negligence principle was an open question in this country when the following landmark case was decided.

Brown v. Kendall

Supreme Judicial Court of Massachusetts, 1850.
6 Cush. (60 Mass.) 292.

This was an action of trespass for assault and battery, originally commenced against George K. Kendall, the defendant, who died pending the suit, and his executrix was summoned in.

It appeared in evidence, on the trial . . . that two dogs, belonging to the plaintiff and the defendant, respectively, were fighting in the presence of their masters; that the defendant took a stick about four feet long, and commenced beating the dogs in order to separate them; that the plaintiff was looking on, at the distance of about a rod, and that he advanced a step or two towards the dogs. In their struggle, the dogs approached the place where the plaintiff was standing. The defendant retreated backwards from before the dogs, striking them as he retreated; and as he approached the plaintiff, with his back towards him, in raising his stick over his shoulder, in order to strike the dogs, he accidentally hit the plaintiff in the eye, inflicting upon him a severe injury.

Whether it was necessary or proper for the defendant to interfere in the fight between the dogs; whether the interference, if called for, was in a proper manner, and what degree of care was exercised by each party on the occasion; were the subject of controversy between the parties, upon all the evidence in the case, of which the foregoing is an outline.

[Under instructions from the trial judge, which are reviewed in the opinion, the jury returned a verdict for the plaintiff and the trial judge entered judgment.]

■ Shaw, C.J. . . .

The facts set forth in the bill of exceptions preclude the supposition, that the blow, inflicted by the hand of the defendant upon the person of the plaintiff, was intentional. The whole case proceeds on the assumption, that the damage sustained by the plaintiff, from the stick held by the defendant, was inadvertent and unintentional; and the case involves the question how far, and under what qualifications, the party by whose unconscious act the damage was done is responsible for it. We use the term "unintentional" rather than involuntary, because in some of the cases, it is stated, that the act of holding and using a weapon or instrument, the movement of which is the immediate cause of hurt to another, is a voluntary act, although its particular effect in hitting and hurting another is not within the purpose or intention of the party doing the act.

It appears to us, that some of the confusion in the cases on this subject has grown out of the long-vexed question, under the rule of the common law, whether a party's remedy, where he has one, should be sought in an action of the case, or of trespass. This is very distinguishable from the question, whether in a given case, any action will lie. The result of these cases is, that if the damage complained of is the immediate effect of the act of the defendant, trespass *vi et armis* lies; if consequential only, and not immediate, case is the proper remedy. [ ]

In these discussions, it is frequently stated by judges, that when one receives injury from the direct act of another, trespass will lie. But we think this is said in reference to the question, whether trespass and not case will lie, assuming that the facts are such, that some action will lie. These *dicta* are no authority, we think, for holding, that damage received by a direct act of force from another will be sufficient to maintain an action of trespass, whether the act was lawful or unlawful, and neither wilful, intentional, or careless. . . .

We think, as the result of all the authorities, the rule is correctly stated by Mr. Greenleaf, that the plaintiff must come prepared with evidence to show either that the *intention* was unlawful, or that the defendant was *in fault;* for if the injury was unavoidable, and the conduct of the defendant was free from blame, he will not be liable. 2 Greenl.Ev. §§ 85 to 92; [ ]. If, in the prosecution of a lawful act, a casualty purely accidental arises, no action can be supported for an injury arising therefrom. [ ]. In applying these rules to the present case, we can perceive no reason why the instructions asked for by the defendant ought not to have been given; to this effect, that if both plaintiff and defendant at the time of the blow were using ordinary care, or if at that time the defendant was using ordinary care, and the plaintiff was not, or if at that time, both the plaintiff and defendant were not using ordinary care, then the plaintiff could not recover.

In using this term, ordinary care, it may be proper to state, that what constitutes ordinary care will vary with the circumstances of cases. In general, it means that kind and degree of care, which prudent and cautious men would use, such as is required by the exigency of the case, and such as is necessary to guard against probable danger. A man, who should have occasion to discharge a gun, on an open and extensive marsh, or in a forest, would be required to use less circumspection and care, than if he were to do the same thing in an inhabited town, village, or city. To make an accident, or casualty, or as the law sometimes states it, inevitable accident, it must be such an accident as the defendant could not have avoided by the use of the kind and degree of care necessary to the exigency, and in the circumstances in which he was placed.

. . . We can have no doubt that the act of the defendant in attempting to part the fighting dogs, one of which was his own, and for the injurious acts of which he might be responsible, was a lawful and proper act, which he might do by proper and safe means. If, then, in doing this act, using due care and all proper precautions necessary to the exigency of the case, to avoid hurt to others, in raising his stick for that purpose, he accidentally hit the plaintiff in his eye, and wounded him, this was the result of pure accident, or was involuntary and unavoidable, and therefore the action would not lie. . . .

The court instructed the jury, that if it was not a necessary act, and the defendant was not in duty bound to part the dogs, but might with propriety interfere or not as he chose, the defendant was responsible for the consequences of the blow, unless it appeared that he was in the exercise of extraordinary care, so that the accident was inevitable, using the word not in a strict but a popular sense. This is to be taken in connection with the charge afterwards given, that if the jury believed, that the act of interference in the fight was unnecessary, (that is, as before explained, not a duty incumbent on the defendant,) then the burden of proving extraordinary care on the part of the defendant, or want of ordinary care on the part of plaintiff, was on the defendant.

The court are of opinion that these directions were not conformable to law. If the act of hitting the plaintiff was unintentional, on the part of the defendant, and done in the doing of a lawful act, then the defendant was not liable, unless it was done in the want of exercise of due care, adapted to the exigency of the case, and therefore such want of due care became part of the plaintiff's case, and the burden of proof was on the plaintiff to establish it. 2 Greenl.Ev. § 85; [ ].

Perhaps the learned judge, by the use of the term extraordinary care, in the above charge, explained as it is by the context, may have intended nothing more than that increased degree of care and diligence, which the exigency of particular circumstances might require, and which men of ordinary care and prudence would use under like circumstances, to guard against danger. If such was the meaning of this part of the charge, then it does not differ from our views, as above explained. But we are of opinion, that the other part of the charge, that the burden of proof was on the defendant, was incorrect. Those facts which are essential to enable the plaintiff to recover, he takes the burden of proving. The evidence may be offered by the plaintiff or by the defendant; the question of due care, or want of care, may be essentially connected with the main facts, and arise from the same proof; but the effect of the rule, as to the burden of proof, is this, that when the proof is all in, and before the jury, from whatever side it comes, and whether directly proved, or inferred from circumstances, if it appears that the defendant was doing a lawful act, and unintentionally hit and hurt the plaintiff, then unless it also appears to the satisfaction of the jury, that the defendant is chargeable with some fault, negligence, carelessness, or want of prudence, the plaintiff fails to sustain the burden of proof, and is not entitled to recover.

New trial ordered.

NOTES AND QUESTIONS

1. How does Chief Justice Shaw resolve the issue of whether the preexisting common law recognized strict liability for unintended harm? Was plaintiff arguing for a strict liability standard? What might the trial court have intended by recognizing a distinct standard of care when defendant's conduct "was not a necessary act"?

2. Apart from the trial court's erroneous reference to necessary acts, how did the jury instruction misstate the law? What, precisely, were the unsettled questions before Brown v. Kendall that Shaw resolved in the opinion?

3. While Brown v. Kendall is generally regarded as a landmark opinion in establishing the fault principle, a handful of state courts had already reached the same conclusion with relatively little difficulty. See, e.g. Harvey v. Dunlop, Lalor Supp. to Hill & Dennis 193 (N.Y.1843), in which one child appears to have unintentionally put out the eye of another in a stone-throwing incident. The court concluded (at p. 194):

> No case or principle can be found, or if found can be maintained, subjecting an individual to liability for an act done without fault on his part. . . . All the cases concede that an injury arising from accident, or, which in law or reason is the same thing, from an act that ordinary human care and foresight are unable to guard against, is but the misfortune of the sufferer, and lays no foundation for legal responsibility.

4. Does Shaw indicate *why* the fault principle establishes the appropriate standard of liability? We have already given brief consideration to two scholarly efforts to justify liability based on negligence. Recall the excerpts from Holmes and Posner in Chapter I. Compare their positions with the following interpretation of Brown v. Kendall in Gregory, Trespass to Negligence to Absolute Liability, 37 Va.L.Rev. 359, 368 (1951):

> While it is pure speculation, one of Chief Justice Shaw's motives underlying his opinion appears to have been a desire to make risk-creating enterprise less hazardous to investors and entrepreneurs than it had been previously at common law. Certainly that interpretation is consistent with his having furthered the establishment of the fellow servant doctrine and the expansion of the assumption-of-risk defense in actions arising out of industrial injuries. Judicial subsidies of this sort to youthful enterprise removed pressure from the pocket-books of investors and gave incipient industry a chance to experiment on low-cost operations without the risk of losing its reserve in actions by injured employees. Such a policy no doubt seems ruthless; but in a small way it probably helped to establish industry, which in turn was essential to the good society as Shaw envisaged it.

Gregory's mention of the fellow servant doctrine refers to Shaw's famous opinion in Farwell v. Boston & Worcester Railroad Corp., 4 Metc. (45 Mass.) 49 (1842), in which an injured worker's suit against his employer was dismissed on the grounds that a master was not vicariously liable for injuries suffered because of a fellow worker's negligence. More broadly, under nineteenth century negligence law the carelessness of a fellow servant was one of many risks that an employee was taken to assume, and which prevented suit against the employer. See Friedman & Ladinsky, Social Change and the Law of Industrial Accidents, 67 Colum.L.Rev. 50 (1967).

Is Gregory's thesis distinctively different from the views of Holmes and Posner? In what sense could the fault principle be viewed as providing a "subsidy" to industry? Why should a dog-fight case involving two neighbors be regarded as relevant to protection of industrial enterprises, whatever Shaw might have decided in other cases? As you study the materials that follow, ask yourself what rationale for the fault principle seems most convincing. Is it likely that a single rationale will be applicable to every type of unintentional harm?

B.   THE CENTRAL CONCEPT

1.   THE STANDARD OF CARE

Until now, we have discussed fault liability without making any effort to give content to the central concept of negligence—apart from referring to it as "unreasonable" conduct. Although we have given brief consideration to moral and economic justifications for the fault principle, we have yet to examine how the system actually operates. What standard does a court utilize in deciding whether the defendant's behavior was "negligent"? We begin by exploring the concept of unreasonable risk.

Adams v. Bullock

Court of Appeals of New York, 1919.
227 N.Y. 208, 125 N.E. 93.

■ CARDOZO, J.   The defendant runs a trolley line in the city of Dunkirk, employing the overhead wire system. At one point, the road is crossed by a bridge or culvert which carries the tracks of the Nickle Plate and Pennsylvania railroads. Pedestrians often use the bridge as a short cut between streets, and children play on it. On April 21, 1916, the plaintiff, a boy of twelve years, came across the bridge, swinging a wire about eight feet long. In swinging it, he brought it in contact with the defendant's trolley wire, which ran beneath the structure. The side of the bridge was protected by a parapet eighteen inches wide. Four feet seven and three-fourths inches below the top of the parapet, the trolley wire was strung. The plaintiff was shocked and burned when the wires came together. He had a verdict at Trial Term, which has been affirmed at the Appellate Division by a divided court.

We think the verdict cannot stand. The defendant in using an overhead trolley was in the lawful exercise of its franchise. Negligence, therefore, cannot be imputed to it because it used that system and not another [   ]. There was, of course, a duty to adopt all reasonable precautions to minimize the resulting perils. We think there is no evidence that this duty was ignored. The trolley wire was so placed that no one standing on the bridge or even bending over the parapet could reach it. Only some extraordinary casualty, not fairly within the area of ordinary prevision, could make it a thing of danger. Reasonable care in the use of a destructive agency imports a high degree of vigilance (Nelson v. Branford L. & W. Co., 75 Conn. 548, 551; Braun v. Buffalo Gen. El. Co., 200 N.Y. 484). But no vigilance, however alert, unless fortified by the gift of prophecy, could have predicted the point upon the route where such an accident would occur. It might with equal reason have been expected anywhere else. At any point upon the route, a mischievous or thoughtless boy might touch the wire with a metal pole, or fling another wire across it [   ]. If unable to reach it from the walk, he might stand upon a wagon or climb upon a tree. No special danger at this bridge warned the defendant that there was need of special measures of precaution. No like accident had occurred before. No custom had been disregarded. We think that ordinary caution did not involve forethought of this extraordinary peril. It has been so ruled in like circumstances by courts in other jurisdictions. [ ] Nothing to the contrary was held in Braun v. Buffalo Gen. El. Co. (200 N.Y. 484) [ ]. In these cases, the accidents were well within the range of prudent foresight [ ]. That was also the basis of the ruling in Nelson v. Branford Lighting & Water Co. (75 Conn. 548, 551). There is, we may add, a distinction, not to be ignored, between electric light and trolley wires. The distinction is that the former may be insulated. Chance of harm, though remote, may betoken negligence, if needless. Facility of protection may impose a duty to protect. With trolley wires, the case is different. Insulation is impossible. Guards here and there are of little value. To avert the possibility of this accident and others like it at one point or another on the route, the defendant must have abandoned the overhead system, and put the wires underground. Neither its power nor its duty to make the change is shown. To hold it liable upon the facts exhibited in this record would be to charge it as an insurer.

The judgment should be reversed. . . .

■ HISCOCK, CH. J., CHASE, COLLIN, HOGAN, CRANE and ANDREWS, JJ., concur.

NOTES AND QUESTIONS

1. What negligence might the jury have found? That in turn will depend on how the trial proceeded and what evidence was introduced. Consider the following observation in Grady, Untaken Precautions, 18 J.Legal Studies 139 (1989):

> Events do not define what negligence analysis will be the case, and the court does not define it either. Instead, by selecting an untaken precaution on which to rely, the plaintiff defines the analysis that everyone else will use—including the defendant, the court that will try the case, and any court that may hear an appeal. . . . The plaintiff makes his choice from among a group of possible contenders and frequently alleges several untaken precautions in the alternative. . . .

What untaken precautions might have avoided the injury in *Adams*? What about insulating the wires? Building some sort of umbrella over the wires when they pass under bridges? Posting signs on the approaches to bridges, in language that children would understand, warning of the danger of twirling long wires? Are some of these more promising than others?

2. In the Braun case, cited by Judge Cardozo, defendant had strung electric wires some 25 feet above a vacant lot. The wires had been strung around 1890 with insulation that was expected to last three years. They were never inspected. Fifteen years later, a building was begun on the lot. When joists reached over 20 feet from the ground, it would be "natural for one desiring to go from one side of the building to the other to raise the wires so that he could pass under or bear down on them so that he could step over.'' The decedent, a carpenter, came in contact with the now-exposed wires and was electrocuted. After the lower courts dismissed the complaint, the court of appeals reversed and remanded for trial. Discussing negligence, the court observed:

> Little need or can be said about the condition of the wires, for if the respondent owed any obligation whatever of making them safe it would scarcely have been more negligent if, instead of allowing them to remain uninspected and unrepaired as it did, it had strung and maintained absolutely naked wires. The only question which is at all close is whether the respondent in the exercise of the reasonable care and foresight should have apprehended that the premises over which the wires were strung might be so used as to bring people in contact with them, and whether, therefore, it should have guarded against such a contingency. As indicated, I think this was fairly a question for the jury. Here was a vacant lot in the midst of a thickly built-up section of a large city. It was no remote or country lot where no buildings could be expected. The neighboring land was covered with buildings. It was the only vacant lot in the vicinity. It fronted on a street and there was plenty of space for a building. Now, what was reasonably to be anticipated—that this lot would be allowed indefinitely to lie unimproved and unproductive, or that it, like other surrounding lots, would be improved by additions to the old building or by the erection of new and independent ones? Was it to be anticipated that its use would be an exception to the rule prevailing in the entire neighborhood or that it would be in conformity therewith? It seems to me that the answer to these questions should have been made by the jury, and that the latter would be justified in saying that the respondent was bound to anticipate what was usual rather than that which was exceptional and act accordingly. It does not appear how much this neighborhood may have changed since the wires were first strung, but assuming that it had materially changed in respect of the use of lots for buildings, such a change in a neighborhood for aught that appears in this case requires some time, and as a basis for responsibility it is not too much to charge a company stringing such wires with notice of gradual changes in the locality through which the wires pass.

Is *Braun* distinguishable from *Adams?*

3. In Greene v. Sibley, Lindsay & Curr Co., 257 N.Y. 190, 177 N.E. 416 (1931), plaintiff was waiting for her change after making a purchase in defendant's store. She noticed, to her right, a mechanic and a floorwalker repairing a cash register. She turned left to get her change and then moved to her right and stumbled over the protruding foot of the mechanic who had just knelt to look at the underside of the register. Plaintiff testified that she had meant to go around the spot where she had seen the mechanic. Judge Cardozo, writing for the five-member majority, ruled that she had failed to establish negligence on the mechanic's part, despite a trial court judgment in her favor and an affirmance by the appellate division:

> Looking back at the mishap with the wisdom born of the event, we can see that the mechanic would have done better if he had given warning of the change of pose. Extraordinary prevision might have whispered to him at the moment that the warning would be helpful. What the law exacted of him, however, was only the ordinary prevision to be looked for in a busy world. He was doing a common and simple act in the plain sight of those around him. The act did not involve a continuing obstruction with the indefinite possibilities of mischief that permanence implies. [ ] It was a matter of minutes or perhaps seconds. A saleswoman who had knocked a package off a counter or a customer dropping a handbag or a glove might have done the same thing. If the kneeling mechanic gave any thought to the plaintiff standing at his side, he must have known that she had seen him at work upon his job. Was he to suppose that she would act as if he were still standing there erect when to his knowledge a mere glance would have told her something else?

How might the judge respond to the claim that a warning from the mechanic would have taken almost no effort? Why not call this a "needless" risk of harm created by the mechanic?

4. What result in Adams v. Bullock if the same thing had happened twice in recent years? How important is it that "no like accident had occurred before"?

5. How is the concept of "ordinary caution" or "reasonable care" referred to in *Adams* and the note cases, conveyed to the jury? Consider the following version recommended for use in California (BAJI 8th ed., 1994, § 3.10):

> Negligence is the doing of something which a reasonably prudent person would not do, or the failure to do something which a reasonably prudent person would do, under circumstances similar to those shown by the evidence.
>
> It is the failure to use ordinary or reasonable care.
>
> Ordinary or reasonable care is that care which persons of ordinary prudence would use in order to avoid injury to themselves or others under circumstances similar to those shown by the evidence.

Does this formulation capture the spirit of these cases?

The formulation suggests two questions that need to be pursued in greater detail. First, is the concept too general to be effectively used by courts and juries? Second, how do the courts construct the "reasonably prudent person" referred to in the charge? We turn to these questions in order.

First, is it feasible to establish a calculus of risk—a more structured approach to the due care inquiry? Consider the approach to defining unreasonable risk suggested by Judge Learned Hand in the following case.

United States v. Carroll Towing Co.

United States Court of Appeals, Second Circuit, 1947.
159 F.2d 169.

[The harbormaster and a deckhand aboard the Carroll, a tug, readjusted the lines holding fast the Anna C, a barge, in the course of their efforts to "drill out" another barge in New York Harbor. Because of their negligence in securing the Anna C, it later broke loose and rammed against a tanker, whose propeller broke a hole near the bottom of the barge. The Anna C soon filled with water and sank, with loss of cargo as well as the vessel itself. In this action for property loss, the question arose whether the damages should be reduced pursuant to admiralty law because the plaintiff's bargee was absent from the Anna C. The evidence indicated that siphoning efforts by other boats present in the area could have kept the barge afloat if the bargee had been aboard to sound a warning.]

■ Before L. Hand, Chase and Frank, Circuit Judges.

■ L. Hand, Circuit Judge.

. . .

It appears from the foregoing review that there is no general rule to determine when the absence of a bargee or other attendant will make the owner of the barge liable for injuries to other vessels if she breaks away from her moorings. . . . It becomes apparent why there can be no such general rule, when we consider the grounds for such a liability. Since there are occasions when every vessel will break from her moorings, and since, if she does, she becomes a menace to those about her, the owner's duty, as in other similar situations, to provide against resulting injuries is a function of three variables: (1) The probability that she will break away; (2) the gravity of the resulting injury, if she does; (3) the burden of adequate precautions. Possibly it serves to bring this notion into relief to state it in algebraic terms: if the probability be called P; the injury, L; and the burden, B; liability depends upon whether B is less than L multiplied by P: i.e., whether $B < PL$. Applied to the situation at bar, the likelihood that a barge will break from her fasts and the damage she will do, vary with the place and time; for example, if a storm threatens, the danger is greater; so it is, if she is in a crowded harbor where moored barges are constantly being shifted about. On the other hand, the barge must not be the bargee's prison, even though he lives aboard; he must go ashore at times. We need not say whether, even in such crowded waters as New York Harbor a bargee must be aboard at night at all, it may be that the custom is otherwise . . . and that, if so, the situation is one where custom should control. We leave that question open; but we hold that it is not in all cases a sufficient answer to a bargee's absence without excuse, during working hours, that he has properly made fast his barge to a pier, when he leaves her. In the case at bar the bargee left at five o'clock in the afternoon of January 3rd, and the flotilla broke away at about two o'clock in the afternoon of the following day, twenty-one hours afterwards. The bargee had been away all the time, and we hold that his fabricated story was affirmative evidence that he had no excuse for his absence. At the locus in quo—especially during the short January days and in the full tide of war activity—barges were being constantly "drilled" in and out. Certainly it was not beyond reasonable expectation that, with the inevitable haste and bustle, the work might not be done with adequate care. In such circumstances we hold—and it is all that we do hold—that it was a fair requirement that the Conners Company should have a bargee aboard (unless he had some excuse for his absence), during the working hours of daylight.

[The court affirmed the reduction of damages.]

NOTES AND QUESTIONS

1. Consider the following comments by Richard Posner on the *Carroll Towing* formula in A Theory of Negligence, 1 J.Legal Studies 29, 32–33 (1972):

> It is time to take a fresh look at the social function of liability for negligent acts. The essential clue, I believe, is provided by Judge Learned Hand's famous formulation of the negligence standard—one of the few attempts to give content to the deceptively simple concept of ordinary care. . . . [The formulation] never purported to be original but was an attempt to make explicit the standard that the courts had long applied. In a negligence case, Hand said, the judge (or jury) should attempt to measure three things: the magnitude of the loss if an accident occurs; the probability of the accident's occurring; and the burden of taking precautions that would avert it. If the product of the first two terms exceeds the burden of precautions, the failure to take those precautions is negligence. Hand was adumbrating, perhaps unwittingly, an economic meaning of negligence. Discounting (multiplying) the cost of an accident if it occurs by the probability of occurrence yields a measure of the economic benefit to be anticipated from incurring the costs necessary to prevent the accident. The cost of prevention is what Hand meant by the burden of taking precautions against the accident. It may be the cost of installing safety equipment or otherwise making the activity safer, or the benefit forgone by curtailing or eliminating the activity. If the cost of safety measures or of curtailment—whichever cost is lower—exceeds the benefit in accident avoidance to be gained by incurring that cost, society would be better off, in economic terms, to forgo accident prevention. A rule making the enterprise liable for the accidents that occur in such cases cannot be justified on the ground that it will induce the enterprise to increase the safety of its operations. When the cost of accidents is less than the cost of prevention, a rational profit-maximizing enterprise will pay tort judgments to the accident victims rather than incur the larger cost of avoiding liability. Furthermore, overall economic value or welfare would be diminished rather than increased by incurring a higher accident-prevention cost in order to avoid a lower accident cost. If, on the other hand, the benefits in accident avoidance exceed the

costs of prevention, society is better off if those costs are incurred and the accident averted, and so in this case the enterprise is made liable, in the expectation that self-interest will lead it to adopt the precautions in order to avoid a greater cost in tort judgments.

Is Posner correct in attributing a strictly economic definition of negligence to Hand? On this score, why does Hand consider it relevant that the bargee must be expected to go ashore at times? Why isn't the question simply how much it would cost the barge owner to hire a second-shift bargee? Similarly, why should the "customary" night-time hours of bargees be relevant? Again, isn't the cost of adequate precaution—hiring a night bargee—the only relevant consideration from an economic standpoint? The role of custom in negligence cases is considered in greater detail later in this Chapter.

2. Is the *Carroll Towing* formula useful in determining whether particular conduct is negligent? How would the formulation apply to *Adams?* To *Braun?* To *Greene?* Does *Greene* (the kneeling mechanic case) present distinct difficulties in applying the *Carroll Towing* formula because it involves a claim of careless *personal behavior,* rather than an allegation of unreasonable business judgment—as in the other cases? Is this a meaningful distinction? Which type of case is *Carroll Towing?* Even in a "business judgment" case such as *Adams,* how would Cardozo have responded to the argument that a warning notice on the bridge would have involved a trivial expense? Should a court assess the cost of such a warning—let alone the kneeling mechanic's "cost"—in purely economic terms? As far as the usefulness of the formula is concerned, does it make a difference that *Carroll Towing* involved property damage and all the other cases involved personal harm?

3. Note Posner's comment that the Hand test was not meant to state a new principle for deciding negligence cases. Compare Chicago, Burlington & Quincy R. Co. v. Krayenbuhl, 65 Neb. 889, 91 N.W. 880 (1902), in which a group of children were playing on the railroad's unlocked turntable. As other children were rotating the turntable, plaintiff's leg got caught and was severed. The court discussed due care in the following terms:

> The business of life is better carried forward by the use of dangerous machinery; hence the public good demands its use, although occasionally such use results in the loss of life or limb. It does so because the danger is insignificant, when weighed against the benefits resulting from the use of such machinery, and for the same reason demands its reasonable, most effective and unrestricted use, up to the point where the benefits resulting from such use no longer outweigh the danger to be anticipated from it. At that point the public good demands restrictions. For example, a turntable is a dangerous contrivance, which facilitates railroading; the general benefits resulting from its use outweigh the exceptional injuries inflicted by it: hence the public good demands its use. We may conceive of means by which it might be rendered absolutely safe, but such means would so inter-

fere with its beneficial use that the danger to be anticipated would not justify their adoption; therefore the public good demands its use without them.   But the danger incident to its use may be lessened by the use of a lock which would prevent children, attracted to it, from moving it;   the interference with the proper use of the turntable occasioned by the use of such a lock is so slight that it is outweighed by the danger to be anticipated from an omission to use it;   therefore the public good, we think, demands the use of the lock.

4.   In McCarty v. Pheasant Run, Inc., 826 F.2d 1554 (7th Cir.1987), plaintiff guest was assaulted in her room at defendant's resort by an intruder who entered by a sliding glass door.   The door, which opened onto a walkway, had not been locked but the security chain had been fastened. The plaintiff's theories of negligence included that the defendant should have made sure the door was locked before renting the room, or should have warned her to keep the door locked; or should have equipped the door with a better lock; or should have had more security guards on duty; or should have made the walkway inaccessible to the rooms; or some combination of these things.

After a jury verdict for defendant, plaintiff moved for judgment notwithstanding the verdict.   The trial court's denial of the motion was affirmed on appeal.   The court, in an opinion by Judge Posner, observed that:

> Ordinarily, and here, the parties do not give the jury the information required to quantify the variables that the Hand Formula picks out as relevant.   That is why the formula has greater analytic than operational significance.   Conceptual as well as practical difficulties in monetizing personal injuries may continue to frustrate efforts to measure expected accident costs with the precision that is possible, in principle at least, in measuring the other side of the equation—the cost or burden of precaution.   [   ]   For many years to come juries may be forced to make rough judgments of reasonableness, intuiting rather than measuring the factors in the Hand Formula; and so long as their judgment is reasonable, the trial judge has no right to set it aside, let alone substitute his own judgment.

Judge Posner recognized that innkeepers frequently know more about some dangers than do their guests and can take reasonable steps to reduce them while the guests can do little to protect themselves.   "Maybe this asymmetry in the parties' position should make the defendant's standard of care higher than it would be in, say, an ordinary collision case.   [   ]   But it does not make the defendant's liability strict.   In this case there was evidence of negligence but not so much as to establish liability as a matter of law or (the plaintiff's alternative argument) to require a new trial."

5.   Mark Grady has identified what he refers to as a pocket of strict liability within the negligence rule, based on the fact that "people face a cost of consistent performance that is higher than the sum of the cost of all individual trials."   He offers the following illustration:

It is impossible to drive a car for any period of time without missing a required precaution. There is evidently a special cost of consistent performance, and people respond to this cost by trying to establish for themselves an efficient rate of error which is (hopefully) low. Nevertheless, in most situations judges do not recognize the special cost of inconsistency. They assess a penalty for every miss, even for those that must be efficient judging from the way reasonable people behave.

Grady refers to this type of negligence, linked to the impossibility of driving—or engaging in any high-repetition precautionary behavior—without an occasional lapse as "compliance error," which he distinguishes from the Learned Hand formula negligence that tends to involve the quality of performance rather than high-repetition situations. Does the distinction make sense? Does it in fact appear to reflect a "pocket of strict liability" within the negligence concept? See Grady, Res Ipsa Loquitur and Compliance Error, 142 U.Pa.L.Rev. 887 (1994).

6. Why not charge the jury in Learned Hand terms? In Gilles, The Invisible Hand Formula, 80 Va.L.Rev. 1016 (1994), the author argues that the Hand formula is "to a significant extent, an unjustifiably underenforced norm," and suggests that the formula can be utilized—without the need for explicit reference—by "comparison between the value the average injurer would assign to precaution costs and the value the average victim would assign to the expected accident costs eliminated by the precaution. Because the average injurer and the average victim, taken together, constitute the average person, the inquiry reduces to whether the average person would take the precaution if he or she bore both the costs and benefits in full." Would this be a useful aid to jury decisionmaking?

7. Another perspective on defining reasonable care is suggested in the following excerpt from the concurring opinion of Lord Reid in Bolton v. Stone, [1951] A.C. 850, in which a member of a visiting team drove the ball out of the defendant's cricket field on to a relatively untravelled road that had a few houses on the far side. Plaintiff happened to be standing in that road near her house and was injured when the ball hit her. In 28 years six balls had been driven over the field's fence but no one had been hurt before. The House of Lords unanimously held that the risk was so small that the defendant club might reasonably disregard it. In his response to plaintiff's claim that at least after a ball had once gone over the fence defendants had a duty to prevent a recurrence, Lord Reid observed:

Once a ball has been driven on to a road without there being anything extraordinary to account for the fact, there is clearly a risk that another will follow, and if it does there is clearly a chance, small though it may be, that someone may be injured. On the theory that it is foreseeability alone that matters it would be irrelevant to consider how often a ball might be expected to land in the road and it would not matter whether the road was the busiest street, or the quietest country lane; the only difference between these cases is in the degree of risk.

It would take a good deal to make me believe that the law has departed so far from the standards which guide ordinary careful people in ordinary life. In the crowded conditions of modern life even the most careful person cannot avoid creating some risks and accepting others. What a man must not do, and what I think a careful man tries not to do, is to create a risk which is substantial. . . . In my judgment the test to be applied here is whether the risk of damage to a person on the road was so small that a reasonable man in the position of the appellants, considering the matter from the point of view of safety, would have thought it right to refrain from taking steps to prevent the danger.

In considering that matter I think that it would be right to take into account not only how remote is the chance that a person might be struck but also how serious the consequences are likely to be if a person is struck; but I do not think that it would be right to take into account the difficulty of remedial measures. If cricket cannot be played on a ground without creating a substantial risk, then it should not be played there at all.

Is Lord Reid's argument persuasive? Why isn't the risk a "needless" one as that term was used in *Adams?* On the other hand, why does he say that in cases of "substantial risk" it would not be "right to take into account the difficulty of remedial measures?" Is he suggesting that one who exposes another to a substantial risk is always negligent for doing so? Do either the Cardozo opinions or Judge Hand's formula suggest any such threshold of harm?

We turn now to the second matter noted above—the construction of the "reasonably prudent person."

2. THE REASONABLE PERSON

As the BAJI jury instruction, supra, indicated, courts traditionally have utilized a hypothetical person whose conduct is taken to measure what is reasonable under the circumstances. Consider the following description from 3 F. Harper, F. James, Jr. and O. Gray, The Law of Torts, pp. 389–90 (2d ed. 1986):

§ 16.2. General formula: Reasonable person; The external as against the subjective standard. We come next to inquire into the nature of the standard below which conduct must not fall if it is to avoid being negligence. This is ordinarily measured by what the reasonably prudent person would do in the circumstances. As everyone knows, this reasonable person is a creature of the law's imagination. He is an abstraction. He has long been the subject of homely phrase and witty epigram. He is no man who has ever lived and is not to be identified with any of the parties nor with any member of the jury. Greer, L.J., has described him as " 'the man in the street,' or 'the man in the Clapham omnibus,' or, as I recently read in an

American author, 'the man who takes the magazines at home, and in the evening pushes the lawn mower in his shirt sleeves.' "

Now this reasonably prudent person is not infallible or perfect. In foresight, caution, courage, judgment, self-control, altruism and the like he represents, and does not excel, the general average of the community. He is capable of making mistakes and errors of judgment, of being selfish, of being afraid—but only to the extent that any such shortcoming embodies the normal standard of community behavior. On the other hand the general practice of the community, in any given particular, does not necessarily reflect what is careful. The practice itself may be negligent. "Neglect of duty does not cease by repetition to be neglect of duty." Thus the standard represents the general level of moral judgment of the community, what it feels ought ordinarily to be done, and not necessarily what is ordinarily done, although in practice the two would very often come to the same thing.

Is "the general level of moral judgment of the community" necessarily the same as "the general average of the community"?

Would matters be helped if juries were guided in their task by a judge who required answers to specific questions rather than general verdicts? Consider Richard A. Posner, The Problems of Jurisprudence 209 (1990)(asserting that asking jurors to explain their verdicts "would be a source of profound embarrassment to the legal system").

As the section heading from Harper, James and Gray suggests, the authors subsequently discuss the question whether reasonable care should be based on an external standard or the defendant's own capacity for care. In fact, the reasonable care inquiry raises two threshold questions: first, whether the salient measuring stick of due care is the conduct or the state of mind of the defendant, and second—if defendant's conduct is the determining factor—whether it is to be measured against the defendant's own capacity or an external standard. Employing a reasonable person test suggests, of course, that defendant's conduct is the critical determinant, and that the conduct is to be measured against external, "objective" norms, rather than "subjective" ability. In adopting this two-fold external standard, the legal system adheres to a definition of "fault" that is arguably at odds with our everyday usage of the term. Is the approach justifiable? The following excerpt discusses this question.

The Common Law

O. W. Holmes.
108–110 (1881).

The standards of the law are standards of general application. The law takes no account of the infinite varieties of temperament, intellect, and education which make the internal character of a given act so different in different men. It does not attempt to see men as God sees them, for more than one sufficient reason. In the first place, the impossibility of nicely measuring a man's powers and limitations is far clearer than that of ascertaining his knowledge of law, which has been thought to account for what is called the presumption that every man knows the law. But a more satisfactory explanation is, that, when men live in society, a certain average of conduct, a sacrifice of individual peculiarities going beyond a certain point, is necessary to the general welfare. If, for instance, a man is born hasty and awkward, is always having accidents and hurting himself or his neighbors, no doubt his congenital defects will be allowed for in the courts of Heaven, but his slips are no less troublesome to his neighbors than if they sprang from guilty neglect. His neighbors accordingly require him, at his proper peril, to come up to their standard, and the courts which they establish decline to take his personal equation into account.

The rule that the law does, in general, determine liability by blameworthiness, is subject to the limitation that minute differences of character are not allowed for. The law considers, in other words, what would be blameworthy in the average man, the man of ordinary intelligence and prudence, and determines liability by that. If we fall below the level in those gifts, it is our misfortune; so much as that we must have at our peril, for the reasons just given. But he who is intelligent and prudent does not act at his peril, in theory of law. On the contrary, it is only when he fails to exercise the foresight of which he is capable, or exercises it with evil intent, that he is answerable for the consequences.

There are exceptions to the principle that every man is presumed to possess ordinary capacity to avoid harm to his neighbors, which illustrate the rule, and also the moral basis of liability in general. When a man has a distinct defect of such a nature that all can recognize it as making certain precautions impossible, he will not be held answerable for not taking them. A blind man is not required to see at his peril; and although he is, no doubt, bound to consider his infirmity in regulating his actions, yet if he properly finds himself in a certain situation, the neglect of precautions requiring eyesight would not prevent his recovering for an injury to himself, and, it may be presumed, would not make him liable for injuring another. So it is held that, in cases where he is the plaintiff, an infant of very tender years is only bound to take the precautions of which an infant is capable; the same principle may be cautiously applied where he is defendant. Insanity is a more difficult matter to deal with, and no general rule can be laid down about it. There is no doubt that in many cases a man may be insane, and yet perfectly capable of taking the precautions, and of being influenced by the motives, which the circumstances demand. But if insanity of a pronounced type exists, manifestly incapacitating the sufferer from complying with the rule which he has broken, good sense would require it to be admitted as an excuse.

Taking the qualification last established in connection with the general proposition previously laid down, it will now be assumed that, on the one hand, the law presumes or requires a man to possess ordinary capacity to avoid harming his neighbors, unless a clear and manifest incapacity be shown; but that, on the other, it does not in general hold him liable for unintentional injury, unless, possessing such capacity, he might and ought to have foreseen the danger, or, in other words, unless a man of ordinary intelligence and forethought would have been to blame for acting as he did. . . .

Notwithstanding the fact that the grounds of legal liability are moral to the extent above explained, it must be borne in mind that law only works within the sphere of the senses. If the external phenomena, the manifest acts and omissions, are such as it requires, it is wholly indifferent to the internal phenomena of conscience. A man may have as bad a heart as he chooses, if his conduct is within the rules. In other words, the standards of the law are external standards, and, however much it may take moral considerations into account, it does so only for the purpose of drawing a line between such bodily motions and rests as it permits, and such as it does not. What the law really forbids, and the only thing it forbids, is the act on the wrong side of the line, be that act blameworthy or otherwise. . . .

NOTES AND QUESTIONS

1. Is Holmes consistent in rejecting strict liability in favor of negligence, on the one hand, and holding injurers to an external standard of reasonable care, on the other? Why should the "hasty and awkward" be held to community standards of reasonable conduct?

2. In the leading case of Vaughan v. Menlove, 3 Bing.N.C. 468, 132 Eng.Rep. 490 (1837), the defendant landowner piled hay in a way that created a fire hazard to neighbors, including plaintiff. A fire occurred and plaintiff sued and won. Defendant's attorney sought a new trial on the ground that instead of charging the standard of ordinary prudence, the judge should have asked the jury to decide whether defendant had acted to the best of his judgment. He emphasized that the "measure of prudence varies so with the varying faculties of men" that it was impossible to say what was negligence "with reference to the standard of what is called ordinary prudence." Perhaps alluding delicately to his client's limitation, the attorney urged that if the defendant had acted to the best of his judgment "he ought not to be responsible for the misfortune of not possessing the highest order of intelligence." The court unanimously rejected the argument on the ground that "it would leave so vague a line as to afford no rule at all, the degree of judgment belonging to each individual being infinitely various."

Is the court's position persuasive? Should cases of distinctive physical handicap—such as blindness, the example used by Holmes—be measured by a standard that takes defendant's disability into account (presumably the reasonable blind person)? Is the problem of degree likely to be manageable in the physical handicap situation?

3. In Roberts v. Ramsbottom, [1980] 1 All E.R. 7 (Q.B.1979), the judge found that the 73–year-old defendant had had a stroke a few minutes before setting out on a drive; that he had had no previous warnings or symptoms; that though his consciousness was impaired he was in sufficient possession of his faculties "(i) to have some, though an impaired, awareness of his surroundings and the traffic conditions and (ii) to make a series of deliberate and voluntary though inefficient movements of his hands and legs to manipulate the controls of his car;" and that the defendant "was at no time aware of the fact that he was unfit to drive; accordingly no moral blame can be attached to him for continuing to do so." After reviewing the English case law, the judge concluded:

> The driver will escape liability if his actions at the relevant time were wholly beyond his control. The most obvious case is sudden unconsciousness. But if he retained some control, albeit imperfect control, and his driving, judged objectively, was below the required standard, he remains liable. His position is the same as a driver who is old or infirm. In my judgment unless the facts establish what the law recognizes as automatism the driver cannot avoid liability on the basis that owing to some malfunction of the brain his consciousness was impaired. Counsel for the plaintiff put the matter accurately, as I see it, when he said "One cannot accept as exculpation anything less than total loss of consciousness."

The judge also accepted the alternative ground of liability based on defendant's failure to realize, after one or two misadventures on the road, that he was unfit to continue driving that day. Had he recognized his condition, he would have stopped driving before he hit the plaintiff's car. Although not morally to blame for failing to realize his inadequacy, the defendant was nonetheless responsible for failing to "appreciate [the] proper significance" of his prior mishaps.

Is the suggestion that the reasonable person standard applies without considering the deficiencies of the elderly or those with relatively minor handicaps? Should it be otherwise?

4. What standard should be used to judge the defendant claiming diminished mental capacity? In Turner v. Caldwell, 36 Conn.Sup. 350, 421 A.2d 876 (1980), defendant motorist contended that "she was suddenly stricken by mental illness which she had no cause to anticipate, thereby rendering it impossible for her to control her vehicle." The court granted plaintiff's motion to strike the defense: "The majority rule . . . is that an insane person is liable for acts of negligence." One commonly accepted rationale is that "where two parties are involved in an accident, one being at fault and mentally ill, and the other being blameless and injured, public policy requires compensation to the faultless party by the culpable one. Another basis . . . is that mental illness, particularly that which is temporary, is difficult of proof and susceptible of being feigned." See Gould v. American Family Mut. Ins. Co., 543 N.W.2d 282 (Wis.1996) (Alzheimer's patient hurts nurse).

5. What standard should the law use in a case involving an unusually skilled, perceptive or prudent person? In Fredericks v. Castora, 241 Pa.Super. 211, 360 A.2d 696 (1976), the defendants were "professionals who drove trucks for a living and had done so for over 20 years." The court refused to hold the truck drivers to a higher standard of care than ordinary motorists:

> An understanding of the ordinary standard of due care applicable to the average motorist under the multitude of changing circumstances likely to confront today's driver is already difficult to grasp and apply justly. To begin to vary the standard according to the driver's experience would render the application of any reasonably uniform standard impossible.

Should the result change if the plaintiff can show that the truck drivers in question received special driver training before being put on the job? Or, is the fact that most adults in the community engage in driving dispositive? Consider that doctors, lawyers and a variety of other "professionals" are, in fact, held to standards of professional skill and capacity, rather than the ability of a reasonable lay person. We will consider the medical malpractice area in detail at p. 97, infra.

With *Fredericks,* compare Restatement (Second) of Torts § 298, Comment *d*:

> *Necessity That Actor Employ Competence Available.* The actor must utilize with reasonable attention and caution not only those qualities and facilities which as a reasonable man he is required to have, but also those superior qualities and facilities which he himself has. Thus a superior vision may enable the actor, if he pays reasonable attention, to perceive dangers which a man possessing only normal vision would not perceive, or his supernormal physical strength may enable him to avoid dangers which a man of normal strength could not avoid.

Is this consistent with Holmes's view? With *Fredericks?*

In connection with *Fredericks,* consider the following excerpt from Harper, James and Gray, § 16.3:

> The law here impinges on actual cases predominantly through the language of instructions to the jury, though it may also bear on the exclusion or admission of evidence, and sometimes leads to taking a case away from the jury. So far as the judge's charge is concerned, it may well be more a matter of finding a form of statement that will be upheld on appeal than a guide to what factors juries actually consider in determining the negligence issue. However objective the test laid down in the charge, the trial of an accident case always furnishes a host of indications as to the subjective factors (as to what kind of people the parties are) and it is hard indeed to believe that these do not weigh heavily with the jury (and for that matter, with the court). In actual practice the personal equation will be very much taken into account. Since appellate courts and lawyers, however, for purposes of appeal, analyze the language of the charge on the assumption that juries can and do follow it, we shall proceed on the same assumption to examine the rules that will be given the jury for determining the

extent to which they are to judge a party's conduct in the light of his own qualities on the one hand, or by applying the community standard on the other.

6. *Emergency situations.* In Rivera v. New York City Transit Authority, 77 N.Y.2d 322, 569 N.E.2d 432, 567 N.Y.S.2d 629 (1991), plaintiff's decedent fell onto a subway track and was killed by an oncoming train. Plaintiff claimed that the motorman of the train had sufficient time to bring the train to a halt after becoming aware of the fall. Plaintiff's judgment, affirmed by the Appellate Division, was reversed, 4–3, for failure to charge on the "emergency doctrine":

> This doctrine recognizes that when an actor is faced with a sudden and unexpected circumstance [due to no fault of the actor] which leaves little or no time for thought, deliberation or consideration, or causes the actor to be reasonably so disturbed that the actor must make a speedy decision without weighing alternative courses of conduct, the actor may not be negligent if the actions taken are reasonable and prudent in the emergency context. [ ] A person in such an emergency situation "cannot reasonably be held to the same accuracy of judgment or conduct as one who has had full opportunity to reflect, even though it later appears that the actor made the wrong decision."

The majority thought the state of the evidence warranted such a charge because of such matters as the motorman's concern for his passengers' safety if "the train were subjected to a sudden emergency stop." The dissenters, accepting the doctrine, thought that the defendant had claimed only that when the motorman saw the person fall it was already too late to avoid the harm. Under that view, there was no occasion to charge the emergency doctrine. What does the emergency doctrine add to the usual instructions that speak of the obligation to act reasonably under all the circumstances?

7. *Children.* A major modification of the concept of the reasonable person has involved children.* Traditionally, children have been held to the standard of conduct reasonable for persons of their actual age, intelligence, and experience. How might such a standard be applied to a child riding a bicycle or throwing a ball? How should we analyze a case involving a child who is unusually rash? Unusually dull? Unusually forgetful? Why should children be treated differently from adults in applying the standard of reasonableness?

In Mastland, Inc. v. Evans Furniture, Inc., 498 N.W.2d 682 (Iowa 1993), the court identified the following role for the jury in judging acts by children:

> [T]he jury's first inquiry is a subjective one: What was the capacity of this particular child—given what the evidence shows about

---

* Apart from statutes making parents liable for malicious mischief committed by their children (up to a usual limit of several hundred dollars), parents are rarely vicariously liable for torts of their children. Parents may, however, be liable for their own negligence in permitting a child to use a dangerous product or in failing to exercise control over a child whom they know or should know is dangerous to others.

his age, intelligence and experience—to perceive and avoid the particular risk involved in this case? Once this has been determined, the focus becomes objective: How would a reasonable child of like capacity have acted under similar circumstances? The particular child in question can be found negligent only if his actions fall short of what may reasonably be expected of children of similar capacity.

Is this an intelligible standard? The issue was to be taken from the jury "only if the child is so young or evidence of incapacity so overwhelming that reasonable minds could not differ on that issue." This was such a case because the child was under three years old.

In Ellis v. D'Angelo, 116 Cal.App.2d 310, 253 P.2d 675 (1953), a four-year-old boy was charged with negligently shoving a babysitter to the floor. The court stated that it was "satisfied from our own common knowledge of the mental development of 4–year–old children that it is proper to hold that they have not at that age developed the mental capacity for foreseeing the possibilities of their inadvertent conduct which would rationally support a finding that they were negligent." See also Smedley v. Piazzolla, 59 A.D.2d 940, 399 N.Y.S.2d 460 (1977)(child under four years of age could not have been negligent in getting behind the wheel of a car and either releasing the emergency brake or putting the car in gear). In Lester v. Sayles, 850 S.W.2d 858 (Mo.1993), a child 4 years 9 months old was held capable of contributory negligence.

A few states cling to conclusive presumptions based on age. In Price v. Kitsap Transit, 125 Wash.2d 456, 886 P.2d 556 (1994), for example, the question was whether a four-year-old who had pushed a button on the dashboard of a moving bus could be found negligent in a suit by an injured passenger. The court adhered to its "conclusive presumption" that children under the age of 6 could not be found negligent and rejected the view that it should be a case-by-case inquiry. Abolition of the conclusive presumption "would subject vulnerable and very young children to the awkward position of their own relatives attempting to prove their stupidity or lack of knowledge. Opening this issue to litigation would also create an evidentiary morass since the capacities of young children change rapidly and evidence could be unreliable."

Most courts that use conclusive presumptions do so for children under 7 and commonly also employ a rebuttable presumption that children between 7 and 14 are incapable of negligent behavior. See Pino v. Szuch, 185 W.Va. 476, 408 S.E.2d 55 (1991), in which the court required the defendant to show that the plaintiff "child's maturity, intelligence, experience, and judgmental capacity is significantly beyond that of the average eight-year-old" to overcome the presumption. "Merely showing that the child is a bright eight-year-old or does well in school does not rebut the presumption, and to hold otherwise would undercut its very foundation." Why?

When children engage in adult activities, courts have applied adult standards. In Dellwo v. Pearson, 259 Minn. 452, 107 N.W.2d 859 (1961), involving a twelve-year-old driving a motor boat, the court said:

While minors are entitled to be judged by standards commensurate with age, experience, and wisdom when engaged in activities appropriate to their age, experience, and wisdom, it would be unfair to the public to permit a minor in the operation of a motor vehicle to observe any other standards of care and conduct than those expected of all others. A person observing children at play with toys, throwing balls, operating tricycles or velocipedes, or engaged in other childhood activities may anticipate conduct that does not reach an adult standard of care or prudence. However, one cannot know whether the operator of an approaching automobile, airplane, or powerboat is a minor or an adult, and usually cannot protect himself against youthful imprudence even if warned. Accordingly, we hold that in the operation of an automobile, airplane, or powerboat, a minor is to be held to the same standard of care as an adult.

Is this sound? *Dellwo* has been especially influential in automobile cases.

In Goss v. Allen, 70 N.J. 442, 360 A.2d 388 (1976), a 17–year–old beginning skier, while attempting to negotiate a turn, collided with plaintiff. The trial judge charged that the defendant should be held to the care that a reasonably prudent person of 17 would have exercised under the same or similar circumstances. On appeal from a jury verdict and judgment for the defendant, the court held that skiing was an activity for persons of all ages and did not qualify as an activity for which minors should be held to an adult standard. The court thought that 18, the age of legal majority, was the appropriate age for holding persons to the adult standard. Although the difference between 17 and 18 was hard to define, the court recognized that no matter what age was selected for adult responsibility the line would seem arbitrary.

What about the fact that defendant was a beginner in Goss v. Allen? Should inexperienced persons, regardless of age, be held to a less demanding standard? Apart from other considerations, are the line-drawing problems insurmountable?

We turn now to a consideration of factors that sometimes circumscribe the role of juries in determining what constitutes due care. After an initial look at the interplay between judge and jury, we examine the roles of custom and statute.

C.   THE ROLES OF JUDGE AND JURY

1.   IN GENERAL

Baltimore & Ohio Railroad Co. v. Goodman

Supreme Court of the United States, 1927.
275 U.S. 66, 48 S.Ct. 24, 72 L.Ed. 167.

■ MR. JUSTICE HOLMES delivered the opinion of the Court.

This is a suit brought by the widow and administratrix of Nathan Goodman against the petitioner for causing his death by running him down at a grade crossing. The defense is that Goodman's own negligence caused the death. At the trial, the defendant asked the Court to direct a verdict for it, but the request, and others looking to the same direction, were refused, and the plaintiff got a verdict and a judgment which was affirmed by the Circuit Court of Appeals. 10 F.2d 58.

Goodman was driving an automobile truck in an easterly direction and was killed by a train running southwesterly across the road at a rate of not less than sixty miles an hour. The line was straight, but it is said by the respondent that Goodman "had no practical view" beyond a section house two hundred and forty-three feet north of the crossing until he was about twenty feet from the first rail, or, as the respondent argues, twelve feet from danger, and that then the engine was still obscured by the section house. He had been driving at the rate of ten or twelve miles an hour, but had cut down his rate to five or six miles at about forty feet from the crossing. It is thought that there was an emergency in which, so far as appears, Goodman did all that he could.

We do not go into further details as to Goodman's precise situation, beyond mentioning that it was daylight and that he was familiar with the crossing, for it appears to us plain that nothing is suggested by the evidence to relieve Goodman from responsibility for his own death. When a man goes upon a railroad track he knows that he goes to a place where he will be killed if a train comes upon him before he is clear of the track. He knows that he must stop for the train, not the train stop for him. In such circumstances it seems to us that if a driver cannot be sure otherwise whether a train is dangerously near he must stop and get out of his vehicle, although obviously he will not often be required to do more than to stop and look. It seems to us that if he relies upon not hearing the train or any signal and takes no further precaution he does so at his own risk. If at the last moment Goodman found himself in an emergency it was his own fault that he did not reduce his speed earlier or come to a stop. It is true as said in Flannelly v. Delaware & Hudson Co., 225 U.S. 597, 603, that the question of due care very generally is left to the jury. But we are dealing with a standard of conduct, and when the standard is clear it should be laid down once for all by the Courts. [   ]

Judgment reversed.

NOTES AND QUESTIONS

1. Under the *Goodman* view, when would plaintiffs win grade crossing cases?

2. Almost a half-century before *Goodman*, Holmes stated his position on the role of the jury in negligence cases in The Common Law (at pp. 123–24):

When a case arises in which the standard of conduct, pure and simple, is submitted to the jury, the explanation is plain. It is that the court, not entertaining any clear views of public policy applicable to the matter, derives the rule to be applied from daily experience, as it has been agreed that the great body of the law of tort has been derived. But the court further feels that it is not itself possessed of sufficient practical experience to lay down the rule intelligently. It conceives that twelve men taken from the practical part of the community can aid its judgment. Therefore it aids its conscience by taking the opinion of the jury.

But supposing a state of facts often repeated in practice, is it to be imagined that the court is to go on leaving the standard to the jury forever? Is it not manifest, on the contrary, that if the jury is, on the whole, as fair a tribunal as it is represented to be, the lesson which can be got from that source will be learned? Either the court will find that the fair teaching of experience is that the conduct complained of usually is or is not blameworthy, and therefore, unless explained, is or is not a ground of liability; or it will find the jury oscillating to and fro, and will see the necessity of making up its mind for itself. . . .

If this be the proper conclusion in plain cases, further consequences ensue. Facts do not often exactly repeat themselves in practice; but cases with comparatively small variations from each other do. A judge who has long sat at *nisi prius* ought gradually to acquire a fund of experience which enables him to represent the common sense of the community in ordinary instances far better than an average jury. He should be able to lead and to instruct them in detail, even where he thinks it desirable, on the whole, to take their opinion. Furthermore, the sphere in which he is able to rule without taking their opinion at all should be continually growing.

Do these arguments justify his position in *Goodman*?

Pokora v. Wabash Railway Co.

Supreme Court of the United States, 1934.
292 U.S. 98, 54 S.Ct. 580, 78 L.Ed. 1149.

[Pokora was driving his truck west across four tracks of defendant's railroad. The easternmost track was a switch track and the one next to that was the main track. A string of boxcars standing on the switch track 5–10 feet north of the crossing cut off plaintiff's view of the track north. As he moved past that track he listened but heard no bell or whistle. As he reached the main track he was struck by a train coming from the north at 25–30 miles per hour. The distance between the western rail of the switch track and the eastern rail of the main track was 8 feet, but 2–3 feet were lost to the overhang of the boxcars. Although there was no showing how far from the front of the truck Pokora was sitting, the opinion suggests "perhaps five feet or even more." Although a view 130 feet north may have been available from a nearby point, the opinion notes that this would not protect plaintiff if the train was 150 feet away when Pokora looked. "For all that appears, he had no view of the main track northward, or none for a substantial distance, till the train was so near that escape had been cut off." Relying on *Goodman,* the court of appeals had upheld a directed verdict for the railroad.]

■ MR. JUSTICE CARDOZO delivered the opinion of the Court.

. . .

In such circumstances the question, we think, was for the jury whether reasonable caution forbade his going forward in reliance on the sense of hearing, unaided by that of sight. No doubt it was his duty to look along the track from his seat, if looking would avail to warn him of the danger. This does not mean, however, that if vision was cut off by obstacles, there was negligence in going on, any more than there would have been in trusting to his ears if vision had been cut off by the darkness of the night. [ ] Pokora made his crossing in the day time, but like the traveler by night he used the faculties available to one in his position. [ ] A jury, but not the court, might say that with faculties thus limited, he should have found some other means of assuring himself of safety before venturing to cross. The crossing was a frequented highway in a populous city. Behind him was a line of other cars, making ready to follow him. To some extent, at least, there was assurance in the thought that the defendant would not run its train at such a time and place without sounding bell or whistle. . . .

The argument is made, however, that our decision in B. & O.R. Co. v. Goodman, supra, is a barrier in the plaintiff's path, irrespective of the conclusion that might commend itself if the question were at large. There is no doubt that the opinion in that case is correct in its result. Goodman, the driver, traveling only five or six miles an hour, had, before reaching the track, a clear space of eighteen feet within which the train was plainly visible.[2] With that opportunity, he fell short of the legal standard of duty established for a traveler when he failed to look and see. This was decisive of the case. But the court did not stop there. It added a remark, unnecessary upon the facts before it, which has been a fertile source of controversy. "In such circumstances it seems to us that if a driver cannot be sure otherwise whether a train is dangerously near he must stop and get out of his vehicle, although obviously he will not often be required to do more than to stop and look."

. . .

Standards of prudent conduct are declared at times by courts, but they are taken over from the facts of life. To get out of a vehicle and reconnoitre is an uncommon precaution, as everyday experience informs us. Besides being uncommon, it is very likely to be futile, and sometimes even dangerous. If the driver leaves his vehicle when he nears a cut or curve, he will learn nothing by getting out about the perils that lurk beyond. By the time he regains his seat and sets his car in motion, the hidden train may be

---

2. For a full statement of the facts, see the opinion of the Circuit Court of Appeals, 10 F.2d 58, 59.

upon him. [ ] Often the added safeguard will be dubious though the track happens to be straight, as it seems that this one was, at all events as far as the station, about five blocks to the north. A train traveling at a speed of thirty miles an hour will cover a quarter of a mile in the space of thirty seconds. It may thus emerge out of obscurity as the driver turns his back to regain the waiting car, and may then descend upon him suddenly when his car is on the track. Instead of helping himself by getting out, he might do better to press forward with all his faculties alert. So a train at a neighboring station, apparently at rest and harmless, may be transformed in a few seconds into an instrument of destruction. At times the course of safety may be different. One can figure to oneself a roadbed so level and unbroken that getting out will be a gain. Even then the balance of advantage depends on many circumstances and can be easily disturbed. Where was Pokora to leave his truck after getting out to reconnoitre? If he was to leave it on the switch, there was the possibility that the box cars would be shunted down upon him before he could regain his seat. The defendant did not show whether there was a locomotive at the forward end, or whether the cars were so few that a locomotive could be seen. If he was to leave his vehicle near the curb, there was even stronger reason to believe that the space to be covered in going back and forth would make his observations worthless. One must remember that while the traveler turns his eyes in one direction, a train or a loose engine may be approaching from the other.

Illustrations such as these bear witness to the need for caution in framing standards of behavior that amount to rules of law. The need is the more urgent when there is no background of experience out of which the standards have emerged. They are then, not the natural flowerings of behavior in its customary forms, but rules artificially developed, and imposed from without. Extraordinary situations may not wisely or fairly be subjected to tests or regulations that are fitting for the common-place or normal. In default of the guide of customary conduct, what is suitable for the traveler caught in a mesh where the ordinary safeguards fail him is for the judgment of a jury. [ ] The opinion in Goodman's case has been a source of confusion in the federal courts to the extent that it imposes a standard for application by the judge, and has had only wavering support in the courts of the states. We limit it accordingly.

The judgment should be reversed and the cause remanded for further proceedings in accordance with this opinion.

NOTES AND QUESTIONS

1. Under the *Pokora* view, is it ever proper to take cases from the jury on the issues of negligence and contributory negligence? Is Justice Cardozo's opinion consistent with his opinions in *Adams* and *Greene?*

2. Plaintiff was hit in the eye by a foul ball while watching a high school baseball game. Her suit against the school district, which owned the field, was dismissed, 4–3. Akins v. Glens Falls City School District, 53

N.Y.2d 325, 424 N.E.2d 531, 441 N.Y.S.2d 644 (1981). The majority observed that the field was equipped with a backstop 24 feet high and 50 feet wide located 60 feet behind home plate. Seats for 120 adults and standing room for others were behind the backstop. In addition, two chain link fences, three feet high, ran from each end of the backstop along the baselines to a point 60 feet behind first and third bases. Plaintiff, who arrived while the game was in progress, stood along the third base line, 10 to 15 feet past the end of the backstop. She was hit ten minutes after arriving.

The majority held that there was no basis for a jury to find defendant negligent. Although "what constitutes reasonable care under the circumstances ordinarily is a question for the jury," not every case was for the jury. On the record here, "the school district fulfilled its duty of reasonable care to plaintiff as a matter of law and, therefore, no question of negligence remained for the jury's consideration."

The dissenters argued that the majority had engaged in "an unfortunate exercise in judicial rule making in an area that should be left to the jury. This attempt to precisely prescribe what steps the proprietor of a baseball field must take to fulfill its duty of reasonable care is unwarranted and unwise." They found the majority's opinion "reminiscent" of the effort in *Goodman* to impose a specific duty on drivers at grade crossings:

> The wisdom of eschewing such blanket rules where negligence is concerned is obvious. In the present context, the majority has held as a matter of law that the proprietor of the baseball field has fulfilled his duty of reasonable care by erecting a backstop that was 24 feet high and 50 feet wide. The court issues this rule with no more expertise available to it than Justice Holmes had in 1927. . . . It has selected one of a variety of forms of protection currently in use . . . and has designated it as sufficient protection as a matter of law.

The dissent thought it "would make as much sense for the court to decree, as a matter of law, what sort of batting helmet or catcher's mask a school district should supply to its baseball team. Baseball . . . is hardly immune from technological change and shifts in public perception of what constitute reasonable safety measures. It has traditionally been the jury that reflects these shifts and changes."

3. Plaintiff was getting her hair bleached in defendant's hairdressing salon. During a break, while plaintiff had absorbent cotton in her hair, she lit a cigarette. The cotton caught fire and she was injured. Her suit claimed that the hairdresser should have warned her about the danger of smoking. The trial court entered judgment on a jury verdict for plaintiff. The appellate division unanimously reversed. The Court of Appeals, in turn, reversed, 4–3. The majority stated:

> It cannot be said, as a matter of law, that [the hairdresser] was not negligent in failing to warn the plaintiff of the dangers of smoking while she was undergoing the complicated hair treatment which he had applied. It was within the province of the jury to determine that he

had failed to act upon a risk which was foreseeable to him. As to contributory negligence, "it was also within the province of the jury, taking into account the positions of the respective parties, to determine that the risk was unforeseeable to her."

Heller v. Encore of Hicksville, Inc., 53 N.Y.2d 716, 421 N.E.2d 824, 439 N.Y.S.2d 332 (1981).

Does the fact that the judges disagree necessarily indicate, in itself, that a jury question exists? What about the fact that eight judges (five in the appellate division and three in the Court of Appeals) voted that no liability exists, while only five (the trial judge and four in the Court of Appeals) found a jury question?

If the jury had returned a verdict for the defendant which was upheld by the trial judge, what arguments would plaintiff have had to make on appeal?

4.   Although motions for summary judgment and for directed verdicts are usually made by defendants in negligence cases, plaintiffs occasionally make such motions. In Andre v. Pomeroy, 35 N.Y.2d 361, 320 N.E.2d 853, 362 N.Y.S.2d 131 (1974), plaintiff daughter was a passenger in a car driven by defendant mother. Defendant, who ran into the car in front of her, admitted that she was driving in heavy traffic, that she knew a car was in front of her, but that she nonetheless took her eyes off the road to look down into her purse. When she looked back at the road, she found that she was too close to the car in front, which had either stopped or slowed significantly, and she could not avoid it.

The court approved granting plaintiff summary judgment as to liability, 4–3. The majority indicated that plaintiffs are entitled to such relief "only in cases in which there is no conflict at all in the evidence [and] the defendant's conduct fell far below any permissible standard of due care. . . ."

When the negligence is so clear, why would plaintiff risk appeal and reversal of a motion for summary judgment instead of relying on the jury?

Andrews v. United Airlines, Inc.

United States Court of Appeals, Ninth Circuit, 1994.
24 F.3d 39.

■ Before: FLETCHER, KOZINSKI and TROTT, CIRCUIT JUDGES.

■ KOZINSKI, CIRCUIT JUDGE.

We are called upon to determine whether United Airlines took adequate measures to deal with that elementary notion of physics—what goes up, must come down. For, while the skies are friendly enough, the ground can be a mighty dangerous place when heavy objects tumble from overhead compartments.

I

During the mad scramble that usually follows hard upon an airplane's arrival at the gate, a briefcase fell from an overhead compartment and seriously injured plaintiff Billie Jean Andrews. No one knows who opened the compartment or what caused the briefcase to fall, and Andrews doesn't claim that airline personnel were involved in stowing the object or opening the bin. Her claim, rather, is that the injury was foreseeable and the airline didn't prevent it.

The district court dismissed the suit on summary judgment, and we review de novo. [ ] This is a diversity action brought in California, whose tort law applies. [ ]

II

The parties agree that United Airlines is a common carrier and as such "owe[s] both a duty of utmost care and the vigilance of a very cautious person towards [its] passengers." Acosta v. Southern Cal. Rapid Transit Dist., 2 Cal. 3d 19, 27 (1970); [ ]. Though United is "responsible for any, even the slightest, negligence and [is] required to do all that human care, vigilance, and foresight reasonably can do under all the circumstances," [ ], it is not an insurer of its passengers' safety, [ ]. "[T]he degree of care and diligence which [it] must exercise is only such as can reasonably be exercised consistent with the character and mode of conveyance adopted and the practical operation of [its] business. . . ." [ ]

To show that United did not satisfy its duty of care toward its passengers, Ms. Andrews presented the testimony of two witnesses. The first was Janice Northcott, United's Manager of Inflight Safety, who disclosed that in 1987 the airline had received 135 reports of items falling from overhead bins. As a result of these incidents, Ms. Northcott testified, United decided to add a warning to its arrival announcements, to wit, that items stored overhead might have shifted during flight and passengers should use caution in opening the bins. This announcement later became the industry standard.

Ms. Andrews's second witness was safety and human factors expert Dr. David Thompson, who testified that United's announcement was ineffective because passengers opening overhead bins couldn't see objects poised to fall until the bins were opened, by which time it was too late. Dr. Thompson also testified that United could have taken additional steps to prevent the hazard, such as retrofitting its overhead bins with baggage nets, as some airlines had already done, or by requiring passengers to store only light-weight items overhead [though—as the court noted in a footnote—Dr. Thompson "recognized that this was not a very practical solution from either the airlines' or the passengers' point of view"].

United argues that Andrews presented too little proof to satisfy her burden [ ]. One hundred thirty-five reported incidents, United points out, are trivial when spread over the millions of passengers travelling on its 175,000 flights every year. Even that number overstates the problem, according to United, because it includes events where passengers merely observed items falling from overhead bins but no one was struck or injured. Indeed, United sees the low incidence of injuries as incontrovertible proof that the safety measures suggested by plaintiff's expert would not merit the additional cost and inconvenience to airline passengers.

III

It is a close question, but we conclude that plaintiff has made a sufficient case to overcome summary judgment. United is hard-pressed to dispute that its passengers are subject to a hazard from objects falling out of overhead bins, considering the warning its flight crews give hundreds of times each day. The case then turns on whether the hazard is serious enough to warrant more than a warning. Given the heightened duty of a common carrier, [ ], even a small risk of serious injury to passengers may form the basis of liability if that risk could be eliminated "consistent with the character and mode of [airline travel] and the practical operation of [that] business. . . ." [ ] United has demonstrated neither that retrofitting overhead bins with netting (or other means) would be prohibitively expensive, nor that such steps would grossly interfere with the convenience of its passengers. Thus, a jury could find United has failed to do "all that human care, vigilance, and foresight reasonably can do under all the circumstances." [ ]

The reality, with which airline passengers are only too familiar, is that airline travel has changed significantly in recent years. As harried travelers try to avoid the agonizing ritual of checked baggage, they hand-carry more and larger items—computers, musical instruments, an occasional deceased relative. [ ] The airlines have coped with this trend, but perhaps not well enough. Given its awareness of the hazard, United may not have done everything technology permits and prudence dictates to eliminate it. See Treadwell v. Whittier, 80 Cal. 574, 600 (1889)("common carriers . . . must keep pace with science, art, and modern improvement"); Valente v. Sierra Ry., 151 Cal. 534, 543 (1907)(common carriers must use the best precautions in practical use "known to any company exercising the utmost care and diligence in keeping abreast with modern improvement in . . . such precautions").

Jurors, many of whom will have been airline passengers, will be well equipped to decide whether United had a duty to do more than warn passengers about the possibility of falling baggage. A reasonable jury might conclude United should have done more; it might also find that United did enough. Either decision would be rational on the record presented to the district court which, of course, means summary judgment was not appropriate.

Reversed and Remanded.

NOTES AND QUESTIONS

1. How would the analysis differ if an airline employee had stowed the bag in the compartment or had opened the compartment at the end of the trip? See Brosnahan v. Western Air Lines, Inc., 892 F.2d 730 (8th Cir.1989), holding that a jury might find airline personnel negligent in failing to adequately supervise the boarding process during which a passenger dropped his carry-on bag on another passenger's head while attempting to stow it in the overhead compartment. See also USAir, Inc. v. United States Dept. of the Navy, 14 F.3d 1410 (9th Cir.1994), holding that a passenger (and his employer) might be held liable for negligently stowing in the overhead compartment a briefcase that fell and hurt another passenger.

2. What is the significance of the fact that this case involves a common carrier? Note the varying phrasings of the duty of a common carrier. How does "any, even the slightest, negligence" differ from the general duty of due care? Can a jury distinguish a "reasonably cautious" person from a "very cautious" person?

Although many courts have articulated this higher obligation for carriers, some have expressed doubt. In McLean v. Triboro Coach Corp., 302 N.Y. 49, 96 N.E.2d 83 (1950), the court noted that given the usual definition of negligence as the failure to employ reasonable care under the circumstances, "it may well be asked whether it is ever practicable for one to use more care than one reasonably can; whether . . . in sum, there can ever be more than one degree of care."

Consider also Stewart v. Motts, 539 Pa. 596, 654 A.2d 535 (1995), involving an accident at an automobile repair shop. Plaintiff appealed an adverse jury verdict on the ground that since the case involved the handling of gasoline the judge should have told the jury that the defendants owed a "high degree of care." The court disagreed, and concluded that the state recognized "only one standard of care in negligence actions involving dangerous instrumentalities—the standard of reasonable care under the circumstances. It is well established by our case law that the reasonable man must exercise care in proportion to the danger involved in his act. [ ] Thus, when a reasonable man is presented with circumstances involving the use of dangerous instrumentalities, he must necessarily exercise a 'higher' degree of care proportionate to the danger." Since the trial judge had told the jury that the care required had to be "in keeping with the degree of danger involved," the charge given was adequate. Is "higher degree of care" as used by the court different from a "higher standard of care"?

On occasion, legislatures have enacted statutes using such terms as gross negligence, recklessness, or willfulness—and courts have occasionally developed such notions themselves. We consider these terms at p. 384, infra. Until then, we shall concern ourselves with the basic negligence formulation of reasonable care.

3. Why does the court demand that United demonstrate that "retrofitting overhead bins with netting . . . would be prohibitively expensive" or that such steps "would grossly interfere with the convenience of its passengers"? If we assume that 35 of the 135 incidents in 1987 involved no harm whatever and that the other 100 involved 60 bruised bodies, 30 broken bones and 10 serious brain damage cases, might that affect the analysis?

4. How would the case differ if the plaintiff's claim had been that the bottom part of the baggage compartment should have been made of transparent material?

5. One quoted passage demands that carriers "must keep pace with science, art, and modern improvement." How does that obligation differ from what is expected of any reasonable company? Another quotation states the duty in terms of what practical steps are "known to any company." Does that imply that if no company knew of a practical step to avoid the harm there would be no liability? These matters are addressed in the next section.

2. THE ROLE OF CUSTOM

Trimarco v. Klein

Court of Appeals of New York, 1982.
56 N.Y.2d 98, 436 N.E.2d 502, 451 N.Y.S.2d 52.

[Plaintiff tenant was very badly cut when he fell through the glass door that enclosed his tub in defendant's apartment building. The door turned out to be ordinary thin glass that looked the same as the tempered glass that plaintiff thought it was. The building had been built, and the shower installed, in 1953.

Plaintiff presented expert evidence that at least since the 1950s a practice of using shatterproof glass in bathroom enclosures had come into common use, so that by 1976, the date of the accident, "the glass door here no longer conformed to accepted safety standards." Defendant's managing agent admitted that at least since 1965, "it was customary for landlords who had occasion to install glass for shower enclosures, whether to replace broken glass or to comply with the request of a tenant or otherwise, to do so with 'some material such as plastic or safety glass.'"

The jury awarded plaintiff damages. A divided appellate division reversed the plaintiff's judgment on the ground that even if "there existed a custom and usage at the time to substitute shatterproof glass" and this was a "better way or a safer method of enclosing showers," no common-law duty devolved on the defendant to replace the glass unless prior notice of the danger came to the defendants either from the plaintiff or by reason of a similar accident in the building. Since plaintiff had made no such showing, the appellate division majority reversed and dismissed the case.

The dissenters observed that in the 1,000–page trial record there was ample showing that landlords generally had known of the danger of ordinary glass for more than ten years before this accident. The dissenters saw no need for specific notice to this landlord either by prior accident in the building or by personal request from the plaintiff.]

■ FUCHSBERG, JUDGE.

. . .

Which brings us to the well-recognized and pragmatic proposition that when "certain dangers have been removed by a customary way of doing things safely, this custom may be proved to show that [the one charged with the dereliction] has fallen below the required standard" (Garthe v. Ruppert, 264 N.Y. 290, 296). Such proof, of course, is not admitted in the abstract. It must bear on what is reasonable conduct under all the circumstances, the quintessential test of negligence.

It follows that, when proof of an accepted practice is accompanied by evidence that the defendant conformed to it, this may establish due care (Bennett v. Long Is. R.R. Co., 163 N.Y. 1, 4 [custom not to lock switch on temporary railroad siding during construction]), and, contrariwise, when proof of a customary practice is coupled with a showing that it was ignored and that this departure was a proximate cause of the accident, it may serve to establish liability (Levine v. Russell Blaine Co., 273 N.Y. 386, 389[custom to equip dumbwaiter with rope which does not splinter]). Put more conceptually, proof of a common practice aids in "formulat[ing] the general expectation of society as to how individuals will act in the course of their undertakings, and thus to guide the common sense or expert intuition of a jury or commission when called on to judge particular conduct under particular circumstances" (Pound, Administrative Application of Legal Standards, 44 ABA Rep. 445, 456–457).

The source of the probative power of proof of custom and usage is described differently by various authorities, but all agree on its potency. Chief among the rationales offered is, of course, the fact that it reflects the judgment and experience and conduct of many [ ]. Support for its relevancy and reliability comes too from the direct bearing it has on feasibility, for its focusing is on the practicality of a precaution in actual operation and the readiness with which it can be employed (Morris, Custom and Negligence, 42 Col.L.Rev. 1147, 1148). Following in the train of both of these boons is the custom's exemplification of the opportunities it provides to others to learn of the safe way, if that the customary one be. [ ].

From all this it is not to be assumed customary practice and usage need be universal. It suffices that it be fairly well defined and in the same calling or business so that "the actor may be charged with knowledge of it or negligent ignorance" [ ].

However, once its existence is credited, a common practice or usage is still not necessarily a conclusive or even a compelling test of negligence [ ]. Before it can be, the jury must be satisfied with its reasonableness, just as the jury must be satisfied with the reasonableness of the behavior which adhered to the custom or the unreasonableness of that which did not (see Shannahan v. Empire Eng. Corp., 204 N.Y. 543, 550). After all, customs and usages run the gamut of merit like everything else. That is why the question in each instance is whether it meets the test of reasonableness. As Holmes' now classic statement on this subject expresses it, "[w]hat usually is done may be evidence of what ought to be done, but what ought to be done is fixed by a standard of reasonable prudence, whether it usually is complied with or not" (Texas & Pacific Ry. Co. v. Behymer, 189 U.S. 468, 470).

So measured, the case the plaintiff presented . . . was enough to send it to the jury and to sustain the verdict reached. The expert testimony, the admissions of the defendant's manager, the data on which the professional and governmental bulletins were based, the evidence of how replacements were handled by at least the local building industry for the better part of two decades, these in the aggregate easily filled that bill. Moreover, it was also for the jury to decide whether, at the point in time when the accident occurred, the modest cost and ready availability of safety glass and the dynamics of the growing custom to use it for shower enclosures had transformed what once may have been considered a reasonably safe part of the apartment into one which, in the light of later developments, no longer could be so regarded.

Furthermore, the charge on this subject was correct. The Trial Judge placed the evidence of custom and usage "by others engaged in the same business" in proper perspective, when, among other things, he told the jury that the issue on which it was received was "the reasonableness of the defendant's conduct under all the circumstances". He also emphasized that the testimony on this score was not conclusive, not only by saying so but by explaining that "the mere fact that another person or landlord may have used a better or safer practice does not establish a standard" and that it was for the jurors "to determine whether or not the evidence in this case does establish a general custom or practice".

[The court reversed the dismissal but ordered a new trial because the trial judge had erroneously admitted certain evidence that had hurt the defense.]

■ CHIEF JUDGE COOKE and JUDGES JASEN, GABRIELLI, JONES, WACHTLER and MEYER concur.

NOTES AND QUESTIONS

1. How did the proof of custom affect the plaintiff's case in *Trimarco?*

2. Recall that in *Carroll Towing,* p. 35, supra, Judge Hand observed that it "may be that the custom" in New York Harbor was not to have bargees on board ships at night and that, if so it may be that "the situation is one where custom should control." Why might custom establish the standard of care? The court did not reach that question, but Judge Hand had stated the basic proposition about the role of custom in an earlier case, The T.J. Hooper, 60 F.2d 737 (2d Cir.), cert. denied 287 U.S. 662 (1932), in which a tug plying the Atlantic coast sank in a storm, causing the loss of barges it was towing and their cargoes. If the tug had had a radio it would have learned about the storm in time to avoid it. The tug owner sought to make the alleged lack of radios on most tugs the standard of care. Judge

Hand observed that some court pronouncements might be read to say that general practice sets the standard. He continued:

> Indeed in most cases reasonable prudence is in fact common prudence; but strictly it is never its measure; a whole calling may have unduly lagged in the adoption of new and available devices. It never may set its own tests, however persuasive be its usages. Courts must in the end say what is required; there are precautions so imperative that even their universal disregard will not excuse their omission. But here there was no custom at all as to receiving sets; some had them; some did not; the most that can be urged is that they had not yet become general. Certainly in such a case we need not pause; when some have thought a device necessary, at least we may say that they were right, and the others too slack.

Except in malpractice cases, courts have rejected the argument that a prevailing custom defines the standard of care. The malpractice situation is discussed at p. 97, infra.

3. Even if prevailing custom does not set the standard of care, adherence to, and deviation from, custom may be important in deciding whether the actor has behaved reasonably.

A defendant who can prove that it has adhered to a prevailing custom may eliminate what might otherwise be a jury question. In the classic article, Morris, Custom and Negligence, 42 Colum.L.Rev. 1147 (1942), the author suggested that such proof alerts the trial court to three main points. First, if an industry adheres to a single way of doing something, the court may be wary of plaintiff's assertion that there are safer ways to do that thing—and may insist that plaintiff clearly demonstrate the feasibility of the asserted alternative. Second, even if the plaintiff can show a feasible alternative, the fact that it may not have been in use anywhere may suggest that it was not unreasonable for the defendant to be unaware of the possibility. Third, the existence of a custom that involves large fixed costs may warn the court of the social impact of a jury or court decision that determines the custom to be unreasonable.

4. In LaVallee v. Vermont Motor Inns, Inc., 153 Vt. 80, 569 A.2d 1073 (1989), plaintiff guest fell in his room during a power outage at defendant's motel. He claimed that the motel was negligent in that it knew about past power failures, had flashlights at the front desk, had emergency lighting in the hallways, and that "inexpensive battery-powered lighting fixtures were available at the time of the accident and could have been installed in the motel rooms. The trial court concluded that this evidence, even if true, was insufficient as a matter of law to show that the motel owner had failed to exercise ordinary care to the plaintiff." The grant of a directed verdict was upheld on appeal. Even though power failures had occurred in the past, no guest had been hurt during an outage. The defendant's general manager had testified, without contradiction, that in his ten years in the industry "I've never seen emergency lighting in a motel room." The court's total discussion of custom was as follows:

> In [directing a verdict] the trial court appropriately considered evidence of the motel industry's practice and custom [ ], noting that no witness knew of any motel or hotel that provided the sort of emergency

lighting that plaintiff claims defendant had a duty to provide. . . . While industry custom is not conclusive in any given case, it is a useful guide, unless it is apparent that under the particular circumstances of the case a reasonable person would not conform to the industry-wide custom.

What if the cost were $1 per unit?

5. On the other hand, as Professor Morris pointed out, a plaintiff will find it useful to prove that the defendant fell below the industry custom because it tends to show that others, usually competitors, found it feasible to do something in a safer manner than did the defendant; that the defendant had ample opportunity to learn about the alternative; and that no great social upheaval will follow a judicial determination that the defendant's failure to follow custom was negligence.

In Levine v. Russell Blaine Co., cited in *Trimarco,* plaintiff cut her hand on a rough rope while operating a dumbwaiter. Infection led to amputation of her arm. She sought to show that the defendant building owner had failed to follow the custom of using smooth ropes in dumbwaiters. The court held that if plaintiff could show that the purpose of the customary use of smooth rope was to avoid such injuries, the evidence of custom was admissible.

6. Note that the plaintiff can achieve some of these goals simply by proving that others in the industry, although not establishing a custom, have developed safer techniques than did defendant. In Garthe v. Ruppert, cited in *Trimarco*, plaintiff slipped on a wet brewery floor. In an effort to show that it was feasible to keep the floors dry, plaintiff sought to show that, although most breweries had slippery floors, one local brewery had a technique that kept floors from getting slippery. The court held that such evidence was inadmissible because it had never "been permitted to take one or two instances as a gauge or guide in place of the custom of the trade." But this evidence might have been relevant if the defendant had tried to argue that it had no way of learning about the techniques that plaintiff claimed it should have used.

In *Andrews*, p. 54, supra, plaintiff's evidence showed that British Airways had begun using restraining netting the year before plaintiff was hurt. What is the significance of the fact that one other airline used baggage nets? Would the plaintiff necessarily have lost if she had been hurt the month before British Airways began using the baggage nets—even if she had proven that such nets were economically and technically feasible? How might the analysis have changed if the plaintiff had proven that more than two thirds of all American carriers used baggage nets at the time of the accident?

7. Should evidence of deviation from custom be usable against a company that is barely profitable—and which would have been unable to continue operations had it made the expenditures necessary to bring it into conformity?

If the larger members of an industry follow a custom, should evidence be admitted showing that smaller companies engaged in the same line of business deviate from that custom? One example might be the different techniques for eliminating flour dust from large and small bakeries.

3.   THE ROLE OF STATUTES

Martin v. Herzog

Court of Appeals of New York, 1920.
228 N.Y. 164, 126 N.E. 814.

■ CARDOZO, J.   The action is one to recover damages for injuries resulting in death.

Plaintiff and her husband, while driving toward Tarrytown in a buggy on the night of August 21, 1915, were struck by the defendant's automobile coming in the opposite direction. They were thrown to the ground, and the man was killed. At the point of the collision the highway makes a curve. The car was rounding the curve when suddenly it came upon the buggy, emerging, the defendant tells us, from the gloom. Negligence is charged against the defendant, the driver of the car, in that he did not keep to the right of the center of the highway (Highway Law, sec. 286, subd. 3; sec. 332; Consol.Laws, ch. 25). Negligence is charged against the plaintiff's intestate, the driver of the wagon, in that he was traveling without lights (Highway Law, sec. 329a, as amended by L.1915, ch. 367). There is no evidence that the defendant was moving at an excessive speed. There is none of any defect in the equipment of his car. The beam of light from his lamps pointed to the right as the wheels of his car turned along the curve toward the left; and looking in the direction of the plaintiff's approach, he was peering into the shadow. The case against him must stand therefore, if at all, upon the divergence of his course from the center of the highway. The jury found him delinquent and his victim blameless. The Appellate Division reversed, and ordered a new trial.

We agree with the Appellate Division that the charge to the jury was erroneous and misleading. The case was tried on the assumption that the hour had arrived when lights were due. It was argued on the same assumption in this court. In such circumstances, it is not important whether the hour might have been made a question for the jury [ ]. A controversy put out of the case by the parties is not to be put into it by us. We say this by way of preface to our review of the contested rulings. In the body of the charge the trial judge said that the jury could consider the absence of light "in determining whether the plaintiff's intestate was guilty of contributory negligence in failing to have a light upon the buggy as provided by law. I do not mean to say that the absence of light necessarily makes him negligent, but it is a fact for your consideration." The defendant requested a ruling that the absence of a light on the plaintiff's vehicle was *"prima facie* evidence of contributory negligence." This request was refused, and the jury were again instructed that they might consider the absence of lights as some evidence of negligence, but that it was not conclusive evidence. The plaintiff then requested a charge that "the fact that the plaintiff's intestate was driving without a light is not negligence in itself," and to this the court acceded. The defendant saved his rights by appropriate exceptions.

We think the unexcused omission of the statutory signals is more than some evidence of negligence. It *is* negligence in itself. Lights are intended for the guidance and protection of other travelers on the highway (Highway Law, sec. 329a). By the very terms of the hypothesis, to omit, willfully or heedlessly, the safeguards prescribed by law for the benefit of another that he may be preserved in life or limb, is to fall short of the standard of diligence to which those who live in organized society are under a duty to conform. That, we think, is now the established rule in this state. [ ]Whether the omission of an absolute duty, not willfully or heedlessly, but through unavoidable accident, is also to be characterized as negligence, is a question of nomenclature into which we need not enter, for it does not touch the case before us. There may be times, when if jural niceties are to be preserved, the two wrongs, negligence and breach of statutory duty, must be kept distinct in speech and thought [ ]. In the conditions here present they come together and coalesce. . . . In the case at hand, we have an instance of the admitted violation of a statute intended for the protection of travelers on the highway, of whom the defendant at the time was one. Yet the jurors were instructed in effect that they were at liberty in their discretion to treat the omission of lights either as innocent or as culpable. They were allowed to "consider the default as lightly or gravely" as they would (Thomas, J., in the court below). They might as well have been told that they could use a like discretion in holding a master at fault for the omission of a safety appliance prescribed by positive law for the protection of a workman [ ]. Jurors have no dispensing power by which they may relax the duty that one traveler on the highway owes under the statute to another. It is error to tell them that they have. The omission of these lights was a wrong, and being wholly unexcused was also a negligent wrong. No license should have been conceded to the triers of the facts to find it anything else.

[At this point Judge Cardozo concluded that the jury could well have found that the absence of the light was causally related to the accident. This portion of the case is reprinted at p. 310, infra.]

We are persuaded that the tendency of the charge and of all the rulings following it, was to minimize unduly, in the minds of the triers of the facts, the gravity of the decedent's fault. Errors may not be ignored as unsubstantial when they tend to such an outcome. A statute designed for the protection of human life is not to be brushed aside as a form of words, its commands reduced to the level of cautions, and the duty to obey attenuated into an option to conform.

The order of the Appellate Division should be affirmed, and judgment absolute directed on the stipulation in favor of the defendant, with costs in all courts.

■ HISCOCK, CH. J., POUND, MCLAUGHLIN, ANDREWS and ELKUS, JJ., concur with CARDOZO, J.; HOGAN, J., reads dissenting opinion [in which he viewed the record as indicating no causal relation between the plaintiff's violation and the crash.—Eds.]

NOTES AND QUESTIONS

1. Plaintiff's stipulation for judgment absolute, mentioned in the final paragraph, meant that if the appellate court found that the plaintiff's judgment could not be reinstated she would not pursue the case. Plaintiff stipulated this to avoid the provision that the court of appeals reviewed only final judgments, making it possible to get a definitive ruling on the critical issue without first having another trial and appeal.

2. On the question of the husband's negligence what did the trial judge charge? What did the defendant ask the trial judge to charge? What does Judge Cardozo say the trial judge should have charged? What distinguishes these formulations? What are the respective roles of the judge and the jury under each view?

3. What kind of penalties do you think the legislature provided for crossing the center line and traveling without lights after dark? Should it matter whether they linked the violation of such requirements to civil liability in personal injury cases? If the legislature failed to do so, why does the court get involved with these statutes at all?

4. In Clinkscales v. Carver, 22 Cal.2d 72, 136 P.2d 777 (1943), defendant ran a stop sign and crashed into plaintiff. The stop sign had been erected under an ordinance that had never become effective because it had not been properly published, which meant that defendant could not be punished criminally for his action. He argued that this made it improper for the trial judge to use the ordinance in his charge. Justice Traynor, writing for the majority, upheld the charge and the plaintiff's judgment:

> Whatever the effect of the irregularity on defendant's criminal liability, it cannot be assumed that the conditions that limit it also limit civil liability. The propriety of taking from the jury the determination of negligence does not turn on defendant's criminal liability. A statute that provides for a criminal proceeding only does not create a civil liability; if there is no provision for a remedy by civil action to persons injured by a breach of the statute it is because the Legislature did not contemplate one. A suit for damages is based on the theory that the conduct inflicting the injuries is a common-law tort. . . . The decision as to what the civil standard should be still rests with the court, and the standard formulated by a legislative body in a police regulation or criminal statute becomes the standard to determine civil liability only because the court accepts it. In the absence of such a standard the case goes to the jury, which must determine whether the defendant has acted as a reasonably prudent man would act in similar circumstances. The jury then has the burden of deciding not only what the facts are but what the unformulated standard is of reasonable

conduct. When a legislative body has generalized a standard from the experience of the community and prohibits conduct that is likely to cause harm, the court accepts the formulated standards and applies them [   ] except where they would serve to impose liability without fault. [   ]

Is this consistent with Martin v. Herzog?

5. Section 286 of the Second Restatement provides:

The court may adopt as the standard of conduct of a reasonable man the requirements of a legislative enactment or an administrative regulation whose purpose is found to be exclusively or in part (a) to protect a class of persons which includes the one whose interest is invaded, and (b) to protect the particular interest which is being invaded, and (c) to protect that interest against the kind of harm which has resulted, and (d) to protect that interest against the particular hazard from which the harm results.

In Sweet v. Sisters of Providence in Washington, 895 P.2d 484 (Alaska 1995), the court noted that even if the criteria of § 286 are met, the trial judge "retains discretion to refuse to adopt the law as the standard of care. [   ] For example, rejection of the legislative enactment is appropriate when the law is so obscure, unknown, outdated, or arbitrary as to make its adoption as a standard of reasonable care inequitable." Why should this be so? Is it consistent with *Martin*?

Tedla v. Ellman

Court of Appeals of New York, 1939.
280 N.Y. 124, 19 N.E.2d 987.

[Two junk collectors, brother and sister, were walking eastward along Sunrise Highway, a major route connecting New York City and Long Island. There were no sidewalks and they could not use the grass center strip because they were transporting junk in baby carriages that would have gotten mired in the soft ground. A 1933 statute provided:

Pedestrians walking or remaining on the paved portion, or traveled part of a roadway shall be subject to, and comply with, the rules governing vehicles, with respect to meeting and turning out, except that such pedestrians shall keep to the left of the center line thereof, and turn to their left instead of right side thereof, so as to permit all vehicles passing them in either direction to pass on their right. Such pedestrians shall not be subject to the rules governing vehicles as to giving signals.

It was Sunday night and "very heavy traffic" was heading westbound back to New York City but there were "very few cars going east." The two were walking eastward on the edge of the eastbound lane when they were hit from behind by defendant's car. The trial judge entered judgment on a plaintiffs' verdict and the appellate division affirmed. On this appeal the defendant does not contest his negligence, but argues that both pedestrians were contributorily negligent as a matter of law.]

■ LEHMAN, J.

. . .

. . . The appellants lean heavily upon [Martin v. Herzog] and kindred cases and the principle established by them.

The analogy is, however, incomplete. The "established rule" should not be weakened either by subtle distinctions or by extension beyond its letter or spirit into a field where "by the very terms of the hypothesis" it can have no proper application. At times the indefinite and flexible standard of care of the traditional reasonably prudent man may be, in the opinion of the Legislature, an insufficient measure of the care which should be exercised to guard against a recognized danger; at times, the duty, imposed by custom, that no man shall use what is his to the harm of others provides insufficient safeguard for the preservation of the life or limb or property of others. Then the Legislature may by statute prescribe additional safeguards and may define duty and standard of care in rigid terms; and when the Legislature has spoken, the standard of the care required is no longer what the reasonably prudent man would do under the circumstances but what the Legislature has commanded. That is the rule established by the courts and "by the very terms of the hypothesis" the rule applies where the Legislature has prescribed safeguards "for the benefit of another that he may be preserved in life or limb." In that field debate as to whether the safeguards so prescribed are reasonably necessary is ended by the legislative fiat. Obedience to that fiat cannot add to the danger, even assuming that the prescribed safeguards are not reasonably necessary and where the legislative anticipation of dangers is realized and harm results through heedless or willful omission of the prescribed safeguard, injury flows from wrong and the wrongdoer is properly held responsible for the consequent damages.

The statute upon which the defendants rely is of different character. It does not prescribe additional safeguards which pedestrians must provide for the preservation of the life or limb or property of others, or even of themselves, nor does it impose upon pedestrians a higher standard of care. What the statute does provide is rules of the road to be observed by pedestrians and by vehicles, so that all those who use the road may know how they and others should proceed, at least under usual circumstances. A general rule of conduct—and, specifically, a rule of the road—may accomplish its intended purpose under usual conditions, but, when the unusual occurs, strict observance may defeat the purpose of the rule and produce catastrophic results.

Negligence is failure to exercise the care required by law. Where a statute defines the standard of care and the safeguards required to meet a recognized danger, then, as we have said, no other measure may be applied in determining whether a person has carried out the duty of care imposed by law. Failure to observe the standard imposed by statute is negligence, as matter of law. On the other hand, where a statutory general rule of conduct fixes no definite standard of care which would under all circumstances tend to protect life, limb or property, but merely codifies or supplements a common-law rule which has always been subject to limitations and exceptions; or where the statutory rule of conduct regulates conflicting rights and obligations in a manner calculated to promote public convenience and safety, then the statute, in the absence of clear language to the contrary, should not be construed as intended to wipe out the limitations and exceptions which judicial decisions have attached to the common-law duty; nor should it be construed as an inflexible command that the general rule of conduct intended to prevent accidents must be followed even under conditions when observance might cause accidents. We may assume reasonably that the Legislature directed pedestrians to keep to the left of the center of the road because that would cause them to face traffic approaching in that lane and would enable them to care for their own safety better than if the traffic approached them from the rear. We cannot assume reasonably that the Legislature intended that a statute enacted for the preservation of the life and limb of pedestrians must be observed when observance would subject them to more imminent danger.

.   .   .

Even under that construction of the statute, a pedestrian is, of course, at fault if he fails without good reason to observe the statutory rule of conduct. The general duty is established by the statute, and deviation from it without good cause is a wrong and the wrongdoer is responsible for the damages resulting from his wrong. [   ]

.   .   .

In each action, the judgment should be affirmed, with costs.

■ CRANE, CH. J., HUBBS, LOUGHRAN and RIPPEY, JJ., concur; O'BRIEN and FINCH, JJ., dissent on the authority of Martin v. Herzog (228 N.Y. 164).

NOTES AND QUESTIONS

1. How does Judge Lehman distinguish Martin v. Herzog? Would his analysis be compromised if in a criminal proceeding against the two pedestrians, the court were to construe the statute as categorical and therefore find them guilty?

2. Might this be a situation in which "the two wrongs, negligence and breach of statutory duty, must be kept distinct in speech and thought"?

3. In Bassey v. Mistrough, 88 App.Div.2d 894, 450 N.Y.S.2d 604 (1982), a vehicle "came to a stop partially on the highway, and the entire electrical system of the car failed to function." While plaintiff was standing in front of his car searching for the source of the electrical trouble, his car was hit from behind and he was hurt. The judge read the jury the statute requiring the illumination of vehicles on the highway. He refused a request to tell the jury about the possibility of an excuse. Judgment was entered on a jury verdict for the defendant. On appeal, the court reversed.

The jury should have been advised that if they found plaintiff "unable to avoid temporarily leaving his stalled, unlighted vehicle on the highway" the violation would be excused.

What if a driver testified that the car's lights failed ten minutes earlier but that the driver continued on while looking for a store to buy a replacement switch and had not passed one? What if plaintiff testified that although the lights failed ten minutes earlier the driver continued on and passed a store with the needed switch in order to take a child to the hospital for emergency treatment? Is there a difference between the type of excuse that Tedla offered and an excuse by the plaintiff in *Martin* that the light had just gone out?

4.   In Bauman v. Crawford, 104 Wash.2d 241, 704 P.2d 1181 (1985), a 14–year–old boy, riding his bicycle after dark without reflectors in violation of the Seattle Municipal Code, was involved in an accident. The boy argued that the common law rules of the negligence of children should apply. The trial judge charged the state's usual negligence per se rules. The supreme court noted the conflict between negligence per se and the special child's standard of care. It resolved the conflict by concluding that a child's relevant statutory violations may be presented to the jury. The jury must then be instructed that the violations "may be considered as evidence of negligence only if the jury finds that a reasonable child of the same age, intelligence, maturity and experience as [this child] would not have acted in violation of the statute under the same circumstances."

Three concurrers used the occasion to urge that the court reexamine the entire doctrine of negligence per se. "Perhaps it is time we stopped selectively placing the negligence question within 'rational judicial control' and place it, in all cases, in the rational control of the trier of fact, where it belongs."

5.   Tedla's brother, Bachek, was deaf. If he had been walking alone might the case have been different?

6.   In Casey v. Russell, 138 Cal.App.3d 379, 188 Cal.Rptr. 18 (1982), two cars collided head-on as they came around a curve on a narrow winding mountain dirt road. Plaintiff passenger in one of the cars sued both drivers, claiming that the drivers had violated a statute that said to stay to the right of the middle, or a statute that said to blow horns on blind curves where the road is too narrow for two cars to pass. The judge told the jury to find that a violation of either statute was negligence unless the apparent violator "proves by a preponderance of the evidence that he did what might reasonably be expected of a person of ordinary prudence, acting under similar circumstances, who desired to comply with the law." The jury returned a verdict for both defendants.

On appeal, the court rejected the charge because it did "not adequately convey that there must be some special circumstances which justify violating the statute. The phrase 'who desired to comply with the law' does not mean one who in general is a law-abiding person, but rather refers to one who, although he desired to comply with the particular statute in issue, was faced with other circumstances which prevented compliance or justified noncompliance." Some examples included the "driver who inspected the tail light and found it in good order a short time before it went out;" a heavy blizzard that prevents a railroad from meeting its statutory duty to keep fences clear of snow; and a driver confronted with an emergency not due to his own misconduct—such as the need to swerve into a lane of oncoming traffic to avoid a child "suddenly darting into the road."

In cases in which excuses are offered for violations of the literal terms of criminal statutes, what should be the respective functions of judge and jury in deciding the validity of these excuses?

7. Consider the potential interplay between the role of custom and statutory violations. In Robinson v. District of Columbia, 580 A.2d 1255 (D.C.App.1990), plaintiff, who had been hit by a police van, was held contributorily negligent for violating a traffic regulation by crossing the street outside of a marked cross walk. She argued that her behavior was reasonable because it was "the common practice of pedestrians at the location of the accident." The court disagreed: there was no basis to "excuse violations of the law where such violations are common practice."

In Langner v. Caviness, 238 Iowa 774, 28 N.W.2d 421 (1947), at a narrow point on a construction road, defendant truck driver travelling downhill with a full load collided with plaintiff's empty truck going uphill. The defendants admitted that their statutory violation could not be justified by a trucking custom calling for uphill trucks to yield in that situation. But they successfully argued that the custom might be used to find plaintiff contributorily negligent even though he had the statutory right of way. The court noted that a motorist who complies with a statute is not necessarily exercising due care because statutes generally prescribe only the minimum of prudent conduct. If it could be shown that plaintiff knew or should have known of the custom here, a jury could find his failure to yield could be found negligent "not because of any statute but by reason of his obligation to use due care."

8. *Statutory Purpose.* Courts have long been unwilling to use statutory violations in cases in which the harm that occurred was different from the harm that the legislature apparently was seeking to prevent.

In Platz v. City of Cohoes, 89 N.Y. 219 (1882), an obstruction in the road, negligently left by the city, led to plaintiffs' injuries while they were violating a statute by riding on Sunday. The only defense was that the plaintiffs would not have been hurt if they had been obeying that statute. After noting several states in which that argument had been upheld, the court rejected it on the ground that the statute was designed to promote public order and not safety.

In De Haen v. Rockwood Sprinkler Co., 258 N.Y. 350, 179 N.E. 764 (1932), a radiator placed about a foot from the edge of an unprotected hoistway on a construction project fell down the shaft and killed a man below. The court, in an opinion by Judge Cardozo, first upheld the liability of Rockwood because its employees had negligently struck the radiator and brought about its fall. The court next upheld liability against LeBeau, whose employees negligently placed the radiator dangerously near the open shaft. The fact that it took the act of another to cause the fall did not exculpate LeBeau. "One may not place an engine of destruction in a position where a heedless touch by someone else will awaken its destructive power." At least, "a jury may so find."

The court then turned to the liability of Turner, the general contractor. Turner had violated a statute by failing to erect a barrier around the hoistway. Two sides were to be rigid. The other two, "which may be used for taking off and putting on materials . . . shall be guarded by an adjustable barrier not less than three nor more than four feet from the floor and not less than two feet from the edges of such shafts or openings."

Although the statute had been violated, that violation "does not establish liability if the statute is intended to protect against a particular hazard, and a hazard of a different kind is the occasion of the injury." Why should that requirement be imposed? The court then sought the purpose of the statute:

> The chief object of this statute is to protect workmen from the hazard of falling into a shaft. We cannot say, however, that no other hazard was within the zone of apprehension. On two sides of the shaft there must be a solid or comparatively solid fence. Only on the other sides where material is taken on or off may there be a single bar. If there was no thought to give protection against falling missiles or debris, the lawmakers might well have stopped with a requirement that there be a single bar on every side. The fact that they did not stop there is evidence of a broader purpose. True, indeed, it is that on two of the four sides the security is only partial and imperfect. A barrier set in place at a height of four feet will often be of little avail in holding back material or rubbish collected on the floor. Even so, security against the hazard of falling objects will not be lacking altogether. One of the requirements of the statute is that the guard shall be placed at least two feet from the edge. In a barrier so fixed there is warning, if no more. Workmen, who may otherwise be tempted to store material in dangerous proximity to the edge of an open shaft will be reminded of the danger and will tend to stand afar. The thoughtless will be checked, though the recklessly indifferent will be free to go their way.

> The potencies of protection that reside in such a barrier have illustration in the case before us. If the hoistway had been guarded, it is unlikely that the radiators thirty-eight inches high would have been placed as they were within falling distance of the edge. It is still less likely that a worker would heedlessly have brushed against them and so brought about the fall. We do not mean to say that these considerations are decisive. Liability is not established by a showing that as chance would have it a statutory safeguard might have avoided the particular hazard out of which an accident ensued. The hazard out of which the accident ensued must have been the particular hazard or

class of hazards that the statutory safeguard in the thought and purpose of the Legislature was intended to correct [ ]. Nonetheless, the sequence of events may help to fix the limits of a purpose that would be obscure if viewed alone. A safeguard has been commanded, but without distinct enumeration of the hazards to be avoided. In the revealing light of experience the hazards to be avoided are disclosed to us as the hazards that ensued.

If the court had concluded that the only purpose of the statute was to keep workers from falling into the open shaft and had refused to use the statute in the case, would Turner necessarily have won the case?

In Darmento v. Pacific Molasses Co., 81 N.Y.2d 985, 615 N.E.2d 1012, 599 N.Y.S.2d 528 (1993), defendant truck driver was following plaintiff too closely in violation of statute. Plaintiff claims that he became so "disconcerted" that he lost control of his car, went into a center guardrail and then careened back into the roadway and into a collision. Although the lower courts had held the statute inapplicable because it was intended only to prevent rear-end accidents, the court reversed: "While a rear-end collision is the most obvious type of accident to occur as a result of tailgating, other types of accidents also may occur."

9. When defendant driver parked outside the pharmacy on the grounds of the Middletown Psychiatric Center, she left her keys in the ignition. "Moments later," a patient drove away in the vehicle and "met his death soon thereafter when it left the road and struck a tree." Plaintiff, the patient's administrator, moved for summary judgment based on violation of the state statute against leaving keys in the ignition of an unattended car. The majority concluded that the statute was enacted to "deter theft and injury from the operation of motor vehicles by unauthorized persons. In our view, however, its provisions were plainly not designed to protect such unauthorized users from the consequences of their own conduct." Two judges thought the purpose was "to protect the public generally from the consequences that foreseeably flow from unauthorized use of motor vehicles." It was "patently unfair to deny to plaintiff the evidentiary weight of such violation and leave him to the more vigorous burden of establishing common law negligence."

The court unanimously concluded that plaintiff could proceed under common law negligence. Why the difference? Rushink v. Gerstheimer, 82 App.Div.2d 944, 440 N.Y.S.2d 738 (1981).

Other state courts have concluded that the purpose of the "key-in-the-ignition" statutes is to reduce thefts, and thus reduce both the time police must spend tracking down stolen cars and the payments insurers must make to owners of such cars. In this view there is no safety purpose and the statute is not invoked in personal injury cases. See Peck, An Exercise Based Upon Empirical Data: Liability for Harm Caused by Stolen Automobiles, 1969 Wis.L.Rev. 909.

10. In violation of the Contagious Diseases Act, defendant shipowner failed to build pens on the deck in order to keep groups of sheep separated.

During the voyage, some sheep were washed overboard. A suit by the owners of the sheep failed. Gorris v. Scott, L.R. 9 Ex. 125 (1874). The court observed that "the damage is of such a nature as was not contemplated at all by the statute, and as to which it was not intended to confer any benefit on the plaintiffs."

11. Licensing statutes have generally not been used to set standards of care. The explanation has been that the purpose of such a statute is to protect the public from actions performed by unskilled persons. If that is the purpose, then plaintiff must prove that the defendant lacked the required skill—in effect proving negligence.

The most common example is a motor vehicle accident involving an unlicensed driver. The lack of a license is irrelevant to the tort claim—whether the unlicensed driver is the plaintiff or the defendant.

Another example occurred in Brown v. Shyne, 242 N.Y. 176, 151 N.E. 197 (1926), in which a chiropractor allegedly hurt plaintiff by undertaking a treatment only licensed physicians could perform. The court held the defendant to the standard of a physician but ruled that the jury should not be told about defendant's violation of the licensing statute.

Are the driving and medical cases comparable? Should a distinction be drawn between a driver who inadvertently allowed a driving license to expire and one who never took the driving test? Should it matter whether a person's medical license was revoked for income tax evasion or for performing an illegal abortion? Or if the person never had a license?

In 1971, the rule of Brown v. Shyne was changed by statute. CPLR § 4504(d) provides that in any action for personal injuries against a person not authorized to practice medicine "the fact that such person practiced medicine without being so authorized shall be deemed prima facie evidence of negligence."

12. Some statutes are interpreted as barring their use in civil cases. Violations of the Occupational Safety and Health Act (OSHA) were held to fall into this category in Hernandez v. Martin Chevrolet, Inc., 72 Ohio St. 3d 302, 649 N.E.2d 1215 (1995). The court relied on the statute's preamble in 29 U.S.C.A. § 653(b)(4):

> Nothing in this chapter shall be construed to supersede or in any manner affect any workmen's compensation law or to enlarge or diminish or affect in any other manner the common law or statutory rights, duties, or liabilities of employers and employees under any law with respect to injuries, diseases, or death of employees arising out of, or in the course of, employment.

13. Should courts treat ordinances in the same way as statutes? In some states they are treated only as "evidence of negligence" rather than as "negligence per se." Why might that be? In others they are treated like statutes. A somewhat related issue arises in cases in which the plaintiff seeks to introduce defendant's violation of a company operating or safety manual to show negligence. See e.g, Sherman v. Robinson, 80 N.Y.2d 483, 606 N.E.2d 1365, 591 N.Y.S.2d 974 (1992), in which the court held that violation of a manual was not only not negligence per se, it was not even admissible as evidence of negligence if the manual's requirements exceeded the standards of due care. What if the manual told drivers always to drive ten miles below the posted limit?

14. *Compliance.* In *Tedla,* is it conceivable that plaintiffs might have been contributorily negligent if they had been walking in compliance with the statute and had been hit by an oncoming car? More generally, should compliance with a safety statute necessarily satisfy the standard of due care? In Hubbard–Hall Chemical Co. v. Silverman, 340 F.2d 402 (1st Cir.1965), plaintiffs were the administrators of the estates of two migrant farm workers who were killed by contact with an insecticide manufactured and distributed by defendant. The Department of Agriculture had found that danger warnings on the sacks conformed to Congressional requirements. Judgments entered for plaintiffs on a jury verdict were affirmed: the "jury could reasonably have believed that defendant should have foreseen that its admittedly dangerous product would be used by, among others, persons like plaintiffs' intestates, who were farm laborers, of limited education and reading ability, and that a warning even if it were in the precise form of the label submitted to the Department of Agriculture would not, because of its lack of a skull and bones or other comparable symbols" be adequate warning. The court found no reason to believe that Congress intended conformity with its requirements to mean that the defendant had "met the possibly higher standard of due care imposed by the common law . . . in actions of tort for negligence."

See also Alvarado v. J.C. Penney Co., 735 F.Supp. 371 (D.Kan.1990), in which the defendant claimed compliance with the Kansas Product Liability Act. Plaintiff was burned when the nightgown and robe she wore were ignited by an open flame gas heater. The court held that compliance with the regulatory standard was not conclusive.

In Espinoza v. Elgin, Joliet and Eastern Ry. Co., 165 Ill.2d 107, 649 N.E.2d 1323 (1995), the plaintiff in a grade-crossing accident claimed, among other things, that the defendant railroad should have had better warning devices at the intersection. The relevant state commission had inspected the crossing before the accident and had approved the existing devices. A state statute said in part that "[l]uminous flashing signal or crossing gate devices installed at grade crossings, which have been approved by the Commission, shall be deemed adequate and appropriate." The court interpreted this to mean that once such approval has been given "a conclusive legal presumption is created which prevents plaintiffs from arguing that the railroad should have installed other warning devices." The railroad was entitled to summary judgment on that issue. Can this case be reconciled with *Hubbard-Hall*? See generally, Dieffert, The Role of Regulatory Compliance in Tort Actions, 26 Harv.J.Legis. 175 (1989).

The question of whether and when courts should defer to legislative and administrative decisions about safety is an important and controversial question, to which we return—in the context of whether federal legislation preempts state tort remedies—in Chapter VIII. In the meantime, evaluate this excerpt from the conclusion of Huber, Safety and the Second Best: The Hazards of Public Risk Management in the Courts, 85 Colum.L.Rev. 277, 334–35 (1985):

> [J]udicial nondeference may make some sense when the administrative regulatory regime is casual or sporadic, as with consumer products. But it is wholly unpersuasive for comprehensively regulated industries. Vaccines, pesticides, aircraft, electric power plants and the like all entail potentially enormous mass-exposure hazards. Precisely because they can create public risks of this nature, these products and services are also subject to the most searching and complete state and federal safety regulation. Administrative agencies may find it politically convenient to disclaim final responsibility for the public risk choices that inhere in such licensing decisions. But the simple fact is that an agency cannot intelligently issue a license for such public-risk activities without comparing the licensee's risks to those of the competition and determining that the new offering represents some measure of progress or, at worst, no measure of regression in the risk market in question.
>
> Once that determination has been made by an expert licensing agency, the courts should respect it. Regulatory agencies are equipped to make the risk comparisons on which all progressive transformation of the risk environment must be based. The courts are simply not qualified to second-guess such decisions; when they choose to do so they routinely make regressive risk choices. Requiring—or at least strongly encouraging—the courts to respect the comparative risk choices made by competent, expert agencies would inject a first, small measure of rationality into a judicial regulatory system that currently runs quite wild.

D.   PROOF OF NEGLIGENCE

Problems of proof occur at virtually every stage of the negligence action. In this section we focus on the plaintiff's burden of proving that the defendant's conduct fell below the standard of reasonable care. This, in turn, involves proving what the defendant actually did or did not do and, at times, the unreasonableness of such behavior.

The most convincing type of proof is usually documentary or "real" evidence: the broken bottle, the flight recorder in an airplane accident, or a videotape of an automobile crash. In few personal injury accidents, however, is such evidence available. A "lucky" plaintiff will be able to present photographs of skid marks or other visible evidence that might serve almost as well as "real" evidence. The plaintiff may also use "direct" evidence: eyewitnesses may testify. Whether the witness describes skid marks or the crash itself, the party hurt by such testimony may seek to undermine it by cross examination in an effort to show erroneous recall of the facts or to cast doubt on the witness's credibility. When documentary and photographic proof are used, accuracy and credibility are less readily challenged.

Negri v. Stop and Shop, Inc.

Court of Appeals of New York, 1985.
65 N.Y.2d 625, 480 N.E.2d 740, 491 N.Y.S.2d 151.

[The trial court entered judgment for the plaintiff in a slip and fall case.   The Appellate Division reversed and dismissed the complaint.]

■ MEMORANDUM.

The order of the Appellate Division, [   ] should be reversed, with costs, and remitted to that court for consideration of the facts and of other issues not previously addressed.

The record contains some evidence tending to show that defendant had constructive notice of a dangerous condition which allegedly caused injuries to its customer.   There was testimony that the injured plaintiff, while shopping in defendant's store, fell backward, did not come into contact with the shelves, but hit her head directly on the floor where "a lot of broken jars" of baby food lay; that the baby food was "dirty and messy"; that a witness in the immediate vicinity of the accident did not hear any jars falling from the shelves or otherwise breaking during the 15 or 20 minutes prior to the accident; and that the aisle had not been cleaned or inspected for at least 50 minutes prior to the accident—indeed, some evidence was adduced that it was at least two hours.

Viewing the evidence in a light most favorable to the plaintiffs and according plaintiffs the benefit of every reasonable inference [   ], it cannot be said, as a matter of law, that the circumstantial evidence was insufficient to permit the jury to draw the necessary inference that a slippery condition was created by jars of baby food which had fallen and broken a sufficient length of time prior to the accident to permit defendant's employees to discover and remedy the condition.   [   ]   Plaintiffs having made out a prima facie case, it was error to dismiss the complaint.   If the jury verdict be deemed by the Appellate Division to be against the weight of the evidence, that court's power is limited to ordering a new trial.   [   ]

■ WACHTLER, C.J., and JASEN, MEYER, SIMONS, KAYE and ALEXANDER, JJ., concur.

Gordon v. American Museum of Natural History

Court of Appeals of New York, 1986.
67 N.Y.2d 836, 492 N.E.2d 774, 501 N.Y.S.2d 646.

■ MEMORANDUM.

The order of the Appellate Division, [   ], should be reversed, with costs, the complaint dismissed and the certified question answered in the negative.

Plaintiff was injured when he fell on defendant's front entrance steps. He testified that as he descended the upper level of steps he slipped on the third step and that while he was in midair he observed a piece of white, waxy paper next to his left foot. He alleges that this paper came from the concession stand that defendant had contracted to have present and which was located on the plaza separating the two tiers of steps and that defendant was negligent insofar as its employees failed to discover and remove the paper before he fell on it. The case was submitted to the jury on the theory that defendant had either actual or constructive notice of the dangerous condition presented by the paper on the steps. The jury found against defendant on the issue of liability. A divided Appellate Division affirmed and granted defendant leave to appeal on a certified question.

There is no evidence in the record that defendant had actual notice of the paper and the case should not have gone to the jury on that theory. To constitute constructive notice, a defect must be visible and apparent and it must exist for a sufficient length of time prior to the accident to permit defendant's employees to discover and remedy it (Negri v. Stop & Shop [ ]). The record contains no evidence that anyone, including plaintiff, observed the piece of white paper prior to the accident. Nor did he describe the paper as being dirty or worn, which would have provided some indication that it had been present for some period of time (cf. [*Negri*] (broken baby food jars were dirty)). Thus, on the evidence presented, the piece of paper that caused plaintiff's fall could have been deposited there only minutes or seconds before the accident and any other conclusion would be pure speculation.

Contrary to plaintiff's contentions, neither a general awareness that litter or some other dangerous condition may be present [ ] nor the fact that plaintiff observed other papers on another portion of the steps approximately 10 minutes before his fall is legally sufficient to charge defendant with constructive notice of the paper he fell on. [Two cited cases] are not to the contrary. In both cases constructive notice was established by other evidence and the issue was whether plaintiffs had presented sufficient evidence on the issue of causation insofar as both plaintiffs failed to specify which step they had fallen on and what condition—wear, wetness or litter—had caused them to slip. In each case, the court concluded that plaintiff had presented a prima facie case because a fall was a natural and probable consequence of the conditions present on the stairs. The defect in plaintiff's case here, however, is not an inability to prove the causation element of his fall but the lack of evidence establishing constructive notice of the particular condition that caused his fall.

■ WACHTLER, C.J., and MEYER, SIMONS, KAYE, ALEXANDER, TITONE and HANCOCK, JJ., concur in memorandum.

NOTES AND QUESTIONS

1. Are *Negri* and *Gordon* distinguishable?

2. What more might plaintiff have done in *Gordon*? Does the court suggest that the judgment below would have been affirmed if Gordon had testified that the paper looked dirty?

3. Recall the difference, noted in *Negri*, between dismissing the complaint (or granting summary judgment) and ordering a new trial. What controls the appropriate appellate response?

4. What would Gordon have had to prove if he had sued the concession? Why might he have decided not to sue the concession?

5. In an omitted footnote in *Gordon*, the court notes that plaintiff did not press at trial a claim that the Museum "created the dangerous condition"—and thus could not rely on it on appeal. What might that theory involve?

6. In some states the supermarket customer may be able to recover on a theory sometimes called "mode of operation" that is based on the notion that by choosing self-service, the owner has agreed to assume responsibility for the conduct of customers who drop items on the floor or are careless. Under this approach there is no need to prove actual or constructive notice "if the proprietor could reasonably anticipate that hazardous conditions would regularly arise." This rule "looks to a business's choice of a particular mode of operation and not events surrounding the plaintiff's accident. Under the rule, the plaintiff is not required to prove notice if the proprietor could reasonably anticipate that hazardous conditions would regularly arise. [ ] In other words, a third person's independent negligence is no longer the source of liability, and the plaintiff is freed from the burden of discovering and proving a third person's actions." Chiara v. Fry's Food Stores of Arizona, Inc., 152 Ariz. 398, 733 P.2d 283 (1987).

Chiara cited cases in other states that were willing to use the rule in cases involving "open food displays." But there was no need to limit it to "produce or pizza." The real issue in the case is whether defendant "could reasonably anticipate that creme rinse would be spilled on a regular basis." Here, employee depositions showed that spills regularly occurred in the store. From these, it was for a jury to determine if "Fry's reasonably could have anticipated that sealed bottles regularly were opened and spilled." If so, the question would be whether Fry's had exercised reasonable care under these circumstances.

Compare Milliken v. City of Lewiston, 580 A.2d 151 (Me.1990), in which plaintiff student slipped on a green pepper while walking by a self-serve salad bar in her junior high school cafeteria. Relying on the language of another court, plaintiff argued:

> In a self-service operation, an owner has for his pecuniary benefit required customers to perform the tasks previously carried out by employees. Thus, the risk of items being dangerously located on the floor, which previously was created by employees, is now created by other customers. But it is the very same risk and the risk has been created by the owner by his choice of mode of operation. He is charged

with the creation of this condition just as he would be charged with the responsibility for negligent acts of his employees.

Plaintiff asserted that "functionally" the defendant had placed the green pepper on the floor "by electing to operate the school cafeteria without waiters." The court rejected the claim because plaintiff had failed to show "that her injury resulted from a recurring condition on the premises and [had] generated no factual issue concerning defendants' actual or constructive knowledge of the presence of the green pepper on the floor." The court "adhere[d] to the rule that [liability is] determined by the existence of actual or constructive knowledge, even in a self-service cafeteria."

7. In Dumont v. Shaw's Supermarkets, Inc., 664 A.2d 846 (Me.1995), plaintiff had slipped on a chocolate-covered peanut in a self-service area. The defendant had placed mats

> next to the displayed grapes, cherries, the ice machine, the salad bar, the bouquet rack, and any place that contains ice. There were no mats, however, on the floor of the area next to the candy bins. In deciding where to place mats, Shaw's weighs the probability of an accident occurring, considers the nature of the product, its slipperiness, the number or customers passing through the area, and its past experience with like items. No evidence was presented that Shaw's was aware of candy being on the floor prior to the present accident.

Does the last sentence refer to evidence about Shaw's awareness of (1) whether any candy had previously fallen to the floor, or (2) the presence of the piece of candy on which plaintiff slipped? The court held that the trial judge erred in failing to give an instruction concerning the "foreseeable risk of a recurring condition." It adhered to its ruling in *Milliken* on the ground that it was unwilling to impute any negligence of the person who dropped the candy to the defendant.

Is there a difference between a "mode of operation" rule that (1) imputes the negligence of one customer to the management whenever a customer slips on something that should not be on the floor and (2) allows that imputation only in a situation in which management is already aware of the dangers and continues to allow customers to help themselves?

8. In Ingersoll v. DeBartolo, Inc., 123 Wash.2d 649, 869 P.2d 1014 (1994), the court had concluded earlier that its manner-of-operation rule applied to the self-service parts of stores if continuous risks existed in those areas. It did not apply to non-self-serve areas. The court now refused to extend the rule to a slip and fall in a public area of a shopping mall. Plaintiff had failed to show such things as how many food places were housed in the mall, how many cleaners defendant mall hired, and how much refuse and of what type they found daily. There was no jury question on whether it was reasonably foreseeable that slippery substances would be found on floors in the area of the accident.

See generally, Comment, Reapportioning the Burden of Uncertainty: Storekeeper Liability in the Self–Service Slip-and-Fall Case, 41 UCLA L.Rev. 861 (1994).

9. *Spoliation of evidence.* Plaintiff's burden of showing negligence is of course made even more difficult if the defendant destroys or refuses, after proper demand, to provide evidence that would show negligence. In recent years, plaintiffs have begun accusing defendants (and occasionally third parties) of negligently or intentionally destroying important evidence. Courts have responded with a variety of remedies. If the person accused of destroying the evidence is already the defendant in a tort action courts tend to conclude that there is no need to create a separate tort; it is enough to alter the rules under which the tort action goes forward. In Sweet v. Sisters of Providence in Washington, 895 P.2d 484 (Alaska 1995), the claim was that essential medical records in the defendant's custody had disappeared. When that was shown the court concluded that in the case pending against the defendant, the burden of persuasion on negligence as well as on causation should be shifted from the plaintiff to the defendant.

Where the person in control of the evidence is not subject to a preexisting claim, courts have created a new tort action for spoliation of evidence. This can be brought at the same time that plaintiff tries to pursue the underlying action for which the evidence is said to be crucial. If the plaintiff wins the underlying action, then the evidence was not essential; if the plaintiff loses the underlying action for want of crucial evidence that the second defendant has negligently (or intentionally) caused to disappear the plaintiff will be able to recover against the second defendant. See Boyd v. Travelers Ins.Co., 166 Ill.2d 188, 652 N.E.2d 267 (1995)(insurer that took custody of and then lost allegedly defective heater can be sued along with manufacturer of heater).

Byrne v. Boadle

Court of Exchequer, 1863.
2 H. & C. 722, 159 Eng.Rep. 299.

At the trial before the learned Assessor of the Court of Passage at Liverpool, the evidence adduced on the part of the plaintiff was as follows:—A witness named Critchley said: "On the 18th July, I was in Scotland Road, on the right side going north, defendant's shop is on that side. When I was opposite to his shop, a barrel of flour fell from a window above in defendant's house and shop, and knocked the plaintiff down. He was carried into an adjoining shop. A horse and cart came opposite the defendant's door. Barrels of flour were in the cart. I do not think the barrel was being lowered by a rope. I cannot say: I did not see the barrel until it struck the plaintiff. It was not swinging when it struck the plaintiff. It struck him on the shoulder and knocked him towards the shop. No one called out until after the accident." The plaintiff said: "On approaching Scotland Place and defendant's shop, I lost all recollection. I felt no blow. I saw nothing to warn me of danger. I was taken home in a cab. I was helpless for a fortnight." (He then described his sufferings.) "I saw the path clear. I did not see any cart opposite defendant's shop." Another witness said: "I saw a barrel falling. I don't know how, but from defendant's." The only other witness was a surgeon, who described the injury which the plaintiff had received. It was admitted that the defendant was a dealer in flour.

It was submitted, on the part of the defendant, that there was no evidence of negligence for the jury. The learned Assessor was of that opinion, and nonsuited the plaintiff, reserving leave to him to move the Court of Exchequer to enter the verdict for him with £50. damages, the amount assessed by the jury.

Littler, in the present Term, obtained a rule nisi to enter the verdict for the plaintiff, on the ground of misdirection of the learned Assessor in ruling that there was no evidence of negligence on the part of the defendant. . . .

■ POLLOCK, C.B. We are all of opinion that the rule must be absolute to enter the verdict for the plaintiff. The learned counsel was quite right in saying that there are many accidents from which no presumption of negligence can arise, but I think it would be wrong to lay down as a rule that in no case can presumption of negligence arise from the fact of an accident. Suppose in this case the barrel had rolled out of the warehouse and fallen on the plaintiff, how could he possibly ascertain from what cause it occurred? It is the duty of persons who keep barrels in a warehouse to take care that they do not roll out, and I think that such a case would, beyond all doubt, afford prima facie evidence of negligence. A barrel could not roll out of a warehouse without some negligence, and to say that a plaintiff who is injured by it must call witnesses from the warehouse to prove negligence seems to me preposterous. So in the building or repairing of a house, or putting pots on the chimneys, if a person passing along the road is injured by something falling upon him, I think the accident alone would be prima facie evidence of negligence. Or if an article calculated to cause damage is put in a wrong place and does mischief, I think that those whose duty it was to put it in the right place are prima facie responsible, and if there is any state of facts to rebut the presumption of negligence, they must prove them. The present case upon the evidence comes to this, a man is passing in front of the premises of a dealer in flour, and there falls down upon him a barrel of flour. I think it apparent that the barrel was in the custody of the defendant who occupied the premises, and who is responsible for the acts of his servants who had the control of it; and in my opinion the fact of its falling is prima facie evidence of negligence, and the plaintiff who was injured by it is not bound to show that it could not fall without negligence, but if there are any facts inconsistent with negligence it is for the defendant to prove them.

■ [The concurring opinion of BARON CHANNELL is omitted. BRAMWELL, B., and PIGOTT, B., concurred without opinion.]

NOTES AND QUESTIONS

1. In the midst of the defendant's argument, Pollock, C.B., interrupted to observe, "There are certain cases of which it may be said res ipsa loquitur, and this seems one of them. In some cases the Courts have held that the mere fact of the accident having occurred is evidence of negligence, as, for instance, in the case of railway collisions." This was apparently the first use of a term that was to become central to negligence litigation. Defense counsel sought to distinguish railway cases as limited to collisions involving two trains of the same railroad company. He then argued that in one case the suit was by a passenger and that there was an implicit contract of safe carriage between the passenger and the railroad. What difference would it have made, Pollock inquired, if the case cited had been brought by a bystander instead of a passenger? Defense counsel responded that because of the contract, "The fact of the accident might be evidence of negligence in the one case, though not in the other." What is the relevance of this exchange to the decision in *Byrne?*

2. Is *Gordon* consistent with *Byrne?*

3. In Larson v. St. Francis Hotel, 83 Cal.App.2d 210, 188 P.2d 513 (1948), plaintiff pedestrian was struck by a chair thrown out of the window of one of defendant's rooms on V–J Day, August 14, 1945. Plaintiff proved this and her injuries and rested. Defendant's motion for a nonsuit at the end of plaintiff's case was granted.

Compare Connolly v. Nicollet Hotel, 254 Minn. 373, 95 N.W.2d 657 (1959), in which the hotel had been taken over by a convention of the National Junior Chamber of Commerce. In the days before plaintiff's injury, the hotel management had learned that objects were being thrown from windows and that vandalism was occurring throughout the hotel. The day before the incident, the general manager sent a memo to the hotel staff saying in part, "We have almost arrived at the end of the most harrowing experience we have had in the way of conventions, at least in my experience. . . . We had no alternative but to proceed and 'turn the other cheek.' . . . " The following night, plaintiff pedestrian lost an eye when hit by an object thrown from a room.

The majority held that the hotel could have been found to have behaved negligently after knowing of the dangers. Management decided not to try to find out who had thrown the earlier objects, because the convention was "out of control." No increased patrolling was instituted, no new guards were hired, and no appeal was made to responsible officers of the convention. Perhaps the most significant step taken was to cut holes in the corners of the hotel's laundry bags to prevent their use as water containers.

The dissenters argued that it was not reasonable to expect the management to enter every room, or at random, or to remain in them to prevent possible misconduct. They relied on *Larson.*

Is the majority relying on a res ipsa argument? Is negligence inferred from the accident itself?

4. In Dermatossian v. New York City Transit Authority, 67 N.Y.2d 219, 492 N.E.2d 1200, 501 N.Y.S.2d 784 (1986), the plaintiff passenger testified that he struck his head on a defective grab handle as he stood up to leave defendant's bus. The claim was that the handle projected straight down from the ceiling instead of "at the customary angle of about 45 degrees." Although the plaintiff presented no evidence of negligence, the trial court held the case sufficient for a jury. A plaintiff's verdict and judgment followed. On appeal, the court of appeals reversed.

The plaintiff "did not establish control of the grab handle by defendant with sufficient exclusivity to fairly rule out the chance that the defect in the handle was caused by some agency other than defendant's negligence. The proof did not adequately exclude the chance that the handle had been damaged by one or more of defendant's passengers who were invited to use it."

Anderson v. Service Merchandise Company, Inc.

Supreme Court of Nebraska, 1992.
240 Neb. 873, 485 N.W.2d 170.

[Plaintiff was injured June 27, 1986, when a light fixture fell 16 feet from the ceiling and hit her while she was waiting to pay at defendant Service Merchandise's store. The premises had been leased in 1978 from Jewel Companies, Inc. In 1985 defendant Sylvania entered into a contract with Service Merchandise to service and maintain the lighting fixtures. Pursuant to the contract, which provided that Service Merchandise had to approve "any and all services" performed by Sylvania, Sylvania did work twice in 1985, and inspected the system in May 1986. What occurred during that May inspection "is undisclosed." During the entire period employees of Service Merchandise changed elements in the light fixtures in the store and changed the lamps when they burned out. The trial court granted both defendants summary judgment. Nothing presented in the summary judgment proceedings suggested "any specific negligence" by either defendant. Further facts are stated in the court's opinion.]

■ Before HASTINGS, C.J., and BOSLAUGH, CAPORALE, SHANAHAN, GRANT and FAHRNBRUCH, JJ.

■ SHANAHAN, JUSTICE.

.   .   .

As expressed in Widga v. Sandell, 236 Neb. 798, 803, 464 N.W.2d 155, 158–59 (1991), concerning the doctrine and elements of res ipsa loquitur:

> [W]hen an instrumentality under the exclusive control and management of the alleged wrongdoer produces an occurrence which would not, in the ordinary course of things, come to pass in the absence of the negligence of the one having such management and control, the occurrence itself, in the absence of explanation by the alleged wrongdoer, affords evidence that the occurrence arose as

the result of the alleged wrongdoer's negligence. [   ]Literally, the "thing speaks for itself." [   ]

Res ipsa loquitur operates as a type of circumstantial evidence, that is, "facts or circumstances, proved or known, from which existence or nonexistence of another fact may be logically inferred or deduced through a rational process." [   ] Regarding res ipsa loquitur,

> [t]he requirement that the occurrence be one which ordinarily does not happen without negligence is of course only another way of stating an obvious principle of circumstantial evidence: that the event must be such that in the light of ordinary experience it gives rise to an inference that someone must have been negligent.

Prosser and Keeton on the Law of Torts, [   ]. As further noted by Prosser and Keeton:

> The plaintiff is not required to eliminate with certainty all other possible causes or inferences, which would mean that the plaintiff must prove a civil case beyond a reasonable doubt. All that is needed is evidence from which reasonable persons can say that on the whole it is more likely that there was negligence associated with the cause of the event than that there was not. It is enough that the court cannot say that the jury could not reasonably come to that conclusion. Where no such balance of probabilities in favor of negligence can reasonably be found, res ipsa loquitur does not apply. [   ]

Thus, res ipsa loquitur is not a matter of substantive law, but, as a form of circumstantial evidence, is a procedural matter. [   ] Consequently, if res ipsa loquitur applies, an inference of a defendant's negligence exists for submission to the fact finder, which may accept or reject the inference in the factual determination whether the defendant is negligent. [   ] As pointed out in Prosser and Keeton [   ]:

> The inference of negligence to be drawn from the circumstances is left to the jury. They are permitted, but not compelled to find it. The plaintiff escapes a nonsuit, or a dismissal of his case, since there is sufficient evidence to go to the jury. . . .
>
>   . . . As a general proposition, however, the procedural effect of res ipsa may be said to be a matter of the strength of the inference to be drawn, which will vary with the circumstances of the case.

Therefore, in Anderson's case, if res ipsa loquitur is inapplicable as a matter of law, there is no material question of fact regarding actionable negligence, and the summary judgments were proper dispositions. However, if res ipsa loquitur is applicable in light of the presentation at the hearing for summary judgments in Anderson's case, the inference of negligence itself presents a question of material fact, and the summary judgments were improper.

Anderson's Res Ipsa Case

"[I]n the ordinary course of things," part of a light fixture attached to a building's ceiling does not, in the absence of negligence, fall and injure an invitee. Thus, in Anderson's case the focal point is "exclusive control," a requisite element for application of res ipsa loquitur. [ ]

Sylvania.

What constituted Sylvania's "inspection" of the lighting system in May 1986, some 7 weeks before the light fixture fell on Anderson, is undisclosed. Therefore, Sylvania's last disclosed physical contact with the lighting system was in September 1985, when Sylvania replaced some lamps and ballasts in the lighting system. Thus, there was a hiatus of approximately 9 months between Sylvania's last physical work on the lighting system and the light fixture's falling on Anderson. Also, independent of Sylvania's involvement with the lighting system, Service Merchandise's employees had unrestricted access to the lighting system and even changed burned-out lamps and elements in the light fixtures. As presented to us, the record fails to indicate Sylvania's control of the lighting system and its fixtures. While Sylvania had a contractual duty to maintain the lighting system in Service Merchandise's store, the record before us shows that Sylvania actually worked on the system a total of only 12 hours over 3 days during the 15–month period before Anderson's accident, with the last occasion being 9 months before the accident. Meanwhile, Service Merchandise and its employees had daily control over the entire premises, including the lighting system. Thus, Sylvania's control of the lighting system in Service Merchandise's store is so attenuated and lacking in continuity that Sylvania's control is nonexistent. Without control, there is no inference of negligence under res ipsa loquitur. . . . Without res ipsa loquitur, . . . the district court properly granted summary judgment to Sylvania.

. . .

Service Merchandise.

Service Merchandise contends that it lacked exclusive control because Service Merchandise had contracted with Sylvania for periodic inspection and service of the store's overhead lighting fixtures, Service Merchandise had not occupied the store throughout the building's existence, and Service Merchandise's landlord had a right to show the premises to prospective purchasers.

[As to the first of these, the court concluded that Sylvania was an independent contractor (recall the discussion in Chapter I) but that Service Merchandise had a nondelegable duty to exercise care for the benefit of customers. "As a business possessor of real estate, Service Merchandise has a duty to exercise reasonable care to keep the premises safe for its business invitees. [ ] Moreover, a business possessor's duty to use reasonable care for invitees on the premises is a nondelegable duty. [ ]; Restatement (Second) of Torts § 422 (1965)." This meant that even if

Sylvania were negligent, Service Merchandise would be responsible for that negligence along with any of its own.]

Service Merchandise's "exclusive control" is similarly not defeated by the fact that the building existed before Service Merchandise's occupancy under its lease or by the fact that Service Merchandise's landlord has some limited right to potential entry under the lease. Service Merchandise's nondelegable duty of safe premises exists as the result of Service Merchandise's unquestioned status as a business possessor of land and Anderson's unquestioned status as a business invitee of Service Merchandise. [   ]

To summarize, Service Merchandise was in "exclusive control" of the premises for purposes of res ipsa loquitur because Service Merchandise possessed and, therefore, controlled the site of the accident and had a nondelegable duty to exercise reasonable care for the protection of Anderson, a business invitee. Since Anderson has established all the elements of res ipsa loquitur, including Service Merchandise's "exclusive control" as an element of res ipsa loquitur, a genuine issue of material fact existed in Anderson's negligence action against Service Merchandise. Therefore, the district court erred by granting a summary judgment to Service Merchandise.

Conclusion

Our decision in no way affects Service Merchandise's action against Sylvania for "indemnity and/or contribution," a matter which is not before the court in Anderson's appeal.   .   .   .

Affirmed in part and in part reversed and remanded for further proceedings.

■ WHITE, J., not participating.

NOTES AND QUESTIONS

1. Do the facts of this case—in the court's quoted words—"give rise to an inference that someone must have been negligent"? From where might such an inference arise? Would this determination be any easier if Service Merchandise had built the building and occupied it from the beginning and had handled all of its lighting matters itself?

2. If one can infer that "someone" must have been negligent, who might that be in this case? Why does the court exculpate Sylvania? What if it had appeared that in May 1986, Sylvania had changed a lamp in the fixture that fell? Had dusted the fixture that fell?

3. Why did the plaintiff present no "specific" evidence of negligence?

4. Recall the *Dermatossian* case, p. 83, supra, involving the grab handle in a bus. Is that analysis consistent with the analysis in *Anderson*?

5. Once the court concludes that res ipsa loquitur applies to the case at hand, it also concludes that an "inference" is created. If no further evidence is presented at trial, how is the jury to decide the negligence question in this case? How does the jury's analysis differ from the process the court went through to decide whether to create the inference in the first place?

6. In Baumann v. Long Island Railroad, 110 App.Div.2d 739, 487 N.Y.S.2d 833 (1985), the plaintiff pedestrian was hurt when the upraised arm of a grade crossing gate broke off its hinges and fell on her. Apparently, the accident occurred when a shear pin in the gate broke. The plaintiff relied on res ipsa loquitur. The defendant presented evidence that it conducted regular monthly inspections of the arms, testing a variety of features. "No visual inspection of the gate's shear pins was made except a check was done to make sure that all the pins were in place. The railroad's inspector testified that even if each shear pin was visually inspected, there would be no way to determine whether the pin was going to break."

[handwritten margin note: Reasonably prudent person would have changed pins.]

The jury returned a defense verdict that was affirmed on appeal. A jury could find that the inference of negligence had been rebutted: "the jury was free to, and obviously did, reject the permissible inference. . . . We cannot say that the verdict was against the weight of the credible evidence."

7. The *Anderson* court notes that the strength of the inference varies from case to case. In some cases, an inference may be so strong that the jury must find negligence if no exculpatory evidence is presented. In Farina v. Pan American World Airlines, Inc., 116 App.Div.2d 618, 497 N.Y.S.2d 706 (1986), plaintiff passenger was injured when the defendant's airplane went off a runway while landing at Kennedy Airport. Although New York generally treats res ipsa as a permissible inference, in this case the showing was "so convincing that the inference of negligence arising therefrom is inescapable if not rebutted by other evidence." In the absence here of any plausible counter-showing, plaintiff was entitled to summary judgment on liability.

8. In some states if res ipsa applies it is a "presumption affecting the burden of producing evidence." This means that if the defendant offers no plausible rebutting evidence the plaintiff is entitled to a directed verdict on liability. If, however, the defendant offers such evidence the jury is to be informed that the plaintiff still bears the burden of persuading the jury that defendant was negligent. See, e.g., Calif. Evidence Code § 646.

9. Can the defendant ever so "conclusively rebut" the plaintiff's case as to obtain judgment as a matter of law? In Leonard v. Watsonville Community Hospital, 47 Cal.2d 509, 305 P.2d 36 (1956), a Kelly clamp, about six inches long, was left inside plaintiff after an abdominal operation. The court held initially that res ipsa loquitur applied against all three participating physicians, the surgical nurse, and the hospital. It then considered the testimony of the physicians in deciding whether judgment had been properly granted to MD3. MD1 and MD2 worked on the upper abdomen, where the Kelly clamp was left, and also on the lower abdomen. MD3 testified that he had worked only on the lower abdomen, had left before the incision was closed, and had used only curved clamps—while Kelly clamps were uncurved. The testimony of MD1 and MD2 corroborated MD3. The court held that since this testimony increased the possibility that MD1 and MD2 would be held liable, the "record indicates no rational ground for disbelieving their testimony." The case against MD3 "was dispelled as a matter of law." The court found testimony of another witness less persuasive because it was consistent with her self-interest to shield her employer and associates from liability. Ordinarily, may juries disbelieve witnesses even though there is no "rational ground" for doing so?

10. Is it appropriate to give the benefit of res ipsa loquitur to a plaintiff who also seeks to prove specific acts of negligence? In Abbott v. Page Airways, Inc., 23 N.Y.2d 502, 245 N.E.2d 388, 297 N.Y.S.2d 713 (1969), plaintiff's husband was killed in the crash of a helicopter owned by defendant and operated by its employee. In addition to relying on res ipsa loquitur, plaintiff presented witnesses who testified that the pilot waved to someone on the ground just before the crash, had flown too low and too slowly, and had taken several drinks before the flight. The trial judge charged that the jury could properly find negligence in the specific acts charged or they "could infer negligence from the happening of the accident." The charge was upheld on appeal. A few courts disagree. See, e.g., Malloy v. Commonwealth Highland Theatres, Inc., 375 N.W.2d 631 (S.D.1985).

11. In a state with well-developed pretrial discovery procedures, is there still a place for res ipsa loquitur? In Fowler v. Seaton, 61 Cal.2d 681, 394 P.2d 697, 39 Cal.Rptr. 881 (1964), the plaintiff was a four-year-old child who went to nursery school one morning in good health but returned that evening with a bump on her forehead, a concussion and crossed eyes. Is this enough for res ipsa loquitur? Having these and other facts, the majority thought it was. Two justices dissented on the ground that plaintiff had an obligation "to present such facts as were available to show that the accident was more probably than not the result of the alleged inadequate supervision by defendant." The dissent then listed several omissions from plaintiff's case and observed that they were "undoubtedly obtainable by discovery." Should it suffice for plaintiff to prove the minimum required to permit the critical inference? Do the facts already stated here suffice? Should all facts available by discovery but not presented be taken as adverse to plaintiff?

In Helton v. Forest Park Baptist Church, 589 S.W.2d 217 (Ky.App. 1979), plaintiffs left their two-and-one-half-year-old daughter with about a dozen other children at the nursery room of their church while they attended services. During the service, the daughter suffered a serious eye injury. The two adults who were supervising the children could not explain what had happened. All toys and furniture were inspected, but "no one could find any object which could have caused such an injury." It could not be determined whether she had been struck in the eye by a thrown object or had fallen on some object.

The court denied plaintiffs the benefit of res ipsa loquitur and upheld a summary judgment for the defense. Res ipsa was "inapplicable where the instrumentality producing the injury or damage is unknown or is not in the exclusive control of the defendant." A jury could "only speculate, surmise or guess as to how Melissa's injury occurred, and for this reason the case is one to be decided by the court as a matter of law."

12. The notion of nondelegability implies that if subsequent proceedings (and additional proof) should indicate that Service Merchandise is ultimately being held liable based on the negligence of Sylvania, Service Merchandise may proceed against the negligent party for indemnity. Recall that the defendant in Maloney v. Rath, p. 8, supra, would have had the same remedy when she was held liable for the negligence of the garage mechanic in working on her brakes. We return to remedies among defendants later.

Automobile Accidents. In Pfaffenbach v. White Plains Express Corp., 17 N.Y.2d 132, 216 N.E.2d 324, 269 N.Y.S.2d 115 (1966), the plaintiff was a passenger in a car that was hit when defendant's oncoming truck came over the center line in rainy or snowy weather. The defendant "offered no explanation for the accident, offered no proof on the issue of negligence, and the jury found a verdict for plaintiff." The court of appeals upheld a judgment entered on that verdict. In such a case, plaintiff's showing is "prima facie sufficient to go to the jury to determine liability. The explanation of the defendant, if he gives one, will also usually be for the jury."

In New York, a suit by an injured passenger against the driver in a one-car crash is handled under the same negligence formula as crashes involving more than one vehicle.* This permitted the court in *Pfaffenbach* to say that the "same rule, open to additional factual evaluation of his own responsibility for events, would apply to the passenger in a car which goes out of control."

The *Pfaffenbach* dictum was relied on in Coury v. Safe Auto Sales, Inc., 32 N.Y.2d 162, 297 N.E.2d 88, 344 N.Y.S.2d 347 (1973), in which the court held that a sleeping passenger made out a prima facie case of negligence against the driver by showing that the car crossed the center line and struck an oncoming vehicle.

In Paul v. Paul, 41 App.Div.2d 560, 339 N.Y.S.2d 901 (1973), plaintiffs were passengers in a car driven by X which was involved in an accident with a car driven by Y. Plaintiffs sued both X and Y. X testified that Y cut sharply in front of him from left to right and that he could not avoid the accident although he tried—and the right front of his car struck the left rear of Y's car. Y testified that he had stopped in the right lane for a traffic light. As he began to make a right turn, he was hit from behind by X. The jury found for both defendants and the trial judge entered

---

* In some states, the one-car crash would be subject to a "guest statute," which provides that the driver will be liable to a "guest" only if the driver has engaged in wilful or reckless conduct or, in some states, been grossly negligent. In such a state, losing control of a car may not, without more, show such serious misconduct. In these states, drivers owe "passengers," such as those in taxis, a general duty of due care.

judgment. The appellate court reversed. In light of the testimony "the jury should have found at least one of the defendants negligent, depending on which version of the accident it believed. Certainly, the jury's verdict in favor of both defendants was contrary to the weight of the evidence."

Ybarra v. Spangard

Supreme Court of California, 1944.
25 Cal.2d 486, 154 P.2d 687.

■ GIBSON, C.J. This is an action for damages for personal injuries alleged to have been inflicted on plaintiff by defendants during the course of a surgical operation. The trial court entered judgments of nonsuit as to all defendants and plaintiff appealed.

On October 28, 1939, plaintiff consulted defendant Dr. Tilley, who diagnosed his ailment as appendicitis, and made arrangements for an appendectomy to be performed by defendant Dr. Spangard at a hospital owned and managed by defendant Dr. Swift. Plaintiff entered the hospital, was given a hypodermic injection, slept, and later was awakened by Doctors Tilley and Spangard and wheeled into the operating room by a nurse whom he believed to be defendant Gisler, an employee of Dr. Swift. Defendant Dr. Reser, the anesthetist, also an employee of Dr. Swift, adjusted plaintiff for the operation, pulling his body to the head of the operating table and, according to plaintiff's testimony, laying him back against two hard objects at the top of his shoulders, about an inch below his neck. Dr. Reser then administered the anesthetic and plaintiff lost consciousness. When he awoke early the following morning he was in his hospital room attended by defendant Thompson, the special nurse, and another nurse who was not made a defendant.

Plaintiff testified that prior to the operation he had never had any pain in, or injury to, his right arm or shoulder, but that when he awakened he felt a sharp pain about half way between the neck and the point of the right shoulder. He complained to the nurse, and then to Dr. Tilley, who gave him diathermy treatments while he remained in the hospital. The pain did not cease, but spread down to the lower part of his arm, and after his release from the hospital the condition grew worse. He was unable to rotate or lift his arm, and developed paralysis and atrophy of the muscles around the shoulder. He received further treatments from Dr. Tilley until March, 1940, and then returned to work, wearing his arm in a splint on the advice of Dr. Spangard.

Plaintiff also consulted Dr. Wilfred Sterling Clark, who had X-ray pictures taken which showed an area of diminished sensation below the shoulder and atrophy and wasting away of the muscles around the shoulder. In the opinion of Dr. Clark, plaintiff's condition was due to trauma or injury by pressure or strain, applied between his right shoulder and neck.

Plaintiff was also examined by Dr. Fernando Garduno, who expressed the opinion that plaintiff's injury was a paralysis of traumatic origin, not arising from pathological causes, and not systemic, and that the injury resulted in atrophy, loss of use and restriction of motion of the right arm and shoulder.

Plaintiff's theory is that the foregoing evidence presents a proper case for the application of the doctrine of res ipsa loquitur, and that the inference of negligence arising therefrom makes the granting of a nonsuit improper. Defendants take the position that, assuming that plaintiff's condition was in fact the result of an injury, there is no showing that the act of any particular defendant, nor any particular instrumentality, was the cause thereof. They attack plaintiff's action as an attempt to fix liability "en masse" on various defendants, some of whom were not responsible for the acts of others; and they further point to the failure to show which defendants had control of the instrumentalities that may have been involved. Their main defense may be briefly stated in two propositions: (1) that where there are several defendants, and there is a division of responsibility in the use of an instrumentality causing the injury, and the injury might have resulted from the separate act of either one of two or more persons, the rule of res ipsa loquitur cannot be invoked against any one of them; and (2) that where there are several instrumentalities, and no showing is made as to which caused the injury or as to the particular defendant in control of it, the doctrine cannot apply. We are satisfied, however, that these objections are not well taken in the circumstances of this case.

The doctrine of res ipsa loquitur has three conditions: "(1) the accident must be of a kind which ordinarily does not occur in the absence of someone's negligence; (2) it must be caused by an agency or instrumentality within the exclusive control of the defendant; (3) it must not have been due to any voluntary action or contribution on the part of the plaintiff." (Prosser, Torts, p. 295.) It is applied in a wide variety of situations, including cases of medical or dental treatment and hospital care. [ ]

There is, however, some uncertainty as to the extent to which res ipsa loquitur may be invoked in cases of injury from medical treatment. This is in part due to the tendency, in some decisions, to lay undue emphasis on the limitations of the doctrine, and to give too little attention to its basic underlying purpose. The result has been that a simple, understandable rule of circumstantial evidence, with a sound background of common sense and human experience, has occasionally been transformed into a rigid legal formula, which arbitrarily precludes its application in many cases where it is most important that it should be applied. If the doctrine is to continue to serve a useful purpose, we should not forget that "the particular force and justice of the rule, regarded as a presumption throwing upon the party charged the duty of producing evidence, consists in the circumstance that the chief evidence of the true cause, whether culpable or innocent, is practically accessible to him but inaccessible to the injured person." (9 Wigmore, Evidence [3d ed.], § 2509, p. 382; [ ]; Maki v. Murray Hospital, 91 Mont. 251 [7 P.2d 228]). In the last-named case, where an unconscious patient in a hospital received injuries from a fall, the court declared that without the doctrine the maxim that for every wrong there is a remedy would be rendered nugatory, "by denying one, patently entitled to damages, satisfaction merely because he is ignorant of facts, peculiarly within the knowledge of the party who should, in all justice, pay them."

The present case is of a type which comes within the reason and spirit of the doctrine more fully perhaps than any other. The passenger sitting awake in a railroad car at the time of a collision, the pedestrian walking along the street and struck by a falling object or the debris of an explosion, are surely not more entitled to an explanation than the unconscious patient on the operating table. Viewed from this aspect, it is difficult to see how the doctrine can, with any justification, be so restricted in its statement as to become inapplicable to a patient who submits himself to the care and custody of doctors and nurses, is rendered unconscious, and receives some injury from instrumentalities used in his treatment. Without the aid of the doctrine a patient who received permanent injuries of a serious character, obviously the result of someone's negligence, would be entirely unable to recover unless the doctors and nurses in attendance voluntarily chose to disclose the identity of the negligent person and the facts establishing liability. [ ]If this were the state of the law of negligence, the courts, to avoid gross injustice, would be forced to invoke the principles of absolute liability, irrespective of negligence, in actions by persons suffering injuries during the course of treatment under anesthesia. But we think this juncture has not yet been reached, and that the doctrine of res ipsa loquitur is properly applicable to the case before us.

The condition that the injury must not have been due to the plaintiff's voluntary action is of course fully satisfied under the evidence produced herein; and the same is true of the condition that the accident must be one which ordinarily does not occur unless someone was negligent. We have here no problem of negligence in treatment, but of distinct injury to a healthy part of the body not the subject of treatment, nor within the area covered by the operation. The decisions in this state make it clear that such circumstances raise the inference of negligence, and call upon the defendant to explain the unusual result. [ ]

The argument of defendants is simply that plaintiff has not shown an injury caused by an instrumentality under a defendant's control, because he has not shown which of the several instrumentalities that he came in contact with while in the hospital caused the injury; and he has not shown that any one defendant or his servants had exclusive control over any particular instrumentality. Defendants assert that some of them were not the employees of other defendants, that some did not stand in any permanent relationship from which liability in tort would follow, and that in view of the nature of the injury, the number of defendants and the different functions performed by each, they could not all be liable for the wrong, if any.

We have no doubt that in a modern hospital a patient is quite likely to come under the care of a number of persons in different types of contractual and other relationships with each other. For example, in the present case it appears that Doctors Swift, Spangard and Tilley were physicians or surgeons commonly placed in the legal category of independent contractors; and Dr. Reser, the anesthetist, and defendant Thompson, the special nurse, were employees of Dr. Swift and not of the other doctors. But we do not believe that either the number or relationship of the defendants alone determines whether the doctrine of res ipsa loquitur applies. Every defendant in whose custody the plaintiff was placed for any period was bound to exercise ordinary care to see that no unnecessary harm came to him and each would be liable for failure in this regard. Any defendant who negligently injured him, and any defendant charged with his care who so neglected him as to allow injury to occur, would be liable. The defendant employers would be liable for the neglect of their employees; and the doctor in charge of the operation would be liable for the negligence of those who became his temporary servants for the purpose of assisting in the operation.

In this connection, it should be noted that while the assisting physicians and nurses may be employed by the hospital, or engaged by the patient, they normally become the temporary servants or agents of the surgeon in charge while the operation is in progress, and liability may be imposed upon him for their negligent acts under the doctrine of *respondeat superior*. Thus a surgeon has been held liable for the negligence of an assisting nurse who leaves a sponge or other object inside a patient, and the fact that the duty of seeing that such mistakes do not occur is delegated to others does not absolve the doctor from responsibility for their negligence.

It may appear at the trial that, consistent with the principles outlined above, one or more defendants will be found liable and others absolved, but this should not preclude the application of the rule of res ipsa loquitur. The control, at one time or another, of one or more of the various agencies or instrumentalities which might have harmed the plaintiff was in the hands of every defendant or of his employees or temporary servants. This, we think, places upon them the burden of initial explanation. Plaintiff was rendered unconscious for the purpose of undergoing surgical treatment by the defendants; it is manifestly unreasonable for them to insist that he identify any one of them as the person who did the alleged negligent act.

The other aspect of the case which defendants so strongly emphasize is that plaintiff has not identified the instrumentality any more than he has the particular guilty defendant. Here, again, there is a misconception which, if carried to the extreme for which defendants contend, would unreasonably limit the application of the res ipsa loquitur rule. It should be enough that the plaintiff can show an injury resulting from an external force applied while he lay unconscious in the hospital; this is as clear a case of identification of the instrumentality as the plaintiff may ever be able to make.

An examination of the recent cases, particularly in this state, discloses that the test of actual exclusive control of an instrumentality has not been strictly followed, but exceptions have been recognized where the purpose of the doctrine of res ipsa loquitur would otherwise be defeated. Thus, the test has become one of right of control rather than actual control. [ ]In the bursting bottle cases where the bottler has delivered the instrumentality to a retailer and thus has given up actual control, he will nevertheless be subject to the doctrine where it is shown that no change in the condition of the bottle occurred after it left the bottler's possession, and it can accordingly be said that he was in constructive control. [ ] Moreover, this court departed from the single instrumentality theory in the colliding vehicle cases, where two defendants were involved, each in control of a separate vehicle. (See Smith v. O'Donnell, 215 Cal. 714 [12 P.2d 933]; Godfrey v. Brown, 220 Cal. 57 [29 P.2d 165, 93 A.L.R. 1072]; Carpenter, 10 So.Cal.L.Rev. 170.) Finally, it has been suggested that the hospital cases may properly be considered exceptional, and that the doctrine of res ipsa loquitur "should apply with equal force in cases wherein medical and nursing staffs take the place of machinery and may, through carelessness or lack of skill, inflict, or permit the infliction of injury upon a patient who is thereafter in no position to say how he received his injuries." (Maki v. Murray Hospital, 91 Mont. 251 [7 P.2d 228, 231]; see, also, Whetstine v. Moravec, 228 Iowa 352 [291 N.W. 425, 435], where the court refers to the "instrumentalities" as including "the unconscious body of the plaintiff.")

In the face of these examples of liberalization of the tests for res ipsa loquitur, there can be no justification for the rejection of the doctrine in the instant case. As pointed out above, if we accept the contention of defendants herein, there will rarely be any compensation for patients injured while unconscious. A hospital today conducts a highly integrated system of activities, with many persons contributing their efforts. There may be, e.g., preparation for surgery by nurses and interns who are employees of the hospital; administering of an anesthetic by a doctor who may be an employee of the hospital, an employee of the operating surgeon, or an independent contractor; performance of an operation by a surgeon and assistants who may be his employees, employees of the hospital, or independent contractors; and post surgical care by the surgeon, a hospital physician, and nurses. The number of those in whose care the patient is placed is not a good reason for denying him all reasonable opportunity to recover for negligent harm. It is rather a good reason for reexamination of the statement of legal theories which supposedly compel such a shocking result.

We do not at this time undertake to state the extent to which the reasoning of this case may be applied to other situations in which the doctrine of res ipsa loquitur is invoked. We merely hold that where a plaintiff receives unusual injuries while unconscious and in the course of medical treatment, all those defendants who had any control over his body or the instrumentalities which might have caused the injuries may properly be called upon to meet the inference of negligence by giving an explanation of their conduct.

The judgment is reversed.

■ SHENK, J., CURTIS, J., EDMONDS, J., CARTER, J., and SCHAUER, J., concurred.

NOTES AND QUESTIONS

1. This opinion quotes Prosser's formulation of res ipsa loquitur that conditions its application upon proof of three factors. In this case how is each of them met? Is that formulation consistent with the passage quoted from Wigmore? Would the plaintiff's case have been stronger, or weaker, under the Prosser approach to res ipsa loquitur if he had sued only Drs. Swift and Spangard?

For an extensive discussion of vicarious liability in the operating room, including the responsibility for negligence in counting sponges, see Truhitte v. French Hospital, 128 Cal.App.3d 332, 180 Cal.Rptr. 152 (1982).

For an extended discussion of the imposition of liability on a hospital for negligence in granting staff privileges and in reviewing the competency of its medical staff, see Strubhart v. Perry Mem. Hosp. Trust Auth., 903 P.2d 263 (Okl.1995).

2. In this case is res ipsa loquitur "a simple, understandable rule of circumstantial evidence, with a sound background of common sense and human experience"? The court relies mainly on a case involving an unconscious patient "patently entitled to damages." Is that true here?

3. On remand the trial judge as trier of fact accepted the testimony of plaintiff's experts and of an independent court-appointed expert that the injury was traumatic in origin and did not result from an infection. Except for the hospital owner, who did not personally attend plaintiff, each defendant testified that he or she "saw nothing occur which could have caused the injury." The trial judge found against all defendants and his ruling was affirmed. The court observed that "There is nothing inherent in direct testimony which compels a trial court to accept it over the contrary inferences which may reasonably be drawn from circumstantial evidence," and quoted Justice Holmes to the effect that "law does not always keep step with logic." Ybarra v. Spangard, 93 Cal.App.2d 43, 208 P.2d 445 (1949). Is this result sensible? Could the trial judge have found some defendants liable and some not liable?

4. In Inouye v. Black, 238 Cal.App.2d 31, 47 Cal.Rptr. 313 (1965), the defendant surgeon implanted stainless steel wire in plaintiff's neck to stabilize it. Although the tension was expected to break the wire, it was expected that the wire would remain in the body and cause no physical damage. The wire fragmented into unexpectedly small pieces that migrated downward toward the lower spine, necessitating further surgery to retrieve the pieces. Plaintiff sued only the surgeon. Uncontroverted medical testimony showed that he had selected the right type of wire; that if he was telling the truth, he had properly inspected it visually and manually before using it; and that the fragmentation was unexpected. The trial judge's grant of a nonsuit was affirmed on appeal. Res ipsa loquitur was inapplicable because common experience "reveals defendant's negligence as one of several available speculations, but not as a probability." It might have been that the surgeon failed to do some of the things he said he did; but it might also have been that the hospital left the wire too long in the supply room or that the wire left the manufacturer's plant with hidden flaws.

The court observed that a "group of persons and instrumentalities may combine in the performance of a medical procedure culminating in an unexpected, mysterious and disastrous result. With the sources of disaster personified in a group of defendants, the demand for evidence pointing the finger of probability at any one of them is relaxed; all may be called upon to give the jury evidence of care," citing *Ybarra* and other cases. The court then noted that since only the surgeon was before the court, that principle did not apply. If all three had been before the court, might the surgeon still have received a nonsuit?

Plaintiff was undergoing surgery for the removal of a disc when a surgical instrument broke and became lodged in his back, causing injuries. He sued the surgeon, the hospital, the manufacturer of the instrument, and the retailer who sold it to the hospital. The jury returned a verdict in favor of all defendants. On appeal, the court held, 4–3, though without a majority opinion, that the case should be reversed. The defendants should be obligated to exculpate themselves and the jury should be charged that it must find at least one defendant liable to the plaintiff. Anderson v. Somberg, 67 N.J. 291, 338 A.2d 1, cert. denied 423 U.S. 929 (1975). On remand, the judge charged as instructed and the jury returned a verdict against the manufacturer and the retailer, which was affirmed on appeal. Anderson v. Somberg, 158 N.J.Super. 384, 386 A.2d 413 (1978).

See Spannaus v. Otolaryngology Clinic, 308 Minn. 334, 242 N.W.2d 594 (1976), refusing to apply the *Ybarra* approach to a case with a similar fact pattern except that the anesthesiologist was not sued.

5. In Fireman's Fund Amer. Ins. Cos. v. Knobbe, 93 Nev. 201, 562 P.2d 825 (1977), plaintiff, a hotel's fire insurer, sued four guests to recover insurance payments it had had to make as the result of a fire that started in the room occupied by two of the guests. That couple and another couple, which was occupying a connecting room, had all been smoking in the room shortly before the fire broke out. Plaintiff was unable to prove which defendant had been negligent and sought to invoke res ipsa loquitur. The court upheld a summary judgment granted the defendants and rejected *Ybarra*. In doing so, it agreed with Justice Traynor who, dissenting in Raber v. Tumin, 36 Cal.2d 654, 226 P.2d 574 (1951), had warned of the danger of extending *Ybarra*. He asserted that under *Ybarra,* a plaintiff "who is struck on the head by a flower pot falling from a multistoried apartment building may recover judgment against all the tenants unless the innocent tenants are able to identify the guilty one."

If you are run over by a negligent hit-and-run driver as you cross the street and all you can tell is the year, make and color of the car, what analysis if you sue jointly all local owners of such cars and rest after your testimony about what happened?

6. It has been suggested that in the Ybarra case each participant in the operation who stated exactly what he or she did should be entitled to a directed verdict. "It is something of a mockery to require the defendant in the name of fairness to offer an explanation and then let a jury ignore the explanation on no other basis than its choice not to believe." The author does recognize, however, that if the explanation is evasive or "suggests mendacity" the case should go to the jury. Jaffe, Res Ipsa Loquitur Vindicated, 1 Buffalo L.Rev. 1, 11 (1951). Is this defensible?

7. In Judson v. Giant Powder Co., 107 Cal. 549, 40 P. 1020 (1895), the defendant's nitroglycerine factory exploded, killing all who could possibly have explained why it happened. In a suit by plaintiff, whose property was damaged, the court held that evidence of the explosion sufficed to withstand a nonsuit. Is this sound in a situation in which rebuttal is impossible?

8. *Ybarra* was flatly rejected in Barrett v. Emanuel Hospital, 64 Or.App. 635, 669 P.2d 835, review denied 296 Or. 237, 675 P.2d 491 (1983). First, "modern discovery practice" casts doubt on the need for the *Ybarra* approach. Second, the inference of res ipsa "is permitted only when the plaintiff is able to establish . . . the probability that a particular defendant's conduct was the cause of the plaintiff's harm." Finally, special protections for unconscious patients could "be achieved in various direct ways which may warrant societal consideration, e.g., strict liability or some form of *respondeat superior* liability. However, we do not think the objective should be pursued by stretching a permissible inference beyond the point where there are underlying facts other than the result from which it can reasonably be drawn." The complaint was dismissed.

E. THE SPECIAL CASE OF MEDICAL MALPRACTICE

In this section we consider special legal and practical problems involved in medical malpractice cases. In the process we review the standard of care, the role of custom, and questions of proof. Consider the following excerpt from Robbins v. Footer, 553 F.2d 123 (D.C.Cir.1977), involving a claim against an obstetrician:

> The conduct of a defendant in a negligence suit is usually measured against the conduct of a hypothetical reasonably prudent person acting under the same or similar circumstances. [ ] In medical malpractice cases, however, courts have required that the specialized knowledge and skill of the defendant must be taken into account. [ ] Although the law had thus imposed a higher standard of care on doctors, it has tempered the impact of that rule by permitting the profession, as a group, to set its own legal standards of reasonable conduct. Whether a defendant has or has not conformed his conduct to a customary practice is generally only evidence of whether he has acted as a reasonably prudent person. [ ] In a malpractice case, however, the question of whether the defendant acted in conformity with the common practice within his profession is the heart of the suit. [ ] As part

of his prima facie case a malpractice plaintiff must affirmatively prove the relevant recognized standard of medical care exercised by other physicians and that the defendant departed from that standard when treating the plaintiff. [   ] In almost all cases the plaintiff must present expert witnesses since the technical complexity of the facts and issues usually prevents the jury itself from determining both the appropriate standard of care and whether the defendant's conduct conformed to that standard. In such cases there can be no finding of negligence without expert testimony to support it. [   ]

Despite the refined standard of care, judges must still be sure to use language in their charges that conveys the objective nature of the inquiry. In Di Franco v. Klein, 657 A.2d 145 (R.I.1995), the court overturned a defense verdict in a malpractice case because the trial judge had likely confused the jury by stating that the defendant was not liable "even if in the exercise of . . . good faith judgment she has made a mistake as to the course of treatment taken" and that a physician "is not liable for damages resulting from an honest mistake or error in judgment."

The following case explores problems of establishing the standard of care through the use of experts.

Jones v. O'Young

Supreme Court of Illinois, 1992.
154 Ill.2d 39, 607 N.E.2d 224.

[Plaintiff husband and wife brought a medical malpractice action against a hospital and several doctors—three of whom remain in the case at this stage: Dr. Kalimuthu, who was board certified in plastic surgery and general surgery; Dr. O'Young, who was an orthopedic surgeon; and Dr. Pacis, who was a general surgeon. Plaintiff husband was hurt in an auto accident. While in the hospital "he developed an infectious process in the fractured leg known as pseudomonas osteomyelitis. Plaintiffs claimed that defendants' negligence led to the amputation of Jones' left leg." In response to a demand by defendants, plaintiffs identified their expert witness as Dr. Malcolm Deam, who was board certified in internal medicine and infectious diseases. The three defendant doctors moved to bar Dr. Deam's testimony as an expert at trial. Following a hearing on Dr. Deam's qualifications, the trial court granted the motion but also, because the court thought appellate opinions were in conflict, certified the following question of law for appeal:

In order to testify concerning the standard of care required of and deviations from the standard of care by a defendant physician specializing in an area of medicine, must the plaintiff's expert also specialize in the same area of medicine as the defendant, so that, in this case, the plaintiff's infectious disease specialist would not be qualified to testify against the defendant plastic surgeon, orthopedic surgeon, or general surgeon with regard to each defendant's care and treatment of the infectious disease, pseudomonas osteo-myelitis?

Defendants' ensuing motions for summary judgment were denied without prejudice pending the result of an appeal.]

■ JUSTICE CLARK delivered the opinion of the court:

. . .

. . . We answer the [certified] question in the negative. We are not reviewing the trial court's decision as to the competency of Dr. Deam to testify and are considering only the question certified by the trial court. [ ]

In Purtill v. Hess (1986), 111 Ill.2d 229, 489 N.E.2d 867, this court articulated the requirements necessary to demonstrate an expert physician's qualifications and competency to testify. First, the physician must be a licensed member of the school of medicine about which he proposes to testify. [ ] Second, "the expert witness must show that he is familiar with the methods, procedures, and treatments ordinarily observed by other physicians, in either the defendant physician's community or a similar community." [ ] Once the foundational requirements have been met, the trial court has the discretion to determine whether a physician is qualified and competent to state his opinion as an expert regarding the standard of care. [ ]

By hearing evidence on the expert's qualifications and comparing the medical problem and the type of treatment in the case to the experience and background of the expert, the trial court can evaluate whether the witness has demonstrated a sufficient familiarity with the standard of care practiced in the case. The foundational requirements provide the trial court with the information necessary to determine whether an expert has expertise in dealing with the plaintiff's medical problem and treatment. Whether the expert is qualified to testify is not dependent on whether he is a member of the same specialty or subspecialty as the defendant but, rather, whether the allegations of negligence concern matters within his knowledge and observation.

If the plaintiff fails to satisfy either of the foundational requirements of *Purtill*, the trial court must disallow the expert's testimony. [ ] The requirements are a threshold beneath which the plaintiff cannot fall without failing to sustain the allegations of his complaint. They monitor the course the plaintiff's action will take, and are sufficiently comprehensive in alerting the trial court to the concerns relevant in determining the admissibility of the expert's testimony.

If the trial court determines that the expert is qualified, the defendant is then in the position to direct the jury's attention to any infirmities in his testimony or his competency to testify. Cross-examination, argument and jury instructions provide defense counsel with the opportunity and means to challenge the expert's qualifications as well as the opinion he offers. Restricting the qualification of experts to those physicians who are members of the same specialty or subspecialty as the defendant would only upset the balance necessary to an adversarial system without any compensating benefit. Accordingly, we reaffirm this court's position in *Purtill* without qualification.

.   .   .

The cause is remanded to the circuit court for further proceedings.

NOTES AND QUESTIONS

1.   How should the trial judge proceed on remand? What steps might the defendants take?

2.   The court asserts that the expert witness must show familiarity with the "defendant physician's community or a similar community." In *Robbins*, the defendant obstetrician argued that local practice in the District of Columbia set the appropriate standard. The issue arose when the trial judge excluded expert testimony of a witness who was not familiar with practice in the District of Columbia. The court reviewed the history of the locality rule:

> Geographic limitations on the appropriate reference group for establishing the standard of care which the law of negligence requires of a doctor first appeared in American decisions of the nineteenth century. As originally formulated, the rule was sometimes interpreted as only holding a physician to the standard of those physicians who actually practiced in his community. . . . The policy behind the rule was to prevent the small town practitioner from being held to the standards of practice of the more sophisticated urban areas. The courts generally assumed that the rural practitioner had less access to the latest medical information and facilities than urban doctors and did not have the benefit of the same breadth of experience. It was also argued that since the cities offered a more lucrative practice, they attracted the most talented doctors and any attempt to hold country doctors to urban standards would only drive rural doctors out of practice, leaving small communities without any doctors.
>
> [It soon became apparent that in towns with only one or a small group of doctors those few would set the standard.] The rule was thus broadened to "the same or similar localities"—the standard applied by the district court in this case.

How should a court determine whether a locality is "similar" for purpose of qualifying an expert? In fact, as we see in the next note, the *Robbins* court rejected "the same or similar localities" rule.

3.   The *Jones* court noted that one of the three defendants was "board-certified" but that played no part in the decision. That fact was central to the resolution of *Robbins*, where the obstetrician was certified:

> Modern medical education and postgraduate training has been nationalized. Scientific information flows freely among medical institutions throughout the country. Professional journals and numerous other networks of continuing education are all national in scope. [ ]

Several courts have . . . established a national standard of care for all physicians, completely abandoning any locality limitation. . . .

Even in jurisdictions which have not adopted a national standard for all malpractice issues, if a physician holds himself out as a specialist, [as defendant had done here], he is held to the general standard of care required of all physicians in the same specialty. [ ] In order to become a certified specialist in obstetrics, a physician must meet nationally uniform educational and residency requirements. [ ] The textbooks used are national textbooks and the required examination is a national exam graded by a body of examiners selected so as to eliminate any regional peculiarities. [ ]After certification, specialists keep abreast of developments in their field through medical specialty journals available throughout the nation and medical specialty societies with national memberships. It seems clear that the medical profession itself has adopted a national standard for membership in one of its certified specialties. If the law remains tied to a locality standard it ignores the reality of modern medicine in favor of an outdated mythology.

Does the court's analysis in *Jones v. O'Young* implicitly reject this approach?

4.   The reference to the same "school" is a reference to the training and practice of the physician. In a case cited by the court, a physician was held unqualified to testify as to the conduct of a podiatrist. The majority concluded that a podiatrist had been trained differently from a physician and defendant was entitled to be judged only by others in that same school. Other courts disagree.

Sometimes "school" is used to differentiate between training that a "physician" has received. See, e.g., Frazier v. Hurd, 380 Mich. 291, 157 N.W.2d 249 (1968)(asserting that an allopathic physician would be permitted to testify against an osteopathic physician if the expert were able to show familiarity with the standards of the osteopathic school).

A third possible meaning of the term is suggested in Sinclair v. Block, 534 Pa. 563, 633 A.2d 1137 (1993), in which plaintiffs claimed malpractice due to the defendant's use of forceps in delivering a baby. The court noted that "the 'two schools of thought' doctrine provides a complete defense to a malpractice claim when the prescribed medical treatment or procedure has been approved by one group of medical experts even though an alternate group recommends another approach, or the experts agree that alternative treatments or procedures are acceptable". The trial judge erred by failing to charge the jury on the "two schools" defense raised by the defendant.

5.   The *Jones* court is concerned about restricting expert testimony in a way that would "upset the balance necessary to an adversarial system without any compensating benefit." What is that balance in this type of case? How might it be affected by restricting experts to the same specialty as the defendant? Is the same concern present in requiring that the expert come from the same locality or from one similar to that of the defendant?

6. How are experts retained and compensated? If witnesses to auto accidents are not paid why should medical experts be paid? In Henning v. Thomas, 235 Va. 181, 366 S.E.2d 109 (1988), the court held that the trial judge committed error by not permitting defendants to show the jury that the plaintiff's expert was a " 'doctor for hire' who was part of a nationwide group that offered themselves as witnesses, on behalf of medical malpractice plaintiffs. Once the jury was made aware of this information it was for the jury to decide what weight, if any, to give to [the expert's] testimony. This was a classic case of an effort to establish bias, prejudice, or relationship." Is it relevant that an expert retained by one side has never rendered an opinion on behalf of the other side? Is it relevant that an expert has testified in 20 cases during the past year—and has seen patients only three weeks during that period?

7. For many years, the usual requirement of expert testimony in malpractice cases was difficult for some plaintiffs to meet for reasons unrelated to the merits of the case. In 1961, a survey of surgeons indicated that only 30 percent would be willing to testify against another surgeon who had removed the wrong kidney. Medical Economics, Aug. 28, 1961. Physicians who criticized colleagues might face expulsion from the local medical society. Bernstein v. Alameda–Contra Costa Medical Ass'n, 139 Cal.App.2d 241, 293 P.2d 862 (1956). See also L'Orange v. Medical Protective Co., 394 F.2d 57 (6th Cir.1968), in which plaintiff alleged that defendant insurer had cancelled his malpractice policy because he had testified in court against a dentist also insured by the defendant.

These concerns undoubtedly induced courts to devise techniques for avoiding the need for experts in certain kinds of cases. One change permitted a plaintiff to call the defendant physician and try to use that testimony to fill gaps in plaintiff's case. Some courts permitted the plaintiff to read treatises to educate the jury.

8. On occasion plaintiffs in malpractice cases do not need experts. For example, it might be shown that without any need for hasty termination of a surgical procedure, a sponge or a surgical instrument was inadvertently left in the plaintiff's abdomen. Or it might be shown that the surgeon operated on the left leg when it was the right leg that needed the treatment. In each case, the court might rule that the case came within a "common knowledge" exception by which lay jurors could be found able to understand the facts and the applicable standard without expert guidance. In such cases, it would necessarily follow that even if an expert testified for the defense that the relevant segment of the medical profession behaved as the defendant did, the jury would not be required to accept that as the proper standard.

Recall Leonard v. Watsonville Community Hospital, p. 87, supra, involving a clamp that was left inside the plaintiff. The court stated that even if the defendants were trying to assert that there was a custom in the relevant community not to count instruments before closing an incision, that would not control the case: "It is a matter of common knowledge . . . that no special skill is required in counting instruments. Although under such circumstances proof of practice or custom is some evidence of what should be done and may assist in the determination of what constitutes due care, it does not conclusively establish the standard of care."

9. Although aspects of the standard of care may be special to medical malpractice, the need for experts is not. When buildings collapse, when factories catch fire, when chemicals escape, the plaintiff will often need an expert to explain the underlying mechanics or technology to the jury so that the judge can be confident that the jury will understand the facts sufficiently to be able to make a rational determination of whether or not there was negligence. We return to expert testimony in Chapter V.

10. For comprehensive treatment of the medical malpractice area, see P. Weiler, Medical Malpractice on Trial (1991); F. Sloan and R. Bovbjerg, Medical Malpractice: Crisis, Response and Effects (1989); Symposium, Medical Malpractice: Can the Private Sector Find Relief? 49 Law & Contemp.Probs. 1–348 (1986). In Chapter XI we consider recent developments and proposals for changing the handling of medical malpractice litigation.

Connors v. University Associates in Obstetrics & Gynecology, Inc.

United States Court of Appeals, Second Circuit, 1993.
4 F.3d 123.

[In an effort to become pregnant, plaintiff underwent surgery. After the surgery she lost all function in her left leg. In this diversity action brought by plaintiff and her husband, the theory of plaintiff's experts was that a retractor used to keep the incision open had impinged on a nerve leading to plaintiff's left leg. Plaintiff's expert testified that the requisite care with this retractor required (1) caution in opening the blades so as not to exert too much force; (2) assuring that the blades not impinge on the muscle, the pelvic wall or various nerves; (3) releasing the retractor during surgery to reduce pressure on these areas; and (4) altering the position of the retractor blades to avoid prolonged pressure on these areas. Plaintiff tried to show that these had not been done carefully. Experts on both sides agreed that the retractors had to be used carefully. They disagreed, however, over whether the injury could still have occurred even if the defendants had been careful with the retractor. Plaintiff's experts testified that the injury would not have occurred in such a case even if plaintiff's nerve had been abnormally situated. Defense experts testified that plaintiff's nerve was "abnormally positioned, an anatomical rarity that the performing physicians could not have anticipated. These experts also testified that nerve injuries in operations of this type were sometimes unavoidable complications not attributable to negligence."

At the first trial the judge refused to charge res ipsa loquitur. After a defense verdict, the judge granted a new trial on the ground that he had erred in refusing to charge res ipsa. More facts are stated in the opinion.]

■ Before: NEWMAN, CHIEF JUDGE, VAN GRAAFEILAND, and ALTIMARI, CIRCUIT JUDGES.

■ ALTIMARI, CIRCUIT JUDGE.

. . .

. . . At the close of the second trial, the district court, over University Associates' objection, issued the following instruction to the jury:

> In ordinary cases, the mere fact that an accident or injury happened does not furnish evidence that it was caused by any person's negligence. And the plaintiff must prove some negligent act or omission on the part of the defendant. This is the method of finding negligence that I have just described to you.

> Nevertheless, I instruct you in this case that you may find the defendant, University Associates, negligent if you find that the plaintiff has proved each of the following elements by a preponderance of the evidence: first, that an injury to the plaintiff [was caused] by the self-retaining retractor used during her surgery; [second], that at the time of the accident or injury, the self-retaining retractor was under the exclusive control or management of Dr. John Brumsted and/or his surgical assistants . . . ; and, third, that in the normal course of events this type of injury would not have occurred without the negligence of the person having control and management of the self-retaining retractor.

> I say that you may so find. You are not compelled to so find. You should consider all the facts and circumstances in evidence and also the defendant's explanation. You are reminded that the plaintiff has the burden of proving the defendant's negligence by a preponderance of the evidence.

At the close of the second trial, the jury returned a verdict for the plaintiffs in the amount of $800,000. University Associates moved for a new trial, arguing that the res ipsa instruction was error. That motion was denied.

University Associates now appeals the result of the second trial, arguing that the district court erred in instructing the jury on res ipsa loquitur where: (1) expert testimony on causation was given; and (2) Connors introduced direct evidence on the cause of the injury. The appeal brings up for review both the correctness of giving a res ipsa loquitur charge at the second trial and the order granting a new trial for lack of a res ipsa loquitur charge at the first trial.

. . .

University Associates has not challenged the district court's ruling that Vermont law would allow a res ipsa instruction in medical malpractice cases generally. However, the defendants-appellees contend that res ipsa should not apply to medical malpractice cases in which expert testimony is presented. The basis for this contention is that res ipsa is a doctrine traditionally grounded on the theory that jurors share a common experience that allows them to make certain inferences of negligence. If expert testimony is needed to support the inference, then the inference does not come from common experience but from uncommon experience (i.e., specialized medical knowledge).

University Associates has raised an issue that has divided jurisdictions across the country. Unless a medical malpractice case is factually simple (i.e., leaving a sponge in the patient), jurors' common experience will not provide them with the requisite insight to determine whether certain injuries can only be the result of negligence. In such non-obvious cases, courts are presented with a choice of either allowing a res ipsa loquitur instruction and permitting the plaintiff to educate the jury through the use of experts, or of disallowing the application of res ipsa loquitur and leaving the plaintiff to demonstrate negligence solely through the opinions of experts.

Although no Vermont court has ruled on the issue, there is a clear split between states in their treatment of res ipsa loquitur charges in medical malpractice cases. Some states allow the plaintiff to come forward with expert testimony to support a res ipsa theory, while others preclude the use of a res ipsa instruction in non-obvious cases and permit its use only in cases where the plaintiff's injury is one that the average citizen can perceive to be a function of negligence based on everyday experience. . . .

We conclude . . . that the district court was correct in predicting that Vermont would permit a plaintiff to utilize expert testimony to "bridge the gap" between the jury's common knowledge and the uncommon knowledge of experts. The Restatement explicitly encourages the use of expert testimony in medical malpractice cases involving res ipsa loquitur:

> In the usual case the basis of past experience from which this conclusion may be drawn is common to the community, and is a matter of general knowledge, which the court recognizes on much the same basis as when it takes judicial notice of facts which everyone knows. It may, however, be supplied by the evidence of the parties; and expert testimony that such an event usually does not occur without negligence may afford a sufficient basis for the inference. Such testimony may be essential to the plaintiff's case where, as for example in some actions for medical malpractice, there is no fund of common knowledge which may permit laymen reasonably to draw the conclusion.

Restatement, § 328D, comment *d*. Moreover, states have increasingly chosen to follow the modern trend in permitting expert testimony, [citing cases from 14 jurisdictions].

The restrictive view of res ipsa loquitur, barring expert testimony, erroneously overstates the importance of the traditional "common knowledge" requirement. Whether the knowledge required to evaluate the likelihood of negligent conduct inferred from an accident comes from common or specialized knowledge, the key question is still whether that accident would normally occur in the ordinary course of events. As the district court stated:

> in this era of constantly developing medical science, cases in which injuries bespeak negligence to the average person occur less and less and complex cases predominate. If courts refuse to allow experts to testify to what is common knowledge within their fields, then they are not being responsive to new conditions nor are they keeping abreast of changes in society.

[ ]. Experts within a field share a common knowledge about whether a certain type of injury could only occur through negligence, just as average citizens can share a common knowledge about whether barrels of flour normally roll out of warehouse windows. [ ] These experts can educate the jurors, essentially training them to be twelve new initiates into a different, higher level of common knowledge. The jurors can then determine for themselves whether the expert opinion is credible, after also considering the defendant's experts' opinions that res ipsa does not apply. . . .

This is clearly the type of case in which expert testimony was appropriate and necessary. To find otherwise would place Connors in a "Catch–22," presenting her with a choice of either introducing expert testimony or forgoing a res ipsa instruction. . . . If the res ipsa instruction were to be given without the expert testimony, the jury would be given the opportunity to find the defendants negligent without proof, but the jury would lack the acumen to be able to determine whether the injury was truly the type that could not occur but for the defendant's negligence.

Alternatively, Connors could introduce the expert testimony but do without the res ipsa charge, as in the first trial. This would give the jurors the ability to evaluate the injury, but would not instruct them that they can make the leap to inferring negligence from the fact of the injury. Expert testimony in this case was not able to prove conclusively that negligence caused Connors' injury. Rather, Connors' experts opined that there was nothing unusual about Connors' anatomy, contrary to the defendant-appellant's suggestion, and that the injury could only have occurred if the doctors had negligently used the retractor. This does not, by itself, support a finding of negligence. A res ipsa instruction was needed to allow the jury to make the inference. The res ipsa loquitur instruction in this case was important guidance to the jurors, informing them that, if they credited the testimony of Connors' experts, they could infer that the physicians were negligent simply because the injury occurred.

A res ipsa loquitur instruction is given in order to allow a plaintiff with no ability to show actual negligence the opportunity to prove negligence through inference. It is especially necessary in medical malpractice cases, since the unconscious plaintiff is in no position to be able to testify about what happened to her in surgery. . . .

[On the second issue the court agreed with the district court that plaintiffs had not "proved themselves out of" res ipsa loquitur by trying to prove specific negligence. The court cited Vermont cases that "comport with the majority rule" that a plaintiff can "couple a res ipsa argument with evidence of specific acts of negligence by the defendant."

The judgment was affirmed.]

NOTES AND QUESTIONS

1. Assume the following evidence. Expert evidence shows that custom and good practice require that retractor pressure be released every 15 minutes. The nurse testifies—and the record supports this—that until near the end of the operation she told the surgeon every time 15 minutes had passed and the surgeon stopped working for a minute or two so that the nurse could release the pressure on the retractor. The last time the nurse informed the surgeon that 15 minutes had passed, the surgeon said that he was almost finished with the surgery and rather than take time to release the pressure he told the nurse to do nothing. This meant that the last time the nurse released the pressure was 23 minutes before the end of the surgery. The plaintiff's expert testifies that the extra eight minutes of pressure probably caused the harm that plaintiff suffered. Does this case involve res ipsa loquitur?

2. Why is there general agreement that res ipsa loquitur is available in the "sponge" cases?

3. Why is there disagreement in cases like *Connors*? Is it realistic to suggest that "experts can educate the jurors, essentially training them to be twelve new initiates into a different, higher level of common knowledge"? What are juries likely to discuss after receiving a res ipsa instruction—that is, after being told that an inference of negligence is permissible—in the following cases:

    a. Byrne v. Boadle.

    b. Hammontree v. Jenner.

    c. Sponge left in a surgery patient—no expert testimony.

    d. The Connors case.

4. If experts testify that out of every 100 operations of a particular type five fail, has plaintiff made out a res ipsa case? What if the testimony is that of those five failures on average three are due to malpractice? Is either of these situations similar to what plaintiff's expert in *Connors* was saying when, based on his experience, he testified that the defendants' use of the retractor was probably negligent—in some undetermined and undeterminable way?

5. What role might experts play in a case brought by home owners who were hurt when their recently built house collapsed in an earthquake?

Might their role extend to helping plaintiff develop a res ipsa case against the contractor?

Korman v. Mallin

Supreme Court of Alaska, 1993.
858 P.2d 1145.

[Plaintiff consulted defendant plastic surgeon to inquire about possible breast reduction surgery. At this initial visit, plaintiff viewed two videotapes—one an overview of the procedure and the other dealing with the procedure itself. Defendant then examined plaintiff briefly. He then, in the presence of his medical assistant, discussed the procedure, including a variety of risks including permanent scarring. Defendant gave plaintiff pamphlets about the procedure to read at home. These restated the risk of permanent scarring. At a second visit, defendant described the surgery and drew a diagram of the procedure. Plaintiff's affidavit stated that when she expressed concern about the scarring, defendant responded in part "I've done . . . don't worry about it. I've done hundreds of them.
 . . . I think that you'll be happy with the results." Plaintiff also alleged that defendant did not tell her that as a smoker she ran a risk of scarring that was 50% greater than that of nonsmokers—though she acknowledged reading about this in the consent form she signed. An affidavit from another assistant stated that plaintiff acknowledged that all her questions had been answered and that she understood that no guarantees were given concerning the outcome of the surgery. After the surgery, which occurred a few days after the second visit, plaintiff was "very unhappy with the result—particularly the broad, wide and painful scars." Plaintiff's suit claimed that defendant had negligently failed to obtain her informed consent to the surgery. The trial court granted defendant summary judgment. Further facts are stated in the opinion.]

■ Before MOORE, C.J., and RABINOWITZ, MATTHEWS and COMPTON, JJ.

■ MOORE, CHIEF JUSTICE.

. . .

Alaska Statute 09.55.556(a) provides that a physician is liable for failure to obtain the informed consent of a patient if

the claimant establishes by a preponderance of the evidence that the provider has failed to inform the patient of the common risks and reasonable alternatives to the proposed treatment or procedure, and that but for that failure the claimant would not have consented to the proposed treatment or procedure. [ ]

. . .

Traditionally, a physician's duty to disclose information concerning treatment has been measured by the professional standard in the field. [ ] This rule reflects the belief that holding a physician to a lay standard of disclosure would interfere with the flexibility a physician must have in determining what therapy would best suit the patient's needs. [ ] In order to establish a prima facie case, a plaintiff must usually present expert testimony of the professional standard of disclosure in the community and of the physician's failure to meet that standard. [ ]

However, the modern trend is to measure the physician's duty of disclosure by what a reasonable patient would need to know in order to make an informed and intelligent decision. The Louisiana Supreme Court has articulated this standard as follows:

Patient's Rule

> The informed consent doctrine is based on the principle that every human being of adult years and sound mind has a right to determine what shall be done to his or her own body. Surgeons and other doctors are thus required to provide their patients with sufficient information to permit the patient to make an informed and intelligent decision on whether to submit to a proposed course of treatment. Where circumstances permit, the patient should be told the nature of the pertinent ailment or condition, the general nature of the proposed treatment or procedure, the risks involved in the proposed treatment or procedure, the prospects of success, the risks of failing to undergo any treatment or procedure at all, and the risks of any alternate methods of treatment.

Hondroulis v. Schuhmacher, 553 So.2d 398, 411 (La.1988). [ ] Under this modern view, expert testimony concerning the professional standard of disclosure is not a necessary element of the plaintiff's case because the scope of disclosure is measured from the standpoint of the patient.

Our recent comments on the nature of the physician-patient relationship echo the concerns outlined by the Hondroulis court:

> The physician-patient relationship is one of trust. Because the patient lacks the physician's expertise, the patient must rely on the physician for virtually all information about the patient's treatment and health. A physician therefore undertakes, not only to treat a patient physically, but also to respond fully to a patient's inquiry about his treatment, i.e., to tell the patient everything that a reasonable person would want to know about the treatment.

Pedersen v. Zielski, 822 P.2d 903, 909 (Alaska 1991)(citations omitted). We are persuaded that the modern view is the better rule and hold that the scope of disclosure required under [the statute] must be measured by what a reasonable patient would need to know in order to make an informed and intelligent decision about the proposed treatment.

Under the reasonable patient rule, a physician must disclose those risks which are "material" to a reasonable patient's decision concerning treatment [ ]:

> The determination of materiality is a two-step process. The first step is to define the existence and nature of the risk and the likelihood of its occurrence. "Some" expert testimony is necessary to establish this aspect of materiality because only a physician or other qualified expert is capable of judging what risk exists and

the likelihood of its occurrence. The second prong of the materiality test is for the trier of fact to decide whether the probability of
that type of harm is a risk which a reasonable patient would
consider in deciding on treatment. The focus is on whether a
reasonable person in the patient's position would attach significance to the specific risk. This determination does not require
expert testimony. [ ].

Evidence of
Objective
theory

We also note that, in certain circumstances, a physician's failure to
disclose a risk may be privileged:

> [T]he physician retains a qualified privilege to withhold informa-
> tion on therapeutic grounds, as in those cases where a complete
> and candid disclosure of possible alternatives and consequences
> might have a detrimental effect on the physical or psychological
> well-being of the patient, or where the patient is incapable of
> giving his consent by reason of mental disability or infancy, or has
> specifically requested that he not be told. Likewise the physician's
> duty to disclose is suspended where an emergency of such gravity
> and urgency exists that it is impractical to obtain the patient's
> consent. Finally disclosure is not required where the risk is either
> known to the patient or is so obvious as to justify presumption of
> such knowledge, nor is the physician under a duty to discuss the
> relatively remote risks inherent in common procedures, when it is
> common knowledge that such risks inherent in the procedure are
> of very low incidence. Conversely, where the physician does not
> know of a risk and should not have been aware of it in the exercise
> of ordinary care, he is under no obligation to make disclosure.

Patient's
Rule
Exceptions

Sard v. Hardy, 281 Md. 432, 379 A.2d 1014, 1022–23 (1977); [ ]. As
noted by the courts which have examined this issue, the burden of going
forward with evidence pertaining to a privilege rests on the physician in
whose hands the necessary evidence ordinarily rests. [ ]

. . .

After deciding which legal standard to apply, the issue becomes whether the information Dr. Mallin provided Korman satisfies this standard as a
matter of law. Although Korman maintains that a patient would have "no
inkling" that painful and unsightly scarring is a normal consequence of
uncomplicated breast reduction surgery after reviewing the pamphlets,
videos and consent forms provided by Dr. Mallin, we cannot agree. Dr.
Mallin's office notes indicate he discussed scarring at both visits. Both the
videos and pamphlets provided by Dr. Mallin emphasize that breast reduction surgery resulted in permanent scars. Finally the consent forms signed
by Korman specifically refer to the risk of "unsightly and painful scarring."
The trial court concluded that the information Dr. Mallin provided Korman
clearly advised her of the scarring risk and therefore granted Dr. Mallin's
motion for summary judgment.

Nonetheless, merely identifying a risk does not necessarily provide a patient with the information necessary for an informed decision.[5] For a trial court to decide on summary judgment that a doctor has disclosed sufficient information to allow a reasonable patient to make an informed decision about treatment, the record must establish that the physician explained to the patient in lay terms the nature and severity of the risk and the likelihood of its occurrence. [ ]

After reviewing the record on appeal, we are unable to conclude that Dr. Mallin's explanation of the risks inherent in this procedure satisfied his duty of disclosure as a matter of law. In her affidavit, Korman states that she requested additional information about the scarring at the second consultation and that, in response, Dr. Mallin told her "not to worry" and that she would be happy with the results. A number of courts have held that a patient's request for more detailed information regarding a risk is a factor in determining whether there has been adequate disclosure. See [ ] (holding that physician's duty of disclosure was "expanded" when patient requested physician to explain the "least likely" complications of proposed surgery); see also Kinikin v. Heupel, 305 N.W.2d 589, 595 (Minn.1981)(holding that where a doctor is aware or should be aware that a patient attaches particular significance to a risk, further disclosure may be required even under the professional community standard). Our own comments in *Pedersen* emphasize a physician's duty to respond fully to a patient's questions concerning treatment. [ ]

Furthermore, although it is undisputed that Korman read that portion of the consent form which states that all risks of the procedure were increased by 50% because she smoked, this information has little meaning in the absence of a base probability figure establishing the average risk to an average patient. The record does not indicate that Dr. Mallin disclosed to Korman the probability that painful and unsightly scarring would occur in her case or explained the increased risk of such scarring attributable to smoking. [ ]

There is no question that an individual contemplating elective cosmetic surgery will attach particular significance to the risk of "unsightly and painful" scarring. Although Dr. Mallin certainly provided Korman with a significant amount of information concerning the proposed procedure and its attendant risks, we cannot say that he satisfied his duty of disclosure as a matter of law in light of the above circumstances. . . . We conclude that it is a factual question whether Dr. Mallin's explanation of the scarring risk was adequate to allow a reasonable patient to make an informed and intelligent decision whether to undergo the procedure.

. . .

---

5. It is meaningless to tell a patient that a given risk is increased by 50% unless the patient is also told the original or baseline risk factor. For example, assuming the risk of unsightly scarring for nonsmokers is 2%, the risk for a smoker rises to 3%. However, if the risk factor for nonsmokers is 20%, the risk for a smoker rises to 30%, a very significant increase. A physician must not only disclose the identity of all known material risks, but also the likelihood of their occurrence in meaningful terms. [ ]

NOTES AND QUESTIONS

1. What are the merits of the professional standard approach? The reasonable patient approach? What role does expert testimony play in each?

2. Is it consistent to focus on what a reasonable patient would want to know—and then to recognize the exceptions that the court notes? Consider the justification for each situation suggested by the court.

3. How is a physician to determine that a patient "attaches particular significance to a risk"?

4. Note that the quoted statute requires plaintiff to prove that "but for" the failure to inform her, she would not have consented to the procedure. After any event that is disappointing a person may have second thoughts. Assume that plaintiff testifies that if told all the material risks she would have declined the procedure; that the jury believes the plaintiff would have behaved as she says; but that the jury is also persuaded that a reasonable person would not have declined. Is it sound to let plaintiff recover on these facts? On the other hand, is using an objective "reasonable patient" approach consistent with the view that these decisions are for the individual patient to make. Almost all courts, even those using the broader disclosure standard, reject the Alaska statute's subjective consent standard.

5. In Pauscher v. Iowa Methodist Medical Center, 408 N.W.2d 355 (Iowa 1987), the patient developed post-delivery problems. After aggressive drug treatment failed, the physician ordered an intravenous procedure that carried some risk of mild reaction and a 1 in 100,000 to 1 in 150,000 risk of death from anaphylactic shock. The court concluded that telling "a patient with a potentially life-threatening illness [that] there was a 1 in 100,000 chance she could die from a diagnostic procedure" could not have affected her decision.

6. In Henderson v. Milobsky, 595 F.2d 654 (D.C.Cir.1978), plaintiff who was to undergo removal of a wisdom tooth was not told of a 1 in 100,000 risk of permanent loss of sensation in an area a half-inch square just below the lower lip. The court concluded that the risk was "undoubtedly troublesome but hardly disabling." No "prudent juror could reasonably have concluded" that the risk was material.

7. Is it negligent not to inform a patient about an experimental therapy alternative to surgery that is not recognized by professors at the state's medical schools as a "practical alternative" to the surgery and that is opposed openly by a number of professional associations, though some unorganized physicians publicly argue that it ought to be accepted? In Moore v. Baker, 989 F.2d 1129 (11th Cir.1993), the court read Georgia law as requiring disclosure only of alternatives that are "generally recognized and accepted by reasonably prudent physicians."

8. Is there an obligation to warn patients of the risks of declining or delaying treatment? In Truman v. Thomas, 27 Cal.3d 285, 611 P.2d 902, 165 Cal.Rptr. 308 (1980), the court, 4–3, held that a physician might be liable for not advising his patient of the dangers of not getting a Pap smear. The patient contracted cervical cancer and died. The court held that the trial court improperly failed to charge that the physician was "liable for any injury legally resulting from the patient's refusal to take the test if a reasonably prudent person in the patient's position would not have refused the test if she had been adequately informed of all the significant perils." The dissenters argued that "when no intrusion takes place, no need for consent—effective or otherwise—arises." They also argued that the value of a Pap smear in spotting cervical cancer was common knowledge.

9. The consent issue is also raised by assertions that health care provider D should not have done the procedure but should have referred the patient to provider T because the collected statistics show that provider D has a 15% rate of adverse outcomes, compared to provider T's rate of 10%. Note that the providers might be hospitals or surgeons. Should the duty to obtain informed consent require that D tell the patient the different statistics (and provide a reasonable and honestly believed explanation for the disparity)? See Twerski & Cohen, Comparing Medical Providers: A First Look at the New Era of Medical Statistics, 58 Brooklyn L.Rev. 15 (1992). The authors suggest that the patient might be awarded 5/15 of the damages sustained in the cited example.

On the questions of whether such comparative statistics benefit the health care delivery system and whether they should be admissible in malpractice cases, see Pauly, The Public Policy Implications of Using Outcome Statistics, 58 Brooklyn L.Rev. 35 (1992); Green, Problems in the Use of Outcome Statistics to Compare Health Care Providers, 58 Brooklyn L.Rev. 55 (1992); Rheingold, The Admissibility of Evidence in Malpractice Cases: The Performance Records of Practitioners, 58 Brooklyn L.Rev. 75 (1992).

10. In some states the use of written consents may avoid this type of litigation. In Allan v. Levy, 109 Nev. 46, 846 P.2d 274 (1993), the trial judge told the jury about the consent statute and the jury returned a defense verdict in a laminectomy case. The statute provided:

A physician . . . has conclusively obtained the consent of a patient for a medical or surgical procedure if he has done the following:

1. Explained to the patient in general terms without specific details, the procedure to be undertaken;

2. Explained to the patient alternative methods of treatment, if any, and their general nature;

3. Explained to the patient that there may be risks, together with the general nature and extent of the risks involved, without enumerating such risks; and

4. Obtained the signature of the patient to a statement containing an explanation of the procedure, alternative methods of treatment and risks involved, as provided in this section.

The court held that since the written consent in the case did not contain what the section required it was error to tell the jury about this defense. Should the statute be interpreted to require that "risks" be quantified?

11. For comprehensive discussion of the informed consent issue, see Schuck, Rethinking Informed Consent, 103 Yale L.J. 899 (1994).

CHAPTER III

THE DUTY REQUIREMENT: PHYSICAL INJURIES

A. INTRODUCTION

In Chapter II we considered a wide variety of cases in which we explored the basic characteristics of the negligence concept. Typically, the defendant did not deny an obligation to behave reasonably toward the plaintiff. We turn now to cases in which the defendant makes precisely that contention—that defendant had no duty to exercise due care in the particular situation. The purpose of this chapter is to explore situations in which such claims are asserted and to determine how they should be resolved. The connection between the "negligence" question of Chapter II and the "duty" question of Chapter III is demonstrated by the fact that "negligence" is often referred to as "breach of duty"—a clear indication that some duty must exist before a defendant can be said to have committed actionable negligence. Although pedagogical reasons favored initial exploration of the negligence issue, it should be evident that, logically, the duty question is an antecedent issue.

An appropriate starting point is the question whether a plaintiff must show that a specific duty governs the context in which the case arose—or whether a general duty of due care exists unless the defendant can invoke an exception. As the materials in this chapter will indicate, there seems to be a clear long-term movement towards recognizing a general duty of due care. But the early historical picture is hazy. In many early cases, specific relationships appeared to be the basis for imposing duties of care. These were the classic relationships, such as innkeeper-guest, carrier-passenger, and the like. Yet, during this period one also finds highway collision cases in which the courts appear to recognize a general obligation of care to others.

The view that duties arose in specific contexts is supported by the fact that *failure* to establish a relational setting was often fatal to the claim that defendant should be held responsible for a lack of due care. A noteworthy example of this restrictive view is the privity doctrine. Under one aspect of that doctrine, courts held that the manufacturer of a product generally owed a duty of due care in its manufacture only to the person who acquired the product from the maker. No general duty of care was owed to remote buyers or users. The survival of the privity doctrine into this century and its eventual demise are traced in MacPherson v. Buick Motor Co., 217 N.Y. 382, 111 N.E. 1050 (1916), reprinted at p. 473, infra, in which the court concluded that a car manufacturer owed a duty of due care to someone who bought a car from a dealer. Judge Cardozo asserted:

> If the nature of a thing is such that it is reasonably certain to place life and limb in peril when negligently made, it is then a thing of danger. Its nature gives warning of the consequences to be expected. If to the element of danger is added knowledge that the thing will be used by persons other than the purchaser, and used without new tests, then, irrespective of contract, the manufacturer of this thing of danger is under a duty to make it carefully. . . . We have put aside the notion that the duty to safeguard life and limb, when the consequences of negligence may be foreseen, grows out of contract and nothing else. We have put the source of the obligation where it ought to be. We have put its source in the law.

As early as 1883, Brett, M.R., in Heaven v. Pender, 11 Q.B.D. 503 (1883), offered a general approach, though one that failed to convey how uneven the landscape remained:

> The proposition which these recognized cases suggest, and which is, therefore, to be deduced from them, is that whenever one person is by circumstances placed in such a position with regard to another that everyone of ordinary sense who did think would at once recognize that if he did not use ordinary care and skill in his own conduct with regard to those circumstances he would cause danger of injury to the person or property of the other, a duty arises to use ordinary care and skill to avoid such danger.

In this chapter, we will examine a number of discrete categories of cases in which Brett's straightforward proposition has been tested by moral and economic considerations—usually of long-standing acceptance—that established limitations on the duty to act reasonably. Related problems, involving invasion of non-physical interests, will be considered in Chapter IV.

B.   OBLIGATIONS TO OTHERS

We begin with a most fundamental inquiry. If an individual is in a situation of danger, should the law impose a duty on others to assist that person? Is there a meaningful distinction between harm arising from action and inaction? Consider the following case.

Harper v. Herman

Supreme Court of Minnesota, 1993.
499 N.W.2d 472.

■ PAGE, JUSTICE.

This case arises upon a reversal by the court of appeals of summary judgment in favor of the defendant. The court of appeals held that defendant, the owner and operator of a private boat on Lake Minnetonka, had a duty to warn plaintiff, a guest on the boat, that water surrounding the boat was too shallow for diving. We reverse and reinstate judgment in favor of defendant.

The facts are undisputed for the purpose of this appeal. On Sunday, August 9, 1986, Jeffrey Harper ("Harper") was one of four guests on Theodor Herman's ("Herman") 26–foot boat, sailing on Lake Minnetonka. Harper was invited on the boat outing by Cindy Alberg Palmer, another guest on Herman's boat. Herman and Harper did not know each other prior to this boat outing. At the time Herman was 64 years old, and Harper was 20 years old. Herman was an experienced boat owner having spent hundreds of hours operating boats on Lake Minnetonka similar to the one involved in this action. As owner of the boat, Herman considered himself to be in charge of the boat and his passengers. Harper had some experience swimming in lakes and rivers, but had no formal training in diving.

After a few hours of boating, the group decided to go swimming and, at Herman's suggestion, went to Big Island, a popular recreation spot. Herman was familiar with Big Island, and he was aware that the water remains shallow for a good distance away from its shore. Harper had been to Big Island on one previous occasion. Herman positioned the boat somewhere between 100 to 200 yards from the island with the bow facing away from the island in an area shallow enough for his guests to use the boat ladder to enter the water, but still deep enough so they could swim. The bottom of the lake was not visible from the boat. After positioning the boat Herman proceeded to set the anchor and lower the boat's ladder which was at its stern.

While Herman was lowering the ladder, Harper asked him if he was "going in." When Herman responded yes, Harper, without warning, stepped onto the side of the middle of the boat and dove into approximately two or three feet of water. As a result of the dive, Harper struck the bottom of the lake, severed his spinal cord, and was rendered a C6 quadriplegic.

Harper then brought suit, alleging that Herman owed him a duty of care to warn him that the water was too shallow for diving. [The trial court granted defendant's motion for summary judgment on the ground that defendant owed plaintiff no duty to warn. The court of appeals held that defendant voluntarily assumed such a duty when he allowed Harper onto his boat.]

The sole issue on appeal is whether a boat owner who is a social host owes a duty of care to warn a guest on the boat that the water is too shallow for diving.

Harper alleges that Herman owed him a duty to warn of the shallowness of the water because he was an inexperienced swimmer and diver, whereas Herman was a veteran boater. Under those circumstances, Harper argues, Herman should have realized that Harper needed his protection.

We have previously stated that an affirmative duty to act only arises when a special relationship exists between the parties. "The fact that an actor realizes or should realize that action on his part is necessary for another's aid or protection does not of itself impose upon him a duty to take such action * * * unless a special relationship exists * * * between the actor and the other which gives the other the right to protection." Delgado v. Lohmar, 289 N.W.2d 479, 483 (Minn.1979), [ ]. Accepting, *arguendo,* that Herman should have realized that Harper needed protection, Harper must still prove that a special relationship existed between them that placed an affirmative duty to act on the part of Herman.

Harper argues that a special relationship requiring Herman to act for his protection was created when Herman, as a social host, allowed an inexperienced diver on his boat. Generally, a special relationship giving rise to a duty to warn is only found on the part of common carriers, innkeepers, possessors of land who hold it open to the public, and persons who have custody of another person under circumstances in which that other person is deprived of normal opportunities of self-protection. Restatement (Second) of Torts § 314A (1965). Under this rule, a special relationship could be found to exist between the parties only if Herman had custody of Harper under circumstances in which Harper was deprived of normal opportunities to protect himself.[2] These elements are not present here.

The record before this court does not establish that Harper was either particularly vulnerable or that he lacked the ability to protect himself. Further, the record does not establish that Herman held considerable power over Harper's welfare, or that Herman was receiving a financial gain by hosting Harper on his boat. Finally, there is nothing in the record which would suggest that Harper expected any protection from Herman; indeed, no such allegation has been made.

The court of appeals found that Herman owed Harper a duty to warn him of the shallowness of the water because Herman knew that it was "dangerously shallow." We have previously stated that "[a]ctual knowledge of a dangerous condition tends to impose a special duty to do something about that condition." Andrade v. Ellefson, 391 N.W.2d 836, 841 (Minn.1986)(holding that county was not immune to charge of improp-

---

2. Prosser describes a circumstance in which one party would be liable in negligence because another party was deprived of normal opportunities for self-protection as occurring when the plaintiff is typically in some respect particularly vulnerable and dependent upon the defendant who, correspondingly, holds considerable power over the plaintiff's welfare. In addition, such relations have often involved some existing or potential economic advantage to the defendant. Fairness in such cases thus may require the defendant to use his power to help the plaintiff, based upon the plaintiff's expectation of protection, which itself may be based upon the defendant's expectation of financial gain. [ ]

er supervision of day care center where children were abused when county knew about overcrowding at the center). However, superior knowledge of a dangerous condition by itself, in the absence of a duty to provide protection, is insufficient to establish liability in negligence. Thus, Herman's knowledge that the water was "dangerously shallow" without more does not create liability. *Andrade* involved a group of plaintiffs who had little opportunity to protect themselves, children in day care, and a defendant to whom the plaintiffs looked for protection. In this case, Harper was not deprived of opportunities to protect himself, and Herman was not expected to provide protection.

"There are many dangers, such as those of fire and water, * * * which under ordinary conditions may reasonably be expected to be fully understood and appreciated by any child * * *." Restatement (Second) of Torts § 339 cmt. *j* (1965). If a child is expected to understand the inherent dangers of water, so should a 20–year-old adult. Harper had no reasonable expectation to look to Herman for protection, and we hold that Herman had no duty to warn Harper that the water was shallow.

Reversed and judgment in favor of defendant reinstated.

NOTES AND QUESTIONS

1. What are the arguments in favor of imposing a duty on the defendant? What are the arguments against such an imposition? When it would be virtually costless for defendant to offer assistance, should there be a distinction between moral and legal obligations? Certainly, moral and legal obligations are not *always* distinct. Is it self-evident why they should diverge in a situation involving, say, a helpless infant lying on a railroad track who could easily be rescued before a train arrives? Consider Epstein, A Theory of Strict Liability, 2 J.Legal Studies 151, 197–98 (1973):

> The common law position on the good Samaritan question does not appeal to our highest sense of benevolence and charity, and it is not at all surprising that there have been many proposals for its alteration or abolition. Let us here examine but one of these proposals. After concluding that the then (1908) current position of the law led to intolerable results, James Barr Ames argued [in Law and Morals, 22 Harv.L.Rev. 97 (1908)], that the appropriate rule should be that:
>
>> One who fails to interfere to save another from impending death or great bodily harm, when he might do so with little or no inconvenience to himself, and the death or great bodily harm follows as a consequence of his inaction, shall be punished criminally and shall make compensation to the party injured or to his widow and children in case of death.
>
> Even this solution, however, does not satisfy the *Carroll Towing* formula. The general use of the cost-benefit analysis required under the economic interpretation of negligence does not permit a person to act on the assumption that he may as of right attach special weight

and importance to his own welfare. Under Ames' good Samaritan rule, a defendant in cases of affirmative acts would be required to take only those steps that can be done "with little or no inconvenience." But if the distinction between causing harm and not preventing harm is to be disregarded, why should the difference in standards between the two cases survive the reform of the law? The only explanation is that the two situations are regarded at bottom as raising totally different issues, even for those who insist upon the immateriality of this distinction. Even those who argue, as Ames does, that the law is utilitarian must in the end find some special place for the claims of egoism which are an inseparable byproduct of the belief that individual autonomy—individual liberty—is a good in itself not explainable in terms of its purported social worth. It is one thing to *allow* people to act as they please in the belief that the "invisible hand" will provide the happy congruence of the individual and the social good. Such a theory, however, at bottom must regard individual autonomy as but a means to some social end. It takes a great deal more to assert that men are *entitled* to act as they choose . . . even though it is certain that there will be cases where individual welfare will be in conflict with the social good. Only then is it clear that even freedom has its costs. . . .

For an article proposing a duty of "easy rescue" and providing a detailed criticism of Epstein's views, see Weinrib, The Case for a Duty to Rescue, 90 Yale L.J. 247 (1980). For a range of other perspectives, see Heyman, Foundations of the Duty to Rescue, 47 Vand.L.Rev. 673 (1994); Adler, Relying Upon the Reasonableness of Strangers: Some Observations about the Current State of Common Law Affirmative Duties to Aid or Protect Others, 1991 Wisc.L.Rev. 867; Levmore, Waiting for Rescue: An Essay on the Evolution and Incentive Structure of the Law of Affirmative Obligations, 72 Va.L.Rev. 879 (1986).

2. Is it relevant that we are told the plaintiff in *Harper* was 20 years old and the defendant 64 years old? What if the ages were reversed? What if defendant had met plaintiff at a party a week earlier and had invited him to join other guests for this trip?

If one were to find that the boat owner owed a duty would the rationale extend to the person who invited plaintiff on to the boat? The other two guests? What about his office mate from work who happens to be passing by on another boat and sees disaster about to happen? What if his mother had been on the passing boat?

Does the rationale of *Harper* necessarily extend to the case of the infant on the railroad tracks?

3. As the court notes, a variety of "special" relationships have led courts to impose duties to act in this type of case. Do the listed relationships suggest a unifying principle for an affirmative obligation?

4. *Nonnegligent injury.* At common law, one who innocently injured another had no duty to take due care for the other's subsequent wellbeing.

See, e.g., Union Pacific Ry. v. Cappier, 66 Kan. 649, 72 P. 281 (1903), in which the court held that there was no duty to do anything to help a victim who was nontortiously run over while trespassing on defendant's railroad tracks.

That attitude is fading. In Maldonado v. Southern Pacific Transp. Co., 129 Ariz. 165, 629 P.2d 1001 (App.1981), plaintiff claimed that as he was attempting to board one of defendant's freight trains, it jerked or bumped and he fell off—and under the wheels, suffering a severed arm and other serious injuries. Alleging that defendant's employees knew about his plight but did nothing to help him, he sued for aggravation of his injuries. The court imposed a duty recognized by § 322 of the Second Restatement:

> If the actor knows or has reason to know that by his conduct, whether tortious or innocent, he has caused such bodily harm to another as to make him helpless and in danger of further harm, the actor is under a duty to exercise reasonable care to prevent such further harm.

5. With respect to motor vehicles, one common reaction to the traditional no-duty view in these situations has been the adoption of criminal statutes. California, for example, provides that "the driver of any vehicle involved in an accident resulting in injury shall render to any person injured in the accident reasonable assistance, including the carrying or the making arrangements for the carrying of such person to a physician, surgeon or hospital . . . if it is apparent that treatment is necessary or if such carrying is requested by the injured person." Cal.Vehicle Code § 20003. This statute has been held applicable regardless of whose negligence, if any, caused the accident in the first place. In this situation in which the common law had imposed no affirmative duty, should the existence of the criminal statute persuade a court to create an analogous common law duty? If the driver was not negligent, why should that driver's duty be any different from that of a bystander?

6. *Nonnegligent creation of risk.* In Simonsen v. Thorin, 120 Neb. 684, 234 N.W. 628 (1931), defendant motorist without fault knocked a utility pole into the street and drove on. In a suit by a motorist who ran into the pole the court held that the defendant had an affirmative duty to use due care to remove the hazard or to warn others of it, though he was not liable for creating the hazard. Why should his duty be any different from that of a bystander who watched the episode?

In Menu v. Minor, 745 P.2d 680 (Colo.App.1987), a driver lost control of his car, it hit the median and came to rest, disabled, blocking a lane of an interstate highway. What might the driver's duties be? A taxicab picked up the driver and drove him away. Some time later, plaintiffs crashed into the disabled car. In a suit against the cab company, plaintiffs contended that the cab should have either stayed at the scene to warn, removed the car, or called the police. The court held that the cab driver had no affirmative duty to do any of these things. The cab driver had not "voluntarily assumed a duty to plaintiffs by acting affirmatively to induce" them to rely on him. Nor had he "created a peril or changed the nature of the existing risk" to them. Transporting the driver from the scene did not change the already existing risk. The knowledge of the danger alone did not create a special relationship.

In Tresemer v. Barke, 86 Cal.App.3d 656, 150 Cal.Rptr. 384 (1978), plaintiff was seriously injured from use of the Dalkon Shield intrauterine device. She never consulted defendant physician after he inserted the device. Within two years, there was medical information about the dangers of using the device, but the plaintiff was unaware of the risk for another year afterwards and suffered injury because of the delay. The court held that she stated a cause of action against the defendant for failure to warn her about the newly-discovered dangers.

Section 321 of the Second Restatement states that one who has done an act and "subsequently realizes or should realize that it has created an unreasonable risk of causing physical harm to another," is under a duty to exercise due care to prevent the risk from occurring even though at the time the actor had no reason to believe that his act would create such a risk.

7. At one point, the *Harper* court notes that plaintiff did not show that he "expected any protection" from defendant. How might Harper have shown that? What if defendant had charged each guest $10 for the trip?

If plaintiff, when coming on board, says to defendant that he knows little about boating and that "I expect you to let me know if you see me doing anything foolish while on board" would that suffice if defendant did not respond? If defendant responded "OK"?

In Morgan v. County of Yuba, 230 Cal.App.2d 938, 41 Cal.Rptr. 508 (1964), the plaintiff's decedent expressed fear of the consequences if the sheriff were to release a man he had arrested for threatening her. Although under no duty to do so, the sheriff's office promised to warn her before any release. They failed to do so and the man, upon his release, killed her. After deciding that the county should be treated as a private person, the court held that liability should exist if the plaintiff could establish that the decedent relied on the promise—and would have acted differently without it. What relationship is this?

Other courts have employed similar reasoning. In Mixon v. Dobbs Houses, Inc., 149 Ga.App. 481, 254 S.E.2d 864 (1979), husband informed the manager of the restaurant where he worked that his wife was pregnant and might call at any time to ask for a ride to the hospital. Since husband did not have access to a phone, the manager promised to tell him if his wife called. When the wife went into labor, she called the restaurant three times, and although the manager received the message that the wife had called, he failed to deliver the message to the husband. When husband returned home, his wife had already given birth to a baby girl, "all alone, unassisted and unmedicated, experiencing total fear and excruciating pain." The court held that the manager was obligated to exercise due care in performing his promise. The lower court's dismissal was reversed.

In Hartley v. Floyd, 512 So.2d 1022 (Fla.App.1987), when her husband did not return from a fishing trip as expected, plaintiff wife called the sheriff's office and asked a deputy to check the boat ramp where her husband had parked his truck before the trip to see if it was still there. Deputy promised to check for the truck and, if it was still there, to alert the Coast Guard to the missing husband. When the wife called back, the deputy, falsely, told her that the ramp had been checked and the truck was not there. Believing that her husband was on the way home, wife did nothing for five hours. It was established that the husband lost his strength and drowned just 30 minutes before a much-delayed Coast Guard search found him. The sheriff's office was held liable for negligently failing to perform its promises because the wife relied on the promises and alleged performance in deciding not to take further action to locate her husband.

In these cases should it matter whether the defendant omitted to take any steps to carry out the promise or took such steps but did so negligently? Some courts reject this entire line of cases. See, e.g., Santy v. Bresee, 129 Ill.App.3d 658, 473 N.E.2d 69 (1984)(rejecting *Morgan* on very similar facts).

8. Regarding legislative change, consider Vt.Stat.Ann., tit. 12, § 519 (1973):

(a) A person who knows that another is exposed to grave physical harm shall, to the extent that the same can be rendered without danger or peril to himself or without interference with important duties owed to others, give reasonable assistance to the exposed person unless that assistance or care is being provided by others.

(b) A person who provides reasonable assistance in compliance with subsection (a) of this section shall not be liable in civil damages unless his acts constitute gross negligence or unless he will receive or expects to receive remuneration. Nothing contained in this subsection shall alter existing law with respect to tort liability of a practitioner of the healing arts for acts committed in the ordinary course of his practice.

(c) A person who willfully violates subsection (a) of this section shall be fined not more than $100.00.

Should a court in a tort action use the statute by analogy to create a civil duty to rescue? The situation is discussed in Franklin, Vermont Requires Rescue: A Comment, 25 Stan.L.Rev. 51 (1972). For the lack of a record of either civil actions or criminal prosecutions under the Vermont statute, see Note, Duty to Aid the Endangered Act: The Impact and Potential of the Vermont Approach, 7 Vt.L.Rev. 143 (1982). A handful of states have followed the Vermont approach. See Ackerman, Tort Law and Communitarianism: Where Rights Meet Responsibilities, 30 Wake Forest L.Rev. 649, 660 (1995).

In D'Amato, The "Bad Samaritan" Paradigm, 70 Nw.U.L.Rev. 798 (1975), the author proposed adoption of a criminal statute similar to Vermont's, with a provision prohibiting any private action based on violation of the criminal statute. In partial explanation, the author states that "There is a need for help from a stranger when an accident occurs, and the law should attempt to meet that need without going so far as to make everyone his brother's insurer." Among the problems surveyed by the author is that of V who decides to dive into a river, even though he can't swim, because S, nearby, can save him. Should S be under a civil obligation to save V? A criminal one? If S yells, "Don't jump" or "If you jump I won't save you" should that change the analysis?

9. *Do Statutes Create Duties?* Before exploring duty further, we consider an institutional question raised by the Vermont statute.

In Chapter II, we considered the role of statutes in cases in which it was clear that one party had a duty of due care to the other. The question was whether the statute should be used to formulate more exact standards for determining the question of breach. Here, however, we may assume that before the statute was adopted Vermont courts would have adhered to the general rejection of a duty to rescue a stranger. Should the passage of this statute cause a change in the civil no-duty rule? The traditional view was expressed in Thayer, Public Wrong and Private Action, 27 Harv.L.Rev. 317 (1914), arguing that criminal statutes did not create civil duties. Their only function in civil cases was the one we have already considered—to make the breach determination more precise.

Another view is presented in Morris on Torts 146–51 (2d ed. 1980), arguing that the passage of criminal legislation removes two reasons for adhering to a no-duty rule. First, the criminal statute gives notice to the public so that retroactive abolition of a no-duty rule will not cause unfair surprise. Second, the nature of the legislative process makes it more likely that the change will be feasible: "A court creating a novel tort liability without investigation runs a risk of demanding impractical or undesirable precaution. But criminal statutes are not likely to interdict conduct which most people cannot forgo in everyday affairs."

On the other hand, Morris argues that civil liability should not automatically follow criminal liability: "Some criminal statutes may be unwisely severe. Potentially ruinous civil liability is often inappropriate for infraction of petty criminal regulations." Also, if the legislation creates an elaborate administrative structure for achieving certain goals, imposing a new civil duty might interfere with the legislature's efforts to achieve a balanced treatment. The Restatement, Second, § 874A provides:

> When a legislative provision protects a class of persons by proscribing or requiring certain conduct but does not provide a civil remedy for the violation, the court may, if it determines that the remedy is appropriate in furtherance of the purpose of the legislation and needed to assure the effectiveness of the provision, accord to an injured member of the class a right of action, using a suitable existing tort action or a new cause of action analogous to an existing tort action.

The Restatement and other authorities are discussed in Miller v. City of Portland, 288 Or. 271, 604 P.2d 1261 (1980).

10. *Implied Right of Action.* A related issue is whether, under some circumstances, a federal civil tort suit should be implied from a federal regulatory statute establishing criminal penalties. In Cort v. Ash, 422 U.S. 66 (1975), involving a shareholder's claim for damages based on allegations that the corporation made campaign contributions in violation of federal law, the Court articulated four criteria for determining whether a civil action would be implied: 1) whether the plaintiff is "one of the class for whose *especial* benefit the statute was enacted"; 2) whether there is "any indication of legislative intent, explicit or implicit, either to create such a remedy or to deny one"; 3) whether it is "consistent with the underlying purposes of the legislative scheme to imply such a remedy for the plaintiff"; and 4) whether the claim is "one traditionally relegated to state law, in an area basically the concern of the states." The Court refused to imply a cause of action in the case.

Is this a helpful test in deciding when a civil cause of action should be implied? For comprehensive discussion of the subject, see Stewart and Sunstein, Public Programs and Private Rights, 95 Harv.L.Rev. 1195 (1982).

On occasion legislation prescribes civil remedies for certain acts or harms. In such cases, the plaintiff proceeds directly under the statutory grant of relief rather than by common law analogy. See, e.g., the civil remedies provision in the Consumer Product Safety Act, 15 U.S.C. § 2072.

Farwell v. Keaton

Supreme Court of Michigan, 1976.
396 Mich. 281, 240 N.W.2d 217.

■ LEVIN, J. There is ample evidence to support the jury determination that David Siegrist failed to exercise reasonable care after voluntarily coming to the aid of Richard Farwell and that his negligence was the proximate cause of Farwell's death. We are also of the opinion that Siegrist, who was with Farwell the evening he was fatally injured and, as the jury found, knew or should have known of his peril, had an affirmative duty to come to Farwell's aid.

I

On the evening of August 26, 1966, Siegrist and Farwell drove to a trailer rental lot to return an automobile which Siegrist had borrowed from a friend who worked there. While waiting for the friend to finish work, Siegrist and Farwell consumed some beer.

Two girls walked by the entrance to the lot. Siegrist and Farwell attempted to engage them in conversation; they left Farwell's car and followed the girls to a drive-in restaurant down the street.

The girls complained to their friends in the restaurant that they were being followed. Six boys chased Siegrist and Farwell back to the lot. Siegrist escaped unharmed, but Farwell was severely beaten. Siegrist found Farwell underneath his automobile in the lot. Ice was applied to

Farwell's head.   Siegrist then drove Farwell around for approximately two hours, stopping at a number of drive-in restaurants.   Farwell went to sleep in the back seat of his car.   Around midnight Siegrist drove the car to the home of Farwell's grandparents, parked it in the driveway, unsuccessfully attempted to rouse Farwell, and left.   Farwell's grandparents discovered him in the car the next morning and took him to the hospital.   He died three days later of an epidural hematoma.

At trial, plaintiff [Farwell's father, in this wrongful death action] contended that had Siegrist taken Farwell to the hospital, or had he notified someone of Farwell's condition and whereabouts, Farwell would not have died.   A neurosurgeon testified that if a person in Farwell's condition is taken to a doctor before, or within half an hour after, consciousness is lost, there is an 85 to 88 per cent chance of survival. Plaintiff testified that Siegrist told him that he knew Farwell was badly injured and that he should have done something.

The jury returned a verdict for plaintiff and awarded $15,000 in damages.   The Court of Appeals reversed, finding that Siegrist had not assumed the duty of obtaining aid for Farwell and that he neither knew nor should have known of the need for medical treatment.

II

. . .

The existence of a duty is ordinarily a question of law.   However, there are factual circumstances which give rise to a duty.   The existence of those facts must be determined by a jury.   . . .

. . .

B.

Without regard to whether there is a general duty to aid a person in distress, there is a clearly recognized legal duty of every person to avoid any affirmative acts which may make a situation worse.   "[I]f the defendant does attempt to aid him, and takes charge and control of the situation, he is regarded as entering voluntarily into a relation which is attended with responsibility.   Such a defendant will then be liable for a failure to use reasonable care for the protection of the plaintiff's interests."   [   ] "Where performance clearly has begun, there is no doubt that there is a duty of care."   [   ]

In a case such as the one at bar, the jury must determine, after considering all the evidence, whether the defendant attempted to aid the victim.   If he did, a duty arose which required defendant to act as a reasonable person.

. . .

There was ample evidence to show that Siegrist breached a legal duty owed Farwell.   Siegrist knew that Farwell had been in a fight, and he attempted to relieve Farwell's pain by applying an ice pack to his head. While Farwell and Siegrist were riding around, Farwell crawled into the back seat and laid down. The testimony showed that Siegrist attempted to rouse Farwell after driving him home but was unable to do so.

[The court summarized testimony of Farwell's father that when he asked Siegrist why he didn't tell someone when he knew that Farwell was badly hurt, Siegrist replied: "I know I should have, I don't know."]

. . .

III

Siegrist contends that he is not liable for failure to obtain medical assistance for Farwell because he had no duty to do so.

Courts have been slow to recognize a duty to render aid to a person in peril. Where such a duty has been found, it has been predicated upon the existence of a special relationship between the parties; in such a case, if defendant knew or should have known of the other person's peril, he is required to render reasonable care under all the circumstances.

. . .

Farwell and Siegrist were companions on a social venture. Implicit in such a common undertaking is the understanding that one will render assistance to the other when he is in peril if he can do so without endangering himself. Siegrist knew or should have known when he left Farwell, who was badly beaten and unconscious, in the back seat of his car that no one would find him before morning. Under these circumstances, to say that Siegrist had no duty to obtain medical assistance or at least to notify someone of Farwell's condition and whereabouts would be "shocking to humanitarian considerations" and fly in the face of "the commonly accepted code of social conduct". "[C]ourts will find a duty where, in general, reasonable men would recognize it and agree that it exists." [Prosser, *Torts*]

Farwell and Siegrist were companions engaged in a common undertaking; there was a special relationship between the parties. Because Siegrist knew or should have known of the peril Farwell was in and could render assistance without endangering himself he had an affirmative duty to come to Farwell's aid.

The Court of Appeals is reversed and the verdict of the jury reinstated.

■ KAVANAGH, C.J., and WILLIAMS, J., concurred with LEVIN, J.

■ LINDEMER and RYAN, JJ., took no part in the decision of this case.

■ FITZGERALD, J. (dissenting).

. . .

The close relationship between defendant and the decedent is said to establish a legal duty upon defendant to obtain assistance for the decedent. No authority is cited for this proposition other than the public policy observation that the interest of society would be benefited if its members were required to assist one another. This is not the appropriate case to establish a standard of conduct requiring one to legally assume the duty of insuring the safety of another.   .   .   .[4]

Plaintiff believes that a legal duty to aid others should exist where such assistance greatly benefits society and only a reasonable burden is imposed upon those in a position to help. He contends further that the determination of the existence of a duty must rest with the jury where questions of foreseeability and the relationship of the parties are primary considerations.

It is clear that defendant's nonfeasance, or the "passive inaction or a failure to take steps to protect [the decedent] from harm" is urged as being the proximate cause of Farwell's death. We must reject plaintiff's proposition which elevates a moral obligation to the level of a legal duty where, as here, the facts within defendant's knowledge in no way indicated that immediate medical attention was necessary and the relationship between the parties imposes no affirmative duty to render assistance.   .   .   .

The relationship of the parties and the question of foreseeability does not require that the jury, rather than the court, determine whether a legal duty exists. We are in agreement with the general principle advanced by plaintiff that the question of negligence is one of law for the court only when the facts are such that all reasonable men must draw the same conclusion. However, this principle becomes operative only after the court establishes that a legal duty is owed by one party to another. Prosser's analysis of the role of the court and jury on questions of legal duty bears repeating:

> "The existence of a duty. In other words, whether, upon the facts in evidence, such a relation exists between the parties that the community will impose a legal obligation upon one for the benefit of the other—or, more simply, whether the interest of the plaintiff which has suffered invasion was entitled to legal protection at the hands of the defendant. This is entirely a question of law, to be determined by reference to the body of statutes, rules, principles and precedents which make up the law; and it must be determined only by the court.   .   .   . A decision by the court that, upon any version of the facts, there is no duty, must necessarily result in judgment for the defendant." Prosser, Torts (4th ed.), § 37, p. 206.

.   .   .

The Court of Appeals properly decided as a matter of law that defendant owed no duty to the deceased.

We would affirm.

---

4. Were a special relationship to be the basis of imposing a legal duty upon one to insure the safety of another, it would most probably take the form of "co-adventurers" who embark upon a hazardous undertaking with the understanding that each is mutually dependent upon the other for his own safety. There is no evidence to support plaintiff's position that decedent relied upon defendant to provide any assistance whatsoever.   .   .   .

■ COLEMAN, J., concurred with FITZGERALD, J.

NOTES AND QUESTIONS

1. As the first paragraph of the opinion indicates, the majority recognizes an obligation of due care on two independent grounds: (1) that Siegrist voluntarily came to the assistance of Farwell and (2) that Siegrist, in any event, had an affirmative duty to aid Farwell on the basis of their pre-existing relationship. We have already examined the second ground in the *Harper* case. How does that apply in *Farwell*? What if Siegrist had never returned, but knew that Farwell had been physically attacked? Would the dissent find a duty on one member of a two-person mountain-climbing team to aid the other? Is *Farwell* different?

2. Compare Ronald M. v. White, 112 Cal.App.3d 473, 169 Cal.Rptr. 370 (1980), in which summary judgment for defendants was affirmed when a group of ten minors, cruising around in an auto, had spent the day together drinking and taking drugs, and defendants—group members who had not been drinking or taken drugs or furnished or paid for any—allegedly failed to restrain the driver before his negligence injured others in the group. Is *Farwell* distinguishable?

3. We return now to the court's first ground of recovery in *Farwell*—the duty Siegrist assumed by voluntarily attempting to aid Farwell. Should a voluntary actor assume the same duty of due care as an actor bound by a pre-existing relationship to the plaintiff? Suppose a passerby had discovered Farwell and "voluntarily acted" by trying to revive him, but then decided not to get further involved and left the scene. Should that passerby be held liable for failing to exercise the due care that might be expected of a close relative?

Section 324 of the Second Restatement provides that one who, being under no duty to do so, takes charge of another who is helpless is subject to liability caused by "(a) the failure of the actor to exercise reasonable care to secure the safety of the other while within the actor's charge, or (b) the actor's discontinuing his aid or protection, if by so doing he leaves the other in a worse position than when the actor took charge of him." The Restatement expresses no opinion as to whether "an actor who has taken charge of a helpless person may be subject to liability for harm resulting from his discontinuance of the aid or protection, where by doing so he leaves the other in no worse position than when the actor took charge of him." A comment states that although "A, who has taken B from a trench filled with poisonous gas, does not thereby obligate himself to pay for B's treatment in a hospital, he cannot throw B back into the same trench, or leave him lying in the street where he may be run over." What about leaving him on the nearby sidewalk? See Parvi v. City of Kingston, 41 N.Y.2d 553, 362 N.E.2d 960, 394 N.Y.S.2d 161 (1977), discussing § 324.

4. Restatement (Second) § 323 comment *e* leaves open the liability of a person who begins the rescue of a drowning swimmer, who pulls him close to shore and then leaves him to drown even though the rescuer could readily have completed the rescue. There were no other potential rescuers around. Should the rescuer be liable? What analysis if a passing sailor pulls a drowning stranger into the sailboat, but then, while bringing the victim back to shore, negligently permits the boat to capsize killing both occupants?

5. In Haben v. Anderson, 232 Ill.App.3d 260, 597 N.E.2d 655 (1992), a university student died from acute alcohol intoxication after participating in an initiation into a club. Part of the case involved a claim against one member of the club alleging that he had placed the decedent in peril by participating as one of 12 in the initiation, allowed other members to place the unconscious decedent on the floor of the member's room, and that the member checked on decedent periodically during the night and heard him gurgling. The court held that the trier of fact could find that the member had assumed a duty to care for the decedent and that he did not act reasonably to prevent harm to the decedent after decedent's placement in his room. Is the member's participation in the initiation essential to sustaining the suit?

6. Referring back to *Farwell,* what role should the jury play in deciding these issues? Is the threshold question of whether a special relationship exists for the jury? What about the question of whether there has been a voluntary undertaking? Or should the jury be limited to determining whether there has been a breach of duty?

7. The *Maldonado* court, p. 121, supra, in which the train ran over the trespasser, also held that plaintiff stated an independent claim under Restatement § 326, in that defendant's employees attempted to dissuade and impede would-be rescuers: "One who intentionally prevents a third person from giving to another aid necessary to prevent physical harm to him, is subject to liability. . . ." Section 327 creates a basis for liability against one who negligently prevents aid.

Consider in this connection, Soldano v. O'Daniels, 141 Cal.App.3d 443, 190 Cal.Rptr. 310 (1983), in which a bartender refused to allow a third party to make an emergency phone call to the police on behalf of a person who had been threatened at another bar across the street. Although the court acknowledged that there was no pre-existing relationship between defendant bartender and the deceased, it asserted that the defendant had interfered with the third party's rescue efforts. The court limited its holding to a request made to deal with an emergency by using a telephone in the public portion of a business establishment.

8. As these materials indicate, the attendant obligations—once a duty of due care has been established—may create a substantial disincentive to render assistance in the first place. The possibility of injury to one's self creates still another disincentive. In addition to the development of judicial exceptions to the general no-duty rules, the legislative branch has also been addressing these problems. Among the early efforts were statutes providing awards to persons hurt while attempting rescues. The object was to indemnify for loss rather than to "reward." See, e.g., Calif.Govt.Code § 13970–74.

In 1959, California provided in Bus. and Prof.Code § 2144 that no physician licensed in the state "who in good faith renders emergency care at the scene of the emergency, shall be liable for any civil damages as a result of acts or omissions by such person in rendering the emergency care." If fear that victims aided in an emergency will sue for malpractice is a major factor in the alleged reluctance of physicians to volunteer, how effective are statutes like California's? How about a statute that protects physicians against liability for negligence but not for gross negligence? Should such statutes be limited to physicians or should all volunteers be similarly protected? What changes in behavior would you expect from such a statute? See Holland, The Good Samaritan Law: A Reappraisal, 16 J.Pub.L. 128, 133 (1967). Some form of Good Samaritan legislation now exists in every state. For a survey of the field, see Mapel & Weigel, Good Samaritan Laws—Who Needs Them?: The Current State of Good Samaritan Protection in the United States, 21 So.Tex.L.J. 327 (1981).

What are the respective merits of creating an affirmative duty of "easy rescue" and the creation of incentives to aid? For another suggestion of a limited duty, see Galligan, Jr., Aiding and Altruism: A Mythopsycholegal Analysis, 27 U.Mich.J.L.Ref. 439 (1995), drawing on experimental studies and other sources to propose that a duty to rescue be developed along the following lines:

> A court, when deciding whether to impose a duty of reasonable action in a particular case, should consider: (1) the number of bystanders present; (2) the degree of attachment, connection, or relationship between all the parties, including the bystanders; (3) the costs of rescue, including potential risk to the rescuer; (4) the degree of empathy that the defendant nonrescuer felt or could reasonably be expected to feel for the person who was not rescued; (5) the extent to which contract values were implicated, or adversely affected, by imposing a duty to rescue; and (6) the defendant's interest in doing what he chooses.

Would this be an improvement over existing law?

9. *The Moch case.* In H.R. Moch Co. v. Rensselaer Water Co., 247 N.Y. 160, 159 N.E. 896 (1928), defendant water works had a contract with the City of Rensselaer to supply water for various purposes, including service at fire hydrants. A building caught fire and the flames spread to plaintiff's warehouse, destroying it. Plaintiff alleged that the water company's failure to supply adequate water permitted the spread of the fire to the warehouse. The court of appeals, in an opinion by Judge Cardozo, held that the complaint should be dismissed. Among other grounds discussed, Cardozo held that there was no common law tort action available to users of the water supplied to the city:

> "It is ancient learning that one who assumes to act, even though gratuitously, may thereby become subject to the duty of acting carefully, if he acts at all" (Glanzer v. Shepard, 233 N.Y. 236, 239, 135 N.E. 275, 276; [   ]). The plaintiff would bring its case within the orbit of that principle. The hand once set to a task may not always be

withdrawn with impunity though liability would fail if it had never been applied at all. A time-honored formula often phrases the distinction as one between misfeasance and nonfeasance. Incomplete the formula is, and so at times misleading. Given a relation involving in its existence a duty of care irrespective of a contract, a tort may result as well from acts of omission as of commission in the fulfillment of the duty thus recognized by law [ ]. What we need to know is not so much the conduct to be avoided when the relation and its attendant duty are established as existing. What we need to know is the conduct that engenders the relation. It is here that the formula, however incomplete, has its value and significance. If conduct has gone forward to such a stage that inaction would commonly result, not negatively merely in withholding a benefit, but positively or actively in working an injury, there exists a relation out of which arises a duty to go forward (Bohlen, Studies in the Law of Torts, p. 87). So the surgeon who operates without pay, is liable though his negligence is in the omission to sterilize his instruments (cf. *Glanzer v. Shepard*, supra); the engineer, though his fault is in the failure to shut off steam [ ]; the maker of automobiles, at the suit of some one other than the buyer, though his negligence is merely in inadequate inspection (Mac-Pherson v. Buick Motor Co., 217 N.Y. 382). The query always is whether the putative wrongdoer has advanced to such a point as to have launched a force or instrument of harm, or has stopped where inaction is at most a refusal to become an instrument for good [ ].

The plaintiff would have us hold that the defendant, when once it entered upon the performance of its contract with the city, was brought into such a relation with every one who might potentially be benefited through the supply of water at the hydrants as to give to negligent performance, without reasonable notice of a refusal to continue, the quality of a tort. . . . We are satisfied that liability would be unduly and indeed indefinitely extended by this enlargement of the zone of duty. . . . What we are dealing with at this time is a mere negligent omission, unaccompanied by malice or other aggravating elements. The failure in such circumstances to furnish an adequate supply of water is at most the denial of a benefit. It is not the commission of a wrong.

How is this case different from the cited examples of the negligent surgeon and the engineer? Note Cardozo's conclusion that the defendant's behavior was "at most the denial of a benefit. It is not the commission of a wrong." How is the distinction between misfeasance and nonfeasance being used here? Is there a danger that the result in *Moch* will reduce incentives toward safety?

Your house catches on fire. Your neighbor has a swimming pool with a pump to allow the water to be drawn from the pool to fight fires. He refuses to allow you to use any of his water to fight your fire. Is this like *Moch*?

Is there a relationship between the misfeasance-nonfeasance point and the existence of the contract relationship with the city? Is the existence of the contract relevant to the question of whether the defendant has denied a benefit or committed a wrong? Does the existence of the contract help or hurt the plaintiff's case?

Strauss v. Belle Realty Co.

Court of Appeals, New York, 1985.
65 N.Y.2d 399, 482 N.E.2d 34, 492 N.Y.S.2d 555.

■ KAYE, J.

On July 13, 1977, a failure of defendant Consolidated Edison's power system left most of New York City in darkness. In this action for damages allegedly resulting from the power failure, we are asked to determine whether Con Edison owed a duty of care to a tenant who suffered personal injuries in a common area of an apartment building, where his landlord—but not he—had a contractual relationship with the utility. We conclude that in the case of a blackout of a metropolis of several million residents and visitors, each in some manner necessarily affected by a 25–hour power failure, liability for injuries in a building's common areas should, as a matter of public policy, be limited by the contractual relationship.

This court has twice before confronted legal questions concerning the 1977 blackout (see, Koch v. Consolidated Edison Co., 62 N.Y.2d 548, cert. denied 469 U.S. 1210; Food Pageant v. Consolidated Edison Co., 54 N.Y.2d 167).

Plaintiff, Julius Strauss, then 77 years old, resided in an apartment building in Queens. Con Edison provided electricity to his apartment pursuant to agreement with him, and to the common areas of the building under a separate agreement with his landlord, defendant Belle Realty Company. As water to the apartment was supplied by electric pump, plaintiff had no running water for the duration of the blackout. Consequently, on the second day of the power failure, he set out for the basement to obtain water, but fell on the darkened, defective basement stairs, sustaining injuries. In this action against Belle Realty and Con Edison, plaintiff alleged negligence against the landlord, in failing to maintain the stairs or warn of their dangerous condition, and negligence against the utility in the performance of its duty to provide electricity.

Plaintiff moved for partial summary judgment against Con Edison (1) to estop it from contesting the charge of gross negligence in connection with the blackout, and (2) to establish that Con Edison owed a duty of care to plaintiff. He argued that Con Edison . . . owed plaintiff a duty even though he was "not a customer of Consolidated Edison in a place where the accident occurred." Con Edison cross-moved for summary judgment dismissing the complaint, maintaining it had no duty to a noncustomer.

The court granted the motion insofar as it sought collateral estoppel regarding gross negligence,[1] and denied Con Edison's cross motion to dismiss the complaint, finding a question of fact as to whether it owed plaintiff a duty of care. The Appellate Division reversed and dismissed the complaint against Con Edison. Citing Moch Co. v. Rensselaer Water Co. [ ], the plurality concluded that "Con Ed did not owe a duty to plaintiff in any compensable legal sense" [ ]. Justice Gibbons dissented, finding extension of the duty tolerable here because "[t]he tenants of the building in question constitute a defined, limited and known group of people" [ ]. On public policy grounds, we now affirm the Appellate Division order dismissing the complaint against Con Edison.

A defendant may be held liable for negligence only when it breaches a duty owed to the plaintiff (Pulka v. Edelman, 40 N.Y.2d 781, 782). The essential question here is whether Con Edison owed a duty to plaintiff, whose injuries from a fall on a darkened staircase may have conceivably been foreseeable, but with whom there was no contractual relationship for lighting in the building's common areas.

Duty in negligence cases is defined neither by foreseeability of injury [ ] nor by privity of contract. As this court has long recognized, an obligation rooted in contract may engender a duty owed to those not in privity, for "[t]here is nothing anomalous in a rule which imposes upon A, who has contracted with B, a duty to C and D and others according as he knows or does not know that the subject-matter of the contract is intended for their use" (MacPherson v. Buick Motor Co., 217 N.Y. 382, 393). In Fish v. Waverly Elec. Light & Power Co. (189 N.Y. 336), for example, an electric company which had contracted with the plaintiff's employer to install ceiling lights had a duty to the plaintiff to exercise reasonable care. And in Glanzer v. Shepard (233 N.Y. 236), a public weigher, hired by a seller of beans to certify the weight of a particular shipment, was found liable in negligence to the buyer. [ ]

But while the absence of privity does not foreclose recognition of a duty, it is still the responsibility of courts, in fixing the orbit of duty, "to limit the legal consequences of wrongs to a controllable degree" [ ], and to protect against crushing exposure to liability [ ]. "In fixing the bounds of that duty, not only logic and science, but policy play an important role" [ ]. The courts' definition of an orbit of duty based on public policy may at times result in the exclusion of some who might otherwise have recovered for losses or injuries if traditional tort principles had been applied.

Considerations of privity are not entirely irrelevant in implementing policy. Indeed, in determining the liability of utilities for consequential damages for failure to provide service—a liability which could obviously be "enormous," and has been described as *"sui generis,"* rather than strictly governed by tort or contract law principles (see, Prosser and Keeton, Torts § 92, at 663 [5th ed.])—courts have declined to extend the duty of care to noncustomers. For example, in Moch Co. v. Rensselaer Water Co. [ ], a

---

1. The collateral estoppel question was decided against Con Edison in [*Koch*].

water works company contracted with the City of Rensselaer to satisfy its water requirements. Plaintiff's warehouse burned and plaintiff brought an action against the water company in part based on its alleged negligence in failing to supply sufficient water pressure to the city's hydrants. The court denied recovery, concluding that the proposed enlargement of the zone of duty would unduly extend liability. Similarly, in Beck v. FMC Corp. (42 N.Y.2d 1027, *affg.* 53 A.D.2d 118), an explosion interrupted a utility's electrical service, which in turn resulted in the loss of a day's pay for hourly workers at a nearby automobile plant. In an action brought by the workers, the court denied recovery on the basis of controlling the unwarranted extension of liability [ ].

Moch involved ordinary negligence, while Con Edison was guilty of gross negligence, but the cases cannot be distinguished on that basis. In reserving the question of what remedy would lie in the case of "reckless and wanton indifference to consequences measured and foreseen" (247 N.Y., at p. 169), the court in *Moch* contemplated a level of misconduct greater than the gross negligence involved here [ ]. The court in *[Food Pageant v. Consolidated Edison Co.],* in upholding the jury's verdict against Con Edison, noted as instances of Con Edison's misconduct its employee's failure to follow instructions to reduce voltage by "shedding load" after lightning had hit the electrical system, and its staffing decisions [ ]. Though found by the jury to constitute gross negligence, this behavior was not so consciously culpable as to fall into the category of conduct contemplated as "reckless and wanton" by the court in *Moch* [ ].

In the view of the Appellate Division dissenter, *Moch* does not control because the injuries here were foreseeable and plaintiff was a member of a specific, limited, circumscribed class with a close relationship with Con Edison. The situation was thought to be akin to White v. Guarente (43 N.Y.2d 356), where an accounting firm was retained by a limited partnership to perform an audit and prepare its tax returns. As the court noted there, the parties to the agreement contemplated that individual limited partners would rely on the tax returns and audit. Refusing to dismiss a negligence action brought by a limited partner against the accounting firm, the court said, "the services of the accountant were not extended to a faceless or unresolved class of persons, but rather to a known group possessed of vested rights, marked by a definable limit and made up of certain components" (id., at p. 361; see also, Glanzer v. Shepard [ ]).

Central to these decisions was an ability to extend the defendant's duty to cover specifically foreseeable parties but at the same time to contain liability to manageable levels. In *White,* for instance, liability stemmed from a single isolated transaction where the parties to the agreement contemplated the protection of identified individuals. Here, insofar as revealed by the record, the arrangement between Con Edison and Belle Realty was no different from those existing between Con Edison and the millions of other customers it serves. . . . When plaintiff's relationship with Con Edison is viewed from this perspective, it is no answer to say that a duty is owed because, as a tenant in an apartment building, plaintiff belongs to a narrowly defined class.[2]

Additionally, we deal here with a system-wide power failure occasioned by what has already been determined to be the utility's gross negligence. If liability could be found here, then in logic and fairness the same result must follow in many similar situations. For example, a tenant's guests and invitees, as well as persons making deliveries or repairing equipment in the building, are equally persons who must use the common areas, and for whom they are maintained. Customers of a store and occupants of an office building stand in much the same position with respect to Con Edison as tenants of an apartment building. In all cases the numbers are to a certain extent limited and defined, and while identities may change, so do those of apartment dwellers (compare, White v. Guarente, 43 N.Y.2d 356, 361, supra ["situation did not involve prospective limited partners, unknown at the time"]). While limiting recovery to customers in this instance can hardly be said to confer immunity from negligence on Con Edison (see, [*Koch*]) permitting recovery to those in plaintiff's circumstances would, in our view, violate the court's responsibility to define an orbit of duty that places controllable limits on liability.

. . .

In sum, Con Edison is not answerable to the tenant of an apartment building injured in a common area as a result of Con Edison's negligent failure to provide electric service as required by its agreement with the building owner. Accordingly, the order of the Appellate Division should be affirmed, with costs.

■ MEYER, J. (dissenting). My disagreement with the majority results not from its consideration of public policy as a factor in determining the scope of Con Ed's duty, but from the fact that in reaching its public policy conclusion it has considered only one side of the equation and based its conclusion on nothing more than assumption. I, therefore, respectfully dissent.

. . .

The majority's blind acceptance of the notion that Consolidated Edison will be crushed if held liable to the present plaintiff and others like him ignores the possibility that through application to the Public Service Commission Con Ed can seek such reduction of the return on stockholders' equity [ ] or increase in its rates, or both, as may be necessary to pay the judgments obtained against it. It ignores as well the burden imposed upon

---

2. In deciding that public policy precludes liability to a noncustomer injured in the common areas of an apartment building, we need not decide whether recovery would necessarily also be precluded where a person injured in the home is not the family bill payer but the spouse. In another context, where this court has defined the duty of a public accounting firm for negligent financial statements, we have recognized that the duty runs both to those in contractual privity with the accountant and to those whose bond is so close as to be, in practical effect, indistinguishable from privity, and we have on public policy grounds precluded wider liability to persons damaged by the accountant's negligence. (See, Credit Alliance Corp. v. Arthur Andersen & Co., 65 N.Y.2d 536.)

the persons physically injured by Con Ed's gross negligence or, as to those forced to seek welfare assistance because their savings have been wiped out by the injury, the State. Doing so in the name of public policy seems particularly perverse, for what it says, in essence, is the more persons injured through a tort-feasor's gross negligence, the less the responsibility for injuries incurred.

. . . There simply is no basis other than the majority's say so for its assumptions [ ], that the impact of a city-wide deprivation of electric power upon the utility is entitled to greater consideration than the impact upon those injured; that a rational boundary cannot be fixed that will include some (apartment tenants injured in common areas, for example), if not all of the injured; that the consequence of imposing some bystander liability will be more adverse to societal interests than will follow from blindly limiting liability for tort to those with whom the tort-feasor has a contractual relationship. Before we grant Con Ed's motion to dismiss, therefore, we should require that a rational basis for such assumptions be established.

Con Ed may well be able to do so, but before its motion is granted at the expense of an unknown number of victims who have suffered injuries the extent and effects of which are also unknown, it should be required to establish that the catastrophic probabilities are great enough to warrant the limitation of duty it seeks [ ].

I would, therefore, deny the summary judgment motions of both sides and remit to Supreme Court for determination of the preliminary fact issues involved.

■ CHIEF JUDGE WACHTLER and JUDGES SIMONS, ALEXANDER and TITONE concur with JUDGE KAYE; JUDGE MEYER dissents and votes to reverse in a separate opinion in which JUDGE JASEN concurs.

NOTES AND QUESTIONS

1. Public Service Commission approval of Con Edison's rate schedule included a proviso that the utility would be liable only for "willful misconduct or gross negligence." See discussion in Food Pageant v. Consolidated Edison Co., cited in the principal case, involving an action by a grocery chain for food spoilage and loss of business due to the blackout. Why was this limitation alone not a sufficient concession to the court's concern about crushing liability?

2. Presumably, if Strauss had fallen (without fault on his part) in a personal residence that he owned he would have been able to collect as a ratepayer of Con Edison. Is *Belle Realty* nonetheless a substantial assurance against crushing liability?

3. Does the dissent persuasively deal with the majority's concern about crushing liability?

4. In Palka v. Servicemaster Management Services Corp., 83 N.Y.2d 579, 634 N.E.2d 189, 611 N.Y.S.2d 817 (1994), plaintiff nurse was hurt when a wall-mounted fan in a patient's room fell. Defendant had contracted with the hospital to perform all maintenance functions. The defendant argued that its only duty was owed to the hospital with which it had contracted. The court disagreed. The unanimous court rejected "an open-ended range of tort duty arising out of contractual breaches." To find a duty the relationship between the defendant's contract obligation and the "injured noncontracting party's reliance and injury must be direct and demonstrable, not incidental or merely collateral [citing *Strauss* and other cases]."

> Here, the functions to be performed by Servicemaster were not directed to a faceless or unlimited universe of persons. Rather, a known and identifiable group—hospital employees, patients and visitors—was to benefit and be protected by safety maintenance protocols assumed and acquired exclusively by Servicemaster. It cannot reasonably claim that it was unaware or that it was entitled to be unaware that individuals would expect some entity's direct responsibility to perform maintenance services with ordinary prudence and care. [ ] In fact, the very "end and aim" of the service contract was that Servicemaster was to become the sole privatized provider for a safe and clean hospital premises (see [*Glanzer*]).

How is *Strauss* different?

5. Does the majority effectively distinguish White v. Guarente, in which the defendants prepared an audit and tax returns for use by a limited number of parties? Should it matter that *White,* as well as many of the other cases cited by the majority limiting liability to a specific, circumscribed class, involved non-physical injury, unlike *Belle Realty* ? The issues involved in deciding whether special treatment should be afforded to non-physical injuries are the subject of Chapter IV.

6. Noting that only four states allowed recovery against water companies in fire cases, Libbey v. Hampton Water Works Co., 118 N.H. 500, 389 A.2d 434 (1978), adopted the majority view of *Moch.* Among other reasons, the court noted that water companies do not charge higher rates in areas of high fire risk. If they did, "water would no longer be a cheap, easily procurable commodity. In areas of high risk, water could become prohibitively expensive." Also, the defendant "cannot be said to have dissuaded the homeowner from selecting another method of protecting his home."

We return to the water company cases from an insurance perspective in Chapter X.

7. In Albala v. City of New York, 54 N.Y.2d 269, 429 N.E.2d 786, 445 N.Y.S.2d 108 (1981), plaintiff alleged that a negligently performed abortion on his mother-to-be in 1971 perforated her uterus and caused him to be born with brain damage in 1975. The court, 5–1, concluded that to recognize this action "would require the extension of traditional tort concepts beyond manageable bounds." The court observed:

> We are not unmindful . . . that at the time Ruth Albala underwent an abortion in 1971 it was foreseeable that she would again

conceive and that the health of children born thereafter could be adversely affected by damage to her uterus. We disagree, however, that this foreseeability alone established a duty to plaintiff on the part of defendants. We determined long ago in a case involving policy issues as sensitive as the ones at bar that foreseeability alone is not the hallmark of legal duty for if foreseeability were the sole test we could not logically confine the extension of liability. (Tobin v. Grossman [ ]; see Pulka v. Edelman [ ]).

The majority also expressed concern that extended liability would lead to "defensive medicine" in which a physician might have to choose between a treatment more likely to save the patient, but with risks to possible offspring, and another treatment somewhat less beneficial to the patient but with no dangers to future generations. If liability ran to future generations "society as a whole would bear the cost of our placing physicians in a direct conflict between their moral duty to patients and the proposed legal duty to those hypothetical future generations outside the immediate zone of danger."

The New York court has adhered to *Albala* in rejecting a claim of a grandchild that the DES taken by her grandmother led to harm to her. The court found no duty to a third-generation victim. Enright v. Eli Lilly & Co., 77 N.Y.2d 377, 570 N.E.2d 198, 568 N.Y.S.2d 550, cert. denied 502 U.S. 868 (1991):

For all we know, the rippling effects of DES exposure may extend for generations. It is our duty to confine liability within manageable limits. [ ] Limiting liability to those who ingested the drug or were exposed to it *in utero* serves this purpose.

The *Albala* approach was rejected in Renslow v. Mennonite Hospital, 67 Ill.2d 348, 367 N.E.2d 1250 (1977), in which plaintiff alleged that when her mother was 13 years old, the defendant hospital and its director of laboratories, negligently transfused her mother with Rh-positive blood. The 13-year-old's Rh-negative blood was incompatible with, and was sensitized by, the new blood. The problem did not become apparent until several years later when the mother became pregnant with plaintiff. As a result of the incompatibility, plaintiff alleged, she needed blood transfusions immediately after birth and suffered severe permanent damage. The court, 4–3, upheld the complaint, with five opinions that explored the appropriate judicial response to claims based on acts alleged to have been committed many years earlier. *Albala* is also rejected in Lough v. Rolla Women's Clinic, Inc., 866 S.W.2d 851 (Mo.1993) involving allegations about negligent reporting of a mother's Rh status in an earlier pregnancy.

8. In Jansen v. Fidelity & Casualty Co., 79 N.Y.2d 867, 589 N.E.2d 379, 581 N.Y.S.2d 156 (1992), defendant was the workers' compensation insurance carrier for plaintiff's employer. Defendant had the right under the insurance contract to, and did, carry out regular inspections of the premises in an effort to reduce the occurrence of worker injuries. Plaintiff worker, who was injured in an accident on the premises, alleged that the defendant had negligently carried out its inspections. and that he had been hurt as a result.   The court rejected a duty because it was "apparent that the safety inspections were undertaken solely for defendant's own underwriting purposes—to reduce the risks that might give rise to liability under the policy."

9.   Next, we consider situations in which the injury victim's claim is that the defendant should have taken action to prevent a third party from engaging in harmful conduct.   Are the duty considerations developed in this section helpful in dealing with these three-party configurations?

C.   Obligations to Control the Conduct of Others

Tarasoff v. Regents of the Univ. of California

Supreme Court of California, 1976.
17 Cal.3d 425, 551 P.2d 334, 131 Cal.Rptr. 14.

[Dr. Moore, a psychologist employed by the University of California, was treating one Poddar.   Poddar killed Tatiana Tarasoff.   Plaintiffs, the parents of Tatiana Tarasoff, allege that Poddar had confided his intention to kill Tarasoff to Dr. Moore;   that after an abortive effort to detain Poddar, he was released;   and that no one warned Tarasoff or plaintiffs of Tarasoff's peril.   The trial judge dismissed the suit that was brought against several therapists and others.]

■ Tobriner, J.

.   .   .

The second cause of action can be amended to allege that Tatiana's death proximately resulted from defendants' negligent failure to warn Tatiana or others likely to apprise her of her danger.   Plaintiffs contend that as amended, such allegations of negligence and proximate causation, with resulting damages, establish a cause of action.   Defendants, however, contend that in the circumstances of the present case they owed no duty of care to Tatiana or her parents and that, in the absence of such duty, they were free to act in careless disregard of Tatiana's life and safety.

In analyzing this issue, we bear in mind that legal duties are not discoverable facts of nature, but merely conclusory expressions that, in cases of a particular type, liability should be imposed for damage done.
.   .   .

In the landmark case of Rowland v. Christian [   ], Justice Peters recognized that liability should be imposed "for injury occasioned to another by his want of ordinary care or skill" as expressed in § 1714 of the Civil Code.   Thus, Justice Peters, quoting from Heaven v. Pender (1883) 11 Q.B.D. 503, 509 stated: " 'whenever one person is by circumstances placed in such a position with regard to another .   .   .   that if he did not use ordinary care and skill in his own conduct .   .   .   he would cause danger of injury to the person or property of the other, a duty arises to use ordinary care and skill to avoid such danger.' "

We depart from "this fundamental principle" only upon the "balancing of a number of considerations"; major ones "are the foreseeability of harm to the plaintiff, the degree of certainty that the plaintiff suffered injury, the closeness of the connection between the defendant's conduct and the injury suffered, the moral blame attached to the defendant's conduct, the policy of preventing future harm, the extent of the burden to the defendant and consequences to the community of imposing a duty to exercise care with resulting liability for breach, and the availability, cost and prevalence of insurance for the risk involved." [citing several cases]

The most important of these considerations in establishing duty is foreseeability. As a general principle, a "defendant owes a duty of care to all persons who are foreseeably endangered by his conduct, with respect to all risks which make the conduct unreasonably dangerous." [ ] As we shall explain, however, when the avoidance of foreseeable harm requires a defendant to control the conduct of another person, or to warn of such conduct, the common law has traditionally imposed liability only if the defendant bears some special relationship to the dangerous person or to the potential victim. Since the relationship between a therapist and his patient satisfies this requirement, we need not here decide whether foreseeability alone is sufficient to create a duty to exercise reasonable care to protect a potential victim of another's conduct.

Although, as we have stated above, under the common law, as a general rule, one person owed no duty to control the conduct of another[5] [ ], nor to warn those endangered by such conduct [ ], the courts have carved out an exception to this rule in cases in which the defendant stands in some special relationship to either the person whose conduct needs to be controlled or in a relationship to the foreseeable victim of that conduct (see Restatement, Second, Torts, supra, §§ 315–320). Applying this exception to the present case, we note that a relationship of defendant therapists to either Tatiana or Poddar will suffice to establish a duty of care; as explained in section 315 of the Restatement Second of Torts, a duty of care may arise from either "(a) a special relation . . . between the actor and the third person which imposes a duty upon the actor to control the third person's conduct, or (b) a special relation . . . between the actor and the other which gives to the other a right of protection."

---

5. This rule derives from the common law's distinction between misfeasance and nonfeasance, and its reluctance to impose liability for the latter. (See Harper & Kime, The Duty to Control the Conduct of Another (1934) 43 Yale L.J. 886, 887.) Morally questionable, the rule owes its survival to "the difficulties of setting any standards of unselfish service to fellow men, and of making any workable rule to cover possible situations where fifty people might fail to rescue. . . ." (Prosser, Torts (4th ed. 1971) § 56, p. 341.) Because of these practical difficulties, the courts have increased the number of instances in which affirmative duties are imposed not by direct rejection of the common law rule, but by expanding the list of special relationships which will justify departure from that rule. [ ]

Although plaintiffs' pleadings assert no special relation between Tatiana and defendant therapists, they establish as between Poddar and defendant therapists the special relation that arises between a patient and his doctor or psychotherapist. Such a relationship may support affirmative duties for the benefit of third persons. Thus, for example, a hospital must exercise reasonable care to control the behavior of a patient which may endanger other persons. A doctor must also warn a patient if the patient's condition or medication renders certain conduct, such as driving a car, dangerous to others.

Although the California decisions that recognize this duty have involved cases in which the defendant stood in a special relationship *both* to the victim and to the person whose conduct created the danger,[9] we do not think that the duty should logically be constricted to such situations. Decisions of other jurisdictions hold that the single relationship of a doctor to his patient is sufficient to support the duty to exercise reasonable care to protect others against dangers emanating from the patient's illness. The courts hold that a doctor is liable to persons infected by his patient if he negligently fails to diagnose a contagious disease [ ], or having diagnosed the illness, fails to warn members of the patient's family [ ].

. . .

Defendants contend, however, that imposition of a duty to exercise reasonable care to protect third persons is unworkable because therapists cannot accurately predict whether or not a patient will resort to violence. In support of this argument amicus representing the American Psychiatric Association and other professional societies cites numerous articles which indicate that therapists, in the present state of the art, are unable reliably to predict violent acts; their forecasts, amicus claims, tend consistently to overpredict violence, and indeed are more often wrong than right. Since predictions of violence are often erroneous, amicus concludes, the courts should not render rulings that predicate the liability of therapists upon the validity of such predictions.

. . .

We recognize the difficulty that a therapist encounters in attempting to forecast whether a patient presents a serious danger of violence. . . . Within the broad range of reasonable practice and treatment in which professional opinion and judgment may differ, the therapist is free to exercise his or her own best judgment without liability; proof, aided by hindsight, that he or she judged wrongly is insufficient to establish negligence.

9. Ellis v. D'Angelo (1953) 116 Cal. App.2d 310 [253 P.2d 675], upheld a cause of action against parents who failed to warn a babysitter of the violent proclivities of their child; Johnson v. State of California (1968) 69 Cal.2d 782, 447 P.2d 352 [73 Cal.Rptr. 240], upheld a suit against the state for failure to warn foster parents of the dangerous tendencies of their ward; Morgan v. County of Yuba (1964) 230 Cal.App.2d 938 [41 Cal. Rptr. 508], sustained a cause of action against a sheriff who had promised to warn decedent before releasing a dangerous prisoner, but failed to do so.

In the instant case, however, the pleadings do not raise any questions as to failure of defendant therapists to predict that Poddar presented a serious danger of violence. On the contrary, the present complaints allege that defendant therapists did in fact predict that Poddar would kill, but were negligent in failing to warn.

Amicus contends, however, that even when a therapist does in fact predict that a patient poses a serious danger of violence to others, the therapist should be absolved of any responsibility for failing to act to protect the potential victim. In our view, however, once a therapist does in fact determine, or under applicable professional standards reasonably should have determined, that a patient poses a serious danger of violence to others, he bears a duty to exercise reasonable care to protect the foreseeable victim of that danger. While the discharge of this duty of due care will necessarily vary with the facts of each case,[11] in each instance the adequacy of the therapist's conduct must be measured against the traditional negligence standard of the rendition of reasonable care under the circumstances. . . .

. . . Weighing the uncertain and conjectural character of the alleged damage done the patient by such a warning against the peril to the victim's life, we conclude that professional inaccuracy in predicting violence cannot negate the therapist's duty to protect the threatened victim.

The risk that unnecessary warnings may be given is a reasonable price to pay for the lives of possible victims that may be saved. We would hesitate to hold that the therapist who is aware that his patient expects to attempt to assassinate the President of the United States would not be obligated to warn the authorities because the therapist cannot predict with accuracy that his patient will commit the crime.

Defendants further argue that free and open communication is essential to psychotherapy. . . . The giving of a warning, defendants contend, constitutes a breach of trust which entails the revelation of confidential communications.

We recognize the public interest in supporting effective treatment of mental illness and in protecting the rights of patients to privacy [ ], and the consequent public importance of safeguarding the confidential character of psychotherapeutic communication. Against this interest, however, we must weigh the public interest in safety from violent assault. The Legislature has undertaken the difficult task of balancing the countervailing concerns. In Evidence Code section 1014, it established a broad rule of privilege to protect confidential communications between patient and psychotherapist. In Evidence Code section 1024, the Legislature created a

---

11. Defendant therapists and amicus also argue that warnings must be given only in those cases in which the therapist knows the identity of the victim. We recognize that in some cases it would be unreasonable to require the therapist to interrogate his patient to discover the victim's identity, or to conduct an independent investigation. But there may also be cases in which a moment's reflection will reveal the victim's identity. The matter thus is one which depends upon the circumstances of each case, and should not be governed by any hard and fast rule.

specific and limited exception to the psychotherapist-patient privilege: "There is no privilege   .   .   .   if the psychotherapist has reasonable cause to believe that the patient is in such mental or emotional condition as to be dangerous to himself or to the person or property of another and that disclosure of the communication is necessary to prevent the threatened danger."

We realize that the open and confidential character of psychotherapeutic dialogue encourages patients to express threats of violence, few of which are ever executed.   Certainly a therapist should not be encouraged routinely to reveal such threats;   such disclosures could seriously disrupt the patient's relationship with his therapist and with the persons threatened. To the contrary, the therapist's obligations to his patient require that he not disclose a confidence unless such disclosure is necessary to avert danger to others, and even then that he do so discreetly, and in a fashion that would preserve the privacy of his patient to the fullest extent compatible with the prevention of the threatened danger. [   ]

The revelation of a communication under the above circumstances is not a breach of trust or a violation of professional ethics; as stated in the Principles of Medical Ethics of the American Medical Association (1957), section 9: "A physician may not reveal the confidence entrusted to him in the course of medical attendance   .   .   .   *unless he is required to do so by law or unless it becomes necessary in order to protect the welfare of the individual or of the community.*"   (Italics added.)   We conclude that the public policy favoring protection of the confidential character of patient-psychotherapist communications must yield to the extent to which disclosure is essential to avert danger to others.   The protective privilege ends where the public peril begins.

Our current crowded and computerized society compels the interdependence of its members.   In this risk-infested society we can hardly tolerate the further exposure to danger that would result from a concealed knowledge of the therapist that his patient was lethal.   If the exercise of reasonable care to protect the threatened victim requires the therapist to warn the endangered party or those who can reasonably be expected to notify him, we see no sufficient societal interest that would protect and justify concealment.   The containment of such risks lies in the public interest.   .   .   .

.   .   .

For the reasons stated, we conclude that plaintiffs can amend their complaints to state a cause of action against defendant therapists by asserting that the therapists in fact determined that Poddar presented a serious danger of violence to Tatiana, or pursuant to the standards of their profession should have so determined, but nevertheless failed to exercise reasonable care to protect her from that danger.

.   .   .

■ WRIGHT, C.J., SULLIVAN, J., and RICHARDSON, J., concurred.

■ Mosk, J., Concurring and Dissenting.—I concur in the result in this instance only because the complaints allege that defendant therapists did in fact predict that Poddar would kill and were therefore negligent in failing to warn of that danger. . . .

. . .

I cannot concur, however, in the majority's rule that a therapist may be held liable for failing to predict his patient's tendency to violence if other practitioners, pursuant to the "standards of the profession," would have done so. The question is, what standards? Defendants and a responsible amicus curiae, supported by an impressive body of literature discussed at length in our recent opinion in People v. Burnick (1975) 14 Cal.3d 306 [535 P.2d 352, 121 Cal.Rptr. 488], demonstrate that psychiatric predictions of violence are inherently unreliable.

. . .

■ [Justice Clark, joined by Justice McComb, dissented. First, he argued that certain legislation indicated an intention that therapists not disclose this information. Entirely apart from the statute, he believed that general tort principles favored nondisclosure. He considered confidentiality critical for three reasons: without such assurances those requiring treatment would be deterred; confidentiality encouraged the full disclosure necessary for effective treatment; and even with full disclosure, confidentiality is necessary to allow the patient to maintain his trust in his psychiatrist. Given the lack of precision in predicting violence, psychiatrists will be tempted either to issue excessive warnings or to commit patients—a practice already used to excess. "We should accept legislative and medical judgment, relying upon effective treatment rather than on indiscriminate warning."]

NOTES AND QUESTIONS

1. The citation to § 315 of the Second Restatement raises several questions. The section itself indicates that the relationship must be one that "imposes a duty upon the actor to control the third person's conduct." The comment declares that these relations "are stated in §§ 316–319." Those sections provide that an actor who knows or should know that he or she has the ability to control the third person and knows or should know of the need for the action, comes under a duty to do so as to parent-child (§ 316); master-servant (§ 317); and possessor of land or chattels-user of the land or chattels (§ 318). Section 319 provides that "One who takes charge of a third person whom he knows or should know to be likely to cause bodily harm to others if not controlled is under a duty to exercise reasonable care to control the third person to prevent him from doing such harm." The illustrations deal with an escape of a homicidal maniac and the negligent release of patients who have contagious diseases. Do any of these sections support *Tarasoff?*

2. So far as § 315 is concerned, consider Lego v. Schmidt, 805 P.2d 1119 (Colo.App.1990), in which the court rejected a duty on a passenger to

warn the driver about an impending danger to a pedestrian that the driver, moving at 5 miles per hour, did not appear to recognize. The court quoted comment *b* of § 315 of the Restatement, which states that in the absence of a special relationship between the actor and either the third person or the person hurt

> the actor is not subject to liability if he fails, either intentionally or through inadvertence, to exercise his ability so to control the actions of the third persons as to protect another from even the most serious harm. This is true although the actor realizes that he has the ability to control the conduct of a third person, and could do so with only the most trivial of efforts and without any inconvenience to himself. Thus if the actor is riding in a third person's car merely as a guest, he is not subject to liability to another run over by the car even though he knows of the other's danger and knows that the driver is not aware of it, and knows that by a mere word, recalling the driver's attention to the road, he would give the driver an opportunity to stop the car before the other is run over.

The passenger, who saw the danger, "rather than shouting or pulling the emergency brake," was said to have "looked away." The court noted that any "attempt on the part of a passenger to direct the driver or to take over control of the brake or wheel could well become negligence itself, and the passenger is trapped into an instantaneous Hobson's choice between action and inaction." The court concluded that there was no duty "to interfere with the driver's control of the car, by either word or deed" and cited other cases including one that it summarized as holding that "passengers had no duty to warn driver that fellow passenger had been thrown from car and was in danger of being run over." The Restatement comment also notes that if the guest is hurt in such a situation the guest's silence may constitute contributory negligence because of the guest's violation of the duty of self-protection. Is this outcome consistent with that in *Tarasoff*?

3. Is the line of cases referred to in the opinion in which a physician failed to warn a patient's family or friends of the patient's contagious condition a closer analogy than the Restatement sections? The courts disagree.

a. *Duty beyond the physician-patient relationship.* In Reisner v. Regents of the University of California, 31 Cal.App.4th 1195, 37 Cal.Rptr.2d 518 (1995), a day after 12-year-old T received a transfusion, her doctor discovered that the blood had been contaminated with HIV antibodies. Although the same doctor continued treating T, he never told her about the situation. Three years later, T became intimate with plaintiff. Two years after that the doctor told T, who died a month later. Shortly thereafter, plaintiff was tested and learned that he was HIV seropositive. The court, relying largely on *Tarasoff*, held that defendant doctor owed a duty to plaintiff despite the lack of a physician-patient relationship. Might the passage of time distinguish the cases? (Note the causal part of plaintiff's case—that if T had been told when she should have been told, she would have warned plaintiff and he would not have been infected.)

In Pate v. Threlkel, 661 So.2d 278 (Fla.1995), defendant surgeon who operated on patient knew or should have known of the likelihood that her adult children would contract the carcinoma involved because it was genetically transferrable. The court imposed a duty to the patient's child who alleged that her cancer would have been discovered sooner and been treatable if her mother had been told about the genetic situation. Since the obligation here was "obviously for the benefit of certain identified third parties and the physician knows of the existence of those third parties, then the physician's duty runs to those third parties."

b. *No duty.* In Clarke v. Hoek, 174 Cal.App.3d 208, 219 Cal.Rptr. 845 (1985), plaintiff argued that defendant doctor was negligent in failing to intervene to prevent malpractice by a surgical team while he was proctoring an operation. Defendant was observing the operation as part of the hospital's determination of whether to grant staff privileges to the operating surgeon. The court affirmed summary judgment for the defendant on the ground that the proctoring physician's role was limited to observing and reporting on the operation and that he had no special relationship to the patient. Is this consistent with *Tarasoff*?

It has also been widely, though not uniformly, held that physicians who are employed by companies (or insurers) to give prospective employees (or insureds) physical examinations owe no duty to tell the person being examined if they find signs of trouble. For an argument against that position, see Squillante, Expanding the Potential Tort Liability of Physicians: A Legal Portrait of "Nontraditional Patients" and Proposals for Change, 40 UCLA L.Rev. 1617 (1993). Recall the *Jansen* case, p. 139, supra.

In Werner v. Varner, Stafford & Seaman, P.A., 659 So.2d 1308 (Fla. App.1995), the court dismissed a claim brought by a motorist who was rear-ended by defendant's patient. The claim was that the physician had failed to tell the patient not to drive while taking anti-epilepsy medicine. The court distinguished *Pate v. Threlkel*, supra, on the ground that the victim here was neither known nor identifiable by the defendant.

In Conboy v. Mogeloff, 172 App.Div.2d 912, 567 N.Y.S.2d 960 (1991), defendant prescribed a drug for his patient and told her she could drive a car while taking it. A few days later, while using the drug, she lost consciousness and the car crashed hurting her children passengers. The court rejected a duty:

> As a general rule, a defendant has no legal duty to control the conduct of third persons so as to prevent them from harming others, (see *Pulka v. Edelman*) [cited in the main case and discussed below]. However, certain relationships may give rise to such a duty, but then only when the defendant has the ability and authority to control the third persons' conduct [   ]. The threshold inquiry here, therefore, is whether defendant had sufficient ability and authority to control the conduct of Dillenbeck so as to give rise to a duty on his part to protect the children. . . . Dillenbeck was free to accept or reject defendant's diagnosis and advice and she was at liberty to seek a second opinion.

In short, she had the right to decide what treatment and advice she would accept or reject. [   ] Contrary to plaintiff's contentions, advice does not equate to control.

The court observed that "there are no allegations . . . of the children's reliance on defendant's conduct or of knowledge by the defendant of any such reliance." Would that have changed matters? See also Tenuto v. Lederle Laboratories, 207 App.Div.2d 541, 616 N.Y.S.2d 391 (1994)(no duty to warn infant's father about dangers of getting polio from coming into contact with excrement of infant recently immunized against polio); Ellis v. Peter, 211 App.Div.2d 353, 627 N.Y.S.2d 707 (1995)(physician who failed to diagnose tuberculosis in patient husband owed no duty to plaintiff wife who contracted the disease from husband). In *Ellis* the majority feared that no line could be drawn to prevent such a duty from extending to "children, co-workers, or even fellow commuters."

4.   The court lists a number of factors that are said to play a role in the determination whether to impose a duty. Does it rely on these factors? What result would the factors suggest in *Tarasoff*?

5.   Later California cases adhered to *Tarasoff* with caution. See Bellah v. Greenson, 81 Cal.App.3d 614, 146 Cal.Rptr. 535 (1978), in which a patient of the defendant psychiatrist committed suicide. The patient's parents claimed that defendant negligently failed to take sufficient measures to prevent the suicide; that he failed to warn plaintiffs, who were out of state, of the seriousness of their daughter's condition; and that she was consorting with heroin addicts. All claims failed. *Tarasoff* does not apply where the risk is "self-inflicted harm or mere property damage."

In Thompson v. County of Alameda, 27 Cal.3d 741, 614 P.2d 728, 167 Cal.Rptr. 70 (1980), the county released James, a violent juvenile offender into his mother's custody although the county knew that he had threatened to kill some unidentified child in the neighborhood. Within 24 hours, James killed plaintiff's son, a boy in his neighborhood. The plaintiffs claimed that the county had been negligent in failing to warn the public, the police, and James's mother.

The trial court's dismissal of the complaint was affirmed, 5–2. There was no identified potential victim. Warnings to the general public were unlikely to do much good because the public is already conditioned to protecting itself against crime and violence and a specific warning might negate the rehabilitative purposes of the probation and parole systems. Nor was a warning to the juvenile's mother likely to be effective. She would not be likely to "inform other neighborhood parents or children that her son posed a general threat to their welfare, thereby perhaps thwarting any rehabilitative effort, and also effectively stigmatizing both the mother and son in the community."

In Hedlund v. Superior Court, 34 Cal.3d 695, 669 P.2d 41, 194 Cal.Rptr. 805 (1983), a young child harmed during a violent assault on his mother was given an action when threats of violence against the mother had been communicated to defendant psychotherapists. Injuries to a child were foreseeable in an assault upon the mother, and consequently fell within the *Tarasoff* principle.

6. After *Tarasoff*, Cal. Civil Code § 43.92 was enacted to provide that therapists are immune from liability for failure to warn "except when the patient has communicated to the psychotherapist a serious threat of physical violence against a reasonably identifiable victim or victims." If there is a duty to warn, it "shall be discharged by the psychotherapist making reasonable efforts to communicate the threat to the victim or victims and to a law enforcement agency."

7. *Tarasoff* has been followed and extended to a broader range of injuries in some jurisdictions. E.g., Peck v. Counseling Service of Addison County, 146 Vt. 61, 499 A.2d 422 (1985)(extending the duty in favor of the patient's parents, whose barn was burned down); but see Cole v. Taylor, 301 N.W.2d 766 (Iowa 1981)(no duty owed to the patient herself who claimed that her psychiatrist had not prevented her from committing a murder for which she was imprisoned). Some states have rejected *Tarasoff*. See, e.g., Nasser v. Parker, 249 Va. 172, 455 S.E.2d 502 (1995)(no duty to warn potential victim of danger from person who had voluntarily committed himself and then checked himself out; psychiatrist had not "taken charge" of the patient).

For a review of the case developments and an empirical study of how the cases have shaped professional behavior, see Rosenhan, Teitelbaum, Teitelbaum & Davidson, Warning Third Parties: The Ripple Effect of *Tarasoff*, 24 Pac.L.J. 1165 (1993).

8. After *Tarasoff*, does a physician who knows that a patient has tested positive for the AIDS virus have a duty to notify the sexual partners of the patient if they are known? California, by Cal.Health & Safety Code § 199.25(c), has provided: "No physician has a duty to notify any person of the fact that a patient is reasonably believed to be infected by the probable causative agent of acquired immune deficiency syndrome." Subsections (a) and (b) provide that, subject to some limitations, no physician shall be held liable for "disclosing to a person reasonably believed to be the [spouse, sexual partner, hypodermic needle sharer, or county health officer] that the patient has tested positive on a test to detect infection by the probable causative agent of" AIDS. The physician must first discuss the matter with the patient and attempt to obtain "voluntary consent for notification of his or her contacts." All persons so notified are to be referred for "appropriate care, counseling, and follow up." The statute, amended to this form in 1988, has yet to be interpreted in a reported case. In *Reisner*, note 3, supra, plaintiff did not claim to be entitled to direct warning from the defendant.

9. What if a regular patron of Joe's Tavern tells the bartender that he has "had it" with his wife's behavior and is going home to kill her? What if he told his dentist explicitly what he was going to do? Are these stronger or weaker cases for imposing a duty than *Tarasoff*?

10. In Pulka v. Edelman, 40 N.Y.2d 781, 358 N.E.2d 1019, 390 N.Y.S.2d 393 (1976), cited in *Strauss,* plaintiff pedestrian was struck by a car while it was being driven out of the defendant's garage and across an adjacent sidewalk by a patron of the garage. A statute required the driver to stop before entering the sidewalk and yield to any pedestrian. A jury found the driver and the garage both liable. The court of appeals held, 4–3, that the claim against the garage should be dismissed.

The majority stated the issue to be whether a garage "has a duty to control the conduct of its patrons for the protection of off-premises pedestrians." No such duty arose from the relationship between the garage and the driver because the garage had no reasonable opportunity to control the conduct of the driver. Although the garage may have taken precautions, it could not be said that it had "a reasonable opportunity to stop drivers from disregarding their own sense of danger to pedestrians." To build a duty on this relationship would place "an unreasonable burden on the garage."

Nor could a duty be based on the relationship between garage and pedestrian, which was "at best somewhat tenuous." It "would be most unfair" to impose a duty on the garage with respect to its patrons because it did not "control the tort-feasor." Providing an action against the garage "would be to create an unnecessary extension of a duty beyond the limits required under the law of negligence as we know it." The court continued:

> If a rule of law were established so that liability would be imposed in an instance such as this, it is difficult to conceive of the bounds to which liability logically would flow. The liability potential would be all but limitless and the outside boundaries of that liability, both in respect to space and the extent of care to be exercised, particularly in the absence of control, would be difficult of definition. Consider a city like New York with its almost countless parking garages and lots. Think especially of those in the theatre districts and around sporting stadiums and convention halls with the mass exoduses that occur upon cessation of the events which draw the crowds. Think also of the parking facilities at some hotels, office buildings and shopping centers. The burden cast on the operators of these parking establishments in order to discharge their responsibilities in respect to patron-operated vehicles beyond the confines of their properties would be an impractical and unbearable one.

The dissenters responded:

> [A garage operator] cannot close his eyes to the duty to pedestrians who are thereby imperiled. The obligation of due care might have been discharged by restricting operation of departing vehicles to garage employees, by cautioning patron drivers of the possible presence of sidewalk pedestrians, by warning the pedestrians themselves, or by some combination of such methods, or by resort to some other means of protecting against injury to passersby. Liability would not necessarily be predicated on an obligation of the garage to control the conduct of its patrons; the responsibility of due care might otherwise have been discharged by the expenditure of some effort and attention. In the

present instance there was no evidence that any attempt was made to protect users of the sidewalk.

Who has the better of the dispute? Are *Pulka* and *Tarasoff* consistent in result?

11. In an omitted part of the *Tarasoff* opinion, Justice Tobriner concluded that the campus police, who detained Poddar for a short while but released him when he appeared rational, and did not warn Tatiana or her parents of any danger, did not owe a duty to the plaintiffs. No special relationship was found between the police and Tatiana or Poddar sufficient to impose upon the police a duty to warn. The affirmative duties of the police and other governmental entities are considered in Section F.

12. Note that these extended duty cases arise primarily in situations in which the immediately responsible party is unlikely to be a solvent defendant. In the *Tarasoff* sequence of cases, for example, clearly doctors and clinics are generally more promising defendants than homicidal psychopaths. Keep this "strategic" consideration in mind as we look at other doctrinal efforts to assign liability beyond the "obvious" defendant.

In J.L. v. Kienenberger, 257 Mont. 113, 848 P.2d 472 (1993), plaintiff sued the parents of a 13–year-old who was alleged to have raped the plaintiff. Section 316 of the Restatement asserts that a "parent is under a duty to exercise reasonable care so to control his minor child as to prevent it from intentionally harming others or from so conducting itself as to create an unreasonable risk of bodily harm to them, if the parent (a) knows or has reason to know that he has the ability to control his child, and (b) knows or should know of the necessity and opportunity for exercising such control." According to § 12 of the Restatement, "has reason to know" means that the person has information from which a "person of reasonable intelligence or of the superior intelligence of the actor would infer that the fact in question exists" or behave as though it exists; "should know" is used to "denote the fact that a person of reasonable prudence and intelligence or of the superior intelligence of the actor would ascertain the fact in question in the performance of his duty to another" or would behave as though the fact exists.

The court rejected the section, 5–2, stating that it did not "find it necessary" to expand the existing limited statutory exceptions to the common law rule of nonliability. The dissenters would have imposed such a duty upon a showing that a parent was "aware" of the dangerous propensity which "caused the harm complained of." See also Brahm v. Hatch, 203 App.Div.2d 640, 609 N.Y.S.2d 956 (1994), in which a 17–year-old shot and killed his father and others. A suit brought by the estates of the others against the estate of the father was rejected in the absence of a showing that the father was aware of a need to control the son.

In Pamela L. v. Farmer, 112 Cal.App.3d 206, 169 Cal.Rptr. 282 (1980), plaintiffs alleged that defendant wife frequently left her house knowing that her husband, who had a record as a sexual offender, planned to sexually molest the minor plaintiffs who came onto the premises to use the swimming pool; that the wife knew that these acts would occur unless she warned the children, their parents or the police. In addition, plaintiffs alleged that the wife invited the children onto the premises knowing what would occur, and told the parents that it was perfectly safe to permit their children to be there when the wife was absent. The allegations of invitation and reassurance were held sufficient to create a special relationship with the children and to sustain an action against the wife. What if the only allegation had been that defendant knew that when she left her home her husband would use the opportunity to molest minors?

13. As the following case suggests, the duty to control the conduct of others is not necessarily limited to business and professional relationships.

Vince v. Wilson

Supreme Court of Vermont, 1989.
151 Vt. 425, 561 A.2d 103.

■ Before ALLEN, C.J., and PECK, GIBSON, DOOLEY and MAHADY, JJ.

■ MAHADY, JUSTICE.

This personal injury action requires us to further refine our definition of the tort of negligent entrustment. Plaintiff, seriously injured in an automobile accident, brought suit against defendant Wilson, who had provided funding for her grandnephew, the driver of the car in which plaintiff was a passenger at the time of the accident, to purchase the vehicle. Subsequently Ace Auto Sales, Inc. and its president Gary Gardner were added as defendants. Ace sold the vehicle to the driver; Gardner was the salesman of the vehicle.

At the close of plaintiff's case, the trial court directed verdicts in favor of defendants Ace and Gardner. Plaintiff appeals from this ruling. The claim against Wilson, on the other hand, was submitted to the jury, which returned a substantial verdict in favor of plaintiff. Wilson appeals from the judgment entered against her on the jury verdict. For the reasons stated below, we hold that the trial court erred in directing verdicts in favor of Ace and Gardner. As to the judgment against Wilson, we affirm the court's decision to submit the question to the jury, and remand for proceedings consistent with this opinion.

I.

The tort of negligent entrustment has long been recognized in Vermont. [ ] In Dicranian v. Foster, 114 Vt. 372, 45 A.2d 650 (1946), we noted that such "liability . . . arises out of the combined negligence of both, the negligence of one in entrusting the automobile to an incompetent driver and of the other in its operation." [ ]

Plaintiff argues that the rule should be applied to a person who knowingly provides funding to an incompetent driver to purchase a vehicle and to a person who knowingly sells a vehicle to an incompetent driver. We have not previously had an opportunity to address this issue. In [an earlier case], the defendant negligently entrusted a firearm and ammunition to his child, who negligently discharged the firearm resulting in the death of the plaintiff's intestate. In *Dicranian*, the defendant negligently entrusted his motor vehicle to an incompetent operator whose negligent operation of the vehicle caused injury to the plaintiff.

Defendants urge us to follow those courts which have limited recovery under a claim of negligent entrustment to situations where the defendant "is the owner or has the right to control" the instrumentality entrusted. [   ] These courts have denied liability where a father sold a car to his son who was known to have a drinking problem but not a driver's license, [   ]; where a vehicle was given to an incompetent operator, [   ]; or where a bailee automobile dealer returned an automobile after repair to its obviously intoxicated owner [   ].

Other courts have applied the rule more broadly. For example, courts have allowed recovery against an automobile dealer who sold a vehicle to an inexperienced and incompetent driver whose driving injured several people when the seller knew or should have known of the incompetency. [   ]. These courts hold that the fact that a defendant had ownership and control over the instrumentality at the time it was turned over to an incompetent individual is sufficient. [   ]. Thus, a father was held liable for funding the purchase of an automobile by a son whom the father knew to be an irresponsible driver, [   ], and a complaint against a father who purchased a vehicle for his epileptic son was held to state a cause of action. Golembe v. Blumberg, 262 A.D. 759, 27 N.Y.S.2d 692 (1941).

Both lines of cases derive their rule from the Restatement of Torts, which provides:

> One who supplies directly or through a third person a chattel for the use of another whom the supplier knows or has reason to know to be likely because of his youth, inexperience, or otherwise, to use it in a manner involving unreasonable risk of physical harm to himself and others whom the supplier should expect to share in or be endangered by its use, is subject to liability for physical harm resulting to them.

Restatement (Second) of Torts § 390 (1965). The comments to the Restatement support those decisions which extend the rule to individuals such as sellers:

> The rule stated applies to anyone who supplies a chattel for the use of another. It applies to sellers, lessors, donors or lenders, and to all kinds of bailors, irrespective of whether the bailment is gratuitous or for a consideration.

Id., comment a.

The cases noted above which restrict the rule to situations where the defendant is the owner or has the right to control the instrumentality have been severely criticized. See [law review comments].

Indeed, the leading commentators on the law of torts have said that such decisions "look definitely wrong," explaining:

It is the negligent entrusting which creates the unreasonable risk; and this is none the less when the goods are conveyed.

Prosser and Keeton on Torts § 104, at 718 (5th ed. 1984). Seen in this light, the issue is clearly one of negligence to be determined by the jury under proper instruction; the relationship of the defendant to the particular instrumentality is but one factor to be considered. The key factor is that "[t]he negligent entrustment theory requires a showing that the entrustor knew or should have known some reason why entrusting the item to another was foolish or negligent." [ ] This approach, based upon traditional negligence analysis, is consistent with our prior decisions. . . .

II.

With regard to plaintiff's claim against defendant Wilson, we must view the evidence in the light most favorable to plaintiff because of the jury's verdict in plaintiff's favor. [ ] With regard to plaintiff's claims against defendants Ace and Gardner, the trial court directed a verdict in favor of the defendants; as such, we must view the evidence in the light most favorable to plaintiff, excluding the effect of any modifying evidence. [ ]

So viewed, the evidence indicates that Wilson knew that the operator for whom she provided funding to purchase the vehicle had no driver's license and had failed the driver's test several times. Indeed, she communicated this fact to defendant Gardner, an agent of defendant Ace, prior to the sale of the vehicle. Defendant Wilson was also aware of the fact that her grandnephew abused alcohol and other drugs. The evidence also tended to show that the operator's inexperience and lack of training contributed to the accident which caused plaintiff's injuries. The evidence was sufficient to make out a prima facie case of negligent entrustment, and the trial court properly submitted the question to the jury.

Verdicts should not have been directed in favor of defendants Ace and Gardner, however. There was evidence which, if believed by the jury, would establish that they knew the operator had no operator's license and that he had failed the driver's test several times. Viewed in the light most favorable to plaintiff, the evidence tends to demonstrate negligence on the part of Ace and Gardner, and the issue should have been determined by the jury. [ ]

. . .

Cause remanded for further proceedings not inconsistent with this opinion [which, for procedural reasons, might include a new trial for Wilson].

NOTES AND QUESTIONS

1. Are there persuasive arguments supporting the notion that lending should produce a different result from selling? From giving? From providing funds for purchase? (Some states impose vicarious liability on car owners who lend their cars even to the best of drivers. Why might these states do this? The subject is considered in Chapter X.)

2. The court suggests that the theory requires the combined negligence of two or more persons. In the case cited by the court in which an adult had entrusted a firearm and ammunition to his child, what if the child had been too young to have behaved negligently? Or if the child was eight years old and acted reasonably for a child that age?

3. After the decision in *Vince,* the parties settled. The New York Times reported that word of Mrs. Wilson's plight had prompted "an outpouring of support and money from people around the country." The plaintiff's lawyer argued that the press coverage "has been missing the point that every single car dealer in the country has been riveted on this case." Mrs. Wilson was quoted as saying that "It's terrible what happened to that boy, but I'm not responsible for what happened." N.Y.Times, Feb. 21, 1990 at A11.

4. If Wilson hadn't mentioned to the seller her grandnephew's failure to secure a driver's license, might the seller nonetheless have been held liable for failing to inquire about the prospective buyer's driving capacity or by demanding to see his driver's license?

In Osborn v. Hertz Corp., 205 Cal.App.3d 703, 252 Cal.Rptr. 613 (1988), the court rejected the claim that a car rental company had a duty to investigate the driving record of a sober customer who had a valid driver's license before entrusting a car to that customer. A search would have shown two prior convictions for drunk driving and one related six-month license suspension. The court cited cases imposing liability for renting a car to a customer who did not hold a valid driver's license.

If D allows a friend who has a spotless record as a driver to use her car overnight—and then coincidentally sees the friend drunk that evening in a restaurant, does D now have a duty to use due care to retrieve the car? See Casebolt v. Cowan, 829 P.2d 352 (Colo.1992)(suggesting a duty in this situation). What if it is a car rental that still has a day to run when the clerk who did the paperwork earlier that day sees the renter drunk in a restaurant?

5. A recurring scenario involves the "key in the ignition" case. A car owner leaves an auto unlocked with the key in the ignition and a thief takes the opportunity to steal it. The thief negligently runs into the plaintiff causing injuries for which a claim is brought against the only solvent party, the car owner, alleging negligence in leaving the car vulnerable to theft. In some states courts derive liability from the violation of a statute. Others reject that approach on the ground that the goal of the statute is not safety but the avoidance of time-consuming and expensive police searches for cars and payments by insurers for their loss. Recall p. 72, supra.

In Palma v. U.S. Industrial Fasteners, 36 Cal.3d 171, 681 P.2d 893, 203 Cal.Rptr. 626 (1984), defendant's driver left a truck unlocked overnight with the key in the ignition in a highly dangerous neighborhood. The court reviewed the leading California cases, which require "special circumstances" in order to find a duty owed by car owners to the general public, and then observed:

> Factors which distinguished the conduct in [Hergenrether v. East, 61 Cal.2d 440, 393 P.2d 164, 39 Cal.Rptr. 4 (1964)] and were held sufficient to establish a duty, are also present here. They included the area in which the truck had been parked—one frequented by persons who had little respect for the rights of others, and populated by alcoholics; the intent that the truck remain in the location for a relatively long period of time—overnight; the size of the vehicle—rendering it capable of inflicting more serious injury or damage if not properly controlled; and the fact that safe operation of a half-loaded two-ton truck was not a matter of common experience. These factors together led to a conclusion there, as similar factors may here, that a foreseeable risk of harm was posed by the truck left with its keys in the ignition or cab warranting imposition of a duty on the owner or operator to refrain from exposing third persons to the risk.

What rationale would limit the duty to "special circumstances"?

6. Related to the idea of negligent entrustment is negligent hiring or retention or supervision. These involve claims that employers were negligent either in initially hiring or in retaining or in supervising an employee who has committed a tort—usually a violent one. Recall Foster v. The Loft, Inc., p. 19, supra, involving the aggressive bartender. Compare McLean v. Kirby Co., 490 N.W.2d 229 (N.D.1992)(duty on vacuum cleaner manufacturer to investigate backgrounds of salesmen hired to enter homes and demonstrate product) with Connes v. Molalla Transport System, Inc., 831 P.2d 1316 (Colo.1992)(no duty owed by trucking company to assaulted hotel clerk to investigate prospective truck driver's nonvehicular criminal background) and Jackson v. Righter, 891 P.2d 1387 (Utah 1995)(no duty owed by wife's employer to husband for negligent retention or supervision for not preventing supervisors from becoming "romantically involved" with wife).

A physician who asks another physician to "cover" on occasion is not vicariously liable for the negligence of the covering physician—but may be liable for negligence in choosing the covering physician. Kavanaugh v. Nussbaum, 71 N.Y.2d 535, 523 N.E.2d 284, 528 N.Y.S.2d 8 (1988).

6. In Peterson v. Halsted, 829 P.2d 373 (Colo.1992), defendant father in 1985 co-signed a financial note so that his adult daughter could get financing for a car. She made all the payments. She caused an accident due to her drunk driving—which plaintiffs alleged defendant knew about all along. The court declined to impose a duty on a co-signer. Because of the large number of variables in financing arrangements, the court thought it "unwise and destructive of flexibility of analysis to classify suppliers of money or credit categorically as suppliers of chattels . . . even though the loan or credit may be essential to the borrower in obtaining possession of the chattel." The court then turned to the question of whether the parents had a general common law duty to refrain from helping their daughter get a car because they knew of her drinking problems. The court held that a duty in this case would not "comport with fairness under contemporary standards." The court emphasized that the accident occurred three years after the co-signing.

7. How great is the difference between lending or giving a car to someone known to drink while driving and serving drinks to a social guest who drove to the house and will be driving away? That issue is raised in the next case.

Kelly v. Gwinnell

Supreme Court of New Jersey, 1984.
96 N.J. 538, 476 A.2d 1219.

■ WILENTZ, C.J.

This case raises the issue of whether a social host who enables an adult guest at his home to become drunk is liable to the victim of an automobile accident caused by the drunken driving of the guest. Here the host served liquor to the guest beyond the point at which the guest was visibly intoxicated. We hold the host may be liable under the circumstances of this case.

[After driving defendant Zak home, defendant Gwinnell spent an hour or two with him before leaving for his own home. During that time, according to Gwinnell, Zak and Zak's wife, he consumed two or three drinks of scotch on the rocks. Zak accompanied Gwinnell to his car and watched him drive off. On the way home, Gwinnell was involved in a head-on collision with plaintiff Marie Kelly in which she was seriously injured. Gwinnell was subjected to a blood alcohol test which indicated a blood alcohol concentration of 0.286 percent. Under New Jersey law, a concentration of 0.10 or higher is a statutory violation. Kelly's expert concluded that Gwinnell had consumed the equivalent of thirteen drinks and that he must have shown unmistakable signs of intoxication when he left the Zaks' home.

The trial court granted the Zaks' motion for summary judgment on the ground that a social host is not liable for the negligence of an adult guest who has become intoxicated at his home. In affirming, the Appellate Division noted that although the state has no Dram Shop Act imposing legislative liability on establishments that sell liquor to an intoxicated person, New Jersey's decisional law does extend civil liability to licensed sellers of liquor under such circumstances. But the court refused to extend common law liability to social hosts. Plaintiff appealed.]

Under the facts here defendant provided his guest with liquor, knowing that thereafter the guest would have to drive in order to get home. Viewing the facts most favorably to plaintiff (as we must, since the complaint was dismissed on a motion for summary judgment), one could reasonably conclude that the Zaks must have known that their provision of liquor was causing Gwinnell to become drunk, yet they continued to serve him even after he was visibly intoxicated. By the time he left, Gwinnell was in fact severely intoxicated. A reasonable person in Zak's position could foresee quite clearly that this continued provision of alcohol to Gwinnell was making it more and more likely that Gwinnell would not be able to operate his car carefully. Zak could foresee that unless he stopped providing drinks to Gwinnell, Gwinnell was likely to injure someone as a result of the negligent operation of his car. The usual elements of a cause of action for negligence are clearly present: an action by defendant creating an unreasonable risk of harm to plaintiff, a risk that was clearly foreseeable, and a risk that resulted in an injury equally foreseeable. Under those circumstances the only question remaining is whether a duty exists to prevent such risk or, realistically, whether this Court should impose such a duty.

In most cases the justice of imposing such a duty is so clear that the cause of action in negligence is assumed to exist simply on the basis of the actor's creation of an unreasonable risk of foreseeable harm resulting in injury. In fact, however, more is needed, "more" being the value judgment, based on an analysis of public policy, that the actor owed the injured party a duty of reasonable care. . . .

When the court determines that a duty exists and liability will be extended, it draws judicial lines based on fairness and policy. In a society where thousands of deaths are caused each year by drunken drivers,[3] where the damage caused by such deaths is regarded increasingly as intolerable, where liquor licensees are prohibited from serving intoxicated adults, and where long-standing criminal sanctions against drunken driving have recently been significantly strengthened to the point where the Governor notes that they are regarded as the toughest in the nation, see Governor's Annual Message to the N.J. State Legislature, Jan. 10, 1984, the imposition of such a duty by the judiciary seems both fair and fully in accord with the State's policy. Unlike those cases in which the definition of desirable policy is the subject of intense controversy, here the imposition of a duty is both consistent with and supportive of a social goal—the reduction of drunken driving—that is practically unanimously accepted by society.

. . .

---

3. From 1978 to 1982 there were 5,755 highway fatalities in New Jersey. Alcohol was involved in 2,746 or 47.5% of these deaths. Of the 629,118 automobile accident injuries for the same period, 131,160, or 20.5% were alcohol related. The societal cost for New Jersey alcohol-related highway deaths for this period has been estimated as $1,149,516,000.00, based on statistics and documents obtained from the New Jersey Division of Motor Vehicles. The total societal cost figure for all alcohol-related accidents in New Jersey in 1981 alone, including deaths, personal injuries and property damage was $1,594,497,898.00. New Jersey Division of Motor Vehicles, Safety, Service, Integrity, A Report on the Accomplishments of the New Jersey Division of Motor Vehicles 45 (April 1, 1982 through March 31, 1983). These New Jersey statistics are consistent with nationwide figures. Presidential Commission on Drunk Driving, Final Report 1 (1983).

The argument is made that the rule imposing liability on licensees is justified because licensees, unlike social hosts, derive a profit from serving liquor. We reject this analysis of the liability's foundation and emphasize that the liability proceeds from the duty of care that accompanies control of the liquor supply. Whatever the motive behind making alcohol available to those who will subsequently drive, the provider has a duty to the public not to create foreseeable, unreasonable risks by this activity.

We therefore hold that a host who serves liquor to an adult social guest, knowing both that the guest is intoxicated and will thereafter be operating a motor vehicle, is liable for injuries inflicted on a third party as a result of the negligent operation of a motor vehicle by the adult guest when such negligence is caused by the intoxication. We impose this duty on the host to the third party because we believe that the policy considerations served by its imposition far outweigh those asserted in opposition. While we recognize the concern that our ruling will interfere with accepted standards of social behavior; will intrude on and somewhat diminish the enjoyment, relaxation, and camaraderie that accompany social gatherings at which alcohol is served; and that such gatherings and social relationships are not simply tangential benefits of a civilized society but are regarded by many as important, we believe that the added assurance of just compensation to the victims of drunken driving as well as the added deterrent effect of the rule on such driving outweigh the importance of those other values. Indeed, we believe that given society's extreme concern about drunken driving, any change in social behavior resulting from the rule will be regarded ultimately as neutral at the very least, and not as a change for the worse; but that in any event if there be a loss, it is well worth the gain.

The liability we impose here is analogous to that traditionally imposed on owners of vehicles who lend their cars to persons they know to be intoxicated. [ ] If, by lending a car to a drunk, a host becomes liable to third parties injured by the drunken driver's negligence, the same liability should extend to a host who furnishes liquor to a visibly drunken guest who he knows will thereafter drive away.

Some fear has been expressed that the extent of the potential liability may be disproportionate to the fault of the host. A social judgment is therein implied to the effect that society does not regard as particularly serious the host's actions in causing his guests to become drunk, even though he knows they will thereafter be driving their cars. We seriously question that value judgment; indeed, we do not believe that the liability is disproportionate when the host's actions, so relatively easily corrected, may result in serious injury or death. The other aspect of this argument is that the host's insurance protection will be insufficient. While acknowledging that homeowners' insurance will cover such liability,[9] this argument notes

---

9. The dissent challenges our assumption that present homeowners' policies cover the liability imposed by this decision. At oral argument, counsel for both sides indicated that they believe typical homeowners' policies would cover such liability. Even if that is so,

the risk that both the host and spouse will be jointly liable. The point made is not that the level of insurance will be lower in relation to the injuries than in the case of other torts, but rather that the joint liability of the spouses may result in the loss of their home and other property to the extent that the policy limits are inadequate.[10] If only one spouse were liable, then even though the policy limits did not cover the liability, the couple need not lose their home because the creditor might not reach the interest of the spouse who was not liable. [ ] We observe, however, that it is common for both spouses to be liable in automobile accident cases. It may be that some special form of insurance could be designed to protect the spouses' equity in their homes in cases such as this one. In any event, it is not clear that the loss of a home by spouses who, by definition, have negligently caused the injury, is disproportionate to the loss of life of one who is totally innocent of any wrongdoing.

Given the lack of precedent anywhere else in the country, however, we believe it would be unfair to impose this liability retroactively. [ ] Homeowners who are social hosts may desire to increase their policy limits; apartment dwellers may want to obtain liability insurance of this kind where perhaps they now have none. The imposition of retroactive liability could be considered unexpected and its imposition unfair. We therefore have determined that the liability imposed by this case on social hosts shall be prospective, applicable only to events that occur after the date of this decision. We will, however, apply the doctrine to the parties before us on the usual theory that to do otherwise would not only deprive the plaintiff of any benefit resulting from her own efforts but would also make it less likely that, in the future, individuals will be willing to claim rights, not yet established, that they believe are just.

.   .   .

We are satisfied that our decision today is well within the competence of the judiciary. Defining the scope of tort liability has traditionally been accepted as the responsibility of the courts. Indeed, given the courts' prior involvement in these matters, our decision today is hardly the radical change implied by the dissent but, while significant, is rather a fairly predictable expansion of liability in this area.

however, says the dissent, the homeowner/social host is unable "to spread the cost of liability." *Post* at 568. The contrast is then made with the commercial licensee who "spreads the cost of insurance against liability among its or her customers." Id. But the critical issue here is not whether the homeowner can pass the cost on or must bear it himself, but whether tort law should be used to spread the risk over a large segment of society through the device of insurance rather than imposing the entire risk on the innocent victim of drunken driving. Obviously there will be some additional insurance premium at some point that homeowners and renters will have to bear. Their inability to pass that cost on to others, however, is no more persuasive than that same argument would be as to the "average citizen's" automobile liability insurance or, for that matter, for homeowners' insurance as it now exists.

10. We need not, and do not, reach the question of which spouse is liable, or whether both are liable, and under what circumstances.

It should be noted that the difficulties posited by the dissent as to the likely consequence of this decision are purely hypothetical. Given the facts before us, we decide only that where the social host directly serves the guest and continues to do so even after the guest is visibly intoxicated, knowing that the guest will soon be driving home, the social host may be liable for the consequences of the resulting drunken driving. We are not faced with a party where many guests congregate, nor with guests serving each other, nor with a host busily occupied with other responsibilities and therefore unable to attend to the matter of serving liquor, nor with a drunken host. [   ] We will face those situations when and if they come before us, we hope with sufficient reason and perception so as to balance, if necessary and if legitimate, the societal interests alleged to be inconsistent with the public policy considerations that are at the heart of today's decision. .   .   .

We recognize, however, that the point of view expressed by the dissent conforms, at least insofar as the result is concerned, with the view, whether legislatively or judicially expressed, of practically every other jurisdiction that has been faced with this question. It seems to us that by now it ought to be clear to all that the concerns on which that point of view is based are minor compared to the devastating consequences of drunken driving. This is a problem that society is just beginning to face squarely, and perhaps we in New Jersey are doing so sooner than others.

For instance, the dissent's emphasis on the financial impact of an insurance premium increase on the homeowner or the tenant should be measured against the monumental financial losses suffered by society as a result of drunken driving. By our decision we not only spread some of that loss so that it need not be borne completely by the victims of this widespread affliction, but, to some extent, reduce the likelihood that the loss will occur in the first place. Even if the dissent's view of the scope of our decision were correct, the adjustments in social behavior at parties, the burden put on the host to reasonably oversee the serving of liquor, the burden on the guests to make sure if one is drinking that another is driving, and the burden on all to take those reasonable steps even if, on some occasion, some guest may become belligerent: those social dislocations, their importance, must be measured against the misery, death, and destruction caused by the drunken driver. Does our society morally approve of the decision to continue to allow the charm of unrestrained social drinking when the cost is the lives of others, sometimes of the guests themselves?

If we but step back and observe ourselves objectively, we will see a phenomenon not of merriment but of cruelty, causing misery to innocent people, tolerated for years despite our knowledge that without fail, out of our extraordinarily high number of deaths caused by automobiles, nearly half have regularly been attributable to drunken driving. [   ] Should we be so concerned about disturbing the customs of those who knowingly supply that which causes the offense, so worried about their costs, so worried about their inconvenience, as if they were the victims rather than the cause of the carnage? And while the dissent is certainly correct that we could learn more through an investigation, to characterize our knowledge as "scant" or insufficient is to ignore what is obvious, and that is that drunken drivers are causing substantial personal and financial destruction in this state and that a goodly number of them have been drinking in homes as well as taverns. Does a court really need to know more? Is our rule vulnerable because we do not know—nor will the Legislature—how much injury will be avoided or how many lives saved by this rule? Or because we do not know how many times the victim will require compensation from the host in order to be made whole?

This Court senses that there may be a substantial change occurring in social attitudes and customs concerning drinking, whether at home or in taverns. We believe that this change may be taking place right now in New Jersey and perhaps elsewhere. It is the upheaval of prior norms by a society that has finally recognized that it must change its habits and do whatever is required, whether it means but a small change or a significant one, in order to stop the senseless loss inflicted by drunken drivers. We did not cause that movement, but we believe this decision is in step with it.

.   .   .

We therefore reverse the judgment in favor of the defendants Zak and remand the case to the Law Division for proceedings consistent with this opinion.

[JUSTICE GARIBALDI dissented, primarily on two grounds: 1) that the need for tort liability was unclear in view of the New Jersey insurance scheme providing compensation for injuries caused by negligent uninsured motorists, and 2) that the fairness of imposing liability on social hosts, as distinguished from commercial establishments, was open to serious question in view of the difficulties that private persons would face in identifying and controlling intoxicated guests, as well as in spreading the costs of liability insurance. Any change should be made by the legislature.]

■ *For reversal and remandment*—CHIEF JUSTICE WILENTZ, and JUSTICES CLIFFORD, SCHREIBER, HANDLER, POLLOCK and O'HERN—6.

■ *Opposed*—JUSTICE GARIBALDI—1.

NOTES AND QUESTIONS

1. On balance, is civil liability on the social host better left to the legislature? Dram Shop Acts, imposing civil liability on commercial establishments that serve intoxicated patrons who subsequently injure others, are currently in force in about a third of the states. In a few states, liability extends to the injured patron as well.

2. Should the courts recognize a distinction between commercial establishments and social hosts?

3. Do the loss-spreading consequences of social host liability constitute an argument in its favor or against it? Should the availability of insurance be a relevant factor in resolving duty questions? Recall that the California duty factors discussed in *Tarasoff* included insurance.

4. In response to *Kelly v. Gwinnell*, the legislature adopted a statute limiting the potential liability of social hosts. The statute establishes social host liability for "willfully and knowingly" providing alcoholic beverages to "a person who was visibly intoxicated in the host's presence . . . under circumstances manifesting reckless disregard of the consequences." There is an irrebuttable presumption that the driver was not visibly intoxicated if the blood alcohol concentration was less than 0.10% and a rebuttable presumption of non-intoxication between 0.10% and 0.15%. The intoxicated driver is not allowed to recover damages from the host in any case, and the social host's liability to a third-person victim is limited to the percentage of fault attributable to the social host. See N.J. Stat. Ann., §§ 2A:15–5.6 to 5.8. Is the statutory scheme preferable to the court's approach?

5. A handful of other state courts have taken the same initiative as New Jersey, but legislative abrogation has generally followed. See generally, Comment, The Continuing Search for Solutions to the Drinking Driver Tragedy and the Problem of Social Host Liability, 82 Nw.U.L.Rev. 403 (1988). In 1978, the California Supreme Court took the position subsequently adopted in Kelly v. Gwinnell, imposing a duty on social hosts. See Coulter v. Superior Court, 21 Cal.3d 144, 577 P.2d 669, 145 Cal.Rptr. 534 (1978). The state legislature was quick to react, overturning the decision, as well as an earlier case that had created civil liability against commercial sellers. Bus. & Prof. Code § 25602.

One part of the California statute provided: "No social host who furnishes alcoholic beverages to any person shall be held legally accountable for damages suffered by such person, or for injury to the person or property, or death of, any third person resulting from the consumption of such beverages." Civil Code § 1714, subd (c). Criminal liability was established for licensed premises that served a person obviously intoxicated and for those who furnish alcoholic beverages to minors. The legislature expressed its desire to return to the state of the law before three named decisions that had permitted licensed premises and social hosts to be held liable for harm done by drunk drivers.

6. Assume that Gwinnell had been drunk before reaching the Zak house. Zak, who realized the situation, had thanked him for the ride and invited him in for coffee. Gwinnell refused. He returned to his car but couldn't start it. He asked Zak for help and Zak complied by supplying the cable for a jump start. Gwinnell drove off—and ran into Kelly. What analysis? See Leppke v. Segura, 632 P.2d 1057 (Colo.App.1981)(person responding to request to help jump-start car of apparent drunk may be liable to those killed by drunk's driving). Could *Leppke* be decided the same way in California with its statute?

7. In O'Gorman v. Antonio Rubinaccio & Sons, Inc., 408 Mass. 758, 563 N.E.2d 231 (1990), Grover Greenleaf walked into defendant's bar and sought a drink. The owner, who knew Greenleaf from before, refused to serve him because he was already drunk, but did give him food—and took his car keys. After two hours, Greenleaf asked for his keys. Defendant tried to dissuade him but to no avail. He returned the keys and Greenleaf drove off and killed a person. Greenleaf's blood count after the accident was still far over the legal intoxication limit.

The court refused to impose a duty. Although it had imposed liability in earlier cases when defendants had served alcohol to a drunk, this case was different. Plaintiff relied on cases in which the court had found a special relationship between police who had stopped a driver and the driving public. That reliance was misplaced here because those cases "concern the alleged failure of public employees to perform tasks required of them by the terms of their employment, with the result that indirect harm is caused to an individual."

8. In a case raising an issue similar to that in *Kelly,* the court in *D'Amico v. Christie,* 71 N.Y.2d 76, 518 N.E.2d 896, 524 N.Y.S.2d 1 (1987), refused to follow New Jersey's lead. It noted that New Jersey did not have a dram shop act and that the court in *Kelly* had emphasized that point. The "very existence of a Dram Shop Act constitutes a substantial argument against expansion of the legislatively-mandated liability. Very simply, when the Legislature has spoken so specifically on the subject and has chosen to make only licensees liable, arguably the Legislature did not intend to impose the same liability on hosts." Since the New York legislature had prohibited the unlawful sale of alcohol generally and had prohibited the unlawful provision of alcohol to minors—but had not imposed liability generally on providers of alcohol, the court in *D'Amico* thought the extension sought in the case was beyond the appropriate reach of adjudication.

9. The vast majority of courts confronting the social host question have, for one reason or another, rejected the approach of Kelly v. Gwinnell. See the list in Ferreira v. Strack, 652 A.2d 965 (R.I.1995). See also Charles v. Seigfried, 165 Ill.2d 482, 651 N.E.2d 154 (1995)(rejecting actions against social hosts by minors who had auto accidents after becoming intoxicated; the various dram shop actions of the state legislature had preempted judicial development of the area).

10. *Some Broader Implications.* Is there any reason to limit the duty to control the actions of third parties to defendants who bear a particularized relationship—such as host or parent—to the dangerous actor? Suppose, instead, that the defendant is responsible for a situation in which dangerous conduct is generally encouraged or facilitated, without reference to any specific risky individual?

In Weirum v. RKO General, Inc., 15 Cal.3d 40, 539 P.2d 36, 123 Cal.Rptr. 468 (1975), defendant radio station, which commanded the largest teenage audience in the Los Angeles area, conducted a contest in which drivers who first reached a peripatetic disk jockey would win a prize. The disk jockey was traveling freeways of the area and stopping at various spots for short times. The station was broadcasting clues that identified specific or general destinations, such as "The Real Don Steele is back on his feet again with some money and he is headed for the Valley." In their efforts to be the first to reach him when he stopped, two minor drivers in separate vehicles were following the disc jockey on a freeway. During the course of their pursuit, one of the drivers negligently forced a car off the highway killing its driver. In a suit against the station, the court unanimously upheld a plaintiff's judgment.

In Olivia N. v. National Broadcasting Co., 126 Cal.App.3d 488, 178 Cal.Rptr. 888 (1981), cert. denied 458 U.S. 1108 (1982), a television network was sued on the claim that it had broadcast a program that contained a particularly vivid scene in which a teenager in a girls' juvenile detention home was "raped" by a group of inmates using a "plumber's helper." Plaintiff, a nine-year-old girl, alleged that some youths who had seen the program had been prompted to reenact the scene a few days later by attacking her with a soda bottle. The defendant's contention that it should not be judged on a negligence standard was upheld on appeal. The analysis stressed the protection of speech and press found in the First and Fourteenth Amendments, which overrode what might otherwise be an appropriate tort duty. See Crump, Camouflaged Incitement: Freedom of Speech, Communicative Torts, and the Borderland of the *Brandenburg* Test, 29 Ga.L.Rev. 1 (1994).

D. LANDOWNERS AND OCCUPIERS

This section deals with duties owed to entrants by those who own, or are in possession of, land. Although the area showed great signs of change some years ago, the situation appears to have stabilized with two distinct views emerging. We begin with the traditional, and still prevailing, view.

Carter v. Kinney

Supreme Court of Missouri, 1995.
896 S.W.2d 926.

■ ROBERTSON, JUDGE.

    .   .   .

Ronald and Mary Kinney hosted a Bible study at their home for members of the Northwest Bible Church. Appellant Jonathan Carter, a member of the Northwest Bible Church, attended the early morning Bible study at the Kinneys' home on February 3, 1990. Mr. Kinney had shoveled snow from his driveway the previous evening, but was not aware that ice had formed overnight. Mr. Carter arrived shortly after 7:00 a.m., slipped on a patch of ice in the Kinneys' driveway, and broke his leg. The Carters filed suit against the Kinneys.

The parties agree that the Kinneys offered their home for the Bible study as part of a series sponsored by their church; that some Bible studies took place at the church and others were held at the homes of church members; that interested church members signed up for the studies on a sheet at the church, which actively encouraged enrollment but did not solicit contributions through the classes or issue an invitation to the general public to attend the studies; that the Kinneys and the Carters had not engaged in any social interaction outside of church prior to Mr. Carter's injury, and that Mr. Carter had no social relationship with the other participants in the class. Finally, the parties agree that the Kinneys received neither a financial nor other tangible benefit from Mr. Carter in connection with the Bible study class.

They disagree, however, as to Mr. Carter's status. Mr. Carter claims he was an invitee; the Kinneys say he was a licensee. And the parties dispute certain facts bearing on the purpose of his visit, specifically, whether the parties intended a future social relationship, and whether the Kinneys held the Bible study class in order to confer some intangible benefit on themselves and others.

On the basis of these facts, the Kinneys moved for summary judgment. The trial court sustained the Kinneys' summary judgment motion on the ground that Mr. Carter was a licensee and that the Kinneys did not have a duty to a licensee with respect to a dangerous condition of which they had no knowledge. This appeal followed.

. . .

As to premises liability, "the particular standard of care that society recognizes as applicable under a given set of facts is a question of law for the courts." Harris v. Niehaus, 857 S.W.2d 222, 225 (Mo.banc 1993). Thus, whether Mr. Carter was an invitee, as he claims, or a licensee is a question of law and summary judgment is appropriate if the defendants' conduct conforms to the standard of care Mr. Carter's status imposes on them.

. . .

Historically, premises liability cases recognize three broad classes of plaintiffs: trespassers, licensees and invitees. All entrants to land are trespassers until the possessor of the land gives them permission to enter. All persons who enter a premises with permission are licensees until the possessor has an interest in the visit such that the visitor "has reason to believe that the premises have been made safe to receive him." [ ] That makes the visitor an invitee. The possessor's intention in offering the invitation determines the status of the visitor and establishes the duty of care the possessor owes the visitor. Generally, the possessor owes a trespasser no duty of care, [ ]; the possessor owes a licensee the duty to make safe dangers of which the possessor is aware, [ ]; and the possessor owes invitees the duty to exercise reasonable care to protect them against both known dangers and those that would be revealed by inspection. [ ] The exceptions to these general rules are myriad, but not germane here.

A social guest is a person who has received a social invitation. [ ] Though the parties seem to believe otherwise, Missouri does not recognize social guests as a fourth class of entrant. [ ] In Missouri, social guests are but a subclass of licensees. The fact that an invitation underlies a visit does not render the visitor an invitee for purposes of premises liability law. This is because "[t]he invitation was not tendered with any material benefit motive" . . . and "[t]he invitation was not extended to the public generally or to some undefined portion of the public from which invitation, . . . entrants might reasonably expect precautions have been taken, in the exercise of ordinary care, to protect them from danger." [ ] Thus, this Court held that there "is no reason for concluding it is unjust to the parties . . . to put a social guest in the legal category of licensee." [ ]

It does not follow from this that a person invited for purposes not strictly social is perforce an invitee. As [cited case] clearly indicates, an entrant becomes an invitee when the possessor invites with the expectation of a material benefit from the visit or extends an invitation to the public generally. See also Restatement (Second) of Torts, § 332[2] (defining an invitee for business purposes) and 65 C.J.S. Negligence, § 63(41)(A person is an invitee "if the premises are thrown open to the public and [the person] enters pursuant to the purposes for which they are thrown open."). Absent the sort of invitation from the possessor that lifts a licensee to invitee status, the visitor remains a licensee as a matter of law.

The record shows beyond cavil that Mr. Carter did not enter the Kinneys' land to afford the Kinneys any material benefit. He is therefore not an invitee under the definition of ["business visitor"] contained in Section 332 of the Restatement. The record also demonstrates that the Kinneys did not "throw open" their premises to the public in such a way as would imply a warranty of safety. The Kinneys took no steps to encourage general attendance by some undefined portion of the public; they invited only church members who signed up at church. They did nothing more than give permission to a limited class of persons—church members—to enter their property.

Mr. Carter's response to the Kinneys' motion for summary judgment includes Mr. Carter's affidavit in which he says that he did not intend to socialize with the Kinneys and that the Kinneys would obtain an intangible benefit, albeit mutual, from Mr. Carter's participation in the class. Mr. Carter's affidavit attempts to create an issue of fact for the purpose of defeating summary judgment. But taking Mr. Carter's statement of the facts as true in all respects, he argues a factual distinction that has no meaning under Missouri law. Human intercourse and the intangible benefits of sharing one's property with others for a mutual purpose are hallmarks of a licensee's permission to enter. Mr. Carter's factual argument makes the legal point he wishes to avoid: his invitation is not of the sort that makes an invitee. He is a licensee.

2. Section 332 [provides that an invitee is either "a public invitee or a business visitor." A public invitee is defined as a "person who is invited to enter or remain on land as a member of the public for a purpose for which the land is held open to the public." "A business visitor" is one who is invited to enter or remain on land "for a purpose directly or indirectly connected with business dealings with the possessor of the land."]

The trial court concluded as a matter of law that Mr. Carter was a licensee, that the Kinneys had no duty to protect him from unknown dangerous conditions, and that the defendants were entitled to summary judgment as a matter of law. In that conclusion, the trial court was eminently correct.

. . .

The judgment of the trial court is affirmed.

■ COVINGTON, C.J., and HOLSTEIN, BENTON, THOMAS, and LIMBAUGH, JJ., concur.

■ PRICE, J., concurs in result.

NOTES AND QUESTIONS

1. What is the justification for treating a social guest as a licensee? Why isn't he an invitee? Consider comment *h* (3) to § 330:

> The explanation usually given by the courts for the classification of social guests as licensees is that there is a common understanding that the guest is expected to take the premises as the possessor himself uses them, and does not expect and is not entitled to expect that they will be prepared for his reception, or that precautions will be taken for his safety, in any manner in which the possessor does not prepare or take precautions for his own safety, or that of the members of his family.

Is this persuasive?

2. Might the categorization change if Mr. Carter regularly gave Mr. Kinney a lift to work in his car after the class? If Mr. Carter regularly brought pastries to the class (while others brought instant coffee or napkins)? What if the list in the church had asked each person signing up to bring the Kinneys "a small token of appreciation for the use of their house"?

3. It is one thing to put the plaintiff into one of the three boxes—though the court notes that there are "myriad" exceptions. It is another to determine what duty is owed to each category. For example, the duty to trespassers is stated in section 333 as "Except as stated in §§ 334–339, a possessor of land is not liable to trespassers for physical harm caused by his failure to exercise reasonable care

(a) to put the land in a condition reasonably safe for their reception, or

(b) to carry on his activities so as not to endanger them."

The listed exceptions create obligations to warn, for example, where the possessor knows that persons "constantly intrude upon a limited area" of the land and may encounter a hidden danger, or when the possessor fails to exercise reasonable care for the safety of a known trespasser. Generally, though, the duty is simply not to wilfully or wantonly harm trespassers. For a discussion of the category of trespasser and the duty owed to trespassers, see Blakely v. Camp Ondessonk, 38 F.3d 325 (7th Cir.1994)(discussing Illinois law).

4. What duty did the Kinneys owe Mr. Carter? Why does the court hold that they met that duty as a matter of law?

5. If Mr. Carter had been categorized as an invitee, what duty would the Kinneys have owed? Section 342 provides so far as the condition of the premises is concerned, an occupier is subject to liability to invitees if the occupier:

> (a) knows or by the exercise of reasonable care would discover the condition, and should realize that it involves an unreasonable risk of harm to such invitees, and

> (b) should expect that they will not discover or realize the danger, or will fail to protect themselves against it, and

> (c) fails to exercise reasonable care to protect them against the danger.

How does this general obligation differ from what the court found was owed to licensees?

6. *Open and obvious dangers.* One issue that has long divided courts involves the duty owed invitees where the danger is "open and obvious." Some courts have concluded that no duty is owed since the danger was apparent to the invitee. Recently, courts have focused more on whether such notice was enough to make the premises reasonably safe. In Tharp v. Bunge Corp., 641 So.2d 20 (Miss.1994), plaintiff was a government grain inspector whose work on defendant's premises involved his having to step from a landing onto sloping ground between 29 and 39 inches below. Plaintiff was 5′ 8″ with a stride of 30 inches.

The court, 5–4, overruled its earlier position that open and obvious dangers did not give rise to liability, and followed § 343 (1), stating in part that a possessor was not liable to invitees for harm from obvious dangers "unless the possessor should anticipate the harm despite such knowledge or obviousness." The court thought it "should discourage unreasonably dangerous conditions rather than fostering them in their obvious form. It is anomalous to find that a defendant has a duty to provide reasonably safe premises and at the same time deny a plaintiff recovery from a breach of that same duty." If the jury finds that both parties behaved unreasonably comparative negligence would apply.

7. The foregoing discussion has focused on the condition of the premises. Another set of questions involves *activities* taking place on the premises. The traditional rule was that licensees and trespassers could not recover for active negligence while they were on the premises. Thus, in Britt v. Allen County Community Junior College, 230 Kan. 502, 638 P.2d 914 (1982), the plaintiff, a Shaklee sales representative, was using defendant's auditorium solely to promote sales. Before the session, she asked the custodian to move a piano from the center of the room to a wall. While he was doing this, he lost control of the piano and it tipped over onto plaintiff's foot. The court first held that plaintiff was a licensee because the entry was solely for Shaklee's benefit. It rejected the claim that the purpose of the meeting was to educate the community. The court then held that she could not establish wilful or wanton injury, refused to adopt a distinction between active and passive negligence, and dismissed the case.

Britt was overruled in Bowers v. Ottenad, 240 Kan. 208, 729 P.2d 1103 (1986), involving a social guest who was burned during the preparation of "flaming Irish coffee":

> We hold . . . that when a licensee, whose presence is known or should be known, is injured or damaged by some affirmative activity conducted upon the property by the occupier of the property the duty owed to such person is one of reasonable care under the circumstances. When the injury or damage results from the condition of the premises as opposed to the activity thereon, the duty of the occupier to the licensee is only to refrain from willfully or wantonly injuring the licensee.

Section 341 of the Second Restatement provides for liability to licensees for failure to carry on activities with due care if, but only if, the occupier should expect that the licensee will not discover or realize the danger and if the licensee does not know or have reason to know of the activities and the risk involved.

Assume that a burglar who is found lurking outside the auditorium of a junior college is brought into the auditorium by the police for investigation. Should the burglar have an action if the custodian carelessly loses control of a piano that he is moving nearby so that it tips over on the burglar's foot?

8. *Child Trespassers.* In Holland v. Baltimore & O. R. Co., 431 A.2d 597 (D.C.App.1981), a nine-year-old boy was injured by a freight train. The court invoked one of the most influential sections of the Restatement, § 339:

> A possessor of land is subject to liability for physical harm to children trespassing thereon caused by an artificial condition upon the land if
>
> (a) the place where the condition exists is one upon which the possessor knows or has reason to know that children are likely to trespass, and
>
> (b) the condition is one of which the possessor knows or has reason to know and which he realizes or should realize will involve an unreasonable risk of death or serious bodily harm to such children, and
>
> (c) the children because of their youth do not discover the condition or realize the risk involved in intermeddling with it or in coming within the area made dangerous by it, and
>
> (d) the utility to the possessor of maintaining the condition and the burden of eliminating the danger are slight as compared with the risk to children involved, and
>
> (e) the possessor fails to exercise reasonable care to eliminate the danger or otherwise to protect the children.

The judge found the section inapplicable because "a moving train is a danger so obvious that any nine-year-old child allowed at large would readily discover it and realize the risk involved in coming within the area made dangerous by it."

The special treatment of children dates to the "turntable" cases, involving injuries to children tampering with railroad track-switching devices. Recall the *Krayenbuhl* case, p. 37, supra. These cases evolved into a broader "attractive nuisance" doctrine which covered injuries to children who were unaware, because of their immaturity, of risks associated with a land occupier's property. Most courts did not require that the child have been enticed onto the land by the sight of the danger. The evolution of the doctrine is discussed in Prosser, Trespassing Children, 47 Calif.L.Rev. 427 (1959).

9. *Recreational Use of Land.* Almost all states have enacted statutes that limit the liability of owners of land used for recreational purposes. The goal is to prevent persons on open land from suing for natural dangers on such land or demanding that warnings be posted of such dangers. Willful misconduct is generally required for liability. See generally Comment, Wisconsin's Recreational Use Statute: Towards Sharpening the Picture at the Edges, 1991 Wisc.L.Rev. 491. For a good summary of the considerations behind this type of legislation, see Bragg v. Genesee County Agricultural Society, 84 N.Y.2d 544, 644 N.E.2d 1013, 620 N.Y.S.2d 322 (1994).

10. *Ice and Snow.* In colder climates slips and falls on ice have been a fertile field for litigation. In Sullivan v. Town of Brookline, 416 Mass. 825, 626 N.E.2d 870 (1994), plaintiff slipped on an icy ramp. The court began by noting that failure to clean ice and snow was not actionable. The law "does not regard the natural accumulation of snow and ice as an actionable property defect, if it regards such weather conditions as a defect at all. [ ] Liability is possible only 'in circumstances where some act or failure to act has changed the condition of naturally accumulated snow and ice, and the elements alone or in connection with the land become a hazard to lawful visitors.' " Plaintiff's claim that the defendant's employees shoveled the snow to expose an icy surface on the ramp and then failed to remove the ice was not actionable. At most it had exposed the ice that was already there. Plaintiff then argued that even if the actions of the town had not worsened the condition of the ramp there was an affirmative obligation to remove the ice or sand it. The court rejected the contention. Some of the cases on which plaintiff relied "involved snow and ice conditions which could be found to have become unnatural due to the passage of time."

In Gamere v. 236 Commonwealth Avenue Condominium Ass'n, 19 Mass.App. 359, 474 N.E.2d 1135 (1985), a pedestrian slipped on the sidewalk. The jury could have found that there were mounds of snow and ice on both sides of the sidewalk—and no sand, salt, or other substance to improve traction. The property owner was in violation of a city ordinance requiring owners to remove ice and snow within certain time limits. The court concluded, as had other states, that such ordinances and statutes were for the benefit of the governmental unit and not for pedestrians. The plaintiff's common law claim against the owner failed because there was no showing the ice was other than a natural accumulation. There was no liability "for a fall on ice caused by the melting of snow which had been shoveled to the edge of the sidewalk" even if some of that pile had melted and formed ice.

Is the distinction between natural and non-natural accumulations different from the distinction between nonfeasance and misfeasance? What seems to be the underlying liability-limiting concern here?

Rowland v. Christian

Supreme Court of California, 1968.
69 Cal.2d 108, 443 P.2d 561, 70 Cal.Rptr. 97.

[The pleadings and affidavits showed that plaintiff, while a social guest in defendant's apartment, severed some tendons and nerves when the porcelain handle on a bathroom faucet cracked in his hand. Although defendant had told her lessor about the handle some weeks earlier, she did not mention it to the plaintiff before he went to the bathroom. Further facts are stated in the opinion. The trial court entered summary judgment for defendant.]

■ PETERS, J. [after stating the facts].

In the instant case, Miss Christian's affidavit and admissions made by plaintiff show that plaintiff was a social guest and that he suffered injury when the faucet handle broke; they do not show that the faucet handle crack was obvious or even nonconcealed. Without in any way contradicting her affidavit or his own admissions, plaintiff at trial could establish that she was aware of the condition and realized or should have realized that it involved an unreasonable risk of harm to him, that defendant should have expected that he would not discover the danger, that she did not exercise reasonable care to eliminate the danger or warn him of it, and that he did not know or have reason to know of the danger. Plaintiff also could establish, without contradicting Miss Christian's affidavit or his admissions, that the crack was not obvious and was concealed. Under the circumstances, a summary judgment is proper in this case only if, after proof of such facts, a judgment would be required as a matter of law for Miss Christian. The record supports no such conclusion.

Section 1714 of the Civil Code provides: "Every one is responsible, not only for the result of his willful acts, but also for an injury occasioned to another by his want of ordinary care or skill in the management of his property or person, except so far as the latter has, willfully or by want of ordinary care, brought the injury upon himself. . . ." . . .

. . .

A departure from this fundamental principle involves the balancing of a number of considerations; the major ones are the foreseeability of harm to the plaintiff, the degree of certainty that the plaintiff suffered injury, the closeness of the connection between the defendant's conduct and the injury suffered, the moral blame attached to the defendant's conduct, the policy of preventing future harm, the extent of the burden to the defendant and consequences to the community of imposing a duty to exercise care with resulting liability for breach, and the availability, cost, and prevalence of insurance for the risk involved. [ ]

One of the areas where this court and other courts have departed from the fundamental concept that a man is liable for injuries caused by his carelessness is with regard to the liability of a possessor of land for injuries to persons who have entered upon that land. It has been suggested that the special rules regarding liability of the possessor of land are due to historical considerations stemming from the high place which land has traditionally held in English and American thought, the dominance and prestige of the landowning class in England during the formative period of the rules governing the possessor's liability, and the heritage of feudalism. (2 Harper and James, The Law of Torts, supra, p. 1432.)

. . .

An increasing regard for human safety has led to a retreat from this position, and an exception to the general rule limiting liability has been made as to active operations where an obligation to exercise reasonable care for the protection of the licensee has been imposed on the occupier of land. [ ] In an apparent attempt to avoid the general rule limiting liability, courts have broadly defined active operations, sometimes giving the term a strained construction in cases involving dangers known to the occupier.

[The court gave examples of such straining. In one case, the maintenance of a dangerous swimming pool was called the "active conduct of a party for a large number of swimmers in the light of knowledge of the dangerous pool."]

Another exception to the general rule limiting liability has been recognized for cases where the occupier is aware of the dangerous condition, the condition amounts to a concealed trap, and the guest is unaware of the trap. . . .

The cases dealing with the active negligence and the trap exceptions are indicative of the subtleties and confusion which have resulted from application of the common law principles governing the liability of the possessor of land. Similar confusion and complexity exist as to the definitions of trespasser, licensee, and invitee. [ ]

. . .

There is another fundamental objection to . . . the common law distinctions based upon the status of the injured party as a trespasser, licensee, or invitee. Complexity can be borne and confusion remedied where the underlying principles governing liability are based upon proper considerations. Whatever may have been the historical justifications for the common law distinctions, it is clear that those distinctions are not justified in the light of our modern society and that the complexity and confusion which has arisen is not due to difficulty in applying the original common law rules—they are all too easy to apply in their original formulation—but is due to the attempts to apply just rules in our modern society within the ancient terminology.

Without attempting to labor all of the rules relating to the possessor's liability, it is apparent that the classifications of trespasser, licensee, and invitee, the immunities from liability predicated upon those classifications, and the exceptions to those immunities, often do not reflect the major factors which should determine whether immunity should be conferred upon the possessor of land. Some of those factors, including the closeness of the connection between the injury and the defendant's conduct, the moral blame attached to the defendant's conduct, the policy of preventing future harm, and the prevalence and availability of insurance, bear little, if any, relationship to the classifications of trespasser, licensee and invitee and the existing rules conferring immunity.

Although in general there may be a relationship between the remaining factors and the classifications of trespasser, licensee, and invitee, there are many cases in which no such relationship may exist. Thus, although the foreseeability of harm to an invitee would ordinarily seem greater than the foreseeability of harm to a trespasser, in a particular case the opposite may be true. The same may be said of the issue of certainty of injury. The burden to the defendant and consequences to the community of imposing a duty to exercise care with resulting liability for breach may often be greater with respect to trespassers than with respect to invitees, but it by no means follows that this is true in every case. In many situations, the burden will be the same, i.e., the conduct necessary upon the defendant's part to meet the burden on exercising due care as to invitees will also meet his burden with respect to licensees and trespassers. The last of the major factors, the cost of insurance, will, of course, vary depending upon the rules of liability adopted, but there is no persuasive evidence that applying ordinary principles of negligence law to the land occupier's liability will materially reduce the prevalence of insurance due to increased cost or even substantially increase the cost.

Considerations such as these have led some courts in particular situations to reject the rigid common law classifications and to approach the issue of the duty of the occupier on the basis of ordinary principles of negligence. [ ] And the common law distinctions after thorough study have been repudiated by the jurisdiction of their birth. (Occupiers' Liability Act, 1957, 5 and 6 Eliz. 2, ch. 31.)

A man's life or limb does not become less worthy of protection by the law nor a loss less worthy of compensation under the law because he has come upon the land of another without permission or with permission but without a business purpose. Reasonable people do not ordinarily vary their conduct depending upon such matters, and to focus upon the status of the injured party as a trespasser, licensee, or invitee in order to determine the question whether the landowner has a duty of care, is contrary to our modern social mores and humanitarian values. The common law rules obscure rather than illuminate the proper considerations which should govern determination of the question of duty.

. . . The proper test to be applied to the liability of the possessor of land in accordance with section 1714 of the Civil Code is whether in the management of his property he has acted as a reasonable man in view of the probability of injury to others, and, although the plaintiff's status as a trespasser, licensee, or invitee may in the light of the facts giving rise to such status have some bearing on the question of liability, the status is not determinative.

Once the ancient concepts as to the liability of the occupier of land are stripped away, the status of the plaintiff relegated to its proper place in determining such liability, and ordinary principles of negligence applied, the result in the instant case presents no substantial difficulties. As we have seen, when we view the matters presented on the motion for summary judgment as we must, we must assume defendant Miss Christian was aware that the faucet handle was defective and dangerous, that the defect was not obvious, and that plaintiff was about to come in contact with the defective condition, and under the undisputed facts she neither remedied the condition nor warned plaintiff of it. Where the occupier of land is aware of a concealed condition involving in the absence of precautions an unreasonable risk of harm to those coming in contact with it and is aware that a person on the premises is about to come in contact with it, the trier of fact can reasonably conclude that a failure to warn or to repair the condition constitutes negligence. Whether or not a guest has a right to expect that his host will remedy dangerous conditions on his account, he should reasonably be entitled to rely upon a warning of the dangerous condition so that he, like the host, will be in a position to take special precautions when he comes in contact with it.

It may be noted that by carving further exceptions out of the traditional rules relating to the liability to licensees or social guests, other jurisdictions reach the same result [ ], that by continuing to adhere to the strained construction of active negligence or possibly, by applying the trap doctrine the result would be reached on the basis of some California precedents [ ], and that the result might even be reached by a continued expansion of the definition of the term "invitee" to include all persons invited upon the land who may thereby be led to believe that the host will exercise for their protection the ordinary care of a reasonable man (cf. O'Keefe v. South End Rowing Club, 64 Cal.2d 729, [ ]). However, to approach the problem in these manners would only add to the confusion, complexity, and fictions which have resulted from the common law distinctions.

The judgment is reversed.

■ TRAYNOR, C.J., TOBRINER, J., MOSK, J., and SULLIVAN, J., concurred.

■ BURKE, J. I dissent. In determining the liability of the occupier or owner of land for injuries, the distinctions between trespassers, licensees and invitees have been developed and applied by the courts over a period of many years. They supply a reasonable and workable approach to the problems involved, and one which provides the degree of stability and predictability so highly prized in the law. The unfortunate alternative, it appears to me, is the route taken by the majority in their opinion in this case; that such issues are to be decided on a case by case basis under the application of the basic law of negligence, bereft of the guiding principles and precedent which the law has heretofore attached by virtue of the relationship of the parties to one another.

Liability for negligence turns upon whether a duty of care is owed, and if so, the extent thereof. Who can doubt that the corner grocery, the large department store, or the financial institution owes a greater duty of care to one whom it has invited to enter its premises as a prospective customer of its wares or services than it owes to a trespasser seeking to enter after the close of business hours and for a nonbusiness or even an antagonistic purpose? I do not think it unreasonable or unfair that a social guest (classified by the law as a licensee, as was plaintiff here) should be obliged to take the premises in the same condition as his host finds them or permits them to be. Surely a homeowner should not be obliged to hover over his guests with warnings of possible dangers to be found in the condition of the home (e.g., waxed floors, slipping rugs, toys in unexpected places, etc., etc.). Yet today's decision appears to open the door to potentially unlimited liability despite the purpose and circumstances motivating the plaintiff in entering the premises of another, and despite the caveat of the majority that the status of the parties may "have some bearing on the question of liability . . . ," whatever the future may show that language to mean.

In my view, it is not a proper function of this court to overturn the learning, wisdom and experience of the past in this field. Sweeping modifications of tort liability law fall more suitably within the domain of the Legislature, before which all affected interests can be heard and which can enact statutes providing uniform standards and guidelines for the future.

I would affirm the judgment for defendant.

■ McComb, J., concurred.

NOTES AND QUESTIONS

1. How would the case have been analyzed using the traditional categories?

2. Within a residential context, assume that a home owner has permitted a living room couch to become dangerously weakened. How would a *Rowland* court analyze a fall through the couch by (a) the owner's business partner, there for a meeting; (b) the owner's neighbor, there for a beer; (c) a burglar, who was hoping to rest after finishing work? Would it matter to the *Rowland* court whether the owner had been aware of the condition before the fall? Might that fact matter to courts following the categorical approach?

3. For a time after *Rowland* it appeared that the case would signal a massive shift among the states. After a handful of states quickly followed California, the movement virtually stopped in its tracks. In Carter v. Kinney, supra, after failing to persuade the court to categorize Mr. Carter as an invitee, the Carters asked the court to overturn the categorical approach and follow California's lead. They noted that nine states had abolished the distinction between licensee and invitee, and that another eleven states had abolished the trespasser category as well. The defendants noted that twelve courts had considered abolition and declined to do it and that eighteen had not addressed the issue since *Rowland*. The court refused to abandon the categories:

> The contours of the legal relationship that results from the possessor's invitation reflect a careful and patient effort by courts over time to balance the interests of persons injured by conditions of land against the interests of possessors of land to enjoy and employ their land for the purposes they wish. Moreover, and despite the exceptions courts have developed to the general rules, the maintenance of the distinction between licensee and invitee creates fairly predictable rules within which entrants and possessors can determine appropriate conduct and juries can assess liability. To abandon the careful work of generations for an amorphous "reasonable care under the circumstances" standard seems—to put it kindly—improvident.

The court quoted a passage from Prosser & Keeton that speculated that the failure of more states to join the "trend"

> may reflect a more fundamental dissatisfaction with certain developments in accident law that accelerated during the 1960's—reduction of whole systems of legal principles to a single, perhaps simplistic, standard of reasonable care, the sometimes blind subordination of other legitimate social objectives to the goals of accident prevention and compensation, and the commensurate shifting of the balance of power to the jury from the judge. At least it appears that the courts are . . . acquiring a more healthy skepticism toward invitations to jettison years of developed jurisprudence in favor of beguiling legal panacea.

The *Carter* court concluded that the "experience of the states that have abolished the distinction between licensee and invitee does not convince us that their idea is a better one. Indeed, we are convinced that they have chosen wrongly."

4. As noted, several of the courts rejecting the categorical approach limited their action to the distinction between invitees and licensees, maintaining the categorical treatment for trespassers. The impact of the *Rowland* approach on trespassers was not tested early because of a lack of suits brought by trespassers. In the early 1980s, however, the legal uncertainties persuaded a California school district to settle a case brought by someone crawling over the roof at night who fell through a skylight that had been painted over. The resulting outcry led to a statute that protected landowners against liability to persons hurt on premises while committing or attempting to commit one of 25 enumerated offenses. The bar applies only upon a charge of a felony and the conviction for that felony or a lesser included felony or misdemeanor. The civil action is to be delayed until the conclusion of the criminal action. Calif.Civil Code § 847. For discussion of a similar approach, see Sun v. State of Alaska, 830 P.2d 772 (Alaska 1992).

5. Is the majority's approach an improvement over the traditional categorical approach? Is the dissent persuasive?

6. *Landlord and Tenant.* What affirmative obligations, if any, does a landlord owe a tenant to protect the latter from harm? The traditional rules of liability for defective conditions have insulated landlords from liability except in a few situations. As summarized in Sargent v. Ross, 113 N.H. 388, 308 A.2d 528 (1973), a landlord was liable in tort only "if the injury is attributable to (1) a hidden danger in the premises of which the landlord but not the tenant is aware, (2) premises leased for public use, (3) premises retained under the landlord's control, such as common stairways, or (4) premises negligently repaired by the landlord."

Liability was much less likely if the landlord had promised to repair but had failed to take any steps to do so. That distinction between bad repairs and no repairs at all is disappearing. In Putnam v. Stout, 38 N.Y.2d 607, 345 N.E.2d 319, 381 N.Y.S.2d 848 (1976), the court overturned its earlier view and imposed a duty where a promise had been made:

> First, the lessor has agreed, for a consideration, to keep the premises in repair; secondly, the likelihood that the landlord's promise to make repairs will induce the tenant to forgo repair efforts which he otherwise might have made; thirdly; the lessor retains a reversionary interest in the land and by his contract may be regarded as retaining and assuming the responsibility of keeping his premises in safe condition; finally, various social policy factors must be considered: (a) tenants may often be financially unable to make repairs; (b) their possession is for a limited term and thus the incentive to make repairs is significantly less than that of a landlord; and (c) in return for his pecuniary benefit from the relationship, the landlord could properly be expected to assume certain obligations with respect to the safety of the others. [   ]

In the cited Sargent v. Ross, the court took a much more dramatic step to increase the liability of landlords. A child visiting a tenant in defendant's residential building fell to her death from a stairway. The claim was that the stairway was too steep and the railing inadequate. (The stairway was not common premises because it went only to the tenant's apartment.) On appeal, the court adopted the following position:

> [A] landlord must act as a reasonable person under all of the circumstances including the likelihood of injury to others, the probable

seriousness of such injuries, and the burden of reducing or avoiding the risk. . . . The questions of control, hidden defects and common or public use, which formerly had to be established as a prerequisite to even considering the negligence of a landlord, will now be relevant only inasmuch as they bear on the basic tort issues such as the foreseeability and unreasonableness of the particular risk of harm.

How does this new approach differ from the *Sargent* court's summary of earlier law?

7. *Criminal Activity.* During the long development of the categorical approach, most cases involved physical conditions of the premises or the negligent conduct of others. Later, plaintiffs began to sue for harms caused them by criminal conduct occurring on the premises. Most commonly, tenants began suing landlords for providing inadequate protection against criminal activity. The major early case was Kline v. 1500 Massachusetts Avenue Apartment Corp., 439 F.2d 477 (D.C.Cir.1970), in which the court imposed a duty of care on the landlord of a large apartment building toward a tenant who had been assaulted in a common hallway of the building. Crime had been occurring on the premises with mounting frequency. Although the owner could take some steps, such as extra heavy locks or guards, "no individual tenant had it within his power to take measures to guard" against these same perils:

> Not only as between landlord and tenant is the landlord best equipped to guard against the predictable risk of intruders, but even as between landlord and the police power of government, the landlord is in the best position to take the necessary protective measures. Municipal police cannot patrol the entryways and the hallways, the garages and the basements of private multiple unit apartment dwellings. They are neither equipped, manned, nor empowered to do so. In the area of the predictable risk which materialized in this case, only the landlord could have taken measures which might have prevented the injuries suffered by appellant.
>
> . . .
>
> . . . We do not hold that the landlord is an insurer of the safety of his tenants. His duty is to take those measures of protection which are within his power and capacity to take, and which can reasonably be expected to mitigate the risk of intruders assaulting and robbing tenants. The landlord is not expected to provide protection commonly owed by a municipal police department; but as illustrated in this case, he is obligated to protect those parts of his premises which are not usually subject to periodic patrol and inspection by the municipal police.

The court recognized that the discharge of this duty might often cause "the expenditure of large sums" and that these costs "will be ultimately passed on to the tenant in the form of increased rents. This prospect, in itself, however, is no deterrent to our acknowledging and giving force to the duty, since without protection the tenant already pays in losses from theft, physical assault and increased insurance premiums." The landlord "is entirely justified in passing on the cost of increased protective measures to his tenant, but the rationale of compelling the landlord to do it in the first place is that he is the only one who is in a position to take the necessary protective measures for overall protection of the premises."

There has been more disagreement when commercial property was involved, as the following case suggests.

Williams v. Cunningham Drug Stores, Inc.

Supreme Court of Michigan, 1988.
429 Mich. 495, 418 N.W.2d 381.

■ CAVANAGH, JUSTICE.

In this case of first impression we are asked to determine whether a store owner must provide armed, visible security guards to protect customers from the criminal acts of third parties.

I

[Plaintiff was shopping in defendant's store "located in a high crime area of the City of Detroit."] A plainclothes security guard was employed by the store, but on the day in question he was sick. Store personnel called the main office to request a substitute, but one was not sent.[1]

While plaintiff was shopping, an armed robbery occurred. During the resulting confusion and panic, plaintiff ran out of the store, directly behind the fleeing robber. As the two men were outside, the robber turned and shot plaintiff [who by this time was outside the store].

[Plaintiff's complaint alleged] that defendant had breached its duty to exercise reasonable care for the safety of its patrons. Specifically, plaintiff alleged that defendant had failed to provide armed, visible security guards and had failed to intercede after having noticed that an armed robbery was in progress. Plaintiff's wife, Cleva Williams, brought a claim of loss of consortium.

[At the close of plaintiff's case, the trial court granted defendant's motion for a directed verdict. The court of appeals affirmed.]

.   .   .

III

The question before us in this case is whether a merchant's duty to exercise reasonable care includes providing armed, visible security guards to protect invitees from the criminal acts of third parties. Plaintiffs

---

1. At trial, defendant Cunningham's director of corporate security testified that the security personnel were employees of defendant and were purposely plainclothed and unarmed. Their primary purpose, in addition to protection of assets, was to summon medical assistance if an injury or illness occurred on the premises. These security personnel were specifically instructed not to intervene in the event of a robbery.

contend that it does and that the trial court erred in granting defendant's motion for a directed verdict rather than allowing the jury to determine whether defendant's conduct met the standard of reasonable care.

In deciding this question, we note that the court and jury perform different functions in a negligence case. Among other things, the court decides the questions of duty and the general standard of care, and the jury determines what constitutes reasonable care under the circumstances. However, in cases in which overriding public policy concerns arise, the court determines what constitutes reasonable care. [ ] Such public policy concerns exist in the present case, and therefore the question whether defendant's conduct constituted reasonable care is one the court should determine as a matter of law.

We agree with the Court of Appeals that a merchant's duty of reasonable care does not include providing armed, visible security guards to deter criminal acts of third parties.[14] We decline to extend defendant's duty that far in light of the degree of control in a merchant's relationship with invitees, the nature of the harm involved, and the public interest in imposing such a duty.[15]

The duty advanced by plaintiffs is essentially a duty to provide police protection. That duty, however, is vested in the government by constitution and statute. We agree with the Court of Appeals in this case that neither the Legislature nor the constitution has established a policy requiring that the responsibility to provide police protection be extended to commercial businesses.

Furthermore, although defendant can control the condition of his premises by correcting physical defects that may result in injuries to his invitees, he cannot control the incidence of crime in the community. Today a crime may be committed anywhere and at any time. To require defendant to provide armed, visible security guards to protect invitees from criminal acts in a place of business open to the general public would require defendant to provide a safer environment on his premises than his invitees would encounter in the community at large. Defendant simply does not have that degree of control and is not an insurer of the safety of his invitees.[17]

---

14. A merchant may voluntarily provide security guards in accordance with the Private Security Guard Act, M.C.L. § 338.1051 et seq.; [ ] We hold today only that he is under no duty to do so.

15. We note that 2 Restatement Torts, 2d, § 344, pp. 223–224, states that a business owner is subject to liability for physical harm caused by the intentional acts of third parties. However, given the public policy concerns underlying our decision in this case, we decline to apply that section to these facts. [ ] We note, however, that some courts have recognized a defendant's duty to protect business invitees in situations similar to the facts of this case. For example, the Supreme Court of Colorado, in a four-to-three decision . . . in the interest of "fairness," affirmed the imposition of liability upon a merchant for failing to take measures to protect invitees from the criminal acts of unknown third persons. See Taco Bell, Inc. v. Lannon, 744 P.2d 43 (Colo.1987).

17. We find that a landlord has more control in his relationship with his tenants than does a merchant in his relationship with his invitees. Should a dangerous condition exist in the common areas of a building

In addition, any duty we might impose on defendant to protect his invitees from the criminal acts of third parties would be inevitably vague, given the nature of the harm involved. Fairness requires that if a merchant could be held liable for the failure to provide security guards, he should be able to ascertain in advance the extent of his duty and whether he has fulfilled it. In this respect, we note the comments of the New Jersey Supreme Court in Goldberg v. Newark Housing Authority, 38 N.J. 578, 589–590, 186 A.2d 291 (1962), a case in which that court held that the municipal housing authority did not have a duty to provide police protection for its tenants:

> And if a prescient owner concludes the duty is his, what measures will discharge it? It is an easy matter to know whether a stairway is defective and what repairs will put it in order. Again, it is fairly simple to decide how many ushers or guards suffice at a skating rink or a railroad platform to deal with the crush of a crowd and the risks of unintentional injury which the nature of the business creates, but how can one know what measures will protect against the thug, the narcotic addict, the degenerate, the psychopath and the psychotic? Must the owner prevent all crime? We doubt that any police force in the friendliest community has achieved that end.

Even if a merchant were not required to prevent all crime, defining a reasonable standard of care short of that goal might well be impossible.

Finally, we note that imposing the duty advanced by plaintiffs is against the public interest. The inability of government and law enforcement officials to prevent criminal attacks does not justify transferring the responsibility to a business owner such as defendant. To shift the duty of police protection from the government to the private sector would amount to advocating that members of the public resort to self-help. Such a proposition contravenes public policy.[19]

IV

We conclude as a matter of law that the duty of reasonable care a merchant owes his invitees does not extend to providing armed, visible security guards to protect customers from the criminal acts of third parties.

which tenants must necessarily use, the tenants can voice their complaints to the landlord. Thus, in Samson v. Saginaw Professional Building, Inc., 393 Mich. 393, 408–411, 224 N.W.2d 843 (1975), we upheld a landlord's duty to investigate and take available preventive measures when informed by his tenants that a possible dangerous condition exists in the common areas of the building, noting that the landlord's duty may be slight. The relationship between a merchant and invitee, however, is distinguishable because the merchant does not have the same degree of control. When the dangerous condition to be guarded against is crime in the surrounding neighborhood, as it is in the present case, the merchant may be the target as often as his invitees. Therefore, there is little the merchant can do to remedy the situation, short of closing his business.

19. Furthermore, shifting the financial loss caused by crime from one innocent victim to another is improper. Davis v. Allied Supermarkets, Inc., 547 P.2d 963, 965 (Okla. 1976).

The merchant is not an insurer of the safety of his invitees, and for reasons of public policy he does not have the responsibility for providing police protection on his premises.   Accordingly, the decision of the Court of Appeals is affirmed.

■ RILEY, C.J., and BRICKLEY, BOYLE, LEVIN and GRIFFIN, JJ., concur.

■ ARCHER, J., concurs in the result.

NOTES AND QUESTIONS

1.   Why is this a question for the court rather than the jury?   Why is it that when "overriding public policy concerns arise, the court determines what constitutes reasonable care"?

2.   Do the differences between physical defects on the premises and the risks in this case warrant different treatment?

3.   In Scott v. Harper Recreation, Inc., 444 Mich. 441, 506 N.W.2d 857 (1993), plaintiff was shot in the parking lot of defendant's night club.   In an effort to avoid the *Williams* approach, he alleged that the club had advertised that it had "Free Ample Lighted Security Parking."   The court thought *Williams* controlled and dismissed the case.   On the night in question, the parking lot was fenced and lighted—and security guards were on the premises.   "To the extent that this defendant voluntarily assumed any obligations, the exact terms of its undertaking were explicitly stated in its advertising.   It promised parking that was (a) free, (b) ample, (c) lighted, and (d) guarded.   But the defendant did not advertise that it would 'make the parking lot safe' or provide a 'lot free of criminal activity'—it never claimed the ability or the intention to create an environment that was guaranteed to be free of crime."

> We reject the notion that a merchant who makes property visibly safer has thereby "increased the risk of harm" by causing patrons to be less anxious.   In 1988, we held in *Williams* that a merchant ordinarily has no obligation to provide security guards or to protect customers against crimes committed by third persons.   Today, we decline to adopt a theory of law under which a merchant would be effectively obliged not to take such measures.

In a footnote the *Scott* court reserved judgment on whether the *Williams* doctrine applied to residential landlord-tenant situations.   Do the differences between residential situations and commercial situations warrant different treatment?

4.   Consider how the Michigan appellate courts have been grappling with the *Williams-Scott* line:

a.   In Mills v. White Castle System, Inc., 167 Mich.App. 202, 421 N.W.2d 631 (1988), plaintiffs observed an unruly group of people in defendant's parking lot.   After eating, plaintiffs were attacked by this group.   A companion reentered the restaurant and asked the manager to call the police.   This was refused—as was a request to let the companion use the phone for that purpose.   While the companion went elsewhere for help, the attack continued. A duty was imposed to call the police or allow use of the phone when defendant knew or should have known about the danger.

b. In Jackson v. White Castle System, Inc., 205 Mich.App. 137, 142, 517 N.W.2d 286 (1994), an unruly crowd earlier in the evening was still milling around when plaintiff entered defendant's restaurant. A man carrying a baseball bat shoved plaintiff as he stood in line and then threatened him. After plaintiff was leaving, the same man reappeared and shot him. A duty was imposed based on the presence earlier of the unruly group. This was closer to *Mills*, supra, as being an "ongoing, prolonged disturbance" providing notice of the need to call the police rather than a "criminal episode so random and instantaneous" that the defendant lacked notice of the immediate danger, as in *Williams*.

c. In Abner v. Oakland Mall Ltd., 209 Mich.App. 490, 531 N.W.2d 726 (1995), an employee at a shop in a shopping center, who was raped as she walked to her car in the parking lot, sued the owners of the center and its security company for negligently failing to make the premises reasonably safe. The case was dismissed because the court thought that the claim was based on the notion that "the safety measures voluntarily undertaken by defendants were less effective than they could or should have been"—and that that theory was precluded by *Scott*. *Jackson* was distinguished on the ground that the danger to the specific plaintiff was apparent.

d. In Mason v. Royal Dequindre, Inc., 209 Mich.App. 514, 531 N.W.2d 797 (1995), plaintiff was injured by T during a brief altercation in the parking lot adjoining defendant's bowling alley and lounge. T had earlier been ejected from the lounge after fighting with plaintiff's friend. Plaintiff was waiting for his friend—who was being kept inside until T had been given time to leave the area, but no employee of defendant ascertained whether in fact T had left the area. The court rejected "this effort to shift blame from wrongdoers to innocent merchants." This case was distinguishable from *Jackson* because there the defendants "had specific knowledge of a substantial danger to their patrons." Here that was lacking because the defendant had no reason to think that T would attack plaintiff since his earlier dispute had been with another person.

5. In the cited Taco Bell, Inc. v. Lannon, the Colorado court affirmed a plaintiff's judgment in a robbery case. The nature of the neighborhood and the history of the specific location made the danger amply foreseeable. Noting that foreseeability alone did not establish a duty, the majority considered the potential gravity of the harm that might result and the burden of taking steps to protect customers. It concluded that although food costs would increase, many potential measures such as "installing highly visible video cameras, keeping small amounts of cash in the registers [and alerting prospective robbers to that fact], training employees in methods for dealing with in-progress robberies, and locking non-public entrances during nighttime hours—are relatively inexpensive." These steps were being listed for illustration only. "They are not intended to be regarded as a complete list of security measures that may be regarded as reasonable.   Nor do we mean to imply by listing these particular measures that a defendant must take all or even any of these measures in order to meet its duty."   These would be questions for the jury.   Does this meet the concern of the *Williams* court about giving notice of obligations in this type of case?

6. *Prior similar incidents.*   Should it matter if the drug store had been the scene of armed robberies ten times within the past year?   In most states a duty would likely be found to take some safety steps in such a situation.   These states generally speak of "prior similar incidents" as being required to trigger the obligation.

In states that require "prior similar incidents" there is often dispute about what qualifies.   In Jacqueline S. v. City of New York, 81 N.Y.2d 288, 614 N.E.2d 723, 598 N.Y.S.2d 160 (1993), plaintiff tenant of one building in a public housing complex was raped by an intruder.   The court, 6–1, held that plaintiff did not have to show prior incidents in that same building; it was enough to show that such incidents had occurred elsewhere in the complex.   The negligence claim here was the lack of adequate locks on the building.   Although there had been no showing of a prior violent incident in plaintiff's building, there was a showing of "drug-related criminal activity in her building and that vagrants and drug addicts readily gained access to and loitered in the corridors, stairwells and on the roof of plaintiff's building.   .   .   .   The Housing Authority was aware that neither the doors to the lobbies of the buildings nor the doors to the utility rooms on the roofs were equipped with locks."

For some years California held that past similar incidents were not required.   See Isaacs v. Huntington Memorial Hospital, 38 Cal.3d 112, 695 P.2d 653, 211 Cal.Rptr. 356 (1985):

> While prior similar incidents are helpful to determine foreseeability, they are not required to establish it.   Other circumstances may also place the landowner on notice of a dangerous condition.   A rule which limits proof of foreseeability to evidence of prior similar incidents automatically precludes recovery to the first-injured victims.   Such a rule is inherently unfair and contrary to public policy.

California retreated from that position in Ann M. v. Pacific Plaza Shopping Center, 6 Cal.4th 666, 863 P.2d 207, 25 Cal.Rptr.2d 137 (1993), in which the court decided as a matter of law that the defendant owed no duty to provide security guards in its mall.   Violent criminal assaults "were not sufficiently foreseeable to impose a duty upon [the owner] to provide security guards in the common areas."

In *Ann M.*, the court concluded that "random, violent crime is endemic in today's society.   It is difficult, if not impossible, to envision any locale open to the public where the occurrence of violent crime seems improbable. Upon further reflection and in light of the increase in violent crime," the earlier rule had to be refined.   The result in *Isaacs* had been correct because there had indeed been similar acts of violence in the past in that case.   The dictum, however, had been misleading.

The "duty in such circumstances is determined by a balancing of 'foreseeability' of the criminal acts against the 'burdensomeness, vagueness, and efficacy' of the proposed security measures." The "monetary cost of hiring security guards is not insignificant. . . . [W]e conclude that a high degree of foreseeability is required in order to find that the scope of a landlords' duty of care includes the hiring of security guards. We further conclude that the requisite degree of foreseeability rarely, if ever, can be proven in the absence of prior similar incidents of violent crime on the landowner's premises."

The plaintiff in *Ann M.* had not provided evidence "to show that, like a parking garage or an all-night convenience store, a retail store located in a shopping center creates 'an especial temptation and opportunity for criminal misconduct.' . . . Therefore, we need not consider in this case whether some types of commercial property are so inherently dangerous that, even in the absence of prior similar incidents, providing security guards will fall within the scope of a landowner's duty of care." For a case discussing parking garages, see Erickson v. Curtis Investment Co., 447 N.W.2d 165 (Minn.1989).

In a case in which a security guard in a McDonald's restaurant was alleged to have behaved negligently in his efforts to defuse a tense situation, a lower court held that *Ann M.* did not apply. There was no need to show prior similar acts because the claim was that the security guard, fully aware of the danger, did not respond reasonably when he escorted one attacker outside while leaving the imperiled plaintiff inside in the midst of several other menacing persons. Trujillo v. G.A.Enterprises, Inc., 36 Cal.App.4th 1105, 43 Cal.Rptr.2d 36 (1995).

7. *Resisting the Robbery and Apprehending Perpetrators.* The foregoing cases dealt with the duty to anticipate and try to avert robberies and other criminal conduct. In fact in each there had been no resistance. Might the proprietor be held liable for trying to thwart the robbers once the robbery has begun?

In Boyd v. Racine Currency Exchange, Inc., 56 Ill.2d 95, 306 N.E.2d 39 (1973), a robber approached the currency exchange's bulletproof window, held a gun to a customer's head, and demanded that the access door be opened. The teller refused to comply and dropped to the floor, and the robber killed the customer. His widow's wrongful death claim asserted that the teller had a duty to obey the robber's demands. The court dismissed her action, concluding that no duty to accede to criminal demands should be placed on robbery victims:

> If a duty to comply exists, the occupier of the premises would have little choice in determining whether to comply with the criminal demand and surrender the money or to refuse the demand and be held liable in a civil action for damages brought by or on behalf of the hostage. The existence of this dilemma and knowledge of it by those who are disposed to commit such crimes will only grant to them additional leverage to enforce their criminal demands. . . . In this particular case the result may appear to be harsh and unjust, but, for

the protection of future business invitees, we cannot afford to extend to the criminal another weapon in his arsenal.

But see Kentucky Fried Chicken of California, Inc. v. Superior Court, 40 Cal.App.4th 798, 47 Cal.Rptr.2d 69 (1995), holding that a restaurant may be liable for exposing a customer hostage to a fear of being killed by not readily opening the register on the robber's demand. The court rejected *Boyd* and a California appellate case that had expressed concern that imposing a duty would lead to increased hostage-taking. The court did not "presume street criminals stay abreast of developments in California tort law. Moreover, the prevailing wisdom has long been that one does not resist an armed robber's demands for money. We do presume that the average robber is aware of that concept." Review has been granted.

In Giant Food, Inc. v. Mitchell, 334 Md. 633, 640 A.2d 1134 (1994), a store employee tried to retrieve a package from a shoplifter. After a short struggle the shoplifter ran out the door—and into plaintiff. A directed verdict was granted to defendant:

> In other words, simply because flight by some shoplifters is foreseeable, a storekeeper is not per se liable when a shoplifter, fleeing apprehension by the storekeeper, collides with a customer. Rather, taking into account all of the circumstances, the degree of risk of flight and the degree of risk of harm to invitees must be weighed against the privilege [of a shopkeeper to use some force to protect its goods] when determining if exercise of the privilege created an unreasonable risk of injury to invitees.

The court noted that the states reached varying results in these cases. Compare Basile v. Union Plaza Hotel & Casino, 110 Nev. 1382, 887 P.2d 273 (1994)(casino might be liable for harm done by "six-foot, two hundred pound" guest who fled and knocked over plaintiff when two guards began to chase him) with Brown v. Jewel Companies, Inc., 175 Ill.App.3d 729, 530 N.E.2d 57 (1988) (no liability when suspected shoplifter, being chased by guards, ran into plaintiff customer since serious injury was not likely; and shoplifters will generally flee when stopped—whether pursued or not).

8. The *Williams* court noted that the harm had occurred off the premises, but that did not play a role in the decision. Should it matter whether the episode begins or ends off the premises? In Waters v. New York City Housing Authority, 69 N.Y.2d 225, 505 N.E.2d 922, 513 N.Y.S.2d 356 (1987), plaintiff was accosted on a public street and forced into defendant's unlocked building where she was taken to the roof and assaulted.

The court asserted that the landlord's duty "exists principally to protect the safety and possessions of the tenants and visitors inside the premises." It rejected the idea that the duty should extend to prevent unsecured buildings from becoming safe havens for crime. It could not "agree that the scope of a landowner's duty should be extended to embrace members of the public at large, with no connection to the premises, who might be victimized by street predators." The court used the *Strauss* and

Pulka cases, pp. 133, 150, supra, to show the importance of relationships in the imposition of duties. It was important here that the landowner had "no control over either the acts of the primary wrongdoer or the conditions on the public byways that make such acts all too commonplace."

Since safety incentives already existed as to locks and other safety features in the duty owed to the tenants and their visitors, "the social benefits to be gained do not warrant the extension of the landowner's duty to maintain secure premises to the millions of individuals who use the sidewalks of New York City each day and are thereby exposed to the dangers of street crime." To similar effect, see Doe v. Manheimer, 212 Conn. 748, 563 A.2d 699 (1989), denying liability against a landowner whose overgrown shrubbery in a high crime neighborhood provided a shielded area to which plaintiff was forcibly taken at the start of an assault. Would you expect a different result if the plaintiff in *Waters* had been a tenant of the building?

In general, landowners and occupiers owe a duty of due care to outsiders—those who walk by on the public road or who own adjoining land—to avoid unreasonable risks from falling cornices or broken branches. Is the situation in *Waters* different?

E.   INTRAFAMILY DUTIES

In this section we consider the impact on duty of the fact that the plaintiff and the defendant are part of the same family unit. The issue of liability within the family unit has been one of much confusion.

Spousal suits. At common law courts quite commonly barred spouses from suing one another for personal injury. The common law view was that husband and wife were a unity for legal purposes—and suits between them were a logical impossibility. But in the 19th century legislatures began adopting so-called "Married Women's Acts" that gave wives the right to own property and to sue over property and contract disputes. With this destruction of the "unity," state courts slowly began eliminating the immunity from tort liability that spouses had enjoyed against being sued by one another.

The first abrogations occurred in suits for intentional torts because these claims showed that any spousal harmony sought to be preserved had probably already dissipated. It was harder to abrogate the immunity in suits for negligence because the courts feared not marital disharmony, but rather fraud and collusion against insurers as one spouse readily admitted negligence in hurting the other spouse. Virtually all remnants of spousal immunity have disappeared as to both intentional and negligent harms. See the discussions in Waite v. Waite, 618 So.2d 1360 (Fla.1993) and Price v. Price, 732 S.W.2d 316 (Tex.1987).

Parent-child suits. The parent-child relationship was never treated as a unity. The immunity of parents to suits by their children can be traced to Hewlett v. George, 68 Miss. 703, 9 So. 885 (1891). The ban was very widely adopted, and has recently been an active area of litigation. We have already considered suits within the family, though they did not involve the ability of the child to sue. Recall Andre v. Pomeroy, p. 54, supra, involving the child's claim against her mother for negligent driving.

Claims by children against parents for intentional harm are almost universally permitted today. For an extended discussion of an "issue of first impression," concluding that a child should be permitted to sue her father for sexual abuse, see Henderson v. Woolley, 230 Conn. 472, 644 A.2d 1303 (1994). The major battleground in parent-child injuries has been over negligently inflicted harms.

The negligence picture is more complicated. The New York history in this area, briefly, was to adopt the immunity; then to lift it in Gelbman v. Gelbman, 23 N.Y.2d 434, 245 N.E.2d 192, 297 N.Y.S.2d 529 (1969), involving parental negligence in driving a car. A few years later, the court decided Holodook v. Spencer, 36 N.Y.2d 35, 324 N.E.2d 338, 364 N.Y.S.2d 859 (1974), consolidating three appeals involving injuries to children. In the first, a four-year-old boy was injured when he fell from an 11–foot–high slide in a playground after his father had allowed him to "stray from his immediate control." In the second, a three-year-old boy playing in a neighbor's backyard had his hand run over by the neighbor's eight-year-old who was using a power lawnmower while the child's mother was inside the neighbor's house. In the third, a four-year-old boy was injured when he ran out from between two parked cars in his mother's presence. The court barred all three suits. The reasons and implications are considered in the next case.

Zikely v. Zikely

Supreme Court of New York, Appellate Division, 1983.
98 App.Div.2d 815, 470 N.Y.S.2d 33.

■ Before DAMIANI, J.P., and THOMPSON, BOYERS and GIBBONS, JJ.

■ MEMORANDUM

The infant plaintiff was injured when the defendant parent turned on a hot water faucet in a tub to prepare a bath and then left the room. The child, left unsupervised, wandered into the bathroom and fell into or otherwise entered the tub, suffering severe burns. The complaint was properly dismissed. The proximate cause of the injury was the negligent supervision of the infant (Nolechek v. Gesuale, 46 N.Y.2d 332, 413 N.Y.S.2d 340, 385 N.E.2d 1268; Holodook v. Spencer [   ]).

The dissenter's position is untenable. The dissent seeks to take this case out of the general *Holodook* principle of nonliability for negligent supervision by a parent of a child by arguing that in this case the dangerous condition was created by the parent. In *Nolechek v. Gesuale* (supra), however, it was determined that a child did not have a cause of action against his parent when the parent gave an unregistered, uninspected motorcycle to his child, who not only lacked any type of operator's license, but who was also blind in one eye and had impaired vision in the other eye.   Although the parent created a dangerous condition by his actions, and the child was then injured as a direct result of those actions (i.e., a motorcycle accident), the Court of Appeals held that the child had no cause of action against the parent.   This same rule of law governs the instant situation.

The dissenter's reading of *Holodook* (supra), would also severely undermine the considered determination of the Court of Appeals that no cause of action for negligent parental supervision exists in this State.   The dissent thus states that the three factual situations presented in *Holodook* derive from situations in which an unsupervised infant was injured by something which was outside the control of the parent.   The Court of Appeals, however, stated:

> We can conceive of few, if any, accidental injuries to children which could not have been prevented, or substantially mitigated, by keener parental guidance, broader foresight, closer protection and better example.   Indeed, a child could probably avoid most physical harm were he under his parents' constant surveillance and instruction, though detriment more subtle and perhaps more harmful than physical injury might result.

Furthermore, to at least some degree the parents in *Holodook* took some affirmative action in creating a danger.   Bringing a young child to a neighbor and letting the child loose in a yard where an eight-year old is playing with a power mower or bringing a child to a playground containing an 11–foot-high slide involves some affirmative behavior on the part of the parent in creating a danger that the child, if left unsupervised, will suffer injury.   If the courts choose to carve out the exception to *Holodook* suggested by the dissent, it becomes too easy to avoid the *Holodook* holding by characterizing some act by a parent as an affirmative step in creating the danger for the child.   Every time a parent plugged in an iron, started a toaster, or boiled a pot of water on the stove, he would be subjected to potential liability if an unsupervised child came in contact with these common, daily household hazards in a manner which resulted in injury.   To accept such a position would be to strip *Holodook* of a significant part of its meaning.

The dissent takes the position that *Holodook* derives from a concern that the courts not second guess decisions involving parental discretion, and that this concern is not involved herein.   *Holodook*, however, expresses a concern not only with a desire to keep the judiciary from excessively interjecting itself into the family relationship, but also with potential fraud problems, [third party] apportionment problems [   ], a desire to preserve family resources for all family members, and a desire to avoid getting the courts involved in the burdensome and difficult task of drawing lines as to the proper level of supervision a parent must exercise over his child in each individual case.   Although not each of these concerns will be involved in every negligent supervision case, the question of the proper level of supervision required for a child while a bath is being prepared for the child implicates these considerations to a sufficient degree to require a conclusion that the facts herein constituted only negligent supervision. Accordingly, the complaint was properly dismissed.

■ DAMIANI, J.P., and THOMPSON and BOYERS, JJ., concur.

■ GIBBONS, JUSTICE, dissents and votes to reverse the order appealed from, and deny the defendant's motion for summary judgment, with the following memorandum.

. . .

The majority disposes of this case as one of negligent parental supervision, which is not actionable in this State [   ]. Parental immunity from liability in cases of negligent supervision is an exception to the abrogation of intra-family immunity for nonwillful torts established in *Gelbman v. Gelbman.* . . .

Assuming the truth of defendant's description of the incident, the injury in the instant case may not have been solely caused by negligent supervision. The injurious instrumentality was the running hot water which was turned on and controlled by the parent. This case is analogous to *Hurst v. Titus* [   ], in which the infant was injured in a fire negligently caused by her mother. Applying *Holodook*, the Fourth Department [in *Titus*] reasoned that the mother could not be held liable if the injuries were caused solely by her failure to rescue the child before calling the fire department, since that omission constituted negligent supervision. However, she could be liable for injuries proximately caused by her negligence in causing the fire in the first instance [in leaving the kitchen and allowing oil used in cooking to catch fire]. . . . In contrast, *Holodook* and its companion cases [   ], all involved situations in which an unsupervised infant was injured by something which was outside the control of the parent. There were no allegations in those cases that the parent had negligently set into motion an instrument which then caused injury.

Holodook derives from a concern that the courts not second guess decisions involving parental discretion in the raising of children [   ]. The facts in this case do not directly involve a parental decision about how much freedom or responsibility to give a child. Rather, this case involves an unconsidered lapse which exposes the child to a dangerous condition created by the parent, independent of and separate from the parent-child relationship. Holding the parent liable for creating that condition does not impinge on the exercise of parental authority and does not involve familial relationships. My colleagues' reliance on [*Nolechek*] is misplaced. In [*Nolechek*] it was determined, as the majority correctly notes, that a child does not have a cause of action against a parent who entrusts the child with a dangerous instrument, such as a motorcycle. . . . [*Nolechek*], is a logical application of the *Holodook* rule, since what to entrust to a child is a major aspect of the parent-child relationship. However, *Holodook* only carved out an exception to *Gelbman v. Gelbman* [   ]. The latter case is the appropriate guide where a parent's alleged negligence does not pertain to the unique activities of parenthood. Thus, a father who stores blasting caps in the basement of the family home may be liable to his son who is thereby injured [   ]. Likewise, having a trap door open may lead to parental liability [   ], or, as already described, negligently causing a fire (*Hurst v. Titus*). Letting scalding water run into a bathtub for an extended period of time falls into this category of activity [   ].

. . .

NOTES AND QUESTIONS

1.   The New York Court of Appeals unanimously affirmed *Zikely* "for reasons stated in the memorandum of the Appellate Division." 62 N.Y.2d 907, 467 N.E.2d 892, 479 N.Y.S.2d 8 (1984). Can any of the cases relied on by Justice Gibbons in his dissent survive this affirmance? What is the distinction that the dissent seeks to draw between this case and the *Holodook* cases?

2.   The majority's discussion of *Holodook* suggests several different justifications. Evaluate each. (We address the third party apportionment point shortly.) Is it clear why New York permits suits against parents who drive negligently? Is there a difference between inadvertently letting a child use an 11-foot slide in a playground and encouraging the child to use that slide in an effort to improve the child's physical prowess? Should a parent be liable for leaving the lawnmower running while going inside to answer the phone? (A court imposed liability in the last example in Grivas v. Grivas, 113 App.Div.2d 264, 496 N.Y.S.2d 757 (1985)).

3.   In Thurel v. Varghese, 207 App.Div.2d 220, 621 N.Y.S.2d 633 (1995), a mother was holding her two-month-old baby in her arms in the back seat of a car rather than using the available infant safety seat. As the result of a crash due to defendant's negligence the baby was ejected out a window and died as a result. The defendant's effort to seek contribution from the mother was rejected. Since the mother as a passenger had no general duty to use due care for the safety of another passenger, her only possible liability here was for negligently supervising her baby—a claim barred by *Holodook*.

Should it make a difference if the mother's conduct endangers herself as well as her child? A mother who crossed a busy street against a red light while carrying plaintiff child in her arms was protected against suit under *Holodook*. Kronengold v. Kronengold, 192 App.Div.2d 487, 598 N.Y.S.2d 698 (1993).

4.   Other states have adopted various positions. In Goller v. White, 20 Wis.2d 402, 122 N.W.2d 193 (1963), the court abrogated parental immunity except in two instances: "(1) where the alleged negligent act involves an exercise of parental authority over the child; and (2) where the negligent act involves an exercise of ordinary parental discretion with respect to the provision of food, clothing, housing, medical and dental services, and other care."

California rejected the Wisconsin view in Gibson v. Gibson, 3 Cal.3d 914, 479 P.2d 648, 92 Cal.Rptr. 288 (1971):

[W]e reject the implication of *Goller* that within certain aspects of the parent-child relationship, the parent has carte blanche to act negligently toward his child. . . . In short, although a parent has the prerogative and the duty to exercise authority over his minor child, this prerogative must be exercised within reasonable limits. The standard to be applied is the traditional one of reasonableness, but viewed in the light of the parental role. Thus, we think the proper test of a parent's conduct is this: what would an ordinarily reasonable and prudent *parent* have done in similar circumstances?

Does this standard suggest that every fact situation discussed so far in this section would be a jury question in California? The *Gibson* court thought that the Wisconsin approach would "inevitably result in the drawing of arbitrary distinctions about when particular parental conduct falls within or without the immunity guidelines." Might the same charge be made against the New York position?

5. The New York courts have been slow to extend *Holodook* protection to others, such as grandparents. In Broome v. Horton, 83 Misc.2d 1002, 372 N.Y.S.2d 909 (1975), affirmed on opinion below 53 App.Div.2d 1030, 386 N.Y.S.2d 156 (1976), the court decided that conclusions based on the "daily parental responsibility to shape and develop an infant's physical, emotional and intellectual growth can hardly be extended, with equal force, to grandparents who take the child for a day." The court analogized grandparents to school teachers, camp directors, baby sitters, and neighbors—all of whom can be sued for negligent supervision. On questions of foster parents and stepparents compare Mitchell v.Davis, 598 So.2d 801 (Ala.1992)(foster parents may assert parental immunity doctrine) with Warren v. Warren, 336 Md. 618, 650 A.2d 252 (1994)(denying immunity to stepparent because stepparent has no duty to support stepchildren and may leave the relationship at will).

In Smith v. Sapienza, 52 N.Y.2d 82, 417 N.E.2d 530, 436 N.Y.S.2d 236 (1981), the court barred a suit by a four-year-old boy against his ten-year-old sibling for negligent supervision on the ground that where "children of the same family unit are forced into essentially adversarial positions in litigation, the potential for disruption and perhaps even irreconcilable conflict is manifest."

6. *Harm to the fetus.* In Bonte v. Bonte, 136 N.H. 286, 616 A.2d 464 (1992), a child born alive was allowed to sue her mother for "catastrophic" injuries sustained when her mother failed "to use reasonable care in crossing the street and fail[ed] to use a designated crosswalk." The court, 3–2, held that since a fetus born alive could sue a third party for harm sustained before birth, and since the court had abolished parental immunity, "it follows" that this action should lie. The majority rejected the notion that fetal injury warranted different treatment from claims brought by a child already born. One of the three justices, urging case-by-case development of this area, concluded that the negligence alleged here was actionable "because a breach of the duty owed to her fetus could foreseeably cause serious harm to an unborn child." (The majority noted in passing that the defendant mother was "represented by counsel provided by her insurance company," but made nothing of that fact in its decision.)

The dissenters thought that the majority had "failed to fully appreciate the extent of the intrusion into the privacy and physical autonomy rights of women." They drew a sharp distinction between a child suing third persons for what happened in the womb and suing the mother. "Third parties . . . are able to continue to act much as they did before the cause of action was recognized." But extending this duty to a pregnant woman "could govern such details of a woman's life as her diet, sleep, exercise, sexual activity, work and living environment, and, of course, nearly every aspect of her health care." The dissenters had "serious doubts" that it was possible to "subject a woman's judgment, action, and behavior as they related to the well-being of her fetus to a judicial determination of reasonableness in a manner that is consistent and free from arbitrary results." They also feared difficult line-drawing problems.

Should a child be permitted to sue a parent for smoking-related harm suffered prior to birth? What about a suit for respiratory harm caused to a child by a smoking parent after birth?

7. In Curlender v. Bio–Science Laboratories, 106 Cal.App.3d 811, 165 Cal.Rptr. 477 (1980), the court had suggested in dictum that parents who conceive with knowledge of a high risk of birth defects might be liable to a child born with such defects. The legislature responded with Calif.Civil Code § 43.6(a), providing that "No cause of action arises against a parent of a child based upon the claim that the child should not have been conceived or, if conceived, should not have been allowed to have been born alive."

8. Should parental duties be mediated by religious beliefs? In Lundman v. McKown, 530 N.W.2d 807 (Minn.App.1995), cert. denied 116 S.Ct. 828 (1996), an 11–year–old boy became ill and died after four days without medical attention. During that period, his condition was easily diagnosable and was treatable by doctors up to two hours before his death. When he first became ill, his mother and his stepfather, who were Christian Scientists, called a local church source and were referred to a practitioner who was "specially trained to provide spiritual treatment through prayer." The mother hired the practitioner to pray for the boy. As the illness progressed a Christian Science nurse was hired who tried to keep the boy clean and comfortable, read hymnals to him, and kept the practitioner informed of the boy's deteriorating condition.

A wrongful death judgment obtained by the boy's father was affirmed against the mother, stepfather, practitioner and nurse. The mother's duty was clear: a "custodial parent" has a special relationship to a dependent and vulnerable child that gives rise to duty to protect the child from harm." The stepfather was held to have assumed a duty by his conduct in participating in the treatment. As to the standard of care, the court rejected any formulation that would "insulate Christian Scientists from tort liability in cases involving children." Then, adopting a standard that took account of " 'good-faith Christian Scientist' beliefs, rather than an unqualified 'reasonable person standard,' " the court held that "that reasonable Christian Science care is circumscribed by an obligation to take the state's (and child's) side in the tension between the child's welfare and the parents' freedom to rely on sprirtual care." A parent's religious belief "must yield when—judged by accepted medical practice—it jeopardizes the life of a child." Was it correct to adopt a mixed standard? Does the mixed standard offer any special protection for exercise of religious beliefs?

The nurse and the practitioner argued that they had been retained by the mother to provide only services consistent with the mother's religious preferences and that the mother controlled the treatment. The court disagreed: this was "an instance where Christian Science professionals should have been aware of the requirement that they yield to the law of the community." They had a "responsibility on these facts to acknowledge that Christian Science care was not succeeding and to persuade mother to call in providers of conventional medicine or, persuasion failing, to override her and personally call for either a doctor or the authorities."

9. *The Impact of Insurance.* In some of these family cases the reason for suit is clear—especially in those cases involving intentional harm committed by one member on another. But in the negligence situation the motivation is not so clear. Indeed, in cases such as *Smith v. Sapienza*, note 5 supra, even though plaintiffs might have been able to sue a family member they have declined to do so—and have attempted full recovery against a third party. It was the third party's joinder claim that brought the allegedly negligent family member into the case. The plaintiff's choices of whether to sue another family member for negligence are likely to be tied closely to considerations of insurance. Although we postpone extensive consideration of insurance until Chapter X, it is appropriate to note some special points related to family suits at this time.

In intra-family cases, what might have been a bitter internal feud over allocation of family assets without liability insurance becomes instead a way to obtain outside assistance when one member has caused injury to another. (Of course, this creates concerns about collusion that have led to the enactment of guest statutes, recall p. 89, supra, and have led insurers to exclude such coverage from their policies.) In some parental immunity cases the result has been dictated by judicial reluctance to get involved in deciding how closely parents should supervise their children at play. Under that rationale, insurance questions would seem beside the point.

In Schlessinger v. Schlessinger, 796 P.2d 1385 (Colo.1990), a challenge to parental immunity in the context of an automobile accident, the court rejected the claim that liability insurance had eliminated the problem. Apart from the possibility that the judgment might exceed the liability limits of the insurance, the court went on to approve the following passage from Mathis v. Ammons, 453 F.Supp. 1033, 1036–37 (E.D.Tenn.1978):

"The existence of liability insurance does not remove the obligation of the parent to cooperate with the insurer, an obligation which will often place a parent who is seeking honestly to cooperate, and his child, in adversarial roles. . . . Assuming, for example, that there are differing versions of the facts of an accident, the public display of disagreement and accusation can only weaken the bond between parent and child. In such a situation, the parent's obligation to the insurer cannot be 'faithfully complied with without disturbing the family relationship which the policy of the law seeks to preserve. . . .' The parent may find himself forced to choose between his child's interests and his obligations to the courts. For this reason, 'The existence of liability insurance does not remove the inherent danger of the destruction of the parent-child relationship' inherent in the setting of a tort action." (Citations omitted).

How would you evaluate the conflicting arguments?

In Principal Casualty Ins. Co. v. Blair, 500 N.W.2d 67 (Iowa 1993), plaintiff mother sued her husband for injuries suffered by their son allegedly due to defendant's negligence in assembling a bicycle. In this part of the case, the insurer sought a declaratory ruling that it was not obligated to defend or pay for this claim. The policy in question explicitly excluded coverage of any claim brought by one member of the family against another. The family argued that the exclusion was void as against public policy. The court disagreed. It had already ruled that such a provision in an automobile insurance policy was permissible. Here it extended that ruling on the ground that the same arguments applied.

Some courts permit insurers to exclude coverage of intrafamily claims in non-auto suits but refuse to allow it in auto suits especially where such insurance is compulsory or strongly encouraged. See the discussion in Horesh v. State Farm Fire & Cas. Co., 265 N.J.Super. 32, 625 A.2d 541 (App.Div.1993) and the three-way split in National County Mut. Fire Ins. Co. v. Johnson, 879 S.W.2d 1 (Tex.1993).

In Ard v. Ard, 414 So.2d 1066 (Fla.1982), when a child sued his mother for negligently allowing him to be run over, the court reaffirmed its adherence to parental immunity, except that it now ruled that immunity was waived "to the extent of the parent's available liability insurance coverage." An earlier case had already upheld the power of a liability insurer to exclude coverage of family members.

For an extended discussion of the problems that emerge in intrafamily suits where insurance coverage is arguably present, see Myers v. Robertson, 891 P.2d 199 (Alaska 1995), in which the defendant parents admitted liability for their son's death. In a suit by the son's estate against the parents, the issues included whether there was sufficient adversity between the parties (yes), whether the parents could benefit from any recovery (no), whether the award should be reduced by an amount that reflected the parents' role in the death (no), and whether juries in the various cases should be told about the role insurance was playing in an apparently intrafamily case (yes).

10. *Contribution.* The issue of parental responsibility can arise when the child's guardian sues a third person, who in turn seeks contribution from the allegedly negligent parent. The question in such a case is usually seen to be whether the child could have sued the parent initially. Does the different procedural posture suggest some new questions about parental liability?

In Barocas v. F.W. Woolworth Co., 207 App.Div.2d 145, 622 N.Y.S.2d 5 (1995), parents bought a toy with movable parts for their child at defendant's store. The box said it was for children over 3 years old. The child at the time was 4½ months shy of that age. Defendant filed a third party action against the parents for negligent supervision and negligent entrustment. The court barred the action. The age disparity was not relevant because the child was considered bright and had played with similar toys that his sister had. The toy was simply not dangerous as were bicycles, skateboards, plastic tricycles and other subjects of previous cases. It would be "incongruous to permit the manufacturer to obtain contribution from parents who unwittingly bring [a] toy into their home, only to have it injure their child." See also Shoemake v. Fogel, Ltd., 826 S.W.2d 933 (Tex.1992)(holding, 5–4, that where child nearly drowns in apartment complex swimming pool, defendant landlord cannot seek contribution from child's mother for negligent supervision).

In a few states, the contribution action is permissible even though a direct action against the parent would not lie. See Bishop v. Nielsen, 632 P.2d 864 (Utah 1981), in which the court viewed "the equities in favor of contribution as far outweighing the benefits to be achieved by a strict application of the doctrine [of family immunity.]" Given parental immunity, what are the merits of the *Bishop* approach to contribution? We explore contribution in detail in Chapter VI.

In *Horesh v. State Farm Fire & Cas. Co.*, supra, plaintiff child was hurt in defendant department store when a free standing display fell on him. The store brought a third party action against the mother for negligent supervision. In this part of the case, the court decided that the insurance company's exclusion of liability for intrafamily torts applied to this third party claim as well. Is it likely that the child's action will still be brought against the department store?

F. GOVERNMENTAL ENTITIES

The doctrine of sovereign immunity, based on the precept that "the King can do no wrong," was a part of the English common law heritage. Despite the absence of a monarch in this country, governmental immunity to tort liability was imported and became firmly established here. Shortly after the turn of the century, in Kawananakoa v. Polyblank, 205 U.S. 349 (1907), Justice Holmes summed up the received wisdom in his characteristically concise fashion: "A sovereign is exempt from suit, not because of any formal conception or obsolete theory, but on the logical and practical ground that there can be no legal right as against the authority that makes the law on which the right depends." See generally, Prosser & Keeton on Torts (5th ed. 1984), § 131.

If the Holmes position sounds suspiciously conclusory, so too did the public policy rationale stating that tax funds ought not to be diverted from the public purposes for which they were collected.[†] Nonetheless, the protective embrace of governmental immunity to suit encompassed federal, state and municipal entities until the end of World War II.[*] In the two succeeding decades, judicial abrogation and legislative refinement went hand-in-hand in reversing the earlier state of affairs: immunity became the exception rather than the rule.

The abrogation of blanket immunity, however, did not lead to uniform treatment of public and private acts causing unintentional harm. This section explores the ramifications of governmental liability from a duty perspective, because duty limitations have in fact been the principal technique for continued recognition of the special character of certain public functions.

1. MUNICIPAL AND STATE LIABILITY

Riss v. City of New York

Court of Appeals of New York, 1968.
22 N.Y.2d 579, 240 N.E.2d 860, 293 N.Y.S.2d 897.

[The facts are taken from the dissenting opinion. Linda Riss was terrorized for six months by one Pugach who had formerly dated her. He warned that if he could not have her, "no one else will have you, and when I get through with you, no one else will want you." She sought police protection unsuccessfully. She then became engaged to another man and

---

[†] For hundreds of years courts protected charities by giving them immunity from liability for the negligent actions of their employees. This limit on respondeat superior was justified on the ground that benefactors gave money to these organizations to further their charitable work and not to be given to those harmed by the work. This protection has virtually disappeared at common law. See, e.g., Albritton v. Neighborhood Centers Ass'n for Child Development, 12 Ohio St.3d 210, 466 N.E.2d 867 (1984). In some states legislative limits have been placed on the amount for which a charity might be held liable and some states condition liability on whether the charity carries liability insurance to cover the risk. See, e.g., Schultz v. Roman Catholic Archdiocese of Newark, 95 N.J. 530, 472 A.2d 531 (1984).

[*] Not without scholarly criticism, however. In the 1920s, Professor Edwin Borchard wrote a series of articles vigorously attacking governmental immunity. See Borchard, Governmental Liability in Tort, 34 Yale L.J. 1, 129, 229 (1924); 36 Yale L.J. 1, 757, 1029 (1926); and Governmental Responsibility in Tort, 28 Colum.L.Rev. 577, 734 (1928).

Another classic article from this period, attacking the feasibility of distinguishing between "governmental" and "proprietary" functions—a distinction under which municipal entities were held responsible when engaged in activities that had a private ("proprietary") counterpart—is Fuller & Casner, Municipal Tort Liability in Operation, 54 Harv.L.Rev. 437 (1941).

at a celebration party she received a call saying that this was her last chance. She again sought police help but was refused. The next day a thug hired by Pugach threw lye in plaintiff's face, leaving her permanently scarred, blind in one eye, and with little vision in the other.]

■ BREITEL, J.   This appeal presents, in a very sympathetic framework, the issue of the liability of a municipality for failure to provide special protection to a member of the public who was repeatedly threatened with personal harm and eventually suffered dire personal injuries for lack of such protection. The facts are amply described in the dissenting opinion and no useful purpose would be served by repetition. The issue arises upon the affirmance by a divided Appellate Division of a dismissal of the complaint, after both sides had rested but before submission to the jury.

It is necessary immediately to distinguish those liabilities attendant upon governmental activities which have displaced or supplemented traditionally private enterprises, such as are involved in the operation of rapid transit systems, hospitals, and places of public assembly. Once sovereign immunity was abolished by statute the extension of liability on ordinary principles of tort law logically followed. To be equally distinguished are certain activities of government which provide services and facilities for the use of the public, such as highways, public buildings and the like, in the performance of which the municipality or the State may be liable under ordinary principles of tort law. The ground for liability is the provision of the services or facilities for the direct use by members of the public.

In contrast, this case involves the provision of a governmental service to protect the public generally from external hazards and particularly to control the activities of criminal wrongdoers. [   ] The amount of protection that may be provided is limited by the resources of the community and by a considered legislative-executive decision as to how those resources may be deployed. For the courts to proclaim a new and general duty of protection in the law of tort, even to those who may be the particular seekers of protection based on specific hazards, could and would inevitably determine how the limited police resources of the community should be allocated and without predictable limits. This is quite different from the predictable allocation of resources and liabilities when public hospitals, rapid transit systems, or even highways are provided.

Before such extension of responsibilities should be dictated by the indirect imposition of tort liabilities, there should be a legislative determination that that should be the scope of public responsibility [   ].

It is notable that the removal of sovereign immunity for tort liability was accomplished after legislative enactment and not by any judicial arrogation of power (Court of Claims Act, § 8). It is equally notable that for many years, since as far back as 1909 in this State, there was by statute municipal liability for losses sustained as a result of riot (General Municipal Law, § 71). Yet even this class of liability has for some years been suspended by legislative action [   ], a factor of considerable significance.

When one considers the greatly increased amount of crime committed throughout the cities, but especially in certain portions of them, with a repetitive and predictable pattern, it is easy to see the consequences of fixing municipal liability upon a showing of probable need for and request for protection. To be sure these are grave problems at the present time, exciting high priority activity on the part of the national, State and local governments, to which the answers are neither simple, known, or presently within reasonable controls. To foist a presumed cure for these problems by judicial innovation of a new kind of liability in tort would be foolhardy indeed and an assumption of judicial wisdom and power not possessed by the courts.

Nor is the analysis progressed by the analogy to compensation for losses sustained. It is instructive that the Crime Victims Compensation and "Good Samaritan" statutes, compensating limited classes of victims of crime, were enacted only after the most careful study of conditions and the impact of such a scheme upon governmental operations and the public fisc [ ]. And then the limitations were particular and narrow.

For all of these reasons, there is no warrant in judicial tradition or in the proper allocation of the powers of government for the courts, in the absence of legislation, to carve out an area of tort liability for police protection to members of the public. Quite distinguishable, of course, is the situation where the police authorities undertake responsibilities to particular members of the public and expose them, without adequate protection, to the risks which then materialize into actual losses (Schuster v. City of New York, 5 N.Y.2d 75).

Accordingly, the order of the Appellate Division affirming the judgment of dismissal should be affirmed.

■ KEATING, J. (dissenting). . . .

     .   .   .

It is not a distortion to summarize the essence of the city's case here in the following language: "Because we owe a duty to everybody, we owe it to nobody." Were it not for the fact that this position has been hallowed by much ancient and revered precedent, we would surely dismiss it as preposterous. To say that there is no duty is, of course, to start with the conclusion. The question is whether or not there should be liability for the negligent failure to provide adequate police protection.

     .   .   .

The fear of financial disaster is a myth. The same argument was made a generation ago in opposition to proposals that the State waive its defense of "sovereign immunity." The prophecy proved false then, and it would now. The supposed astronomical financial burden does not and would not exist. No municipality has gone bankrupt because it has had to respond in damages when a policeman causes injury through carelessly driving a police car or in the thousands of other situations where, by judicial fiat or legislative enactment, the State and its subdivisions have been held liable for the tortious conduct of their employees. . . . [Judge Keating then observed that less than two-tenths of 1% of the city's annual budget was being allocated to payment of tort claims.] That Linda Riss should be asked to bear the loss, which should properly fall on the city if we assume, as we must, in the present posture of the case, that her injuries resulted from the city's failure to provide sufficient police to protect Linda is contrary to the most elementary notions of justice.

The statement in the majority opinion that there are no predictable limits to the potential liability for failure to provide adequate police protection as compared to other areas of municipal liability is, of course, untenable. When immunity in other areas of governmental activity was removed, the same lack of predictable limits existed. Yet, disaster did not ensue.

Another variation of the "crushing burden" argument is the contention that, every time a crime is committed, the city will be sued and the claim will be made that it resulted from inadequate police protection. . . . The argument is . . . made as if there were no such legal principles as fault, proximate cause or foreseeability, all of which operate to keep liability within reasonable bounds. No one is contending that the police must be at the scene of every potential crime or must provide a personal bodyguard to every person who walks into a police station and claims to have been threatened. They need only act as a reasonable man would under the circumstances. At first there would be a duty to inquire. If the inquiry indicates nothing to substantiate the alleged threat, the matter may be put aside and other matters attended to. If, however, the claims prove to have some basis, appropriate steps would be necessary.

. . .

More significant, however, is the fundamental flaw in the reasoning behind the argument alleging judicial interference. It is a complete over-simplification of the problem of municipal tort liability. What it ignores is the fact that indirectly courts are reviewing administrative practices in almost every tort case against the State or a municipality, including even decisions of the Police Commissioner. Every time a municipal hospital is held liable for malpractice resulting from inadequate record-keeping, the courts are in effect making a determination that the municipality should have hired or assigned more clerical help or more competent help to medical records or should have done something to improve its record-keeping procedures so that the particular injury would not have occurred. Every time a municipality is held liable for a defective sidewalk, it is as if the courts are saying that more money and resources should have been allocated to sidewalk repair, instead of to other public services.

. . .

The truth of the matter, however, is that the courts are not making policy decisions for public officials. In all these municipal negligence cases, the courts are doing two things. First, they apply the principles of vicarious liability to the operations of government. Courts would not insulate the city from liability for the ordinary negligence of members of the highway department.   There is no basis for treating the members of the police department differently.

Second, and most important, to the extent that the injury results from the failure to allocate sufficient funds and resources to meet a minimum standard of public administration, public officials are presented with two alternatives: either improve public administration or accept the cost of compensating injured persons.   Thus, if we were to hold the city liable here for the negligence of the police, courts would no more be interfering with the operations of the police department than they "meddle" in the affairs of the highway department when they hold the municipality liable for personal injuries resulting from defective sidewalks, or a private employer for the negligence of his employees.   In other words, all the courts do in these municipal negligence cases is require officials to weigh the consequences of their decisions.   If Linda Riss' injury resulted from the failure of the city to pay sufficient salaries to attract qualified and sufficient personnel, the full cost of that choice should become acknowledged in the same way as it has in other areas of municipal tort liability.   Perhaps officials will find it less costly to choose the alternative of paying damages than changing their existing practices.   That may be well and good, but the price for the refusal to provide for an adequate police force should not be borne by Linda Riss and all the other innocent victims of such decisions.

.   .   .

No doubt in the future we shall have to draw limitations just as we have done in the area of private litigation, and no doubt some of these limitations will be unique to municipal liability because the problems will not have any counterpart in private tort law.   But if the lines are to be drawn, let them be delineated on candid considerations of policy and fairness and not on the fictions or relics of the doctrine of "sovereign immunity."   Before reaching such questions, however, we must resolve the fundamental issue raised here and recognize that, having undertaken to provide professional police and fire protection, municipalities cannot escape liability for damages caused by their failure to do even a minimally adequate job of it.

.   .   .

■ CHIEF JUDGE FULD and JUDGES BURKE, SCILEPPI, BERGAN and JASEN concur with JUDGE BREITEL; JUDGE KEATING dissents and votes to reverse in a separate opinion.

NOTES   AND   QUESTIONS

1.   Safeguarding the personal security of the community is, of course, one of the traditional functions of government.   *Riss* has been a pivotal case because it raises fundamental issues about police responsibility to the public at large.   Consider the following cases that arguably pose more focused questions of government responsibility for personal security.

In the earlier case of Schuster v. City of New York, cited by Judge Breitel, Schuster provided information to the police that led to the capture of a noted criminal, Willie Sutton. Schuster recognized Sutton from an FBI flyer that had been posted in his father's store. Shortly after he supplied the information to the police his life was threatened, and three weeks later he was killed. The court, 4–3, sustained plaintiff's claim that the police were under a legal duty to respond reasonably to Schuster's request for protection. The court remarked:

> In a situation like the present, government is not merely passive; it is active in calling upon persons "in possession of any information regarding the whereabouts of" Sutton, quoting from the FBI flyer, to communicate such information in aid of law enforcement. Where that has happened, as here, or where the public authorities have made active use of a private citizen in some other capacity in the arrest or prosecution of a criminal, it would be a misuse of language to say that the law enforcement authorities are merely passive. They are active in calling upon the citizen for help, and in utilizing his help when it is rendered.

Is there a satisfying distinction between *Schuster* and *Riss* ?

Consider Davidson v. City of Westminster, 32 Cal.3d 197, 649 P.2d 894, 185 Cal.Rptr. 252 (1982), refusing to find the requisite relationship in a case in which police were keeping a laundromat under surveillance to catch a man who had attacked several women earlier in this and other nearby laundromats. He had escaped a trap the night before. This time, police saw someone they thought was the attacker enter and leave the laundromat several times. Then he returned and stabbed plaintiff. The police, who had hoped to be able to arrest the man after he did something criminal but before he hurt anyone, had not warned the plaintiff before the attack.

The court refused to find a special relationship involving either defendant and plaintiff or defendant and attacker. Is the case more closely aligned to *Riss* or to *Schuster*?

2. Sorichetti v. City of New York, 65 N.Y.2d 461, 482 N.E.2d 70, 492 N.Y.S.2d 591 (1985), involved a suit on behalf of a young child who was badly mutilated by her father while he was exercising his visitation rights. The father had a long history of violent and abusive behavior towards his ex-wife, the child's mother, which had led the Family Court to issue a series of protective orders (which, by statute, gave the police broad discretion to take Sorichetti into custody at the petition of his ex-wife). On the weekend in question when Sorichetti picked up his daughter he threatened to kill his wife, and as for the child, he shouted "You see Dina; you better do the sign of the cross before this weekend is up." His ex-wife made repeated efforts to initiate police intervention to get the child, but the officers refused to take action on the basis of Sorichetti's verbal threats, and told her to go home. An hour after Sorichetti was to have returned the child on Sunday evening, he severely injured her in a drunken rage.

In allowing recovery for the police inaction, the court distinguished *Riss* on the basis of the protective orders, Sorichetti's history of violent behavior, and the front-desk officer's assurance that at some point the police would take action. Is *Riss* distinguishable?

3. In Cuffy v. City of New York, 69 N.Y.2d 255, 505 N.E.2d 937, 513 N.Y.S.2d 372 (1987), the court of appeals attempted to establish guidelines for its continuing line of police protection cases. Plaintiff Cuffys sought police protection on a number of occasions from their downstairs neighbors (and tenants) the Aitkins, with whom they had had a number of skirmishes. After Mr. Aitkins physically attacked Ms. Cuffy, Mr. Cuffy finally received assurance from the police that something would be done—possibly an arrest—"first thing in the morning." The next evening, when Ralston Cuffy, a son, came to visit, Aitkins attacked him with a baseball bat, and Ms. Aitkins slashed Ms. Cuffy and Cyril Cuffy, another son who lived at home, with a knife. In the interim, the police had done nothing, and the three Cuffys subsequently sued the city for their injuries.

The court stated the general rule to be no tort duty to provide police protection, but recognized an exception in cases of "special relationship"—the elements of which were stated to be: "1) an assumption by the municipality through promises or action, of an affirmative duty to act on behalf of the party who was injured; 2) knowledge on the part of the municipality's agents that inaction could lead to harm; 3) some form of direct contact between the municipality's agents and the injured party; and 4) that party's justifiable reliance on the municipality's undertaking."

Under these principles, Ralston Cuffy was denied recovery because he could establish neither direct contact nor reliance on the police promise—indeed he apparently didn't even know about the promise when he came to visit—and the other Cuffys were denied recovery because by the evening, when the harm occurred, they were no longer relying on a police promise to respond that morning.

Do the four "elements" seem a fair summary of the standards used in deciding the cases in this section? Do they seem to have been properly applied in *Cuffy*? Keep the elements in mind as you read on.

4. *Municipal transport.* The court followed *Riss* in Weiner v. Metropolitan Transportation Authority, 55 N.Y.2d 175, 433 N.E.2d 124, 448 N.Y.S.2d 141 (1982). The court ruled that a public transportation authority "owes no duty to protect a person on its premises from assault by a third person, absent facts establishing a special relationship between the authority and the person assaulted. That a nongovernmental common carrier would be liable under the same factual circumstances is not determinative of the authority's liability." The difference was that imposing a duty on the public authority would necessarily have an impact upon the utilization of the transit authority's resources. *Riss* made clear that "the allocation of police resources to protection from criminal wrongdoing is a legislative-executive decision for which there is no liability." Why is *Riss* more compelling than the analogy of the nongovernmental common carrier?

Weiner is distinguished in Crosland v. New York City Transit Authority, 68 N.Y.2d 165, 498 N.E.2d 143, 506 N.Y.S.2d 670 (1986), in which a Transit Authority employee allegedly witnessed the attack on the plaintiff and failed to summon assistance even though he could have done so without personal risk. Compare Clinger v. New York City Transit Authority, 85 N.Y.2d 957, 650 N.E.2d 855, 626 N.Y.S.2d 1008 (1995), in which plaintiff was raped behind construction materials, including a large metal plate, in a city subway pedestrian tunnel. The court characterized plaintiff's claim as involving "a proprietary act (the location of the metal plate) [that] intersected with a governmental act (the failure either to close the tunnel or to properly police it), to create the conditions under which she was attacked". Summary judgment for defendant was sustained on the basis that the act was "overwhelmingly governmental." Is this a logical extension of *Weiner*? *Riss*?

Compare Lopez v. Southern California Rapid Transit District, 40 Cal.3d 780, 710 P.2d 907, 221 Cal.Rptr. 840 (1985), in which a bus driver for the public transit system failed to take any action to assist plaintiffs when a fight broke out on the bus. The court refused to distinguish between public and private carriers in the application of a statute requiring "the utmost care and diligence." Moreover, the court held that cases involving the police were inapposite because a "special relationship" existed here. Finally, the court swept aside resource allocation arguments, asserting that bus companies can adopt reasonable precautionary measures that involve minimal resource expenditures. Is bus safety a special case?

5. *The 911 Call.* As municipalities set up emergency phone numbers, the question of liability followed quickly. In De Long v. County of Erie, 60 N.Y.2d 296, 457 N.E.2d 717, 469 N.Y.S.2d 611 (1983), a woman called 911 to report a burglar outside. The court treated a 911 operator's assurance that help was being sent "right away" as the assumption of a duty to respond with due care to the victim's call for help.

But both direct communication and reliance by the caller are needed to create the special relationship that New York requires for that duty. In Merced v. City of New York, 75 N.Y.2d 798, 551 N.E.2d 589, 552 N.Y.S.2d 96 (1990), a 911 case in which the caller apparently was not the victim, the court held that the required relationship "cannot be established without proof that the injured party had direct contact with the municipality's agents and justifiably relied to his or her detriment on the municipality's assurances that it would act on that party's behalf."

In Kircher v. City of Jamestown, 74 N.Y.2d 251, 543 N.E.2d 443, 544 N.Y.S.2d 995 (1989), witnesses who saw the victim being abducted, got the license number and tried to follow the car. They lost it in traffic but gave all the information to a police officer who promised to report it. He did not and the victim sued for the ensuing assault. The court, 5–2, concluded that no special relationship had been established because the victim had not been in direct communication with the police and had not relied on a promise that help was forthcoming.

6. *Other Custodial Relationships.* The police department undertook to provide school crossing guards whenever the regular crossing guard was ill. The child's mother took the child both ways across one busy street every day during the first two weeks of school. She noticed the guard, decided that further effort was unnecessary, and took a job. The first day she did not accompany the child the guard was absent and the police, though notified, did not guard the crossing. The child was run down crossing the street. In a suit against the city, the court held that the undertaking to provide a substitute guard was enough to impose a duty of care for the safety of children crossing that street. Florence v. Goldberg, 44 N.Y.2d 189, 375 N.E.2d 763, 404 N.Y.S.2d 583 (1978). What if the parent had sent the child alone each day and had taken her job without knowing that there usually was a guard at the corner?

7. In Hoyem v. Manhattan Beach City School Dist., 22 Cal.3d 508, 585 P.2d 851, 150 Cal.Rptr. 1 (1978), a ten-year-old student slipped away from school during the day and was run over by a motorcyclist four blocks from the school. The court, 4–3, reversed dismissal of the complaint and held that the defendant school district owed a duty of due care in supervising the plaintiff.

Justice Tobriner's opinion for the majority stressed that the alleged negligence occurred on the school premises even though the injury occurred elsewhere. The decision did not require "truant-proof" schools: "We require ordinary care, not fortresses; schools must be reasonably supervised, not truant-proof." The majority relied on Bryant v. United States, 565 F.2d 650 (10th Cir.1977), in which three boys slipped away from a New Mexico boarding school and later were trapped in a snowstorm. They suffered extreme frostbite and each student had to have both legs amputated. The court, applying state law, imposed a duty to use due care to supervise the students. Are the cases comparable?

The dissenters in *Hoyem* thought it odd that a truant had a lawsuit when a student who had attended all day and was run over after school did not. Using the array of factors discussed in the Rowland case, p. 172, supra, two of the dissenters argued against a duty: "These 'considerations of policy' . . . include the fundamental function, purpose, and role of a school and its staff, the nature and probable degree of supervision required to prevent truancy, the physical variables of entrances and exits to school grounds, the financial costs of adequate supervision to prevent truancy, the relative moral culpability of pupil, parent and school administration, the historical experience of schools in the supervision of pupils, truant and nontruant, the expense of adequate insurance to cover the extension of liability herein, and other factors." They wanted to limit the district's liability to students injured on school property or in school-related activities off the premises.

8. Compare Pratt v. Robinson, 39 N.Y.2d 554, 349 N.E.2d 849, 384 N.Y.S.2d 749 (1976), in which the seven-year-old plaintiff was run over by a truck while crossing a street after having been left off at the school bus stop about five blocks from her house—the closest designated stop. The accident occurred at a busy intersection three blocks from the stop. The complaint against the school district was dismissed, 4–3, on the grounds that the duty terminated when the child left the bus at a designated stop. The district did not have to run a door-to-door service.

Is the majority view in *Pratt* fundamentally at odds with *Hoyem,* or are the two cases distinguishable? Do the school cases raise a distinctive issue because of concern about interfering with "the discretionary nature of the functions of planning and allocation of resources" in governmental activities? On this score, reconsider *Schuster* and *Riss.*

The allocation of resources argument has not prevented the court of appeals from affirming a judgment in favor of two high school students against school authorities, based on negligent supervision, for injuries suffered in an altercation with a hostile gang in the school building. See Mirand v. City of New York, 84 N.Y.2d 44, 637 N.E.2d 263, 614 N.Y.S.2d 372 (1994), finding a breach of the duty of adequate supervision despite detailed evidence of the security measures taken by the school. Suppose the altercation—based on in-school threats—had taken place as the threatened students walked home from school?

9. *Educational Malpractice.* A graduate of a San Francisco public high school sued the school district for, among other things, its negligent failure to teach him to read above fifth-grade level. Peter W. v. San Francisco Unified School Dist., 60 Cal.App.3d 814, 131 Cal.Rptr. 854 (1976). After noting that the district had no governmental immunity, the court stated that the problem was one of duty, but cases involving the duty of a school to exercise due care for the physical safety of the students did not control this situation:

> On occasions when the Supreme Court has opened or sanctioned new areas of tort liability, it has noted that the wrongs and injuries involved were both comprehensible and assessable within the existing judicial framework. [ ] This is simply not true of wrongful conduct and injuries allegedly involved in educational malfeasance. Unlike the activity of the highway or the market place, classroom methodology affords no readily acceptable standards of care, or cause, or injury. The science of pedagogy itself is fraught with different and conflicting theories of how or what a child should be taught, and any layman might—and commonly does—have his own emphatic views on the subject. The "injury" claimed here is plaintiff's inability to read and write. Substantial professional authority attests that the achievement of literacy in the schools, or its failure, are influenced by a host of factors which affect the pupil subjectively, from outside the formal teaching process, and beyond the control of its ministers. They may be physical, neurological, emotional, cultural, environmental; they may be present but not perceived, recognized but not identified.
>
> We find in this situation no conceivable "workability of a rule of care" against which defendants' alleged conduct may be measured, [ ], no reasonable "degree of certainty that . . . plaintiff suffered injury" within the meaning of the law of negligence (see Rest.2d Torts,

§ 281), and no such perceptible "connection between the defendant's conduct and the injury suffered," as alleged, which would establish a causal link between them within the same meaning. [   ]

These recognized policy considerations alone negate an actionable "duty of care" in persons and agencies who administer the academic phases of the public educational process. Others, which are even more important in practical terms, command the same result. Few of our institutions, if any, have aroused the controversies, or incurred the public dissatisfaction, which have attended the operation of the public schools during the last few decades. Rightly or wrongly, but widely, they are charged with outright failure in the achievement of their educational objectives; according to some critics, they bear responsibility for many of the social and moral problems of our society at large. Their public plight in these respects is attested in the daily media, in bitter governing board elections, in wholesale rejections of school bond proposals, and in survey upon survey. To hold them to an actionable "duty of care," in the discharge of their academic functions, would expose them to the tort claims—real or imagined—of disaffected students and parents in countless numbers. They are already beset by social and financial problems which have gone to major litigation, but for which no permanent solution has yet appeared. [   ] The ultimate consequences, in terms of public time and money, would burden them—and society—beyond calculation.

The Supreme Court of California denied a hearing. How might the damages be measured?

New York took a different path to the same result. In Donohue v. Copiague Union Free School District, 47 N.Y.2d 440, 391 N.E.2d 1352, 418 N.Y.S.2d 375 (1979), the plaintiff alleged that although he attended the defendant's high school for four years and was graduated, he lacks the ability to comprehend written English sufficiently to enable him to complete applications for employment.

The court recognized that if other professionals are held to a duty to the public they serve, nothing precludes similar treatment of professional educators. Creating a standard for judging such performance did not pose an insurmountable problem. Even if proximate causation might be difficult to establish "it perhaps assumes too much to conclude that it could never be established." Damages were clear. Despite this, the court concluded that public policy dictated that courts not entertain such claims. To entertain an action for educational malpractice "would require the courts not merely to make judgments as to the validity of broad educational policies—a course we have unalteringly eschewed in the past—but, more importantly, to sit in review of the day-to-day implementation of these policies. Recognition in the courts of this cause of action would constitute blatant interference with the responsibility for the administration of the public school system lodged by Constitution and statute in school administrative agencies." The court noted that it was holding open the possibility of recourse in cases of "gross violations of defined public policy." Finally, the court noted that administrative procedures were available to any person aggrieved by any "official act or decision" of any school official or board.

Two judges concurred on the ground that the practical problems of administration are so great as to justify concluding that the complaint did not state a cognizable cause of action. The main point was the difficulty of showing causal relation because factors such as "the student's attitude, motivation, temperament, past experience and home environment may all play an essential and immeasurable role in learning."

In Hoffman v. Board of Education, 49 N.Y.2d 121, 400 N.E.2d 317, 424 N.Y.S.2d 376 (1979), plaintiff alleged that at age five he was negligently determined by defendant's psychologist to be retarded. Although the psychologist (because plaintiff had a serious speech defect) was sufficiently unsure of his diagnosis to recommend that plaintiff be retested in two years, plaintiff spent 12 years in classes for the retarded before defendant recognized that he was not retarded.

A judgment of $500,000 was reversed, 4–3. The majority followed *Donohue.* The lower courts had distinguished *Donohue* on the ground that it had involved nonfeasance while *Hoffman* involved misfeasance. The court of appeals thought both cases involved negligent acts and omissions. The principle of judicial noninterference in school administration controlled in both cases. The court refused to substitute its judgment for that of the board as to the type of tests to be given and their frequency. "Such a decision would allow a court or jury to second-guess the determinations of each of plaintiff's teachers. To do so would open the door to an examination of the propriety of each of the procedures used in the education of every student in our school system." Again, recourse was available through the administrative process.

The dissenters found "discernible affirmative negligence on the part of the board of education in failing to carry out the recommendation for re-evaluation within a period of two years."

The Court adhered to *Donohue* and *Hoffman* in Torres v. Little Flower Children's Services, 64 N.Y.2d 119, 474 N.E.2d 223, 485 N.Y.S.2d 15 (1984), involving a Spanish-speaking child whose inability to understand English was misdiagnosed as borderline retardation with educational consequences that allegedly left him functionally illiterate.

10. In Williams v. State, 34 Cal.3d 18, 664 P.2d 137, 192 Cal.Rptr. 233 (1983), the plaintiff was injured when a piece of the brake drum from a passing truck was propelled through the window of the car in which she was riding. Defendant police officers came to the scene of the accident and investigated, but failed to identify other witnesses, injured parties, or the driver responsible for her injuries. Plaintiff based her claim against the police on their alleged negligence which resulted in the lost opportunity to sue the party primarily responsible for her harm.

A majority of the court refused to recognize an affirmative duty on the part of the police to secure information or preserve evidence for civil litigation, remarking that:

> The officers did not create the peril in which plaintiff found herself; they took no affirmative action which contributed to, increased, or changed the risk which would have otherwise existed; there is no indication that they voluntarily assumed any responsibility to protect plaintiff's prospects for recovery by civil litigation; and there are no allegations of the requisite factors to a finding of special relationship, namely detrimental reliance by the plaintiff on the officers' conduct, statements made by them which induced a false sense of security and thereby worsened her position.

Do these circumstances adequately distinguish the case from the protective relationships discussed in the preceding notes?

Friedman v. State of New York

Court of Appeals of New York, 1986.
67 N.Y.2d 271, 493 N.E.2d 893, 502 N.Y.S.2d 669.

[Three personal injury actions involving crossover collisions were consolidated in this appeal. All were brought under the Court of Claims Act, which provides for court hearing without a jury. In Friedman v. State of New York, plaintiff's car was sideswiped on a viaduct causing her to swerve into the oncoming traffic where she was hit head-on. She claimed that the state was negligent in failing to construct a median barrier. The state Department of Transportation (DOT) had studied the question five years earlier and decided that a median barrier should be constructed. But at the time of the accident no action had been taken. Although the state attempted to justify its non-action by pointing to funding priorities and project revisions, it did not offer concrete evidence in support of its claims. The Appellate Division affirmed a judgment for plaintiff.

Both Cataldo v. New York State Thruway Authority and Muller v. State of New York involved accidents on the Tappan Zee bridge. Once again, the plaintiffs claimed negligence in failing to construct a median barrier that would have prevented the crossover accidents. In these cases, however, departmental studies between 1962 and 1972 had determined that the risks of rear-end collisions from "bounce-back" occurrences and stranded autos if a barrier were constructed exceeded the dangers of crossover collisions without a barrier. Cataldo's accident occurred shortly after the last of these studies. Her claim that the studies reached the wrong conclusion was rejected by the Appellate Division on the ground that the agency decision "was premised on a reasonable public safety plan." By the time Muller was injured, however, the department had changed its mind and decided to construct a barrier. More than three years had passed with no further action taken. Nonetheless, the Appellate Division held that the delay was not unreasonable and dismissed Muller's claim.]

■ ALEXANDER, J.

. . .

We now affirm the orders of the Appellate Division in *Friedman* and *Cataldo,* and reverse the order appealed from in *Muller.*

It has long been held that a municipality " 'owe[s] to the public the absolute duty of keeping its streets in a reasonably safe condition' "(Weiss v. Fote, 7 N.Y.2d 579, 584, [ ]). While this duty is nondelegable, it is measured by the courts with consideration given to the proper limits on intrusion into the municipality's planning and decision-making functions. Thus, in the field of traffic design engineering, the State is accorded a qualified immunity from liability arising out of a highway planning decision [ ]. In the seminal *Weiss* case, we recognized that "[t]o accept a jury's verdict as to the reasonableness and safety of a plan of governmental services and prefer it over the judgment of the governmental body which originally considered and passed on the matter would be to obstruct normal governmental operations and to place in inexpert hands what the Legislature has seen fit to entrust to experts" [ ]. The *Weiss* court examined a municipality's decision to design a traffic light with a four-second interval between changing signals, and concluded that there was no indication that "due care was not exercised in the preparation of the design or that no reasonable official could have adopted it" [ ]. We went on to note that "something more than a mere choice between conflicting opinions of experts is required before the State or one of its subdivisions may be charged with a failure to discharge its duty to plan highways for the safety of the traveling public" [ ].

Under this doctrine of qualified immunity, a governmental body may be held liable when its study of a traffic condition is plainly inadequate or there is no reasonable basis for its traffic plan (Alexander v. Eldred, 63 N.Y.2d 460, 466, [municipality's traffic engineer's mistaken belief that the city had no authority to place a stop sign on a private road]). Once the State is made aware of a dangerous traffic condition it must undertake reasonable study thereof with an eye toward alleviating the danger [ ]. Moreover, after the State implements a traffic plan it is "under a continuing duty to review its plan in the light of its actual operation" [ ].

Before analyzing the cases before us in light of these principles, it is pertinent to discuss the procedural posture in which they are presented. In *Friedman v. State of New York*, there is an affirmed finding of fact that the State breached its duty by its unreasonable delay in acting to remedy a known dangerous highway condition once the decision to do so had been made. This finding must be upheld if supported by evidence in the record [ ]. In both *Cataldo v. New York State Thruway Auth.* and *Muller v. State of New York*, however, the intermediate appellate courts reached the factual conclusion, contrary to the respective trial courts, that the duty to the claimants was not breached. Thus, the scope of our review is limited to determining whether the evidence of record in each of these cases more nearly comports with the trial court's findings or with those of the Appellate Division [ ].

In *Cataldo* and *Muller* it is clear that no liability can flow from the Authority's initial decision in 1962 not to construct median barriers on the tangent section of the bridge. This decision was consistent with the opinions that were expressed by experts in the Authority's employ and was a rational response to valid safety concerns. The claimants argue, however, that by failing to reevaluate the barrier issue between 1962 and 1972 the Authority breached its "continuing duty to review its plan in the light of its actual operation" (*Weiss v. Fote*, [   ]). They contend that this inactivity was inexcusable given the changes in the state of the art of highway design occurring during that time. While this position might have some force if urged with respect to an accident occurring during the 10–year period of inactivity, such is not the case at bar. Here, both accidents occurred after the Authority reviewed its plan in 1972 and again reached the conclusion that the public's safety would be better served by not installing median barriers.

Claimants argue, however, that the 1972 engineer's reports upon which the Authority's decision was made were the product of inadequate study of the issue [see *Alexander*]. The gravamen of this assertion is that the reports failed to consider the history of the west curve barrier since its installation in 1962 and attached inordinate importance to operational difficulties that would be incurred while downplaying safety concerns to an inappropriate degree.

Strong policy considerations underpin the qualified immunity doctrine set forth in *Weiss* (*supra*), and, in cases such as these where a governmental body has invoked the expertise of qualified employees, the *Weiss* directive should not be lightly discounted. Appellants would have us examine the criteria that were considered by the State's professional staff, emphasize factors allegedly overlooked, and, with the benefit of hindsight, rule that the studies were inadequate as a matter of law. We decline this invitation, for to do so, as the Appellate Division correctly concluded, "would constitute the type of judgment substitution that *Weiss v. Fote* (*supra*) prohibits" [   ].

Because the Authority's decisions prior to the *Cataldo* accident in 1973 not to install median barriers were based on reasonable public safety considerations the Appellate Division properly dismissed the claim in that case. The Authority fulfilled its duty under *Weiss* by studying the dangerous condition, determining that design changes were not advisable and later reaching the same conclusion upon reevaluation of its decision.

In *Friedman* and *Muller,* however, a further basis upon which the defendants may be held liable is tendered: that once a decision has been reached to go forward with a plan intended to remedy a dangerous condition, liability may result from a failure to effectuate the plan within a reasonable period of time. Although this precise question has not been specifically addressed by this court, several Appellate Division decisions have held that when the State is made aware of a dangerous highway condition and does not take action to remedy it, the State can be held liable for resulting injuries [   ]. This conclusion flows logically from the premise that the State has a nondelegable duty to maintain its roads in a reasonably safe condition [   ], and it applies even if the design in question complied with reasonable safety standards at the time of construction. Of course as we have said, when a municipality studies a dangerous condition and determines as part of a reasonable plan of governmental services that certain steps need not be taken, that decision may not form the basis of liability [   ]. When, however, as in *Friedman* and *Muller,* analysis of a hazardous condition by the municipality results in the formulation of a remedial plan, an unjustifiable delay in implementing the plan constitutes a breach of the municipality's duty to the public just as surely as if it had totally failed to study the known condition in the first instance.

In *Friedman,* there is evidence to support the affirmed finding that the State unreasonably delayed its remedial action. The State failed to demonstrate at trial either that the five-year delay between DOT's recognition of the hazardous condition on the viaduct and its project proposal and the Friedman accident was necessary in order to study and formulate a reasonable safety plan, that the delay was itself part of a considered plan of action taken on the advice of experts, or that the delay stemmed from a legitimate ordering of priorities with other projects based on the availability of funding [   ].

Similarly, in *Muller,* we conclude that the record evidence more nearly comports with the trial court's finding that the three-year delay between the Authority's decision in 1974 to construct median barriers and the Muller accident in 1977 was unreasonable. This is not to say that the study and resolution of issues surrounding the concurrent installation of a traffic control system and the optimum location of the barrier, the ostensible cause of the delay, was not warranted. Indeed, a reasonable delay justified by design considerations, as with one resulting from a legitimate claim of funding priorities, would not be actionable. Our review of the evidence, however, reveals that the period of consideration in this case was marked by only intermittent spurts of study and evaluation and long gaps of inactivity, wholly inconsistent with the project's designation in an Authority press release as one having a "high priority" for which "[n]o significant delay [wa]s expected."

. . .

We conclude, therefore, that the order of the Appellate Division in *Cataldo* should be affirmed, with costs. The order appealed from in *Muller* should be reversed, with costs, and the judgment of the Court of Claims reinstated. In *Friedman,* the order of the Appellate Division should be affirmed. . . .

■ CHIEF JUDGE WACHTLER and JUDGES MEYER, SIMONS, KAYE, TITONE and HANCOCK, JR., concur.

NOTES AND QUESTIONS

1. The court quotes the leading case of *Weiss v. Fote* for the proposition that government liability turns on whether "due care was not exercised in the preparation of the design or that no reasonable official could have adopted it." How does this standard, or the court's more detailed discussion of governmental immunity, differ from the ordinary test of negligence applicable to private parties? In what sense does the state transportation agency have a "qualified immunity"?

2. Suppose the plaintiff's injury resulted from a large pothole in the road that was known to the highway department but which had been designated for repair six months later because of funding shortages. Does the nature of the risk bear on the legal obligation to repair? For a discussion of municipal obligations to maintain roadways and sidewalks under common law negligence principles and legislative notice requirements, see Note, New York City's Pothole Law: In Need of Repair, 10 Ford.Urban L.J. 323 (1982).

3. Do these planning and maintenance cases raise different issues, so far as government immunity is concerned, from the police protection and custodial cases considered in conjunction with *Riss*?

4. The Friedman case consolidates two distinct types of claims. Should a court exercise a different degree of oversight when an agency has allegedly delayed action inordinately as opposed to a situation in which the agency has purportedly made the wrong decision?

5. Should it matter that municipal negligence cases are ordinarily tried to a jury? Consider the following passage from *Weiss v. Fote*:

> To accept a jury's verdict as to the reasonableness and safety of a plan of governmental services and prefer it over the judgment of the governmental body which originally considered and passed on the matter would be to obstruct normal governmental operations and to place in inexpert hands what the Legislature has seen fit to entrust to experts. Acceptance of this conclusion, far from effecting revival of the ancient shibboleth that "the king can do no wrong," serves only to give expression to the important and continuing need to preserve the pattern of distribution of governmental functions prescribed by constitution and statute.

Is the separation of powers argument of lesser force in cases such as *Friedman*, brought against the state and heard by a court of claims without the right to a jury?

6. In abrogating sovereign immunity, state legislatures have created statutory frameworks governing the terms on which the state may be sued. Often, the grant of jurisdiction preserves state immunity for "discretionary functions." Illustrative is Estate of Arrowwood v. State, 894 P.2d 642 (Alaska 1995), in which the claims were based on the state's failure to close a highway after receiving many reports of icy conditions that had made driving very dangerous—and that caused plaintiff to lose control of her vehicle leading to serious personal injuries and the death of her son. The court held that the state's decision to keep the highway open was "a planning-level decision which falls within the discretionary function excep-

tion [provided in the Alaska Tort Claims Act]." Keep the case in mind as you are reading the next section on the Federal Tort Claims Act.

7. Claims of agency impropriety are most commonly reviewed through direct appeal to the courts from an administrative decision, rather than after personal injury has occurred. The body of statutory and case law that has resulted from these supervisory and oversight functions is the subject of the law school course in Administrative Law.

2.   FEDERAL TORT CLAIMS ACT

The federal government waived its general tort immunity in 1946 in the Federal Tort Claims Act, 28 U.S.C. §§ 1346(b), 2402, 2671 et seq. The most significant sections follow:

§ 1346(b). [T]he district courts . . . shall have exclusive jurisdiction of civil actions on claims against the United States, for money damages, accruing on and after January 1, 1945, for injury or loss of property, or personal injury or death caused by the negligent or wrongful act or omission of any employee of the Government while acting within the scope of his office or employment, under circumstances where the United States, if a private person, would be liable to the claimant in accordance with the law of the place where the act or omission occurred.

§ 2402. Any action against the United States under section 1346 shall be tried by the court without a jury. . . .

§ 2674. The United States shall be liable, respecting the provisions of this title relating to tort claims, in the same manner and to the same extent as a private individual under like circumstances, but shall not be liable for interest prior to judgment or for punitive damages.

§ 2678. No attorney shall charge, demand, receive, or collect for services rendered, fees in excess of 25 per centum of any judgment rendered [under § 1346(b)]. . . .

§ 2679(b). The remedy against the United States . . . for injury or loss of property, or personal injury or death, arising or resulting from the negligent or wrongful act or omission of any employee of the Government while acting within the scope of his office or employment is exclusive of any other civil action or proceeding for money damages by reason of the same subject matter against the employee whose act or omission gave rise to the claim or against the estate of such employee. Any other civil action or proceeding for money damages arising out of or relating to the same subject matter against the employee or the employee's estate is precluded without regard to when the act or omission occurred.

§ 2680. The provisions of this chapter and section 1346(b) of this title shall not apply to—

(a) Any claim based upon an act or omission of an employee of the Government, exercising due care, in the execution of a statute or regulation, whether or not such statute or regulation be valid, or based upon the exercise or performance or the failure to exercise or perform a discretionary function or duty on the part of a federal agency or an employee of the Government, whether or not the discretion involved be abused.

(b) Any claim arising out of the loss, miscarriage, or negligent transmission of letters or postal matter.

. . .

(h) [a list of exceptions for intentional torts, discussed at p. 872, infra].

(i) Any claim for damages caused by the fiscal operations of the Treasury or by the regulation of the monetary system.

(j) Any claim arising out of the combatant activities of the military or naval forces, or the Coast Guard, during time of war.

(k) Any claim arising in a foreign country.

What might justify each of the exceptions listed?

The exception for "discretionary functions" was read broadly in Dalehite v. United States, 346 U.S. 15 (1953), involving hundreds of cases that resulted from an explosion in the loading of a shipment of fertilizer. In denying liability, the Court drew a distinction between "planning decisions," which are policy oriented, and "operational decisions," which are of a nondiscretionary nature. Unfortunately the distinction between the categories, as used in the cases, has often been less than clear. The Court sought to clarify its position in the following case.

Berkovitz v. United States

Supreme Court of the United States, 1988.
486 U.S. 531, 108 S.Ct. 1954, 100 L.Ed.2d 531.

■ JUSTICE MARSHALL delivered the opinion of the Court.

The question in this case is whether the discretionary function exception of the Federal Tort Claims Act (FTCA or Act), 28 U.S.C. § 2680(a), bars a suit based on the Government's licensing of an oral polio vaccine and on its subsequent approval of the release of a specific lot of that vaccine to the public.

I

On May 10, 1979, Kevan Berkovitz, then a 2–month–old infant, ingested a dose of Orimune, an oral polio vaccine manufactured by Lederle Laboratories. Within one month, he contracted a severe case of polio. The disease left Berkovitz almost completely paralyzed and unable to breathe without the assistance of a respirator. The Communicable Disease Center, an agency of the Federal Government, determined that Berkovitz had contracted polio from the vaccine.

Berkovitz, joined by his parents as guardians, subsequently filed suit against the United States in Federal District Court.[1] The complaint alleged that the United States was liable for his injuries under the FTCA, 28 U.S.C. §§ 1346(b), 2674, because the Division of Biologic Standards (DBS), then a part of the National Institutes of Health, had acted wrongfully in licensing Lederle Laboratories to produce Orimune and because the Bureau of Biologics of the Food and Drug Administration (FDA) had acted wrongfully in approving release to the public of the particular lot of vaccine containing Berkovitz's dose. According to petitioners, these actions violated federal law and policy regarding the inspection and approval of polio vaccines.

The Government moved to dismiss the suit for lack of subject-matter jurisdiction on the ground that the agency actions fell within the discretionary function exception of the FTCA. The District Court denied this motion, concluding that neither the licensing of Orimune nor the release of a specific lot of that vaccine to the public was a "discretionary function" within the meaning of the FTCA. [ ] . . .

A divided panel of the Court of Appeals reversed. . . .

We granted certiorari, [ ] to resolve a conflict in the Circuits regarding the effect of the discretionary function exception on claims arising from the Government's regulation of polio vaccines. [ ] . . . We now reverse the Third Circuit's judgment.

II

[The Court began its analysis by setting out the general authorization to sue the United States in § 1346(b) and the exception for discretionary functions in § 2680(a).] This exception, as we stated in our most recent opinion on the subject, "marks the boundary between Congress' willingness to impose tort liability upon the United States and its desire to protect certain governmental activities from exposure to suit by private individuals." [United States v. Varig Airlines, 467 U.S. 797 (1984).]

The determination of whether the discretionary function exception bars a suit against the Government is guided by several established principles. This Court stated in *Varig* that "it is the nature of the conduct, rather than the status of the actor, that governs whether the discretionary function exception applies in a given case." [*Varig*] In examining the nature of the challenged conduct, a court must first consider whether the action is a matter of choice for the acting employee. This inquiry is mandated by the language of the exception; conduct cannot be discretionary unless it involves an element of judgment or choice. See *Dalehite v. United States*, [ ] (stating that the exception protects "the discretion of

---

1. Petitioners also sued Lederle Laboratories in a separate civil action. That suit   was settled before the instant case was filed.

the executive or the administrator to act according to one's judgment of the best course"). Thus, the discretionary function exception will not apply when a federal statute, regulation, or policy specifically prescribes a course of action for an employee to follow. In this event, the employee has no rightful option but to adhere to the directive. And if the employee's conduct cannot appropriately be the product of judgment or choice, then there is no discretion in the conduct for the discretionary function exception to protect. [ ]

Moreover, assuming the challenged conduct involves an element of judgment, a court must determine whether that judgment is of the kind that the discretionary function exception was designed to shield. The basis for the discretionary function exception was Congress' desire to "prevent judicial 'second-guessing' of legislative and administrative decisions grounded in social, economic, and political policy through the medium of an action in tort." [Varig] The exception, properly construed, therefore protects only governmental actions and decisions based on considerations of public policy. . . .

This Court's decision in [Varig] illustrates these propositions. The two cases resolved in that decision were tort suits by the victims of airplane accidents who alleged that the Federal Aviation Administration (FAA) had acted negligently in certifying certain airplanes for operation. The Court characterized the suits as challenging the FAA's decision to certify the airplanes without first inspecting them and held that this decision was a discretionary act for which the Government was immune from liability. In reaching this result, the Court carefully reviewed the statutory and regulatory scheme governing the inspection and certification of airplanes. Congress had given the Secretary of Transportation broad authority to establish and implement a program for enforcing compliance with airplane safety standards. In the exercise of that authority, the FAA, as the Secretary's designee, had devised a system of "spot-checking" airplanes for compliance. This Court first held that the establishment of that system was a discretionary function within the meaning of the FTCA because it represented a policy determination as to how best to "accommodat[e] the goal of air transportation safety and the reality of finite agency resources." [Varig] The Court then stated that the discretionary function exception also protected "the acts of FAA employees in executing the 'spot-check' program" because under this program the employees "were specifically empowered to make policy judgments regarding the degree of confidence that might reasonably be placed in a given manufacturer, the need to maximize compliance with FAA regulations, and the efficient allocation of agency resources." [Varig] Thus, the Court held the challenged acts protected from liability because they were within the range of choice accorded by federal policy and law and were the results of policy determinations.[3]

---

3. The decision in Indian Towing Co. v. United States, 350 U.S. 61 (1955), also illuminates the appropriate scope of the discretionary function exception. The plaintiff in that case sued the Government for failing to maintain a lighthouse in good working order.

In restating and clarifying the scope of the discretionary function exception, we intend specifically to reject the Government's argument, pressed both in this Court and the Court of Appeals, that the exception precludes liability for any and all acts arising out of the regulatory programs of federal agencies.   That argument is rebutted first by the language of the exception, which protects "discretionary" functions, rather than "regulatory" functions.   The significance of Congress' choice of language is supported by the legislative history.   As this Court previously has indicated, the relevant legislative materials demonstrate that the exception was designed to cover not all acts of regulatory agencies and their employees, but only such acts as are "discretionary" in nature. [ ] . . .

. . .   To the extent we have not already put the Government's argument to rest, we do so now.   The discretionary function exception applies only to conduct that involves the permissible exercise of policy judgment.   The question in this case is whether the governmental activities challenged by petitioners are of this discretionary nature.

III

Petitioners' suit raises two broad claims.   First, petitioners assert that the DBS violated a federal statute and accompanying regulations in issuing a license to Lederle Laboratories to produce Orimune.   Second, petitioners argue that the Bureau of Biologics of the FDA violated federal regulations and policy in approving the release of the particular lot of Orimune that contained Kevan Berkovitz's dose.   We examine each of these broad claims by reviewing the applicable regulatory scheme and petitioners' specific allegations of agency wrongdoing.   Because the decision we review adjudicated a motion to dismiss, we accept all of the factual allegations in petitioners' complaint as true and ask whether, in these circumstances, dismissal of the complaint was appropriate.

A

Under federal law, a manufacturer must receive a product license prior to marketing a brand of live oral polio vaccine. [ ]   In order to become eligible for such a license, a manufacturer must first make a sample of the vaccine product. [ ]   This process begins with the selection of an original virus strain.   The manufacturer grows a seed virus from this strain; the seed virus is then used to produce monopools, portions of which are combined to form the consumer-level product.   Federal regulations set forth safety criteria for the original strain, [ ] the seed virus, [ ] and the vaccine monopools.   Under the regulations, the manufacturer must conduct a variety of tests to measure the safety of the product at each stage of

---

The Court stated that the initial decision to undertake and maintain lighthouse service was a discretionary judgment. See id., at 69. The Court held, however, that the failure to maintain the lighthouse in good condition subjected the Government to suit under the FTCA. See ibid. The latter course of conduct did not involve any permissible exercise of policy judgment.

the manufacturing process. [ ] Upon completion of the manufacturing process and the required testing, the manufacturer is required to submit an application for a product license to the DBS. [ ] In addition to this application, the manufacturer must submit data from the tests performed and a sample of the finished product. [ ]

In deciding whether to issue a license, the DBS is required to comply with certain statutory and regulatory provisions. The Public Health Service Act provides:

> "Licenses for the maintenance of establishments for the propagation or manufacture and preparation of products [including polio vaccines] may be issued only upon a showing that the establishment and the products for which a license is desired meet standards, designed to insure the continued safety, purity, and potency of such products, prescribed in regulations, and licenses for new products may be issued only upon a showing that they meet such standards. All such licenses shall be issued, suspended, and revoked as prescribed by regulations. . . ." [ ]

. . . These statutory and regulatory provisions require the DBS, prior to issuing a product license, to receive all data the manufacturer is required to submit, examine the product, and make a determination that the product complies with safety standards.

Petitioners' first allegation with regard to the licensing of Orimune is that the DBS issued a product license without first receiving data that the manufacturer must submit showing how the product, at the various stages of the manufacturing process, matched up against regulatory safety standards. [ ] The discretionary function exception does not bar a cause of action based on this allegation. The statute and regulations described above require, as a precondition to licensing, that the DBS receive certain test data from the manufacturer relating to the product's compliance with regulatory standards. [ ] The DBS has no discretion to issue a license without first receiving the required test data; to do so would violate a specific statutory and regulatory directive. Accordingly, to the extent that petitioners' licensing claim is based on a decision of the DBS to issue a license without having received the required test data, the discretionary function exception imposes no bar.

Petitioners' other allegation regarding the licensing of Orimune is difficult to describe with precision. Petitioners contend that the DBS licensed Orimune even though the vaccine did not comply with certain regulatory safety standards. [ ] This charge may be understood in any of three ways. First, petitioners may mean that the DBS licensed Orimune without first making a determination as to whether the vaccine complied with regulatory standards. Second, petitioners may intend to argue that the DBS specifically found that Orimune failed to comply with certain regulatory standards and nonetheless issued a license for the vaccine's manufacture. Third, petitioners may concede that the DBS made a determination of compliance, but allege that this determination was incorrect.

Neither petitioners' complaint nor their briefs and argument before this Court make entirely clear their theory of the case.

If petitioners aver that the DBS licensed Orimune either without determining whether the vaccine complied with regulatory standards or after determining that the vaccine failed to comply, the discretionary function exception does not bar the claim. Under the scheme governing the DBS's regulation of polio vaccines, the DBS may not issue a license except upon an examination of the product and a determination that the product complies with all regulatory standards. [ ] The agency has no discretion to deviate from this mandated procedure. Petitioners' claim, if interpreted as alleging that the DBS licensed Orimune in the absence of a determination that the vaccine complied with regulatory standards, therefore does not challenge a discretionary function. Rather, the claim charges a failure on the part of the agency to perform its clear duty under federal law. When a suit charges an agency with failing to act in accord with a specific mandatory directive, the discretionary function exception does not apply.

If petitioners' claim is that the DBS made a determination that Orimune complied with regulatory standards, but that the determination was incorrect, the question of the applicability of the discretionary function exception requires a somewhat different analysis. In that event, the question turns on whether the manner and method of determining compliance with the safety standards at issue involve agency judgment of the kind protected by the discretionary function exception. Petitioners contend that the determination involves the application of objective scientific standards, [ ] whereas the Government asserts that the determination incorporates considerable "policy judgment." [ ] In making these assertions, the parties have framed the issue appropriately; application of the discretionary function exception to the claim that the determination of compliance was incorrect hinges on whether the agency officials making that determination permissibly exercise policy choice. The parties, however, have not addressed this question in detail, and they have given us no indication of the way in which the DBS interprets and applies the regulations setting forth the criteria for compliance. Given that these regulations are particularly abstruse, we hesitate to decide the question on the scanty record before us. We therefore leave it to the District Court to decide, if petitioners choose to press this claim, whether agency officials appropriately exercise policy judgment in determining that a vaccine product complies with the relevant safety standards.

B

The regulatory scheme governing release of vaccine lots is distinct from that governing the issuance of licenses. The former set of regulations places an obligation on manufacturers to examine all vaccine lots prior to distribution to ensure that they comply with regulatory standards. [ ]These regulations, however, do not impose a corresponding duty on the Bureau of Biologics. Although the regulations empower the Bureau to examine any vaccine lot and prevent the distribution of a noncomplying lot, [ ] they do not require the Bureau to take such action in all cases. The regulations generally allow the Bureau to determine the appropriate manner in which to regulate the release of vaccine lots, rather than mandating certain kinds of agency action. The regulatory scheme governing the release of vaccine lots is substantially similar in this respect to the scheme discussed in [*Varig*].

Given this regulatory context, the discretionary function exception bars any claims that challenge the Bureau's formulation of policy as to the appropriate way in which to regulate the release of vaccine lots. Cf. [*Varig*] (holding that discretionary function exception barred claim challenging FAA's decision to establish a spot-checking program). In addition, if the policies and programs formulated by the Bureau allow room for implementing officials to make independent policy judgments, the discretionary function exception protects the acts taken by those officials in the exercise of this discretion. Cf. [*Varig*] (holding that discretionary function exception barred claim that employees charged with executing the FAA's spot-checking program made negligent policy judgments respecting the proper inspection of airplanes). The discretionary function exception, however, does not apply if the acts complained of do not involve the permissible exercise of policy discretion. Thus, if the Bureau's policy leaves no room for an official to exercise policy judgment in performing a given act, or if the act simply does not involve the exercise of such judgment, the discretionary function exception does not bar a claim that the act was negligent or wrongful. Cf. *Indian Towing Co. v. United States*, [ ] (holding that a negligent failure to maintain a lighthouse in good working order subjected Government to suit under the FTCA even though the initial decision to undertake and maintain lighthouse service was a discretionary policy judgment).

Viewed in light of these principles, petitioners' claim regarding the release of the vaccine lot from which Kevan Berkovitz received his dose survives the Government's motion to dismiss. Petitioners allege that, under the authority granted by the regulations, the Bureau of Biologics has adopted a policy of testing all vaccine lots for compliance with safety standards and preventing the distribution to the public of any lots that fail to comply. Petitioners further allege that notwithstanding this policy, which allegedly leaves no room for implementing officials to exercise independent policy judgment, employees of the Bureau knowingly approved the release of a lot that did not comply with safety standards. [ ] Thus, petitioners' complaint is directed at a governmental action that allegedly involved no policy discretion. Petitioners, of course, have not proved their factual allegations, but they are not required to do so on a motion to dismiss. If those allegations are correct—that is, if the Bureau's policy did not allow the official who took the challenged action to release a noncomplying lot on the basis of policy considerations—the discretionary function exception does not bar the claim.[13] Because petitioners may yet show, on

13. The Government's own argument before this Court provides some support for petitioners' allegation regarding the Bureau's policy. The Government indicated that the

the basis of materials obtained in discovery or otherwise, that the conduct challenged here did not involve the permissible exercise of policy discretion, the invocation of the discretionary function exception to dismiss petitioners' lot release claim was improper.

IV

For the foregoing reasons, the Court of Appeals erred in holding that the discretionary function exception required the dismissal of petitioners' claims respecting the licensing of Orimune and the release of a particular vaccine lot. The judgment of the Court of Appeals is accordingly reversed, and the case is remanded for further proceedings consistent with this opinion.

NOTES AND QUESTIONS

1. The Court expressly rejects the Government's argument that all acts arising out of the federal regulatory programs are covered by the discretionary function exception. Is the Government's argument plausible? Putting aside legislative history, is it flawed?

2. Is the decision in this case consistent with the Court's determination in *Varig* that the FAA's spot-check system fell within the discretionary function exception?

3. The Court says that an "incorrect" determination by the agency that Orimune complied with applicable licensing standards might, in fact, fall within the discretionary function exception. How could such an agency determination be regarded as a "policy judgment"? Is the Court taking a position consistent with the rest of its opinion on this point?

4. Does the discretionary function exception, as interpreted by the Court in *Berkovitz*, express a different set of policy concerns from those just considered in municipal and state liability cases?

5. Does *Berkovitz* give us any guidance as to how the Court would decide a negligence claim against an air controller for incorrect flight instructions?

6. Suppose the FDA licenses a vaccine in violation of specific test regulations, but does so in the belief that equally safe alternative safety measures are warranted to avoid delay—and consequent adverse health effects—which would result from following the letter of the law. Should the discretionary function exception apply? In In re Sabin Oral Polio Vaccine Products Liability Litigation, 984 F.2d 124 (4th Cir.1993), the court interpreted *Berkovitz* as providing a negative answer.

Bureau reviews each lot of vaccine and decides whether it complies with safety standards. [ ] The Government further suggested that if an employee knew that a lot did not comply with these standards, he would have no discretion to approve the release of the lot. [ ]

7. In United States v. Gaubert, 499 U.S. 315 (1991), plaintiff argued that the negligence of the Federal Home Loan Bank Board in supervising the day-to-day activities of a now-defunct savings and loan association had caused damages that were recoverable as "operational actions" of the agency. The court rejected the claim, holding that "[d]ay-to-day management of banking affairs, like the management of other businesses, regularly requires judgment as to which of a range of permissible courses is the wisest."

8. The range of cases testing the breadth of the discretionary function exception is suggested by Galloway Farms, Inc. v. United States, 834 F.2d 998 (Fed. Cir.1987)(government not liable to farmers who claimed an unconstitutional taking of property because of grain embargo of Soviet Union); Piechowicz v. United States, 885 F.2d 1207 (4th Cir.1989)(claim dismissed against government for failure to protect two federal witnesses who were murdered by contract killer); Hart v. United States, 894 F.2d 1539 (11th Cir.1990)(government's efforts to identify American flyer shot down over Laos and the decision as to when to discontinue the search for military personnel are discretionary); and Autery v. United States, 992 F.2d 1523 (11th Cir.1993)(claims for injuries from falling tree in national park dismissed because agency's design and implementation of tree inspection program falls within exception).

9. *The Feres Doctrine.* The Court broadened the armed services exception beyond claims "arising out of the combatant services of the military" in Feres v. United States, 340 U.S. 135 (1950), to encompass *all* injuries that arise out of or in the course of military service. The Court adhered to the doctrine, explained its rationale (including a restatement of the traditional concern about maintaining military discipline and effectiveness), and expanded its reach in United States v. Johnson, 481 U.S. 681 (1987), a case in which *Feres* was invoked to bar a surviving wife's claim against the FAA for negligence in providing guidance to a military helicopter pilot who died in a rescue mission. For a lucid analysis of the history and evolution of the Feres doctrine, see Taber v. United States, 45 F.3d 598 (2d Cir.1995)(opinion by Judge Calabresi).

In Stencel Aero Engineering Corp. v. United States, 431 U.S. 666 (1977), the Court decided that a government contractor who was held liable to military personnel for a defective product could not get indemnity from the government. The point was to avoid an end run around *Feres*. A related question is whether the government contractor can claim a defense against primary liability. The government contractor defense is considered in Chapter VIII.

10. Actions against federal officials for violation of constitutional rights generally involve claims of intentional wrongdoing. Although most intentional harms are exempted under the FTCA, a constitutional tort, independent of the act, was recognized in Bivens v. Six Unknown Named Agents, 403 U.S. 388 (1971), discussed in Chapter XII.

11. Similar claims against state and municipal officials, under the Civil Rights Act of 1871, 42 U.S.C. § 1983, are discussed in Chapter XII.

The interplay between the issues arising in § 1983 cases and issues considered in this section, as well as the earlier section in this chapter on duties of affirmative action, is illustrated by DeShaney v. Winnebago County Dept. of Social Services, 489 U.S. 189 (1989), in which plaintiff, a young boy suffered serious permanent brain damage from beatings administered by his father. The § 1983 claim against defendant social services agency was based on a failure to intervene and remove plaintiff from his father's custody despite notice from concerned parties on various occasions. The Court denied the claim of constitutional denial of liberty under the due process clause, holding that there is no affirmative duty on the part of the state to protect individuals against invasion by other private parties.

CHAPTER IV

THE DUTY REQUIREMENT: NONPHYSICAL HARM

In this chapter we deal with protection against non-physical harms. The focus will be on the *types* of harm that plaintiffs suffer. The common law distinguished situations in which the only harm suffered was psychic or economic from the classic physical injury, and developed limited or no-duty rules for reasons that we will explore. We begin with a type of harm generically referred to as "emotional harm." Historically, this type of harm was far less widely protected than the interest in being free from physical harm. Nonetheless, by the early twentieth century courts had begun to protect plaintiffs against intentional extreme and outrageous conduct that produced "only" this type of harm. We explore that subject in Chapter XII. Here, we consider the circumstances in which the courts protect non-physical interests against negligent interference.

A. EMOTIONAL HARM

K.A.C. v. Benson

Supreme Court of Minnesota, 1995.
527 N.W.2d 553.

[Plaintiff T.M.W. and about 50 other patients sued defendant gynecologist when informed that defendant had performed two gynecological procedures on plaintiff while he was infected with HIV and had open sores on his hands and forearms. Dr. Benson consulted a dermatologist about his lesions and was diagnosed as having a variety of skin disorders. Upon learning that he was HIV positive, defendant sought guidance from the State Board of Medical Examiners. He complied with restrictions they imposed, including wearing two pairs of gloves and refraining from performing surgery. After this meeting, defendant examined T.M.W. twice. After the second exam, he again met with the board, which imposed further restrictions and had Dr. Benson write to 336 patients to inform them of the situation. He wrote plaintiff that at the time of her two exams, he did not realize there was any risk. "I am now aware that even with gloves, an extremely minimal risk still existed." None of the patients, including T.M.W., tested HIV positive.

[handwritten margin note: Gynecologist was HIV+ and examined patients with open sores on hands. Patients sued for emotional harm.]

The trial court granted summary judgments for failure to allege "actual exposure to HIV." The court of appeals reversed on the ground that there was a question of fact whether defendant placed his patients in a "zone of danger." It also limited plaintiffs' damages for emotional distress to the "'reasonable window of anxiety' between the time they learned of Dr. Benson's illness until they received negative HIV test results." All the cases except T.M.W.'s were settled during this appeal.]

■ STRINGER, JUSTICE.

. . .

a.   Negligent Infliction of Emotional Distress

The first issue presented on appeal is whether plaintiff must allege actual exposure to the body fluids of an HIV-infected individual to recover emotional distress damages. To establish a claim for negligent infliction of emotional distress, plaintiff must show she: (1) was within a zone of danger of physical impact; (2) reasonably feared for her own safety; and (3) suffered severe emotional distress with attendant physical manifestations. Stadler v. Cross, 295 N.W.2d 552, 553 (Minn.1980). T.M.W. argues that although she cannot prove actual exposure to HIV occurred, it is possible she was exposed to a body fluid transfer. Thus, T.M.W. in effect alleges her proximity to Dr. Benson's HIV-infected body fluids put her within the "zone of danger" of physical impact. She offers the affidavit of Dr. Sanford Kuvin, who would testify that gloves are inadequate protection against HIV transmission. We are not persuaded by this argument, and hold, as a matter of law, for the reasons stated hereafter, that plaintiff was beyond the "zone of danger" for purposes of a claim of negligent infliction of emotional distress.

In Purcell v. St. Paul City Ry. Co., 48 Minn. 134, 50 N.W. 1034 (1892), this court first ruled that actual physical impact is not necessary to sustain a claim for emotional distress damages. There, plaintiff suffered a miscarriage after the cable car on which she was a passenger narrowly avoided a collision with another cable car. [ ] The court adopted the "zone of danger" test, noting the impending cable car collision "seemed so imminent, and was so nearly caused, that the incident and attending confusion of ringing alarm-bells and passengers rushing out of the car caused to plaintiff sudden fright and reasonable fear of immediate death or great bodily injury * * *." [ ] The zone of danger test has remained the law in Minnesota for over 100 years.

We adhered to the "zone of danger" test in Okrina v. Midwestern Corp., 282 Minn. 400, 401, 165 N.W.2d 259, 261 (1969), where plaintiff was in a dressing room at a J.C. Penney store when "she heard what sounded like a bomb and witnessed the collapse of the wall." [ ] Plaintiff ultimately escaped "without being physically struck by debris other than dust." [ ] This court held that plaintiff was within the zone of danger. The court of appeals applied the "zone of danger" test in Quill v. Trans World Airlines, Inc., 361 N.W.2d 438 (Minn.App.1985), pet. for rev. denied, (Minn., Apr. 18, 1985), where the aircraft on which plaintiff was a passen-

[handwritten margin notes:] Appeals court limited damages to the time between learning of Dr's infection and their negative test.

[handwritten margin note:] beyond "zone of danger"

ger suddenly rolled and plunged toward the earth. [ ] The pilot regained control of the craft only seconds before it would have struck the ground. [ ]

This court has limited the zone of danger analysis to encompass plaintiffs who have been in some actual personal physical danger caused by defendant's negligence. [ ] Whether plaintiff is within a zone of danger is an objective inquiry. [ ]

Thus, cases permitting recovery for negligent infliction of emotional distress are characterized by a reasonable anxiety arising in the plaintiff, with attendant physical manifestation, from being in a situation where it was abundantly clear that plaintiff was in grave personal peril for some specifically defined period of time. Fortune smiled and the imminent calamity did not occur. Here, the situation is quite different. The facts as alleged by T.M.W. indicate that Dr. Benson's actions never did place T.M.W. in "apparent, imminent peril" of contracting HIV because she was not actually exposed to the AIDS virus. [ ] Transmission of HIV from Dr. Benson to plaintiff was, fortunately, never more than a very remote possibility.

That T.M.W.'s risk of contracting HIV was no more than a remote possibility is acknowledged by the numerous resource materials referred to by the district court and the parties. HIV is transmitted through direct fluid-to-fluid contact with the blood, semen, vaginal secretions, or breast milk of an HIV-infected individual. . . .

Documented modes of HIV transmission include: unprotected sexual intercourse with an HIV-infected person; using contaminated needles; contact with HIV-infected blood, blood components, or blood products by parenteral mucous membrane or nonintact skin; transplants of HIV-infected organs and/or tissues; transfusions of HIV-infected blood; artificial insemination of HIV-infected semen; and perinatal transmission from mother to child around the time of birth.

Ninety-nine percent of reported AIDS cases are transmitted by sexual intercourse, intravenous drug abuse, or perinatal transmission.[8]

This court has long recognized that a person within the zone of danger of physical impact who reasonably fears for his or her own safety during the time of exposure, and who consequently suffers severe emotional distress with resultant physical injury, may recover emotional distress damages whether or not physical impact results. [ ] However, a remote possibility of personal peril is insufficient to place plaintiff within a zone of danger for purposes of a claim of negligent infliction of emotional distress.

---

8. [ ]. Even if a person is exposed to HIV-infected body fluids or tissues, transmission of HIV may not necessarily occur. The theoretical risk of HIV transmission from an infected health-care worker to a patient during invasive procedures is minute. Indeed, "a modeled risk estimation by the CDC was that transmission could occur in one of 2.4 million to one of 24 million surgical procedures." [ ] In 1991, the CDC estimated the theoretical risk of HIV transmission from an HIV-infected patient to a health-care worker following actual percutaneous exposure to HIV-infected blood is approximately 0.3 percent per exposure. [ ]

Consequently, we hold that a plaintiff who fails to allege actual exposure to HIV is not, as a matter of law, in personal physical danger of contracting HIV, and thus not within a zone of danger for purposes of establishing a claim for negligent infliction of emotional distress.

The actual exposure requirement we adopt today is consistent with the court's historical caution regarding emotional distress claims. Concerns about unintended and unreasonable results prompted this court to limit negligent infliction of emotional distress claims to persons who experienced personal physical danger as a result of defendant's negligence. We determined the "zone-of-danger rule" would lead to reasonable and consistent results because courts and juries can objectively determine whether plaintiffs were within the zone of danger. [ ] The standard we adopt today, requiring a plaintiff to allege actual exposure to HIV as a predicate to recovery, retains the objective component this court has long deemed necessary to ensure stability and predictability in the disposition of emotional distress claims.

Actual exposure to HIV

We also find persuasive several policy considerations articulated by the California Court of Appeal on remand in Kerins v. Hartley (Kerins II), 27 Cal.App.4th 1062, 33 Cal.Rptr.2d 172 (1994):

> The magnitude of the potential class of plaintiffs seeking emotional distress damages for negligent exposure to HIV or AIDS cannot be overstated. * * * "[t]he devastating effects of AIDS and the widespread fear of contamination at home, work, school, health-care facilities and elsewhere are, sadly, too well known to require further discussion at this point." Proliferation of fear of AIDS claims in the absence of meaningful restrictions would run an equal risk of compromising the availability and affordability of medical, dental and malpractice insurance, medical and dental care, prescription drugs, and blood products. Juries deliberating in fear-of-AIDS lawsuits would be just as likely to reach inconsistent results, discouraging early resolution or settlement of such claims. Last but not least, the coffers of defendants and their insurers would risk being emptied to pay for the emotional suffering of the many plaintiffs uninfected by exposure to HIV or AIDS, possibly leaving inadequate compensation for plaintiffs to whom the fatal AIDS virus was actually transmitted. [ ] (citations omitted).

Although our decision is based upon existing Minnesota case law, we note that it is consistent with the majority of jurisdictions that have addressed the issue of emotional distress damages arising from a plaintiff's fear of contracting HIV. The majority of courts that have decided fear of HIV exposure cases hold the plaintiff must allege actual exposure to HIV to recover emotional distress damages. We concur with the majority of jurisdictions and reject plaintiff's claim in this case. . . .

[The court also rejected claims based on intentional infliction of emotional distress, battery, negligent nondisclosure, and consumer fraud.]

■ COYNE, J., took no part.

■ [JUSTICE PAGE dissented on the battery point because a jury could find that T.M.W. had shown a "substantial mistake concerning the nature of the invasion . . . or the extent of the harm to be expected from it and the mistake is known to the other or is induced by the other's misrepresentation. . . ." (quoting Restatement § 892B(2)). The majority rejected this claim because the defendant performed the procedure that the parties had agreed upon and his conduct "did not significantly increase the risk that T.M.W. would contract HIV."]

NOTES AND QUESTIONS

1. The court notes that in 1892 it decided that "actual physical impact" was not crucial to recovery. Other courts took longer to eliminate the requirement. In Falzone v. Busch, 45 N.J. 559, 214 A.2d 12 (1965), plaintiff claimed that defendant's car had veered across the highway, and, heading in her direction, came "so close to plaintiff as to put her in fear for her safety." The court understood two main reasons to support the impact rule which was being challenged in the case. The first was that it was "not 'probable or natural' for persons of normal health to suffer physical injuries, when subjected to fright, and that since a person whose acts cause fright alone could not reasonably anticipate that physical harm would follow, such acts cannot constitute negligence as to the frightened party." The court responded that this was a question for medical evidence in each case; courts had long recognized that "great emotion, may, and sometimes does, produce physical effects."

The second was that "proof or disproof of fear-induced physical suffering would be so difficult that recovery would often be based on mere conjecture and speculation, and that the door would be opened to extensive litigation in a class of cases where injury is easily feigned." But this problem was not unique to non-impact cases and "occurs in all types of personal injury litigation." As to fraud, courts "should not deny recovery for a type of wrong which may result in serious harm because some people may institute fraudulent actions. Our trial courts retain sufficient control, through the rules of evidence and the requirements as to the sufficiency of evidence, to safeguard against the danger that juries will find facts without legally adequate proof."

As to the fear of a "flood of litigation," the court responded that "fear of an expansion of litigation should not deter courts from granting relief in meritorious cases; the proper remedy is an expansion of the judicial machinery, not a decrease in the availability of justice."

The court did recognize that the lack of impact might mean that plaintiff's suit might come as a surprise to the defendant who would not be able to remember events on what the defendant thought was an uneventful day. To meet this concern, the court stated that the trial judge might charge the jury that an "undue delay in notifying the defendant of the incident and the resulting injury may weigh heavily in determining the truth of the plaintiff's claim." It was unnecessary to decide whether dismissal might sometimes be warranted.

The requirement of impact has virtually disappeared today. For a rare insistence on impact, see R.J. v. Humana of Florida, Inc., 652 So.2d 360 (Fla.1995), in which plaintiff alleged that due to defendants' negligence he was diagnosed as HIV positive and remained under that impression until he was retested 18 months later. The court held that plaintiff would be able to state an actionable claim only if treatments or injections had harmed him.

How might a Florida court analyze *Falzone*? *Benson*? What if the car in *Falzone* had brushed the plaintiff?

2. What role does the "zone of danger" play in the *Benson* court's analysis? Why does the court say that this is an "objective inquiry"? Why does the court require "actual exposure" to the zone of danger rather than ask whether the plaintiff reasonably feared such an exposure? Why is the scientific probability of infection more relevant than what the reasonable patient might have feared on receipt of the letter?

Consider Brzoska v. Olson, 668 A.2d 1355 (Del.1995), in which the court denied recovery to patients for their anxiety based on learning that their dentist had treated them after having been diagnosed as HIV positive. If plaintiffs were understood to be asserting the lack of informed consent, their action failed for want of actual exposure:

> AIDS is a disease that spawns widespread public misperception based upon the dearth of knowledge concerning HIV transmission. Indeed, plaintiffs rely upon the degree of public misconception about AIDS to support their claim that their fear was reasonable. To accept this argument is to contribute to the phobia. Were we to recognize a claim for the fear of contracting AIDS based upon a mere allegation that one may have been exposed to HIV, totally unsupported by any medical evidence or factual proof, we would open a Pandora's Box of "AIDS-phobia" claims by individuals whose ignorance, unreasonable suspicions or general paranoia cause them apprehension over the slightest contact with HIV-infected individual or objects. Such patients would recover for their fear of AIDS, no matter how irrational. [ ] We believe the better approach is to assess the reasonableness of a plaintiff's fear of AIDS according to the plaintiff's actual—not potential—exposure to HIV.

Consider these possibilities: (1) medical science determines that there is virtually no risk to the public from some substance but the findings have not yet been widely publicized; (2) the findings have been widely publicized but are not accepted by the general public; and (3) the findings have been accepted by the mass of the public but some small pockets of the public remain unconvinced.

We consider claims for emotional distress in toxic tort and other mass exposure situations in Chapter V.

3. Why does the court deny recovery in *Benson*? The court notes that it is following the majority view. For a distinct minority view, see Faya v. Almaraz, 329 Md. 435, 620 A.2d 327 (1993), permitting patients to recover in the *Benson* situation for anxiety sustained during the window of uncertainty before they received the results of their tests.

4. The court notes that even where recovery is permitted in this type of case it would be limited to "a reasonable window of anxiety." Recall the case, supra, in which the plaintiff thought he was HIV positive for 18 months.

Another "window" situation is pregnancy. See Jones v. Howard University, Inc., 589 A.2d 419 (D.C.App.1991), upholding a mother's claim for the mental distress she suffered as a result of defendant hospital's negligence in giving her an x-ray exam while she was pregnant. The mother alleged that she suffered emotional distress during her pregnancy term due to the possibility that the radiation had harmed her unborn twins and the chance that she might experience severe pregnancy complications. See also Harris v. Kissling, 80 Or.App. 5, 721 P.2d 838 (1986)(upholding mother's verdict for emotional distress suffered during pregnancy as a result of hospital's negligent failure to conduct Rh blood tests). Does the existence of finite periods of distress make it easier or more difficult to recognize this type of claim?

5. Most courts have allowed recovery where plaintiff was aware of impending death or injury even if the period of time has been very short. See e.g., Solomon v. Warren, 540 F.2d 777 (5th Cir.1976), cert. dismissed 434 U.S. 801 (1977)(claim for passenger in plane that was running low on fuel over the open sea and was never seen again). These cases are quite fact-specific. Compare Shatkin v. McDonnell Douglas Corp., 727 F.2d 202 (2d Cir.1984)(insufficient evidence to show that passenger on right side of plane was even aware of impending disaster until just before the crash) with Shu–Tao Lin v. McDonnell Douglas Corp., 742 F.2d 45 (2d Cir.1984)(upholding judgment of $10,000 for pre-impact fright for passenger in seat over left wing on same flight where jury might reasonably have found that the passenger saw "the left engine and a portion of the wing break away at the beginning of the flight, which lasted some thirty seconds between takeoff and crash").

What if the pilot at the last minute pulls out of what appeared to be a fatal crash? In the cited *Quill* case, the court upheld an award of $50,000 to a passenger in an airplane that plunged 34,000 feet in an uncontrolled tailspin before pilots regained control, and then continued to shake and shudder for 40 minutes until it could be brought to a safe emergency landing. The plaintiff's claim for negligent infliction of emotional distress was grounded in the severe anxiety he experienced after the accident whenever he took an airplane flight. The court held that the plaintiff had made out a prima facie case:

> the unusually disturbing experience plaintiff endured combined with his physical symptoms assure that his claim is real. There can be few experiences as terrifying as being pinned to a seat by gravity forces as

an airplane twists and screams towards earth at just under the speed of sound.

Five other passengers settled with the airline for amounts ranging from $2,000 to $70,000, with the highest awards going to passengers who claimed they were no longer able to fly as a result of the incident. See Leebron, "Final Moments: Damages for Pain and Suffering Prior to Death," 64 N.Y.U.L.Rev. 256, 299 (1989). How might *Quill* be analyzed in an impact state?

The phenomenon of pre-impact fright is not limited to airplane cases. In Nelson v. Dolan, 230 Neb. 848, 434 N.W.2d 25 (1989), the court permitted such a recovery in a case in which defendant motorist negligently collided with plaintiff motorcyclist in such a way that the vehicles interlocked and plaintiff's motorcycle was carried 268 feet before he was killed when his motorcycle hit a light post and went under the automobile. The court estimated that five seconds had passed between the original collision and the death.

6. In Air Crash Disaster Near Cerritos, 973 F.2d 1490 (9th Cir.1992), plaintiffs were at home when they heard a loud crash, followed by another one. The first was two airliners colliding overhead; the second turned out to be the crash of wreckage alleged to have been 100 yards from their home. They alleged a variety of emotional injuries severe enough to require medical attention and "to cause problems in the Di Costas' marriage amounting to a loss of consortium." The court, 2–1, refused to dismiss the complaint. It concluded that persons "in the path of negligent conduct" who reasonably fear for their safety may recover for resulting emotional distress as direct victims. To the dissent's assertion that "noise alone is neither threatening nor dangerous," the majority responded that "the fear is caused by the fact that extremely loud, explosive noise is frequently not 'noise alone.' The Di Costas may reasonably have been put in fear by such a noise, even without knowing whether it was produced by a colliding airplane or some other nearby exploding object."

7. Compare Heiner v. Moretuzzo, 73 Ohio St.3d 80, 652 N.E.2d 664 (1995), in which plaintiff alleged that defendant laboratory incorrectly reported that plaintiff's blood had tested HIV positive and that when it did a retest it improperly used the original sample. Again it reported the result as positive. Some two months after the first test, plaintiff was tested again by a different tester and was reported negative. This was confirmed by a fourth test. Plaintiff's claim for emotional distress was rejected, 5–2, on the ground that the "claimed negligent diagnosis never placed [plaintiff] or any other person in real physical peril, since [plaintiff] was, in fact, HIV negative." This distinguished the present case from others in which the person seeking recovery "had been aware of a real and existing physical peril." The court concluded by noting that it had "no doubt that the emotional injuries suffered by [plaintiff] were real and debilitating. However, the facts of this case remind us that not every wrong is deserving of a legal remedy."

8. Why does the *Benson* court list "attendant physical manifestations" as one element of plaintiff's claim? The court says nothing more than that plaintiff sought to recover for "emotional damages she allegedly suffered" upon receiving the letter. What would be added to the case if plaintiff alleged that she had vomited or developed persistent headaches after reading the letter? Note also that *Falzone* required a showing of "substantial bodily injury or sickness" to support the action. We return to the need for physical manifestations after the following case, in which there was no threat to plaintiff's personal safety.

Gammon v. Osteopathic Hospital of Maine, Inc.

Supreme Judicial Court of Maine, 1987.
534 A.2d 1282.

[Plaintiff's father, Linwood, died in defendant hospital. Plaintiff asked defendant funeral home to make the arrangements. He alleged that the defendants negligently conducted their operations so that he received a bag that was supposedly personal effects, but which in fact contained "a bloodied leg, severed below the knee, and bluish in color." He yelled "Oh my God, they have taken my father's leg off." He ran into the kitchen where an aunt testified that he "was as white as a ghost." In fact the leg was a pathology specimen removed from another person. Thereafter, plaintiff "began having nightmares for the first time in his life, his personality was affected and his relationship with his wife and children deteriorated." After several months Gammon's emotional state began to improve, although he still had occasional nightmares. He sought no medical or psychiatric attention and offered no medical evidence at trial.

The trial court granted a directed verdict on count I—plaintiff's negligence claim for severe emotional distress. On other counts, not directly relevant here, the judge had charged the jury that "severe emotional distress" was distress "such that no reasonable man should be expected to endure it."]

■ Before MCKUSICK, C.J., and NICHOLS, ROBERTS, WATHEN, SCOLNIK and CLIFFORD, JJ.

■ ROBERTS, JUSTICE. [after stating the facts].

The issue is whether, in these circumstances, Gammon has established a claim, in tort, for negligent infliction of severe emotional distress. A person's psychic well-being is as much entitled to legal protection as is his physical well-being. We recognize as much and provide compensation when the emotional distress is intentionally or recklessly inflicted, when the emotional distress results from physical injury negligently inflicted, or when negligently inflicted emotional distress results in physical injury. In order to ensure that a claim for emotional distress without physical injury is not spurious, we have previously required a showing of physical impact, objective manifestation, underlying or accompanying tort, or special circumstances. In the case before us, we conclude that these more or less arbitrary requirements should not bar Gammon's claim for compensation for severe emotional distress.

[At this point the court reviewed eight emotional distress cases it had decided over a period of 100 years.]

No useful purpose would be served by more detailed analyses of our prior decisions or by consideration of whether the holdings of these cases follow a consistent trend.   They demonstrate in a variety of ways the difficulty courts have had dealing with psychic injury.[5] They also demonstrate the frailty of supposed lines of demarcation when they are subjected to judicial scrutiny in the context of varying fact patterns.   Moreover, these cases disclose our awareness of the extensive criticism aimed at the artificial devices used by courts to protect against fraudulent claims and against undue burden on the conduct of defendants.

The analyses of commentators and the developing trend in case law encourage us to abandon these artificial devices in this and future tort actions and to rely upon the trial process for protection against fraudulent claims.   In addition, the traditional tort principle of foreseeability relied upon in [two earlier cases] provides adequate protection against unduly burdensome liability claims for emotional distress.   Jurors or trial judges will be able to evaluate the impact of psychic trauma with no greater difficulty than pertains to assessment of damages for any intangible injury. We do not foresee any great extension of tort liability by our ruling today. We do not provide compensation for the hurt feelings of the supersensitive plaintiff—the eggshell psyche.   A defendant is bound to foresee psychic harm only when such harm reasonably could be expected to befall the ordinarily sensitive person.[8]

We have previously recognized that courts in other jurisdictions have allowed recovery for mental distress alone for negligent mishandling of corpses.   [ ]   In recognizing that Gammon has made out a claim in the instant case, we do not find it necessary to rely on an extension of this exception.   Instead, we look to the rationale supporting the exception. Courts have concluded that the exceptional vulnerability of the family of recent decedents makes it highly probable that emotional distress will result from mishandling the body.   [ ]   That high probability is said to provide sufficient trustworthiness to allay the court's fear of fraudulent claims.   [ ]   This rationale, it seems, is but another way of determining that the defendant reasonably should have foreseen that mental distress would result from his negligence.   By the same token, on the record before us, a jury could conclude that the hospital and the mortician reasonably

---

5. When discussing this type of injury, the courts of other jurisdictions and the commentators have used as the adjective either "emotional, mental, nervous or psychic" together with the noun "distress, pain, injury, harm, trauma, disturbance or shock." These phrases have not become words of art although each, with varying degrees of accura-cy, seems to refer to non-tactile trauma resulting in injury to the psyche.

8. We described serious mental distress in [an earlier case] as being "where a reasonable person, normally constituted, would be unable to adequately cope with the mental stress engendered by the circumstances of the event." [ ]

should have foreseen that members of Linwood Gammon's family would be vulnerable to emotional shock at finding a severed leg in what was supposed to be the decedent's personal effects. Despite the defendants' argument to the contrary, we hold that the evidence in this case would support a jury finding that either or both defendants failed to exercise reasonable care to prevent such an occurrence.

Although the analysis in the instant case may impact upon the rationale of our recent cases, we do not find it necessary to overrule those cases. We do not hold that any prior case was wrongly decided. Rather, we recognize that the elimination of some barriers to recovery for negligent infliction of severe emotional distress may compel further evaluation of other policy considerations. . . .

On the facts and circumstances of the case before us, however, we find no sound basis to preclude potential compensation to Gammon. We hold, therefore, that the trial court erred in directing a verdict on Gammon's claim for negligent infliction of severe emotional distress.[9] Accordingly, we vacate the judgment in favor of the defendants on Count I.

Remanded for further proceedings consistent with the opinion herein.

NOTES AND QUESTIONS

1. Is this a situation involving death and the special sensitivity of families after a death? If not, are there any limits to the type of situation that may give rise to a claim like plaintiff's?

Building on § 868 of the Restatement, some states permit recovery without physical injury in cases of mishandled corpses and botched burials and some states agree. For a recent rejection of recovery in a case alleging that defendants negligently failed to provide a proper burial for a newborn baby, and left it in a refrigerated drawer at the hospital morgue for two months, see Gonzalez v. Metropolitan Dade County Public Health Trust, 651 So.2d 673 (Fla.1995):

> While we recognize that cases involving negligent mishandling of corpses entail real and palpable injury to feelings, and it may even be true that the "special circumstances" guarantee the authenticity of the claim, there is no accurate method of separating the natural grief resulting from the death of a loved one from the additional grief suffered as a result of mishandling of the body.

Are there other reasons to deny recovery in such cases? To permit it?

A second situation that leads a significant number of states to permit recovery without physical injury involves the emotional distress that arises

---

9. By virtue of the pleadings and the jury finding in the case before us, our holding necessarily is limited to negligently inflicted severe emotional distress. We do not decide whether a defendant shall be liable for negligently inflicted emotional distress of any lesser degree.

when a telegram arrives that negligently and incorrectly announces that a family member has died.

2. Is the *Gammon* court's discussion of the nature of the harm required likely to keep the action from expanding to anyone suffering emotional harm from any negligent act?

3. In Chizmar v. Mackie, 896 P.2d 196 (Alaska 1995), plaintiff alleged that defendant physician incorrectly and negligently informed her that she was HIV positive and that this news had caused severe emotional distress. The court upheld an action in this situation. Is there impact? Is there a risk to plaintiff's safety? The court also concluded that the harm in this type of case may well last past the date on which she learns that she is negative. For other misdiagnosis cases, recall *Heiner,* p. 233, supra, and see Weidlich, Suits by Patients Surge in Misdiagnosed AIDS Cases, Natl. L.J., Aug. 7, 1995 at A12. How might the *Gammon* court analyze this case?

4. In Nieman v. Upper Queens Medical Group, 220 N.Y.S.2d 129 (City Ct. 1961), the defendant negligently reported to plaintiff's physician that plaintiff's sperm count indicated sterility. The physician passed the results on to the plaintiff who sued for severe mental distress. The court upheld the complaint. Do you agree? How might the *Gammon* court analyze this case?

5. In Holliday v. Jones, 215 Cal.App.3d 102, 264 Cal.Rptr. 448 (1989) a client's conviction for involuntary manslaughter had been reversed in an earlier appeal based on the incompetence of his privately retained counsel. On retrial, with a different lawyer, the client was acquitted. The client subsequently sued the attorney who had been found incompetent seeking, among other items, damages for emotional distress. The court upheld a judgment for the client on the ground that he had a special relationship with the attorney. Suits by the client's children for emotional distress were rejected on the ground that they had "no contractual or other relationship with" the attorney. How might the *Gammon* court decide *Holliday?*

6. Even courts like *Gammon* that recognize actions where there is no risk of physical danger, may disagree about whether the plaintiff must show some residual physical manifestations from the distress. In *Chizmar,* supra, involving the false diagnosis that plaintiff was HIV positive, the court noted that in such cases it had generally held that emotional distress without physical manifestations was not actionable. Here, however, the professional relationship between physician and patient, and the patient's reliance on the expertise of the physician, justified an exception that tracked the one for wrongful death telegrams: if a state does not require physical manifestations when one receives false news of the death of a close relative, the same rule should apply when the plaintiff receives false news that she herself will soon die.

7. How can a jury or a judge identify "severe emotional distress?" Is the trial judge's suggested standard in *Gammon* adequate? What does the *Benson* court mean by an "ordinarily sensitive person"?

The *Chizmar* court, supra, adopted the standard of Rodrigues v. State, 52 Haw. 156, 472 P.2d 509 (1970) that where "severe" or "serious" emotional distress suffices, it is shown "where a reasonable man, normally constituted, would be unable to adequately cope with the mental stress engendered by the circumstances of the case." *Chizmar* then added that "examples of serious emotional distress may include 'neuroses, psychoses, chronic depression, phobia, and shock.' [ ] However, temporary fright, disappointment or regret does not suffice. . . ." Although "some jurisdictions have required claims of emotional distress to be 'medically diagnosable or objectifiable,' we do not believe that such a limitation is necessary or desirable." The existence of the required distress was a matter of proof for the trier of fact.

8. In Sullivan v. Boston Gas Co., 414 Mass. 129, 605 N.E.2d 805 (1993), the two plaintiffs, McDonald and Sullivan, stood across the street as their house burned to the ground allegedly due to defendant's negligence. (Note that property loss was the alleged trigger of this distress.) In an earlier case the court had said that in emotional distress cases the plaintiff need generally show, in addition to other items, "physical harm manifested by objective symptomatology." The court paraphrased Restatement section 436, which rejected the line between physical and mental harm in this area and concluded that "repeated hysterical attacks" are illnesses sufficient to corroborate the existence of the claimed distress; that "headaches or nausea" could qualify if they "lasted for a substantial period of time," but that "transient symptoms such as vomiting" did not qualify "even though they clearly involve physical functions of the body."

Plaintiff McDonald alleged that she suffered from posttraumatic stress disorder that sometimes occurred as often as once or twice a week, the symptoms of which were diarrhea and heart palpitation. In addition, she asserted that she had experienced "sleeplessness, weeping, depression, and feelings of despair." Sullivan alleged that he had experienced tension headaches, muscle tenderness in the back of his head, and problems with concentration and reading, as well as "sleeplessness, gastrointestinal distress, upset stomach, nightmares, depression, feelings of despair, difficulty in driving and working, and an over-all 'lousy' feeling" from the explosion. Both were held to meet the required standard, which was seen as an attempt to strike a balance between "our desire to ferret out fraudulent claims and our duty to grant deserving plaintiffs a chance to present their case to a fact finder."

Portee v. Jaffee

Supreme Court of New Jersey, 1980.
84 N.J. 88, 417 A.2d 521.

[Plaintiff and her seven-year-old son, Guy, lived in an apartment building owned by Jaffee. One afternoon Guy became trapped in the building's elevator between its outer door and the wall of the elevator shaft. The elevator was activated and the boy was dragged up to the third floor. Another child ran to seek help. Plaintiff and police arrived and the police worked for four and one-half hours to free the child. While their efforts continued, plaintiff "watched as her son moaned, cried out and flailed his arms. Much of the time she was restrained from touching him, apparently to prevent interference with the attempted rescue." Guy suffered multiple bone fractures and internal injuries. He died while still trapped, "his mother a helpless observer." Companies involved in designing and maintaining the elevator were also sued.

After Guy's death, plaintiff became severely depressed and self-destructive. She slashed her wrist in a suicide attempt and required physical therapy for her wrist and extensive counseling and psychotherapy. The trial court granted summary judgment for defendants on claims by plaintiff for mental and emotional distress. The dismissal was reviewed directly by the supreme court.]

The opinion of the Court was delivered by

■ PASHMAN, J. [after stating the facts].

. . .

On many occasions, the law of negligence needs no other formulation besides the duty of reasonable care. Other cases, however, present circumstances rendering application of that general standard difficult, if not impossible. Without adequate guidance, juries may impose liability that is not commensurate with the culpability of defendant's conduct.

This difficulty has been recognized when courts considered liability for mental and emotional distress. We have noted the traditional argument, rejected by this Court in *Falzone*, that the imposition of such liability unoccasioned by any physical impact would lead to "mere conjecture and speculation." [ ] Even where the causal relationship between conduct and emotional harm was clear, courts would deny liability unless the fault of defendant's conduct could be demonstrated by the occurrence of physical harm to the plaintiff. [ ] Under *Falzone*, it became clear that the creation of a risk of physical harm would be a sufficient indication that defendant's conduct was unreasonable. Without such an indication, it might be argued that a jury could not form a reliable judgment regarding negligence. The question now before us is whether we are left to "mere conjecture and speculation" in assessing the culpability of conduct that creates neither the risk nor the occurrence of physical harm.

The task in the present case involves the refinement of principles of liability to remedy violations of reasonable care while avoiding speculative results or punitive liability. The solution is close scrutiny of the specific personal interests assertedly injured. By this approach, we can determine whether a defendant's freedom of action should be burdened by the imposition of liability. In the present case, the interest assertedly injured is more than a general interest in emotional tranquility. It is the profound and abiding sentiment of parental love. The knowledge that loved ones are

safe and whole is the deepest wellspring of emotional welfare. Against that
reassuring background, the flashes of anxiety and disappointment that mar
our lives take on softer hues. No loss is greater than the loss of a loved
one, and no tragedy is more wrenching than the helpless apprehension of
the death or serious injury of one whose very existence is a precious
treasure. The law should find more than pity for one who is stricken by
seeing that a loved one has been critically injured or killed.

Courts in other jurisdictions which have found liability in the circumstances before us have placed limits on this type of negligence liability
consistent with their view of the individual interest being injured. In
Dillon v. Legg, 68 Cal.2d 728, 441 P.2d 912, 69 Cal.Rptr. 72 (1968), the
California Supreme Court identified three factors which would determine
whether an emotional injury would be compensable because "foreseeable":

> (1) Whether plaintiff was located near the scene of the accident as
> contrasted with one who was a distance away from it. (2) Wheth-
> er the shock resulted from a direct emotional impact upon plaintiff
> from the sensory and contemporaneous observance of the accident,
> as contrasted with learning of the accident from others after its
> occurrence. (3) Whether plaintiff and the victim were closely
> related, as contrasted with an absence of any relationship or the
> presence of only a distant relationship. [   ]

We agree that the three factors described in *Dillon* together create a
strong case for negligence liability. In any given case, as physical proximity between plaintiff and the scene of the accident becomes closer, the
foreseeable likelihood that plaintiff will suffer emotional distress from
apprehending the physical harm of another increases. The second requirement of "direct . . . sensory and contemporaneous observance" appears to reflect a limitation of the liability rule to traumatic distress
occasioned by immediate perception. The final criterion, that the plaintiff
be "closely related" to the injured person, also embodies the judgment that
only the most profound emotional interests should receive vindication for
their negligent injury.

Our analysis of the specific emotional interest injured in this case—a
fundamental interest in emotional tranquility founded on parental love—
reveals where the limits of liability would lie. Addressing the *Dillon*
criteria in reverse order, we find the last—the existence of a close relationship—to be the most crucial. It is the presence of deep, intimate, familial
ties between the plaintiff and the physically injured person that makes the
harm to emotional tranquility so serious and compelling. The genuine
suffering which flows from such harm stands in stark contrast to the
setbacks and sorrows of everyday life, or even to the apprehension of harm
to another, less intimate person. The existence of a marital or intimate
familial relationship is therefore an essential element of a cause of action
for negligent infliction of emotional distress. In the present case, the
instinctive affection of a mother for her seven-year-old son would be a
sufficiently intimate bond on which to predicate liability.

The second requirement—that the plaintiff witness the incident which resulted in death or serious injury—is equally essential. We recognize that to deny recovery solely because the plaintiff was not subjected to a risk of physical harm would impose an arbitrary barrier that bears no relation to the injury to his basic emotional stability. [ ] Yet avoiding arbitrary distinctions does not entail that a cause of action should exist for all emotional injuries to all the close relatives of the victim. This expansive view would extend judicial redress far beyond the bounds of the emotional interest entitled to protection. To avoid imposing liability in excess of culpability, the scope of recovery must be circumscribed to negligent conduct which strikes at the plaintiff's basic emotional security.

Discovering the death or serious injury of an intimate family member will always be expected to threaten one's emotional welfare. Ordinarily, however, only a witness at the scene of the accident causing death or serious injury will suffer a traumatic sense of loss that may destroy his sense of security and cause severe emotional distress. . . . Such a risk of severe emotional distress is present when the plaintiff observes the accident at the scene. Without such perception, the threat of emotional injury is lessened and the justification for liability is fatally weakened. The law of negligence, while it redresses suffering wrongfully caused by others, must not itself inflict undue harm by imposing an unreasonably excessive measure of liability. Accordingly, we hold that observing the death or serious injury of another while it occurs is an essential element of a cause of action for the negligent infliction of emotional distress.

The first factor discussed in *Dillon*—that the plaintiff be near the injured person—embodies the same observations made concerning the other requirements of direct perception and close familial relationship. Physical proximity may be of some relevance in demonstrating the closeness of the emotional bond between plaintiff and the injured family member. For example, one would generally suppose that the risk of emotional distress to a brother who is halfway across the country is not as great as to a mother who is at the scene of the accident. The proximity of the plaintiff to the accident scene increases the likelihood that he will witness the event causing the death or serious injury of a loved one. Yet it appears that if the plaintiff must observe the accident that causes death or serious injury, a requirement of proximity is necessarily satisfied. The risk of emotional injury exists by virtue of the plaintiff's perception of the accident, not his proximity to it.

An additional factor yet undiscussed is the severity of the physical injury causing emotional distress. The harm we have determined to be worthy of judicial redress is the trauma accompanying the observation of the death or serious physical injury of a loved one. While any harm to a spouse or a family member causes sorrow, we are here concerned with a more narrowly confined interest in mental and emotional stability. When confronted with accidental death, "the reaction to be expected of normal persons," [ ], is shock and fright. We hold that the observation of either death or this type of serious injury is necessary to permit recovery. Since the sense of loss attendant to death or serious injury is typically not present following lesser accidental harm, perception of less serious harm would not ordinarily result in severe emotional distress. Thus, the risk of an extraordinary reaction to less serious injury is not sufficient to result in liability. To impose liability for any emotional consequence of negligent conduct would be unreasonable; it would also be unnecessary to protect a plaintiff's basic emotional stability. Therefore, a cause of action for emotional distress would require the perception of death or serious physical injury.

The cause of action we approve today for the negligent infliction of emotional distress requires proof of the following elements: (1) the death or serious physical injury of another caused by defendant's negligence; (2) a marital or intimate familial relationship between plaintiff and the injured person; (3) observation of the death or injury at the scene of the accident; and (4) resulting severe emotional distress. We find that a defendant's duty of reasonable care to avoid physical harm to others extends to the avoidance of this type of mental and emotional harm. . . .

. . .

[The trial court judgment was reversed.]

■ For *reversal*—CHIEF JUSTICE WILENTZ, and JUSTICES SULLIVAN, PASHMAN, CLIFFORD, SCHREIBER, HANDLER and POLLOCK—7.

For *affirmance*—none.

NOTES AND QUESTIONS

1. At several points, the *Portee* court expresses concern that "juries may impose liability that is not commensurate with the culpability of defendant's conduct." Is this more of a concern in cases producing nonphysical harm than in those involving broken bones and death?

2. The *Dillon–Portee* elements of proximity to the scene and sensory impact are closely related to each other, but are not overlapping. In Scherr v. Las Vegas Hilton, 168 Cal.App.3d 908, 214 Cal.Rptr. 393 (1985), plaintiff wife, in California, saw live television coverage of a fire then taking place at the Las Vegas Hilton Hotel. She knew her husband was attending a meeting at that hotel and that he was supposed to be in the hotel at that time. She never saw him on camera and did not discover until later that he had in fact been hurt in the fire. The court found that plaintiff had failed to come within the sensory perception requirement. Her perception "of endangerment, while potentially stressful, is insufficient to cause legally cognizable harm, for the stress has not yet ripened into disabling shock." The court did not reach the television aspect of the case. What if the plaintiff had watched her husband, about to be enveloped by flames, jump from a balcony on a high floor and hit the ground? See also Gain v. Carroll Mill Co., Inc., 114 Wash.2d 254, 787 P.2d 553 (1990), a case apparently involving a televised viewing of an event, but avoiding decision on that ground.

3. What if the mother in *Portee* had arrived at the scene a half hour after Guy had died, because she had been shopping and could not be found immediately? In Ferriter v. Daniel O'Connell's Sons, Inc., 381 Mass. 507, 413 N.E.2d 690 (1980), the wife and children of an accident victim first observed him in the hospital paralyzed from the neck down. On summary judgment, the court thought that "we may infer that the shock occurred immediately after the accident. A plaintiff who rushes onto the accident scene and finds a loved one injured has no greater entitlement to compensation for the shock than a plaintiff who rushes instead to the hospital. So long as the shock follows closely on the heels of the accident, the two types of injury are equally foreseeable."

In Stockdale v. Bird & Son, Inc., 399 Mass. 249, 503 N.E.2d 951 (1987), plaintiff was the mother of a 21–year–old son who had been killed by the alleged negligence of defendant. She learned of the death from the police four hours after it had occurred. She first saw the body 24 hours later in a funeral home. The plaintiff sustained physical and mental suffering that began shortly after learning of the death. The son had lived at home until his death. A unanimous court rejected the claim for negligently inflicted emotional distress. The two lengths of time distinguished the case from *Ferriter*. Does the likelihood of serious emotional harm depend on how soon after the accident the plaintiff learns of the consequences?

4. The *Portee* court adds another element of death or serious injury to the victim. In Barnhill v. Davis, 300 N.W.2d 104 (Iowa 1981), the plaintiff and his mother were driving one behind the other to the same destination. After plaintiff cleared an intersection, he looked in the rear view mirror and saw his mother's car hit on the driver's side by the defendant's car. In fact, the mother was only slightly injured. Plaintiff alleged serious emotional and physical harm from his concern before he learned how slight the injury was. The court said the proper test was whether a reasonable person would believe, and the plaintiff did believe, that his mother would be seriously injured by the type of accident that occurred.

Compare Barnes v. Geiger, 15 Mass.App. 365, 446 N.E.2d 78 (1983), involving a mother who reasonably but mistakenly thought that her child had been horribly injured in an accident that she had witnessed. The victim of that accident was in fact an unrelated child. The mother died the next day from trauma alleged to have resulted from her experience. The court denied recovery:

> Daily life is too full of momentary perturbation. Injury to a child and the protracted anguish placed upon the witnessing parent is, on the scale of human experience, tangible and predictable. Distress based on mistake as to the circumstances is ephemeral and will vary with the disposition of a person to imagine that the worst has happened. We are unwilling to expand the circle of liability [established in earlier cases] to such an additional dimension, because to do so expands unreasonably the class of person to whom a tortfeasor may be liable.

In Sell v. Mary Lanning Memorial Hospital Assn., 243 Neb. 266, 498 N.W.2d 522 (1993), plaintiff mother had been incorrectly and negligently informed that her son had been killed. After two days of planning the funeral, she learned that there had been a case of mistaken identity. Plaintiff's suit for emotional distress was rejected, 4–3, even though Nebraska has indicated a broader approach than the *Portee-Dillon* line.

The majority held that plaintiff's reactions—continual crying, trouble eating and sleeping, and some medication—were inadequate. "Without minimizing plaintiff's apparent and understandable heartache upon being told of her son's death," she had not met the required standard. According to a concurring judge "we should shed tears for the loss of [the dead youth], empathize with the grief of his family and friends, rejoice in Scott Sell's life, and move on." The dissenters thought no further evidence was needed where a mother thought her child had been killed. "I hope our society has not reached the point where we need a doctor to tell us what emotional impact results from loss of a child."

5.   After a period of expansion, California has narrowed its decisions in this area. Contrast the various opinions, all supporting recovery, in *Ochoa v. Superior Court,* 39 Cal.3d 159, 703 P.2d 1, 216 Cal.Rptr. 661 (1985)(mother watched child in juvenile hall deteriorate from apparently serious illness when medical staff would not respond to the emergency; he died after she left for the night) with *Thing v. La Chusa,* 48 Cal.3d 644, 771 P.2d 814, 257 Cal.Rptr. 865 (1989)(mother, who was nearby, neither heard nor saw accident injuring her child, but was told about it and rushed to the scene to see the child's bloody and unconscious body lying in the roadway). The court in *Thing* concluded after extensive discussion that the three factors set forth in *Dillon* were defining elements and not simply guidelines:

> We conclude . . . that a plaintiff may recover damages for emotional distress caused by observing the negligently inflicted injury of a third person if, but only if [the three factors are present.]

> The dictum in *Ochoa* suggesting that the factors noted in the *Dillon* guidelines are not essential in determining whether a plaintiff is a foreseeable victim of defendant's negligence should not be relied on. . . . Experience has shown that, contrary to the expectation of the *Dillon* majority, . . . there are clear judicial days on which a court can foresee forever and thus determine liability but none on which that foresight alone provides a socially and judicially acceptable limit on recovery of damages for that injury.

In elaborating on the three elements, the court stated that "absent exceptional circumstances, recovery should be limited to relatives residing in the same household, or parents, siblings, children, and grandparents of the victim." As to the second element, the viewing of "consequences" of an accident was insufficient—even if they were, as the dissent had argued, "immediate consequences." As to the third element, the court identified the requisite distress as "a reaction beyond that which would be anticipated in a disinterested witness and which is not an abnormal response to the circumstances." Is it superfluous to require that plaintiff be in a close relationship with the victim and then to require a reaction beyond "that which would be anticipated in a disinterested witness"?

6. Many states have not moved as far as the multi-factor tests for bystander recovery adopted in *Dillon* and *Portee.* One of those is New York. Early on, Tobin v. Grossman, 24 N.Y.2d 609, 249 N.E.2d 419, 301 N.Y.S.2d 554 (1969), rejected *Dillon,* concluding that it would be difficult if not impossible to draw lines limiting the action. No recovery for emotional distress was to be permitted in such cases. In Bovsun v. Sanperi, 61 N.Y.2d 219, 461 N.E.2d 843, 473 N.Y.S.2d 357 (1984), the court, 4–3, overruled *Tobin's* total refusal to allow an action, and extended a duty to members of the "immediate family" who were themselves in the zone of physical danger:

> The zone-of-danger rule, which allows one who is himself or herself threatened with bodily harm in consequence of the defendant's negligence to recover for emotional distress resulting from viewing the death or serious physical injury of a member of his or her immediate family, is . . . premised on the traditional negligence concept that by unreasonably endangering the plaintiff's physical safety the defendant has breached a duty owed to him or her for which he or she should recover all damages sustained including those occasioned by witnessing the suffering of an immediate family member who is also injured by the defendant's conduct. Recognition of this right to recover for emotional distress attributable to observation of injuries suffered by a member of the immediate family involves a broadening of the duty concept but—unlike the *Dillon* approach—not the creation of a duty to a plaintiff to whom the defendant is not already recognized as owing a duty to avoid bodily harm. In so doing it permits recovery for an element of damages not heretofore allowed. Use of the zone-of-danger rule thus mitigates the possibility of unlimited recovery, an overriding apprehension expressed in *Tobin,* by restricting liability in a much narrower fashion than does the *Dillon* rule. Additionally, the circumstances in which a plaintiff who is within the zone of danger suffers serious emotional distress from observing severe physical injury or death of a member of the immediate family may not be altogether common.

In addition, the emotional distress had to be "serious and verifiable." The dissenters would have adhered to *Tobin.* Do you consider either the *Tobin* or the *Bovsun* approach preferable to the *Dillon–Portee* approach?

7. *Gammon reprised.* After deciding *Gammon,* p. 234, supra, the Maine court, which had previously adopted a *Dillon-Portee* approach to bystander cases, was urged to shift to the foreseeability approach without the constraints of required elements. In Cameron v. Pepin, 610 A.2d 279 (Me.1992), the plaintiffs had first seen their fatally injured son in the hospital "shortly" after the accident and had stayed with him for the six days until he died. The court adhered to the distinction between "direct" and "indirect" victims. Rejecting the plaintiffs' argument that this would amount to an "arbitrary and artificial device contrary to *Gammon*'s principle," the court stressed that duty was not necessarily coextensive with foreseeability.

In *Gammon*, the court saw no reasons to impose added limits. Here, however, the court was concerned about "unlimited liability and liability out of all proportion to culpability." This led the court to reject "the pure foreseeability standard" and to recognize that the "scope of defendant's duty should be limited to the emotional vulnerability that arises in parents upon actually witnessing their child receiving an injury. The impact of such an experience is surely qualitatively and quantitatively different from the distress occasioned by a subsequent visit to the hospital."

How would a "pure foreseeability" court analyze a case in which a class of kindergarten children on a trip to a museum see a car go through a red light and kill two of their classmates? Would it be different if senior citizen residents of a retirement home had such an experience?

In 1995, the following accident occurred in New York City. As a man held the door of an elevator for an exiting woman on the second floor, a second woman caught her foot. As the man moved to free her, the elevator suddenly lurched upward with its doors still open. The movement decapitated the man sending his body to the hallway floor while the elevator continued up to the ninth floor with other passengers and the decapitated man's head—with his Walkman earphones still attached. S.F. Examiner, Jan. 7, 1995, at 2. How would current law handle suits by the passengers—and their spouses? How should it handle such suits?

8. *Unmarried Couples and Emotional Distress.* In Elden v. Sheldon, 46 Cal.3d 267, 758 P.2d 582, 250 Cal.Rptr. 254 (1988), Richard was hurt in an auto accident allegedly caused by the defendant's negligence. This case involved claims for his emotional distress from witnessing the death of Linda who was in Richard's car and with whom Richard alleged he had an "unmarried cohabitation relationship . . . which was both stable and significant and parallel to a marital relationship." The court, 6–1, relying on three "policy reasons," affirmed dismissal of claims for emotional distress and also for loss of consortium.

The first was that "the state has a strong interest in the marriage relationship; to the extent unmarried cohabitants are granted the same rights as married persons, the state's interest in promoting marriage is inhibited. . . . The policy favoring marriage is 'rooted in the necessity of providing an institutional basis for defining the fundamental relational rights and responsibilities of persons in organized society.' [ ] Formally married couples are granted significant rights and bear important responsibilities toward one another which are not shared by those who cohabit without marriage." The court cited property rights and support obligations, among others.

The second justification for rejecting the claim was that acceptance of such claims would impose "a difficult burden on the courts" requiring inquiry into whether the relationship "was stable and significant" and into such matters as "sexual fidelity."

The third justification was the need to "limit the number of persons to whom a negligent defendant owes a duty of care." Since every injury has ramifying consequences "the problem for the law is to limit the legal consequences of wrongs to a controllable degree." Here it was enough to allow recovery to those in close family relationships. A "bright line in this area of the law is essential."

The dissenter, in addition to responding to the three points, noted that the majority would presumably preclude "any gay or lesbian plaintiff from stating a *Dillon* cause of action based on the injury of his or her partner. [ ] Clearly the state's interest in marriage is not advanced by precluding recovery to couples who could not in any case choose marriage."

The *Elden* approach was rejected in Dunphy v. Gregor, 136 N.J. 99, 642 A.2d 372 (1994), involving a claim by a woman who witnessed the death of her fiancé. They had been engaged two years earlier and had set the wedding for four years hence. Plaintiff alleged that at the time of the death they had been living together for two years, had taken out life-insurance policies making each other beneficiaries; maintained a joint checking account from which they paid their bills, and had jointly purchased an automobile. In addition, she alleged that the decedent "had asked her several times to elope with him, and he had introduced her in public as his wife."

The court, 5–1, after reviewing *Portee v. Jaffee* and its progeny at length, was "convinced that the solution to the posed question lies not in a hastily-drawn 'bright line' distinction between married and unmarried persons but in the 'sedulous application' of the principles of tort law." The nature and extent of the harm was to be judged by inquiring into such matters as "the duration of the relationship, the degree of mutual dependence, the extent of common contributions to a life together, the extent and quality of shared experience, and, [quoting the court below] 'whether the plaintiff and the injured person were members of the same household, their emotional reliance on each other, the particulars of their day to day relationship, and the manner in which they related to each other in attending to life's mundane requirements.'" The court said that these inquiries must be made in the case of married couples in emotional distress and in loss of consortium cases to assess the harm done to that relationship.

9. *Loss of Consortium.* Interference with the marital relationship has been the subject of legal concern for centuries. Early on, courts recognized two actions for intentional interference with the relation. The action for "criminal conversation" involved "sexual intercourse of an outsider with husband or wife," and is the tort action based on adultery. Historically, the action was available only to husbands because of the early property rights approach to the relationship between husband and wife. In recent times some states have extended the action to wives as well. But some 20 states have abolished the action entirely either legislatively or judicially. The details of these claims are explored in Chapter XII dealing with intentional harm.

10. *Negligent interference with consortium.* The history of liability to one spouse for seriously injuring the other is traced in the following extended excerpt from the opinion of Justice Kaplan in Diaz v. Eli Lilly & Co., 364 Mass. 153, 302 N.E.2d 555 (1973):

In olden days, when married women were under legal disabilities corresponding to their inferior social status, any action for personal or other injuries to the wife was brought in the names of the husband and wife, and the husband was ordinarily entitled to the avails of the action as of his own property. The husband had, in addition, his own recourse by action without even nominal joinder of the wife against those who invaded the conjugal relationship, for example, by criminal conversation with or abduction of his wife. At one time the gravamen of the latter claims for loss of consortium was the deprivation of the wife's services conceived to be owing by the wife to the husband; the action was similar to that of a master for enticement of his servant. Later the grounds of the consortium action included loss of the society of the wife and impairment of relations with her as a sexual partner, and emphasis shifted away from loss of her services or earning capacity. The defendant, moreover, need not have infringed upon the marital relation by an act of adultery or the like, for he could inflict similar injuries upon the husband in the way of loss of consortium by an assault upon the wife or even a negligent injury. Meanwhile, what of the wife's rights? She had none analogous to the husband's. The husband was of course perfectly competent to sue without joinder of the wife for injuries to himself, and there was no thought that the wife had any legal claim to the husband's services or his sexual or other companionship—any claim, at any rate, in the form of a cause of action for third-party damage to the relationship.

With the coming in of the married women's acts in the mid-nineteenth century, the wife became competent to sue in her own name for injuries to herself and could retain the proceeds of those actions. Her injuries for which she could recover judgment included loss of her capacity to render services in the home as well as to earn money on the outside; the husband, in Massachusetts at least, no longer had a claim even for household help required because of his wife's disablement. The question naturally arose whether after the married women's acts the husband's actions above described for loss of consortium should be ruled obsolete or whether, on the contrary, they should be held to survive in substantial dimension and be complemented by analogous remedies extended to the wife. To be sure, loss of the wife's services or earnings could no longer figure in a right of consortium on the part of the husband, but the other components of the right—the wife's society or companionship or assistance and her sexual availability—could remain. It was held very widely that husbands still retained their consortium rights, the element of loss of wives' services and earnings, however, being excluded from the husbands' recoveries as belonging to the wives themselves. And it was generally held that the new status of married women implied at least some rights of consortium on their part. If adultery with or alienation of the affections of a wife was a wrong to the husband, similar traffic of another woman with the husband should be actionable by the wife. Wives were readily accorded these rights of action.

However, there was difficulty about wives' recovery for acts of third parties not so plainly attacking the marriage relation, say acts of negligence toward the husband injuring him in such a way as to deprive the wife of his society and sexual comfort. The difficulty was perhaps traceable in the end to the reluctance of judges to accept the women's emancipation acts as introducing a broad general premise for fresh decision. . . .

[After reviewing the course of decisions in Massachusetts, Justice Kaplan turned to the situation in the rest of the country.]

. . .   Without attempting a count of the decisions, we may summarize the position roughly as follows. The right of the husband has long been acknowledged in a very substantial majority of the jurisdictions. The right of the wife, first confirmed in Hitaffer v. Argonne Co., Inc., 183 F.2d 811, cert. den. sub nom., Argonne Co. Inc. v. Hitaffer, 340 U.S. 852 (1950), . . .   has now been established in perhaps half the American jurisdictions; the result has been achieved in some States by overruling relatively recent precedent in point. In certain jurisdictions the wife's right has been denied although the husband's right is still affirmed—a regrettable solecism. A few jurisdictions have followed our Feneff case or another route to a conclusion denying the right both to husband and wife. Having in the first Restatement of Torts published in 1938 affirmed the husband's right and denied the wife's in accordance with the then weight of authority, the American Law Institute in Restatement Second [states] that husband and wife have the right on equal terms, adding the requirement—in recognition of the significant procedural point—that where possible the consortium claim must be joined with the claim for bodily injury [to minimize concerns about double recovery]. This resolution of the problem conforms to the prevailing ideas of the commentators.

To a few critics the idea of a right of consortium seems no more than an anachronism harking back to the days when a married woman was a chattel slave, and in a formulation such as that of the new Restatement they would find a potential for indefinite expansion of a questionable liability. But that formulation, reflecting a strong current of recent decisions, is a natural expression of a dominant (and commonplace) theme of our modern law of torts, namely, that presumptively there should be recourse for a definite injury to a legitimate interest due to a lack of the prudence or care appropriate to the occasion. That it would be very difficult to put bounds on an interest and value it is a possible reason for leaving it without protection at least in the form of money damages. But the law is moderately confident about the ability of the trier (subject to the usual checks at the trial and appellate levels) to apply common sense to the question. The marital interest is quite recognizable and its impairment may be definite, serious, and enduring, more so than the pain and suffering or mental or psychic distress for which recovery is now almost routinely allowed in various tort actions. The valuation problem here may be difficult but is not less manageable. Nor does it follow that if the husband-wife relationship is protected as here envisaged, identical protection must be afforded by analogy to other relationships from that of parent-child in a lengthy regress to that of master-servant; courts will rather proceed from case to case with discerning caution.   .   .   .

———————

To update Justice Kaplan's opinion, over the intervening years virtually all states have come to recognize the loss of consortium action for both spouses. For a counter example, see Boucher By Boucher v. Dixie Medical Center, 850 P.2d 1179 (Utah 1992)(rejecting the action). Today's questions concern the extension to couples that are not legally married and to the question Justice Kaplan alluded to at the end—the extension of similar actions to other relationships.

In Borer v. American Airlines, Inc., 19 Cal.3d 441, 563 P.2d 858, 138 Cal.Rptr. 302 (1977), the court refused to extend this type of action to young children whose mother had been injured to such an extent that she was unable to provide the usual parental care. The financial aspects of this loss were recoverable in the mother's action. The mother could also recover the emotional aspects of this loss of ability to care for her children if she were conscious of that loss. See generally, Ridgeway, Loss of Consortium and Loss of Services Actions: A Legacy of Separate Spheres, 50 Mont.L.Rev. 349 (1989).

In Ferriter v. Daniel O'Connell's Sons, Inc., 381 Mass. 507, 413 N.E.2d 690 (1980), the children of a paralyzed accident victim pressed a *Borer* claim. The court was "skeptical" of any suggestion that the children's interests were any less intense than the wife's. The court reviewed and rejected the reasons offered by the majority in *Borer* and held that the children "have a viable claim for loss of parental society if they can show that they are minors dependent on the parent, Michael Ferriter. This dependence must be rooted not only in economic requirements, but also in filial needs for closeness, guidance, and nurture."

Shortly thereafter, the Supreme Court of Michigan followed suit, in a case involving harm to the parent of a severely retarded and physically handicapped child. Berger v. Weber, 411 Mich. 1, 303 N.W.2d 424 (1981). The defendant argued that recognizing this lawsuit would increase the burden on the public due to increased insurance premiums. The majority responded that "compensating a child who has suffered emotional problems because of the deprivation of a parent's love and affection may provide the child with the means of adjustment to the loss. The child receives the immediate benefit of the compensation, but society will also benefit if the child is able to function without emotional handicap." This might more than offset any increase in premiums. See also Hay v. Medical Center Hospital of Vermont, 145 Vt. 533, 496 A.2d 939 (1985).

In *Elden v. Sheldon*, discussed in note 8, the court relied on the many cases that had refused to extend loss of consortium beyond the legal relationship of marriage. The primary justifications were "the state's interest in promoting the responsibilities of marriage and the difficulty of assessing the emotional, sexual and financial relationship of cohabiting parties to determine whether their arrangement would be equivalent of a marriage." Nothing in the decisions permitting unmarried cohabiting couples to enforce express and implied contracts warranted a different result here. The court concluded that "it is evident from what we say above that our determination here is not based on a value judgment regarding the morality of unmarried cohabitation relationships."

The dissenter would also have allowed an action for loss of consortium. As he noted, initially the action was available only to husbands who had lost the services of their wives and this conveyed something of a property notion:

> The modern view regards consortium as a package of relational interests, including love, companionship, emotional support, and sexual relations. The marital status of the plaintiff has no more bearing on his or her standing to claim injury to these interests than does age or socioeconomic status. Accordingly, there is no principled reason to perpetuate the fiction that only marital partners suffer compensable loss of consortium.

He concluded that by failing to "harmonize the law with present societal conditions," the majority had abdicated its responsibility for the upkeep of the common law.

We discuss related issues regarding recovery for loss of companionship in wrongful death, as contrasted with serious injury, cases in Chapter X.

No claim will lie against a negligent spouse for depriving the other spouse of consortium by negligent conduct, such as driving. See Plain v. Plain, 307 Minn. 399, 240 N.W.2d 330 (1976). See also General Motors Corp. v. Doupnik, 1 F.3d 862 (9th Cir.1993)(involving a negligent defendant's attempt to recover from a negligent (and injured) spouse the damages for lost consortium that the defendant had had to pay the uninjured spouse).

Very shortly after deciding the *Bovsun* case, discussed in note 6, the New York court decided another emotional distress claim.

Johnson v. Jamaica Hospital

Court of Appeals of New York, 1984.
62 N.Y.2d 523, 467 N.E.2d 502, 478 N.Y.S.2d 838.

[Plaintiffs' daughter, Kawana, was born in defendant hospital. After the plaintiff mother was discharged, Kawana was kept for further treatment. When the mother visited a week later, Kawana was discovered missing. She apparently had been abducted that day—a day on which the hospital received two bomb threats. While she was missing plaintiffs brought suit for the emotional distress brought about by defendant's negligence. Kawana was recovered by the police and returned to plaintiffs after four and one-half months. A separate suit was brought on Kawana's behalf, which is not part of this appeal. The trial court denied defendant's motion to dismiss the parents' action for failure to state a cause of action. The Appellate Division affirmed by a divided vote and certified the question whether it had acted properly.]

■ KAYE, JUDGE [after stating the facts].

Assuming the allegations of plaintiffs' complaint to be true [ ], no cause of action is stated. Plaintiff parents may not recover damages from defendant hospital for any mental distress or emotional disturbances they may have suffered as a result of the direct injury inflicted upon their daughter by defendant's breach of its duty of care to her. [ ] Although in Bovsun v. Sanperi, [ ], we recently decided that damages may be recovered for such indirect "psychic injuries" in limited circumstances, plaintiffs have stated no basis for recovering under the standard set forth in *Bovsun* in that they have not alleged that they were within the zone of danger and that their injuries resulted from contemporaneous observation of serious physical injury or death caused by defendant's negligence. Plaintiffs contend, and the courts below concluded, that their complaint states a cause of action because the defendant hospital owed a duty directly to them, as parents, to care properly for their child, and that it was or should have been foreseeable to defendant that any injury to Kawana, such as abduction, would cause them mental distress. There is no basis for establishing such a direct duty. This court has refused to recognize such a duty on the part of a hospital to the parents of hospitalized children (Kalina v. General Hosp., 13 N.Y.2d 1023, 245 N.Y.S.2d 599, 195 N.E.2d 309), and there is no reason to depart from that rule here.

In *Kalina,* the plaintiffs, an observant Jewish couple, gave express instructions to the defendant hospital that their newborn son was to be ritualistically circumcised on his eighth day by a mohel in accordance with the tenets of their religion. Instead, due to the alleged negligence and malpractice of the hospital, the baby was circumcised on his fourth day by a physician. The plaintiff parents sought recovery for their mental pain and suffering caused by the assault and battery upon their son. Special Term granted defendants' motion to dismiss the complaint [ ], and we ultimately affirmed on Special Term's opinion. In that opinion, the parents of the hospitalized child were held to be "interested bystanders" to whom no direct duty was owed.

> Both of the pleadings are insufficient because the plaintiffs as individuals, apart from their status as representatives of their son, do not have a legally protected interest under these circumstances [ ]. To paraphrase the language of [Palsgraf v. Long Island R. Co., reprinted in Chapter V], the conduct of the defendants, if a wrong in relation to the son, was not a wrong in its relation to the plaintiffs, remote from the event. Rights are not abstractions but exist only correlatively with duties. Everyone who has been damaged by an interruption in the expected tenor of his life does not have a cause of action. The law demands that the equation be balanced; that the damaged plaintiff be able to point the finger of

responsibility at a defendant owing, not a general duty to society, but a specific duty to him.

The defendants here in accepting a relationship with the son assumed the risk of liability for a tortious performance to him. They did not assume any risk of liability that their acts might violate the personal sensibilities of others, be they the son's parents, his coreligionists or the community at large. [ ]

Jamaica Hospital owed no more of a direct duty to the plaintiff parents to refrain from causing them psychic injury than did the defendants in *Kalina* [and three other cases]. The direct injury allegedly caused by defendant's negligence—abduction—was sustained by the infant, and plaintiffs' grief and mental torment which resulted from her disappearance are not actionable. The foreseeability that such psychic injuries would result from the injury to Kawana does not serve to establish a duty running from defendant to plaintiffs (Albala v. City of New York, 54 N.Y.2d 269, 273, 445 N.Y.S.2d 108, 429 N.E.2d 786; Pulka v. Edelman, [discussed at p. 150, supra]), and in the absence of such a duty, as a matter of law there can be no liability [ ]. That sound policy reasons support these decisions is evident here, for to permit recovery by the infant's parents for emotional distress would be to invite open-ended liability for indirect emotional injury suffered by families in every instance where the very young, or very elderly, or incapacitated persons experience negligent care or treatment.

[The court rejected duties based on the contractual relationship and on a *loco parentis* relationship.]

Finally, our prior holdings in Johnson v. State of New York, [ ], and Lando v. State of New York, [ ], provide no basis for recovery. In neither case was liability based upon a hospital's breach of care to its patient causing direct injury to the patient resulting in emotional injury to relatives of the patient. In *Johnson* the defendant hospital negligently sent a telegram to plaintiff notifying her of her mother's death when in fact her mother had not died, and in *Lando* the defendant hospital negligently failed to locate a deceased patient's body for 11 days, when it was found in an advanced state of decomposition. Each case presented exceptional circumstances in which courts long ago recognized liability for resultant emotional injuries: a duty to transmit truthfully information concerning a relative's death or funeral [ ] which the hospital assumed by sending the message [ ], and the mishandling of or failure to deliver a dead body with the consequent denial of access to the family [ ]. Neither exception is applicable here.

In summary, Jamaica Hospital, even if negligent in caring for Kawana and directly liable to her, is not liable for emotional distress suffered by plaintiffs as a consequence of the abduction. This is in accord with the majority rule in this country. [ ] There is no duty owing from defendant to plaintiffs to refrain from negligently causing such injury. To hold otherwise would be to invite the very sort of boundless liability for indirect emotional injury that we have consistently rejected.

[The court rejected a dissent argument that liability here can be circumscribed by limiting any duty owed to those parents whose custodial rights have been interfered with because this was not a common occurrence. The majority responded that "any right to recover for emotional injury sustained by plaintiffs because of defendant's negligence in the 'care, custody and management' of their child cannot rationally be refused to other parents, relatives or custodians of persons to whom caretakers of various types, such as schools and day care centers, are alleged to have breached a similar duty."] Accordingly, the order of the Appellate Division should be reversed, the certified question answered in the negative, and the complaint dismissed.

■ MEYER, JUDGE (dissenting).

I had thought that the fear of "open-ended liability for indirect emotional injury" [   ], had long ago been laid to rest [*Battalla*], and that Bovsun v. Sanperi, [   ], with its recognition that serious and verifiable emotional disturbance [   ], suffered by an immediate family member [   ], was a compensable injury, marked the beginning of a rationale for determining just when "[f]reedom from mental disturbance is . . . a protected interest in this State" [   ]. . . .

[In an extended opinion the two dissenters asserted that the burden on the courts was not to be considered because it was, quoting Prosser, "the business of the law to remedy wrongs that deserve it, even at the expense of a 'flood of litigation.'" Moreover, a flood was unlikely here because "interference with the right of custody [was] not a common occurrence." As to fear of disproportionate burden on defendant, this case came to the court on a motion to dismiss and there was "nothing before the court to indicate what, if any, change in hospital procedures would be required were there imposed upon it a duty to exercise reasonable care not to permit a newborn baby to be removed from the hospital by someone other than the parents or a person having the parents' permission to do so, or how great a burden in time or cost such a duty would impose. Clearly, however, it cannot simply be presumed that the burden would be so great as to foreclose imposition of liability, the more particularly so in view of the fact that it is a matter of common knowledge that hospitals already have a checkout procedure."

Kalina was said to be distinguishable because the hospital had not assumed "any risk of liability that their acts might violate the personal sensibilities of others." Here, however, the hospital interfered with the custodial rights of the parents. Finally, for courts to deny a duty here "is a pitiful confession of incompetence on the part of courts of justice."]

■ COOKE, C.J., and JONES, WACHTLER and SIMONS, JJ., concur with KAYE, J.

■ MEYER, J., dissents and votes to affirm in a separate opinion in which JASEN, J., concurs.

NOTES AND QUESTIONS

1. As the court notes, Kawana's own action is not involved at this time. Does she have a claim if she is returned in good health? Is the court overlooking the deterrence function?

2. Is there a meaningful distinction between "direct" and "indirect" harms in these emotional distress cases?

3. In two recent cases, courts have viewed the mother who is claiming negligent infliction of emotional distress resulting from giving birth as a special case. She is not seen as a direct victim since the alleged malpractice was on the fetus; she is not a bystander because she is so close to the event as to be part of it. The mother has an action whether conscious at the time or not. (There was concern that the use of anesthetic might become more common in deliveries if the courts barred suits when the mother was not aware of the negligence at the time it occurred.) In one case, Carey v. Lovett, 132 N.J. 44, 622 A.2d 1279 (1993), the father was said to come under the bystander approach; in the other he would "probably" be treated as a bystander. Burgess v. Superior Court (Gupta), 2 Cal.4th 1064, 831 P.2d 1197, 9 Cal.Rptr.2d 615 (1992). How might New York analyze this type of case?

4. How does *Bovsun* apply here? Is this a stronger or weaker case for recovery than a zone-of-danger case in which a child is suddenly hurt before a parent's eyes?

5. The dissent argued, among other points, that the limits of this case could be held. What about a suit by a grandparent? By a seven year old sibling of Kawana? By an aunt who had been living with the parents for several years?

6. Is *Kalina* controlling? If the court had recognized a duty in the main case would it have had to overrule *Kalina?*

7. In Oresky v. Scharf, 126 App.Div.2d 614, 510 N.Y.S.2d 897 (1987), plaintiffs, who were sisters, placed their mother in defendants' nursing home. Plaintiffs alleged that all parties knew that the mother had Alzheimer's Disease. Six months after her arrival, the mother disappeared from the nursing home and, by the time of this appeal, was still missing.

The court traced the same arguments as those raised in the main case and rejected plaintiffs' claim. *Bovsun* did not apply because plaintiffs had "not alleged that they were in the zone of danger or that their alleged emotional injuries resulted from contemporaneous observation of serious physical injury or death caused by the defendants' negligence." The case of the kidnapped baby was said to be "dispositive." Efforts to obtain further review failed.

Is the case of the kidnapped baby stronger (or weaker) than one involving a disappearing parent? What type of action might be brought on behalf of the missing parent?

8. *Property.* Is the harm "direct" or "indirect" if the cause of the emotional distress is alleged to have been triggered by concern over the loss of plaintiff's property or pet animal?

In Rodrigues v. State, 52 Haw. 156, 472 P.2d 509 (1970), plaintiffs had built their house with their own hands. Due to the state's negligence, water flooded the house to a depth of six inches causing damage. In addition to recovery for property damage, the plaintiffs would be able to recover damages for their emotional distress upon a showing that "a reasonable man normally constituted, would be unable adequately to cope with the mental stress engendered by the circumstances of the case." Two of the five justices dissented on the ground that it was inappropriate to award such damages as a result of harm to property. For the denial of recovery where water damaged a home that plaintiffs had not built with their own hands, see Dobbins v. Washington Suburban Sanitary Comm'n, 338 Md. 341, 658 A.2d 675 (1995).

In Campbell v. Animal Quarantine Station, 63 Haw. 557, 632 P.2d 1066 (1981), plaintiffs learned over the telephone that their dog had died because of the negligence of defendant, which had occurred on the same island in Hawaii. Recovery of $200 for each of five plaintiffs was upheld after a finding that they had each suffered severe emotional distress.

But see Roman v. Carroll, 127 Ariz. 398, 621 P.2d 307 (App.1980), in which plaintiff alleged that she sustained emotional distress from "watching defendants' St. Bernard dismember plaintiff's poodle while she was walking the dog near her home." The poodle died two days later. The court rejected plaintiff's effort to use bystander analysis because a dog "is personal property" and "distress from witnessing injury to property" did not give rise to an action.

The results in *Rodrigues* and *Campbell* were affected by 1986 legislation in Hawaii that barred recovery for negligent infliction of emotional distress arising from damage to "property or material objects" unless the distress resulted in "physical injury to or mental illness of the person who experiences the emotional distress or disturbance." H.R.S. § 663–8.9.

9. Other cases from Hawaii have been receptive to claims for emotional distress. In addition to *Rodrigues* and *Campbell*, consider the following:

a. Leong v. Takasaki, 55 Haw. 398, 520 P.2d 758 (1974). A ten-year-old boy was walking hand-in-hand with his stepfather's mother. She walked into a crosswalk but plaintiff held back because of an oncoming vehicle. He was allowed to recover for the emotional distress of witnessing the ensuing accident. The lack of a blood relationship was not controlling because "Hawaiian and Asian families of this state have long maintained strong ties among members of the same extended family group." The court also concluded that no physical symptoms were required.

b. Kelley v. Kokua Sales & Supply, Ltd., 56 Haw. 204, 532 P.2d 673 (1975). A man in California suffered emotional distress when he was informed by telephone that his daughter and granddaughter had been killed in an auto accident in Hawaii. The court, 4–1, refused to recognize a duty on the ground that the scene of the accident was too remote for the defendants to have reasonably foreseen these consequences of their conduct.

c. Masaki v. General Motors Corp., 71 Haw. 1, 780 P.2d 566 (1989). Plaintiff parents heard that their son had been hurt in an accident. They resided on the same island and went immediately to the hospital where they saw the consequences of the accident and were told that their son would never again walk. The fact that they did not witness the accident was not a bar to recovery but rather "a factor in determining the degree of mental stress suffered. Whether the degree of stress engendered by the circumstances of this case was beyond that with which a reasonable man can be expected to cope is a question for the jury."

Is the Hawaii approach preferable to others we have considered?

10.   Another group of cases decided under *Johnson v. Jamaica Hospital* involves incorrect medical diagnoses. In Jacobs v. Horton Memorial Hospital, 130 A.D.2d 546, 515 N.Y.S.2d 281 (1987), plaintiff alleged that defendant had negligently diagnosed her husband as having pancreatic cancer with a prognosis of only six months to live. This diagnosis was conveyed to plaintiff who alleged that she suffered emotional distress. The court denied recovery on the ground that a duty was owed only to those "directly injured by the act of malpractice." The court cited a similar result in a case in which the wrong diagnosis of a child was conveyed to the parents. Only the child had an action. (What if the child was too young to understand the situation?) To hold otherwise would invite the danger of "boundless liability for indirect emotional injury that we have consistently rejected," quoting *Johnson*.

11.   The consequences of being categorized as either direct or bystander are still being developed. In Huggins v. Longs Drug Stores California Inc., 6 Cal.4th 124, 862 P.2d 148, 24 Cal.Rptr.2d 587 (1993), plaintiff parents followed an incorrect label and gave their infant an excessive dose of medicine. The child was not permanently injured. The parents' claim against the pharmacist was rejected, 5–2. The goal of the transaction was to provide medication for the baby: "Because plaintiffs were not the patients for whom defendant dispensed the prescribed medication, they cannot recover as direct victims of defendant's negligence." One dissenter thought plaintiffs were "direct victims," since they were "necessary parties to the administration" of the medicine. The other dissenter emphasized the guilt that parents feel when they are the—even innocent—instruments of harm to their children: "It is this additional injury that renders the parent a direct victim."

B.   WRONGFUL BIRTH AND WRONGFUL LIFE

Greco v. United States

Supreme Court of Nevada, 1995.
111 Nev. 405, 893 P.2d 345.

■ SPRINGER, JUSTICE.

In this case we certify to the United States District Court for the District of Maryland that a mother has a tort claim in negligent malpractice against professionals who negligently fail to make a timely diagnosis of gross and disabling fetal defects, thereby denying the mother her right to terminate the pregnancy. We further certify that the child born to this mother has no personal cause of action for what is sometimes called "wrongful life."

[Plaintiff mother, suing individually and for her son, claimed that as a result of negligence by physicians at Nelles Air Force Base in Nevada during plaintiff's prenatal care, her son was born with a variety of disabling conditions and that he "has paraplegia with no sensation from the hips down and suffers permanent fine and gross motor retardation and mental retardation."]

These kinds of tort claims have been termed "wrongful birth" when brought by a parent and "wrongful life" when brought on behalf of the child for the harm suffered by being born deformed.

THE CHILD'S CAUSE OF ACTION: "WRONGFUL LIFE"

We decline to recognize any action by a child for defects claimed to have been caused to the child by negligent diagnosis or treatment of the child's mother. The Grecos' argument is conditional and narrowly put, so: if this court does not allow Sundi Greco to recover damages for Joshua's care past the age of majority, it should allow Joshua to recover those damages by recognizing claims for "wrongful life." Implicit in this argument is the assumption that the child would be better off had he never been born. These kinds of judgments are very difficult, if not impossible, to make. Indeed, most courts considering the question have denied this cause of action for precisely this reason. Recognizing this kind of claim on behalf of the child would require us to weigh the harms suffered by virtue of the child's having been born with severe handicaps against "the utter void of nonexistence"; this is a calculation the courts are incapable of performing. . . . We conclude that Nevada does not recognize a claim by a child for harms the child claims to have suffered by virtue of having been born.

THE MOTHER'S CAUSE OF ACTION

With regard to Sundi Greco's claim against her physician for negligent diagnosis or treatment during pregnancy, we see no reason for compounding or complicating our medical malpractice jurisprudence by according this particular form of professional negligence action some special status apart from presently recognized medical malpractice or by giving it the new name of "wrongful birth." Sundi Greco either does or does not state a claim for medical malpractice; and we conclude that she does.

Medical malpractice, like other forms of negligence, involves a breach of duty which causes injury. To be tortiously liable a physician must have departed from the accepted standard of medical care in a manner that results in injury to a patient. . . .

It is difficult to formulate any sound reason for denying recovery to Sundi Greco in the case at hand. Sundi Greco is saying, in effect, to her doctors:

"If you had done what you were supposed to do, I would have known early in my pregnancy that I was carrying a severely deformed baby. I would have then terminated the pregnancy and would not have had to go through the mental and physical agony of delivering this child, nor would I have had to bear the emotional suffering attendant to the birth and nurture of the child, nor the extraordinary expense necessary to care for a child suffering from such extreme deformity and disability."

The United States advances two reasons for denying Sundi Greco's claim: first, it argues that she has suffered no injury and that, therefore, the damage element of negligent tort liability is not fulfilled; second, the United States argues that even if Sundi Greco has sustained injury and damages, the damages were not caused by her physicians. To support its first argument, the United States points out that in Szekeres v. Robinson, 102 Nev. 93, 715 P.2d 1076 (1986), this court held that the mother of a normal, healthy child could not recover in tort from a physician who negligently performed her sterilization operation because the birth of a normal, healthy child is not a legally cognizable injury.[6] The United States argues that no distinction can be made between a mother who gives birth to a healthy child and a mother who gives birth to a child with severe deformities and that, therefore, *Szekeres* bars recovery.

Szekeres can be distinguished from the instant case. Unlike the birth of a normal child, the birth of a severely deformed baby of the kind described here is necessarily an unpleasant and aversive event and the cause of inordinate financial burden that would not attend the birth of a normal child. The child in this case will unavoidably and necessarily require the expenditure of extraordinary medical, therapeutic and custodial care expenses by the family, not to mention the additional reserves of physical, mental and emotional strength that will be required of all concerned. Those who do not wish to undertake the many burdens associated with the birth and continued care of such a child have the legal right, under *Roe v. Wade* and codified by the voters of this state, to terminate their pregnancies. Roe v. Wade, 410 U.S. 113 (1973); NRS 442.250 (codifying by referendum the conditions under which abortion is permitted in this state). Sundi Greco has certainly suffered money damages as a result of her physician's malpractice.

We also reject the United States' second argument that Sundi Greco's physicians did not cause any of the injuries that Sundi Greco might have suffered. We note that the mother is not claiming that her child's defects were caused by her physicians' negligence; rather, she claims that her physicians' negligence kept her ignorant of those defects and that it was

---

6. We did observe that the mother might have a contractual remedy against the physician for failure to do what he promised to do—sterilize his patient. [   ]

this negligence which caused her to lose her right to choose whether to carry the child to term. The damage Sundi Greco has sustained is indeed causally related to her physicians' malpractice.

Sundi Greco's claim here can be compared to one in which a physician negligently fails to diagnose cancer in a patient. Even though the physician did not cause the cancer, the physician can be held liable for damages resulting from the patient's decreased opportunity to fight the cancer, and for the more extensive pain, suffering and medical treatment the patient must undergo by reason of the negligent diagnosis. . . .[7] If we were to deny Sundi Greco's claim, we would, in effect, be groundlessly excepting one type of medical malpractice from negligence liability. We see no reason to treat this case any differently from any other medical malpractice case. Sundi Greco has stated a prima facie claim of medical malpractice under Nevada law.

DAMAGE ISSUES

The certified question requires us to decide specifically what types of damages the mother may recover if she succeeds in proving her claim. Courts in these cases have struggled with what items of damages are recoverable because, unlike the typical malpractice claim, claims such as Sundi Greco's do not involve a physical injury to the patient's person. We consider each of Sundi Greco's claimed items of damage separately.

Extraordinary Medical and Custodial Expenses

This claim for damages relates to the medical, therapeutic and custodial costs associated with caring for a severely handicapped child. There is nothing exceptional in allowing this item of damage. It is a recognized principle of tort law to "afford compensation for injuries sustained by one person as the result of the conduct of another." [ ] Extraordinary care expenses are a foreseeable result of the negligence alleged in this case, and Sundi Greco should be allowed to recover those expenses if she can prove them. This leads us to the question of how to compensate for these kinds of injuries.

Sundi Greco correctly observes that Nevada law requires the parents of a handicapped child to support that child beyond the age of majority if the child cannot support itself. [ ] Nevada recognizes the right of a parent to recover from a tortfeasor any expenses the parent was required to pay because of the injury to his or her minor child. [ ] Accordingly, Sundi Greco claims the right to recover damages for these extraordinary costs for a period equal to Joshua's life expectancy. Other states which require parents to care for handicapped children past the age of majority allow plaintiffs to recover these types of damages for the lifetime of the child or until such time as the child is no longer dependent on her or his parents.

---

7. . . . Whether the mother may have "wanted" the child, despite its infirmities, is a factual issue for the trier of fact. Obviously, if the mother would have elected to have the baby, notwithstanding its condition, she would suffer no damage from the loss of the opportunity to terminate the pregnancy.

We agree with these authorities and conclude that Sundi Greco may recover extraordinary medical and custodial expenses associated with caring for Joshua for whatever period of time it is established that Joshua will be dependent upon her to provide such care.

The United States contends that if this court allows the mother to recover such extraordinary medical and custodial expenses, then it should require the district court to offset any such award by the amount it would cost to raise a non-handicapped child. To do otherwise, argues the United States, would be to grant the mother a windfall. See, e.g., Smith v. Cote, 128 N.H. 231, 513 A.2d 341, 349–50 (1986)(adopting offset rule).

The offset rule has its origins in two doctrines: the "avoidable consequences rule," which requires plaintiffs to mitigate their damages in tort cases, and the expectancy rule of damages employed in contract cases, which seeks to place the plaintiff in the position he or she would have been in had the contract been performed. [ ] We conclude that neither of these doctrines is applicable to the case at bar. To enforce the "avoidable consequences" rule in the instant case would impose unreasonable burdens upon the mother such as, perhaps, putting Joshua up for adoption or otherwise seeking to terminate her parental obligations. [ ]

With regard to the expectancy rule, it would unnecessarily complicate and limit recovery for patients in other malpractice cases if we were to begin intruding contract damage principles upon our malpractice jurisprudence. The rule for compensatory damages in negligence cases is clear and workable, and we decline to depart from it.

Loss of Services and Companionship

The United States contends that Sundi Greco should not be allowed to recover any damages for the services of her child lost due to the child's handicap, because Sundi Greco claims that but for the negligence of her physician she would never have carried her pregnancy to term. It follows then, that if the child had not been born, Sundi Greco would have had far less in terms of service and companionship than what she can currently expect from her handicapped child. Amicus NTLA attempts to rebut the United States' argument by analogizing Sundi Greco's situation to that of the wife in General Electric Co. v. Bush, 88 Nev. 360, 498 P.2d 366 (1972). In that case a wife was permitted to recover damages from a tortfeasor for loss of the services and companionship of her husband, who was still alive but had become a permanent invalid. The General Electric case exemplifies the problems relating to Sundi Greco's request for these sorts of damages in the instant case. In General Electric, the wife lost the services of a healthy, productive individual; here, the crux of Sundi Greco's claim is that she would have aborted the fetus had she been given the opportunity to do so. In that case, she would have had no services or companionship at all. We thus conclude that Sundi Greco may not recover for lost services or companionship.

Damages for Emotional Distress

Sundi Greco asserts that she is suffering and will continue to suffer tremendous mental and emotional pain as a result of the birth of Joshua. Several jurisdictions allow plaintiffs such as Sundi Greco to recover such damages. In line with these cases, we agree that it is reasonably foreseeable that a mother who is denied her right to abort a severely deformed fetus will suffer emotional distress, not just when the child is delivered, but for the rest of the child's life.[10] Consequently, we conclude that the mother in this case should have the opportunity to prove that she suffered and will continue to suffer emotional distress as a result of the birth of her child.

We reject the United States' argument that this court should follow an "offset" rule with regard to damages for emotional distress. Cf. Blake v. Cruz, 108 Idaho 253, 258, 698 P.2d 315, 320 (1984)(requiring damages for emotional distress to be offset by "the countervailing emotional benefits attributable to the birth of the child"). Any emotional benefits are simply too speculative to be considered by a jury in awarding emotional distress damages. As Dean Prosser observes:

> In the case of the wrongful birth of a severely impaired child, it would appear that the usual joys of parenthood would often be substantially overshadowed by the emotional trauma of caring for the child in such a condition, so that application of the benefit rule would appear inappropriate in this context.

[ ] It is beyond cavil, for example, that "[t]here is no joy in watching a child suffer and die from cystic fibrosis." Schroeder v. Perkel, 87 N.J. 53, 432 A.2d 834, 842 (1981). Moreover, it would unduly complicate the jury's task to require it to weigh one intangible harm against another intangible benefit.

. . .

■ STEFFEN, C.J., and YOUNG, J., concur.

■ SHEARING, J., with whom ROSE, J. joins, concurring in part and dissenting in part:

I agree with the majority that a mother should have a malpractice claim against professionals who negligently fail to make a timely diagnosis of fetal defects. However, I would also allow the impaired child a cause of action, with the measure of damages being the extraordinary expenses attributable to the child's impairment.

. . .

10. Both parties argue by analogy to *Dillon v. Legg*, [ ]. Nevada law recognizes the right of a parent to recover emotional distress damages if the factors set forth by the California Supreme Court in Dillon are met. [ ] Those factors are: the proximity of the plaintiff to the scene of the injury; whether the plaintiff actually observed the injury; and the degree of relationship between the plaintiff and victim. Although these factors are met in the case at bar, we find any reliance on *Dillon v. Legg* misplaced. Greco seeks to recover for a direct and personal injury, not because of mental distress occasioned by an injury to Joshua.

The majority, along with other courts, rejects the impaired child's cause of action after wrestling with the question of whether damages exist when that determination requires the comparison of the value of an impaired life to the value of no life at all. . . .

However, not all courts have taken the view that these difficulties are so great as to overcome the public policy objectives of tort law—to compensate injured parties and to deter future wrongful conduct. In Turpin v. Sortini, 31 Cal.3d 220, 643 P.2d 954, 182 Cal.Rptr. 337 (1982), the California Supreme Court quoted with approval a lower court opinion which stated:

> "The reality of the 'wrongful life' concept is that such a plaintiff exists and suffers, due to the negligence of others. It is neither necessary nor just to retreat into meditation on the mysteries of life. We need not be concerned with the fact that had defendants not been negligent, the plaintiff might not have come into existence at all. The certainty of genetic impairment is no longer a mystery. In addition, a reverent appreciation of life compels recognition that plaintiff, however impaired she may be, has come into existence as a living person with certain rights."

. . . .

> Although it is easy to understand and to endorse these decisions' desire to affirm the worth and sanctity of less-than-perfect life, we question whether these considerations alone provide a sound basis for rejecting the child's tort action. To begin with, it is hard to see how an award of damages to a severely handicapped or suffering child would "disavow" the value of life or in any way suggest that the child is not entitled to the full measure of legal and nonlegal rights and privileges accorded to all members of society. [   ]

The California Supreme Court . . . allowed only the claim for medical expenses and extraordinary expenses for specialized teaching, training and equipment required because of the impairment. [   ]

The New Jersey Supreme Court has taken a similar approach [on behalf of the child], stating in Procanik by Procanik v. Cillo, 97 N.J. 339, 478 A.2d 755 (1984):

. . .

> The crux of the problem is that there is no rational way to measure non-existence or to compare non-existence with the pain and suffering of his impaired existence. Whatever theoretical appeal one might find in recognizing a claim for pain and suffering is outweighed by the essentially irrational and unpredictable nature of that claim. Although damages in a personal injury action need not be calculated with mathematical precision, they require at their base some modicum of rationality.

. . .

We believe that the interests of fairness and justice are better served through more predictably measured damages—the cost of the extraordinary medical expenses necessitated by the infant plaintiff's handicaps. Damages so measured are not subject to the same wild swings as a claim for pain and suffering and will carry a sufficient sting to deter future acts of medical malpractice. [   ]

. . .

I would allow the child the cost of the extraordinary expenses attributable to the impairment. The claims of the child and the parents are mutually dependent; it would be unfair to deny compensation to the child if the parent or parents are not available to make their claim. While there can be no duplication of recovery, either action should lie.

NOTES AND QUESTIONS

1. What is the precise claim of negligence in the case? In what way might it be said to differ from the typical medical malpractice claim? Should the name given to this action affect the analysis of the claim? What if the claim is brought against a testing laboratory that failed to detect a genetic defect?

2. In the mother's suit, what are the strongest reasons for accepting the claim? Rejecting it?

3. Consider each item of damages for which the mother is suing. How can each one be justified?

4. Consider how a court should analyze a case in which the genetic counselor negligently tells a couple that they are at great risk of conceiving a child with a very serious, usually fatal, disease. As a result (a) the man and woman decide not to marry; (b) they marry but decide not to have children. In each case, after ten years the man and woman get a second opinion that correctly assures them that there is no genetic risk.

In Martinez v. Long Island Jewish Hillside Medical Center, 70 N.Y.2d 697, 512 N.E.2d 538, 518 N.Y.S.2d 955 (1987), plaintiff alleged that defendants negligently advised her that her baby would be born either with no brain or a small brain. She submitted to an abortion, believing that it was justified under the extraordinary circumstances. Afterward, she learned that the advice had been incorrect and that no abortion had been necessary. At trial, plaintiff and her psychiatrist testified that plaintiff considered abortion to be a sin except under exceptional circumstances; but that when she discovered the truth, she suffered mental anguish and depression from her awareness that "she had needlessly committed an act in violation of her deep-seated convictions."

The court concluded that the breach was of a "duty owed directly to her in giving her erroneous advice on which she affirmatively acted." The emotional distress for which she sought recovery "derives from the psychological injury" tied to her having acted against her beliefs—and not from the loss of the baby. On remand, a judgment of $125,000 for the wife and

$25,000 for the husband was affirmed. 133 App.Div.2d 264, 519 N.Y.S.2d 53 (1987). Is the result consistent with *Johnson v. Jamaica Hospital,* supra?

5. *Healthy children.* As suggested by the discussion of the *Szekeres* case, a separate but related recent development has been the claim arising from failed contraceptive procedures. Contrary to the Nevada position, most courts have imposed a tort duty. See, e.g., Zehr v. Haugen, 318 Or. 647, 871 P.2d 1006 (1994).

a. If the child has been born healthy, should any tort action lie for the unexpected and initially (at least) unwanted child? Should the duty question be affected by the reason contraception was sought in the first place? Should it matter whether the surgeon performing the procedure knows the reasons for the choice? Consider these situations:

1. The couple have one child and wanted originally to have another but now conclude that they cannot afford any more children.

2. The couple already have two children and do not wish to have any more because they believe their family is large enough given their parenting skills and other interests.

3. The couple have one child who was born with a serious genetic defect and have been advised that there is a high risk that any future child will have a similar problem.

b. If a duty should be imposed in at least some of these cases, consider the recoverable damages:

1. Expenses incurred in connection with the unwanted pregnancy, including the medical expenses of the delivery; the wife's loss of earnings, if any; the costs of child care incurred while the wife was incapacitated; and the costs of a sterilization procedure after the birth.

2. The wife's pain and suffering during the pregnancy and any subsequent sterilization procedure.

3. The husband's loss of consortium during the pregnancy and thereafter.

4. The expenses of food, shelter, clothing and similar expenses incurred for the benefit of the child; the expenses of college education for that child.

5. The emotional distress of the husband and wife over the added expenses and changes to their life plans that have been caused by the negligence.

c. Might an action lie for damages sustained by the existing children from the birth of their sibling?

6. *Offset.* In both the healthy and the unhealthy child cases, the issue of offset has frequently arisen. Did the *Greco* court handle the issue soundly as to custodial expenses? As to emotional distress? Much of the debate has sprung from section 920 of the Second Restatement which provides:

When the defendant's tortious conduct has caused harm to the plaintiff or to his property and in so doing has conferred a special benefit to the interest of the plaintiff that was harmed, the value of the benefit conferred is considered in mitigation of damages, to the extent that this is equitable.

Would that section authorize a mitigation of custodial expenses in the principal case? Of damages for emotional distress?

Perhaps the strongest result for plaintiff in the healthy baby situation is Marciniak v. Lundborg, 153 Wis.2d 59, 450 N.W.2d 243 (1990), involving a negligent sterilization of a woman. The couple already had two children and wanted no more. First, the court rejected an array of defense arguments against liability for the expenses in raising the child. The court saw no reason to deviate from the rule that made defendants liable for those damages foreseeably flowing from the tort. In rejecting the argument of psychological harm to the child, the court stated:

> The suit is for the costs of raising the child, not to rid themselves of an unwanted child. They obviously want to keep the child. The love, affection, and emotional support any child needs they are prepared to give. But the love, affection, and emotional support they are prepared to give do not bring with them the economic means that are also necessary to feed, clothe, educate and otherwise raise the child. That is what this suit is about and we trust the child in the future will be well able to distinguish the two. Relieving the family of the economic costs of raising the child may well add to the emotional well-being of the entire family, including this child, rather than bring damage to it.

> Nor did the suit "debase the sanctity of human life." The court did not "perceive that the Marciniaks in bringing this suit are in any way disparaging the value of their child's life. They are, to the contrary, attempting to enhance it."

The court also rejected the claim that the plaintiffs had not mitigated their damages by placing the child for adoption or aborting the fetus. "We do not consider it reasonable to expect parents to essentially choose between the child and the cause of action. . . . [D]ecisions concerning abortion or adoption are highly personal matters and involve deeply held moral or religious convictions. For these reasons, courts have typically rejected the argument that parents must select either abortion or adoption as a method of mitigation, and we concur."

As to offset, the Wisconsin court quoted a comment from § 920 that "Damages for pain and suffering are not diminished by showing that the earning capacity of the plaintiff has been increased by the defendant's act." Thus, economic benefit would be set off only against economic harm, and emotional benefits only against emotional harm. Here the defendants were trying to set off emotional benefits against economic harm. The parents' decision not to have a child included a decision to forgo emotional benefits that might flow from another child. "When parents make the decision to forgo this opportunity for emotional enrichment, it hardly seems equitable to not only force this benefit upon them but to tell them they must pay for it as well by offsetting it against their proven economic damages. With respect to economic benefits, the same argument prevails. In addition, any economic advantages the child might confer upon the parents are ordinarily insignificant.''

7. *Roe v. Wade.* If the law should change to permit states to regulate or ban abortions (at least in the types of cases we have been considering in this section), how many of the results might change in a state that enacted a restrictive statute? Would the illegality of the procedure mean, for example, that a physician would be under no duty to warn a pregnant woman that an already conceived fetus is almost certain to be born with severe birth defects? Would it mean that there was no duty to check for such defects in the first place? For discussion of statutes limiting the tort remedy, see Ryan, Wrongful Birth: False Representations of Women's Reproductive Lives, 78 Minn.L.Rev. 857 (1994); Note, Wrongful Birth Actions: The Case Against Legislative Curtailment, 100 Harv. L.Rev. 2017 (1987).

State statutes barring actions for the birth of healthy children have been upheld. See Edmonds v. Western Pennsylvania Hospital Radiology Assoc., 414 Pa.Super. 567, 607 A.2d 1083 (1992), cert. denied 114 S.Ct. 63 (1993). See also Musk v. Nelson, 647 A.2d 1198 (Me.1994)(applying statute providing that ''no person may maintain a claim for relief or receive an award for damages based on the claim that the birth and rearing of a healthy child resulted in damages to him'').

8. In Welzenbach v. Powers, 139 N.H. 688, 660 A.2d 1133 (1995), an earlier paternity suit had established that the man had fathered the child in question—while he was married to another woman—and awarded support against the man. In this case, the man sued the mother for misrepresenting to him that she was practicing contraception. The claimed damages included the extent of the support award. The court rejected the claim on the ground that allowing such a suit would violate the state's public policy favoring support for such children. It also agreed that the interest in privacy of sexual relationships prevailed in this type of case.

In C.A.M. v. R.A.W., 237 N.J.Super. 532, 568 A.2d 556 (1990), plaintiff who had given birth to a healthy child sued defendant father claiming that he had falsely assured her that he had had a vasectomy. The court, 2–1, after reviewing the extensive litigation in this area, held that ''the birth of a normal, healthy child as a consequence of a sexual relationship between consenting adults precludes inquiry by the courts into representations that may have been made before or during that relationship by either of the partners concerning birth control.'' Why might that be?

The *C.A.M.* court distinguished J.P.M. v. Schmid Laboratories, Inc., 178 N.J.Super. 122, 428 A.2d 515 (1981), in which a husband and wife sued a manufacturer of condoms claiming that a defect in one of defendant's condoms had led to the birth of normal twins. The court permitted the defendant to file a cross-claim against the husband for negligent use of the condom. How might the cases be distinguished?

The *Welzenbach* court did note that where children were not involved and one partner had given the other a sexually transmitted disease, the public policy of controlling such diseases had led some courts to impose duties of due care to disclose the condition or otherwise protect the plaintiff. See Kathleen K. v. Robert B., 150 Cal.App.3d 992, 198 Cal.Rptr. 273 (1984)(genital herpes).

A second exception to the barrier to suit has developed in cases in which the plaintiff alleges that the defendant's misrepresentation caused physical harm. See Barbara A. v. John G., 145 Cal.App.3d 369, 193 Cal.Rptr. 422 (1983) (woman who had ectopic pregnancy and was forced to undergo surgery that rendered her sterile, alleged that man who impregnated her falsely claimed that he was sterile).

As the court noted in *Kathleen K.*, both exceptions are triggered by the observation that the "right of privacy is not absolute, and in some cases is subordinate to the state's fundamental right to enact laws which promote public health, welfare and safety, even though such laws may invade the offender's right of privacy."

9. *Wrongful Life.* In several cases, suits have been brought on behalf of children like Joshua claiming that they have a distinct claim for the pain and suffering sustained during their lifetimes. Are the reasons for denying recovery for this part of the claim persuasive? For arguments supporting a tort action, see Laudor, In Defense of Wrongful Life: Bringing Political Theory to the Defense of a Tort, 62 Ford.L.Rev. 1675 (1994).

Where the child was expected to have a fairly normal life expectancy, some cases, e.g. *Turpin v. Sortini*, cited in the dissent in *Greco*, involving congenital deafness, have awarded the child the future expenses that will likely be incurred in coping with the disability during majority (the parents being able to recover for those expenses they will incur during the child's minority). Note, though that if the condition is more disabling than deafness, the parents may have to support the child throughout its life. Is there a danger of double recovery?

C.   ECONOMIC HARM

In this section, we consider cases in which the defendant has exposed plaintiff only to the risk of economic harm. The defendant's conduct threatens no personal injury or property damage to the plaintiff. Initially, we will look at cases in which no personal injury or property damage is threatened to anyone—situations such as a creditor who makes a loan in reliance on negligently prepared financial statements or a beneficiary who fails to get an inheritance because of a defectively drawn will.

As with emotional distress, the courts have not protected economic interests as extensively as those involving physical security of person and property—even when the harm was inflicted intentionally, by fraud. We consider intentional misrepresentation at length in Chapter XV. In this chapter we continue our focus on identifying the situations in which courts do, or should, impose duties of due care—the obligation to use due care to acquire and communicate information.

After considering cases that threaten only economic harm, we will examine a variety of situations in which threatened or actual personal injury or property damage not directed at the plaintiff nonetheless causes economic loss to the plaintiff (for example, when a negligently caused explosion in the vicinity of plaintiff's business causes a loss of profits because customers can no longer reach the shop).

Prudential Ins. Co. v. Dewey Ballantine, Bushby, Palmer & Wood

Court of Appeals of New York, 1992.
80 N.Y.2d 377, 605 N.E.2d 318, 590 N.Y.S.2d 831.

■ TITONE, J.

[U.S. Lines told its creditor Prudential Ins. Co. and others that it was having trouble meeting its obligations. It sought to restructure its debt with a new mortgage. Prudential told U.S. Lines that before it would consider restructuring its claim of $92,885,000 it needed a favorable legal opinion on the impact of the proposal. At the direction of U.S. Lines the Gilmartin law firm drafted and delivered to Prudential an opinion letter containing an assurance that the mortgage documents to be recorded (which had been prepared by other counsel) represented "legal, valid and binding" obligations of U.S. Lines. The letter also stated that neither federal nor state law would interfere "with the practical realization of the benefits of the security intended to be provided" by those documents. Prudential ultimately accepted Gilmartin's opinion letter as satisfactory, and permitted the recording of those mortgage documents. One of those documents erroneously stated the outstanding balance of the mortgage securing the debt as $92,885—rather than the correct sum of $92,885,000. In the proceedings that followed when U.S. Lines filed for bankruptcy, Prudential lost its protected lien status for the amount over $92,885.]

Prudential thereafter commenced this action against Gilmartin, contending that the law firm's opinion letter had falsely assured it that the mortgage documents in question would fully protect its existing $92,885,-000 security interest. Although Prudential acknowledged that it was not actually in privity with Gilmartin, it nevertheless contended that the relationship between them was sufficiently close so as to support a cause of action in negligence. Alternatively, it maintained that Gilmartin could be held liable to it, in contract, on a third party beneficiary theory.

Following joinder of issue, Gilmartin moved for summary judgment on both causes of action. [The trial court granted the motion, concluding that no duty was owed and that the plaintiff was not a third party beneficiary. The Appellate Division affirmed, and granted leave for further appeal.]

II

Initially, it must be stressed that attorneys, like other professionals, may be held liable for economic injury arising from negligent representation. Although the defendants in many of the prior cases addressing this issue have been accountants, there is no reason to arbitrarily limit the potentially liable defendants to that class of professionals (see, Ossining Union Free School District v. Anderson LaRocca Anderson, 73 N.Y.2d 417, 424). Indeed, liability was imposed on engineering consultants in *Ossining*, and in Ultramares Corp. v. Touche (255 N.Y. 170, 188) and Glanzer v. Shepard (233 N.Y. 236, 240), it was suggested that in the right circumstances pecuniary recovery might be had from lawyers. We now conclude that in circumstances such as these, a theoretical basis for liability against legal professionals can be presented. Gilmartin contends that Canons 4 and 5 of the Code of Professional Responsibility, regarding the preservation of client loyalty and client confidences, argue against imposing liability on attorneys in these circumstances. However, where, as here, the negligent acts, i.e., the creation of an opinion letter and the transmission of that letter to a third party for the party's own use, were carried out by the lawyer at the client's express direction, the ethical considerations of Canons 4 and 5 are insufficient reason to insulate attorneys from liability. [   ]

III

Having concluded that legal professionals are not immune from liability in these cases, we turn now to the question whether liability may attach in the present circumstances. This Court has long held that before a party may recover in tort for pecuniary loss sustained as a result of another's negligent misrepresentations there must be a showing that there was either actual privity of contract between the parties or a relationship so close as to approach that of privity (see, e.g., [*Ossining*]; Credit Alliance Corp. v. Arthur Andersen & Co., 65 N.Y.2d 536; [*Ultramares*; *Glanzer*]). Such a requirement is necessary in order to provide fair and manageable bounds to what otherwise could prove to be limitless liability [   ].

Since Prudential concedes that it was not in direct privity with Gilmartin, we must determine whether the relationship between Prudential and Gilmartin was sufficiently close to support liability. For that purpose, we must look first to the substantial body of decisional law delineating the boundaries of liability to parties not in privity. In Glanzer v. Shepard (233 N.Y. 236 [1922]) a bean seller retained public weighers and directed them to furnish one copy of the weight certificate to a particular prospective buyer. The certificate was inaccurate and, as a result, the buyer suffered a loss. In language that is as applicable now as it was then, this Court concluded that the law imposed a duty on the weighers in favor of the buyer, despite the absence of privity between them, because the representations at issue had been made "for the very purpose of inducing action" on the part of the buyer [   ]. In other words, the buyer's use of the certificates was "not an indirect or collateral consequence" of the action of the weighers. Rather, it was a consequence which, to the weighers' knowledge, was the "end and aim of the transaction" [ ].

By contrast, in Ultramares Corp. v. Touche (255 N.Y. 170 [1931]), where accountants had prepared a certified balance sheet for their client and provided some 32 copies to be exhibited generally to "banks, creditors, stockholders, purchasers or sellers, according to the needs of the occasion" [ ], the accountants were not liable to third parties who may have relied on the financial information to their detriment. That was so because the accountants' report was primarily intended as a convenient instrument for the client's use in developing its business and only "incidentally or collaterally" was it expected to assist those to whom the client "might exhibit it thereafter" [ ].

In White v. Guarente (43 N.Y.2d 356 [1977]), accountants had contracted with a limited partnership to perform an audit and prepare the partnership's tax returns. It was clear that the accountants' services were obtained to benefit the specific members of the partnership, "a known group possessed of vested rights, marked by a definable limit and made up of certain components" [ ]. In these circumstances, this Court held that the relationship between the parties, accountants and a limited partner, was clearly one approaching privity.

Similar conclusions were reached in the more recent cases dealing with this issue. In *Credit Alliance* [1985], where we held the allegations insufficient to establish a relationship approaching privity between the plaintiffs and defendant accountants, there were no direct dealings between the plaintiffs and defendants, no specific agreement by the defendants to prepare the report for the plaintiffs' use or according to the plaintiffs' requirements, no specific promise to provide the plaintiffs with a copy of the report, and no actual provision of the report to the plaintiffs by the defendants. In sum, the necessary link between the relevant parties simply did not exist and there was no basis for liability.

Conversely, in the companion case (European American Bank and Trust Company v. Strauhs & Kaye, 65 N.Y.2d 536 [1985]), the prerequisites for the cause of action in negligence, as well as in gross negligence, were fully satisfied because the defendant accounting firm was well aware that a primary "end and aim" of its auditing process was to provide the third party plaintiff with the financial information it required. Not only did the accountants know the identity of the specific nonprivy party who would be relying on their reports, but they were also aware of the particular purpose for their services and they engaged in conduct creating an unmistakable relationship with the plaintiff, including having direct written, oral and in-person communications with the plaintiff's representatives. Significantly, the opinion in *Credit Alliance* distilled the principles emerging from the prior case law and identified three critical criteria for imposing liability: (1) an awareness by the maker of the statement that it is to be used for a particular purpose; (2) reliance by a known party on the statement in furtherance of that purpose; and (3) some conduct by the maker of the statement linking it to the relying party and evincing its understanding of that reliance [   ].

. . .

The *Credit Alliance* criteria and the cases on which those criteria are based clearly support the imposition of [a duty] here. First, it is undisputed that Gilmartin was well aware that the opinion letter which U.S. Lines directed it to prepare was to be used by Prudential in deciding whether to permit the debt restructuring. Thus, the end and aim of the opinion letter was to provide Prudential with the financial information it required. Indeed, [the deal] made Prudential's receipt of the opinion letter a condition precedent to closing. Second, as fully expected by Gilmartin, Prudential unquestionably relied on the opinion letter in agreeing to the debt restructuring. Specifically, Prudential focused on certain statements in the letter which assured it, generally, that the mortgage documents represented "legal, valid and binding" obligations of U.S. Lines which, once recorded, would be enforceable against it "in accordance with [their] respective terms." Finally, by addressing and sending the opinion letter directly to Prudential, Gilmartin clearly engaged in conduct which evinced its awareness and understanding that Prudential would rely on the letter, and provided the requisite link between the parties. Accordingly, contrary to the conclusion of the courts below, the bond between Gilmartin and Prudential was sufficiently close to establish a duty of care running from the former to the latter. Since this determination disposes of the question of Gilmartin's [duty], we find it unnecessary to reach Prudential's alternative contract claim.

IV

Having concluded that Gilmartin owed Prudential a duty of care, we now turn to the question of whether Prudential has demonstrated that there is a triable issue of fact as to whether that duty was breached here [   ]. In support of its claim that Gilmartin breached a duty owing to it, Prudential contends that the opinion letter falsely assured it that the mortgage documents in question would continue to fully protect its existing $92,885,000 security interest.

Initially, it should be stressed that the purpose of an opinion letter, as correctly spelled out by defendant, is to offer assurances to the creditor about the inner workings of the borrower's business, in particular, that no further corporate formalities are necessary to make the loan documents valid; that the documents are fully authorized under applicable law; that the terms, as written, are enforceable against the borrower; and that the proposed transaction does not violate some other obligation by which the borrower is bound. An examination of the opinion letter reveals that, although it did not make the specific assurance of a dollar amount of security, it did fulfill its purpose of assuring procedural regularity in forming its opinion. The opinion letter initially made clear that, in rendering its opinion, Gilmartin had relied in part upon certificates of certain public officials and corporate officers, and upon corporate documents and records, with respect to the accuracy of material factual matters which were not independently established. Then, with reference to the mortgage documents in issue, the letter simply stated that those documents represented "legal, valid and binding" obligations of U.S. Lines, which, when recorded, would be enforceable against it "in accordance with [their] respective terms," whatever those terms might be. No specific dollar amount was assured.

[The court noted that Gilmartin had qualified its opinion in several ways.]

In sum, a duty of care was owed to Prudential in these circumstances, and the facts do not prove a breach of that duty. In preparing the opinion letter, Gilmartin represented that it took the particular procedural measures, as discussed above, in investigating and substantiating the mortgage documents in question. After taking those measures, Gilmartin made certain general assurances to Prudential in the opinion letter. Those assurances did not set forth a specific dollar amount as securing the debt. It was agreed that the letter was to be in a form satisfactory to Prudential, which condition was satisfied when Prudential accepted the letter containing no more than general assurances. We can only conclude on these facts, where neither procedural nor substantive misrepresentations were made by Gilmartin, that the law firm was properly awarded summary judgment.

Accordingly, the order of the Appellate Division should be affirmed. . . .

■ SIMONS, ACTING C.J., and KAYE, HANCOCK and BELLACOSA, JJ., concur. SMITH, J., took no part.

NOTES AND QUESTIONS

1. *Privity.* Before analyzing the due care obligations that an attorney may owe to third parties—the issue raised in *Prudential*—we consider the duty of due care when an attorney gives incorrect advice to a client.

Meeting filing deadlines. Questions of legal malpractice tend to arise in two contexts. One involves cases in which attorneys fail to file complaints within the statute of limitations or in some other way clearly fail to perform a nonjudgmental task. In such cases, the client may have a good legal claim for malpractice if it is possible to show that the action, if filed, had a good chance for success.

Making strategic choices. The second type of claim arises from judgmental decisions that usually occur during litigation—when a strategic choice turns out badly. Here, the courts are not likely to second-guess the attorney's decision unless it lacked any plausible justification. As in the medical situation, attorneys are not expected to "be perfect or infallible," nor "must they always secure optimum outcomes for their clients." In both situations, an expert is usually needed to show the jury the standard and the deviation.

The strategy question extends beyond how to conduct litigation—to whether and on what terms to settle pending litigation. Advice to settle a claim for too little may lead to liability for malpractice. See Grayson v. Wofsey, Rosen, Kweskin & Kuriansky, 231 Conn. 168, 646 A.2d 195 (1994)(upholding an action where the attorney was alleged to have negligently valued the marital estate so as to induce his client to settle for too little).

Clients in criminal cases may face an extension of the requirement of a valid case. In Shaw v. State of Alaska, 861 P.2d 566 (Alaska 1993), plaintiff alleged that his public defender negligently failed to make constitutional arguments that would have prevented his conviction for burglary and larceny. He was freed after ten years when another lawyer made those arguments. The court concluded that the case should fail if the plaintiff was "actually guilty of the original charges." Why not permit recovery for the ten years in prison if it can be shown that a reasonably careful attorney would have avoided that result? See also, Peeler v. Hughes & Luce, 868 S.W.2d 823 (Tex.App.1993).

2. In *Prudential*, the court's references to Canons 4 and 5 are to the American Bar Association Model Code of Professional Responsibility, adopted in New York and other states. (More recently, the ABA has promulgated—and states have adopted—the Model Rules of Professional Conduct.) Canon 4 states that a "lawyer should preserve the confidences and secrets of a client." Canon 5 states that a "lawyer should exercise independent professional judgment on behalf of a client." Each is elaborated upon in rules and comments. How might either be relevant in the *Prudential* case?

3. *Emotional distress*. In these cases it is unusual for the awards to include recovery for the client's emotional distress. In Pleasant v. Celli, 18 Cal.App.4th 841, 22 Cal.Rptr.2d 663 (1993), an attorney missed the statute of limitations on what the jury could find would have been a successful medical malpractice case. The claim against the attorney properly included economic harm, but an award of $500,000 for emotional distress was reversed. The plaintiff in such a case must show that she sustained "highly foreseeable shock stemming from an abnormal event." Missing the statute of limitations did not suffice.

Other courts have suggested that when the purpose of the attorney's retention is for non-economic purposes, such as criminal defense, adoption proceedings, or marital dissolution, damages for emotional distress may be foreseeable and may be recovered as one item of damages. See, e.g., Kohn v. Schiappa, 281 N.J.Super. 235, 656 A.2d 1322 (Law Div.1995)(lawyer representing clients seeking to adopt a child reveals their names to the natural mother); Wagenmann v. Adams, 829 F.2d 196 (1st Cir.1987) (malpractice led to client's involuntary incarceration in psychiatric hospital). Is this consistent with the general treatment of negligent infliction of emotional distress that we considered earlier?

In a few cases distraught clients have committed suicide allegedly due to the attorneys' malpractice. E.g., McPeake v. William T. Cannon, 381

Pa.Super. 227, 553 A.2d 439 (1989)(client found guilty of rape, among other charges, jumped through closed fifth floor courtroom window). The court denied recovery, expressing concern that liability here would discourage attorneys "from representing what may be a sizeable number of depressed or unstable criminal defendants." As we shall see, p. 350, infra, claims for suicide have met more judicial resistance than claims for emotional distress.

4. The Restatement identifies the duty owed the client in the following terms in section 552(1) of the Second Restatement, which has been quite influential:

(1) One who, in the course of his business, profession or employment, or in any other transaction in which he has a pecuniary interest, supplies false information for the guidance of others in their business transactions, is subject to liability for pecuniary loss caused to them by their justifiable reliance upon the information, if he fails to exercise reasonable care or competence in obtaining or communicating the information.

Does this accord with the attorney malpractice decisions we have been considering? The range of persons owing a duty of the type set forth in § 552(1) stretches well beyond accountants and attorneys. Consider the following cases:

a. In Aesoph v. Kusser, 498 N.W.2d 654 (S.D.1993), plaintiff farmers alleged that they asked defendant insurance agent about getting federal crop insurance and that he incorrectly responded that they were not eligible. To determine eligibility apparently required reading and understanding seven single spaced pages of a manual. The court asserted that a duty existed if "the relationship of the parties arising out of contract or otherwise, [is] such that in morals and good conscience the one has the right to rely upon the other for information, and the other giving the information to give it with care." When asked, defendant "had no obligation to provide any answer. However, when he chose to provide an answer he changed the relationship and undertook a duty to exercise care in providing the answer" since the subject was "the complex matter of eligibility for federal crop insurance." Is "morals and good conscience" comparable to the language of section 552?

b. In Mohr v. Commonwealth, 421 Mass. 147, 653 N.E.2d 1104 (1995), adoptive parents alleged that the defendant social service agency, after learning that the child's mother had suffered from schizophrenia, made negligent misrepresentations to plaintiffs regarding the child's emotional and medical history. The court, after tracing the development of this type of claim, upheld a "wrongful adoption" action for the adoptive parents. An adoption agency, whether public or private, has "an affirmative duty to disclose to adoptive parents information about a child that will enable them to make a knowledgeable decision about whether to accept the child for adoption." The award was for economic harm that would be sustained in providing "the structured, residential placement that Elizabeth will need throughout her lifetime." Should damages for emotional distress be recoverable in this type of case? See also Gibbs v. Ernst, 538 Pa. 193, 647 A.2d 882 (1994), imposing a duty of disclosure in adoption cases but rejecting an affirmative duty on the agency to investigate the child's background.

c. The situation is not so clear when the parties are in an arm's length bargaining situation and one of the parties carelessly misrepresents.

In Onita Pacific Corp. v. Trustees of Bronson, 315 Or. 149, 843 P.2d 890 (1992), purchasers sued their vendors for harm arising when they relied on the vendors' allegedly negligent misrepresentations about when certain lots would be released to the plaintiffs. The court held, 5–2, that such claims are not actionable in arm's length transactions. Plaintiffs could have avoided the problem by "insisting that the [crucial] provision be included in the written agreements" rather than relying on an alleged representation.

A dissenter observed that "Oregon's future commercial interests, including its prospect for international trade growth, are not likely to be served by an outmoded rule that one party in a business transaction may not rely on what she, he, or it is told by the other party. Oregon will be best served by requiring care to not mislead your business 'partners.' I think Oregonians believe and expect that the best business is where both sides to a transaction make a profit and are able to invest in new activities." The majority approach was "based on an urban savagery where all are divided by the 'limiting notion' of 'us versus them.'"

Although the no-duty approach was once the dominant view, it is rejected by most courts today. In Williams Ford, Inc. v. Hartford Courant Co., 232 Conn. 559, 657 A.2d 212 (1995), a newspaper allegedly misrepresented terms to prospective advertisers. Defendant argued that "between two sophisticated commercial parties with full access to information concerning a business transaction" there was no duty of due care. The court disagreed. It found Onita "unpersuasive" and found "very little justification for not extending liability to all parties and agents to a bargaining transaction for making misrepresentations negligently."

Recall that intentional misrepresentations are explored in Chapter XV.

5. *Attorneys and Third Parties.* *Prudential* addresses the question of how far beyond the attorney-client relation duty should be extended. In Biakanja v. Irving, 49 Cal.2d 647, 320 P.2d 16 (1958), the defendant notary public drew up plaintiff's brother's will giving plaintiff the entire estate. Because of the notary's negligent failure to have the will properly witnessed, the will failed and the brother's property passed by law to other relatives, so that plaintiff got only one-eighth of the estate. Her recovery against the notary for the difference was affirmed:

> The determination whether in a specific case the defendant will be held liable to a third person not in privity is a matter of policy and involves the balancing of various factors, among which are the extent to which the transaction was intended to affect the plaintiff, the foreseeability of harm to him, the degree of certainty that the plaintiff

suffered injury, the closeness of the connection between the defendant's conduct and the injury suffered, the moral blame attached to the defendant's conduct, and the policy of preventing future harm. [ ] Here, the "end and aim" of the transaction was to provide for the passing of Maroevich's estate to plaintiff. (See *Glanzer v. Shepard* [ ].) Defendant must have been aware from the terms of the will itself that, if faulty solemnization caused the will to be invalid, plaintiff would suffer the very loss which occurred.

In Lucas v. Hamm, 56 Cal.2d 583, 364 P.2d 685, 15 Cal.Rptr. 821 (1961), cert. denied 368 U.S. 987 (1962), a will was invalid because it violated the rule against perpetuities. In a malpractice action, the court denied that liability "would impose an undue burden" on the legal profession because "although in some situations liability could be large and unpredictable in amount, this is also true of an attorney's liability to his client." The *Lucas* court ultimately concluded, however, that the legal error did not demonstrate negligence because the rule was so difficult to understand and apply.

The *Biakanja–Lucas* line was continued in Heyer v. Flaig, 70 Cal.2d 223, 449 P.2d 161, 74 Cal.Rptr. 225 (1969), involving another will failure. The court observed that in "some ways, the beneficiary's interests loom greater than those of the client. After the latter's death, a failure in his testamentary scheme works no practical effect except to deprive his intended beneficiaries of the intended bequests." Also, as *Lucas* recognized, "unless the beneficiary could recover against the attorney in such a case, no one could do so and the social policy of preventing future harm would be frustrated."

See also Petrillo v. Bachenberg, 139 N.J. 472, 655 A.2d 1354 (1995), imposing a duty of due care on a seller's attorney in connection with an arguably misleading percolation-test report given to the prospective buyer. The court extended the opinion-letter line to other kinds of information that the attorney knows or should know will influence a non-client because the "objective purpose of documents such as opinion letters, title reports, or offering statements," is to induce others to rely on them.

See Note, Expanding Legal Malpractice to Nonclient Third Parties—At What Cost?, 23 Colum.J. of Law & Soc. Probs. 1 (1989), indicating that many states continue to adhere to a privity limitation, criticizing the California "balance of factors" approach, and proposing a duty to third parties limited to situations of intentional wrongdoing.

6. *Accountants' Liability.* As the court's discussion of earlier cases suggests, most have involved the liability of accounting firms for harm caused to those who have loaned money to the accountant's clients based on statements prepared by the accountants. Tracing the *Ultramares, Guarente, Credit Alliance,* and *European American Bank* sequence, what emerges as the cornerstone of liability? Do the same considerations apply to the cases involving lawyers? In a famous sentence in *Ultramares,* Judge Cardozo observed that if the accountant were to be held liable for negligence, they would be exposed to "liability in an indeterminate amount for an indeterminate time to an indeterminate class." Is that more true for accountants than for attorneys?

7. *Approaches to accountants' liability.* States have developed three basic approaches to the question of the duty owed by accountants to those not in privity with them.

a. The New York view is followed by some ten states. As indicated in *Prudential*, New York demands a "linking" between the accountant and the relying party that requires more than notice from the relying party to the accountant. How *much* more is the question. In William Iselin & Co. v. Mann Judd Landau, 71 N.Y.2d 420, 522 N.E.2d 21, 527 N.Y.S.2d 176 (1988) the court denied recovery to plaintiff creditor who had been sent a copy of the financial statements by the defendant accountant at the client-borrower's request. That single act would not satisfy the requirement of showing that defendant knew that plaintiff would rely on the report.

In Security Pacific Business Credit, Inc. v. Peat Marwick Main & Co., 79 N.Y.2d 695, 597 N.E.2d 1080, 586 N.Y.S.2d 87 (1992), plaintiff lender claimed that it was owed a duty of due care by defendant auditor based essentially on a "single unsolicited phone call" that plaintiff's vice-president made to defendant after it had completed the field audit of the client but before the final report had been prepared. At most defendant responded to the call by saying that "nothing untoward had been uncovered in the course of the audit." The court held that a lender could not meet the requirements of *Credit Alliance* and impose "negligence liability of significant commercial dimension and consequences by merely interposing and announcing its reliance in this fashion." If this single call could suffice,

> "then every lender's due diligence list will in the future mandate such a telephone call. For the small price of a phone call, [the lender] would in effect acquire additional loan protection by placing the auditor in the role of an insurer or guarantor of loans extended to its clients." The facile acquisition of deep pocket surety coverage, with no opportunity for actuarial assessment and self-protection, by the party sought to be charged, at the mere cost of a telephone call by the lender, is a bargain premium rate indeed.

What if the plaintiff had made the phone call after the client had requested the audit but before the defendant had agreed to do the work?

b. Modified foreseeability. In H. Rosenblum, Inc. v. Adler, 93 N.J. 324, 461 A.2d 138 (1983), the court held that accountants owed a duty of due care to third parties who had obtained the allegedly negligently prepared statements from the client of the accountant. A handful of states have adopted an approach close to general foreseeability. Is it consistent with a foreseeability test for the New Jersey court to have insisted that the plaintiff have obtained the statement from the client? Would you expect accountants in New Jersey to exercise greater care in their work than those in New York? If so, would the higher degree of care exercised be desirable? In 1995, New Jersey adopted legislation that brought it closer to the New York position. N.J.S.A. 2A:53A–25.

c. The Restatement view. Some 15–20 states follow the approach developed in section 552. At p. 275, supra, we noted the duty imposed by subsection (1). Subsections (2) and (3) indicate to whom that duty is owed:

(2) Except as stated in Subsection (3), the liability stated in Subsection (1) is limited to loss suffered

(a) by the person or one of a limited group of persons for whose benefit and guidance he intends to supply the information or knows that the recipient intends to supply it; and

(b) through reliance upon it in a transaction that he intends the information to influence or knows that the recipient so intends or in a substantially similar transaction.

(3) The liability of one who is under a public duty to give the information extends to loss suffered by any of the class of persons for whose benefit the duty is created, in any of the transactions in which it is intended to protect them.

Consider the following examples suggested by comments and illustrations to that section:

1. The client asks D to prepare an audit so that the client can show it "to Bank B" to get a loan of $50,000. D prepares the requested statements. Bank B fails and, without telling D, the client shows the statements to Bank A, which lends $50,000 in reliance and loses the money when the client goes bankrupt. D owes no duty to Bank A. Why not? What result if the client had not told D the prospective use of the statements?

2. If the client had told D that it intended to seek a loan of $50,000 from an unidentified bank, D would owe a duty to any bank that lends the money—even if the client had Bank X in mind at the time but later goes to Bank Y. Why? What if the loan is for $250,000?

3. The client tells D that the documents are to help get a loan of $50,000 from B. Instead, B decides to buy an interest in the client for $250,000. The client soon collapses and B loses everything. D does not owe a duty to B.

How would each of these examples be analyzed in New York? Under *Rosenblum*?

d. Federal securities law. Some professional liability is controlled by federal securities law—the Securities Act of 1933 and the Securities Exchange Act of 1934. This regulatory scheme is discussed in Bily v. Arthur Young & Co., 3 Cal.4th 370, 834 P.2d 745, 11 Cal.Rptr.2d 51 (1992), and applied in O'Melveny & Myers v. Federal Deposit Ins.Corp., 114 S.Ct. 2048 (1994). This subject is pursued in upper class courses.

8. The *Bily* court, after reviewing and critiquing the various state positions, decided to adopt an approach close to that of the Restatement. The case involved claims by investors in Osborne Computer Corp. who claimed reliance on financial statements defendants prepared for Osborne.

Defendant delivered 100 copies of the professionally-printed report to Osborne.

The court rejected the New York approach because it saw "no rationale for the distinct 'linking'" that it required. It also rejected a foreseeability standard because it feared that an auditor would face "potential liability far out of proportion to its fault" because the "client, its promoters, and its managers have generally left the scene, headed in most cases for government-supervised liquidation or the bankruptcy court." Moreover, the court was skeptical about the claims of reliance. Here, the plaintiffs "perceived an opportunity to make a large sum of money in a very short time by investing in a company they believed would (literally within months) become the dominant force in the new personal computer market. Although hindsight suggests they misjudged a number of major factors (including, at a minimum, the product, the market, the competition, and the company's manufacturing capacity), plaintiffs' litigation-focused attention is now exclusively on the auditor and its report."

The *Bily* court also thought the area might be more effectively regulated through contract and self-help than through tort. Third parties "should be encouraged to rely on their own prudence, diligence, and contracting power, as well as other informational tools. This kind of self-reliance promotes sound investment and credit practices and discourages the careless use of monetary resources." On the other hand, if liability based on foreseeability were imposed, this might lead accountants to "rationally respond to increased liability by simply reducing audit services in fledgling industries where the business failure rate is high, reasoning that they will inevitably be singled out and sued when their client goes into bankruptcy regardless of the care or detail of their audits."

Finally, "investors and creditors can limit the impact of losses by diversifying investments and loan portfolios. They effectively constitute a 'broad social base upon which the costs of accounting errors can be spread.'"

Two dissenters would have used foreseeability on the ground that there was "apparently no reason for preferring a foreseen user over a foreseeable one. Neither party pays for the audit, and neither party is owed a greater duty of care from the accountant. Since modern auditors fully expect third parties to rely on their opinions, the distinction is simply indefensible."

9. Do you think that *Glanzer* would have been decided differently if the defendant had negligently failed to discover that his scales were defective and had made a hundred inaccurate weighings? If the weigher had not delivered the statement to the buyer, might the weigher have been protected by writing into its contract with the seller that the information was provided only for the benefit of the seller?

10. Professor Bishop argues that the nonliability of accountants and other providers of information can be justified on the ground that suppliers of information cannot capture the benefit of their "product" once it has entered the stream of commerce. He concludes that liability "should be restricted when (a) the information is of a type that is valuable to many potential users, (b) the producer of the information cannot capture in his prices the benefits flowing to all users of the information, and (c) the imposition of liability to all persons harmed would raise potential costs significantly enough to discourage information production altogether. When these three conditions are met the court should impose liability on the defendant in relation to a limited class only." Bishop, Negligent Misrepresentation Through Economists' Eyes, 96 L.Q.Rev. 360 (1980). Do you agree? Judge Posner discusses Bishop's thesis in Greycas, Inc. v. Proud, 826 F.2d 1560 (7th Cir.1987), cert. denied 484 U.S. 1043 (1988).

11. In Bronstein v. GZA GeoEnvironmental, Inc., 665 A.2d 369 (N.H. 1995), a prospective buyer of property retained defendant to do an environmental study of the property. The contract provided that the report was "for the exclusive use of [the party requesting the report]." It could be given to the lender and the title insurer but other dissemination was barred. Similar language was incorporated into the final report itself. After receiving the report, the prospective buyer, without notifying the defendant, assigned his rights under the purchase contract to plaintiffs who immediately purchased the land. When plaintiffs tried to sell the land, another environmental firm discovered hazardous substances. Although New Hampshire normally ties duty closely to foreseeability in this type of case, the court rejected this claim on the ground that the parties had never dealt directly and that, because of the contractual restrictions, "it was not reasonably foreseeable that [the prospective buyer] would furnish the information to [the actual buyer] or that [they] would rely on the report." Can other suppliers of information use this device?

12. *Physicians and Economic Harm.* Although we tend to think of carelessness by physicians in terms of physical consequences, a series of cases has shown that carelessness may also have an economic impact. In Aufrichtig v. Lowell, 85 N.Y.2d 540, 650 N.E.2d 401, 626 N.Y.S.2d 743 (1995), the court decided that a physician could be sued for understating the severity of plaintiff patient's medical condition in an affidavit. This led the patient to settle her case against her insurer for less than its value. There is a duty of due care to speak truthfully if one speaks at all in this relationship. See also Greinke v. Keese, 82 Misc.2d 996, 371 N.Y.S.2d 58 (1975)(allowing claim where physician negligently told patient he had only 12–18 months to live, plaintiff relied and took early retirement from his job and sustained substantial financial loss).

In Arato v. Avedon, 5 Cal.4th 1172, 858 P.2d 598, 23 Cal.Rptr.2d 131 (1993), the widow and children of a patient who died of pancreatic cancer sued treating physicians on the ground that they failed to disclose information regarding the poor life expectancy of patients with this type of cancer. If they had done so, and the patient had realized the odds, he would have put his affairs in better order. One claim was for the economic loss sustained by the survivors due to the condition in which the decedent left his affairs. The court rejected the claim. The main point was that the physicians had met their obligation of obtaining informed consent—and that this did not require the use of statistical life expectancy data. Moreover, there was no duty to disclose information that might be material to the patient's nonmedical interests. Why might this be so?

13. As *Prudential* and the note cases indicate, the risk in virtually all these cases has been exclusively economic. Should the analysis differ where the economic harm results from threatened or actual physical harm? Keep this question in mind while reading the next case and the notes that follow it.

People Express Airlines, Inc. v. Consolidated Rail Corp.

Supreme Court of New Jersey, 1985.
100 N.J. 246, 495 A.2d 107.

■ HANDLER, J.

This appeal presents a question that has not previously been directly considered: whether a defendant's negligent conduct that interferes with a plaintiff's business resulting in purely economic losses, unaccompanied by property damage or personal injury, is compensable in tort. The appeal poses this issue in the context of the defendants' alleged negligence that caused a dangerous chemical to escape from a railway tank car, resulting in the evacuation from the surrounding area of persons whose safety and health were threatened. The plaintiff, a commercial airline, was forced to evacuate its premises and suffered an interruption of its business operations with resultant economic losses.

I.

Because of the posture of the case—an appeal taken from the grant of summary judgment for the defendant railroad, subsequently reversed by the Appellate Division, [ ]—we must accept plaintiff's version of the facts as alleged. The facts are straight-forward.

On July 22, 1981, a fire began in the Port Newark freight yard of defendant Consolidated Rail Corporation (Conrail) when ethylene oxide manufactured by defendant BASF Wyandotte Company (BASF) escaped from a tank car, punctured during a "coupling" operation with another rail car, and ignited. The tank car was owned by defendant Union Tank Car Company (Union Car) and was leased to defendant BASF.

The plaintiff asserted at oral argument that at least some of the defendants were aware from prior experiences that ethylene oxide is a highly volatile substance; further, that emergency response plans in case of an accident had been prepared. When the fire occurred that gave rise to this lawsuit, some of the defendants' consultants helped determine how much of the surrounding area to evacuate. The municipal authorities then evacuated the area within a one-mile radius surrounding the fire to lessen the risk to persons within the area should the burning tank car explode. The evacuation area included the adjacent North Terminal building of

Newark International Airport, where plaintiff People Express Airlines' (People Express) business operations are based. Although the feared explosion never occurred, People Express employees were prohibited from using the North Terminal for twelve hours.

The plaintiff contends that it suffered business-interruption losses as a result of the evacuation. These losses consist of cancelled scheduled flights and lost reservations because employees were unable to answer the telephones to accept bookings; also, certain fixed operating expenses allocable to the evacuation time period were incurred and paid despite the fact that plaintiff's offices were closed. No physical damage to airline property and no personal injury occurred as a result of the fire.

[The trial court granted a motion for summary judgment entered by one of the defendants. On appeal, the Appellate Division reversed, holding that recovery of negligently caused economic loss was not automatically barred by the absence of any property damage or personal injury. The question was certified for consideration by the Supreme Court.]

II.

The single characteristic that distinguishes parties in negligence suits whose claims for economic losses have been regularly denied by American and English courts from those who have recovered economic losses is, with respect to the successful claimants, the fortuitous occurrence of physical harm or property damage, however slight. It is well-accepted that a defendant who negligently injures a plaintiff or his property may be liable for all proximately caused harm, including economic losses. [ ]Nevertheless, a virtually *per se* rule barring recovery for economic loss unless the negligent conduct also caused physical harm has evolved throughout this century, based, in part, on Robins Dry Dock & Repair Co. v. Flint, 275 U.S. 303 (1927), and Cattle v. Stockton Waterworks Co., 10 Q.B. 453 (1875). This has occurred although neither case created a rule absolutely disallowing recovery in such circumstances. See, e.g., Stevenson v. East Ohio Gas Co., 73 N.E.2d 200 (Ohio.Ct.App.1946)(employee who was prohibited from working at his plant, which was closed due to conflagration begun by negligent rupture of stored liquified natural gas at nearby utility, could not recover lost wages); Byrd v. English, 117 Ga. 191, 43 S.E. 419 (1903) (plaintiff who owned printing plant could not recover lost profits when defendant negligently damaged utility's electrical conduits that supplied power to the plant); see also Restatement (Second) of Torts § 766C (1979)(positing rule of nonrecovery for purely economic losses absent physical harm). But see In re Kinsman Transit Co., 388 F.2d 821, 824 (2d Cir.1968) [*Kinsman II*] (after rejecting an inflexible rule of nonrecovery, court applied traditional proximate cause analysis to claim for purely economic losses).

The reasons that have been advanced to explain the divergent results for litigants seeking economic losses are varied. Some courts have viewed the general rule against recovery as necessary to limit damages to reasonably foreseeable consequences of negligent conduct. This concern in a

[handwritten margin note: Employees can't sue in most, if not all jurisdictions]

given case is often manifested as an issue of causation and has led to the requirement of physical harm as an element of proximate cause. In this context, the physical harm requirement functions as part of the definition of the causal relationship between the defendant's negligent act and the plaintiff's economic damages; it acts as a convenient clamp on otherwise boundless liability. [ ] The physical harm rule also reflects certain deep-seated concerns that underlie courts' denial of recovery for purely economic losses occasioned by a defendant's negligence. These concerns include the fear of fraudulent claims, mass litigation, and limitless liability, or liability out of proportion to the defendant's fault. [ ]

The assertion of unbounded liability is not unique to cases involving negligently caused economic loss without physical harm. Even in negligence suits in which plaintiffs have sustained physical harm, the courts have recognized that a tortfeasor is not necessarily liable for *all* consequences of his conduct. While a lone act can cause a finite amount of physical harm, that harm may be great and very remote in its final consequences. A single overturned lantern may burn Chicago. Some limitation is required; that limitation is the rule that a tortfeasor is liable only for that harm that he proximately caused. Proximate or legal cause has traditionally functioned to limit liability for negligent conduct. Duty has also been narrowly defined to limit liability. Compare the majority and dissenting opinions in [*Palsgraf*, discussed in Chapter V]. Thus, we proceed from the premise that principles of duty and proximate cause are instrumental in limiting the amount of litigation and extent of liability in cases in which no physical harm occurs just as they are in cases involving physical injury.

Countervailing considerations of fairness and public policy have led courts to discard the requirement of physical harm as an element in defining proximate cause to overcome the problem of fraudulent or indefinite claims. See *Portee v. Jaffee*. . . .

The troublesome concern reflected in cases denying recovery for negligently-caused economic loss is the alleged potential for infinite liability, or liability out of all proportion to the defendant's fault. . . . The answer to the allegation of unchecked liability is not the judicial obstruction of a fairly grounded claim for redress. Rather, it must be a more sedulous application of traditional concepts of duty and proximate causation to the facts of each case. [ ]

It is understandable that courts, fearing that if even one deserving plaintiff suffering purely economic loss were allowed to recover, all such plaintiffs could recover, have anchored their rulings to the physical harm requirement. While the rationale is understandable, it supports only a limitation on, not a denial of, liability. The physical harm requirement capriciously showers compensation along the path of physical destruction, regardless of the status or circumstances of individual claimants. Purely economic losses are borne by innocent victims, who may not be able to absorb their losses. See Comment, 88 Harv.L.Rev. 444, 449–50 (1974). In the end, the challenge is to fashion a rule that limits liability but permits adjudication of meritorious claims. The asserted inability to fix chrystal-line formulae for recovery on the differing facts of future cases simply does not justify the wholesale rejection of recovery in all cases.

Further, judicial reluctance to allow recovery for purely economic losses is discordant with contemporary tort doctrine. The torts process, like the law itself, is a human institution designed to accomplish certain social objectives. One objective is to ensure that innocent victims have avenues of legal redress, absent a contrary, overriding public policy. [ ] This reflects the overarching purpose of tort law: that wronged persons should be compensated for their injuries and that those responsible for the wrong should bear the cost of their tortious conduct.

Other policies underlie this fundamental purpose. Imposing liability on defendants for their negligent conduct discourages others from similar tortious behavior, fosters safer products to aid our daily tasks, vindicates reasonable conduct that has regard for the safety of others, and, ultimately, shifts the risk of loss and associated costs of dangerous activities to those who should be and are best able to bear them. Although these policies may be unevenly reflected or imperfectly articulated in any particular case, we strive to ensure that the application of negligence doctrine advances the fundamental purpose of tort law and does not unnecessarily or arbitrarily foreclose redress based on formalisms or technicalisms. Whatever the original common law justifications for the physical harm rule, contempo-rary tort and negligence doctrine allow—indeed, impel—a more thorough consideration and searching analysis of underlying policies to determine whether a particular defendant may be liable for a plaintiff's economic losses despite the absence of any attendant physical harm. [ ]

III.

We may appropriately consider two relevant avenues of analysis in defining a cause of action for negligently-caused economic loss. The first examines the evolution of various exceptions to the rule of nonrecovery for purely economic losses, and suggests that the exceptions have cast consider-able doubt on the validity of the current rule and, indeed, have laid the foundation for a rule that would allow recovery. The second explores the elements of a suitable rule and adopts the traditional approach of foresee-ability as it relates to duty and proximate cause molded to circumstances involving a claim only for negligently-caused economic injury.

A.

Judicial discomfiture with the rule of nonrecovery for purely economic loss throughout the last several decades has led to numerous exceptions in the general rule. Although the rationalizations for these exceptions differ among courts and cases, two common threads run throughout the excep-tions. The first is that the element of foreseeability emerges as a more appropriate analytical standard to determine the question of liability than a *per se* prohibitory rule. The second is that the extent to which the defendant knew or should have known the particular consequences of his negligence, including the economic loss of a particularly foreseeable plaintiff, is dispositive of the issues of duty and fault.

One group of exceptions is based on the "special relationship" between the tortfeasor and the individual or business deprived of economic expectations. Many of these cases are recognized as involving the tort of negligent misrepresentation, resulting in liability for specially foreseeable economic losses. Importantly, the cases do not involve a breach of contract claim between parties in privity; rather, they involve tort claims by innocent third parties who suffered purely economic losses at the hands of negligent defendants with whom no direct relationship existed. Courts have justified their finding of liability in these negligence cases based on notions of a special relationship between the negligent tortfeasors and the foreseeable plaintiffs who relied on the quality of defendants' work or services, to their detriment. The special relationship, in reality, is an expression of the courts' satisfaction that a duty of care existed because the plaintiffs were particularly foreseeable and the injury was proximately caused by the defendant's negligence.

The special relationship exception has been extended to auditors, see *H. Rosenblum, Inc. v. Adler*, [ ] (independent auditor whose negligence resulted in inaccurate public financial statement held liable to plaintiff who bought stock in company for purposes of sale of business to company; stock subsequently proved to be worthless); surveyors, [ ](surveyor whose negligence resulted in error in depicting boundary of lot held liable to remote purchaser); termite inspectors, [ ] (termite inspectors whose negligence resulted in purchase of infested home liable to out-of-privity buyers); engineers, [ ] (engineers whose negligence resulted in successful bidder's losses in performing construction contract held liable); attorneys, see Lucas v. Hamm, 56 Cal.2d 583, 15 Cal.Rptr. 821, 364 P.2d 685 (1961), cert. den., 368 U.S. 987 (1962)(attorney whose negligence caused intended beneficiary to be deprived of proceeds of the will [owed duty] to beneficiary); notaries public, [ ]; Biakanja v. Irving, 49 Cal.2d 647, 320 P.2d 16 (1958)(notaries public whose negligence caused out-of-privity mortgagee and intended beneficiary of will, respectively, to be deprived of expected proceeds held liable); architects, [ ] (architects whose negligence resulted in use of defective concrete liable to out-of-privity prime contractor); weighers, see Glanzer v. Shepard, 233 N.Y. 236, 135 N.E. 275 (1922)(public weigher whose negligence caused remote buyer's losses was liable for loss); and telegraph companies, [ ] (telegraph company whose negligent transmission caused plaintiff not to obtain contract was liable); see also W. Prosser, The Law of Torts § 107, at 705 (4th ed.1971); Restatement (Second) of Torts § 552 (1977)(positing recovery for negligent misrepresentation). [ ]

. . .

Courts have found it fair and just in all of these exceptional cases to impose liability on defendants who, by virtue of their special activities, professional training or other unique preparation for their work, had particular knowledge or reason to know that others, such as the intended beneficiaries of wills (e.g., *Lucas v. Hamm*, supra) or the purchasers of stock who were expected to rely on the company's financial statement in the prospectus (e.g., *H. Rosenblum, Inc. v. Adler*, supra), would be economically harmed by negligent conduct. In this group of cases, even though the particular plaintiff was not always foreseeable, the particular class of plaintiffs was foreseeable as was the particular type of injury.

A very solid exception allowing recovery for economic losses has also been created in cases akin to private actions for public nuisance. Where a plaintiff's business is based in part upon the exercise of a public right, the plaintiff has been able to recover purely economic losses caused by a defendant's negligence. See, e.g., Louisiana ex rel. Guste v. M/V Testbank, 752 F.2d 1019 (5th Cir.1985)(en banc)(defendants responsible for ship collision held liable to all commercial fishermen, shrimpers, crabbers and oystermen for resulting pollution of Mississippi River); Union Oil Co. v. Oppen, 501 F.2d 558 (9th Cir.1974)(fishermen making known commercial use of public waters may recover economic losses due to defendant's oil spill); [ ]. The theory running throughout these cases, in which the plaintiffs depend on the exercise of the public or riparian right to clean water as a natural resource, is that the pecuniary losses suffered by those who make direct use of the resource are particularly foreseeable because they are so closely linked, through the resource, to the defendants' behavior.

Particular knowledge of the economic consequences has sufficed to establish duty and proximate cause in contexts other than those already considered. In Henry Clay v. Jersey City, 74 N.J.Super. 490 (Ch.Div.1962), aff'd, 84 N.J.Super. 9 (App.Div.1964), for example, a lessee-manufacturer had to vacate the building in which its business was located because of the defendant city's negligent failure to maintain its sewer line while the line was repaired. While there was some property damage, the court treated the tenant's and owner's claims separately; the tenant's claims were purely economic, stemming from the loss of use of its property right, as in the instant case. Further, the city had had notice of the leak since 1957 and should have known about it even earlier. Duty, breach and proximate cause were found to exist; the plaintiff-tenant recovered lost profits and expenses incurred during the shut-down. See also J'Aire Corp. v. Gregory, 24 Cal.3d 799, 157 Cal.Rptr. 407, 598 P.2d 60 (1979)(contractor who undertook construction work for owner of building had duty to tenants to complete construction on time to avoid resultant economic losses).

These exceptions expose the hopeless artificiality of the *per se* rule against recovery for purely economic losses. When the plaintiffs are reasonably foreseeable, the injury is directly and proximately caused by defendant's negligence, and liability can be limited fairly, courts have endeavored to create exceptions to allow recovery. . . .

. . .

. . .   The foreseeability standard that may be synthesized from these cases is one that posits liability in terms of where, along a spectrum ranging from the general to the particular, foreseeability is ultimately found. [   ] A broad view of these cases reasonably permits the conclusion that the extent of liability and degree of foreseeability stand in direct proportion to one another. The more particular is the foreseeability that economic loss will be suffered by the plaintiff as a result of defendant's negligence, the more just is it that liability be imposed and recovery allowed.

We hold therefore that a defendant owes a duty of care to take reasonable measures to avoid the risk of causing economic damages, aside from physical injury, to particular plaintiffs or plaintiffs comprising an identifiable class with respect to whom defendant knows or has reason to know are likely to suffer such damages from its conduct. A defendant failing to adhere to this duty of care may be found liable for such economic damages proximately caused by its breach of duty.

We stress that an identifiable class of plaintiffs is not simply a foreseeable class of plaintiffs. For example, members of the general public, or invitees such as sales and service persons at a particular plaintiff's business premises, or persons travelling on a highway near the scene of a negligently-caused accident, such as the one at bar, who are delayed in the conduct of their affairs and suffer varied economic losses, are certainly a foreseeable class of plaintiffs. Yet their presence within the area would be fortuitous, and the particular type of economic injury that could be suffered by such persons would be hopelessly unpredictable and not realistically foreseeable. Thus, the class itself would not be sufficiently ascertainable. An identifiable class of plaintiffs must be particularly foreseeable in terms of the type of persons or entities comprising the class, the certainty or predictability of their presence, the approximate numbers of those in the class, as well as the type of economic expectations disrupted. [   ]

We recognize that some cases will present circumstances that defy the categorization here devised to circumscribe a defendant's orbit of duty, limit otherwise boundless liability and define an identifiable class of plaintiffs that may recover. In these cases, the courts will be required to draw upon notions of fairness, common sense and morality to fix the line limiting liability as a matter of public policy, rather than an uncritical application of the principle of particular foreseeability. [   ]

[The court concluded that plaintiff had shown the requisite proximate causal connection between the negligence and the harm—a discussion we consider in Chapter V at p. 381.]

IV.

We are satisfied that our holding today is fully applicable to the facts that we have considered on this appeal. Plaintiff has set forth a cause of action under our decision, and it is entitled to have the matter proceed to a plenary trial. Among the facts that persuade us that a cause of action has been established is the close proximity of the North Terminal and People Express Airlines to the Conrail freight yard; the obvious nature of the plaintiff's operations and particular foreseeability of economic losses resulting from an accident and evacuation; the defendants' actual or constructive knowledge of the volatile properties of ethylene oxide; and the existence of an emergency response plan prepared by some of the defendants (alluded to in the course of oral argument), which apparently called for the nearby area to be evacuated to avoid the risk of harm in case of an explosion. We do not mean to suggest by our recitation of these facts that actual knowledge of the eventual economic losses is necessary to the cause of action; rather, particular foreseeability will suffice. The plaintiff still faces a difficult task in proving damages, particularly lost profits, to the degree of certainty required in other negligence cases. The trial court's examination of these proofs must be exacting to ensure that damages recovered are those reasonably to have been anticipated in view of the defendants' capacity to have foreseen that this particular plaintiff was within the risk created by their negligence.

. . .

■ For modification and affirmance—CHIEF JUSTICE WILENTZ, and JUSTICES CLIFFORD, HANDLER, O'HERN, GARIBALDI and STEIN—6.

For reversal—None.

NOTES AND QUESTIONS

1. The court refers to the cases that we have just considered involving third-party loss from the activities of accountants, lawyers and the like, as exceptions to the no-recovery rule based on "special relationships"—citing its *Rosenblum* decision (discussed earlier at p. 278, supra), among others. Is *People Express* similar to the various special relationship cases cited by the court?

2. Does *People Express* appear to raise the same issue as *Union Oil Co. v. Oppen*, cited in the opinion at p. 287, supra, in which commercial fishermen sought to recover lost profits as a consequence of the Santa Barbara oil spill?

3. What is the difference between a foreseeability standard and a "particular foreseeability" standard? Is the latter test likely to be helpful in deciding the limits on recovery for economic loss resulting from threatened or actual physical harm? Does the court's approach apply to any defendant other than the railroad?

4. Would the court now reach a different result on the facts of the landmark no-recovery cases of Stevenson v. East Ohio Gas Co. and Byrd v. English, cited in the opinion?

5. In Koch v. Consolidated Edison Co. of New York, Inc., 62 N.Y.2d 548, 468 N.E.2d 1, 479 N.Y.S.2d 163 (1984), cert. denied 469 U.S. 1210 (1985), the City of New York attempted to recover damages for various economic losses suffered as a result of the 1977 blackout discussed at p. 133, supra. The court held that the city stated a cause of action as to whether damages caused by looting and vandalism were recoverable, but dismissed plaintiff's claims for recovery of emergency wages paid to city personnel such as police and fire officers and municipal revenues lost as a

consequence of the blackout. What considerations might have led the New York court to its conclusions about recovery? What recovery might have been allowed under the *People Express* test?

6. In Milliken & Co. v. Consolidated Edison Co., 84 N.Y.2d 469, 644 N.E.2d 268, 619 N.Y.S.2d 686 (1994), tenants of commercial buildings sued defendant utility for economic losses suffered when power failed in the garment district during a crucial sales week. Although these tenants had no direct contractual relation with the utility, their leases required them to pay their landlords a proportionate share of the landlord's utility bills. The unanimous court thought that was inadequate to ground a duty of due care. Relying heavily on *Strauss v. Belle Realty*, p. 133 supra, and the *Moch* case, p. 131, supra, the court concluded that it followed "a general policy and approach [that] declined to leapfrog duties, over directly juridically related parties, to noncontractually related consumers of a utility's service or product." Tenants as such "are not a sufficiently 'narrowly defined class.' "

The tenants tried to distinguish *Strauss* on the ground that the harm here occurred inside the leased premises rather than in common areas. The court thought the plaintiff in *Strauss* was in an identical situation. The court rejected the location argument "because it would hold regulated utilities liable to every tenant in every one of the countless skyscrapers comprising the urban skyline. This would unwisely subject utilities to loss potentials of uncontrollable and unworkable dimensions."

A third-party beneficiary theory also failed. The court distinguished one case in which it had allowed such a claim on the ground that there the utility "had expressly undertaken a contractual duty to supply electricity for the needs of [the contracting party's] customers."

7. The court in *People Express* acknowledges a "troublesome concern" about "liability out of all proportion to the defendant's fault." Does its standard give adequate weight to that concern? See generally, Rabin, Tort Recovery for Negligently Inflicted Economic Loss: A Reassessment, 37 Stan.L.Rev. 1513 (1985).

8. In Robins Dry Dock & Repair Co. v. Flint, 275 U.S. 303 (1927), liability was denied to the time charterers of a boat for loss of use due to negligent repairs. Justice Holmes observed that the damage to the ship "was no wrong" to the plaintiffs, whose loss arose only from a contract with the owners:

> It seems to have been thought that perhaps the whole might have been recovered by the owners, that in that event the owners would have been trustees for the respondents to the extent of the respondents' share and that no injustice would be done to allow the respondents to recover their share by direct suit. But justice does not permit that the petitioner be charged with the full value of the loss of use unless there is some one who has a claim to it as against the petitioner. The respondents have no claim either in contract or in tort, and they cannot get standing by the suggestion that if some one else had

recovered it he would have been bound to pay over a part by reason of his personal relations with the respondents.

The *Robins* doctrine was attacked in Federal Commerce & Navigation Co. v. M/V Marathonian, 528 F.2d 907 (2d Cir.1975), in which a time charterer was denied recovery for damages of $700,000 caused by the defendant's negligence in colliding with the chartered ship. The court quoted the criticism of *Robins* in James, Limitations on Liability for Economic Loss Caused by Negligence: A Pragmatic Appraisal, 25 Vand. L.Rev. 43, 56 (1972), which observed that an owner who lost the vessel's use could recover for that loss measured by its reasonable value. James saw no reason why the negligent defendant should escape liability simply because that loss was suffered by someone who had no proprietary interest in the ship.

The court stated that if free to do so, "we might question whether at least the damage to the principal time charterer is not so reasonably to be expected as to justify recovery. [ ] But there are arguments to the contrary, such as the difficulty in drawing the line in a field where successive subcharterers are not uncommon and rapid and wide fluctuations of rates of charter hire not unknown." Any change in *Robins* would have to come from the Supreme Court—which denied certiorari. 425 U.S. 975 (1976).

For a discussion of the thesis that courts have denied liability in cases in which a party suffering physical harm exists who might have indemnified the victim of economic loss through a "channeling contract" (a contract that would reduce the amount of litigation by allowing the victim of physical harm to recover economic losses as well), see Rizzo, A Theory of Economic Loss in the Law of Torts, 11 J.Legal Studies 281 (1982).

9. Can a life insurance company maintain an action against a defendant who negligently caused the premature death of the insured? In the leading case of Connecticut Mutual Life Ins. Co. v. New York & N.H. R.R., 25 Conn. 265 (1856), the court said it could not. Does the holding remain sound?

10. In Rickards v. Sun Oil Co., 23 N.J.Misc. 89, 41 A.2d 267 (1945), discussed in an omitted portion of *People Express,* defendant's barge negligently destroyed a bridge that was the only means of access to a group of plaintiffs' retail businesses. The court distinguished *Rickards* as a case of general rather than particular foreseeability. Is this sound? See also Dundee Cement Co. v. Chemical Laboratories, Inc., 712 F.2d 1166 (7th Cir.1983) and Leadfree Enters., Inc. v. United States Steel Corp., 711 F.2d 805 (7th Cir.1983).

In Bishop, Economic Loss in Tort, 2 Oxford J. Legal Studies 1 (1982), the author argues that many economic loss situations involve no net social costs. Although these situations involve private costs to the victims, the net effect is a mere redistribution of wealth with no consequent loss to society. Thus, as long as excess capacity exists, the disappointed vacationers in *Rickards* will simply satisfy their needs elsewhere. Private costs occur, but they are in the nature of transfer payments from the disappointed suppliers of goods and services to others who fill the breach, and, as a consequence, liability is appropriately denied.

Is Bishop's thesis generally applicable to the cases in this chapter? When it is applicable, does it follow that the supplier of goods or service ought to be denied recovery?   For a highly critical view, see Rizzo, The Economic Loss Problem: A Comment on Bishop, 2 Oxford J. Legal Stud. 197 (1982).   See in response, Bishop, Economic Loss: A Reply to Professor Rizzo, 2 Oxford J. Legal Stud. 207 (1982).

11. At early common law, a master was allowed an action for the damages he suffered as the result of injury to a servant. Although based on the philosophy of the era of cottage industry, the action long survived in some states for servants generally, and in others for servants who were members of the master's household. But the general trend is to treat servant cases like other cases. See, e.g., Phoenix Professional Hockey Club, Inc. v. Hirmer, 108 Ariz. 482, 502 P.2d 164 (1972), in which the plaintiff's regular goalie was injured in an automobile accident allegedly due to the defendant's negligence. In an effort to avoid the defense that its claim was too speculative, the plaintiff did not sue for general damages for injuries to the employee or for lost profits. Instead, it sued only for out-of-pocket expenses incurred in "hiring and employing a substitute goalie during the remainder of the term" of the injured goalie's contract. The court agreed that the claim was not unduly speculative, but nonetheless dismissed it. Although a negligent wrongdoer "should be held responsible for the natural and probable consequences of his wrong," to protect contract interests from "negligent interference would place an undue burden on freedom of action and could impose a severe penalty on one guilty of mere negligence."

CHAPTER V

CAUSATION

In earlier chapters we addressed questions that asked whether the defendant owed a duty of due care to the plaintiff and whether defendant had violated that duty. In this chapter we ask whether the defendant's negligence "caused" the harm for which the plaintiff is suing. This inquiry is a compound of two quite different questions.

First, we consider whether "cause in fact" ("actual cause") has been established. This inquiry seeks to tie the defendant's conduct to the plaintiff's harm in an almost physical or scientific way.

The second question concerns a very different—and often more problematic—issue called "proximate" or "legal" causation. Here, the question is whether, granting that defendant's negligence has been an actual cause of the plaintiff's harm, the injury occurred under circumstances that allow the defendant to argue plausibly against being required to compensate the plaintiff for that harm. In our consideration of proximate causation we return to some of the aspects of duty that we explored in Chapter IV.

A. CAUSE IN FACT

1. BASIC DOCTRINE

From the outset of the book we have implicitly accepted the notion that a defendant who behaves negligently should not have to compensate an injured plaintiff unless the plaintiff's injury is causally connected to the defendant's negligent conduct. Can you justify a system in which a driver who runs a red light or who drives recklessly (but hits no one) should compensate a person who, several blocks away, at that very moment is struck by lightning? Or is hit by an insolvent reckless driver?

Judicial decisions have accepted the need for some connection between the plaintiff's harm and the defendant's negligent conduct before imposing tort liability on the defendant. Courts have denied liability when it is clear that the connection was missing. Consider a situation in which a motorist should have sounded the car's horn when going around a dangerous bend that has a sign requiring that the horn be sounded. The negligence is clear. But the causal connection is missing if the lone motorist coming the other way was deaf and would not have heard the horn even if it had been sounded.

In Rinaldo v. McGovern, 78 N.Y.2d 729, 587 N.E.2d 264, 579 N.Y.S.2d 626 (1991), involving an errant golf shot, one claim was that the golfer negligently failed to shout "fore" before hitting the ball. On this point, the court concluded that a warning "would have been all but futile." Even if the defendant had shouted, "it is unlikely that plaintiffs, who were driving in a vehicle on a nearby roadway, would have heard, much less had the opportunity to act upon, the shouted warning." The chance was "too 'remote' to justify submission of the case to the jury."

Sometimes the lack of actual cause is shown in a different, but equally clear, way. Defendant may be negligent for not maintaining a dam so that it could withstand an ordinary rainfall. If such a normal rain had fallen, the dam would have given way and the defendant's liability for the downstream flooding would have been clear. In fact, however, the next rainfall is not of the ordinary variety; it is an unprecedented deluge beyond anything that the courts would require dam keepers to anticipate. The dam bursts—even a well-constructed dam would have burst—and downstream flooding occurs—doing roughly the same type and amount of harm as would have been done if the dam had burst under the anticipated rain. What arguments support liability on the dam owner? What arguments cut the other way?

In these cases we know all the relevant facts. Sometimes, however, the problem results from uncertainty about what happened.

Stubbs v. City of Rochester

Court of Appeals of New York, 1919.
226 N.Y. 516, 124 N.E. 137.

[Defendant supplied Hemlock system water for drinking and Holly system water for firefighting. The evidence indicated that through the city's negligence in May, 1910, the systems had become intermingled near the Brown Street Bridge. The Hemlock water became contaminated by sewage known to be present in the Holly water, but this was not discovered until October. Plaintiff contracted typhoid fever in September and attributed it to the city's negligence. By a 3–2 vote, without opinion, the Appellate Division affirmed a nonsuit granted by the trial judge at the close of plaintiff's case. Other facts are stated in the opinion.]

■ HOGAN, J. [after stating the facts].

The important question in this case is—did the plaintiff produce evidence from which inference might reasonably be drawn that the cause of his illness was due to the use of contaminated water furnished by defendant. Counsel for respondent argues that even assuming that the city may be held liable to plaintiff for damages caused by its negligence in furnishing contaminated water for drinking purposes, (a) that the evidence adduced by plaintiff fails to disclose that he contracted typhoid fever by drinking contaminated water; (b) that it was incumbent upon the plaintiff to establish that his illness was not due to any other cause to which typhoid fever may be attributed for which defendant is not liable. The evidence does disclose several causes of typhoid fever which is a germ disease, the germ being known as the typhoid bacillus, which causes may be classified as follows:

First. Drinking of polluted water. *Second.* Raw fruits and vegetables in certain named localities where human excrement is used to fertilize the soil are sometimes sources of typhoid infection. *Third.* The consumption of shell fish, though not a frequent cause. *Fourth.* The consumption of infected milk and vegetables. *Fifth.* The house fly in certain localities. *Sixth.* Personal contact with an infected person by one who has a predilection for typhoid infection and is not objectively sick with the disease. *Seventh.* Ice if affected with typhoid bacilli. *Eighth.* Fruits, vegetables, etc., washed in infected water. *Ninth.* The medical authorities recognize that there are still other causes and means unknown. This fact was developed on cross-examination of physicians called by plaintiff.

[Counsel argues first] that the evidence fails to disclose that plaintiff contracted typhoid fever by drinking contaminated water. The plaintiff having been nonsuited at the close of his case is entitled to the most favorable inference deducible from the evidence. That plaintiff on or about September 6th, 1910, was taken ill and very soon thereafter typhoid fever developed is not disputed. That he was employed in a factory located one block distant from the Brown street bridge in which Hemlock lake water was the only supply of water for potable and other purposes, and that the water drawn from faucets in that neighborhood disclosed that the water was roily and of unusual appearance is not questioned. And no doubt prevails that the Holly system water was confined to the main business part of the city for use for fire purposes and sprinkling streets and is not furnished for domestic or drinking purposes.

The evidence of the superintendent of water works of the city is to the effect that Hemlock lake water is a pure wholesome water free from contamination of any sort at the lake and examinations of the same are made weekly; that the Holly water is not fit for drinking purposes taken as it is from the Genesee river. Further evidence was offered by plaintiff by several witnesses, residents in the locality of Brown street bridge, who discovered the condition of the water at various times during July, August and September and made complaint to the water department of the condition of the same. Dr. Goler, a physician and health officer of the city, was called by plaintiff and testified that in September when complaint was made to him by a resident of the district he went to the locality, visited houses in the immediate neighborhood, found that the water drawn from the faucet of the Hemlock supply looked badly and smelled badly. He took a sample of the water to the laboratory and had it examined by a chemist who found that it contained an increase in solids and very many times, that is twenty to thirty times as much chlorine or common salt as is found in the domestic water supply—the presence of chlorine in excessive quantities indicates contamination in that quantity, bad contamination and usually sewage contamination. Further examination followed in the district. Water was collected from various houses and a large number of samples, perhaps less than one hundred, but over twenty-five. . . . About the following day, the source of contamination having been discovered, the doctor made an investigation as to the reported cases of typhoid fever in the city in the months of August, September and October for the purpose of determining the number of cases, where the cases came from, what gave rise to it, and he stated that in his opinion the outbreak of typhoid was due to polluted water, contaminated as he discovered afterwards by sewage. In answer to a hypothetical question embracing generally the facts asserted by plaintiff the witness testified that he had an opinion as to the cause of the infection of plaintiff and such opinion was that it was due to contaminated water.

Doctor Dodge, of the faculty of the University of Rochester, a professor of biology, also bacteriologist of the city of Rochester, about October first made an analysis of samples of water. . . . While his examination did not disclose any colon bacillus, it did disclose some evidence of the same. Dr. Brady, the physician who attended the plaintiff, and Dr. Culkin both testified that in their opinion the plaintiff contracted typhoid fever from drinking polluted water.

Plaintiff called a witness who resided on Brown street about two minutes' walk from the bridge and proved by her that she drank water from the Hemlock mains in the fall of 1910 and was ill with typhoid fever. Thereupon counsel for defendant stipulated that fifty-seven witnesses which the plaintiff proposed to call will testify that they drank water from the Hemlock taps in the vicinity of the district west of the Genesee river and north of Allen street in the summer and fall of 1910 and during said summer and fall suffered from typhoid fever, that in view of the stipulation such witnesses need not be called by plaintiff and the stipulation shall have the same force and effect as though the witnesses had been called and testified to the facts.

The plaintiff resided with his wife some three miles distant from the factory where he was employed. The water consumed by him at his house outside the infected district was Hemlock water. The only water in the factory was Hemlock water and he had there an individual cup from which he drank. He was not outside of the city during the summer of 1910. Therefore, the only water he drank was in the city of Rochester.

A table of statistics as to typhoid fever in the city of Rochester for the years 1901–1910, inclusive, was produced by the health officer and received in evidence. . . . The statistics disclose that the number of typhoid cases in the city in 1910 was 223, an excess of 50 cases of any year of the nine years preceding. Recalling that complaints as to water commenced in the summer of 1910 and as shown by the evidence that typhoid fever does not develop until two or three weeks after the bacilli have been taken into the system, in connection with the fact that the course of contamination was not discovered until October, the statistics disclose that of the 223 cases of typhoid in the city in the year 1910, 180 cases appear during the months of August, September, October and November as against forty-three cases during the remaining eight months; thirty-five of which were prior to August and eight in the month of December, two months after the source of contamination of the water was discovered.

The evidence on the trial discloses that at least fifty-eight witnesses, residents of the district, drank the contaminated water and suffered from typhoid fever in addition to plaintiff; thus one-third of the 180 cases during the months stated were shown to exist in that district.

Counsel for respondent asserts that there was a failure of proof on the part of plaintiff in that he did not establish that he contracted disease by drinking contaminated water and in support of his argument cites a rule of law, that when there are several possible causes of injury for one or more of which a defendant is not responsible, plaintiff cannot recover without proving that the injury was sustained wholly or in part by a cause for which defendant was responsible. He submits that it was essential for plaintiff to eliminate all other of seven causes from which the disease might have been contracted. If the argument should prevail and the rule of law stated is not subject to any limitation the present case illustrates the impossibility of a recovery in any case based upon like facts. One cause of the disease is stated by counsel to be "personal contact with typhoid carriers or other persons suffering with the disease, whereby bacilli are received and accidentally transferred by the hands or some other portion of the person or clothes to the mouth." Concededly a person is affected with typhoid some weeks before the disease develops. The plaintiff here resided three miles distant from his place of employment and traveled to and from his work upon the street car. To prove the time when he was attacked with typhoid, then find every individual who traveled on the same car with him and establish by each one of them that he or she was free from the disease even to his or her clothing is impossible. Again the evidence disclosed that typhoid fever was caused by sources unknown to medical science. If the word of the rule stated is to prevail plaintiff would be required to eliminate sources which had not yet been determined or ascertained. I do not believe the rule stated to be as inflexible as claimed for. If two or more possible causes exist, for only one of which a defendant may be liable, and a party injured establishes facts from which it can be said with reasonable certainty that the direct cause of the injury was the one for which the defendant was liable the party has complied with the spirit of the rule.

The plaintiff was employed in the immediate locality where the water was contaminated. He drank the water daily. The consumption of contaminated water is a very frequent cause of typhoid fever. In the locality there were a large number of cases of typhoid fever and near to sixty individuals who drank the water and had suffered from typhoid fever in that neighborhood appeared as witnesses on behalf of plaintiff. The plaintiff gave evidence of his habits, his home surroundings and his method of living, and the medical testimony indicated that his illness was caused by drinking contaminated water. Without reiteration of the facts disclosed on the trial I do not believe that the case on the part of plaintiff was so lacking in proof as matter of law that his complaint should be dismissed. On the contrary the most favorable inferences deducible from the plaintiff were such as would justify a submission of the facts to a jury as to the reasonable inferences to be drawn therefrom, and a verdict rendered thereon for either party would rest not in conjecture but upon reasonable possibilities.

The judgment should be reversed and a new trial granted, costs to abide the event.

■ CARDOZO, POUND and ANDREWS, JJ., concur; HISCOCK, CH. J., CHASE and McLAUGHLIN, JJ., dissent [without opinion].

NOTES AND QUESTIONS

1. Why is it the plaintiff's burden to show the causal relationship?

2. Each party pays for its expert witnesses and the preparation of its statistics. Who should pay for these expenses?

3. Why is it relevant that 58 persons who drank the water got typhoid? Didn't they also sleep and get typhoid, or drink milk and get typhoid? Might they all have been bitten by houseflies and gotten typhoid? What further data would be helpful?

4. If each of the other 57 victims sued one at a time, would it be possible for 35 juries to hold for the plaintiffs and 22 juries for the defendant if the evidence was essentially the same in each case?

5. In Wolf v. Kaufmann, 227 App.Div. 281, 237 N.Y.S. 550 (1929), the "deceased was shown to have entered the premises and was heard by tenants upon the stairs and in the hallway. Following a thud, also heard by tenants, he was found at the foot of the stairs. No one saw him fall." The stairways were shown to have been dark and unlighted due to negligence. The court ruled that "without further proof it would be solely a conjecture for a jury to draw the conclusion that the deceased fell down the stairs because of the absence of light." Later, it observed that "there is nothing to show that the accident occurred in the use of the stairs in the ordinary manner. In the absence of such proof, there are many possible conjectures for the accident." The case was dismissed. What proof might have helped plaintiff? Is Wolf consistent with Stubbs ?

In Hinman v. Sobocienski, 808 P.2d 820 (Alaska 1991), a tenant who was found injured at the foot of a flight of stairs proved only that the flight was "unreasonably dangerous and that she was found injured at its bottom. She introduced no further evidence, however, tending to show that the condition of the stairway contributed to her injuries." The trial court granted directed verdict for the defendant landlord because there was no showing that she had fallen due to the condition rather than that she was thrown down the stairs or had jumped—though nothing in the record suggested these possibilities. The supreme court, 4–1, reversed. The court observed:

> Common experience . . . suggests that the presence in a bar/apartment building of a dangerous, dimly lighted staircase greatly increases the chances that a patron or resident will accidentally fall

and suffer injury. When a resident is then found injured at the bottom of those stairs, a reasonable inference is that the dangerous condition more likely than not played a substantial part in the mishap. "The court can scarcely overlook the fact that the injury which has in fact occurred is precisely the sort of thing that proper care on the part of the defendant would be intended to prevent." [   ] The absence of evidence that the plaintiff fell—rather than jumped or was pushed—does not negate the reasonableness of the inference.

6. In the absence of further evidence, is one of these analyses superior to the other: (a) although we know that individuals often fall down lighted stairways, falls occur more frequently on dark stairways so that plaintiff's proof in *Wolf* is adequate; or (b) since individuals often fall down lighted stairs we have no reason to assume that the darkness had anything to do with this fall in the absence of some showing to that effect by plaintiff?

7. Suppose all 58 residents of the district who contracted typhoid fever sued. Suppose the historical data—from earlier years when there was no intermixing of the water supplies—further suggest that ten residents of the district would have contracted typhoid fever from one of the other causes. All 58 residents might well collect full damages, even though it seems clear that ten should not recover—liability exceeding its responsibility is being assigned to the City of Rochester, creating overdeterrence. Is this an insoluble dilemma?

One solution to this problem that has been suggested in recent years as toxic tort cases have become more prevalent is "proportional recovery." Thus, it would be possible to compensate each of the 58 victims for 48/58 of their damages. Do you see problems with this approach? See Farber, Toxic Causation, 71 Minn.L.Rev. 1229, 1220, n. 9 (1987) for references to the literature. Might a proportionate recovery scheme be employed at the time of exposure, even before actual harm was experienced? These issues are discussed again at p. 311, infra, in the context of the asbestos cases.

8. In Wilson v. Circus Circus Hotels, Inc., 101 Nev. 751, 710 P.2d 77 (1985), a young boy contracted salmonella poisoning following ingestion of food at defendant's hotel restaurant. The plaintiff's proof included expert testimony that there was an 80% chance that the boy was poisoned by defendant's food if he ate only at the defendant hotel during the 52 hours before the onset of symptoms; if no member of the family ate certain items that the boy ate at the hotel; if no member of the family got ill from non-hotel foods that the boy and other family members had eaten; and if the hotel's cups of tartar sauce had been left unrefrigerated for too long. The court noted the difficulties of proving causation in food cases and cited other cases in which courts had ruled that "mere correlation between ingestion and illness is insufficient as a matter of law to establish causation." Here, however, the court concluded that the plaintiff had presented enough to reach a jury. The showing of almost exclusive ingestion at the hotel during the incubation period and the negation of other causes was sufficient.

9. In Mitchell v. Pearson Enterprises, 697 P.2d 240 (Utah 1985), a guest in defendant's hotel was murdered in his room by an unknown person. The motive appeared to be robbery. There were no signs of a forced entry. Local police had several hypotheses. Some centered on a person entering the room with a passkey and then being surprised by the guest. Another suggested a gangland killing in which the guest was accosted in the hallway or elevator. The suit claimed inadequate security measures.

Accepting that the plaintiff had made a sufficient showing of negligence, the court affirmed summary judgment for the defendant on the ground that proof of causation was lacking. It was not known how the murderer first encountered the guest or whether they had a prior relationship. The lack of forced entry "could be probative of entrance by a person using an unauthorized master or room key. However, it could also be probative of entrance, at [the deceased's] invitation, by a friend or colleague. Any supposition, therefore, as to the manner of entrance to [the deceased's] room or the identity of the assailant would be totally speculative. A jury cannot be permitted to engage in such speculation."

10. In Hancock v. R.A. Earnhardt Textile Machinery Div., 139 N.H. 356, 653 A.2d 558 (1995), plaintiff worker was hurt on a machine that was one of four his employer had bought from a supply company. Records showed that the supply company had acquired three of the four from defendant—but could not determine whether the defective unit was one of those three. The court held that the jury could not reasonably find that the defendant was more likely than not the supplier of the defective machine. Why not?

Falcon v. Memorial Hospital

Supreme Court of Michigan, 1990.
436 Mich. 443, 462 N.W.2d 44.

[Moments after Nena Falcon, 19 years old, gave birth to a healthy baby, she suffered a sudden and complete respiratory and cardiac collapse, and died soon thereafter. The autopsy indicated that she had sustained an amniotic fluid embolism, "an unpreventable complication that occurs in approximately one of ten or twenty thousand births." In such an event, amniotic fluid enters the mother's circulatory system and particles from the fluid lodge in the lungs. In a suit against the hospital and Falcon's physician by her administratrix, plaintiff's expert testified by deposition that it was negligent not to have inserted an intravenous line in Falcon before giving her anesthesia and that, if such a line had been introduced, Falcon would have had a 37.5 percent chance to survive.

The trial court dismissed the complaint because plaintiff failed to show that the introduction of the line would have made it more probable than not that Falcon would have survived. The court of appeals reversed. In the following opinion, the supreme court recognizes that most courts and commentators speak of this issue as involving the "loss of a chance."

Justice Levin, however, preferred the word "opportunity." Citing dictionary sources, he observed that "chance" included "the absence of any cause of events that can be predicted, understood, or controlled." On the other hand, "opportunity" includes "a situation or condition favorable for attainment of a goal."]

■ LEVIN, JUSTICE.

.   .   .

The defendants contend that because the proofs at a trial of Falcon's claim would not show that it was probable, measured as more than fifty percent, that Nena Falcon would have avoided physical harm had the procedure not been omitted, Falcon cannot show that the asserted negligence of defendants caused her physical harm.   .   .   .

II

Some courts disallow recovery for lost opportunity unless the plaintiff can establish that the patient would not have suffered the physical harm but for the defendant's negligence, or, at least, that it is more probable, measured as more than fifty percent, that, but for such negligence, the patient would not have suffered the physical harm.

[margin note: but for D's negligence]

Under the more probable, measured as more than fifty percent, approach to causation, a plaintiff who establishes that the patient would have had more than a fifty percent opportunity of not suffering physical harm had the defendant not acted negligently, recovers one hundred percent of the damages. The better than even opportunity is compensated as if it were a certainty, although the patient's chances of a better result are significantly less than one hundred percent.

[margin note: 50% chance of not suffering]

To say that a patient would have had a ninety-nine percent opportunity of survival if given proper treatment, does not mean that the physician's negligence was the cause in fact if the patient would have been among the unfortunate one percent who would have died. A physician's carelessness may, similarly, be the actual cause of physical harm although the patient had only a one percent opportunity of surviving even with flawless medical attention.

[margin note: 99% chance of ok, but doctor negligence, perhaps p was part of 1%]

All this is simply to say that the more probable than not standard, as well as other standards of causation, are analytic devices—tools to be used in making causation judgments. They do not and cannot yield ultimate truth. Absolute certainty in matters of causation is a rarity.

III

Other courts have permitted recovery for physical harm on a showing that the lost opportunity was a substantial, albeit fifty percent or less, factor in producing the harm.   .   .   .

Some courts have held that the plaintiff need only show that the defendant's conduct was a substantial factor in producing the physical harm. Other courts allow recovery for loss of a fifty percent or less opportunity of achieving a better result without clearly articulating the standard of causation. A number of courts have so held on the basis of language in the Restatement Torts, 2d.[13]

. . .

V

The question whether a defendant caused an event is not readily answered, and is especially perplexing in circumstances such as those present in the instant case where the defendant's failure to act is largely responsible for the uncertainty regarding causation.

Had the defendants in the instant case inserted an intravenous line, one of two things would have happened, Nena Falcon would have lived, or she would have died. There would be no uncertainty whether the omissions of the defendants caused her death. Falcon's destiny would have been decided by fate and not possibly by her health care providers. The United States Court of Appeals for the Fourth Circuit, observed:

"When a defendant's negligent action or inaction has effectively terminated a person's chance of survival, it does not lie in the defendant's mouth to raise conjectures as to the measure of the chances that he has put beyond the possibility of realization. If there was any substantial possibility of survival and the defendant has destroyed it, he is answerable. Rarely is it possible to demonstrate to an absolute certainty what would have happened in circumstances that the wrongdoer did not allow to come to pass. The law does not in the existing circumstances require the plaintiff to show to a *certainty* that the patient would have lived had she been hospitalized and operated on promptly. [ ]." Hicks v. United States, 368 F.2d 626, 632 (C.A.4, 1966)(Emphasis in original.)

VI

In an ordinary tort action seeking recovery for physical harm, the defendant is a stranger to the plaintiff and the duty imposed by operation of law is imposed independently of any undertaking by the defendant. In an action claiming medical malpractice, however, the patient generally is not a stranger to the defendant. Generally, the patient engaged the services of the defendant physician. The physician undertook to perform services for the patient, and the patient undertook to pay or provide payment for the services.

The scope of the undertakings by a physician or hospital to the patient and by the patient to the physician or hospital is not generally a matter of express agreement. There is, however, an understanding that the law

---

13. "One who undertakes, gratuitously or for consideration, to render services to another which he should recognize as necessary for the protection of the other's person or things, is subject to liability to the other for physical harm resulting from his failure to exercise reasonable care to perform his undertaking, if (a) his failure to exercise such care increased the risk of such harm. . . ." [§ 323]

enforces in the absence of express agreement. The patient expects a physician to do that which is expected of physicians of like training in the community, and the physician expects the patient to pay or provide payment for the services, whether the likelihood of there in fact being any benefit to the patient is only one through fifty percent or is greater than fifty percent.

.   .   .

Patients engage the services of doctors, not only to prevent disease or death, but also to delay death and to defer or ameliorate the suffering associated with disease or death. If the trier of fact were to decide, on the basis of expert testimony, that the undertaking of the defendant physician included the implementation of tasks and procedures that, in the case of Nena Falcon, would have enabled the physician and other medically trained persons, who were present at the time of delivery, to provide her, in the event of the medical accident that occurred, an opportunity to survive the accident, a failure to do so was a breach of the understanding or undertaking.

.   .   .

Women gave birth to children long before there were physicians or hospitals or even midwives. A woman who engages the services of a physician and enters a hospital to have a child does so to reduce pain and suffering and to increase the likelihood of her surviving and the child surviving childbirth in a good state of health even though the likelihood of the woman and child not surviving in good health without such services is far less than fifty percent. That is why women go to physicians. That is what physicians undertake to do. That is what they are paid for. They are, and should be, subject to liability if they fail to measure up to the standard of care.

VII

A number of courts have recognized, as we would, loss of an opportunity for a more favorable result, as distinguished from the unfavorable result, as compensable in medical malpractice actions. Under this approach, damages are recoverable for the loss of opportunity although the opportunity lost was less than even, and thus it is not more probable than not that the unfavorable result would or could have been avoided.[26]

---

26. Professor King explains:

"[C]onsider the case in which a doctor negligently fails to diagnose a patient's cancerous condition until it has become inoperable. Assume further that even with a timely diagnosis the patient would have had only a 30% chance of recovering from the disease and surviving over the long term. There are two ways of handling such a case. Under the traditional approach, this loss of a not-better-than-even chance of recovering from cancer would not be compensable because it did not appear more likely than not that the patient would have survived with proper care. Recoverable damages, if any, would depend on the extent to which it appeared that cancer killed the patient sooner than it would have with timely diagnosis and treatment, and on the extent to which the delay in diagnosis aggravated the patient's condition, such as by causing additional pain. A more rational approach, however, would allow recovery for

Under this approach, the plaintiff must establish more-probable-than-not causation. He must prove, more probably than not, that the defendant reduced the opportunity of avoiding harm.

. . .

The Supreme Court of Washington permitted the personal representative of the patient to maintain an action where there was expert testimony of a fourteen percentage point reduction—from thirty-nine percent to twenty-five percent—in the patient's opportunity for survival, which was claimed to have resulted from a delay in diagnosis of lung cancer. Herskovits v. Group Health Cooperative of Puget Sound, 99 Wash.2d 609, 664 P.2d 474 (1983). The majority, in two separate opinions, agreed, that recovery for "[c]ausing reduction of the opportunity to recover (loss of chance) by one's negligence, however, does not necessitate a total recovery against the negligent party for all damages caused by the victim's death."

. . .

VIII

The defendants contend, that the injury for which Falcon sought to maintain this wrongful death action, the failure to protect Nena Falcon's opportunity of avoiding physical harm, cannot be maintained because the proofs at trial will not show that it is probable, measured as more than fifty percent, that, had they protected her opportunity of living, she would not have died. Recognizing loss of a substantial opportunity of avoiding physical harm as actionable makes it unnecessary to consider whether Falcon's action for medical malpractice can be maintained as an action for wrongful death. Falcon may maintain a survival action against the defendants for their failure to protect Nena Falcon's opportunity of living.

The harm resulting from defendants' asserted malpractice occurred immediately before Nena Falcon's death when the medical accident occurred and, by reason of the failure to have inserted an intravenous line, it became certain that she would die. At that moment, immediately before her death, Nena Falcon had a cause of action for the harm, the denial of any opportunity of living, that had been caused her. Her claim therefor survived her death because "[a]ll actions and claims survive death." [ ]

We are persuaded that loss of a 37.5 percent opportunity of living constitutes a loss of a substantial opportunity of avoiding physical harm.[43]

the loss of the chance of cure even though the chance was not better than even. The probability of long-term survival would be reflected in the amount of damages awarded for the loss of the chance. While the plaintiff here could not prove by a preponderance of the evidence that he was denied a cure by the defendant's negligence, he could show by a preponderance that he was deprived of a 30% chance of cure." [King, Causation, Valuation, and Chance in Personal Injury Torts Involving Preexisting Conditions and Future Consequences, 90 Yale L.J. 1353, 1363–64 (1981)].

43. While in Nena Falcon's case the time interval between the loss of an opportunity for a better result and the resulting physical harm, her death, was relatively short, in other cases the time interval between the loss or reduction of the opportunity for a better result and the occurrence of physical harm will be considerably longer, as

We need not now decide what lesser percentage would constitute a substantial loss of opportunity.

IX

In the instant case, while Nena Falcon's cause of action accrued before her death, she did not suffer conscious pain and suffering from the failure to implement the omitted procedures between the moment that the medical accident occurred and the time of her death a few minutes later—she was sedated throughout the entire time period. In this case, 37.5 percent times the damages recoverable for wrongful death would be an appropriate measure of damages.

. . .

We would affirm the Court of Appeals reversal of the entry of summary judgment for the defendants, and remand the case for trial.

■ ARCHER, J., concurs.

■ BOYLE, JUSTICE (concurring).

I concur in the recognition of "lost opportunity to survive" as injury for which tort law should allow recovery in proportion to the extent of the lost chance of survival, provided that the negligence of the defendant more probably than not caused the loss of opportunity. However, I would emphasize that the Court today is called upon to decide the viability of a claim for "lost opportunity" only where the ultimate harm to the victim is death. Thus, any language in the lead opinion suggesting that a similar cause of action might lie for a lost opportunity of avoiding lesser physical harm is dicta. Whether the social and policy factors which justify compensation for a lost chance of survival would justify recovery for the loss of a chance to avoid some lesser harm is a question for another day.

■ CAVANAGH, J., concurs.

■ RILEY, CHIEF JUSTICE (dissenting).

I would hold that a wrongful death action may not survive a motion for summary disposition where it is uncontested that the plaintiff cannot show that defendant's negligence caused the decedent's death, and will produce evidence only that the decedent would have had an increased chance of survival if the defendant, as in this case, had not negligently failed to insert an intravenous line before or immediately after administering saddle block anaesthesia. Where plaintiff cannot show that defendants' omission was

where there is a failure to diagnose or a misdiagnosis. The resulting physical harm, pain resulting from the spread of a disease that might have been avoided, pain resulting from medical treatment that might have been avoided, pain and suffering resulting from anxiety that might have been avoided, may extend over a prolonged period of time until death, remission, or a cure. A patient who suffers such harm as a result of a failure to diagnose or misdiagnosis has an actionable claim for damages without regard to whether death ensues. [ ]

The accrual of a cause of action for loss of an opportunity of achieving a better result does not, thus, depend on whether death ensues as a result. The cause of action accrues when harm and damages result from the loss of a substantial opportunity for a better result. . . . .

probably a cause of the death of Nena Falcon, the degree of certitude which would justify the imposition of liability on defendants is lacking. The recognition of mere chance as a recoverable item of loss fundamentally contradicts the essential notion of causation. By definition, the lost chance theory would compensate plaintiff for a mere possibility that defendants' omission caused the death of Nena Falcon.

. . .

IV

The lost chance of survival theory does more than merely lower the threshold of proof of causation; it fundamentally alters the meaning of causation.

The most fundamental premise upon which liability for a negligent act may be based is cause in fact. [   ] "An act or omission is not regarded as a cause of an event if the particular event would have occurred without it." [   ] If the defendant's acts did not actually cause the plaintiff's injury, then there is no rational justification for requiring the defendant to bear the cost of the plaintiff's damages. Thus, it is the plaintiff's burden to show a causal connection between negligence and injury. [   ] "A case cannot go to a jury supported merely by sheer speculation that something might have been a cause, or, going one step further, that there was a possibility that something was the cause." [   ]

The recognition of a lost chance as a cognizable injury is necessarily based on the reasoning that but for the defendant's negligence, the plaintiff might possibly have avoided an adverse result. Thus, recognition of lost chance as a recoverable interest contradicts the very notion of cause in fact. Professor King aptly characterizes a lost chance as a "raffle ticket" destroyed by the defendant's negligence. [   ] King advocates compensation for "statistically demonstrable losses," [   ], so that a person deprived of a forty percent chance of survival should be compensated for forty percent of the compensable value of his life. [   ] Thus, tort law is transformed from a compensatory system to a payout scheme on the basis of a statistical chance that the defendant caused the plaintiff's death. It is no answer that full compensation based on less than a certainty that a plaintiff would have survived is overcompensation. Professor King criticizes the probability standard of causation because, in his view, it treats the better-than-even chance as a certainty, "as though it had materialized or were certain to do so." [   ] Clearly, causation can never be proven to a certainty; the law settles for less in determining that a defendant should be held liable for damages to a plaintiff. Thus, Professor McCormick describes the preponderance of the evidence standard of proof in terms of "probability":

> "The most acceptable meaning to be given to the expression, proof by a preponderance, seems to be proof which leads the jury to find that the existence of the contested fact is more probable than its nonexistence. Thus the preponderance of the evidence

becomes the trier's belief in the preponderance of probability." McCormick, Evidence (3d ed.), § 339, p. 957.

McCormick notes that some courts are "shocked at the suggestion that a verdict, a truth-finding, should be based on nothing stronger than an estimate of probabilities." [ ] This statement reveals the very foundation of the tort system.   Imperfect as it may be, our legal system attempts to ascertain facts to arrive at the truth.   To protect the integrity of that goal, there must be some degree of certainty regarding causation before a jury may determine as fact that a medical defendant did cause the plaintiff's injury and should therefore compensate the plaintiff in damages.   To dispense with this requirement is to abandon the truth-seeking function of the law.   Professor King is willing to do so in his attempt to compensate for the precise magnitude of any lost chance.   Professor King's criticism of the more likely than not standard for causation, like the lost chance theory itself, is based on the erroneous premise that it is the purpose of tort law to compensate for lost chances.   But tort law should not operate by the same principles that govern lotteries and insurance policies.   If the acts of the defendants did not actually cause plaintiff's injury, then there is no rational justification for requiring defendants to bear the cost of plaintiff's damages.

.   .   .

.   .   .   If liability is to be imposed in proportion to any chance at survival, then the medical profession will be subjected to a burden which is not imposed on any other group of defendants.   [ ]   I submit that nothing is to be gained by extracting payment from a defendant who cannot be shown to have caused the adverse result.   Such a rule will not serve the deterrence function of tort law.   It more likely will encourage the practice of costly defensive medicine in an attempt to avoid practically certain liability in the event of an unfavorable outcome.

.   .   .

■ GRIFFIN and BRICKLEY, JJ., concur.

NOTES AND QUESTIONS

1.   What is the alleged negligence of the defendants?

2.   Consider the difference between the following two formulations:

a.   The plaintiff is being awarded 40 percent of the value of decedent's life because there is a 40 percent chance that the defendant caused the decedent's death.

b.   The plaintiff is being awarded 40 percent of the value of decedent's life because the plaintiff has proven that the defendant more probably than not deprived the plaintiff of a 40 percent chance of survival.

Which formulation does the majority appear to be using?

3.   If this complication occurs in eight births in 80,000, and there is the same proof of a ⅜ (37.5%) chance of surviving with an intravenous line, how would the dissent resolve these eight cases? How would Justice Levin resolve them?

Suppose that after deciding *Falcon,* the court were to be confronted with a different type of medical malpractice case in which the lost opportunity to survive had been ⅝ (62.5%). How much should Justice Levin award to each of the victims? How would Chief Justice Riley resolve this type of case?

Is there anything about the case that might justify limiting it to death, as opposed to loss of a limb or loss of a house or the loss of a chance to win a lottery?

4. Part VI of the opinion suggests that the result is being justified by the nature of the doctor-patient relationship. Recall the *Farwell* case, p. 125, supra, in which the expert testified that prompt attention would have given the victim an 85% opportunity to survive. If the expert testimony had instead placed that number at 40%, would the rationale of *Falcon* apply against Siegrist?

The dissent suggests that the decision affects only the medical profession and not any other group of defendants. If that is correct, does the majority present persuasive arguments for that result?

The dissent argues that the decision is likely to "encourage the practice of costly defensive medicine." Does that concern go to the question of breach or of causation? Is it a valid concern in this case? Does the dissent's approach provide adequate deterrence?

5. The dissent argues that "tort law is transformed from a compensatory system to a payout scheme on the basis of a statistical chance that the defendant caused the plaintiff's death." Is that a cause for concern?

6. Other arguments supporting the dissent are offered in Fennell v. Southern Maryland Hospital Center, Inc., 320 Md. 776, 580 A.2d 206 (1990). The court denied all recovery in a case in which the plaintiff had shown that the hospital's negligence deprived the decedent of a 40 percent chance of survival. First, the court thought that the logic of the loss-of-a-chance theory dictated some recovery if a defendant's negligence reduced a plaintiff's chance of survival from 40 percent to 10 percent—even if the plaintiff later survived. Is this correct? What if the victim has to wait six months before learning that she will survive? What if the negligent reduction in the chance of survival occurs in a situation in which the physician and patient will know within a minute whether the patient will survive? Second, the court was concerned about the conduct of trials:

> The use of statistics in trials is subject to criticism as being unreliable, misleading, easily manipulated, and confusing to a jury. When large damage awards will be based on the statistical chance of survival before the negligent treatment, minus the statistical chance of survival after the negligent treatment, times the value of the lost life, we can imagine the bewildering sets of numbers with which the jury will be confronted, as well as the difficulties juries will have in assessing the

comparative reliability of the divergent statistical evidence offered by each side.

Third, the court identified a fairness concern: "If a plaintiff whose decedent had a 49% chance of survival, which was lost through negligent treatment, is permitted to recover 49% of the value of the decedent's life, then a plaintiff whose decedent had a 51% chance of survival which was lost through negligent treatment, perhaps ought to have recovery limited to 51% of the value of the life lost."

Finally, the court stressed the impact of a change in the law on the costs of the delivery of medical services.

Which, if any, of these arguments are persuasive?

Falcon was also rejected in Kramer v. Lewisville Memorial Hospital, 858 S.W.2d 397 (Tex.1993). The court, 6–3, asserted that any claim must come under either the survival statute or the wrongful death statute—and both require a showing of causation. Otherwise, courts would have to award damages to those whose chances of recovery are lowered but who "beat the lower odds" and recover. The court also feared extension to lawyers whose negligence reduces a 40% chance of recovery to 15%. The court disavowed an earlier decision in which the plaintiff had won an award when the defendant railroad delayed a hog's arrival at a contest so that the hog lost weight and plaintiff failed to win the first prize. Finally, the court rejected various formulations that sought to mitigate the *Falcon* concerns: such as sending the case to the jury on a "reasonable probability" charge without requiring evidence on the issue, and using an increased risk analysis. The court's count indicated that 17 states had accepted *Falcon* and eight had rejected it. Does *Falcon* necessarily allow malpractice against attorneys in the situation mentioned?

7. Recall that in the quoted *Hicks* case the court says that it does not "lie in the defendant's mouth to raise conjectures" about the cause of the death. Is the basis for the decision one of probability or one of fairness? If fairness or proof questions are at the heart of the problem, why does the court insist that the lost opportunity have been a "substantial possibility"? How much is the *Hicks* court likely to award for the lost chance?

A few courts have awarded full damages for loss of life in a case in which the plaintiff showed at most the loss of a 40 percent chance of survival. E.g., Kallenberg v. Beth Israel Hosp., 45 App.Div.2d 177, 357 N.Y.S.2d 508 (1974), aff'd 37 N.Y.2d 719, 337 N.E.2d 128, 374 N.Y.S.2d 615 (1975). Can this course be justified?

11. How far should the analysis of the majority be carried? If the jury in a case involving solely a credibility dispute concludes that it is 80 percent likely that the plaintiff is the one telling the truth, should it be told to award the plaintiff 80 percent of the agreed-upon damages? See generally, Levmore, Probabilistic Recoveries, Restitution, and Recurring Wrongs, 19 J.Legal Studies 691 (1990).

12. The court noted that the time between the loss of opportunity to survive and the resulting harm was short and that the patient was unaware of her plight. In other cases, though, the period would be longer and give rise to claims for pain from physical harm or medical treatments that might have been avoided, as well as "pain and suffering resulting from anxiety that might have been avoided, [and that] may extend over a prolonged period of time until death, remission, or a cure." It would be plaintiff's burden to establish by expert testimony "the difference between the course of the disease and treatment had there been a correct diagnosis, and the course of the disease and treatment as a result of failure to diagnose or misdiagnosis."

13. Although plaintiff normally must show causation, the rule is otherwise where the defendant's liability is rooted in an unexcused statutory violation. In *Martin v. Herzog*, p. 63, supra, Judge Cardozo observed that such a violation also makes a "case, *prima facie* sufficient, of negligence contributing to the result. There may indeed be times when the lights on a highway are so many and so bright that lights on a wagon are superfluous. If that is so, it is for the offender to go forward with the evidence. . . ."

14. The discussion to this point has suggested that the actual causation question would disappear, or at least be less difficult, if we could only learn certain facts about the actual episode or about what would have happened if defendant had acted differently. A strain of scholarship spurred by Professor Wex Malone has suggested that the issues are much more subtle, at least in close cases. See Malone, Ruminations on Cause–in–Fact, 9 Stan.L.Rev. 60 (1956). Consider the problems raised when a child darts into the path of a drunk and speeding driver in a situation in which even a careful, skilled driver could not have avoided hitting the child. In Thode, The Indefensible Use of the Hypothetical Case to Determine Cause in Fact, 46 Texas L.Rev. 423 (1968), the author suggested that a court would not, as a matter of law, hold that plaintiff had failed to show causation:

> My judgment is that the court would strive mightily to uphold a jury finding of cause in fact. Why? Basically I think it is because the public policy against drunken, high-speed driving in residential areas is so strong and the risk of injury to children so great that the court would decide that the defendant should have the potential for liability even though plaintiff is unable to produce evidence that a sober man, driving carefully, would not have caused the same injury. This kind of argument cannot logically be made by the court under the cause in fact issue, hence the straitjacket.

Thode also noted that in the real world a jury would strain very hard to find a causal link between the driver's negligence and the injury if the judge charged that such a link was needed. If the jury found that link, the trial and appellate judges would "strive mightily" to uphold the verdict.

The same issue was addressed in Pedrick, Causation, The "Who Done It" Issue and Arno Becht, 1978 Wash.U.L.Q. 645, 655–60. Pedrick asserted that "It is probably not possible nor always sensible, regardless of how we frame the rules of causation, to wholly separate questions of physical causation from questions of policy and policy implementation." He agreed with Professor Thode that "in the real world" the driver is likely to be held liable. In a debate with a personal injury lawyer, Pedrick had "characterized this case as one where the law of negligence would impose no liability because of lack of causal connection between the defendant's negligence and the child's injury. The practitioner's response was simple and effective: 'Just let me try that case and I'll get you a plaintiff's verdict.'" What about a plaintiff's judgment?

Mauro v. Raymark Industries, Inc.

Supreme Court of New Jersey, 1989.
116 N.J. 126, 561 A.2d 257.

1. What injuries are compensable?
2. Is it reasonable to call injury compensable because of increase probability?
① r hasn't happened yet?

3. link b/w causation and policy.

[Plaintiff was employed at a state hospital as a repairman and then as a plumber-steamfitter. From 1964 until the mid-to-late 1970s he used or was exposed to materials containing asbestos manufactured by defendants. In 1981, plaintiff and his co-workers were tested by the state health department, and he was informed that although the results of his physical examination were "normal," he had bilateral thickening of both chest walls and calcification of the diaphragm. He was informed in writing that "your exposure to asbestos has been significant and there is some evidence that this exposure may increase the risk of development of lung cancer." Plaintiff feared contracting cancer because his mother and a prior employer had died of the disease. He has been examined every six months since 1982.

Plaintiff's primary witness, Dr. Guidice, first examined plaintiff in 1986. He testified that plaintiff had "pleural asbestosis," based on the lung lining, pleural plaque formation, and the diaphragm's calcification. He testified that asbestos exposure can cause cancer and identified four areas of the body in which asbestos-related cancer was most likely to occur: lungs, lung linings, larynx, and the entire gastrointestinal tract. He acknowledged that he was not testifying that it was "probable that Mauro would contract cancer." He did say: "There's a risk. . . . I certainly can't predict he's going to get cancer. All I can say is there's a high probability he's at risk because he's a young man and therefore he's at increased risk . . . for developing cancer."

Plaintiff's effort to have an expert quantify the enhanced risk at 20–43% was rejected by the trial judge on the ground that the expert's written report had not cited the statistical or epidemiological studies on which he later wanted to rely.

The trial judge barred the jury from awarding damages for the enhanced risk of developing cancer. The jury was permitted to consider damages for emotional distress relating to plaintiff's fear of getting cancer provided the jury found an asbestos-related injury. The jury was also permitted to award damages for continued medical surveillance and for damages attributable to his current condition.

The jury awarded $7,500 and denied recovery to his wife on her claim for loss of consortium. The appellate division affirmed.]

■ STEIN, J.

In Ayers v. Jackson Township, 106 N.J. 557, 525 A.2d 287 (1987), we declined to recognize a cause of action under the New Jersey Tort Claims Act, [ ], to recover damages for an unquantified enhanced risk of disease resulting from exposure to toxic chemicals. We are now asked to consider whether a claim for enhanced risk of disease is cognizable in a case involving personal injury claims against *private*-entity defendants asserted by a plaintiff with present injuries attributed to asbestos exposure. The plaintiff's expert testified that there was a "high probability" that plaintiff had *an increased risk* of contracting cancer during his lifetime. The expert was unable to testify that it was *probable* that plaintiff would *contract* cancer, and evidence of statistical studies offered to show a correlation between asbestos-related disease and cancer was excluded. Thus, there is no evidence in the record of the likelihood that plaintiff will contract cancer. . . .

. . .

To set a context for our consideration of the enhanced-risk question posed by this record, we restate the inquiry we posed in *Ayers* as a preface to our analysis of the issues in that litigation:

> Our evaluation of the enhanced risk . . . claim [ ] requires that we focus on a critical issue in the management of toxic tort litigation: at what stage in the evolution of a toxic injury should tort law intercede by requiring the responsible party to pay damages? [ ]

It is important to recognize at the outset that the rule of law advocated by plaintiffs, i.e., that tort victims should have a present cause of action for a significant but unquantified enhanced risk of future injury, represents a significant departure from traditional, prevailing legal principles. The general rule is that set forth in the Restatement:

> When an injured person seeks to recover for harms that may result in the future, he is entitled to damages based upon the probability that harm of one sort or another will ensue and upon its probable seriousness if it should ensue. When a person has suffered physical harm that is more or less permanent in nature . . . he is entitled to recover damages not only for harm already suffered, but also for that which probably will result in the future. [§ 912 comment e]

[ ]

The long-standing rule in New Jersey is that prospective damages are not recoverable unless they are reasonably probable to occur. [The court discussed an earlier case that justified the rule on the ground that "the law cannot be administered so as to do reasonably efficient justice if conjecture and speculation are to be used as a measure of damages." The *Mauro* court then noted that although most courts have followed this rule in "toxic-tort cases," commentators disagreed. "Generally, advocates of an enhanced-risk cause of action endorse the view that 'common-law tort doctrines are ill-suited to the resolution of [toxic-tort] injury claims, and that some form of statutorily-authorized compensation procedure is required if the injuries sustained by victims of chemical contamination are to be fairly redressed.' Specifically, recognition of an enhanced-risk cause of action is urged primarily to avoid the bar posed by statutes of limitation and the entire-controversy rule, and to afford plaintiffs exposed to toxic chemicals a basis for recovering medical surveillance and emotional distress damages."]

We recently addressed several of the arguments supporting recognition of enhanced-risk claims in [*Ayers*]. With respect to the statute of limitations and the single-controversy doctrine, we held that in toxic-tort cases

> neither the single controversy doctrine nor the statute of limitations, [ ], will preclude a timely-filed cause of action for damages prompted by the future "discovery" of a disease or injury related to the tortious conduct at issue in this litigation. The bar of the statute of limitations is avoided because, under New Jersey's discovery rule, the cause of action does not accrue until the victim is aware of the injury or disease and of the facts indicating that a third party is or may be responsible. Moreover, the single controversy rule, intended " 'to avoid the delays and wasteful expense of the multiplicity of litigation which results from the splitting of a controversy,' " cannot sensibly be applied to a toxic-tort claim filed when disease is manifested years after the exposure, merely because the same plaintiff sued previously to recover for property damage or other injuries. In such a case, the rule is literally inapplicable since, as noted, the second cause of action does not accrue until the disease is manifested; hence, it could not have been joined with the earlier claims. [ ]

In *Ayers,* we also explained the significant distinctions between a claim for damages based on enhanced risk of injury and a claim for medical-surveillance damages. . . .

Although we rejected the enhanced-risk claim in *Ayers,* partially on the basis that the action was brought under the New Jersey Tort Claims Act, [ ], we upheld the right of plaintiffs with an unquantified enhanced risk of disease due to exposure to toxic chemicals to recover for medical-surveillance expenses:

> Accordingly, we hold that the cost of medical surveillance is a compensable item of damages where the proofs demonstrate, through reliable expert testimony predicated upon the significance and extent of exposure to chemicals, the toxicity of the chemicals, the seriousness of the diseases for which individuals are at risk, the relative increase in the chance of onset of disease in those exposed, and the value of early diagnosis, that such surveillance to monitor the effect of exposure to toxic chemicals is reasonable and

necessary. In our view, this holding is thoroughly consistent with our rejection of plaintiffs' claim for damages based on their en-hanced risk of injury. That claim seeks damages for the impair-ment of plaintiffs' health, without proof of its likelihood, extent, or monetary value. In contrast, the medical surveillance claim seeks reimbursement for the specific dollar costs of periodic examina-tions that are medically necessary notwithstanding the fact that the extent of plaintiffs' impaired health is unquantified. [ ]

Nor is there any question concerning the right of a plaintiff who has sustained physical injury because of exposure to toxic chemicals to recover damages for emotional distress based on a reasonable concern that he or she has an enhanced risk of further disease. [ ] The trial court in this case submitted plaintiff's emotional-distress claim to the jury. On appeal, defendants urged that the claim was not cognizable because of a lack of physical symptoms evidencing plaintiff's distress. The Appellate Division upheld the trial court, noting that "[p]roof that emotional distress has resulted in 'substantial bodily injury or sickness' is not required when plaintiff suffers from a present physical disease attributable to defendant's tortious conduct." [ ] Defendants also advanced this issue in their cross-petition for certification, which we denied. [ ] Hence, although we need not and do not reach the question whether exposure to toxic chemicals without physical injury would sustain a claim for emotional-distress dam-ages based on a reasonable fear of future disease, such a damage claim is clearly cognizable where, as here, plaintiff's exposure to asbestos has resulted in physical injury.

. . .

[The claim for enhanced risk] is a claim for damages based on a prospective injury, conceptually analogous to the claim of a personal-injury plaintiff with a damaged knee to recover damages for the prospective onset of an arthritic condition that may result from the knee injury. See Jackson v. Johns–Manville Sales Corp., 781 F.2d 394, 412 (5th Cir.)(describing General Motors Acceptance Corp. v. Layton, 353 So.2d 749 (Miss.1977)—where plaintiff with bruised knee recovered damages for prospective arthri-tis—as "indistinguishable" from asbestos plaintiffs' claim for prospective cancer), cert. denied, 478 U.S. 1022 (1986). Under our case law, the personal-injury plaintiff conceivably could claim medical-surveillance dam-ages and emotional-distress damages on the basis that the knee injury might cause arthritis, but could not recover damages for the prospective arthritic condition—the "enhanced risk" of arthritis—unless its occurrence was established as a matter of reasonable medical probability. [ ] Thus, the fact that Mauro's claims for medical surveillance and emotional dis-tress, attributable to his enhanced risk of cancer, were submitted to the jury does not exhaust his claim for damages based on the prospective occurrence of cancer—the "enhanced risk" of cancer. [ ] The question before us is whether that component of the claim should have been submitted to the jury in the absence of evidence establishing the future occurrence of cancer as a reasonable medical probability. We hold that the prospective-cancer component of plaintiff's enhanced-risk claim was properly withheld from the jury.

We first observe that the decided cases throughout the country that have considered the question, both in the context of asbestos litigation and claims based on exposure to other toxic chemicals, are almost uniform in their conclusion that in order to recover damages, plaintiff must prove that the prospective disease is at least reasonably probable to occur. [summarizing 20 cases].

Although the weight of authority compellingly argues against recognition of an enhanced-risk-of-cancer claim by a plaintiff with an asbestos-related injury absent proof that satisfies the standard of reasonable medical probability, our analysis would be incomplete without consideration of policy arguments that oppose the general rule. Foremost among these is the concern that deferral of the prospective-injury claim may preclude any recovery when the disease eventually occurs because of the substantial difficulties inherent in attempting to prove causation in toxic-tort cases. See [Ayers]. If the enhanced-risk claim is deferred, a plaintiff asserting the claim when the second injury occurs will inevitably confront the defense that the injury did not result from exposure to toxic chemicals but was "the product of intervening events or causes." [ ]

Recognition of a claim for significantly enhanced risk of disease would also enhance the tort-law's capacity to deter the improper use of toxic chemicals and substances, thereby addressing the contention that tort law cannot deter polluters who view the cost of proper use or disposal as exceeding the risk of tort liability. [Ayers]

The rule of reasonable medical probability is also challenged as an artificial, all-or-nothing standard that rejects future-injury claims supported by substantial evidence that barely falls short of the required quantum of proof. . . .

Other considerations weigh in favor of limiting recognition of enhanced-risk claims to those that prove to a reasonable medical probability the likelihood of future injury. Those claims that fail to meet this standard, if presented to juries, would require damage awards for diseases that are prospective, speculative, and less than likely to occur. The more speculative the proof of future disease, the more difficult would be the juries' burden of calculating fair compensation. Inevitably, damage awards would be rendered for diseases that will never occur, exacting a societal cost in the form of higher insurance premiums and higher product costs.

The vast number of asbestos-related claims now pending in state and federal courts throughout the country is a matter of public record. The formidable burden of litigating such claims would be significantly greater if a substantial percentage of these cases also involved disposition of damage claims for the relatively unquantified enhanced risk of future disease.

Equally persuasive to this Court, however, is the availability of a future opportunity to assert such claims if and when the disease occurs, combined with the present availability of medical surveillance and emotional distress damages in appropriate cases. In our view, removal of the statute-of-limitations and single-controversy doctrines as a bar to the institution of suit when the disease for which plaintiff is at risk ultimately occurs enhances the quality of the remedy that tort law can provide in such cases. If the disease never occurs, presumably there will be no claim and no recovery. If it does occur, the resultant litigation will involve a tangible claim for present injury, rather than a speculative claim for future injury. Hence, juries will be better able to award damages in an amount that fairly reflects the nature and severity of the plaintiff's injury.

We acknowledge that our resolution of this issue is imperfect. In asbestos cases, for example, the available statistical evidence correlating asbestos-related disease with the future onset of cancer appears to fall short—as was evident from the evidence proffered in this case—of establishing the occurrence of cancer as a matter of reasonable medical probability. [ ] Undoubtedly, there will be individual cases in which statistical evidence, combined with the particular degree of exposure and injury sustained by the plaintiff, will establish the likelihood of future disease as a matter of probability. [ ] With respect to those cases in which the evidence that future disease will occur falls substantially short of the reasonable-medical-probability standard, we are satisfied that the interests of justice are well served by excluding such claims from jury consideration. Of course, there will be close cases, and for their resolution our use of the reasonable-medical-probability standard "to draw judicial lines beyond which liability will not be extended is fundamentally * * * an instrument of fairness and policy."   . . .

. . .

Judgment affirmed.

■ HANDLER, J., dissenting.

. . .

. . . The traditional rule [of damage measurement], at least considered in the context of this case, can no longer be reconciled with the knowledge and experience that has emerged in recent years. . . .

. . .

The Court . . . bases its decision on public-policy considerations. First, it finds that there are vast numbers of asbestos-related claims in courts and that litigating enhanced-risk claims would be "too burdensome." Why? The claim based on the enhanced risk of cancer would be only one element of damages that would be presented with other medical and relevant proofs relating to a plaintiff's injuries and general condition. The Court does not bother to explain how evidence relating to this one element, in addition to admissible proofs relating to plaintiff's current disease and its future consequences, shortened life expectancy, the need for medical surveillance, his or her emotional distress and mental anguish, economic losses, per quod claims and the like, all of which are concededly allowable, would unduly complicate or burden this litigation. Nor does the Court explain whether its solution will and can avoid burdening the legal system, if not today, surely tomorrow. The Court proposes to reserve for the future any claims relating to cancer attributable to the current toxic exposure. Such an action brought long after the current actions are concluded will present enormous procedural and administrative obstacles. Many such actions will be undertaken when evidence will have vanished, witnesses will be gone, memories dimmed, and transcripts, needed for purposes of preparation, discovery, examination and cross-examination, and record reconstruction, will have disappeared. The problems that will arise from such future lawsuits do not bode well for the administration of justice.

. . .

In my view, the majority's solution of allowing the plaintiff to sue defendant later if he develops cancer is unfair and unjust and does not comport with broader notions of sound public policy. In light of current knowledge and experience, there is no valid reason why plaintiff's enhanced risk of cancer should not be considered an element of a present injury caused by the defendant and to be compensated now. See [*Ayers,* (Handler, J., dissenting)]. Due to this injury, plaintiff may have to alter his lifestyle to avoid cancer-causing agents that may be present in foods or the environment and atmosphere to prevent the likelihood of developing cancer. Plaintiff may also be prevented from obtaining certain jobs—such as in chemical factories—because his enhanced risk of cancer make him more vulnerable to other workplace injuries. In addition, his health and life insurance premiums will be greater because the insurance companies will charge plaintiff for his enhanced risk of developing cancer.

I return to the fairness and feasibility of permitting a current recovery for the present risk of cancer. It seems disingenuous, if not callous, to suggest that plaintiff's risk of cancer is not palpable and serious—why quibble between probable and possible when it is agreed that the risk is significant? When the reality of this risk is confirmed by the fact that plaintiff is now required to submit to bi-annual cancer medical examinations and defendant is more than willing to pay for the cost of this medical surveillance? If the rest of the society treats plaintiff's enhanced risk of cancer as a present injury, why should the courts deny its existence by denying its compensability? Plaintiff does not ask for damages for having cancer, he only wants to recover for the unusual risk to his health and life and the tangible and significant likelihood of developing cancer. He seeks only fair compensation, which a jury should be quite capable of assessing.

. . .

We should, on balance, encourage plaintiffs to sue in current actions for all elements of a claim for relief consistent with the principles of comprehensiveness, finality, and repose that we invoke in determining and concluding litigation. These principles are reflected in the evolution of the entire controversy doctrine and statutes of limitations. [ ] If a plaintiff were required, or permitted, to sue in a current action for the risk of future cancer, he or she would not have it both ways. Such a plaintiff should be barred from again asserting a claim for the disease even if it becomes manifest. The litigation should be put at rest.

In my opinion, Mr. Mauro, like the plaintiffs from Jackson Township, has a cognizable injury in the form of a palpable and serious risk of incurring cancer that should be compensated for now.

■ For affirmance—JUSTICES CLIFFORD, POLLOCK, O'HERN, GARIBALDI and STEIN—5.

■ Dissenting—JUSTICE HANDLER—1.

NOTES AND QUESTIONS

1. What are the strongest reasons supporting the majority's approach? The dissent's approach?

2. Does the court's analysis of the statute of limitations justify the denial of the present claim?

3. Justice Handler identifies several current costs that Mauro has sustained, such as change in life style, higher insurance premiums to get new coverage, and greater difficulty in getting certain jobs. Would these be currently recoverable under the majority's approach?

4. *Enhanced Risk of Future Harm.*

a. In Petriello v. Kalman, 215 Conn. 377, 576 A.2d 474 (1990), defendant obstetrician negligently performed a procedure on plaintiff, as the result of which plaintiff suffered some immediate injury and also an 8–16 percent chance of specific future injury. The court upheld a jury instruction that permitted an award for the increased risk:

> If this increased risk was more likely than not the result of the bowel resection necessitated by the defendant's actions, we conclude that there is no legitimate reason why she should not recover present compensation based upon the likelihood of the risk becoming a reality. When viewed in this manner, the plaintiff was attempting merely to establish the extent of her present injuries. She should not be burdened with proving that the occurrence of a future event is more likely than not, when it is a present risk, rather than a future event for which she claims damages. In our judgment, it was fairer to instruct the jury to compensate the plaintiff for the increased risk . . . rather than to ignore that risk completely.

> Such a system would also be fairer to a defendant "who should be required to pay damages for a future loss based upon the statistical probability that such a loss will be sustained rather than upon the assumption that the loss is a certainty because it is more likely than not. We hold, therefore, that in a tort action, a plaintiff who has established a breach of duty that was a substantial factor in causing a present injury which has resulted in an increased risk of future harm is entitled to compensation to the extent that the future harm is likely to occur."

How might the *Mauro* majority respond to the Connecticut court's approach? Is it significant that the Connecticut case does not involve a toxic tort claim? Is it significant that Connecticut has a statute of limitations with a proviso "that no [tort] action may be brought more than three years from the date of the act or omission complained of?"

b. Does the logic of the Connecticut court require proportionate—rather than full—recovery in cases in which the plaintiff establishes a greater than 51 percent likelihood of future harm?

c. Under the Connecticut approach should the plaintiff have the option to decide whether to sue now for a small percentage or to wait until getting the disease? Does Justice Handler address this issue? If the latency period is 30 years might the plaintiff choose to sue in the tenth year? Recall the Connecticut proviso that suits be brought within three years of the act or omission.

d. A number of courts have followed *Mauro* in adopting a more-likely-than-not standard in enhanced risk cases. See e.g., Abuan v. General Electric Co., 3 F.3d 329 (9th Cir.1993), denying future risk claims to plaintiffs allegedly exposed to toxic chemicals. In contrast to *Mauro*—and in sharp contrast to *Petriello*—the court in Marinari v. Asbestos Corp., Ltd., 417 Pa.Super. 440, 612 A.2d 1021 (1992), involving asbestos claims for present pleural thickening and future risk of lung cancer, enunciated a "two-disease" approach, barring any recovery for enhanced risk until the anticipated condition develops:

> The speculative nature of the prediction of future damages—that a person with asbestosis will someday contract cancer—may lead to several inequitable results. First, the plaintiff who does not contract cancer gets a windfall—cancer damages without cancer. Second, and perhaps worse, an asbestosis plaintiff who is unsuccessful in his efforts to recover risk of cancer damages, but later contracts cancer, has the disease but no damages. Third, even plaintiffs who later contract cancer and who recovered some amount of risk of cancer damages may emerge with an inequitable award, since the jury, cognizant of the less than one hundred percent chance that the plaintiff will contract cancer, likely will have awarded less than one hundred percent damages. Finally, inequitable awards are more likely to result from a future damages action simply because the damages cannot be known. If the disease has advanced—or even come into existence—the actual financial needs of the plaintiff can obviously be more accurately assessed.

See also Giffear v. Johns–Manville Corp., 429 Pa.Super. 327, 632 A.2d 880 (1993), appeal granted. How might the *Mauro* majority respond? Justice Handler? Which of the preceding approaches seems most desirable?

e. Do these probabilistic harm questions raise different issues in the future damage cases than arise in the lost-opportunity cases?

5. *Medical surveillance.*

a. The court seems clear that Mauro can recover his medical surveillance costs after he has been injured. Assume that the normal risk in a community of 100,000 is that some disease will strike two persons in their lifetimes. After an escape of gas from defendant's plant, the risk is shown to have risen to five in 100,000. Does this mean that everyone in the community will be entitled to medical surveillance costs for the rest of their lives? In the hypothetical, note that the defendant has more than doubled the exposure risk of the entire community. Suppose proper surveillance in such cases involves expensive scanning and laboratory tests? Would the majority and dissent in *Mauro* disagree over the resolution of this issue?

b. In Theer v. Philip Carey Co., 133 N.J. 610, 628 A.2d 724 (1993), plaintiff's husband had spent his "lifetime" as an asbestos worker and had recently died from asbestos-related diseases. Here, plaintiff widow, a smoker for 36 years, whose exposure to asbestos came from laundering her husband's clothes, apparently for many years, sought medical surveillance costs. The jury had found "no asbestos-related injury." In the course of denying recovery, the court elaborated on its medical surveillance standard:

> [such] damages are not available for plaintiffs who have not experienced direct and hence discrete exposure to a toxic substance and who have not suffered an injury or condition resulting from that exposure and whose risk of cancer cannot be limited and related specifically and tangibly to that exposure.

Plaintiff's exposure was "indirect." It was "impossible to approximate or to quantify the extent to which she may have encountered the substance, given that her exposure was essentially 'second-hand.'" Moreover, her smoking suggests "that there may be multiple factors that contribute to any future injuries that she may have."

c. Hansen v. Mountain Fuel Supply Co., 858 P.2d 970 (Utah 1993), involving an asbestos exposure while doing renovation work at a building, purports to adopt the New Jersey approach and adds a requirement that the plaintiff prove "that by reason of the exposure to the toxic substance caused by the defendant's negligence, a reasonable physician would prescribe for her or him a monitoring regime different than the one that would have been prescribed in the absence of that particular exposure." Is this a helpful addition?

6. *Emotional distress from enhanced likelihood of physical harm.* The majority concludes that when physical injury is present, damages for emotional distress may be recoverable for fear of future harm. For a similar result, see Sterling v. Velsicol Chemical Corp., 855 F.2d 1188 (6th Cir.1988). Should the presence of existing injury be essential to this type of claim? The *Mauro* court leaves the question open.

In Potter v. Firestone Tire and Rubber Co., 6 Cal.4th 965, 863 P.2d 795, 25 Cal.Rptr.2d 550 (1993), plaintiffs were exposed to carcinogens over a prolonged period due to defendant's dumping of toxic wastes into a landfill near its plant site. While none of the plaintiffs suffered from any current condition they faced "an enhanced but unquantified risk of developing cancer in the future due to the exposure." The court held that:

> . . . in the absence of a present physical injury or illness, damages for fear of cancer may be recovered only if the plaintiff pleads and proves that 1) as a result of the defendant's negligent breach of a duty

owed to the plaintiff, the plaintiff is exposed to a toxic substance which threatens cancer, *and* 2) the plaintiff's fear stems from a knowledge, corroborated by reliable medical or scientific opinion, that it is more likely than not that the plaintiff will develop the cancer in the future due to the toxic exposure.

The court went on to add that the plaintiff must further show "a serious fear that the toxic ingestion or exposure was of such magnitude and proportion as to likely result in the feared cancer." Since the claim in these cases is based on emotional distress, not the likelihood of actually contracting cancer, why shouldn't this "serious fear" requirement be the exclusive test for liability? This issue is often characterized as a question of whether a duty is owed to compensate for negligent infliction of emotional distress. Reconsider *Benson*, p. 226 supra, requiring actual exposure to the HIV virus before permitting a claim for emotional distress from the fear of getting AIDS.

The *Potter* court offered a number of reasons for its holding—that "all of us are exposed to carcinogens every day;" that wider liability would have "an unduly detrimental impact" on the health field; that wider liability would have a detrimental impact on the likelihood of recovery for those who actually develop cancer or other physical injuries later on; and that any other test would lack the certainty of the more-likely-than-not standard. Are these reasons persuasive? (The court also held that if plaintiff could establish "oppression, fraud or malice"—the standard for punitive damages established in the California Civil Code—then a showing that the plaintiff's fear is "serious, genuine and reasonable," would suffice.)

See also San Diego Gas and Electric v. Superior Court, 32 Cal.App.4th 1062, 38 Cal.Rptr.2d 811 (1995), hearing granted, in which a lower court denied a claim for fear of contracting cancer from exposure to electric and magnetic fields on the basis of *Potter*.

7. On the variety of issues discussed in the preceding notes, see generally, Wells, The Grin Without a Cat: Claims for Damages from Toxic Exposures, 18 Wm. & Mary J. Envtl. L. 285 (1994). See also, Comment, Curing Cancerphobia: Reasonableness Redefined, 62 U.Chi.L.Rev. 1113 (1995), rejecting judicial requirements of "physical injury," "physical manifestation of cancerphobia," "traditional 'reasonableness,'" and the "more-likely-than-not" standard of *Potter*. With 14 million workers who have been significantly exposed to asbestos, plus other situations giving rise to fear of cancer, some screening device is needed in cancerphobia cases. The author argues that each of the listed traditional approaches is unsatisfying as a screening device, and urges a "substantial probability" standard—one that emphasizes the increased risk to plaintiff "over the societal rate based on general levels of exposure."

8. *Establishing causation through reliance on expert testimony: The Daubert case.* In virtually every case involving a toxic exposure claim, plaintiffs rely on science experts to establish that the exposure was in fact the cause of the plaintiff's harm. As toxic tort litigation has proliferated, there has been great controversy over threshold questions of standards of reliability and relevance that are to guide the trial court in determining expert qualifications. For sharp criticism of the courts, see P. Huber, Galileo's Revenge: Junk Science in the Courtroom (1991).

Traditionally, the dominant approach to admissibility has been the *Frye* test, which was fashioned in Frye v. United States, 293 Fed. 1013 (D.C.Cir.1923), requiring that scientific evidence be based on techniques generally regarded as reliable in the scientific community. But in Daubert v. Merrell Dow Pharmaceuticals, Inc., 113 S.Ct. 2786 (1993), involving one of the many cases in which Bendectin, a morning-sickness drug, was alleged to cause subsequent limb reduction birth defects, the Court held that Federal Rule of Evidence 702 set a more easily-satisfied standard of qualification. The rule provides:

> If scientific, technical, or other specialized knowledge will assist the trier of fact to understand the evidence or to determine a fact in issue, a witness qualified as an expert by knowledge, skill, experience, training, or education, may testify thereto. . . .

In the Court's view, Rule 702 entailed "a preliminary assessment of whether the reasoning or methodology underlying the testimony is scientifically valid and of whether that reasoning or methodology properly can be applied to the facts in issue"—a judicial "gatekeeping role" that might take general scientific acceptability into account, but that dictated an inquiry beyond scientific orthodoxy in the search for relevance and reliability.

On remand to the Ninth Circuit panel that had initially granted summary judgment under the *Frye* test, the court once again dismissed the case. Daubert v. Merrell Dow Pharmaceuticals, Inc., 43 F.3d 1311 (9th Cir.), cert. denied 116 S.Ct. 189 (1995). On the issue of reliability of the plaintiffs' experts, Judge Kozinski remarked, "Bendectin litigation has been pending in the courts for over a decade, yet the only review the plaintiffs' experts' work has received has been by judges and juries, and the only place their theories and studies have been published is in the pages of federal and state reporters." On the question of relevance, the court found no evidence offered that Bendectin ingestion more than doubled the incidence of limb reduction—the necessary threshold for establishing that Bendectin was more probably than not the cause of harm.

For a detailed examination of the background in the Bendectin controversy, as well as a useful summary of the scientific techniques used to establish causation in toxic exposure cases, see Sanders, From Science to Evidence: The Testimony on Causation in the Bendectin Cases, 46 Stan. L. Rev. 1 (1993).

2. AN INTRODUCTION TO JOINT AND SEVERAL LIABILITY

The basic doctrine. So far we have been dealing with cases in which the focus was on the causal contribution of a single defendant. We turn now to cases in which more than one relevant cause may be involved in the harm that befell plaintiff. One example would be a case in which two cars collide and one of the cars goes up on the sidewalk and hits a pedestrian. The proof shows that if either driver had been careful the accident would have been averted. In other words, the negligence of each driver was essential to plaintiff's harm.

In this type of case the two drivers were traditionally held subject to "joint and several liability." This meant that the plaintiff might sue them together or separately and recover the full extent of the damages against either one. If plaintiff's harm was $50,000, and both defendants were found negligent, the judgment traditionally provided that the plaintiff was to recover $50,000 against D1 and D2. Plaintiff could then collect the entire $50,000 from whichever defendant plaintiff chose—usually the one from whom it was easier to collect the entire award. The plaintiff did not care whether one of the defendants was insolvent because any solvent defendant was liable for the entire award. (Originally, the two defendants were held equally responsible between themselves—so that one of the two defendants who paid the plaintiff the full $50,000 would be entitled to recoup $25,000 from the other. As we shall see in Chapter VI, that pattern gave way to a system in which the defendants shared on the basis of their respective percentages of fault.)

The doctrine operated in situations beyond those in which multiple defendants combined to cause the same harm. Consider Ravo v. Rogatnick, 70 N.Y.2d 305, 514 N.E.2d 1104, 520 N.Y.S.2d 533 (1987), a case in which plaintiff suffered severe brain damage at birth. The evidence supported the view that the harm could have come from the obstetrician's negligence in delivery or from the pediatrician's negligence immediately thereafter, or from both causes. The jury found eight acts of malpractice by the obstetrician and three by the pediatrician. The trial judge instructed the jury that if they found both defendants negligent and that both had caused a single injury to the plaintiff that could not be apportioned between the defendants, the jury could find each liable for the whole harm. The jury was also told to apportion the fault in the case on the basis of 100%.

The jury returned a verdict finding for plaintiff against both defendants. It also apportioned the fault 80% to the obstetrician and 20% to the pediatrician. The pediatrician asserted that he should be liable for no more than 20% of the award. The court disagreed:

> When two or more tort-feasors act concurrently or in concert to produce a single injury, they may be held jointly and severally liable. [ ] This is so because such concerted wrongdoers are considered "joint tort-feasors" and in legal contemplation, there is a joint enterprise and a mutual agency, such that the act of one is the act of all and liability for all that is done is visited upon each. [ ] On the other hand, where multiple tort-feasors "neither act in concert nor contribute concurrently to the same wrong, they are not joint tort-feasors; rather their wrongs are independent and successive." [ ] Under successive and independent liability, of course, the initial tort-feasor may well be liable to the plaintiff for

the entire damage proximately resulting from his own wrongful acts. [ ] The successive tort-feasor, however, is liable only for the separate injury or the aggravation his conduct has caused. [ ]

It is sometimes the case that tort-feasors who neither act in concert nor concurrently may nevertheless be considered jointly and severally liable. This may occur in the instance of certain injuries which, because of their nature, are incapable of any reasonable or practicable division or allocation among multiple tort-feasors. [ ]

The court thought the same reasoning applied to this case. Although the second defendant is not to be held jointly and severally liable "in every case where it is difficult, because of the nature of the injury, to separate the harm done" by each defendant, the evidence here showed that the brain damage was a single indivisible injury.

The fact that the jury allocated only 20% of the negligence to the second defendant did not alter the analysis. This "aspect of the jury's determination of culpability merely defines the amount of contribution defendants may claim from each other, and does not impinge upon plaintiff's right to collect the entire judgment from either defendant."

Recent changes. Since the advent of comparative negligence two changes have occurred that alter the basic doctrine. The first has already been noted—having the defendants obtain contribution from each other in proportion to their fault in the accident. Thus, if D1 was held 75% at fault and D2 25% at fault for the harm suffered by the pedestrian, the victim could still get full damages from either defendant, but they would ultimately share the loss in a 75–25 ratio if both were solvent.

The second recent change in the traditional pattern has been much more significant—questioning the very idea of "joint and several liability." Joint and several liability has come under fire in recent years because of perceived unfairness in certain situations in which one of the two defendants is unable to bear his or her share of the judgment. The problem is suggested by the situation above in which the jury holds D1 75% to blame for an accident. Under the common law each would be jointly and severally liable for the entire judgment—with contribution to follow—if both defendants were solvent. If both were solvent, there was little sense of unfairness. But if either driver turned out to be insolvent, the entire loss would rest on the other one. Thus, the defendant who was 25% at fault might be out of pocket for 100% of the damages.

The advent of comparative negligence, discussed in detail in Chapter VI, was meant to modify the perceived harshness of the all-or-nothing aspect of contributory negligence. But once comparisons were permitted between plaintiff and defendant, the argument was put forward that it was at least as desirable to make similar comparisons among defendants—and then to have each party to the accident bear only the share attributable to his or her fault. Again, if everyone is solvent, there is little reason for concern. But in reality, insolvency often intrudes on the nature of tort liability. (We have seen some implicit examples in *Tarasoff*, p. 140, supra, *Vince v. Wilson*, p. 152 supra, and *Kelly v. Gwinnell*, p. 157 supra).

Since the early 1980s, some forty states have made major legislative changes in the operation of joint and several liability. It is hard to capture the array of changes but they fit roughly into the following categories:

1. About ten states have abolished the doctrine, leaving a solvent defendant responsible only for his or her percentage of fault.

2. About ten have abolished the doctrine in cases in which the defendant is less than a certain percentage at fault. In most of these the threshold is 50%.

3. Somewhat fewer states have abolished the doctrine in many kinds of torts but have retained it in a few areas—most commonly toxic and environmental torts. (New York, for example, retains the doctrine in several listed situations, including motor vehicle and motorcycle cases, recklessness cases, and a variety of environmental cases.)

4. A few states, including California, have retained joint and several liability for economic damages but have abolished it for non-economic damages.

5. A handful of states have abolished the doctrine where the plaintiff is partially at fault, but have retained it when the plaintiff was not at fault.

6. About ten states have enacted more than one of the changes listed above.

Which if any of these changes would you favor?

We return to joint and several liability and related topics in detail in Chapter VI. For now, though, it is enough to have a basic understanding of the implications of holding two or more defendants jointly and severally liable.

3. MULTIPLE DEFENDANTS

Summers v. Tice

Supreme Court of California, 1948.
33 Cal.2d 80, 199 P.2d 1.

[Plaintiff and defendants Tice and Simonson were hunting quail when both defendants fired in plaintiff's direction. One shot struck plaintiff's eye and another his lip. Both defendants were using the same gauge shotgun and the same size shot. The trial judge, sitting without a jury, found both defendants negligent and found that plaintiff was in no way at fault. Unable to decide which defendant's shot hit the plaintiff, the judge awarded judgment against both defendants, who appealed.]

■ CARTER, J. [after stating the facts and upholding the negligence determinations].

The problem presented in this case is whether the judgment against both defendants may stand. It is argued by defendants that they are not joint tort feasors, and thus jointly and severally liable, as they were not acting in concert, and that there is not sufficient evidence to show which defendant was guilty of the negligence which caused the injuries—the shooting by Tice or that by Simonson. Tice argues that there is evidence to show that the shot which struck plaintiff came from Simonson's gun because of admissions allegedly made by him to third persons and no evidence that they came from his gun. Further in connection with the latter contention, the court failed to find on plaintiff's allegation in his complaint that he did not know which one was at fault—did not find which defendant was guilty of the negligence which caused the injuries to plaintiff.

Considering the last argument first, we believe it is clear that the court sufficiently found on the issue that defendants were jointly liable and that thus the negligence of both was the cause of the injury or to that legal effect. It found that both defendants were negligent and "That as a direct and proximate result of the shots fired by *defendants, and each of them,* a birdshot pellet was caused to and did lodge in plaintiff's right eye and that another birdshot pellet was caused to and did lodge in plaintiff's upper lip." In so doing the court evidently did not give credence to the admissions of Simonson to third persons that he fired the shots which it was justified in doing. It thus determined that the negligence of both defendants was the legal cause of the injury—or that both were responsible. Implicit in such finding is the assumption that the court was unable to ascertain whether the shots were from the gun of one defendant or the other or one shot from each of them. The one shot that entered plaintiff's eye was the major factor in assessing damages and that shot could not have come from the gun of both defendants. It was from one or the other only.

It has been held that where a group of persons are on a hunting party, or otherwise engaged in the use of firearms, and two of them are negligent in firing in the direction of a third person who is injured thereby, both of those so firing are liable for the injury suffered by the third person, although the negligence of only one of them could have caused the injury. [   ] Oliver v. Miles, 144 Miss. 852 [110 So. 666; 50 A.L.R. 357]; [   ] The same rule has been applied in criminal cases [   ] and both drivers have been held liable for the negligence of one where they engaged in a racing contest causing an injury to a third person [   ]. These cases speak of the action of defendants as being in concert as the ground of decision, yet it would seem they are straining that concept and the more reasonable basis appears in *Oliver v. Miles,* supra. There two persons were hunting together. Both shot at some partridges and in so doing shot across the highway injuring plaintiff who was traveling on it. The court stated they were acting in concert and thus both were liable. The court then stated: "We think that .   .   .   each is liable for the resulting injury to the boy, although no one can say definitely who actually shot him. *To hold otherwise would be to exonerate both from liability, although each was negligent, and the injury resulted from such negligence.''* [Emphasis added.]

. . .

When we consider the relative position of the parties and the results that would flow if plaintiff was required to pin the injury on one of the defendants only, a requirement that the burden of proof on that subject be shifted to defendants becomes manifest. They are both wrongdoers—both negligent toward plaintiff. They brought about a situation where the negligence of one of them injured the plaintiff, hence it should rest with them each to absolve himself if he can. The injured party has been placed by defendants in the unfair position of pointing to which defendant caused the harm. If one can escape the other may also and plaintiff is remediless. Ordinarily defendants are in a far better position to offer evidence to determine which one caused the injury. This reasoning has recently found favor in this court. In a quite analogous situation this court held that a patient injured while unconscious on an operating table in a hospital could hold all or any of the persons who had any connection with the operation even though he could not select the particular acts by the particular person which led to his disability. *Ybarra v. Spangard*, [   ]. There the court was considering whether the patient could avail himself of res ipsa loquitur, rather than where the burden of proof lay, yet the effect of the decision is that plaintiff has made out a case when he has produced evidence which gives rise to an inference of negligence which was the proximate cause of the injury. It is up to defendants to explain the cause of the injury. It was there said: "If the doctrine is to continue to serve a useful purpose, we should not forget that 'the particular force and justice of the rule, regarded as a presumption throwing upon the party charged the duty of producing evidence, consists in the circumstance that the chief evidence of the true cause, whether culpable or innocent, is practically accessible to him but inaccessible to the injured person.' " (P. 490). Similarly in the instant case plaintiff is not able to establish which of defendants caused his injury.

. . .

It is urged that plaintiff now has changed the theory of his case in claiming a concert of action; that he did not plead or prove such concert. From what has been said it is clear that there has been no change in theory. The joint liability, as well as the lack of knowledge as to which defendant was liable, was pleaded and the proof developed the case under either theory. We have seen that for the reasons of policy discussed herein, the case is based upon the legal proposition that, under the circumstances here presented, each defendant is liable for the whole damage whether they are deemed to be acting in concert or independently.

The judgment is affirmed.

■ GIBSON, C.J., SHENK, J., EDMONDS, J., TRAYNOR, J., SCHAUER, J., and SPENCE, J., concurred.

NOTES AND QUESTIONS

1. If the damages are $20,000, who will pay how much to whom under the doctrine of joint and several liability?

2. Is it essential to the analysis that the two defendants were hunting as a team? What if they had been independent negligent hunters who never met one another until after the accident?

3. How should the cause issue be analyzed if the judge found that although either pellet might have hit the plaintiff, only Tice's behavior had been negligent, so that the innocent Simonson could not be liable to plaintiff even if his pellet had done the harm? In Garcia v. Joseph Vince Co., 84 Cal.App.3d 868, 148 Cal.Rptr. 843 (1978), plaintiff fencer was hurt by a defective saber. Plaintiff could not identify which of two manufacturers was the source of the defective saber because it had been put back into a pile of sabers. His effort to invoke *Summers v. Tice* was rejected and the case was dismissed.

4. What result would the court reach if Tice had fired two shots and Simonson only one? What if three defendants had fired negligently at the same time? What if only two of the three had been negligent?

5. Are the differences between *Ybarra* and *Summers* significant? Which decision is more justifiable? This question is discussed and *Ybarra* criticized, in Seavey, Res Ipsa Loquitur: Tabula in Naufragio, 63 Harv. L.Rev. 643 (1950).

6. In a subsequent multiple-shooting case, should a plaintiff who cannot prove anyone's negligence, be able to invoke *Ybarra* and then use *Summers*?

7. Suppose P is injured in a highway accident when D1 negligently swerves into P's car and that then D2 negligently piles into the tangled autos. Does it follow from the reasoning of *Summers v. Tice* that the burden shifts to each defendant to show that his collision was not the cause of the plaintiff's injuries? See Copley v. Putter, 93 Cal.App.2d 453, 207 P.2d 876 (1949), treating virtually simultaneous impacts under the *Summers v. Tice* approach.

8. In Basko v. Sterling Drug, Inc., 416 F.2d 417 (2d Cir.1969), the plaintiff was allegedly blinded after taking two drugs manufactured by the defendant. Under one view of the case, the defendant would have been liable if the blinding had been caused by its Triquin but not if caused by its Aralen. The blinding might have been caused by either one or a combination of the drugs. The court noted that ordinarily cause can be analyzed in terms of a "but for" test: "defendant's negligence is a cause in fact of an injury where the injury would not have occurred *but for* defendant's negligent conduct. [ ] The test will not work, however, in the situation where two independent forces concur to produce a result which either of them alone would have produced. In such a situation, either force can be said to be the cause in fact of the harm, despite the fact that the same harm would have resulted from either force acting alone." The causation element would be satisfied by a finding that the defendant's negligence was a "substantial factor" in producing the harm:

> The reason for imposing liability in such a situation, as Harper and James explain, is that the "defendant has committed a wrong and this has been *a* cause of the injury; further, such negligent conduct will be more effectively deterred by imposing liability than by giving the wrongdoer a windfall in cases where an all-sufficient innocent cause happens to concur with his wrong in producing the harm." [ ] Similarly, in Navigazione Libera T. S. A. v. Newtown Creek Towing Co., 98 F.2d 694, 697 (2d Cir.1938), Judge Learned Hand stated that "the single tortfeasor cannot be allowed to escape through the meshes of a logical net. He is a wrongdoer; let him unravel the casuistries resulting from his wrong." See also Malone, Ruminations on Cause-In-Fact, 9 Stan.L.Rev. 60, 88–94 (1956). The contrary arguments have been rejected by the Restatement, and there is good reason to believe that the Connecticut courts would follow the Restatement approach. [ ]

Is the court's resolution persuasive?

9. Analyze a case in which two negligent defendants independently race their motorcycles past plaintiff's horse—which bolts and runs away. The act of either defendant alone would have sufficed to cause the harm. See Corey v. Havener, 182 Mass. 250, 65 N.E. 69 (1902). What if one of the motorcyclists had not been negligent?

In Peaslee, Multiple Causation and Damage, 47 Harv.L.Rev. 1127 (1934), the author argued that the but-for rule should bar liability where one concurrent cause is innocent. Otherwise, the plaintiff would be made "better off than he would have been if the defendant had done no wrong. . . . Causation is matter of fact, and that which is not in fact causal ought not to be deemed so in law."

Peaslee's approach was criticized in Carpenter, Concurrent Causation, 83 U.Pa.L.Rev. 941 (1935). Setting out some "elementary, if not almost self-evident, principles," Carpenter stated that the defendant "does not escape liability for a damage to which his wrongful cause substantially contributed either because of the fact that other causes contributed or because some other causes were innocent."

Hymowitz v. Eli Lilly & Co.

Court of Appeals of New York, 1989.
73 N.Y.2d 487, 539 N.E.2d 1069, 541 N.Y.S.2d 941.
Cert. denied, 493 U.S. 944 (1989).

■ WACHTLER, CHIEF JUDGE.

Plaintiffs in these appeals allege that they were injured by the drug diethylstilbestrol (DES) ingested by their mothers during pregnancy. They seek relief against defendant DES manufacturers. While not class actions, these cases are representative of nearly 500 similar actions pending in the courts in this State; the rules articulated by the court here, therefore, must do justice and be administratively feasible in the context of this mass litigation. . . .

I.

The history of the development of DES and its marketing in this country has been repeatedly chronicled [ ]. Briefly, DES is a synthetic substance that mimics the effect of estrogen, the naturally formed female hormone. It was invented in 1937 by British researchers, but never patented.

In 1941, the Food and Drug Administration (FDA) approved the new drug applications (NDA) of 12 manufacturers to market DES for the treatment of various maladies, not directly involving pregnancy. In 1947, the FDA began approving the NDAs of manufacturers to market DES for the purpose of preventing human miscarriages; by 1951, the FDA had concluded that DES was generally safe for pregnancy use, and stopped requiring the filing of NDAs when new manufacturers sought to produce the drug for this purpose. In 1971, however, the FDA banned the use of DES as a miscarriage preventative, when studies established the harmful latent effects of DES upon the offspring of mothers who took the drug. Specifically, tests indicated that DES caused vaginal adenocarcinoma, a form of cancer, and adenosis, a precancerous vaginal or cervical growth.

Although strong evidence links prenatal DES exposure to later development of serious medical problems, plaintiffs seeking relief in court for their injuries faced two formidable and fundamental barriers to recovery in this State; not only is identification of the manufacturer of the DES ingested in a particular case generally impossible, but, due to the latent nature of DES injuries, many claims were barred by the Statute of Limitations before the injury was discovered.

The identification problem has many causes. All DES was of identical chemical composition. Druggists usually filled prescriptions from whatever was on hand. Approximately 300 manufacturers produced the drug, with companies entering and leaving the market continuously during the 24 years that DES was sold for pregnancy use. The long latency period of a DES injury compounds the identification problem; memories fade, records are lost or destroyed, and witnesses die. Thus the pregnant women who took DES generally never knew who produced the drug they took, and there was no reason to attempt to discover this fact until many years after ingestion, at which time the information is not available.

. . .

The second barrier to recovery, involving the Statute of Limitations, arose from the long-standing rule in this State that the limitations period accrued upon exposure in actions alleging personal injury caused by toxic substances. [Following a case in which the court refused to change that rule for DES cases, the legislature provided that the statute began to run upon the discovery of "the latent effects of exposure to any substance," and for one year revived causes of action for exposure to DES that had been barred.]

It is estimated that eventually 800 DES cases will be brought under the revival portion of this recent statute. . . .

The present appeals are before the court in the context of summary judgment motions. In all of the appeals defendants moved for summary judgment dismissing the complaints because plaintiffs could not identify the manufacturer of the drug that allegedly injured them. In three of the appeals defendants also moved on Statute of Limitations grounds, arguing that the revival of the actions was unconstitutional under the State and Federal Constitutions, and that the complaints, therefore, are time barred and should be dismissed. The trial court denied all of these motions. On the Statute of Limitations issue, the trial court also granted plaintiffs' cross motions, dismissing defendants' affirmative defenses that the actions were time barred. The Appellate Division affirmed in all respects and certified to this court the questions of whether the orders of the trial court were properly made. [ ] We answer these questions in the affirmative.

II.

In a products liability action, identification of the exact defendant whose product injured the plaintiff is, of course, generally required [ ]. In DES cases in which such identification is possible, actions may proceed under established principles of products liability [ ]. The record now before us, however, presents the question of whether a DES plaintiff may recover against a DES manufacturer when identification of the producer of the specific drug that caused the injury is impossible.

A.

As we noted [ ], the accepted tort doctrines of alternative liability and concerted action are available in some personal injury cases to permit recovery where the precise identification of a wrongdoer is impossible. However, we agree with the near unanimous views of the high State courts that have considered the matter that these doctrines in their unaltered common-law forms do not permit recovery in DES cases [ ].

The paradigm of alternative liability is found in the case of Summers v. Tice, [ ]. In *Summers,* plaintiff and the two defendants were hunting, and defendants carried identical shotguns and ammunition. During the hunt, defendants shot simultaneously at the same bird, and plaintiff was struck by bird shot from one of the defendants' guns. The court held that where two defendants breach a duty to the plaintiff, but there is uncertainty regarding which one caused the injury, "the burden is upon each such actor to prove that he has not caused the harm" [ ]; cf., Ravo v. Rogatnick, ([ ] [successive tort-feasors may be held jointly and severally liable for an indivisible injury to the plaintiff]). The central rationale for shifting the burden of proof in such a situation is that without this device both defendants will be silent, and plaintiff will not recover; with alternative liability, however, defendants will be forced to speak, and reveal the culpable party, or else be held jointly and severally liable themselves. Consequently, use of the alternative liability doctrine generally requires that the defendants have better access to information than does the plaintiff, and that all possible tort-feasors be before the court [   ]. It is also recognized that alternative liability rests on the notion that where there is a small number of possible wrongdoers, all of whom breached a duty to the plaintiff, the likelihood that any one of them injured the plaintiff is relatively high, so that forcing them to exonerate themselves, or be held liable, is not unfair [   ].

In DES cases, however, there is a great number of possible wrongdoers, who entered and left the market at different times, and some of whom no longer exist. Additionally, in DES cases many years elapse between the ingestion of the drug and injury. Consequently, DES defendants are not in any better position than are plaintiffs to identify the manufacturer of the DES ingested in any given case, nor is there any real prospect of having all the possible producers before the court. Finally, while it may be fair to employ alternative liability in cases involving only a small number of potential wrongdoers, that fairness disappears with the decreasing probability that any one of the defendants actually caused the injury. This is particularly true when applied to DES where the chance that a particular producer caused the injury is often very remote [   ]. Alternative liability, therefore, provides DES plaintiffs no relief.

Nor does the theory of concerted action, in its pure form, supply a basis for recovery. This doctrine, seen in drag racing cases, provides for joint and several liability on the part of all defendants having an understanding, express or tacit, to participate in "a common plan or design to commit a tortious act" [   ]. As . . . the present record reflects, drug companies were engaged in extensive parallel conduct in developing and marketing DES [   ]. There is nothing in the record, however, beyond this similar conduct to show any agreement, tacit or otherwise, to market DES for pregnancy use without taking proper steps to ensure the drug's safety. Parallel activity, without more, is insufficient to establish the agreement element necessary to maintain a concerted action claim [   ]. Thus this theory also fails in supporting an action by DES plaintiffs.

In short, extant common-law doctrines, unmodified, provide no relief for the DES plaintiff unable to identify the manufacturer of the drug that injured her. This is not a novel conclusion; in the last decade a number of courts in other jurisdictions also have concluded that present theories do not support a cause of action in DES cases. Some courts, upon reaching this conclusion, have declined to find any judicial remedy for the DES plaintiffs who cannot identify the particular manufacturer of the DES ingested by their mothers (see, Zafft v. Eli Lilly & Co., 676 S.W.2d 241 [Mo][en banc]; Mulcahy v. Eli Lilly & Co., 386 N.W.2d 67 [Iowa] [stating that any change in the law to allow for recovery in nonidentification DES cases should come from the Legislature]). Other courts, however, have found that some modification of existing doctrine is appropriate to allow for relief for those injured by DES of unknown manufacture (e.g., [Sindell v.

Abbott Labs., 26 Cal.3d 588, 607 P.2d 924, 163 Cal.Rptr. 132, cert. denied 449 U.S. 912 (1980); Collins v. Eli Lilly & Co., 116 Wis.2d 166, 342 N.W.2d 37, cert. denied 469 U.S. 826 (1984); Martin v. Abbott Labs., 102 Wash.2d 581, 689 P.2d 368 (1984)]).

We conclude that the present circumstances call for recognition of a realistic avenue of relief for plaintiffs injured by DES. These appeals present many of the same considerations that have prompted this court in the past to modify the rules of personal injury liability, in order "to achieve the ends of justice in a more modern context" [   ], and we perceive that here judicial action is again required to overcome the " 'inordinately difficult problems of proof' " caused by contemporary products and marketing techniques [   ].

Indeed, it would be inconsistent with the reasonable expectations of a modern society to say to these plaintiffs that because of the insidious nature of an injury that long remains dormant, and because so many manufacturers, each behind a curtain, contributed to the devastation, the cost of injury should be borne by the innocent and not the wrongdoers. This is particularly so where the Legislature consciously created these expectations by reviving hundreds of DES cases. Consequently, the ever-evolving dictates of justice and fairness, which are the heart of our common-law system, require formation of a remedy for injuries caused by DES [   ].

We stress, however, that the DES situation is a singular case, with manufacturers acting in a parallel manner to produce an identical, generically marketed product, which causes injury many years later, and which has evoked a legislative response reviving previously barred actions. Given this unusual scenario, it is more appropriate that the loss be borne by those that produced the drug for use during pregnancy, rather than by those who were injured by the use, even where the precise manufacturer of the drug cannot be identified in a particular action. We turn then to the question of how to fairly and equitably apportion the loss occasioned by DES, in a case where the exact manufacturer of the drug that caused the injury is unknown.

B.

The past decade of DES litigation has produced a number of alternative approaches to resolve this question. Thus, in a sense, we are now in an enviable position; the efforts of other courts provided examples for contending with this difficult issue, and enough time has passed so that the actual administration and real effects of these solutions now can be observed. With these useful guides in hand, a path may be struck for our own conclusion.

[The court decided to adopt a version of the market share concept. In *Sindell*—the first case to adopt such an approach—the "central justification" was the "belief that limiting a defendant's liability to its market share will result, over the run of cases, in liability on the part of a defendant roughly equal to the injuries the defendant actually caused."

After *Sindell* the California court held, in Brown v. Superior Court, 44 Cal.3d 1049, 751 P.2d 470, 245 Cal.Rptr. 412 (1988), that a manufacturer's liability is several only, and, in cases in which all manufacturers in the market are not joined for any reason, liability will still be limited to market share, resulting in a less than 100% recovery for a plaintiff. The *Hymowitz* court also noted that determining the market shares in the years after *Sindell* "proved difficult and engendered years of litigation. After attempts at using smaller geographical units, it was eventually determined that the national market provided the most feasible and fair solution, and this national market information was compiled."

The court then traced the variations on *Sindell* developed in Wisconsin and Washington, involving such issues as how to determine market shares; how to handle absent defendants; when to allow named defendants to exculpate themselves; and whether to make liability joint and several or only several.]

Turning to the structure to be adopted in New York, we heed both the lessons learned through experience in other jurisdictions and the realities of the mass litigation of DES claims in this State. Balancing these considerations, we are led to the conclusion that a market share theory, based upon a national market, provides the best solution. As California discovered, the reliable determination of any market smaller than the national one likely is not practicable. Moreover, even if it were possible, of the hundreds of cases in the New York courts, without a doubt there are many in which the DES that allegedly caused injury was ingested in another State. Among the thorny issues this could present, perhaps the most daunting is the spectre that the particular case could require the establishment of a separate market share matrix. We feel that this is an unfair, and perhaps impossible burden to routinely place upon the litigants in individual cases.

[The court rejected approaches that required "individualized and open-ended assessment" in each case because it feared the that the large number of cases pending in New York would unduly burden the courts.]

Consequently, for essentially practical reasons, we adopt a market share theory using a national market. We are aware that the adoption of a national market will likely result in a disproportion between the liability of individual manufacturers and the actual injuries each manufacturer caused in this State. Thus our market share theory cannot be founded upon the belief that, over the run of cases, liability will approximate causation in this State [ ]. Nor does the use of a national market provide a reasonable link between liability and the risk created by a defendant to a particular plaintiff [ ]. Instead, we choose to apportion liability so as to correspond to the over-all culpability of each defendant, measured by the amount of risk of injury each defendant created to the public-at-large. Use of a national market is a fair method, we believe, of apportioning defendants' liabilities according to their total culpability in marketing DES for use during pregnancy. Under the circumstances, this is an equitable way to provide plaintiffs with the relief they deserve, while also rationally distributing the responsibility for plaintiffs' injuries among defendants.

To be sure, a defendant cannot be held liable if it did not participate in the marketing of DES for pregnancy use; if a DES producer satisfies its burden of proof of showing that it was not a member of the market of DES sold for pregnancy use, disallowing exculpation would be unfair and unjust. Nevertheless, because liability here is based on the over-all risk produced, and not causation in a single case, there should be no exculpation of a defendant who, although a member of the market producing DES for pregnancy use, appears not to have caused a particular plaintiff's injury. It is merely a windfall for a producer to escape liability solely because it manufactured a more identifiable pill, or sold only to certain drugstores. These fortuities in no way diminish the culpability of a defendant for marketing the product, which is the basis of liability here.

Finally, we hold that the liability of DES producers is several only, and should not be inflated when all participants in the market are not before the court in a particular case. We understand that, as a practical matter, this will prevent some plaintiffs from recovering 100% of their damages. However, we eschewed exculpation to prevent the fortuitous avoidance of liability, and thus, equitably, we decline to unleash the same forces to increase a defendant's liability beyond its fair share of responsibility.[29]

III.

The constitutionality of the revival statute remains to be considered [   ]. This section revives, for the period of one year, actions for damages caused by the latent effects of DES, tungsten-carbide, asbestos, chlordane, and polyvinylchloride. Defendants argue that the revival of barred DES claims was unconstitutional as a denial of both due process and equal protection, under the State and Federal Constitutions. . . .

---

29. . . . . We are confronted here with an unprecedented identification problem, and have provided a solution that rationally apportions liability. We have heeded the practical lessons learned by other jurisdictions, resulting in our adoption of a national market theory with full knowledge that it concedes the lack of a logical link between liability and causation in a single case. The dissent ignores these lessons, and, endeavoring to articulate a theory it perceives to be closer to traditional law, sets out a construct in which liability is based upon chance, not upon the fair assessment of the acts of defendants. Under the dissent's theory, a manufacturer with a large market share may avoid liability in many cases just because it manufactured a memorably shaped pill. Conversely, a small manufacturer can be held jointly liable for the full amount of every DES injury in this State simply because the shape of its product was not remarkable, even though the odds, realistically, are exceedingly long that the small manufacturer caused the injury in any one particular case. Therefore, although the dissent's theory based upon a "shifting the burden of proof" and joint and several liability is facially reminiscent of prior law, in the case of DES it is nothing more than advocating that bare fortuity be the test for liability. When faced with the novel identification problem posed by DES cases, it is preferable to adopt a new theory that apportions fault rationally, rather than to contort extant doctrines beyond the point at which they provide a sound premise for determining liability.

[handwritten margin note: Marketing the product was negligent and the companies are liable; no exculpation for drug co. allowed]

[handwritten margin note: Liability is not joint, therefore I can only collect from those drug companies still around based on % of the market those companies controlled]

[After extended discussion, the court rejected the constitutional challenges.]

Accordingly, in each case the order of the Appellate Division should be affirmed, with costs, and the certified question answered in the affirmative.

■ MOLLEN, JUDGE (concurring in *Hymowitz* and *Hanfling;* and dissenting in part in *Tigue* and *Dolan.*)

. . .

. . . I would adopt a market share theory of liability, based upon a national market, which would provide for the shifting of the burden of proof on the issue of causation to the defendants and would impose liability upon all of the defendants who produced and marketed DES for pregnancy purposes, except those who were able to prove that their product could not have caused the injury. Under this approach, DES plaintiffs, who are unable to identify the actual manufacturer of the pill ingested by their mother, would only be required to establish, (1) that the plaintiff's mother ingested DES during pregnancy; (2) that the plaintiff's injuries were caused by DES; and (3) that the defendant or defendants produced and marketed DES for pregnancy purposes. Thereafter, the burden of proof would shift to the defendants to exculpate themselves by establishing, by a preponderance of the evidence, that the plaintiff's mother could not have ingested their particular pill. Of those defendants who are unable to exculpate themselves from liability, their respective share of the plaintiff's damages would be measured by their share of the national market of DES produced and marketed for pregnancy purposes during the period in question.

I would further note that while, on the one hand, the majority would not permit defendants who produced DES for pregnancy purposes to exculpate themselves, the majority at the same time deprives the plaintiffs of the opportunity to recover fully for their injuries by limiting the defendants' liability for the plaintiff's damages to several liability. In my view, the liability for the plaintiff's damages of those defendants who are unable to exculpate themselves should be joint and several thereby ensuring that the plaintiffs will receive full recovery of their damages, as they are entitled to by any fair standard. . . .

. . .

. . . [T]his approach, unlike that taken by the majority, does not represent an unnecessary and radical departure from basic principles of tort law. By characterizing this approach as "nothing more than advocating that bare fortuity be the test for liability" [ ], the majority fails to perceive that this is no more and no less than a basic principle of tort law; i.e., a plaintiff may not recover for his or her injuries from a defendant who could not have caused those injuries. When the majority eliminates this fundamental causative factor as a basis for recovery, it effectively indulges in the act of judicial legislating. . . .

Judged by the aforesaid standard, I conclude that the trial courts' orders in [*Tigue* and *Dolan*] to the extent that they denied the summary judgment motions of the defendant The Upjohn Company (Upjohn) in both actions and the defendant Rexall Drug Company (Rexall) in the *Tigue* action, were improper. In *Tigue*, Mrs. Tigue, the plaintiff's mother, testified that the DES pill she ingested while she was pregnant with the plaintiff was a white, round tablet [ ]. Similarly, Myrna Margolies' mother testified that the DES pill she ingested was a dark red, hard, round pill [ ]. Mr. Margolies, the plaintiff's father, also recalled that the pills were a reddish color and Mrs. Margolies' obstetrician stated that the DES pill he prescribed to his patients was not an Upjohn product. Moreover, in the *Dolan* action, Mrs. Dolan, the plaintiff's mother, stated that the DES pill she took was a white, round, hard tablet [ ]. This fact was corroborated by Mr. Dolan's testimony [ ]. Finally, it was established that Upjohn's DES pill which was produced and marketed for pregnancy purposes, was in the form of a "perle" which is a pharmaceutical term for a dose form consisting of a soft elastic capsule containing a liquid center [ ]. Based on the evidence submitted in support of Upjohn's summary judgment motions in these two cases, I would conclude that the plaintiffs have failed to adduce sufficient proof in admissible form to raise a triable issue of fact as to whether their mothers ingested an Upjohn DES pill. Accordingly, Upjohn's motion for summary judgment in those actions should have been granted.

Additionally, in [*Tigue*], Rexall's motion for summary judgment should have been granted since the plaintiffs failed to raise a triable issue of fact as to whether their mothers could have ingested a Rexall DES product during the pregnancies in question. The evidence submitted in support of Rexall's motion established that until 1978, Rexall sold its products, including its DES pill, exclusively to Rexall Drug Stores [ ]. The testimony of the plaintiffs' parents, Mrs. Tigue and Mr. and Mrs. Margolies established that they had purchased their DES prescriptions from non-Rexall pharmacies during the periods of their respective pregnancies, i.e., 1960 and 1953. Based on this uncontroverted evidence demonstrating Rexall's noninvolvement in these plaintiffs' injuries, Rexall's motion for summary judgment should have been granted.

. . .

■ ALEXANDER, TITONE and HANCOCK, JJ., concur with WACHTLER, C.J.

■ MOLLEN, J., [concurring and dissenting].

■ SIMONS, KAYE and BELLACOSA, JJ., taking no part.

NOTES AND QUESTIONS

1. The various state courts have had to consider a market-share analysis because they almost uniformly rejected the traditional theories plaintiffs put forth. In addition to rejecting *Summers v. Tice,* the court, as noted, also rejected the "concert of action" theory. This theory has been used more broadly than in the drag race cases. In Orser v. George, 252 Cal.App.2d 660, 60 Cal.Rptr. 708 (1967), for example, several men negligently fired in the plaintiff's direction. D1 and D2 alternately fired with the gun that was identified as the one causing the fatal injury. D3 was firing at the same time with a different gun. D3 was held jointly and severally liable with the others—although his bullet could not have caused the injury—because he knew the others were acting tortiously and encouraged them by doing the same thing.

The *Sindell* court in the influential California DES case rejected the concert-of-action analogy on the ground that in cases like *Orser* there was an allegation that the defendant knew others were acting tortiously. In *Sindell*, however, there was no allegation that "each defendant knew the other defendants' conduct was tortious toward plaintiff, and that they assisted and encouraged one another to inadequately test DES and to provide inadequate warnings. Indeed, it seems dubious whether liability on the concert of action theory can be predicated upon substantial assistance and encouragement given by one alleged tortfeasor to another pursuant to a tacit understanding to fail to perform an act." All the cases cited by plaintiff had involved "conduct by a small number of individuals whose actions resulted in a tort against a single plaintiff, usually over a short span of time, and the defendant held liable was either a direct participant in the acts which caused damages, or encouraged and assisted the person who directly caused the injuries by participating in a joint activity."

A third theory rejected by the DES cases has been industry-wide liability or "enterprise liability." The plaintiff relied on Hall v. E.I. Du Pont De Nemours & Co., Inc., 345 F.Supp. 353 (E.D.N.Y.1972), in which the defendants were six blasting cap manufacturers "comprising virtually the entire blasting cap industry in the United States" and their trade association. The claim resulted from blasts allegedly due to inadequate warnings and other safety precautions. The *Sindell* court, for example, saw *Hall* as a case in which "there was evidence that defendants, acting independently, had adhered to an industry-wide standard with regard to the safety features of blasting caps, that they had in effect delegated some functions of safety investigation and design, such as labelling, to their trade association, and that there was industry-wide cooperation in the manufacture and design of blasting caps."

Hall itself had cautioned against application of the doctrine to large numbers of producers. The difference between six and 200 was too great. Moreover, there was no showing of delegation in the DES situation. There was one further distinction, according to the *Sindell* court:

> Equally important, the drug industry is closely regulated by the Food and Drug Administration, which actively controls the testing and manufacture of drugs and the methods by which they are marketed, including the contents of warning labels. To a considerable degree, therefore, the standards followed by drug manufacturers are suggested or compelled by the government. Adherence to those standards cannot, of course, absolve a manufacturer of liability to which it would otherwise be subject. [ ] But since the government plays such a pervasive role in formulating the criteria for the testing and marketing of drugs, it would be unfair to impose upon a manufacturer liability for

injuries resulting from the use of a drug which it did not supply simply because it followed the standards of the industry.

Do the distinctions recognized by the *Sindell* court require the exploration of a new theory for DES cases?

2.   The majority in *Hymowitz* refers to the "reasonable expectations of a modern society." What might they be in this type of case? The separate opinion seeks to "ensure that these plaintiffs receive full recovery for their damages, as they are properly entitled to by any fair standard." What is the source of that entitlement?

3.   The judges agree on using a national market share. What are the benefits of that approach? The drawbacks?

Conley v. Boyle Drug Co., 570 So.2d 275 (Fla.1990), decided that the market "should be as narrowly defined as the evidence in a given case allows. Thus, where it can be determined that the DES ingested by the mother was purchased from a particular pharmacy, that pharmacy should be considered the relevant market." This definition was consistent with allowing exculpation by defendants who did not market in the region in which the DES was purchased. Also, the narrower the market "the greater the likelihood that liability will be imposed only on those drug companies who could have manufactured the DES which caused the plaintiff's injuries."

Conley demanded that plaintiff show due diligence in trying to find the specific source of the DES before she would be allowed to bring a market share action. Market share liability was a "theory of last resort" to be used only where need can be shown.

How does the *Conley* approach compare to the *Sindell* and the *Hymowitz* approaches in terms of fairness? Administrative feasibility? All market-share approaches were rejected in Smith v. Eli Lilly & Co., 137 Ill.2d 222, 560 N.E.2d 324 (1990) as "too great a deviation from our existing tort principles."

In the cited *Martin* case, the court used a rebuttable presumption that all defendants had an equal (local) market share totalling one hundred percent; each could rebut this by proof of its actual market share; those who could not do so had their shares inflated to return the group total to one hundred percent.

4.   The judges in *Hymowitz* disagree over whether each defendant should be permitted to try to exculpate itself. Who has the better of that argument?

5.   The judges disagree over whether to use several liability or joint and several liability. Who has the better of that argument?

6.   *Other possible applications.* In the wake of the DES cases, plaintiffs have tried to extend market share liability to other products, with mixed success. Is there a common theme?

a.   *Asbestos.* In Goldman v. Johns–Manville Sales Corp., 33 Ohio St.3d 40, 514 N.E.2d 691 (1987), the court observed that the essential condition required for market share treatment was "fungibility"—all the products made pursuant to a single formula. "In contrast, asbestos is not a 'product,' but rather a generic name for a family of minerals." Asbestos-containing products "do not create similar risks of harm because there are several varieties of asbestos fibers, and they are used in various quantities, even in the same class of products." In one example, the court noted that a tape made by one company was 95% asbestos by weight, while tapes from another company varied from 80 to 100%, and those made by a third company were 15% asbestos and 85% sodium silicate.

Compare Wheeler v. Raybestos–Manhattan, 8 Cal.App.4th 1152, 11 Cal.Rptr.2d 109 (1992), in which the court extended the market share approach to manufacturers of brake pads that used asbestos fibers because the pads were sufficiently fungible and their asbestos content was similar.

b. *Lead paint.* In Santiago v. Sherwin Williams Co., 3 F.3d 546 (1st Cir.1993), a child who was allegedly harmed by exposure to lead paint sued several manufacturers. He was born in 1972 and lived in the same house until 1978. An expert tied the child's hyperactivity and motor skill problems to lead in the house, which had been painted several times between 1917 (when it was built) and 1970. An expert testified that one layer of lead paint was applied between 1933 and 1939; and another layer between 1956 and 1969. The court thought this was not sufficiently precise for Massachusetts to impose market share liability on this group of paint companies—some were not making lead paint during part of this period. Moreover, there were other sources of lead: airborne, food, water, soil and dust. The neighborhood in question had "heavily contaminated" soil.

c. *Childhood vaccine.* In Shackil v. Lederle Laboratories, 116 N.J. 155, 561 A.2d 511 (1989), the court, 4–2, refused to extend market share liability to manufacturers of diphtheria-typhoid-pertussis vaccine in a personal injury suit in which plaintiff could not identify the producer of the particular dose. The court noted that the pertussis portion of the vaccine causes almost all the adverse reactions. There were then three major types of that part of the vaccine, each with a different risk factor. Although one version was most likely responsible for the child's illness, at least one of the defendants also marketed one of the other vaccines at the same time. Should plaintiff have sought market share liability against only those who marketed the likely cause? One of the cases on which *Shackil* relied concluded that public policy goals would be subverted by allowing market share liability for producers of vital vaccines.

d. *Blood clotting factors.* A blood coagulant used by hemophiliacs may give rise to market share liability even though the product "does not have the constant quality of DES [because] the donor source of the plasma is not a constant." The plasma in question came from donors infected with HIV. If all defendants were negligent in their acquisition and production methods, the court thought it appropriate to develop "new rules of causation, for otherwise innocent plaintiffs would be left without a remedy." The court adopted a national market. Smith v. Cutter Biological, Inc., 72 Haw. 416, 823 P.2d 717 (1991).

e. *Paint shop products.* The doctrine was rejected in Setliff v. E.I.Du Pont de Nemours & Co., 32 Cal.App.4th 1525, 38 Cal.Rptr.2d 763 (1995), involving a plaintiff who worked in a paint shop and claimed he was harmed by volatile organic compounds (VOCs). He sued 40 defendants who had supplied products that included VOCs but he could not identify which compound had caused his harm. Market share analysis was rejected because there was no allegation that the products alleged to have caused the harm were fungible in their harmful capacity—only that VOCs were common to paint and other related products.

7. For an extended discussion of the possible justifications for *Sindell* and an exploration of possible extensions, see Robinson, Multiple Causation in Tort Law: Reflections on the DES Cases, 68 Va.L.Rev. 713 (1982). The author suggests that "As long as liability is proportionate to the risks created by a defendant, there is no reason why the *Sindell* liability rule cannot be applied to cases involving multiple and *different* risk-creating activities." He posits a victim who has contracted cancer and three events that contributed to the risk of his developing cancer: he worked as an asbestos installer for 20 years; then he worked 10 years at a chemical plant where he was exposed to chemical wastes; and he took medication that created a risk of cancer. Robinson suggests that if the estimates of these three contributions to cancer were 60/20/20 each might be held liable in those percentages under a modest extension of *Sindell*. Would it be preferable to put all liability on the asbestos company?

Although other causes might have produced the cancer, Robinson suggests that it is not necessary to bring all, or even most, possible causes before the court. In such cases the "plaintiff would bear the costs associated with the unidentified causal agenda." The same result would follow for identified but non-actionable causes. Would this pattern be an improvement over current treatment of causation?

4. A POSTSCRIPT ON TOXIC HARM

The causal relation issue has been central to a wide variety of extensively publicized recent concerns about toxics in the environment: among others, claims based on asbestos, Agent Orange, hazardous wastes, and atomic test fallout. These environmental harm controversies, along with related drug cases such as DES and Bendectin, have posed a number of distinctive issues for the tort system which are discussed in the following excerpt.

Environmental Liability and the Tort System

Robert L. Rabin.
24 Houston Law Review 27, 27–32 (1987).

. . .

. . . Essentially, environmental liability stands out in bold relief from the generality of everyday risks embraced by tort law because of three critical characteristics that are found, singly or in combination, in every case of harm from toxics or other pollutants. I will refer to these characteristics of environmental liability as problems of *identification, boundaries* and *source.*

(1) *Problems of Identification.* Through the centuries of common law development, the identification of a tortious injury has hardly ever been a problem. At earliest common law, it was the unwanted intrusion on the land of another or the physical violation of a right to bodily integrity. Well into the twentieth century, one finds remarkably little change on this score. Auto accidents and overcharged coke bottles are the modern-day counterpart of trespassers and runaway buggies from the pre-industrial era. The focus is consistently on an accidental injury, the relatively sudden event in which the victim's bodily security or property is violated. If problems of causation exist, they are ordinarily of the "whodunit" variety, rather than issues of whether the victim actually suffered identifiable harm that can be isolated from the everyday risks of living.

But it is precisely this latter inquiry which characterizes the case of environmental harm. Toxics of all sorts—impure water, hazardous chemicals, defective synthetics—often breed disease rather than cause immediate injury. As a consequence, the tort system is severely tested. Since diseases do not occur instantaneously, there are serious time-lag issues. And because diseases are frequently a product of the background risks of living (or at least intertwined with those risks), technical information is essential to establish attribution. Thus, *identification,* ordinarily a routine issue of cause in fact at common law, is a costly enterprise that relies on types of evidence and probability judgments which can be regarded as ill-suited to traditional resolution through the adversary process.

(2) *Problems of Boundaries.* Let us assume that through epidemiological studies, laboratory tests or rough mortality data it can be established that a particular widespread incidence of disease was "caused" by the release of an identifiable toxic substance. At first blush, environmental liability may then appear to be similar to a classical mass tort episode— akin to a commercial airline disaster or the collapse of a hotel balcony. But appearances are deceiving; once again, the case of environmental harm frequently creates problems that place special stress on the tort system.

The crux of the matter, again, is the accident/disease distinction. The harm suffered in an airplane crash is extensive but it is also bounded. Most of the victims die, and, apart from derivative loss, there are virtually no post-generational consequences. Contrast the toxic tort scenario. In cases like Agent Orange and hazardous waste dump exposure, the claims are potentially unbounded. Victims of exposure not yet ill fear that it is only a matter of time before they show signs of pathology, *in utero* exposure is an overriding concern, and generations not yet conceived may suffer genetic damage.

Moreover, these are only the most peripheral claims. Even with respect to first-generation, identifiable victims, the *ex ante* assessment of limits on liability is often highly open-ended. Unlike an airplane or public facilities disaster, the aggregate exposure can be hard to define in advance. In addition, the extent of harm may be unpredictable because the need for post-exposure treatment is extensive (degeneration rather than instant death is, by and large, far more common in toxic tort episodes than mass accident cases) and the array of disorders is far more wide-ranging.

By *boundaries,* then, I have in mind an *ex ante* assessment of the magnitude of harm. Mass accident torts are rare at common law, and in fact, put the flexibility of the tort system to the test when they occur. But they pose nothing like the challenge of unconfined liability intrinsic to many environmental harms. In common law terms, valuation of damages is the crux of the matter. Asbestos and the emerging toxic tort cases claim victims in the thousands, not the low hundreds. And, the intrinsic vagaries of chemically-induced diseases introduce bizarre pathologies that are costly to treat and raise intergenerational concerns which vex a torts process designed for more modest purposes. In sum, it is both the two-party structure of traditional tort litigation and the underlying premise of sudden accidental injury that are confounded by environmental harm.

(3) *Problems of Source.* A generation ago, tort lawyers viewed the frontiers of causal responsibility as defined by cases like *Summers v. Tice,* the classic accident situation in which the victim could not identify which of his two careless hunting companions fired the shotgun pellet which entered his eye. *Summers* seems almost an ancient artifact bearing witness to the practices of an earlier epoch when compared with the source-related issues presented by toxic tort and pollution cases. To venture for a moment into the world of conjecture (or, perhaps, nightmare), suppose at some future date uncertainty over the harmful effects of chlorofluorocarbon emissions is resolved through an extraordinarily sharp rise in the incidence of skin cancer. To continue in a speculative vein, assume that the multitude of victims can properly pursue a class action. Would the action be appropriately brought against the thousands of emitters of chlorofluoro-carbons including the producers of aerosols, foams, solvents, freezers and insulation materials? Should the multinational chemical companies producing the constituent products be joined? What about the host governments that approve (or, at least, allow) the processes to be undertaken? The prospects stagger the imagination.

But one need not create a parade of future horribles to illustrate the problem. The vast array of asbestos producers and insurers, or the typical participants in the hazardous waste chain of distribution—generators, transporters and operators of sites—are present-day examples of the singular difficulties in dealing with problems of *source* in environmental liability cases.

Here, too, the long-standing premises of tort law are challenged by the rise of toxic and pollutant harms. Because tort law has traditionally been concerned with accidents, the search for a responsible source has never raised overwhelming difficulties. At most, the classic single-party focus of responsibility is extended slightly along a horizontal axis in cases like *Summers v. Tice* or a multi-car collision. Under other circumstances, the single-party focus may be extended slightly along a vertical (production/distribution) axis in cases where a defective product may be the responsibility of an assembler and manufacturers of component parts. But these modest variations on the two-party tort configuration in which some*one* is responsible for the harm clearly are of small consequence to the system.

By contrast, environmental torts evoke an entirely different perspective on liability, one which is virtually unknown at common law. Frequently, environmental harm is a consequence of the aggregate risk created by a considerable number of independently acting enterprises. It may be that the risk generated by any single source is, in fact, inconsequential. Or, it may be that the risk inherent in the product is substantial, but it soon merges into a common pool. Whatever the case, environmental harm is very often *collective* harm.

Acid rain, chlorofluorocarbons, Agent Orange, and asbestos fibers confound the private law perspective in a dual sense. Not only are they potentially the source of widespread harm, but they are frequently produced by a vast number of discrete enterprises, each making independent decisions about the extent to which they will degrade or endanger the commons. Traditional tests of causal responsibility—the but-for principle, substantial factor causation, *pro rata* joint-and-several liability—are operating in foreign territory when they are employed in such cases. They are premised on a wrongful act that in itself triggers accidental harm, an act that can be isolated and pinned down as consequential.

In view of these distinctive characteristics, it is small wonder that environmental liability has achieved special recognition in discourse about standards of liability and the efficacy of the torts process. Automobiles and power lawnmowers may wreak havoc, but their dangers are readily cognizable. We understand how they work and why they go awry. Toxic substances evoke the special apprehensions of unseen risks. They emanate from sources that are hard to identify. They attack us unawares, planting the seeds of future debilitating disease. They run a course that we cannot discern. Translated into legal terms, they pose unique challenges to a tort system premised on adversary treatment of easily identifiable two-party accidents.

NOTES AND QUESTIONS

1. In a following section, the article points out that not all cases of environmental harm exhibit the same distinctive characteristics. The article discusses three scenarios: (1) individualized harm such as Ferebee v. Chevron Chemical Co., 736 F.2d 1529 (D.C.Cir.1984), in which an agricultural worker claimed toxic poisoning from exposure to a herbicide; (2) multiple party harm in which injuries occurred to residents of a discrete and limited geographical area; and (3) mass tort claims such as the thousands of cases arising from asbestos exposure.

The latter category, in particular, places singular strains on the tort system—partly because of causation-related issues, but also due to the procedural difficulties created by the enormous volume of cases. For illustration of the complexities in aggregating mass tort claims, see Castano v. American Tobacco Co., 160 F.R.D. 544 (E.D.La.1995), appeal pending (smokers' class action against the tobacco industry); In the Matter of Rhone-Poulenc Rorer, Inc., 51 F.3d 1293 (7th Cir.), cert. denied 116 S.Ct. 184 (1995) (HIV infected hemophiliacs' class action against blood solids suppliers); Coffee, Class Wars: The Dilemma of the Mass Tort Class Action, 95 Colum.L.Rev. 1343 (1995).

2. Would causation issues be more fairly and efficiently decided under an administrative scheme than through tort litigation? See Rabin, Some Thoughts on the Efficacy of a Mass Toxics Administrative Compensation Scheme, 52 Md.L.Rev. 951 (1993). No-fault and social insurance replacements for the tort system are discussed generally in Chapter XI.

3. For further discussion, see Rosenberg, The Causal Connection Issue in Mass Exposure Cases: A "Public Law" Vision of the Tort System, 97 Harv.L.Rev. 851 (1984) and Note, The Inapplicability of Traditional Tort Analysis to Environmental Risks: The Example of Toxic Waste Pollution Victim Compensation, 35 Stan.L.Rev. 575 (1983). For useful case studies, in addition to Brodeur, see P. Schuck, Agent Orange on Trial: Mass Toxic Disasters in the Courts (1986)(Agent Orange); H. Ball, Justice Downwind (1986)(Nevada atomic tests); and M. Mintz, At Any Cost (1985)(Dalkon Shield).

B. PROXIMATE CAUSE

In the cases presented in this section, either the plaintiff has made out the elements previously discussed—duty, violation of duty, and cause in fact—or else they are sufficiently in dispute that the defendant cannot establish the absence of any of them as a matter of law. Instead, the defendant will argue that even a negligent defendant who actually caused the harm in question should not be liable for the plaintiff's harm. The legal formulation of the claim is that the defendant's admitted or assumed negligence was not the proximate cause (or "legal cause") of the plaintiff's harm. The cases in which this claim is given serious consideration tend to have one feature in common—something quite unexpected has contributed either to the occurrence of the harm or to its severity.

1. UNEXPECTED HARM

Steinhauser v. Hertz Corp.

United States Court of Appeals, Second Circuit, 1970.
421 F.2d 1169.

■ Before FRIENDLY, SMITH and ANDERSON, CIRCUIT JUDGES.

■ FRIENDLY, CIRCUIT JUDGE:

On September 4, 1964, plaintiff Cynthia Steinhauser, a New Jersey citizen then 14 years old, her mother and father were driving south through Essex County, N.Y. A northbound car, owned by defendant Hertz Corporation, a Delaware corporation authorized to do business in New York, and operated by defendant, Ponzini, a citizen of New York, crossed over a double yellow line in the highway into the southbound lane and struck the Steinhauser car heavily on the left side. The occupants did not suffer any bodily injuries.

The plaintiffs' evidence was that within a few minutes after the accident Cynthia began to behave in an unusual way. Her parents observed her to be "glassy-eyed," "upset," "highly agitated," "nervous" and "disturbed." When Ponzini came toward the Steinhauser car, she jumped up and down and made menacing gestures until restrained by her father. On the way home she complained of a headache and became uncommunicative. In the following days things went steadily worse. Cynthia thought that she was being attacked and that knives, guns and bullets were coming through the windows. She was hostile toward her parents and assaulted them; becoming depressed, she attempted suicide.

The family physician recommended hospitalization. After observation and treatment in three hospitals, with a final diagnosis of "schizophrenic reaction—acute—undifferentiated," she was released in December 1964 under the care of a psychiatrist, Dr. Royce, which continued until September 1966. His diagnosis, both at the beginning and at the end, was of a chronic schizophrenic reaction; he explained that by "chronic" he meant that Cynthia was not brought to him because of a sudden onset of symptoms. She then entered the Hospital of the University of Pennsylvania and, one month later, transferred to the Institute of Pennsylvania Hospital for long-term therapy. Discharged in January 1968, she has required the care of a psychiatrist. The evidence was that the need for this will continue, that reinstitutionalization is likely, and that her prognosis is bad.

As the recital makes evident, the important issue was the existence of a causal relationship between the rather slight accident and Cynthia's undoubtedly serious ailment. The testimony was uncontradicted that prior to the accident she had never displayed such exaggerated symptoms as thereafter. However, she had fallen from a horse about two years earlier and suffered what was diagnosed as a minor concussion; she was not hospitalized but missed a month of school. The other evidence relied on by the defendants to show prior psychiatric abnormality was derived largely from the history furnished, apparently in large part by Cynthia, at her admission to the first of the three hospitals on September 20, 1964, which we set out in the margin.[2]

2. She was a normal child except one incident when at the age of nine one of the friends of her uncle molested her three times. Two years before while in camp she fell down from a horse. There she liked one horse called Silverfox, which she wanted to buy and

Dr. Royce testified that a person may have a predisposition to schizophrenia which, however, requires a "precipitating factor" to produce an outbreak. As a result of long observation he believed this to have been Cynthia's case—that "she was a rather sensitive child and frequently exaggerated things and distorted things that happened within the family" but that the accident was "the precipitating cause" of her serious mental illness.   Under cross-examination he stated that prior to the accident Cynthia had a "prepsychotic" personality but might have been able to lead a normal life.   Dr. Stevens, attending psychiatrist at the Institute of Pennsylvania Hospital, who had treated Cynthia, in answer to a hypothetical question which included the incidents relied on by the defendants to show prior abnormality, was of the opinion that the accident "was the precipitating cause of the overt psychotic reaction," "the last straw that breaks the camel's back."   In contrast defendants' expert, Dr. Brock, while agreeing that "with a background of fertile soil" schizophrenia can be induced by emotional strain, was of the opinion, based largely on the matters recited in footnote 2, that Cynthia was already schizophrenic at the time of the accident.

At the conclusion of the evidence the judge remarked to counsel, outside the presence of the jury, that, as he saw it, the sole question in the case was whether plaintiff had established that defendants caused Cynthia's condition or aggravated a pre-existing one. . . .

The charge followed the black-and-white pattern prefigured in the colloquy.   The judge said the plaintiffs claimed the accident caused the schizophrenia whereas defendants contended "that this plaintiff has had this disease all along."   Defendant was not liable unless it "proximately caused" the disease.   "Proximately . . . is just a big word for what people use for cause."   If there was a "logical relationship" between the accident and plaintiffs' "psychotic injuries," defendants were responsible. But "if the child had this condition or disease all along and this defendant did not cause it," the defendants were not liable.   Damages could be awarded only if the accident caused the schizophrenic condition but not if Cynthia "already had the disease."

After several hours of deliberation the jury propounded the following question:

> If we find the auto accident was the precipitating factor, but not the cause of the illness (schizophrenia) must we find for the plaintiff?

felt much attached to him.   Against her wishes, she saw that horse sold to another party.   She felt depressed.   Food seemed the only answer.   She ate and felt better.   As a result of it she became fat and felt further depressed.   Later on she felt attached to a Riviera automobile but the family bought a Cadillac, which she hated very much.   "Horses go away, car goes away but food never does."   One year before she got involved with "hoods."   They were fast and did everything—also in quotes.   Quote, I felt much better among them.   I wished to be liked and did everything to please them, unquote.

There was evidence that in fact the first incident was exposure by the brother of an uncle rather than molestation.

The judge responded by rereading what he had already said on proximate cause. Ten minutes later the jury brought in a defendants' verdict.

It is plain enough that plaintiffs were deprived of a fair opportunity to have the jury consider the case on the basis of the medical evidence they had adduced. The testimony was that before the accident Cynthia was *neither* a "perfectly normal child" *nor* a schizophrenic, but a child with some degree of pathology which was activated into schizophrenia by an emotional trauma although it otherwise might not have blossomed. Whatever the medical soundness of this theory may or may not be, and there does not seem in fact to have been any dispute about it, see Guttmacher and Weihofen, Psychiatry and the Law 43–55 (1952), plaintiffs were entitled to have it fairly weighed by the jury. They could not properly be pinioned on the dilemma of having either to admit that Cynthia was already suffering from active schizophrenia or to assert that she was wholly without psychotic tendencies. The jury's question showed how well they had perceived the true issue. When they were told in effect that plaintiffs could recover only if, contrary to ordinary experience, the accident alone produced the schizophrenia, the result was predestined.

It is unnecessary to engage in exhaustive citation of authority sustaining the legal validity of plaintiffs' theory of the case. Since New York law governs, the oft-cited decision in McCahill v. New York Transportation Co., 201 N.Y. 221, 94 N.E. 616, 48 L.R.A.,N.S. 131 (1911), which plaintiffs' appellate counsel has discovered, would alone suffice. There the defendant's taxicab negligently hit McCahill, broke his thigh and injured his knee. After being hospitalized, he died two days later of delirium tremens. A physician testified that "the injury precipitated his attack of delirium tremens, and understand I mean precipitated not induced;" he explained that by "precipitated," he meant "hurried up,"—just what plaintiffs' experts testified to be the role of the accident here. The Court of Appeals allowed recovery for wrongful death. In Champlin Refining Co. v. Thomas, 93 F.2d 133, 136 (10 Cir.1937), the court held that "where one who has tubercular germs in his system suffers injuries due to the negligence of another, and the injuries so weaken the resistance of the tissue that as a direct consequence tubercular infection sets up therein, the negligence is the proximate cause of the tubercular infection and renders the negligent person liable in damages therefor." There was no suggestion that plaintiff was required either to admit that he already "had" tuberculosis or to assert that the accident "caused" the development of the germs. [ ]

. . .

We add a further word that may be of importance on a new trial. Although the fact that Cynthia had latent psychotic tendencies would not defeat recovery if the accident was a precipitating cause of schizophrenia, this may have a significant bearing on the amount of damages. The defendants are entitled to explore the probability that the child might have developed schizophrenia in any event. While the evidence does not demonstrate that Cynthia already had the disease, it does suggest that she was a good prospect. Judge Hiscock said in *McCahill*, "it is easily seen that the probability of later death from existing causes for which a defendant was not responsible would probably be an important element in fixing damages, but it is not a defense." 201 N.Y. at 224, 94 N.E. at 617. In Evans v. S. J. Groves & Sons Company, [315 F.2d 335] we noted that if a defendant "succeeds in establishing that the plaintiff's pre-existing condition was bound to worsen . . . an appropriate discount should be made for the damages that would have been suffered even in the absence of the defendant's negligence." 315 F.2d at 347–348. See also the famous case of Dillon v. Twin State Gas & Electric Co., 85 N.H. 449, 163 A. 111 (1932), and 2 Harper & James, supra, at 1128–1131. It is no answer that exact prediction of Cynthia's future apart from the accident is difficult or even impossible. However taxing such a problem may be for men who have devoted their lives to psychiatry, it is one for which a jury is ideally suited.

Reversed for a new trial.

NOTES AND QUESTIONS

1. What should the trial judge have told the jury?

2. In the cited Dillon v. Twin State case, a boy lost his balance while sitting on the girder of a bridge. In an effort to avoid falling, he came in contact with an exposed wire and was electrocuted. The court concluded that if it were found that the boy would have been killed or severely injured by the fall without regard to the wire, any award against the defendant for the exposed wire should be reduced drastically. Is that applicable to *Steinhauser?*

3. In Benn v. Thomas, 512 N.W.2d 537 (Iowa 1994), decedent, who had a history of coronary disease and diabetes, died of a heart attack six days after suffering a bruised chest and fractured ankle due to defendant's negligent driving. The estate's expert referred to the accident as "the straw that broke the camel's back." Other medical evidence indicated that the accident did not cause the death. The trial judge refused to charge that if the decedent had a "prior heart condition making him more susceptible to injury than a person in normal health, then the Defendant is responsible for all injuries and damages which are experienced by [decedent] proximately caused by the Defendant's actions, even though the injuries claimed produced a greater injury than those which might have been experienced by a normal person under the same circumstances."

The refusal was reversible error. If the jury concluded that the accident had been an actual cause of the heart attack, the defendant should be held liable for the death. The charge actually did not "adequately convey to the jury the eggshell plaintiff rule," which "rejects the limit of foreseeability that courts ordinarily require in the determination of proximate cause."

4. In Bartolone v. Jeckovich, 103 App.Div.2d 632, 481 N.Y.S.2d 545 (1984), plaintiff was slightly injured in a four-car chain reaction collision suffering primarily from whiplash, and back strain for which he was treated with muscle relaxants and physical therapy. He was a single 48–

year old man who worked as a carpenter. He was "very proud of his physique and his strength, spending an average of four hours daily . . . engaged in body building." On weekends, he painted, sang, and played music. Since the accident plaintiff had been withdrawn, hostile, delusional, heard voices, refused to cut his hair, shave or bathe, and no longer participated in any of his former interests.

It appeared at the trial that plaintiff's mother and sister had died of cancer at early ages and that plaintiff had probably acquired a fear and dislike of physicians. His body building was being done to avoid doctors and ward off illness. After the accident, he perceived that his "bodily integrity was impaired and that he was physically deteriorating." This led to psychological and social deterioration as well. The consensus of the plaintiff's experts was that plaintiff had "suffered from a pre-existing schizophrenic illness which had been exacerbated by the accident [and] was now in a chronic paranoid schizophrenic state which is irreversible."

The trial judge cut plaintiff's award of $500,000 to $30,000. The appellate court, relying on *Steinhauser,* reinstated the verdict. A defendant "must take a plaintiff as he finds him and hence may be liable in damages for aggravation of a preexisting illness."

5. *Suicide.* Courts have shown an increasing willingness to allow recoveries where the defendant's negligence has severely injured a person who later commits suicide. In Fuller v. Preis, 35 N.Y.2d 425, 322 N.E.2d 263, 363 N.Y.S.2d 568 (1974), the victim was a 43–year–old surgeon who sustained injuries in an automobile accident that left him subject to seizures and caused a physical deterioration. Meanwhile, his wife, who had been partially paralyzed by polio, suffered "nervous exhaustion." Seven months after the crash he learned that his mother had cancer. One of his suicide notes warned his family to destroy it because "it would alter the outcome of the 'case'—i.e., it's worth a million dollars to you all." Chief Judge Breitel declared that an "irresistible impulse" does not necessarily mean a "sudden impulse." The jury could find that the irresistible impulse that "caused decedent to take his life also impelled the acquisition of the gun and the writing of the suicide notes."

See also Zygmaniak v. Kawasaki Motors Corp., 131 N.J.Super. 403, 330 A.2d 56 (1974)(defendant liable for the death of a victim who was shot and killed at his own request by his brother after defendant's negligence had rendered the victim a quadriplegic); Stafford v. Neurological Medicine, Inc., 811 F.2d 470 (8th Cir.1987)(defendant liable for suicide after negligently permitting patient to receive mail indicating incorrectly that she was suffering from a brain tumor). But recall the reluctance of courts to hold negligent attorneys liable for the suicides of disappointed clients, p. 275, supra.

6. *Secondary harm.* In Stoleson v. United States, 708 F.2d 1217 (7th Cir.1983), plaintiff worked in a munitions plant and was found to have suffered heart problems from negligently being exposed to nitroglycerine. Although the harm was temporary and should have stopped when plaintiff ceased working at the factory, she developed hypochondria after the episode and was unable to function normally. The court adverted to the possibility that the plaintiff's condition was brought about by medical advice given her after the exposure to nitroglycerine had ended:

> If a pedestrian who has been run down by a car is taken to a hospital and because of the hospital's negligence incurs greater medical expenses or suffers more pain and suffering than he would have if the hospital had not been negligent, he can collect his incremental as well as his original damages from the person who ran him down, since they would have been avoided if that person had used due care.

Is the original wrongdoer liable if the hospital staff reasonably chooses a course of treatment that does not work—if it later appears that another reasonable choice would in fact have done the job? What if the staff surgeon is drunk and operates on the wrong leg?

7. Plaintiff, who was seriously injured by defendant's negligence, died when the ambulance driver transporting him to a hospital suffered a heart attack and the ambulance swerved into a tree. The trial judge charged that the defendant was liable for the further injuries resulting from "normal efforts of third persons in rendering aid . . . which the other's injury reasonably requires irrespective of whether such acts are done in a proper or in a negligent manner." The charge was upheld on appeal from a plaintiff's judgment. Pridham v. Cash & Carry Bldg. Center, Inc., 116 N.H. 292, 359 A.2d 193 (1976). If medical services "are rendered negligently, the rule based on questions of policy makes the negligence of the original tortfeasor a proximate cause of the subsequent injuries suffered by the victim." Since such services are generally rendered in hospitals, the ambulance trip was a "necessary step in securing medical services required by the accident at Cash & Carry. Therefore the rule holding the original tortfeasor liable for additional harm from medical care rendered because of the original injury should be extended to, and include, injuries sustained while being transported to a hospital where medical services can be obtained."

8. Consider the following variations on *Pridham:*

a. D's negligence caused serious harm and emergency efforts were required to get P to the hospital quickly. The ambulance driver has a heart attack.

b. D's negligence causes only a broken leg and the ambulance is returning to the hospital in the ordinary stream of traffic when the driver has a heart attack.

c. Under either (a) or (b) the ambulance is in a collision when an oncoming driver has a heart attack and the car careens into the ambulance. What if the oncoming driver is negligently driving?

d. The ambulance attendant examines P at the scene and tells P that he appears to have sustained only a badly twisted wrist. P can come back to the hospital by ambulance or can see his own doctor. P decides to see his own doctor and calls a taxicab. The taxi driver has a heart attack. What if an oncoming driver has the heart attack?

e. P, who has been badly hurt by D's negligence, has been recuperating in the hospital for 18 days. The doctors decide to transfer P to a hospital that has better physical therapy facilities. As he is being transferred by ambulance the driver has an epileptic seizure and the ambulance crashes. Lucas v. City of Juneau, 127 F.Supp. 730 (D.Alaska 1955).

In these cases, should it matter whether the crash aggravates the original injury or causes totally new harm?

9. In Wagner v. Mittendorf, 232 N.Y. 481, 134 N.E. 539 (1922), the defendant negligently broke plaintiff's leg. While plaintiff was recovering, through no fault of his own his crutch slipped and the leg was rebroken. The court held the defendant liable for that aggravation. Why?

The Polemis case. In the English case of *In re Polemis*, [1921] 3 K.B. 560, [1921] All.E.R. 40 (Ct.App.1921), while stevedores were moving benzine from one hold to another on the ship Thrasyvoulos, a worker carelessly dropped a wooden board into the hold. Fire broke out and the ship was destroyed. The case centered on whether those responsible for the acts of the careless stevedore were liable for the loss of the ship. A panel of arbitrators, whose fact findings were binding, found "that the fire arose from a spark igniting petrol vapour in the hold; that the spark was caused by the falling board coming into contact with some substance in the hold; . . . [and] that the causing of the spark could not reasonably have been anticipated from the falling of the board though some damage to the ship might reasonably have been anticipated." The court of appeal affirmed an award of the full loss to the owners. Lord Justice Bankes noted that a split existed:

> According to the one view, the consequences which may reasonably be expected to result from a particular act are material only in reference to the question whether the act is or is not a negligent act; according to the other view, those consequences are the test whether the damages resulting from the act, assuming it to be negligent, are or are not too remote to be recoverable.

He adopted the first view, observing that the "fire appears to me to have been directly caused by the falling of the plank. Under these circumstances I consider that it is immaterial that the causing of the spark by the falling of the plank could not have been reasonably anticipated." Lord Justice Scrutton, in his opinion, stated:

> Once the act is negligent, the fact that its exact operation was not foreseen is immaterial. . . . In the present case it was negligent in discharging cargo to knock down the planks of the temporary staging, for they might easily cause some damage either to workmen, or cargo, or the ship. The fact that they did directly produce an unexpected result, a spark in an atmosphere of petrol

vapour which caused a fire, does not relieve the person who was negligent from the damage which his negligent act directly caused.

Polemis played a central role in the following case.

Overseas Tankship (U.K.) Ltd. v. Morts Dock & Engineering Co., Ltd. (The Wagon Mound)

Privy Council, 1961.
[1961] A.C. 338.

[Plaintiffs-respondents, a ship-repairing firm, owned a wharf in Sydney Harbour, Australia, and were refitting the ship Corrimal. At a different wharf, about 600 feet away, the ship Wagon Mound, chartered by defendants, was taking on bunkering oil. A large quantity of bunkering oil spilled into the bay and some of it concentrated near plaintiff's property. Defendants set sail, making no effort to disperse the oil. When plaintiffs' manager became aware of the condition he stopped all welding and burning until he could assess the danger. Based on discussions with the manager at the Wagon Mound berth and his own understanding about furnace oil in open waters, he felt he could safely order activities to be resumed with all precautions taken to prevent flammable material from falling off the wharf into the oil.

For two days work proceeded and there was no movement of the oil. Then, oil under or near the wharf was ignited and a fire spread, causing extensive damage to the wharf and plaintiffs' equipment. The trial judge found that floating on the oil underneath the wharf was a piece of debris on which lay some cotton waste or rag that had caught fire from molten metal falling from the wharf, and that this set the floating oil afire either directly or by first setting fire to a wooden pile coated with oil.

The trial judge awarded judgment to the plaintiff and the Full Court of the Supreme Court of New South Wales dismissed the defendants' appeal.]

■ VISCOUNT SIMONDS [after stating the facts].

The trial judge also made the all-important finding, which must be set out in his own words: "The *raison d'être* of furnace oil is, of course, that it shall burn, but I find the defendant did not know and could not reasonably be expected to have known that it was capable of being set afire when spread on water." This finding was reached after a wealth of evidence, which included that of a distinguished scientist, Professor Hunter. It receives strong confirmation from the fact that at the trial the respondents strenuously maintained that the appellants had discharged petrol into the bay on no other ground than that, as the spillage was set alight, it could not be furnace oil. An attempt was made before their Lordships' Board to limit in some way the finding of fact, but it is clear that it was intended to cover precisely the event that happened.

One other finding must be mentioned. The judge held that apart from damage by fire the respondents had suffered some damage from the spillage of oil in that it had got upon their slipways and congealed upon them and interfered with their use of the slips.   He said: "The evidence of this damage is slight and no claim for compensation is made in respect of it. Nevertheless it does establish some damage, which may be insignificant in comparison with the magnitude of the damage by fire, but which nevertheless is damage which, beyond question, was a direct result of the escape of the oil."   It is upon this footing that their Lordships will consider the question whether the appellants are liable for the fire damage.   . . .

. . .

There can be no doubt that the decision of the Court of Appeal in *Polemis* plainly asserts that, if the defendant is guilty of negligence he is responsible for all the consequences whether reasonably foreseeable or not. The generality of the proposition is perhaps qualified by the fact that each of the Lords Justices refers to the outbreak of fire as the direct result of the negligent act.   There is thus introduced the conception that the negligent actor is not responsible for consequences which are not "direct," whatever that may mean.   . . .

. . .   If the line of relevant authority had stopped with *Polemis*, their Lordships might, whatever their own views as to its unreason, have felt some hesitation about overruling it.   But it is far otherwise.   . . .

. . .

Enough has been said to show that the authority of *Polemis* has been severely shaken though lip-service has from time to time been paid to it. In their Lordships' opinion it should no longer be regarded as good law.   It is not probable that many cases will for that reason have a different result, though it is hoped that the law will be thereby simplified, and that in some cases, at least, palpable injustice will be avoided.   For it does not seem consonant with current ideas of justice or morality that for an act of negligence, however slight or venial, which results in some trivial foreseeable damage the actor should be liable for all consequences however unforeseeable and however grave, so long as they can be said to be "direct."   It is a principle of civil liability, subject only to qualifications which have no present relevance, that a man must be considered to be responsible for the probable consequences of his act.   To demand more of him is too harsh a rule, to demand less is to ignore that civilized order requires the observance of a minimum standard of behaviour.

This concept applied to the slowly developing law of negligence has led to a great variety of expressions which can, as it appears to their Lordships, be harmonized with little difficulty with the single exception of the so-called rule in *Polemis*.   For, if it is asked why a man should be responsible for the natural or necessary or probable consequences of his act (or any other similar description of them) the answer is that it is not because they are natural or necessary or probable, but because, since they have this quality, it is judged by the standard of the reasonable man that he ought to have foreseen them.   Thus it is that over and over again it has happened that in different judgments in the same case, and sometimes in a single judgment, liability for a consequence has been imposed on the ground that it was reasonably foreseeable or, alternatively, on the ground that it was natural or necessary or probable. The two grounds have been treated as coterminous, and so they largely are. But, where they are not, the question arises to which the wrong answer was given in *Polemis*. For, if some limitation must be imposed upon the consequences for which the negligent actor is to be held responsible—and all are agreed that some limitation there must be—why should that test (reasonable foreseeability) be rejected which, since he is judged by what the reasonable man ought to foresee, corresponds with the common conscience of mankind, and a test (the "direct" consequence) be substituted which leads to nowhere but the never-ending and insoluble problems of causation.   .   .   .

.   .   .

It is, no doubt, proper when considering tortious liability for negligence to analyze its elements and to say that the plaintiff must prove a duty owed to him by the defendant, a breach of that duty by the defendant, and consequent damage. But there can be no liability until the damage has been done. It is not the act but the consequences on which tortious liability is founded. Just as (as it has been said) there is no such thing as negligence in the air, so there is no such thing as liability in the air. Suppose an action brought by A for damage caused by the carelessness (a neutral word) of B, for example, a fire caused by the careless spillage of oil. It may, of course, become relevant to know what duty B owed to A, but the only liability that is in question is the liability for damage by fire. It is vain to isolate the liability from its context and to say that B is or is not liable, and then to ask for what damage he is liable. For his liability is in respect of that damage and no other. If, as admittedly it is, B's liability (culpability) depends on the reasonable foreseeability of the consequent damage, how is that to be determined except by the foreseeability of the damage which in fact happened—the damage in suit? And, if that damage is unforeseeable so as to displace liability at large, how can the liability be restored so as to make compensation payable?

But, it is said, a different position arises if B's careless act has been shown to be negligent and has caused some foreseeable damage to A. Their Lordships have already observed that to hold B liable for consequences however unforeseeable of a careless act, if, but only if, he is at the same time liable for some other damage however trivial, appears to be neither logical nor just. This becomes more clear if it is supposed that similar unforeseeable damage is suffered by A and C but other foreseeable damage, for which B is liable, by A only. A system of law which would hold B liable to A but not to C for the similar damage suffered by each of them could not easily be defended. Fortunately, the attempt is not necessary. For the same fallacy is at the root of the proposition. It is irrelevant to the question whether B is liable for unforeseeable damage that he is liable for foreseeable damage, as irrelevant as would the fact that he had trespassed on Whiteacre be to the question whether he has trespassed on Blackacre. Again, suppose a claim by A for damage by fire by the careless act of B. Of what relevance is it to that claim that he had another claim arising out of the same careless act? It would surely not prejudice his claim if that other claim failed: it cannot assist it if it succeeds. Each of them rests on its own bottom, and will fail if it can be established that the damage could not reasonably be foreseen. . . .

Their Lordships conclude this part of the case with some general observations. They have been concerned primarily to displace the proposition that unforeseeability is irrelevant if damage is "direct." In doing so they have inevitably insisted that the essential factor in determining liability is whether the damage is of such a kind as the reasonable man should have foreseen. This accords with the general view thus stated by Lord Atkin in Donoghue v. Stevenson: "The liability for negligence, whether you style it such or treat it as in other systems as a species of 'culpa,' is no doubt based upon a general public sentiment of moral wrongdoing for which the offender must pay." It is a departure from this sovereign principle if liability is made to depend solely on the damage being the "direct" or "natural" consequence of the precedent act. Who knows or can be assumed to know all the processes of nature? But if it would be wrong that a man should be held liable for damage unpredictable by a reasonable man because it was "direct" or "natural," equally it would be wrong that he should escape liability, however "indirect" the damage, if he foresaw or could reasonably foresee the intervening events which led to its being done. . . . Thus foreseeability becomes the effective test. In reasserting this principle their Lordships conceive that they do not depart from, but follow and develop, the law of negligence as laid down by Baron Alderson in Blyth v. Birmingham Waterworks Co.

. . .

Their Lordships will humbly advise Her Majesty that this appeal should be allowed, and the respondents' action so far as it related to damage caused by the negligence of the appellants be dismissed with costs. . . . The respondents must pay the costs of the appellants of this appeal and in the courts below.

NOTES AND QUESTIONS

1. The Judicial Committee of the Privy Council has jurisdiction over appeals from the Commonwealth courts, whereas the House of Lords has jurisdiction over appeals from British courts. In the House of Lords, each judge delivers an opinion, but the Privy Council at the time of this case delivered but one opinion—and no dissents. Since the Privy Council was advising Her Majesty on the disposition, a single opinion was thought more useful. Rumor has it that the Privy Council split 3–2 in *Wagon Mound*. See The Foresight Saga 3 (Haldane Society 1962).

2. The court observes that "all are agreed" that there must be some limitation upon the consequences for which the negligent actor is held responsible. Would setting such a limit be facilitated by ascertaining its purpose?

3. What is the basis of the court's decision? Is it dictated by logic?

4. What might Viscount Simonds have said if the fire had occurred shortly after the discharge of the oil and before the plaintiff had reason to know of any oil in the area?

5. In Smith v. Leech Brain & Co., [1962] 2 Q.B. 405, through the defendant's negligence in providing inadequate shielding, a worker was burned on the lip by a piece of molten metal. The burn was treated but did not heal. It ulcerated, developed into cancer which spread, and the worker died of cancer three years later. The judge found that the worker had probably become pre-disposed to cancer by ten years of work in the gas industry earlier in his life. He held that *Wagon Mound* did not alter the principle that a defendant must take his victim as he finds him:

> The test is not whether these employers could reasonably have foreseen that a burn would cause cancer and he would die. The question is whether these employers could reasonably foresee the type of injury he suffered, namely, the burn. What, in the particular case, is the amount of damage which he suffers as a result of that burn, depends upon the characteristics and constitution of the victim.

Is this approach consistent with *Wagon Mound?* After *Wagon Mound,* is there room for a distinction between the "type" and the "extent" of harm?

6. Suppose the defendant is driving negligently through skid row and runs down a person who appears to be one of the derelicts on the street. In fact the victim is a successful and highly paid athlete who was posing as a derelict to work among the area's residents. How might Viscount Simonds respond to the defendant's argument that he could reasonably expect to have done only minor harm—and not the great harm suffered by this prosperous athlete and his or her family?

Is this different from a defendant arguing that he could foresee only a small fire resulting from his negligence but that totally unexpected events, such as an unprecedented wind, caused a much greater fire?

7. Assume that the foreseeable cloggage could be expected to affect 10 feet of slipway and to cause $10,000 worth of damage. What if an unprecedented wind occurs after the negligence with the result that the slipway is clogged for 30 feet with a loss of $30,000? How might Viscount Simonds analyze this? What about $50,000 worth of unforeseeable fire damage? $5,000 worth of unforeseeable fire damage?

8. Viscount Simonds puts the example of A and C who suffer damage at the hands of B. He suggests that a system that allowed A to recover for the negligently inflicted unforeseeable harm but denied such recovery to C "could not easily be defended." Why not? Is the problem allowing A to recover or not allowing C to recover?

9. In Blyth v. Birmingham Waterworks Co., 11 Exch. 781 (1856), cited at the end of *Wagon Mound,* the defendant's water main sprang a leak during an unprecedented frost and the escaping water damaged plaintiff's house. On appeal from a jury verdict for the plaintiff, Baron Alderson concluded: "Such a state of circumstances constitutes a contingency against which no reasonable man can provide. The result was an accident for which the defendants cannot be held liable." How does this opinion support the *Wagon Mound* court?

10. The owners of the Corrimal brought a separate action against the charterers of the Wagon Mound. The trial judge held against plaintiffs on the negligence claim. The Privy Council reversed. Overseas Tankship (U.K.), Ltd. v. Miller Steamship Co. (Wagon Mound No. 2), [1967] 1 A.C. 617. The Privy Council read the trial judge's findings as suggesting that the defendants might have foreseen a very slight danger of fire, contrasting this with the finding in No. 1 that the defendant "did not know and could not reasonably be expected to have known that [the oil] was capable of being set afire when spread on water." The Privy Council reconciled the two findings on the ground that in No. 1 if the plaintiffs "had set out to prove that it was foreseeable by the engineers of the Wagon Mound that this oil could be set alight, they might have had difficulty in parrying the reply that then this must also have been foreseeable by their manager. Then there would have been contributory negligence" which would have been a complete defense. Does this suggest something about the nature of the adversary process and the purposes of litigation?

There was no such embarrassment in this case and the Privy Council saw the new finding as raising a question akin to that presented in the cricket case, *Bolton v. Stone*, p. 39, supra, in which the risk was not totally unforeseeable but rather was judged too small to dictate evasive action. "But it does not follow that, no matter what the circumstances may be, it is justifiable to neglect a risk of such a small magnitude. A reasonable man would only neglect such a risk if he had some valid reason for doing so: e.g., that it would involve considerable expense to eliminate the risk." The Council found liability because discharging the oil could not be justified since it also caused a major loss to defendants: "If the ship's engineer had thought about the matter there could have been no question of balancing the advantages and disadvantages. From every point of view it was both his duty and his interest to stop the discharge immediately."

11. In Ventricelli v. Kinney System Rent A Car, 45 N.Y.2d 950, 383 N.E.2d 1149, 411 N.Y.S.2d 555 (1978), plaintiff's rented car had a defective rear trunk lid that flew up while plaintiff was driving. Plaintiff pulled the car over into a regular parking space along the city street and was trying to get the lid to stay down when he was hit by a car. The lessor was held not liable. In a later case, the court explained its result in *Ventricelli* by stating that although the lessor's negligence "undoubtedly served to place the injured party at the site of the accident, the intervening act was divorced from and not the foreseeable risk associated with the original negligence. And the injuries were different in kind than those which would have normally been expected from a defective trunk. In short, the negligence of the renter merely furnished the occasion for an unrelated act to cause injuries not ordinarily anticipated." The quotation is from Derdiarian v. Felix Contracting Corp., 51 N.Y.2d 308, 414 N.E.2d 666, 434 N.Y.S.2d 166 (1980).

See Betancourt v. Manhattan Ford Lincoln Mercury Inc., 195 App. Div.2d 246, 607 N.Y.S.2d 924 (1994), refusing to apply *Ventricelli* where a defective car is forced to pull over to the side of a busy highway—as opposed to stopping in a legal parking space.

Consider Harpster v. Hetherington, 512 N.W.2d 585 (Minn.1994), in which plaintiff, as a favor, went onto defendants' property to feed their dog. She let the dog out into a fenced area as she prepared the food. When she went to get the dog she discovered that it had escaped through a hole in the fence. Plaintiff went to the front door to shout for the dog. As she stepped out on the front stoop she slipped and fell on ice, which had developed after the defendants had left earlier that morning. The claimed negligence was the hole in the fence. It was accepted by all sides that if the fence had not been in disrepair the accident would not have occurred. The court ordered judgment for the defendants. Plaintiff's argument was "much like arguing that if one had not got up in the morning, the accident would not have happened. . . . The problem with the 'but for' test . . . is that with a little ingenuity it converts events both near and far, which merely set the stage for an accident, into a convoluted series of 'causes' of the accident. . . . Not only does the 'but for' test obfuscate the legal doctrine of causation, but it distorts the basic tort concept of duty."

In Berry v. Sugar Notch Borough, 191 Pa. 345, 43 A. 240 (1899), defendant motorman's speeding brought a trolley car to a point at the precise moment at which a tree along the track fell on the trolley car injuring passengers. Assume the injuries were no more serious than they would have been if the tree had fallen on a trolley going at the proper speed. Should liability be imposed? See also Whinery v. Southern Pacific Co., 6 Cal.App.3d 126, 85 Cal.Rptr. 649 (1970). The issue is discussed in Shavell, An Analysis of Causation and the Scope of Liability in the Law of Torts, 9 J.Legal Studies 463 (1980). How might the *Polemis* court analyze this type of case?

12. Recall *DeHaen,* p. 70, supra, in which Judge Cardozo thought it important to identify the purposes behind the statute's requirement of a barrier around an open hole at a construction site. Is the statutory purpose question analogous to the proximate cause question presented in these cases?

2. UNEXPECTED MANNER

In the previous section, we considered situations in which the defendant claimed that the harm that resulted was unexpected given the nature of the negligent act. In this section, the defendant contends that although the harm that occurred was of the sort that might have been expected, the manner of its occurrence justifies exculpating the defendant. In one illustrative case, for example, plaintiff alleged that the defendant Los Angeles Transit had negligently allowed a wooden power pole on a main road to deteriorate to such an extent that when a negligent driver crashed into it, it fell over onto the plaintiff who was walking by at the time.

Gibson v. Garcia, 96 Cal.App.2d 681, 216 P.2d 119 (1950). The court rejected the defendant's argument that, although it might be liable if the pole had simply fallen by itself, it should not be liable when the fall was caused by a negligent driver. Do you agree with the court? If so, can you imagine any situation in which you would exculpate the defendant because of what caused the pole to come down?

McLaughlin v. Mine Safety Appliances Co.

Court of Appeals of New York, 1962.
11 N.Y.2d 62, 181 N.E.2d 430, 226 N.Y.S.2d 407.

[Plaintiff was removed unconscious from a lake after nearly drowning. The local fire department brought blankets but more heat was needed and a fireman gave a nurse at the scene heating blocks marketed by defendant. The blocks were covered in "flocking" that resembled flannel. Attached to the flocking was a label containing the block's trade name and the defendant's name and design. On the cardboard container was written, "Always Ready for Use" and, in much smaller print, instructions for use—the last one of which said "Wrap in insulation medium, such as pouch, towel, blanket or folded cloth."

One fireman at the scene, Traxler, testified that he recalled having been told by defendant's representative at a training session some five years earlier that the block must be insulated before use, that he was fully aware of the need for insulation, and that he had told the nurse to wrap the blocks before using. Then the nurse applied the blocks directly to the plaintiff's body while Traxler, who had activated the blocks, stood next to her and watched. The plaintiff's aunt could recall hearing no warning about insulation from Traxler to the nurse. Plaintiff received third degree burns from the blocks.

On appeal from a judgment for plaintiff, the appellate division affirmed after plaintiff agreed to a reduction in damages.]

■ FOSTER, J.

.   .   .

The jury, under the court's instructions, could have found that a hidden or latent danger existed in the use of the product, or at least that the form and design of the product itself, together with the printing on the container, could mislead ultimate users as to the need for further insulation. [ ] The blocks were dressed in "flocking" and appeared to be insulated, and the bold lettering on the containers revealed that the blocks were "ALWAYS READY FOR USE" and "ENTIRELY SELF CON-TAINED", all of which seemed to indicate that nothing extrinsic to the contents of the package was needed. And inasmuch as the blocks were designed for use on the human body, and if improperly used could cause severe injuries, the jury was justified in finding that the final sentence of the instructions, found in small print on the back side of the containers, advising use of a further insulating medium, was totally inadequate as a warning commensurate with the risk; indeed, they were entitled to find that the *instructions,* not particularly stressed, did not amount to a *warning of the risk at all,* and that it was foreseeable that the small print instruction might never be read, and might be disregarded even if read [   ]. It also was foreseeable, and the jury could have found, that the blocks would be reused ultimately by persons without notice of the risks involved in failing to insulate, long after the cardboard containers bearing the so-called "warning" had been dispensed with, and that the distributor would be liable to such unwarned ultimate users. The containers themselves encouraged such reuse, and told how new "charges" could be obtained.

But the true problem presented in this case is one of proximate causation, and not one concerning the general duty to warn or negligence of the distributor. In this regard the trial court instructed the jury that the defendant would not be liable if "an actual warning was conveyed to the person or persons applying the blocks that they should be wrapped in insulation of some kind before being placed against the body" for in that event the "failure to heed that warning would be a new cause which intervened." Subsequently, and after the jury retired, they returned and asked this question: "Your Honor, if we, the jury, find that the M.S.A. Company was negligent in not making any warning of danger on the heat block itself, but has given proper instructions in its use up to the point of an intervening circumstance (the nurse who was not properly instructed), is the M.S.A. Company liable?"

The trial court answered as follows: "Ladies and gentlemen of the jury, if you find from the evidence that the defendant, as a reasonably prudent person under all of the circumstances should have expected use of the block by some person other than those to whom instruction as to its use had been given, either by the wording on the container or otherwise, and that under those circumstances a reasonably prudent person would have placed warning words on the heat block itself, and if you find in addition to that that the nurse was not warned at the scene and that a reasonably prudent person in the position of the nurse, absent any warning of the block itself, would have proceeded to use it without inquiry as to the proper method of use, then the defendant would be liable." Counsel for the defendant excepted to that statement. The jury then returned its verdict for the plaintiffs.

From the jury's question, it is obvious that they were concerned with the effect of the fireman's knowledge that the blocks should have been wrapped, and his apparent failure to so advise the nurse who applied the blocks in his presence. The court in answering the jury's question instructed, in essence, that the defendant could still be liable even though the fireman had knowledge of the need for further insulation, if it was reasonably foreseeable that the blocks, absent the containers, would find their way from the fireman to unwarned third persons.

We think that the instruction, as applied to the facts of this case, was erroneous. In [cases discussed by the court], the manufacturer or distributor failed to warn the original vendee of the latent danger, and there were no additional acts of negligence intervening between the failure to warn and the resulting injury or damage. This was not such a case, or at least the jury could find that it was not. Nor was this simply a case involving the negligent failure of the vendee to inspect and discover the danger; in such a case the intervening negligence of the immediate vendee does not necessarily insulate the manufacturer from liability to third persons, nor supersede the negligence of the manufacturer in failing to warn of the danger (Rosebrock v. General Elec. Co., 236 N.Y. 227; Sider v. General Elec. Co., 203 App.Div. 443, affd. 238 N.Y. 64).

In the case before us, the jury obviously believed that the fireman, Traxler, had actual knowledge of the need for further insulation, and the jury was preoccupied with the effect of his failure to warn the nurse as she applied the blocks to the plaintiff's person. The jury also could have believed that Traxler removed the blocks from the containers, thereby depriving the nurse of *any* opportunity she might have had to read the instructions printed on the containers, and that Traxler actually activated the blocks, turned them over, uninsulated, to the nurse for her use, and stood idly by as they were placed directly on the plaintiff's wet skin.

Under the circumstances, we think the court should have charged that if the fireman did so conduct himself, without warning the nurse, his negligence was so gross as to supersede the negligence of the defendant and to insulate it from liability. This is the rule that prevails when knowledge of the latent danger or defect is *actually* possessed by the original vendee, who then deliberately passes on the product to a third person without warning (see Stultz v. Benson Lbr. Co., 6 Cal.2d 688; Catlin v. Union Oil Co., 31 Cal.App. 597; [   ]).

In short, whether or not the distributor furnished ample warning on his product to third persons in general was not important here, if the jury believed that Traxler had actual notice of the danger by virtue of his presence at demonstration classes or otherwise, and that he deprived the nurse of her opportunity to read the instructions prior to applying the blocks. While the distributor might have been liable if the blocks had found their way into the hands of the nurse in a more innocent fashion, the distributor could not be expected to foresee that its demonstrations to the firemen would callously be disregarded by a member of the department. . . .

Here, the jury might have found that the fireman not only had the means to warn the nurse, but further that, by his actions, he prevented any warning from reaching her, and, indeed, that he actually had some part in the improper application of the blocks. Such conduct could not have been foreseen by the defendant.

. . . .

The judgment should be reversed and a new trial granted, with costs to abide the event.

■ Van Voorhis, J. (dissenting). The recovery by plaintiff should not, as it seems to us, be reversed on account of lack of foreseeability or a break in the chain of causation due to any intervening act of negligence on the part of a volunteer fireman. These heat blocks were dangerous instrumentalities unless wrapped in "insulating" media, "such as pouch, towel, blanket or folded cloth" as the instructions on the container directed. What happened here was that the container, with the instructions on it, was thrown away, and the nurse who applied the heat block was unaware of this safety requirement. In our minds the circumstances that the fireman who knew of the danger failed to warn the nurse, even if negligent, did not affect the fact, as the jury found it, that this was a risk which the manufacturer of the heat block ought to have anticipated in the exercise of reasonable care, nor intercept the chain of causation. The jury found by their verdict that a duty was imposed on the manufacturer to inscribe the warning on the heat block for the reason that in the exercise of reasonable care it should have anticipated that the warning written on the container might be lost or discarded under circumstances similar to those surrounding this injury.

The rule is not absolute that it is not necessary to anticipate the negligence or even the crime of another. It has been said in the Restatement of Torts (§ 449): "If the realizable likelihood that a third person may act in a particular manner is the hazard or one of the hazards which makes the actor negligent, such an act whether innocent, negligent, intentionally tortious or criminal does not prevent the actor from being liable for harm caused thereby." It is further provided by section 447: "The fact that an intervening act of a third person is negligent in itself or is done in a negligent manner does not make it a superseding cause of harm to another which the actor's negligent conduct is a substantial factor in bringing about, if (a) the actor at the time of his negligent conduct should have realized that a third person might so act". [ ]

The judgment appealed from should be affirmed.

■ JUDGES FULD, FROESSEL and BURKE concur with JUDGE FOSTER; JUDGE VAN VOORHIS dissents in an opinion in which JUDGE DYE concurs; CHIEF JUDGE DESMOND taking no part.

NOTES AND QUESTIONS

1. What negligence on MSA's part might the jury reasonably have found?

2. What if Traxler had testified, and was believed, that:

   a. He remembered about the wrapping and warned the nurse.

   b. He thought he remembered but wasn't sure and assumed the nurse knew best.

   c. He forgot—the course had been many years earlier and had been quite short.

   d. He forgot even though the course had been only a short time before.

      e.   He remembered about the wrapping but stayed silent because the victim was a person who had been bothering him over the years.

     In Cohen v. St. Regis Paper Co., 65 N.Y.2d 752, 481 N.E.2d 562, 492 N.Y.S.2d 22 (1985), a worker was killed by exposure to dry ice. In a claim against the supplier of the ice, the supplier argued that even if it had failed to provide a warning of the dangers involved, it was not liable because the employer knew the danger and did not warn the worker. The court rejected the argument: "there is here no evidence of gross negligence such as there was in *McLaughlin*, where the warnings that might otherwise have been seen were removed and the remover stood idly by while the decedent was exposed to danger." It was for the jury to decide whether the employer's "negligent failure to warn" relieved the supplier of liability.

     3.   Is it essential to the majority that Traxler may have removed the block from the container? What if the nurse removed the block without reading the container—but a person standing in the crowd knew how to use the block, realized the nurse was misusing it, and said nothing? Is the problem the fireman's possible contribution to the harm or the callousness of a person who watched another get burned?

     4.   How are the Restatement sections that the dissent quotes relevant to the case? In Hines v. Garrett, 131 Va. 125 108 S.E. 690 (1921), a train improperly carried the 18–year-old plaintiff a mile past her stop. The conductor told her to walk back to the depot, even though he knew she would have to walk through a disreputable area known as Hoboes' Hollow. In her action against the railroad for damages for rape, the court held that the intervening criminal conduct did not insulate the railroad from liability. Is *Hines* comparable to the principal case?

     5.   Consider the relevance of Restatement (Second) § 435, which provides as follows:

     (1) If the actor's conduct is a substantial factor in bringing about harm to another, the fact that the actor neither foresaw nor should have foreseen the extent of the harm or the manner in which it occurred does not prevent him from being liable.

     (2) The actor's conduct may be held not to be a legal cause of harm to another where after the event and looking back from the harm to the actor's negligent conduct, it appears to the court highly extraordinary that it should have brought about the harm.

How might each opinion have used § 435?

     6.   In Addis v. Steele, 38 Mass.App. 433, 648 N.E.2d 773 (1995), guests at an inn were injured when forced to jump from a second floor window to escape a late-night fire. Their claim of negligent failure to provide lights or reasonable escape paths withstood defendant's claim that it was not liable because the fire was set by an arsonist. The defendant's obligation was to anticipate fire from whatever source. It had failed in that respect and the actual source of this fire was irrelevant. Would the analysis be the same if the fire was started by the first recorded lightning in the region?

Compare Johnson v. Kosmos Portland Cement Co., 64 F.2d 193 (6th Cir.), cert. denied 290 U.S. 641 (1933), in which the defendant allowed a barge to become and remain full of potentially explosive petroleum gases that exploded, hurting nearby workers. Is such conduct negligent? Should it matter whether the cause of the spark was ordinary lightning? Unprecedented lightning? An arsonist? Should the cause of the explosion be relevant to the defendant's liability?

Why not say that the defendant's obligation in *MSA* was to anticipate burns from whatever source?

7. In the cited Catlin case, the defendant negligently delivered a mixture of gasoline and kerosene to Riley's store in response to an order for kerosene. Riley sold quantities of the mixture to customers who immediately complained that something was wrong. Riley tested their purchases and the other containers that defendant had delivered and decided that some of the delivered containers had been pure kerosene, some pure gasoline, and some a mixture. He called defendant, who agreed to take back this delivery. Shortly afterward, Catlin asked for kerosene and Riley sold him a quantity of the liquid from the disputed delivery in the belief that this container was pure kerosene. In fact there was some gasoline mixed in with the kerosene. When Catlin sought to use the liquid at home, it exploded and burned him fatally. Pure kerosene would not have exploded under those conditions. The court held that defendant was not liable because Riley had become aware of the problem.

8. If foreseeability is to play a role in these cases, we must first decide what it is that needs to be foreseeable. Professor Clarence Morris has addressed this question in considering the role of unusual details in these cases:

> For example, in Hines v. Morrow,[17] two men were sent out in a service truck to tow a stalled car out of a mud hole. One of them, the plaintiff, made a tow rope fast and tried to step from between the vehicles as the truck started. His artificial leg slipped into the mud hole in the road, which would not have been there had defendant-railroad not disregarded its statutory duty to maintain this part of the highway. He was unable to pull out his peg-leg and was in danger of being run over by the stalled car. He grabbed the tailgate of the service truck to use its forward force to pull him loose. A loop in the tow rope lassoed his good leg, tightened, and broke his good leg. As long as these details are considered significant facts of the case, the accident is unforeseeable. No doubt some judges would itemize the facts and hold that the railroad's neglect was not the proximate cause of the injury. As a matter of fact, courts have on occasion ruled that much less freakish injuries were unforeseeable. But in the peg-leg case, the court quoted with approval the plaintiff's lawyer's "description" of the "facts," which was couched in these words, "The case, stated in the briefest form, is simply this: Appellee was on the

---

17. 236 S.W. 183 (Tex.Civ.App.1921).

highway, using it in a lawful manner, and slipped into this hole, created by appellant's negligence, and was injured in undertaking to extricate himself." The court also adopted the injured man's answer to the railroad's attempt to stress unusual details: "Appellant contends [that] it could not reasonably have been foreseen that slipping into this hole would have caused the appellee to have become entangled in a rope, and the moving truck, with such dire results. The answer is plain: The exact consequences do not have to be foreseen."

In this . . . class of cases, foreseeability can be determined only after the significant facts of the case have been described. If official description of the facts of the case as formulated by the court is detailed, the accident can be called unforeseeable; if it is general, the accident can be called foreseeable. Since there is no authoritative guide to the proper amount of specificity in describing the facts, the process of holding that a loss is—or is not—foreseeable is fluid and often embarrasses attempts at accurate prediction.

Professor Morris cautioned that an advocate who pushes too far hurts rather than helps the cause: "A plaintiff's lawyer who insists on a too-general description appears to be trying to suppress important facts; a defense counsel who insists on a too-specific description appears to be taking advantage of mere technicality." Morris on Torts, 164–66 (2d ed. 1980).

3. Unexpected Victim

Palsgraf v. Long Island Railroad Co.

Court of Appeals of New York, 1928.
248 N.Y. 339, 162 N.E. 99.

[Appeal from a judgment entered on a plaintiff's verdict. The Appellate Division affirmed, 3–2.]

■ Cardozo, Ch. J. Plaintiff was standing on a platform of defendant's railroad after buying a ticket to go to Rockaway Beach. A train stopped at the station, bound for another place. Two men ran forward to catch it. One of the men reached the platform of the car without mishap, though the train was already moving. The other man, carrying a package, jumped aboard the car, but seemed unsteady as if about to fall. A guard on the car, who had held the door open, reached forward to help him in, and another guard on the platform pushed him from behind. In this act, the package was dislodged, and fell upon the rails. It was a package of small size, about fifteen inches long, and was covered by a newspaper. In fact it contained fireworks, but there was nothing in its appearance to give notice of its contents. The fireworks when they fell exploded. The shock of the explosion threw down some scales at the other end of the platform, many feet away. The scales struck the plaintiff, causing injuries for which she sues.

The conduct of the defendant's guard, if a wrong in its relation to the holder of the package, was not a wrong in its relation to the plaintiff, standing far away. Relatively to her it was not negligence at all. Nothing in the situation gave notice that the falling package had in it the potency of peril to persons thus removed. Negligence is not actionable unless it involves the invasion of a legally protected interest, the violation of a right. "Proof of negligence in the air, so to speak, will not do" (Pollock, Torts [11th ed.], p. 455; [ ]). "Negligence is the absence of care, according to the circumstances" (Willes, J., in Vaughan v. Taff Vale Ry. Co., 5 H. & N. 679, 688; [ ]; Adams v. Bullock, 227 N.Y. 208, 211; Parrot v. Wells, Fargo & Co., 15 Wall. [82 U.S.] 524). The plaintiff as she stood upon the platform of the station might claim to be protected against intentional invasion of her bodily security. Such invasion is not charged. She might claim to be protected against unintentional invasion by conduct involving in the thought of reasonable men an unreasonable hazard that such invasion would ensue. These, from the point of view of the law, were the bounds of her immunity, with perhaps some rare exceptions, survivals for the most part of ancient forms of liability, where conduct is held to be at the peril of the actor (Sullivan v. Dunham, 161 N.Y. 290). If no hazard was apparent to the eye of ordinary vigilance, an act innocent and harmless, at least to outward seeming, with reference to her, did not take to itself the quality of a tort because it happened to be a wrong, though apparently not one involving the risk of bodily insecurity, with reference to some one else. "In every instance, before negligence can be predicated on a given act, back of the act must be sought and found a duty to the individual complaining, the observance of which would have averted or avoided the injury" (McSherry, C.J., in West Virginia Central & P. Ry. Co. v. State, 96 Md. 652, 666; [ ]). "The ideas of negligence and duty are strictly correlative" (Bowen, L.J., in Thomas v. Quartermaine, 18 Q.B.D. 685, 694). The plaintiff sues in her own right for a wrong personal to her, and not as the vicarious beneficiary of a breach of duty to another.

A different conclusion will involve us, and swiftly too, in a maze of contradictions. A guard stumbles over a package which has been left upon a platform. It seems to be a bundle of newspapers. It turns out to be a can of dynamite. To the eye of ordinary vigilance, the bundle is abandoned waste, which may be kicked or trod on with impunity. Is a passenger at the other end of the platform protected by the law against the unsuspected hazard concealed beneath the waste? If not, is the result to be any different, so far as the distant passenger is concerned, when the guard stumbles over a valise which a truckman or a porter has left upon the walk? The passenger far away, if the victim of a wrong at all, has a cause of action, not derivative, but original and primary. His claim to be protected against invasion of his bodily security is neither greater nor less because the act resulting in the invasion is a wrong to another far removed. In this case, the rights that are said to have been violated, the interests said to have been invaded, are not even of the same order. The man was not injured in his person nor even put in danger. The purpose of the act, as well as its effect, was to make his person safe. If there was a wrong to him at all, which may very well be doubted, it was a wrong to a property interest only, the safety of his package. Out of this wrong to property, which threatened injury to nothing else, there has passed, we are told, to the plaintiff by derivation or succession a right of action for the invasion of an interest of another order, the right to bodily security. The diversity of interests emphasizes the futility of the effort to build the plaintiff's right upon the basis of a wrong to some one else. The gain is one of emphasis, for a like result would follow if the interests were the same. Even then, the orbit of the danger as disclosed to the eye of reasonable vigilance would be the orbit of the duty. One who jostles one's neighbor in a crowd does not invade the rights of others standing at the outer fringe when the unintended contact casts a bomb upon the ground. The wrongdoer as to them is the man who carries the bomb, not the one who explodes it without suspicion of the danger. Life will have to be made over, and human nature transformed, before prevision so extravagant can be accepted as the norm of conduct, the customary standard to which behavior must conform.

The argument for the plaintiff is built upon the shifting meanings of such words as "wrong" and "wrongful," and shares their instability. What the plaintiff must show is "a wrong" to herself, i.e., a violation of her own right, and not merely a wrong to some one else, nor conduct "wrongful" because unsocial, but not "a wrong" to any one. We are told that one who drives at reckless speed through a crowded city street is guilty of a negligent act and, therefore, of a wrongful one irrespective of the consequences. Negligent the act is, and wrongful in the sense that it is unsocial, but wrongful and unsocial in relation to other travelers, only because the eye of vigilance perceives the risk of damage. If the same act were to be committed on a speedway or a race course, it would lose its wrongful quality. The risk reasonably to be perceived defines the duty to be obeyed, and risk imports relation; it is risk to another or to others within the range of apprehension [ ]. This does not mean, of course, that one who launches a destructive force is always relieved of liability if the force, though known to be destructive, pursues an unexpected path. "It was not necessary that the defendant should have had notice of the particular method in which an accident would occur, if the possibility of an accident was clear to the ordinarily prudent eye" (Munsey v. Webb, 231 U.S. 150, 156; [ ]). Some acts, such as shooting, are so imminently dangerous to any one who may come within reach of the missile, however unexpectedly, as to impose a duty of prevision not far from that of an insurer. Even today, and much oftener in earlier stages of the law, one acts sometimes at one's peril [ ]. Under this head, it may be, fall certain cases of what is known as transferred intent, an act willfully dangerous to A resulting by misadventure in injury to B (Talmage v. Smith, 101 Mich. 370, 374). These cases aside, wrong is defined in terms of the natural or probable, at least when unintentional (Parrot v. Wells, Fargo & Co. [The Nitro–Glycerine Case], 15 Wall. [82 U.S.] 524). The range of reasonable apprehension is at times a question for the court, and at times, if varying inferences are possible, a question for the jury. Here, by concession, there was nothing in the situation to suggest to the most cautious mind that the parcel wrapped in newspaper would spread wreckage through the station. If the guard had thrown it down knowingly and willfully, he would not have threatened the plaintiff's safety, so far as appearances could warn him. His conduct would not have involved, even then, an unreasonable probability of invasion of her bodily security. Liability can be no greater where the act is inadvertent.

Negligence, like risk, is thus a term of relation. Negligence in the abstract, apart from things related, is surely not a tort, if indeed it is understandable at all [ ]. Negligence is not a tort unless it results in the commission of a wrong, and the commission of a wrong imports the violation of a right, in this case, we are told, the right to be protected against interference with one's bodily security. But bodily security is protected, not against all forms of interference or aggression, but only against some. One who seeks redress at law does not make out a cause of action by showing without more that there has been damage to his person. If the harm was not willful, he must show that the act as to him had possibilities of danger so many and apparent as to entitle him to be protected against the doing of it though the harm was unintended. Affront to personality is still the keynote of the wrong. Confirmation of this view will be found in the history and development of the action on the case. Negligence as a basis of civil liability was unknown to mediaeval law (8 Holdsworth, History of English Law, p. 449; Street, Foundations of Legal Liability, vol. 1, pp. 189, 190). For damage to the person, the sole remedy was trespass and trespass did not lie in the absence of aggression, and that direct and personal [ ]. Liability for other damage, as where a servant without orders from the master does or omits something to the damage of another, is a plant of later growth [ ]. When it emerged out of the legal soil, it was thought of as a variant of trespass, an offshoot of the parent stock. This appears in the form of action, which was known as trespass on the case [ ]. The victim does not sue derivatively, or by right of subrogation, to vindicate an interest invaded in the person of another. Thus to view his cause of action is to ignore the fundamental difference between tort and crime (Holland, Jurisprudence [12th ed.], p. 328). He sues for breach of a duty owing to himself.

The law of causation, remote or proximate, is thus foreign to the case before us. The question of liability is always anterior to the question of the measure of the consequences that go with liability. If there is no tort to be redressed, there is no occasion to consider what damage might be recovered if there were a finding of a tort. We may assume, without deciding, that negligence, not at large or in the abstract, but in relation to the plaintiff, would entail liability for any and all consequences, however novel or extraordinary ([ ]; Smith v. London & S.W. Ry. Co., L.R. 6 C.P. 14; [ ]; cf. Matter of Polemis, L.R.1921, 3 K.B. 560; [ ]). There is room for argument that a distinction is to be drawn according to the diversity of interests invaded by the act, as where conduct negligent in that it threatens an insignificant invasion of an interest in property results in an unforeseeable invasion of an interest of another order, as, e.g., one of bodily security. Perhaps other distinctions may be necessary. We do not go into the question now. The consequences to be followed must first be rooted in a wrong.

The judgment of the Appellate Division and that of the Trial Term should be reversed, and the complaint dismissed, with costs in all courts.

■ ANDREWS, J. (dissenting). Assisting a passenger to board a train, the defendant's servant negligently knocked a package from his arms. It fell between the platform and the cars. Of its contents the servant knew and could know nothing. A violent explosion followed. The concussion broke some scales standing a considerable distance away. In falling they injured the plaintiff, an intending passenger.

This is Modern Trend

Upon these facts may she recover the damages she has suffered in an action brought against the master? The result we shall reach depends upon our theory as to the nature of negligence. Is it a relative concept— the breach of some duty owing to a particular person or to particular persons? Or where there is an act which unreasonably threatens the safety of others, is the doer liable for all its proximate consequences, even where they result in injury to one who would generally be thought to be outside the radius of danger? This is not a mere dispute as to words. We might not believe that to the average mind the dropping of the bundle would seem to involve the probability of harm to the plaintiff standing many feet away whatever might be the case as to the owner or to one so near as to be likely to be struck by its fall. If, however, we adopt the second hypothesis we have to inquire only as to the relation between cause and effect. We deal in terms of proximate cause, not of negligence.

. . .

But we are told that "there is no negligence unless there is in the particular case a legal duty to take care, and this duty must be one which is owed to the plaintiff himself and not merely to others." (Salmond, Torts [6th ed.], 24.) This I think too narrow a conception. Where there is the unreasonable act, and some right that may be affected there is negligence whether damage does or does not result. That is immaterial. Should we drive down Broadway at a reckless speed, we are negligent whether we strike an approaching car or miss it by an inch. The act itself is wrongful. It is a wrong not only to those who happen to be within the radius of danger but to all who might have been there—a wrong to the public at large. Such is the language of the street. . . .

It may well be that there is no such thing as negligence in the abstract. "Proof of negligence in the air, so to speak, will not do." In an empty world negligence would not exist. It does involve a relationship between man and his fellows. But not merely a relationship between man and those whom he might reasonably expect his act would injure. Rather, a relationship between him and those whom he does in fact injure. If his act has a tendency to harm some one, it harms him a mile away as surely as it does those on the scene. We now permit children to recover for the negligent killing of the father. It was never prevented on the theory that no duty was owing to them. A husband may be compensated for the loss of his wife's services. To say that the wrongdoer was negligent as to the husband as well as to the wife is merely an attempt to fit facts to theory. An insurance company paying a fire loss recovers its payment of the negligent incendiary. We speak of subrogation—of suing in the right of the insured. Behind the cloud of words is the fact they hide, that the act, wrongful as to the insured, has also injured the company. Even if it be true that the fault of father, wife or insured will prevent recovery, it is because we consider the original negligence not the proximate cause of the injury. [　]

In the well-known Polemis Case (1921, 3 K.B. 560), Scrutton, L.J., said that the dropping of a plank was negligent for it might injure "workman or cargo or ship." Because of either possibility the owner of the vessel was to be made good for his loss. The act being wrongful the doer was liable for its proximate results. Criticized and explained as this statement may have been, I think it states the law as it should be and as it is. [　]

The proposition is this: Every one owes to the world at large the duty of refraining from those acts that may unreasonably threaten the safety of others. Such an act occurs. Not only is he wronged to whom harm might reasonably be expected to result, but he also who is in fact injured, even if he be outside what would generally be thought the danger zone. There needs be duty due the one complaining but this is not a duty to a particular individual because as to him harm might be expected. Harm to some one being the natural result of the act, not only that one alone, but all those in fact injured may complain. We have never, I think, held otherwise. . . .

If this be so, we do not have a plaintiff suing by "derivation or succession." Her action is original and primary. Her claim is for a breach of duty to herself—not that she is subrogated to any right of action of the owner of the parcel or of a passenger standing at the scene of the explosion.

The right to recover damages rests on additional considerations. The plaintiff's rights must be injured, and this injury must be caused by the negligence. We build a dam, but are negligent as to its foundations. Breaking, it injures property down stream. We are not liable if all this happened because of some reason other than the insecure foundation. But when injuries do result from our unlawful act we are liable for the consequences. It does not matter that they are unusual, unexpected, unforeseen and unforeseeable. But there is one limitation. The damages must be so connected with the negligence that the latter may be said to be the proximate cause of the former.

These two words have never been given an inclusive definition. What is a cause in a legal sense, still more what is a proximate cause, depend in each case upon many considerations, as does the existence of negligence itself. Any philosophical doctrine of causation does not help us. A boy throws a stone into a pond. The ripples spread. The water level rises. The history of that pond is altered to all eternity. It will be altered by other causes also. Yet it will be forever the resultant of all causes combined. Each one will have an influence. How great only omniscience can say. You may speak of a chain, or if you please, a net. An analogy is of little aid. Each cause brings about future events. Without each the future would not be the same. Each is proximate in the sense it is essential. But that is not what we mean by the word. Nor on the other hand do we mean sole cause. There is no such thing.

Should analogy be thought helpful, however, I prefer that of a stream. The spring, starting on its journey, is joined by tributary after tributary. The river, reaching the ocean, comes from a hundred sources. No man may say whence any drop of water is derived. Yet for a time distinction may be possible. Into the clear creek, brown swamp water flows from the left. Later, from the right comes water stained by its clay bed. The three may remain for a space, sharply divided. But at last, inevitably no trace of separation remains. They are so commingled that all distinction is lost.

As we have said, we cannot trace the effect of an act to the end, if end there is. Again, however, we may trace it part of the way. A murder at Sarajevo may be the necessary antecedent to an assassination in London twenty years hence. An overturned lantern may burn all Chicago. We may follow the fire from the shed to the last building. We rightly say the fire started by the lantern caused its destruction.

A cause, but not the proximate cause. What we do mean by the word "proximate" is, that because of convenience, of public policy, of a rough sense of justice, the law arbitrarily declines to trace a series of events beyond a certain point. This is not logic. It is practical politics. Take our rule as to fires. Sparks from my burning haystack set on fire my house and my neighbor's. I may recover from a negligent railroad. He may not. Yet the wrongful act has directly harmed the one as the other. We may regret that the line was drawn just where it was, but drawn somewhere it had to be. We said the act of the railroad was not the proximate cause of our neighbor's fire. Cause it surely was. The words we used were simply indicative of our notions of public policy. Other courts think differently. But somewhere they reach the point where they cannot say the stream comes from any one source.

Take the illustration given in an unpublished manuscript by a distinguished and helpful writer on the law of torts. A chauffeur negligently collides with another car which is filled with dynamite, although he could not know it. An explosion follows. A, walking on the sidewalk nearby, is killed. B, sitting in a window of a building opposite, is cut by flying glass. C, likewise sitting in a window a block away, is similarly injured. And a further illustration. A nursemaid, ten blocks away, startled by the noise, involuntarily drops a baby from her arms to the walk. We are told that C may not recover while A may. As to B it is a question for court or jury. We will all agree that the baby might not. Because, we are again told, the chauffeur had no reason to believe his conduct involved any risk of injuring either C or the baby. As to them he was not negligent.

But the chauffeur, being negligent in risking the collision, his belief that the scope of the harm he might do would be limited is immaterial. His act unreasonably jeopardized the safety of any one who might be affected by it. C's injury and that of the baby were directly traceable to the collision. Without that, the injury would not have happened. C had the right to sit in his office, secure from such dangers. The baby was entitled to use the sidewalk with reasonable safety.

The true theory is, it seems to me, that the injury to C, if in truth he is to be denied recovery, and the injury to the baby is that their several injuries were not the proximate result of the negligence. And here not what the chauffeur had reason to believe would be the result of his conduct, but what the prudent would foresee, may have a bearing. May have some bearing, for the problem of proximate cause is not to be solved by any one consideration.

It is all a question of expediency. There are no fixed rules to govern our judgment. There are simply matters of which we may take account. We have in a somewhat different connection spoken of "the stream of events." We have asked whether that stream was deflected—whether it was forced into new and unexpected channels. [ ] This is rather rhetoric than law. There is in truth little to guide us other than common sense.

There are some hints that may help us. The proximate cause, involved as it may be with many other causes, must be, at the least, something without which the event would not happen. The court must ask itself whether there was a natural and continuous sequence between cause and effect. Was the one a substantial factor in producing the other? Was there a direct connection between them, without too many intervening causes? Is the effect of cause on result not too attenuated? Is the cause likely, in the usual judgment of mankind, to produce the result? Or by the exercise of prudent foresight could the result be foreseen? Is the result too remote from the cause, and here we consider remoteness in time and space. (Bird v. St. Paul F. & M. Ins. Co., 224 N.Y. 47, where we passed upon the construction of a contract—but something was also said on this subject.) Clearly we must so consider, for the greater the distance either in time or space, the more surely do other causes intervene to affect the result. When a lantern is overturned the firing of a shed is a fairly direct consequence. Many things contribute to the spread of the conflagration—the force of the wind, the direction and width of streets, the character of intervening structures, other factors. We draw an uncertain and wavering line, but draw it we must as best we can.

Once again, it is all a question of fair judgment, always keeping in mind the fact that we endeavor to make a rule in each case that will be practical and in keeping with the general understanding of mankind.

Here another question must be answered. In the case supposed it is said, and said correctly, that the chauffeur is liable for the direct effect of the explosion although he had no reason to suppose it would follow a collision. "The fact that the injury occurred in a different manner than that which might have been expected does not prevent the chauffeur's negligence from being in law the cause of the injury." But the natural results of a negligent act—the results which a prudent man would or should foresee—do have a bearing upon the decision as to proximate cause.

We have said so repeatedly. What should be foreseen? No human fore-sight would suggest that a collision itself might injure one a block away. On the contrary, given an explosion, such a possibility might be reasonably expected. I think the direct connection, the foresight of which the courts speak, assumes prevision of the explosion, for the immediate results of which, at least, the chauffeur is responsible.

It may be said this is unjust. Why? In fairness he should make good every injury flowing from his negligence. Not because of tenderness toward him we say he need not answer for all that follows his wrong. We look back to the catastrophe, the fire kindled by the spark, or the explosion. We trace the consequences—not indefinitely, but to a certain point. And to aid us in fixing that point we ask what might ordinarily be expected to follow the fire or the explosion.

This last suggestion is the factor which must determine the case before us. The act upon which defendant's liability rests is knocking an apparent-ly harmless package onto the platform. The act was negligent. For its proximate consequences the defendant is liable. If its contents were broken, to the owner; if it fell upon and crushed a passenger's foot, then to him. If it exploded and injured one in the immediate vicinity, to him also as to A in the illustration. Mrs. Palsgraf was standing some distance away. How far cannot be told from the record—apparently twenty-five or thirty feet. Perhaps less. Except for the explosion, she would not have been injured. We are told by the appellant in his brief "it cannot be denied that the explosion was the direct cause of the plaintiff's injuries." So it was a substantial factor in producing the result—there was here a natural and continuous sequence—direct connection. The only intervening cause was that instead of blowing her to the ground the concussion smashed the weighing machine which in turn fell upon her. There was no remoteness in time, little in space. And surely, given such an explosion as here it needed no great foresight to predict that the natural result would be to injure one on the platform at no greater distance from its scene than was the plaintiff. Just how no one might be able to predict. Whether by flying fragments, by broken glass, by wreckage of machines or structures no one could say. But injury in some form was most probable.

Under these circumstances I cannot say as a matter of law that the plaintiff's injuries were not the proximate result of the negligence. That is all we have before us. The court refused to so charge. No request was made to submit the matter to the jury as a question of fact, even would that have been proper upon the record before us.

The judgment appealed from should be affirmed, with costs.

■ POUND, LEHMAN and KELLOGG, JJ., concur with CARDOZO, CH. J.; ANDREWS, J., dissents in opinion in which CRANE and O'BRIEN, JJ., concur.

NOTES AND QUESTIONS

1. Motion for reargument was denied, 249 N.Y. 511, 164 N.E. 564 (1928), with the following opinion:

If we assume that the plaintiff was nearer the scene of the explosion than the prevailing opinion would suggest, she was not so near that injury from a falling package, not known to contain explosives, would be within the range of reasonable prevision.

How close would have been close enough for the majority? The denial was unanimous with the three dissenters concurring in the result.

2. In what way do the facts of *Palsgraf* differ from those of *Polemis and Wagon Mound*? How might the facts of *Wagon Mound* be altered to resemble *Palsgraf*?

3. Are there differences between the approach taken by Judge Cardozo and that taken by Viscount Simonds in *Wagon Mound*? Compare the reasons for limiting liability for negligence offered by Viscount Simonds and Judge Andrews.

4. How might Judge Cardozo analyze the hypothetical involving A, B, and C that is discussed in the next-to-last paragraph of *Wagon Mound*? How would Judge Andrews analyze it?

5. What is the role of proximate cause in *Wagon Mound*? In the Cardozo analysis?

6. How are the functions of judge and jury allocated under the Cardozo view? Under the Andrews view?

7. In what types of cases are Cardozo and Andrews most likely to reach different results?

8. How might Judge Cardozo's suggested distinction between the risk of an insignificant invasion of property and the occurrence of bodily injury work? He suggests other distinctions might be desirable. Assume plaintiff is standing four feet from the railroad agents. Instead of the package falling on P's foot it hits the ground and explodes, taking out one of P's eyes. Would it make sense to distinguish between a risk to the feet and a risk to the eyes?

9. Toward the end of his opinion, Judge Cardozo says that to permit the plaintiff to sue "derivatively" to "vindicate an interest invaded in the person of another" would be to "ignore the fundamental difference between tort and crime." What does he mean?

10. Do the *Palsgraf* facts suggest any other theory on which plaintiff might have been more successful in a suit against the railroad? How should the case have been analyzed if plaintiff had argued that the railroad's negligence was the failure to secure adequately the weighing scale?

11. *Recurring fact patterns of causation questions.* Even though proximate cause cases individually seem freakish, some fact patterns have emerged with some regularity. Consider the following.

a. *Rescue.* Judge Cardozo had previously decided a case in which plaintiff was hurt while trying to rescue his cousin who had fallen from defendant's train due to the negligence of the crew. Wagner v. International Railway Co., 232 N.Y. 176, 133 N.E. 437 (1921). The trial judge had charged that the negligence toward the cousin would not lead to liability to the rescuer unless the jury found that the train conductor had invited the plaintiff to partake in the rescue and had accompanied him with a lantern. Rejecting that approach, Judge Cardozo wrote:

> Danger invites rescue. The cry of distress is the summons to relief. The law does not ignore these reactions of the mind in tracing conduct to its consequences. It recognizes them as normal. It places their effects within the range of the natural and probable. The wrong that imperils life is a wrong to the imperilled victim; it is a wrong also to his rescuer. . . . The risk of rescue, if only it be not wanton, is born of the occasion. The emergency begets the man. The wrongdoer may not have foreseen the coming of a deliverer. He is accountable as if he had.

Is this consistent with *Palsgraf*? What about a case in which the area is so desolate that the defendant could not reasonably anticipate anyone around to attempt to rescue someone defendant is negligently harming or threatening? Judge Cardozo then turned to another issue:

> The defendant says that we must stop, in following the chain of causes, when action ceases to be "instinctive." By this, is meant, it seems, that rescue is at the peril of the rescuer, unless spontaneous and immediate. If there has been time to deliberate, if impulse has given way to judgment, one cause, it is said, has spent its force, and another has intervened. In this case, the plaintiff walked more than four hundred feet in going to Herbert's aid. He had time to reflect and weigh; impulse had been followed by choice; and choice, in the defendant's view, intercepts and breaks the sequence. We find no warrant for thus shortening the chain of jural causes. We may assume, though we are not required to decide, that peril and rescue must be in substance one transaction; that the sight of the one must have aroused the impulse to the other; in short, that there must be unbroken continuity between the commission of the wrong and the effort to avert its consequences. If all this be assumed, the defendant is not aided. Continuity in such circumstances is not broken by the exercise of volition. . . . The law does not discriminate between the rescuer oblivious of peril and the one who counts the cost. It is enough that the act, whether impulsive or deliberate, is the child of the occasion.

In his Cogitations on Torts 35 (1954), Seavey doubts "that an airplane pilot who negligently crashes on a mountain, would be liable to an injured and non-negligent member of a rescue party." Is that consistent with *Wagner*? Is it sound? Might it matter whether the rescuer is bitten by a snake, struck by lightning, or hurt in the crash of a helicopter that has joined the search? Injuries to professional rescuers are discussed at p. 425, infra.

In Moore v. Shah, 90 App.Div.2d 389, 458 N.Y.S.2d 33 (1982), the court refused to extend the rescuer doctrine to an adult son who donated a kidney to his father. The kidney was needed because of the defendant's alleged malpractice. The court refused to impose a duty simply because it was foreseeable that a close relative would be likely to donate a needed organ. Here, the action was not spontaneous or instantaneous. Instead, the son's action was "deliberate and reflective, not made under the pressures of an emergency situation, and significantly, at a time after defendant's alleged negligent acts." Is *Wagner* sufficiently distinguished?

b. *Time.* In Firman v. Sacia, 7 App.Div.2d 579, 184 N.Y.S.2d 945 (1959), plaintiff alleged that as the result of defendant's negligent driving, he struck a three-year-old boy named Springstead who sustained serious brain injuries that induced him, seven years later, to shoot the plaintiff. Plaintiff alleged that at the time of the shooting Springstead was "unable to realize the nature and consequences of his act, was not able to resist pulling the trigger of the rifle, and was deprived of capacity to govern his conduct in accordance with reason"—though insanity or incompetency was not claimed. The trial judge's dismissal of the complaint was upheld on appeal:

> Assuming, as we must, that defendant's conduct was negligent as it related to the rights of the Springstead child, the fact of negligence was not, of course, thereby established for all purposes or as necessarily definitive of defendant's relationship to others. If, in his conduct, there was no risk of danger to this infant plaintiff "reasonably to be perceived", there was no breach of duty, or negligence, as to him. [*Palsgraf*] In this case, the order and judgment seem to us sustainable on the grounds that, as in *Palsgraf*, the risk was not "within the range of apprehension". [ ]

Does a long time interval between wrongful act and injury necessarily mean the risk is outside "the range of apprehension?" Recall the discussions in *Albala,* p. 138, supra, involving the negligently performed abortion and in *Hymowitz,* p. 329, supra.

Cases involving long time periods between the act and the harm are not usually barred by the statute of limitations. Tort limitations usually start to run at the time of the plaintiff's injury. They have traditionally been even longer in the case of injuries to minors, sometimes allowing the minor to wait until majority before suing. Recently, several states, especially in medical malpractice cases, have shortened the period for minors (and also for adults). On the other hand, as *Hymowitz* indicates, several states, either by statute or by judicial decision, have lengthened some statutes of limitation to protect plaintiffs who may not realize that they have been injured. This is especially likely to occur with conditions that have long incubation periods, such as asbestosis or slowly developing cancers. For further discussion, see Rheingold, The Hymowitz Decision—Practical Aspects of New York DES Litigation, 55 Bklyn.L.Rev. 883 (1989); Green, The Paradox of Statutes of Limitations in Toxic Standards Litigation, 76 Calif.L.Rev. 965 (1988).

c. *Distance.* Defendant negligently collided with another car and careened off the road, hitting a box that contained the master traffic signal devices for several intersections including one two miles away. The lights at that intersection jammed and in the ensuing confusion, plaintiff was hurt in a collision. Liability was imposed. Ferroggiaro v. Bowline, 153 Cal.App.2d 759, 315 P.2d 446 (1957).

     d. *Fire.* The fire rule to which Judge Andrews referred is unique to New York and originated in Ryan v. New York Central R. Co., 35 N.Y. 210 (1866). Sparks from defendant's negligently maintained engine ignited one of its sheds and the fire spread to other buildings, including plaintiff's. The court denied recovery:

> I prefer to place my opinion upon the ground that, in the one case, to wit, the destruction of the building upon which the sparks were thrown by the negligent act of the party sought to be charged, the result was to have been anticipated the moment the fire was communicated to the building; that its destruction was the ordinary and natural result of its being fired. In the second, third or twenty-fourth case, as supposed, the destruction of the building was not a natural and expected result of the first firing. That a building upon which sparks and cinders fall should be destroyed or seriously injured must be expected, but that the fire should spread and other buildings be consumed, is not a necessary or [a] usual result. That it is possible, and that it is not unfrequent, cannot be denied. The result, however, depends, not upon any necessity of a further communication of the fire, but upon a concurrence of accidental circumstances, such as the degree of the heat, the state of the atmosphere, the condition and materials of the adjoining structures and the direction of the wind. These are accidental and varying circumstances. The party has no control over them, and is not responsible for their effects.

Later New York cases have extended the liability somewhat, but the fundamental limitation remains. Does Judge Andrews adequately distinguish this line of cases? Virtually all other states reject this limitation.

     For further reading on *Palsgraf*, see J. Noonan, Persons and Masks of the Law, Ch. 4 (1976); Green, The Palsgraf Case, 30 Colum.L.Rev. 789 (1930); Prosser, Palsgraf Revisited, 52 Mich.L.Rev. 1 (1953); Seavey, Mr. Justice Cardozo and the Law of Torts, 39 Colum.L.Rev. 20 (1939); 52 Harv.L.Rev. 372 (1939); 48 Yale L.J. 390 (1939).

     The Kinsman cases. Several of the issues raised in the foregoing proximate cause cases came together in Petition of Kinsman Transit Co., 338 F.2d 708 (2d Cir.1964), cert denied 380 U.S. 944 (1965). The Buffalo River "with many turns and bends" was full of floating ice in winter. A thaw had begun and two ice jams were moving downstream under strong current. Because its crew responded inadequately to the impending danger, the Shiras, owned by Kinsman, was torn loose from its moorings at the Concrete Elevator dock operated by Continental and began floating downstream. The Shiras crashed into a properly moored ship, the Tewksbury, tearing it loose, and both ships (one 525 feet long and the other 425 feet long) careened down the river (whose channel was 177 feet wide) toward a lift bridge operated by the city, situated three miles from the Continental dock. Because of the city's negligence, the bridge was not raised, and the two ships crashed into it, destroying it and some surrounding property. The wreckage of the ships and the bridge formed a dam that caused the ice and the water to back up causing property to sustain flooding damage as far back upstream as the Continental dock. This case involves claims for the property damage. In a complex group of rulings, the trial judge found liability against Continental, Kinsman, and the City of Buffalo.

The court of appeals, in an opinion by Judge Friendly, affirmed (over a dissent as to the city). As to Kinsman, the timing of the negligence of the crew was such that what followed was foreseeable. (What new question would have been raised if the flooding had damaged property upstream from the dock?) As to the city, the majority once again concluded that the conditions that day made it reasonably foreseeable that a dam might be created at the bridge if the span were not lifted in time and that upriver flooding might result. (How would you analyze a case against the city brought by flooded property owners upstream from the dock?)

The difficult case was Continental, which was negligent because of failure to inspect a "deadman" device at its dock over an extended period of time. The court thought that the negligence in failing to maintain equipment was not time-specific. This raised the question of the liability of a defendant who could have foreseen the ships crashing into property as they made their way down the river, but not the flooding that actually occurred. Although Judge Friendly stated his agreement with the result in *Wagon Mound* because the defendant there "had no reason to believe that the floating furnace oil would burn," his opinion also conveyed the spirit of *Polemis*:

> On that view [*Wagon Mound*] simply applies the principle which excludes liability where the injury sprang from a hazard different from that which was improperly risked, [ ]. Although some language in the judgment goes beyond this, we would find it difficult to understand why one who had failed to use the care required to protect others in the light of expectable forces should be exonerated when the very risks that rendered his conduct negligent produced other and more serious consequences to such persons than were fairly foreseeable when he fell short of what the law demanded. Foreseeability of danger is necessary to render conduct negligent; where as here the damage was caused by just those forces whose existence required the exercise of greater care than was taken—the current, the ice, and the physical mass of the Shiras—the incurring of consequences other and greater than foreseen does not make the conduct less culpable or provide a reasoned basis for insulation.[9]

9. The contrasting situation is illustrated by the familiar instances of the running down of a pedestrian by a safely driven but carelessly loaded car, or of the explosion of unlabeled rat poison, inflammable but not known to be, placed near a coffee burner.

[ ] Exoneration of the defendant in such cases rests on the basis that a negligent actor is responsible only for harm the risk of which was increased by the *negligent aspect* of his conduct. [ ]

. . .

> The weight of authority in this country rejects the limitation of damages to consequences foreseeable at the time of the negligent conduct when the consequences are "direct," and the damage, although other and greater than expectable, is of the same general sort that was risked. . . .

> We see no reason why an actor engaging in conduct which entails a large risk of small damage and a small risk of other and greater damage, of the same general sort, from the same forces, and to the same class of persons, should be relieved of responsibility for the latter simply because the chance of its occurrence, if viewed alone, may not have been large enough to require the exercise of care.

Was the harm that occurred due to the crew's negligence of the "same general sort" as might have been reasonably expectable from that negligence? Are you persuaded that the *Kinsman* facts are different from the cases in the court's footnote 9?

After quoting the phrase from Judge Andrews that decisions in these cases were "all a question of expediency . . . of fair judgment," Judge Friendly observed that it "would be pleasant if greater certainty were possible, [ ], but the many efforts that have been made at defining the *locus* of the 'uncertain and wavering line' [Andrews], are not very promising; what courts do in such cases makes better sense than what they, or others, say." Would Judge Cardozo agree? Viscount Simonds?

Kinsman II.   Another set of claims arose from the closure of the bridge. 388 F.2d 821 (2d Cir.1968). Here the court rejected claims based on the higher costs of unloading ships due to the inability of tugs to reach them, and the costs of obtaining substitute grain to fulfil contracts when grain could not be moved to elevators above the bridge. The "instant claims occurred only because the downed bridge made it impossible to move traffic along the river. Under all the circumstances of this case, we hold that the connection between the defendants' negligence and the claimants' damages is too tenuous and remote to permit recovery":

> In the final analysis, the circumlocution whether posed in terms of "foreseeability," "duty," "proximate cause," "remoteness," etc. seems unavoidable. As we have previously noted [in *Kinsman I*], we return to Justice Andrews' frequently quoted statement [in *Palsgraf*] "It is all a question of expediency . . . of fair judgment, always keeping in mind the fact that we endeavor to make a rule in each case that will be practical and in keeping with the general understanding of mankind."

Kinsman II was distinguished in *People Express*, p. 282, supra. Although tortfeasors "are liable only for the results falling within the foreseeable risks of their negligent conduct," that condition was satisfied in *People Express*. The economic losses in *People Express* were "the natural and probable consequences of a defendant's negligence in the sense that they are reasonably to be anticipated in view of defendant's capacity to have foreseen that the particular plaintiff or identifiable class of plaintiff, is demonstrably within the risk created by defendant's negligence." For the court in *People Express*, proximate causation "is that combination of 'logic, common sense, justice, policy and precedent' that fixes a point in a chain of events, some foreseeable and some unforeseeable, beyond which the law will bar recovery. [   ] The standard of particular foreseeability may be successfully employed to determine whether the economic injury was proximately caused, i.e., whether the particular harm that occurred is compensable, just as it informs the question whether a duty exists." In which types of cases do duty and proximate cause raise substantially the same issue?

For further reading on proximate cause, see Green, Rationale of Proximate Cause (1927); H. Hart and A. Honore, Causation in the Law (1959); C. Morris and C. Robert Morris, Morris on Torts, Ch. VII (2d ed. 1980); Calabresi, Concerning Cause and the Law of Torts: An Essay for Harry Kalven, Jr., 43 U.Chi.L.Rev. 69 (1975); Kelley, Proximate Cause in Negligence Law: History, Theory, and the Present Darkness, 69 Wash. U.L.Q. 49 (1991).

CHAPTER VI

DEFENSES

A. THE PLAINTIFF'S FAULT

The foregoing chapters have explored the prima facie case that the plaintiff must present in order to establish liability for negligence (except for damages, a subject discussed in Chapter X). But the common law has recognized several defenses against the plaintiff's claim. By far the most common is the defendant's contention that even if defendant was negligent toward the plaintiff, the plaintiff was careless about his or her own safety and was "contributorily" negligent. This defense appears as early as 1809 in England and seems to be well established in this country by 1850—the time of Brown v. Kendall, p. 26, supra. We have already encountered the defense in a number of cases, such as the *Goodman–Pokora* sequence, p. 48, supra.

1. CONTRIBUTORY NEGLIGENCE

The common law elements of the defense parallel those of the basic negligence claim—except in the sense that any duty owed is to one's self rather than to others. An adapted risk calculus is used to determine the reasonableness of the plaintiff's conduct. The conduct must be an actual cause of the plaintiff's harm. This is illustrated by Hightower v. Paulson Truck Lines, Inc., 277 Or. 65, 559 P.2d 872 (1977), in which plaintiff's recovery was not affected, despite his having followed too closely on the highway, because defendant "suddenly slowed" without warning. A jury could have found that even if the plaintiff had been following at a reasonably safe distance, he still could not have stopped in time.

The plaintiff's negligence must also be a proximate cause of the plaintiff's harm. For example, assume P is warned not to stand on a high platform because it is shaky and may not hold P's weight. Without justification P disregards the advice, stands on the platform, and is hurt when an adjacent wall collapses as the result of defendant's negligence and knocks P from the platform to the ground below. Assuming P is hurt, his or her negligence may have causally contributed to the injury, but was it a proximate cause or was the unexpected result one that absolves plaintiff of the unreasonableness?

Similarly, what if the plaintiff who claims malpractice in the emergency room of a hospital was there because he drove carelessly, or was shot committing a crime, or botched a suicide attempt? See Whitehead v. Linkous, 404 So.2d 377 (Fla.App.1981)(suicide attempt irrelevant to malpractice claim).

Recall the assertion in Brown v. Kendall that the plaintiff had the burden of proving freedom from contributory negligence. Many states have switched that burden to the defendant. Is one approach more clearly appropriate than the other?

When the defense of contributory negligence was established, the effect was a total bar to recovery. Thus, the traditional negligence law operated on an all-or-nothing basis. As we shall soon see, this feature of the system produced a range of legal doctrines to ease the impact of the contributory negligence defense on certain plaintiffs.

Despite the apparent symmetry, courts sometimes have appeared to make contributory negligence more difficult to establish than the elements might suggest. Rescuers who are hurt going to the aid of others would often be barred by a straightforward application of the risk calculus because the risks attending the attempted rescue often clearly outweigh the expected gain both to the victim and the rescuer. Nevertheless, the courts usually allow these cases to reach juries by declaring them to involve issues on which reasonable persons could differ.*

Some courts have not imposed the reasonable person standard on plaintiffs with mental or psychological difficulties who have hurt themselves due in part to their limitations. In Cowan v. Doering, 111 N.J. 451, 545 A.2d 159 (1988), a patient known to be suicidal jumped to her death while in the care of defendant physicians and nurses. The court imposed a duty on the part of defendants that included taking into account the plaintiff's known tendencies. On the question of contributory negligence, the court refused to use the reasonable person standard. It noted that the "modern trend appears to favor the use of a capacity-based standard for the contributory negligence of mentally disturbed plaintiffs." This standard "tolerates a reduced standard of care for such persons." It measures the conduct of a mentally disturbed plaintiff in light of his or her capacity. Such a rule did not eliminate contributory negligence—but judged it on a "capacity-based standard." To impose a due care standard in this type of case might "enable a tortfeasor to escape liability, [and] can indirectly lessen responsibility for wrongful conduct and defeat the goals of tort law."

How would this court analyze a case in which two bicyclists collided—if it turned out that the one who was hurt was "mentally disturbed"? What if the one who was not hurt was the one who was mentally disturbed? What is the justification for this asymmetry? Would it apply in a two-car crash in which both drivers are hurt and in which one is "mentally disturbed"?

---

* Might a lack of due care for one's own safety create liability toward others? In Carney v. Buyea, 271 App.Div. 338, 65 N.Y.S.2d 902 (1946), defendant parked her car on an incline, walked about twenty feet in front of the car and bent down to remove something from the road. Her car started downhill and plaintiff, standing nearby, rushed to her rescue, and was struck by the car while pushing her to safety. Can you develop a theory for establishing negligence? See also Talbert v. Talbert, 22 Misc.2d 782, 199 N.Y.S.2d 212 (1960), in which plaintiff was hurt while attempting to prevent the defendant's suicide attempt.

In fact, however, the court in *Cowan* did not apply this approach in the case itself because "the plaintiff's inability to exercise reasonable self-care attributable to her mental ability was itself subsumed within the duty of care defendants owed her." The result was that contributory negligence was eliminated from the case. What does "subsumed" mean here?

Statutes. A similar result to *Cowan* is reached by statute in a small number of cases in which the statutory command is understood to be an effort to protect some group against its own inability to protect itself. In those cases, courts have disregarded the contributory negligence of a member of that group. See, e.g. Chainani v. Board of Education, 1995 WL 641390 (N.Y.1995), discussing a statute requiring school bus operators to instruct students in crossing streets, to flash red lights, and to wait until students disembarking from the bus had crossed the street. The court had already decided that the purpose was to protect the school children against their own negligence, and that that purpose would be thwarted if a child's contributory negligence were a defense.

Relatively few statutes have been given such effect. In Feisthamel v. State, 89 App.Div.2d 756, 453 N.Y.S.2d 904 (1982), a nine-year-old girl was badly cut when she tried to walk through the glass drum that was wrapped around a revolving glass door. The girl had mistakenly believed that she had reached an exit point from the revolving door. The state, which had violated a statutory obligation to mark glass revolving doors, asserted contributory negligence. The trial court accepted the defense and reduced damages by half. On appeal, the court, 3–2, concluded that the statute "was not enacted for the protection of a definite class of persons from a hazard which they themselves are incapable of avoiding." The dissenters argued that the statute's purpose was to protect users of glass doors from colliding with the glass due to their inability to perceive it as such. They would have awarded full damages. See generally, Prosser, Contributory Negligence as Defense to Violation of Statute, 32 Minn.L.Rev. 105 (1948).

Even if contributory negligence was found in a particular case, several rules emerged over the years that limited the applicability of the defense.

Recklessness. Virtually all courts decided that contributory negligence was a defense only in cases of negligence. If the misconduct of the defendant was found to be more serious—recklessness or willful misconduct—the appropriate defense would have been "contributory recklessness" or "contributory willful misconduct." Contributory negligence was totally irrelevant in such cases and the plaintiff recovered all of his or her damages. Why?

Consider Restatement (Second) § 500, which provides the following approach to the common law aspects of recklessness, usually considered to be synonymous with willful or wanton misconduct:

> The actor's conduct is in reckless disregard of the safety of another
> if he does an act or intentionally fails to do an act which it is his
> duty to the other to do, knowing or having reason to know of facts

which would lead a reasonable man to realize, not only that his conduct creates an unreasonable risk of physical harm to another, but also that such risk is substantially greater than that which is necessary to make his conduct negligent.

Apart from making contributory negligence inapplicable, recklessness has been most important in connection with guest statute cases, discussed at p. 89, supra, and with the possibility that plaintiff might obtain punitive damages, discussed at p. 650, infra.

Last Clear Chance.   Contributory negligence was also disregarded under circumstances which came to be called "last clear chance." In these cases the plaintiff behaved carelessly and got into a dangerous situation that led to injury. In response to the defense of contributory negligence, the plaintiff claimed that even though he was careless for his own safety, the defendant had, but failed to utilize, the "last clear chance" to avoid the injury to plaintiff. The doctrine is first mentioned in Davies v. Mann, 10 M. & W. 546, 152 Eng.Rep. 588 (1842), in which defendant ran into a donkey that plaintiff had carelessly left tied in the roadway.

Two types of dangerous situations triggered the doctrine of last clear chance. In one, the plaintiff had gotten into a position of "helpless peril" and was no longer able to take protective steps. In that situation most courts invoked last clear chance against a defendant who knew or should have known of the plaintiff's plight while still able to avoid the harm by the exercise of due care. The other type of last clear chance case involved a plaintiff who was oblivious to the danger but who could, if behaving reasonably, become aware of it and avoid harm up to the last minute. Here most courts required that before the doctrine could be applied the defendant driver had to have actual knowledge of plaintiff's danger in time to avoid harm by the exercise of due care.

Generally, the doctrine was regarded as having a chronological aspect. Thus, a claim that the defendant could not stop in time because of brake failure would not have invoked last clear chance because most courts required that the defendant be able to do something in the period after the plaintiff's peril starts. These intricacies are discussed in detail in Restatement (Second) of Torts §§ 479 and 480.

When last clear chance was held applicable, the fact that the plaintiff was contributorily negligent became totally irrelevant and the plaintiff recovered all appropriate damages with no offset.

Refusal to Impute Contributory Negligence.   We have already observed that on occasion the law will impute the negligence of one person to another. The most significant example of imputed primary negligence is respondeat superior, the doctrine that has given rise to the imposition of liability on employers. On the plaintiff's side, we have also seen examples of cases in which the courts have reached a similar result by calling one action derivative from another, thus giving the person bringing the second action only the rights that the first person had.

These imputation rules do not necessarily reflect a single ethical or economic rationale. Respondeat superior, for example, served the important function of providing a class of defendants who were more likely than their servants to be able to respond to the damage awards that the courts were imposing and might be able to make the entire operation safer. On the other hand, calling an action "derivative" rather than "independent" in the consortium and wrongful death cases appears to spring more from a notion of regarding the cluster of plaintiffs as a group, and then finding it "unfair" for the defendant to owe a greater obligation to some "indirect" plaintiffs than to the original victim.

Many of the rules that impute negligence to persons as defendants do not have the same effect when the person becomes a plaintiff. The most important of these arises in automobile accidents. This is discussed in Continental Auto Lease Corp. v. Campbell, 19 N.Y.2d 350, 227 N.E.2d 28, 280 N.Y.S.2d 123 (1967), in which Kamman, who rented a car from plaintiff, was involved in an accident with Shepard. Both drivers were negligent. Continental sued Shepard for the property damage to its car. The court rejected the claim that Kamman's negligence should be imputed to Continental. The court noted that the goal of vicarious liability against defendants was to protect the injured plaintiff but that imputing negligence to defeat actions had the effect of leaving innocent victims uncompensated. Nor was it relevant that Continental was benefiting financially from the rental. It had no control or interest in where the car was driven nor did it have a right to control the driver.

Imputation of contributory negligence reached its peak in the late nineteenth century. Its two most significant manifestations were (a) imputing the negligence of a driver or engineer to all the passengers on the vehicle, preventing their suits against other parties whose negligence contributed to the collision; and (b) imputing to the child a parent's negligence in failing to protect that child.

If a child is hurt through the combined negligence of its mother and a stranger, we generally no longer impute the mother's negligence to bar the child's action. Indeed, as we have seen, we may even permit the child to sue the mother as well as the stranger, or we may permit the child to sue the stranger and then—depending on other considerations—allow the stranger to try to obtain contribution from the mother. See the discussion of these various issues in LaBier v. Pelletier, 665 A.2d 1013 (Me.1995)(refusing to impute a mother's negligence to her child in an action against a stranger and noting that the stranger may file a third-party claim against the mother; even if the parents might "realize some incidental benefit from the child's recovery, it is unfair to remedy that problem by shifting the windfall to the nonparental tortfeasor.")

The "derivative" questions aside, virtually all imputed contributory negligence has been eliminated over the years. The rigors of the contributory negligence doctrine and the changing perceptions of the relationships involved have undoubtedly played important roles in its demise.

The Jury's Role. Surely the most modern technique for ameliorating the perceived harshness of the all-or-nothing contributory negligence rule (prior to the adoption of comparative negligence) was the increased frequency with which courts found that reasonable persons could differ over the characterization of the plaintiff's conduct—so that a jury question was presented. Observers asserted that most juries rejected the judge's instruction to return a defense verdict if they found any contributory negligence—even the most minimal contributory fault, so long as it proximately related to the harm. The belief was that the jury simply reduced the plaintiff's damages by some amount rather than returning a defense verdict. Consider the following passage from Alibrandi v. Helmsley, 63 Misc.2d 997, 314 N.Y.S.2d 95 (1970), in which, in a trial to the court, the judge assumed that defendant was negligent and concluded that the plaintiff was contributorily negligent. He then continued:

> Plaintiff's injuries were not trivial. I am as confident as one can be about these matters that, had the case been tried to a jury, the jury would have determined the sum of plaintiff's damages in a substantial amount, deducted a portion equivalent to the degree of his negligence, and returned a verdict for the difference. In short, as every trial lawyer knows, the jury would likely have ignored its instructions on contributory negligence and applied a standard of comparative negligence.

> It would be comfortable for me simply to guess what the jury's verdict would have been and then file a one-sentence decision holding defendants liable in that amount. Comfortable but false. My duty is to apply the law as I understand it, and I do not understand that, no matter what a jury might do, a Judge may pretend to make a decision on the basis of contributory negligence while actually deciding on comparative negligence.

Did the judge reach the right decision? Did the plaintiff's attorney commit malpractice by not demanding a jury in the case? Does the judge's analysis reflect badly on the legal system? The jury system?

From the plaintiff's standpoint, a basic problem was that sometimes contributory negligence was so clear that no self-respecting judge could permit the issue to go to the jury. In other words, the device of sending a close case to the jury worked only when the closeness was in the question of whether plaintiff had been negligent at all—not in cases in which plaintiff's negligence was clear, but relatively minor. Of course, plaintiffs also faced the prospect that some juries might actually follow the judge's instructions!

2. COMPARATIVE NEGLIGENCE

Until the late 1960s, only a handful of states had abandoned the all-or-nothing contributory negligence approach. These few states adopted a system called "comparative negligence" in which a negligent plaintiff's recovery depended on how serious P's negligence was compared to the defendant's. Three principal versions were employed. In one, called "pure" comparative negligence, the plaintiff who was 90 percent to blame for an accident could recover 10 percent of the damages from the defendant who was found to be 10 percent at fault. (A defendant who was also hurt in the accident could recover 90 percent of damages from the plaintiff.) The second and third versions were lumped together as a "modified" system. Under one variant, a plaintiff who was at fault could recover as under the pure system but only so long as that negligence was "not as great as" the defendant's. Under the other variant, plaintiff could recover as under the pure system but only so long as that negligence was "no greater than" the defendant's. What distinguishes these two modified variants?

In addition to the states, the federal statute regulating injuries to railroad workers, discussed in detail at p. 752, infra, used a pure system. Still, comparative negligence remained largely a reform proposal at the beginning of the 1970s.

Today, virtually all states have adopted some version of comparative negligence. In Williams v. Delta Int'l Machinery Corp., 619 So.2d 1330 (Ala.1993), the court concluded that although 46 states had adopted comparative negligence, it would decline: after "exhaustive study and these lengthy deliberations, the majority of this Court, for various reasons, has decided that we should not abandon the doctrine of contributory negligence, which has been the law in Alabama for approximately 162 years."

Of the states that have adopted comparative negligence, about a dozen use the "pure" version, and almost all the others are divided between those adhering to the "not as great as" and the "no greater than" variants. This flood of legislation was undoubtedly due in part to growing unhappiness with the harshness of contributory negligence. But the flood seems to have received a considerable boost from efforts to undermine proponents of no-fault auto insurance, who were arguing that too many auto accident victims were getting no tort compensation because of the contributory negligence rule. We discuss the no-fault approach in Chapter XI.

Although most of the action in the 1970s and early 1980s occurred in state legislatures, some major courts, including those of California, Florida, and Illinois adopted comparative negligence by judicial decision. See, e.g., Li v. Yellow Cab Co., 13 Cal.3d 804, 532 P.2d 1226, 119 Cal.Rptr. 858 (1975), discussing at length the propriety of judicial action in this area. Those courts willing to change the rule have emphasized the fact that the original doctrine was judicially created and thus was amenable to judicial change. They also stress the power of the common law to grow and develop in response to newly perceived needs. In contrast, those courts that have refused to make the change have emphasized that the doctrine has been such a central part of negligence law for 100 years that legislative consideration should occur before it is changed. Who has the better of this argument?

Recall that in *Hammontree v. Jenner,* p. 3, supra, the court rejected the plaintiff's suggestion that the court abandon the negligence approach in favor of strict liability principles. Is there a distinction between the two situations? Is it possible to generalize from these two cases about the circumstances in which judicial reform of basic tort doctrine—as opposed to legislative reform—is appropriate?

In the states that proceeded by legislation, the statutes were usually quite short and simply announced which version of comparative negligence was being adopted—most frequently a modified, rather than pure, version. No attempt was made to anticipate the many questions that would arise after any such basic change in the system was enacted. By contrast, virtually all the states that proceeded by judicial decision adopted the "pure version"—in large part because the choice of either modified version involved what might have appeared to be an arbitrary selection.

Implementation Issues. The courts, though perhaps discussing some of the impending problems more than the legislatures, also did not anticipate many of the complications that have emerged. We will explore the central issues raised by a comparative fault approach through consideration of a model statute and discussion of the judicial issues that have arisen in the area. The statute, which is more elaborate than any state act, is the Uniform Comparative Fault Act promulgated by the National Conference of Commissioners on Uniform State Laws in 1977.

Read the statute to learn the rights of your client C in the following situations (disregard insurance):

a. There has been an accident in which A has suffered damages of $40,000 and has brought suit against B, C, and D. A trial has established that the relative shares of fault are A–40%; B–30%; C–10%; and D–20%. Assume all are solvent.

b. At trial it appears that D is insolvent. Now what?

c. Same as (a) except that C has also been hurt and has sustained damages of $25,000.

Uniform Comparative Fault Act

12 Uniform Laws Annotated 33 (1981 Supp.).

Section 1.   [Effect of contributory fault]

(a) In an action based on fault seeking to recover damages for injury or death to person or harm to property, any contributory fault chargeable to the claimant diminishes proportionately the amount awarded as compensatory damages for an injury attributable to the claimant's contributory fault, but does not bar recovery. This rule applies whether or not under prior law the claimant's contributory fault constituted a defense or was disregarded under applicable legal doctrines, such as last clear chance.

(b) "Fault" includes acts or omissions that are in any measure negligent or reckless toward the person or property of the actor or others, or that subject a person to strict tort liability. The term also includes breach of warranty, unreasonable assumption of risk not constituting an enforceable express consent, misuse of a product for which the defendant otherwise would be liable, and unreasonable failure to avoid an injury or to mitigate damages. Legal requirements of causal relation apply both to fault as the basis for liability and to contributory fault.

Section 2. [Apportionment of damages]

(a) In all actions involving fault of more than one party to the action, including third-party defendants and persons who have been released under Section 6, the court, unless otherwise agreed by all parties, shall instruct the jury to answer special interrogatories or, if there is no jury, shall make findings, indicating:

(1) the amount of damages each claimant would be entitled to recover if contributory fault is disregarded; and

(2) the percentage of the total fault of all of the parties to each claim that is allocated to each claimant, defendant, third-party defendant, and person who has been released from liability under Section 6. For this purpose the court may determine that two or more persons are to be treated as a single party.

(b) In determining the percentages of fault, the trier of fact shall consider both the nature of the conduct of each party at fault and the extent of the causal relation between the conduct and the damages claimed.

(c) The court shall determine the award of damages to each claimant in accordance with the findings, subject to any reduction under Section 6, and enter judgment against each party liable on the basis of rules of joint-and-several liability. For purposes of contribution under Sections 4 and 5, the court also shall determine and state in the judgment each party's equitable share of the obligation to each claimant in accordance with the respective percentages of fault.

(d) Upon motion made not later than [one year] after judgment is entered, the court shall determine whether all or part of a party's equitable share of the obligation is uncollectible from that party, and shall reallocate any uncollectible amount among the other parties, including a claimant at fault, according to their respective percentages of fault. The party whose liability is reallocated is nonetheless subject to contribution and to any continuing liability to the claimant on the judgment.

Section 3. [Set-off]

A claim and counterclaim shall not be set off against each other, except by agreement of both parties. On motion, however, the court, if it finds that the obligation of either party is likely to be uncollectible, may order that both parties make payment into court for distribution. The court shall distribute the funds received and declare obligations discharged as if the payment into court by either party had been a payment to the other party and any distribution of those funds back to the party making payment had been a payment to him by the other party.

Section 4.   [Right of contribution]

(a) A right of contribution exists between or among two or more persons who are jointly and severally liable upon the same indivisible claim for the same injury, death, or harm, whether or not judgment has been recovered against all or any of them. It may be enforced either in the original action or by a separate action brought for that purpose. The basis for contribution is each person's equitable share of the obligation, including the equitable share of a claimant at fault, as determined in accordance with the provisions of Section 2.

(b) Contribution is available to a person who enters into a settlement with a claimant only (1) if the liability of the person against whom contribution is sought has been extinguished and (2) to the extent that the amount paid in settlement was reasonable.

Section 5.   [Enforcement of contribution]

(a) If the proportionate fault of the parties to a claim for contribution has been established previously by the court, as provided by Section 2, a party paying more than his equitable share of the obligation, upon motion, may recover judgment for contribution.

(b) If the proportionate fault of the parties to the claim for contribution has not been established by the court, contribution may be enforced in a separate action, whether or not a judgment has been rendered against either the person seeking contribution or the person from whom contribution is being sought.

(c) If a judgment has been rendered, the action for contribution must be commenced within [one year] after the judgment becomes final. If no judgment has been rendered, the person bringing the action for contribution either must have (1) discharged by payment the common liability within the period of the statute of limitations applicable to the claimant's right of action against him and commenced the action for contribution within [one year] after payment, or (2) agreed while action was pending to discharge the common liability and, within [one year] after the agreement, have paid the liability and commenced an action for contribution.

Section 6.   [Effect of release]

A release, covenant not to sue, or similar agreement entered into by a claimant and a person liable discharges that person from all liability for contribution, but it does not discharge any other persons liable upon the same claim unless it so provides. However, the claim of the releasing person against other persons is reduced by the amount of the released person's equitable share of the obligation, determined in accordance with the provisions of Section 2.

NOTES AND QUESTIONS

1. *Pure or Modified Version?* The introductory notes by the commissioners make three arguments against the modified version. First, a party

more at fault than the other who has to bear his or her own losses and also a share of the other party's losses, is worse off than at common law. Second, if several parties are at fault, the modified version creates chaos—especially if the plaintiff's share of the fault is greater than that of some defendants but less than that of others. This problem is discussed further in note 7, infra. Third, if a plaintiff whose fault is greater than the defendant's is excluded from the benefits of the statute and is relegated to traditional common law, plaintiff might, in some cases, such as last clear chance, recover full damages: "The anomaly therefore arises that he may be better off if his negligence is found to be greater than that of the defendant and he thus recovers full damages. . . ." Are these persuasive attacks on the modified version? What are the problems of the "pure" version?

In Sutton v. Piasecki Trucking, Inc., 59 N.Y.2d 800, 451 N.E.2d 481, 464 N.Y.S.2d 734 (1983), plaintiff driver disregarded a stop sign and was hit by an approaching truck. Plaintiff was allocated 99% of the fault—and received 1% of his damages. Is such an award repugnant?

2. *What is to be compared?* The comments to § 2 of the UCFA state that in setting fault percentages, the trier of fact should consider:

> such matters as (1) whether the conduct was mere inadvertence or engaged in with an awareness of the danger involved, (2) the magnitude of the risk created by the conduct, including the number of persons endangered and the potential seriousness of the injury, (3) the significance of what the actor was seeking to attain by his conduct, (4) the actor's superior or inferior capacities, and (5) the particular circumstances, such as the existence of an emergency requiring a hasty decision.

Making this comparison sometimes can produce widely varying appraisals. In Wright v. City of Knoxville, 898 S.W.2d 177 (Tenn.1995), for example, plaintiff girlfriend was riding in a car driven by defendant boyfriend. At an extremely busy intersection, the green arrow came on and boyfriend began to make a left turn when he heard a siren. Because he could not locate the siren, he continued making the turn—and he collided with a police car that was driving east in the westbound lane to avoid traffic backed up at the light. The officer, who was responding to a call of "an accident with injuries," was moving at 10–15 miles per hour. Plaintiff sued both her boyfriend and the officer driving the police car. The trial judge allocated 75% of the fault to the officer and 25% to the boyfriend. The court of appeals found that the boyfriend had violated a number of Tennessee traffic regulations and allocated 100% of the fault to him. The Supreme Court held that the officer should be assigned 25% of the fault because she had driven on the wrong side of the road with full knowledge that drivers would be turning directly at her.

Despite the result in the Knoxville case, courts generally are reluctant to reassess the fact finder's allocation of percentages unless they are totally indefensible.

3. *Fault and causation.* Comments to the UCFA also provide that in determining fault the fact-finder should consider "the relative closeness of the causal relationship of the negligent conduct of the defendants and the harm to the plaintiff. Degrees of fault and proximity of causation are inextricably mixed, as a study of last clear chance indicates, and that common law doctrine has been absorbed into this Act." Does this mean that a system of comparative negligence has no room for proximate cause analysis because a jury can always take into account the attenuated nature of defendant's negligence in reaching its determination of fault percentages? Or should the jury compare only conduct that has at least some minimal level of causal connection to the harm? In other words, should the question of proximate cause be antecedent to the allocation of fault rather than being inextricably mixed with it?

In Carlotta v. Warner, 601 F.Supp. 749 (E.D.Ky.1985), 19–year-old plaintiff was injured when he attempted to dive through an inner-tube that he had placed in defendant apartment house owner's pool. Plaintiff claimed that defendant was negligent for failing to provide someone to supervise the pool in accordance with state regulations. In barring the plaintiff's suit, the district court observed:

> The doctrine of comparative negligence does not mean that plaintiff is entitled to a recovery in some amount in every situation in which he can show some negligence of the defendant, however slight. If the plaintiff fails to establish that defendant's negligent act or omission was a substantial factor in causing harm to the plaintiff, or if there was a superseding cause, defendant will not be liable in any amount. Where, as here, the defendant's negligence is very slight in relation to the negligence of the plaintiff or some other party, or to some force of nature, the law of causation becomes of paramount importance. . . . I am well aware of the danger of allowing the doctrine of sole proximate cause, if over-employed, to eviscerate the enlightened doctrine of comparative negligence adopted by the Supreme Court of Kentucky.
>
> Nevertheless, the use of sole proximate cause remains viable under comparative negligence, although it will be a rare case where the comparative fault is not submitted to the jury for apportionment. This is, however, one of those rare cases.

The court found it significant that the plaintiff had himself created the risk by personally placing the inner tube into the pool. It suggested that the result would have been different if, for example, the plaintiff had negligently dived into an object that had been in the pool for some time. Why might that be?

The court was influenced by Prosser & Keeton, *Torts* (5th ed. 1984), p. 474–75:

> Once causation in fact has been established, however, the determination of proximate or legal cause remains a question of policy that may be susceptible to proportionate division. A court which is able to

award an injured plaintiff substantially diminished damages may thus be willing to extend the traditional boundaries of proximate cause and permit a limited recovery against a remotely negligent defendant. . . . In any event, at either end of the fault continuum, where one party's negligence approaches one hundred percent and the other party's approaches zero, the court may rule or the jury find that the conduct of the plaintiff or of the defendant was the "sole proximate cause" of the plaintiff's harm, so that damages will not be awarded—or reduced—at all.

This analysis may explain several New York cases that have denied recovery from pool owners, pool manufacturers, property owners and municipalities to plaintiffs who knowingly dove into shallow water or dove from platforms that they had not tested. The courts have concluded that the diver's reckless behavior was a "superseding act of negligence absolving defendants." Lionarons v. General Electric Co., 626 N.Y.S.2d 321 (App. Div.), aff'd for reasons stated below, 86 N.Y.2d 832, 658 N.E.2d 214, 634 N.Y.S.2d 436 (1995); Amatulli v. Delhi Const. Corp., 77 N.Y.2d 525, 571 N.E.2d 645, 569 N.Y.S.2d 337 (1991). But see Kendrick v. Ed's Beach Service, Inc., 577 So.2d 936 (Fla.1991)("foolhardy conduct by diving into four feet of water" is to be compared with defendant's negligence).

4. *Reckless conduct.* What types of conduct should be compared? Under contributory negligence, the plaintiff's negligence generally was overlooked when the defendant's conduct had been reckless. The Uniform Act's sweep in § 1(b) is quite broad, reaching matters of liability and of damage measurement. Even though few courts have adopted this draft legislation, virtually all states with pure versions have concluded that reckless conduct should be compared with negligence. E.g. Sorensen v. Allred, 112 Cal.App.3d 717, 169 Cal.Rptr. 441 (1980)(comparing defendant's drunk and speeding driving (55%) with plaintiff's careless left turn in front of defendant (45%)); Zavala v. Regents of the University of California, 125 Cal.App.3d 646, 178 Cal.Rptr. 185 (1981)(comparing 80% plaintiff's fault with defendant's 20%). In states with modified versions, the comparison cannot be made when the plaintiff has been reckless and the defendant negligent.

Some courts appear reluctant to follow the logic of comparison when the plaintiff's conduct is thought to be socially offensive. See Barker v. Kallash, 63 N.Y.2d 19, 468 N.E.2d 39, 479 N.Y.S.2d 201 (1984), in which the 15–year-old plaintiff was hurt when a pipe bomb that he was making exploded in his hands. His suit against various defendants was totally barred, 5–2, even though the state had adopted pure comparative negligence: "when the plaintiff has engaged in activities prohibited, as opposed to regulated, by law, the courts will not entertain the suit if the plaintiff's conduct constituted a serious violation of the law and the injuries for which he seeks recovery were the direct result of that violation." Contra, Ashmore v. Cleanweld Products, Inc., 66 Or.App. 62, 672 P.2d 1230 (1983), also involving a 15–year-old bomb maker, in which the court relied on § 889 of the Second Restatement, providing in part that "One is not barred from recovery for an interference with his legally protected interests merely because at the time of the interference he was committing a tort or a crime." The strong public policy against illegal manufacture of explosives "is best effectuated . . . through penal laws."

In Symone T. v. Lieber, 205 App.Div.2d 609, 613 N.Y.S.2d 404 (1994), a 12–year-old patient who obtained an abortion 24.7 weeks after conception brought a malpractice action for neurological damage caused by an embolism. The court, 4–1, relying on *Barker v. Kallash*, held that plaintiff would be "barred from recovering if she willfully submitted to an abortion which she knew to be illegal":

> While recovery will not be barred in every case where the injury is sustained while engaging in illegal activity, a plaintiff cannot seek compensation for the loss where the injury is a 'direct result of his [or her] knowing and intentional participation in a criminal act . . . if the criminal act is judged to be so serious an offense as to warrant denial of recovery.' [ ] Submitting to an illegal abortion has been held to be such a serious offense, so that one cannot recover damages for medical malpractice for injuries sustained as the result.

The case was remanded for fact finding. One judge insisted that as a matter of law knowledge could not be imputed "to a 12–year-old girl who had been made pregnant by rape, and who is taken to the hospital by her mother." He thought the majority holding here was "an unwarranted extension" of *Barker*.

Should one compare when both defendants are negligent but not when they are both reckless? How would the Uniform Act handle this? "Reckless" and "willful and wanton" are of course complex notions. See Poole v. City of Rolling Meadows, 167 Ill.2d 41, 656 N.E.2d 768 (1995), in which four justices divided willful and wanton misconduct into two categories: the one closer to negligence would bear comparison with negligence, but the one closer to intentional harm would not. The other three justices concluded that all willful and wanton misconduct involved "acts performed in conscious disregard of a known risk or with utter indifference to the consequences" and should not be compared with negligence. See also Lewis v. Miller, 374 Pa.Super. 515, 543 A.2d 590 (1988) (court will not compare claim by one drag racer against another).

5. *The interplay of intent and negligence.* Although the vast majority of states will compare the plaintiff's negligence with the defendant's recklessness, what should they do when the defendant has committed an intentional tort or crime? The comments to § 1 of the Uniform Act state that although the Act does not include intentional torts, courts are not precluded from making comparisons in such cases if they find it appropriate. Of the few states that have addressed the issue, most have refused to compare the negligence of a plaintiff with the intentional tort of a defendant on the ground that intentional conduct is different "in kind" from negligent or reckless conduct and therefore may not be compared.

Does it raise different questions to ask whether a court should compare the intentional actions of the plaintiff with the negligence of a defendant? Compare Hickey v. Zezulka, 440 Mich. 1203, 487 N.W.2d 106 (1992)(negligent campus police officer, who had failed to remove decedent's belt from holding cell, entitled to comparative fault instruction so jury could compare officer's negligence with decedent's fault in intentionally committing suicide) with Loeb v. Rasmussen, 822 P.2d 914 (Alaska 1991)(liquor store owner not entitled to comparative fault defense against minor for her act in buying liquor illegally before having an accident).

A very important related issue arises when the case involves two defendants—one negligent and one a criminal. In Reichert v. Atler, 117 N.M. 623, 875 P.2d 379 (1994), a bartender was negligent in failing to protect one patron from the foreseeable killing by another patron. The court held the bar liable for one third and the killer liable for two thirds of the award. The court thought its result consistent with the state's abolition of joint and several liability for all damages: "each individual tortfeasor should be held responsible only for his or her percentage of the harm."

Compare this approach with Veazey v. Elmwood Plantation Associates, Ltd., 650 So.2d 712 (La.1994), in which the plaintiff was raped in her apartment and brought an action against the management company for failure to exercise due care for the safety of residents. The trial judge refused to permit any allocation of fault to the unidentified nonparty rapist. In defendant's appeal from a plaintiff's judgment for the full amount of the damages, the supreme court split three ways. The majority concluded that it might be appropriate to compare negligence and intentional fault in some cases but that this case was not one of them.

Three reasons motivated the majority. First, the defendant's duty to provide a safe place to live encompassed the very risk that injured plaintiff, and the defendant should not be able to reduce its liability when its failure brought about the very harm feared. Second, any comparison would be against public policy because it would reduce the safety incentives of the management company, especially here since any "rational juror" would apportion most of the fault to the rapist at the "innocent plaintiff's expense." Finally, the court concluded that intentional torts are "fundamentally different" from negligence and the two cannot be compared in many situations, including this one.

The concurring justice asserted that the two types of torts could never be compared and that the trial judge reached the right result. The dissenters thought that the two types of harm could be compared and should be compared in this case. One dissenter asserted that this "result—holding the negligent tortfeasor(s) responsible for the entirety of the damages because of the mere happenstance that a co-tortfeasor committed an intentional, as opposed to a negligent wrongdoing—is anomalous." That justice concluded that the fault should be apportioned 90 percent to the rapist and 10 percent to the defendant. Under the state law of joint and several liability this would mean that the defendant was liable for half the plaintiff's damages. Which of the three views seems soundest? Does your view depend on the state's approach to joint and several liability?

For another case refusing to compare these two faults, see Kansas State Bank & Trust Co. v. Specialized Transportation Services, Inc., 249 Kan. 348, 819 P.2d 587 (Kan.1991), in which plaintiff brought suit on behalf of a mentally retarded six-year-old girl against a school bus driver, the school bus transportation service and the school district for the bus driver's alleged sexual molestation. The supreme court held that negligent tortfeasors should not be allowed to reduce their fault by the intentional fault of another that they had a duty of care to prevent.

In a state that allows comparison, is a jury ever justified in allocating more fault to the negligent defendant than the defendant who committed an intentional tort? How is the jury to compare the two? In Scott v. County of Los Angeles, 27 Cal.App.4th 125, 32 Cal.Rptr.2d 643 (1994), the trial court entered judgment in favor of an abused child on a jury's apportionment of fault 99% to the county and the social worker and 1% to the abusive parent. On appeal, the court rejected that allocation. It referred to a recent case in which another court had overturned a jury's allocation of 95% of the fault to a landlord who had been negligent in not protecting tenants from assaults and 5% against the two rapists. Compare Rosh v. Cave Imaging Systems, Inc., 26 Cal.App.4th 1225, 32 Cal.Rptr.2d 136 (1994)(upholding an apportionment of 25% against a former employee who shot the manager who fired him and 75% against the security firm that, against orders, had permitted the employee to enter the company's premises where the shooting occurred). Recall the California approach to joint and several liability, p. 325, supra.

6. *Should the negligence of one plaintiff be imputed to another plaintiff?*

a. Loss of consortium. Does the Act speak to the question of an action for loss of consortium where the injured spouse and the defendant were both at fault? Most states that have addressed this question have treated the claim as derivative and have imputed the negligence of the injured spouse to the other spouse. This rule emerged during the days of contributory negligence and was criticized by commentators. Now that comparative negligence has become virtually universal, these states have retained the rule but now find it easier to defend. In Blagg v. Illinois F.W.D. Truck & Equip. Co., 143 Ill.2d 188, 572 N.E.2d 920 (1991), the court noted that one reason to treat the action as derivative was that the action of the negligent spouse "harms not only the marital interest of the other spouse, but also affects the unity of the familial entity which is in fact an 'economic unit.'" A second reason was that imputation was the "simplest and most efficient way to reach a just result."

In a situation in which the spouse was 15% at fault and the stranger 85%, how might imputation produce a "just result"? With these numbers the court in Eggert v. Working, 599 P.2d 1389 (Alaska 1979), chose the derivative approach. The goal of pure comparative negligence was that "the loss resulting from an accident is best distributed among those whose negligence caused it in proportion to the fault of each of them." In the "ideal" solution, the wife would recover her full loss, 85% from the defendant and 15% from her husband. Imputing the husband's negligence, though not "ideal," was "very close to the same thing, because the evidence is clear that [the husband and wife] are in effect if not in law, an economic unit. That, it seems to us, is likely to be the case in most instances where substantial loss of consortium damages are suffered." Should it matter whether the wife can sue the husband directly? Whether the state allows contribution against the husband?

For the minority approach, see the discussion in Huber v. Hovey, 501 N.W.2d 53 (Iowa 1993), in which the court concluded that from the "vantage point of the negligent defendant, [the plaintiff] is simply a foreseeable plaintiff to whom he owes a separate duty of care." The *Huber* court extended that analysis by refusing to bind an absent wife to the terms of an exculpatory agreement signed by her husband—who was then hurt and held barred from recovery.

b. Wrongful death. Do the same considerations apply in a wrongful death action? Most courts treat the action as derivative. E.g., Bevan v. Vassar Farms, Inc., 117 Idaho 1038, 793 P.2d 711 (1990). In Griffin v. Gehret, 17 Wash.App. 546, 564 P.2d 332 (1977), the court, in rejecting a parent's argument that his child's negligence should not be imputed to him, noted that under comparative negligence the parent's claim was not barred. But if the decedent's negligence were not imputed, then "the parents of a 17–year–old minor decedent who was 99 percent negligent would be entitled to recover 100 percent from a 17–year–old tort-feasor who was only 1 percent negligent." Why not treat the parents as independent foreseeable plaintiffs who are owed a separate duty?

c. Bystander emotional distress. How about an action for emotional distress? In Meredith v. Hanson, 40 Wash.App. 170, 697 P.2d 602 (1985), the infant plaintiffs sued for their emotional distress at seeing their stepfather struck and killed by a passing car. The court distinguished *Griffin*, supra: "If the present action was a survival action or for wrongful death, the contributory negligence of the decedent would be at issue. [ ] It is neither. The case at bench concerns the emotional distress suffered by the plaintiffs due to [the defendant's] negligence. It makes no difference whether [the stepfather] was negligent so long as his negligence was not the sole proximate cause of the accident. The plaintiffs do not seek compensation for [the stepfather's] death. [His] negligence should not have been imputed to the children." What if the stepfather's negligence was 99%?

In Portee v. Jaffee, p. 238, supra, the court took the contrary position in an omitted part of the opinion: "to allow a plaintiff seeking damages for emotional injuries to recover a greater proportion than the injured party would surely create liability in excess of the defendant's fault." Any award was to be reduced by the negligence of the injured victim "as well as, of course, any contributing negligence of the plaintiff himself."

Should it matter whether the state has pure or modified comparative negligence? What reasons might the *Meredith* court have for distinguishing between wrongful death plaintiffs and emotional distress plaintiffs? Is the distinction sound?

d. Parent-child. Recall that under contributory negligence, later courts refused to impute the negligence of parents to children, p. 386, supra. The emergence of comparative negligence has not changed that approach. Should it?

7. *Should the fault of multiple defendants be combined?* In states following a modified version of comparative negligence, it becomes critical to decide whether to compare the plaintiff's negligence with the aggregated negligence of the defendants (or all negligent actors) or whether it is to be compared with the negligence of each defendant individually. Most states with modified versions compare the plaintiff's fault to the combined fault of the defendants. Consider these two distributions of negligence:

(1) P 30%; D1 60%; D2 10%

(2) P 40%; D1 30%; D2 30%

In a state that imposes joint and several liability, what are the implications of your choice for comparison? What are the implications of your choice in a state that has only several liability? What if all three parties are hurt in the accident and sue each other? These problems are discussed in Wong v. Hawaiian Scenic Tours, Ltd., 64 Hawaii 401, 642 P.2d 930 (1982).

It is in this kind of situation that one can see the underlying philosophy of the few states that retain joint and several liability in cases in which the plaintiff has not been at fault, but abolish the doctrine in cases in which the plaintiff has been negligent and invokes comparative negligence. Recall p. 325, supra.

8. *Should the judgments be set off against each other?* The denial of set-offs in the Uniform Act is designed to cover situations in which insurance exists on both sides so that injured parties will maximize their recoveries. The issue arose in Jess v. Herrmann, 26 Cal.3d 131, 604 P.2d 208, 161 Cal.Rptr. 87 (1979), in which the court, 4–3, denied set-off: if both drivers were adequately insured, the "setoff produces results detrimental to the interests *of both parties* and accords the insurance companies of the parties a fortuitous windfall simply because each insured happens to have an independent claim against the person he has injured."

9. *What if one defendant is insolvent?* Example (b) at the outset of the statute suggests how the Uniform Act handles insolvencies. In most states, however, the treatment will depend on the state's law on joint and several liability. Most states that retain the doctrine, spread the loss due to one defendant's insolvency among the remaining defendants. With several liability, the plaintiff will bear the loss.

10. *Contribution and indemnity.* Recall that in states that retain joint and several liability in all or some cases, there will be questions about contribution and indemnity where one defendant has paid more than its fair share. As noted in Chapter I, traditionally, contribution and indemnity were treated quite separately despite their obvious relationship. Contribution was not available at common law, and many of the statutes permitting contribution provided limits on its availability. Indemnity, on the other hand, was available at common law and allowed one party to obtain full reimbursement from another. The classic situation was master-servant, in which the master, who was liable only as a matter of law under respondeat superior, could seek indemnification. That right was extended to what the courts called "active-passive" negligence situations, in which the party asserted to have been negligent in a "passive" manner could obtain indemnity from the "actively" negligent party.

11. *What should happen when one defendant settles?* A longstanding question even before comparative negligence became common was how to resolve cases in which one or more defendants have settled before trial and another goes to trial and verdict. For example, consider the situation in which plaintiff sues D1 and D2 claiming $50,000 for an injury for which both are allegedly liable. D1 settles for $10,000.

a. D2 proceeds to trial and the jury finds that D2 is negligent and the total damages are $30,000. The jury assesses fault at 50% for D1 and 50% for D2. Under the Uniform Act, how much should D2 pay to P? What impact does the trial outcome have on D1? Is this a sensible outcome?

Another way to look at the matter—called the pro tanto rule—would be to require D2 to pay P $20,000 ($30,000 less the $10,000 P has already gotten from D1). Is that superior to the approach of the Uniform Act?

b. In the trial the jury finds damages of $30,000, but this time finds D2 to be 90% at fault and D1 10% at fault. Under the Uniform Act, how much should D2 pay to P? What impact does the trial outcome have on D1? Is this a sensible outcome?

The pro tanto rule would require D2 to pay P $20,000 ($30,000 less the $10,000 P has already gotten from D1). Is that superior to the approach of the Uniform Act? New York sets off the larger of the two measures. See Didner v. Keene Corp., 82 N.Y.2d 342, 624 N.E.2d 979, 604 N.Y.S.2d 884 (1993)(adopting an aggregate approach to all the settlements in the case). In California a good faith settlement releases the settling defendant and gives the remaining defendant credit for the amount of the settlement. In Mattco Forge, Inc. v. Arthur Young & Co., 38 Cal.App.4th 1337, 45 Cal.Rptr.2d 581 (1995), the court rejected the claim of good faith settlement where the settling defendant had paid less than 1% of the plausible value of the plaintiff's claim, still had a large amount of liability insurance available, and stated that the purpose of the settlement was to avoid the costs of defending a cross-complaint from the remaining defendant. Does the Uniform Act avoid this problem? Does New York's approach?

Consider McDermott, Inc. v. AmClyde, 114 S.Ct. 1461 (1994), holding that P's recovery in court should be reduced by the percentages of fault the jury found against the settling parties no matter how much they paid to settle. In response to concern that under this approach the plaintiff might collect more than the damages assessed by the jury, the Supreme Court stated:

> It seems to us that a plaintiff's good fortune in striking a favorable bargain with one defendant gives other defendants no claim to pay less than their proportionate share of the total loss. In fact, one of the virtues of the proportionate share rule is that, unlike the pro tanto rule, it does not make a litigating defendant's liability dependent on the amount of a settlement negotiated by others without regard to its interests.

Does this approach also present risks to plaintiffs?

12. *Should the jury be told the relevant law?* States disagree over whether juries should know the implications of their decisions. Compare Roman v. Mitchell, 82 N.J. 336, 413 A.2d 322 (1980)(tell the jury) with McGowan v. Story, 70 Wis.2d 189, 234 N.W.2d 325 (1975) (contra). Is it sound to argue that juries are now sophisticated enough to wonder about the legal consequences of their verdicts—and that courts should try to avoid decisions based on erroneous guesses? Did juries in the past simply follow instructions without worrying about the consequences? Or was the situation so simple that everyone knew the contributory negligence rule without being told—and damages were rarely high enough to produce insolvent defendants?

The outcome question arises in other contexts as well. See, e.g., Kaeo v. Davis, 68 Hawaii 447, 719 P.2d 387 (1986), in which the jury allocated 99% of the fault for an accident to the driver of the car in which plaintiff was a passenger, and 1% to the city because of a winding road at the point of the accident. The jury was not told about joint and several liability. A new trial was ordered at which the jury would be informed "of the possible legal consequences of a verdict apportioning negligence among joint tortfeasors." If an "outcome" charge is appropriate in the comparative negligence area, why is it not appropriate in any area in which a jury's verdict might have consequences not comprehended by ordinary jurors?

13. *Other Changes Wrought by Comparative Negligence.* The introduction of comparative negligence has forced courts to reconsider almost every aspect of the negligence system. Some defenses, such as last clear chance, were eliminated. Some other changes include:

a. Res ipsa loquitur. Under comparative negligence what if the evidence clearly shows undeniable contributory negligence on plaintiff's part? In Montgomery Elevator Co. v. Gordon, 619 P.2d 66 (Colo.1980), the court asserted that res ipsa could be used if the plaintiff's evidence showed only the first two conditions. Then, once "the trial court rules that the doctrine is applicable, the jury must then compare any evidence of negligence of the plaintiff with the inferred negligence of the defendant and decide what percentage of negligence is attributable to each party." See Giles v. City of New Haven, 228 Conn. 441, 636 A.2d 1335 (1994).

b. Rescue. Since the introduction of comparative negligence, defendants have argued that rescuers—who were not held at fault earlier unless rash or reckless—no longer need special protection. Most courts have agreed. But see Ouellette v. Carde, 612 A.2d 687 (R.I.1992), in which the court held that comparative negligence "does not fully protect the rescue doctrine's underlying policy of promoting rescue." The law "places a premium on human life, and one who voluntarily attempts to save a life of another should not be barred from complete recovery." Since the defendant did not allege that the plaintiff had acted rashly or recklessly, the trial judge should not have charged at all on the issue of plaintiff's negligence.

   c.   The drinking plaintiff. In Estate of Kelley v. Moguls, Inc., 160 Vt. 531, 632 A.2d 360 (1993), the court held that the estate of a person who has killed himself by driving while drunk may have a common law negligence action against the licensed vendor who supplied the alcohol. The defendant argued that this would encourage drunk driving and allow a wrongdoer to profit from his own wrong. The court responded that under comparative negligence plaintiff would not be made whole and that it was appropriate that both parties in this situation be deterred from their conduct. Contra, Estate of Kelly v. Falin, 127 Wash.2d 31, 896 P.2d 1245 (1995)(allowing suit by intoxicated adult against vendor of alcohol would foster irresponsibility and reward drunk driving).

3.   AVOIDABLE CONSEQUENCES

   During the era of contributory negligence there existed side by side a related doctrine called "avoidable consequences," which addressed the measure of damages but not issues of liability. Even if the accident was entirely the defendant's fault, the plaintiff's recovery might be reduced by failure to exercise due care to mitigate the harm done.

   The clearest form of avoidable consequences issue involved the plaintiff's failure to get medical attention or to follow medical advice. Courts quite generally refused to award damages for complications that could have been avoided by the exercise of due care after the accident. This situation may raise particularly sensitive problems. In Hall v. Dumitru, 250 Ill. App.3d 759, 620 N.E.2d 668 (1993), the court held a person under no duty to undergo surgery to mitigate the damages caused by defendant's negligence. Refusing to distinguish between major and minor surgery, the court thought the crucial line was between treatments that involved a "recognized risk" and those that did not. The duty to mitigate applied in the latter case, but not in the former:

> [I]f the proposed treatment could result in an aggravation of the existing condition or the development of an additional condition of ill health, or if the prospect for improved health is slight, then there should be no duty to undergo the treatment. If the risk is clearly remote, the exception should not apply. But the risk need not be significant or even probable in order to trigger the exception.

   Once the grounds for an exception are established, the plaintiff need not articulate reasons for rejecting the procedure. "It is not the place of the court or the jury to evaluate a patient's reasons for declining surgery or treatment, if the risks are recognized." In the actual case the proposed surgery was a tubal ligation that involved "general anesthetic which alone has attendant risks which can be potentially harmful and life threatening. The procedure itself involves the use of a sharp instrument in close proximity to vital organs necessitating the use of carbon dioxide to inflate the abdomen. It is apparent from the record that a tubal ligation surgery involves risks to a woman's life or member. [ ] Therefore, the plaintiff was under no duty to undergo the surgery to mitigate her damages. . . ."

The reluctance to mitigate by treatment raises special problems when the reasons are based on religious beliefs. In Munn v. Algee, 924 F.2d 568 (5th Cir.1991), the court held that the decedent's religious beliefs would not justify her failure to accept a blood transfusion. The case is criticized in Note, Reason, Religion, and Avoidable Consequences: When Faith and the Duty to Mitigate Collide, 67 N.Y.U.L.Rev. 1111 (1992), which develops a "reasonable believer" notion under which the jury would be "instructed to assess the reasonableness of a plaintiff's mitigation efforts according to the standard of a reasonable, sincere adherent of the plaintiff's religious tenets." The note suggests an analogy to "eggshell skull. . . . From a policy standpoint . . . a victim of another's tortious conduct—whose religion constrains her from taking what others might deem reasonable, ameliorative steps—ought not be forced to choose between being spiritually or financially whole." But see Simons, The Puzzling Doctrine of Contributory Negligence, 16 Cardozo L.Rev. 1693, 1730 (1995), suggesting that the result in *Munn* is better explained on the ground that although "decedent's decision to honor her religious beliefs is *not* unreasonable, defendant has no duty to subsidize her choice to sacrifice her life in the name of religion."

In Tanberg v. Ackerman Investment Co., 473 N.W.2d 193 (Iowa 1991), plaintiff sustained a back injury due to defendant's negligence. His physician advised him to lose weight to mitigate the back pain. A jury could have found that plaintiff failed to make a reasonable effort to lose weight, and that plaintiff was 70% at fault for his damage compared to 30% for the tortfeasor. Under the state's modified rule plaintiff recovered nothing and the court affirmed. How would the Uniform Act handle this situation?

One heavily litigated current aspect of the avoidable consequences issue involves the failure to use seat belts or safety belts in automobiles or helmets with motorcycles. Although traditional obligations to mitigate arose only after the original injury, these new cases raise what might be called an issue of "anticipatory avoidable consequences." Under the regime of contributory negligence, efforts by defendants to bar recovery under that doctrine generally failed. With the emergence of comparative fault, the issue has become quite complicated. The problem is posed by assuming some numbers:

a. Defendant was solely to blame for a two-car crash in which the plaintiff, the other driver, was not wearing an available seat belt. Defendant offers unrebutted expert testimony that use of the belt would have kept the damages at $20,000 instead of $200,000.

  b. Does anything change if the defendant was a drunk driver?

  c. What if the plaintiff was 20% at fault in causing the initial accident? 90%?

The states have responded to these issues in a variety of ways. Some legislatures, when making it a crime not to use a belt or helmet, have added a provision that makes the violation inadmissible in any civil action. Others have provided that the violation, if causally related to the harm, may affect civil damages but by no more than a small percentage. See, e.g., Meyer v. City of Des Moines, 475 N.W.2d 181 (Iowa 1991), discussing the Iowa statute that limits the reduction in the plaintiff's recovery to 5%. See also LaHue v. General Motors Corp., 716 F.Supp. 407 (W.D.Mo.1989)(maximum reduction in Missouri of 1%). When statutes have commanded use of these safety devices but have said nothing about civil consequences, some courts have chosen to treat the failure to use belts or helmets as a species of fault.

In the absence of controlling statutes on the appropriate approach, courts have disagreed. Some, including California and New York, allow the failure to use safety devices to fully reduce recoverable damages, though the defendant is likely to bear the burden of showing what part of plaintiff's harm was due to the failure to use the safety equipment. See the extended discussion in Law v. Superior Court, 157 Ariz. 147, 755 P.2d 1135 (1988). Others reject any reduction. See Swajian v. General Motors Corp., 559 A.2d 1041 (R.I.1989):

> We recognize the safety-belt defense for what it is worth—a manifestation of public policy. This court believes that any attempt at reducing highway fatalities through promoting the increased use of safety belts is best accomplished by legislative action. Recent studies indicate that the vast majority of Rhode Islanders refuse to buckle up. [   ] If we were to impose a duty to wear safety belts, in essence this court would be condemning most motor-vehicle occupants as negligent. Such a determination, if desirable, is properly left to the Legislature. . . . Moreover, should recent safety-belt-use studies prove reliable, it could be argued that manufacturers should design vehicles in a manner safe for those who foreseeably will not wear safety belts. The above discussion smacks of public-policy considerations more appropriately addressed by the Legislature. In any event, we are doubtful that a contrary holding would encourage increased use of safety belts.

In the *Meyer* case, supra, which involved the failure to wear a helmet, the state legislature had not addressed that question. The court noted that under the state's comparative negligence statute a plaintiff who was more than 50% at fault would get nothing. If failure to wear a helmet were treated as fault for this purpose, the plaintiff might get no recovery whatever—and the doctrine of avoidable consequences would be operating as comparative fault. This was one among several reasons for excluding evidence of the failure to use a helmet.

For an attempt to weave an intermediate course in which the plaintiff will lose some portion of the damages attributable to the failure to wear the belt or helmet, but cannot lose more than half the actual damages by such conduct, see Waterson v. General Motors Corp., 111 N.J. 238, 544 A.2d 357 (1988).

Is the problem one of comparing faults? Is it one of causation—so that the plaintiff should bear the full consequences of allowing what would otherwise have been a relatively minor injury to become a catastrophe? Consider Rodgers v. American Honda Motor Co., 46 F.3d 1 (1st Cir.1995), in which the plaintiff was hurt when thrown from an all-terrain vehicle (ATV). In plaintiff's claim against the manufacturer, Maine's comparative negligence statute was understood to provide that if plaintiff's fault was "equally responsible for the damage sustained or more responsible for the damages sustained than the defendant, the claimant shall not recover." The proof showed that plaintiff, an experienced ATV rider, was not wearing a helmet at the time he sustained "brain-crippling injuries." The jury's defense verdict was upheld. The statute made the lack of a helmet admissible on the question of liability and the result followed because virtually all of the damage sustained was due to the failure to wear the helmet.

Another current aspect of the doctrine of avoidable consequences occurs in the world of synergistic interactions. In Champagne v. Raybestos–Manhattan, Inc., 212 Conn. 509, 562 A.2d 1100 (1989), plaintiff's job brought him into contact with asbestos. After being tested in 1975, he was warned that his chest x-ray had shown change and was "strongly advised [to] discontinue cigarette smoking." The jury could have found that plaintiff had continued smoking until his death despite repeated warnings. He left work in 1979, developed lung cancer in late 1984 or early 1985, and died in 1985 at age 60. An expert testified that the most likely cause of the cancer was "asbestos exposure along with the incidence of smoking." His basis for such an opinion was that the incidence of cancer in smokers exposed to asbestos is "from ten to sixty times more than the incidence of cancer in nonsmokers exposed to asbestos." The judge's charge allowed the jury to allocate comparative responsibility. The jury found for plaintiff but reduced the award by 75 percent. This part of the case was affirmed on appeal. The court held that the jury could reasonably have concluded that the decedent knew or should have known that his conduct was not reasonable and, consequently, there was no basis for upsetting the jury's decision.

B.   ASSUMPTION OF RISK

1.   EXPRESS AGREEMENTS

Parties sometimes agree in advance that the defendant need not exercise due care for the safety of the plaintiff—generally in a more-or-less formal written contract, usually called an exculpatory or a hold-harmless agreement. If the plaintiff is later hurt by what is claimed to be defendant's negligence, the contract is usually at the center of any ensuing litigation. Such litigation generally raises two types of questions: (1) will the courts enforce even the most clearly drafted contract given the type of activity involved, and (2) if so, is the contract in question sufficiently clear. The following case suggests the nature of the inquiries.

Dalury v. S–K–I, Ltd.

Supreme Court of Vermont, 1995.
670 A.2d 795.

[While skiing at defendants' resort, plaintiff was badly hurt when he collided with a metal pole that formed part of the control maze for a ski lift line. Before the season had started plaintiff had purchased a season pass and signed a form that provided in relevant part:

RELEASE FROM LIABILITY AND CONDITIONS OF USE

1. I accept and understand that Alpine Skiing is a hazardous sport with many dangers and risks and that injuries are a common and ordinary occurrence of the sport. As a condition of being permitted to use the ski area premises, I freely accept and voluntarily assume the risks of injury or property damage and release Killington Ltd., its employees and agents from any and all liability for personal injury or property damage resulting from negligence, conditions of the premises, operations of the ski area, actions or omissions of employees or agents of the ski area or from my participation in skiing at the area, accepting myself the full responsibility for any and all such damage or injury of any kind which may result.

Plaintiff also signed a photo identification card that contained the same language. The trial judge granted defendant summary judgment.]

■ Before ALLEN, C.J., and GIBSON, DOOLEY, MORSE and JOHNSON, JJ.

■ JOHNSON, JUDGE.

. . .

On appeal, plaintiffs contend that the release was ambiguous as to whose liability was waived and that it is unenforceable as a matter of law because it violates public policy. We agree with defendants that the release was quite clear in its terms. Because we hold the agreement is unenforceable, we proceed to a discussion of the public policy that supports our holding.

I.

This is a case of first impression in Vermont. While we have recognized the existence of a public policy exception to the validity of exculpatory agreements, see [   ]; in most of our cases, enforceability has turned on whether the language of the agreement was sufficiently clear to reflect the parties' intent. See [ ]; [ ] (broad exculpatory language at end of limited warranty clause insufficient to release defendant for negligent design); [ ] (agreement in entirety sufficiently clear to show experienced, professional freestyle skier intended to hold ski area harmless); [ ] (language of contract sufficiently clear to show parties' intent to hold railroad harmless for its own negligence).

Even well-drafted exculpatory agreements, however, may be void because they violate public policy. Restatement (Second) of Torts Sec. 496B comment *e* (1965). According to the Restatement, an exculpatory agreement should be upheld if it is (1) freely and fairly made, (2) between parties who are in an equal bargaining position, and (3) there is no social interest with which it interferes. Sec. 496B comment *b*. The critical issue here concerns the social interests that are affected.

Courts and commentators have struggled to develop a useful formula for analyzing the public policy issue. The formula has been the "subject of great debate" during "the whole course of the common law," and it had proven impossible to articulate a precise definition because the "social forces that have led to such characterization are volatile and dynamic." Tunkl v. Regents of Univ. of Cal., 383 P.2d 441, 444 (Cal.1963).

The leading judicial formula for determining whether an exculpatory agreement violates public policy was set forth by Justice Tobriner of the California Supreme Court [in *Tunkl*]. An agreement is invalid if it exhibits some or all of the following characteristics:

> [1.] It concerns a business of a type generally thought suitable for public regulation. [2.] The party seeking exculpation is engaged in performing a service of great importance to the public, which is often a matter of practical necessity for some members of the public. [3.] The party holds [it]self out as willing to perform this service for any member of the public who seeks it, or at least for any member coming within certain established standards. [4.] As a result of the essential nature of the service, in the economic setting of the transaction, the party invoking exculpation possesses a decisive advantage of bargaining strength against any member of the public who seeks [the party's] services. [5.] In exercising a superior bargaining power the party confronts the public with a standardized adhesion contract of exculpation, and makes no provision whereby a purchaser may pay additional reasonable fees and obtain protection against negligence. [6.] Finally, as a result of the transaction, the person or property of the purchaser is placed under the control of the seller, subject to the risk of carelessness by the seller or [the seller's] agents.

[handwritten margin note: Tunkl decision sets up rules when exculpatory clauses are invalid]

[ ]. Applying these factors, the court concluded that a release from liability for future negligence imposed as a condition for admission to a charitable research hospital was invalid. Id. at 449. Numerous courts have adopted and applied the *Tunkl* factors. See Wagenblast v. Odessa Sch. Dist. No. 105–157–166J, 758 P.2d 968, 971–73 (Wash.1988)(release for

school district's interscholastic athletics violated public policy); Kyriazis v. University of W.Va., 450 S.E.2d 649, 654–55 (W.Va.1994)(release for state university-sponsored club rugby was invalid because "[w]hen a state university provides recreational activities to its students, it fulfills its educational mission, and performs a public service").

Other courts have incorporated the *Tunkl* factors into their decisions. The Colorado Supreme Court has developed a four-part inquiry to analyze the validity of exculpatory agreements: (1) existence of a duty to the public, (2) the nature of the service performed, (3) whether the contract was fairly entered into, and (4) whether the intention of the parties is expressed in clear and unambiguous language. Jones v. Dressel, 623 P.2d 370, 376 (Colo.1981). In the Jones case, the court concluded, based on the *Tunkl* factors, that no duty to the public was involved in air service for a parachute jump, because that sort of service does not affect the public interest. [ ] Using a similar formula, the Wyoming Supreme Court concluded that a ski resort's sponsorship of an Ironman Decathlon competition did not invoke the public interest. Milligan v. Big Valley Corp., 754 P.2d 1063, 1066–67 (Wyo.1988).

On the other hand, the Virginia Supreme Court recently concluded, in the context of a "Teflon Man Triathlon" competition, that a preinjury release from liability for negligence is void as against public policy because it is simply wrong to put one party to a contract at the mercy of the other's negligence. Hiett v. Lake Barcroft Community Ass'n, 418 S.E.2d 894, 897 (Va.1992). The court stated: "'[T]o hold that it was competent for one party to put the other parties to the contract at the mercy of its own misconduct . . . can never be lawfully done where an enlightened system of jurisprudence prevails. Public policy forbids it, and contracts against public policy are void.'" [ ]

Having reviewed these various formulations of the public policy exception, we accept them as relevant considerations, but not as rigid factors that, if met, preclude further analysis. Instead, we recognize that no single formula will reach the relevant public policy issues in every factual context. Like the court in Wolf v. Ford, 644 A.2d 522, 527 (Md.1994), we conclude that ultimately, the "determination of what constitutes the public interest must be made considering the totality of the circumstances of any given case against the backdrop of current societal expectations."

II.

Defendants urge us to uphold the exculpatory agreement on the ground that ski resorts do not provide an essential public service. They argue that they owe no duty to plaintiff to permit him to use their private lands for skiing, and that the terms and conditions of entry ought to be left entirely within their control. Because skiing, like other recreational sports, is not a necessity of life, defendants contend that the sale of a lift ticket is a purely private matter, implicating no public interest. See, e.g., *Milligan*, [ ] ("Generally, a private recreational business does not qualify as a service demanding a special duty to the public, nor are its services of a special, highly necessary or essential nature.") We disagree.

Whether or not defendants provide an essential public service does not resolve the public policy question in the recreational sports context. The defendants' area is a facility open to the public. They advertise and invite skiers and nonskiers of every level of skiing ability to their premises for the price of a ticket. At oral argument, defendants conceded that thousands of people buy lift tickets every day throughout the season. Thousands of people ride lifts, buy services, and ski the trails. Each ticket sale may be, for some purposes, a purely private transaction. But when a substantial number of such sales take place as a result of the seller's general invitation to the public to utilize the facilities and services in question, a legitimate public interest arises.

The major public policy implications are those underlying the law of premises liability. In Vermont, a business owner has a duty "of active care to make sure that its premises are in safe and suitable condition for its customers." [ ] This duty of care "increases proportionately with the foreseeable risks of the operations involved." [ ] The business invitee "ha[s] a right to assume that the premises, aside from obvious dangers, [are] reasonably safe for the purpose for which he [is] upon them, and that proper precaution [has] been taken to make them so." [ ] We have already held that a ski area owes its customers the same duty as any other business—to keep its premises reasonably safe. [ ]

The policy rationale is to place responsibility for maintenance of the land on those who own or control it, with the ultimate goal of keeping accidents to the minimum level possible. Defendants, not recreational skiers, have the expertise and opportunity to foresee and control hazards, and to guard against the negligence of their agents and employees. They alone can properly maintain and inspect their premises, and train their employees in risk management. They alone can insure against risks and effectively spread the cost of insurance among their thousands of customers. Skiers, on the other hand, are not in a position to discover and correct risks of harm, and they cannot insure against the ski area's negligence.

If defendants were permitted to obtain broad waivers of their liability, an important incentive for ski areas to manage risk would be removed, with the public bearing the cost of the resulting injuries. [ ] It is illogical, in these circumstances, to undermine the public policy underlying business invitee law and allow skiers to bear risks they have no ability or right to control.

. . . We do not accept the proposition that because ski resorts do not provide an essential public service, such agreements do not affect the public interest. [ ] A recognition of the principles underlying the duty to business invitees makes clear the inadequacy of relying upon the essential public service factor in the analysis of public recreation cases. While interference with an essential public service surely affects the public interest, those services do not represent the universe of activities that implicate public concerns.

Moreover, reliance on the private nature of defendants' property would be inconsistent with societal expectations about privately owned facilities that are open to the general public. Indeed, when a facility becomes a place of public accommodation, it "render[s] a 'service which has become of public interest' in the manner of the innkeepers and common carriers of old." [ ] Defendants are not completely unfettered, as they argue, in their ability to set the terms and conditions of admission. Defendants' facility may be privately owned, but that characteristic no longer overcomes a myriad of legitimate public interests. Public accommodations laws that prohibit discrimination against potential users of the facility are just one example of limitations imposed by law that affect the terms and conditions of entry. See 9 V.S.A. Sec. 4502 (prohibiting discrimination in place of public accommodation).

Defendants argue that the public policy of the state, as expressed in the "Acceptance of inherent risks" statute, 12 V.S.A. 1037 ["a person who takes part in any sport accepts as a matter of law the damages that inhere therein insofar as they are obvious and necessary"] indicates a willingness on the part of the Legislature to limit ski area liability. Therefore, they contend that public policy favors the use of express releases such as the one signed by plaintiff. On the contrary, defendants' allocation of responsibility for skiers' injuries is at odds with the statute. The statute places responsibility for the "inherent risks" of any sport on the participant, insofar as such risks are obvious and necessary. [ ] A ski area's own negligence, however, is neither an inherent risk nor an obvious and necessary one in the sport of skiing. Thus, a skier's assumption of the inherent risks of skiing does not abrogate the ski area's duty "'to warn of or correct dangers which in the exercise of reasonable prudence in the circumstances could have been foreseen and corrected.'" [ ]

Reversed and remanded.

NOTES AND QUESTIONS

1. *Tunkl* involved a release required of all patients entering a hospital. Is the court suggesting that the same analysis should apply to skiing? How do the *Tunkl* factors play out here?

2. Why is the law of premises liability appropriate here? Is this situation comparable to that of a department store or a park?

3. The court invokes the "ultimate goal of keeping accidents to the minimum level possible." Does that suggest that the ski resort would be liable here for having slopes that are more than minimal? To require that no skier be allowed to start down a slope until a signal has been received from below that the last skier has safely cleared the slope?

4. On the other hand, why should a ski resort be allowed to place an unpadded metal pole in a skier's path?

5. What is the role of the statute discussed in the last paragraph of the opinion?

6. Compare Barnes v. New Hampshire Karting Ass'n, Inc., 128 N.H. 102, 509 A.2d 151 (1986), in which the court upheld a release-from-negligence agreement signed as a condition of participating in Karting races. Plaintiff was under no serious disadvantage in bargaining power even though he had to sign the release in order to be able to race. He was under "no physical or economic compulsion" to sign the release and the activity involved was "not an essential one." See also Okura v. United States Cycling Federation, 186 Cal.App.3d 1462, 231 Cal.Rptr. 429 (1986)(upholding release covering negligence required for participation in bicycle race; the case did not come within the *Tunkl* factors).

7. No matter what the situation, courts generally agree that gross negligence or recklessness may never be disclaimed by agreement no matter what words are used. Sommer v. Federal Signal Corp., 79 N.Y.2d 540, 593 N.E.2d 1365, 583 N.Y.S.2d 957 (1992)(fire alarm company's failure to relay alarm). Why should this be so if the activity is not one that implicates the *Tunkl* factors?

8. Even where valid, the ability of adults to sign releases that bind members of their family is in serious doubt. See Scott v. Pacific West Mountain Resort, 119 Wash.2d 484, 834 P.2d 6 (1992)(refusing to enforce ski release signed by parent against injured child); Huber v. Hovey, 501 N.W.2d 53 (Iowa 1993)(refusing to enforce against wife release signed by husband).

9. *Drafting the contract.* Even in jurisdictions that are willing to permit exculpatory agreements in certain situations, the actual form must meet certain criteria. New York, for example, requires that the agreement state "unambiguously" that it involves an exemption from liability for negligence. See Gross v. Sweet, 49 N.Y.2d 102, 400 N.E.2d 306, 424 N.Y.S.2d 365 (1979).

In Krazek v. Mountain River Tours, Inc., 884 F.2d 163 (4th Cir.1989), the release executed before a river rafting trip stated:

> I am aware that during [the trip] certain substantial risks and dangers may occur, including but not limited to, hazards of traveling on a rubber raft in rough river conditions, hiking in tough terrain, accidents or illnesses in remote places without medical facilities, the forces of nature, and travel by automobile, bus or other conveyance.

> In consideration of and as part payment for the right to participate in such river trips or other activities and the services and food, if any, arranged for me by Mountain River Tours, Inc., its agents, employees and associates, I have and do hereby assume all of the above risks, and release, and will hold harmless from any and all liability actions, causes of action, debts, claims and demand of every kind and nature whatsoever which I now have or which may arise out of or in connection with my trip or participation in any other activity. The terms hereof shall serve as a release, indemnification, and assumption of risk for my heirs, executors and administrators and for all members of my family, including any minors accompanying me.

During plaintiff's trip a severe hail storm began. The rafter guide, an employee of defendant, ordered the rafters into the river to protect them from the hail. "While in the river Ms. Krazek was swept away by the current, thrown up against rocks, and injured." Her claim was that the form did not specifically mention negligence and thus she had not waived her right to pursue that remedy. The court disagreed. Applying West Virginia law, it began by noting that exculpatory clauses must be clear and definite and that contracts releasing a party from liability due to his own negligence "are looked upon with disfavor, and are strictly construed against the releasee." Additionally, "any ambiguities in a contract will be strictly construed against the preparer."

Nonetheless, the court concluded that this form was clear enough to protect the defendant from negligence liability—particularly the phrase waiving any claim "of every kind or nature whatsoever." To fail to bar this action "would create a requirement that to bar negligence claims all releases must include the words 'negligence' or 'negligent act.' We decline, however, to formulate a rule that requires the use of specific 'magic words' in contracts such as this one." The court also enforced the contract's indemnification provision to require plaintiff to reimburse the defendant for its costs in defending this action.

Compare Kissick v. Schmierer, 816 P.2d 188 (Alaska 1991), in which three prospective passengers on a private plane belonging to an aviation club were required to agree that they would not sue for negligence that caused "any loss, damage or injury to my person or my property." The passengers were killed. The court held that the agreement did not bar suits for death. A dissenter was "incredulous."

For a case in which defendant took extraordinary steps, see Johnson v. Paraplane Corp., 460 S.E.2d 398 (S.C.App.1995), upholding a release signed by a plaintiff who was hurt when defendant's flying powered parachute crashed. The exculpatory agreement was extensive, including provisions stating the "unavoidable and unprecedented dangers involved;" that "parachutes and engines do not always work;" that the release included "hidden, latent or obvious defects" in the equipment; that disclaimed liability for negligence and barred suit for negligence; and that "I agree that powered parachute flight activities are of little value to the public and no one has to engage in them." In addition plaintiff was required to watch a video that explained the release in everyday language and stressed the dangers and included such statements as "Now, you notice this discharge is as complete as it's possible to do under the law."

10. Before we turn to cases in which defendants claim that plaintiff's conduct shows an implied assumption of the risk, we should note briefly an intermediate area—cases in which defendants claim that a contract exists by virtue of a sign posted on defendant's land combined with plaintiff's conduct. The typical case involves a bailment at a parking lot with a large sign that announces that all cars are left at owner's risk. When the car is stolen the courts reject the claim that the bailment contract included the disclaimer, in the absence of a showing that the limitation—whether on a sign or on a claim check—was drawn to the plaintiff's attention.   See, e.g., Allright, Inc. v. Schroeder, 551 S.W.2d 745 (Tex.Civ.App.1977);   Allen v. Southern Pacific Co., 117 Utah 171, 213 P.2d 667 (1950)(limitation sign in railroad checkroom).

For a review of the area in the context of non-profit activities, see King, Exculpatory Agreements for Volunteers in Youth Activities—the Alternative to "Nerf"(R) Tiddlywinks, 53 Ohio St.L.J. 683 (1992), arguing that denying immunity will deter volunteers.   The "choice for many may be between youth activities without a right to sue and no organized youth activities at all."   He suggests that immunity even for acts of gross negligence and recklessness may be appropriate here because it is difficult to predict how actions will be judged in advance and because volunteers are not motivated by greed to endanger others.

2.   IMPLIED ASSUMPTION OF RISK

In this section, no express language or agreement indicates the intentions or understandings of the parties.   The area is quite controversial, in part because of disagreement over whether the term plays any useful role in negligence litigation.   Throughout the materials in this section consider whether the doctrine serves a purpose distinct from other aspects of the negligence framework we have considered up to this point.

Murphy v. Steeplechase Amusement Co.

Court of Appeals of New York, 1929.
250 N.Y. 479, 166 N.E. 173.

Appeal from a judgment of the Appellate Division of the Supreme Court, affirming a judgment in favor of plaintiff entered upon a verdict.

■ CARDOZO, CH. J.   The defendant, Steeplechase Amusement Company, maintains an amusement park at Coney Island, New York.

One of the supposed attractions is known as "The Flopper."   It is a moving belt, running upward on an inclined plane, on which passengers sit or stand.   Many of them are unable to keep their feet because of the movement of the belt, and are thrown backward or aside.   The belt runs in a groove, with padded walls on either side to a height of four feet, and with padded flooring beyond the walls at the same angle as the belt.   An electric motor, driven by current furnished by the Brooklyn Edison Company, supplies the needed power.

Plaintiff, a vigorous young man, visited the park with friends.   One of them, a young woman, now his wife, stepped upon the moving belt. Plaintiff followed and stepped behind her.   As he did so, he felt what he describes as a sudden jerk, and was thrown to the floor.   His wife in front and also friends behind him were thrown at the same time.   Something more was here, as every one understood, than the slowly-moving escalator that is common in shops and public places.   A fall was foreseen as one of the risks of the adventure.   There would have been no point to the whole thing, no adventure about it, if the risk had not been there. The very name above the gate, the Flopper, was warning to the timid. If the name was not enough, there was warning more distinct in the experience of others. We are told by the plaintiff's wife that the members of her party stood looking at the sport before joining in it themselves. Some aboard the belt were able, as she viewed them, to sit down with decorum or even to stand and keep their footing; others jumped or fell. The tumbling bodies and the screams and laughter supplied the merriment and fun. "I took a chance," she said when asked whether she thought that a fall might be expected.

Plaintiff took the chance with her, but, less lucky than his companions, suffered a fracture of a knee cap. He states in his complaint that the belt was dangerous to life and limb in that it stopped and started violently and suddenly and was not properly equipped to prevent injuries to persons who were using it without knowledge of its dangers, and in a bill of particulars he adds that it was operated at a fast and dangerous rate of speed and was not supplied with a proper railing, guard or other device to prevent a fall therefrom. No other negligence is charged.

We see no adequate basis for a finding that the belt was out of order. It was already in motion when the plaintiff put his foot on it. He cannot help himself to a verdict in such circumstances by the addition of the facile comment that it threw him with a jerk. One who steps upon a moving belt and finds his heels above his head is in no position to discriminate with nicety between the successive stages of the shock, between the jerk which is a cause and the jerk, accompanying the fall, as an instantaneous effect. There is evidence for the defendant that power was transmitted smoothly, and could not be transmitted otherwise. If the movement was spasmodic, it was an unexplained and, it seems, an inexplicable departure from the normal workings of the mechanism. An aberration so extraordinary, if it is to lay the basis for a verdict, should rest on something firmer than a mere descriptive epithet, a summary of the sensations of a tense and crowded moment [   ]. But the jerk, if it were established, would add little to the case. Whether the movement of the belt was uniform or irregular, the risk at greatest was a fall. This was the very hazard that was invited and foreseen [   ].

Volenti non fit injuria. One who takes part in such a sport accepts the dangers that inhere in it so far as they are obvious and necessary, just as a fencer accepts the risk of a thrust by his antagonist or a spectator at a ball game the chance of contact with the ball [   ]. The antics of the clown are not the paces of the cloistered cleric. The rough and boisterous joke, the horseplay of the crowd, evokes its own guffaws, but they are not the pleasures of tranquillity. The plaintiff was not seeking a retreat for meditation. Visitors were tumbling about the belt to the merriment of onlookers when he made his choice to join them. He took the chance of a like fate, with whatever damage to his body might ensue from such a fall. The timorous may stay at home.

A different case would be here if the dangers inherent in the sport were obscure or unobserved ([   ]; Tantillo v. Goldstein Bros. Amusement Co., 248 N.Y. 286), or so serious as to justify the belief that precautions of some kind must have been taken to avert them [   ]. Nothing happened to the plaintiff except what common experience tells us may happen at any time as the consequence of a sudden fall. Many a skater or a horseman can rehearse a tale of equal woe. A different case there would also be if the accidents had been so many as to show that the game in its inherent nature was too dangerous to be continued without change. The president of the amusement company says that there had never been such an accident before. A nurse employed at an emergency hospital maintained in connection with the park contradicts him to some extent. She says that on other occasions she had attended patrons of the park who had been injured at the Flopper, how many she could not say. None, however, had been badly injured or had suffered broken bones. Such testimony is not enough to show that the game was a trap for the unwary, too perilous to be endured. According to the defendant's estimate, two hundred and fifty thousand visitors were at the Flopper in a year. Some quota of accidents was to be looked for in so great a mass. One might as well say that a skating rink should be abandoned because skaters sometimes fall.

There is testimony by the plaintiff that he fell upon wood, and not upon a canvas padding. He is strongly contradicted by the photographs and by the witnesses for the defendant, and is without corroboration in the testimony of his companions who were witnesses in his behalf. If his observation was correct, there was a defect in the equipment, and one not obvious or known. The padding should have been kept in repair to break the force of any fall. The case did not go to the jury, however, upon any such theory of the defendant's liability, nor is the defect fairly suggested by the plaintiff's bill of particulars, which limits his complaint. The case went to the jury upon the theory that negligence was dependent upon a sharp and sudden jerk.

The judgment of the Appellate Division and that of the Trial Term should be reversed.   .   .   .

◼ POUND, CRANE, LEHMAN, KELLOGG and HUBBS, JJ., concur; O'BRIEN, J., dissents on the authority of Tantillo v. Goldstein Brothers Amusement Co. (248 N.Y. 286).

NOTES AND QUESTIONS

1. Why does Judge Cardozo say that even if the belt had jerked unexpectedly this would not help plaintiff's case? What might he have said if such a jerk made everyone on the belt fall and suffer broken limbs?

2. In the Tantillo case cited, judgment was affirmed in favor of a 14–year–old plaintiff who was admitted to defendant's show without paying in return for his agreement to participate in a vaudeville act. He was hurt when one of the performers failed to catch him as he was tossed through the air. How is *Tantillo* relevant to *Murphy?*

3.   What was the defendant's negligence in *Murphy?*

4.   Judge Cardozo suggests that *Murphy* might have been different if the Flopper caused so many accidents that its "inherent nature" made it "too dangerous to be continued without change." If one of every three patrons suffered a broken bone and such information was posted conspicuously at the entrance to the Flopper and each prospective customer had to watch for ten minutes before getting on, how would that case differ from *Murphy?*

5.   More generally, should the supplier of a product, service or activity be insulated from liability for known risks—no matter how serious—as long as the information is clearly provided to the potential victim? Note that this issue is distinct from the question in the preceding section where the claim was that the victim expressly agreed not to sue. We will reconsider the present issue in Chapter VIII, when we discuss product liability cases.

6.   *Participants.* In recent years, there has been a sudden spurt of litigation between participants in amateur sports. The first major case was decided in California. In Knight v. Jewett, 3 Cal.4th 296, 834 P.2d 696, 11 Cal.Rptr.2d 2 (1992), plaintiff alleged that during halftime of a Super Bowl telecast, she and her friends decided to play an informal game of touch football on an adjoining dirt lot, using a "peewee" football. Each side included both men and women. No rules were explicitly discussed before the game. Plaintiff alleged that defendant, one of her opponents, played aggressively and that on the play before she was hurt, she told him to "be careful" or she would stop playing. On the next play, he knocked plaintiff over from behind while defending on a pass play—and stepped on her hand, injuring it. The trial judge granted defendant summary judgment.

On appeal, the court affirmed, 6–1, but split 4–3 on the right way to approach these cases. The majority asserted that the crucial analysis was on the duty defendant owed the plaintiff. If the defendant has met whatever duty was owed the plaintiff, the defendant is not liable to plaintiff for anything. If, on the other hand, the defendant has violated the duty owed plaintiff, the defendant will be liable, subject to a reduction for whatever contributory negligence might be shown. (The four justices taking this view split over terminology. Three wanted to continue to call the part focusing on duty "primary assumption of the risk" and the part focusing on possible defenses after breach "secondary assumption of the risk." The fourth judge wanted to eliminate all use of "assumption of risk" in favor of duty and comparative negligence.) For the majority:

> . . .   [I]n the heat of an active sporting event like baseball or football, a participant's normal energetic conduct often includes accidentally careless behavior. . . . [V]igorous participation in such sporting events likely would be chilled if legal liability were to be imposed on a participant on the basis of his or her ordinary careless conduct. . . . [E]ven when a participant's conduct violates a rule of the game and may subject the violator to internal sanctions prescribed by the sport itself, imposition of legal liability for such conduct might well alter fundamentally the nature of the sport by deterring

participants from vigorously engaging in activity that falls close to, but on the permissible side, of a prescribed rule.

Liability would flow "only if the participant intentionally injures another player or engages in conduct that is so reckless as to be totally outside the range of the ordinary activity involved in the sport." The defendant's behavior here was at most careless and summary judgment was properly granted.

Three justices argued that the proper approach to this type of case centered on the notion of the plaintiff's "consent" to accept specific risks. Two of them found that consent here because plaintiff admitted that she expected to receive contact and "bumps and bruises." The third did not find that consent and dissented.

A different result was reached in Lestina v. West Bend Mut.Ins.Co., 176 Wis.2d 901, 501 N.W.2d 28 (1993), involving a soccer injury. The court, 4–3, held that negligence should be the governing principle. The majority rejected the notion that vigorous participation would be chilled by invocation of negligence:

> To determine whether a player's conduct constitutes actionable negligence (or contributory negligence), the fact finder should consider such material factors as the sport involved, the rules and regulations governing the sport; the generally accepted customs and practices of the sport (including the types of contact and the level of violence generally accepted); the risks inherent in the game and those that are outside the realm of anticipation; the presence of protective equipment or uniforms; and the facts and circumstances of the particular case, including the ages and physical attributes of the participants, the participants' respective skills at the game, and the participants' knowledge of the rules and customs.

The dissenters rejected the idea that "negligence was flexible enough to be applied under any set of circumstances." Applied to contact sports the negligence standard would chill vigorous participation. Why might the court's formulation of considerations chill participants?

In Crawn v. Campo, 136 N.J. 494, 643 A.2d 600 (1994), arising when a base runner in an informal softball game either ran into or slid into the catcher, the court unanimously held that "the duty of care applicable to participants in informal recreational sports is to avoid the infliction of injury caused by reckless or intentional conduct." Justice Handler cited two "policy reasons" for this result: "One is the promotion of vigorous participation in athletic activities . . . The other is to avoid a flood of litigation." He responded to the lower court's reliance on the Wisconsin case as follows:

> The problem with the court's analysis lies in the extraordinary difficulty in judging conduct that is based on limitless variables with respect to how the same game is played among different groups of people. The relationship among sports participants is derived from a consensual arrangement that involves both articulated and unarticulat-

ed rules, obvious and obscure conventions, and clear and not-so-clear expectations. Some rules are broken, yet their transgression is tolerated. Certain practices are customary yet others are followed inconsistently. Some conventions are well understood, others are not always known or appreciated by all participants. Each player's expectations are often subjective, and may not be shared or experienced by others in the same way.

Are fouls in basketball rule violations that should be tolerated? What if a player is hurt when he falls after being fouled? Is there a distinction between "regular" fouls and "flagrant" fouls? On the "flood of litigation" point, Justice Handler noted:

> One might well conclude that something is terribly wrong with a society in which the most commonly-accepted aspects of play—a traditional source of a community's conviviality and cohesion—spur litigation. The heightened-recklessness standard recognizes a common-sense distinction between excessively harmful conduct and the more routine rough-and-tumble of sports that should occur freely on the playing fields and should not be second-guessed in courtrooms.

In Freeman v. Hale, 30 Cal.App.4th 1388, 36 Cal.Rptr.2d 418 (1994), plaintiff skier was injured in a collision with defendant drunken skier. In response to defendant's argument that collisions are an inherent risk of skiing, the court relied on *Knight* in upholding actions in situations in which prohibiting the conduct in question "would neither deter vigorous participation in the sport nor otherwise fundamentally alter the nature of the sport." Although defendant "did not have a duty to avoid an inadvertent collision with [plaintiff], he did have a duty to avoid increasing the risk of such a collision. [ ] He did not establish that, by drinking alcohol while he was skiing, he did not increase that risk."

Compare Connelly v. Mammoth Mountain Ski Area, 39 Cal.App.4th 8, 45 Cal.Rptr.2d 855 (1995), in which the plaintiff, an advanced skier, was skiing down an "advanced intermediate" run when his ski bindings released and he fell and slid downhill into a large metal tower that supported the ski lift. The court denied recovery under *Knight v. Jewett,* noting that the tower was visible for 200 yards and that the run was fairly wide at the point at which the tower bisected it. In response to plaintiff's claim that the tower's padding was not at snow level and was inadequate in any event to cushion the blow, the court said that on previous occasions it had identified some of the inherent dangers of skiing to include "variations in terrain, surface or subsurface snow or ice conditions; bare spots; rocks, trees and other forms of natural growth or debris; collision with ski lift towers and their components, with other skiers, or with properly marked or plainly visible snow-making or snow-grooming equipment." The risk in this case was inherent in skiing. Ski operators had no duty to pad their clearly visible towers and it "would be anomalous to hold an operator who padded its towers—as Mammoth did here—more liable than an operator who failed to do so." There was no claim that defendant had done anything that caused plaintiff to collide with the tower: "colliding with a ski lift tower while skiing is an inherent risk within the doctrine of primary assumption of risk, and Mammoth owed no duty to Connelly to protect him from this inherent risk." Recall the Dalury case, p. 406, supra, involving express assumption of risk questions in a similar accident.

In Turcotte v. Fell, 68 N.Y.2d 432, 502 N.E.2d 964, 510 N.Y.S.2d 49 (1986), plaintiff, an experienced professional jockey, was hurt in a racing accident. His suit against the jockeys who allegedly acted negligently was dismissed. The court concluded that "by participating in the race, plaintiff consented that the duty of care owed him by defendants was no more than a duty to avoid reckless or intentionally harmful conduct." The court observed that in horse races jockeys try to control half-ton horses whose speeds reach 40 miles per hour. Every jockey is trying to win and the horses have no prescribed lanes. During races "speeding horses lawfully and properly come within inches of other horses and frequently bump each other. [Plaintiff] conceded that there is a fine line between what is lawful and unlawful in the movement of a horse on the track during a race." Because of these dangers, the plaintiff consented to relieve other jockeys "of the legal duty to use reasonable care to avoid crossing into his lane of travel."

7. *Baseball spectators.* In Davidoff v. Metropolitan Baseball Club, 61 N.Y.2d 996, 463 N.E.2d 1219, 475 N.Y.S.2d 367 (1984), the 14–year-old plaintiff was sitting in the first row behind first base during a professional game at Shea Stadium when she was badly injured by a foul ball. The court, 5–2, affirmed defendant stadium owner's summary judgment:

> Claims involving injuries sustained by spectators from misdirected baseballs were traditionally decided—and dismissed—on the ground of assumption of risk. However, with the enactment of [comparative negligence] in 1975, the absolute defense was no longer applicable and it became necessary to define the duty of care owed by a proprietor of a baseball field to its spectators. This we did [in *Akins*, p. 52,]
>
> > [W]here a proprietor of a ball park furnishes screening for the area of the field behind home plate where the danger of being struck by a ball is greatest and that screening is of sufficient extent to provide adequate protection for as many spectators as may reasonably be expected to desire such seating in the course of an ordinary game, the proprietor fulfills the duty of care imposed by law and, therefore, cannot be liable in negligence.
>
> Here, there has been no showing by plaintiff that (1) defendants failed to erect a screen behind home plate providing adequate protection in that area, and (2) there are not sufficient seats behind the screen to accommodate as many spectators as reasonably may be expected to desire such seating. No evidence that the screen was inadequate was presented, and it is undisputed that there were unoccupied seats behind the screen at Shea on the day plaintiff was injured.

The fact that others have been injured in this unscreened area did not matter. Plaintiff's claim that notice of danger should raise a jury question "would require a baseball field proprietor to operate as an insurer of spectators unless there was a protective screen shielding every seat. We held in *Akins* that a proprietor should be allowed to satisfy the desires of the many spectators who prefer to view the game from a seat unobstructed by fences or protective screening. No sound reason has been shown why the rule of policy set forth in *Akins* should be changed."

The dissenters argued that requiring screening only behind home plate "does nothing more than to artificially limit the liability of ball park owners." Moreover, even if the majority's focus on unoccupied screened seats made sense in a sandlot where spectators may move around, it "is utterly out of place when the setting is a major sports stadium where . . . all seats are individually assigned or allocated to a specific area." A fan who is "unable to secure a seat behind home plate must go home or fully assume responsibility for any consequences of remaining at the ball park no matter how unreasonable the risk of injury."

Would the result or the analysis change if the plaintiff had been a foreign tourist who had heard about baseball but did not know about its dangers? Does it matter whether the spectator is hurt during the first two minutes after taking a seat or after one hour?

In Neinstein v. Los Angeles Dodgers, Inc., 185 Cal.App.3d 176, 229 Cal.Rptr. 612 (1986), the court followed a similar approach, observing that imposing a duty to protect all spectators would require owners either (1) to place "all spectators behind a protective screen thereby reducing the quality of everyone's view" and preventing spectators from catching balls, or (2) to continue the status quo and increase ticket prices to cover the cost of compensating those hurt. The latter course would mean that "persons of meager means might be 'priced out' of enjoying the great American pastime." The introduction of comparative fault did not change the court's analysis.

The court also observed that but for the constraint of an earlier decision, "we would not be persuaded that there is a need to impose a duty to provide *any* screened seats. A person who fears injury always has the option of refraining from attending a baseball game or of sitting in a part of the park which is out of reach of balls traveling with sufficient velocity to cause harm." How would prospective spectators learn about the total absence of screening?

Legislation. After adverse judgments against both the Chicago Cubs and White Sox, the Illinois legislature adopted protective legislation. Essentially, owners and operators of stadiums are not liable to anyone hit by a ball or bat unless they were sitting behind a negligently defective screen or they were hurt as the result of willful or wanton conduct. 745 I.L.C.S. 38/10. Colorado adopted similar legislation just as it got its first major league team. The legislation, Colo.Rev.Stat. § 13–21–120, asserts that professional baseball is a "wholesome and healthy family activity which should be encouraged," that the "state will derive economic benefit from spectators" attending the games, and that it is thus in the state's interest to "encourage attendance at professional baseball games." Limiting the civil liability of team owners and stadium owners "will help contain costs, keeping ticket prices more affordable."

10. *Hockey.* The baseball analysis was applied to amateur hockey in Gilchrist v. City of Troy, 113 App.Div.2d 271, 495 N.Y.S.2d 781 (1985), affirmed 67 N.Y.2d 1034, 494 N.E.2d 1382, 503 N.Y.S.2d 717 (1986). The rink had plexiglass screening at each end, but none in the middle third of the rink. The plaintiff's son was hit by a puck while standing behind the boards in the unscreened part. See also Rosa v. County of Nassau, 153 App.Div.2d 618, 544 N.Y.S.2d 652 (1989)(finding the duty met in a hockey case by a three foot wooden fence surmounted by a three foot plexiglass fence).

Before television, the risks of hockey were not as widely known as they are now. What duty might a proprietor staging a professional hockey game have owed to spectators in California in the 1930s? See Thurman v. Ice Palace, 36 Cal.App.2d 364, 97 P.2d 999 (1939), in which plaintiff, who knew nothing about hockey, was hit by a puck within ten minutes after arriving at her seat in an unprotected area. The court upheld the action on the ground that ice hockey was "practically a new" game in California and the risk of a flying puck was not "common knowledge."

1st Semester

Gonzalez v. Garcia

Court of Appeal of California, Second District, 1977.
75 Cal.App.3d 874, 142 Cal.Rptr. 503.

[Plaintiff, defendant, and Longest were co-workers who shared a car pool. They got off work at 6 a.m. and went drinking. "It was their custom to stop for a few drinks, but on this particular day they stayed longer and consumed more alcohol than usual." Defendant resumed driving his car and plaintiff passenger fell asleep. When he awoke he twice asked to be taken home. During a stop at a liquor store, plaintiff called his wife to come and get him but there was no answer. He assumed she was with her mother who was ill—and he did not want to call there because it would disturb her mother. Defendant and Longest shared a bottle of tequila and, over plaintiff's protests, went to another bar. A disturbance broke out and police were called. An officer told plaintiff, who appeared to be the least intoxicated, that he should drive. He did so and they dropped Longest at his home. Then defendant insisted on driving. Plaintiff again tried to reach his wife but failed. After further talk, defendant got behind the wheel and plaintiff got into the passenger's seat—and fell asleep. The car crashed, injuring plaintiff. Although plaintiff testified that defendant seemed all right, the driver was "unquestionably intoxicated."

The trial judge charged on comparative negligence but he refused to charge on assumption of risk. The jury found that the defendant was 80% at fault and plaintiff 20%. On appeal, defendant argued that assumption of risk should have been charged.]

■ STEPHENS, J.

. . .

The defense of assumption of risk was a late development in the law of negligence. The elements most frequently cited as essential to find assumption of risk are that the plaintiff have actual knowledge of the specific risk, appreciate the magnitude of the danger and freely and voluntarily encounter it. [ ]

Most commentators recognize at least three kinds of assumption of risk: (1) express—where plaintiff, in advance, gives consent to relieve defendant of a legal duty and to take his chances of injury from a known risk; (2) implied—where plaintiff acts reasonably in voluntarily encountering a risk with the knowledge that defendant will not protect him; and (3) implied—where the plaintiff acts unreasonably in voluntarily exposing himself to a risk created by defendant's negligence. [ ] Others define implied assumption of risk as being divided into primary, where defendant cannot be held negligent because he is under no duty to plaintiff or there has been no breach of duty because plaintiff's conduct has limited the duty owed him by defendant, and secondary, which is used as an affirmative defense to an established breach of duty. (Meistrich v. Casino Arena Attractions, Inc. (1959) 31 N.J. 44 [155 A.2d 90].)

So long as contributory negligence and assumption of risk were both complete bars to recovery, the distinction between the two was never completely clarified, especially with implied assumption of risk. Usually, if a distinction was made, it was based upon the fact that assumption of risk requires knowledge of the danger and intelligent and deliberate acquiescence, whereas contributory negligence is concerned with fault or departure from the reasonable man standard of conduct, frequently inadvertently. [ ] Also the standard for determining whether the defense is available is different—assumption of risk using a subjective standard of the particular individual and circumstances and contributory negligence using an objective, reasonably prudent man standard with which to compare plaintiff's conduct. [ ]

Assumption of risk has been rather unpopular due to the harshness of the "all or nothing" recovery, and there has been considerable effort to abolish it completely, particularly in view of the emergence of the comparative negligence doctrine. [ ] Nevertheless, where the doctrine of comparative negligence has been accepted, there have been three different approaches to assumption of risk—completely abolishing it as a defense, as in the federal Employers' Liability Act, [ ], as interpreted in Tiller v. Atlantic Coast Line R. Co. (1943) 318 U.S. 54; maintaining it as a complete and separate defense, [ ], or merging it to some extent with contributory negligence, [ ]. In those states which have merged the defenses, there has frequently been a complete merger of implied assumption of risk and contributory negligence, with express assumption of risk remaining as a separate defense. . . .

. . .

Regardless of the extent of assumption of risk which still exists as a separate defense and complete bar to recovery, in this case plaintiff's conduct clearly falls into the overlapping area, the area of choosing an unreasonable alternative when reasonable ones were available, thereby evidencing a lack of due care for his own safety. Plaintiff had actual knowledge that defendant was intoxicated, he had been advised by a police officer that he should drive, he demonstrated that he probably had knowledge of the risk by his attempts to contact his wife, he had alternatives of remaining at Longest's house or calling a cab and yet he chose to ride with defendant. Where there is a reasonably safe alternative open, the plaintiff's free choice of the more dangerous way is unreasonable and amounts to both contributory negligence and assumption of the risk. [ ] To that extent the doctrines are merged . . . into the doctrine of comparative negligence.

The facts do not justify even an inference that the acts of plaintiff included an element in addition to negligence such as waiver of duty, agreement, or other element not a variant of contributory negligence.

There was no error in the court's refusal to give the instruction on assumption of risk as requested.

The judgment is affirmed.

■ KAUS, P.J., and ASHBY, J., concurred.

NOTES AND QUESTIONS

1. What, if anything, remains of assumption of risk? Does anything in *Gonzalez* suggest that the court might allow the plaintiff some recovery in the "Flopper" case? The baseball cases?

2. New Jersey was the first state clearly to reject the existence of the term assumption of risk—and did so well before comparative negligence became popular. The history is set forth in McGrath v. American Cyanamid Co., 41 N.J. 272, 196 A.2d 238 (1963):

> In Meistrich v. Casino Arena Attractions, Inc., [ ], we pointed out that assumption of the risk was theretofore used in two incongruous senses: in one sense it meant the defendant was not negligent, while in its other sense it meant the plaintiff was contributorily negligent. We said that in truth there are but two issues—negligence and contributory negligence—both to be resolved by the standard of the reasonably prudent man, and that it was erroneous to suggest to the jury that assumption of the risk was still another issue.
>
> . . .
>
> In *Meistrich* we said the terminology of assumption of the risk should not be used when it is projected in its secondary sense, i.e., that of contributory negligence [ ]. We thought, however, that "[p]erhaps a well-guarded charge of assumption of risk in its primary sense will aid comprehension" [ ]. . . . Experience, however, indicates the term "assumption of risk" is so apt to create mist that it is better

banished from the scene. We hope we have heard the last of it. Henceforth let us stay with "negligence" and "contributory negligence."

Does the emergence of comparative negligence affect the analysis?

3. Consider the following article from page 3 of the San Francisco Daily Journal, Dec. 17, 1993:

> Assumption of Risk: The justices [of the California Supreme Court] let stand a $240,000 jury award in favor of a woman who was injured while orally copulating a man driving a car in 1988.
>
> The motorist, who veered off the road and hit a telephone pole near Modesto after closing his eyes, contended she assumed the risk of injury and her suit should be barred. But both a Stanislaus County trial judge and the Court of Appeal rejected the assumption of risk defense and none of the Supreme Court justices voted to review the unpublished decision in *Gehrt v. Costanza*, [ ].

Why is assumed risk not a total bar? Should it have been a partial bar?

4. *The Employment Context.* The doctrine of assumed risk was of major significance in nineteenth century industrial injury cases—before workers' compensation legislation replaced the tort system. In fact, the doctrine proved to be such an effective bar to employee tort suits that it played a key role in triggering the workers' compensation movement. See generally Friedman and Ladinsky, Social Change and the Law of Industrial Accidents, 67 Colum.L.Rev. 50 (1967). Utilization of the doctrine in employment cases has been justified on economic grounds—as a tool in facilitating freedom of contract. See Posner, A Theory of Negligence, 1 J.Legal Studies 29, 45 (1972). Consider the following response in Rabin, The Historical Development of the Fault Principle: A Reinterpretation, 15 Ga.L.Rev. 925, 940 (1981)*:

> With regard to assumed risk, Posner has argued that the courts, by effecting a trade-off between higher wages and an injury premium, were giving explicit recognition to the worker's desire to market his taste for risk. Resting this argument, as he does, on freedom of contract is obviously circular. The empirical question is whether workers in relatively dangerous occupations possessed the autonomy and mobility to effect trade-offs between safety and wages in their negotiations with employers, or whether they simply were impelled by circumstances to confront unwanted hazards. Posner offers no evidence on this score. As Gary Schwartz has indicated, there is some historical documentation to suggest the contrary.[55] In a similar vein, a leading contemporaneous authority on industrial injury law remarked:

---

* This article was originally published in 15 Ga.L.Rev. No. 4 and is reprinted by permission.

55. See Schwartz, Tort Law and the Economy in Nineteenth Century America: A Reinterpretation, 90 Yale L.J. 1717, 1769 & nn. 389–90 (1981). [ ]

Upon the average man it is certain that the fear of the disagreeable, and it may be, frightful consequences which will almost certainly ensue from the failure to obtain work or from the loss of a position, must always operate as a very strong coercive influence, indeed. To speak of one whom that fear drives into or detains in a dangerous employment as being a voluntary agent is a mere trifling with words.[56]

Moreover, the history of workmen's compensation reform is singularly free of any reference to laborers protesting against the legislation on the grounds that a compulsory safety premium was likely to have a depressing effect on wages. Where were the risk-preferring workers when their wage premiums were under siege? If the historical record is to be believed, they were unappreciatively on the side of unseating their judicial protectors.

Any trace of harmonization between the fault principle and assumed risk is further weakened when one examines the scope of the doctrine closely, for it was by no means limited to well-understood risks of the workplace. To the contrary, Labatt points out that the doctrine was applied to abnormal or transitory risks of the employment as well as "normal" hazards. Moreover, Schwartz, in his study of New Hampshire cases, concludes that the risks assumed were not limited to those immediately apparent in the employment situation.

Workers' compensation legislation is given detailed treatment in Chapter XI.

Zanghi v. Niagara Frontier Transportation Commission

Court of Appeals of New York, 1995.
85 N.Y.2d 423, 649 N.E.2d 1167, 626 N.Y.S.2d 23.

■ TITONE, JUDGE.

In Cooper v. City of New York, [1995], we held that, pursuant to the firefighter rule, police and firefighters may not recover in common-law negligence for line-of-duty injuries resulting from risks associated with the particular dangers inherent in that type of employment. These three appeals require us to determine the scope of this bar to recovery. We conclude that the firefighter rule precludes a police officer or firefighter from recovering in tort when the performance of his or her duties increased the risk of the injury happening, and did not merely furnish the occasion for the injury. Applying that test in each of these cases before us, we hold that all three plaintiffs are barred from recovering on their common-law negligence claims. [In one case a statutory claim was reinstated.]

I. Background

[In *Zanghi*, plaintiff police officer was assigned to defendant's bus terminal during a bus driver strike. He "slipped and fell on a snow-

---

56. 3 C. Labatt, Master and Servant § 963, at 2490 (1913).

covered metal plate as he was approaching a picketer who was packing snowballs, presumably to throw at departing buses." In *Raquet v. Braun*, one firefighter was killed and another injured when the wall of a burning building collapsed outward rather than inward due to alleged construction defects. In *Ruocco v. New York City Tr.Auth.*, two police officers were injured when they fell while "rushing down a flight of stairs leading into the subway in response to a radio call for assistance from another officer." They claimed that defendant failed to properly maintain the stairs, which were alleged to be "cracked, worn, uneven, dirty and wet." All three trial courts refused to dismiss the claims "citing the 'separate and apart' exception to the firefighter rule, which would permit a common-law negligence action to go forward if the conduct causing the injury was independent of the conduct for which the officers and firefighters had been summoned." All three common-law rulings were reversed by the Appellate Division on the ground that the *Cooper* case had rejected that basis for liability.]

We affirm the dismissal of the negligence claims in all three cases [and modify a statutory ruling in the second case].

II. Common–Law Negligence Claims

The "firefighter's rule," a product of this State's long-standing common law, precludes firefighters and police officers from recovering damages for injuries caused by "negligence in the very situations that create the occasion for their services." [ ] The rule is applied to bar common-law negligence claims where "the injury sustained is related to the particular dangers which police officers [and firefighters] are expected to assume as part of their duties" [*Cooper*].

The rationale for applying the firefighter rule has evolved from the initial theory that public safety officers, as licensees entering upon the land, took the property as they found it. With that rationale undermined by Basso v. Miller, [in which New York abolished the distinction between invitees and licensees], subsequent cases retained the firefighter rule by reliance on the doctrine of assumption of risk—i.e., that persons who accept employment as firefighters or police assume the risks of fire-related or crime-fighting-related injuries, including the risk that property owners and occupants may negligently maintain their premises [ ]. Continued application of the bar is presently grounded on the public policy against awarding damages to firefighters and police for hazards "that create a need for their services" and which they are hired, specially trained and compensated to confront (Santangelo v. State of New York, 71 N.Y.2d, at 397, 521 N.E.2d 770, 526 N.Y.S.2d 812 (1988)).

In an apparent effort to abate the harsh effects of the firefighter rule, some courts in this State created an exception to the bar of common-law negligence claims where the negligent act causing the injury was "separate and apart" from the act occasioning the need for the officer's services [ ]. As the Appellate Division in each of the cases before us correctly stated, however, that exception was rejected by this Court in [*Cooper*.]

In *Cooper*, this Court explained that the "determinative factor" in applying the firefighter rule's bar is "whether the injury sustained is related to the particular dangers which police officers [and firefighters] are expected to assume as part of their duties" [ ]. In these three cases we are essentially asked to define when the requisite "connection" exists between the plaintiff's injury and the special hazards associated with police and fire duties [ ]. We hold that that necessary connection is present where the performance of the police officer's or firefighter's duties increased the risk of the injury happening, and did not merely furnish the occasion for the injury. In other words, where some act taken in furtherance of a specific police or firefighting function exposed the officer to a heightened risk of sustaining the particular injury, he or she may not recover damages for common-law negligence. By contrast, a common-law negligence claim may proceed where an officer is injured in the line of duty merely because he or she happened to be present in a given location, but was not engaged in any specific duty that increased the risk of receiving that injury. For example, if a police officer who is simply walking on foot patrol is injured by a flower pot that fortuitously falls from an apartment window, the officer can recover damages because nothing in the acts undertaken in the performance of police duties placed him or her at increased risk for that accident to happen. On the other hand, if an officer is injured by a suspect who struggles to avoid an arrest, the rule precludes recovery in tort because the officer is specially trained and compensated to confront such dangers.

Applying the pertinent principles to the cases before us, we conclude that the common-law negligence claims in all three cases were properly dismissed. In *Zanghi*, which involved the police officer who slipped on the snow-covered metal plate, the officer's own trial testimony established that he was focused solely on quickly reaching the picketer who was packing the snowball. Thus, the emergent circumstances exposed plaintiff Zanghi to the risk of injury from slipping on the plate concealed by patches of snow— a risk similar to that faced by the police officers in *Cooper*, who drove in excess of the speed limit and without regard for the attendant weather and lighting conditions. Accordingly, the risk of slipping while approaching the strikers was one of the particular risks of employment that plaintiff Zanghi was compensated to confront.

Likewise, injury to a firefighter due to the collapse of a burning building is one of the particular risks firefighters are asked to brave by their employment. Without doubt, the performance of the firefighting duties by plaintiffs Spoth and Raquet [ ] increased the risk of being injured by the collapse of the roof and exterior wall.

Also, police officers are commonly called to render assistance to other officers, and may respond in a variety of ways. The primary goal of the officers is to reach the fellow servant quickly and to render assistance; care and caution in the steps taken to reach that location are naturally compromised. The risk that an officer may be injured during the response, due to the loss of footing, a blow out on a tire, or a car collision at an intersection is inherent in police duties. Thus, the officers in *Ruocco*, who were rushing down stairs to reach a co-worker in need of assistance, were at an increased risk of injury precisely because of the nature of the duty they were performing—responding to a call for backup—and are barred from recovering damages for common-law negligence by the firefighter rule.

[The court upheld a statutory action in the firefighter case. The two police cases were affirmed and the firefighter case was modified.]

■ KAYE, C.J., and SIMONS, BELLACOSA, SMITH, LEVINE and CIPARICK, JJ., concur.

NOTES AND QUESTIONS

1. How was the rule justified before the distinction between invitee and licensee was abolished? How was it justified after abolition?

Is there an intelligible distinction between the rejected "separate and apart" exception and the adopted "related to the particular dangers" rule? In Sharkey v. Mitchell's Newspaper Delivery, Inc., 165 App.Div.2d 664, 560 N.Y.S.2d 140 (1990), plaintiff police officer was injured by defendant while directing traffic at the scene of an earlier accident. The court permitted the suit because the "defendant's negligence was separate and apart from the act which occasioned the services of plaintiff as a police officer." The "determinative factor" was said to be the "degree of separation between the negligent act directly causing the injury and the act which occasioned the police officer's services." How should this case be analyzed under *Zanghi*?

2. Is the fact that the plaintiffs in these cases were paid to undertake these risks a separate justification?

3. Is the court suggesting that a police officer hurt while struggling with a suspect cannot recover from the suspect? What if the suspect shoots the plaintiff?

4. In each of the cases can you suggest changes in the facts that might warrant different results under the court's analysis? Suppose, for example, that in the first case the shifts change and plaintiff is hurt walking away from the site? What if he was hurrying because he was very cold from the long hours at the strike site?

5. In Neighbarger v. Irwin Industries, Inc., 8 Cal.4th 532, 882 P.2d 347, 34 Cal.Rptr.2d 630 (1994), the court refused to extend the bar to safety employees of a private firm who were hurt while fighting a fire started by defendant's negligence. The court reviewed the justifications offered for the special rule for public employees and concluded that "it is unfair to charge the defendant with a duty of care to prevent injury to the plaintiff arising from the very condition or hazard the defendant has contracted with the plaintiff to remedy or confront."

The court then turned to whether this should apply to private security and safety workers. Although there was an initial similarity in terms of the jobs being performed, this faded when the public aspect was considered:

When the firefighter is publicly employed, the public, having secured the services of the firefighter by taxing itself, stands in the shoes of the person who hires a contractor to cure a dangerous condition. In effect, the public has purchased exoneration from the duty of care and should not have to pay twice, through taxation and through individual liability, for that service. [   ] But when a safety employee is privately employed, a third party lacks the relationship that justifies exonerating him or her from the usual duty of care. The third party, unlike the public with its police and fire departments, has not provided the services of the private safety employee. Nor has the third party paid in any way to be relieved of the duty of care toward such a private employee. Having no relationship with the employee, and not having contracted for his or her services, it would not be unfair to charge the third party with the usual duty of care towards the private safety employee.

If workers in private industry receive a hazard premium for dangerous occupations should that affect the analysis in *Neighbarger*?

6. The *Neighbarger* court observed that the public pays one way or the other in the public firefighter situation—and that allowing suits "would involve the parties in costly litigation over rights of subrogation without substantially benefiting the firefighter, who is compensated either by the retirement system or the worker's compensation system." We consider worker's compensation in some detail in Chapter XI. At this point it is enough to know that that system does not provide recovery for "pain and suffering." In light of that fact how can the court say that the public firefighter does not "substantially benefit" more from one approach than the other?

New Jersey has abolished the firefighter's rule by statute. N.J.S.A. 2A:62A–21. See the discussion in Boyer v. Anchor Disposal, 135 N.J. 86, 638 A.2d 135 (1994). What will change?

7. Neighbarger rejected Holland v. Crumb, 26 Cal.App.4th 1844, 32 Cal.Rptr.2d 366 (1994), which had applied "the firefighter's rule to the claim of a privately employed tow truck driver on the theory that a tow truck driver must assume the foreseeable risks of such hazardous employment. It is certainly not the case, as the Court of Appeal suggested in *Holland*, that private employees assume all the foreseeable risks of their employment. As we have explained above, *Knight* [   ], requires a closer analysis, focusing not on the foreseeability of the hazard or the plaintiff's subjective awareness of risk, but on the defendant's duty of care and the relationship of the parties."

Despite that passage, a court of appeal after *Neighbarger* rejected a claim by a private tow truck driver who was run into on the highway while he was trying to remove a car immobilized by the defendant driver's drunk driving. Bryant v. Glastetter, 32 Cal.App.4th 770, 38 Cal.Rptr.2d 291 (1995). The supreme court denied review.

Would it be appropriate to treat the private tow truck driver as a professional rescuer?   See Maltman v. Sauer, 84 Wash.2d 975, 530 P.2d 254 (1975), denying recovery against a negligent motorist when a professional rescue helicopter crashed on its way to rescue him in a remote area.   An effort to limit *Maltman* to cases involving public employees failed in Black Industries, Inc. v. Emco Helicopters, Inc., 19 Wash.App. 697, 577 P.2d 610 (1978): "public policy demands that recovery be barred whenever a person, fully aware of a hazard created by another's negligence, voluntarily confronts the risk for compensation."   Why?

8.   What analysis if a student driver crashes the car, hurting the driving instructor?   Might it matter what kind of error, if any, the student made?   How experienced the student was?

What if an Alzheimer's patient hurts a nurse who is taking care of him?   See Gould v. American Family Mut. Ins. Co., 543 N.W.2d 282 (Wis. 1996).

9.   Suppose A tries to rewire his home, thinking that it isn't really all that hard.   After some time he realizes that he doesn't know what he is doing and becomes frightened.   He calls an electrician and describes what he has done.   Shortly after beginning work, the electrician is electrocuted. What if it can be shown that A's work created a danger that the electrician had failed to anticipate?   See Salima v. Scherwood South, Inc. 38 F.3d 929 (7th Cir.1994), in which the court found no duty on a land occupier to tell a handyman (who was later electrocuted) about what management had learned in its prior unsuccessful attempts to locate the source of an electrical problem.

10.   In Chapter VIII we consider defective-product claims brought by employees against third parties.

CHAPTER VII

STRICT LIABILITY

In the first part of this Chapter, we will consider the doctrinal developments that have led to the concept of strict liability for certain types of activities. In tracing the evolution of this traditional form of strict liability, we will see the courts venturing beyond isolated cases—such as escaping fires, rampaging wild animals and straying cattle—to fashion a more comprehensive principle of liability without fault. It should be said, however, that there is no clear demarcation of the emergence of traditional strict liability. In the late nineteenth century, for instance, continued reference to "the blasting cases" indicates the judicial affinity for narrow categorization. But as the leading case of *Rylands v. Fletcher*, along with the cases that follow, should demonstrate, the courts were quite consciously drawing on a principle that they regarded as contrary to negligence liability when they invoked the doctrine of strict liability for ultrahazardous, or abnormally dangerous, activity.

In the second part of the Chapter, we examine a variety of scholarly efforts to establish the theoretical underpinnings of strict liability. This literature consists of efforts both to identify the strands of strict liability in the case law and to advocate a broader reliance on strict liability for normative reasons. An examination of the theories should serve as a reprise on the tension between strict liability and negligence, as well as providing a bridge to the analysis of defective products cases in the next Chapter.

A. DOCTRINAL DEVELOPMENT

Fletcher v. Rylands

Exchequer Chamber, 1866.
L.R. 1. Ex. 265.

[Plaintiff Fletcher was a tenant mining coal under agreement with the landowner. Defendant Rylands was a tenant operating a cotton mill on nearby land.]

■ The judgment of the Court (WILLES, BLACKBURN, KEATING, MELLOR, MONTAGUE SMITH, and LUSH, JJ.), was delivered by BLACKBURN, J. This was a special case stated by an arbitrator, under an order of nisi prius, in which the question for the court is stated to be whether the plaintiff is entitled to recover any, and, if any, what damages from the defendants, by reason of the matters therein before stated.

In the Court of Exchequer, the Chief Baron and Martin, B., were of opinion that the plaintiff was not entitled to recover at all, Bramwell, B., being of a different opinion. The judgment in the Exchequer was consequently given for the defendants, in conformity with the opinion of the majority of the court. The only question argued before us was whether this judgment was right, nothing being said about the measure of damages in case the plaintiff should be held entitled to recover. We have come to the conclusion that the opinion of Bramwell, B., was right, and that the answer to the question should be that the plaintiff was entitled to recover damages from the defendants, by reason of the matters stated in the case, and consequently, that the judgment below should be reversed, but we cannot at present say to what damages the plaintiff is entitled.

It appears from the statement in the case, that the plaintiff was damaged by his property being flooded by water, which, without any fault on his part, broke out of a reservoir constructed on the defendants' land by the defendants' orders, and maintained by the defendants.

It appears from the statement in the case that the coal under the defendants' land had, at some remote period, been worked out; but this was unknown at the time when the defendants gave directions to erect the reservoir, and the water in the reservoir would not have escaped from the defendants' land, and no mischief would have been done to the plaintiff, but for this latent defect in the defendants' subsoil. And it further appears, that the defendants selected competent engineers and contractors to make their reservoir, and themselves personally continued in total ignorance of what we have called the latent defect in the subsoil; but that these persons employed by them in the course of the work became aware of the existence of the ancient shafts filled up with soil, though they did not know or suspect that they were shafts communicating with old workings.

It is found that the defendants, personally, were free from all blame, but that in fact proper care and skill was not used by the persons employed by them, to provide for the sufficiency of the reservoir with reference to these shafts. The consequence was, that the reservoir when filled with water burst into the shafts, the water flowed down through them into the old workings, and thence into the plaintiff's mine, and there did the mischief.

The plaintiff, though free from all blame on his part, must bear the loss, unless he can establish that it was the consequence of some default for which the defendants are responsible. The question of law therefore arises, what is the obligation which the law casts on a person who, like the defendants, lawfully brings on his land something which, though harmless whilst it remains there, will naturally do mischief if it escape out of his land. It is agreed on all hands that he must take care to keep in that which he has brought on the land and keeps there, in order that it may not escape and damage his neighbors, but the question arises whether the duty which the law casts upon him, under such circumstances, is an absolute duty to keep it in at his peril, or is, as the majority of the Court of Exchequer have thought, merely a duty to take all reasonable and prudent precautions, in order to keep it in, but no more. If the first be the law, the person who has brought on his land and kept there something dangerous, and failed to keep it in, is responsible for all the natural consequences of its escape. If the second be the limit of his duty, he would not be answerable except on proof of negligence, and consequently would not be answerable for escape arising from any latent defect which ordinary prudence and skill could not detect.

Supposing the second to be the correct view of the law, a further question arises subsidiary to the first, viz., whether the defendants are not so far identified with the contractors whom they employed, as to be responsible for the consequences of their want of care and skill in making the reservoir in fact insufficient with reference to the old shafts, of the existence of which they were aware, though they had not ascertained where the shafts went to.

We think that the true rule of law is, that the person who for his own purposes brings on his lands and collects and keeps there anything likely to do mischief if it escapes, must keep it in at his peril, and, if he does not do so, is prima facie answerable for all the damage which is the natural consequence of its escape. He can excuse himself by showing that the escape was owing to the plaintiff's default; or perhaps that the escape was the consequence of vis major, or the act of God; but as nothing of this sort exists here, it is unnecessary to inquire what excuse would be sufficient. The general rule, as above stated, seems on principle just. The person whose grass or corn is eaten down by the escaping cattle of his neighbor, or whose mine is flooded by the water from his neighbour's reservoir, or whose cellar is invaded by the filth of his neighbour's privy, or whose habitation is made unhealthy by the fumes and noisome vapours of his neighbour's alkali works, is damnified without any fault of his own; and it seems but reasonable and just that the neighbour, who has brought something on his own property which was not naturally there, harmless to others so long as it is confined to his own property, but which he knows to be mischievous if it gets on his neighbour's, should be obliged to make good the damage which ensues if he does not succeed in confining it to his own property. But for his act in bringing it there no mischief could have accrued, and it seems but just that he should at his peril keep it there so that no mischief may accrue, or answer for the natural and anticipated consequences. And upon authority, this we think is established to be the law whether the things so brought be beasts, or water, or filth, or stenches.

The case that has most commonly occurred, and which is most frequently to be found in the books, is as to the obligation of the owner of cattle which he has brought on his land, to prevent their escaping and doing mischief. The law as to them seems to be perfectly settled from early times; the owner must keep them in at his peril, or he will be answerable for the natural consequences of their escape; that is with regard to tame beasts, for the grass they eat and trample upon, though not for any injury

[handwritten margin note: P's default. Act of God has to be shown to relieve liability]

to the person of others, for our ancestors have settled that it is not the general nature of horses to kick, or bulls to gore; but if the owner knows that the beast has a vicious propensity to attack man, he will be answerable for that too.

. . .

. . . But it was further said by Martin, B., that when damage is done to personal property, or even to the person, by collision, either upon land or at sea, there must be negligence in the party doing the damage to render him legally responsible; and this is no doubt true, and as was pointed out by Mr. Mellish during his argument before us, this is not confined to cases of collision, for there are many cases in which proof of negligence is essential, as for instance, where an unruly horse gets on the footpath of a public street and kills a passenger [ ]; or where a person in a dock is struck by the falling of a bale of cotton which the defendant's servants are lowering [ ]; and many other similar cases may be found. But we think these cases distinguishable from the present. Traffic on the highways, whether by land or sea, cannot be conducted without exposing those whose persons or property are near it to some inevitable risk; and that being so those who go on the highway, or have their property adjacent to it, may well be held to do so subject to their taking upon themselves the risk of injury from that inevitable danger; and persons who by the license of the owner pass near to warehouses where goods are being raised or lowered, certainly do so subject to the inevitable risk of accident. In neither case, therefore, can they recover without proof of want of care or skill occasioning the accident; and it is believed that all the cases in which inevitable accident has been held an excuse for what prima facie was a trespass, can be explained on the same principle, viz., that the circumstances were such as to show that the plaintiff had taken that risk upon himself. But there is no ground for saying that the plaintiff here took upon himself any risk arising from the uses to which the defendants should choose to apply their land. He neither knew what these might be, nor could he in any way control the defendants, or hinder their building what reservoirs they liked, and storing up in them what water they pleased, so long as the defendants succeeded in preventing the water which they there brought from interfering with the plaintiff's property.

The view which we take of the first point renders it unnecessary to consider whether the defendants would or would not be responsible for the want of care and skill in the persons employed by them, under the circumstances stated in the case.

. . .

Judgment for the plaintiff.

NOTES AND QUESTIONS

1. The independent contractor question was difficult because there had as yet been no decision holding the employer of an independent contractor liable for the contractor's negligence. That did not come until

Bower v. Peate, 1 Q.B.D. 321 (1876). Recall the discussion of vicarious liability in Chapter I.

Fletcher did not sue the contractor directly—probably because earlier cases had concluded that in such situations the contractor would be held to owe a duty only to the employer and not to strangers. The leading case was Winterbottom v. Wright, 10 M. & W. 109, 152 Eng.Rep. 402 (1842), discussed at p. 476, infra.

2. In the Court of Exchequer, the defendant prevailed, 2–1. The majority found that the traditional actions for interference with real property—trespass and nuisance—were inapplicable. Trespass required direct and immediate invasion of the plaintiff's land, while in this case the water flowed down and through intervening shafts and land. If the water had been cast upon plaintiff's land that would have amounted to a trespass. Nuisance, which is an interference with the plaintiff's use and enjoyment of his land, failed because a reservoir was lawful and the defendants had no reason to expect that any damage was likely to ensue. Furthermore, nuisances were usually continuing harm, such as noxious fumes, rather than a single occurrence. Martin, B., emphasized the fault requirement in collision cases and concluded that to "hold the defendant liable without negligence would be to constitute him an insurer, which, in my opinion, would be contrary to legal analogy and principle." Trespass and nuisance are discussed in Chapter IX. Bramwell, B., dissented in an opinion in which he argued that the plaintiff had a "right to be free from what has been called 'foreign' water, that is, water artificially brought or sent to him directly, or indirectly by its being sent to where it would flow to him." Defendants' knowledge of the danger was irrelevant.

3. What was the reason for Justice Blackburn's ruling?

4. At one point he emphasizes that "but for" the defendants' act no mischief would have resulted. Is he saying that cause-in-fact suffices for finding liability for any act that harms another's land?

5. If the reservoir had been made exclusively from material on the defendants' land and had been filled only with rain water that fell on the land, would this be covered by Justice Blackburn's opinion?

6. Are the trespassing animal cases relevant to this case?

7. Is the rule about potentially vicious animals relevant here?

8. Might the analysis have been different if the plaintiff had been working in his mine and had been drowned by the water? What if the drowned man had been an employee of plaintiff?

9. How successful are Justice Blackburn's efforts to distinguish the highway injury cases, in which he admits that negligence must be shown? Recall that the falling barrel case, p. 80, supra, had been decided only three years earlier. What analysis if the flooding had caused part of a public highway to collapse, injuring a traveler? Or destroying a wagon?

10. Defendants appealed to the House of Lords.

Rylands v. Fletcher

House of Lords, 1868.
L.R. 3 H.L. 330.

■ THE LORD CHANCELLOR (Lord Cairns) [after stating the facts.]

My Lords, the principles on which this case must be determined appear to me to be extremely simple. The Defendants treating them as the owners or occupiers of the close on which the reservoir was constructed, might lawfully have used that close for any purpose for which it might in the ordinary course of the enjoyment of land be used; and if, in what I may term the natural user of that land, there had been any accumulation of water, either on the surface or underground, and if, by the operation of the laws of nature, that accumulation of water had passed off into the close occupied by the Plaintiff, the Plaintiff could not have complained that that result had taken place. If he had desired to guard himself against it, it would have lain upon him to have done so, by leaving, or by interposing, some barrier between his close and the close of the Defendants in order to have prevented that operation of the laws of nature.

.   .   .

On the other hand if the Defendants, not stopping at the natural use of their close, had desired to use it for any purpose which I may term a non-natural use, for the purpose of introducing into the close that which in its natural condition was not in or upon it, for the purpose of introducing water either above or below ground in quantities and in a manner not the result of any work or operation on or under the land,—and if in consequence of their doing so, or in consequence of any imperfection in the mode of their doing so, the water came to escape and to pass off into the close of the Plaintiff, then it appears to me that that which the Defendants were doing they were doing at their own peril; and, if in the course of their doing it, the evil arose to which I have referred, the evil, namely, of the escape of the water and its passing away to the close of the Plaintiff and injuring the Plaintiff, then for the consequence of that, in my opinion, the Defendants would be liable.   .   .   .

My Lords, these simple principles, if they are well founded, as it appears to me they are, really dispose of this case.

The same result is arrived at on the principles, referred to by Mr. Justice Blackburn. [Lord Cairns here quotes in full the paragraph starting "We think that the true rule of law is.   .   .   ."—Eds.]

My Lords, in that opinion, I must say I entirely concur. Therefore, I have to move your Lordships that the judgment of the Court of Exchequer Chamber be affirmed, and that the present appeal be dismissed with costs.

■ LORD CRANWORTH:—My Lords, I concur with my noble and learned friend in thinking that the rule of law was correctly stated by Mr. Justice Blackburn in delivering the opinion of the Exchequer Chamber. If a person brings, or accumulates, on his land anything which, if it should escape, may cause damage to his neighbour, he does so at his peril. If it does escape, and cause damage, he is responsible, however careful he may have been, and whatever precautions he may have taken to prevent the damage.

. . .

Judgment of the Court of Exchequer Chamber affirmed.

NOTES AND QUESTIONS

1. *Rylands* has inspired a vast literature, including the following: Bohlen, The Rule in Rylands v. Fletcher, 59 U.Pa.L.Rev. 298, 373, 423 (1911); Goodhart, Rylands v. Fletcher Today, 72 L.Q.Rev. 184 (1956); 3 Harper, James & Gray, The Law of Torts, §§ 14.2–14.5 (2d ed.1986); Molloy, Fletcher v. Rylands—A Reexamination of Juristic Origins, 9 U.Chi. L.Rev. 266 (1941); Prosser, The Principle of Rylands v. Fletcher, in Prosser, Selected Topics in the Law of Torts 134 (1954); Simpson, Legal Liability for Bursting Reservoirs: The Historical Context of Rylands v. Fletcher, 13 J. Legal Studies 209 (1984). Particularly interesting are the views of Bohlen, arguing that "in England, the dominant class was the landed gentry, whose opinion the judges, who either sprang from this class or hoped to establish themselves and their families within—naturally reflected" (p. 318), and Molloy, reporting social and biographical data on the judges in *Rylands* that contradicts the "landed gentry" thesis.

2. Is there a difference between Justice Blackburn's "not naturally there" and Lord Cairns's "non-natural use"? Does Lord Cranworth agree with Lord Cairns?

3. Where does Justice Blackburn's rationale stand after the decision of the House of Lords?

4. Is *Rylands* limited in time and place to the social conditions in mid-nineteenth century England? From the outset, most American courts were less than enthusiastic about recognizing a broad principle of strict liability, on the basis of *Rylands,* that would apply to cases involving neighboring landowners. Consider the leading case of Losee v. Buchanan, 51 N.Y. 476 (1873), in which defendant's steam boiler—used in connection with a paper manufacturing business—exploded and was catapulted onto plaintiff's land and through several of his buildings. Rejecting *Rylands,* as well as the line of cases recognizing strict liability for harm caused by straying wild animals, the court extolled the virtues of the fault principle in an industrializing society:

> By becoming a member of civilized society, I am compelled to give up many of my natural rights, but I receive more than a compensation from the surrender by every other man of the same rights and the security, advantage and protection which the laws give me. So, too, the general rules that I may have the exclusive and undisturbed use and possession of my real estate, and that I must so use my real estate as not to injure my neighbor, are much modified by the exigencies of the social state. We must have factories, machinery, dams, canals and

railroads. They are demanded by the manifold wants of mankind, and lay at the basis of all our civilization. If I have any of these upon my lands, and they are not a nuisance and are not so managed as to become such, I am not responsible for any damage they accidentally and unavoidably do my neighbor. He receives his compensation for such damage by the general good, in which he shares, and the right which he has to place the same things upon his lands. I may not place or keep a nuisance upon my land to the damage of my neighbor, and I have my compensation for the surrender of this right to use my own as I will by the similar restriction imposed upon my neighbor for my benefit. I hold my property subject to the risk that it may be unavoidably or accidentally injured by those who live near me; and as I move about upon the public highways and in all places where other persons may lawfully be, I take the risk of being accidentally injured in my person by them without fault on their part. Most of the rights of property, as well as of person, in the social state, are not absolute but relative, and they must be so arranged and modified, not unnecessarily infringing upon natural rights, as upon the whole to promote the general welfare.

See also Brown v. Collins, 53 N.H. 442 (1873), another leading contemporaneous American decision, similarly rejecting the strict liability rule of *Rylands* because it would "impose a penalty upon efforts, made in a reasonable, skillful, and careful manner, to rise above a condition of barbarism" and would serve as "an obstacle in the way of progress and improvement." But compare the favorable reception in Massachusetts dating back to 1868, which is traced to the present in Clark–Aiken Co. v. Cromwell–Wright Co., Inc., 367 Mass. 70, 323 N.E.2d 876 (1975).

5. More particularly, on the escape of impounded water, contrast the *Rylands* view with Turner v. Big Lake Oil Co., 128 Tex. 155, 96 S.W.2d 221 (1936):

. . . what use of land is or may be a natural use, one within the contemplation of the parties to the original grant of land, necessarily depends upon the attendant circumstances and conditions which obtain in the territory of the original grants, or the initial terms of those grants.

In Texas we have conditions very different from those which obtain in England. A large portion of Texas is an arid or semi-arid region. West of the 98th meridian of longitude, where the rainfall is approximately 30 inches, the rainfall decreases until finally, in the extreme western part of the State, it is only about 10 inches. This land of decreasing rainfall is the great ranch or live stock region of the State, water for which is stored in thousands of ponds, tanks, and lakes on the surface of the ground. The country is almost without streams; and without the storage of water from rainfall in basins constructed for the purpose, or to hold waters pumped from the earth, the great livestock industry of West Texas must perish. No such condition obtains in England. With us the storage of water is a natural or necessary and common use of the land, necessarily within the contemplation of the State and its grantees when grants were made, and obviously the rule announced in Rylands v. Fletcher, predicated upon different conditions, can have no application here.

Compare Cities Service Co. v. State, 312 So.2d 799 (Fla.App.1975). Cities Service operated a phosphate rock mine in which it collected phosphate slimes in settling ponds. When a dam broke, one billion gallons of slime escaped into a creek and then into a river "killing countless numbers of fish and inflicting other damage." In this damage action the court concluded that the doctrine of Rylands v. Fletcher should be applied in Florida: "In a frontier society there was little likelihood that a dangerous use of land could cause damage to one's neighbor. Today our life has become more complex. Many areas are overcrowded, and even the non-negligent use of one's land can cause extensive damages to a neighbor's property. Though there are still many hazardous activities which are socially desirable, it now seems reasonable that they pay their own way."

6. As *Cities Service Co.* implies, *Rylands* may have gained new life as an environmental harm principle. In particular, consider State, Dept. of Environmental Protection v. Ventron Corp., 94 N.J. 473, 468 A.2d 150 (1983). The State Department of Environmental Protection brought a damage action against Ventron and others for the cost of cleanup and removal of mercury pollution emanating from a tract of land on which defendants had conducted mercury processing for almost fifty years. The operations had raised the mercury content of a nearby tidal estuary to the highest found in fresh water sediments anywhere in the world. Among other theories, plaintiff argued for liability on the basis of *Rylands*. The court responded affirmatively:

> We believe it is time to recognize expressly that the law of liability has evolved so that a landowner is strictly liable to others for harm caused by toxic wastes that are stored on his property and flow onto the property of others. Therefore, we overrule [an earlier case rejecting *Rylands*] and adopt the principle of liability originally declared in *Rylands v. Fletcher.* The net result is that those who use, or permit others to use, land for the conduct of abnormally dangerous activities are strictly liable for resultant damages.

Is this a logical extension of *Rylands*? *Rylands* has not fared nearly so well in its land of origin. See Fleming, Comment: The Fall of a Crippled Giant, 3 Tort L. Rev. 56 (1995).

7. Despite the mixed reception given *Rylands*, the concept of strict liability for harm caused by entrepreneurial activity was not unknown to American courts at the time. The following case provides the context.

Sullivan v. Dunham

Court of Appeals of New York, 1900.
161 N.Y. 290, 55 N.E. 923.

[Defendant land owner employed two men to dynamite a 60–foot tree on the land. The blast hurled a fragment of wood 412 feet onto a highway where it struck plaintiff's decedent and killed her. The two blasters were also sued. The trial judge charged that negligence need not be proven to establish liability. Defendants appealed from a judgment entered on a plaintiff's verdict and affirmed by the appellate division.]

■ VANN, J. The main question presented by this appeal is whether one who, for a lawful purpose and without negligence or want of skill, explodes a blast upon his own land and thereby causes a piece of wood to fall upon a person lawfully traveling in a public highway, is liable for the injury thus inflicted.

The statute authorizes the personal representative of a decedent to "maintain an action to recover damages for a wrongful act, neglect, or default, by which the decedent's death was caused, against a natural person who, or a corporation which, would have been liable to an action in favor of the decedent, by reason thereof, if death had not ensued." (Code Civ.Pro. § 1902.) It covers any action of trespass upon the person, which the deceased could have maintained if she had survived the accident. Stated in another form, therefore, the question before us is whether the defendants are liable as trespassers.

This is not a new question, for it has been considered, directly or indirectly, so many times by this court that a reference to the earlier authorities is unnecessary. In the leading case upon the subject, the defendant, in order to dig a canal authorized by its charter, necessarily blasted out rocks from its own land with gunpowder, and thus threw fragments against the plaintiff's house, which stood upon the adjoining premises. Although there was no proof of negligence, or want of skill, the defendant was held liable for the injury sustained. All the judges concurred in the opinion of Gardiner, J., who said: "The defendants had the right to dig the canal. The plaintiff the right to the undisturbed possession of his property. If these rights conflict, the former must yield to the latter, as the more important of the two, since, upon grounds of public policy, it is better that one man should surrender a particular use of his land, than that another should be deprived of the beneficial use of his property altogether, which might be the consequence if the privilege of the former should be wholly unrestricted. The case before us illustrates this principle. For if the defendants in excavating their canal, in itself a lawful use of their land, could, in the manner mentioned by the witnesses, demolish the stoop of the plaintiff with impunity, they might, for the same purpose, on the exercise of reasonable care, demolish his house, and thus deprive him of all use of his property. The use of land by the proprietor is not therefore an absolute right, but qualified and limited by the higher right of others to the lawful possession of their property. To this possession the law prohibits all direct injury, without regard to its extent or the motives of the aggressor. . . . He may excavate a canal, but he cannot cast the dirt or stones upon the land of his neighbor, either by human agency or the force of gunpowder. If he cannot construct the work without the adoption of such means, he must abandon that mode of using his property, or be held responsible for all damages resulting therefrom. He will not be permitted to accomplish a legal object in an unlawful manner." (Hay v. Cohoes Co., 2 N.Y. 159)[1849].

This case was followed immediately by Tremain v. Cohoes Co. (2 N.Y. 163), a similar action against the same defendant, which offered to show upon the trial "that the work was done in the best and most careful manner." It was held that the evidence was properly excluded because the manner in which the defendant performed its work was of no consequence, as what it did to the plaintiff's injury was the sole question.

These were cases of trespass upon lands, while the case before us involves trespass upon the person of a human being, when she was where she had the same right to protection from injury as if she had been walking upon her own land. As the safety of the person is more sacred than the safety of property, the cases cited should govern our decision unless they are no longer the law.

The Hay case was reviewed by the Commission of Appeals in Losee v. Buchanan (51 N.Y. 476, 479) [1873], where it was held that one who, without negligence and with due care and skill, operates a steam boiler upon his own premises, is not liable to his neighbor for the damages caused by the explosion thereof. That was not a case of intentional but of accidental explosion. A tremendous force escaped, so to speak, from the owner, but was not voluntarily set free. The court, commenting upon the Hay case, said: "It was held that the defendant was liable for the injury, although no negligence or want of skill in executing the work was alleged or proved. This decision was well supported by the clearest principles. The acts of the defendant in casting the rocks upon plaintiff's premises were direct and immediate. The damage was the necessary consequence of just what the defendant was doing, and it was just as much liable as if it had caused the rocks to be taken by hand, or any other means, and thrown directly upon plaintiff's land."

The Hay case was expressly approved and made the basis of judgment in St. Peter v. Denison (58 N.Y. 416) [1874], where a blast, set off by a contractor with the state in the enlargement of the Erie canal, threw a piece of frozen earth against the plaintiff when he was at work upon the adjoining premises for the owner thereof. . . .

This case is analogous to the one before us, because the person injured did not own the land upon which he stood when struck, but he had a right to stand there the same as the plaintiff's intestate had a right to walk in the highway. We see no distinction in principle between the two cases.

. . .

When the injury is not direct, but consequential, such as is caused by concussion, which, by shaking the earth, injures property, there is no liability in the absence of negligence.

. . .

We think that the Hay case has always been recognized by this court as a sound and valuable authority. After standing for fifty years as the law of the state upon the subject it should not be disturbed, and we have no inclination to disturb it. It rests upon the principle, founded in public policy, that the safety of property generally is superior in right to a particular use of a single piece of property by its owner. It renders the enjoyment of all property more secure by preventing such a use of one piece by one man as may injure all his neighbors. It makes human life safer by tending to prevent a landowner from casting, either with or without negligence, a part of his land upon the person of one who is where he has a right to be. It so applies the maxim of *sic utere tuo* as to protect person and property from direct physical violence, which, although accidental, has the same effect as if it were intentional. It lessens the hardship by placing absolute liability upon the one who causes the injury. The accident in question was a misfortune to the defendants, but it was a greater misfortune to the young woman who was killed. The safety of travelers upon the public highway is more important to the state than the improvement of one piece of property, by a special method, is to its owner.   .   .   .

.   .   .

The judgment is right and should be affirmed, with costs.

■ All concur, except GRAY, J., not voting.

NOTES AND QUESTIONS

1. Judge Vann states that courts will apply the maxim of *sic utere* so "as to protect person and property from direct physical violence, which, although accidental, has the same effect as if it were intentional." Is this consistent with *Losee?*

2. How might the *Sullivan* facts have been analyzed by Justice Blackburn? By Lord Cairns?

3. Did the court in *Losee* adequately distinguish the Hay case? What analysis in *Losee* if the defendant had been testing this boiler's capacity by increasing the pressure until it exploded?

4. The difference in treatment accorded harms caused by debris and by concussion was justified by one view of the history of the writ system. Direct harm from debris might give rise to a trespass action, in which intent and fault were once irrelevant; concussion damage was viewed as indirect, or consequential, harm for which only an action on the case would lie—and a fault component developed here earlier than in trespass. Can this distinction be supported on other grounds? In the leading case of Booth v. Rome, W. & O.T.R.R. Co., 140 N.Y. 267, 35 N.E. 592 (1893), the court held the 1849 Hay case inapplicable to harm suffered by concussion because there the defendant's act had caused direct harm to the plaintiff's property and was thus a trespass. In *Booth,* the court emphasized that the defendant was engaged in a "lawful act" on its own land. "The immediate act was confined to its own land, but the blasts, by setting the air in motion, or in some other unexplained way, caused an injury to plaintiff's house.   .   .   .   The blasting was necessary, was carefully done, and the

injury was consequential. There was no technical trespass." The court added that "to exclude the defendant from blasting to adapt its lot to the contemplated uses, at the instance of the plaintiff, would not be a compromise between conflicting rights, but an extinguishment of the right of the one for the benefit of the other." Again, "public policy is sustained by the building up of towns and cities and the improvement of property. Any unnecessary restraint on freedom of action of a property owner hinders this." The New York cases are discussed in detail, along with the roughly contemporaneous decisions in *Brown v. Kendall* and *Rylands v. Fletcher*, in Gregory, Trespass to Negligence to Absolute Liability, 37 Va.L.Rev. 359 (1951).

The distinction between debris and concussion has virtually disappeared. It survived in New York until Spano v. Perini Corp., 25 N.Y.2d 11, 250 N.E.2d 31, 302 N.Y.S.2d 527 (1969) in which, referring to the second set of reasons in *Booth,* the court said:

> This rationale cannot withstand analysis. The plaintiff in *Booth* was not seeking, as the court implied, to "exclude the defendant from blasting" and thus prevent desirable improvements to the latter's property. Rather, he was merely seeking compensation for the damage which was inflicted upon his own property as a result of that blasting. The question, in other words, was not *whether* it was lawful or proper to engage in blasting but *who* should bear the cost of any resulting damage—the person who engaged in the dangerous activity or the innocent neighbor injured thereby. Viewed in such a light, it clearly appears that *Booth* was wrongly decided and should be forthrightly overruled.

5. The Restatement sought to generalize from these pockets of liability in sections 519 and 520. In the first Restatement the covered activity was described as "ultrahazardous," which was defined as involving a risk that "cannot be eliminated by the exercise of the utmost care" and "is not a matter of common usage." The Second Restatement reframed the approach by providing that one who "carries on an abnormally dangerous activity is subject to liability for harm   .   .   .   resulting from the activity, although he has exercised the utmost care to prevent the harm." In determining whether an activity is "abnormally dangerous," section 520 listed six factors for consideration:

(a) existence of a high degree of risk of some harm to the person, land or chattels of others;

(b) likelihood that the harm that results from it will be great;

(c) inability to eliminate the risk by the exercise of reasonable care;

(d) extent to which the activity is not a matter of common usage;

(e) inappropriateness of the activity to the place where it is carried on; and

(f) extent to which its value to the community is outweighed by its dangerous attributes.

This section is central to the case that follows.

Indiana Harbor Belt Railroad Co. v. American Cyanamid Co.

United States Court of Appeals, Seventh Circuit. 1990.
916 F.2d 1174.

■ Before POSNER, MANION and KANNE, CIRCUIT JUDGES.

■ POSNER, CIRCUIT JUDGE.

American Cyanamid Company, the defendant in this diversity tort suit governed by Illinois law, is a major manufacturer of chemicals, including acrylonitrile, a chemical used in large quantities in making acrylic fibers, plastics, dyes, pharmaceutical chemicals, and other intermediate and final goods. On January 2, 1979, at its manufacturing plant in Louisiana, Cyanamid loaded 20,000 gallons of liquid acrylonitrile into a railroad tank car that it had leased from the North American Car Corporation. The next day, a train of the Missouri Pacific Railroad picked up the car at Cyanamid's siding. The car's ultimate destination was a Cyanamid plant in New Jersey served by Conrail rather than by Missouri Pacific. The Missouri Pacific train carried the car north to the Blue Island railroad yard of Indiana Harbor Belt Railroad, the plaintiff in this case, a small switching line that has a contract with Conrail to switch cars from other lines to Conrail, in this case for travel east. The Blue Island yard is in the Village of Riverdale, which is just south of Chicago and part of the Chicago metropolitan area.

The car arrived in the Blue Island yard on the morning of January 9, 1979. Several hours after it arrived, employees of the switching line noticed fluid gushing from the bottom outlet of the car. The lid on the outlet was broken. After two hours, the line's supervisor of equipment was able to stop the leak by closing a shut-off valve controlled from the top of the car. No one was sure at the time just how much of the contents of the car had leaked, but it was feared that all 20,000 gallons had, and since acrylonitrile is flammable at a temperature of 30 degrees Fahrenheit or above, highly toxic, and possibly carcinogenic [ ], the local authorities ordered the homes near the yard evacuated. The evacuation lasted only a few hours, until the car was moved to a remote part of the yard and it was discovered that only about a quarter of the acrylonitrile had leaked. Concerned nevertheless that there had been some contamination of soil and water, the Illinois Department of Environmental Protection ordered the switching line to take decontamination measures that cost the line $981,-022.75, which it sought to recover by this suit.

[After some procedural tangles, the district judge granted plaintiff summary judgment on its strict liability claim and dismissed plaintiff's negligence claim. Defendant appealed and plaintiff cross-appealed.]

The question whether the shipper of a hazardous chemical by rail should be strictly liable for the consequences of a spill or other accident to the shipment en route is a novel one in Illinois [despite earlier confusion that might have suggested otherwise].

The parties agree that the question whether placing acrylonitrile in a rail shipment that will pass through a metropolitan area subjects the shipper to strict liability is, as recommended in Restatement (Second) of Torts § 520, comment l (1977), a question of law, so that we owe no particular deference to the conclusion of the district court. They also agree . . . that the Supreme Court of Illinois would treat as authoritative the provisions of the Restatement governing abnormally dangerous activities. The key provision is section 520, which sets forth six factors to be considered in deciding whether an activity is abnormally dangerous and the actor therefore strictly liable.

The roots of section 520 are in nineteenth-century cases. The most famous one is Rylands v. Fletcher, 1 Ex. 265, aff'd, L.R. 3 H.L. 300 (1868), but a more illuminating one in the present context is Guille v. Swan, 19 Johns. (N.Y.) 381 (1822). A man took off in a hot-air balloon and landed, without intending to, in a vegetable garden in New York City. A crowd that had been anxiously watching his involuntary descent trampled the vegetables in their endeavor to rescue him when he landed. The owner of the garden sued the balloonist for the resulting damage, and won. Yet the balloonist had not been careless. In the then state of ballooning it was impossible to make a pinpoint landing.

Guille is a paradigmatic case for strict liability. (a) The risk (probability) of harm was great, and (b) the harm that would ensue if the risk materialized could be, although luckily was not, great (the balloonist could have crashed into the crowd rather than into the vegetables). The confluence of these two factors established the urgency of seeking to prevent such accidents. (c) Yet such accidents could not be prevented by the exercise of due care; the technology of care in ballooning was insufficiently developed. (d) The activity was not a matter of common usage, so there was no presumption that it was a highly valuable activity despite its unavoidable riskiness. (e) The activity was inappropriate to the place in which it took place—densely populated New York City. The risk of serious harm to others (other than the balloonist himself, that is) could have been reduced by shifting the activity to the sparsely inhabited areas that surrounded the city in those days. (f) Reinforcing (d), the value to the community of the activity of recreational ballooning did not appear to be great enough to offset its unavoidable risks.

These are, of course, the six factors in section 520. They are related to each other in that each is a different facet of a common quest for a proper legal regime to govern accidents that negligence liability cannot adequately control. The interrelations might be more perspicuous if the six factors were reordered. One might for example start with (c), inability to eliminate the risk of accident by the exercise of due care. [ ] The baseline common law regime of tort liability is negligence. When it is a workable regime, because the hazards of an activity can be avoided by being careful (which is to say, nonnegligent), there is no need to switch to strict liability.

Sometimes, however, a particular type of accident cannot be prevented by taking care but can be avoided, or its consequences minimized, by shifting the activity in which the accident occurs to another locale, where the risk or harm of an accident will be less (e), or by reducing the scale of the activity in order to minimize the number of accidents caused by it (f). [ ] By making the actor strictly liable—by denying him in other words an excuse based on his inability to avoid accidents by being more careful—we give him an incentive, missing in a negligence regime, to experiment with methods of preventing accidents that involve not greater exertions of care, assumed to be futile, but instead relocating, changing, or reducing (perhaps to the vanishing point) the activity giving rise to the accident. [ ] The greater the risk of an accident (a) and the costs of an accident if one occurs (b), the more we want the actor to consider the possibility of making accident-reducing activity changes; the stronger, therefore, is the case for strict liability. Finally, if an activity is extremely common (d), like driving an automobile, it is unlikely either that its hazards are perceived as great or that there is no technology of care available to minimize them; so the case for strict liability is weakened.

The largest class of cases in which strict liability has been imposed under the standard codified in the Second Restatement of Torts involves the use of dynamite and other explosives for demolition in residential or urban areas. [ ] Explosives are dangerous even when handled carefully, and we therefore want blasters to choose the location of the activity with care and also to explore the feasibility of using safer substitutes (such as a wrecking ball), as well as to be careful in the blasting itself. Blasting is not a commonplace activity like driving a car, or so superior to substitute methods of demolition that the imposition of liability is unlikely to have any effect except to raise the activity's costs.

Against this background we turn to the particulars of acrylonitrile. Acrylonitrile is one of a large number of chemicals that are hazardous in the sense of being flammable, toxic, or both; acrylonitrile is both, as are many others. A table in the record, [ ], contains a list of the 125 hazardous materials that are shipped in highest volume on the nation's railroads. Acrylonitrile is the fifty-third most hazardous on the list . . . . The plaintiff's lawyer acknowledged at argument that the logic of the district court's opinion dictated strict liability for all 52 materials that rank higher than acrylonitrile on the list, and quite possibly for the 72 that rank lower as well, since all are hazardous if spilled in quantity while being shipped by rail. Every shipper of any of these materials would therefore be strictly liable for the consequences of a spill or other accident that occurred while the material was being shipped through a metropolitan area. The plaintiff's lawyer further acknowledged the irrelevance, on her view of the case, of the fact that Cyanamid had leased and filled the car that spilled the acrylonitrile; all she thought important is that Cyanamid introduced the product into the stream of commerce that happened to pass through the Chicago metropolitan area. Her concession may have been incautious. One might want to distinguish between the shipper who merely places his goods on his loading dock to be picked up by the carrier and the shipper who, as in this case, participates actively in the transportation. But the concession is illustrative of the potential scope of the district court's decision.

No cases recognize so sweeping a liability. Several reject it, though none has facts much like those of the present case. . . .

[The court discussed Siegler v. Kuhlman, 81 Wash.2d 448, 502 P.2d 1181 (1972), in which the trailer of defendant's gasoline truck broke away and rolled down onto a highway on which plaintiff motorist was traveling. Plaintiff's car went into a pool of gasoline spilled from the trailer and the resulting explosion "obliterated the plaintiff's decedent and her car"—and evidence of what happened. Although the *Siegler* court used strict liability, Judge Posner suggested that res ipsa loquitur would have sufficed. He also noted that the suit was against the transporter of the gasoline rather than its manufacturer.]

So we can get little help from precedent, and might as well apply section 520 to the acrylonitrile problem from the ground up. To begin with, we have been given no reason, whether the reason in *Siegler* or any other, for believing that a negligence regime is not perfectly adequate to remedy and deter, at reasonable cost, the accidental spillage of acrylonitrile from rail cars. [ ] Acrylonitrile could explode and destroy evidence, but of course did not here, making imposition of strict liability on the theory of the *Siegler* decision premature. More important, although acrylonitrile is flammable even at relatively low temperatures, and toxic, it is not so corrosive or otherwise destructive that it will eat through or otherwise damage or weaken a tank car's valves although they are maintained with due (which essentially means, with average) care. No one suggests, therefore, that the leak in this case was caused by the inherent properties of acrylonitrile. It was caused by carelessness—whether that of the North American Car Corporation in failing to maintain or inspect the car properly, or that of Cyanamid in failing to maintain or inspect it, or that of the Missouri Pacific when it had custody of the car, or that of the switching line itself in failing to notice the ruptured lid, or some combination of these possible failures of care. Accidents that are due to a lack of care can be prevented by taking care; and when a lack of care can (unlike *Siegler*) be shown in court, such accidents are adequately deterred by the threat of liability for negligence.

. . . For all that appears from the record of the case or any other sources of information that we have found, if a tank car is carefully maintained the danger of a spill of acrylonitrile is negligible. If this is right, there is no compelling reason to move to a regime of strict liability, especially one that might embrace all other hazardous materials shipped by rail as well. . . . If the vast majority of chemical spills by railroads are preventable by due care, the imposition of strict liability should cause only a slight, not as [amici] argue a substantial, rise in liability insurance rates, because the incremental liability should be slight. The amici have momentarily lost sight of the fact that the feasibility of avoiding accidents simply by being careful is an argument against strict liability.

.   .   .

The district judge and the plaintiff's lawyer make much of the fact that the spill occurred in a densely inhabited metropolitan area.   Only 4,000 gallons spilled; what if all 20,000 had done so?   Isn't the risk that this might happen even if everybody were careful sufficient to warrant giving the shipper an incentive to explore alternative routes?   Strict liability would supply that incentive.   But this argument overlooks the fact that, like other transportation networks, the railroad network is a hub-and-spoke system.   And the hubs are in metropolitan areas.   Chicago is one of the nation's largest railroad hubs.   In 1983, the latest year for which we have figures, Chicago's railroad yards handled the third highest volume of hazardous-material shipments in the nation.   East St. Louis, which is also in Illinois, handled the second highest volume.   [   ]   With most hazardous chemicals (by volume of shipments) being at least as hazardous as acrylonitrile, it is unlikely—and certainly not demonstrated by the plaintiff—that they can be rerouted around all the metropolitan areas in the country, except at prohibitive cost.   Even if it were feasible to reroute them one would hardly expect shippers, as distinct from carriers, to be the firms best situated to do the rerouting.   Granted, the usual view is that common carriers are not subject to strict liability for the carriage of materials that make the transportation of them abnormally dangerous, because a common carrier cannot refuse service to a shipper of a lawful commodity.   Restatement, supra, § 521.   Two courts, however, have rejected the common carrier exception.   National Steel Service Center, Inc. v. Gibbons, 319 N.W.2d 269 (Iowa 1982); Chavez v. Southern Pacific Transportation Co., 413 F.Supp. 1203, 1213–14 (E.D.Cal.1976).   If it were rejected in Illinois, this would weaken still further the case for imposing strict liability on shippers whose goods pass through the densely inhabited portions of the state.

The difference between shipper and carrier points to a deep flaw in the plaintiff's case.   Unlike *Guille* and unlike *Siegler*, and unlike the storage cases, beginning with *Rylands* itself, here it is not the actors—that is, the transporters of acrylonitrile and other chemicals—but the manufacturers, who are sought to be held strictly liable.   [   ]   A shipper can in the bill of lading designate the route of his shipment if he likes, 49 U.S.C. § 11710(a)(1), but is it realistic to suppose that shippers will become students of railroading in order to lay out the safest route by which to ship their goods?   Anyway, rerouting is no panacea.   Often it will increase the length of the journey, or compel the use of poorer track, or both.   When this happens, the probability of an accident is increased, even if the consequences of an accident if one occurs are reduced; so the expected accident cost, being the product of the probability of an accident and the harm if the accident occurs, may rise.   [   ]   It is easy to see how the accident in this case might have been prevented at reasonable cost by greater care on the part of those who handled the tank car of acrylonitrile. It is difficult to see how it might have been prevented at reasonable cost by a change in the activity of transporting the chemical.   This is therefore not an apt case for strict liability.

[Although an argument might have been made that Cyanamid should be treated as a "shipper-transporter" subject to rules more onerous than those imposed on "shippers" the court found it had not been made in this case and was waived.] Which is not to say that had it not been waived it would have changed the outcome of the case. The very fact that Cyanamid participated actively in the transportation of the acrylonitrile imposed upon it a duty of due care and by doing so brought into play a threat of negligence liability that, for all we know, may provide an adequate regime of accident control in the transportation of this particular chemical.

In emphasizing the flammability and toxicity of acrylonitrile rather than the hazards of transporting it, as in failing to distinguish between the active and the passive shipper, the plaintiff overlooks the fact that ultra-hazardousness or abnormal dangerousness is, in the contemplation of the law at least, a property not of substances, but of activities: not of acrylonitrile, but of the transportation of acrylonitrile by rail through populated areas. . . . Whatever the situation under products liability law (section 402A of the Restatement), the manufacturer of a product is not considered to be engaged in an abnormally dangerous activity merely because the product becomes dangerous when it is handled or used in some way after it leaves his premises, even if the danger is foreseeable. [ ]The plaintiff does not suggest that Cyanamid should switch to making some less hazardous chemical that would substitute for acrylonitrile in the textiles and other goods in which acrylonitrile is used. Were this a feasible method of accident avoidance, there would be an argument for making manufacturers strictly liable for accidents that occur during the shipment of their products (how strong an argument we need not decide). Apparently it is not a feasible method.

. . . Brutal though it may seem to say it, the inappropriate use to which land is being put in the Blue Island yard and neighborhood may be, not the transportation of hazardous chemicals, but residential living. The analogy is to building your home between the runways at O'Hare.

. . .

[Although the improper grant of summary judgment normally requires a remand for trial of that part of the case, this case was different because no new facts were suggested that would warrant strict liability. Defendant conceded that if the strict liability claim fell, the negligence claim had to be remanded for trial.]

The judgment is reversed (with no award of costs in this court) and the case remanded for further proceedings, consistent with this opinion, on the plaintiff's claim for negligence.

NOTES AND QUESTIONS

1. Why might manufacturing, transportation, and storage be treated as different activities for purposes of strict liability?

2. Why is the Restatement section framed in terms of activities rather than "acts", as in negligence? (We will consider liability for defective products shortly.)

3. The first Restatement used the term "ultrahazardous" instead of "abnormally dangerous" activity and framed the liability as a rule instead of using a list of factors. According to that version, strict liability was to be imposed if the activity

> (a) necessarily involves a risk of serious harm to the person, land or chattels of others which cannot be eliminated by the exercise of the utmost care, and

> (b) is not a matter of common usage.

How does this version differ from the one used by the court? Would its use have altered the result of the principal case?

4. A few courts have rejected the approach of the Restatement. See e.g., Yukon Equipment, Inc. v. Fireman's Fund Ins. Co., 585 P.2d 1206 (Alaska 1978), involving the explosion of a building used to store explosives. The court insisted that the use and storage of dynamite warranted the imposition of strict liability no matter how valuable the activity might be to the community and even if there were no safer place to store it:

> The reasons for imposing absolute liability on those who have created a grave risk of harm to others by storing or using explosives are largely independent of considerations of locational appropriateness. We see no reason for making a distinction between the right of a homesteader to recover when his property has been damaged by a blast set off in a remote corner of the state, and the right to compensation of an urban resident whose home is destroyed by an explosion originating in a settled area. In each case, the loss is properly to be regarded as a cost of the business of storing or using explosives. Every incentive remains to conduct such activities in locations which are as safe as possible, because there the damages resulting from an accident will be kept to a minimum.

How might Judge Posner respond?

5. In Torchia v. Fisher, 95 N.J. 43, 468 A.2d 1061 (1983), the court held the owner of a stolen airplane liable for ground damage to plaintiffs under a statute construed to create "absolute liability." The court asserted that "as between an unsuspecting homeowner or person on the ground and the plane's owner, the Legislature could rationally decide to place the loss on the owner, for whom the plane served some purpose."

Contrary to a view taken in the First Restatement, most courts now refuse to hold owners or pilots of falling aircraft strictly liable for harm to land, persons or chattels on the ground. See e.g. Crosby v. Cox Aircraft Co. of Washington, 109 Wash.2d 581, 746 P.2d 1198 (1987). The framers of the Second Restatement, however, after much debate, adopted a special provision making the owner and operator of any aircraft liable for harm caused to land, persons or chattels on the ground by the aircraft itself or any object falling therefrom "even if he has exercised the utmost care to prevent it." A comment to the section observed that despite great strides the safety records did not indicate "that the ordinary rules of negligence should be applied." The comment also stressed that those on the ground have "no place to hide from falling aircraft and are helpless to select any locality for their residence or business in which they will not be exposed to the risk, however minimized it may be." § 520A. Is this a unique hazard?

For a capsule view of the evolving judicial treatment of aircraft cases in New York, see Guille v. Swan, 19 Johns. (N.Y.) 381 (1822)(discussed in the principal case); Rochester Gas & Elec. Corp. v. Dunlop, 148 Misc. 849, 266 N.Y.S. 469 (1933); and Wood v. United Air Lines, Inc., 32 Misc.2d 955, 223 N.Y.S.2d 692 (1961), affirmed without opinion 16 App.Div.2d 659, 226 N.Y.S.2d 1022 (1962), appeal dismissed 11 N.Y.2d 1053, 184 N.E.2d 180, 230 N.Y.S.2d 207 (1962).

6. In 1973, an explosion occurred in the Southern Pacific yards near Roseville, California. Eighteen boxcars laden with bombs, all belonging to the United States, exploded, causing widespread damage and injury, and triggering several lawsuits. In Chavez v. Southern Pacific Transp. Co., 413 F.Supp. 1203 (E.D.Cal.1976), cited by Judge Posner, the railroad argued that where a carrier is required to accept dangerous cargo, it is "unjust" to impose strict liability. The judge concluded that California courts would not create such an exception even though the Second Restatement's § 521 did reject strict liability in such a situation:

> If California predicated liability solely upon the "fairness" rationale appearing in [Green v. General Petroleum Corp., 205 Cal. 328, 270 P. 952 (1928)], it might well find that strict liability was inappropriate. Under the *Green* rationale strict liability is imposed because the ultrahazardous factor intentionally exposes others to a serious danger—an anti-social act is being redressed. Where the carrier has no choice but to accept dangerous cargo and engage in an ultrahazardous activity, it is the public which is requiring the carrier to engage in the anti-social activity. The carrier is innocent.
>
> But, there is no logical reason for creating a "public duty" exception when the rationale for subjecting the carrier to absolute liability is the carrier's ability to distribute the loss to the public. Whether the carrier is free to reject or bound to take the explosive cargo, the plaintiffs are equally defenseless. Bound or not, Southern Pacific is in a position to pass along the loss to the public. Bound or not, the social and economic benefits which are ordinarily derived from strict liability are achieved. . . . A more efficient allocation of resources results. Thus, the reasonable inference to be drawn from the adoption of the risk distribution rationale in Smith v. Lockheed Propulsion Co., [247 Cal.App.2d 774, 56 Cal.Rptr. 128 (1967)] is that California would . . . find carriers engaging in ultrahazardous activity are subject to strict liability.

For an extensive discussion of the carrier issue, see National Steel Service Center, Inc. v. Gibbons, 319 N.W.2d 269 (Iowa 1982), also rejecting the Second Restatement's position.

7. In Laird v. Nelms, 406 U.S. 797 (1972), the Court, 6–2, concluded that "wrongful" as used in 28 U.S.C. § 1346(b) of the Federal Tort Claims Act did not permit recovery against the government on a strict liability theory. See p. 215, supra. That section gives district courts jurisdiction to hear tort claims against the government for harm caused "by negligent or wrongful act or omission" of a government employee. The Nelms case involved property damage caused by sonic booms from military planes. Although state law might recognize an action on a strict liability theory, the statute did not permit imposition of such liability on the government. See Peck, Laird v. Nelms: A Call for Review and Revision of the Federal Tort Claims Act, 48 Wash.L.Rev. 391 (1973) and Note, Utility, Fairness and the Takings Clause: Three Perspectives on Laird v. Nelms, 59 Va.L.Rev. 1034 (1973).

See also In re Bomb Disaster at Roseville, California, 438 F.Supp. 769 (E.D.Cal.1977), in which the court concluded that Laird v. Nelms barred recovery against the United States for the explosions that occurred.

8. *Defenses.* There have been relatively few cases involving defenses in this branch of strict liability. Why might this be? Restatement (Second) of Torts § 523 states that plaintiff's assumption of the risk of harm from the activity "bars his recovery for the harm." An illustration states that if a person drives along the public highway knowing that a magazine of explosives is adjacent to the highway, he is not barred by assumption of the risk if the magazine explodes as he is driving past. Why not?

Another illustration asserts that if a flagman warns P about an impending blast down the road and asks P to wait five minutes, P will be barred by assumption of the risk if he refuses to wait the five minutes.

Section 524 states that contributory negligence is not a defense to strict liability except when the plaintiff's conduct involves "knowingly and unreasonably subjecting himself to the risk of harm from the activity . . . ." An illustration to § 524 states that if a driver is so intent on passing the truck in front of him that he fails to see "Danger, Dynamite" plainly marked on the truck, and collides with the truck causing an explosion, he is not barred by his contributory negligence. If the driver has read the sign, however, he is barred from recovery. Why? What if no explosion follows the collision?

In a jurisdiction not following comparative fault notions, do these defenses make sense? Should a state that has adopted comparative fault for negligence cases, extend it to this type of strict liability case? This issue is discussed in the context of liability for defective products at p. 559, infra.

9. *Handguns.* The question of whether traditional strict liability, as it has developed from *Rylands* through the Restatement, is limited to situations in which one engages in an abnormally dangerous activity or whether it also applies to cases involving the manufacture of a highly dangerous product has been addressed in litigation against the makers of small, easily concealable handguns. In Burkett v. Freedom Arms, 299 Or. 551, 704 P.2d 118 (1985), a person shot during a jail break sued the manufacturer of the weapon used by the escaping convict. The court relied on a number of precedents from other jurisdictions in holding that strict liability for abnormally dangerous activities did not extend to the marketing of handguns.

In Kelley v. R.G. Industries, Inc., 304 Md. 124, 497 A.2d 1143 (1985), the court similarly held that strict liability under the Restatement's abnormally dangerous approach was inapplicable to the claim of a gunshot victim of a grocery store robbery against the manufacturer of the weapon. The court asserted that in Maryland the theory applied only to landowners and occupiers. However, the court then reviewed federal and state gun control legislation and decided that it was "entirely consistent with public policy" to adopt strict liability against a delimited category of handgun manufacturers:

> This type of handgun, commonly known as a "Saturday Night Special," presents particular problems for law enforcement officials. Saturday Night Specials are generally characterized by short barrels, light weight, easy concealability, low cost, use of cheap quality materials, poor manufacture, inaccuracy and unreliability. These characteristics render the Saturday Night Special particularly attractive for criminal use and virtually useless for the legitimate purposes of law enforcement, sport, and protection of persons, property and businesses.

Does *Kelley* suggest a substantial expansion of the strict liability concept? Can you think of other non-defective products that are likely candidates for similar treatment. (Liability for defective products is given detailed treatment in the next Chapter.) Six months after the case was decided, R.G. Industries announced that it was terminating its handgun business because of liability insurance costs. See Nat'l L.J., June 2, 1986, p. 8, discussing a $400,000 settlement of a Texas case and "a string of products liability suits" that had been brought against the company.

The Maryland legislature subsequently overruled *Kelley* by statute. Md. Code, Art. 27, § 36-I (1992) provides:

> h) Liability for damages.—1) A person or entity may not be held strictly liable for damages of any kind resulting from injuries to another person sustained as a result of the criminal use of any firearm by a third person, unless the person or entity conspired with the third person to commit, or wilfully aided, abetted, or caused the commission of the criminal act in which the firearm was used.

> 2) This section may not be construed to otherwise negate, limit, or modify the doctrine of negligence or strict liability relating to abnormally dangerous products or activities and defective products.

Kelley has also been rejected by a number of federal and state courts that have confronted the issue of strict liability for handgun manufacture, attacking its logic for, among other things, discriminating against the poor and setting up an unworkable test; see e.g., Delahanty v. Hinckley, 686 F.Supp. 920 (D.D.C.1986) and Richardson v. Holland, 741 S.W.2d 751 (Mo.App.1987). Efforts to pin liability on the handgun manufacturer based on a theory of negligence in promoting the product and in failing to warn distributors about the characteristics of potential dangerous users have also failed. See First Commercial Trust Co. v. Lorcin Engineering, Inc., 321 Ark. 210, 900 S.W.2d 202 (1995).

By contrast, in 1991 the voters of the District of Columbia overwhelmingly adopted an initiative whose major provision states:

> Any manufacturer, importer, or dealer of an assault weapon or machine gun shall be held strictly liable in tort, without regard to fault or proof of defect, for all direct and consequential damages that arise from bodily injury or death if the bodily injury or death proximately results from the discharge of the assault weapon or machine gun in the District of Columbia.

The enactment, D.C. Code § 6–2392 (1995), has survived a number of subsequent legal challenges.

B.   THEORETICAL PERSPECTIVES

Strict liability can be seriously regarded as a comprehensive alternative to the fault principle only if it is grounded in a broader-based foundation than the cases involving abnormally dangerous activities. The various formulations of enterprise liability adopted by the courts, initially in the abnormally dangerous activity cases but more extensively in defective products litigation supply the basic elements for such a theory. These elements, along with other insights drawn from economics and moral theory, served as the basis for a substantial body of tort scholarship in recent years aimed at illuminating the principles of strict liability.

A central figure in developing the economic approach to optimal behavior and safety has been Judge Guido Calabresi, formerly professor and dean at Yale Law School. The following excerpt traces the elements of his conception of general, or market, deterrence which is at the core of his influential writing on the subject. At the outset, Calabresi carefully notes that considerations of justice may override the commitment to reach an economically optimal level of accident costs. But justice is hard to define, and, without denigrating its importance, he turns to an analysis of the economic side of the problem.

The Costs of Accidents

Guido Calabresi.
26–29, 68–75 (1970).

Reduction of Accident Costs

Apart from the requirements of justice, I take it as axiomatic that the principal function of accident law is to reduce the sum of the costs of accidents and the costs of avoiding accidents. (Such incidental benefits as providing a respectable livelihood for a large number of judges, lawyers, and insurance agents are at best beneficent side effects.) This cost, or loss, reduction goal can be divided into three subgoals.

The first is reduction of the number and severity of accidents. This "primary" reduction of accident costs can be attempted in two basic ways. We can seek to forbid specific acts or activities thought to cause accidents, or we can make activities more expensive and thereby less attractive to the extent of the accident costs they cause. These two methods of primary reduction of accident costs are not clearly separable; a number of difficulties of definition will become apparent as we consider them in detail. But the distinction between them is useful because from it flow two very different approaches toward primary reduction of accident costs, the "general deterrence" or market method and the "specific deterrence" or collective method.

The second cost reduction subgoal is concerned with reducing neither the number of accidents nor their degree of severity. It concentrates instead on reducing the societal costs resulting from accidents. I shall attempt to show that the notion that one of the principal functions of accident law is the compensation of victims is really a rather misleading, though occasionally useful, way of stating this "secondary" accident cost reduction goal. The fact that I have termed this compensation notion secondary should in no way be taken as belittling its importance. There is no doubt that the way we provide for accident victims *after* the accident is crucially important and that the real societal costs of accidents can be reduced as significantly here as by taking measures to avoid accidents in the first place. This cost reduction subgoal is secondary only in the sense that it does not come into play until after earlier primary measures to reduce accident costs have failed.

The secondary cost reduction goal can be accomplished through the two methods outlined in [an earlier chapter], both of which usually involve a shifting of accident losses: the risk (or loss) spreading method and the deep pocket method.[6]

The third subgoal of accident cost reduction is rather Pickwickian but very important nonetheless. It involves reducing the costs of administering our treatment of accidents. It may be termed "tertiary" because its aim is to reduce the costs of achieving primary and secondary cost reduction. But in a very real sense this "efficiency" goal comes first. It tells us

---

6. Economists, unlike lawyers, tend to treat secondary cost reduction under the rubric of justice. [ ] The reason, the same given for treating collective desires under justice, is that reduction of secondary costs usually entails interpersonal comparisons of utility and hence is not amenable to traditional economic efficiency analysis. I treat it under cost reduction because what can be said about reducing secondary costs is much more concrete than what can be said about the catchall of goals we deal with under justice. As a result we are willing to have trade-offs between spreading and economic efficiency, while we would not tolerate trade-offs between justice and economic efficiency. . . .

to question constantly whether an attempt to reduce accident costs, either by reducing accidents themselves or by reducing their secondary effects, costs more than it saves. By forcing us to ask this, it serves as a kind of general balance wheel to the cost reduction goal.

.   .   .

It should be noted in advance that these subgoals are not fully consistent with each other. For instance, a perfect system of secondary cost reduction is, as we shall see, inconsistent with the goals of reducing primary accident costs. We cannot have more than a certain amount of reduction in one category without forgoing some of the reduction in the other, just as we cannot reduce all accident costs beyond a certain point without incurring costs in *achieving* the reduction that are greater than the reduction is worth. Our aim must be to find the best combination of primary, secondary, and tertiary cost reduction taking into account what must be given up in order to achieve that reduction.

.   .   .

As suggested earlier, the primary way in which a society may seek to reduce accident costs is to discourage activities that are "accident prone" and substitute safer activities as well as safer ways of engaging in the same activities. But such a statement suggests neither the degree to which we wish to discourage such activities nor the means for doing so. As we have seen, we certainly do not wish to avoid accident costs at all costs by forbidding all accident-prone activities. Most activities can be carried out safely enough or be sufficiently reduced in frequency so that there is a point at which their worth outweighs the costs of the accidents they cause. Specific prohibition or deterrence of most activities would cost society more than it would save in accident costs prevented. We want the fact that activities cause accidents to influence our choices among activities and among ways of doing them. But we want to limit this influence to a degree that is justified by the cost of these accidents. The obvious question is, how do we do this?

There are two basic approaches to making these difficult "decisions for accidents," and our society has always used both, though not always to the same degree. The first, which I have termed the specific deterrence or collective approach, will be discussed later. At present it suffices to say that it involves deciding collectively the degree to which we want any given activity, who should participate in it, and how we want it done. These decisions may or may not be made solely on the basis of the accident costs the activity causes. The collective decisions are enforced by penalties on those who violate them.

The other approach, and the one I wish to discuss first, involves attempting instead to decide what the accident costs of activities are and letting the *market* determine the degree to which, and the ways in which, activities are desired given such costs. Similarly, it involves giving people freedom to choose whether they would rather engage in the activity and pay the costs of doing so, including accident costs, or, given the accident costs, engage in safer activities that might otherwise have seemed less desirable. I call this approach general, or market, deterrence.

The crucial thing about the general deterrence approach to accidents is that it does not involve an *a priori* collective decision as to the correct number of accidents. General deterrence implies that accident costs would be treated as one of the many costs we face whenever we do anything. Since we cannot have everything we want, individually or as a society, whenever we choose one thing we give up others. General deterrence attempts to force individuals to consider accident costs in choosing among activities. The problem is getting the best combination of choices available. The general deterrence approach would let the free market or price system tally the choices.

Theoretical Basis

The theoretical basis of general deterrence is not hard to find. The problem posed is simply the old one of allocation of resources which for years has been studied in the branch of economics called welfare economics; the free market solution is the one traditionally given by welfare economics. This solution presupposes certain postulates. The most important of these, and the only one we need consider now, is the notion that no one knows what is best for individuals better than they themselves do. If people want television sets, society should produce television sets; if they want licorice drops, then licorice drops should be made. The proportion of television sets to licorice drops, as well as the way in which each is made, should also be left up to individual choices because, according to the postulate, as long as individuals are adequately informed about the alternatives and as long as the cost to society of giving them what they want is reflected in the cost to the individual, the individual can decide better than anyone else what he wants. Thus the function of the prices of various goods must be to reflect the relative costs to society of producing them, and if prices perform this function properly, the buyer will cast an informed vote in making his purchases; thus the best combination of choices available will be achieved.

The general deterrence approach treats accident costs as it does any other costs of goods and activities—such as the metal, or the time it takes, to make cars. If all activities reflect the accident costs they "cause," each individual will be able to choose for himself whether an activity is worth the accident costs it "causes." The sum of these choices is, *ex hypothesis*, the best combination available and will determine the degree to which accident-prone activities are engaged in (if at all), how they are engaged in, and who will engage in them.[2] Failure to include accident costs in the

2. The sum of individual choices will not necessarily be the best combination available, however, if the activities' other costs are not reflected in their prices. Thus if the petroleum industry were subsidized, we might have too much driving as against walking, even though both driving and walking bore their proper share of the costs of accidents. And some economists would contend that once one cost is not reflected properly, the reflection of other costs may even worsen the overall result in terms of proper resource allocation. [ ]

prices of activities will, according to the theory, cause people to choose more accident-prone activities than they would if the prices of these activities made them pay for these accident costs, resulting in more accident costs than we want. Forbidding accident-prone activities *despite* the fact that they can "pay" their costs would, in theory, bring about an equally bad result from the resource allocation point of view. Either way, the postulate that individuals know best for themselves would be violated.

A hypothetical example may help clarify this. In Athens, accident costs are in some way or other charged to the activity that engenders them. Sparta is a society in which all accident costs are borne by the state and come out of general taxes. C.J. Taney, a businessman in Athens, has one car and is considering buying a used car in addition. The cost of owning the second car would come to about $200 a year, plus an addition to his insurance bill of another $200. Alternatively, the cost of train fares, the taxis he would occasionally need to take, and the other expenses incurred to make up for not having a second car come to about $250. Contrasting the $400 expense of owning a second car with the $250 expense of riding in trains and taxis, he decides to forgo the car.

If Taney lived in Sparta, on the other hand, he would have to pay a certain sum in taxes as his share of Sparta's general accident program. Short of moving out of Sparta, he could not avoid this cost whatever he did. As a result, the comparative costs in Sparta would be $200 per year for the car as contrasted with $250 for train and taxi fares. Chances are Taney would buy the car. In purchasing a second car in Sparta, he is not made to pay the full $400 that it costs society. In fact, he must pay *part* of that cost whether or not he buys one. He will, therefore, buy a car. If he had to carry the full burden of a second car, he would use trains and taxis, spending the money saved on something else—television, or perhaps a rowboat.

For the theory to make some sense there is no need to postulate a world made up of economic men who consciously consider the relative costs of each different good and the relative pleasure derived from each. If the cost of all automobile accidents were suddenly to be paid out of a general social insurance fund, the expense of owning a car would be a good deal lower than it is now since people would no longer need to worry about buying insurance. The result would be that some people would buy more cars. Perhaps they would be teenagers who can afford $100 for an old jalopy but who cannot afford—or whose fathers cannot afford—the insurance. Or they might be people who could only afford a second car so long as no added insurance was involved. In any event, the demand for cars would increase, and so would the number of cars produced. Indeed, the effect on car purchases would be much the same as if the government suddenly chose to pay the cost of the steel used by automobile manufacturers and to raise the money out of general taxes. In each case the objection would be the same. In each, an economist would say, resources are misallocated in that goods are produced that the consumer would not want if he had to pay the full extent of their cost to society, whether in terms of the physical components of the product or in terms of the expense of accidents associated with its production and use.

As I shall show later, I do not believe resource allocation theory in its extreme or pure form can find much acceptance today, especially as applied to accidents. Its inherent limitations, together with those added by its application to accident costs, are simply too great. But this is far from saying that the theory is useless. It has always had, in fact, a remarkable practical appeal and tenacity. It can even stand substantial modification of its basic ethical postulate—that individuals know what is best for themselves by and large—and still play an important role, albeit a more limited one, in highly welfaristic or socialistic societies. Indeed, it is hard to imagine a society where, somewhere along the line, the market deterrence approach to primary accident cost control would not be significant. All that is needed for the approach to have some influence is acceptance of the notion that *sometimes* people know best for themselves, even if for no other reason than that the choices involved arise too frequently for adequate collective decisions. To make the reasons for the appeal of general deterrence even clearer, it may be useful to discuss how it operates to reduce accident costs and how it would do so even in a society not committed to free enterprise.

How Costs Are Reduced by General Deterrence

The general deterrence approach operates in two ways to reduce accident costs. The first and more obvious one is that it creates incentives to engage in safer activities. Some people who would engage in a relatively dangerous activity at prices that did not reflect its accident costs will shift to a safer activity if accident costs *are* reflected in prices. The degree of the shift will depend on the relative difference in accident costs and on how good a substitute the safer activity is. Whatever the shift, however, it will reduce accident costs, since a safer activity will to some degree have been substituted for a dangerous one.

The second and perhaps more important way general deterrence reduces accident costs is that it encourages us to make activities safer. This is no different from the first if every variation in the way an activity is carried out is considered to be a separate activity, but since that is not how the term activity is used in common language, it may be useful to show how general deterrence operates to cause a given activity to become safer. Taney drives a car. His car causes, on the average, $200 per year in accident costs. If a different kind of brake were used in the car, this would be reduced to $100. The new kind of brake costs the equivalent of $50 per year. If the accident costs Taney causes are paid either by the state out of general taxes or by those who are injured, he has no financial incentive to put in the new brake. But if Taney has to pay, he will certainly put the new brake in. He will thus bear a new cost of $50 per year, but it will be less than the $100 per year in accident costs he will avoid. As a result, the cost of accidents to society will have been reduced by $50.

This example of how general deterrence operates to reduce costs is, of course, highly simplified. It assumes, for instance, that we know that Taney "causes" the $200 in accident costs. It also assumes that the government or the victims, if they bear the losses, cannot cause the brakes to be installed as readily as Taney. Indeed, the assumptions are so simple that they lead one to ask why we do not simply make all Taneys install the new brakes. Why, in short, do we not specifically deter the "dangerous conduct" instead of bothering with so cumbersome a method as general deterrence?

Mentioning a few more of the many complications inherent in the situation may make clearer why general deterrence is worthwhile. Suppose that Marshall, who uses old-style brakes, has only $25 worth of accidents per year. It is not worth our while to force him to install the new brakes. Indeed, if he were made to install new brakes and if we can assume our measurements of costs to be accurate (a matter calling for a good deal of discussion later), forcing Marshall to install new brakes would add an unnecessary $25 to our cost burden. Yet we would still wish to have Taney install the brakes in order to get his $50 saving. It will be expensive, if not impossible, to make collective decisions distinguishing the Taneys from the Marshalls. It will, in fact, be much easier if we let the distinction be made by Taney and Marshall themselves by letting them choose between paying for the accidents and paying for the new brakes.

Another complication may be even more significant. Suppose we do not yet have the safe brakes, and requiring such brakes is therefore impossible. Placing the cost on cars may still bring about general deterrence in the form of a continuous pressure to develop something—such as new brakes—that would avoid the accident costs and would be cheaper to make and sell than paying the accident costs. General deterrence creates a market for this cost-saving substitute and, therefore, an incentive for someone to develop it and bring about a cost reduction.

———————

In a lengthy review of "The Costs of Accidents," Professor Frank Michelman offered a general critique of the theory, as well as a detailed application to the problem of air pollution. In the review, Michelman provides a particularly useful summary of a critical issue in Calabresi's analysis, the problem of deciding which activity is to be assigned the costs of liability.

Pollution as a Tort: a Non–accidental Perspective on Calabresi's *Costs*

Frank I. Michelman.
80 Yale Law Journal 647, 654–57 (1971).

. . .

a. Assignment of Liability—Cheapest Cost Avoiders and Externalization

What-is-a-cost-of-what is the decision about which activity, of the two or more whose convergence results in given accident costs, should be said to have "caused" (or, in the Calabresian usage, should be "held liable" for) those costs. To say that law is in any sense deployed for purposes of controlling primary accident costs is precisely to say that what-is-a-cost-of-what is being decided collectively. There is no escape, because leaving costs on victims is itself a choice. This choice may be adopted because it is thought optimal for primary-cost control—because, for example, rotary-mower dismemberments are thought best controlled by pressuring users to wear protective shoes—but that is to say that a collective decision has been made about whether liability for such accidents is better assigned to manufacture and/or sale of mowers or, alternatively, to ill-shod use of them.

Since, then . . . the idea of strict manufacturer's (or "enterprise") liability provides no sure guide to how liability ought to be allocated for general-deterrence purposes, what *is* the principle which ought to be followed? In developing his own conclusion—that rules should be set so that liability will come to rest on "the cheapest cost-avoider"—Calabresi draws heavily on a seminal article by economist Ronald Coase.[17] The starting point is that in a world where voluntary transactions could be arranged costlessly, primary-cost optimization would result irrespective of the initial placement of liability and we could therefore (except for possible concern about secondary costs or justice) leave it on victims. Thus, suppose it to be clear that the cheapest means to significant reduction of rotary-mower accidents are those, such as altered design, lying within the control of manufacturers. Manufacturers would, then, by definition be the "cheapest cost-avoiders." But no collective shift of liability to manufacturers would be required because, by our hypothesis that product alteration is a cheaper method of accident-cost avoidance than protective clothing or reduced use of mowers, the victims on whom accident costs initially fall would find it worth their while to compensate ("bribe") manufacturers for the cost of altering the product—if, but only if, that cost were less than the costs of accidental injuries thereby avoided. The market would, indeed, function just as efficaciously if we decided that mower-accident costs should be placed initially on rock musicians. Holding our other assumptions constant, we can assume that the musicians would in due course figure out that (a) there is nothing much they can do directly about the problem (*they* are not the cheapest cost-avoiders)(Calabresi calls this step an "initial rough guess"); (b) a dollar spent compensating manufacturers for altering the product saves more accident costs than one spent compensating users for wearing protective clothing or giving up mowing; and (c) dollars spent thus compensating manufacturers are (or are not) worth their savings in accident-cost liabilities. Depending on which conclusion is reached on item

17. Coase, The Problem of Social Cost, 3 J.Law & Econ. 1 (1960).

(c), manufacturers will (or will not) be bribed by musicians to alter the product—which is the efficient solution.

It should be obvious that the reason for not taking such a complacent view of the market's ability to optimize is the falsity of our starting assumption that transactions are costless. If we know for sure that manufacturers are the cheapest cost-avoiders, there is no reason for incurring the tertiary costs of transactions required before a liability placed initially on mower-users or rock musicians will come to rest on manufacturers, where it "belongs." Indeed, by not placing the liability directly on manufacturers, we run the risk that the efficient solution will be lost, because the transaction costs of shifting liabilities become so large for, say, rock musicians, that it is cheaper all told for them just to pay the accident bills.

Unfortunately, it is not always quite obvious who the cheapest cost avoider is. What should we do if in doubt as between rotary-mower manufacturers and users? Calabresi offers a number of "guidelines" for handling this problem. An important one is to avoid "externalization." In our mower case we might note that if mower-accident costs are placed on users, users—responding to the marketing practices of the insurance industry—may tend to classify these costs among the general risks of personal injury associated with being alive and active, and so leave them to be taken care of by general accident and health insurance. The costs of such insurance do not reflect specifically the frequency or severity of mower accidents, and so exert no particular pressure towards behavior modifications (like heavy shoes or reduced mower consumption) specifically adapted to mower accident cost reduction. For any user who carries accident and health insurance anyway, the question of investing in mower-proof shoes depends how their costs compare with the risks to him of mower-accident costs, considering that the insurance benefits will be available. In short, some of the desired accident-cost pressure has been allowed to escape from decision-making about mower use (been "externalized") and thereby deprived of its deterrent effect. Any likelihood that this will happen, Calabresi suggests, would argue for initial placement of liability on manufacturers because they seem very likely to be, among imaginable cost avoiders, the "cheapest" who are reasonably susceptible of being deterred by market pressures.

b.   Assignment of Liability—The Need for Prospective Rules

The inescapable collective decision of what-is-a-cost-of-what may, as Calabresi shows, be made on a highly individual basis with reference to each costly incident as it arises, or on a less individualized basis with reference to classes of incidents resulting from similar interactions of general categories of activity. The difference can be illustrated through Calabresi's argument that the latter sort of decision-making is to be preferred for general deterrence in the accident field. His basic point seems to be that the proper cost pressures cannot adequately be brought to bear on accident-prone activities by leaving it to individual actors to extrapolate from a series of retrospective liability-placing decisions the statistical cost of which is thereby being loaded onto "their" activities. Not enough information is conveyed (at the stage where decisions "for accidents" or against them must be made) by a rule placing liability on that activity retrospectively judged to be the cheapest cost-avoider in the particular case. Prospective (i.e., categorical) rules are necessary for this purpose, probably couched in terms of fairly broad classes of activity (driving, driving while intoxicated, selling cars, walking on the streets at dusk), and in terms of classes of accidents involving pairs of these activity classes ("Cars are liable for costs of collisions between cars and bicycles."). Stated another way, in order to exert effective deterrent pressures liability rules must define insurable classes of activity; and a class such as "activity which, in a given case, is retrospectively determined to have been the cheapest cost-avoider" obviously will not do. Having gotten this far, it is easy for Calabresi to go on and show that categorization will in any event occur (through private insurance) despite insistence by the official system on case-by-case identification of the cheapest cost-avoider—so that the official case-by-case determination involves wasteful tertiary expenditure, unless we (absurdly) prohibit insurance and rely (stupidly) on extrapolation of costs by individual actors.

NOTES AND QUESTIONS

1. *Guidelines.* In Views and Overviews, 1967 U.Ill.L.F. 600, Calabresi, in the context of automobile accidents, discussed "guidelines" for determining who, in practice, is the best cost avoider. First, he noted that one of the parties may have better information about the accident risks involved in the situation: "to an individual the chance of being injured or of injuring is an unknown; to an auto manufacturer it is a known statistic." (In his book at p. 56, he suggested that even if the individual learns the accurate statistics, he will consistently undervalue the risk: "people cannot estimate rationally their chances of suffering death or catastrophic injury.")

The second guideline is that one activity may be able to insure against the danger more cheaply than another. Third, "placing the cost on one activity may be more likely to result in efficient allocation of the cost to subcategories of activities than placing the cost on the other." If liability is placed on auto manufacturers the subcategories most likely to emerge would include makes of cars and whether they have safety features, but it would be difficult to develop categories relating to age of the driver or previous driving record. Although in theory the more useful categorization should emerge from any starting point, in practice it may not be so easy because of transaction costs.

The fourth guideline involved the externalization point mentioned by Michelman: "placing the cost on one activity rather than another may result, for political or practical reasons, in removing it from both, thus destroying market deterrence altogether. If liability is placed on drivers, but they insure inadequately and as a result fail to pay damages, or if the government steps in and pays the damages out of a generalized social insurance fund, neither the drivers nor the manufacturers will include these damages in future prices." In his book Calabresi treats all four guidelines as aspects of externalization.

Calabresi suggests that these guidelines are necessary in practice even in situations in which the parties are in a bargaining situation. If they are not in such a relationship, the problem is more difficult because the same criteria still apply plus a new one: "Suppose we have guessed wrong and allocated the costs to the wrong activity? Which mistaken allocation can be cured most cheaply by parties entering into transactions with each other in the market? If we place costs of auto-pedestrian accidents on pedestrians and the cheapest way of avoiding these is to change how cars are made, it would cost too much for pedestrians to gather together in the market to pay car makers to change how cars are made. It would be much cheaper for car makers to pay pedestrians to wear flashing lights, if car makers had wrongly been held liable and flashing lights, instead of differently made cars, avoided the cost most cheaply." Unless we are sure which activity is the cheapest cost avoider, "we should put the burden on the party which can cure a mistake most cheaply if one has been made, and thus help the market to operate as effectively as possible."

2. In a subsequent article, Calabresi and Hirschoff, Toward a Test for Strict Liability in Torts, 81 Yale L.J. 1055 (1972), the authors expand upon Calabresi's approach. They note that the Learned Hand negligence test would minimize the sum of accident costs "if it were applied perfectly" because "it would put the costs of the accident on the injurer when and only when it was cheaper for him to avoid the accident costs by appropriate safety measures than to pay those costs." But contributory negligence was not handled correctly because in theory a plaintiff who could have avoided the accident by less costly means than defendant would be barred—even though the defendant could have avoided it more cheaply. Thus, if read literally, the contributory negligence test would bar a plaintiff who could avoid an accident cost of $100 by spending $60—even though the defendant might have avoided that same accident cost by spending only $40. The authors concluded that "the *correct* optimizing rule, under the Learned Hand test, would be to have a doctrine of contributory negligence, but to apply it only where the cost of injurer avoidance exceeds the cost of victim avoidance."

The authors urged that instead of requiring the courts to decide the difficult question of who could avoid an accident more cheaply in a case-by-case setting, as required by negligence law, the legal system should decide only "which of the parties to the accident is in the best position to make the cost-benefit analysis between accident costs and accident avoidance costs and to act on that decision once it is made. . . . The issue becomes not *whether* avoidance is worth it, but which of the parties is relatively more likely to find out whether avoidance is worth it. This judgment is by no means an easy one, but we would suggest that in practice it is usually easier to make correctly than is the judgment required under . . . the Learned Hand test."

3. The Calabresi and Hirschoff article used "assumption of risk" in cases in which the plaintiff is determined to be the cheapest cost avoider:

> The doctrine of assumption of risk—though grossly misapplied by courts which have not looked realistically to whether the plaintiff in practice had the requisite knowledge and possibility of choice the doctrine implied—is essential to an understanding of a non-fault world. It is, and always has been, a kind of plaintiff's strict liability—the other side of the coin of defendant's strict liability. . . . Just as the employer may be in a better position to evaluate the costs and benefits of a piece of equipment given the likelihood of occasional employee negligence (defendant's strict liability), so a spectator at a baseball game may be best suited to evaluate the desirability of sitting in an unscreened bleacher given the likelihood of occasional negligent wild throws by the players during the game which may result in the spectator's being hit on the head (plaintiff's strict liability, or assumption of risk). In both these situations the conclusion as to whether an accident cost should be shifted depends not on whether a party was negligent, but rather on a judgment as to which party was in a better position to make the cost-benefit analysis irrespective of the other's negligence.

4. This focus leads, as the excerpts have noted, to a call for generalized liability rules using broad categories—a departure from the case-by-case approach of the fault system. Calabresi and Hirschoff discuss how broad the categories might be in the context of blasting. As we saw, although blasters are generally held strictly liable for harm done by their blasts, some courts reject strict liability when the blasting occurs in a remote area. The authors understand these courts to be saying that the victim "is better suited to gauge the costs of making his presence in such an unusual place known as against the costs of taking whatever risk may be attendant upon being in a place unexpectedly. But some judges have in effect reasoned that such an exception, precisely because it would require more individualized judgments, might not be worth making. Perhaps an occasional victim would be better suited to make the cost-benefit analysis, but the administrative cost of dealing with such instances would not be worthwhile, given their presumed rarity."

5. Under certain circumstances, the most efficient solution to an accident problem may require joint action to reduce the cost of harm. Assume, for example, a potential accident cost of $100. P alone could avoid it only by a cost of $150. D alone could avoid it only at a cost of $130. But if P spent $30 and D spent $40, the accident could be avoided. Calabresi discusses this problem in Optimal Deterrence and Accidents, 84 Yale L.J. 656 (1975). Professor Schwartz suggests that the problem can be resolved through the use of a comparative negligence system in which, since liability is divided, there is an incentive for P and D to cooperate in avoiding the accident. See Schwartz, Contributory and Comparative Negligence, 87 Yale L.J. 697, 705 (1978). The appropriateness of a comparative fault defense in strict liability for defective product cases is discussed at p. 559, infra.

6. Among those who agree on the utility of economic analysis in tort law, not all have subscribed without qualification to the case for strict liability. Consider the following excerpt.

Economic Analysis of Law

Richard A. Posner.
175–79 (4th ed. 1992).

Strict liability means that someone who causes an accident is liable for the victim's damages even if the injury could not have been avoided by the exercise of due care (PL might be $150 and B $300). As a first approximation, strict liability has the same effects on safety as negligence liability, provided that there is a defense of contributory negligence, as there usually is though often under a different name. (Why is this proviso more important for strict liability than for negligence?) If B is smaller than PL, the strictly liable defendant will take precautions to avoid the accident, just as the defendant in a negligence system will, in order to reduce his net costs. Less obviously, if B is larger than PL, the strictly liable defendant will not take precautions, just as under negligence. True, he will have to pay the victim's damages. But those damages, discounted by the probability of the accident, are less than the cost of avoidance; in other words, the expected cost of liability ($= PL$) is less than the cost of avoidance, so avoidance doesn't pay.

And yet there are significant economic differences between negligence and strict liability. . . .

Judicial inability to determine optimal activity levels except in simple cases is potentially a serious shortcoming of a negligence system. Suppose railroads and canals are good substitutes in transportation but railroads inflict many accidents that cannot be avoided by being careful and canals none. Were it not for these accident costs railroads would be 10 percent cheaper than canals, but when these accident costs are figured in, railroads are actually 5 percent more costly. Under a rule of negligence liability, railroads will displace canals even though they are the socially more costly method of transportation.

In contrast, potential injurers subject to a rule of strict liability will automatically take into account possible changes in activity level, as well as possible changes in expenditures on care in deciding whether to prevent accidents. . . .

The problem with using this analysis to support a general rule of strict liability is that changes in activity level by victims are also a method of accident avoidance, and one that is encouraged by negligence liability but discouraged by strict liability. Suppose that the cost to the railroad of preventing damage to the farmer's crops, whether by more care or less activity, is greater than $150, the expected loss, so that the railroad will do nothing, but that the farmer could prevent the loss by switching to a fire-resistant crop at a cost of $100. Under a rule of strict liability, he will have no incentive to do so, because his failure to change his activity will not be deemed contributory negligence and therefore the railroad will have to pay for the damage. But under a regime of negligence liability, since the railroad will not be liable for the damage, the farmer will switch to the fire-resistant crop, a switch that will now give him an expected gain of $50. Thus, strict liability encourages activity-level changes by potential injurers but discourages them by potential victims, while negligence liability encourages activity-level changes by potential victims but discourages them by potential injurers.

So, if a class of activities can be identified in which activity level changes by potential injurers appear to be the most efficient method of accident prevention, there is a strong argument for imposing strict liability on the people engaged in those activities. And, conversely, if there is a class of activities in which activity-level changes by potential victims are the most efficient method of accident prevention, there is a strong argument for no liability, as by applying the doctrine of assumption of risk to participation in dangerous sports. Through the concept of ultrahazardous activities, the tort law imposes strict liability on activities that involve a high degree of danger that cannot feasibly be prevented by the actor's being careful or potential victims' altering their behavior. . . .

. . .

The distinction between care and activity is not the only dimension along which negligence and strict liability differ. Another . . . has to do with the costs of administering these different rules. The trial of a strict liability case is simpler than that of a negligence case because there is one less issue, negligence; and the fewer the issues, the easier it should be to settle the case without a trial. On both counts we can expect litigation costs to be lower under strict liability than under negligence—for the same number of claims. But the number may not be the same. In principle, under strict liability, every accident to which there is more than one party gives rise to a claim, not just every accident in which the defendant may have been negligent. This makes it important, before one chooses strict liability, to assess the responsiveness of the accident rate to the incentives that such liability will create. If the accident rate in some activity will fall dramatically if strict liability is imposed, because accident costs exceed the costs of avoiding them through changes in the level of the activity, there may well be fewer claims under strict liability, and, since the average cost of processing claims should be lower under strict liability, the substitution of strict liability for negligence will be an unequivocal economic gain. On the other hand, if most of the accidents that occur in some activity are unavoidable in an economic sense either by taking greater care or by reducing the amount of the activity (because the costs of greater care, or less activity, exceed any savings in reduced accident costs), the main effect of switching from negligence to strict liability will be to increase the number of damages claims.

Another difference is that strict liability operates to insure victims of unavoidable accidents. But this is a gain only if the cost of insurance through the tort system is less than the cost to potential victims of buying accident insurance policies in the insurance market; and almost certainly it is greater. All sides of the no-fault debate agree that the tort system is a very costly method of providing insurance; the debate is over whether it provides another good, the deterrence of non-cost-justified accidents. . . . A related point is that . . . the size of, and economic rents earned in, an industry subject to strict liability will be smaller than if the industry were subject to negligence. In sum, strict liability differs from negligence in the incentives imparted to injurers and victims to avoid accidents through changes in activity levels, in information and claims costs, in the provision of insurance, and in the size and profitability of the liable activity. Given these many differences, we would not expect the tort system to opt all for negligence or all for strict liability, nor would we expect the balance between the two regimes to be the same at all times.

.   .   .

NOTES AND QUESTIONS

1. Does the Posner excerpt undermine Calabresi's main arguments? Do other major differences between the consequences of strict liability and negligence occur to you?

2. A useful supplement to the Calabresi–Posner dialogue is Shavell, Strict Liability versus Negligence, 9 J.Legal Studies 1 (1980), arguing that economic analysis of liability rules has not been sufficiently sensitive to the distinction between measuring injurer-victim conduct on a case-by-case basis as compared to injurer-victim decisions to engage in a different level of activity—including no involvement at all. For more general treatments of economic analysis of tort issues, see W. Landes & R. Posner, The Economic Structure of Tort Law (1987) and S. Shavell, Economic Analysis of Accident Law (1987). See also Rizzo, Law Amid Flux: The Economics of Negligence and Strict Liability in Tort, 9 J.Legal Studies 291 (1980), criticizing economic efficiency analysis on the ground that information costs and market imperfections make it unworkable.

3. Gary Schwartz has systematically reviewed the empirical evidence bearing on the economists' claims for the deterrent effect of tort law and their many critics' claims that tort law does not effectively deter in Schwartz, Reality in the Economic Analysis of Tort Law: Does Tort Law Really Deter?, 42 UCLA L. Rev. 377 (1994). He concludes that neither polar position is correct: "tort law, while not as effective as economic models suggest, may still be somewhat successful in achieving its stated deterrence goals." For discussion of the psychological literature on the deterrent effect of tort sanctions, see Shuman, The Psychology of Deterrence in Tort Law, 42 Kans.L.Rev. 115 (1993).

4. *Moral Theories.* Several writers have objected to the focus on economics because other values have been diluted or disregarded. Among the critics of the economic approach to tort liability is Professor George Fletcher. In Fairness and Utility in Tort Theory, 85 Harv.L.Rev. 537 (1972), he objected that "the thrust of the academic literature is to convert the tort system into something other than a mechanism for determining the just distribution of accident losses. . . . Discussed less and less are precisely those questions that make tort law a unique repository of intuitions of corrective justice: What is the relevance of risk-creating conduct to the just distribution of wealth? What is the rationale for an individual's 'right' to recover for his losses? What are the criteria for justly singling out some people and making them, and not their neighbors, bear the costs of accidents?"

Fletcher developed an approach that built on a variety of cases, including the Rylands case, the ultrahazardous group, and Vincent v. Lake Erie Transp. Co., p. 847, infra. "The general principle expressed in all of these situations governed by diverse doctrinal standards is that a victim has a right to recover for injuries caused by a risk greater in degree and different in order from those created by the victim and imposed on the defendant—in short, for injuries resulting from nonreciprocal risks . . . . For example, a pilot or an airplane owner subjects those beneath the path of flight to nonreciprocal risks of harm. Conversely, cases of nonliability are those of reciprocal risks, namely those in which the victim and the defendant subject each other to roughly the same degree of risk. For example, two airplanes flying in the same vicinity subject each other to reciprocal risks of a mid-air collision. Of course, there are significant problems in determining when risks are nonreciprocal. . . ."

Professor Fletcher then sketched a paradigm of reasonableness opposing the paradigm of reciprocity. The reasonableness paradigm "represents a rejection of non-instrumentalist values and a commitment to the community's welfare as the criterion for determining both who is entitled to receive and who ought to pay compensation. Questions that are distinct under the paradigm of reciprocity—namely, is the risk nonreciprocal and was it unexcused—are collapsed in this paradigm into a single test: was the risk unreasonable?"

Although the paradigm of reciprocity bears resemblance to strict liability and that of reasonableness to negligence, Fletcher asserted that the reciprocity cases cut across these lines and that many negligence cases lend themselves to analysis under both categories—in particular, because liability is warranted between reciprocal risk-creators when one party negligently harms the other. Much of the article was devoted to analyzing groups of cases to suggest how they fit into one or the other of the paradigms.

At one point Fletcher flatly rejected assignments of liability based on access to insurance or ability to invoke the market mechanism to distribute losses: "This is an argument of distributive rather than corrective justice, for it turns on the defendant's wealth and status, rather than his conduct. Using the tort system to redistribute negative wealth (accident losses) violates the premise of corrective justice, namely that liability should turn on what the defendant has done, rather than on who he is. [ ] What is at stake is keeping the institution of taxation distinct from the institution of tort litigation."

Calabresi responded to Fletcher in Calabresi and Hirschoff, Toward a Test for Strict Liability in Torts, 81 Yale L.J. 1055 (1972). Posner responded in Strict Liability: A Comment, 2 J.Legal Studies 205 (1973).

5. In Fletcher, Corrective Justice for Moderns, 106 Harv. L. Rev. 1658 (1993), he revisits his thesis, now arguing that tort law should be understood as a "middle position" between criminal law and contract law:

> . . . cases of strict liability reflect criminal law. The influence begins early in the law of torts under the writ of trespass and carries forward in the various situations in which we perceive the defendant's action as aggression that dominates the interests of a plaintiff insulated by her rights. In contrast, the influence of private law thinking breaks through in the collaborative principle underlying the law of negligence. By entering into certain spheres of risk-taking, plaintiff and defendant both come under duties to act with a view to the costs and benefits of their actions. They become a unit, acting under an implicit obligation to optimize the consequences of their actions.

He elaborates on the distinction between dominance and collaboration with three airplane operators' liability examples. In the first two, where harm occurs to passengers or owners of other planes, the parties have entered into a collaborative enterprise and thus fall under a negligence system. In the third, involving homeowners in the path of flight, the situation is one of dominance and strict liability applies. Does the dominance-collaboration perspective seem consistent with Fletcher's earlier non-reciprocity-reciprocity perspective?

6. The economic approach (and Fletcher's right-based reciprocity analysis) were rejected by Professor Epstein in favor of a strict liability approach that relied heavily on notions of causation, which he introduced in:

> four distinct paradigm cases covered by the proposition "A caused B harm." These paradigms are not the only way in which we can talk about torts cases. They do, however, provide modes of description which best capture the ordinary use of causal language. Briefly put, they are based upon notions of force, fright, compulsion and dangerous conditions. . . . [D]espite the internal differences, it can, I believe, be demonstrated that each of these paradigms, when understood, exhibits the features that render it relevant to the question of legal responsibility. [2 J.Legal Studies at 166]

Epstein developed applications of the paradigm cases and defenses in Epstein, A Theory of Strict Liability, 2 J.Legal Studies 151 (1973), and Defenses and Subsequent Pleas in a System of Strict Liability, 3 J.Legal Studies 165 (1974). The theory was further elaborated in Epstein, Nuisance Law: Corrective Justice and Its Utilitarian Constraints, 8 J.Legal Studies 49 (1979).

The theories developed by Epstein and Fletcher are criticized in Schwartz, The Vitality of Negligence and the Ethics of Strict Liability, 15 Ga.L.Rev. 963, 977–1005 (1981). See also Posner, The Concept of Corrective Justice in Recent Theories of Tort Law, 10 J.Legal Studies 187 (1981) and Borgo, Causal Paradigms in Tort Law, 8 J.Legal Studies 419 (1979). Epstein responded in Causation and Corrective Justice: A Reply to Two Critics, 8 J.Legal Studies 477 (1979). Subsequently, however, he took the position that his theory of strict liability may be excessively formalistic and insufficiently sensitive to the social consequences of liability rules. See, Epstein, Causation—In Context: An Afterword, 63 Chi–Kent L.Rev. 653 (1987), an essay appearing in a wide-ranging collection of papers addressing the role of causation in tort law from many perspectives. See Symposium on Causation in the Law of Torts, 63 Chi–Kent L.Rev. 397–680 (1987).

7. More recent contributions to the corrective justice literature can be found in E. Weinrib, The Idea of Private Law (1995) (positing a formalist theory of corrective justice, which draws principally on Aristotle and Kant, to articulate a foreseeability-based system of negligence liability) and J. Coleman, Risks and Wrongs (1992) (arguing that tort law serves a rectification function in repairing wrongful losses and annulling wrongful gains). Weinrib's theoretical writing has triggered two wide-ranging symposia on corrective justice featuring a number of corrective justice theorists: Corrective Justice and Formalism: The Care One Owes One's Neighbors, 77 Iowa L.Rev. 403–863 (1992) and Symposium on Legal Formalism, 16 Harv.J.L. & Pub.Pol. 583–679 (1993).

8. For historical analysis of tort developments, see Rabin, The Historical Development of the Fault Principle: A Reinterpretation, 15 Ga.L.Rev. 925 (1981); Schwartz, Tort Law and the Economy in Nineteenth–Century America: A Reinterpretation, 90 Yale L.J. 1717 (1981), The Character of Early American Tort Law, 36 UCLA L.Rev. 641 (1989), and The Beginning and the Possible End of the Rise of Modern American Tort Law, 26 Ga. L.Rev. 601 (1992); and G. White, Tort Law in America (1980). See also L. Friedman, A History of American Law, Chap. 6 (2d ed. 1985), and M. Horwitz, The Transformation of American Law 1780–1860, 85–101 (1977).

Special attention is given to the enterprise liability phenomenon in two contrasting historical interpretations, Priest, The Invention of Enterprise Liability: A Critical History of the Intellectual Foundations of Modern Tort Law, 14 J.Legal Studies 461 (1985) and V. Nolan and E. Ursin, Understanding Enterprise Liability: Rethinking Tort Reform for the Twenty-first Century (1995).

9. For extensive readings on economic, moral, historical and other approaches to the analysis of tort law, see the collection of essays in R. Rabin, Perspectives on Tort Law (4th ed. 1995). See also S. Levmore, Foundations of Tort Law (1994).

10. Should the choice of theory affect damages? Courts considering damages in strict liability cases have thus far failed to draw any distinction. In one of the few explicit references to this problem, Justice O'Connell, in Wights v. Staff Jennings, Inc., 241 Or. 301, 405 P.2d 624 (1965), was reluctant to adopt a general strict liability approach in a products case in part because

> Although we believe that it is the function of the judiciary to modify the law of torts to fit the changing needs of society, we feel that the judicial extension of the theory of strict liability to all cases where it is convenient for those engaged in commerce to spread the risk would not be advisable. If enterprise liability is to be so extended, there is a strong argument for limiting the victim's measure of recovery to some scheme of compensation similar to that employed in workmen's compensation. The legislature alone has the power to set up such a compensation scheme. The court cannot put a limit upon the jury's verdict.

Consider Nolan and Ursin, cited in the preceding note, proposing an extension of strict liability to "business premises enterprise liability" combined with a limitation on recovery of pain and suffering damages in business premises cases. The subjects of damages and damage reform are discussed in detail in Chapters X and XI.

Why should the measure of recovery change if strict liability replaces negligence as the basis for recovery? Why cannot a court limit the amount of a jury verdict? Why has the award of common law damages in strict liability situations produced little comment? Does this imply that strict liability is still perceived as a species of fault? See R. Keeton, Conditional Fault in the Law of Torts, 72 Harv.L.Rev. 401 (1959). Might one explanation be that until the emergence of a discrete area of strict liability for defective products, activities creating strict liability usually caused property damage alone and did not raise the question of pain and suffering? *Wights* is discussed further at p. 558, infra.

CHAPTER VIII

LIABILITY FOR DEFECTIVE PRODUCTS

A. INTRODUCTION

No area of personal injury law has changed as dramatically in this century as the law governing liability for defective products. Nineteenth century products liability law languished in the shadow of the privity doctrine, which required a contractual relationship between the parties as the basis for a duty of due care. As the following landmark case indicates, the privity requirement was eventually undermined by a cluster of categorical exceptions created in response to the growing influence of the negligence principle. But as we shall see, the judicial impulse to refashion the liability rules in this area was not exhausted by consolidation of the negligence principle. Instead, the courts soon began to construct a system of strict liability—a process that continues to lend a dynamic, and controversial, quality to defective products law. The materials in this section, then, provide an excellent opportunity for exploring the fundamental resource allocation issues underlying competing systems of tort liability. At the same time, products liability is of particular interest because of the interplay between contract and tort law in shaping the approach to the subject.

MacPherson v. Buick Motor Co.

Court of Appeals of New York, 1916.
217 N.Y. 382, 111 N.E. 1050.

Appeal, by permission, from a judgment of the Appellate Division . . . affirming a judgment in favor of plaintiff entered upon a verdict.

■ CARDOZO, J. The defendant is a manufacturer of automobiles. It sold an automobile to a retail dealer. The retail dealer resold to the plaintiff. While the plaintiff was in the car, it suddenly collapsed. He was thrown out and injured. One of the wheels was made of defective wood, and its spokes crumbled into fragments. The wheel was not made by the defendant; it was bought from another manufacturer. There is evidence, however, that its defects could have been discovered by reasonable inspection, and that inspection was omitted. There is no claim that the defendant knew of the defect and willfully concealed it. The case, in other words, is not brought within the rule of Kuelling v. Roderick Lean Mfg. Co.

(183 N.Y. 78). The charge is one, not of fraud, but of negligence. The question to be determined is whether the defendant owed a duty of care and vigilance to any one but the immediate purchaser.

The foundations of this branch of the law, at least in this state, were laid in Thomas v. Winchester (6 N.Y. 397). A poison was falsely labeled. The sale was made to a druggist, who in turn sold to a customer. The customer recovered damages from the seller who affixed the label. "The defendant's negligence," it was said, "put human life in imminent danger." A poison falsely labeled is likely to injure any one who gets it. Because the danger is to be foreseen, there is a duty to avoid the injury. Cases were cited by way of illustration in which manufacturers were not subject to any duty irrespective of contract. The distinction was said to be that their conduct, though negligent, was not likely to result in injury to any one except the purchaser. We are not required to say whether the chance of injury was always as remote as the distinction assumes. Some of the illustrations might be rejected today. The *principle* of the distinction is for present purposes the important thing.

Thomas v. Winchester became quickly a landmark of the law. In the application of its principle there may at times have been uncertainty or even error. There has never in this state been doubt or disavowal of the principle itself. The chief cases are well known, yet to recall some of them will be helpful. Loop v. Litchfield (42 N.Y. 351) is the earliest. It was the case of a defect in a small balance wheel used on a circular saw. The manufacturer pointed out the defect to the buyer, who wished a cheap article and was ready to assume the risk. The risk can hardly have been an imminent one for the wheel lasted five years before it broke. In the meanwhile the buyer had made a lease of the machinery. It was held that the manufacturer was not answerable to the lessee. Loop v. Litchfield was followed in Losee v. Clute (51 N.Y. 494), the case of the explosion of a steam boiler. That decision has been criticized [   ]; but it must be confined to its special facts. It was put upon the ground that the risk of injury was too remote. The buyer in that case had not only accepted the boiler, but had tested it. The manufacturer knew that his own test was not the final one. The finality of the test has a bearing on the measure of diligence owing to persons other than the purchaser [   ].

These early cases suggest a narrow construction of the rule. Later cases, however, evince a more liberal spirit. First in importance is Devlin v. Smith (89 N.Y. 470). The defendant, a contractor, built a scaffold for a painter. The painter's servants were injured. The contractor was held liable. He knew that the scaffold, if improperly constructed, was a most dangerous trap. He knew that it was to be used by the workmen. He was building it for that very purpose. Building it for their use, he owed them a duty, irrespective of his contract with their master, to build it with care.

From Devlin v. Smith we pass over intermediate cases and turn to the latest case in this court in which Thomas v. Winchester was followed. That case is Statler v. George A. Ray Mfg. Co. (195 N.Y. 478, 480). The defendant manufactured a large coffee urn. It was installed in a restaurant. When heated, the urn exploded and injured the plaintiff. We held that the manufacturer was liable. We said that the urn "was of such a character inherently that, when applied to the purposes for which it was designed, it was liable to become a source of great danger to many people if not carefully and properly constructed."

It may be that Devlin v. Smith and Statler v. George A. Ray Mfg. Co. have extended the rule of Thomas v. Winchester. If so, this court is committed to the extension. The defendant argues that things imminently dangerous to life are poisons, explosives, deadly weapons—things whose normal function it is to injure or destroy. But whatever the rule in Thomas v. Winchester may once have been, it has no longer that restricted meaning. A scaffold (Devlin v. Smith, supra) is not inherently a destructive instrument. It becomes destructive only if imperfectly constructed. A large coffee urn (Statler v. Ray Mfg. Co., supra) may have within itself, if negligently made, the potency of danger, yet no one thinks of it as an implement whose normal function is destruction. What is true of the coffee urn is equally true of bottles of aerated water (Torgesen v. Schultz, 192 N.Y. 156). . . .

. . .

We hold, then, that the principle of Thomas v. Winchester is not limited to poisons, explosives, and things of like nature, to things which in their normal operation are implements of destruction. If the nature of a thing is such that it is reasonably certain to place life and limb in peril when negligently made, it is then a thing of danger. Its nature gives warning of the consequences to be expected. If to the element of danger there is added knowledge that the thing will be used by persons other than the purchaser, and used without new tests, then, irrespective of contract, the manufacturer of this thing of danger is under a duty to make it carefully. That is as far as we are required to go for the decision of this case. There must be knowledge of a danger, not merely possible, but probable. It is *possible* to use almost anything in a way that will make it dangerous if defective. That is not enough to charge the manufacturer with a duty independent of his contract. Whether a given thing is dangerous may be sometimes a question for the court and sometimes a question for the jury. There must also be knowledge that in the usual course of events the danger will be shared by others than the buyer. Such knowledge may often be inferred from the nature of the transaction. But it is possible that even knowledge of the danger and of the use will not always be enough. The proximity or remoteness of the relation is a factor to be considered. We are dealing now with the liability of the manufacturer of the finished product, who puts it on the market to be used without inspection by his customers. If he is negligent, where danger is to be foreseen, a liability will follow. We are not required at this time to say that it is legitimate to go back of the manufacturer of the finished product and hold the manufacturers of the component parts. To make their negligence a cause of imminent danger, an independent cause must often intervene; the manufacturer of the finished product must also fail in *his* duty of

[handwritten margin notes:]
1) knowledge of probable danger
2) usual course of events the danger will be shared by others than the buyer
3) proximity or remoteness of the relation is a factor to be considered

inspection. It may be that in those circumstances the negligence of the earlier members of the series is too remote to constitute, as to the ultimate user, an actionable wrong [ ]. We leave that question open. We shall have to deal with it when it arises. The difficulty which it suggests is not present in this case. There is here no break in the chain of cause and effect. In such circumstances, the presence of a known danger, attendant upon a known use, makes vigilance a duty. We have put aside the notion that the duty to safeguard life and limb, when the consequences of negligence may be foreseen, grows out of contract and nothing else. We have put the source of the obligation where it ought to be. We have put its source in the law.

From this survey of the decisions, there thus emerges a definition of the duty of a manufacturer which enables us to measure this defendant's liability. Beyond all question, the nature of an automobile gives warning of probable danger if its construction is defective. This automobile was designed to go fifty miles an hour. Unless its wheels were sound and strong, injury was almost certain. It was as much a thing of danger as a defective engine for a railroad. The defendant knew the danger. It knew also that the car would be used by persons other than the buyer. This was apparent from its size; there were seats for three persons. It was apparent also from the fact that the buyer was a dealer in cars, who bought to resell. The maker of this car supplied it for the use of purchasers from the dealer just as plainly as the contractor in Devlin v. Smith supplied the scaffold for use by the servants of the owner. The dealer was indeed the one person of whom it might be said with some approach to certainty that by him the car would not be used. Yet the defendant would have us say that he was the one person whom it was under a legal duty to protect. The law does not lead us to so inconsequent a conclusion. Precedents drawn from the days of travel by stage coach do not fit the conditions of travel to-day. The principle that the danger must be imminent does not change, but the things subject to the principle do change. They are whatever the needs of life in a developing civilization require them to be.

.   .   .

In England the limits of the rule are still unsettled. Winterbottom v. Wright (10 M. & W. 109)[1842] is often cited. The defendant undertook to provide a mail coach to carry the mail bags. The coach broke down from latent defects in its construction. The defendant, however, was not the manufacturer. The court held that he was not liable for injuries to a passenger. .   .   .

There is nothing anomalous in a rule which imposes upon A, who has contracted with B, a duty to C and D and others according as he knows or does not know that the subject-matter of the contract is intended for their use. We may find an analogy in the law which measures the liability of landlords. If A leases to B a tumble-down house he is not liable, in the absence of fraud, to B's guests who enter it and are injured. This is because B is then under the duty to repair it, the lessor has the right to suppose that he will fulfill that duty, and, if he omits to do so, his guests must look to him (Bohlen, supra, at p. 276). But if A leases a building to be used by the lessee at once as a place of public entertainment, the rule is different. There injury to persons other than the lessee is to be foreseen, and foresight of the consequences involves the creation of a duty (Junkermann v. Tilyou R. Co., 213 N.Y. 404, and cases there cited).

. . .

We think the defendant was not absolved from a duty of inspection because it bought the wheels from a reputable manufacturer. It was not merely a dealer in automobiles. It was a manufacturer of automobiles. It was responsible for the finished product. It was not at liberty to put the finished product on the market without subjecting the component parts to ordinary and simple tests [ ]. Under the charge of the trial judge nothing more was required of it. The obligation to inspect must vary with the nature of the thing to be inspected. The more probable the danger, the greater the need of caution. There is little analogy between this case and Carlson v. Phenix Bridge Co. (132 N.Y. 273), where the defendant bought a tool for a servant's use. The making of tools was not the business in which the master was engaged. Reliance on the skill of the manufacturer was proper and almost inevitable. But that is not the defendant's situation. Both by its relation to the work and by the nature of its business, it is charged with a stricter duty.

Other rulings complained of have been considered, but no error has been found in them.

The judgment should be affirmed with costs.

■ Hiscock, Chase and Cuddeback, JJ., concur with Cardozo, J., and Hogan, J., concurs in result; Willard Bartlett, Ch. J., reads dissenting opinion; Pound, J., not voting.

[The dissenting opinion stressed that the earlier cases could all be explained by the "inherently dangerous" analysis and that the court should not go beyond that formulation.]

NOTES AND QUESTIONS

1. Earlier analyses had understood the English case of Winterbottom v. Wright to stand for the proposition that manufacturers, suppliers, and repairers of chattels could be liable for their negligence only to those with whom they had contracted. Lord Abinger stated:

> There is no privity of contract between these parties; and if the plaintiff can sue, every passenger, or even any person passing along the road, who was injured by the upsetting of the coach, might bring a similar action. Unless we confine the operation of such contracts as this to the parties who entered into them, the most absurd and outrageous consequences, to which I can see no limit, would ensue.

How might Judge Cardozo respond to that assertion?

2. What is your understanding of the state of the law before the *MacPherson* decision? What was Judge Cardozo's contribution? Recall the discussion at the outset of Chapter III, p. 115, supra.

3. What is the meaning of the requirement that there "must be knowledge of a danger, not merely possible, but probable"? Was that met here?

4. Assess the significance of Judge Cardozo's statement that "We have put the source of the obligation where it ought to be. We have put its source in the law."

5. What arguments might justify imposing a duty on Buick but not on the wheel manufacturer? In Smith v. Peerless Glass Co., 259 N.Y. 292, 181 N.E. 576 (1932), a soda bottle exploded and hurt plaintiff. The court treated the bottle maker as the manufacturer of a component part and brought it within the *MacPherson* principle. Might there be proximate cause problems in such cases?

6. Is the rationale of *MacPherson* entirely congruent with the notions of due care we have already developed? The doctrine of *MacPherson* came to be accepted generally throughout the United States. It covered injuries to bystanders including pedestrians hurt by a careening car or tire, property damage, duty of repairers as well as manufacturers, and cases where damage was not "reasonably certain."

Other developments included holding a retailer who sold a product under its own brand name as though it were the manufacturer and thus liable for negligent manufacture. Also, manufacturers who incorporated component parts in the final product were liable for the negligence of the subcontractors. Eventually, courts began holding architects and builders liable for negligence in construction that hurt patrons or tenants.

7. *Warranty Development.* But as these extensions of *MacPherson* were taking place, a new approach to the area was taking shape.

Warranty law had been an integral part of sales law for many years before the common law of sales was codified in the Uniform Sales Act and then in the Uniform Commercial Code. For the most part, sales law dealt with products that did not meet the purposes for which they were bought or were otherwise unsatisfactory, rather than products that caused personal injury. Nevertheless, occasionally the latter were involved and the operation of modern warranty law in such cases can be seen in Ryan v. Progressive Grocery Stores, Inc., 255 N.Y. 388, 175 N.E. 105 (1931), in which Mrs. Ryan asked the defendant storekeeper for a loaf of Ward's bread. Her husband was seriously injured when he swallowed a pin embedded in a slice of the bread. Judge Cardozo held the shopkeeper liable for breach of the implied warranty of merchantability, ruling that a loaf of bread with a pin in it was not of such quality. He noted in imposing such liability on the retailer without any finding of fault that "the burden may be heavy. It is one of the hazards of business." At the same time he rejected plaintiff's claim for breach of an implied warranty of fitness for a particular purpose, in which the buyer relies on the seller's choice of product to meet a need stated by the buyer. Because Mrs. Ryan asked for a specific brand of bread there was no such reliance.

Finally Judge Cardozo rejected the argument that liability be limited to the difference in value between a good loaf and a bad one. Rather he used the basic contract rule permitting higher damages where the seller had "notice from the nature of the transaction that the bread was to be eaten." These implied warranties were codified in the Uniform Sales Act, § 15, and remain in its successor, the Uniform Commercial Code, §§ 2–314, 2–315.

Warranties traditionally ran only between parties in contract privity. In *Ryan,* this might have presented a problem because the person hurt was not the person who bought the bread from the retailer. Judge Cardozo resolved this problem in his first sentence by saying that the plaintiff "through his wife, who acted as his agent, bought a loaf of bread." In efforts to permit warranty recoveries courts resorted to many devices to avoid the lack-of-privity barrier: one author catalogued 29 theories used to achieve the result, mostly in food cases. Gillam, Products Liability in a Nutshell, 37 Or.L.Rev. 119, 153–155 (1957).*

8. These developments notwithstanding, a tension between negligence and strict liability in tort became more evident, as the following case suggests.

Escola v. Coca Cola Bottling Co. of Fresno

Supreme Court of California, 1944.
24 Cal.2d 453, 150 P.2d 436.

[Plaintiff, a waitress, was injured when a soda bottle broke in her hand as she moved it from the case to the refrigerator. She testified that she had handled it carefully. The defendant bottler used pressure to bottle carbonated beverages. An engineer from the bottle manufacturer (which was not sued) testified at the trial about how bottles are tested and called these tests "pretty near" infallible. The majority affirmed a plaintiff's judgment and held that plaintiff had properly benefitted from res ipsa loquitur in her negligence action:

It thus appears that there is available to the industry a commonly-used method of testing bottles for defects not apparent

---

* The UCC eliminated the traditional requirement of privity. Its drafters offered three versions of § 2–318 from which the states were to pick one. Under all three versions whatever warranties the seller does extend with the product are statutorily extended to certain classes of people who may reasonably be expected to "use, consume or be affected by the goods." Version A extends the warranties to "any natural person who is in the family or household of his buyer or who is a guest in his home . . . who is injured in person. . . ." Version B extends to "any natural person . . . who is injured in person. . . ." Version C extends to "any person . . . who is injured. . . ."

Most state legislatures adopted Version A, but in some of these states the courts considered themselves free to expand such protection.

to the eye, which is almost infallible. Since Coca Cola bottles are subjected to these tests by the manufacturer, it is not likely that they contain defects when delivered to the bottler which are not discoverable by visual inspection. Both new and used bottles are filled and distributed by defendant. The used bottles are not again subjected to the tests referred to above, and it may be inferred that defects not discoverable by visual inspection do not develop in bottles after they are manufactured. Obviously, if such defects do occur in used bottles there is a duty upon the bottler to make appropriate tests before they are refilled, and if such tests are not commercially practicable the bottles should not be re-used. This would seem to be particularly true where a charged liquid is placed in the bottle. It follows that a defect which would make the bottle unsound could be discovered by reasonable and practicable tests.

Although it is not clear in this case whether the explosion was caused by an excessive charge or a defect in the glass, there is a sufficient showing that neither cause would ordinarily have been present if due care had been used. Further, defendant had exclusive control over both the charging and inspection of the bottles. Accordingly, all the requirements necessary to entitle plaintiff to rely on the doctrine of res ipsa loquitur to supply an inference of negligence are present.

It is true that defendant presented evidence tending to show that it exercised considerable precaution by carefully regulating and checking the pressure in the bottles and by making visual inspections for defects in the glass at several stages during the bottling process. It is well settled, however, that when a defendant produces evidence to rebut the inference of negligence which arises upon application of the doctrine of res ipsa loquitur, it is ordinarily a question of fact for the jury to determine whether the inference has been dispelled.

One justice concurred separately:]

■ TRAYNOR, J. I concur in the judgment, but I believe the manufacturer's negligence should no longer be singled out as the basis of a plaintiff's right to recover in cases like the present one. In my opinion it should now be recognized that a manufacturer incurs an absolute liability when an article that he has placed on the market, knowing that it is to be used without inspection, proves to have a defect that causes injury to human beings. MacPherson v. Buick Motor Co. [ ], established the principle, recognized by this court, that irrespective of privity of contract, the manufacturer is responsible for an injury caused by such an article to any person who comes in lawful contact with it. [ ] In these cases the source of the manufacturer's liability was his negligence in the manufacturing process or in the inspection of component parts supplied by others. Even if there is no negligence, however, public policy demands that responsibility be fixed wherever it will most effectively reduce the hazards to life and health inherent in defective products that reach the market. It is evident that the manufacturer can anticipate some hazards and guard against the recurrence of others, as the public cannot. Those who suffer injury from defective products are unprepared to meet its consequences. The cost of an injury and the loss of time or health may be an overwhelming misfortune to the person injured, and a needless one, for the risk of injury can be insured by the manufacturer and distributed among the public as a cost of doing business. It is to the public interest to discourage the marketing of products having defects that are a menace to the public. If such products nevertheless find their way into the market it is to the public interest to place the responsibility for whatever injury they may cause upon the manufacturer, who, even if he is not negligent in the manufacture of the product, is responsible for its reaching the market. However intermittently such injuries may occur and however haphazardly they may strike, the risk of their occurrence is a constant risk and a general one. Against such a risk there should be general and constant protection and the manufacturer is best situated to afford such protection.

The injury from a defective product does not become a matter of indifference because the defect arises from causes other than the negligence of the manufacturer, such as negligence of a submanufacturer of a component part whose defects could not be revealed by inspection [ ] or unknown causes that even by the device of res ipsa loquitur cannot be classified as negligence of the manufacturer. The inference of negligence may be dispelled by an affirmative showing of proper care. If the evidence against the fact inferred is "clear, positive, uncontradicted, and of such a nature that it cannot rationally be disbelieved, the court must instruct the jury that the nonexistence of the fact has been established as a matter of law." (Blank v. Coffin, 20 Cal.2d 457, 461 [126 P.2d 868].) An injured person, however, is not ordinarily in a position to refute such evidence or identify the cause of the defect, for he can hardly be familiar with the manufacturing process as the manufacturer himself is. In leaving it to the jury to decide whether the inference has been dispelled, regardless of the evidence against it, the negligence rule approaches the rule of strict liability. It is needlessly circuitous to make negligence the basis of recovery and impose what is in reality liability without negligence. If public policy demands that a manufacturer of goods be responsible for their quality regardless of negligence there is no reason not to fix that responsibility openly.

. . .

The retailer, even though not equipped to test a product, is under an absolute liability to his customer, for the implied warranties of fitness for proposed use and merchantable quality include a warranty of safety of the product. [ ] This warranty is not necessarily a contractual one [ ], for public policy requires that the buyer be insured at the seller's expense against injury. [ ] The courts recognize, however, that the retailer cannot bear the burden of this warranty, and allow him to recoup any losses by means of the warranty of safety attending the wholesaler's or manufacturer's sale to him. [   ] Such a procedure, however, is needlessly circuitous and engenders wasteful litigation. Much would be gained if the injured person could base his action directly on the manufacturer's warranty.

The liability of the manufacturer to an immediate buyer injured by a defective product follows without proof of negligence from the implied warranty of safety attending the sale. Ordinarily, however, the immediate buyer is a dealer who does not intend to use the product himself, and if the warranty of safety is to serve the purpose of protecting health and safety it must give rights to others than the dealer. In the words of Judge Cardozo in the MacPherson case: "The dealer was indeed the one person of whom it might be said with some approach to certainty that by him the car would not be used. Yet, the defendant would have us say that he was the one person whom it was under a legal duty to protect. The law does not lead us to so inconsequent a solution." While the defendant's negligence in the MacPherson case made it unnecessary for the court to base liability on warranty, Judge Cardozo's reasoning recognized the injured person as the real party in interest and effectively disposed of the theory that the liability of the manufacturer incurred by his warranty should apply only to the immediate purchaser. It thus paves the way for a standard of liability that would make the manufacturer guarantee the safety of his product even when there is no negligence.

This court and many others have extended protection according to such a standard to consumers of food products, taking the view that the right of a consumer injured by unwholesome food does not depend "upon the intricacies of the law of sales" and that the warranty of the manufacturer to the consumer in absence of privity of contract rests on public policy. [   ] Dangers to life and health inhere in other consumers' goods that are defective and there is no reason to differentiate them from the dangers of defective food products. [   ]

In the food products cases the courts have resorted to various fictions to rationalize the extension of the manufacturer's warranty to the consumer: that a warranty runs with the chattel; that the cause of action of the dealer is assigned to the consumer; that the consumer is a third party beneficiary of the manufacturer's contract with the dealer. They have also held the manufacturer liable on a mere fiction of negligence: "Practically he must know it [the product] is fit, or bear the consequences if it proves destructive." [   ] Such fictions are not necessary to fix the manufacturer's liability under a warranty if the warranty is severed from the contract of sale between the dealer and the consumer and based on the law of torts [   ] as a strict liability. [   ]Warranties are not necessarily rights arising under a contract. An action on a warranty "was, in its origin, a pure action of tort," and only late in the historical development of warranties was an action in assumpsit allowed. (Ames, The History of Assumpsit, 2 Harv.L.Rev. 1, 8; 4 Williston on Contracts (1936) § 970.)   . . .

As handicrafts have been replaced by mass production with its great markets and transportation facilities, the close relationship between the producer and consumer of a product has been altered. Manufacturing processes, frequently valuable secrets, are ordinarily either inaccessible to or beyond the ken of the general public. The consumer no longer has means or skill enough to investigate for himself the soundness of a product, even when it is not contained in a sealed package, and his erstwhile vigilance has been lulled by the steady efforts of manufacturers to build up confidence by advertising and marketing devices such as trade marks. [   ] Consumers no longer approach products warily but accept them on faith, relying on the reputation of the manufacturer or the trade mark. [   ] Manufacturers have sought to justify that faith by increasingly high standards of inspection and a readiness to make good on defective products by way of replacements and refunds. (See Bogert and Fink, Business Practices Regarding Warranties In The Sale of Goods, 25 Ill.L.Rev. 400.) The manufacturer's obligation to the consumer must keep pace with the changing relationship between them; it cannot be escaped because the marketing of a product has become so complicated as to require one or more intermediaries. Certainly there is greater reason to impose liability on the manufacturer than on the retailer who is but a conduit of a product that he is not himself able to test.

The manufacturer's liability should, of course, be defined in terms of the safety of the product in normal and proper use, and should not extend to injuries that cannot be traced to the product as it reached the market.

NOTE AND QUESTIONS

1. What were the majority's justifications for using res ipsa loquitur? What were Justice Traynor's objections?

2. Consider separately each sentence in the first paragraph of Justice Traynor's opinion. What justifications for strict liability are presented? Are other justifications presented elsewhere in the opinion?

3. How does *MacPherson* support Justice Traynor's theory of liability here?

4. Warranty doctrine as a basis for strict liability recovery in tort remained largely limited to the food cases until 1960 when the New Jersey Supreme Court decided the influential case of Henningsen v. Bloomfield Motors, Inc., 32 N.J. 358, 161 A.2d 69 (1960). A defect in the steering mechanism of a recently-acquired Plymouth caused the car to spin out of control, seriously injuring plaintiff driver. Echoing Justice Traynor's language in *Escola*, the court held "under modern marketing conditions, when a manufacturer puts a new automobile in the stream of trade and promotes its purchase by the public, an implied warranty that it is reasonably suitable for use as such accompanies it into the hands of the ultimate purchaser. Absence of agency between the manufacturer and the dealer who makes the ultimate sale is immaterial." For related reasons, the court went on to strike down express disclaimers limiting liability that were "imposed upon the automobile consumer" in "a standardized form designed for mass use" as contrary to public policy.

For the moment, it appeared that the move beyond negligence to strict liability might be grounded in warranty, rather than the tort theory urged by Traynor. See the classic contemporaneous article, Prosser, The Assault on the Citadel, 69 Yale L.J. 1099 (1960). But Traynor was to have the final word on this issue.

5. *Subsequent California Developments.* Beginning in the early 1960s, a series of California decisions foreshadowed similar developments in other jurisdictions that have now become accepted by the overwhelming majority of states.

a. Greenman v. Yuba Power Products, Inc., 59 Cal.2d 57, 377 P.2d 897, 27 Cal.Rptr. 697 (1963). Plaintiff's wife bought from a retailer a Shopsmith power tool made by defendant. While using the tool as a lathe with the necessary attachment, plaintiff was hurt when the piece of wood flew up and struck him in the forehead. Plaintiff's judgment against the manufacturer, based on negligence and express warranty claims, was affirmed by Justice Traynor writing for a unanimous court. Experts had testified that the lathe was of defective design because the set screws were inadequate to hold the wood given the lathe's normal vibrations, and that better fastening of the machine's parts would have prevented the harm. From this Justice Traynor concluded that the jury could have found negligence as well as breach of the express warranty that included the assertion that "every component has positive locks that hold adjustments through rough or precision work."

Since there was a general verdict, the manufacturer sought a new trial contending that it was not liable for breach of express (or any) warranties because of the plaintiff's failure to comply with a statutory requirement that notice of the alleged breach be given "within a reasonable time" after it is discovered. Justice Traynor disagreed. Warranty notice requirements should not apply when the plaintiff and the manufacturer have not dealt directly with one another because the injured party would probably be unaware of such an obligation. Moreover, echoing his concurrence in *Escola*, Justice Traynor concluded that a "manufacturer is strictly liable in tort when an article he places on the market, knowing that it is to be used without inspection for defects, proves to have a defect that causes injury to a human being." In addition to his other reasons, he noted that the "purpose of such liability is to insure that the costs of injuries resulting from defective products are borne by the manufacturers that put such products on the market rather than by the injured persons who are powerless to protect themselves. Sales warranties serve this purpose fitfully at best."

b. Vandermark v. Ford Motor Co., 61 Cal.2d 256, 391 P.2d 168, 37 Cal.Rptr. 896 (1964). Plaintiff bought a new Ford from defendant retailer Maywood Bell Ford. The brakes soon locked pulling the car to the right and into a pole, hurting plaintiff and his sister, who also sued. Expert testimony suggested a wrong-sized part or improper assembly or adjustment. The trial judge nonsuited plaintiffs on both negligence and breach of implied warranty against the manufacturer, Ford, and on a warranty count against Maywood Bell. The jury returned a verdict for Maywood Bell on the negligence count.

On appeal Justice Traynor, speaking for a unanimous court, upheld the jury verdict on Maywood Bell's negligence but reversed the other three rulings. Ford could not insulate itself by delegating final inspection and adjustment to Maywood Bell. The "warranty" count against Ford should not have been dismissed because of the evidence of the defect and of its existence at the time of delivery to plaintiff. The negligence count against Ford should stand because the evidence suggested manufacturing negligence.

Maywood Bell's disclaimer in the sales contract limited its liability to replacement "of such parts as shall be returned to the Dealer and as shall be acknowledged by Dealer to be defective. . . . This warranty is expressly in lieu of all other warranties, express or implied, and of all other obligations on the part of Dealer." (The crash occurred within the warranty period.) Since Maywood Bell was "an integral part of the overall producing and marketing enterprise," and the retailer may be able to ensure product safety or to put pressure on the manufacturer toward that end, and was often the one link in the chain that plaintiff could conveniently sue, Justice Traynor concluded that the retailer "is strictly liable in tort for personal injuries caused by defects in cars sold by it." He noted that this provided maximum protection for the plaintiff but did no injustice to the defendants since "they can adjust the costs of such protection between them in the course of their continuing business relationship." Contractual disclaimers were immaterial: "Regardless of the obligations it assumed by contract, it is subject to strict liability in tort because it is in the business of selling automobiles, one of which proved to be defective and caused injury to human beings."

c. *Elmore v. American Motors Corp.*, 70 Cal.2d 578, 451 P.2d 84, 75 Cal.Rptr. 652 (1969). Plaintiff Elmore purchased a new Rambler manufactured by one defendant and sold by the other. It veered across the road and into the oncoming car of Waters. Occupants of both cars were hurt or killed and suits were brought against both defendants. The cases were consolidated for trial, at which there was testimony that just before the crash the drive shaft had fallen out of Elmore's car, which was almost new. Nonsuits for both defendants were unanimously reversed on appeal in an opinion by Justice Peters. First, the evidence was sufficient to permit a jury to find that the drive shaft did fall out, that this was due to a defect that had been present at the time of sale, and that it caused the crash. He then observed that bystanders such as Waters were entitled to the same strict liability protections as those in the Elmore car:

If anything, bystanders should be entitled to greater protection than the consumer or user where injury to bystanders from the defect is reasonably foreseeable. Consumers and users, at least, have the opportunity to inspect for defects and to limit their purchases to articles manufactured by reputable manufacturers and sold by reputable retailers, whereas the bystander ordinarily has no such opportunities. . . .

An automobile with a defectively connected drive shaft constitutes a substantial hazard on the highway not only to the driver and passenger of the car but also to pedestrians and other drivers. The public policy which protects the driver and passenger of the car should also protect the bystander, and where a driver or passenger of another car is injured due to defects in the manufacture of an automobile and without any fault of their own, they may recover from the manufacturer of the defective automobile.

Finally, for the reasons suggested in *Vandermark,* the court concluded that the retailer was liable to bystanders as well as customers.

6. *Extensions to others.* Strict liability has also been extended greatly on the defendant's side to include a wide variety of suppliers and those who aid suppliers.

a. *Bailors and lessors of goods.* Most courts have extended the seller's liability to include bailors and lessors of goods. In Price v. Shell Oil Co., 2 Cal.3d 245, 466 P.2d 722, 85 Cal.Rptr. 178 (1970), defendant had leased a gasoline tank truck to plaintiff's employer. Plaintiff was injured when a defective ladder on the truck collapsed. The court held that there was "no significant difference between a manufacturer or retailer who places an article on the market by means of a sale and a bailor or lessor who accomplishes the same result by means of a lease."

Even with sellers and lessors, courts tend not to apply strict liability to incidental transactions. In Stiles v. Batavia Atomic Horseshoes, Inc., 81 N.Y.2d 950, 613 N.E.2d 572, 597 N.Y.S.2d 666 (1993), the court refused to impose strict liability on the defendant for harm caused by a used punch press that it sold to plaintiff's employer. Defendant's normal business was making horseshoes and it was not a regular seller of used products.

b. *Dealers in used goods.* The courts have been much less willing to impose strict liability on sellers of used goods—even when the claim is that the product has had the defect in question since it was first marketed. In Tillman v. Vance Equipment Co., 286 Or. 747, 596 P.2d 1299 (1979), the court noted that of its three reasons for strict liability—spreading the risk, satisfying reasonable buyer expectations, and risk reduction—only the first applied to dealers in used products. The second did not apply since these sellers generally make no particular representations about the quality of their goods. The third did not apply since these dealers have no direct relationship to the manufacturers or distributors of the goods. Providing an adequate remedy for the victim "cannot provide the sole justification for imposing liability without fault on a particular class of defendants." The analogy to strict liability for lessors did not apply:

The lessor chooses the products which he offers in a significantly different way than does the typical dealer in used goods; the fact that he offers them repeatedly to different users as products he has selected may constitute a representation as to their quality; and it may well be that he has purchased them, either new or used, from a dealer who is directly related to the original distribution chain.

What is the difference between dealers in used goods and commercial lessors?

c. *Landlords.* In 1985, California extended strict liability to landlords who were liable for harm sustained by tenants due to defective premises. Becker v. IRM Corp., 38 Cal.3d 454, 698 P.2d 116, 213 Cal.Rptr. 213 (1985)(imposing strict liability on purchaser of apartment house when tenant was hurt by shower door that was in defective condition at time defendant purchased the building). In 1995, the court overruled *Becker,* which had been virtually alone in this extension. Peterson v. Superior Court, 10 Cal.4th 1185, 899 P.2d 905, 43 Cal.Rptr.2d 836 (1995)(denying strict liability claim against hotel owner for guest who slipped in defective bathtub).

The court noted that defects in buildings may have been created by builders, subcontractors, or suppliers of fixtures, among others. "Because the landlord or hotel owner generally has no continuing business relationship, or other ready channel of communication, with any of these persons or entities, only in rare cases would the imposition of strict liability upon the landlord or hotel owner create an impetus to manufacture safer products." Nor was there any "implied representation of safety." Tenants may reasonably expect that the landlord has inspected the rental dwelling and corrected any defects disclosed by that inspection or of which he has actual or constructive notice. "But a tenant cannot reasonably expect that the landlord will have eliminated defects in a rented dwelling of which the landlord was unaware and which would not have been disclosed by a reasonable inspection." Nor was it likely that landlords or hotel owners would have expert knowledge "of the myriad of components which comprise the leased dwelling." Plaintiff retained a strict liability action against the supplier of the bathtub, and also a negligence claim against the hotel.

d. *Financiers.* Under some arrangements those who finance commercial transactions become "lessors." If the product being financed is defective should the rules applicable to suppliers apply to the financier? In Nath v. National Equipment Leasing Corp., 497 Pa. 126, 439 A.2d 633 (1981), the court, 4–3, refused to apply the doctrine in favor of a worker whose hand was injured in the machine his employer had leased. A party "merely financing the transaction has no control over its manufacture, is not involved in the selection of the product nor in any way makes a representation as to its quality or soundness. Between the financier and the ultimate purchaser, it is usually the latter who selects the goods, negotiates for its purchase and has control over its use." In addition to expressing concern over the impact on financial institutions, the majority noted that financiers lack a continuous relationship with upstream suppliers and thus cannot influence their conduct.

The dissenters stressed that a major goal of the area was to relieve consumers from intolerable burdens and to shift them to "those whose

Dissent
Financier should
be liable because
part of stream
of commerce

business it is to traffic in commerce." The lack of control over the product was irrelevant because strict liability "is imposed without reference to whether caution was exercised or disregarded, if *in fact* the product was defective." The goal of spreading costs over society at large was being thwarted.

e. *Franchisors.* Franchisors may be held liable for defects in their products under some circumstances. Plaintiff picked up a carton of 7–Up and carried it under her arm toward the checkout counter. On the way, one bottle dropped out and broke. A piece of glass flew up into plaintiff's eye as she looked down. Her claim against the Seven–Up Co., the franchisor of the operation, was that the carton had been defectively designed because it was planned only for those who held it by the top rather than those who held it under their arms. The court noted that the defendant kept control over carton design and specifically approved the one in question. "The franchisor's sponsorship, management and control of the system for distributing 7–Up, plus its specific consent to the use of the cartons, in our view, places the franchisor in the position of a supplier of the product for purposes of tort liability." Kosters v. Seven–Up Co., 595 F.2d 347 (6th Cir.1979).

f. *Successor liability.* What happens when a supplier that sells a defective product is no longer in existence when a victim is hurt? Under state corporation law the dissolved manufacturer's shareholders are generally not liable. Traditionally, corporation law held that the successor company was also not liable for products it did not design, manufacture or sell—subject to four exceptions: 1) if the purchasing company expressly or implicitly agreed to accept liability, 2) if the successor company resulted from a de facto merger, rather than a sale of assets, 3) if the purchaser was merely a continuation of the seller corporation, or 4) if the transaction was a fraudulent attempt to escape liability.

In Ray v. Alad, 19 Cal.3d 22, 560 P.2d 3, 136 Cal.Rptr. 574 (1977), the court developed a new "strict tort liability" exception: if the purchasing company continued to manufacture and market the same "product line" from which the injuries resulted, the successor company would be held liable. *Ray* has been rejected in all but a handful of states. See, e.g., Guzman v. MRM/Elgin, 409 Mass. 563, 567 N.E.2d 929 (1991), asserting that the "product line" exception is a matter for legislative decision. The question is discussed in Roe, Mergers, Acquisitions, and Tort: A Comment on the Problem of Successor Corporation Liability, 70 Va.L.Rev. 1559 (1984).

g. *Contractors.* One cluster of cases raises the question of duties owed by contractors and rebuilders who are asked to make or rebuild products according to the specifications of the designer or original manufacturer or owner of the product. For example, in Michalko v. Cooke Color & Chemical Corp., 91 N.J. 386, 451 A.2d 179 (1982), plaintiff's employer, Elastimold, contracted with Cubby for the latter to carry out redesigns of Elastimold's 35–ton presses according to drawings and specifications supplied by Elastimold. Cubby failed to install feasible safety devices or warn about the known dangers of operating this type of press without a safety device. Plaintiff lost a hand in the machine.

The court held that the principles applicable to manufacturers of complete machines were also applicable to those hired to rebuild machines according to plans provided them: Otherwise, "it would leave the determination as to the safety of the product and investment allocation in safety to the private marketplace." Where the commercial marketplace does not generate a "safety stimulus, courts can contribute to that end."

How about repairers? Should strict liability be imposed on a vacuum cleaner repairer who does not install a new safety device for the vacuum that has been developed since the vacuum was originally marketed? Or advise the customer that it is now possible to add such a safety device? Does it matter how extensively the vacuum cleaner was overhauled at the shop? Is there a distinction between repairers and rebuilders?

h. *Government contractors.* In Boyle v. United Technologies Corp., 487 U.S. 500 (1988), a Marine helicopter co-pilot drowned when his helicopter crashed in the ocean and he was unable to escape from it before it sank. His father's suit against the manufacturer alleged a design defect in the escape hatch because it opened outward, and could not be opened against the pressure of the water. The Supreme Court, 5–4, held that a private contractor who followed government specifications in making a product could not be held liable for inadequacies in the design as long as certain requirements were met. It remanded for further consideration of whether the requisite elements had been satisfied in this case.

For the majority, Justice Scalia held that federal law controlled the obligations to and from the United States under its contracts and that questions of liability of federal officials for actions taken in the scope of their official duties are generally governed by federal law. The imposition of liability in this type of case "will directly affect the terms of Government contracts: either the contractor will decline to manufacture the design specified by the Government, or it will raise its price. Either way, the interests of the United States will be directly affected." A state's effort to impose a duty of product design conflicted with the duty imposed by the Government contract—to deliver helicopters with the sort of escape mechanisms called for in the specifications. In such a case

> Liability for design defects in military equipment cannot be imposed, pursuant to state law, when (1) the United States approved reasonably precise specifications; (2) the equipment conformed to those specifications; and (3) the supplier warned the United States about the dangers in the use of the equipment that were known to the supplier but not to the United States.

The first two elements were to show that the design feature was considered by the Government and not only by the contractor. This would make the situation analogous to the exception in the Federal Tort Claims Act, p. 215, supra, that bars liability against the Government when the official was exercising a "discretionary function." The third condition was necessary because its absence might give contractors incentives to withhold knowledge of risks "since conveying that knowledge might disrupt the contract but withholding it would produce no liability."

The dissenters, led by Justice Brennan, relied heavily on the lack of any action by Congress to legislate such a defense. Justice Stevens dissented separately. Should Congress be obliged to enact a government contractor immunity in order to shield the federal government from indirect tort liability? Is the judicially fashioned defense consistent with the thrust of the Federal Tort Claims Act? Recently, suppliers of Agent Orange have lost their efforts to force the federal government to reimburse them for settlement costs and legal expenses they incurred in the litigation over that product. See Hercules Inc. v. United States, 116 S.Ct. 981 (1996).

For a broad discussion of the government contractor problem, see Cass & Gillette, The Government Contractor Defense: Contractual Allocation of Public Risk, 77 Va.L.Rev. 257 (1991). The government contractor defense played a particularly interesting role throughout the mass tort litigation against the manufacturers of Agent Orange. For discussion, see the case study, P. Schuck, Agent Orange on Trial: Mass Toxics Disasters in the Courts (enlarged edition, 1987).

7. *The Restatement.* Early in the development of the modern approach, the American Law Institute promulgated § 402A of the Restatement (Second) of Torts, a most influential section that provided an early black letter formulation of the new approach. The section, published in 1965, though available earlier in tentative draft, provided:

> (1) One who sells any product in a defective condition unreasonably dangerous to the user or consumer or to his property is subject to liability for physical harm thereby caused to the ultimate user or consumer, or to his property, if
>
> (a) the seller is engaged in the business of selling such a product, and
>
> (b) it is expected to and does reach the user or consumer without substantial change in the condition in which it is sold.
>
> (2) The rule stated in Subsection (1) applies although
>
> (a) the seller has exercised all possible care in the preparation and sale of his product, and
>
> (b) the user or consumer has not bought the product from or entered into any contractual relation with the seller.

The Institute noted three caveats—situations on which it took no position: whether the section applied to victims other than users or consumers; whether it applied to a seller of a product that was expected to be "processed or otherwise substantially changed" before it reached the consumer; and whether it applied to a seller of component parts.

The mixed contract-tort heritage of strict products liability, suggested in *Escola,* is reflected in the Restatement's definition of a defect. Plaintiff must demonstrate that the product causing the injuries was in a "defective condition unreasonably dangerous" to person or property at the time it left defendant's possession. The Restatement's comments define the requisite defective state in terms of a consumer's expectations—the traditional contract approach. Comment *g* to § 402A posits a defective condition as one "not contemplated by the ultimate consumer, which will be unreasonably dangerous to him." Comment *i* provides that to be "unreasonably dangerous" the article sold "must be dangerous to an extent beyond that which would be contemplated by the ordinary consumer who purchases it, with the ordinary knowledge common to the community as to its characteristics."

Although both defectiveness and unreasonableness are defined by expectation, not all unexpected product aberrations that cause harm are suitable for recovery under § 402A. Suppose the button of a shirt made by defendant is insecurely attached to the material. Plaintiff buys the shirt and wears it to work, where he turns out candlesticks on a high-speed lathe. The button drops off, allowing the shirt to sag into the machine. It gets caught by the spinning axle, and plaintiff is yanked into the machine. Would § 402A allow plaintiff to recover from the shirt manufacturer or retailer? Or again, consider an eraser that is poorly anchored to the base of a wooden pencil. While plaintiff is vigorously erasing a mistake, the eraser snaps free and flies into, and injures, her eye. The uncertain analysis of such claims under the Restatement suggests that unreasonableness retains some meaning beyond "reasonable expectation."

Before beginning our consideration of this area, it is appropriate to note that § 402A emerged at the outset of the incipient judicial change in this area. As a result, it was an unrefined statement of the law that failed to address distinctions among various types of product claims that became apparent later. Although it has been much cited by courts, there has been considerable confusion, and some outright rejection of its core definitions. In response, a new effort of the American Law Institute, the Restatement (Third) of the Law of Torts: Products Liability, has been undertaken. As of late 1995, the central framework in § 1 provided that suppliers of products were liable for harm caused by a product defect—and identified three types of defects, which are defined in § 2:

For purposes of determining liability under § 1:

   (a) a product contains a manufacturing defect when the product departs from its intended design even though all possible care was exercised in the preparation and marketing of the product;

   (b) a product is defective in design when the foreseeable risks of harm posed by the product could have been reduced or avoided by the adoption of a reasonable alternative design by the seller or other distributor, or a predecessor in the commercial chain of distribution, and the omission of the alternative design renders the product not reasonably safe;

(c) a product is defective because of inadequate instructions or warnings when the foreseeable risks of harm posed by the product could have been reduced or avoided by the provision of reasonable instructions or warnings by the seller or other distributor, or a predecessor in the commercial chain of distribution, and the omission of the instructions or warnings renders the product not reasonably safe.

What appear to be the essential differences between the two approaches? Keep both in mind as we consider recent developments in liability for defective products.

B. MANUFACTURING DEFECTS

The most common and straight-forward cases of defective products involve the aberrational mass-produced item that has come off the assembly line different from (and more dangerous than) the intended product. The defect is generally apparent in the flawed unit by the time of trial, and courts have concluded that strict liability should follow. These dangers are almost always latent. There are not many open and obvious ("patent") manufacturing defect cases, either because modern manufacturing processes can identify them or because retailers who find them while preparing goods for sale will take them off the shelves. Whatever the reason, patent manufacturing defects have not led to much litigation. The issue is much more complex with design defects, as we shall see shortly.

The issues in manufacturing defect claims are more likely to be practical than theoretical. In Welge v. Planters Lifesavers Co., 17 F.3d 209 (7th Cir.1994), for example, plaintiff was hurt when a glass jar of peanuts smashed as he tried to re-fasten its plastic lid. The fragments of the jar were preserved and the experts agreed that it "must have contained a defect but they could not find the fracture that had precipitated the shattering of the jar and they could not figure out when the defect . . . had come into being." The case revolved around efforts to identify the cause of the failure. Defendants, the jar manufacturer, Planters who filled the jar, and K–Mart, the retailer, argued that actions of plaintiff and the person with whom he boarded had created the weakness; plaintiff's evidence suggested that nothing untoward had occurred to the jar after purchase. Summary judgment against plaintiff was inappropriate:

> The strict liability element in modern products liability law comes precisely from the fact that a seller subject to that law is liable for defects in his product even if those defects were introduced, without the slightest fault of his own for failing to discover them, at some anterior stage of production. [ ] So the fact that K–Mart sold a defective jar of peanuts to Karen Godfrey would be conclusive of K–Mart's liability. . . . In exactly the same way, Planter's liability would be unaffected by the fact, if it is a fact, that the defect was due to [the jar manufacturer] rather than to itself. To repeat an earlier and fundamental point, a seller who is

subject to strict products liability is responsible for the consequences of selling a defective product even if the defect was introduced without any fault on his part by his supplier or by his supplier's supplier.

Would res ipsa loquitur apply in this case? If a defective product has been made from scratch and marketed directly by the manufacturer to the consumer who is hurt, might "strict liability" be explained as simply a conclusive presumption that the manufacturer was negligent at some point in the process?

As an indication of the practical problems confronting plaintiffs in cases alleging manufacturing defects, consider Price v. General Motors Corp., 931 F.2d 162 (1st Cir.1991). Plaintiffs alleged a sudden swerve of the car from the highway into a utility pole. The car had been "inadvertently destroyed" before major investigation could be conducted. The court upheld summary judgment for defendant:

> Even if the Price vehicle leaked power steering fluid, the leak could as well have been due to inadequate maintenance, improper repairs to any of several hoses and seals, or defective non-GM replacement parts, as it could to an original [manufacturing defect]. The Prices purchased their 1981 Citation second-hand in 1983, after it had been driven more than 63,000 miles; they drove it approximately 15,000 additional miles. Appellants offered no evidence relating to the maintenance and repair history of the vehicle prior to their purchase. . . . Finally, appellants' own expert conceded that he had no way of knowing whether any of the mechanical parts in the power steering mechanism were original.

The failure to preserve the product is not always fatal to plaintiff's case if there is enough evidence of the malfunction to permit an inference of defect. See, e.g., Daniels v. GNB, Inc., 629 So.2d 595 (Miss.1993)(plaintiff's testimony about exploding auto battery together with expert who said that plaintiff's version of the accident, if accurate, was consistent with a product defect, sufficed to withstand summary judgment). This area has also given rise to claims of spoliation of evidence. Recall p. 80, supra.

C.   DESIGN DEFECTS

In Cronin v. J.B.E. Olson Corp., 8 Cal.3d 121, 501 P.2d 1153, 104 Cal.Rptr. 433 (1972), the driver of a nine-year-old bakery truck was forced off the road as he tried to pass another vehicle. The impact of running into a ditch broke a safety hasp holding bread trays in place directly behind plaintiff. The unrestricted trays came forward, struck plaintiff in the back, and propelled him through the front windshield. Plaintiff sued the seller of the truck for personal injuries, alleging that the hasp was defective. Defendant appealed from a judgment for plaintiff on the ground that the trial judge's charge on strict liability omitted the requirement that any defect in the product must be found to be "unreasonably dangerous." The court noted that in its original formulation in *Greenman* no "unreasonably dangerous" element was required. It "crept into our jurisprudence without fanfare after its inclusion in section 402A of the Restatement Second of Torts in 1965":

> Prosser, the reporter for the Restatement, suggests that the "unreasonably dangerous" qualification was added to foreclose the possibility that the manufacturer of a product with inherent possibilities for harm (for example, butter, drugs, whiskey and automobiles) would become "automatically responsible for all the harm that such things do in the world." [ ]

The court thought the phrase "burdened the injured plaintiff with proof of an element which rings of negligence. . . . A bifurcated standard is of necessity more difficult to prove than a unitary one. But merely proclaiming that the phrase 'defective condition unreasonably dangerous' requires only a single finding would not purge that phrase of its negligence complexion":

> We recognize that the words "unreasonably dangerous" may also serve the beneficial purpose of preventing the seller from being treated as the insurer of its products. However, we think that such protective end is attained by the necessity of proving that there was a defect in the manufacture or design of the product and that such defect was a proximate cause of the injuries.

Although the court assumed that *Greenman* had involved a manufacturing defect, it saw "no difficulty in applying the *Greenman* formulation to the full range of products liability situations, including those involving 'design defects.' A defect may emerge from the mind of the designer as well as from the hand of the workman." Although it may be "easier to see the 'defect' in a single imperfectly fashioned product than in an entire line badly conceived, a distinction between manufacture and design defects is not tenable." It rejected the Restatement's "unreasonably dangerous" standard in both contexts.

A large number of states have followed *Cronin* in dropping the "unreasonably dangerous" phrase from the definition of defect. When will the results differ from those indicated by the formulation in § 402A? How might California analyze the loose button and the eraser examples? How might the broken hasp be analyzed under the Restatement?

The Barker case. In Barker v. Lull Engineering Co., Inc., 20 Cal.3d 413, 573 P.2d 443, 143 Cal.Rptr. 225 (1978), plaintiff was hurt when the high-lift loader he was operating overturned on a slope. The court reversed a defense judgment because the trial judge, ruling before *Cronin* had been decided, used the "unreasonably dangerous" language. The court also found error in the trial judge's limitation of liability to situations in which the product was used in the "intended" manner. Such a limitation would prevent liability in cases of automobile crashes or in situations in which products are widely used for purposes for which they are not "intended," such as standing on chairs or using a screwdriver to pry up the lid of a tin. The appropriate limiting phrase would require the product to be used in the "intended or a reasonably foreseeable manner."

The court then discussed how plaintiffs might show that a product was defectively designed. "First, our cases establish that a product may be found defective in design if the plaintiff demonstrates that the product failed to perform as safely as an ordinary consumer would expect when used in an intended or reasonably foreseeable manner."

But this could not be the exclusive yardstick because in many situations consumers "have no idea how safe the product could be made." This led to a second formulation: that design defect could be shown "if through hindsight the jury determines that the product's design embodies 'excessive preventable danger,' or, in other words, if the jury finds that the risk of danger inherent in the challenged design outweighs the benefits of such design." The jury was to consider "among other relevant factors, the gravity of the danger posed by the challenged design, the likelihood that such danger would occur, the mechanical feasibility of a safer alternative design, the financial cost of an improved design, and the adverse consequences to the product and to the consumer that would result from an alternative design."

On this second prong, the defendant had the burden of persuading the trier of fact that the product should not be judged defective. Plaintiff and amicus argued that this second prong was equivalent to demanding a showing of negligence. The court disagreed. In many cases it is true that a showing of defect "may also demonstrate that the manufacturer was negligent in choosing such a design. As we have indicated, however, in a strict liability case, as contrasted with a negligent design action, the jury's focus is properly directed to the condition of the product itself, and not to the reasonableness of the manufacturer's conduct."

The *Barker* case plays a central role in the case that follows and is discussed further in the case.

Soule v. General Motors Corporation

Supreme Court of California, 1994.
8 Cal.4th 548, 882 P.2d 298, 34 Cal.Rptr.2d 607.

■ BAXTER, JUSTICE.

Plaintiff's ankles were badly injured when her General Motors (GM) car collided with another vehicle. She sued GM, asserting that defects in her automobile allowed its left front wheel to break free, collapse rearward, and smash the floorboard into her feet. GM denied any defect and claimed that the force of the collision itself was the sole cause of the injuries. Expert witnesses debated the issues at length. Plaintiff prevailed at trial, and the Court of Appeal affirmed the judgment.

We granted review to resolve three questions. First, may a product's design be found defective on grounds that the product's performance fell below the safety expectation of the ordinary consumer (see [*Barker*]), if the question of how safely the product should have performed cannot be answered by the common experience of its users? [The second question was whether it was error to deny GM's requested instruction that even if a defect is found it "cannot be a legal cause of injury if the accident would have produced the same injury even without the defect" and the third was whether an erroneous denial of an instruction was always reversible error.]

We reach the following conclusions: The trial court erred by giving an "ordinary consumer expectations" instruction in this complex case. Moreover, the court should have granted GM's request for a special instruction explaining its correct theory of legal cause. However, neither error warrants reversal unless it caused actual prejudice, and both errors were harmless on this record. We will therefore affirm the Court of Appeal's judgment.

[During a slight drizzle one afternoon, plaintiff was driving her Camaro on the street "apparently" not wearing her seat belt. An approaching Datsun suddenly skidded into plaintiff's path. The Datsun's left rear quarter struck plaintiff's car in the area of the left front wheel at a combined closing speed estimated variously at from 30 to 70 miles per hour. "The collision bent the Camaro's frame adjacent to the wheel and tore loose the bracket that attached the wheel assembly (specifically, the lower control arm) to the frame. As a result, the wheel collapsed rearward and inward. The wheel hit the underside of the 'toe pan'—the slanted floorboard area beneath the pedals—causing the toe pan to crumple, or 'deform,' upward into the passenger compartment." In addition to various minor injuries, plaintiff sustained two fractured ankles, including a compound compression fracture of her left ankle, which caused permanent injury.

The "failed bracket" was retrieved but the rest of the Camaro was acquired by a salvage dealer, repaired and resold. In the ensuing suit, plaintiff "asserted a theory of strict tort liability for a defective product. She claimed the severe trauma to her ankles was not a natural consequence of the accident, but occurred when the collapse of the Camaro's wheel caused the toe pan to crush violently upward against her feet. Plaintiff attributed the wheel collapse to a manufacturing defect, the substandard quality of the weld attaching the lower control arm bracket to the frame. She also claimed that the placement of the bracket, and the configuration of the frame, were defective designs because they did not limit the wheel's rearward travel in the event the bracket should fail."

The "available physical and circumstantial evidence left room for debate about the exact angle and force of the impact and the extent to which the toe pan had actually deformed. The issues of defect and causation were addressed through numerous experts produced by both sides in such areas as biomechanics, metallurgy, orthopedics, design engineering, and crash-test simulation."

Plaintiff presented evidence of improper welding techniques and of a design on Ford Mustangs of comparable years that were said to "provide protection against unlimited rearward travel of the wheel should a bracket assembly give way." GM denied the claims of poor welding and design defect, and argued that the Ford design was "not distinctly safer for all collision stresses to which the vehicle might be subjected." One witness asserted that at least one recent Ford product had adopted the Camaro's design. GM also argued that the force of the collision was the sole cause of the ankle injuries—that plaintiff's unrestrained body went forward and downward at the moment of impact, causing the ankle injury "before significant deformation of the toe pan occurred."

The trial court gave a conventional "ordinary consumer expectations" charge that required plaintiff to show "(1) the manufacturer's product failed to perform as safely as an ordinary consumer would expect, (2) the defect existed when the product left the manufacturer's possession, (3) the defect was a 'legal cause' of plaintiff's 'enhanced injury,' and (4) the product was used in a reasonably foreseeable manner." As noted earlier, the judge denied GM's requested instruction on causation.

The jury made special findings that the Camaro contained a "defect (of unspecified nature) which was a 'legal cause' of plaintiff's 'enhanced injury.'" The jury found that plaintiff was at fault for not wearing a seat belt but that it was not a legal cause of her enhanced injuries. The jury awarded $1.65 million. The court of appeal affirmed.]

DISCUSSION

. . .

In *Barker*, we offered two alternative ways to prove a design defect, each appropriate to its own circumstances. The purposes, behaviors, and dangers of certain products are commonly understood by those who ordinarily use them. By the same token, the ordinary users or consumers of a product may have reasonable, widely accepted minimum expectations about the circumstances under which it should perform safely. Consumers govern their own conduct by these expectations, and products on the market should conform to them.

In some cases, therefore, "ordinary knowledge . . . as to . . . [the product's] characteristics" [Restatement], may permit an inference that the product did not perform as safely as it should. If the facts permit such a conclusion, and if the failure resulted from the product's design, a finding of defect is warranted without any further proof. The manufacturer may not defend a claim that a product's design failed to perform as safely as its ordinary consumers would expect by presenting expert evidence of the design's relative risks and benefits.[3]

---

3. For example, the ordinary consumers of modern automobiles may and do expect that such vehicles will be designed so as not to explode while idling at stoplights, experience sudden steering or brake failure as they leave the dealership, or roll over and catch fire in two-mile-per-hour collisions. If the plaintiff in a product liability action proved that a vehicle's design produced such a result, the jury could find forthwith that the car failed to perform as safely as its ordinary consumers would expect, and was therefore defective.

However, as we noted in *Barker*, a complex product, even when it is being used as intended, may often cause injury in a way that does not engage its ordinary consumers' reasonable minimum assumptions about safe performance. For example, the ordinary consumer of an automobile simply has "no idea" how it should perform in all foreseeable situations, or how safe it should be made against all foreseeable hazards. [*Barker*]

An injured person is not foreclosed from proving a defect in the product's design simply because he cannot show that the reasonable minimum safety expectations of its ordinary consumers were violated. Under *Barker*'s alternative test, a product is still defective if its design embodies "excessive preventable danger" [   ], that is, unless "the benefits of the . . . design outweigh the risk of danger inherent in such design" [   ]. But this determination involves technical issues of feasibility, cost, practicality, risk, and benefit [   ], which are "impossible" to avoid [   ]. In such cases, the jury must consider the manufacturer's evidence of competing design considerations [   ] and the issue of design defect cannot fairly be resolved by standardless reference to the "expectations" of an "ordinary consumer."

As we have seen, the consumer expectations test is reserved for cases in which the everyday experience of the product's users permits a conclusion that the product's design violated minimum safety assumptions, and is thus defective regardless of expert opinion about the merits of the design. It follows that where the minimum safety of a product is within the common knowledge of lay jurors, expert witnesses may not be used to demonstrate what an ordinary consumer would or should expect. Use of expert testimony for that purpose would invade the jury's function [   ], and would invite circumvention of the rule that the risks and benefits of a challenged design must be carefully balanced whenever the issue of design defect goes beyond the common experience of the product's users.[4]

By the same token, the jury may not be left free to find a violation of ordinary consumer expectations whenever it chooses. Unless the facts actually permit an inference that the product's performance did not meet the minimum safety expectations of its ordinary users, the jury must

---

4. Plaintiff insists that manufacturers should be forced to design their products to meet the "objective" safety demands of a "hypothetical" reasonable consumer who is fully informed about what he or she should expect. Hence, plaintiff reasons, the jury may receive expert advice on "reasonable" safety expectations for the product. However, this function is better served by the risk-benefit prong of *Barker*. There, juries receive expert advice, apply clear guidelines, and decide accordingly whether the product's design is an acceptable compromise of competing considerations. On the other hand, appropriate use of the consumer expectations test is not necessarily foreclosed simply be-cause the product at issue is only in special-ized use, so that the general public may not be familiar with its safety characteristics. If the safe performance of the product fell be-low the reasonable, widely shared minimum expectations of those who do use it, perhaps the injured consumer should not be forced to rely solely on a technical comparison of risks and benefits. By the same token, if the ex-pectations of the product's limited group of ordinary consumers are beyond the lay expe-rience common to all jurors, expert testimony on the limited subject of what the product's actual consumers do expect may be proper. [   ]

engage in the balancing of risks and benefits required by the second prong of *Barker*.

Accordingly, as *Barker* indicated, instructions are misleading and incorrect if they allow a jury to avoid this risk-benefit analysis in a case where it is required. [ ] Instructions based on the ordinary consumer expectations prong of *Barker* are not appropriate where, as a matter of law, the evidence would not support a jury verdict on that theory. Whenever that is so, the jury must be instructed solely on the alternative risk-benefit theory of design defect announced in *Barker*.[5]

GM suggests that the consumer expectations test is improper whenever "crashworthiness," a complex product, or technical questions of causation are at issue. Because the variety of potential product injuries is infinite, the line cannot be drawn as clearly as GM proposes. But the fundamental distinction is not impossible to define. The crucial question in each individual case is whether the circumstances of the product's failure permit an inference that the product's design performed below the legitimate, commonly accepted minimum safety assumptions of its ordinary consumers.

GM argues at length that the consumer expectations test is an "unworkable, amorphic, fleeting standard" which should be entirely abolished as a basis for design defect. In GM's view, the test is deficient and unfair in several respects. First, it defies definition. Second, it focuses not on the objective condition of products, but on the subjective, unstable, and often unreasonable opinions of consumers. Third, it ignores the reality that ordinary consumers know little about how safe the complex products they use can or should be made. Fourth, it invites the jury to isolate the particular consumer, component, accident, and injury before it instead of considering whether the whole product fairly accommodates the competing expectations of all consumers in all situations [ ]. Fifth, it eliminates the careful balancing of risks and benefits which is essential to any design issue.

In its amicus curiae brief, the Product Liability Advisory Council, Inc. (Council) makes similar arguments. The Council proposes that all design defect claims be resolved under a single risk-benefit analysis geared to "reasonable safety."

We fully understand the dangers of improper use of the consumer expectations test. However, we cannot accept GM's insinuation that ordinary consumers lack any legitimate expectations about the minimum safety of the products they use. In particular circumstances, a product's design may perform so unsafely that the defect is apparent to the common reason, experience, and understanding of its ordinary consumers. In such cases, a lay jury is competent to make that determination.

---

5. Plaintiff urges that any limitation on use of the consumer expectations test contravenes *Greenman*'s purpose to aid hapless consumers. But we have consistently held that manufacturers are not insurers of their products; they are liable in tort only when "defects" in their products cause injury. . . .

Nor are we persuaded by the Council's proposal. In essence, it would reinvest product liability claims with the requirement of "unreasonable danger" that we rejected in *Cronin* and *Barker*.

When use of the consumer expectations test is limited as *Barker* intended, the principal concerns raised by GM and the Council are met. Within these limits, the test remains a workable means of determining the existence of design defect. We therefore find no compelling reason to overrule the consumer expectations prong of *Barker* at this late date, and we decline to do so.[7]

Applying our conclusions to the facts of this case, however, we agree that the instant jury should not have been instructed on ordinary consumer expectations. Plaintiff's theory of design defect was one of technical and mechanical detail. It sought to examine the precise behavior of several obscure components of her car under the complex circumstances of a particular accident. The collision's exact speed, angle, and point of impact were disputed. It seems settled, however, that plaintiff's Camaro received a substantial oblique blow near the left front wheel, and that the adjacent frame members and bracket assembly absorbed considerable inertial force.

An ordinary consumer of automobiles cannot reasonably expect that a car's frame, suspension, or interior will be designed to remain intact in any and all accidents. Nor would ordinary experience and understanding inform such a consumer how safely an automobile's design should perform under the esoteric circumstances of the collision at issue here. Indeed, both parties assumed that quite complicated design considerations were at issue, and that expert testimony was necessary to illuminate these matters. Therefore, injection of ordinary consumer expectations into the design defect equation was improper.

We are equally persuaded, however, that the error was harmless, because it is not reasonably probable defendant would have obtained a more favorable result in its absence. . . .

[The court stressed that "the consumer expectations theory was never emphasized at any point." The case was "tried on the assumption that the alleged design defect was a matter of technical debate. Virtually all the evidence and argument on design defect focused on expert evaluation of the strengths, shortcomings, risks, and benefits of the challenged design, as compared with a competitor's approach." Neither "plaintiff's attorney nor any expert witness on her behalf told the jury that the Camaro's design violated the safety expectations of the ordinary consumer."]

Under these circumstances, we find it highly unlikely that a reasonable jury took that path. We see no reasonable probability that the jury

---

7. GM observes that some other states have rejected the consumer expectations test. (E.g., Prentis v. Yale Mfg. Co. (1984) 421 Mich. 670, 365 N.W.2d 176, 185–186 [adopting pure negligence theory for product injury]; [   ]). But a substantial number of jurisdictions expressly recognize, consistent with *Barker*, that a product's design is defective if it either violates the minimum safety expectations of an ordinary consumer or contains dangers which outweigh its benefits. [   ]

disregarded the voluminous evidence on the risks and benefits of the Camaro's design, and instead rested its verdict on its independent assessment of what an ordinary consumer would expect. Accordingly, we conclude, the error in presenting that theory to the jury provides no basis for disturbing the trial judgment.[8]

[The court then turned to GM's requested causation instruction, concluding that it should have been given, but that the failure to give it was harmless error. Overruling several cases that had called for automatic reversal when a request to charge was erroneously granted or refused, the court concluded that "there is no rule of automatic reversal or 'inherent' prejudice applicable to any category of civil instructional error, whether of commission or omission."]

Instructional error in a civil case is prejudicial "where it seems probable" that the error "prejudicially affected the verdict." [   ]

.   .   .

The trial court erred when it instructed on the consumer expectations test for design defect, and when it refused GM's special instruction on causation. However, neither error caused actual prejudice. Accordingly, the judgment of the Court of Appeal, upholding the trial court judgment in favor of plaintiff, is affirmed.

■ KENNARD, GEORGE, WERDEGAR and BOREN (assigned) JJ,, concur.

■ MOSK, ACTING CHIEF JUSTICE, concurring [addressing the issue of reversals for instructional errors].

■ ARABIAN, JUSTICE, concurring and dissenting [agreeing with the majority on the first two grounds but concluding that the failure to give GM's requested charge was reversible error].

NOTES AND QUESTIONS

1. What is the difference in this case between plaintiff's claim based on a manufacturing defect and her claim based on a design defect? Does the distinction affect any of the defense arguments raised by GM?

8. In a separate argument . . . both GM and the Council urge us to reconsider *Barker*'s holding . . . that under the risk-benefit test, the manufacturer has the burden of proving that the utility of the challenged design outweighs its dangers. [ ] We explained in *Barker* that placement of the risk-benefit burden on the manufacturer is appropriate because the considerations which influenced the design of its product are "peculiarly within . . . [its] knowledge." . . . GM argues that *Barker* unfairly requires the manufacturer to "prove a negative"—i.e., the absence of a safer alternative design. The Council suggests our "peculiar knowledge" rationale is unrealistic under liberal modern discovery rules. We are not persuaded. *Barker* allows the evaluation of competing designs, but it does not require proof that the challenged design is the safest possible alternative. The manufacturer need only show that given the inherent complexities of design, the benefits of its chosen design outweigh the dangers. Moreover, modern discovery practice neither redresses the inherent technical imbalance between manufacturer and consumer nor dictates that the injured consumer should bear the primary burden of evaluating a design developed and chosen by the manufacturer. GM and the Council fail to convince us that *Barker* was incorrectly decided in this respect.

2. Consider how the four elements of the consumer expectations test listed by the trial judge would work in a case like Campbell v. General Motors Corp. 32 Cal.3d 112, 649 P.2d 224, 184 Cal.Rptr. 891 (1982), in which a bus passenger, was thrown from her seat and injured during a sharp turn. She claimed a defective design because there was no "grab bar" within easy reach of her seat. Plaintiff presented no expert testimony but did present photographs of the interior of the bus.

The court held that it was enough for Campbell to show "the objective conditions of the product" so that the jurors could employ "[their] own sense of whether the product meets ordinary expectations as to its safety under the circumstances presented by the evidence. Since public transportation is a matter of common experience, no expert testimony was required to enable the jury to reach a decision on this part of the *Barker* inquiry."

How might *Campbell* be analyzed under the second prong of *Barker*?

3. What is the basis for GM's argument that the consumer expectations test should be eliminated? Which of the five reasons offered seems strongest?

4. The court suggests that some car accidents are properly subject to the consumer expectations test. What do they have in common? Why doesn't this case fit within that category?

5. Few states have joined California in shifting the burden of proof to defendants on the issue of "excessive preventable danger." What are the arguments for and against such a shift?

6. In Morton v. Owens–Corning Fiberglas Corp., 33 Cal.App.4th 1529, 40 Cal.Rptr.2d 22 (1995), a former insulation installer sued asbestos suppliers after getting mesothelioma. Plaintiff succeeded before the jury on a consumer expectations approach. On appeal, defendant argued that such a test was inapplicable in an asbestos case because of its complexity.

The court held the consumer expectations test applicable. The question was whether "the circumstances of the product's failure permit an inference that the product's design performed below the legitimate, commonly accepted minimum safety assumptions of its ordinary consumers." Quoting an earlier case [Sparks v. Owens–Illinois, Inc., 32 Cal.App.4th 461, 38 Cal.Rptr.2d 739 (1995), in which this same court had upheld a plaintiff's judgment in an asbestos case], the court concluded that asbestos involved "neither 'complicated design considerations,' nor 'obscure components,' nor 'esoteric circumstances' surrounding the 'accident,' " and the product failure was not "beyond the 'legitimate, commonly accepted minimum safety assumptions of its ordinary consumers.' " Individuals who worked around asbestos were capable of formulating minimum expectations. Plaintiff's witnesses were coworkers from 1959 to 1961 who testified that they believed the insulation materials they were working with in building the carrier Kitty Hawk "were safe and that they had no expectations that exposure to such products would make them ill."

7. In Bresnahan v. Chrysler Corp., 32 Cal.App.4th 1559, 38 Cal. Rptr.2d 446 (1995), plaintiff was hurt when she was rear-ended by another car at low speed. Her "air bag inflated, forcing her left arm and hand upward. Her hand struck the car's overarching windshield, cracking it, and her elbow apparently impacted the windshield's side pillar." Plaintiff sought to proceed solely under the consumer expectations test; defendant sought to proceed exclusively under the risk-utility test. Is each strategy understandable? The court held that it was plaintiff's choice: "We believe that, on the showing before us, an ordinary consumer would be capable of forming an expectation, one way or the other, about whether the design of the highly publicized and by now commonplace product of an air bag-equipped automobile satisfied minimal safety expectations in causing that result." *Soule*'s situation was "complex and murky" compared to what should be expected from a "side windshield assembly and air bag in a minor rear-end collision."

8. In Ewen v. McLean Trucking Co., 300 Or. 24, 706 P.2d 929 (1985), a pedestrian was struck by a truck while crossing the street. In a claim against the truck's manufacturer the pedestrian claimed that a defective design prevented the driver from seeing pedestrians just in front and to the right of the truck. In charging the jury, the judge used the reasonable consumer expectations test. A plaintiff's judgment was reversed on appeal because it was improper to use the consumer expectation approach for "everyone who might be affected by the product." Is the consumer expectations test meaningless in bystander cases?

9. *Causation.* As with manufacturing defects, the supplier must anticipate uses that were not intended. In Price v. Blaine Kern Artista, Inc., 111 Nev. 515, 893 P.2d 367 (1995), plaintiff entertainer had bought an oversized caricature head mask of then-President George Bush made by defendant. While entertaining in Las Vegas plaintiff either tripped or was pushed from behind and was hurt by the shifting weight of the mask when he fell. His negligence action claimed a defective design in that the mask did not have a safety harness to support the head and neck in case of a fall. Defendant argued that if plaintiff had been deliberately pushed by a drunk or by a political foe of President Bush that was not a foreseeable use of the mask. The court disagreed: a fact question was presented whether defendant should have foreseen the possibility of some sort of violent reaction by intoxicated or politically volatile persons, "ignited by the oversized caricature of prominent political figures." What if it had been shown that the plaintiff had tripped over a wire? Been bumped into accidentally?

10. Some states have emphasized the consumer expectations test. Others have tended to emphasize the risk-benefit approach, referred to in *Barker* as a search for "excessive preventable danger." Some states have tended to let the plaintiff choose—or try both. A preliminary draft of the new Restatement goes beyond *Soule* and, except for harm from food products, eliminates the consumer expectations test, relying exclusively on risk-benefit analysis.

Part of the food exception drew on cases involving customers choking on chicken bones in chicken salad or on fish bones in chowder. Though plaintiffs in these cases might have claimed a manufacturing defect, it was difficult to tell if this was an aberration from a norm or an intrinsic (albeit unwanted) part of a designed dish. Here a consumer expectations test "relies upon culturally defined, widely shared standards that food products ought to meet." § 2 comment *g*. Might that be true in other contexts as well?

Should consumer expectations—whether narrowly or broadly defined—be retained? Or should exclusive reliance be placed on risk-benefit analysis? Consider the following case.

Camacho v. Honda Motor Co., Ltd.

Supreme Court of Colorado, 1987.
741 P.2d 1240, cert. dismissed 485 U.S. 901 (1988).

[In March, 1978, plaintiff bought a new Honda Hawk motorcycle. In an intersection accident with a car, plaintiff suffered severe leg injuries. Plaintiff and his wife sued the various parties in the chain of distribution, claiming that the absence of crash bars to protect the legs made the product defective under a strict liability analysis. Negligence and breach-of-warranty claims were not before the court. Two mechanical engineers supplied depositions asserting that "the state of the art in mechanical engineering and motorcycle design was such that effective leg protection devices were available in March 1978 and that several manufacturers other than Honda had made such devices available as optional equipment; that, although room for further improvement of crash bars existed in March 1978, crash bars then available from manufacturers other than Honda provided some protection in low-speed collisions and, in particular, would have reduced or completely avoided the serious leg injuries" that plaintiff suffered. The trial court granted Honda summary judgment. The court of appeals affirmed on the ground that the danger " 'would have been fully anticipated by or within the contemplation of' the ordinary user or consumer."]

■ KIRSHBAUM, JUSTICE.

.   .   .

In Roberts v. May, 41 Colo.App. 82, 583 P.2d 305 (1978), the Court of Appeals recognized the applicability of the "crashworthiness" doctrine in Colorado. Under this doctrine, a motor vehicle manufacturer may be liable in negligence or strict liability for injuries sustained in a motor vehicle accident where a manufacturing or design defect, though not the cause of the accident, caused or enhanced the injuries. [ ] The doctrine was first recognized in the landmark case of Larsen v. General Motors Corp., 391 F.2d 495 (8th Cir.1968), in which the court noted that a manufacturer's duty encompassed designing and building a product reasonably fit and safe for its intended use, that automobiles are intended for use on the roadways and that injury-producing collisions are a frequent, foreseeable and statistically expectable result of such normal use. Incumbent upon the automobile manufacturer was a duty of reasonable care in the design and manufacture of its product, including a duty to use reasonable care to minimize the injurious effects of a foreseeable collision by employing commonsense safety features. [ ] The crashworthiness doctrine has been adopted by the vast majority of courts in other jurisdictions which have considered the issue. [ ] We agree with the reasoning of those decisions, as did the Court of Appeals in its consideration of this case, and adopt the crashworthiness doctrine for this jurisdiction.

The crashworthiness doctrine has been applied to accidents involving motorcycles. [ ] Honda argues, however, that motorcycles are inherently dangerous motor vehicles that cannot be made perfectly crashworthy and, therefore, that motorcycle manufacturers should be free of liability for injuries not actually caused by a defect in the design or manufacture of the motorcycle. We find no principled basis to conclude that liability for failure to provide reasonable, cost-acceptable safety features to reduce the severity of injuries suffered in inevitable accidents should be imposed upon automobile manufacturers but not upon motorcycle manufacturers. The use of motorcycles for transportation over roadways is just as foreseeable as the use of automobiles for such purpose. The crashworthiness doctrine does not require a manufacturer to provide absolute safety, but merely to provide some measure of reasonable, cost-effective safety in the foreseeable use of the product. [ ] Honda acknowledges that motorcycle accidents are just as foreseeable as automobile accidents and that motorcycle riders face a much greater risk of injury in the event of an accident than do occupants of automobiles. In view of the important goal of encouraging maximum development of reasonable, cost-efficient safety features in the manufacture of all products, the argument that motorcycle manufacturers should be exempt from liability under the crashworthiness doctrine because serious injury to users of that product is foreseeable must be rejected. [ ]

III.

In determining the extent of liability of a product manufacturer for a defective product, this court has adopted the doctrine of strict products liability as set forth in [§ 402A].

Honda asserts that as a matter of law a motorcycle designed without leg protection devices cannot be deemed "in a defective condition unreasonably dangerous to the user" because the risk of motorcycle accidents is foreseeable to every ordinary consumer and because it is obvious that motorcycles do not generally offer leg protection devices as a standard item. In support of this argument Honda relies on comment *i* to section 402A, which states in pertinent part:

i. Unreasonably dangerous. The rule stated in this Section applies only where the defective condition of the product makes it unreasonably dangerous to the user or consumer.

. . . .

The article sold must be dangerous to an extent beyond that which would be contemplated by the ordinary consumer who purchases it, with the ordinary knowledge common to the community as to its characteristics.

The trial court and the Court of Appeals in essence applied this consumer contemplation test in dismissing the Camachos' claims.

In Cronin v. J.B.E. Olson Corp., [ ], the California Supreme Court declined to require an injured person to establish that a product is unreasonably dangerous as a requisite to recovery for injuries in a strict liability design defect context. In Union Supply Co. v. Pust, 196 Colo. 162, 583 P.2d 276 (1978), this court rejected the *Cronin* rationale, recognizing that requiring a party who seeks recovery on the basis of an alleged defective product to establish that the product is unreasonably dangerous appropriately places reasonable limits on the potential liability of manufacturers. However, we also held in *Pust* that the fact that the dangers of a product are open and obvious does not constitute a defense to a claim alleging that the product is unreasonably dangerous. We noted that adoption of such a principle would unfairly elevate the assumption of risk defense to a question of law.[6] The obvious and foreseeable consumer contemplation test employed by the trial court and approved by the Court of Appeals is substantially similar to the open and obvious standard specifically rejected in *Pust*. It is not the appropriate standard in Colorado for measuring whether a particular product is in a defective condition unreasonably dangerous to the consumer or user.

A consumer is justified in expecting that a product placed in the stream of commerce is reasonably safe for its intended use, and when a product is not reasonably safe a products liability action may be maintained. [ ] Of course, whether a given product is reasonably safe and, therefore, not unreasonably dangerous, necessarily depends upon many circumstances. Any test, therefore, to determine whether a particular product is or is not actionable must consider several factors. While reference to "reasonable" or "unreasonable" standards introduces certain negligence concepts into an area designed to be free from these concepts [ ], that difficulty is much less troublesome than are the problems inherent in attempting to avoid dealing with the competing interests involved in allocating the risk of loss in products liability actions. . . .

These considerations strongly suggest that the consumer contemplation concept embodied in comment *i*, while illustrative of a particular problem, does not provide a satisfactory test for determining whether particular products are in a defective condition unreasonably dangerous to

---

6. Where the obviousness of the danger inherent in the ordinary use of a product is not dispositive of whether the product is unreasonably dangerous, the plaintiff's appreciation of the danger may nonetheless rise to the level of assumption of the risk. Assumption of the risk is an affirmative defense to strict liability, requiring a showing of more than ordinary contributory negligence in that the plaintiff must have voluntarily and un-reasonably proceeded to encounter a known danger the specific hazards of which the plaintiff had actual subjective knowledge. [ ] The question of whether a plaintiff had actual knowledge of the specific hazards comprising the danger is ordinarily a fact question which should be left for the jury and not precluded by the conclusion that the danger should have been obvious. . . .

the user or consumer. In the final analysis, the principle of products liability contemplated by section 402A is premised upon the concept of enterprise liability for casting defective products into the stream of commerce. [ ] The primary focus must remain upon the nature of the product under all relevant circumstances rather than upon the conduct of either the consumer or the manufacturer. [ ] Total reliance upon the hypothetical ordinary consumer's contemplation of an obvious danger diverts the appropriate focus and may thereby result in a finding that a product is not defective even though the product may easily have been designed to be much safer at little added expense and no impairment of utility. [ ] Uncritical rejection of design defect claims in all cases wherein the danger may be open and obvious thus contravenes sound public policy by encouraging design strategies which perpetuate the manufacture of dangerous products. [ ]

In Ortho Pharmaceutical Corp. v. Heath, 722 P.2d 410 (Colo.1986), we recently recognized that exclusive reliance upon consumer expectations is a particularly inappropriate means of determining whether a product is unreasonably dangerous under section 402A where both the unreasonableness of the danger in the design defect and the efficacy of alternative designs in achieving a reasonable degree of safety must be defined primarily by technical, scientific information.[8] Moreover, manufacturers of such complex products as motor vehicles invariably have greater access than do ordinary consumers to the information necessary to reach informed decisions concerning the efficacy of potential safety measures. [ ] The principles that have evolved in the law of products liability have in part been developed to encourage manufacturers to use information gleaned from testing, inspection and data analysis to help avoid the "massive problem of product accidents." [ ]

. . . In *Ortho* we noted that the following factors are of value in balancing the attendant risks and benefits of a product to determine whether a product design is unreasonably dangerous:

> (1) The usefulness and desirability of the product—its utility to the user and to the public as a whole.

8. Honda asserts that the application of the consumer expectation test is particularly appropriate in the context of motorcycle design defect claims because the motorcycle purchaser who is injured in an accident has bargained for the condition about which he complains and because the element of conscious consumer choice is invariably present in contradistinction to those claims involving accidents occurring in the workplace. We cannot agree that the purchaser of a motorcycle bargains for the risk of serious leg injury; rather, the purchaser bargains for a motorized vehicle the purpose of which is to provide an economical, open-air, maneuverable form of transportation on the roadways. Cf. Wade, On the Nature of Strict Liability for Products, 44 Miss.L.J. 825, 839–40 (1973)(noting that a plaintiff who has cut his finger on a sharp knife should not be able to maintain a cause of action against the manufacturer of the knife on the theory that the knife was unsafe because it was sharp, because the very purpose of a knife is to cut); Page, Generic Product Risks: The Case Against Comment *k* and For Strict Tort Liability, 58 N.Y.U.L.Rev. 853, 857 (1983). . . .

(2) The safety aspects of the product—the likelihood that it will cause injury and the probable seriousness of the injury.

(3) The availability of a substitute product which would meet the same need and not be as unsafe.

(4) The manufacturer's ability to eliminate the unsafe character of the product without impairing its usefulness or making it too expensive to maintain its utility.

(5) The user's ability to avoid danger by the exercise of care in the use of the product.

(6) The user's anticipated awareness of the dangers inherent in the product and their avoidability because of general public knowledge of the obvious condition of the product, or of the existence of suitable warnings or instructions.

(7) The feasibility, on the part of the manufacturer, of spreading the loss by setting the price of the product or carrying liability insurance.

[*Ortho,*] (relying on [Wade's article]). The factors enumerated in *Ortho* are applicable to the determination of what constitutes a product that is in a defective unreasonably dangerous condition. By examining and weighing the various interests represented by these factors, a trial court is much more likely to be fair to the interests of both manufacturers and consumers in determining the status of particular products.

The question of the status of the motorcycle purchased by Camacho involves in part the interpretation of mechanical engineering data derived from research and testing—interpretation which necessarily includes the application of scientific and technical principles. In addition, the question posed under the crashworthiness doctrine is not whether the vehicle was obviously unsafe but rather whether the degree of inherent dangerousness could or should have been significantly reduced. The record contains some evidence to support the conclusion that Honda could have provided crash bars at an acceptable cost without impairing the motorcycle's utility or substantially altering its nature and Honda's failure to do so rendered the vehicle unreasonably dangerous under the applicable danger-utility test. It is far from certain, however, that the ultimate answer to this question can be determined on the basis of the limited facts thus far presented to the trial court.

. . .

The Camachos proffered evidence that the Honda Hawk motorcycle could have been equipped with crash bars which would mitigate injuries in low-speed, angled-impact collisions such as the one in which Camacho was involved. The Camachos' expert witnesses' interpretation of research and testing data indicated that the maneuverability of the motorcycle could be retained by making the crash bars no wider than the handlebars, that the stability of the motorcycle could be retained by mounting the crash bars relatively close to the center of gravity and that the addition of crash bars would not impair the utility of the motorcycle as a fuel efficient, open-air vehicle nor impair the safety of the motorcycle in accidents which varied in kind from the accident involving Camacho. These conclusions are all strenuously disputed by Honda. However, precisely because the factual conclusions reached by expert witnesses are in dispute, summary judgment as to whether the design strategies of Honda were reasonable is improper.

The judgment is reversed, and the case is remanded to the Court of Appeals with directions to remand the case to the trial court for further proceedings consistent with the views expressed in this opinion.

■ [Three justices concurred in Justice KIRSHBAUM'S opinion.]

■ VOLLACK, JUSTICE, dissenting:

Because I believe that the court of appeals correctly affirmed the trial court's order, I respectfully dissent.

The issue before the court is what test should apply in determining whether a product has a design defect causing it to be in a defective condition that is unreasonably dangerous. After arriving at the appropriate test, we must decide whether the court of appeals correctly affirmed the trial court's summary judgment order.   .   .   .

.   .   .

II.

We have not before decided what test should apply in determining whether a product is "unreasonably dangerous" in a design defect case. I believe the appropriate test is defined in [comment *i* to § 402A]: "The article sold must be dangerous to an extent beyond that which would be contemplated by the ordinary consumer who purchases it, with the ordinary knowledge common to the community as to its characteristics" [hereinafter the consumer contemplation test].

Some jurisdictions have adopted this test; others have adopted it in part or rejected it. [   ]

.   .   .

Other jurisdictions have adopted a variation of the consumer expectation test. Dart v. Wiebe Mfg., Inc., 147 Ariz. 242, 709 P.2d 876 (1985)(where consumer expectation test is sufficient to resolve a case, that test is to be used; where that test "fails to provide a complete answer," application of risk/benefit factors is appropriate [   ]); Nichols v. Union Underwear Co., 602 S.W.2d 429 (Ky.1980)(consumer expectation or knowledge is just one factor to be considered by a jury in determining whether a product is unreasonably dangerous. [   ]); Knitz v. Minster Machine Co., 69 Ohio St.2d 460, 432 N.E.2d 814 (1982)(product is of defective design "if (1) it is more dangerous than an ordinary consumer would expect when used in an intended or reasonably foreseeable manner, or (2) if the benefits of the challenged design do not outweigh the risk inherent in such design." [   ]).

Other states have rejected the consumer expectation test. Prentis v. Yale Mfg. Co., 421 Mich. 670, 365 N.W.2d 176 (1984)("[W]e adopt, forthrightly, a pure negligence, risk-utility test in products liability actions against manufacturers of products, where liability is predicated upon defective design." [ ]); Turner v. General Motors Corp., 584 S.W.2d 844 (Tex.1979)(risk-utility test will be applied "when the considerations of utility and risk are present in the state of the evidence." [ ]).

III.

. . .

The cases discussed demonstrate that states have taken a variety of approaches to resolve this question. Because of the nature of the product here, I believe the appropriate test is the consumer contemplation or consumer expectation test. The facts presented in this case differ from cases which involve the defective condition of products such as automobile brakes, prescription drugs, and gas tanks. With those types of products, the ordinary consumer is not capable of assessing the danger of the product. On the other hand, an ordinary consumer is necessarily aware that motorcycles can be dangerous. The plaintiff had the choice to purchase other motorcycles by other manufacturers which carried additional safety features, and instead elected to purchase this particular motorcycle and ride it without leg protection devices. The conclusion follows that the trial court's ruling and the court of appeals' decision were correct.

. . .

I also believe the majority incorrectly relies on [*Ortho*]. I believe the risk-benefit test cited by the majority and applied in *Ortho* is an appropriate test for products such as drugs, because their danger "is defined primarily by technical, scientific information," and because some drugs are unavoidably unsafe in some respect. [ ] A consumer of drugs cannot realistically be expected to foresee dangers in prescribed drugs which even scientists find to be complex and unpredictable. On the other hand, the purchaser of a motorcycle knows that the purchase and use of "an economical, open-air, maneuverable form of transportation," [ ], presents the risk of accidents and resulting injuries due to the open-air nature of the motorcycle.

Because I believe that the correct test under facts such as these is the consumer-contemplation test, I would affirm the court of appeals' decision. Accordingly, I respectfully dissent.

■ I am authorized to state that JUSTICE ERICKSON and JUSTICE ROVIRA join in this dissent.

NOTES AND QUESTIONS

1. On the crashworthiness issue, what is the argument for applying the doctrine in the case of automobiles? Do these considerations justify extending it to motorcycles?

2. Is it justifiable to use the risk/benefit test when the danger is as "open and obvious" as it was in this case? If a state uses the consumer expectations test can the victim ever win a case when hurt by a danger that was "open and obvious"? In Luque v. McLean, 8 Cal.3d 136, 501 P.2d 1163, 104 Cal.Rptr. 443 (1972), defendant manufactured a power lawnmower that cut grass with a single revolving blade and ejected it through an open, unprotected hole in the front. Printed next to the hole was the word "caution." While mowing, plaintiff stepped in front of the running mower to remove a carton from its path. He slipped on wet grass and, as he fell backward, his hand slid into the unguarded hole and was mangled by the rotary blade spinning at 100 revolutions per second. How might this case be analyzed under *Camacho*? What test is appropriate if the mower's unguarded hole occasionally permitted stones to fly out and hit pedestrians?

3. Under the risk/benefit test how do the *Barker* factors differ from the seven-factor test used in *Camacho*? More generally, does a court that rejects *Barker* in favor of an "unreasonably dangerous" standard, necessarily adopt a substantively different approach?

4. The court says that "the record contains some evidence to support the conclusion that Honda could have provided crash bars at an acceptable cost without impairing the motorcycle's utility or substantially altering its nature." If the motorcycle cost $5,000, how much could the crash bars cost and still be an "acceptable cost"?

5. What is the relevance of the discussion in footnote 8 about plaintiff's motivations in buying the model he chose? Courts that rely exclusively on the consumer expectations test reject plaintiffs' claims in comparable fact situations. See, e.g., Kutzler v. AMF Harley–Davidson, 194 Ill.App.3d 273, 550 N.E.2d 1236, appeal denied 132 Ill.2d 546, 555 N.E.2d 377 (1990).

6. What is the significance of the fact that other manufacturers offered the crash bars? Is it relevant that they offered it as optional equipment?

7. When analyzing risk-benefit cases, comparisons among products must consider only comparable products. See Dyson v. General Motors Corp., 298 F.Supp. 1064 (E.D.Pa.1969), refusing to hold a hard-top car defective because it was less protective than a full-frame sedan. But one hard-top car should not be "appreciably less safe" than other hard-tops. See also Curtis v. General Motors Corp., 649 F.2d 808 (10th Cir.1981).

8. In Dreisonstok v. Volkswagenwerk, A.G., 489 F.2d 1066 (4th Cir.1974), plaintiff passengers were hurt when the microbus in which they were riding left the road and ran into a tree. One distinctive feature of the microbus was that its passenger compartment was at the very front of the vehicle. Plaintiffs' negligence claim alleged that the design was defective because it provided less protection than that available in a "standard American made vehicle, which is a configuration with the passengers in the middle and the motor in the front." The court, reversing a plaintiffs' judgment, rejected the claim. After quoting *Dyson* on the need to distinguish types of vehicles, it continued:

> Price is, also, a factor to be considered, for, if a change in design would appreciably add to cost, add little to safety, and take an article out of the price range of the market to which it was intended to appeal, it may be "unreasonable" as well as "impractical" for the courts to require the manufacturer to adopt such change. Of course, if an article can be made safer and the hazard of harm may be mitigated "by an alternate design or device at no substantial increase in price", then the manufacturer has a duty to adopt such a design but a Cadillac may be expected to include more in the way of both conveniences and "crashworthiness" than the economy car. Moreover, in a "crashworthy" case, it is necessary to consider the circumstances of the accident itself. As *Dyson* puts it, "it could not reasonably be argued that a car manufacturer should be held liable because its vehicle collapsed when involved in a head-on collision with a large truck, at high speed." In summary, every case such as this involves a delicate balancing of many factors in order to determine whether the manufacturer has used ordinary care in designing a car, which, giving consideration to the market purposes and utility of the vehicle, did not involve unreasonable risk of injury to occupants within the range of its "intended use."

> Applying the foregoing principles to the facts of this particular case, it is clear that there was no violation by the defendant of its duty of ordinary care in the design of its vehicle. The defendant's vehicle, described as "a van type multipurpose vehicle," was of a special type and particular design. This design was uniquely developed in order to provide the owner with the maximum amount of either cargo or passenger space in a vehicle inexpensively priced and of such dimensions as to make possible easy maneuverability. To achieve this, it advanced the driver's seat forward, bringing such seat in close proximity to the front of the vehicle, thereby adding to the cargo or passenger space. This, of course, reduced considerably the space between the exact front of the vehicle and the driver's compartment. All of this was readily discernible to any one using the vehicle; in fact, it was, as we have said, the unique feature of the vehicle. The usefulness of the design is vouchsafed by the popularity of the type. It was of special utility as a van for the transportation of light cargo, as a family camper, as a station wagon and for use by passenger groups too large for the average passenger car. It was a design duplicated in the construction of the large trucking tractors, where there was the same purpose of extending the cargo space without unduly lengthening the tractor-trailer coupling. There was no evidence in the record that there was any practical way of improving the "crashability" of the vehicle that would have been consistent with the peculiar purposes of its design.

The court concluded that the microbus was to be compared only with comparable vehicles. Here, the defense had presented unrefuted testimony that the safety of the microbus "was equal to or superior to that of other vehicles of like type."

See Bittner v. American Honda Motor Co., 194 Wis.2d 122, 533 N.W.2d 476 (1995), in which plaintiff was hurt when his 3–wheel ATV overturned going around a corner on a mowed grass path. Defendant was properly permitted to compare safety records of this ATV with other products intended for similar purposes—snowmobiles, minibikes, trailbikes and 4–wheel ATVs—to suggest that the accident in question was more likely attributable to the operator than to the product. But Honda should not have been allowed to introduce evidence on the risks of "dissimilar products and activities"—sky-diving, skiing, bicycle riding, scuba diving, football, and passenger automobiles—to show that ATVs were not unreasonably dangerous. Such evidence could not help the jury decide whether the product at issue was reasonably safe. The manufacturer's obligations "persist whether or not the product has a high rate of injury associated with it." In some cases a high rate of injury associated with a product might help the defense because it might permit the jury "to infer plaintiff's contributory negligence." We consider the role of this sort of defense at p. 559 infra.

9. In Fitzpatrick v. Madonna, 424 Pa.Super. 473, 623 A.2d 322 (1993), a carelessly operated motorboat ran over a swimmer, who died after being badly cut by the unguarded propeller on the outboard motor. In a suit against the manufacturer of the propeller, the court, 2–1, overturned a jury verdict and held that the motor had no design defect. Although it was technologically possible to guard or shroud an outboard motor, this produced "other undesirable effects. For instance, a propeller guard would reduce a vessel's speed and would thereby reduce its efficient use of fuel. In addition, a propeller guard will affect the maneuverability of a boat." Plaintiff's expert was quoted as saying that a guard would have "a substantial degrading effect on boat performance." A guard or shroud would also create a "larger target area" for swimmers to encounter, creating the "possibility . . . that human limbs may become wedged between a shroud and the propeller, exposing a swimmer to even greater injury."

The majority's final concern was that buyers would remove guards to gain power and fuel economy. If the motor had been made more powerful to overcome the impact of a guard, the guard's removal would push the speed to more than its power rating and would create handling difficulties. The value of the open propeller was great and when the boat is handled in a "common sense manner" the danger to bystanders is "not great." The majority did not quantify any of the "undesirable effects" that it discussed. The dissenter simply listed the factors to be considered in a risk-benefit analysis under state law and concluded that plaintiff's evidence was strong enough to sustain a jury verdict.

10. Do *Soule* and *Camacho* require, or permit, differentiating between products that may be dangerous only to the users, such as food, drink and microbuses, and those that might be dangerous to bystanders as well, such as snowmobiles, and power mowers that toss rocks beyond the lawn? If a manufacturer has achieved a huge cost reduction by the sacrifice of a small amount of safety, should bystanders be subjected to the additional danger without hope of recovering damages under a balancing test, when they receive no direct benefit from the reduced price?

11. Would either *Soule* or *Camacho* be decided differently under a negligence analysis?

12. Some cases raise the question whether it is desirable to have uniform design standards—at least with regard to a particular product line. The issue is discussed in Dawson v. Chrysler Corp., 630 F.2d 950 (3d Cir.1980), cert. denied 450 U.S. 959 (1981). The court, applying New Jersey law, upheld a judgment for $2 million for a driver who was crushed after his car skidded sideways into a pole and wrapped around it. Evidence showed that using a firmer side frame would have added 200–250 pounds to the weight of the car and $300 to the cost. The court noted that even though the car's design complied with the National Traffic and Motor Vehicle Safety Act, that fact did not exempt the manufacturer from liability under state common law. It went on to point out that:

> The result of such arrangement is that while the jury found Chrysler liable for not producing a rigid enough vehicular frame, a factfinder in another case might well hold the manufacturer liable for producing a frame that is too rigid. Yet, as pointed out at trial, in certain types of accidents—head-on collisions—it is desirable to have a car designed to collapse upon impact because the deformation would absorb much of the shock of the collision, and divert the force of deceleration away from the vehicle's passengers. In effect, this permits individual juries applying varying laws in different jurisdictions to set nationwide automobile safety standards and to impose on automobile manufacturers conflicting requirements. It would be difficult for members of the industry to alter their design and production behavior in response to jury verdicts in such cases, because their response might well be at variance with what some other jury decides is a defective design. Under these circumstances, the law imposes on the industry the responsibility of insuring vast numbers of persons involved in automobile accidents.

> Equally serious is the impact on other national social and economic goals of the existing case-by-case system of establishing automobile safety requirements. As we have become more dependent on foreign sources of energy, and as the price of that energy has increased, the attention of the federal government has been drawn to a search to find alternative supplies and the means of conserving energy. More recently, the domestic automobile industry has been struggling to compete with foreign manufacturers which have stressed smaller, more fuel-efficient cars. Yet, during this same period, Congress has permitted a system of regulation by ad hoc adjudications under which a jury can hold an automobile manufacturer culpable for not producing a car that is considerably heavier, and likely to have less fuel efficiency.

The court concluded that letting individual juries impose liability for defective designs was neither "fair nor efficient." Since Congress had permitted the common law to continue, and "because Congress is the body best suited to evaluate and, if appropriate, to change that system, we decline today to do anything in this regard except to bring the problem to the attention of the legislative branch."

What about under warranty analysis? In a recent ruling, New York's highest court has held that design claims under tort and warranty are not identical—that one is "subtly different" from the other. Denny v. Ford Motor Co., 1995 WL 722844 (N.Y.1995). The court, 6–1, concluded that it was not inconsistent for a jury in a highway rollover accident involving a Bronco II to find that the product was not "defective" for tort purposes but that the warranty of fitness had been breached.

The evidence showed that since it was designed as an off-road vehicle the engineers could not build into it the same stability as for the conventional highway vehicle. Indeed, "Ford's own engineer stated that he would not recommend the vehicle to someone whose primary interest was to use it as a passenger car, since the features of a four-wheel-drive utility vehicle were not helpful for that purpose and the vehicle's design made it inherently less stable." The evidence also showed that Ford's marketing manual suggested that the vehicle was "suitable to contemporary life styles" and that sales presentations might take into account the vehicle's suitability "for commuting and for suburban and city driving." Also, the manual noted that the vehicle might "be particularly appealing to women who may be concerned about driving in snow and ice with their children." The plaintiffs were not at all interested in the vehicle's off-road utility.

The majority stressed that tort law used a risk/utility focus and that warranty law "focuses on the expectations for the performance of the product when used in the customary, usual and reasonably foreseeable manner." Recovery could be had "without regard to the feasibility of alternative designs or the manufacturer's 'reasonableness' in marketing it in that unsafe condition":

> This distinction between the "defect" analysis in breach-of-implied-warranty actions and the "defect" analysis in strict-products-liability actions is explained by the differing etiology and doctrinal underpinnings of the two distinct theories. The former class of actions originates in contract law, which directs its attention to the purchaser's disappointed expectations; the latter originates in tort law, which traditionally has concerned itself with social policy and risk allocation by means other than those dictated by the marketplace.

Even if persuaded that the two analyses should be merged, the majority was unable to do so because the warranty approach was legislative in origin through the UCC and its focus on consumer expectation was beyond judicial change. The court observed that although the distinction was not likely to matter frequently, here it did matter. On a tort analysis the instability of the vehicle might well have been justified on a risk/utility basis—but the consumer expectation was that the vehicle would perform on paved roads as well as ordinary vehicles. It might be found not to have been "merchantable" or "fit" for its ordinary purposes. Might a sales pitch be worked into a tort risk/utility analysis?

The dissenter agreed that the legal terms were not identical but concluded that the two verdicts were not reconcilable. He thought that the consumer expectation approach was appropriate to commercial transactions but had "no place in personal injury litigation alleging a design defect . . . . Whether a product has been defectively designed should be determined in a personal injury action by a risk/utility analysis." The tort and contract remedies "developed from separate legal doctrines but are not materially different when applied to personal injury claims involving design defects."

In sum, although procedural distinctions may remain because mandated by the Legislature's enactment of various provisions of the Uniform Commercial Code, [ ], strict liability and breach of implied warranty causes of action are substantively similar and impose liability without fault [ ]. It makes little sense, therefore, to perpetuate a legal distinction between them based upon the method for determining defectiveness, particularly when the flaws in the consumer expectation standard for measuring defectiveness are recognized.

Jones v. Ryobi, Ltd

United States Court of Appeals, Eighth Circuit, 1994.
37 F.3d 423.

■ Before FAGG, CIRCUIT JUDGE, HEANEY, SENIOR CIRCUIT JUDGE, and LOKEN, CIRCUIT JUDGE.

■ FAGG, CIRCUIT JUDGE.

Jennifer Jones was employed at Business Cards Tomorrow (BCT) as the operator of a small printing press known as an offset duplicator. Jones seriously injured her left hand when she caught it in the moving parts of the press. Alleging negligence and strict product liability for defective design, Jones brought this diversity lawsuit against Ryobi, Ltd. (the manufacturer) and A.B. Dick Corporation (the distributor). At trial, Jones dropped her negligence claims but she later moved to amend her complaint to reassert her negligence claim against the distributor. The district court denied Jones's motion to amend. At the close of Jones's case, the manufacturer and the distributor moved for judgment as a matter of law (JAML). The district court granted the manufacturer's and the distributor's motions for JAML. Jones appeals and we affirm.

The press involved in Jones's injury operates by passing blank paper through several moving parts, imprinting an image on the paper, and dispensing the printed paper through upper and lower "eject wheels." To avoid streaking the freshly printed image, on each job the operator must adjust the eject wheels to ensure the wheels do not touch the freshly printed area. The press was manufactured and sold to BCT equipped with both a plastic guard that prevented the operator from reaching into the moving parts to adjust the eject wheels, and an electric interlock switch that automatically shut off the press if the guard was opened. Sometime after the press was manufactured and delivered to BCT, the guard was removed and the interlock switch was disabled to allow the press to run without the guard. Because this modification increased production by saving the few seconds required to stop and to restart the press when the operator adjusted the eject wheels, the modification was a common practice in the printing industry.

Jones learned to operate the press by watching other BCT employees. Jones testified she knew the guard was missing and knew it was dangerous to have her hands near the unguarded moving parts, but her supervisor pressured her to save time by adjusting the eject wheels while the press was running. Jones feared she would be fired if she took the time to stop the press. While Jones was adjusting the eject wheels on the running press, a noise startled her. Jones jumped and her left hand was caught in the press's moving parts and crushed.

In granting the manufacturer's and the distributor's motions for JAML, the district court relied on the open and obvious nature of the asserted danger. See Restatement (Second) of Torts § 402A cmt. *i* (1965)(consumer expectation test). The district court did not reach the manufacturer's and the distributor's other grounds for JAML. We review the district court's grant of JAML de novo; thus, we may affirm on another ground. [ ] Because we conclude the district court's grant of JAML was proper on an alternate ground, we need not consider the ground relied on by the district court.

To recover on a theory of strict liability for defective design under Missouri law, Jones must prove she was injured as a direct result of a defect that existed when the press was sold. [ ] Jones had the burden to show the press had not been modified to create a defect that could have proximately caused her injury. [ ] Jones failed to meet this burden because her evidence showed the press had been substantially modified by removing the safety guard and disabling the interlock switch, and showed the modification caused her injury. When a third party's modification makes a safe product unsafe, the seller is relieved of liability even if the modification is foreseeable. [ ] Jones did not show who modified the press, but her evidence clearly showed that a third party, not the manufacturer or the distributor, was responsible for the modification.

3rd party modification relieves manu. of liability

Although the manufacturer provided tools for general maintenance of the press that could also be used to remove the guard, we do not believe this made the manufacturer responsible for the guard's removal. Jones produced no evidence that any representative of the manufacturer or the distributor removed the guard or instructed BCT to remove the guard from the press involved in Jones's injury. Indeed, the distributor's service representative testified he told BCT's owner several times the guard should be replaced, but BCT's owner shrugged off the suggestion. Because BCT knew the guard was missing and the interlock switch was disabled, but did not follow the distributor's advice to repair the disabled safety features, the distributor's service work on the press did not extend the distributor's liability to defects that were not present when the press was sold. [   ]

Jones argues the modification rule does not apply because the press was not safe even before the modification. We disagree. The press was safe before the modification because the press would not run without the safety guard covering the moving parts. The fact BCT encouraged Jones to operate the press without the safety features to increase production does not show the press was sold "in a defective condition [and thus] was unreasonably dangerous when put to a reasonably anticipated use." [   ] Although several witnesses testified the press operated more efficiently without the safety guard and interlock switch, other witnesses testified similar presses operated satisfactorily with the designed safety features intact. The press could be operated safely without removing the guard because the eject wheels did not have to be adjusted while the press was running. Jones's expert witness opined the press was unsafe as designed, but the expert based his view on the printing industry's tendency to disable the press's safety features to achieve greater production. Thus, the expert's testimony does not show the press was unreasonably dangerous when used in the same condition as when it was sold. [   ]

Because Jones's evidence showed a third party's modification, not a defect existing when the press was sold, was the sole cause of her injury, her strict product liability claim for defective design fails as a matter of law. [   ] The district court thus properly granted the manufacturer's and the distributor's JAML motions.

Finally, Jones contends the district court committed error in refusing to allow her to amend her complaint to reassert her negligence claim against the distributor. We disagree. The district court did not abuse its discretion to deny the amendment because the evidence presented did not show colorable grounds for Jones's negligence theory. [   ]

Accordingly, we affirm.

■ HEANEY, SENIOR CIRCUIT JUDGE, dissenting.

Viewing the evidence in the light most favorable to Jones, as we must, I cannot subscribe to the majority's opinion that the offset duplicator was safe as originally manufactured.

The rule to which Missouri adheres, as correctly stated by the majority, is that a manufacturer is not liable where a modification is foreseeable, but the modification renders a safe product unsafe. . . .

. . . The critical question, thus, is whether the duplicator as manufactured was unreasonably dangerous.

The testimony of Dr. Creighton, Jones's expert witness, is alone sufficient to support the inference that the offset duplicator was not safe as originally designed. Dr. Creighton testified that the electric interlock device was wired backwards and was not "fail-safe." He testified that the duplicator's guard, in addition to not being fail-safe, was made of material "that will break . . . readily," did not allow for proper ventilation of the internal components of the machine, and invited removal. He further testified that the design of the eject wheels, which essentially requires operators to make manual adjustments while the offset duplicator is running, was "absolutely not safe," indeed "the worst of situations from a human factors standpoint." The duplicator could have been equipped, he noted, with external adjustment handles to enable operators to make adjustments to the eject wheels without placing their hands in close proximity to the moving parts of the machine.

Further, although not direct proof that the duplicator was defectively designed, the fact that an overwhelming majority of machines had their guards removed after their delivery is evidence that the duplicator was incapable of operating efficiently according to industry standards. According to ITEK [the former distributor of the product] representative Brad Gruenewald, nearly ninety-eight percent of all machines he came into contact with had their safety covers removed. [ ] Indeed, Gruenewald testified that he told duplicator operators in effect to remove the guard in order to alleviate problems with ink emulsification that occurred as a result of humidity which frequently became trapped inside the plastic shield. [ ]

The majority does not address (nor need it, given the focus of its opinion) the open-and-obvious defense on which the district court relied in granting the defendants' motion for judgment as a matter of law. I touch on it briefly [to show that it will not support affirmance.]

We have held that the obviousness of a defect or danger is material to the issue of whether a product is unreasonably dangerous. [ ] It does not, however, alone constitute a defense to a submissible case of strict liability under section 402A. [The question under Missouri law] is not simply whether the danger was open and obvious, but whether the product was unreasonably dangerous taking into account the obviousness of the danger.

There is no question in my mind that there was sufficient evidence from which a jury, taking into account the obviousness of the conceded danger, could conclude that the offset duplicator was unreasonably dangerous. . . .

In my judgment there was sufficient evidence to support the inference that the offset duplicator was unreasonably dangerous and thus was defectively designed. This case should have met its fate in the hands of the jury members, not the district court's and not now ours.

NOTES AND QUESTIONS

1. How would you analyze the trial judge's basis for dismissing the case—open and obvious danger?

2. What is the significance of the fact that defendant distributor knew that BCT had removed the guard and tried "several times" to persuade management to put it back? Even if it did not know about BCT's practices, should it be enough that the manufacturer knew of the "common practice" in the industry to remove the guards? Suppose the distributor's representatives tried to sell the machine by encouraging buyers to remove the guard?

3. Is it relevant why the industry removed the guards? Does it matter whether it was to (a) save ten seconds three times a day, (b) increase production by 20 percent, (c) save one hour a day by preventing overheating because the guard impaired the ventilation, (d) improve the quality of the end product? Does the Missouri bar to recovery "even if [the alteration] is foreseeable" leave any room for recovery in any of these cases? What does it mean to say that a guard "invites removal"?

4. What is the difference between saying that "one who markets a safe machine cannot be rendered legally liable if someone later makes it unsafe by modifications, even if they are foreseeable" and saying that "one who designs a machine has a duty to consider whether it will be safe when used"?

How might the plaintiff show that the duplicator was "not safe" when it left the hands of the manufacturer and the distributor?

5. Several witnesses testified that the machine "operated more efficiently" without the safety devices, while "other witnesses testified similar presses operated satisfactorily" with the devices intact. Why does this not present a jury question?

6. Other courts have responded differently to the alteration problem. Compare Piper v. Bear Medical Systems, Inc., 180 Ariz. 170, 883 P.2d 407 (App.1993), involving the death of a patient who had been using a breathing ventilator. The machine was made to prevent the misconnecting of its parts—but it was also made without a bacterial filter. "It was common for respiratory therapists to modify the [ventilator unit by adding] bacterial filters. This was a common and well-known practice . . . and [the manufacturer] knew its ventilators were being [modified."] The modification required some new parts and—for the first time—made it possible to misconnect parts. As a result of such a misconnection the patient was unable to exhale and died. Defendant admitted that "economically feasible technology existed" at the time that would have prevented the harm, but argued that it need not adopt it because its machine was designed with parts that could not be misconnected. It argued that its knowledge about modifications was irrelevant.

The court disagreed. It acknowledged that there was "general agreement that where misuse or modification of a product is unforeseeable and causes injury," the manufacturer cannot be liable. (Is that because the product is not defective? Or is it lack of proximate causation?) But courts disagree about the "effect of foreseeable product modifications on a manufacturer's liability." In some states responsibility does not extend beyond the "time of sale, and the foreseeability of a substantial modification of its product is irrelevant to the manufacturer's liability." But the *Piper* court followed the other view in which foreseeability of modification was the central issue. A manufacturer that knows that its product is being modified frequently must take that into account in designing the product. (What arguments support this greater duty?) Here a jury could find that the manufacturer was aware that modification was taking place and was introducing a new danger into the product that did not exist when it was sold.

The requisite foreseeability could be found in the widespread action of the respiratory therapy industry that defendant actually knew about. (It would probably have been enough to show only the widespread modification—because a manufacturer is expected to keep abreast of how its machines are being used in the industry.)

In other cases the requisite foreseeability may be found in the fact that a machine guard is easily removed, or difficult to replace, or must be removed frequently for cleaning, or that the guard inhibits the task the machine is to perform. See Spurgeon v. Julius Blum, Inc., 816 F.Supp. 1317 (C.D.Ill.1993) summarizing Illinois law as follows:

> As a matter of law, a manufacturer is liable for all intended use and any reasonably foreseeable misuse of the machine. . . . Generally, where a safety shield is easily removable and hinders use of the product, a jury is entitled to determine whether its removal was reasonably foreseeable. [ ] Conversely, a manufacturer will not be held liable for injury due to an unforeseeable alteration to its product. [ ] For instance, when a safety shield is difficult to remove and cannot be removed by the operator, summary judgment should be granted for the manufacturer because its removal would not be reasonably foreseeable.

In the actual case, involving a door-hinging machine, there was no dispute that there was no guard on the machine on the day of the accident. The "evidence could support a finding, for either party, that the shield was removed because it prevented some operators from doing their best work." Since it could also support a conclusion that removal was not reasonably foreseeable, the case was for the jury.

Most of these cases involve alteration or modification in a factory setting—and indirectly raise questions about the responsibility of the employer. That question is discussed in Chapter XI in the context of workers' compensation.

7. *Statutory change.* Although most courts disagree with *Ryobi*, the situation is less clear when statutory developments are considered. As we have noted in connection with joint and several liability, p. 322, supra, and as will be noted more generally in Chapter XI, legislative changes to common law tort decisions have become quite common recently. About a quarter of the states have adopted statutes aimed at protecting suppliers of goods that have been altered after the supplier distributed them. Some statutes protect suppliers only when the alteration was not foreseeable. But several others apply to any substantial alteration.

In La Plante v. American Honda Motor Co., 27 F.3d 731 (1st Cir.1994), involving an ATV accident, Honda had presented evidence that at the time of the accident, the ATV's "front brakes were inoperable, its rear brakes were faulty, its right rear tire was overinflated, its front forks were bent, and it pulled to the right." The denial of Honda's requested charge under Rhode Island's statute was held reversible error. The statute provided that "no manufacturer or seller of a product shall be liable for product liability damages where a substantial cause of the [harm] was a subsequent alteration or modification" which, in turn, was defined as conduct that "altered, modified, or changed the purpose, use, function, design, or manner of use of the product from that originally designed, tested or intended by the manufacturer, . . . or for which such product was originally designed, tested or manufactured." It was irrelevant whether the alteration was made by an intermediary or by the plaintiff. The statute does not distinguish between foreseeable and unforeseeable alterations.

Plaintiff argued that the statute applied only to "deliberate" changes and not to changes resulting from "inadequate maintenance." The court disagreed. It noted that none of the several other state statutes drew such a distinction, and that some explicitly treated the two similarly. Kentucky's statute, for example, included "failure to observe routine care and maintenance but shall not include ordinary wear and tear." Moreover, the court could "see no reason why the Rhode Island legislature would provide a defendant with a complete defense where an ATV owner disconnected his front brakes, but not where the front brakes were inoperative due to the owner's failure to perform routine maintenance." Can you see such a reason? How would the ATV case be analyzed in a state without such a statute?

D. INSTRUCTIONS AND WARNINGS

1. WORDS THAT REDUCE RISK

We have already seen that defects in products may be found in the intrinsic design of the product itself. We now turn to the search for defects in the words—labels, instructions, warnings—that accompany the product. These may reduce risk by instructing the user in how to obtain the benefits from the product's intended use and by alerting users to the dangers of using the product in ways unintended by the manufacturer.

Hahn v. Sterling Drug, Inc.

United States Court of Appeals, Eleventh Circuit, 1986.
805 F.2d 1480.

[Plaintiff's four-year-old daughter ingested over an ounce of defendant's Campho–Phenique, an "over-the-counter topical analgesic." Earlier in the evening, the plaintiffs had allowed their seven-year-old daughter to use the product and she had evidently misplaced the lid after using it. In this suit "sound[ing] in tort and strict liability" for the younger daughter's convulsions, the trial judge directed a verdict for the defendants.]

■ Before KRAVITCH and CLARK, CIRCUIT JUDGES, and MORGAN, SENIOR CIRCUIT JUDGE.

■ PER CURIAM:

. . .

. . . The warning label on the defendant's product contains the following:

> WARNING: Keep this and all medicines out of children's reach. In case of accidental ingestion, seek professional assistance or contact a poison control center immediately. DIRECTIONS: For external use: apply with cotton three or four times daily.

Appellants contend that they produced evidence from which a jury could conclude that the danger posed by the product when ingested by small children was great enough to require a more stringent warning. The Hahns rely principally on the testimony of their toxicology expert, Dr. Albert P. Rauber, Professor of Pediatrics at Emory University and also Medical Director of the Georgia Poison Center. Dr. Rauber testified that the warning was very general and that its effect is "watered down" by the fact that the same warning appears on numerous products that are not harmful (i.e., Flintstone Vitamins and Hydrocortisone Cream). Rauber said he was not "satisfied" with the Campho–Phenique label.

The Hahns point to several other facts which could have led a jury to believe that the warning was inadequate. First, the Hahns themselves testified that they had read the label in its entirety and were still unaware that the product could harm their child if ingested. Second, Sterling was aware that many children had been injured after ingesting the product, yet the product continued to use the same warning. Third, the product was known to be quite toxic, and as such it required a more dramatic warning. Fourth, the warning was in a smaller print than other messages on the label. The Hahns say that this was confusing even though the warning was in bold-face type. Fifth, the direction "for external use" was not followed by the word "only." Sixth, the label stated that the product may be used on the gums, possibly indicating to a reasonable person that internal use might be acceptable. Seventh, the label was silent as to the possibility of seizures and respiratory failure if taken internally. Eighth, the warning to contact the poison control center was insufficient since it would have been just as easy to put the word "poison" on the label. Also, the warning is said to be more like a "helpful hint meant merely to please and placate a concerned parent and not a clue that the contents of the bottle are poisonous."

Appellee, of course, argues that no reasonable person could find that the warning on the Campho–Phenique label was inadequate. Sterling relies on Dr. Rauber's admission during cross examination that the warning advised a reasonable person that the product was potentially toxic and that ingestion might create "grave danger." The district court agreed. The court below held that both the references to external use and to the poison control center in combination with the reference to keep this and all medicines out of the reach of children were sufficient to convey the message to an average adult that there is a risk of serious harm if the child swallows the medicine.

At oral argument, Sterling's attorneys conceded that they could not refer to the court any case decided in the Eleventh Circuit or in the Georgia courts which held that the adequacy of a product manufacturer's warning is a proper subject for a directed verdict. There are, however, three products liability cases decided in recent years that present the issue of the adequacy of warnings to Georgia consumers. In Stapleton v. Kawasaki Heavy Indus., Ltd., 608 F.2d 571 (5th Cir.1979), modified on other grounds, 612 F.2d 905 (5th Cir.1980), we held that "whether adequate efforts were made to communicate a warning to the ultimate user and whether the warning if communicated was adequate are uniformly held questions for the jury." 608 F.2d at 573. Stapleton v. Kawasaki Heavy Indus., Ltd., supra was followed by [two other cases].

We see no reason to elaborate on this principle of law. Appellee in its argument sought to make a distinction in this case because the Hahns were well-educated, had read the label, undoubtedly understood the meaning of "ingestion," and, according to their testimony, knew of the necessity of keeping medicines away from children. As we understand the decided cases in this area of law, the simple question is whether the warning is adequate, given the unsafe nature of the product. It is appropriate for a jury to determine that adequacy. While the jury may or may not consider the intelligence and experience of the consumer-plaintiff, that does not play a part in our rationale in determining whether or not the question should or should not be presented to a jury. Since our authorities are clear and unanimous, we reverse and remand on the basis of these authorities.

. . . .

NOTES AND QUESTIONS

1. Note that "warnings" may be divided into two major groups. In the first, as in *Hahn,* the words used perform the function of safety instructions that are intended to make the product less dangerous if the instructions are followed. In the second, a warning may simply notify the buyer or user that certain dangers inhere in the product without reducing, or offering any chance to reduce, those dangers other than by abstaining from using the product. We discuss cases involving this second usage in the next section. For a comprehensive treatment of warnings issues, see Henderson and Twerski, Doctrinal Collapse in Products Liability: The Empty Shell of Failure to Warn, 65 N.Y.U. L.Rev. 265 (1990).

2. *Adequacy.* What are the strongest arguments for inadequacy in *Hahn*? Is the court suggesting that every issue of the adequacy of a safety instruction is a jury question? Might plaintiff have had a claim against her parents or her sister? What is the relationship between any such claim and the theory on which Sterling is being sued?

Several cases have developed criteria for determining the adequacy of a warning. Consider this summary from Pittman v. Upjohn Co., 890 S.W.2d 425 (Tenn.1994):

> A reasonable warning not only conveys a fair indication of the dangers involved, but also warns with the degree of intensity required by the nature of the risk. [ ] Among the criteria for determining the adequacy of a warning are: 1. the warning must adequately indicate the scope of the danger; 2. the warning must reasonably communicate the extent or seriousness of the harm that could result from misuse of the drug; 3. the physical aspects of the warning must be adequate to alert a reasonably prudent person to the danger; 4. a simple directive warning may be inadequate when it fails to indicate the consequences that might result from failure to follow it and, . . . 5. the means to convey the warning must be adequate. [ ]

Are these appropriate factors? How does the warning in *Hahn* fare under them?

The adequacy of a warning may be a question even where the plaintiff did not read the warning that was given. In Johnson v. Johnson Chemical Co., 183 App.Div.2d 64, 588 N.Y.S.2d 607 (1992), plaintiff was hurt when an anti-roach fogger exploded while plaintiff was using it in the kitchen— with the pilot light on the stove still lit, despite a warning to shut off pilot lights among other possible sources of flame. When defendant argued that the adequacy of the warning was irrelevant when nothing was read, the court responded:

> This argument loses its persuasive force, however, once it is understood that the intensity of the language used in the text of a warning is only one of the factors to be considered in deciding whether such warning is adequate. A second factor to be considered is the prominence with which such language is displayed. [ ]. For example, the warning "harmful if swallowed" is less intense than the warning, "swallowing will result in death"; however, the former, less intense warning, when displayed prominently in block letters on the front label of a product, may be ultimately more effective than the latter, more intense warning, when [the latter is] displayed unobtrusively in small letters in the middle of a 10–page package insert [ ]. A consumer such as Ms. Kono who, by her own admission, tends to ignore one sort of label, might pay heed to a different, more prominent or more dramatic label.

Although the question of adequacy has generally been held to be a question of fact, courts recognize that in clear cases it may become one of law. See Martin v. Hacker, 83 N.Y.2d 1, 628 N.E.2d 1308, 607 N.Y.S.2d 598 (1993), involving a warning accompanying the drug reserpine. The court reviewed the text at length and, using the same factors listed in *Pittman*, found no question for a jury. Some courts treat the issue as one of law in the first instance on the ground that the text of the warning is before the court and it can make that decision. See, e.g., Mackowick v. Westinghouse Electric Corp., 525 Pa. 52, 575 A.2d 100 (1990).

3. *Safety Instructions.* Words that can help make the product safer might include statements that certain uses should be avoided or more specific directions about how to use or apply a product. Consider the following examples.

a. In Moran v. Fabergé, Inc., 273 Md. 538, 332 A.2d 11 (1975), two teenagers decided to try to scent a candle by pouring cologne on it somewhat below the flame. As one did this, the cologne, containing 82% alcohol, instantly ignited causing serious burns to the other teenager. After the jury found defendant negligent for failing to warn of the cologne's flammability, the trial judge granted judgment n.o.v. The appellate court reinstated the verdict. Although this particular accident was unforeseeable, other similar accidents, such as a woman accidentally spilling the cologne onto a lighted candle, might warrant a warning. The "cost of giving an adequate warning is usually so minimal, amounting only to the expense of adding some more printing to a label, that this balancing process will almost always weigh in favor of an obligation to warn of latent dangers, if the manufacturer is otherwise required to do so." Is it relevant that the cologne had not caused a known accident in 27 years? What might the safety directions say? Might the defendant also need to warn against ingesting? Against keeping it within reach of infants? Against not cleaning it up after it spills?

b. In Burch v. Amsterdam Corp., 366 A.2d 1079 (D.C.App.1976), directions on an adhesive glue for interior use said only "Do Not Use Near Fire Or Flame." Plaintiff forgot about the pilot light on his stove—and an explosion occurred. Summary judgment for defendant was reversed on the ground that a jury could find that the wording did not adequately alert users to the dangers.

c. Even the most explicit language may not suffice. See Campos v. Firestone Tire & Rubber Co., 98 N.J. 198, 485 A.2d 305 (1984), suggesting that a jury might find that pictorial messages were required if the product was likely to be used by migrant workers who did not speak English. Compare Ramirez v. Plough, Inc., 6 Cal.4th 539, 863 P.2d 167, 25 Cal. Rptr.2d 97 (1993), rejecting a claim that safety instructions on children's aspirin had to be in Spanish when the manufacturer advertised in Spanish in areas that were predominantly Spanish-speaking. Any duty to warn of dangers in administering the product to children suffering from respiratory illness was satisfied by the distribution in English of such warnings as were required by the FDA.

d. In Argubright v. Beech Aircraft Corp., 868 F.2d 764 (5th Cir.1989), the student pilot and his instructor were killed when the student pilot's seat slid back suddenly during the takeoff and he lost control of the plane. The survivors claimed that defendant had failed to remind the pilot adequately of the need to anchor the seat firmly before takeoff. (The seats function similarly to front seats in automobiles.) The defendant had listed this step in a checklist sent owners of the plane. But plaintiffs argued that a stronger more immediate reminder was needed in the cockpit. The trial court entered judgment for plaintiffs on a jury verdict.

The court of appeals reversed and dismissed on the ground that no reasonable jury could find an inadequate warning here. The practice of relying on checklists undermined the plaintiff's contention that some additional reminder was needed: "The whole point of the checklist procedure, however, is to replace individualized judgments about danger with a routine responsive to those dangers. The use of such a routine only underscores the absence of any duty upon Beech to direct pilots' attention back to open and obvious dangers."

4. In Cotton v. Buckeye Gas Prods. Co., 840 F.2d 935 (D.C.Cir.1988), plaintiff was hurt when propane tanks on the job site exploded. He argued that the labels were inadequate. In the course of rejecting the claims, the court observed:

> According to plaintiff, this warning was inadequate because it failed (1) to warn about the explosive properties of propane; (2) to instruct users to shut the valves on used cylinders; (3) to advise users not to use or store the cylinders in enclosed, unventilated areas; and (4) to warn that gas might escape from used cylinders believed to be empty.
>
> Failure-to-warn cases have the curious property that, when the episode is examined in hindsight, it appears as though addition of warnings keyed to a particular accident would be virtually cost free. What could be simpler than for the manufacturer to add the few simple items noted above? The primary cost is, in fact, the increase in time and effort required for the user to grasp the message. The inclusion of each extra item dilutes the punch of every other item. Given short attention spans, items crowd each other out; they get lost in fine print. Here, in fact, Buckeye responded to the information-cost problem with a dual approach: a brief message on the canisters themselves and a more detailed one in the [trade association's] pamphlet delivered to [the employer] (and posted on the bulletin board at the Leesburg Pike construction site where [plaintiff] was employed).
>
> Plaintiff's analysis completely disregards the problem of information costs. He asserts that "it would have been neither difficult nor costly for Buckeye to have purchased or created for attachment to its propane cylinders a clearer, more explicit label, such as the alternatives introduced at trial, warning of propane's dangers and instructing how to avoid them." Brief for Appellant at 25. But he offers no reason to suppose that any alternative package of warnings was preferable. He discounts altogether the warnings in the pamphlet, without even considering what the canister warning would have looked like if Buckeye had supplemented it not only with the special items he is personally interested in—in hindsight—but also with all other equally valuable items (i.e., "equally" in terms of the scope and probability of the danger likely to be averted and the incremental impact of the information on user conduct). If every foreseeable possibility must be

covered, "[T]he list of foolish practices warned against would be so long, it would fill a volume." [   ]

How should product suppliers choose between alerting consumers or users to the most likely (even if not the most dangerous) errors in using a product and the most dangerous (even if highly unlikely) risks of harm? Might it be "dangerous" to supply too much safety information?

5. *The addressee.* An important question in judging the need for, and adequacy of, warnings is who they are to reach. The normal rule is that they must reach the person who is likely to use the product. Sometimes, though, that may not be feasible, as where children may be users. One cluster of cases involves the claim that BIC cigarette lighters are dangerous because they were likely to fall into the hands of very young children who could easily get them to work. In addition to attacks on the design, claims were also made that a warning was needed. Compare Bean v. BIC Corp., 597 So.2d 1350 (Ala.1992)(jury question whether warnings on package and lighter were adequate) with Kirk v. Hanes Corp., 16 F.3d 705 (6th Cir.1994)(Michigan law imposes no duty to warn since danger of lighter is obvious to buyers).

Beyond children, two major exceptions have developed to the general duty to warn users—the "learned intermediary" and the "bulk supplier."

6. *The learned intermediary.* Courts generally hold that remote suppliers of prescription drugs fulfil their duty to warn by warning the physician. Why should that suffice?

Courts have developed exceptions to the exception—cases in which a warning to the physician will not suffice. One occurs when the physician is unlikely to make an individualized recommendation—as in mass vaccination programs. See Allison v. Merck & Co., 110 Nev. 762, 878 P.2d 948 (1994), involving vaccine against measles, mumps, and rubella, in which the court observed that the manufacturer of such a drug may choose to delegate its warning function to those conducting mass vaccination programs, but that will not relieve it of "ultimate responsibility for assuring that its unsafe product is dispensed with a proper warning."

A few courts go further and insist that warning reach the patient directly even in cases of individualized treatment—especially when a government agency requires warnings to reach the patient. See MacDonald v. Ortho Pharmaceutical Corp., 394 Mass. 131, 475 N.E.2d 65, cert. denied 474 U.S. 920 (1985)(requiring that warnings about dangers of contraceptive pills reach the ultimate user—as required by FDA regulations—and judging the adequacy of such warning by the standards of such a reader).

7. *The bulk supplier.* A second exception to the duty to warn users has developed when one company supplies a product in bulk to a large enterprise where it will be used by many workers. Some examples follow. Consider how this question differs from those involving the remote supplier in *Ryobi*, p. 516, supra.

a. In Adams v. Union Carbide, 737 F.2d 1453 (6th Cir.), cert. denied 469 U.S. 1062 (1984), the plaintiff sued Union Carbide for failing to provide direct warnings of dangers associated with toluene diisocyanate (TDI) that it supplied to her employer, General Motors. Union Carbide had warned GM about the dangers and had relied on GM to communicate these warnings to its employees. The court, using Ohio law, held that no direct warnings were necessary. GM was held to be a sophisticated buyer on whom Union Carbide could rely.

b. In McCullock v. H.B. Fuller Co., 981 F.2d 656 (2d Cir. 1992), defendant supplied hot melt glue to plaintiff's employer, a book bindery. Plaintiff claimed that fumes from the glue had harmed her. Defendant had warned the employer of the need for adequate ventilation by affixing labels on each box that complied with OSHA regulations and warned of dangers and referred the purchaser to a data sheet that defendant in fact had sent to the employer. Plaintiff claimed that she never saw any warning because she did not transfer the glue from the shipping box to the glue pot. She also claimed that a representative of defendant visited the bindery every few weeks and "knew that the glue pot was unventilated." Applying Vermont law, the court used the consumer expectations approach and relied on a state case that had asserted that a manufacturer's duty to warn was not "limited to purchasers but extended to employees of purchasers as well."

c. In Apperson v. E.I. Du Pont de Nemours & Co., 41 F.3d 1103 (7th Cir. 1994), defendant supplied Teflon to a company that planned to use it in making implants for persons who suffered from problems with their temporomandibular joints—the joint connecting the upper and lower jaw. After many implants failed, the patients sued the remote supplier on the ground that it should have warned physicians and their patients that the product was not suitable for the use to which the intermediary was putting it. The court, using Illinois law, disagreed. The warnings to the intermediary were adequate as a matter of law and the product had no "inherent dangers" that required warning to the public. The problem was not in the Teflon itself but in the use to which the intermediary put it.

Approximately 1,000 cases arose from the 25,000 patients who received these TMJ implants before trouble was reported. One article reports that the manufacturer went bankrupt and that Du Pont was currently on a string of 47 straight summary judgments plus summary judgment in an interdistrict federal litigation of 300 cases. Du Pont's defense has "emphasized its role as a bulk supplier for a sophisticated purchaser regulated by the FDA." One plaintiff's judgment for $468,000 is on appeal in Oregon. Du Pont has settled "many cases for a standard award of $950 per case." About 50 of the cases remained open as of mid–1995. Du Pont reported that about five cents worth of Teflon was used in each implant. The litigation has led to estimated Du Pont legal fees of $40 million. Taylor, A Discovery by Du Pont: Hidden Costs of Winning, Nat'l L.J. March 27, 1995, at B1. Should it matter whether Du Pont knew the use to which its Teflon was being put by the implant manufacturer?

d. For a case in which the manufacturer of a dangerous liquid bulk product was held to owe at a minimum a duty to stop supplying downstream repackagers who omitted necessary warnings, see Hunnings v. Texaco, Inc., 29 F.3d 1480 (11th Cir.1994) (applying Florida law). Plaintiff's claim could also encompass a requirement that defendant instruct "downstream distributors to notify retailers to discontinue the practice of packaging mineral spirits in milk containers, [ ], or curtailing business with customers who were known to distribute the product to errant retailers."

8. Would the differences between strict liability and negligence affect the analysis of safety instruction cases?

9. When, if ever, can the supplier choose to give a safety instruction instead of making the intrinsic product safer? If a safety instruction says in giant-sized print to give the widget two complete turns before starting the engine or else an explosion might occur, is it relevant that the product itself could have been designed to avoid the risk of explosion entirely by adding one percent to its price? Fifteen percent?

Assume that Honda, rejecting the advice of its marketing department, had placed in large print on every item that lacked leg guards the following conspicuous statement: "WARNING. THIS PRODUCT CONTAINS NO LEG GUARDS. ANY ACCIDENT IS LIKELY TO CAUSE THE OCCU-PANT SERIOUS LEG INJURIES." Might this have affected the result in *Camacho*? Suppose the statement were supplemented by language stating that the guards were available as optional equipment? On the more expensive models of Honda motorcycles? On specified models sold by competitors? What if the statement indicated the number of motorcyclists who had suffered leg injuries during the preceding year? Would it have mattered whether the leg guards could have been added for a cost that was lower than the expected benefits?

States that follow the rule that products with open and obvious dangers cannot be defective would follow the dissent in *Camacho* and deny liability using either that rule itself or a consumer expectations test. For a discussion of events that led to a state overruling its "open and obvious" rule in a motorcycle leg guard case, see Satcher v. Honda Motor Co., 52 F.3d 1311 (5th Cir.1995)(Mississippi law).

10. *Causation.* The question of whether the user would have acted differently if there had been an adequate warning has been vexing. Some courts have required the victim to prove that causal element. In Haesche v. Kissner, 229 Conn. 213, 640 A.2d 89 (1994), the court held as a matter of law that failure to warn a child about the dangers of a BB gun were not causally related to the harm to his victim. The gun user had wilfully disobeyed his parents's explicit warnings about safety and was unlikely to have obeyed warnings conveyed with the gun.

Several recent cases have invoked a "heeding presumption"—requiring the party responsible for the inadequate warning to show that the user would not have heeded an adequate warning. See Coffman v. Keene Corp., 133 N.J. 581, 628 A.2d 710 (1993), listing states that apply the presumption. The defendant argued that the presumption could not be justified empirically because "it is nearly impossible to go through a day without consciously ignoring warnings designed to protect health and safety." The court accepted that assertion but concluded that the presumption was justified because it would operate as a "powerful incentive" to manufacturers. If they omitted needed warnings they could no longer argue that the plaintiff might not have heeded one even if it had been there. A possible subject for "speculation" was removed from the jury's consideration.

In Richter v. Limax Int'l, Inc., 45 F.3d 1464 (10th Cir.1995), the court applied the Kansas heeding presumption against a supplier who failed to warn about the risks of stress fractures in using a minitrampoline. The plaintiff was relieved from having to persuade the jury that she would have behaved differently if the absent warning had been there—and she did not have to prove what wording would have been adequate. Instead, causation was presumed to be present.

Compare General Motors Corp. v. Saenz, 873 S.W.2d 353 (Tex.1993), in which the court rejected a heeding presumption where plaintiffs claimed that they had not been adequately warned about the dangers of overloading a truck. Although warnings to that effect were placed in the owner's manual and in the door jamb, plaintiffs argued that the wording was inadequate. There was no reason to conclude that if the wording had been better the accident would not have happened.

Note that a heeding presumption generally also operates to provide that if an adequate warning is given, the supplier is entitled to assume that it will be heeded and the harm averted.

11. *Misuse.* As *Camacho* and *Hahn* suggest, injuries often result from "unintended" uses of the product. As these cases and *Soule* make clear, this is not a complete defense if the "misuse" or "unintended use" was one that was reasonably foreseeable. At its simplest, a manufacturer of screwdrivers is expected to know that its product is widely used to pry open the lids of tins and other containers. So, too, a supplier of chairs must anticipate that many people use them to stand on instead of using ladders. How wide a range of uses must suppliers anticipate? Consider these examples and whether a warning would have mattered.

a. In Ellsworth v. Sherne Lingerie, Inc., 303 Md. 581, 495 A.2d 348 (1985), plaintiff wore a nightgown manufactured by defendant inside out, so that the pockets were "flapping or protruding." As she put a tea kettle on the front burner of her electric stove, she reached above the stove for a coffee filter. Her nightgown ignited and she was severely burned. A defense judgment entered on a jury verdict was reversed on appeal. The court agreed that the question of misuse was part of the plaintiff's case on defectiveness. In this case:

> Clearly, and concededly, Appellant was using the nightgown for a reasonably foreseeable purpose. We conclude that her manner of use of the nightgown, though possibly careless, was reasonably foreseeable as a matter of law. It certainly may be foreseen that wearing apparel, such as nightgowns and robes, will occasionally be worn inside out. It

is also foreseeable that a loosely fitting gown will come into contact with sources of ignition in the environment where it may be expected to be worn, and particularly when worn in the kitchen and near a stove. Momentary inattention or carelessness on the part of the user, while it may constitute contributory negligence, does not add up to misuse of the product under these circumstances.

If misuse is established should it be a complete bar to recovery? The role of contributory fault in defective product cases is discussed at p. 559, infra.

b. A young child threw a beer bottle against a telephone pole. The bottle broke and hurt the child. Venezia v. Miller Brewing Co., 626 F.2d 188 (1st Cir.1980). The manufacturer was absolved of liability because this was held not to be a "foreseeable" use of the bottle. Would the analysis differ if the plaintiff was hurt when the bottle fell from his grasp and landed on a concrete floor?

c. Sometimes the question of defect is affected by the marketing scheme. In Lugo v. LJN Toys, Ltd., 75 N.Y.2d 850, 552 N.E.2d 162, 552 N.Y.S.2d 914 (1990), a playmate threw a detachable part of a doll made by defendant into the eye of plaintiff. The claim was that the doll was a replica of a well-known television cartoon character, Voltron, who overcame enemies by hurling his shield at them. The detachable part of the doll that was thrown was variously described as a "shield," "blade," or "star."

The court held that summary judgment was properly denied. Product suppliers had to anticipate uses that were "unintended but reasonably foreseeable." Here, plaintiff "has submitted expert evidence that, based upon customs and standards in the toy safety community, the part was defective because detachable from the doll and that throwing it was foreseeable because of the extensive television exposure in which Voltron did so."

How is the issue of "misuse" related to the issue of "alteration" discussed in *Ryobi*, supra?

2. WARNINGS OF INTRINSIC RISK

We have been considering language whose main purpose was to make the product safer by advising users what to do or what not to do, or both. We turn now to warnings whose main purpose is to alert potential users to some risks that inhere in the product as made and that cannot be eliminated or reduced at a cost that equals or is lower than the expected benefits.

Is any warning needed? The first question is whether any warning at all is needed for the particular product. Could defendant have argued that point in *Hahn*?

In Brown Forman Corp. v. Brune, 893 S.W.2d 640 (Tex.App.1994), the court held that no notice was required on a bottle of tequila to warn against the dangers of drinking a large quantity in a short period of time. The underage plaintiff, already intoxicated from other drinking, died after drinking unmixed tequila from a glass, and then the bottle, "heavily and rapidly." The dangers were apparent even to an 18–year-old person. No warning would have averted what happened.

Compare Hon v. Stroh Brewery Co., 835 F.2d 510 (3d Cir.1987), in which the 26–year-old decedent drank two or three cans of defendant's beer nightly an average of four nights per week over six years. Plaintiff claimed that decedent had died of pancreatitis as a result of the drinking. The product was alleged to be defective for lack of a warning because although "medical science has now established that *either* excessive *or* prolonged, even though moderate, use of alcohol may result in diseases of many kinds, including pancreatic disease," this was not commonly understood by consumers. The trial judge's grant of summary judgment to Stroh was reversed. On the record a jury could properly have found that although the amount consumed "was potentially lethal, that fact was known neither to [decedent] nor to the consuming public."

In Benedi v. McNeil–P.P.C., Inc., 66 F.3d 1378 (4th Cir.1995), the court upheld plaintiff's negligence award after his liver failed when he used defendant's Tylenol for a few days while drinking some three or four glasses of wine per evening. Defendant argued that it had had no notice of the danger before plaintiff took the tablets—a claim the court held that the jury could properly have rejected. Once the defendant makes that argument can it also argue that no warning was needed?

Whether a warning is needed at all is related to the earlier discussion of whether design dangers are "open and obvious." Even in states in which an open danger is not actionable, a frequent issue is whether the danger met that standard. That issue addresses the appearance of the object and the nature of its dangers, the same questions that arise in warning cases. In Emery v. Federated Foods, Inc., 262 Mont. 83, 863 P.2d 426 (1993), 2½-year-old Chad choked on marshmallows. Because the Heimlich maneuver and other efforts failed to dislodge the obstruction, Chad suffered permanent brain damage before a hospital could suction "a small liquified piece of marshmallow from Chad's airway." The claim was based on the lack of warning about the dangers of allowing children under the age of three to eat marshmallows. Plaintiff's experts testified that marshmallows were "particularly dangerous in that they change their characteristics and consistency when they are soaked with liquid secretions that are present in the breathing tubes of the lungs." Further, an "aspirated piece of marshmallow can be very difficult to dislodge. Because it continues to expand after entering the airway it can efficiently obstruct a large breathing passage. . . . An aspirated marshmallow fragment might not be reachable with a finger and could be difficult to dislodge with a Heimlich maneuver."

The trial court's summary judgment for defendant was reversed on appeal, 5–2. There were disputed issues of fact about whether parents would realize this danger without a warning. The dissenters asserted that if "marshmallows are unreasonably dangerous to eat without a warning, then so would be nearly every conceivable food item that a two-and-one-half-year-old child would try to eat; and I submit that children of that age will try to eat anything and everything. The possibility of a small child choking on nearly all food items is, or should be, a matter of common knowledge to all adults." How much did you know about marshmallows before reading this note? Might that be relevant in deciding the legal issue?

In Sheckells v. AGV–USA Corp., 987 F.2d 1532 (11th Cir.1993), a motorcyclist sued a helmet manufacturer over harm he sustained in an accident. The experts on both sides agreed that no helmet provided "any assurance of protecting the wearer from facial or brain injury at speeds of 30 to 45 miles an hour." Plaintiff's expert added that "the average buyer of a helmet would not know that." The court, applying Georgia law, concluded that a jury could find that a warning was required. Turning to the adequacy of what was stated, the court concluded that despite the manufacturer's inclusion of a general statement that helmets cannot protect against all foreseeable impacts, a jury might conclude that a more specific warning was required—especially in light of the fact that defendant did include a statement with the product that called the helmet "the single most important piece of safety equipment you own."

Allergy. A manufacturer ordinarily has no duty to change a product's design to guard against allergic reactions when the product's benefit to the public outweighs the harm it may cause to the idiosyncratic few. Liability for failure to warn may be imposed, however, where the number of allergic sufferers is substantial. Beyond that, where the potential for serious harm from the reaction is foreseeable, some courts have required warnings even where the reaction occurs in fewer than one in a million users. See generally, Henderson, Process Norms in Products Litigation: Liability for Allergic Reactions, 51 U.Pitt.L.Rev. 761 (1990).

Brown v. Superior Court (Abbott Laboratories)

Supreme Court of California, 1988.
44 Cal.3d 1049, 751 P.2d 470, 245 Cal.Rptr. 412.

■ MOSK, JUSTICE.

[The trial court ruled that defendants could be held liable for the alleged defect in DES "but only for their failure to warn of known or knowable side effects of the drug." It also held for defendants on separate market share and warranty questions. The court of appeal upheld the lower court's rulings. The supreme court granted review to examine the conclusions of the Court of Appeal and its potential conflict with Kearl v. Lederle Laboratories (1985) 172 C.A.3d 812, 218 Cal.Rptr. 453, on the issue of strict liability of a drug manufacturer for a defect in the design of a prescription drug.]

I.   Strict Liability

A.   Strict Liability in General

[The court reviewed the development of strict liability in California, from *Escola* through *Barker*. Note that this principal case was decided before *Soule*.]

B.   Strict Liability and Prescription Drugs

Even before *Greenman* was decided, the members of the American Law Institute, in considering whether to adopt a rule of strict liability, pondered whether the manufacturer of a prescription drug should be subject to the doctrine. [   ] During a rather confusing discussion of a draft of what was to become section 402A, a member of the institute proposed that drugs should be exempted from strict liability on the ground that it would be "against the public interest" to apply the doctrine to such products because of "the very serious tendency to stifle medical research and testing." Dean Prosser, who was the reporter for the Restatement Second of Torts, responded that the problem was a real one, and that he had it in mind in drafting section 402A. A motion to exempt prescription drugs from the section was defeated on the suggestion of Dean Prosser that the problem could be dealt with in the comments to the section. However, a motion to state the exemption in a comment was also defeated. [   ] At the next meeting of the institute in 1962, section 402A was approved together with comment *k* thereto. [   ]

chilling effect [handwritten margin note]

The comment provides that the producer of a properly manufactured prescription drug may be held liable for injuries caused by the product only if it was not accompanied by a warning of dangers that the manufacturer knew or should have known about. It declares:

comment K Important [handwritten margin note]

> *k*.   Unavoidably unsafe products. There are some products which, in the present state of human knowledge, are quite incapable of being made safe for their intended and ordinary use. These are especially common in the field of drugs. An outstanding example is the vaccine for the Pasteur treatment of rabies, which not uncommonly leads to very serious and damaging consequences when it is injected. Since the disease itself invariably leads to a dreadful death, both the marketing and use of the vaccine are fully justified, notwithstanding the unavoidable high degree of risk which they involve. Such a product, properly prepared, and accompanied by proper directions and warning, is not defective, nor is it unreasonably dangerous. The same is true of many other drugs, vaccines, and the like, many of which for this very reason cannot legally be sold except to physicians, or under the prescription of a physician. It is also true in particular of many new or experimental drugs as to which, because of lack of time and opportunity for sufficient medical experience, there can be no assurance of safety, or perhaps even of purity of ingredients, but such experience as there is justifies the marketing and use of the drug notwithstanding a medically recognizable risk. The seller of such products, again with the qualification that they are properly prepared and marketed, and proper warning is given, where the situation calls for it, is not to be held to strict liability for

unfortunate consequences attending their use, merely because he has undertaken to supply the public with an apparently useful and desirable product, attended with a known but apparently reasonable risk.

Comment *k* has been analyzed and criticized by numerous commentators. While there is some disagreement as to its scope and meaning, there is a general consensus that, although it purports to explain the strict liability doctrine, in fact the principle it states is based on negligence. [ ] That is, comment *k* would impose liability on a drug manufacturer only if it failed to warn of a defect of which it either knew or should have known. This concept focuses not on a deficiency in the product—the hallmark of strict liability—but on the fault of the producer in failing to warn of dangers inherent in the use of its product that were either known or knowable—an idea which "rings of negligence," in the words of *Cronin*, [ ].[4]

Comment *k* has been adopted in the overwhelming majority of jurisdictions that have considered the matter. [ ] In California, several decisions of the Courts of Appeal have embraced the comment *k* exemption [ ], but this court has never spoken to the issue.

. . .

We appear, then, to have three distinct choices: (1) to hold that the manufacturer of a prescription drug is strictly liable for a defect in its product because it was defectively designed, as that term is defined in *Barker*, or because of a failure to warn of its dangerous propensities even though such dangers were neither known nor scientifically knowable at the time of distribution;[8] (2) to determine that liability attaches only if a manufacturer fails to warn of dangerous propensities of which it was or should have been aware, in conformity with comment *k*; or (3) to decide, like *Kearl* and [another case], that strict liability for design defects should apply to prescription drugs unless the particular drug which caused the injury is found to be "unavoidably dangerous."

We shall conclude that (1) a drug manufacturer's liability for a defectively designed drug should not be measured by the standards of strict

---

4. The test stated in comment *k* is to be distinguished from strict liability for failure to warn. Although both concepts identify failure to warn as the basis of liability, comment *k* imposes liability only if the manufacturer knew or should have known of the defect at the time the product was sold or distributed. Under strict liability, the reason why the warning was not issued is irrelevant, and the manufacturer is liable even if it neither knew nor could have known of the defect about which the warning was required. Thus, comment *k*, by focussing on the blameworthiness of the manufacturer, sets forth a test which sounds in negligence, while imposition of liability for failure to warn without regard to the reason for such failure is consistent with strict liability since it asks only whether the product that caused injury contained a defect. [ ]

8. We agree with the suggestion of a commentator that a manufacturer's knowledge should be measured at the time a drug is distributed because it is at this point that the manufacturer relinquishes control of the product. (Wade, On the Effect in Product Liability of Knowledge Unavailable Prior to Marketing (1983) 58 N.Y.U.L.Rev. 734, 753–754.)

liability; (2) because of the public interest in the development, availability, and reasonable price of drugs, the appropriate test for determining responsibility is the test stated in comment k; and (3) for these same reasons of policy, we disapprove the holding of *Kearl* that only those prescription drugs found to be "unavoidably dangerous" should be measured by the comment k standard and that strict liability should apply to drugs that do not meet that description.

1. Design defect

Barker, as we have seen, set forth two alternative tests to measure a design defect. . . .

Defendants assert that neither of these tests is applicable to a prescription drug like DES. As to the "consumer expectation" standard, they claim, the "consumer" is not the plaintiff but the physician who prescribes the drug, and it is to him that the manufacturer's warnings are directed. A physician appreciates the fact that all prescription drugs involve inherent risks, known and unknown, and he does not expect that the drug is without such risks. We agree that the "consumer expectation" aspect of the *Barker* test is inappropriate to prescription drugs. While the "ordinary consumer" may have a reasonable expectation that a product such as a machine he purchases will operate safely when used as intended, a patient's expectations regarding the effects of such a drug are those related to him by his physician, to whom the manufacturer directs the warnings regarding the drug's properties.[9] The manufacturer cannot be held liable if it has provided appropriate warnings and the doctor fails in his duty to transmit these warnings to the patient or if the patient relies on inaccurate information from others regarding side effects of the drug.

The second test, which calls for the balancing of risks and benefits, is inapposite to prescription drugs, according to defendants, because it contemplates that a safer alternative design is feasible. While the defective equipment in *Barker* and other cases involving mechanical devices might be "redesigned" by the addition of safety devices, there is no possibility for an alternative design for a drug like DES, which is a scientific constant compounded in accordance with a required formula. [ ]

We agree with defendants that *Barker* contemplates a safer alternative design is possible, but we seriously doubt their claim that a drug like DES cannot be "redesigned" to make it safer. For example, plaintiff might be able to demonstrate at trial that a particular component of DES rendered it unsafe as a miscarriage preventative and that removal of that component would not have affected the efficacy of the drug. Even if the resulting product, without the damaging component, would bear a name other than DES, it would do no violence to semantics to view it as a "redesign" of DES.

9. It is well established that a manufacturer fulfills its duty to warn if it provides adequate warning to the physician. [ ]

Or plaintiff might be able to prove that other, less harmful drugs were available to prevent miscarriage; the benefit of such alternate drugs could be weighed against the advantages of DES in making the risk/benefit analysis of *Barker*. As the Court of Appeal observed, defendants' attempt to confine the issue to whether there is an "alternative design" for DES poses the problem in an "unreasonably narrow" fashion. [   ]

Of course, the fact that a drug with dangerous side effects may be characterized as containing a defect in design does not necessarily mean that its producer is to be held strictly liable for the defect. The determination of that issue depends on whether the public interest would be served by the imposition of such liability. As we have seen, the fundamental reasons underlying the imposition of strict liability are to deter manufacturers from marketing products that are unsafe, and to spread the cost of injury from the plaintiff to the consuming public, which will pay a higher price for the product to reflect the increased expense of insurance to the manufacturer resulting from its greater exposure to liability.

These reasons could justify application of the doctrine to the manufacturers of prescription drugs. It is indisputable, as plaintiff contends, that the risk of injury from such drugs is unavoidable, that a consumer may be helpless to protect himself from serious harm caused by them, and that, like other products, the cost of insuring against strict liability can be passed on by the producer to the consumer who buys the item. Moreover, as we observe below, in some cases additional testing of drugs before they are marketed might reveal dangerous side effects, resulting in a safer product.

But there is an important distinction between prescription drugs and other products such as construction machinery [   ], a lawnmower [   ], or perfume [   ], the producers of which were held strictly liable. In the latter cases, the product is used to make work easier or to provide pleasure, while in the former it may be necessary to alleviate pain and suffering or to sustain life. Moreover, unlike other important medical products (wheelchairs, for example), harm to some users from prescription drugs is unavoidable. Because of these distinctions, the broader public interest in the availability of drugs at an affordable price must be considered in deciding the appropriate standard of liability for injuries resulting from their use.

Perhaps a drug might be made safer if it was withheld from the market until scientific skill and knowledge advanced to the point at which additional dangerous side effects would be revealed. But in most cases such a delay in marketing new drugs—added to the delay required to obtain approval for release of the product from the Food and Drug Administration—would not serve the public welfare. Public policy favors the development and marketing of beneficial new drugs, even though some risks, perhaps serious ones, might accompany their introduction, because drugs can save lives and reduce pain and suffering.

If drug manufacturers were subject to strict liability, they might be reluctant to undertake research programs to develop some pharmaceuticals that would prove beneficial or to distribute others that are available to be marketed, because of the fear of large adverse monetary judgments. . . .

. . .

The possibility that the cost of insurance and of defending against lawsuits will diminish the availability and increase the price of pharmaceuticals is far from theoretical. Defendants cite a host of examples of products which have greatly increased in price or have been withdrawn or withheld from the market because of the fear that their producers would be held liable for large judgments.

For example, according to defendant E.R. Squibb & Sons, Inc., Bendectin, the only antinauseant drug available for pregnant women, was withdrawn from sale in 1983 because the cost of insurance almost equalled the entire income from sale of the drug. Before it was withdrawn, the price of Bendectin increased by over 300 percent. [ ]

Drug manufacturers refused to supply a newly discovered vaccine for influenza on the ground that mass inoculation would subject them to enormous liability. The government therefore assumed the risk of lawsuits resulting from injuries caused by the vaccine. [ ] One producer of diphtheria-tetanus-pertussis vaccine withdrew from the market, giving as its reason "extreme liability exposure, cost of litigation and the difficulty of continuing to obtain adequate insurance." [ ] There are only two manufacturers of the vaccine remaining in the market, and the cost of each dose rose a hundredfold from 11 cents in 1982 to $11.40 in 1986, $8 of which was for an insurance reserve. The price increase roughly paralleled an increase in the number of lawsuits from one in 1978 to 219 in 1985. [ ] Finally, a manufacturer was unable to market a new drug for the treatment of vision problems because it could not obtain adequate liability insurance at a reasonable cost. [ ]

There is no doubt that, from the public's standpoint, these are unfortunate consequences. And they occurred even though almost all jurisdictions follow the negligence standard of comment *k*. It is not unreasonable to conclude in these circumstances that the imposition of a harsher test for liability would not further the public interest in the development and availability of these important products.

We decline to hold, therefore, that a drug manufacturer's liability for injuries caused by the defective design of a prescription drug should be measured by the standard set forth in *Barker*.

2. Failure to warn

For these same reasons of policy, we reject plaintiff's assertion that a drug manufacturer should be held strictly liable for failure to warn of risks inherent in a drug even though it neither knew nor could have known by the application of scientific knowledge available at the time of distribution that the drug could produce the undesirable side effects suffered by the plaintiff.

*Majority rule:
duty to disclose
actual + constructive
knowledge of
risk at time
of sale*

Numerous cases have recognized that a product may be defective because of the absence of a warning that was necessary to allow its safe use. [ ]While some decisions apply strict liability principles to such a defect by holding that it is irrelevant whether the manufacturer knew of the danger or should have known of it [ ], most jurisdictions hold to the contrary. That is, liability is conditioned on the actual or constructive knowledge of the risk by the manufacturer as of the time the product was sold or distributed. [ ] This rule is consistent with comment *j* to section 402A, which confines the duty to warn to a situation in which the seller "has knowledge, or by the application of reasonable, developed human skill and foresight should have knowledge of . . . the danger."

. . .

3. The *Kearl* test

One further question remains in this aspect of the case. Comment *k*, as we have seen, provides that the maker of an "unavoidably unsafe" product is not liable for injuries resulting from its use if the product is "properly prepared, and accompanied by proper directions and warning." With the few exceptions noted above, the courts which have adopted comment *k* have viewed all prescription drugs as coming within its scope.

[*Kearl* adopted a three-part test to decide whether a drug came within comment *k*: the judge should take evidence out of the jury's presence on "(1) whether, when distributed, the product was intended to confer an exceptionally important benefit that made its availability highly desirable; (2) whether the then-existing risk posed by the product was both 'substantial' and 'unavoidable'; and (3) whether the interest in availability (again measured as of the time of distribution) outweighs the interest in promoting enhanced accountability through strict liability design defect review." An affirmative answer led to application of comment *k*. Although the *Brown* court saw good reason not to "grant the same protection from liability to those who gave us thalidomide as to the producers of penicillin," it rejected *Kearl* because it necessarily discouraged development of new drugs. The three-part test gave "a drug manufacturer no assurance that a product he places on the market will be measured by the liability standard of comment *k* because" the trial judge might not find the drug's benefits to be "exceptionally important" or that its availability was "highly desirable." The manufacturer had to know the liability standard before distribution. The court was also concerned that different trial judges might reach different conclusions about the same drug, and that in the same case a judge's determination on this question might differ from that of the jury when it used risk-benefit factors in deciding the "defect" question.]

*Held ↑
for
majority*

In conclusion, and in accord with almost all our sister states that have considered the issue, we hold that a manufacturer is not strictly liable for injuries caused by a prescription drug so long as the drug was properly prepared and accompanied by warnings of its dangerous propensities that were either known or reasonably scientifically knowable at the time of distribution.[12]

[The court then concluded on the other issues that actions for fraud were not available under the market share approach because states of mind of particular manufacturers would have to be shown, and that allowing a warranty claim would be "inconsistent with our determination on the issue of strict liability for design defects."].

The judgment of the Court of Appeal is affirmed.

■ LUCAS, C.J., and BROUSSARD, PANELLI, ARGUELLES, EAGLESON and KAUFMAN, JJ., concur.

NOTES AND QUESTIONS

1. What does the court regard as the appropriate standard for prescription drugs? What does comment *k* add? (Note the court's ruling that any obligation to warn involves reaching the prescribing physician.)

2. What arguments might be made in favor of the *Kearl* approach? Against it? As the court notes, virtually no court has imposed "real" strict liability, as spelled out in the court's footnote 4, where prescription drugs are concerned. In light of this fact what is the significance of the vast increase in vaccine and drug prices recounted in *Brown*?

3. In Tansy v. Dacomed Corp., 890 P.2d 881 (Okla.1994), plaintiff's penile implant failed due to fatigue when metal parts rubbed against each other. The failure caused minor harm to plaintiff's penis and required the implant's surgical removal. The accompanying literature reported a failure rate of 3.7 to 6 percent, far lower than that of the previous generation of implants whose failure rates ran as high as 40 percent. Defendant's implant model was unique in its capability to "impart rigidity or flaccidity on demand." Plaintiff's claim was based on the failure to use stronger metal cables. This was technologically possible but defendant presented evidence that the result with heavier metal cables was deemed "unsatisfactory because it decreased the ability of the penis to appear flaccid."

Plaintiff, appealing from an adverse jury verdict and judgment, attacked the judge's charge that the product was not unreasonably dangerous if it was unavoidably unsafe as long as it was marketed with proper directions and warnings of dangers. The charge was upheld on appeal. In accord with virtually all courts, this court held that comment *k* was applicable to prescription medical devices as well as to drugs. Also, it applied to both alleged defects as well as to "side effects." Should

---

12. Our conclusion does not mean, of course, that drug manufacturers are free of all liability for defective drugs. They are subject to liability for manufacturing defects, as well as under general principles of negligence, and for failure to warn of known or reasonably knowable side effects. It should also be noted that the consumers of prescription drugs are afforded greater protection against defects than consumers of other products, since "the drug industry is closely regulated by the Food and Drug Administration, which actively controls the testing and manufacture of drugs and the method by which they are marketed, including the contents of warning labels." [*Sindell*]

defendant have been obligated to market the model with stronger cables to give consumers a choice? Should any warning in this type of case have to be given to the patient? Reconsider the discussion of the "learned intermediary," p. 528, supra.

4. *The New Jersey experience.* Should the *Brown* court's approach to the question of unknown and scientifically unknowable risks on prescription drugs apply also to other products? Consider the pair of important cases from New Jersey addressing this issue.

In Beshada v. Johns–Manville Products Corp., 90 N.J. 191, 447 A.2d 539 (1982), workers injured by handling asbestos products before 1960 sued the manufacturers of asbestos. Defendants argued that the medical profession did not recognize these particular health hazards from asbestos until the 1960s. Plaintiffs responded that, even if true, this fact was no defense to a strict liability claim. The court agreed: "Strict liability focuses on the product, not the fault of the manufacturer."

This result was said to be consistent with the three main reasons the court had adopted strict liability—risk spreading, accident avoidance, and reducing administrative costs by avoiding "complicated, costly, confusing and time-consuming" trials about the distant past. On the second point, the court asserted that the " 'state of the art' at a given time is partly determined by how much industry invests in safety research. By imposing on manufacturers the costs of failure to discover hazards, we create an incentive for them to invest more actively in safety research." In addition, "fairness" suggested that "manufacturers not be excused from liability because their prior inadequate investment in safety rendered the hazards of their product unknowable."

In Feldman v. Lederle Laboratories, 97 N.J. 429, 479 A.2d 374 (1984), the court reversed course. Plaintiff's teeth were discolored by a drug that was prescribed for respiratory infections. No warning was given about this side effect until late in the course of the plaintiff's use of the product. Defendant claimed that the danger had only then become apparent and could not have been warned about earlier. The court noted that once knowledge of danger is imputed to a supplier "strict liability analysis becomes almost identical to negligence analysis in its focus on the reasonableness of the defendant's conduct." The issue was the imputation. The court concluded that as to design and warning questions, "generally conduct should be measured by knowledge at the time the manufacturer distributed the product." The courts should ask when the manufacturer had "actual or constructive knowledge of the danger." In making this determination the manufacturer should be "held to the standard of an expert in the field." This implied the "notion that at least in some fields, such as those impacting on public health, a manufacturer may be expected to be informed and affirmatively to seek out information concerning the public's use of its own product." The court's focus, however, appeared to be on singling out asbestos for distinctive treatment rather than setting out a special protection for prescription drugs:

Many commentators have criticized this [knowledge-is-irrelevant] aspect of the *Beshada* reasoning and the public policies on which it is based. [ ] The rationale of *Beshada* is not applicable to this case. We do not overrule *Beshada,* but restrict *Beshada* to the circumstances giving rise to its holding. . . . We note, in passing, that, although not argued and determined in *Beshada,* there were or may have been data and other information generally available, aside from scientific knowledge, that arguably could have alerted the manufacturer at an early stage in the distribution of its product to the dangers associated with its use.

The *Feldman* court did, however, shift the burden of proof to the defendant on the question whether and when the relevant technical information became available:

> The defendant is in a superior position to know the technological material or data in the particular field or specialty. The defendant is the expert, often performing self-testing. It is the defendant that injected the product in the stream of commerce for its economic gain. As a matter of policy the burden of proving the status of knowledge in the field at the time of distribution is properly placed on the defendant.

D. is better position to know info

Does the shift in the burden of proof and the emphasis on the defendant as "an expert in the field" undermine any practical difference between *Beshada* and *Feldman*? See generally, Rabin, Indeterminate Risk and Tort Reform, 14 J.Legal Studies 633 (1985). Is the *Feldman* court's ruling applicable only to prescription drugs or is it applicable to all products except asbestos?

5. *Beyond drugs in California.* Although *Brown* dealt only with prescription drugs it necessarily raised the issue of other products as well. Recall that *Brown* suggested that if the court were going to adopt strict liability (as it implied it would for at least some other products), it would judge defectiveness as of the time the product was distributed—see the court's footnote 8, referring to Professor Wade's view. Why is that the right time for judging defectiveness, rather than the time of injury or the time of trial? If a product is distributed at a time when all the experts think it entirely safe, but injury reports suddenly begin coming in shortly after distribution, should the first victims win?

The California court addressed this question in Anderson v. Owens–Corning Fiberglas Corp., 53 Cal.3d 987, 810 P.2d 549, 281 Cal.Rptr. 528 (1991), involving asbestos, in which it asserted that it was applying strict liability:

> [A] reasonably prudent manufacturer might reasonably decide that the risk of harm was such as not to require a warning as, for example, if the manufacturer's own testing showed a result contrary to that of others in the scientific community. Such a manufacturer might escape liability under negligence principles. In contrast, under strict liability principles the manufacturer has no such leeway; the manufacturer is liable if it failed to give warning of dangers that were known to the

scientific community at the time it manufactured or distributed the product. Whatever may be reasonable from the point of view of the manufacturer, the user of the product must be given the option either to refrain from using the product at all or to use it in such a way as to minimize the degree of danger.

Is this likely to be a meaningful distinction? Some of the confusion between negligence and strict liability may be traceable to the use of "state of the art" by many courts. In fact, the term's meaning has varied greatly. As stated at page 88 of Tent.Draft No.2 (1995) of the Third Restatement:

> The term "state-of-the-art" has been variously defined by a multitude of courts. For some it refers to industry custom or industry practice; for others it means the safest existing technology that has been adopted for use; for others it means cutting edge technology.

Consider these meanings of "state of the art" in a situation in which the evidence shows that in the months before a product with an unknown risk is marketed in this country, a small company in Finland had discovered that risk and, without public announcement, had begun preparing a new product that avoided the risk. What if a few months before defendant's product was marketed, the risk had first been reported in a Finnish scientific journal? Should "negligence principles" and "strict liability principles" lead to different results in these cases?

The *Anderson* court asserted that its conclusion accorded with the "considerations of policy that underlie the doctrine of strict liability." Although it recognized that "an important goal of strict liability is to spread the risks and costs of injury to those most able to bear them . . . it was never the intention of the drafters of the doctrine to make the manufacturer or distributor the insurer of the safety of their products. It was never their intention to impose absolute liability." In this passage the court inserted the following footnote:

> 14. The suggestion that losses arising from unknowable risks and hazards should be spread among all users of the product, as are losses from predictable injuries or negligent conduct, is generally regarded as not feasible. Not the least of the problems is insurability. ([ ]; Wade, On the Effect in Product Liability of Knowledge Unavailable Prior to Marketing (1983) 58 N.Y.U.L.Rev. 734.) Dean Wade stated the dilemma, but provided no solution: "How does one spread the potential loss of an unknowable hazard? How can insurance premiums be figured for this purpose? Indeed, will insurance be available at all? Spreading the loss is essentially a compensation device rather than a tort concept. Providing compensation should not be the sole basis for imposing tort liability, and this seems more emphatically so in the situation where the defendant is no more able to insure against unknown risks than is the plaintiff." [ ]

As a result of *Anderson* and *Brown*, are prescription drugs being treated differently from other products on the question of unknown dangers?

In *Anderson*, the court observed that its ruling was limited to questions of warning:

> [W]hile a manufacturing or design defect can be evaluated without reference to the conduct of the manufacturer [ ], the giving of a warning cannot. The latter necessarily requires the communicating of something to someone. How can one warn of something that is unknowable? If every product that has no warning were defective per se and for that reason subject to strict liability, the mere fact of injury by an unlabelled product would automatically permit recovery. That is not, and has never been, the purpose and goal of the failure-to-warn theory of strict liability.

Has it been the "purpose and goal" of manufacturing defect theory? Of design defect theory?

On the question of unknown and scientifically unknowable risks, should there be a different analytical framework for claims based on design defect as opposed to those based on failure to warn?

6. *The special case of asbestos.* It is ironic that the crucial cases that have not involved prescription drugs *have* involved asbestos. The defendants in *Beshada* and in *Anderson* asserted that they had no knowledge of danger at the time the plaintiff in question was hurt. This position is still asserted. See *Morton*, p. 502, supra. Yet, during this period, other courts were finding that the behavior of the asbestos defendants was so egregious that most courts were allowing juries to award massive punitive damage awards. See the discussion of punitive awards in asbestos cases in the *Fischer* case, reported at p. 658, infra.

Indeed, as *Feldman* suggests, the assumption underlying *Beshada* was suspect from the beginning. See generally, P. Brodeur, Outrageous Misconduct: The Asbestos Industry on Trial (1985). Although *Feldman* involved prescription drugs, the court's approach was one of distinguishing asbestos from all other products, including prescription drugs.

7. Very few courts have followed *Beshada* in cases in which the facts did not show that defendant had a basis for knowing about the danger. One is Johnson v. Raybestos–Manhattan, Inc., 69 Hawaii 287, 740 P.2d 548 (1987), an asbestos case, in which the court answered a certified question from the federal court by asserting that in a strict products liability action "the issue of whether the seller knew or reasonably should have known of the dangers inherent in his or her product is irrelevant to the issue of liability." It followed that "in a strict products liability action, state-of-the-art evidence is not admissible for the purpose of establishing whether the seller knew or reasonably should have known of the dangerousness of his or her product."

The court rejected the defendants' argument that this approach made it "absolutely" liable for all harm caused by the product. "The defendants are not liable for any harm caused by their products unless the plaintiff shows that the product is dangerously defective, i.e., that it does not meet the reasonable expectations of the ordinary consumer or user as to its safety." In the case of a danger proven to have been beyond the ability of well-informed industry experts to anticipate, can plaintiff possibly fail to satisfy the consumer expectations test as to defect? Does that mean the plaintiff should win the case?

8. *Discovery of danger after distribution.* Whether or not defendants are liable for the first totally unexpected injuries that occur after their product is marketed, what is their obligation when the first hint of trouble does appear?

Consider Patton v. Hutchinson Wil–Rich Manufacturing Co., 253 Kan. 741, 861 P.2d 1299 (1993), in which a large farm cultivator was discovered to present the totally unexpected danger of a failing part after it was marketed. The machine that injured plaintiff was bought from an HWR dealer in 1977 and the injury occurred in 1987. The court summarized the situation as follows:

> These accidents appear to have occurred as early as 1983. HWR was aware of these accidents. Patton admits that prior to 1977, HWR had no notice of accidents involving cultivator wings falling when the mechanical lock pin on the wing was removed. A secondary safety latch which was developed in 1983 by Deere & Company, one of HWR's competitors, was unknown to cultivator manufacturers in 1976. Similarly, the other safety devices which Patton alleges should have been on the cultivator were unknown in the industry in 1976. Deere & Company instituted a mandatory safety improvement program for [this type of cultivator] in October, 1983. The Deere retrofit program became known to John Kehrwald, Vice President of Engineering and Manufacturing at HWR, at some point four or five years after it was initiated. Kehrwald recognized his company had problems with the cultivator wings in 1983. Kerhwald indicated that he believed it was an acceptable risk to choose not to retrofit the HWR cultivators.

The federal court asked whether on these facts (1) Kansas recognized a continuing duty on manufacturers to warn ultimate consumers through retailers who have continuing contact with the consumers, (2) whether Kansas recognized a continuing duty on manufacturers to warn ultimate consumers directly, (3) whether Kansas imposed a duty to retrofit, and (4) whether Kansas imposed a duty to recall the product.

Plaintiff asserted that these obligations were owed when a product was dangerous when made even though the danger was not recognized at that time. Plaintiff did *not* argue that a manufacturer whose product contained a known danger but whose product was nonetheless considered "safe at the time of manufacture, under then current standards, must later warn prior purchasers when safety standards are upgraded." Is this distinction clear? Tenable?

As to the first two questions, the Kansas court concluded "a qualified yes." The court concluded that negligence was the appropriate standard to use in post-sale cases. Where a more effective safety device becomes available, the court agreed with plaintiff's implied concession that no duty arose to "seek out past customers and notify them of changes in the state of the art." The court reviewed various state positions in cases in which the danger was discovered only after sale. Some recognized a full duty; others only with consumer goods. This court decided to impose a duty to warn ultimate consumers "who can be readily identified or traced when a defect, which originated at the time the product was manufactured and was unforeseeable at the point of sale, is discovered to present a life threatening hazard."

The Kansas court quoted approvingly from another court that had imposed such a duty in a case involving a sausage stuffing machine but warned that it would not do so generally:

> A sausage stuffer and the nature of that industry bears no similarity to the realities of manufacturing and marketing household goods such as fans, snowblowers or lawn mowers which have become increasingly hazard proof with each succeeding model. It is beyond reason and good judgment to hold a manufacturer responsible for a duty of annually warning of safety hazards on household items, mass produced and used in every American home, when the product is 6 to 35 years old and outdated by some 20 newer models equipped with every imaginable safety innovation known in the state of the art.

The Kansas court listed eight factors (at a minimum) to be considered on the duty question: (1) the nature of the harm that may result without notice; (2) the likelihood that harm will occur; (3) how many persons are affected; (4) the economic burden on the manufacturer of giving notice; (5) the nature of the industry; (6) the type of product involved; (7) the number of units manufactured or sold; and (8) steps taken to correct the problem other than giving notice. These factors will also address the question of whether the notice should be given directly to consumers or indirectly through retailers.

[handwritten margin note: 8 factors for duty to warn to consumers? or to retailers?]

Finally, the court rejected any duty to retrofit or to recall on these facts. Recalls were "properly the business of administrative agencies as suggested by the federal statutes that expressly delegate recall authority." These institutions "are better able to weigh the benefits and costs involved in locating, recalling, and retrofitting products." Do you agree? Compare the responses of Deere & Company and of HWR to the discovery of this danger. Who is to pay in a recall or retrofit situation? Does *Patton* seem a sensible resolution of the post-sale problem? See also Gregory v. Cincinnati Inc., 450 Mich. 1, 538 N.W.2d 325 (1995), in which a split court addresses this same set of questions.

How different is this question from the case of a physician who acts reasonably at the time, but later discovers that the conduct created an unexpected danger to the patient, p. 122, supra?

9. *The known danger of the generic product.* One nagging issue has involved products whose dangers are known and often great, but for which there are no ready substitutes. The case that sharpened this issue was O'Brien v. Muskin, 94 N.J. 169, 463 A.2d 298 (1983), involving an above-ground swimming pool that was properly filled with 3½ feet of water. "At one point, the outer wall of the pool bore the logo of the manufacturer, and below it a decal that warned 'DO NOT DIVE' in letters roughly one-half inch high." The plaintiff, an uninvited visitor, dove into the pool. As his outstretched hands hit the vinyl-lined pool bottom they slid apart because of the slipperiness of the vinyl. Plaintiff struck his head on the bottom, sustaining serious injuries. The trial judge refused to submit a claim of design defect, but did submit to the jury the adequacy of the warning. The jury found against the plaintiff. The supreme court ordered a new trial:

> The assessment of the utility of a design involves the consideration of available alternatives. If no alternatives are available, recourse to a unique design is more defensible.   .   .   .
>
> The evaluation of the utility of a product also involves the relative need for that product; some products are essentials, while others are luxuries. A product that fills a critical need and can be designed only one way should be viewed differently from a luxury item. Still other products, including some for which no alternative exists, are so danger-ous and of such little use that under the risk-utility analysis, a manufacturer would bear the cost of liability of harm to others. That cost might dissuade a manufacturer from placing the product on the market, even if the product has been made as safely as possible. Indeed, plaintiff contends that above-ground pools with vinyl liners are such products and that manufacturers who market those pools should bear the cost of injuries they cause to foreseeable users.
>
>   .   .   .   The trial judge should have permitted the jury to consider whether, because of the dimensions of the pool and slipperiness of the bottom, the risks of injury so outweighed the utility of the product as to constitute a defect.   .   .   .   Viewing the evidence in the light most favorable to plaintiff, even if there are no alternative methods of making bottoms for above-ground pools, the jury might have found that the risk posed by the pool outweighed its utility.
>
> [In developing the risk-utility analysis] the plaintiff might seek to establish that pools are marketed primarily for recreational, not thera-peutic purposes; that because of their design, including their configu-ration, inadequate warnings, and the use of vinyl liners, injury is likely; that, without impairing the usefulness of the pool or pricing it out of the market, warnings against diving could be made more prominent and a liner less dangerous.

Is the court casting doubt on the jury's conclusion that the warning was adequate? The majority then turned to emphasize a main difference between them and the dissenter:

> [The dissenter] would find that no matter how dangerous a product may be, if it bears an adequate warning, it is free from design defects if there is no known alternative. Under that hypothesis, manufacturers, merely by placing warnings on their products, could insulate them-selves from liability regardless of the number of people those products

[Handwritten margin note: Court sees a difference in essential products and luxury products; risk-utility analysis might dissuade marketing]

maim or kill. By contrast, the majority concludes that the judicial, not the commercial, system is the appropriate forum for determining whether a product is defective, with the resultant imposition of strict liability upon those in the commercial chain.

What does "defective" mean in this context? What analysis if, after several years of warnings that all reasonable people recognize as more than adequate in substance, size and placement, ten people per year in New Jersey still dive into these pools and are paralyzed? Recall the *Dreisonstok* case, p. 511, supra, in which the court refused to compare the microbus design with that of dissimilar—safer—vehicles. Is that case inconsistent with *O'Brien*?

What if 1,000 people accidentally cut themselves badly on sharp knives in New Jersey each year? In the *Barker* case, p. 494, supra, the court noted that it need not consider "whether a product that entails a substantial risk of harm may be found defective even if no safer alternative design is feasible." It cited a law review article in which Justice Traynor suggested liability might be imposed for products "whose norm is danger." Reconsider Judge Cardozo's analysis of the "Flopper," p. 413, supra. What about a baseball stadium in which the proprietor refuses to use any screens and fully warns all customers of the dangers before selling tickets in sections that had traditionally been screened?

Other states have rejected the analysis in *O'Brien* as a matter of common law. In Baughn v. Honda Motor Co., Ltd., 107 Wash.2d 127, 727 P.2d 655 (1986), for example, the court held that a manufacturer of "minitrail bikes" could not be held liable for injuries suffered when the bikes were used on public roads in disregard of explicit warnings against such usage. Plaintiff relied on *O'Brien* for the proposition that the case should go to the jury to weigh the risk and utility of the bikes. The court insisted that the product was not defective as a matter of law when its warnings (which were found adequate) were followed.

How should the case be analyzed if it appears that the warning against use on public roads is disregarded by 20 percent of all users, most of whom get hurt in road accidents? Is this like the case of the "Do Not Dive" warning in the pool case?

In New Jersey the legislature sought to restrict *O'Brien* by providing that there is no liability when there is no "practical and technically feasible alternative design that would have prevented the harm without substantially impairing the reasonably anticipated or intended function of the product." An exception was created where the court found by "clear and convincing evidence" that "(1) the product is egregiously unsafe or ultrahazardous; (2) the ordinary user or consumer of the product cannot reasonably be expected to have knowledge of the product's risks, or the product poses a risk of serious injury to persons other than the user or consumer; and (3) the product has little or no usefulness." N.J.S.A. 2A:58C–3.

See the discussion of the statute in Dewey v. R.J.Reynolds Tobacco Co., 121 N.J. 69, 577 A.2d 1239 (1990), noting that the statute overturned as much of *O'Brien* and another case "as endorsed the application of the 'risk-utility' analysis when a plaintiff is unable to establish a defect under the 'consumer expectations' text." It was no longer possible in New Jersey to avoid the consumer expectations test in design defect cases. A related change affected the notion of "obvious danger." Under cases like *O'Brien* the obviousness of the danger had been one factor among many in determining whether a defect existed. After the statute it was a "defense, except in instances involving industrial machinery or other workplace equipment."

The issue has recurred during the drafting of the new Restatement. As we have seen, p. 491, supra, the drafters had proposed that to prevail in a design defect case, the plaintiff had to present a "reasonable alternative design" for the product that was alleged to be defective. During early debates, and over the objections of the drafters, a provision was inserted to permit liability without such a showing in cases in which the value of the product at issue is deemed to be minimal. These were identified as generic products whose designs are "manifestly unreasonable, in that they have low social utility and high degree of danger." § 2, comm. *d* (Tent.Draft No. 2, 1995). Would that apply to above-ground pools? All-terrain vehicles? "Saturday Night Specials"?

See generally, Bogus, War on the Common Law: The Struggle at the Center of Products Liability, 60 Mo.L.Rev. 1 (1995).

E. BEYOND PRODUCTS?

Hoven v. Kelble

Supreme Court of Wisconsin, 1977.
79 Wis.2d 444, 256 N.W.2d 379.

[Plaintiff husband suffered cardiac arrest while undergoing a lung biopsy. The surgeon, the anesthesiologist, and the hospital were sued for negligence and strict liability. The trial judge sustained demurrers to the strict liability claims, which had alleged that the services rendered by each defendant were "defective when so rendered."]

■ ABRAHAMSON, J.

.   .   .

Plaintiffs' "strict liability" causes of action are modeled after the requirements of Dippel v. Sciano, 37 Wis.2d 443, 155 N.W.2d 55 (1967), in which this court adopted in products liability cases the rule of strict liability in tort set forth in Restatement of the Law, Torts 2d, sec. 402A.   .   .   .

Application of this standard of liability to the rendition of medical services of course would require that some definition of a "defective" medical service be formulated. Plaintiff's briefs suggest that a suitable and acceptable governing principle is the "reasonable expectations of the consumer," as described by Greenfield in Consumer Protection in Service Transactions—Implied Warranties and Strict Liability in Tort, 1974 Utah L.Rev. 661.

Greenfield attacks the goods/services distinction and advocates strict liability for both. He asserts that the measure of a defective service should be the reasonable expectation of the consumer, breaking service transactions into three parts and applying the test to each: (1) analysis to ascertain the cause of the problem; (2) selection or fabrication of a solution; and (3) application of the solution. The basic idea of Greenfield's test is possibility—unless attainment of the solution or goal is impossible, expecting it to be attained is reasonable, and nonattainment results in liability. Id. at 698. The author illustrates the operation of his theory by the following discussion of its application to the medical profession:

"With respect to the first component of services, analysis of the problem to ascertain its cause, a doctor would not be liable for erroneously diagnosing a patient's ailment if the cause of the ailment is incapable of being ascertained under the present state of knowledge in the profession. If, however, the disease is capable of correct diagnosis, even though it is extremely rare and typically overlooked or misdiagnosed, then the doctor would be strictly liable. If the cause *can* be determined, then the consumer's expectation that it *will* be determined is reasonable. As a practical matter, the rarer the disease, the less frequently the doctor will be exposed to the risk of misdiagnosing it. The more common the disease, the likelier it is that the doctor will have been negligent in failing to diagnose it correctly, in which event he is liable under present law. So, on the one hand, the increase in the liability of the doctor would not seem to be substantial, and, on the other hand, those patients injured by the doctor's error would receive compensation.

"Applied to the second component of services, selection of solution to the problem, the doctrine of strict liability would impose liability for injuries caused by the selection of a wrong course of treatment. The injury could take the form either of a deterioration of the patient's health or of a failure to cure him. There may be some resistance to the idea that a doctor is liable for mere failure to cure. If, however, the physician fails to select a known treatment for a particular illness, there is no reason why strict liability should not apply. The existence of a known cure for the ailment makes reasonable the consumer's expectation that it will be selected and applied in his case, and the doctor's failure to select the proper treatment is a defect in the services. On the other hand, if there is no known cure for the ailment, or if the cure is not generally available to members of the profession, the doctor would not be held liable for his selection of a treatment that fails to cure it.   The consumer, however, may reasonably expect that a course of treatment selected and administered by a person in the business of providing relief from physical ailments will effect a cure in his particular case.   Therefore, the physician's non-liability when there is no known or generally available treatment should be subject to the requirement that the doctor fully inform the patient that there is no known cure and that the proposed course of treatment may not actually provide a cure.   In the absence of this disclosure, the doctor's services should be viewed as defective, even though there is no known cure.

"With respect to the third component of services, application of the solution, the doctrine of strict liability would impose liability on a doctor who, for example, erroneously injects into a muscle a drug that is supposed to be injected into subcutaneous tissue. Strict liability is especially appropriate for mechanical tasks, which are typically so easily done correctly."   Id. at 699, 700.

At oral argument plaintiffs' counsel appeared to advocate a somewhat more restricted test than Greenfield's.   Nevertheless, the essence of plaintiffs' position appears to be that if a plaintiff could show that a hypothetical virtually perfectly informed doctor, working in a perfectly equipped hospital, could have avoided the untoward result, the plaintiff could recover, notwithstanding that the defendants exercised reasonable care in all respects.   If attainment of the goal, or avoidance of the maloccurrence is possible, then failure to attain the goal or to avoid the maloccurrence renders the service defective.

This court has stated in respect to products that the doctrine of strict liability does not make the seller an insurer.   [   ] Plaintiffs in the case at bar recognize this and deny that the theory they advocate would have any such effect.   Under plaintiffs' theory if there is no known cure the plaintiffs would not recover.   However, it is apparent that adoption of the plaintiffs' theory of liability, which we have discussed above, would set the standard of performance for the entire medical profession at the zenith of that profession's achievement, a level at which by definition virtually no one could perform all the time.   That which might possibly have been done would be required, or liability would result, and inevitably, the matter would be judged with the acuity of vision which hindsight provides.

.   .   .

To date this court has not applied the *Dippel* test of strict liability beyond the context of damages resulting from the sale of a defective and unreasonably dangerous product.   Other courts have, however, extended the doctrine of strict liability to transactions which did not involve a sale of goods but which were found analogous to the sale of goods.   For example, the doctrine has been extended to chattel lease transactions and to the sale or use of buildings.   A number of decisions in other jurisdictions have allowed recovery on the basis of strict liability (or the closely related doctrine of implied warranty) where the injury was due to a defective product supplied or used in the course of rendering a service to the plaintiff. Several cases have allowed recovery on the basis of strict liability or implied warranty where "defective services" have been rendered, but these services have been of a relatively routine or simple nature. Where "professional" services are in issue the cases uniformly require that negligence be shown.[12] We have found no decision of any court applying strict liability to the rendition of professional medical services.

. . .

Two . . . decisions on which plaintiffs rely can also be distinguished from the case at bar. Newmark v. Gimbel's, Inc., 54 N.J. 585, 258 A.2d 697 (1969), which applied strict liability to services rendered by a beauty parlor operator in applying permanent wave solution to a customer, differentiated the services involved in that case from the services of a doctor or a dentist. The court concluded that the policy considerations favoring strict liability applied with diminished force in the context of professional services and were outweighed by the need for free availability of the essential services the medical profession supplies. Again in Broyles v. Brown Engineering Co., 275 Ala. 35, 151 So.2d 767 (1963), the court discussed why implied warranties of a particular result, while imposed in that case on defendants submitting defective drainage plans, are not imposed upon doctors, lawyers and architects, among others.

. . .

. . . [I]t may be admitted that many of the justifications for strict liability have force regarding professional medical services.

The provider of medical services appears to stand in substantially the same position with respect to the patient as the seller of goods does with the consumer. The typical purchaser of medical services cannot evaluate

12. . . . See also . . . Magrine v. Krasnica, 94 N.J.Super. 228, 227 A.2d 539 (Law Div.1967), aff'd sub nom. Magrine v. Spector, 100 N.J.Super. 223, 241 A.2d 637 (App.Div.1968), aff'd 53 N.J. 259, 250 A.2d 129 (1969)(plaintiff could not recover against his dentist on a strict liability theory for injuries suffered when a hypodermic needle being used to inject a local anesthetic snapped off, due to no fault of the dentist, while in the plaintiff's jaw); [ ].

Professor Kalven comments on the present expansion of products liability from its historic connection with warranty and the consumer to a broader doctrine, no longer associated with a *product* but with an enterprise.

"The idea of enterprise liability has been in the wind for years, originally in an effort to explain the doctrines of agency. On this view what is important is that the defendant is an enterprise, that is, *systematically* engaged in generating the risks, *and* has access to the mechanism of *the market*. The first characteristic is thought to make him a good target for the deterrence of the tort sanction, liability is imposed in the quest for safety and accident prevention; the second characteristic is thought to make him a superior risk-bearer able to pass on the loss into channels of wide distribution. There is undoubted power in these policy notions and this is not the place to debate them seriously. We would merely note that the premises now have considerable reach, and if we are serious about enterprise liability, a good part of contemporary tort law will need to be revised accordingly, and very little of its once spacious domain is likely to be left to the negligence principle." Kalven, Tort Law–Tort Watch, 34 J. of Am.Trial Lawyers, 1, 57 (1972).

the quality of care offered because medical services are complex and infrequently bought. The medical care market gives the purchaser little assistance in enabling the purchaser to evaluate what he or she is buying. It is generally the physician—not the patient—who determines the kind of services to be rendered and how often. It is the physician not the patient who prescribes other goods and services, e.g., drugs, therapy, and hospitalization, that should supplement the physician's services. The physician is in a better position than the patient to determine and improve the quality of the services, and the patient's reliance on the doctor's skill, care and reputation is perhaps greater than the reliance of the consumer of goods. The difficulties faced by plaintiffs in carrying the burden of proving negligence on the part of a doctor are well known. [   ] The hospital and doctor are in a better position than the patient to bear and distribute the risk of loss.[16]

However, other considerations call for caution in moving in the direction the plaintiffs advocate. There are differences between the rendition of medical services and transactions in goods (or perhaps other types of services as well). Medical and many other professional services tend often to be experimental in nature, dependent on factors beyond the control of the professional, and devoid of certainty or assurance of results. Medical services are an absolute necessity to society, and they must be readily available to the people. It is said that strict liability will inevitably increase the cost for medical services, which might make them beyond the means of many consumers, and that imposition of strict liability might hamper progress in developing new medicines and medical techniques.[17]

It is true that concepts of tort liability have expanded in recent years. . . . However, before a change in the law is made, a court, if it is to act responsibly, must be able to foresee with reasonable clarity the results of its decision and to say with reasonable certainty that the change will serve the best interests of society.

. . .

. . . Several commentators have proposed "no-fault liability" in lieu of negligence or strict-liability concepts. The ability of the judicial system to create a scheme of strict liability or no-fault liability rules for medical accidents has been questioned. Because of the unknown costs and the

---

16. Malpractice insurance is already costly, however, and the increased costs of insurance, if any, if strict liability were imposed, are unknown. The availability of insurance is one factor justifying the imposition of strict liability.

17. " . . . These arguments, however, are not fully persuasive. First, the production and sale of food and drugs, which are as essential as medical services, are subject to strict liability doctrine. Secondly, special treatment for doctors because of the essential nature of their services can be justi-

fied only if the imposition of strict liability would either make doctors unwilling to provide the same range of services they now provide or cause such an increase in the cost of medical services that people now seeking medical services would be deterred from seeking them. Neither assumption has been demonstrated to be true, and it is doubtful whether either assumption has proven true with respect to essential (or even nonessential) goods." Greenfield, supra note 14, at p. 687.

inability to assess the results, commentators have shied away from advocating the adoption of full programs of strict liability or no-fault liability in the medical service area and have suggested that the legislature and private groups establish experimental and elective techniques to deal with injuries occurring from medical services.   .   .   .

We have no doubt that concepts of tort liability will continue to change and that service industries including the medical profession may be affected by such change.   However, at this time the consequences of the step the plaintiffs urge cannot be predicted with sufficient clarity to permit that step to be taken.

By the Court.—Order affirmed.

NOTES AND QUESTIONS

1.   Which of the justifications for strict liability apply most strongly in this case? Which are the weakest?

2.   What is the underlying basis for Professor Greenfield's approach?

3.   Under his approach what would keep the defendants from becoming insurers?

4.   In Murphy v. E.R. Squibb & Sons, Inc., 40 Cal.3d 672, 710 P.2d 247, 221 Cal.Rptr. 447 (1985), the court, 4–3, rejected a strict liability action against a pharmacist who filled prescriptions for DES. The court had already concluded that doctors who prescribed the drug were not strictly liable: "the doctor prescribed the medication only as an aid to effect a cure and was not in the business of selling the drug." Here, plaintiff asserted that the pharmacist simply reads a prescription, fills the container with the proper dosage, types the label, attaches it to the container, and exchanges the container for payment. The plaintiff concluded that a pharmacist was the functional equivalent of "an experienced clerk at a hardware store." The defense stressed the professional aspects of pharmacists.

The plurality expressed concern that if strict liability were imposed, some pharmacists would refuse to stock drugs that carried even remote risks. Furthermore, a pharmacist who has a choice might stock only the more expensive products of an established manufacturer in order to be able to secure indemnity. Although some pharmacies were owned by large chains, most were not. One concurring justice, although recognizing that most customers used pharmacists as retailers, rejected strict liability because drugs are dispensed "only at the direction of a prescriber who is himself exempt from such liability." The dissenters found the focus on professional status "elitist." For them, the sale aspect dominated the transaction and all the policies of strict liability would be furthered by imposing it here.

For negligence applications against pharmacists see Hooks SuperX, Inc. v. McLaughlin, 642 N.E.2d 514 (Ind.1994), (imposing a duty not to refill a prescription for a habit-forming drug if the pharmacist should reasonably realize that the patient is using the drug at an improperly fast rate based on what the physician had prescribed) and Frye v. Medicare–Glaser Corp., 153 Ill.2d 26, 605 N.E.2d 557 (1992)(absolving a pharmacist who warned of some dangers but failed to warn against drinking while taking a drug because the warning "offended so many people that I would think that they might drink").

5. Plaintiffs have had some success in "hybrid" cases involving both products and services. A sequence of cases from New Jersey suggests the approach.

In the Magrine case, cited in footnote 12 in *Hoven,* the court rejected strict liability against a dentist for a broken needle. Then in *Newmark,* also cited in *Hoven,* the same court imposed strict liability on a beauty salon that applied defective hair solution to a patron. The court explained the difference:

> It was held that the strict liability in tort doctrine was not applicable to the professional man, such as a dentist, because the essence of the relationship with his patient was the furnishing of professional skill and services. We accepted the view that a dentist's bill for services should be considered as representing pay for that alone. The use of instruments, or the administration of medicines or the providing of medicines for the patient's home consumption cannot give the ministrations the cast of a commercial transaction. Accordingly the liability of the dentist in cases involving the ordinary relationship of doctor and patient must be tested by principles of negligence, i.e., lack of due care and not by application of the doctrine of strict liability in tort.
>
> Defendants suggest that there is no doctrinal basis for distinguishing the services rendered by a beauty parlor operator from those rendered by a dentist or a doctor, and that consequently the liability of all three should be tested by the same principles. On the contrary there is a vast difference in the relationships. The beautician is engaged in a commercial enterprise; the dentist and doctor in a profession. The former caters publicly not to a need but to a form of aesthetic convenience or luxury, involving the rendition of non-professional services and the application of products for which a charge is made. The dentist or doctor does not and cannot advertise for patients; the demand for his services stems from a felt necessity of the patient. In response to such a call the doctor, and to a somewhat lesser degree the dentist, exercises his best judgment in diagnosing the patient's ailment or disability, prescribing and sometimes furnishing medicines or other methods of treatment which he believes, and in some measure hopes, will relieve or cure the condition. His performance is not mechanical or routine because each patient requires individual study and formulation of an informed judgment as to the physical or mental disability or condition presented, and the course of treatment needed. Neither medicine nor dentistry is an exact science; there is no implied warranty of cure or relief. There is no representation of infallibility and such professional men should not be held to

such a degree of perfection. There is no guaranty that the diagnosis is correct. Such men are not producers or sellers of property in any reasonably acceptable sense of the term. In a primary sense they furnish services in the form of an opinion of the patient's condition based upon their experienced analysis of the objective and subjective complaints, and in the form of recommended and, at times, personally administered medicines and treatment. . . . Thus their paramount function—the essence of their function—ought to be regarded as the furnishing of opinions and services. Their unique status and the rendition of these *sui generis* services bear such a necessary and intimate relationship to public health and welfare that their obligation ought to be grounded and expressed in a duty to exercise reasonable competence and care toward their patients. In our judgment, the nature of the services, the utility of and the need for them, involving as they do, the health and even survival of many people, are so important to the general welfare as to outweigh in the policy scale any need for the imposition on dentists and doctors of the rules of strict liability in tort.

Are the suggested distinctions persuasive? Is it significant that the law now permits professionals to advertise?

In Dixon v. Four Seasons Bowling Alley, Inc., 176 N.J.Super. 540, 424 A.2d 428 (1980), plaintiff was hurt when she fell while bowling and cut her finger on defendant's chipped bowling ball. The court refused to invoke strict liability because the use of the alley's ball was "incidental to the use of defendant's premises and the supplying of such equipment should not result in imposition of liability on defendant on any basis other than liability for injuries caused by conditions of the premises." The court stressed that plaintiff selected the ball from over 240; the defect was no less obvious to her than to the alley; there was no separate charge for the ball; the possession was intended to last for a very short term; and the ball was to be used only on defendant's premises. Since the defendant had not placed the ball "in the stream of commerce," the invitee duty was the more appropriate model. The court thought that the beauty salon case had been influenced by the plaintiff's reliance on the salon's expertise. Are the three New Jersey cases consistent?

6. The service of food in a restaurant may give rise to strict liability. See Shaffer v. Victoria Station, Inc., 91 Wash.2d 295, 588 P.2d 233 (1978), extending such liability to a defective wine glass that shattered in a restaurant patron's hand. Is this distinguishable from the case involving the bowling ball?

7. As noted earlier, p. 503, supra, the consumer expectations test is still widely used when food causes the harm. Although some early cases held that providing food in restaurants was a service that did not produce warranties (or products liability in tort), courts have now virtually all agreed that these cases come within the product notion—but difficulties continue. See, e.g., Mexicali Rose v. Superior Court, 1 Cal.4th 617, 822 P.2d 1292, 4 Cal.Rptr.2d 145 (1992), in which plaintiff was injured when he swallowed a chicken bone while eating a chicken enchilada at defendant's restaurant. The court unanimously agreed that plaintiff should be able to sue in negligence, but rejected, 4–3, defective products and breach of warranty theories. The majority would have permitted all three theories if the harm had been caused by a "foreign" object, such as a piece of glass or wire. Why the difference?

8.   Soon after the movement toward strict liability began, one court hesitated. In Wights v. Staff Jennings, Inc., 241 Or. 301, 405 P.2d 624 (1965), the wife of the purchaser sued the manufacturer for injuries suffered when a pleasure boat exploded. Although reversing a judgment for the defendant, Justice O'Connell declined to follow the approach taken by Justice Traynor in *Escola* and *Greenman:*

> Substantially the same reasons for imposing strict liability upon sellers of defective chattels have been advanced in several other cases and in various texts and articles. Summarized, the thesis is that a loss resulting from the use of defendant's defective goods "is a casualty produced by the hazards of defendant's enterprise, so that the risk of loss is properly a risk of that enterprise,"[9] a view commonly described as the theory of enterprise liability.[10] The theory is a corollary of the broader thesis urged by some writers, particularly Harper and James on Torts, that compensation of the victim rather than fault of the defendant should be the objective in the adjudication of accident cases.[11]
>
> . . .
>
> The rationale of risk spreading and compensating the victim has no special relevancy to cases involving injuries resulting from the use of defective goods. The reasoning would seem to apply not only in cases involving personal injuries arising from the *sale* of defective goods, but equally to any case where an injury results from the risk creating conduct of the seller in any stage of the production and distribution of goods. Thus a manufacturer would be strictly liable even in the absence of fault for an injury to a person struck by one of the manufacturer's trucks being used in transporting his goods to market. It seems to us that the enterprise liability rationale employed in the Escola case proves too much and that if adopted would compel us to apply the principle of strict liability in all future cases where the loss could be distributed.

9.   James, General Products—Should Manufacturers be Liable Without Negligence?, 24 Tenn.L.Rev. 923, 926 (1957).

10.   Ehrenzweig, Negligence Without Fault, 4 (1951); [ ].

11.   "It is the principal job of tort law today to deal with these [human] losses. They fall initially on people who as a class can ill afford them, and this fact brings great hardship upon the victims themselves and causes unfortunate repercussions to society as a whole. The best and most efficient way to deal with accident loss, therefore, is to assure accident victims of substantial compensation, and to distribute the losses involved over society as a whole or some very large segment of it. Such a basis for administering losses is what we have called social insurance." 2 Harper and James, Law of Torts, § 13.2, pp. 762–63 (1956).

How substantial is this concern? Can it be answered? Are the safety considerations of *Escola* applicable to driving a truck? Oregon soon adopted the emerging law of defective products.

F. DEFENSES

Since products cases have raised different issues in the prima facie case from those we have previously considered, it should not be surprising that different considerations might apply to defenses as well. We have already noted that in some states any "substantial alteration or modification" of the product—even if foreseeable—will bar liability against suppliers who distributed the product before it was altered. Recall p. 516, supra. In this section we consider two quite different defenses. The first involves the role of plaintiff's fault. The second involves the impact of federal regulatory developments on state tort law—the question of preemption.

1. PLAINTIFF'S FAULT

The nature of the defenses available in suits alleging defective products is as complex as the question of what is so special about products liability cases in the first place. Given the underlying tension between negligence and strict liability as the basis of liability, one should expect a similar tension over the nature of the permissible defenses. As we review the development of this area, several points might be kept in mind. First, unlike the cases involving abnormally dangerous activities, the victims in products cases are often intimately involved in using the product. Although bystanders and strangers do get hurt in some cases, the interaction of suppliers and users is the most common pattern of injury. Second, just as the law of strict liability for defective products was being developed, comparative negligence was being introduced in negligence cases. Thus, even if a clear body of law had emerged on the question of all-or-nothing defenses in products cases, it would soon have been confronted with the question of how, if at all, to integrate comparative negligence into the picture. Third, tort law and warranty law had historically developed in different ways with different language and different defenses. Now that they may be integrated in important respects, courts have been concerned to mesh the defenses as well.

Before comparative negligence emerged as a major doctrine, the Second Restatement offered only the following comment to § 402A on defenses:

> *n. Contributory Negligence.* Since the liability with which this Section deals is not based upon negligence of the seller, but is strict liability, the rule applied to strict liability cases (see § 524) applies. Contributory negligence of the plaintiff is not a defense when such negligence consists merely in a failure to discover the defect in the product, or to guard against the possibility of its existence. On the other hand the form of contributory negligence which consists in voluntarily and unreasonably proceeding to

encounter a known danger, and commonly passes under the name of assumption of risk, is a defense under this Section as in other cases of strict liability. If the user or consumer discovers the defect and is aware of the danger, and nevertheless proceeds unreasonably to make use of the product and is injured by it, he is barred from recovery.

This meager paragraph reflected the early 1960s understanding of contributory negligence and its relationship to assumption of risk. But as we saw in Chapter VI changes in both areas were already afoot. If a court finds a product defective (under whatever test) and finds that the victim foreseeably misused the product, with knowledge of the danger, a total bar is no longer applied.

The situation is captured in Milwaukee Elec. Tool Corp. v. Superior Court, 15 Cal.App.4th 547, 19 Cal.Rptr.2d 24 (1993), in which plaintiff worker alleged that he was hurt because of a defect while using defendant's power drill. Since plaintiff failed to follow instructions to "always use the side handle," defendant argued that plaintiff had assumed the risk of harm. The court, following *Knight*, p. 416, supra, the case that involved touch football, concluded that in so-called assumed risk cases, the first question was whether defendant had a duty to make a product free from defects. Accepting the justifications underlying the law of products liability, the court concluded that manufacturers owed such a duty. This led to rejection of defendant's "implied consent" argument. The court also rejected any analogy to the firefighter's rule, p. 425, supra, because what happened here was not a "risk that is inherent" in the plaintiff's job.

After the court imposed the duty, it concluded that if the plaintiff " 'proceeds to encounter a known risk imposed by the defendant's breach of duty,' [ ] assumption of risk is merged into the comparative fault scheme so that a trier of fact may consider the relative responsibility of the parties in apportioning the loss and damage resulting from the injury." Is there any reason to analyze "assumption of risk," "implied consent," or the firefighter's rule differently where the claim is a defective product rather than non-products related negligence?

More importantly, how is one to make comparisons between a defective product and the plaintiff's negligence in using the product? The following seminal case explores whether to consider a plaintiff's negligence in a defective product case and, if so, how it might be done.

Daly v. General Motors Corporation

Supreme Court of California, 1978.
20 Cal.3d 725, 575 P.2d 1162, 144 Cal.Rptr. 380.

■ RICHARDSON, J. The most important of several problems which we consider is whether the principles of comparative negligence expressed by us in Li v. Yellow Cab Co. (1975) [ ] apply to actions founded on strict products liability. . . .

The Facts and the Trial

Although there were no eyewitnesses, the parties agree, generally, on the reconstruction of the accident in question. In the early hours of October 31, 1970, decedent Kirk Daly, a 36–year–old attorney, was driving his Opel southbound on the Harbor Freeway in Los Angeles. The vehicle, while travelling at a speed of 50–70 miles per hour, collided with and damaged 50 feet of metal divider fence. After the initial impact between the left side of the vehicle and the fence the Opel spun counterclockwise, the driver's door was thrown open, and Daly was forcibly ejected from the car and sustained fatal head injuries. It was equally undisputed that had the deceased remained in the Opel his injuries, in all probability, would have been relatively minor.

Plaintiffs, who are decedent's widow and three surviving minor children, sued General Motors Corporation, Boulevard Buick, Underwriter's Auto Leasing, and Alco Leasing Company, the successive links in the Opel's manufacturing and distribution chain. The sole theory of plaintiffs' complaint was strict liability for damages allegedly caused by a defective product, namely, an improperly designed door latch claimed to have been activated by the impact. It was further asserted that, but for the faulty latch, decedent would have been restrained in the vehicle and, although perhaps injured, would not have been killed. Thus, the case involves a so-called "second collision" in which the "defect" did not contribute to the original impact, but only to the "enhancement" of injury.

At trial the jury heard conflicting expert versions as to the functioning of the latch mechanism during the accident. Plaintiffs' principal witness testified that the Opel's door was caused to open when the latch button on the exterior handle of the driver's door was forcibly depressed by some protruding portion of the divider fence. It was his opinion that the exposed push button on the door constituted a design "defect" which caused injuries greatly in excess of those which Daly would otherwise have sustained. Plaintiffs also introduced evidence that other vehicular door latch designs used in production models of the same and prior years afforded substantially greater protection. Defendants' experts countered with their opinions that the force of the impact was sufficiently strong that it would have caused the door to open resulting in Daly's death even if the Opel had been equipped with door latches of the alternative designs suggested by plaintiffs.

Over plaintiffs' objections, defendants were permitted to introduce evidence indicating that: (1) the Opel was equipped with a seat belt-shoulder harness system, and a door lock, either of which if used, it was contended, would have prevented Daly's ejection from the vehicle; (2) Daly used neither the harness system nor the lock; (3) the 1970 Opel owner's manual contained warnings that seat belts should be worn and doors locked when the car was in motion for "accident security;" and (4) Daly was intoxicated at the time of collision, which evidence the jury was advised was admitted for the limited purpose of determining whether decedent had used the vehicle's safety equipment. After relatively brief deliberations the jury returned a verdict favoring all defendants, and plaintiffs appeal from the ensuing adverse judgment.

Strict Products Liability and Comparative Fault

. . .

Those counseling against the recognition of comparative fault principles in strict products liability cases vigorously stress, perhaps equally, not only the conceptual, but also the semantic difficulties incident to such a course. The task of merging the two concepts is said to be impossible, that "apples and oranges" cannot be compared, that "oil and water" do not mix, and that strict liability, which is not founded on negligence or fault, is inhospitable to comparative principles. The syllogism runs, contributory negligence was only a defense to negligence, comparative negligence only affects contributory negligence, therefore comparative negligence cannot be a defense to strict liability. [ ] While fully recognizing the theoretical and semantic distinctions between the twin principles of strict products liability and traditional negligence, we think they can be blended or accommodated.

. . .

Given all of the foregoing, we are, in the wake of *Li* [p. 388, supra] disinclined to resolve the important issue before us by the simple expedient of matching linguistic labels which have evolved either for convenience or by custom. Rather, we consider it more useful to examine the foundational reasons underlying the creation of strict products liability in California to ascertain whether the purposes of the doctrine would be defeated or diluted by adoption of comparative principles. We imposed strict liability against the manufacturer and in favor of the user or consumer in order to relieve injured consumers "from *problems of proof* inherent in pursuing negligence . . . and warranty . . . remedies, . . ." [ ] As we have noted, we sought to place the burden of loss on manufacturers rather than " . . . injured persons *who are powerless to protect themselves.* . . ." [ ]

The foregoing goals, we think, will not be frustrated by the adoption of comparative principles. Plaintiffs will continue to be relieved of proving that the manufacturer or distributor was negligent in the production, design, or dissemination of the article in question. Defendant's liability for injuries caused by a defective product remains strict. The principle of protecting the defenseless is likewise preserved, for plaintiff's recovery will be reduced *only* to the extent that his own lack of reasonable care contributed to his injury. The cost of compensating the victim of a defective product, albeit proportionately reduced, remains on defendant manufacturer, and will, through him, be "spread among society." However, we do not permit plaintiff's own conduct relative to the product to escape unexamined, and as to that share of plaintiff's damages which flows from his own fault we discern no reason of policy why it should, following *Li,* be borne by others. Such a result would directly contravene the principle announced in *Li*, that loss should be assessed equitably in proportion to fault.

. . .

A second objection to the application of comparative principles in strict products liability cases is that a manufacturer's incentive to produce safe products will thereby be reduced or removed. While we fully recognize this concern we think, for several reasons, that the problem is more shadow than substance. First, of course, the manufacturer cannot avoid its continuing liability for a defective product even when the plaintiff's own conduct has contributed to his injury. The manufacturer's liability, and therefore its incentive to avoid and correct product defects, remains; its exposure will be lessened only to the extent that the trier finds that the victim's conduct contributed to his injury. Second, as a practical matter a manufacturer, in a particular case, cannot assume that the user of a defective product upon whom an injury is visited will be blameworthy. Doubtless, many users are free of fault, and a defect is at least as likely as not to be exposed by an entirely innocent plaintiff who will obtain full recovery. In such cases the manufacturer's incentive toward safety both in design and production is wholly unaffected. Finally, we must observe that under the present law, which recognizes assumption of risk as a complete defense to products liability, the curious and cynical message is that it profits the manufacturer to make his product so defective that in the event of injury he can argue that the user had to be aware of its patent defects. To that extent the incentives are inverted. We conclude, accordingly, that no substantial or significant impairment of the safety incentives of defendants will occur by the adoption of comparative principles.

. . .

A third objection to the merger of strict liability and comparative fault focuses on the claim that, as a practical matter, triers of fact, particularly jurors, cannot assess, measure, or compare plaintiff's negligence with defendant's strict liability. We are unpersuaded by the argument and are convinced that jurors are able to undertake a fair apportionment of liability.

. . .

We note that the majority of our sister states which have addressed the problem, either by statute or judicial decree, have extended comparative principles to strict products liability.

. . .

Having examined the principal objections and finding them not insurmountable, and persuaded by logic, justice, and fundamental fairness, we conclude that a system of comparative fault should be and it is hereby extended to actions founded on strict products liability. In such cases the separate defense of "assumption of risk," to the extent that it is a form of contributory negligence, is abolished. While, as we have suggested, on the particular facts before us, the term "equitable apportionment of loss" is more accurately descriptive of the process, nonetheless, the term "comparative fault'' has gained such wide acceptance by courts and in the literature that we adopt its use herein.

. . .

The Safety Equipment and Intoxication Evidence

We must determine whether admission of evidence of decedent's failure to use available safety devices and of his intoxication constituted prejudicial error under rules heretofore applicable to strict liability cases. We conclude that it did.

While initially evidence bearing on decedent's intoxication was excluded, other evidence pertaining to the decedent's alleged failure to employ seat belts and door locks was admitted, apparently on the ground that nonuse of safety devices bore on the issues of proximate cause and mitigation of damages.   Plaintiffs contended that evidence of Daly's intoxication, or of his failure to use available safety devices, was wholly inadmissible since contributory negligence was not a defense to an action founded in strict liability for a defective product.   [   ]   The trial court ultimately admitted the intoxication evidence, ruling that such evidence related to decedent's failure to use the Opel's safety devices, which failure, the court reasoned, would bar recovery on the theory of product misuse "aside from any question of contributory negligence."   .   .   .

. . .

Substantial time was spent on the nonuse and intoxication issues, reasonably suggesting to the jury their central importance to the defense case.   There can be little doubt that the evidence of Daly's intoxication was inflammatory.   The only restrictions placed on the jury's consideration of the intoxication evidence was that it bore on the "nonuse" of safety devices in general.   No limitation was placed on the conclusions which the jury could draw either from a finding of "nonuse" itself, or as to the effect on its deliberations of a finding of "nonuse."   In the absence of any such restrictions, we think the jury could well have concluded that decedent's negligent failure, induced by intoxication, to use the belts and locks constituted negligent conduct which *completely barred* recovery for his death.   We do not think it reasonable to conclude that plaintiffs waived their objection by failing to request limiting instructions.

In summary, our review of the record convinces us that, notwithstanding that plaintiffs' case was founded on strict products liability, evidence of decedent's failure to use available seat belts and door locks, and of his intoxication at the time of the fatal collision, may have been improperly regarded by the jury as authorizing a defense verdict.   It appears reasonably probable that, had such evidence been either excluded or its effect confined, a result more favorable to plaintiffs would have been reached. Reversal is therefore required.   [   ]

. . .

■ TOBRINER, J., CLARK, J., and MANUEL, J., concurred.

CLARK, J.   The reasoning of Li v. Yellow Cab Co. [   ], as the majority point out, is equally applicable to strict liability cases and compels applying comparative fault in those cases.   [   ]   Under the compulsion of *Li,* I have signed the majority opinion.

Nevertheless, again we must recognize the difficulties inherent in comparing fault.   [   ]   Relying on the apples and oranges argument, Justices Mosk and Jefferson point out that comparative fault cannot be applied logically and consistently in strict liability cases.   The difficulty, however, is not limited to comparing strict liability with negligence.   The same difficulty persists in almost every case in which we attempt to compare parties' negligence.   [   ]

.   .   .

Li effectively pointed out that the existing contributory negligence system placed on one party the entire burden of a loss for which two were responsible [   ] and today's majority opinion effectively points out that the negligent plaintiff is responsible and should not recover as much as an innocent one.

Those principles do not require a comparative fault system.   Can they not be satisfied by a system which establishes a uniform index factor, such as 30, 50 or 70 percent?   A uniform discount of the negligent plaintiff's recovery would eliminate the necessity of the often impossible task of comparing fault.   A discount system would bring about consistency and predictability where neither now exists, permitting evaluation and settlement of claims.

.   .   .

■ JEFFERSON, J.   I concur in part and dissent in part.

I agree with the majority's result that the judgment should be reversed because of the prejudicial error in admitting evidence of decedent's intoxication and of his failure to use available safety devices.   Otherwise, I part company with the majority's views.

.   .   .

I consider the majority conclusion a case of wishful thinking and an application of an impractical, ivory-tower approach.   The majority's assumption that a jury is capable of making a fair apportionment between a plaintiff's negligent conduct and a defendant's defective product is no more logical or convincing than if a jury were to be instructed that it should add a quart of milk (representing plaintiff's negligence) and a metal bar three feet in length (representing defendant's strict liability for a defective product), and that the two added together equal 100 percent—the total fault for plaintiff's injuries; that plaintiff's quart of milk is then to be assigned its percentage of the 100 percent total and defendant's metal bar is to be assigned the remaining percentage of the total.   Either the jury or the trial judge will then subtract from the total amount of plaintiff's damages an amount equal to the percentage of total fault allocated to plaintiff.

. . .

The majority's decision herein will require the jury, on the one hand, to follow *Barker* and focus on the manufacturer's *product*—disregarding all questions of whether the manufacturer acted unreasonably or negligently—in order to determine defendant manufacturer's liability. On the other hand, the jury must next focus on plaintiff's *conduct,* in order to find that plaintiff was negligent. The jury must then *compare* its focus on plaintiff's negligent *conduct* with its focus on defendant's defective *product*—eliminating, as irrelevant, any consideration of whether defendant's conduct was unreasonable or negligent—to determine the amount of the reduction in plaintiff's total damages. The end result of this configurational analysis by a jury, I submit, based as it must be—on a comparison of noncomparables—will necessarily constitute a patently unfair result.

. . .

It appeals to my sense of reason, justice and equity that we continue the existing legal principle which permits manufacturers to spread through society the costs of compensating injured plaintiffs *fully,* rather than the adoption of an untenable legal principle which will result in *reducing* the total costs to be spread by manufacturers, but at the expense of injured plaintiffs by reducing their recovery *below* the full losses sustained through the necessarily fortuitous, conjectural and haphazard determinations to be made by juries.

■ BIRD, C.J., concurred.

■ MOSK, J.   I dissent.

This will be remembered as the dark day when this court, which heroically took the lead in originating the doctrine of products liability [*Greenman*] and steadfastly resisted efforts to inject concepts of negligence into the newly designed tort [*Cronin*] inexplicably turned 180 degrees and beat a hasty retreat almost back to square one. The pure concept of products liability so pridefully fashioned and nurtured by this court for the past decade and a half is reduced to a shambles.

. . .

The defective product is comparable to a time bomb ready to explode; it maims its victims indiscriminately, the righteous and the evil, the careful and the careless. Thus when a faulty design or otherwise defective product is involved, the litigation should not be diverted to consideration of the negligence of the plaintiff. The liability issues are simple: was the product or its design faulty, did the defendant inject the defective product into the stream of commerce, and did the defect cause the injury? The conduct of the ultimate consumer-victim who used the product in the contemplated or foreseeable manner is wholly irrelevant to those issues.

. . .

NOTES AND QUESTIONS

1. In an omitted part of the opinion, the majority also decided that in considering the question of "defect," the jury should consider not only the alleged problems with the latching mechanism but also the other safety features that the defendant had built into the car, such as the harness belts and the inside door locks. The question was not the defectiveness of the latch but rather the adequacy of the car's overall safety package.

2. Are manufacturers likely to have reduced incentives after this case? Retailers? Motorists?

3. How applicable is Justice Mosk's observation that a "defective product is comparable to a time bomb ready to explode; it maims its victims indiscriminately, the righteous and the evil, the careful and the careless"? Is *Daly* an appropriate case for the majority's statement that "as to that share of plaintiff's damages which flows from his own fault we discern no reason of policy why it should . . . be borne by others"?

4. One author suggests that the way to apportion damages "is to compare the plaintiff's conduct with how he should have conducted himself (the objective standard of the reasonable man) and reduce his recovery according to the extent of his fault." Fischer, Products Liability—Applicability of Comparative Negligence, 43 Mo.L.Rev. 431 (1978). How does this differ from *Daly* ? Is it easier for a jury to understand?

Compare the approach taken in Sandford v. Chevrolet Division, 292 Or. 590, 642 P.2d 624 (1982). Plaintiff suffered burns when a pickup truck she was driving caught fire. The defendants alleged that plaintiff's negligence had caused the injuries. Oregon's modified comparative fault statute was interpreted to require that plaintiff's negligence be considered in a products liability case "unless the user's alleged negligence consists in the kind of unobservant, inattentive, ignorant, or awkward failure to discover or guard against the defect that goes toward making the product dangerously defective in the first place."

The court then turned to the question of how to "compare" the faults of the parties. The proper approach was to compare each party's fault "against behavior that would have been faultless under the circumstances." The product supplier's norm involved "the magnitude of the defect rather than negligence or moral 'blameworthiness' ":

> In this comparison, the benchmark for assessing a defendant's fault for marketing a product which is dangerously defective in design, manufacture, or warning is what the product should have been without the defect. The benchmark for the injured claimant's fault is conduct which would not be unlawful or careless in any relevant respect.

Drawing on Pearson, Apportionment of Losses Under Comparative Fault Laws—An Analysis of Alternatives, 40 La.L.Rev. 346 (1980), the court decided that the deviation from the benchmark for each party could be thought of as a "fault line" with the absence of fault being zero and the deliberate wrongdoing having a value of ten. Each party's deviation would be determined individually. Then they would be compared and apportioned in percentages. For example, if the product defect rated a 3 and the plaintiff's fault a 2, these numbers would be converted to a defendant's "fault" of 60% and plaintiff's of 40%.

In such a situation might the plaintiff feel it necessary to try to show traditional negligence on the defendant in order to fare better in any comparison?

5. How different is the comparison called for in this case from comparing a plaintiff's speeding and a defendant's inattention in an auto collision case?

6. *Apportionment.* If the plaintiff is claiming only enhancement damages it becomes important to separate the harm caused by the initial impact from the harm caused by the fact (when established) that the car was not crashworthy. Who should bear the burden on this apportionment? What if it cannot be made? Is it clear that the two harms should be kept separate?

In Whitehead v. Toyota Motor Corp., 897 S.W.2d 684 (Tenn.1995), plaintiff was entirely responsible for a two car crash in which he was hurt. He sued Toyota for enhanced injuries allegedly due to a defective seat belt system. The court first concluded, as have the "overwhelming majority of states," that it was appropriate to consider the plaintiff's conduct in products cases: "a plaintiff's ability to recover in a strict products liability case should not be unaffected by the extent to which his injuries result from his own fault."

Would the court's view be sound if the claim had been that the Toyota pulled sharply to the right when the brakes were engaged suddenly? Is it sound where the claim is only for enhanced injuries? Might plaintiff's incentives toward safety be too few if the court did not consider the causes of the underlying accident in the suit for enhancement injuries?

Whitehead thought it appropriate that "the fault of the defendant and of the plaintiff should be compared with each other with respect to all damages and injuries for which the conduct of each party is a cause in fact and a proximate cause." Why "all"? Is the plaintiff's fault in the crash a "proximate cause" of the harm attributable to lack of a crashworthy car?

A minority is contra, barring evidence about the cause of the accident in a case brought for enhancement injuries. See, e.g, Reed v. Chrysler Corp., 494 N.W.2d 224 (Iowa 1992), barring evidence of the cause of the accident, primarily on the ground that the "plaintiff's initial negligence in causing an accident is not a proximate cause of his enhanced injuries."

7. The vast majority of courts in states that have adopted a modified version of comparative negligence for use in negligence cases, have concluded that in products liability cases they should use a pure version. The result is that if the plaintiff can show a product defect, the plaintiff will recover something in the case. The *Whitehead* court reached a different result, concluding that modified comparative negligence should apply in strict liability products cases. This creates the possibility that in some cases such a plaintiff will recover nothing although a defective product caused or enhanced the injuries. What might justify a distinct rule for products cases?

8. Some courts refuse to invoke comparative negligence where the plaintiff's only negligence was in failing to discover or guard against a defect in the product. Where the plaintiff has knowingly but foreseeably misused the product, or continued to use it after discovering a defect, most courts have allowed comparative negligence principles to be used to reduce the plaintiff's recovery. The array is discussed in V. Schwartz, Comparative Negligence, §§ 12.1–12.8 (2d ed. 1986 & Supp.).

9. A developing line of cases is related to the *Daly* problem but does not involve defenses. Instead, it involves a driver who was not at fault in causing the accident and who was wearing a safety belt. The crash occurred because T negligently rear-ended the driver, whose injury was enhanced because of a crashworthiness defect. Can the manufacturer reduce its liability (in a state that no longer uses joint and several liability) by blaming the initial impact on T?

That was the issue in Smothers v. General Motors Corp., 34 Cal. App.4th 629, 40 Cal.Rptr.2d 618 (1995), where T admitted full responsibility for rear-ending plaintiff. At trial GM tried to show that T had been drunk. (GM also sought to show that all the harm was due to the first impact and not to the condition of the car.) The trial court excluded the evidence of drunkenness and the jury apportioned liability 20% to T and 80% to GM—apparently on the basis of "fault" rather than of causation.

10. After *Daly,* the same court decided that the comparative fault principle should also be used to apportion liability between two defendants, one of whom was held strictly liable and the other of whom was held liable by the jury on both strict liability and negligence theories. The jury apportioned liability 20% to the first defendant and 80% to the second. Is this different from "comparing" a plaintiff's negligence and a defendant's strict liability? See Safeway Stores, Inc. v. Nest–Kart, 21 Cal.3d 322, 579 P.2d 441, 146 Cal.Rptr. 550 (1978).

11. Where the plaintiff has prevailed against the retailer and the manufacturer in the case of a metal sliver in a can of tuna fish, how should the liability be apportioned?

What if the defective product is a car with a loose wheel that should have been found by the retailer during its final check before delivering the car? The plaintiff has recovered a judgment against both the manufacturer and the retailer.

12. *Employment Setting.* As we have seen, many defective product cases arise in employment settings. In such a setting they have presented questions different from those that emerged in the cases involving injuries to ultimate consumers. Similar differences pervade the defense aspects of the action.

In Cremeans v. Willmar Henderson Manufacturing Co., 57 Ohio St.3d 145, 566 N.E.2d 1203 (1991), plaintiff's job was to load fertilizer at Sohio's plant. The loader had been designed by defendant Willmar to be sold with a protective cage for the driver. Since the loader could not fit into the fertilizer room—where it was needed—if it had the cage, Sohio ordered it without the cage. In the bill of sale the defendant insisted that Sohio assume any liability arising from the removal of the cage. "Cremeans continued to operate the [uncaged] loader in the fertilizer bins even though he was aware of the potential for an avalanche. Cremeans continued to operate the loader because it was his job." If the loader had had its cage, plaintiff "would not have sustained his injury."

The trial court granted summary judgment on the ground that plaintiff had assumed the risk of injury. The court of appeals reversed finding a genuine issue of fact. A divided supreme court affirmed. The plurality thought that

The record in this case demonstrates that Cremeans encountered the risks associated with the use of the Willmar loader because he was required to do so in the normal performance of his job duties and responsibilities and that Cremeans was injured during the execution of such duties and responsibilities. Therefore, his assumption of the risk was neither voluntary nor unreasonable and, hence, . . . Cremeans is not barred from recovery on his products liability claim based upon strict liability in tort. This is so regardless of the fact that it was Cremeans's employer, and not Willmar, who required Cremeans to perform the particular job duty which resulted in the injury. Given the facts of this case, to wit, that Willmar knew that the loader it was selling to Sohio was not equipped with a necessary safety device and, in fact, demanded indemnity from Sohio before agreeing to make the sale, the issue is even clearer.

. . . Thus, Cremeans was put at risk either solely as a result of the product defect, or by the combination of the defect and the conduct of Cremeans's employer, Sohio. In either event, the economic pressures associated with the reality of today's workplace inevitably came to bear on Cremeans's decision to encounter the risk. As such, we believe that it would be incongruous to conclude that the defense of assumption of risk should be available to Willmar and not to Cremeans's employer when the decision to encounter the risk was equally involuntary regardless of who commissioned the employee to perform his or her job duty.

For the dissenters "[t]he unbelievably bad result of the majority opinion here is that the manufacturer becomes an insurer of his product whenever an employer coerces his workers into exposing themselves to unconscionable risk of injury."

Since Willmar entered into an indemnification agreement with Sohio, why should there be any concern about holding the defendant responsible? If there had been no indemnification agreement, would your view be influenced by whether the state allowed the manufacturer a third-party action against an employer insulated from primary tort liability under the workers' compensation statute? The states differ on this issue, which is discussed in Chapter XI. On the other hand, suppose Willmar can establish that Cremeans was receiving premium pay for a hazardous job. Should that affect plaintiff's right of recovery?

Cremeans was decided under common law. Ohio now has legislation providing in part that when plaintiff establishes a strict liability defect, a showing that the victim "expressly or impliedly assumed the risk" is a "complete bar" to recovery of damages. Would that alter the result in *Cremeans?*

At this point, recall the materials at pp. 516-22, supra, on misuse and alteration. Are the issues sufficiently distinct in these various employment scenarios to warrant different analysis?

2. PREEMPTION

Talbott v. C.R.Bard, Inc.

United States Court of Appeals, First Circuit, 1995.
63 F.3d 25.

■ Before STAHL, CIRCUIT JUDGE, CAMPBELL, SENIOR CIRCUIT JUDGE, and JOHN R. GIBSON, SENIOR CIRCUIT JUDGE.

■ CAMPBELL, SENIOR CIRCUIT JUDGE.

Section 360k(a) of the Medical Device Amendments ("MDA") to the Food, Drug and Cosmetic Act ("FDCA") provides:

[N]o State or political subdivision of a State may establish or continue in effect with respect to a device intended for human use any requirement—

(1) which is different from, or in addition to, any requirement applicable under this chapter to the device, and

(2) which relates to the safety or effectiveness of the device or to any other matter included in a requirement applicable to the device under this chapter.

21 U.S.C. § 360k(a)(1988). This appeal presents two questions: (1) whether the above provision applies to state tort law claims asserted against a medical device manufacturer; and (2) if so, whether there is an exception to the preemption clause where the manufacturer fails to comply with the MDA. We hold that the answers to the two questions are, respectively, yes and no. We therefore affirm the district court's dismissal of this case for failure to state a claim under Fed. R. Civ. P. 12(b)(6).

I.

. . . On December 28, 1988, Eunice Beavers died on the operating table during an angioplasty procedure when a heart catheter failed to deflate while inserted in one of her coronary arteries. Her heirs, Linda Talbott et al., sued the manufacturer of the heart catheter, C.R. Bard, Inc. ("Bard"), and two members of its management for wrongful death, alleging numerous state tort claims: negligence, breach of express and implied warranties, punitive damages, negligent infliction of emotional distress, fraudulent misrepresentation and concealment, negligent hiring, civil conspiracy, unfair trade practices. [The heart catheter had been approved for use by the FDA under the Medical Device Amendments.] The district court dismissed the complaint.   .   .   .

II.

To determine whether federal law preempts state law, we look to the intent of Congress: congressional intent to displace state law must be "clear and manifest" before preemption is found. [ ] Such intent may be expressed either explicitly, in the language of a statute, or implicitly, through passage of a statutory scheme that extensively occupies the field or where the purpose and objectives of federal law would be frustrated by state law. Here, Congress has manifested its intention in an explicit preemption clause, § 360k(a). Thus, absent any "general, inherent conflict" between state and federal law, we need only ascertain the preemption Congress intended. Freightliner Corp. v. Myrick, 115 S.Ct. 1483, 1488 (1995); Cipollone v. Liggett Group, 505 U.S. 504 (1992). We review the district court's reading of the clause *de novo*, taking all of plaintiffs' factual averments as true.   .   .   .

A.   State Tort Law Imposes Requirements

Plaintiffs insist that the district court erred in concluding that state tort law imposes a "requirement" as that term is used in § 360k(a). Plaintiffs argue that Congress meant "requirement" to include only the state's positive enactments—such as statutes and regulations—and not common law causes of action. This issue, however, has been resolved against plaintiffs in this circuit in two decisions: King v. Collagen Corp., 983 F.2d 1130, 1135–36 (1st Cir.), cert. denied, 114 S.Ct. 84 (1993), and Mendes v. Medtronic, Inc., 18 F.3d 13, 16 (1st Cir.1994). In both, this court has ruled that Congress understood state tort law to impose a "requirement" such as to subject state tort law to the MDA's preemption clause. Where the requirement is "different from, or in addition to" the requirement imposed by the MDA, state tort law will be preempted. A like construction has been adopted by every other circuit court that has considered the issue. [ ] [The court refused to consider overruling the circuit's two earlier cases because one panel could not overrule another panel in this type of case.]

B.   No Exception For Non–Compliance

Plaintiffs next argue that, even assuming § 360k(a) applies to state tort law generally, the district court erred in holding that it applies where a manufacturer has failed to comply with the provisions of the MDA by fraudulently obtaining approval from the Food and Drug Administration ("FDA"). Plaintiffs argue that, in enacting § 360k(a), Congress intended to preempt only state laws that sought to impose liability on manufacturers who were already complying with the MDA. Congress did not, plaintiffs assert, intend to afford such protection to manufacturers who failed to comply with the provisions of the MDA. Such a result would conflict, in plaintiffs' view, with the MDA's basic purpose of protecting individuals from unreasonably dangerous and defective medical devices. Where a manufacturer has failed to comply with the MDA, state tort liability would merely impose additional state sanctions for noncompliance with the MDA. Here, plaintiffs argue, Bard clearly violated the provisions of the MDA by submitting false data to the FDA in order to obtain approval of its heart catheters.

As the district court explained, [ ], Bard pled guilty in an earlier proceeding to a criminal indictment charging it with conspiring to defraud the FDA in connection with applications for pre-market approval of its heart catheters. Bard was eventually forced to pay civil and criminal fines totaling $61 million. [ ] . . . [F]or present purposes we shall assume that Bard fraudulently obtained approval for the heart catheter by submitting false information to the FDA. The question is whether § 360k(a) applies despite such fraudulent activity.

. . .

We hold that Congress did not intend to provide for an exception to the MDA's preemption clause where a manufacturer fails to comply with the provisions of the MDA by fraudulently obtaining approval of its device from the FDA. In so holding, we reach the same result reached by the *King* concurrence and by the two circuit courts of appeal that have expressly addressed this exact issue. [ ]

Section 360k(a) preempts broadly any state tort law "requirement" that is "different from, or in addition to" the comprehensive and detailed requirements set forth by federal law. The terms of the statute make no distinction based upon whether or not a manufacturer has in fact complied with the federal standard. We find nothing to indicate that preemption is conditional upon satisfactory compliance with the federal standard. Section 360k(a) does not mention compliance at all. As § 360k(a) reads, the relevant inquiry is simply whether, in the abstract, the state tort law requirement is "different from, or in addition to" the federal requirement. If a device manufacturer fails to meet the federal requirements, it will be subject to federal penalties as set forth in the MDA. Nothing in § 360k(a) suggests that the state requirements are somehow revived by this failure to comply with the federal standard.

Plaintiffs argue that state tort claims would not impose a "requirement" that is "different from, or in addition to" federal requirements so long as the state judge instructs the jury that a manufacturer's obligations under state tort law were defined by the provisions of the MDA. Given such an instruction, plaintiffs say, state tort law would not be imposing any additional requirements, but would only compensate the victim *ex post* for failure to meet the MDA standards. This theory of cooperative preemption, however, was expressly rejected, albeit in dictum, in *Mendes*:

> One way to ensure that a [state] factfinder applies a standard not adding to or differing from FDA regulations is to supplant the common law standard with FDA's requirements. We find nothing to support that Congress intended such a radical, unwieldy form of

preemption, however, particularly where Congress did not intend to create a private right of action under the Federal Food, Drug, and Cosmetic Act.

[The court noted that other courts of appeals have disagreed on this question.]

Allowing an exception for noncompliance would disturb the balance Congress struck between the competing goals of protecting individuals from unreasonably dangerous medical devices and spurring innovation by ensuring that device manufacturers are subject to uniform, nationwide standards. [ ] To see how this is so, we need only imagine how such an exception would operate in practice. If state tort claims were allowed to go forward, a state court would initially have to determine whether the manufacturer had complied with the MDA. If, as in this case, the plaintiff claimed that the manufacturer had defrauded the FDA, the state court would need to determine whether the FDA had in fact been defrauded and whether the FDA would have approved the device absent the fraud. Under this scheme, a device manufacturer could potentially be subject to numerous inconsistent interpretations and applications of the MDA across different states, thus undermining the MDA's goal of uniformity. Moreover, if state courts erred in their application of the MDA, they would effectively be imposing requirements "different from, or in addition to" those imposed by federal law. [ ]

To avoid the possibility of disuniform treatment, Congress placed enforcement authority in the FDA. The FDA has the broad power: to withdraw approval of a device if it determines that the device is unsafe or its labelling inadequate, 21 U.S.C. § 360e(e); to order a recall of the device, § 360h(e); and to initiate criminal prosecutions against manufacturers, as it did in this case against Bard. [ ]. Centrally situated and with the requisite expertise, the FDA is in the best position to determine whether the provisions of the MDA have in fact been violated and to ensure that the law is applied in a uniform manner. [ ] Given the FDA's central enforcement role, the preemptive scope of § 360k(a) becomes clear. . . .

The United States, as amicus curiae, argues that such reasoning, while perhaps applicable in *King*, is not applicable in this case, because the FDA has already determined that Bard failed to comply with the requirements of the MDA by submitting fraudulent data to the FDA. Thus, the concerns about disuniformity are not implicated in this case. Under the United States' scheme, then, a plaintiff would simply need to prove, not that the manufacturer failed to comply with the MDA, but that the FDA had determined that the manufacturer failed to comply.

Although this may be a workable arrangement, it still does not get around the problem that neither the language of § 360k(a) nor the legislative history give any hint of congressional intent to create such a unique exception to the MDA's preemption clause. It may or may not be that allowing injured plaintiffs to recover in state actions when the FDA has determined that a manufacturer violated the MDA would be a desirable rule, from a policy standpoint. Congress, however has not provided for such a remedy, choosing instead to place sole enforcement authority in the hands of the FDA. See, e.g., *Mendes*, [　] (no federal private right of action under the MDA).　.　.　.

The absence of a non-compliance exception does not mean that individuals injured by noncompliance will always be without compensation. In a criminal judgment against a manufacturer, a court may, as part of any sentence, award restitution to those harmed. See 18 U.S.C. § 3663(a)(1); [　]. While the district court accepted a binding plea agreement from Bard that contained no restitution provision, it did so, in part, because it erroneously believed that civil proceedings could provide appropriate compensation. [　]. Courts in future criminal proceedings will, or should, be aware that restitution may be the only redress for those harmed by manufacturers who have failed to comply with the provisions of the MDA.

Like the court below, we cannot find any exception to § 360k(a) where a manufacturer of a Class III device has failed to comply with the requirements of the MDA.

C. Application of Preemption Clause

Having held that the MDA's preemption clause applies to state tort law, whether or not the manufacturer has complied with the provisions of the MDA, we must next determine whether the requirements imposed by plaintiffs' numerous state law claims are "different from, or in addition to" the ones imposed by the MDA. In its opinion below, the district court did a thorough job of analyzing each of plaintiffs' claims, finding that each of them imposed additional requirements and was therefore preempted. As we agree with the district court's analysis and as we see no reason to repeat it here, we adopt those portions of the district court's opinion. [　] We hold that all of plaintiffs' claims are preempted by § 360k(a).

[The court noted that in one MDA case the Third Circuit had preserved claims for express warranty and also for fraudulent advertising.]

III.

Because all of plaintiffs' claims are preempted by § 360k(a) of the MDA, we affirm the district court's dismissal of this suit. We end with this quotation from the district court's opinion:

> This is a particularly poignant case in which the heirs of a woman who died during angioplasty are being found not to have the right to seek compensation for the damages they have undoubtedly suffered. The government has vigorously enforced the applicable criminal and civil laws. Nevertheless this decision may cause some, including those who enacted the law, to question whether complete preemption of private rights of action is the most fair and effective means of balancing the legitimate, competing interests of promoting innovation and reasonably assuring the safety of complex medical devices. It is axiomatic, however, that the courts must faithfully give effect to the intentions of Congress when they are clearly expressed by statute, as they have been in

this case.   Defendants' motion to dismiss, therefore, must be granted.   [   ]

Affirmed.

NOTES AND QUESTIONS

1.   As the case suggests, the courts of appeals today frequently confront preemption claims.   The results are not consistent, as this court notes at several points.   As federal regulation of safety and health increases, assertions of preemption follow.   The topic is vast and growing.   This case and these notes are only an introduction to the world of preemption. A petition for certiorari was filed in *Talbott* in February, 1996.

2.   Virtually every court confronted with the question has read "requirement" in preemption statutes to include common law tort liability. In the cited *Cipollone* case, the Supreme Court faced a similar argument under the 1965 cigarette labeling act.   It responded first by noting that the broad language of the statute in question "suggests no distinction between positive enactments and common law."   Moreover, it was clear that "regulation can be as effectively exerted through an award of damages as through some form of preventive relief.   The obligation to pay compensation can be, indeed is designed to be, a potent method of governing conduct and controlling policy."   What is the opposing argument?

3.   What is the difference between express preemption and implied preemption?   Which does the court find here?   Why?

4.   If there had been no FDA determination of fraud and no criminal proceeding what would justify a determination of preemption?   On the actual facts of the case what justifies a determination of preemption?

5.   The court notes that other courts have determined that Congress did not expressly create a private federal action for violation of this statute—nor do the courts imply such an action from criminal violation of the statute.   Why might that be?   Recall the discussion of *Cort v. Ash*, p. 125, supra, on when a federal damage action might be implied for violation of a federal statute or regulation.

6.   In the cited *Cipollone* case, involving a claim for lung cancer against a tobacco company, the Court concluded that claims alleging failure to warn were preempted under the federal cigarette warning legislation, but that claims based on express warranty, fraud, and misrepresentation were not preempted.

7.   In the cited *Myrick* case, the Court held that a state law claim that a tractor-trailer was defectively designed because it lacked air brakes was not preempted by federal regulation.   Although regulations promulgated under the National Highway Traffic Safety Act did not address the subject of air brakes, the defendant manufacturer argued that the absence of regulation was itself indicative of an intent to preclude state regulation. That argument has prevailed where the courts have found that "Congress intended to centralize all authority over the regulated area in one decisionmaker: the Federal Government." But in *Myrick*, the Court found no such intent.

The Court also rejected an argument of implied preemption due to an "actual conflict with federal law." Here, a claim of preemption failed, first, because it was possible for defendant to comply with both state and federal regulation. Second, the tort claim here could not be said to "frustrate 'the accomplishment and execution of the full purposes and objectives of Congress.'"

8. Many statutes in these cases, in addition to raising question of express and implied preemption, also include a so-called "savings clause," with general language asserting that nothing in the act is meant to supersede various aspects of state law. It might appear that the clarity of at least some savings clauses would make those cases simple. In fact, however, the case law indicates that a "savings clause should not be read to save those common law rights 'the continued existence of which would be absolutely inconsistent with the provisions of the act.' [ ] A general remedies savings clause 'cannot be allowed to supersede the specific substantive preemption provision.'" Carstensen v. Brunswick Corp., 49 F.3d 430 (8th Cir.), cert. denied 116 S.Ct. 182 (1995)(claim for design defect based on lack of propeller guard on boat motor is preempted by the Federal Boat Safety Act).

9. The preemption battleground covers many areas that had previously been litigated as common-law tort cases, as suggested in the following cases: see, e.g., Anguiano v. E.I.Du Pont De Nemours & Co., 44 F.3d 806 (9th Cir.1995)(TMJ design claim is not preempted by the 1976 Medical Devices Amendments to the Food Drug & Cosmetic Act); Harris v. American Airlines, Inc., 55 F.3d 1472 (9th Cir.1995)(claim that airline failed to stop passenger from directing rude and obnoxious racially-motivated remarks toward plaintiff passenger was preempted by the Airline Deregulation Act); Hodges v. Delta Airlines, Inc., 44 F.3d 334 (5th Cir. en banc 1995)(negligence claim by passenger hit by falling case of rum against airline for allowing case to be stored in overhead bin was not preempted by Airline Deregulation Act); Bice v. Leslie's Poolmart, Inc., 39 F.3d 887 (8th Cir.1994)(claim of inadequate labeling on chemical swimming pool maintenance product was preempted by Federal Insecticide, Fungicide, and Rodenticide Act "FIFRA"); Greenlaw v. Garrett, 59 F.3d 994 (9th Cir.1995)(federal employee's state claims against former employer for sex discrimination were preempted by federal Civil Service Reform Act).

10. Two important recent preemption cases are pending. In Tebbetts v. Ford Motor Co., 665 A.2d 345 (N.H.1995), the court held that a claim of defective design for lack of a driver's side airbag was not preempted by the National Traffic and Motor Vehicle Safety Act of 1966. Ford argued that the majority of courts faced with this issue had found preemption in the manufacturer's compliance with the statute. The court rejected that argument on the ground that the cited cases had been decided before *Cipollone* "clarified preemption analysis." The Supreme Court denied certiorari, 116 S.Ct. 773 (1996).

In Lohr v. Medtronic, Inc., 56 F.3d 1335 (11th Cir.1995), the plaintiff sued for harm sustained when defendant's pacemaker failed and had to be removed in emergency surgery. Her physician asserted that the failure was caused by a defect in the pacemaker "lead"—a wire carrying electrical impulses from the pacemaker to the heart tissues. In 1976 Congress passed the Medical Device Amendments (MDA). Briefly, three categories were established: Class III covers almost all life-sustaining devices and requires intensive FDA premarket approval. One possible exception to premarket approval existed if the FDA determined that the proposed device was the "substantial equivalent" of a device already on the market, including one that had been grandfathered into the market by virtue of having been introduced into the market before the effective date of the amendments. The pacemaker at issue here was determined to be the "substantial equivalent" of a grandfathered pacemaker. As a result it never underwent the intensive premarketing approval process.

The court held that state law claims of negligent manufacture and failure to warn were preempted but that claims for design defect and "strict liability" were not. Both parties sought certiorari. The Supreme Court granted both petitions, 116 S.Ct. 806 (1996).

G. THE INTERSECTION OF TORT AND THE UNIFORM COMMERCIAL CODE

So far we have been focusing on the role of tort law when victims have been hurt by allegedly defective products. By contrast, the course in contracts involves cases in which plaintiffs with disappointed economic expectations seek damages under common law contract or UCC theories. Although these are the two major categories of cases, two smaller but important categories remain: claims in tort by plaintiffs seeking to recover for economic harm, and claims in contract and under the UCC for personal injury. As we turn first to the role of tort law in product-related economic harm cases, recall the discussion of such cases in the negligence context in Chapter IV.

East River Steamship Corp. v. Transamerica Delaval Inc.

Supreme Court of the United States, 1986.
476 U.S. 858, 106 S.Ct. 2295, 90 L.Ed.2d 865.

[Defendant Delaval made turbines, each costing $1.4 million, for four supertankers, each costing $125 million. East River and three other plaintiffs were the separate charterers of each ship for 20–22 years from the owner. Each charterer assumed responsibility for the cost of any repairs. When the first ship made its maiden voyage, the high-pressure turbine malfunctioned, but the ship was able to get to port. Inspection revealed that an essential ring had virtually disintegrated and had caused additional damage to other parts of the turbine. Eventually, the ship was permanently and satisfactorily repaired. As a result of this experience, the second and third ships were inspected. The same condition was discovered and satisfactory repairs were made. These problems are involved in the first three counts of the complaint. (The fourth count, involving another design claim, is not relevant here.)

The problem with the fourth ship was that a valve between the high-pressure and low-pressure turbines was installed backwards. Because of that error, steam entered the low-pressure turbine and damaged it. This condition was repaired. This episode is the subject of the fifth count—which alleged negligence.

The charterers' complaints invoked the admiralty jurisdiction and set forth tort claims for the cost of repairing the ships and for income lost while the ships were out of service. The district court granted Delaval summary judgment and the court of appeals affirmed. The Supreme Court granted certiorari to resolve a conflict among the courts of appeals sitting in admiralty.]

■ JUSTICE BLACKMUN delivered the opinion of the Court.

In this admiralty case, we must decide whether a cause of action in tort is stated when a defective product purchased in a commercial transaction malfunctions, injuring only the product itself and causing purely economic loss. The case requires us to consider preliminarily whether admiralty law, which already recognizes a general theory of liability for negligence, also incorporates principles of products liability, including strict liability. Then, charting a course between products liability and contract law, we must determine whether injury to a product itself is the kind of harm that should be protected by products liability or left entirely to the law of contracts.

[The Court concluded that the claims fell within the admiralty jurisdiction since the wrongs alleged occurred on or near the high seas or navigable waters. This meant that admiralty substantive law applied. Absent a statute, the general maritime law, as developed by the judiciary from state and federal sources, applied. The Supreme Court joined the courts of appeals in recognizing concepts of products liability based on both negligence and strict liability. But this acceptance of products liability into maritime law "is only the threshold determination to the main issue in this case."]

IV.

Products liability grew out of a public policy judgment that people need more protection from dangerous products than is afforded by the law of warranty. See Seely v. White Motor Co., 63 Cal.2d 9, 15, 403 P.2d 145, 149 (1965). It is clear, however, that if this development were allowed to progress too far, contract law would drown in a sea of tort. See G. Gilmore, The Death of Contract 87–94 (1974). We must determine whether a commercial product injuring itself is the kind of harm against which public policy requires manufacturers to protect, independent of any contractual obligation.

A

The paradigmatic products-liability action is one where a product "reasonably certain to place life and limb in peril," distributed without reinspection, causes bodily injury. See, *e.g.*, [*MacPherson*]. The manufacturer is liable whether or not it is negligent because "public policy demands that responsibility be fixed wherever it will most effectively reduce the hazards to life and health inherent in defective products that reach the market." [*Escola*](concurring opinion).

For similar reasons of safety, the manufacturer's duty of care was broadened to include protection against property damage. [ ] Such damage is considered so akin to personal injury that the two are treated alike. See [*Seely*].

In the traditional "property damage" cases, the defective product damages other property. In this case, there was no damage to "other" property. Rather, the first, second, and third counts allege that each supertanker's defectively designed turbine components damaged only the turbine itself. Since each turbine was supplied by Delaval as an integrated package, each is properly regarded as a single unit. "Since all but the very simplest of machines have component parts, [a contrary] holding would require a finding of 'property damage' in virtually every case where a product damages itself. Such a holding would eliminate the distinction between warranty and strict products liability." Northern Power & Engineering Corp. v. Caterpillar Tractor Co., 623 P.2d 324, 330 (Alaska 1981). The fifth count also alleges injury to the product itself. Before the high-pressure and low-pressure turbines could become an operational propulsion system, they were connected to piping and valves under the supervision of Delaval personnel. [ ] Delaval's supervisory obligations were part of its manufacturing agreement. The fifth count thus can best be read to allege that Delaval's negligent manufacture of the propulsion system—by allowing the installation in reverse of the astern guardian valve—damaged the propulsion system. [ ] Obviously, damage to a product itself has certain attributes of a products-liability claim. But the injury suffered—the failure of the product to function properly—is the essence of a warranty action, through which a contracting party can seek to recoup the benefit of its bargain.

B

The intriguing question whether injury to a product itself may be brought in tort has spawned a variety of answers. At one end of the spectrum, the case that created the majority land-based approach, *Seely* (defective truck), held that preserving a proper role for the law of warranty precludes imposing tort liability if a defective product causes purely monetary harm. [ ]

At the other end of the spectrum is the minority land-based approach, whose progenitor, Santor v. A and M Karagheusian, Inc., 44 N.J. 52, 66–67, 207 A.2d 305, 312–313 (1965)(marred carpeting), held that a manufacturer's duty to make nondefective products encompassed injury to the product itself, whether or not the defect created an unreasonable risk of harm. The courts adopting this approach, including the majority of the Courts of Appeals sitting in admiralty that have considered the issue, [ ] find that the safety and insurance rationales behind strict liability apply equally where the losses are purely economic. These courts reject the *Seely* approach because they find it arbitrary that economic losses are recoverable if a plaintiff suffers bodily injury or property damage, but not if a product injures itself. They also find no inherent difference between economic loss and personal injury or property damage, because all are proximately caused by the defendant's conduct. Further, they believe recovery for economic loss would not lead to unlimited liability because they think a manufacturer can predict and insure against product failure. [ ]

Between the two poles fall a number of cases that would permit a products-liability action under certain circumstances when a product injures only itself. These cases attempt to differentiate between "the disappointed users . . . and the endangered ones," Russell v. Ford Motor Co., 281 Ore. 587, 595, 575 P.2d 1383, 1387 (1978), and permit only the latter to sue in tort. The determination has been said to turn on the nature of the defect, the type of risk, and the manner in which the injury arose. [ ] The Alaska Supreme Court allows a tort action if the defective product creates a situation potentially dangerous to persons or other property, and loss occurs as a proximate result of that danger and under dangerous circumstances. [ ]

We find the intermediate and minority land-based positions unsatisfactory. The intermediate positions, which essentially turn on the degree of risk, are too indeterminate to enable manufacturers easily to structure their business behavior. Nor do we find persuasive a distinction that rests on the manner in which the product is injured. We realize that the damage may be qualitative, occurring through gradual deterioration or internal breakage. Or it may be calamitous. [ ] But either way, since by definition no person or other property is damaged, the resulting loss is purely economic. Even when the harm to the product itself occurs through an abrupt, accident-like event, the resulting loss due to repair costs, decreased value, and lost profits is essentially the failure of the purchaser to receive the benefit of its bargain—traditionally the core concern of contract law. See E. Farnsworth, Contracts § 12.8, pp. 839–840 (1982).

We also decline to adopt the minority land-based view espoused by [*Santor* and other cases]. Such cases raise legitimate questions about the theories behind restricting products liability, but we believe that the countervailing arguments are more powerful. The minority view fails to account for the need to keep products liability and contract law in separate spheres and to maintain a realistic limitation on damages.

C

Exercising traditional discretion in admiralty, [   ], we adopt an approach similar to *Seely* and hold that a manufacturer in a commercial relationship has no duty under either a negligence or strict products-liability theory to prevent a product from injuring itself.

"The distinction that the law has drawn between tort recovery for physical injuries and warranty recovery for economic loss is not arbitrary and does not rest on the 'luck' of one plaintiff in having an accident causing physical injury. The distinction rests, rather, on an understanding of the nature of the responsibility a manufacturer must undertake in distributing his products." [*Seely*] When a product injures only itself the reasons for imposing a tort duty are weak and those for leaving the party to its contractual remedies are strong.

The tort concern with safety is reduced when an injury is only to the product itself. When a person is injured, the "cost of an injury and the loss of time or health may be an overwhelming misfortune," and one the person is not prepared to meet. [*Escola*](concurring opinion). In contrast, when a product injures itself, the commercial user stands to lose the value of the product, risks the displeasure of its customers who find that the product does not meet their needs, or, as in this case, experiences increased costs in performing a service. Losses like these can be insured. [   ] Society need not presume that a customer needs special protection. The increased cost to the public that would result from holding a manufacturer liable in tort for injury to the product itself is not justified. Cf. United States v. Carroll Towing Co., 159 F.2d 169, 173 (C.A.2 1947).

Damage to a product itself is most naturally understood as a warranty claim. Such damage means simply that the product has not met the customer's expectations, or, in other words, that the customer has received "insufficient product value." [   ] The maintenance of product value and quality is precisely the purpose of express and implied warranties. See UCC § 2–313 (express warranty), § 2–314 (implied warranty of merchantability), and § 2–315 (warranty of fitness for a particular purpose). Therefore, a claim of a nonworking product can be brought as a breach-of-warranty action. Or, if the customer prefers, it can reject the product or revoke its acceptance and sue for breach of contract. See UCC §§ 2–601, 2–608, 2–612.

Contract law, and the law of warranty in particular, is well suited to commercial controversies of the sort involved in this case because the parties may set the terms of their own agreements. The manufacturer can restrict its liability, within limits, by disclaiming warranties or limiting remedies. See UCC §§ 2–316, 2–719. In exchange, the purchaser pays less for the product. Since a commercial situation generally does not involve large disparities in bargaining power, [   ] we see no reason to intrude into the parties' allocation of the risk.

While giving recognition to the manufacturer's bargain, warranty law sufficiently protects the purchaser by allowing it to obtain the benefit of its bargain. [   ] The expectation damages available in warranty for purely economic loss give a plaintiff the full benefit of its bargain by compensating for forgone business opportunities. [   ] Recovery on a warranty theory would give the charterers their repair costs and lost profits, and would place them in the position they would have been in had the turbines functioned properly.[9] [   ] Thus, both the nature of the injury and the resulting damages indicate it is more natural to think of injury to a product itself in terms of warranty.

A warranty action also has a built-in limitation on liability, whereas a tort action could subject the manufacturer to damages of an indefinite amount. The limitation in a contract action comes from the agreement of the parties and the requirement that consequential damages, such as lost profits, be a foreseeable result of the breach. See Hadley v. Baxendale, 9 Ex. 341, 156 Eng.Rep. 145 (1854). In a warranty action where the loss is purely economic, the limitation derives from the requirements of foreseeability and of privity, which is still generally enforced for such claims in a commercial setting. [   ]

In products-liability law, where there is a duty to the public generally, foreseeability is an inadequate brake. Cf. Petitions of Kinsman Transit Co., 388 F.2d 821 (C.A.2 1968). [   ] Permitting recovery for all foreseeable claims for purely economic loss could make a manufacturer liable for vast sums. It would be difficult for a manufacturer to take into account the expectations of persons downstream who may encounter its product. In this case, for example, if the charterers—already one step removed from the transaction—were permitted to recover their economic losses, then the companies that subchartered the ships might claim their economic losses from the delays, and the charterers' customers also might claim their economic losses, and so on. "The law does not spread its protection so far." Robins Dry Dock & Repair Co. v. Flint, 275 U.S. 303, 309 (1927).

And to the extent that courts try to limit purely economic damages in tort, they do so by relying on a far murkier line, one that negates the charterers' contention that permitting such recovery under a products-liability theory enables admiralty courts to avoid difficult linedrawing. Cf. Ultramares Corp. v. Touche, 255 N.Y. 170, 174 N.E. 441 (1931); [   ].

D

For the first three counts, the defective turbine components allegedly injured only the turbines themselves. Therefore, a strict products-liability theory of recovery is unavailable to the charterers. Any warranty claims would be subject to Delaval's limitation, both in time and scope, of its warranty liability. . . .

. . .

---

9. In contrast, tort damages generally compensate the plaintiff for loss and return him to the position he occupied before the injury. [   ] Tort damages are analogous to reliance damages, which are awarded in contract when there is particular difficulty in measuring the expectation interest. [   ]

Similarly, in the fifth count, alleging the reverse installation of the astern guardian valve, the only harm was to the propulsion system itself rather than to persons or other property. Even assuming that Delaval's supervision was negligent, as we must on this summary judgment motion, Delaval owed no duty under a products-liability theory based on negligence to avoid causing purely economic loss. [ ] Thus, whether stated in negligence or strict liability, no products-liability claim lies in admiralty when the only injury claimed is economic loss.

. . . . [W]e affirm the entry of judgment for Delaval.

NOTES AND QUESTIONS

1. What is the impact of choosing between tort and contract in this type of case? Although it is not binding on state courts, *East River* has been widely accepted.

2. In *Seely*, a dissenting judge said that he found it "hard to understand how one might . . . award a traveling salesman lost earnings if a defect in his car causes his *leg* to break in an accident but deny that salesman his lost earnings if the defect instead disables only his *car* before any accident occurs." How might Justice Blackmun respond?

3. What are the strengths and weaknesses of the *Santor* approach? Of the "intermediate" approach? Of the Court's approach?

Can the *Santor* position be justified when the buyer is an individual? Consider Jones, Product Defects Causing Commercial Loss: The Ascendancy of Contract over Tort, 44 U.Miami L.Rev. 731 (1990), concluding that when individual consumers are the buyers, "because of limitations on consumer knowledge and because of disparities in consumer wealth, it cannot be said that contractual reallocations of risk are economically efficient and socially acceptable in the general run of manufacturer-consumer transactions." But when the buyer is a commercial enterprise that economic efficiency exists and any social concerns are minimal. In such cases, the role of tort law is "redundant and perverse. It is used by litigants and courts to undermine allocations of risks agreed to by the parties and to substitute judicial solutions for contractual arrangements that are almost certainly superior in terms of both fairness and efficiency."

4. In Bocre Leasing Corp. v. General Motors Corp., 84 N.Y.2d 685, 645 N.E.2d 1195, 621 N.Y.S.2d 497 (1995), plaintiff was a "four-times removed downstream purchaser of a helicopter" that defendant had made and sold some 15 years earlier. Plaintiff bought it from a broker "as is." As the result of an alleged engine defect the helicopter experienced a power loss in flight but landed safely, causing damage only to the helicopter itself "with no damage whatsoever to persons or other property." The court rejected a tort claim despite the fact that the alleged defect created a serious risk of personal injury. Plaintiff here could have bargained with its vendor for warranty protections and acquired insurance against harm to the property and lost profits, such as lost rentals and air time. The denial of tort did not undercut safety: since "any product put into the stream of commerce has the theoretical potential to injure persons and property, the incentive to provide safe products is always present." One judge would have allowed a tort action for the property damage to the helicopter but not for the economic loss. How would the case be analyzed under an *East River* analysis?

For an extreme statement of the economic loss doctrine, see Airport Rent–A–Car, Inc. v. Prevost Car, Inc., 660 So.2d 628 (Fla.1995), in which plaintiff alleged that it owned several buses manufactured by defendant that it had bought from a company that was not a "merchant" under the UCC (and thus against whom no warranty actions would lie). Two buses caught fire and were destroyed—one while transporting school children. The court held that no tort action lay for the loss of the buses because of the "economic loss rule." It was irrelevant that a warranty action might be unavailable or that the losses were sudden calamities.

East River 's analysis was rejected in Washington Water Power Co. v. Graybar Electric Co., 112 Wash.2d 847, 774 P.2d 1199 (1989) on the ground that the "increased certainty [of identifying the line between tort and contract] comes at too high a price." The court preferred the "risk of harm" approach because it encouraged greater attention to product safety.

5. How similar are the problems in cases like *East River* and those raised in the People Express case, p. 282, supra?

6. *Tort liability for innocent misrepresentations.* Although tort law has fastened on § 402A as a crucial Restatement section, the use of "A" suggests that there is a "B"—and indeed there is. According to § 402B of the Second Restatement, a seller of chattels who "makes to the public a misrepresentation of a material fact concerning the character or quality of a chattel sold by him is subject to liability for physical harm to a consumer of the chattel caused by justifiable reliance upon the misrepresentation, even though (a) it is not made fraudulently or negligently, and (b) the consumer has not bought the chattel from or entered into any contractual relation with the seller."

Note that some states may not require reliance and some do not require that the representation be made to the public. Also note that the product might well have been held to be nondefective but for the representation the seller made about it. The basis for liability under § 402B is found in the representational words used to describe the product—not any defect in the product itself or an inadequacy in instructions or warnings.

7. *Introduction to personal injury litigation outside of tort law.* The remaining category involves suits for personal injury that do not arise as tort claims. These are typically brought under a warranty provision of the UCC.

a. *Implied warranties.* The implied warranty sections, §§ 2–314 and 2–315, generally involve aberrationally defective products—so-called manufacturing defects. Recall the *Ryan* case, p. 478, supra, involving a pin in a loaf of bread. Why might a plaintiff prefer to go on a warranty theory rather than tort law—especially where the contract theories may offer privity problems and less attractive damage awards because of limits on punitive damages or on non-pecuniary awards? One answer is the statute of limitations. The Code's statute of limitations is four years from the delivery of the goods, § 2–725. The tort limitation may be shorter but generally runs only from the time of the plaintiff's injury or perhaps discovery of that injury. It is not difficult to imagine situations in which plaintiffs might find one avenue barred while the other is still open. Also, if the claim is for property damage the contract limits on recoverable damages are not a serious impediment.

b. *Express warranty.* This is a potentially very important basis for liability under the Code—with a tort analogue. If a manufacturer makes an express warranty about the quality or attributes of the product, anyone hurt if such a representation or warranty turns out to be false may recover damages—even without fault on the maker's part. In some states this may be true even though the victim did not know about the warranty and did not rely on it in using the product. See §§ 2–313, 2–316. See Note, Express Warranties Under the Uniform Commercial Code: Is There a Reliance Requirement?, 66 N.Y.U.L.Rev. 468 (1991). Note that the product need not be defective; it may be perfectly adequate. The claim is based on the failure of the product to live up to what the supplier claimed for it.

For an extended consideration of the warranty theories and their relation to § 402B, see American Safety Equipment Corp. v. Winkler, 640 P.2d 216 (Colo.1982); Hauter v. Zogarts, 14 Cal.3d 104, 534 P.2d 377, 120 Cal.Rptr. 681 (1975), involving a plaintiff injured by the operation of the "Golfing Gizmo," a training device intended to help unskilled golfers improve their games.

8. *Introduction to Warranty Defenses.* We have seen that courts tend to use a comparative approach to defenses in tort cases. What happens when the case is brought under the Code? The Code nowhere contemplates shared responsibility: it speaks in terms of proximate cause, suggesting that once a buyer discovers a defect or should reasonably have discovered it, there can no longer be reasonable reliance on the warranty, and thus no recovery. See § 2–314 comment 13; § 2–316 comment 8; § 2–715 comment 5.

A few courts have adopted this approach. See Erdman v. Johnson Bros. Radio & Television Co., 260 Md. 190, 271 A.2d 744 (1970)(no warranty liability for fire where plaintiffs continued using a television set after seeing sparks coming from it).

Other courts have developed a comparative fault approach to warranty cases analogous to what the state would do in the tort action. See West v. Caterpillar Tractor Co., 547 F.2d 885 (5th Cir.1977)(developing a partial defense to avoid the anomaly of permitting negligent defendants sued in tort to reduce their liability under comparative negligence, but not permitting innocent defendants sued in warranty a similar reduction where the plaintiff carelessly failed to observe the danger).

9. *The Magnuson–Moss Act.* In 1975, Congress entered the warranty field with the Magnuson–Moss Warranty Act, 15 U.S.C. § 2300 et seq. Although a seller need give no warranties, one who does so must make them either "full" or "limited." The applicable rules tend to fall almost exclusively in the domain of contract because they involve purely economic harm. In most cases, there is no recovery under the Act for personal injuries arising out of a breach of an implied warranty. 15 U.S.C. § 2311(b)(2). See Maillet v. ATF–Davidson Co., 407 Mass. 185, 552 N.E.2d 95 (1990)(Congress left state law central in personal injury cases).

CHAPTER IX

TRESPASS AND NUISANCE

Trespass and nuisance are related doctrines protecting interests in, respectively, the exclusive possession, and the use and enjoyment, of land. In an earlier era, trespass came to be regarded primarily as a safeguard against physical intrusions on land. By contrast, nuisance actions have a long history of affording protection against obnoxious uses of neighboring land. As we shall see, however, in modern times the distinctions between the situations in which the cases arise begin to blur.

Because of the special importance that the law traditionally placed on protection of interests in land, strict liability has been a dominant feature of the law in this area. As the mixed reception of Rylands v. Fletcher, p. 437, supra, indicated, however, great confusion and debate exist over the "strictness" of liability for harms to interests in land.

The subject is given separate consideration here for two main reasons. Most important, as this brief introduction suggests, the courts have long regarded interests in land as a functionally distinct category. As a consequence, trespass and nuisance actions cut across the boundaries of the intentional and unintentional tort categories that we have been examining. In addition, the modern cases, in particular, provide the common-law foundation for analyzing environmental disputes. For both of these reasons, the judicially-fashioned liability rules in this area deserve special attention.

Our brief treatment of basic doctrine will place considerable emphasis on the Restatement approach, which has brought some semblance of order to a confused body of case law.

A. TRESPASS

At early common law, every unauthorized entry by a person or object onto another's land that resulted from a voluntary act was subject to liability as a trespass. Obviously, a person who was carried against his will onto the land of another would not have satisfied the requirement of voluntary conduct, and could therefore not be held to have committed a trespass. Such narrow instances aside, however, a person who nonnegligently but incorrectly believed that particular property was his own, or that he was authorized to go upon it, would nonetheless be liable for trespass because he intended to enter the property.

As the New York blasting cases, p. 439, supra, indicated, many courts required actual physical entry by a tangible object, since the interest that plaintiff sought to protect was the exclusive possession of his land. Once this requirement was satisfied, however, any technical invasion could serve as the basis for an action, since trespass was the principal method by which a lawful possessor of land could vindicate his property rights and ensure that a continuing trespass did not ripen into a prescriptive right. Because the gist of the action was considered to be the intrusion or "breaking of the close," demonstrable harm was not required for at least nominal damages to be assessed.

As plaintiffs came to allege trespassory invasions resulting from objects—such as exploding boilers and flying debris—rather than people, many courts began to distinguish between "direct" and "indirect," or trespassory and non-trespassory harms. This distinction, borrowed from the common-law writ system, where it was not limited to invasions of land, created great confusion. Again, the New York cases, considered earlier, serve as an example.

Modern trespass doctrine has largely obliterated the historical distinction between direct and indirect trespassory invasions of land. But a distinction of another kind—a present day differentiation between intentional and unintentional trespasses—has continuing vitality. The Restatement (Second) of Torts § 165 states that unintended intrusions—those resulting from reckless or negligent conduct or from abnormally dangerous activities—will be subjected to liability only if the intrusion causes actual harm.

By contrast, partly because actions for trespass remain an important means of maintaining the integrity of a possessory interest in land, intentional trespasses retain much of their common-law strict liability character. Section 158 states that one is liable to another in trespass for an intentional intrusion, irrespective of harm caused. In this context, "intent" refers to the intent to enter the land, not necessarily to invade another's interest in the exclusive possession of land. Thus, a mistaken, non-negligent entry can result in liability—as at earlier common law—even if no harm occurred.

The strictness of the intentional trespass action is mitigated to some extent through a series of privileges that shield from liability activity that would otherwise constitute a trespass. These privileges may arise out of the consent of the possessor (§§ 167–175), or may be afforded as a matter of law because of the purposes for which the actor enters the premises (§§ 176–211). The scope of these privileges, however, is in general quite narrow and limited to specific types of situations. Thus, despite the increased flexibility these privileges afford to defendants, no overarching principle of reasonableness has yet developed in the area of intentional, as compared to unintentional, trespasses.

With this background in mind, consider the following case.

Martin v. Reynolds Metals Co.

Supreme Court of Oregon, 1959.
221 Or. 86, 342 P.2d 790, cert. denied 362 U.S. 918 (1960).

[Plaintiffs sued for trespass, claiming damage to their farm land from the operation of defendant's nearby aluminum reduction plant. The trial judge awarded plaintiffs $71,500 for damages to their land, which could no longer be used to raise livestock because the cattle were poisoned by ingesting the fluoride compounds that became airborne from the plant and settled on the plaintiff's land. (The daily emanation of fluorides from the plant averaged 800 pounds.) The judge also awarded $20,000 for the deterioration of the land through growth of brush and weeds resulting from the lack of grazing. The judge rejected punitive damages. The damages covered the period from August 1951 through the end of 1955. If the action were properly brought in trespass, with its six-year statute of limitations, the award was permissible. But if the action were one of nuisance, then damages were recoverable for only 1954 and 1955, because of the two-year statute of limitations.]

■ O'CONNELL, J.

.   .   .

The gist of the defendant's argument is as follows: a trespass arises only when there has been a "breaking and entering upon real property," constituting a direct, as distinguished from a consequential, invasion of the possessor's interest in land; and the settling upon the land of fluoride compounds consisting of gases, fumes and particulates is not sufficient to satisfy these requirements.

Before appraising the argument we shall first describe more particularly the physical and chemical nature of the substance which was deposited upon plaintiffs' land. In reducing alumina (the oxide of aluminum) to aluminum the alumina is subjected to an electrolytic process which causes the emanation of fluoridic compounds consisting principally of hydrogen fluoride, calcium fluoride, iron fluoride and silicon tetrafluoride. The individual particulates which form these chemical compounds are not visible to the naked eye. A part of them were captured by a fume collection system which was installed in November, 1950; the remainder became airborne and a part of the uncaptured particles eventually were deposited upon plaintiffs' land.

.   .   .

Trespass and private nuisance are separate fields of tort liability relating to actionable interference with the possession of land. They may be distinguished by comparing the interest invaded; an actionable invasion of a possessor's interest in the exclusive possession of land is a trespass; an actionable invasion of a possessor's interest in the use and enjoyment of his land is a nuisance. [   ]

The same conduct on the part of a defendant may and often does result in the actionable invasion of both of these interests, in which case the choice between the two remedies is, in most cases, a matter of little consequence. Where the action is brought on the theory of nuisance alone the court ordinarily is not called upon to determine whether the conduct would also result in a trespassory invasion. In such cases the courts' treatment of the invasion solely in terms of the law of nuisance does not mean that the same conduct could not also be regarded as a trespass. Some of the cases relied upon by the defendant are of this type; cases in which the court holds that the interference with the plaintiff's possession through soot, dirt, smoke, cinders, ashes and similar substances constitute a nuisance, but where the court does not discuss the applicability of the law of trespass to the same set of facts. [ ]

However, there are cases which have held that the defendant's interference with plaintiff's possession resulting from the settling upon his land of effluents emanating from defendant's operations is exclusively nontrespassory. [ ] Although in such cases the separate particles which collectively cause the invasion are minute, the deposit of each of the particles constitutes a physical intrusion and, but for the size of the particle, would clearly give rise to an action of trespass. The defendant asks us to take account of the difference in size of the physical agency through which the intrusion occurs and relegate entirely to the field of nuisance law certain invasions which do not meet the dimensional test, whatever that is. In pressing this argument upon us the defendant must admit that there are cases which have held that a trespass results from the movement or deposit of rather small objects over or upon the surface of the possessor's land.

[The court cites examples such as molten lead, soot, and gunshot pellets.]

And liability on the theory of trespass has been recognized where the harm was produced by the vibration of the soil or by the concussion of the air which, of course, is nothing more than the movement of molecules one against the other. . . . The view recognizing a trespassory invasion where there is no "thing" which can be seen with the naked eye undoubtedly runs counter to the definition of trespass expressed in some quarters. [ ] It is quite possible that in an earlier day when science had not yet peered into the molecular and atomic world of small particles, the courts could not fit an invasion through unseen physical instrumentalities into the requirement that a trespass can result only from a *direct* invasion. But in this atomic age even the uneducated know the great and awful force contained in the atom and what it can do to a man's property if it is released. In fact, the now famous equation $E = mc^2$ has taught us that mass and energy are equivalents and that our concept of "things" must be reframed. If these observations on science in relation to the law of trespass should appear theoretical and unreal in the abstract, they become very practical and real to the possessor of land when the unseen force cracks the foundation of his house. The force is just as real if it is chemical in nature and must be awakened by the intervention of another agency before it does harm.

If, then, we must look to the character of the instrumentality which is used in making an intrusion upon another's land we prefer to emphasize the object's energy or force rather than its size. Viewed in this way we may define trespass as any intrusion which invades the possessor's protected interest in exclusive possession, whether that intrusion is by visible or invisible pieces of matter or by energy which can be measured only by the mathematical language of the physicist.

We are of the opinion, therefore, that the intrusion of the fluoride particulates in the present case constituted a trespass.

.   .   .

.   .   . The modern law of trespass can be understood only as it is seen against its historical background. Originally all types of trespass, including trespass to land, were punishable under the criminal law because the trespasser's conduct was regarded as a breach of the peace. When the criminal and civil aspect of trespass were separated, the civil action for trespass was colored by its past, and the idea that the peace of the community was put in danger by the trespasser's conduct influenced the courts' ideas of the character of the tort. Therefore, relief was granted to the plaintiff where he was not actually damaged, partly at least as a means of discouraging disruptive influences in the community. Winfield on Torts (4th ed.) p. 305 expresses the idea as follows:

"The law, on the face of it, looks harsh, but trespass was so likely in earlier times to lead to a breach of the peace that even unwitting and trivial deviations on to another person's land were reckoned unlawful. At the present day there is, of course, much greater respect for the law in general and appreciation of the security which it affords, and the theoretical severity of the rules as to land trespass is hardly ever exploited in practice."

.   .   . If then, we find that an act on the part of the defendant in interfering with the plaintiff's possession, does, or is likely to result in arousing conflict between them, that act will characterize the tort as a trespass, assuming of course that the other elements of the tort are made out.   .   .   .

Probably the most important factor which describes the nature of the interest protected under the law of trespass is nothing more than a feeling which a possessor has with respect to land which he holds. It is a sense of ownership; a feeling that what one owns or possesses should not be interfered with, and that it is entitled to protection through law. This being the nature of the plaintiff's interest, it is understandable why actual damage is not an essential ingredient in the law of trespass. As pointed out in 1 Harper & James, Torts, § 1.8, p. 26, the rule permitting recovery in spite of the absence of actual damages "is probably justified as a vindicatory right to protect the possessor's proprietary or dignitary interest in his land."

We think that a possessor's interest in land as defined by the considerations recited above may, under the appropriate circumstances, be violated by a ray of light, by an atomic particle, or by a particulate of fluoride and, contrariwise, if such interest circumscribed by these considerations is not violated or endangered, the defendant's conduct, even though it may result in a physical intrusion, will not render him liable in an action of trespass. [ ]

We hold that the defendant's conduct in causing chemical substances to be deposited upon the plaintiffs' land fulfilled all of the requirements under the law of trespass.

The defendant contends that trespass will not lie in this case because the injury was indirect and consequential and that the requirement that the injury must be direct and immediate to constitute a trespass was not met. We have held that the deposit of the particulates upon the plaintiff's land was an intrusion within the definition of trespass. That intrusion was direct. The damages which flowed from it are consequential, but it is well established that such consequential damage may be proven in an action of trespass. [ ] The distinction between direct and indirect invasions where there has been a physical intrusion upon the plaintiff's land has been abandoned by some courts. [ ] Since the invasion in the instant case was direct it is not necessary for us to decide whether the distinction is recognized in this state.

. . .

It is also urged that the trial court erred in failing to enter a special finding requested by the defendant. The requested finding in effect stated that it was impossible in the operation of an aluminum reduction plant to capture all fluorides which are created in the manufacturing process; that the fume collection system was in operation during the period in question; and that it was the most efficient of the systems known in aluminum reduction plants in the United States.

It is argued that since the trial court elected to enter special rather than general findings it was required by ORS 17.430 to enter findings on all material issues which, it is claimed, would include the issue defined in the requested findings. The complaint alleged that the defendant "carelessly, wantonly and willfully continuously caused to be emitted," from its plant the poisonous compounds. This allegation was denied in the defendant's answer. The issue thus raised, as to the character of defendant's conduct in making the intrusion upon plaintiffs' land, would be material only with respect to the claim for punitive damages which, as we have already indicated, was rejected by the trial court. Since we hold that the intrusion in this case constituted a trespass it is immaterial whether the defendant's conduct was careless, wanton and willful or entirely free from fault. Therefore, the refusal to enter the requested finding is not error.

The judgment of the lower court is affirmed.

■ [The concurring opinion of MCALLISTER, C.J., is omitted.]

NOTES AND QUESTIONS

1. Is aluminum production an ultrahazardous activity? Is the theory of liability here different from that of the New York blasting cases in Chapter VII?

2. Why is it irrelevant whether the defendant's fume collection system constituted a reasonable effort to capture the fluoride particulates? Is the case distinguishable from *Losee v. Buchanan*, p. 437, supra?

3. Can *Martin* be viewed as an application of the doctrine of *Rylands v. Fletcher*?

4. Under the court's expansive view of the trespass action, what types of cases would be exclusively nuisance actions? Is there a meaningful distinction between "exclusive possession" and "use and enjoyment" of land? If the plant had emitted a noxious stench, would the court have regarded the harm as actionable in trespass? In nuisance? What about a continuing abrasive level of noise? See Wilson v. Interlake Steel Co., 32 Cal.3d 229, 649 P.2d 922, 185 Cal.Rptr. 280 (1982), in which the court asserted that "intangible intrusions, such as noise, odor, or light alone, are dealt with as nuisance cases, not trespass." Compare Ream v. Keen, 314 Or. 370, 838 P.2d 1073 (1992), in which the Oregon court relied on *Martin* to find liability for trespass in a case involving "intrusion of smoke and its lingering odor" from defendant farmer's burning of grass stubble on his field.

Martin is adopted and the question of overlap between trespass and nuisance discussed at length in Borland v. Sanders Lead Co., Inc., 369 So.2d 523 (Ala.1979)(action in trespass for lead pollution). See also Bradley v. American Smelting and Refining Co., 104 Wash.2d 677, 709 P.2d 782 (1985), adopting *Martin* in a case involving deposit of airborne particles from a copper smelter, but rejecting the Restatement view that an intentional trespass entitles a landowner to damages irrespective of actual harm; the court required a showing of "actual and substantial damage" as a safeguard against mass trivial claims by neighboring landowners.

B.   NUISANCE

The confusion attending the law of nuisance is indicated by the frequent references to Prosser's comment that "[t]here is no more impenetrable jungle in the entire law than that which surrounds the word 'nuisance'." Some of this confusion can be avoided by distinguishing at the outset between public and private nuisance. Despite the overlapping terminology, the interests protected by each action and the corresponding elements in establishing a prima facie case are quite different. Although private nuisance is our primary concern, private individuals may, under certain circumstances, employ public nuisance doctrine to protect against harm to person and property. We begin with a brief discussion of the action for public nuisance.

1.   PUBLIC NUISANCE

The historical origins of public nuisance are found in criminal interferences with the rights of the Crown, such as encroachments on the royal domain or on public highways. Subsequently, invasions of the rights of the public—represented by the Crown—became actionable as well. At common law, public nuisance came to cover a broad group of minor criminal offenses that involved unreasonable interferences with some right of the general public. These "included interference with the public health, as in the keeping of diseased animals . . . ; with the public safety, as in the case of storage of explosives in the midst of a city . . . ; with the public morals, as in houses of prostitution . . . ; with the public peace as by loud and disturbing noises; with the public comfort, as in the case of widely disseminated bad odors, dust, and smoke; with the public convenience as by obstruction of a public highway or navigable stream; and with a wide variety of miscellaneous public rights of a similar kind." Restatement (Second) of Torts § 821B comment *b*. Most states, having abolished common law crimes, now have broadly-phrased statutes providing criminal penalties for public nuisances, or have enacted specific statutes declaring certain kinds of conduct to be public nuisances. It does not follow, however, that public nuisance actions have become superfluous. Consider, for example, State v. Schenectady Chemicals, Inc. 103 App.Div.2d 33, 479 N.Y.S.2d 1010 (1984), in which the court found that the migration of chemical wastes over a thirty-year period did not constitute a "discharge" within the meaning of a relevant statute, but did constitute the basis for a public nuisance action initiated by the state. See generally, Note, Chemical Discharge: Application of Public Nuisance Theory as a Remedy for Environmental Law Violations, 26 Suffolk L. Rev. 51 (1992).

Traditionally, the tort of public nuisance required the element of criminality to justify private relief. The Second Restatement, however, has eliminated the reference to a "criminal interference." The motivation for the change was concern that the criminality requirement would limit too severely the usefulness of public nuisance doctrine as a means of protecting the environment, which had become of increasing public concern. Instead, § 821B(1) defines public nuisance as "an unreasonable interference with a right common to the general public," and in subsection (2) lists circumstances that could make an interference unreasonable. These include: a significant interference with the public health, safety, peace, comfort, or convenience; the existence of a statute or ordinance proscribing the conduct; or conduct of a continuing nature or of long-lasting effect that the "actor knows or has reason to know has a significant effect upon the public right."

Private litigants attempting to bring public nuisance suits must overcome strict standing requirements. At early common law, a public nuisance action, in keeping with its criminal character, could be maintained only by a public official. Beginning in the sixteenth century, a private individual who could show special harm different in kind, and not just degree, from that suffered by the general public was allowed to bring a private tort suit. The usual justification for this requirement was that a defendant should not be subjected to the numerous actions that could result from a widespread interference with common rights.

Section 821C(1) retains special harm as a prerequisite for recovery of damages in an individual action. According to § 821C(2), standing to bring such an action requires that parties other than public officials either have suffered special harm or "have standing to sue as a representative of the general public, as a citizen in a citizen's action, or as a member of a class in a class action." The requirement may be relaxed, however, in an injunctive action against a public nuisance. Comment *j* explains that the reasons for the special-harm rule are less applicable to injunctive actions and that there are indications of possible change in the courts. Several commentators have suggested that the special-harm requirement be abandoned, again primarily in response to the possibility of using nuisance doctrine as a means of controlling environmental pollution.

The requirement of specific harm to the claimant is reaffirmed and discussed with reference to a variety of illustrative cases in Stop & Shop Companies, Inc. v. Fisher, 387 Mass. 889, 444 N.E.2d 368 (1983). The individualized harm requirement may be overcome in some cases, particularly in the environmental field, by relying upon a statutory special injury requirement. See, e.g., Florida Wildlife Federation v. State Department of Environmental Regulation, 390 So.2d 64 (Fla.1980), relying on the state Environmental Protection Act.

In some cases, the distinction between public and private nuisance (next to be discussed) may be less than clear. See Lew v. Superior Court, 20 Cal.App.4th 866, 25 Cal.Rptr.2d 42 (1993), involving successful claims for damages by neighboring residents against the owner of an apartment complex whose tenants were heavily involved in drug dealing activities on the premises. In granting recovery, the court referred to defendant's conduct as both a public and private nuisance.

See generally, Abrams & Washington, The Misunderstood Law of Public Nuisance: A Comparison with Private Nuisance Twenty Years After *Boomer,* 54 Alb.L.Rev. 359 (1990); Hodas, Private Actions for Public Nuisance: Common Law Suits for Relief from Environmental Harm, 16 Ecol.L.Q. 883 (1989); Bryson and MacBeth, Public Nuisance, The Restatement (Second) of Torts and Environmental Law, 2 Ecol.L.Q. 241 (1972).

2.   PRIVATE NUISANCE

Section 822 states the general rule that one is subject to liability for conduct that is a legal cause of an invasion of another's interest in the private use and enjoyment of land if the invasion is either: (a) intentional and unreasonable, or (b) unintentional and arising out of negligent or reckless conduct or abnormally dangerous conditions or activities. The latter category, unintentional nuisances, is governed primarily by the rules relating to the underlying negligence, recklessness, or abnormally dangerous activity on which the nuisance is based, with the added requirement that the injury be related to an invasion of interests in the use and enjoyment of land.

By far the more significant category of nuisances is that which the Restatement defines as intentional. Section 825 extends that category to situations in which there is knowledge that the conduct is invading, or is substantially certain to invade, another's interest in the use and enjoyment of land. Virtually all conduct of a continuing nature then, such as the typical instances of industrial pollution, would be intentional after an initial invasion.

An intentional invasion satisfies the "unreasonableness" requirement, according to § 826, if "(a) the gravity of the harm outweighs the utility of the actor's conduct, or (b) the harm caused by the conduct is serious and the financial burden of compensating for this and similar harm to others would not make the continuation of the conduct not feasible." "Gravity of harm" and the "utility of the conduct" are in turn elaborated as follows:

§ 827 Gravity of Harm—Factors Involved

In defining the gravity of the harm from an intentional invasion of another's interest in the use and enjoyment of land, the following factors are important:

(a) The extent of the harm involved;

(b) the character of the harm involved;

(c) the social value that the law attaches to the type of use or enjoyment invaded;

(d) the suitability of the particular use or enjoyment invaded to the character of the locality; and

(e) the burden on the person harmed of avoiding the harm.

§ 828 Utility of the Conduct—Factors Involved

In determining the utility of conduct that causes an intentional invasion of another's interest in the use and enjoyment of land, the following factors are important:

(a) The social value that the law attaches to the primary purpose of the conduct;

(b) the suitability of the conduct to the character of the locality; and

(c) the impracticability of preventing or avoiding the invasion.

These lists of factors are not intended to be exhaustive, and the relative weight to be given each factor is dependent on the circumstances of the particular case. Obviously, this formulation gives the courts very considerable discretion in determining the final outcome of a balancing test.

The first Restatement of Torts included only the test for unreasonableness contained in Restatement (Second) § 826(a)—whether the gravity of the harm outweighs the utility of the conduct. If this were the sole standard, it could be questioned whether there would be much difference between the tests for intentional and unintentional nuisance—even though "unreasonableness" is to be determined, in the case of intentional nuisances, with reference to the gravity of the harm actually suffered, and in the case of unintended harm, with reference to the likelihood of injury multiplied by the prospective extent of the harm. As comment k to § 822 explains, the negligent, reckless, and abnormally dangerous standards of unintentional nuisances incorporate in some form a balancing of harm against the utility of the conduct, as in the concept of unreasonable risk. And this balancing is made explicit for intentional invasions in § 826.

But § 826(a) is not the sole test in the Second Restatement. An intentional invasion may now be unreasonable under § 826(b) even though the utility of the conduct outweighs the gravity of the harm, if the harm is serious and the defendant could afford to compensate the plaintiff and others similarly harmed while continuing to be engaged in its activity. Similarly, § 829A declares that the gravity of an invasion outweighs its utility (and hence is unreasonable under § 826) whenever the harm caused is both substantial and greater than the plaintiff "should be able to bear without compensation." Thus, an invasion, particularly one causing harm "physical in character," may be so grievous that it outweighs as a matter of law any utility arising from the activity.

At this point it should be evident that substantial similarities exist between the Restatement approach to trespass and nuisance—particularly as the rules governing intentional nuisance come to be strongly influenced by strict liability. Apart from the standards of liability, however, what remedies are available to an aggrieved party? Although trespasses traditionally tended to involve individual instances of harm, equity courts were willing to award injunctive relief when the threat of continued trespassory activity existed. In the nuisance context, the question of remedial alternatives often is critical, since continuing diminution of the plaintiff's use and enjoyment of land is usually present. Should injunctive relief be generally available? The following case deals with this important issue, and also provides the opportunity to go beyond this general introduction and explore in greater detail some fundamental questions about the threshold rules of liability.

Boomer v. Atlantic Cement Co.

Court of Appeals of New York, 1970.
26 N.Y.2d 219, 257 N.E.2d 870, 309 N.Y.S.2d 312.

■ BERGAN, J. Defendant operates a large cement plant near Albany. These are actions for injunction and damages by neighboring land owners alleging injury to property from dirt, smoke and vibration emanating from the plant. A nuisance has been found after trial, temporary damages have been allowed; but an injunction has been denied.

The public concern with air pollution arising from many sources in industry and in transportation is currently accorded ever wider recognition accompanied by a growing sense of responsibility in State and Federal Governments to control it. Cement plants are obvious sources of air pollution in the neighborhoods where they operate.

But there is now before the court private litigation in which individual property owners have sought specific relief from a single plant operation. The threshold question raised by the division of view on this appeal is whether the court should resolve the litigation between the parties now before it as equitably as seems possible; or whether, seeking promotion of the general public welfare, it should channel private litigation into broad public objectives.

A court performs its essential function when it decides the rights of parties before it. Its decision of private controversies may sometimes greatly affect public issues. Large questions of law are often resolved by the manner in which private litigation is decided. But this is normally an incident to the court's main function to settle controversy. It is a rare exercise of judicial power to use a decision in private litigation as a purposeful mechanism to achieve direct public objectives greatly beyond the rights and interests before the court.

Effective control of air pollution is a problem presently far from solution even with the full public and financial powers of government. In large measure adequate technical procedures are yet to be developed and some that appear possible may be economically impracticable.

It seems apparent that the amelioration of air pollution will depend on technical research in great depth; on a carefully balanced consideration of the economic impact of close regulation; and of the actual effect on public health. It is likely to require massive public expenditure and to demand more than any local community can accomplish and to depend on regional and interstate controls.

A court should not try to do this on its own as a by-product of private litigation and it seems manifest that the judicial establishment is neither equipped in the limited nature of any judgment it can pronounce nor prepared to lay down and implement an effective policy for the elimination of air pollution. This is an area beyond the circumference of one private lawsuit. It is a direct responsibility for government and should not thus be undertaken as an incident to solving a dispute between property owners and a single cement plant—one of many—in the Hudson River valley.

The cement making operations of defendant have been found by the court at Special Term to have damaged the nearby properties of plaintiffs in these two actions. That court, as it has been noted, accordingly found defendant maintained a nuisance and this has been affirmed at the Appellate Division. The total damage to plaintiffs' properties is, however, relatively small in comparison with the value of defendant's operation and with the consequences of the injunction which plaintiffs seek.

The ground for the denial of injunction, notwithstanding the finding both that there is a nuisance and that plaintiffs have been damaged substantially, is the large disparity in economic consequences of the nuisance and of the injunction. This theory cannot, however, be sustained without overruling a doctrine which has been consistently reaffirmed in several leading cases in this court and which has never been disavowed here, namely that where a nuisance has been found and where there has been any substantial damage shown by the party complaining an injunction will be granted.

The rule in New York has been that such a nuisance will be enjoined although marked disparity be shown in economic consequence between the effect of the injunction and the effect of the nuisance.

The problem of disparity in economic consequence was sharply in focus in Whalen v. Union Bag & Paper Co. (208 N.Y. 1). A pulp mill entailing an investment of more than a million dollars polluted a stream in which plaintiff, who owned a farm, was "a lower riparian owner". The economic loss to plaintiff from this pollution was small. This court, reversing the Appellate Division, reinstated the injunction granted by the Special Term against the argument of the mill owner that in view of "the slight advantage to plaintiff and the great loss that will be inflicted on defendant" an injunction should not be granted (p. 2). "Such a balancing of injuries cannot be justified by the circumstances of this case," Judge Werner noted (p. 4). He continued: "Although the damage to the plaintiff may be slight as compared with the defendant's expense of abating the condition, that is not a good reason for refusing an injunction" (p. 5).

Thus the unconditional injunction granted at Special Term was reinstated. The rule laid down in that case, then, is that whenever the damage resulting from a nuisance is found not "unsubstantial", viz., $100 a year, injunction would follow. This states a rule that had been followed in this court with marked consistency [   ].

.   .   .

Although the court at Special Term and the Appellate Division held that injunction should be denied, it was found that plaintiffs had been damaged in various specific amounts up to the time of the trial and damages to the respective plaintiffs were awarded for those amounts. The effect of this was, injunction having been denied, plaintiffs could maintain successive actions at law for damages thereafter as further damage was incurred.

The court at Special Term also found the amount of permanent damage attributable to each plaintiff, for the guidance of the parties in the event both sides stipulated to the payment and acceptance of such permanent damage as a settlement of all the controversies among the parties. The total of permanent damages to all plaintiffs thus found was $185,000. This basis of adjustment has not resulted in any stipulation by the parties.

This result at Special Term and at the Appellate Division is a departure from a rule that has become settled; but to follow the rule literally in these cases would be to close down the plant at once. This court is fully agreed to avoid that immediately drastic remedy: the difference in view is how best to avoid it.*

One alternative is to grant the injunction but postpone its effect to a specified future date to give opportunity for technical advances to permit defendant to eliminate the nuisance; another is to grant the injunction conditioned on the payment of permanent damages to plaintiffs which would compensate them for the total economic loss to their property present and future caused by defendant's operations. For reasons which will be developed the court chooses the latter alternative.

If the injunction were to be granted unless within a short period—e.g., 18 months—the nuisance be abated by improved methods, there would be no assurance that any significant technical improvement would occur.

The parties could settle this private litigation at any time if defendant paid enough money and the imminent threat of closing the plant would build up the pressure on defendant. If there were no improved techniques found, there would inevitably be applications to the court at Special Term for extensions of time to perform on showing of good faith efforts to find such techniques.

Moreover, techniques to eliminate dust and other annoying by-products of cement making are unlikely to be developed by any research the defendant can undertake within any short period, but will depend on the total resources of the cement industry nationwide and throughout the world. The problem is universal wherever cement is made.

For obvious reasons the rate of the research is beyond control of defendant. If at the end of 18 months the whole industry has not found a technical solution a court would be hard put to close down this one cement plant if due regard be given to equitable principles.

On the other hand, to grant the injunction unless defendant pays plaintiffs such permanent damages as may be fixed by the court seems to do justice between the contending parties. All of the attributions of economic loss to the properties on which plaintiffs' complaints are based will have been redressed.

The nuisance complained of by these plaintiffs may have other public or private consequences, but these particular parties are the only ones who have sought remedies and the judgment proposed will fully redress them. The limitation of relief granted is a limitation only within the four corners of these actions and does not foreclose public health or other public agencies from seeking proper relief in a proper court.

It seems reasonable to think that the risk of being required to pay permanent damages to injured property owners by cement plant owners would itself be a reasonably effective spur to research for improved techniques to minimize nuisance.

---

* Respondent's investment in the plant is in excess of $45,000,000. There are over 300 people employed there.

The power of the court to condition on equitable grounds the continuance of an injunction on the payment of permanent damages seems undoubted. [   ]

The damage base here suggested is consistent with the general rule in those nuisance cases where damages are allowed. "Where a nuisance is of such a permanent and unabatable character that a single recovery can be had, including the whole damage past and future resulting therefrom, there can be but one recovery" (66 C.J.S., Nuisances, § 140, p. 947). It has been said that permanent damages are allowed where the loss recoverable would obviously be small as compared with the cost of removal of the nuisance [   ].

. . .

Thus it seems fair to both sides to grant permanent damages to plaintiffs which will terminate this private litigation. The theory of damage is the "servitude on land" of plaintiffs imposed by defendant's nuisance. (See United States v. Causby, 328 U.S. 256, 261, 262, 267, where the term "servitude" addressed to the land was used by Justice Douglas relating to the effect of airplane noise on property near an airport.)

The judgment, by allowance of permanent damages imposing a servitude on land, which is the basis of the actions, would preclude future recovery by plaintiffs or their grantees.

This should be placed beyond debate by a provision of the judgment that the payment by defendant and the acceptance by plaintiffs of permanent damages found by the court shall be in compensation for a servitude on the land.

Although the Trial Term has found permanent damages as a possible basis of settlement of the litigation, on remission the court should be entirely free to re-examine this subject. It may again find the permanent damage already found; or make new findings.

The orders should be reversed, without costs, and the cases remitted to Supreme Court, Albany County to grant an injunction which shall be vacated upon payment by defendant of such amounts of permanent damage to the respective plaintiffs as shall for this purpose be determined by the court.

■ JASEN, J. (dissenting). I agree with the majority that a reversal is required here, but I do not subscribe to the newly enunciated doctrine of assessment of permanent damages, in lieu of an injunction, where substantial property rights have been impaired by the creation of a nuisance.

It has long been the rule in this State, as the majority acknowledges, that a nuisance which results in substantial continuing damage to neighbors must be enjoined. [   ]

To now change the rule to permit the cement company to continue polluting the air indefinitely upon the payment of permanent damages is, in my opinion, compounding the magnitude of a very serious problem in our State and Nation today.

In recognition of this problem, the Legislature of this State has enacted the Air Pollution Control Act (Public Health Law, §§ 1264–1299–m) declaring that it is the State policy to require the use of all available and reasonable methods to prevent and control air pollution (Public Health Law, § 1265).

The harmful nature and widespread occurrence of air pollution have been extensively documented. Congressional hearings have revealed that air pollution causes substantial property damage, as well as being a contributing factor to a rising incidence of lung cancer, emphysema, bronchitis and asthma.

The specific problem faced here is known as particulate contamination because of the fine dust particles emanating from defendant's cement plant. The particular type of nuisance is not new, having appeared in many cases for at least the past 60 years. [ ] It is interesting to note that cement production has recently been identified as a significant source of particulate contamination in the Hudson Valley. This type of pollution, wherein very small particles escape and stay in the atmosphere, has been denominated as the type of air pollution which produces the greatest hazard to human health. We have thus a nuisance which not only is damaging to the plaintiffs, but also is decidedly harmful to the general public.

I see grave dangers in overruling our long-established rule of granting an injunction where a nuisance results in substantial continuing damage. In permitting the injunction to become inoperative upon the payment of permanent damages, the majority is, in effect, licensing a continuing wrong. It is the same as saying to the cement company, you may continue to do harm to your neighbors so long as you pay a fee for it. Furthermore, once such permanent damages are assessed and paid, the incentive to alleviate the wrong would be eliminated, thereby continuing air pollution of an area without abatement.

It is true that some courts have sanctioned the remedy here proposed by the majority in a number of cases, but none of the authorities relied upon by the majority are analogous to the situation before us. In those cases the courts, in denying an injunction and awarding money damages, granted their decision on a showing that the use to which the property was intended to be put was primarily for the public benefit. Here, on the other hand, it is clearly established that the cement company is creating a continuing air pollution nuisance primarily for its own private interest with no public benefit.

This kind of inverse condemnation [ ] may not be invoked by a private person or corporation for private gain or advantage. Inverse condemnation should only be permitted when the public is primarily served in the taking or impairment of property. [ ] The promotion of the interests of the polluting cement company has, in my opinion, no public use or benefit.

Nor is it constitutionally permissible to impose servitude on land, without consent of the owner, by payment of permanent damages where the continuing impairment of the land is for a private use. [   ] This is made clear by the State Constitution (art. I, § 7,subd. [a]) which provides that "[p]rivate property shall not be taken for *public use* without just compensation" (emphasis added). It is, of course, significant that the section makes no mention of taking for a *private* use.

In sum, then, by constitutional mandate as well as by judicial pronouncement, the permanent impairment of private property for private purposes is not authorized in the absence of clearly demonstrated public benefit and use.

I would enjoin the defendant cement company from continuing the discharge of dust particles upon its neighbors' properties unless, within 18 months, the cement company abated this nuisance.

It is not my intention to cause the removal of the cement plant from the Albany area, but to recognize the urgency of the problem stemming from this stationary source of air pollution, and to allow the company a specified period of time to develop a means to alleviate this nuisance.

I am aware that the trial court found that the most modern dust control devices available have been installed in defendant's plant, but, I submit, this does not mean that *better* and more effective dust control devices could not be developed within the time allowed to abate the pollution.

Moreover, I believe it is incumbent upon the defendant to develop such devices, since the cement company, at the time the plant commenced production (1962), was well aware of the plaintiffs' presence in the area, as well as the probable consequences of its contemplated operation. Yet, it still chose to build and operate the plant at this site.

In a day when there is a growing concern for clean air, highly developed industry should not expect acquiescence by the courts, but should, instead, plan its operations to eliminate contamination of our air and damage to its neighbors.

Accordingly, the orders of the Appellate Division, insofar as they denied the injunction, should be reversed, and the actions remitted to Supreme Court, Albany County to grant an injunction to take effect 18 months hence, unless the nuisance is abated by improved techniques prior to said date.

■ CHIEF JUDGE FULD and JUDGES BURKE and SCILEPPI concur with JUDGE BERGAN; JUDGE JASEN dissents in part and votes to reverse in a separate opinion; JUDGES BREITEL and GIBSON taking no part.

NOTES AND QUESTIONS

1. In *Boomer* the defendant argued at the trial level that it was not committing a nuisance. The trial judge found that the defendant "took every available and possible precaution to protect the plaintiffs from dust," but he found a nuisance because the "discharge of large quantities of dust upon each of the properties and excessive vibration from blasting deprived each party of the reasonable use of his property and thereby prevented his enjoyment of life and liberty therein." 55 Misc.2d 1023, 287 N.Y.S.2d 112 (1967). In *Boomer* the defendant knew to a substantial certainty that those nearby would be subjected to dust and vibration, and continued the operation after having actual knowledge of the harm. Notice that by this analysis the overwhelming majority of alleged industrial nuisances are "intentional." In what sense is the harm intended here? Is there a difference between defendant's conduct in this case and that of a product manufacturer who knows to a substantial certainty that one widget out of ten thousand he produces will cause injury?

2. The fact that the vast majority of industrial nuisances are "intentional" makes all the more important the question whether, in addition to being intentional, the activity is also "unreasonable." This problem was explored at length in Jost v. Dairyland Power Cooperative, 45 Wis.2d 164, 172 N.W.2d 647 (1969), in which sulphur dioxide gas was discharged into the atmosphere by defendant's power plant, damaging nearby crops. The farmers sued and the defendant sought to prove that it had used due care in the construction and operation of its plant and that the "social and economic utility of the Alma plant outweighed the gravity of damage to the plaintiffs." The trial judge's rejection of such proof as to liability was affirmed. The court found crop damage of several hundred dollars and then, turning to liability, concluded:

> that the court properly excluded all evidence that tended to show the utility of the Dairyland Cooperative's enterprise. Whether its economic or social importance dwarfed the claim of a small farmer is of no consequence in this lawsuit. It will not be said that, because a great and socially useful enterprise will be liable in damages, an injury small by comparison should go unredressed. We know of no acceptable rule of jurisprudence that permits those who are engaged in important and desirable enterprises to injure with impunity those who are engaged in enterprises of lesser economic significance. Even the government or other entities, including public utilities, endowed with the power of eminent domain—the power to take private property in order to devote it to a purpose beneficial to the public good—are obliged to pay a fair market value for what is taken or damaged. To contend that a public utility, in the pursuit of its praiseworthy and legitimate enterprise, can, in effect, deprive others of the full use of their property without compensation, poses a theory unknown to the law of Wisconsin, and in our opinion would constitute the taking of property without due process of law.

Is the court's reasoning consistent with the approach taken in the initial Restatement p. 597, supra? In the Second Restatement? In *Boomer* ? For a comprehensive discussion of the case law and law review literature on *Boomer* and private nuisance in the succeeding two decades (including a tally of the cases adopting some version of the Second Restatement approach to balancing the utilities), see Lewin, *Boomer* and the American Law of Nuisance: Past, Present, and Future, 54 Alb.L.Rev. 189 (1990). For a case providing the flavor of nuisance controversies—and resolutions—prior to the adoption of strict liability analysis, see Waschak v. Moffat, 379 Pa. 441, 109 A.2d 310 (1954).

3. Recall that the trial court in *Rylands*, p. 431, supra, decided that there was no nuisance because the act was not a continuing harm. Although most nuisances have been accompanied by continuing harm, this is no longer considered an essential element.

4. The Boomer case also suggests the overlap between nuisance and trespass. Reconsider Martin v. Reynolds Metals Co., p. 590, supra. Under the *Boomer* approach, does it matter for purposes of liability whether defendant's conduct is characterized as nuisance or trespass? Compare Wood v. Picillo, 443 A.2d 1244 (R.I.1982), in which the court enjoined the further operation of a chemical dump on the defendant's property on nuisance grounds, remarking that "it could well be argued that one who utilizes his land for abnormally dangerous activities or for storage of abnormally dangerous substances may be strictly liable for resultant injuries, even in the absence of a finding of nuisance or negligence," and citing *Rylands v. Fletcher*.

5. The law of private nuisance has occasionally been characterized as a form of judicial zoning. Although the court of appeals in *Boomer* does not mention it, the appellate division opinion notes that the area was zoned. 30 App.Div.2d 480, 294 N.Y.S.2d 452 (1968). Apparently before the defendant began operations in 1962, the town zoned the defendant's property to permit quarrying and business, so that defendant's activity was lawful. Should the zoning be relevant to whether the defendant is liable for any nuisance? Is it proper for a court to find a common-law nuisance when the defendant has obeyed legislative zoning requirements? For an extensive discussion of the subject, see Ellickson, Alternatives to Zoning: Covenants, Nuisance Rules, and Fines as Land Use Controls, 40 U.Chi. L.Rev. 681 (1973).

Boomer was held inapplicable in Little Joseph Realty, Inc. v. Town of Babylon, 41 N.Y.2d 738, 363 N.E.2d 1163, 395 N.Y.S.2d 428 (1977), in which plaintiff sued to enjoin the construction and operation of an asphalt plant on defendant's adjoining property. The lower court determined that the plant, which violated the town's zoning ordinance, was a nuisance, and ordered it enjoined unless certain remedial devices were installed—and they were. On appeal, reversed. New York's longstanding rule that structures built on adjoining or nearby property in violation of zoning ordinances were enjoinable at the demand of a specially-damaged neighbor, was not changed by *Boomer*.

Boomer involved a private dispute between two parties in which it was proper to adjust "competing uses with a view towards maximizing the social value of each." But zoning "is far more comprehensive. Its design is, on a planned basis, to serve as a 'vital tool for maintaining a civilized form of existence' for the benefit and welfare of an entire community. . . . It follows that, when a continuing use flies in the face of a valid zoning restriction, it must, subject to the existence of any appropriate equitable defenses, be enjoined unconditionally." This does not mean that "risk-utility considerations have not entered into the adoption of a zoning law's restriction on use. It is rather that presumptively they have already been weighed and disposed of by the Legislature which enacted them."

6. A considerable body of nuisance law deals with land use disputes that lack the broader environmental aspects of the Boomer case. Typically, these cases deal with the loss of commercial value of adjoining property, such as Fontainebleau Hotel Corp. v. Forty–Five Twenty–Five, Inc., 114 So.2d 357 (Fla.App.1959), in which an injunction was sought by a Miami Beach hotel to prevent the construction of a 14–floor addition to a neighboring hotel (cutting off a considerable amount of sunlight from plaintiff's property), or a loss of economic value of residential property, such as the numerous efforts to enjoin a funeral parlor from locating in a neighborhood. See, e.g., Travis v. Moore, 377 So.2d 609 (Miss.1979). Hard feelings and spiteful behavior are not uncommon in these cases. Consider Coty v. Ramsey Associates, 149 Vt. 451, 546 A.2d 196, cert. denied 487 U.S. 1236 (1988), in which defendants were held liable after establishing a pig farm next to the property of neighbors who had successfully opposed the defendants' effort to build a motel on their land; contrast Wernke v. Halas, 600 N.E.2d 117 (Ind.App.1992), in which the court held that nailing a toilet seat to a tree and placing offensive graffiti on a fence facing the plaintiffs' property might constitute "unsightliness or lack of aesthetic virtue" but did not rise to the level of a nuisance.

For a case merging the environmental and commercial aspects of nuisance law, see Prah v. Maretti, 108 Wis.2d 223, 321 N.W.2d 182 (1982), in which the court upheld the claim of the owner of a solar-heated residence against a neighbor's proposed construction that would have interfered with the plaintiff's solar access. Detailed consideration of these dimensions of nuisance law are beyond the scope of a Torts course; the residential and commercial aspects of nuisance law—and zoning law, as well—are taken up in courses in Land Use and Property.

7. In *Boomer,* the defendant came to the area more recently than the plaintiffs. Is this relevant? Sometimes the defendant establishes himself in an isolated area only to find the nearby town expanding and others moving closer to him. The question raised is whether the plaintiff is barred from suing because he has knowingly encountered the nuisance. Restatement (Second) of Torts § 840D says that this is "not in itself sufficient to bar his action, but it is a factor to be considered in determining whether the nuisance is actionable." How might this be a relevant factor? Might there be an underlying concern about first-comers exercising extraterritorial controls over large areas of land? Might the price plaintiff paid for his or her land be relevant? The issue is discussed in Wittman, First Come, First Served: An Economic Analysis of "Coming to the Nuisance," 9 J.Legal Studies 557 (1980).

8. Turning now to questions of remedy for private nuisance, what relief did the trial judge award in *Boomer*? How did the court of appeals alter the remedy granted by the lower courts?

9. In the Jost case the court also awarded damages:

We see no basis for the jury's conclusion that the market value of one of the farms was reduced by $500 and the value of the others not at all. Such a result—although there could have been a differential—is completely unsupported by the evidence.

We conclude that the plaintiffs are entitled to recover for the crops and damage to vegetation for the years complained of—1965 and 1966—as found by the jury, but after those years recovery cannot again be for specific items of damage on a year-by-year basis. Their avenue for compensation is for permanent and continuing nuisance as may be reflected in a diminution of market value. Of course, permitting a recovery now for a permanent loss of market value presupposes that the degree of nuisance will not increase. If such be the case, an award of damages for loss of market value is final. If, however, the level of nuisance and air pollution should be increased above the level that may now be determined by a jury, with a consequent additional injury the plaintiffs would have the right to seek additional permanent damage to compensate them for the additional diminished market value.

What is the justification for reopening the case if the defendant increases the amount of sulphur dioxide it emits? Is this similar to cases in which after final judgment the plaintiff's injury turns out to be more serious than previously believed?

10. What should happen in *Boomer* and *Jost* if, after paying permanent damages, the defendant reduces the harm being inflicted—either by closing down the operation or by installing newly developed control devices? But what is the defendant's incentive in *Boomer* to install any new devices at all? What if the plaintiff in *Jost* switches to crops that are less profitable but impervious to sulphur dioxide gas?

11. Is the majority persuasive in its reasons for denying an injunction? The appellate division upheld the trial court's denial, relying upon "the zoning of the area, the large number of persons employed by the defendant, its extensive business operations and substantial investment in plant and equipment, its use of the most modern and efficient devices to prevent offensive emissions and discharges, and its payment of substantial sums of real property and school taxes." 30 App.Div.2d 480, 294 N.Y.S.2d 452. Are these factors relevant to the remedy question? The liability question?

Further litigation ensued over the damage measurement. The opinions discuss extensively the role of experts in land valuation problems. Boomer v. Atlantic Cement Co., 72 Misc.2d 834, 340 N.Y.S.2d 97 (1972), affirmed in Kinley v. Atlantic Cement Co., 42 App.Div.2d 496, 349 N.Y.S.2d 199 (1973).

12. In Adams v. Star Enterprise, 51 F.3d 417 (4th Cir.1995), property owners brought suit against defendant oil distribution facility for a major discharge of oil that created a plume extending underground to near their property—although not yet actually contaminating their property. They sought damages for emotional distress and diminished property value on, among other theories, private nuisance. Applying Virginia law, the court held that there could be no recovery on a nuisance theory absent some evidence of physically perceptible harm. Here the plume was "incapable of detection" from plaintiffs' properties.

To the same effect, see Adkins v. Thomas Solvent Co., 440 Mich. 293, 487 N.W.2d 715 (1992) and Berry v. Armstrong Rubber Co. 989 F.2d 822 (5th Cir.1993), cert denied, 114 S.Ct. 1067 (1994). Would continuing noxious odors, high noise levels or strong vibrations constitute physically perceptible harm?

13. In an influential article, Property Rules, Liability Rules, and Inalienability: One View of the Cathedral, 85 Harv.L.Rev. 1089 (1972), Calabresi and Melamed discuss a framework of rules that the law uses to protect "entitlements" (decisions regarding which of two or more conflicting parties will prevail). Since an entitlement can be given to either the defendant or plaintiff, four possible rules emerge which yield the traditional results of no liability, damages, or injunctive relief.

An entitlement is protected by a "property" rule when a person who wishes to obtain the entitlement must purchase it at a price determined by the holder. Thus, the New York rule regarding injunctions for nuisances, before *Boomer,* provided an entitlement in cases of "not unsubstantial" damage to the neighbors of a polluter that was protected by a property rule: A polluter who wished to continue operations had to buy the right to do so. Alternatively, an entitlement protected by a property rule could be given to the polluter. This would be the case if the courts adopted a rule of no liability for pollution damage.

Two other results are possible. The entitlement held by the polluter or by the neighbors might be protected only by a "liability" rule, which is the case when one of the parties in conflict can purchase the entitlement at an objectively determined price. This rule corresponds to the imposition of damages by a court. *Boomer* is an example of an entitlement in the plaintiffs protected by a liability rule—defendant polluter can continue operations as long as damages are paid in satisfaction of the entitlement.

The fourth alternative, giving the polluter an entitlement protected by a liability rule, is rarely recognized as a possibility. The leading nuisance case employing this approach, Spur Industries, Inc. v. Del E. Webb Development Co., 108 Ariz. 178, 494 P.2d 700 (1972), involved a conflict between defendant's pre-existing cattle feedlot operation and plaintiff's residential subdivision, which expanded towards the feedlot until the flies and odors drifting onto the development made sale of more units impossible and provoked numerous complaints from existing residents. The court found that the feedlot was an enjoinable nuisance, but held that because of the "coming to the nuisance" aspect of the case, plaintiff developer would be required to indemnify defendant Spur for the cost of "moving or shutting down." The court reasoned:

> It does not seem harsh to require a developer, who has taken advantage of the lesser land values in a rural area as well as the availability of large tracts of land on which to build and develop a new town or city in the area, to indemnify those who are forced to leave as a result.

The court emphasized, however, that:

> this relief to Spur is limited to a case wherein a developer has, with foreseeability, brought into a previously agricultural or industrial area the population which makes necessary the granting of an injunction against a lawful business and for which the business has no adequate relief.

Is the remedy the court awarded in *Spur* likely to be useful or applicable in many cases? Consider that here the homeowners' individual interests were represented by the development company. If an action were brought by an individual or by a class, how would compensation to the feedlot be apportioned among all the homeowners affected? What about homeowners who failed to join in the action?

What factors should be considered in deciding who gets an entitlement? In deciding whether the entitlement should be protected by a property rule or a liability rule? See generally, E. Rabin, Nuisance Law: Rethinking Fundamental Assumptions, 63 Va.L.Rev. 1299 (1977); Lewin, Compensated Injunctions and the Evolution of Nuisance Law, 71 Iowa L. Rev. 775 (1986).

14. Is it helpful to analyze these cases in terms of causal responsibility? See Epstein, Nuisance Law: Corrective Justice and Its Utilitarian Constraints, 8 J. Legal Studies 49 (1979).

Contrast the following views. Professor Fletcher, in the article discussed at p. 469, supra, argues that a victim of harm

> has a right to recover for injuries caused by a risk greater in degree and different in order from those created by the victim and imposed on the defendant—in short, for injuries resulting from nonreciprocal risks.

In a seminal article, Coase, The Problem of Social Cost, 3 J. of Law & Econ. 1 (1960), the author challenges widely-accepted notions of causal direction:

> The question is commonly thought of as one in which A inflicts harm on B and what has to be decided is: how should we restrain A? But this is wrong. We are dealing with a problem of a reciprocal nature. To avoid the harm to B would inflict harm on A. The real question that has to be decided is: should A be allowed to harm B or should B be allowed to harm A? . . . [An] example is afforded by the problem of straying cattle which destroy crops on neighboring land. If it is inevitable that some cattle will stray, an increase in the supply of meat can only be obtained at the expense of a decrease in the supply of crops. The nature of the choice is clear: meat or crops.

Is one of these formulations more helpful than the other in thinking about nuisance cases? Do they address the issue of appropriate remedy as well as initial right (entitlement)? Does *Spur* reflect the idea that the feedlot and the development impose reciprocal costs on each other?

15. In The Problem of Social Cost, Coase goes on to argue that in the absence of transaction costs (i.e., costs associated with striking a bargain) the rule of liability does not matter from an economic efficiency standpoint. In a *Boomer* situation, if the polluter is liable he will invest more in pollution control measures only when doing so is cheaper than paying damages or going out of business. If the polluter is not liable, the victim will "bribe" him to invest in pollution control equipment where doing so costs less than the damage the victim would otherwise suffer. Whatever the liability rule, the choice between pollution control measures and victim harm will result in precisely the same amount of resources being invested in elimination of the harm—although, of course, the distributional consequences will differ.

Since there are almost invariably transaction costs—consider the costs of getting the parties together in *Boomer,* and the potential "holdout" problems if a "property" rule (injunctive relief) were granted—the rights and remedies recognized by nuisance law do generally make a considerable difference. The economic consequences under various assumptions about bargaining behavior are systematically explored in Polinsky, Resolving Nuisance Disputes: The Simple Economics of Injunctive and Damage Remedies, 32 Stan.L.Rev. 1075 (1980).

16. In the *Union Bag* case, cited in *Boomer,* the plaintiff's harm was assessed at $100 per year. Plaintiff enforced his injunction and the mill, which represented an investment of $1,000,000, was permanently closed. Why was the pre-*Boomer* New York rule on injunctive relief on its face so favorable to plaintiffs? Did it embody a distinctive view about property rights in land? Is the majority in *Boomer* correct in its assertion that the court's essential function is to decide "the rights of the parties before it"? Does the dissent disagree?

17. One legislative remedy available in New York against air pollution was Public Health Law §§ 1264–98, establishing an administrative body to determine standards for pollution and to promulgate regulations accordingly. The Commissioner of Health was to investigate and determine violations. His conclusions were subject to administrative and judicial review. Failure to take corrective action subjected the offender to penalties not to exceed $1,000 plus $200 for each day of continued violation. The Commissioner could also seek an injunction. The act expressly stated that it was supplementary to any other existing remedies, but at the same time provided that the rules and regulations promulgated under the statute were "not intended to create in any way new or enlarged rights or to enlarge existing rights." Any determination by the Commissioner that pollution existed or that a regulation had been violated "shall not create by reason thereof any presumption of law or finding of fact which shall inure to or be for the benefit of any person other than the state." New York had also entered interstate compacts to combat water and air pollution. (N.Y. Public Health Law §§ 1299–1299s.) Does the existence of these procedures affect your views of the majority decision?

18.   Since 1970, the federal government has assumed a major presence in the field of regulatory control of air pollution. Comprehensive legislation, the Clean Air Act Amendments of 1970, was passed that year and amended in 1977, see 42 U.S.C. §§ 1857 et seq. (1977), and again in 1990, see 42 U.S.C. §§ 7401 et seq. (1990). A wide variety of other statutory schemes dealing with water pollution and hazardous wastes were also enacted in the 1970s, and later—and constitute a more comprehensive approach to controlling environmental harm than private nuisance actions. For the most part, these enactments have not been interpreted as preempting state common law, but there are exceptions. In International Paper Co. v. Ouellette, 479 U.S. 481 (1987), the Supreme Court held that the Clean Water Act preempts state nuisance law when applied to an out-of-state source. See also Note, National Audubon Society v. Department of Water and Power: The Ninth Circuit Disallows Federal Common Law Nuisance Claim for Mono Lake Water and Air Pollution, 20 Golden Gate L. Rev. 209 (1990).

Although the regulatory approach to environmental pollution cannot be explored in a Torts course, it is important to be aware of the fact that a distinctly different way of dealing with health and safety issues does exist— an approach that has its counterpart in other areas, such as regulation of product safety, occupational safety, and motor vehicle safety, as well.

CHAPTER X

DAMAGES AND INSURANCE

Our emphasis so far has been on the doctrinal development of negligence and strict liability, with principal attention to legal liability in various fact patterns. By and large, tort defendants are less concerned with the concept of liability than with the consequences of that liability—the imposition of damages. The defendant charged with professional malpractice may be quite concerned with liability because a small adverse judgment or even the filing of suit may tarnish a physician's reputation in some communities. More typically, however, corporations and businesses treat tort liability as a cost of doing business and discount its tarnishing effect. They are concerned with the total annual cost of tort liability.

We begin this Chapter with an introduction to the basic items of recoverable damages and highlight the central problems of damage measurement. We then examine the institution of insurance to see how it operates and the critical role it plays in contemporary tort liability and litigation.

A. DAMAGES

1. COMPENSATORY DAMAGES

The fundamental goal of damage awards in the unintentional tort area is to return the plaintiff as closely as possible to his or her condition before the accident. This is achieved by measuring certain items of harm in past and future terms. The total amount of these past and future damages is usually awarded in a single judgment. Since the plaintiff generally may sue no more than once for all items of damage arising from the event in question, to the extent that the plaintiff is not completely healed by the time of trial, some predictions must be made.

It would be possible to provide that every few years the plaintiff must sue anew to recover for the damages shown to have been suffered since the last payment. There are obvious advantages and disadvantages to such a procedure. One drawback is the concern that victims of accidents who are told that their award will depend on how quickly or slowly they recover from the original injury may tend to appear not to recover too quickly. This may not be conscious malingering as much as a subconscious fear that they will be found in later hearings to be better than they actually are, and thus have their damages unfairly reduced or terminated. In workers' compensation, as we shall see, this may also be a problem, but the danger there is somewhat reduced by the fact that the periodic awards are meant to provide no more than two-thirds of lost wages and many awards do not continue indefinitely. In tort law, the damages are theoretically to compensate fully for both amount and duration of loss. In such a system, the rules should encourage speedy recovery. This may be best achieved by a one-time-only recovery that tells the plaintiff what compensation has been recovered and that there is no more to come.

The best explanation for the single-judgment approach, though, has undoubtedly been the administrative difficulty of handling periodic recoveries. In the early days of the common law, the judiciary was incapable of handling such cases. Today such techniques exist. See generally, Henderson, Designing a Responsible Periodic–Payment System for Tort Awards, 32 Ariz.L.Rev.21 (1990). The principal cases in this Chapter all involve the single-judgment and single-payment approach.

Seffert v. Los Angeles Transit Lines

Supreme Court of California, 1961.
56 Cal.2d 498, 364 P.2d 337, 15 Cal.Rptr. 161.

■ PETERS, J. Defendants appeal from a judgment for plaintiff for $187,-903.75 entered on a jury verdict. Their motion for a new trial for errors of law and excessiveness of damages was denied.

At the trial plaintiff contended that she was properly entering defendants' bus when the doors closed suddenly catching her right hand and left foot. The bus started, dragged her some distance, and then threw her to the pavement. Defendants contended that the injury resulted from plaintiff's own negligence, that she was late for work and either ran into the side of the bus after the doors had closed or ran after the bus and attempted to enter after the doors had nearly closed.

The evidence supports plaintiff's version of the facts. Several eyewitnesses testified that plaintiff started to board the bus while it was standing with the doors wide open. Defendants do not challenge the sufficiency of the evidence. They do contend, however, that prejudicial errors were committed during the trial and that the verdict is excessive.

[Here Justice Peters rejected the defendants' contention that the trial judge had made certain erroneous legal rulings during the trial. He continued:]

One of the major contentions of defendants is that the damages are excessive, as a matter of law. There is no merit to this contention.

The evidence most favorable to the plaintiff shows that prior to the accident plaintiff was in good health, and had suffered no prior serious injuries. She was single, and had been self-supporting for 20 of her 42 years. The accident happened on October 11, 1957. The trial took place in July and August of 1959.

As already pointed out, the injury occurred when plaintiff was caught in the doors of defendants' bus when it started up before she had gained full entry. As a result she was dragged for some distance. The record is uncontradicted that her injuries were serious, painful, disabling and permanent.

The major injuries were to plaintiff's left foot. The main arteries and nerves leading to that foot, and the posterior tibial vessels and nerve of that foot, were completely severed at the ankle. The main blood vessel which supplies blood to that foot had to be tied off, with the result that there is a permanent stoppage of the main blood source. The heel and shin bones were fractured. There were deep lacerations and an avulsion[3] which involved the skin and soft tissue of the entire foot.

These injuries were extremely painful. They have resulted in a permanently raised left heel, which is two inches above the floor level, caused by the contraction of the ankle joint capsule. Plaintiff is crippled and will suffer pain for life.[4] Although this pain could, perhaps, be alleviated by an operative fusion of the ankle, the doctors considered and rejected this procedure because the area has been deprived of its normal blood supply. The foot is not only permanently deformed but has a persistent open ulcer on the heel, there being a continuous drainage from the entire area. Medical care of this foot and ankle is to be reasonably expected for the remainder of plaintiff's life.

Since the accident, and because of it, plaintiff has undergone nine operations and has spent eight months in various hospitals and rehabilitation centers. These operations involved painful skin grafting and other painful procedures. One involved the surgical removal of gangrenous skin leaving painful raw and open flesh exposed from the heel to the toe. Another involved a left lumbar sympathectomy in which plaintiff's abdomen was entered to sever the nerves affecting the remaining blood vessels of the left leg in order to force those blood vessels to remain open at all times to the maximum extent. Still another operation involved a cross leg flap graft of skin and tissue from plaintiff's thigh which required that her left foot be brought up to her right thigh and held at this painful angle, motionless, and in a cast for a month until the flap of skin and fat, partially removed from her thigh, but still nourished there by a skin connection, could be grafted to the bottom of her foot, and until the host site could develop enough blood vessels to support it. Several future operations of this nature may be necessary. One result of this operation was to leave a defective area of the thigh where the normal fat is missing and the muscles exposed, and the local nerves are missing. This condition is permanent and disfiguring.

Another operation called a debridement, was required. This involved removal of many small muscles of the foot, much of the fat beneath the skin, cleaning the end of the severed nerve, and tying off the severed vein and artery.

---

3. Defined in Webster's New International Dictionary (2d ed.) as a "tearing asunder; forcible separation."

4. Her life expectancy was 34.9 years from the time of trial.

The ulcer on the heel is probably permanent, and there is the constant and real danger that osteomyelitis may develop if the infection extends into the bone. If this happens the heel bone would have to be removed surgically and perhaps the entire foot amputated.

Although plaintiff has gone back to work, she testified that she has difficulty standing, walking or even sitting, and must lie down frequently; that the leg is still very painful; that she can, even on her best days, walk not over three blocks and that very slowly; that her back hurts from walking; that she is tired and weak; that her sleep is disturbed; that she has frequent spasms in which the leg shakes uncontrollably; that she feels depressed and unhappy, and suffers humiliation and embarrassment.

Plaintiff claims that there is evidence that her total pecuniary loss, past and future, amounts to $53,903.75. This was the figure used by plaintiff's counsel in his argument to the jury, in which he also claimed $134,000 for pain and suffering, past and future. Since the verdict was exactly the total of these two estimates, it is reasonable to assume that the jury accepted the amount proposed by counsel for each item.

The summary of plaintiff as to pecuniary loss, past and future, is as follows:

Doctor and Hospital Bills	$10,330.50	
Drugs and other medical expenses stipulated to in the amount of	2,273.25	
Loss of earnings from time of accident to time of trial	5,500.00	$18,103.75
Future Medical Expenses:		
$2,000 per year for next 10 years	20,000.00	
$200 per year for the 24 years thereafter	4,800.00	
Drugs for 34 years.........................	1,000.00	25,800.00
		43,903.75
Possible future loss of earnings		10,000.00
Total Pecuniary Loss		$53,903.75

There is substantial evidence to support these estimates. The amounts for past doctor and hospital bills, for the cost of drugs, and for a past loss of earnings, were either stipulated to, evidence was offered on, or is a simple matter of calculation. These items totaled $18,103.75. While the amount of $25,800 estimated as the cost of future medical expense, for loss of future earnings and for the future cost of drugs, may seem high, there was substantial evidence that future medical expense is certain to be high. There is also substantial evidence that plaintiff's future earning capacity may be substantially impaired by reason of the injury. The amounts estimated for those various items are not out of line, and find support in the evidence.

This leaves the amount of $134,000 presumably allowed for the nonpecuniary items of damage, including pain and suffering, past and future. It is this allowance that defendants seriously attack as being excessive as a matter of law.

It must be remembered that the jury fixed these damages, and that the trial judge denied a motion for new trial, one ground of which was excessiveness of the award.   These determinations are entitled to great weight.   The amount of damages is a fact question, first committed to the discretion of the jury and next to the discretion of the trial judge on a motion for new trial.   They see and hear the witnesses and frequently, as in this case, see the injury and the impairment that has resulted therefrom. As a result, all presumptions are in favor of the decision of the trial court. [   ]   The power of the appellate court differs materially from that of the trial court in passing on this question.   An appellate court can interfere on the ground that the judgment is excessive only on the ground that the verdict is so large that, at first blush, it shocks the conscience and suggests passion, prejudice or corruption on the part of the jury.   The proper rule was stated in Holmes v. Southern Cal. Edison Co., 78 Cal.App.2d 43, 51[177 P.2d 32], as follows: "The powers and duties of a trial judge in ruling on a motion for new trial and of an appellate court on an appeal from a judgment are very different when the question of an excessive award of damages arises.   The trial judge sits as a thirteenth juror with the power to weigh the evidence and judge the credibility of the witnesses.   If he believes the damages awarded by the jury to be excessive and the question is presented it becomes his duty to reduce them.   [Citing cases.]   When the question is raised his denial of a motion of new trial is an indication that he approves the amount of the award.   An appellate court has no such powers. It cannot weigh the evidence and pass on the credibility of the witnesses as a juror does.   To hold an award excessive it must be so large as to indicate passion or prejudice on the part of the jurors."   . . .

[handwritten margin note: standard for reversal of award by appellate court]

There are no fixed or absolute standards by which an appellate court can measure in monetary terms the extent of the damages suffered by a plaintiff as a result of the wrongful act of the defendant.   . . .   The amount to be awarded is "a matter on which there legitimately may be a wide difference of opinion" [   ].   . . .

While the appellate court should consider the amounts awarded in prior cases for similar injuries, obviously, each case must be decided on its own facts and circumstances.   Such examination demonstrates that such awards vary greatly.   (See exhaustive annotations in 16 A.L.R.2d 3, and 16 A.L.R.2d 393.)   Injuries are seldom identical and the amount of pain and suffering involved in similar physical injuries varies widely.   These factors must be considered.   [   ]   Basically, the question that should be decided by the appellate courts is whether or not the verdict is so out of line with reason that it shocks the conscience and necessarily implies that the verdict must have been the result of passion and prejudice.

In the instant case, the nonpecuniary items of damage include allowances for pain and suffering, past and future, humiliation as a result of being disfigured and being permanently crippled, and constant anxiety and fear that the leg will have to be amputated.   While the amount of the award is high, and may be more than we would have awarded were we the trier of the facts, considering the nature of the injury, the great pain and suffering, past and future, and the other items of damage, we cannot say, as a matter of law, that it is so high that it shocks the conscience and gives rise to the presumption that it was the result of passion or prejudice on the part of the jurors.

Defendants next complain that it was prejudicial error for plaintiff's counsel to argue to the jury that damages for pain and suffering could be fixed by means of a mathematical formula predicated upon a per diem allowance for this item of damages. The propriety of such an argument seems never to have been passed upon in this state. In other jurisdictions there is a sharp divergence of opinion on the subject. [ ]It is not necessary to pass on the propriety of such argument in the instant case because, when plaintiff's counsel made the argument in question, defendants' counsel did not object, assign it as misconduct or ask that the jury be admonished to disregard it. Moreover, in his argument to the jury, the defendants' counsel also adopted a mathematical formula type of argument. This being so, even if such argument were error (a point we do not pass upon), the point must be deemed to have been waived, and cannot be raised properly, on appeal. [ ]

The judgment appealed from is affirmed.

■ GIBSON, C.J., WHITE, J., and DOOLING, J., concurred.

■ TRAYNOR, J. I dissent.

Although I agree that there was no prejudicial error on the issue of liability, it is my opinion that the award of $134,000 for pain and suffering is so excessive as to indicate that it was prompted by passion, prejudice, whim, or caprice.

Before the accident plaintiff was employed as a file clerk at a salary of $375 a month. At the time of the trial she had returned to her job at the same salary and her foot had healed sufficiently for her to walk. At the time of the accident she was 42 years old with a life expectancy of 34.9 years.

During closing argument plaintiff's counsel summarized the evidence relevant to past and possible future damages and proposed a specific amount for each item. His total of $187,903.75 was the exact amount awarded by the jury.

His proposed amounts were as follows:

. . .

Total Pecuniary Loss		$ 53,903.75
Pain and Suffering:		
From time of accident to time of trial (660 days) @ $100 a day	$66,000.00	
For the remainder of her life (34 years) @ $2,000 a year	68,000.00	134,000.00
Total proposed by counsel		$187,903.75

The jury and the trial court have broad discretion in determining the damages in a personal injury case. [ ] A reviewing court, however, has responsibilities not only to the litigants in an action but to future litigants and must reverse or remit when a jury awards either inadequate or excessive damages. [ ]

The crucial question in this case, therefore, is whether the award of $134,000 for pain and suffering is so excessive it must have resulted from passion, prejudice, whim or caprice. "To say that a verdict has been influenced by passion or prejudice is but another way of saying that the verdict exceeds any amount justified by the evidence." (Zibbell v. Southern Pacific Co., 160 Cal. 237, 254 [116 P. 513]; [ ].)

There has been forceful criticism of the rationale for awarding damages for pain and suffering in negligence cases. [ ] Such damages originated under primitive law as a means of punishing wrongdoers and assuaging the feelings of those who had been wronged. [ ] They become increasingly anomalous as emphasis shifts in a mechanized society from ad hoc punishment to orderly distribution of losses through insurance and the price of goods or of transportation. Ultimately such losses are borne by a public free of fault as part of the price for the benefits of mechanization. [ ]

Nonetheless, this state has long recognized pain and suffering as elements of damages in negligence cases [ ]; any change in this regard must await reexamination of the problem by the Legislature. Meanwhile, awards for pain and suffering serve to ease plaintiffs' discomfort and to pay for attorney fees for which plaintiffs are not otherwise compensated.

It would hardly be possible ever to compensate a person fully for pain and suffering. " 'No rational being would change places with the injured man for an amount of gold that would fill the room of the court, yet no lawyer would contend that such is the legal measure of damages.' " (Zibbell v. Southern Pacific Co., supra, 160 Cal. 237, 255; see 2 Harper and James, The Law of Torts 1322.) "Translating pain and anguish into dollars can, at best, be only an arbitrary allowance, and not a process of measurement and consequently the judge can, in his instructions give the jury no standard to go by; he can only tell them to allow such amount as in their discretion they may consider reasonable. . . . The chief reliance for reaching reasonable results in attempting to value suffering in terms of money must be the restraint and common sense of the jury. . . ." (McCormick, Damages, § 88, pp. 318–319.) Such restraint and common sense were lacking here.

A review of reported cases involving serious injuries and large pecuniary losses reveals that ordinarily the part of the verdict attributable to pain and suffering does not exceed the part attributable to pecuniary losses. [ ] The award in this case of $134,000 for pain and suffering exceeds not only the pecuniary losses but any such award heretofore sustained in this state even in cases involving injuries more serious by far than those suffered by plaintiff. [ ] In McNulty v. Southern Pacific Co. [ ], the court reviewed a large number of cases involving injuries to legs and feet, in each of which the total judgment, including both pecuniary loss and pain and suffering did not exceed $100,000. Although excessive damages is "an issue which is primarily factual and is not therefore a matter which can be decided upon the basis of awards made in other cases" [ ] awards for similar injuries may be considered as one factor to be weighed in determining whether the damages awarded are excessive. [ ].

The excessive award in this case was undoubtedly the result of the improper argument of plaintiff's counsel to the jury. Though no evidence was introduced, though none could possibly be introduced on the monetary value of plaintiff's suffering, counsel urged the jury to award $100 a day for pain and suffering from the time of the accident to the time of trial and $2,000 a year for pain and suffering for the remainder of plaintiff's life.

The propriety of counsel's proposing a specific sum for each day or month of suffering has recently been considered by courts of several jurisdictions. (See 19 Ohio St.L.J. 780; 33 So.Cal.L.Rev. 214, 216.) The reasons for and against permitting "per diem argument for pain and suffering" are reviewed in Ratner v. Arrington (Fla.App.), 111 So.2d 82, 85–90[1959 Florida decision holding such argument is permissible] and Botta v. Brunner, 26 N.J. 82 [138 A.2d 713, 718–725, 60 A.L.R.2d 1331] [1958 New Jersey decision holding such argument to be an "unwarranted intrusion into the domain of the jury"].

The reason usually advanced for not allowing such argument is that since there is no way of translating pain and suffering into monetary terms, counsel's proposal of a particular sum for each day of suffering represents an opinion and a conclusion on matters not disclosed by the evidence, and tends to mislead the jury and result in excessive awards. The reason usually advanced for allowing "per diem argument for pain and suffering" is that it affords the jury as good an arbitrary measure as any for that which cannot be measured.

Counsel may argue all legitimate inferences from the evidence, but he may not employ arguments that tend primarily to mislead the jury. [ ] A specified sum for pain and suffering for any particular period is bound to be conjectural. Positing such a sum for a small period of time and then multiplying that sum by the number of days, minutes or seconds in plaintiff's life expectancy multiplies the hazards of conjecture. Counsel could arrive at any amount he wished by adjusting either the period of time to be taken as a measure or the amount surmised for the pain for that period.

.   .   .

The misleading effect of the per diem argument was not cured by the use of a similar argument by defense counsel. Truth is not served by a clash of sophistic arguments. (See Michael and Adler, The Trial of an Issue of Fact, 34 Colum.L.Rev. 1224, 1483–1484.) Had defendant objected to the improper argument of plaintiff's counsel this error would be a sufficient ground for reversal whether or not the award was excessive as a matter of law. Defendant's failure to object, however, did not preclude its appeal on the ground that the award was excessive as a matter of law or preclude this court's reversing on that ground and ruling on the impropriety of counsel's argument to guide the court on the retrial. [ ]

I would reverse the judgment and remand the cause for a new trial on the issue of damages.

■ SCHAUER, J., and McCOMB, J., concurred.

NOTES AND QUESTIONS

1. *Past Pecuniary Losses.* The clearest category of recoverable damages is past pecuniary losses—in *Seffert* those incurred for doctors, hospitals, drugs, and lost earnings. Most of the medical expenses are documented by bills; the lost earnings may be a bit more complicated to establish, especially for self-employed persons, but can usually be reconstructed without much difficulty.

One recurrent problem in awarding lost earnings is the question of taxation. Although some percentage of the gross wages lost would have been taxed if the plaintiff had in fact earned them, Congress has decided that compensatory damage awards are not taxable. What, if anything, should the judge charge the jury on this question? Some courts say nothing and let the jury think whatever it might on the subject. Others charge the jury that the award of lost earnings is not taxable and that the jury should not worry about being sure that plaintiff gets enough to pay the taxes. See Lanzano v. City of New York, 71 N.Y.2d 208, 519 N.E.2d 331, 524 N.Y.S.2d 420 (1988). In an effort to remove the ambiguity about when and how the jury should be told about the tax implications, one court has decided that "the measurement of after-tax income is the 'more accurate and therefore proper, measure of damages'" and that the plaintiff has the burden of proving that sum. Caldwell v. Haynes, 136 N.J. 422, 643 A.2d 564 (1994).

2. *Future Pecuniary Losses.* As *Seffert* shows, these same items may cause losses into the future. To take the easiest case, the evidence shows that the plaintiff will need a specific drug for the next five years. There are of course as yet no bills. But the jury must calculate the cost now. How much will the drug cost over the next five years? What will inflation look like in the prescription drug market? If the plaintiff requires physical therapy or psychological counselling in the future, how long will the course of treatment be needed? If any of these expenses appear likely to be lifelong, life expectancy tables will be used. Should the trier then consider health factors unrelated to the accident, such as smoking, and reduce plaintiff's life expectancy accordingly?

Even more complicated than figuring out future medical expenses is the task of calculating the plaintiff's future earnings. For instance, assume that at the time of her injury, the plaintiff had been earning $30,000 a year and would never be able to work again. (Of course, in some litigation the permanence of plaintiff's disability will be hotly contested, but assume our plaintiff is completely disabled.) In order to decide how large her award should be, the court must first determine how many years she would have worked had she not been injured. The plaintiff might have died in an unrelated accident the next day, in which case she hardly would have worked at all, or she could live into her nineties and have a long, productive career. This question is further complicated by the increasing unpredictability of retirement ages. Given these uncertainties, attorneys may begin with the average work career of an employee in plaintiff's field and present evidence on whether there is reason to believe the plaintiff's career would have varied from the norm.

Once a predicted retirement date has been set, the plaintiff's award cannot be set by multiplying her current wage by the number of years she had left to work. A worker's wages rarely remain stable over the course of a lifetime. What about promotions and merit raises? Even without these personal achievements, the plaintiff's wages could be expected to rise. Since World War II, increases in productivity have resulted in an overall rise in wages for workers as a class. Apart from these "real" increases in workers' wages, many workers have contractual "cost of living adjustments" that automatically increase their wages in relation to the consumer price index so that general inflation drives wages up. And what about fringe benefits such as medical coverage, pensions, and retirement plans?

The defense is likely to present countervailing considerations. Shouldn't the plaintiff, who no longer has to commute, or buy business clothes or uniforms, and thus no longer incurs the cost of these expenses, have them deducted from her award for future earnings? Moreover, as mentioned above, the plaintiff's lump-sum award is tax-free, so in figuring her lost future earnings, it can be argued that only after-tax earnings should be considered. Often a court will offset some of these variables, declaring, for instance, that lost fringe benefits will be roughly equal to the decrease in work-related expenses.

3. *Discounting to Present Value.* Assume that after considering all these factors, the trier of fact determines that the plaintiff would have worked for the next five years and that her after-tax salary in those years would be $30,000, $32,000, $34,000, $36,000 and $38,000 for a total of $170,000. Our calculations are not yet done. To award the plaintiff a lump sum of $170,000 would be to overcompensate her, because by investing the total amount at the outset, she could earn interest on the lump sum that, combined with the initial amount of principal, would be in excess of her lost future earnings. To adjust for this earning potential, the court must reduce the plaintiff's award to its present value. In other words, the trier of fact must determine the amount of money the plaintiff should be awarded today so that, if invested prudently, it will earn interest bringing the total award to $170,000 after five years. Although the original lump-sum award is tax free, the interest earned on it is not, so the original award will have to be high enough to earn interest that will cover the taxes and still provide $30,000 for the first year, $32,000 for the second year, etc., and be exhausted after the last payment.

Thus in order to determine the proper award, the court must decide upon a discount rate, which is in effect the estimated return on prudent investment for the next five years. Each party will present evidence as to why its estimate of this uncertain figure is the better one. Adding to the complexity is the inflation rate. Although the plaintiff may earn additional money through interest, that money may be worth less because of inflation. Plaintiff will argue that her award should not be discounted because the inflation rate and the return on investment cancel each other out. Courts are divided on how to handle this issue. Some accept this "total offset" rationale. See Kaczkowski v. Bolubasz, 491 Pa. 561, 421 A.2d 1027 (1980)("As a matter of law . . . future inflation shall be presumed equal to future interest rates with those factors offsetting").

Other courts adopt the theory that the market interest rate reflects three factors: risk, protection from inflation, and the "real interest rate." The risk element should not be considered in the tort award, because the plaintiff should make only safe investments to ensure compensation. That leaves the real market rate and the inflationary rate. In determining the discount rate for a tort award, these courts believe that the real interest rate is the proper discount rate, letting inflation be offset by the "inflationary interest rate." Otherwise, a total offset would overcompensate the plaintiff.

For a more detailed discussion of these issues, see Jones & Laughlin Steel Corp. v. Pfeifer, 462 U.S. 523 (1983) and Brady, Inflation, Productivity, and the Total Offset Method of Calculating Damages for Lost Future Earnings, 49 U.Chi.L.Rev. 1003 (1982).

4.   *Pain and Suffering.* We turn now to the nonpecuniary losses that formed the core of the *Seffert* case. What is the theoretical justification for awarding damages in this type of case for pain and suffering?

Among the articles cited by Justice Traynor, Jaffe's offered the sharpest attack on pain and suffering awards. Jaffe, Damages for Personal Injury: The Impact of Insurance, 18 Law & Contemporary Probs. 219 (1953). Jaffe recognized that when the defendant's conduct is "reprehensible, damages are an apt instrument of punishment" because criminal law is a clumsy way to handle "unsocial activity. . . . To pay money to one's victim is a salutary humiliation." But justification was harder when the defendant's behavior was negligent rather than willful. The usual justification here is that, although there is no way to measure the loss in question, plaintiff has in fact lost "something" and the wrongdoer should not escape liability because of the difficulty of valuation.

But Jaffe challenged this by asking what justified any award. It could not be returning to plaintiff something that was his or her own for that was an economic notion based on "maintaining the integrity of the economic arrangements which provide the normally expectable basis for livelihood in our society. Pain is a harm, an 'injury,' but neither past pain nor its compensation has any consistent economic significance. The past experience is not a loss except in so far as it produced present deterioration." He continued:

I am aware, however, that though the premise may elude detection, some deep intuition may claim to validate this process of evaluating the imponderable. One who has suffered a violation of his bodily integrity may feel a sense of continuing outrage. This is particularly true where there has been disfigurement or loss of a member (even though not giving rise to economic loss). Because our society sets a high value on money it uses money or price as a means of recognizing the worth of non-economic as well as economic goods. If, insists the plaintiff, society really values my personality, my bodily integrity, it will signify its sincerity by paying me a sum of money. Damages thus may somewhat reestablish the plaintiff's self-confidence, wipe out his sense of outrage. Furthermore, though money is not an equivalent it may be a consolation, a solatium. These arguments, however, are most valid for disfigurements or loss of member giving rise to a continuing sense of injury. (And in such cases there may be potential economic injury which cannot be established.) It is doubtful that past pain figures strongly as present outrage. And even granting these arguments there must be set over against them the arbitrary indeterminateness of the evaluation. Insurance aside, it is doubtful justice seriously to embarrass a defendant, though negligent, by real economic loss in order to do honor to plaintiff's experience of pain. And insurance present, it is doubtful that the pooled social fund of savings should be charged with sums of indeterminate amount when compensation performs no specific economic function. This consideration becomes the stronger as year after year the amounts set aside for the security account become a larger proportion of the national income.

As to those arguments he discusses, is Jaffe persuasive? Are there other arguments supporting recovery for pain and suffering that are not mentioned here? Is it useful to distinguish between transitory physical pain and permanent disfigurement or loss of function? See Ogus, Damages for Lost Amenities: For a Foot, a Feeling or a Function?, 35 Mod.L.Rev. 1 (1972).

Compare Kwasny v. United States, 823 F.2d 194 (7th Cir.1987), in which the court affirmed an award under the Federal Tort Claims Act. In passing, Judge Posner observed:

> We disagree with those students of tort law who believe that pain and suffering are not real costs and should not be allowable items of damages in a tort suit. No one likes pain and suffering and most people would pay a good deal of money to be free of them. If they were not recoverable in damages, the cost of negligence would be less to the tortfeasors and there would be more negligence, more accidents, more pain and suffering, and hence higher social costs.

Do you agree? Is the deterrence argument more powerful than the compensation argument for retaining pain and suffering? Can pain and suffering be justified on deterrence grounds even if people would not insure, in advance, against the prospect of such losses? For useful discussion of these issues, see Leebron, Final Moments: Damages for Pain and

Suffering Prior to Death, 64 N.Y.U. L.Rev. 256, 270–78 (1989); Schwartz, Proposals for Products Liability Reform: A Theoretical Synthesis, 97 Yale L.J. 353, 362–67 (1988); Croley and Hanson, The Nonpecuniary Costs of Accidents: Pain-and-Suffering Damages in Tort Law, 108 Harv.L.Rev. 1785 (1995).

5. Consider the following very large damage awards for pain and suffering, and the logic that lies behind each.

a. In Sternemann v. Langs, 93 App.Div.2d 819, 460 N.Y.S.2d 614 (1983), the court considered an award for pain and suffering sustained by a 26–year-old mother of three, with a life expectancy of 53 years:

> [Plaintiff] will suffer constant, excruciating and unremitting pain in her right arm for the balance of her life. . . . As a result, the plaintiff has effectively lost much of the use of her right arm, has been deprived of a social life, can no longer properly care for her young children, has great difficulty sleeping, and cannot even sleep lying down. In fact, the only way that the plaintiff can continue to function is by the constant administration of narcotic medication in ever-increasing quantities, which medication not only affects her perception and serves to render her groggy and depressed, but has caused her to become a narcotics addict who will require prolonged institutionalization, on the order of three to six months out of every year, for detoxification the remainder of her life. . . . [I]t simply cannot be said that the award of $1,000,000 in damages for a lifetime of pain and suffering was excessive.

How should the court have reacted to a verdict of $5,000,000 for this item?

b. In Haines v. Raven Arms, 536 Pa. 452, 640 A.2d 367 (1994), the 14–year-old plaintiff, Tamika, was negligently struck in the head by a bullet. During the next five years she "underwent six additional operations including removal of the bullet in 1988, long periods of hospitalization, rehabilitation therapy, outpatient treatment, and special schooling for handicapped children." According to the majority:

> Prior to trial, Tamika was diagnosed as suffering the following permanent injuries. She has weakness in one side of her body, impairment of vision on her right side, and loss of cognitive skills which impairs her ability to communicate ideas, her ability to do mathematics, her memory, and her orientation to environment. Her right foot turns inward to some extent, affecting her ability to walk normally. Experts opined that she will require 24–hour supervision for the rest of her life due to impaired physical condition, analytical and differential thinking, memory, and judgment. [Her life expectancy was 55 years from time of trial.]

The jury had returned a verdict of $8 million for pain and suffering as part of a total verdict of over $11 million. A three-judge en banc trial-level court that included the trial judge reduced the pain and suffering award to $5 million.

The court, 4–3, upheld the reduction. The majority said the question was "whether the award of damages falls within the uncertain limits of fair and reasonable compensation or whether the verdict so shocks the sense of justice as to suggest that the jury was influenced by partiality, prejudice, mistake or corruption." The court noted that the en banc court "understandably avoided an assertion that the verdict shocked its sense of justice." The en banc court had stated:

> As noted, Tamika Haines suffered catastrophic injuries. In essence she has been deprived of the ability to have normal relationships with other human beings. She suffered major memory loss, loss of cognitive abilities, and has trouble walking and using her arms. She had seven major surgeries. She cannot be left alone for long, for fear that she will wander off and be taken advantage of by anyone who comes along. At the same time, she remembers that she was once normal and has difficulty relating to those who she considers "retarded." Clearly, this warrants a significant award.
>
> On the other hand, she is not in any physical pain, does relate to her family, goes by herself to remedial classes, and can carry out some activities. She is not in the same class as someone who is a quadriplegic or in great constant pain that cannot be treated.

The en banc court explained its reduction by noting that although the consensus was that the verdict was excessive "considering this case in light of other kinds of catastrophic injuries, the consensus also was that $5,000,000 was not excessive. However, it is asking a great deal of a lay jury to fix a figure in a case like this with no experience and precious little guidance. At least the three judges have a long background from which to draw when determining what is excessive and what is not excessive."

The dissent thought the correct standard was whether the award "shocks the conscience" and that the en banc court and the supreme court majority had admitted that this award did not do that. The dissent added "uncontradicted medical testimony" to the effect that plaintiff is blind in one eye, that her I.Q score had dropped from the 37th percentile to the first percentile, and that she had suffered

> an extreme loss of inhibition, rendering Tamika highly impulsive. This loss of inhibition, in conjunction with a lack of mature judgment, leaves Tamika very vulnerable generally, and particularly vulnerable sexually. Further, and perhaps most tragically, Tamika does not understand that she is limited physically, mentally, and emotionally. She desires the same relationships, opportunities and responsibilities she enjoyed before the accident, and does not understand why they are no longer available to her. This difference between Tamika's true abilities and her unrealistic perception of her abilities causes a continual mixture of boredom, anger, sadness, and frustration for Tamika.

The dissent also noted that given her life expectancy of 61 years from date of injury, the jury's award was $131,000 per year; after the reduction it was $82,000 per year. The dissent noted that although the en banc court included three "very experienced" judges, two of them were operating on a "cold record" much as this court was doing. The dissent would have accepted the jury's verdict.

c.   Can a verdict be so "excessive" as to call for reduction if it does not shock the judicial conscience?   In the mid–1980s a New York statute directed the appellate division to "determine that an award is excessive or inadequate if it deviates materially from what would be reasonable compensation."   N.Y. CPLR § 5501(c).   See the extended discussion of the standard in Consorti v. Armstrong World Industries, Inc., 64 F.3d 781 (2d Cir.1995), concluding in a diversity asbestos case that New York's statute sets "a standard less deferential to the jury's appraisal" than the one that speaks of "shocking the judicial conscience."   Plaintiff's condition was summarized as follows:

> He developed a tumor which gradually enveloped his spine.   The tumor pressed against his vocal cords, causing him to lose his voice and choke.   It interfered with eating, swallowing, even breathing.   His circulatory system was impaired, causing painful and disfiguring swelling of his head and neck.   And, as his disease progressed, it became increasingly difficult (later impossible) for him to walk or to care for himself.   His pain grew worse as time passed, and was, of course, deepened by the certainty of imminent death.   We take it as a given that reasonable people of his age, in good mental and physical health, would not have traded one-quarter of his suffering for a hundred million dollars, much less twelve.

The *Consorti* court explained that courts could not leave this damage item to jury decision.   From the plaintiff's perspective, wide variation among juries was common and created unfairness among plaintiffs with regard to the size of awards, as well as the unfairness—especially in asbestos cases—of early plaintiffs getting compensated while later plaintiffs will likely get nothing.   From the defendant's side, failure to reduce excessive verdicts will "make it difficult for risk bearers to structure their behavior to efficiently manage risk."   When courts "fail to exercise the responsibility to curb excessive verdicts, the effects are uncertainty and an upward spiral. . . . Unbridled, spiraling, excessive judgments predictably impose huge costs on society."

The court used the state standard to reduce the jury's award of $12 million for pain and suffering to $3.5 million, based largely on a series of rulings made by a state trial judge who was supervising awards in asbestos cases.   Plaintiff has filed a petition for certiorari.

6.   *Per diems and other monetary guides.*   Courts are divided over the wisdom of giving the jury some monetary guidelines when they consider pain and suffering.   Most states permit arguments using monetary guidelines.   A few permit the argument but without numbers.   E.g., Friedman v. C & S Car Service, 108 N.J. 72, 527 A.2d 871 (1987).   On the other hand, in Carchidi v. Rodenhiser, 209 Conn. 526, 551 A.2d 1249 (1989), the court, noting that it had already barred plaintiffs from naming the amount sought in the complaint, and did not permit *per diem* arguments, barred the plaintiff's attorney in closing arguments from giving the jury any number that would be an appropriate award for pain and suffering because of the "risk of improper influence upon a jury." *Carchidi* was overturned by a statute providing that in any damage action counsel for any party "shall be entitled to specifically articulate to the trier of fact during closing arguments, in lump sums or by mathematical formulae, the amount of past and future economic and noneconomic damages claimed to be recoverable." The jury is to be told that the numbers are arguments but not evidence. See Vajda v. Tusla, 214 Conn. 523, 572 A.2d 998 (1990).

In *Consorti*, supra, the defendant suggested that the jury might award between $750,000 and $1 million for pain and suffering. The plaintiff's attorney responded with a suggestion of $8 million for the first 28 months of symptoms and $4 million for the expected four months remaining of plaintiff's life at time of trial—figures the jury accepted. On appeal, the court asserted that "specifying target amounts for the jury to award is disfavored." Although not yet willing to call this reversible error, "[w]e encourage trial judges to bar such recommendations."

7. *Discounting awards for intangible losses.* However the sum is arrived at, there is the further question of discounting. The *Friedman* court, note 6, supra, rejected discounting. The "great majority" of courts do not discount these awards because of the "incongruity of discounting to present value damages that are, by their very nature, so speculative and imprecise." The use of time-unit arguments may lend an "aura of rationality" to this type of award but does not convert the award into one for economic loss. To allow discounting here "would add to the time, expense, and complexity of civil trials without any corresponding enhancement of the reliability, accuracy, or fairness of damages awards." But see, Gretchen v. United States, 618 F.2d 177 (2d Cir.1980)(discounting the award). A similar issue regarding loss of society in death cases is discussed shortly.

8. In Blumstein, Bovbjerg, & Sloan, Beyond Tort Reform: Developing Better Tools for Assessing Damages for Personal Injury, 8 Yale J. Regulation 171 (1991), the authors argue that liability decisions rely on precedent to narrow the range of choice, but that with damages we give jurors no guidance from prior results. Prior awards should be collected and analyzed. Information "on the spectrum of prior damage awards should be provided to juries, judges, or both, as an aid to decisionmaking." The jury should be told that if it wants to make an award in the top (or bottom) quartile of past results it must justify that result by pointing to facts in its case that tilt it to the high (or low) side of the range:

> The middle range of prior awards of a similar nature should be given "presumptive" validity. That is, awards that fall in the middle range of the distribution should be deemed presumptively valid. In contrast, where valuations in a case differ significantly from prior results, tort valuations should be subject to both a burden of explanation by the jury and heightened review by the court. . . . An unexplained outlier should constitute a prima facie case for either

remittitur or additur by the trial judge or an appellate holding of inadequacy or excessiveness of the judgment.

For a similar approach, using the analogy of prison sentencing guidelines, see Levin, Pain and Suffering Guidelines: A Cure for Damages Measurement "Anomie," 22 J.L.Reform 303 (1989). Do these efforts resemble Justice Traynor's view in *Seffert*?

Should juries be given information gained from surveying people about their willingness to pay to avoid various kinds of disabling injuries? What about studies analyzing wage differentials for hazardous activities in the labor market? For empirical analyses, see Miller, Willingness to Pay Comes of Age: Will the System Survive?, 83 Nw.U.L.Rev. 876 (1989); Viscusi, Pain and Suffering in Product Liability Cases: Systematic Compensation or Capricious Awards?, 8 Int'l.Rev. L. & Econ. 203 (1988).

For a study rethinking the role of pain and suffering, see McCaffery, Kahneman & Spitzer, Framing the Jury: Cognitive Perspectives on Pain and Suffering, 81 Va.L.Rev. 1341 (1995). Using experimental data, the authors compared the implications of thinking about compensating specific injuries from an *ex post* perspective of "making whole" and an *ex ante* perspective of how much money healthy persons would want to sell their good health for the same injuries. Those viewing the matter from the *ex ante* perspective tended to award about twice as much as those viewing the injury from the "making whole" perspective. See also Geistfeld, Placing a Price on Pain and Suffering: A Method for Helping Juries Determine Tort Damages for Nonmonetary Injuries, 83 Calif.L.Rev. 775 (1995).

9. *Statutory change—caps on awards for intangible losses.* In an effort to reduce the size of damage awards, some states set maximum amounts that may be awarded for "pain and suffering." The movement began in the mid–1970s when California enacted Civil Code § 3333.2, which limited pain and suffering awards in cases brought against health care providers to $250,000. Others have followed with limits—some of which are also limited to malpractice cases, but many of which are applicable across tort actions. For example, Colorado enacted a cap of $250,000 for pain and suffering in all cases unless the plaintiff could show by clear and convincing evidence that the award should exceed that sum, in which case it might reach a maximum of $500,000. Colo.Rev.Stat. § 13–21–102.5(3)(a). Maryland adopted a limit of $350,000. Md.Code.Ann. § 11–108. Most have been upheld against constitutional challenge. But see Sofie v. Fibreboard Corp., 112 Wash.2d 636, 771 P.2d 711 (1989)(cap on pain and suffering violated the state's constitutional protection for trial by jury); Brannigan v. Usitalo, 134 N.H. 50, 587 A.2d 1232 (1991) (statutory cap of $875,000 on noneconomic loss violates state's equal protection clause). We revisit statutory change in a later discussion of incremental tort reform, at p. 720, infra.

10. *Some large total awards.* The combined damage award in *Seffert* for major suffering was so small as to be almost quaint by today's standards. Although some of the cases involving pain and suffering produce large amounts, the very largest are likely to include major components of both economic and noneconomic losses. The following are not typical by any means, but they suggest the current high end of awards to surviving plaintiffs.

In Aves v. Shah, 997 F.2d 762 (10th Cir.1993), a jury found that defendant physician had committed obstetrical malpractice and was responsible for $21.2 million, 90% of the total damages sustained. The court's short summary indicated that the child "suffers from epilepsy, cerebral palsy, mental retardation, cortical blindness and small head size. Medical and economic experts testified for the plaintiffs concerning the staggering cost of caring for [the child] for the remainder of her life. Such costs will include therapy, prescription drugs, medical testing, education and group home placement." The award was "well within the range" that plaintiff's economist presented. The "constellation of problems, especially her blindness and inclination to suffer seizures, may make future care difficult and expensive. There was testimony that she will experience frustration and that her mobility, as well as her mental capacity, is severely limited. To be sure, the award is large; however, given the record before us, the amount does not shock the conscience of the court."

In Firestone v. Crown Center Redevelopment Corp., 693 S.W.2d 99 (Mo.1985), the plaintiff was hurt in the collapse of suspended skyways in the Hyatt Regency in Kansas City, which killed 114 people. Plaintiff was a 34–year–old unmarried woman who was making $33,000 per year, including fringe benefits, as a computer repairer for IBM. She was rendered quadriplegic as a result of the accident. The court upheld a compensatory award of $15 million.

In Herold v. Burlington Northern, Inc., 761 F.2d 1241 (8th Cir.), cert. denied 474 U.S. 888 (1985), the court upheld a jury assessment of $9,425,-000 as the damages sustained by a truck driver who was rendered a "spastic quadriplegic and suffered brain damage" as a result of a collision with a train.

In Pay v. State, 213 App.Div.2d 991, 625 N.Y.S.2d 770 (1995), appeal pending, the court affirmed a trial judge's award of $10 million in favor of a child injured in utero by the state's negligence who was born with missing and malformed extremities, partial deafness, and a speech impediment. Plaintiff, 17 years old at trial, showed the motor skills of a four year old and was expected to be unable to obtain an intellectual level above the sixth grade. Because of problems with walking she will likely wear out her "hips, knees and feet, requiring her to undergo repeated surgeries throughout her lifetime"—a life expectancy of 80 years. She will also need "audiological, speech, physical, occupational, and psychological evaluation and therapy." The award for pain and suffering was $2 million, with $6.65 million awarded for future residential care for the rest of her life. Neither award was held excessive. Compare the pain and suffering award with that in *Haines*, supra.

11. *Statutory change—caps on total awards.* Although most state legislation has been addressed to capping noneconomic loss, a few have capped the total award in certain types of cases. See Fairfax Hosp.Sys.,

Inc. v. Nevitt, 249 Va. 591, 457 S.E.2d 10 (Va.1995) for a discussion of Virginia's $1 million cap on the total recovery in any medical malpractice case. Colorado capped the total recovery available against governmental units at $150,000 per person and $400,000 per occurrence. The limitation was upheld in State v. DeFoor, 824 P.2d 783 (Colo.), cert. denied 506 U.S. 981 (1992), in which nine bus passengers were killed and 19 injured when a 6.7–ton boulder being moved by a state road crew fell onto a tourist bus passing below. Some of these caps are tied to changes in the consumer price index.

12. *Contingent Fees.* The court in *Seffert* discusses the damage award as though it will go entirely to the plaintiff. In fact, this was almost certainly not the case; plaintiffs' attorneys are retained in tort cases on a contingent fee basis and take a fee ranging from 20%–50% of the final award or settlement amount in the case. Typically, the fee will be one third of the final award, but a variety of factors may lead to deviance from the informal norm: in an especially high risk case, or one requiring trial and appellate work, an attorney may charge more than the norm; in certain types of cases—airline crash claims are an example—the fee charged may ordinarily be near the low end of the scale. See J. Kakalik, E. King, M. Traynor, P. Ebener, & L. Picus, Costs and Compensation Paid in Aviation Accident Litigation (1988).

Does the likelihood that Seffert had to pay one-third of the award to her attorney affect your view of the merits of redressing pain and suffering in addition to out-of-pocket loss? Are there arguments for the contingent fee that seem compelling?

As early as the mid–1970s, critics of the tort system aimed their fire at the contingent fee; see the California Medical Injury Compensation Reform Act, which set a sliding scale of decreasing maximum percentages for plaintiffs' contingent fees, linked to the size of the damage award. A dozen states have adopted such proposals. Recently, a proposal to create an "early offer" mechanism to limit fees in cases settled at an early stage in the case has received considerable attention. See Horowitz, Making Ethics Real, Making Ethics Work: A Proposal for Contingency Fee Reform, 44 Emory L.J. 173 (1995), discussing the proposal which he co-authored with Professors Jeffrey O'Connell and Lester Brickman. The main features of the proposal are: (1) that when defendant makes an offer within 60 days of receipt from plaintiff of a demand for compensation and the offer is accepted, "plaintiffs' counsel fees are limited to hourly rate charges and are capped at 10% of the first $100,000 of the offer and 5% of any greater amount;" (2) that if the early offer is rejected by plaintiff, "contingency fees may only be charged against net recoveries in excess of those offers;" and (3) that if there is no defendant's offer "contingency fee contracts are unaffected by the proposal." Does this seem a sensible reform? For criticism of the proposal, see Silver, Control Fees? No, Let the Market Do Its Job, Natl. L.J., April 18, 1994 at A17. California will vote on a fee initiative along these lines in March, 1996.

McDougald v. Garber

Court of Appeals of New York, 1989.
73 N.Y.2d 246, 536 N.E.2d 372, 538 N.Y.S.2d 937.

[Defendants' malpractice left plaintiff in a "permanently comatose condition." In her suit for damages the parties agreed that, if liability were established, she would be entitled to the usual pecuniary damage items—past and future loss of earning capacity, and medical expenses, including custodial care. The parties also agreed that plaintiff could not recover damages for conscious pain and suffering unless she were found to have been aware of experiencing them, but they disagreed over whether she had the requisite level of awareness. "At trial, defendants sought to show that Mrs. McDougald's injuries were so severe that she was incapable of either experiencing pain or appreciating her condition. Plaintiffs, on the other hand, introduced proof that Mrs. McDougald responded to certain stimuli to a sufficient extent to indicate that she was aware of her circumstances."

The judge charged that to "experience suffering" there must be "some level of awareness. . . . If, however, you conclude that there is some level of perception or that she is capable of an emotional response at some level, then damages for pain and suffering should be awarded." In addition, the judge charged:

> Damages for the loss of the pleasures and pursuits of life, however, require no awareness of the loss on the part of the injured person. Quite obviously, Emma McDougald is unable to engage in any of the activities which constitute a normal life, the activities she engaged in prior to her injury * * *. Loss of the enjoyment of life may, of course, accompany the physical sensation and emotional responses that we refer to as pain and suffering, and in most cases it does. It is possible, however, for an injured person to lose the enjoyment of life without experiencing any conscious pain and suffering. Damages for this item of injury relate not to what Emma McDougald is aware of, but rather to what she has lost. What her life was prior to her injury and what it has been since September 7, 1978 and what it will be for as long as she lives.

Defendants objected that this item was not a separate recoverable item and, in any event, required awareness of loss.

In addition to pecuniary awards, the jury awarded $1 million for conscious pain and suffering and $3.5 million for loss of enjoyment of life. The judge reduced these amounts to a single award of $2 million. The appellate division affirmed the award as modified. The only issues now before the court on appeal involve "nonpecuniary damages," which the court defined as those damages "awarded to compensate an injured person for the physical and emotional consequences of the injury, such as pain and suffering and the loss of the ability to engage in certain activities."]

■ WACHTLER, CHIEF JUDGE.

. . .

We begin with the familiar proposition that an award of damages to a person injured by the negligence of another is to compensate the victim, not to punish the wrongdoer [   ]. The goal is to restore the injured party, to the extent possible, to the position that would have been occupied had the wrong not occurred [   ]. To be sure, placing the burden of compensation on the negligent party also serves as a deterrent, but purely punitive damages—that is, those which have no compensatory purpose—are prohibited unless the harmful conduct is intentional, malicious, outrageous, or otherwise aggravated beyond mere negligence [   ].

Damages for nonpecuniary losses are, of course, among those that can be awarded as compensation to the victim. This aspect of damages, however, stands on less certain ground than does an award for pecuniary damages. An economic loss can be compensated in kind by an economic gain; but recovery for noneconomic losses such as pain and suffering and loss of enjoyment of life rests on "the legal fiction that money damages can compensate for a victim's injury" [   ]. We accept this fiction, knowing that although money will neither ease the pain nor restore the victim's abilities, this device is as close as the law can come in its effort to right the wrong. We have no hope of evaluating what has been lost, but a monetary award may provide a measure of solace for the condition created [   ].

Our willingness to indulge this fiction comes to an end, however, when it ceases to serve the compensatory goals of tort recovery. When that limit is met, further indulgence can only result in assessing damages that are punitive. The question posed by this case, then, is whether an award of damages for loss of enjoyment of life to a person whose injuries preclude any awareness of the loss serves a compensatory purpose. We conclude that it does not.

Simply put, an award of money damages in such circumstances has no meaning or utility to the injured person. An award for the loss of enjoyment of life "cannot provide [such a victim] with any consolation or ease any burden resting on him * * * He cannot spend it upon necessities or pleasures. He cannot experience the pleasure of giving it away" [   ].

We recognize that, as the trial court noted, requiring some cognitive awareness as a prerequisite to recovery for loss of enjoyment of life will result in some cases "in the paradoxical situation that the greater the degree of brain injury inflicted by a negligent defendant, the smaller the award the plaintiff can recover in general damages" [   ]. The force of this argument, however—the temptation to achieve a balance between injury and damages—has nothing to do with meaningful compensation for the victim. Instead, the temptation is rooted in a desire to punish the defendant in proportion to the harm inflicted. However relevant such retributive symmetry may be in the criminal law, it has no place in the law of civil damages, at least in the absence of culpability beyond mere negligence.

Accordingly, we conclude that cognitive awareness is a prerequisite to recovery for loss of enjoyment of life. We do not go so far, however, as to require the fact finder to sort out varying degrees of cognition and determine at what level a particular deprivation can be fully appreciated. With respect to pain and suffering, the trial court charged simply that there must be "some level of awareness" in order for plaintiff to recover. We think that this is an appropriate standard for all aspects of nonpecuniary loss.   No doubt the standard ignores analytically relevant levels of cognition, but we resist the desire for analytical purity in favor of simplicity.   A more complex instruction might give the appearance of greater precision but, given the limits of our understanding of the human mind, it would in reality lead only to greater speculation.

We turn next to the question whether loss of enjoyment of life should be considered a category of damages separate from pain and suffering.

IV.

There is no dispute here that the fact finder may, in assessing nonpecuniary damages, consider the effect of the injuries on the plaintiff's capacity to lead a normal life.   Traditionally, in this State and elsewhere, this aspect of suffering has not been treated as a separate category of damages; instead, the plaintiff's inability to enjoy life to its fullest has been considered one type of suffering to be factored into a general award for nonpecuniary damages, commonly known as pain and suffering.

Recently, however, there has been an attempt to segregate the suffering associated with physical pain from the mental anguish that stems from the inability to engage in certain activities, and to have juries provide a separate award for each. [   ]

Some courts have resisted the effort, primarily on the ground that duplicative and therefore excessive awards would result [   ].   Other courts have allowed separate awards, noting that the types of suffering involved are analytically distinguishable [   ].   Still other courts have questioned the propriety of the practice but held that, in the particular case, separate awards did not constitute reversible error [   ].

In this State, the only appellate decisions to address the question are the decision . . . now under review and the decision of the Second Department in Nussbaum v. Gibstein [which the court reverses at the same time it decides *McDougald*].   Those courts were persuaded that the distinctions between the two types of mental anguish justified separate awards and that the potential for duplicative awards could be mitigated by carefully drafted jury instructions.   In addition, the courts opined that separate awards would facilitate appellate review concerning the excessiveness of the total damage award.

We do not dispute that distinctions can be found or created between the concepts of pain and suffering and loss of enjoyment of life.   If the term "suffering" is limited to the emotional response to the sensation of pain, then the emotional response caused by the limitation of life's activities may be considered qualitatively different [   ].   But suffering need not be so limited—it can easily encompass the frustration and anguish caused by the inability to participate in activities that once brought pleasure.   Traditionally, by treating loss of enjoyment of life as a permissible factor in assessing pain and suffering, courts have given the term this broad meaning.

If we are to depart from this traditional approach and approve a separate award for loss of enjoyment of life, it must be on the basis that such an approach will yield a more accurate evaluation of the compensation due to the plaintiff. We have no doubt that, in general, the total award for nonpecuniary damages would increase if we adopted the rule. That separate awards are advocated by plaintiffs and resisted by defendants is sufficient evidence that larger awards are at stake here. But a larger award does not by itself indicate that the goal of compensation has been better served.

The advocates of separate awards contend that because pain and suffering and loss of enjoyment of life can be distinguished, they must be treated separately if the plaintiff is to be compensated fully for each distinct injury suffered. We disagree. Such an analytical approach may have its place when the subject is pecuniary damages, which can be calculated with some precision. But the estimation of nonpecuniary damages is not amenable to such analytical precision and may, in fact, suffer from its application. Translating human suffering into dollars and cents involves no mathematical formula; it rests, as we have said, on a legal fiction. The figure that emerges is unavoidably distorted by the translation. Application of this murky process to the component parts of nonpecuniary injuries (however analytically distinguishable they may be) cannot make it more accurate. If anything, the distortion will be amplified by repetition.

Thus, we are not persuaded that any salutary purpose would be served by having the jury make separate awards for pain and suffering and loss of enjoyment of life. We are confident, furthermore, that the trial advocate's art is a sufficient guarantee that none of the plaintiff's losses will be ignored by the jury.

. . .

[A new trial was ordered as to nonpecuniary damages.]

■ TITONE, JUDGE (dissenting).

The majority's holding represents a compromise position that neither comports with the fundamental principles of tort compensation nor furnishes a satisfactory, logically consistent framework for compensating nonpecuniary loss. Because I conclude that loss of enjoyment of life is an objective damage item, conceptually distinct from conscious pain and suffering, I can find no fault with the trial court's instruction authorizing separate awards and permitting an award for "loss of enjoyment of life" even in the absence of any awareness of that loss on the part of the injured plaintiff. Accordingly, I dissent.

It is elementary that the purpose of awarding tort damages is to compensate the wronged party for the actual loss he or she has sustained [   ]. Personal injury damages are awarded "to restore the injured person to the state of health he had prior to his injuries because that is the only way the law knows how to recompense one for personal injuries suffered" [   ]. Thus, this court has held that "[t]he person responsible for the injury must respond for all damages resulting directly from and as a natural consequence of the wrongful act" [   ].

The capacity to enjoy life—by watching one's children grow, participating in recreational activities, and drinking in the many other pleasures that life has to offer—is unquestionably an attribute of an ordinary healthy individual.   The loss of that capacity as a result of another's negligent act is at least as serious an impairment as the permanent destruction of a physical function, which has always been treated as a compensable item under traditional tort principles [   ].   Indeed, I can imagine no physical loss that is more central to the quality of a tort victim's continuing life than the destruction of the capacity to enjoy that life to the fullest.

Unquestionably, recovery of a damage item such as "pain and suffering" requires a showing of some degree of cognitive capacity.   Such a requirement exists for the simple reason that pain and suffering are wholly subjective concepts and cannot exist separate and apart from the human consciousness that experiences them.   In contrast, the destruction of an individual's capacity to enjoy life as a result of a crippling injury is an objective fact that does not differ in principle from the permanent loss of an eye or limb.   As in the case of a lost limb, an essential characteristic of a healthy human life has been wrongfully taken, and, consequently, the injured party is entitled to a monetary award as a substitute, if, as the majority asserts, the goal of tort compensation is "to restore the injured party, to the extent possible, to the position that would have been occupied had the wrong not occurred" [   ].

Significantly, this equation does not suggest a need to establish the injured's awareness of the loss.   The victim's ability to comprehend the degree to which his or her life has been impaired is irrelevant, since, unlike "conscious pain and suffering," the impairment exists independent of the victim's ability to apprehend it.   Indeed, the majority reaches the conclusion that a degree of awareness must be shown only after injecting a new element into the equation.   Under the majority's formulation, the victim must be aware of the loss because, in addition to being compensatory, the award must have "meaning or utility to the injured person." [   ]   This additional requirement, however, has no real foundation in law or logic. "Meaning" and "utility" are subjective value judgments that have no place in the law of tort recovery, where the primary goal is to find ways of quantifying, to the extent possible, the worth of various forms of human tragedy.

Moreover, the compensatory nature of a monetary award for loss of enjoyment of life is not altered or rendered punitive by the fact that the unaware injured plaintiff cannot experience the pleasure of having it.   The fundamental distinction between punitive and compensatory damages is that the former exceed the amount necessary to replace what the plaintiff lost [   ].   As the Court of Appeals for the Second Circuit has observed, "[t]he fact that the compensation [for loss of enjoyment of life] may inure as a practical matter to third parties in a given case does not transform the nature of the damages" (Rufino v. United States, 2nd Cir., 829 F.2d 354, 362).

. . .

In the final analysis, the rule that the majority has chosen is an arbitrary one, in that it denies or allows recovery on the basis of a criterion that is not truly related to its stated goal. In my view, it is fundamentally unsound, as well as grossly unfair, to deny recovery to those who are completely without cognitive capacity while permitting it for those with a mere spark of awareness, regardless of the latter's ability to appreciate either the loss sustained or the benefits of the monetary award offered in compensation. In both instances, the injured plaintiff is in essentially the same position, and an award that is punitive as to one is equally punitive as to the other. Of course, since I do not subscribe to the majority's conclusion that an award to an unaware plaintiff is punitive, I would have no difficulty permitting recovery to both classes of plaintiffs.

Having concluded that the injured plaintiff's awareness should not be a necessary precondition to recovery for loss of enjoyment of life, I also have no difficulty going on to conclude that loss of enjoyment of life is a distinct damage item which is recoverable separate and apart from the award for conscious pain and suffering. . . .

In fact, while "pain and suffering compensates the victim for the physical and mental discomfort caused by the injury; * * * loss of enjoyment of life compensates the victim for the limitations on the person's life created by the injury", a distinctly objective loss [ ]. In other words, while the victim's "emotional response" and "frustration and anguish" are elements of the award for pain and suffering, the "limitation of life's activities" and the "inability to participate in activities" that the majority identifies are recoverable under the "loss of enjoyment of life" rubric. Thus, there is no real overlap, and no real basis for concern about potentially duplicative awards where, as here, there is a properly instructed jury.

Finally, given the clear distinction between the two categories of nonpecuniary damages, I cannot help but assume that permitting separate awards for conscious pain and suffering and loss of enjoyment of life would contribute to accuracy and precision in thought in the jury's deliberations on the issue of damages. Indeed, the view that itemized awards enhance accuracy by facilitating appellate review has already been expressed by the Legislature in enacting [some special verdict procedures]. In light of the concrete benefit to be gained by compelling the jury to differentiate between the specific objective and subjective elements of the plaintiff's nonpecuniary loss, I find unpersuasive the majority's reliance on vague concerns about potential distortion owing to the inherently difficult task of computing the value of intangible loss. My belief in the jury system, and in the collective wisdom of the deliberating jury, leads me to conclude that we may safely leave that task in the jurors' hands.

. . . . Accordingly, I would affirm the order below affirming the judgment.

■ SIMONS, KAYE, HANCOCK and BELLACOSA, JJ., concur with WACHTLER, C.J. TITONE, J., dissents and votes to affirm in a separate opinion in which ALEXANDER, J., concurs.

NOTES AND QUESTIONS

1. At one point the majority talks of efforts to "segregate the suffering associated with physical pain from the mental anguish that stems from the inability to engage in certain activities." This makes clear that New York seeks to compensate both the pain and the loss of the pleasure under the same rubric.

Other states, however, segregate these items, calling the loss of pleasure "loss of enjoyment of life." In Fantozzi v. Sandusky Cement Prod. Co., 64 Ohio St.3d 601, 597 N.E.2d 474 (1992), the court approved a separate charge to the jury addressing "the plaintiff's inability, presently and prospectively, to perform the usual activities of life, such as the basic mechanical bodily movements that accommodate walking, climbing stairs, feeding oneself, driving a car, etc."

> The claim for damages for deprivation or impairment of life's usual activities has, in other jurisdictions, been applied to a wide variety of pleasurable activities shown to have been curtailed by the injuries received by the plaintiff. Such damages include loss of ability to play golf, dance, bowl, play musical instruments, engage in specific outdoor sports, along with other activities. These types of experiences are all positive sensations of pleasure, the loss of which could provide a basis for an award of damages to the plaintiff in varying degrees depending upon his involvement, as shown by the evidence. Such proof differs from the elements of mental suffering occasioned by the plaintiff's injury such as nervousness, grief, shock, anxiety, and so forth. Although the loss of the ability to engage in a usual pleasant activity of life is an emotional experience, it is a loss of a positive experience rather than the infliction of a negative experience.

The court thought that the use of more and smaller categories "would help the jury understand exactly what claimed damages it is addressing. This adds more clarity and objectivity to this part of the jury determination." To avoid double recoveries, the court mandated an elaborate two-paragraph instruction detailing how the jury should avoid double counting. Do you think this separation will create more rational jury discussions of intangible loss? Is it relevant that plaintiffs generally press for recognition of new damage categories while defendants argue against them?

How would the court handle the case of a woman with a scar across her face that deters her from playing golf—something she did weekly for 20 years before the accident? Suppose she has no scar but cannot play as well as she did before? Does it matter whether this is because her arm hurts every time she swings or whether her coordination has suffered?

2. How does the compensatory role of tort law fit into the discussion in *McDougald*? Is it a "paradoxical situation" that the worse a person is hurt the less likely that person may be able to recover anything for pain and suffering? Might this also be true in wrongful death cases?

3. The dissent addresses the issue of who is likely to get to spend the pain and suffering award in this type of case. Should that matter? What role does the majority's concern about the "utility" of the award play? Under the dissent's approach what is recoverable if the victim died instantly?

4. Omitted parts of the dissent raised two other issues:

a. that the majority has compromised its declared goal by allowing any "level of awareness" to suffice for an award. How might this compromise the majority view?

b. that the time frames differ for the two considerations. Damages for pain and suffering are available only during the period of cognitive awareness. But damages for loss of enjoyment of life are to compensate for losses "over a natural life span." With respect to the latter, the dissent asked, is plaintiff "entitled to recover an award representing his entire lifetime's loss notwithstanding that he was conscious of the loss for only a few moments before lapsing into cognitive oblivion?" How might the majority analyze such a case? Might it limit recovery to the period of awareness?

5. For further discussion of issues raised by *McDougald,* see Wilt v. Buracker, 191 W.Va. 39, 443 S.E.2d 196 (1993), cert. denied 114 S.Ct. 2137 (1994)(discussing at length the nature of expert economic testimony in this type of case that values life by drawing on studies about willingness to pay to avoid injury, and rejecting such testimony in favor of treating hedonic damages as part of general damages); Montalvo v. Lapez, 77 Haw. 282, 884 P.2d 345 (1994)(same); and Note, Hedonic Damages for Wrongful Death: Are Tortfeasors Getting Away with Murder?, 78 Geo.L.J. 1687 (1990).

6. *Death Cases—Survival Actions.* Much of what we have been discussing is equally applicable to survival cases. The measurement of past lost income and medical expense—that is, loss suffered between the time of injury and the time of death—is similar. The survival action also typically allows recovery for pain and suffering sustained by the decedent. In a case in which the plaintiff is very badly burned as a result of the defendant's negligence, remains conscious in excruciating pain for a day or two, and then dies, why should anyone else receive compensation for that pain? Is there an answer other than deterrence?

In Wellborn v. Sears, Roebuck & Co., 970 F.2d 1420 (5th Cir.1992), a 14–year-old boy was caught under a descending automatic garage door that pinned him to the ground. The evidence showed that he had been alive and probably conscious for as short a time as three to five minutes to as long as "several hours." The coroner's estimate was 30 minutes. The jury's award of $1 million for pre-death pain and suffering was upheld on appeal. See also Guzman v. Guajardo, 761 S.W.2d 506 (Tex.App.1988)(upholding award of $600,000 for 15 minutes of child's severe pain before death).

In Sander v. Geib, Elston, Frost, P.A., 506 N.W.2d 107 (S.D.1993), defendant's negligence in reading a pap smear test led to a failure to detect cervical cancer until it was too late to save decedent, a 34–year-old wife and mother of three children. She underwent some radiation therapy but was found unsuitable for any radical procedures because the cancer was too far advanced. The court does not recount evidence of physical pain in its opinion. In a suit for her death, the jury made an award that was assumed to include $1 million for her pain and suffering. In rejecting a claim of excessiveness, the court responded:

> [Decedent] greatly suffered many faces of pain during the year follow-ing the realization that she would die from the very disease which the pap smear was designed to detect. The enormity of [decedent's] knowledge of her impending, unalterable doom, her confusion, fear, misery, depression, helplessness, physical pain and mental terror, her sure knowledge that she would never live to witness the adulthood of her children or old age with her husband, all were proper consider-ations for the jury and surely had a powerful influence upon it.

Is each of these considerations proper? What if the jury had returned a verdict on this item of $3 million? $300,000? The defendant's strategy was to focus on denying liability. As a result it "did not argue damages in closing arguments to the jury." Was this a mistake?

In Yowell v. Piper Aircraft Corp., 703 S.W.2d 630 (Tex.1986), the court upheld an award of $500,000 to the estates of each of four decedents for mental anguish suffered as a result of their airplane's mid-air break-up. The award was for the time from the break-up, at 10,000 feet, to the time the plane hit the ground. Has the discussion of pain and suffering changed your views on the propriety of recovery? Recall p. 232, supra, discussing similar cases.

By statute California has barred the award of pain and suffering in cases in which the victim dies before judgment. See the discussion in Williamson v. Plant Insulation Co., 23 Cal.App.4th 1406, 28 Cal.Rtpr.2d 751 (1994), denying such a recovery where the victim died a few days before final judgment was entered. The court suggests that if the statute seems to be drawing an arbitrary line that harms plaintiffs' estates, they may benefit from that line if a plaintiff who has been awarded future pain and suffering based on a long life expectancy should die one day after obtaining judgment.

7. *Death Cases—Wrongful Death Actions.* In wrongful death actions, the major item of damages traditionally has been the economic loss to the beneficiaries, because only "pecuniary" loss is available under most stat-utes. Since the beneficiaries were to recover only their loss, however defined, an additional measurement had to be made in the economic loss category—they could not be awarded the decedent's lost wages as such.

From that lost income figure the amount the decedent would have spent personally for food, clothing and other habitual items had to be deducted.

In DeLong v. County of Erie, 60 N.Y.2d 296, 457 N.E.2d 717, 469 N.Y.S.2d 611 (1983), a jury could have found that the plaintiff underwent up to 12 minutes of terror before being stabbed to death by an intruder. The county's liability was based on its delayed response to a 911 call caused by the dispatcher's failure to get the right address. The court upheld a survival award of $200,000 for conscious pain and suffering. The trial judge had properly charged that the jury should consider plaintiff's "fear and apprehension" in assessing damages. The court also upheld a wrongful death award of $600,000 to the beneficiaries of the 28–year–old mother of three, who was not employed outside the home. The court approved the use of an economist to evaluate the replacement cost for cooking, cleaning, housekeeping, and bookkeeping.

Whether loss of companionship—a variant on "pain and suffering," experienced by survivors—can be recovered in a wrongful death action is an independent issue. (Recall that we considered loss of companionship actions involving injury, as distinguished from death, in the emotional harm section; see p. 247, supra.) Frequently, the text of the statute controls the analysis. In Liff v. Schildkrout, 49 N.Y.2d 622, 404 N.E.2d 1288, 427 N.Y.S.2d 746 (1980), the court concluded that the state's wrongful death statute did not permit recovery for loss of consortium. The language stated in relevant part that the damages awardable in death cases are such sum as the trier "deems to be fair and just compensation for the pecuniary injuries resulting from the decedent's death to the persons for whose benefit the action is brought." The phrase "pecuniary injuries" had been in the statute since 1847 and had consistently been construed to exclude recovery for "grief, and loss of society, affection and conjugal fellowship." The line of cases was of such long standing that any change was for the legislature. Nor did the common law permit recovery for this harm.

Recall *Sander*, supra, involving the wrongful death of the woman whose pap smear was misread. Among the damages that the court assumed the jury to have made on the wrongful death part of the case was $388,000 as the pecuniary value of decedent's loss to the family (perhaps such items as housekeeping, buying necessities, bookkeeping, cooking, gardening); $480,000 to each of her three children for lost advice, companionship, moral training, and education (the children were 15, 12, and 8 at the time of death); and $890,000 for the pecuniary value to her husband (perhaps advice, companionship). These sums were not challenged.

In Drews v. Gobel Freight Lines, Inc., 144 Ill.2d 84, 578 N.E.2d 970 (1991), decedent was a 32–year-old father of two children. The trial judge refused to tell the jury to discount any award for loss of consortium to present value. The jury returned an award of $8.3 million for wrongful death and $150,000 for decedent's pain and suffering. "Loss of consortium" (permitted by some states in death cases) included "society, companionship, conjugal relationship, money, goods and services the decedent might reasonably have been expected to contribute to the widow and two sons." The court observed that some states discount all damage awards to present value. Others discount the economic awards but not the noneconomic awards. A few courts distinguish between loss of consortium and pain and suffering by reducing the former to present value but not the latter. Illinois had already decided not to discount recoveries for pain and suffering, disability, and disfigurement. The damages at issue in this case were held to be closer to pain and suffering than to economic loss and were to be treated the same way: "Clearly, as both pain and suffering, loss of society, and other noneconomic damages are incapable of being determined with any arithmetic certainty, present cash value analysis is completely inappropriate in determining an award."

The court also rejected the claim that the wrongful death award of $8.3 million was excessive. The court recited decedent's earning record—he had developed a "positive reputation as an insurance salesman, and in 1985 he had been selected outstanding young insurance salesman in Illinois; and testimony showed that he was the leading salesman out of 3,000 agents in a three-State area for one company." The jury "could have reasonably believed that the decedent would reap large financial gains in the future." On the family side, he was depicted as a "romantic husband and caring father" who personally built the family house with his wife. He was described by neighbors as "eager to help others—the All–American guy." This evidence indicated that the "loss of society and consortium suffered by the decedent's wife and young children was catastrophic." The lump sum award was "not outside the limits of fair and reasonable compensation."

One justice dissented. He observed that the decedent's income at his death was about $60,000 and that his work expectancy was somewhat less than 39 years. An award of $1 million invested at 6% would yield his current income and still leave the $1 million intact. Since the attorneys fee was likely to be one-third, the $1 million should be increased to $1.5 million. This meant to the dissenter that almost $7 million must have been for loss of society. (What about the "large financial gains" in the future?)

> This case is illustrative of the irrational tort system under which we operate. . . . [T]he law falsely pretends that [pain and suffering and loss of society] have a cash value when they clearly do not. . . . These are real losses and real suffering. But they cannot be quantified with a dollar sign. . . .
>
> By refusing to recognize any limits on such damage awards, litigants, with the assistance of their attorneys, are turning the court system into a giant gambling casino. Pain, suffering, or the loss of a loved one may produce incalculable wealth if only the person causing the injury is wealthy enough or carries enough insurance. Although these awards are passed off as compensation, they are really a form of punitive damages under another name. . . .
>
> . . . It is time for the courts to recognize that damages such as pain and suffering and loss of society do not have a quantifiable dollar

value. If society is to allow compensation for such injuries, then society has a duty to limit recovery to some rule of reasonableness. This can be done by the State legislature with legislative limits or it can be done by the courts through ordering a reduction in jury verdicts by remittitur in appropriate cases. This is an appropriate case. The jury award is clearly excessive. While the exact dollar amount of the award may always be subject to disputation and is incapable of scientific measurement, I do believe that the jury award in this case should be subject to a remittitur of $6.5 million. That is to say, I would reduce the award of $8,493,100 to $1,993,100.

What is to be said for the dissent's approach? Against it?

8. *Wrongful Death of a Child.* In Green v. Bittner, 85 N.J. 1, 424 A.2d 210 (1980), involving the wrongful death of a high school senior, the measure of recovery was controlled by the state's statute limiting recovery to "pecuniary injuries." The trial judge told the jury to consider the services the child had performed around the house to date and those that she might have undertaken to provide her parents as she grew older. From this, the jury was to subtract the value of food, clothing, and education that the family would have spent on her until her majority. The jury returned a verdict of no damages. The trial judge upheld the verdict, observing that the "jury in this particular case followed literally the language of the statute." On appeal, the court reversed. The court, though staying within the constraint of the statute, greatly expanded the recoverable damages in such cases:

> We hold that [in addition to the usual items] the jury should be allowed, under appropriate circumstances, to award damages for the parents' loss of their child's companionship as they grow older, when it may be most needed and valuable, as well as the advice and guidance that often accompanies it. As noted later, these other losses will be confined to their pecuniary value, excluding emotional loss. Given this expansion of permissible recovery, a verdict finding no damages for the death of a child should ordinarily be set aside by the trial court and a new trial ordered. To sustain such a verdict "would result in a return to the outmoded doctrine that a child is a liability—not an asset." [   ]

In discussing the nature of the recoverable loss of "guidance, advice and counsel," the court stressed:

> The loss of guidance, advice and counsel is similarly to be confined to its pecuniary element. It is not the loss simply of the exchange of views, no matter how perceptive, when child and parent are together; it is certainly not the loss of the pleasure which accompanies such an exchange. Rather it is the loss of that kind of guidance, advice and counsel which all of us need from time to time in particular situations, for specific purposes, perhaps as an aid in making a business decision, or a decision affecting our lives generally, or even advice and guidance needed to relieve us from unremitting depression. It must be the kind of advice, guidance or counsel that could be purchased from a business adviser, a therapist, or a trained counselor, for instance. That some of

us obtain the same benefit without charge from spouses, friends or children does not strip it of pecuniary value.

The court also noted that the proportion of elderly people is growing. "We suspect that there are many more children aged 45 to 55 who are faced with their parents' need for care and guidance than there were in the past. . . . Nursing homes are not the only vehicle for this assistance. The parents' need is real, and when a middle-aged son or daughter is not there because of a wrongful death, a prospective pecuniary advantage of the aged or infirm parent has been lost." The fact that many of these services were likely to be rendered only in the distant future presented no special problem. Ascertaining their present value involves the same discounting process whether the event is two years away or 20.

One survey of the states indicated that 35 jurisdictions allowed loss of companionship to parents in wrongful death actions. Fourteen of these states had statutes that were traditionally interpreted as providing for pecuniary loss only. The rest explicitly allowed for non-economic loss. See Siciliano v. Capitol City Shows, Inc., 124 N.H. 719, 475 A.2d 19 (1984).

9. Should the plaintiff be able to introduce "grief experts" to testify about the impact of wrongful death on the family? This question split the court three ways in Angrand v. Key, 657 So.2d 1146 (Fla.1995), involving the death of a woman due to negligent diagnosis during pregnancy. The trial court, believing that it had no discretion, admitted testimony from the expert, who had a "a Ph.D. in sociology and has conducted postdoctoral studies in grief and bereavement." He taught college courses on death and dying and had taught seminars on grief. He has acted as a consultant to groups that work with the terminally ill. He has also "produced several publications and books on the subject of grief." State law did not allow recovery for "grief," but permits it for "loss of the decedent's companionship and protection and for mental pain and suffering." A minor child could recover for "lost parental companionship, instruction, and guidance and for mental pain and suffering."

The majority concluded that admissibility was in the trial judge's discretion—on the general principle that expert testimony should be admitted when "it will assist the trier of fact in understanding the evidence or in determining a fact in issue." Sometimes "the experience, age, and other relevant information about the jurors or the facts in a particular case could provide a basis for the trial judge to conclude that [the expert] or a person with similar expertise, training, and education would assist the jury in understanding the evidence or in deciding the appropriate damages." But the discretion is not boundless. Experts should not be used where the matters "are within the common experience of the jurors or to summarize what the expert has been told by lay witnesses." Since the trial judge had not exercised discretion here the case had to be remanded for retrial. Two concurring justices observed that the discretion should be reserved for "unusual circumstances" because grief is a "subject generally understood by the average person."

Three dissenters argued that although "we probably all have some knowledge and understanding of grief, . . . that knowledge may vary widely among a group of jurors, some of whom, because of age or good fortune, may have never suffered the loss of a loved one, while some less fortunate or older may have suffered greatly." They thought there was much more justification for the expert in death cases than in an earlier case in which the court had permitted a "human factors expert to explain the dynamics of a 'complicated intersection.' Jurors are much more likely to have worked their way through complicated highway intersections than to have worked their way through a serious episode of grief."

10. *Interplay of damage actions and wrongful death actions.* Most states hold that recovery in a personal injury action bars a later wrongful death claim. In Rummo v. Celotex Corp., 726 F.Supp. 426 (E.D.N.Y.1989), the court, noting that New York followed this majority rule, held that damages for lost future earnings in the personal injury action should be measured by the plaintiff's pre-tort life expectancy, rather than the one year expectancy he had at the time of trial. For a minority view, see Thompson v. Wing, 70 Ohio St.3d 176, 637 N.E.2d 917 (1994), holding that the wrongful death action is "an independent cause of action" that belongs to the beneficiaries, though defenses available against the injured plaintiff are available as well in the wrongful death claim. Recall p. 397, supra. Are there items of damage that cannot be recovered in the victim's action that would be recoverable in a wrongful death action?

The minority approach raises questions of avoiding double recoveries. See Monias v. Endal, 330 Md. 274, 623 A.2d 656 (1993), holding that in actions for personal injury the plaintiff's recovery for lost future earnings is to be based on a pre-accident work/life expectancy but that a recovery for loss of ability to render services to her family was to be based on a post-accident expectancy. Any recovery for loss beyond that period should occur in a wrongful death action brought by those who lost the benefits of the decedent's services.

We turn now to situations in which the victim has received aid from another source.

Bandel v. Friedrich

Supreme Court of New Jersey, 1991.
122 N.J. 235, 584 A.2d 800.

[Plaintiff obtained judgment against two physicians for malpractice that left him, after post-operative complications, permanently disabled. The trial court refused to charge that plaintiff could recover for the value of gratuitous nursing services provided by his mother. The Appellate Division reversed and remanded for a new trial on damages.]

■ HANDLER, J.

. . .

The complications rendered plaintiff permanently disabled to the extent that he requires twenty-four-hour care. He has only limited use of his right leg and no use of his right arm. He has difficulty communicating with others and cannot understand completely what others say to him. Although he can tend to some rudimentary needs such as basic bodily functions and has limited ability to move, plaintiff cannot cook or do laundry. He also should not shower without standby supervision and may need assistance to get out of bed and select clothing. He cannot be left alone in his dwelling. During the three-plus years preceding trial, plaintiff's mother, Bessie Bandel, almost exclusively had provided that care and supervision. Mrs. Bandel received no compensation for her assistance.

The trial court . . . did allow plaintiff to introduce proof of the reasonable value of future services to be provided, presumably because Mrs. Bandel could not forever nurse her son. That lack of evidence of the value of home health care may have influenced the jury's assessment of damages. In his closing argument, defense counsel stressed both the lack of proof of expense of home health care and Mrs. Bandel's testimony that she would care for plaintiff "as long as I have to. I have no choice, he's my son." Defense counsel told the jury: "(T)here has not been any expense at all to date. We don't know when, if ever, there is going to be one. . . ."

We acknowledge ourselves as latecomers to the issue of an injured plaintiff's entitlement to recover the value of gratuitously provided health care as an element of compensatory damages. The majority of jurisdictions that have considered the issue recognize that a plaintiff may recover the value of those services. [ ] Some have expressed the view that a failure to account for the value of such services amounts to an undeserved windfall or benefit to the tortfeasor. Thus, Oddo v. Cardi, 100 R.I. 578, 218 A.2d 373 (1966), citing Coyne v. Campbell, 11 N.Y.2d 372, 183 N.E.2d 891, 894, 230 N.Y.S.2d 1, 5 (1962)(Fuld, J., dissenting), reasoned that the "fortuitous circumstance" of free assistance should not reduce recovery. Judge Fuld's dissent further noted that barring compensation for gratuitously rendered services could discriminate against the poor, who presumably would be affected more than the rich, who could afford nursing services. [ ] Hudson v. Lazarus, 217 F.2d 344, 346 (D.C.Cir.1954), expressed the rationale that the victim deserves to benefit more than the tortfeasor because legal compensation often fails to compensate fully for injuries suffered. Other courts have recognized that the value of such services can serve as a partial measure of the plaintiff's injury and loss. The Arizona Court of Appeals thus observed that the "plaintiff receiving these gratuitous services is actually detrimented. It is a well-known fact that persons wear out their 'welcome' with friends and even with relatives unless favors are returned." [ ]

Jurisdictions holding that gratuitous services should not be reflected in a recovery of compensatory damages stress the absence of actual loss in material or monetary terms. They reason that the plaintiff has incurred "no expense, obligation, or liability in obtaining the services for which he seeks compensation." Peterson v. Lou Bachrodt Chevrolet Co., 76 Ill.2d 353, 362, 392 N.E.2d 1, 5 (1979); [ ].

The majority position permitting recovery of gratuitously provided health-care services as an element of a personal injury award comports with the views reflected generally in our decisions concerning compensatory damages. Defendant does not and cannot dispute that a plaintiff's incapacity to care for himself or herself constitutes an aspect of personal injury and a proper element of damages. Our courts repeatedly have held that the inability to participate in physical activity constitutes one aspect of compensable harm. Compensation referable to that kind of harm may be awarded for "disability to or impairment of plaintiff's faculties, health or ability to participate in activities." [ ] The "ability to participate in activities," by definition, must include the most basic capacity to perform the mundane tasks necessary and incidental to daily existence.

. . .

Defendant stresses that Mrs. Bandel was under no obligation to care for her son and, further, that she did not require any payments from her son for the services rendered. Based on these factors, defendant asserts that the collateral source rule bars recovery of the value of these services as an element of damages. The collateral source rule, according to defendant, precludes such a recovery in situations where a third party has no duty to pay plaintiff for such care or where a third party directly provides services as opposed to paying for their cost. We disagree. In our view, the collateral source rule does not, in these circumstances, operate as a bar to a recovery that includes the value of such services.

"[O]rdinarily a tortfeasor may not set up in mitigation of damages payments made to injured persons from collateral sources." Long v. Landy, 35 N.J. 44, 55, 171 A.2d 1 (1961). The traditional collateral source rule provides that a plaintiff's recovery of damages should include the costs of injury-necessitated services even when he or she does not pay for them. Our courts have applied that rule in various contexts. E.g., [ ] (damages in wrongful death action not affected by remarriage of surviving spouse); [ ] (wife's recovery in her suit against deceased husband's estate not reduced by inheritance or available insurance). We have explained that "[a]n injured person is entitled to be made whole. It should not concern the tortfeasor that someone else is obligated to aid his victim because of a duty assumed by contract or imposed by law." [ ]

The collateral source rule historically has recognized that the tortfeasor cannot escape his or her duty to make the victim whole because of the fortuitous independent provision of aid by a third person to the victim. [ ] The rule does not differentiate between situations in which the provider has a duty to pay for the victim's care and those in which a friend or relative gratuitously funds such services. The amount paid to plaintiff from various sources "regardless of whether paid pursuant to contract or as a gratuity, cannot operate to reduce the damages recoverable against a tortfeasor." [ ]

We similarly find no distinction that can be extrapolated from the common-law collateral source rule between the gratuitous payment for a third party's services and free provision of such home health-care services. In both situations, the payor/provider ensures that the tort victim receives the necessary assistance to overcome his or her incapacity and indirectly compensates for a part of the victim's loss attributable to the injuries.   .   .   .

.   .   .

In concluding that the common-law collateral source rule does not bar the inclusion of health-care services as an element of damages, we also point out that the valuation of such services is a familiar process and poses no obstacle to recovery.   Thus, in the somewhat analogous area involving the recovery of the pecuniary value of a child's companionship under Wrongful Death Act, N.J.S.A. 2A:31–5, the Court dealt with the valuation of such services.   See Green v. Bittner, [   ].   The Court there observed that services involving cooking, cleaning, administering to basic needs, administering medication, and other basis chores of nursing were "substantially equivalent to services provided by nurses or practical nurses," and should be valued by "what the marketplace would pay a stranger with similar qualifications for performing such services."   [   ]

In this case, Bessie Bandel's care for her son does not alter, indeed, it confirms, the fact that plaintiff has lost the capacity to care for himself. The gratuitous provision of such services neither abates nor diminishes defendant's obligation to pay full compensatory damages that include the value of such services as a measure of plaintiff's lost capacity.   .   .   .

We affirm the Appellate Division judgment remanding the case for a new trial on the issue of damages.

■ For affirmance—CHIEF JUSTICE WILENTZ, and JUSTICES CLIFFORD, HANDLER, POLLOCK, O'HERN, GARIBALDI and STEIN—7.

Opposed—None.

NOTES AND QUESTIONS

1.   What are the underlying justifications offered in *Bandel* for the "collateral source" rule?   What are the arguments against it?

2.   Should the rule treat differently money given to the victim by a rich relative that is used to buy nursing services and services rendered directly to the victim, as in *Bandel*?   In the cited *Peterson* case the court, recognizing that it was adopting a minority position, refused to permit plaintiff to recover for the value of medical services he had received at a Shriners' Hospital: "The purpose of compensatory damages is to compensate [   ]; it is not the purpose of such damages to punish defendants or bestow a windfall upon plaintiffs."   The dissenters asserted that the donors to the hospital "intended that the plaintiff, not the tortfeasor, be the beneficiary of their largess."

3. Should it matter whether the collateral source is bound by contract to provide the benefit or whether it is offered gratuitously? Contract payments are quite common where the victim is protected by health or medical insurance or by wage protection insurance. What if the nursing services in this case had been provided under plaintiff's medical insurance coverage? Would it matter whether plaintiff paid the premiums himself or whether his employer provided the medical coverage as a fringe benefit? These topics, as well as subrogation claims by the provider of the benefit, are considered in detail at p. 680, infra.

4. Would defendant's argument have, as the court suggests, a disparate impact on poor victims? It is often asserted that various damage rules and current efforts to change them affect different groups unequally. See, e.g., Koenig & Rustad, His and Her Tort Reform: Gender Injustice in Disguise, 70 Wash.L.Rev. 1 (1995); Chamallas, Questioning the Use of Race–Specific and Gender–Specific Economic Data in Tort Litigation: A Constitutional Argument, 63 Fordham L.Rev. 73 (1994); Note, Caps on Noneconomic Damages and the Female Plaintiff: Heeding the Warning Signs, 44 Case W.Res.L.Rev. 197 (1994). Keep this issue in mind as we explore current damage rules and proposed changes.

5. In Molzof v. United States, 6 F.3d 461 (7th Cir.1993), the court, applying Wisconsin law, held that the plaintiff, who was suing under the Federal Tort Claims Act for negligent treatment at a Veterans Administration hospital, could recover for future medical expenses even though, as a veteran, he was entitled to free medical care from the VA.

The court noted that although it was most unusual to have a single defendant paying twice for the same item, this result had occurred in other cases, such as where an HMO was held liable for negligence. The important point was not that the defendant was the same, but whether the capacities in which the money was being paid were the same. In *Molzof*, future medical services were due to plaintiff because he was a veteran; and similar services were due him because the government was a tortfeasor. To allow offset in the HMO example would allow "the defendant to reap a windfall by allowing it to avoid its contractual obligations to the plaintiff." The *Molzof* court thought that just as customers pay for insurance coverage, "the veteran has contributed to the medical benefits."

Some cases denying tort recovery were distinguished on the ground that they involved *past* medical expenses while this case involved *future* expenses. The court was reluctant to "deny the plaintiff the freedom to choose his medical provider and, in effect, to compel him to undergo treatment from his tortfeasor." In fact, the veteran had been comatose at the trial at which his future medical expenses were assessed at almost $1.3 million. He had since died. The court observed that the award here will be a "windfall to Molzof, or should we say, to his estate and his attorneys. But that is the nature of the collateral source rule. The state of Wisconsin could abolish the rule; Congress with respect to FTCA claims, could require such awards to be offset. Even if we were so inclined, however, we are in no position to bring about such a change."

6. The availability of public institutions raises similar questions. In Washington v. Barnes Hospital, 897 S.W.2d 611 (Mo.1995), as a result of defendant's malpractice, plaintiff brain-damaged child would need special education for life. Plaintiff proved what such a private education would cost. The court held that the defendant was improperly prevented from arguing that public education was available for that need. Although most courts had sided with the plaintiff, this court disagreed:

> Here plaintiffs need not purchase the public school benefits, nor work for them as an employment benefit, nor contract for them. Hence the "benefit of the bargain" rationale does not apply. Nor are these benefits provided as a gift by a friend or family member to assist plaintiffs specifically, such that it would be inequitable to transfer the value of the benefit from plaintiffs to defendants. Nor is this a benefit that is dependent upon plaintiffs' indigence or other special status. Instead, public school programming is available to all by law. While to some extent public schools are funded by plaintiffs' tax dollars, they are also funded by defendants' tax dollars and no windfall results to either. We reject the concept that the collateral source rule should be utilized solely to punish the defendant. Damages in our tort system are compensatory not punitive.

On the remand, plaintiffs "of course, may respond to this evidence with arguments of its inadequacy, the risk of its continued availability, etc."

7. *Statutory change.* The collateral source rule has been the subject of statutory change in about a dozen states. The nature of these changes is considered at p. 692, infra.

2. PUNITIVE DAMAGES

Until now we have been exploring the nature of compensatory damages. We turn now to the question of whether damages that do not seek to compensate should also be available in certain kinds of cases. Almost all the states have concluded that sometimes damages may be awarded to punish the defendant or to make an example of that defendant so that others will avoid this very serious kind of misconduct. At the extreme, intentional unjustified conduct would warrant this type of treatment. We consider this when we consider intentional torts in Chapter XII. Many states have expanded the availability of punitive damages to other types of misbehavior. For example, under California Civil Code § 3294, "where the defendant has been guilty of oppression, fraud, or malice, express or implied, the plaintiff, in addition to actual damages, may recover damages for the sake of example and by way of punishing the defendant." Even in states that sometimes permit punitive damages, the jury has total discretion about whether or not to award them.

The following case explores generally the nature of punitive damages in the context of drunk driving.

Taylor v. Superior Court

Supreme Court of California, 1979.
24 Cal.3d 890, 598 P.2d 854, 157 Cal.Rptr. 693.

[Taylor sued Stille for compensatory and punitive damages arising from a collision between their cars. Plaintiff alleged that Stille had "acted with a conscious disregard" for plaintiff's safety. Stille moved to dismiss the claim for punitive damages. The trial judge agreed and dismissed that part of the complaint. Plaintiff then sought a writ of mandate to require the judge to reinstate the claim for punitive damages.]

■ RICHARDSON, J.

. . .

. . . In pertinent part, the complaint alleged that the car driven by Stille collided with plaintiff's car, causing plaintiff serious injuries; that Stille is, and for a substantial period of time had been, an alcoholic "well aware of the serious nature of his alcoholism" and of his "tendency, habit, history, practice, proclivity, or inclination to drive a motor vehicle while under the influence of alcohol"; and that Stille was also aware of the dangerousness of his driving while intoxicated.

The complaint further alleged that Stille had previously caused a serious automobile accident while driving under the influence of alcohol; that he had been arrested and convicted for drunken driving on numerous prior occasions; that at the time of the accident herein, Stille had recently completed a period of probation which followed a drunk driving conviction; that one of his probation conditions was that he refrain from driving for at least six hours after consuming any alcoholic beverage; and that at the time of the accident in question he was presently facing an additional pending criminal drunk driving charge.

In addition, the complaint averred that notwithstanding his alcoholism, Stille accepted employment which required him both to call on various commercial establishments where alcoholic beverages were sold, and to deliver or transport such beverages in his car. Finally, it is alleged that at the time the accident occurred, Stille was transporting alcoholic beverages, "was simultaneously driving . . . while consuming an alcoholic beverage," and was "under the influence of intoxicants."

. . .

Although we rarely grant extraordinary relief at the pleading stage of a lawsuit, mandamus will lie when it appears that the trial court has deprived a party of an opportunity to plead his cause of action or defense, and when extraordinary relief may prevent a needless and expensive trial and reversal. (Coulter v. Superior Court (1978) 21 Cal.3d 144, 148 [145 Cal.Rptr. 534, 577 P.2d 669]); [   ]. Such a combination of circumstances is herein presented and, accordingly, we examine the propriety of the trial court's ruling in the light of applicable statutory and decisional law.

Section 3294 of the Civil Code authorizes the recovery of punitive damages in noncontract cases "where the defendant has been guilty of oppression, fraud, or malice, express or implied. . . .'' As we recently explained, "This has long been interpreted to mean that malice in fact, as opposed to malice implied by law, is required. [Citations.] The malice in fact, referred to . . . as animus malus, may be proved under section 3294 either expressly (by direct evidence probative on the existence of hatred or ill will) or by implication (by indirect evidence from which the jury may draw inferences). [Citation.]'' (Bertero v. National General Corp. (1974) 13 Cal.3d 43, 66 [118 Cal.Rptr. 184, 529 P.2d 608, 65 A.L.R.3d 878].)

Other authorities have amplified the foregoing principle. Thus it has been held that the "malice" required by section 3294 "implies an act conceived in a spirit of mischief or with criminal indifference towards the obligations owed to others." [ ]; see Gombos v. Ashe (1958) 158 Cal. App.2d 517, 527 [322 P.2d 933]; [ ]. In Dean Prosser's words: "Where the defendant's wrongdoing has been intentional and deliberate, and has the character of outrage frequently associated with crime, all but a few courts have permitted the jury to award in the tort action 'punitive' or 'exemplary' damages. . . . [¶] Something more than the mere commission of a tort is always required for punitive damages. There must be circumstances of aggravation or outrage, such as spite or 'malice,' or a fraudulent or evil motive on the part of the defendant, *or such a conscious and deliberate disregard of the interests of others that his conduct may be called wilful or wanton.*'' [ ]

Defendant's successful demurrer to the complaint herein was based upon plaintiff's failure to allege any actual intent of defendant to harm plaintiff or others. Is this an essential element of a claim for punitive damages? . . .

. . .

We note that when *Gombos* was decided it was unclear whether, as a general principle, an award of punitive damages could be based upon a finding of defendant's conscious disregard of the safety of others. In the evolution of this area of tort law during the ensuing 20 years it has now become generally accepted that such a finding is sufficient. Examining the pleadings before us, we have no difficulty concluding that they contain sufficient allegations upon which it may reasonably be concluded that defendant consciously disregarded the safety of others. There is a very commonly understood risk which attends every motor vehicle driver who is intoxicated. . . . The effect may be lethal whether or not the driver had a prior history of drunk driving incidents.

The allowance of punitive damages in such cases may well be appropriate because of another reason, namely, to deter similar future conduct, the "incalculable cost" of which is well documented. (E.g., *Coulter,* supra, p. 154.) Section 3294 expressly provides that punitive damages may be recovered "for the sake of example." . . .

We are not unmindful of the speedy legislative response to our *Coulter* holding as evidenced by the very recent enactment of Business and Professions Code section 25602, subdivisions (a) and (c), which absolve the server of alcoholic beverages, commercial or social, from any civil liability to third persons no matter how dangerous or obvious the condition of the consumer of the alcohol. . . . We discern no valid reason whatever for immunizing the driver himself from the exposure to punitive damages given the demonstrable and almost inevitable risk visited upon the innocent public by his voluntary conduct as alleged in the complaint. Indeed, under another recent amendment enacted following our *Coulter* decision, the Legislature has expressly acknowledged that "the consumption of alcoholic beverages is the proximate cause of injuries inflicted upon another by an intoxicated person." (Civ.Code, § 1714, subd. (b).)

Since the filing of *Coulter* we have had the enactment of section 25602. There also has appeared a graphic illustration of the magnitude of the danger in question. In June 1978, the Secretary of Health, Education, and Welfare filed the Third Special Report to the U.S. Congress on Alcohol and Health. We take judicial notice of, and extract the following from, this extensive and very recent official study: "Traffic accidents are the greatest cause of violent death in the United States, and approximately one-third of the ensuing injuries and *one-half of the fatalities are alcohol related.* In 1975, as many as *22,926 traffic deaths involved alcohol.* . . ."

. . .

It is crystal clear to us that courts in the formulation of rules on damage assessment and in weighing the deterrent function must recognize the severe threat to the public safety which is posed by the intoxicated driver. The lesson is self-evident and widely understood. Drunken drivers are extremely dangerous people.

. . .

Defendant's final contention is that many instances of simple negligent conduct not involving consumption of alcoholic beverages could also be alleged to involve a conscious disregard of the safety of others. For example, one who wilfully disobeys traffic signals or speed limit laws arguably possesses such a state of mind and culpability. That case is not before us and we express no opinion on it. . . .

. . .

Let a peremptory writ of mandate issue directing the trial court to overrule defendant Stille's demurrer.

■ TOBRINER, J., MOSK, J., and MANUEL, J., concurred.

■ BIRD, C.J.—Although I concur in the judgment of the court, I must respectfully dissent from that portion of the majority opinion which allows a cause of action for punitive damages in every case where a person has driven under the influence of alcohol. . . .

. . .

In this particular case the defendant is charged with repeatedly driving while intoxicated after his own experience has made him completely aware of the possible consequences of his act. Therefore, in this particular case it may be possible for a jury to conclude that "the second time was no accident."

. . .

■ NEWMAN, J., concurred.

■ CLARK, J.—I share the majority's dismay at the carnage on our highways. And if today's decision would significantly reduce the number of accidents involving drunk drivers, the majority might be justified in changing the law relating to punitive damage. However, today's decision clearly will not reduce the number of drunk drivers on our highways. . . .

. . .

The reasons for hesitancy in awarding punitive damages are obvious. First, the plaintiff is fully compensated for injury by compensatory damages. An additional award or fine from the defendant may constitute unjust enrichment. . . .

Second, civil law is concerned with vindicating rights and compensating persons for harm suffered when those rights are invaded. Criminal law is concerned with punishing wrongdoers. In our tripartite system of government, the Legislature prescribes punishment for criminal conduct. . . .

. . . Moreover, when the defendant's conduct also constitutes a crime for which he has been or will be punished, the punitive award constitutes double punishment—potentially in excess of the maximum punishment specified in the Penal Code and a dubious exception to the prohibition against multiple punishment. (Pen.Code, § 654.)

Third, punitive damage trials interfere with policies governing trial procedures. Punishment ordinarily serves as a deterrent to future conduct. As Justice Peters pointed out, if the plaintiff can place punitive damages in issue, it means "that the plaintiffs can offer evidence of the financial status of the defendant. This would convert personal injury cases where intoxication or wilful misconduct are involved from the trial of a negligence case into a field day in which the financial standing of the defendant would become a major issue." (Gombos v. Ashe, supra, 158 Cal.App.2d at p. 528.)

. . .

Fourth, although situations do exist where punitive awards have a substantial deterrent effect, others exist in which deterrence is marginal at best. Because restitution only requires a wrongdoer give up his unjustified gains, compensatory damage will not always constitute deterrence. If the conduct while clearly wrongful is not criminal, a punitive award may be necessary to deter. Otherwise persons contemplating the wrongful conduct may feel they are in a no-lose situation, only gaining by the wrongful conduct. [ ]

On the other hand, deterrent effect of a punitive award may be minimal or marginal where the conduct already constitutes a crime and the criminal statute is regularly and effectively enforced. Deterrence by punitive award is also marginal where wrongful conduct is as likely to result in injury to the wrongdoer as to others. [   ]

. . .

Fifth, the prevalence of liability insurance in our society, requires that any evaluation of punitive damage in accident cases, especially in the context of deterrence, must consider the insurance factor.

Under the traditional view, an award of punitive damage nullifies all insurance coverage. An insurer is not liable for loss intentionally caused by the insured, and any contract providing for liability is void as being against public policy. (Ins. Code § 533; Civ.Code § 1668; [   ].)[1] . . .

. . .

Sixth, creation of the new punitive award appears contrary to the solicitude for injured wrongdoers reflected by the recent adoption of comparative fault. [   ] A plaintiff guilty of wilful misconduct may not recover any damages against a negligent defendant [   ]. Because malice imports wilfulness, intoxicated drivers will be barred from any recovery against negligent defendants.

The foregoing six considerations suggest we adhere rigidly to Justice Peters' fundamental principle that punitive damage should be awarded with "the greatest caution" in accident cases.

. . .

NOTES AND QUESTIONS

1. Was this an "open-and-shut" case of statutory construction? If not, what brought the court to its conclusion?

2. What is the relevance of a showing that half of all traffic deaths are "alcohol related"? Should it depend on the proportion of drunk drivers who are actually involved in traffic accidents? Is it a "windfall" for a plaintiff to recover punitive damages when injured by a drunken driver rather than simply a negligent driver? Are all punitive damage awards "windfalls"? See Note, An Economic Analysis of the Plaintiff's Windfall from Punitive Damage Litigation, 105 Harv.L.Rev. 1900 (1992).

3. What is the crucial difference between the concurring judges and the majority?

4. Since this decision, federal bankruptcy law has been amended to deny discharges for judgments against drunk drivers. 11 U.S.C. § 523(a).

---

1. Insurance Code section 533 provides: "An insurer is not liable for a loss caused by the wilful act of the insured; but he is not exonerated by the negligence of the insured, or of the insured's agents or others."

Civil Code section 1668 provides: "All contracts which have for their object, directly or indirectly, to exempt anyone from responsibility for his own fraud, or wilful injury to the person or property of another, or violation of law, whether wilful or negligent, are against the policy of the law."

Does this support the dissent? When would the dissenter allow punitive damages in drunk driving cases?

5. Note that the dissent's sixth point involving comparative negligence was altered by later cases permitting a reckless plaintiff to obtain partial recovery against a negligent defendant, p. 394, supra. The fifth point, concerning insurance coverage, is addressed at p. 678, infra.

6. Several years after *Taylor* the text of section 3294 was amended to require that the oppression, fraud or malice be "proven by clear and convincing evidence." In addition those three terms were defined as follows:

(1) "Malice" means conduct which is intended by a defendant to cause injury to the plaintiff or despicable conduct which is carried on by the defendant with a willful and conscious disregard of the rights or safety of others.

(2) "Oppression" means despicable conduct that subjects a person to cruel and unjust hardship in conscious disregard of that person's rights.

(3) "Fraud" means an intentional misrepresentation, deceit, or concealment of a material fact known to the defendant with the intention on the part of the defendant of thereby depriving a person of property or legal rights or otherwise causing injury.

Would these definitions change the analysis of *Taylor?* In addition, the legislature provided in section 3295 that, on request, the court must exclude evidence of defendant's profits or financial condition until "after the trier of fact returns a verdict for plaintiff awarding actual damages" and finding the requisite behavior under section 3294. This type of bifurcation is particularly important when the defendant might be exposed to multiple claims for punitive damages, see p. 666, infra.

7. *Defendant's wealth.* In Herman v. Sunshine Chemical Specialties, Inc., 133 N.J. 329, 627 A.2d 1081 (1993), the plaintiff was required to make a prima facie showing of a case for punitive damages before being able even to discover the defendant's financial condition. A statute providing that the jury "shall consider all relevant evidence, including, but not limited to . . . the financial condition of the tortfeasor," was read as "requiring" such a showing. In Adams v. Murakami, 54 Cal.3d 105, 813 P.2d 1348, 284 Cal.Rptr. 318 (1991), the court, 5–2, held that evidence of the defendant's financial condition was a prerequisite to any award of punitive damages and that the plaintiff bore the burden of introducing such evidence.

Once wealth is known, what are the implications? See Michelson v. Hamada, 29 Cal.App.4th 1566, 36 Cal.Rptr.2d 343 (1994), reversing a punitive award for 25 percent of defendant surgeon's net worth for cheating another surgeon. The court asserted that roughly 10 percent was the maximum possible under California law. Do the same concerns exist when measuring compensatory damages?

8. The majority view is that in a comparative fault state, the plaintiff's compensatory award should be reduced to reflect any fault, but punitive awards should not be reduced. Campbell v. Van Roekel, 347 N.W.2d 406 (Iowa 1984). Why might that be?

9. Some courts have concluded that punitive damages should not be recoverable in derivative cases because the directly injured party was able to recover such damages in the main case. See Hammond v. North American Asbestos Corp., 97 Ill.2d 195, 454 N.E.2d 210 (1983), stressing that the main suit had already concluded when this suit for loss of consortium was brought. To allow another punitive recovery would provide "a double windfall to the injured party and the spouse." Would the same analysis apply if the main action and the consortium action were tried together?

10. *Employer liability for punitive damages.* When plaintiffs seek to impose punitive damages on employers, the states have adopted varying positions. In some states, punitive damages flow with vicarious liability. Other states follow the Second Restatement § 909, which provides:

> Punitive damages can properly be awarded against a master or other principal because of an act by an agent if, but only if,
>
> (a) the principal or a managerial agent authorized the doing and the manner of the act, or
>
> (b) the agent was unfit and the principal or a managerial agent was reckless in employing or retaining him, or
>
> (c) the agent was employed in a managerial capacity and was acting in the scope of employment, or
>
> (d) the principal or a managerial agent of the principal ratified or approved the act.

California's approach in § 3294(b) is that no employer is liable for punitive damages based on an employee's actions "unless the employer had advance knowledge of the unfitness of the employee and employed him or her with a conscious disregard of the rights or safety of others or authorized or ratified the wrongful conduct for which the damages are awarded or was personally guilty of oppression, fraud, or malice." In the case of corporate employers, the advance knowledge and the conscious disregard must be on the "part of an officer, director, or managing agent of the corporation." Which view is preferable?

11. *Liability for punitive damages where tortfeasor or victim dies.* The overwhelming majority of states deny recovery of punitive damages from the estate of a deceased tortfeasor. Comment, Punitive Damages and the Deceased Tortfeasor, 98 Dickinson L.Rev. 329 (1994). Is this view consistent with the theory underlying punitive damages? Recall the discussion of whether a victim's estate should be able to recover for the pain and suffering sustained by the victim before death, p. 640, supra. Are the considerations the same for punitive damages when the victim dies before judgment? See Urbaniak v. Newton, 226 Cal.App.3d 1128, 277 Cal.Rptr.

354 (1991), noting that the same statute that bars pain and suffering in survival actions explicitly permits the recovery of punitive damages.

Punitive damages are not recoverable under most wrongful death statutes because, as we have seen, they are generally worded to allow recovery for the losses of the beneficiaries. But see, e.g., Portwood v. Copper Valley Elec. Ass'n, 785 P.2d 541 (Alaska 1990)(allowing estate to recover punitive damages where no statutory beneficiaries existed).

12. What do the purposes of punitive damages suggest about holding the government liable for such damages? Calif. Govt. Code § 818 provides that "a public entity is not liable for damages awarded under § 3294 of the Civil Code or other damages imposed primarily for the sake of example and by way of punishing the defendant." Why not? But see Calif. Govt. Code § 825 permitting the public entity to indemnify officials held liable for such damages under certain conditions.

Is there any reason why a city should not be able to recover punitive damages? See City of Sanger v. Superior Court, 8 Cal.App.4th 444, 10 Cal.Rptr.2d 436 (1992)(allowing city to recover punitive damages for contamination of its water system).

13. *Burden of proof.* The courts are split over the burden of proof plaintiff must meet on the issue of punitive damages. In about half the states that permit such damages, preponderance of the evidence still suffices. Flockhart v. Wyant, 467 N.W.2d 473 (S.D.1991); Glasscock v. Armstrong Cork Co., 946 F.2d 1085 (5th Cir.1991)(upholding a punitive award of $6 million and concluding that preponderance meets the constitutional standard). Recently, through statutory reform many states have declared that claims for such damages must be shown by "clear and convincing" evidence. See, e.g., Hoch v. Allied–Signal, Inc., 24 Cal.App.4th 48, 29 Cal.Rptr.2d 615 (1994)(extended discussion of standard).

14. *Taxability.* We have seen that Congress explicitly declared that the compensatory part of a personal injury award was not taxable. No such clarity exists on the question of taxing punitive damages. Almost all federal courts have concluded that they are taxable, but one has disagreed. Compare O'Gilvie v. United States, 66 F.3d 1550 (10th Cir.1995) cert. granted (taxable) with Horton v. Commissioner, 33 F.3d 625 (6th Cir. 1994)(not taxable).

Fischer v. Johns–Manville Corporation

Supreme Court of New Jersey, 1986.
103 N.J. 643, 512 A.2d 466.

■ CLIFFORD, J.

Plaintiff James Fischer and Geneva Fischer, his wife, brought suit against multiple defendants seeking to recover damages for lung diseases suffered by James Fischer as a result of his exposure to asbestos. The complaint sought compensatory and punitive damages from defendants-suppliers of asbestos under negligence, breach of warranty, and strict products liability theories. Plaintiffs elected to press at trial only the strict liability cause of action for compensatory damages, while at the same time they sought punitive damages. There were dismissals of numerous defendants before and during trial, leaving at the close of trial only the Johns–Manville defendants (hereinafter Johns–Manville or defendant) and Bell Asbestos Mines, Ltd. (Bell).

The case was tried to a jury. At the close of trial, the jury awarded compensatory damages of $86,000 to James Fischer and $5,000 to Geneva Fischer. The jury found Johns–Manville eighty percent liable and Bell twenty percent liable. The jury also awarded James Fischer $300,000 in punitive damages, of which $240,000 was assessed against Johns–Manville and $60,000 against Bell. Both defendants appealed and the Appellate Division affirmed in its entirety the judgment of the trial court. [ ]

. . .

[The court reviewed in detail evidence that tended to show that the defendant knew as early as 1933 that asbestos posed serious health risks but had decided that at least for the time being "our past policy of keeping this matter confidential is to be pursued." In response to Johns–Manville's contention that a punitive damage award is inconsistent with a claim of strict products liability, the court held that no such incompatibility exists as long as the award is based on a showing that the defendants' knowledge or conduct meets the test for punitive damages in other cases of wrongful activity.]

III

Having determined that no theory of law forecloses the award of punitive damages in a failure-to-warn, strict products liability action, we turn to the policy concerns that defendant poses as obstacles to our decision. Our discussion applies to asbestos mass-tort litigation, inasmuch as it is in that context that defendant chooses to present the issue.

One characteristic of this kind of litigation is that it occurs years after the exposure to asbestos, and hence long after the underlying tortious conduct that creates liability. Asbestos-related diseases generally have long latency periods. For example, asbestosis manifests itself ten to forty years after exposure, and pulmonary and bronchogenic carcinoma (lung cancer) typically occurs fifteen to thirty-five years after exposure.

The remoteness of the tortious conduct spawns arguments that it would be inequitable to impose punitive damages in litigation that does not take place until years after the offending event. One such argument posits that changing social values render punishable conduct that would never have been punished at the time it occurred. Professor David Owen cautions against overlooking the prevailing moral and business standards of the time involved. Owen, "Problems in Assessing Punitive Damages Against Manufacturers of Defective Products," 49 U.Chi.L.Rev. 1, 13–14 (1982) (*Owen II*). In an earlier article Professor Owen grouped "manufacturer misconduct" into five categories: (1) fraudulent-type, affirmative conduct designed to mislead the public, (2) knowing violations of safety standards, (3) inadequate testing and quality-control, manufacturing procedures, (4) failure to warn of known dangers, and (5) post-marketing failures to remedy known dangers. [   ]

We do not perceive that any "changing social values" are implicated in this case, which we view as falling within Professor Owen's categories one and four. Punitive damages were available in this state well before James Fischer was exposed to asbestos. [   ] We cannot imagine that the conduct proven in this case would have been viewed as any less egregious in the 1940's, when the exposure commenced, than it is today. . . .

Another concern created by the time gap between exposure and litigation is that the corporate personnel who made the decisions at the time of the exposure are no longer with the defendant company, possibly no longer alive. From this fact it is argued that punitive damages are inappropriate because they will not punish the true wrongdoers. But as many courts have observed, this contention ignores the nature of a corporation as a separate legal entity. . . .

A related argument, which similarly ignores the legal nature of corporations, is that punitive damages unfairly punish innocent shareholders. This argument has been rejected repeatedly. [   ] It is the corporation, not the individual shareholders, that is recognized as an ongoing legal entity engaged in manufacturing and distributing products. True, payment of punitive damages claims will deplete corporate assets, which will possibly produce a reduction in net worth and thereby result in a reduction in the value of individual shares. But the same is true of compensatory damages. . . . These are the risks and rewards that await investors. Also, we would not consider it harmful were shareholders to be encouraged by decisions such as this to give close scrutiny to corporate practices in making investment decisions.

Another characteristic of asbestos litigation is found in the startling numbers that reflect the massive amount of litigation generated by exposure to asbestos. Although we are mindful of the fact that the case before us involves one worker, whose exposure to asbestos caused legally compensable injury to him and his wife—it is not a class action, not a "mass" case—nevertheless we would be remiss were we to ignore the society-wide nature of the asbestos problem. Recognizing the mass-tort nature of asbestos litigation, we address the concerns that that characteristic of the litigation brings to a decision to allow punitive damages.

Studies show that between eleven million and thirteen million workers have been exposed to asbestos. [   ] More than 30,000 lawsuits have been filed already for damages caused by that exposure, with no indication that there are no more victims who will seek redress. Of the multitude of lawsuits that are faced by asbestos defendants as a group, Johns–Manville alone has been named in more than 11,000 cases. New claims are stayed because Johns–Manville is attempting reorganization under federal bankruptcy law. [   ]

Defendant argues that the amount of compensatory damages assessed and to be assessed is so great that it will effectively serve the functions of punitive damages—that is, defendants are more than sufficiently punished and deterred. We are not at all satisfied, however, that compensatory damages effectively serve the same functions as punitive damages, even when they amount to staggering sums. Compensatory damages are often foreseeable as to amount, within certain limits difficult to reduce to a formula but nonetheless familiar to the liability insurance industry. Anticipation of these damages will allow potential defendants, aware of dangers of a product, to factor those anticipated damages into a cost-benefit analysis and to decide whether to market a particular product. The risk and amount of such damages can, and in some cases will, be reflected in the cost of a product, in which event the product will be marketed in its dangerous condition.

. . .

Defendant argues further that the cumulative effect of punitive damages in mass-tort litigation is "potentially catastrophic." The Johns–Manville bankruptcy is offered as proof of this effect. We fail to see the distinction, in the case of Johns–Manville, between the effect of compensatory damages and that of punitive damages. The amount of punitive damages and the determination that they would cause insolvency that could be avoided in their absence are so speculative as to foreclose any sound basis for judicial decision. . . .

Heretofore the typical setting for punitive damage claims has been the two-party lawsuit in which, more often than not, a punitive damages award was supported by a showing of some element of malice or intentional wrongdoing, directed by a defendant to the specific plaintiff. Even if the actual object of the malicious conduct was unknown to defendant, the conduct nevertheless was directed at a single person or a very limited group of potential plaintiffs.

Punishable conduct in a products liability action, on the other hand, will often affect countless potential plaintiffs whose identities are unknown to defendant at the time of the culpable conduct. We agree with the Illinois court that the mere fact that a defendant, "through outrageous misconduct, . . . manage[s] to seriously injure a large number of persons" should not relieve it of liability for punitive damages. [ ]

Of greater concern to us is the possibility that asbestos defendants' assets may become so depleted by early awards that the defendants will no longer be in existence and able to pay compensatory damages to later plaintiffs. Again, it is difficult if not impossible to ascertain the additional impact of punitive damages as compared to the impact of mass compensatory damages alone.

Many of the policy arguments against punitive damages in mass tort litigation cases can be traced to Roginsky v. Richardson–Merrell, Inc., 378 F.2d 832 (2d Cir.1967). The Roginsky court denied punitive damages to a plaintiff who suffered cataracts caused by MER/29, an anti-cholesterol drug. Although the denial of punitive damages rested on a determination that the evidence was insufficient to send the matter to the jury, the court expressed several concerns over allowing punitive damages for injuries to multiple plaintiffs. The fear that punitive damages would lead to "overkill" turned out to be unfounded in the MER/29 litigation. Approximately 1500 claims were made, of which only eleven were tried to a jury verdict. Punitive damages were awarded in only three of those cases, one of which was reversed on appeal. [ ] While we do not discount entirely the possibility of punitive damage "overkill" in asbestos litigation, we do recognize that the vast majority of cases settle without trial.

Accepting the possibility of punitive damage "overkill," we turn to means of addressing that problem. Because the problem is nationwide, several possible remedial steps can be effective only on a nationwide basis, and hence are beyond our reach. One such solution is the setting of a cap on total punitive damages against each defendant. E.g., [*Owen II*]. Such a cap would be ineffective unless applied uniformly. To adopt such a cap in New Jersey would be to deprive our citizens of punitive damages without the concomitant benefit of assuring the availability of compensatory damages for later plaintiffs. This we decline to do.

Perhaps the most likely solution to the problem of cumulative punitive damages lies in the use of a class action for those damages. [ ] Several courts have recognized the need to streamline and consolidate issues that come up repeatedly in asbestos litigation. For instance, the non-availability of the state-of-the-art defense was decided in a consolidated case governing all asbestos cases in the federal district of New Jersey. [ ] Another federal district court certified a class of all plaintiffs in personal injury asbestos cases pending in the Eastern District of Texas, for purposes of determining both the availability of a state-of-the-art defense and punitive damages. [ ]

. . .

Defendants as well as plaintiffs can seek class certification. [ ] In addition, the asbestos industry itself is free to—and has begun to—develop alternatives and supplements to federal class action. A step in this direction is the establishment of the Asbestos Claims Facility pursuant to the Wellington Agreement, an organization whose purpose is to establish expeditious and uniform settlement, payment, or defense of asbestos-related claims.

At the state court level we are powerless to implement solutions to the nationwide problems created by asbestos exposure and litigation arising from that exposure. That does not mean, however, that we cannot institute some controls over runaway punitive damages. . . . We conclude that a reasonable imposition of those limits would permit a defendant to introduce evidence of other punitive damage awards already assessed against and paid by it, as well as evidence of its own financial status and the effect a punitive award would have. . . .

We realize that defendants may be reluctant to alert juries to the fact that other courts or juries have assessed punitive damages for conduct similar to that being considered by the jury in a given case. Although the evidence may convince a jury that a defendant has been sufficiently punished, the same evidence could nudge a jury closer to a determination that punishment is warranted. That is a risk of jury trial. The willingness to accept that risk is a matter of strategy for defendant and its counsel, no different from other strategy choices facing trial lawyers every day.

When evidence of other punitive awards is introduced, trial courts should instruct juries to consider whether the defendant has been sufficiently punished, keeping in mind that punitive damages are meant to punish and deter defendants for the benefit of society, not to compensate individual plaintiffs.

A further protection may be afforded defendants by the judicious exercise of remittitur. . . .

IV

Defendant argues that even if punitive damages are allowed in strict products liability, mass tort actions, they should not have been assessed against Johns–Manville in this action. We disagree.

We hold that punitive damages are available in failure-to-warn, strict products liability actions when a manufacturer is (1) aware of or culpably indifferent to an unnecessary risk of injury, and (2) refuses to take steps to reduce that danger to an acceptable level. . . .

Judge Brody alerted the jury, at the very outset of the charge, that plaintiffs' claims for punitive damages "involve considerations which in some respects are quite different from your concern with respect to compensatory damages." This careful approach was adhered to throughout the charge. The court informed the jury of the purposes of compensatory damages and admonished the jurors not to use punitive damages to compensate the plaintiffs. . . .

[The evidence in support of punitive damages was found to be "indeed overwhelming."]

V

Even though defendant challenged neither the trial court's charge to the jury nor the amount of punitive damages awarded in this case, we consider those issues of sufficient importance to warrant the following comments as a guide in future cases.

. . .

The purpose and nature of punitive damages must be carefully explained to the jury. In determining whether a defendant's conduct was sufficiently egregious to justify punitive damages, fact-finders should consider the seriousness of the hazard to the public; the degree of the defendant's awareness of the hazard and of its excessiveness; the cost of correcting or reducing the risk; the duration of both the improper marketing behavior and its cover-up; the attitude and conduct of the enterprise upon discovery of the misconduct; and the defendant's reasons for failing to act. See [Owen, Punitive Damages in Products Liability Litigation, 74 Mich.L.Rev. 1257 (1976)].

If a fact-finder decides to award punitive damages, additional considerations can guide a determination of the appropriate amount. Punitive damages should bear some reasonable relationship to actual injury, but we have consistently declined to require a set numerical ratio between punitive and compensatory damages. [ ] The reasonableness of the relationship of punitive damages to actual injury must be considered in light of other factors in each case. For example, some particularly egregious conduct may generate only minimal compensatory damages. In such cases higher punitive damages would be justified than when substantial compensatory damages are awarded. The profitability of the marketing misconduct, where it can be determined, is relevant. Other factors to be considered include the amount of the plaintiff's litigation expenses, the financial condition of the enterprise and the probable effect thereon of a particular judgment, and the total punishment the enterprise will probably receive from other sources.

Finally, there looms the question of the quality of proof required to sustain a punitive damages award. Our dissenting colleagues urge adoption of a "clear and convincing" standard to replace New Jersey's traditional "preponderance of the evidence" rule. The dissent makes a persuasive argument to support such a change and has cited policy considerations that deserve careful consideration.

However, the fact remains that the parties have not briefed or argued that issue, nor have the courts below addressed it. So significant a shift in our law should come, if at all, only after it has been fully litigated. Under the circumstance we are content to leave for another day the definitive resolution of so portentous a question.

Judgment affirmed.

■ O'HERN, J., dissenting.

But for its decision not to have the jury in this case consider the punitive damages claims in light of the principles it suggests today, I would join the opinion of the Court. With the exception that I believe that the jury should be clearly convinced that the proofs measure up to the standard, I find myself in basic accord with the Court's emphasis on the need to instruct juries on the purposes of punitive damages, the consideration of proportion in an award, the nature of conduct to be sanctioned, and the effect of prior awards in their deliberations. I also agree with the Court's recognition of the importance of possible class disposition. I am also in accord with the Court's view that the manufacturer's conduct here would meet its test of " 'utter and reckless disregard of (the user's) safety and well-being,' " [ ], or my own view of the test as involving "a conscious and outrageous indifference to the risks of marketing, manufacturing, or producing its product."   [   ]   I find in the conduct a conscious indifference to the worker's well-being.

. . .

■ For affirmance—JUSTICES CLIFFORD, HANDLER and POLLOCK—3.

■ For reversal—JUSTICES O'HERN and GARIBALDI—2.

NOTES AND QUESTIONS

1. Does the opinion suggest that punitive damages may lie for an incorrect risk/utility analysis?   Is there a difference between making a risk/utility decision that is later found mistaken and making one that is later found to have been groundless?   On liability for making risk/utility decisions, see Schwartz, The Myth of the Ford Pinto Case, 43 Rutgers L.Rev. 1013 (1991).

In Hillrichs v. Avco Corp., 514 N.W.2d 94 (Iowa 1994), the court upheld a compensatory award against the manufacturer of a corn picking machine in favor of a farmer whose hand was caught in the machine. Evidence showed that the manufacturer had known of the danger and had consciously decided not to install an emergency stop device nearby because of the "so-called 'dependency hypothesis,' the theory that the product as designed would discourage farmers from making contact with the roller bed and that the plaintiff's proposed device would invite farmers to unreasonably depend on it despite the dangerousness of the husking roller bed."   A jury might disagree with this judgment but that evidence also shows "that an award of punitive damages is inappropriate when room exists for reasonable disagreement over the relative risks and utilities of the conduct and device at issue."   There was no showing that defendant's act was "in disregard of a risk that was so great as to make it highly probable that harm would follow."

2. Should the long passage of time between act and injury influence the availability of punitive damages?   The court limits part III of its opinion to asbestos cases.   Might one argue that the result should differ in other types of cases?   Is it realistic to suggest that investors carefully study the past practices of a corporation before investing in it?

3. The availability of punitive damages may be affected by some of the other legal questions that we have discussed earlier.   Thus, some courts that either permit market share liability in the DES situation or help plaintiffs in other ways when they cannot identify the culpable defendant have concluded that in such cases punitive damages are not recoverable.   E.g., Collins v. Eli Lilly Co., 116 Wis.2d 166, 342 N.W.2d 37, cert. denied 469 U.S. 826 (1984)(insisting that punitive damages are not recoverable unless it is "certain that the wrongdoer being punished because of his conduct actually caused the plaintiff's injuries.")   Why should this be so?   Accord, Magallanes v. Superior Court, 167 Cal.App.3d 878, 213 Cal. Rptr. 547 (1985).

4. Does the large number of claims for the same conduct argue against the availability of punitive damages? Has the court adequately resolved the concern about the "overkill" problem?

5. Toward the end of the opinion, the court develops two lists of factors: one for the question whether to award punitive damages and one for measuring the appropriate size of the recovery. Are the two sets sufficiently different for their different purposes?

6. *Repeated awards.* In W.R. Grace & Co. v. Waters, 638 So.2d 502 (Fla.1994), a mass tort action involving asbestos products, the court refused to bar multiple awards of punitive damages. The court noted that other courts have "unanimously" rejected the idea that such damages be awarded only once—perhaps to the first successful plaintiff:

> We acknowledge the potential for abuse when a defendant may be subjected to repeated punitive damage awards arising out of the same conduct. Yet, like the many other courts which have addressed the problem, we are unable to devise a fair and effective solution. Were we to adopt the position advocated by Grace, our holding would not be binding on other state courts or federal courts. This would place Floridians injured by asbestos on an unequal footing with the citizens of other states with regard to the right to recover damages from companies who engage in extreme misconduct. Any realistic solution to the problems caused by the asbestos litigation in the United States must be applicable to all fifty states. It is our belief that such a uniform solution can only be effected by federal legislation.

Although the lower court had suggested that Grace could use the fact of prior awards as mitigation before this jury, "advising the jury of previous punitive damage awards would actually hurt its cause" as it tries to argue that it should not be punished at all. The *Grace* court sought to meet this concern by ordering lower courts to bifurcate the proceeding. The first step would permit evidence on (1) liability, (2) the amount of compensatory damages and (3) liability for punitive damages. If the jury determines that punitive damages are appropriate, the second step would permit evidence on the amount of such damages, including any prior awards. This would permit defendant to "build a record for a due process argument based on the cumulative effect of prior awards." More than a dozen states use this type of bifurcation.

For an extended consideration of the problem of exposure to repeated punitive awards, see Dunn v. HOVIC, 1 F.3d 1371 (3d Cir. en banc), cert. denied 114 S.Ct. 650 (1993), holding 8–5, that repeated awards are not per se unconstitutional, though repeated awards may be relevant in assessing constitutional attacks on the awards—either on the ground that the total sum is too high or on the ground that the particular defendant cannot afford to pay them. The dissenting opinion of Judge Weis emphasized that even within a single state early punitive awards risked leaving later victims without recovery for even their compensatory damages. This point was also made by Justice O'Hern in an omitted part of his dissent in *Fischer:*

"why, for example, should a few Dalkon Shield users, receive several millions in punitive-damage awards, while others receive nothing from the bankrupt A.H.Robins Co.?"

7.   The following excerpt reviews the current status of punitive damage awards and also provides a useful bibliography.   A particularly interesting set of perspectives can be found in the Alabama Law Review symposium cited in Note 2.

Enterprise Responsibility for Personal Injury Vol. II, Approaches to Legal and Institutional Change

Report to the American Law Institute (1991).
pp. 232–36.

The conundrums relating to punitive damages are no longer simply a matter for scholarly debate.[2]   The topic has surfaced in the public and political arena as people have become aware of occasionally huge jury verdicts—such as the $125 million award against Ford Motor Company in the Pinto case[3] and the $3 *billion* award against Texaco arising out of the Pennzoil litigation.[4]   News stories have fueled a general impression that punitive awards are now being rendered in far more tort cases and in far greater amounts.   Since the whole punitive damages regime appears anomalous and questionable when placed alongside the elaborate set of standards and procedures developed for the criminal justice system, it is little wonder that more and more voices are calling for major overhauls of this area of tort law and that over half of the states have responded with legislative action.[5]

Even casual readers of the case reports will notice regular appearances of multimillion-dollar punitive awards by juries, a substantial number of

---

2.   Nevertheless, the last decade witnessed a flourishing of scholarship on this topic, exemplified by two broad-ranging symposia on punitive damages: the first in 56 Southern California Law Review 1 (1982), and the second in 40 Alabama Law Review 687 (1989).   Among the notable pieces published between these symposia were Sales and Code, "Punitive Damages: A Relic That Has Outlived Its Origins," 37 Vand.L.Rev. 1117 (1984); Johnston, "Punitive Liability: A New Paradigm of Efficiency in Tort Law," 87 Colum.L.Rev. 1385 (1987); and Abraham and Jeffries, "Punitive Damages and the Rule of Law: The Role of Defendant's Wealth," 18 J.Legal Studies 415 (1989).

3.   Grimshaw v. Ford Motor Co., 174 Cal.Rptr. 348 (Ct.App.1981)(affirming trial judge's remittitur to $3.5 million from jury award of $125 million).

4.   See Texaco, Inc. v. Pennzoil Co., 729 S.W.2d 768 (Tex.Ct.App. 1987) ($3 billion punitive award by jury reduced on appeal to $1 billion), cert. dismissed, 485 U.S. 994 (1988).

5.   See J. Ghiardi and J. Kircher, Punitive Damages: Law and Practice (1985 & Supp. 1989), in particular Chapter 21, "Reform Proposals and Legislation."   Two recent and systematic reanalyses of punitive damages are Report of the Special Committee of Punitive Damages, Section of Litigation, American Bar Association, *Punitive Damages: A Constructive Examination* (1986)[*ABA Report*]; and the American College of Trial Lawyers, *Report on Punitive Damages of the Committee on Special Prob-*

which escape judicial scrutiny unscathed.[6] Discussion of this subject assumes that these cases reflect a general increase in the frequency and severity of punitive damages awarded to personal injury claimants, especially in product liability cases. That perception is only partly borne out, however, by the empirical evidence. A 1986 RAND Corporation study,[7] commissioned by the American Bar Association as part of its review of punitive damage issues, found that over the period 1960 to 1984 in San Francisco County, California, and Cook County, Illinois, there was a marked increase in the levying of punitive damages awards. In the 1980's about one-half of all punitive damage awards were against business defendants, awards against business defendants were more than ten times as large as the amount typically assessed against individual defendants, and the ratio of punitive damages to compensatory damages for business defendants has been rising steadily.

However, the RAND study also found that most of the growth in punitive damages was not in the product liability or medical malpractice areas, as is often suggested, but in intentional torts and business contract disputes, including wrongful dismissal, insurer bad faith, and other commercial litigation. The incidence of punitive damage awards in personal injury cases was quite small throughout the 25–year period in both Cook County (on average, less than three such awards a year) and San Francisco County (one per year). Over the entire period, punitive damages were awarded in only four product liability cases in San Francisco County and two in Cook County. However, although the number of punitive damage awards for personal injury cases barely increased in the 1980's, the amount of money awarded rose sharply—that is, a handful of cases received exceptionally large awards. At the same time, median punitive damage awards are far lower than mean awards, implying that a small subset of punitive awards accounts for the bulk of total punitive payouts. These findings reflect initial jury verdicts, but about half of the punitive damage awards from 1979 to 1983 that were analyzed were reduced after trial. In fact, defendants taken as a group eventually paid only about 50 percent of

lems in the Administration of Justice (1989)[ACTL Report].

6. From the enterprise setting in particular come some recent and noteworthy cases: Mason v. Texaco, Inc., 741 F.Supp. 1472 (D.Kan.1990)($25 million punitive award by jury upheld); O'Gilvie v. International Playtex, Inc., 821 F.2d 1438 (10th Cir. 1987)($10 million punitive damages verdict upheld), cert. denied sub nom. Playtex Holdings, Inc. v. O'Gilvie, 486 U.S. 1032 (1988); Masaki v. General Motors Corp., 780 P.2d 566 (Hawaii 1989)($11 million jury verdict sent back for new trial on higher standard of proof); Batteast v. Wyeth Laboratories, Inc., 560 N.E.2d 315 (Ill.1990); Loitz v. Remington Arms Co., 532 N.E.2d 1091 (Ill.App. 1988)($1.6 million verdict upheld), app. al-

lowed, 563 N.E.2d 397 (Ill.1990); Tetuan v. A.H. Robins Co., 738 P.2d 1210 (Kan. 1987)($7.5 million verdict upheld); Kociemba v. G.D. Searle & Co., 707 F.Supp. 1517 (D.Minn.1989)($7 million punitive verdict upheld); Hodder v. Goodyear Tire & Rubber Co., 426 N.W.2d 826 (Minn.1988)($12.5 million punitive verdict reduced to $4 million), cert. denied, 109 S.Ct. 3265 (1989); Mercy Hospital of Laredo v. Rios, 776 S.W.2d 626 (Tex.Ct.App. 1989)($1 million verdict upheld); Hospital Authority of Gwinnett County v. Jones, 259 Ga. 759, 386 S.E.2d 120 (1989)($1.3 million verdict upheld).

7. M. Peterson, S. Sarma, and M. Shanley, Punitive Damages: Empirical Findings (1987).

the punitive damages initially awarded, and only 38 percent of the damages initially awarded in personal injury cases.

The general pattern that emerged from the RAND findings was confirmed by a study conducted by Landes and Posner[8] of 220 federal appeals court product liability cases decided between 1982 and mid–1985, and 139 state court product liability cases decided in 1984 and 1985 (including all 20 cases decided in New York and California). Out of the total of 359 cases, punitive damages were allowed in only 7, or 2 percent of the cases.

These more systematic surveys provide a helpful perspective on the somewhat distorted perception one gets from reading about only the largest and most questionable punitive awards. The findings do not come close to providing full consolation to the targets of such awards, however. The pattern depicted by the empirical research appears to be that enterprises are subject to an occasional risk of what may turn out to be a very large punitive award: an award that may be multiplied if a single business decision about, say, a product design or warning leads to numerous successful tort claims, each with its own punitive damage component.

It is precisely this huge variance in the risk presented by the tort system that moved more than thirty states during the 1980's to enact reforms designed to circumscribe both the circumstances in which punitive damages may be awarded and the size of possible awards. These reforms take a wide variety of forms, from outright abolition of punitive damages to tighter definitions of the kinds of conduct that may attract such awards, more stringent burdens of proof, monetary caps on the size of punitive damage awards or fixed ratios between punitive and compensatory damages, the partial escheat of awards to government agencies, and various procedural reforms such as bifurcated trials, or having judges rather than juries fix awards.

NOTES AND QUESTIONS

1. What are the most persuasive points of the excerpt? The least?

2. In mid–1995, the Justice Department released a study based on a sample of over 6,000 cases, estimating that in the 12,000 trials that developed from 762,000 civil cases, 364 resulted in punitive damages. The cases covered the year from mid–1991 to mid–1992 in the nation's 75 largest counties. Almost 80 percent of the total cases were tort cases. Plaintiffs won 50 percent of the tort jury cases and received punitive damages in 4 percent of these. Three of the 142 plaintiffs who won products cases got punitive awards, as did thirteen of the 202 successful plaintiffs in toxic cases. The results of this study are consistent with several other recent studies that show very few tort cases yielding punitive damages. Of the total sum of money recovered by all tort plaintiffs 10

---

8. W. Landes and R. Posner, *The Economic Structure of Tort Law* 302–07 (1987). A much broader-based study that appeared shortly before this Report went into print, Daniels and Martin, "Myth and Reality in Punitive Damages," 75 *Minnesota Law Review* 1 (1990), provides further corroboration of the empirical picture presented in the text.

percent—$267.8 million—was for punitive damages. The study is reported at 23 Prod.Safety & Liab.Rptr. 756 (1995). Do any of these numbers cast doubt upon points made in the excerpt?

3. *Statutory change.* As the end of the excerpt notes, statutory change has occurred in more than half the states. A handful have abolished punitive damages, joining another handful that had long taken that position. A few states require that plaintiffs share their punitive awards with the state; others have increased the burden of proof to "clear and convincing;" and a dozen or so have set maximum dollar amounts or ratios above which punitive damages may not be recovered—such as a cap of $250,000 or three times compensatory damages, whichever is higher.

Perhaps the most drastic cap on punitive damages (short of abolition) is Colorado's, which provides that "exemplary damages shall not exceed an amount which is equal to the amount of the actual damages awarded to the injured party." See Lira v. Davis, 832 P.2d 240 (Colo.1992). What if the only damage is to a $10 pair of glasses?

Some states have made several changes. For a broad legislative package—addressing both products cases and punitive damages cases— consider Georgia's approach. In State v. Moseley, 263 Ga. 680, 436 S.E.2d 632 (1993) and Mack Trucks, Inc. v. Conkle, 263 Ga. 539, 436 S.E.2d 635 (1993), the court upheld the constitutionality of a statute providing that 75 percent of any punitive damages awarded in a products liability case was to go to the state. In a non-products case punitive damages were recoverable without limit if plaintiff could show that defendant acted "with specific intent to cause harm." In all other non-products cases, punitive damages were capped at $250,000.

To obtain punitive damages in a products case, the plaintiff had to provide "clear and convincing" evidence that defendant acted with "conscious indifference to consequences." Moreover, although there was no cap on punitive damages in a products case, "only one award of punitive damages may be recovered in a court in this state from a defendant for any act or omission if the cause of action arises from product liability, regardless of the number of causes of action which may arise from such act or omission." Does this provision mesh well with the sharing provision?

In *Conkle*, the record showed that for four years before plaintiff was hurt, Mack knew about the problems with the truck model in question and took no action. The marketing division had "vetoed a proposal by the engineering division to reinforce the frames on newly built trucks at a cost of $103. The record further shows that there was no notification to the purchasers of these trucks of the problems associated with the frame rails." The jury's award of $2 million in punitive damages was upheld.

After reading the materials in this section, which—if any—of the various reform proposals mentioned in the last paragraph of the excerpt seem warranted?

4. *Constitutional Questions.* Since the late 1980s the Supreme Court has reviewed several punitive damage cases in which the awards have been claimed to violate various constitutional provisions. Although no sharp lines have emerged, the Court has demonstrated its willingness to permit punitive damage awards under appropriate procedural safeguards.

In Pacific Mutual Life Ins. Co. v. Haslip, 499 U.S. 1 (1991), involving a life insurance agent who continued taking premiums from the insured after the policy had been cancelled, the Court held that a punitive award that was more than four times greater than the compensatory award did not violate the Due Process Clause of the Constitution. The Court did warn that unlimited jury discretion "may invite extremes that jar one's constitutional sensibilities." But the Court admitted that it could not define a "mathematical bright line between the constitutionally acceptable and the constitutionally unacceptable that would fit every case." In Browning-Ferris v. Kelco Disposal, Inc., 492 U.S. 257 (1989), the Court had already held that the Eighth Amendment prohibition on excessive fines did not apply to punitive damage awards in civil cases.

In TXO Prod. Corp. v. Alliance Resources Corp., 509 U.S. 443 (1993), involving an oil and gas developer's unjustifiable litigation to gain economic leverage, the Court upheld a West Virginia punitive award of $10 million, 526 times larger than the compensatory award of $19,000. The Court rejected a constitutional challenge based on the disparity. There was no maximum ratio that one part of the award had to bear to the other. The Court quoted approvingly a passage from an earlier West Virginia case:

> For instance, a man wildly fires a gun into a crowd. By sheer chance, no one is injured and the only damage is to a $10 pair of glasses. A jury reasonably could find only $10 in compensatory damages, but thousands of dollars in punitive damages in order to discourage future bad acts.

Might it be millions if the defendant was very wealthy and the behavior truly outrageous?

In Honda Motor Co., Ltd., v. Oberg, 114 S.Ct. 2331 (1994), involving an ATV accident, the Court held unconstitutional a section of the Oregon constitution providing that punitive damages were not subject to judicial review unless the reviewing court can say that there is "no evidence to support the verdict."

In BMW of North America, Inc. v. Gore, 646 So.2d 619 (Ala.1994), cert. granted 115 S.Ct. 932 (1995), BMW failed to disclose that the paint finish on a new automobile had been damaged and was repaired before sale. At trial plaintiff was awarded compensatory damages of $4,000 and punitive damages of $4 million. On appeal some punitive award was held justified on a showing that 983 vehicles were sold in this manner, but the amount was reduced to $2 million.

In Pulla v. Amoco Oil Co., 72 F.3d 648 (8th Cir.1995), plaintiff's co-worker had to cover for plaintiff when he took what she thought to be excessive sick leave. She checked his credit card charges and discovered that he was charging at restaurants and bars on days that he was taking sick leave. She told their common superior who admonished her against such checking but then forwarded the material to the defendant's human resources department. A jury found defendant liable for invasion of privacy and assessed damages of $1 for past pain and suffering, $1 for future pain and suffering and $500,000 punitive damages. On appeal, the court vacated the punitive award and remanded for further consideration.

In an opinion by retired Justice White, the panel concluded that the trial judge had failed to consider the fact that this was an isolated incident, and thus the threatened harm was limited, and that the level of offensiveness was far below that in *TXO* in which the Court had upheld a punitive award that was 526 times the compensatory award. The trial judge had also overlooked the "limited actual harm suffered by" plaintiff. Given "the limited offensiveness of Amoco's actions and the unlikelihood of any serious potential harm from its conduct, we hold that the 250,000:1 ratio between punitive and actual damages is excessive, unreasonable and violative of due process."

5. One of the crucial differences between compensatory and punitive damages involves the role of liability insurance. Do insurers agree to cover punitive damages? If so, does public policy permit such coverage? We turn now to the crucial role of insurance in tort law.

B.   INTRODUCTION TO INSURANCE

Inevitably a course on tort law emphasizes accidental injuries caused by others. In the real world, however, we often accidentally hurt ourselves or suffer injury at the hands of natural forces that are not subject to tort law. As society has grown more affluent, more and more individuals have sought to insure themselves and their families against the financial burden of these misfortunes. The institution of life insurance, which is several hundred years old, was developed to permit a person to protect others against the insured's premature death. (Since death is inevitable, many view life insurance was a form of savings rather than insurance.) Insurance against loss of property is older than life insurance. This century has seen the emergence of insurance against the expenses of hospitalization, unusual medical expenses, disruption of income as the result of an accident or illness, and disability. In each of these forms of insurance, the insured is seeking protection against the financial consequences of the occurrence of an undesired event—without regard to any legal rules of tort liability. This is called "first-party" insurance: protection of the insured or the insured's family from the direct adverse economic effects of a particular event. Liability insurance, taken out to protect the insured against the economic impact of having to pay damages to another person, is called "third-party" insurance because the insurer pays a third person for a loss the insured has caused. Liability insurance did not appear until the end of the 19th century.

Although third-party and first-party insurance come into play in different situations and serve different goals, they may co-exist in the same insurance policy. The conventional automobile insurance policy contains provisions of both types. The following breakdown and explanation is drawn from Appendix A of Standards of No–Fault Motor Vehicle Accident Benefits Act—Report of the Senate Committee on Commerce, Science and Transportation on S. 1381 (95th Cong.2d Sess., 1978):

Auto insurance policies in general.—The typical auto insurance policy contains both first-party and third-party coverages:

First-party coverages:

Medical payments (Med.Pay.)

Collision.

Uninsured Motorists (UM).

Comprehensive (Comp).

Personal Injury Protection (PIP)(explained [elsewhere]; available only in no-fault States).

Third-party coverages:

Bodily Injury Liability (BI).

Property Damage Liability (PD).

Medical Payments (Med.Pay.) coverage provides protection against specified amounts of hospital and medical costs for each person injured in the policyholder's vehicle (usually a relatively small amount, e.g., $1,500–$2,000).

Collision insurance covers the cost of repairs to a policyholder's car after an accident, regardless of whether the policyholder is at fault.

Uninsured Motorists (UM) coverage provides specified amounts of protection to the policyholder and occupants of his or her car against bodily injury and property damage losses incurred in an accident in which the other driver is uninsured and is determined to be at fault. [Underinsured motorist coverage operates in a similar fashion.]

Comprehensive (Comp.) coverage protects the policyholder's car against the perils of fire, theft, flood, vandalism or malicious mischief.

All first-party coverages except Uninsured Motorists coverage are offered with a variety of coverage limitations and deductible amounts. No deductibles are available under third-party coverages.

Bodily Injury Liability (BI) is the coverage that compensates the economic and non-economic bodily losses of third parties resulting from accidents in which the policyholder (or other lawful operator) is found to be at fault. It is usually sold in varying multiples of thousands of dollars of coverage per person and per occurrence. For example, BI coverage of $25,000/$50,000 would provide protection up to $25,000 for each person, and up to $50,000 for all persons, injured in an accident in which the policyholder (or other lawful operator) is at fault. BI coverage also obligates the insurer to defend the policyholder against third-party bodily injury claims.

Property Damage Liability (PD) coverage compensates third parties for loss of or damage to their property (whether a picket fence or a car) inflicted by the policyholder's vehicle under circumstances in which the policyholder (or other lawful operator) is found to be at fault. Here, too, the insurer is obligated to defend the policyholder against third-party claims.

Similarly homeowner's insurance has both first-party and third-party aspects. Briefly, this coverage is primarily what homeowners buy to protect the value of their property against loss by fire or, in some cases, earthquake. If the owner has a mortgage its purchase may not be optional since lenders demand it to secure the value of the loan. There is, however, a third-party aspect to the policy—a liability coverage that protects the insured against liability that is incurred in non-vehicular contexts. This aspect is at the center of the *Lalomia* case, p. 702, infra.

Before exploring the impact of first-party and third-party insurance on tort law, we first consider some important questions of when and whether it is permissible to buy protection against certain risks. These restrictions may be found either in the insurance contract itself or may be imposed by law.

Contractual restrictions on coverage. The most important contractual restriction on coverage for tort law purposes is the common insurer goal of covering only "accidents." The contract language either limits coverage to "accidents," defined as a "sudden event . . . neither expected or intended by the insured," or offers broad coverage and then excludes coverage of actions that are "intentional." Two lines of cases have emerged and are summarized in Cooperative Fire Ins. Ass'n v. Combs, 648 A.2d 857 (Vt.1994) involving a shooting death and an insurance policy that excludes coverage of liability resulting from "an intentional act of an Insured." It was stipulated that the shooter-insured was "insane." One line of cases holds that "an insane person cannot act intentionally as a matter of law" for insurance purposes and the second holds that "so long as there is evidence that the insured understood the physical nature and consequences of his action, he is capable of intent even though he may not be capable of distinguishing between right and wrong or of controlling his conduct." Even under this second view "there will be coverage if the insured is so mentally ill that he does not, in fact, know what he is doing, as when, for instance, he points a pistol thinking he is peeling a banana." The court adopted the first view. What are the consequences to the victims, the insured, and the insurer of adopting the first view?   The second view?

The reasons for the various positions are explored in Hanover Ins. Co. v. Talhouni, 413 Mass. 781, 604 N.E.2d 689 (1992)(coverage for insured who assaulted stranger while on "bad trip" from LSD and who "was completely out of touch with reality, was hallucinating and delusional, and did not know that he was assaulting another human being"); Municipal Mut. Ins. Co. v. Mangus, 191 W.Va. 113, 443 S.E.2d 455 (1994)(no coverage where insured shot neighbor: "he knew he was picking up a gun and not a banana; that when he went outside with that gun, he knew he was pointing the gun at a man and knew that man was Rickey Fields"); Auto–Owners Ins. Co. v. Churchman, 440 Mich. 560, 489 N.W.2d 431 (1992) (holding that even though "an insane or mentally ill insured may be unable to form the criminal intent necessary to be charged with murder, such an individual can still intend or expect the results of the injuries he causes" and insurance coverage is excluded).

Sexual abuse.   In Allstate Ins. Co. v. Mugavero, 79 N.Y.2d 153, 589 N.E.2d 365, 581 N.Y.S.2d 142 (1992), the insured, who had been sued for damages for the sexual molestation of two children, wanted the insurer to defend the claims.   The victims' complaint alleged (1) that the insured acted with "force and violence, and against the consent" of the children; (2) that the molestation occurred "without intending the resultant serious injuries"; and (3) that the abuse was committed "negligently and careless-ly, and with wanton disregard of others."   (Claims against the wife are discussed shortly.)   The insurer, whose policy stated "We do not cover bodily injury . . . intentionally caused by an insured person," claimed that the policy did not cover the events.   The children and the insured joined in arguing for coverage.

The court, 4–3, denied coverage.   The insured argued that the exclu-sion did not apply because "it requires that the harm be intended rather than the act causing it.   And they insist that theoretically the perpetrator can lack the subjective intent of causing harm while committing an act of sodomy or sexual abuse on a young child."   The court disagreed because sexual abuse usually caused severe damage.   To allow coverage here would be to permit the insured "to transfer the responsibility for his deeds onto the shoulders of other homeowners in the form of higher insurance premi-ums."

"Assault and battery."   The question of coverage does not stop with the perpetrator of intentional harm.   Issues may arise as well in a negli-gence context.   In U.S. Underwriters Ins. Co. v. Val–Blue Corp., 85 N.Y.2d 821, 647 N.E.2d 1342, 623 N.Y.S.2d 834 (1995), Val–Blue employed a retired police office as a security guard at its nightclub.   One night he shot Hanley, an off-duty police officer.   There was dispute about whether Hanley told the guard that he was an off-duty officer before the two shots were fired.   When Hanley sued the club and the guard, the club turned the suit over to its liability insurer for defense.   Hanley claimed (1) that the guard "negligently, carelessly and recklessly" shot him, (2) that the club was liable under respondeat superior and (3) that the club was negligent in hiring, supervising and training employees. The insurer declined to defend on the ground that the policy barred coverage under an "Assault and Battery Exclusion Endorsement" that stated:

> It is agreed that no coverage shall apply under this policy for any claim, demand or suit based on Assault and Battery, and Assault and Battery shall not be deemed an accident, whether or not committed by or at the direction of the insured.

In this declaratory judgment action the court concluded that the exclusion was unambiguous and the insurer need not defend the suit. Plaintiff claimed there was no intentional tort because the guard never intended to shoot a police officer. The court responded that the underlying claim against the guard was for an assault and battery and came within the exclusion. The other claims, such as negligent hiring, "are all 'based on' that assault and battery without which Hanley would have no cause of action."

What if the claim was that the nightclub had insufficient guards as the result of which a patron was assaulted in the rest room by a person other than the insured or an employee of the insured? In Mount Vernon Fire Ins.Co. v. Creative Housing Ltd., 70 F.3d 720 (2d Cir.1995), plaintiff sued the owner of her apartment house for negligent supervision and control after she was assaulted by a person identified by the court as a "third party wholly unconnected to the insured." The policy had a clause very similar to that in *Val-Blue*. The court thought this issue had not been resolved by *Val-Blue* and certified the question to the New York Court of Appeals, where it is pending.

When the abuse victims in *Mugavero*, supra, sued the wife (also an insured) for her negligence as a baby sitter in allowing her husband access to the children, the court denied coverage on the ground that the harm was "caused" by an excluded act—even if it was not one committed by the wife.

"Sudden." Policies involving potential toxic or pollution situations often require that to be covered, the harm must be "sudden"—a common term especially in pollution contexts. In Truck Ins. Exchange v. Pozzuoli, 17 Cal.App.4th 856, 21 Cal.Rptr.2d 650 (1993), the court held that liability for a long-term leak of gasoline from a tank on the premises of the insured's gas station was not covered by its policy. That policy used the standard language for "accident," but also contained a standard "pollution exclusion" clause under which coverage was excluded for damage "arising out of the discharge . . . of . . . liquids . . . into or upon the land, . . . but this exclusion does not apply if such discharge . . . is sudden and accidental." "Sudden" was defined as "not continuous or repeated in nature." If the tank had exploded and spewed gasoline over neighboring property, the court asserted that there would have been coverage.

Often the insurer accepts a risk in reliance upon the applicant's responses to questions. If the applicant is dishonest in an application for first-party insurance the insurer is often permitted to decline to cover the risk. But if an applicant for automobile liability coverage misrepresents his prior driving records, the situation may be different. In Barrera v. State Farm Mutual Automobile Ins. Co., 71 Cal.2d 659, 456 P.2d 674, 79 Cal.Rptr. 106 (1969), the court required the insurer to cover the liability in such a case. The basic policy of the state's Financial Responsibility Law (discussed infra) is "to make owners of motor vehicles financially responsible to those injured by them in the operation of such vehicles." Insurers who are held liable in such situations may be able to obtain indemnity from solvent insureds. See Reliance Ins. Cos. v. Daly, 41 N.Y.2d 930, 363 N.E.2d 361, 394 N.Y.S.2d 637 (1977)(affirming an insurer's judgment entered on a jury verdict against an insured who failed to disclose, in response to a question, that he had had four moving violations in the preceding 39 months).

Permissive exclusions. Sometimes legislation authorizes insurers to write specific exclusions if doubt exists about permissibility at common law of the exclusion. The most important of these involves reluctance to cover intrafamily claims. Pursuant to statutory authorization, an auto policy excluded coverage of any insured for harm to any relative who lived in the same household. The statute's constitutionality was upheld when a wife sued her husband for his alleged negligent driving. Farmers Ins. Exchange v. Cocking, 29 Cal.3d 383, 628 P.2d 1, 173 Cal.Rptr. 846 (1981). The legislature had several rational bases for its passage, including fear of collusion. To require this coverage might lead to "substantial increases" in premiums and might lead to an undesired increase in the number of uninsured motorists. See also Shannon v. Shannon, 150 Wis.2d 434, 442 N.W.2d 25 (1989)(holding that this exclusion serves a legitimate purpose in protecting insurers "from situations where an insured might not completely cooperate and assist an insurance company's administration of the case").

Legal restrictions on insurance. Although the development of insurance took place primarily in the private sector as new kinds of contracts were developed in response to demand, and many cases involve contract interpretation, some coverages and provisions have received legislative attention. We explore two important ones here.

1. *Insurable interest.* As new first-party coverages developed, some critics saw these as creating temptations: life insurance was a form of gambling, fire insurance was an invitation to arson. Among several safeguards developed to allay such concerns, was the concept of an "insurable interest," which limits what may be insured by whom. A person may insure his or her own life, those closely related to that person may do so, and creditors may protect their loans by taking out life insurance on the debtor. This avoids the "moral hazard" that would exist if, for example, one were permitted to insure a stranger's house against fire or a neighbor's life. Perhaps the dangers are best suggested by Liberty National Life Ins. Co. v. Weldon, 267 Ala. 171, 100 So.2d 696 (1957), in which the defendant issued a life insurance policy on a young child to her aunt who, under state

law, did not have the requisite insurable interest in the child. The aunt killed the child in an attempt to recover the insurance proceeds. (The court upheld an award to the child's parents in their wrongful death action against the insurance company for its negligence in issuing the illegal policy to the aunt.)

2. *Intentional and criminal conduct.* Most third-party (liability) coverage has been written to cover the insured's liability for "all sums" for which the insured is held legally liable. As we have seen, insurers commonly limit coverage to "accidents." Other policies exclude certain types of damage awards. Although these are often overlapping categories, they must be kept distinct. If the policy does not exclude such harm, different legal questions arise.

In California, as we saw in *Taylor*, p. 651, supra, section 533 of the Insurance Code provides that an insurer is not liable for a "wilful act of the insured," which state courts have equated with an intent to harm. The section "reflects a fundamental public policy of denying coverage for willful wrongs. [ ] The parties to an insurance policy therefore cannot contract for such coverage." J.C. Penney Casualty Ins. Co. v. M.K., 52 Cal.3d 1009, 804 P.2d 689, 278 Cal.Rptr. 64 (1991)(even if policy is not interpreted to exclude coverage of a claim for sexual molestation, the state's public policy bars insurance coverage of such a claim).

Even if the insurance policy does not exclude coverage of a claim, New York has decided that its "public policy precludes insurance indemnification for punitive damages awards, whether the punitive damages are based on intentional actions or actions which, while not intentional, amount to 'gross negligence, recklessness, or wantonness' [ ] or 'conscious disregard of the rights of others or for conduct so reckless as to amount to such disregard' [ ]." Home Ins. Co. v. American Home Products Corp., 75 N.Y.2d 196, 550 N.E.2d 930, 551 N.Y.S.2d 481 (1990). If the injury has been "intentionally" caused, the state's policy further forbids the insurer from paying any part of the compensatory award as well. Recall the *Mugavero* case, supra, in which coverage of sexual abuse was analyzed as an issue of contract interpretation. If the court had interpreted the contract to provide coverage of the claims, would New York's public policy have permitted the insurer to cover the husband? The wife?

Some states permit coverage of sexual abuse cases. In St. Paul Fire & Marine Ins. Co. v. F.H., 55 F.3d 1420 (9th Cir.1995), the question was whether the insurer had to defend a sexual molestation case brought by children against an employee of the insured charitable organization. The court, applying Alaska law, construed the policy to provide coverage and then concluded that such coverage would not offend public policy:

> Several courts have held that, when liability insurance is designed to compensate innocent third parties for injuries caused by the intentional misconduct of insureds, it may indemnify without violating public policy. This exception is particularly applicable where it is unlikely that insurance coverage induced the insured to engage in misconduct.

When might insureds be induced to commit torts because insurance coverage exists?

A few states try to avoid this dilemma by enforcing an insurance contract that is interpreted to cover intentional harm or punitive damages, and then allowing the liability insurer to recover over against the tortfeasor-insured. See Continental Cas. Co. v. Kinsey, 499 N.W.2d 574 (N.D. 1993); Ambassador Ins. Co. v. Montes, 76 N.J. 477, 388 A.2d 603 (1978). Is this an improvement over the alternatives?

Just as some litigants shape their complaints to avoid contract exclusions, others do so to avoid legislative exclusion. See, e.g., American Employer's Ins. Co. v. Smith, 105 Cal.App.3d 94, 163 Cal.Rptr. 649 (1980), in which an arsonist was sued for negligence. The defense argued that the action should be dismissed since the insured clearly was guilty of intentional wrongdoing. The court concluded that "it is not a defense to negligence to contend that the conduct was willful or the harm intended." But the court left open the question of whether the plaintiff could satisfy any judgment through the defendant's insurance. The tort liability question was separate from the insurability question.

An extraordinary example is Boyles v. Kerr, 855 S.W.2d 593 (Tex. 1993), in which defendant secretly taped his sexual relations with plaintiff. Plaintiff later learned about the tape and sued. Before the case went to the jury, plaintiff expressly dropped all claims of intentional misconduct and relied exclusively on negligent infliction of emotional distress. The court suggests that the plaintiff was trying to frame a claim that would come within defendant's liability insurance coverage for both compensatory and punitive damages.

Critics have been concerned about two cross-currents in the law of punitive damages and insurance. Some argue that states have been permitting punitive damages too readily, including allowing them for gross negligence and in vicarious liability situations, and have not been reviewing jury awards sufficiently carefully. Recall the discussion earlier in this chapter.

The second strand, as we have just seen, is that the law of several states forbids the insurability of punitive damages. These states probably developed these rules at a time when the award signified outrageous behavior. But if it is now possible to be held liable for punitive damages for conduct that is not "all that different" from negligence, is noninsurability still defensible?

See Restivo, Insuring Punitive Damages, Nat'l.L.J., July 24, 1995, at C1, discussing this issue and listing state positions on these questions. In these cases, the plaintiff is in effect saying that the conduct is bad enough to warrant punishment—but the defendant will not be punished because it is covered by insurance. Is that an inconsistent position? On a related point, is it defensible for an insurer to write a policy that does not exclude either intentional harm or punitive damages, collect the premiums—and then argue that it would be unconscionable to pay out in such a case? Is there a difference between a case of murder and one of drunk driving?

———

Beyond the voluntarily acquired first-party insurance already discussed, compulsory governmental programs protect individuals against certain dangers. These include some coverage of medical costs for those over age 65, benefit programs for disabled persons of whatever age—some stressing long term disabilities and others temporary conditions—and attempts to cushion the financial shocks of unemployment and retirement. Still other government programs help those injured in accidents. We discuss workers' compensation in Chapter XI.

All studies indicate that non-tort first-party sources of aid are already significant and becoming more so as first-party insurance becomes more popular. For example, major medical insurance, which covered 32.6 million persons in 1960, covered over 170 million by the late 1980s. Membership in health maintenance organizations (HMOs) rose from 6 million in 1976 to some 50 million by 1995. In 1991, a major survey indicated that almost 60 percent of the 23 million people receiving compensation for accident losses report some payment from their own health insurance and 10 percent report some payment from their own auto insurance. Only 10 percent of all accident victims report receipt of tort payments, which in turn constituted only 7 percent of the total accident compensation paid for economic loss in nonfatal accidents. The percentages are considerably higher for auto accidents—almost one third of these victims received some tort compensation which constituted 22 percent of total payments. D. Hensler, et al., Compensation for Accidental Injuries in the United States (1991).

In many law schools, a course on Insurance is offered as a regular upper-class elective. Several multi-volume treatises cover the subject. The following pages seek only to introduce students to some of the ways in which insurance may affect tort law. For an extended discussion of some of the most basic questions of insurance, including the roles of efficiency and equity, and practical and theoretical problems of coverage, see K. Abraham, Distributing Risk—Insurance, Legal Theory, and Public Policy (1986).

1. LOSS INSURANCE, COLLATERAL SOURCES AND SUBROGATION

Our immediate question is what impact, if any, these private and governmental programs do, and should, have on assessing the damages to be awarded in a tort action. The virtually universal common-law rule in this country, as we saw in *Bandel*, p. 645, supra, has been to treat first-party benefits that plaintiff has received as "collateral" to the defendant's responsibility and not relevant to tort law's determination of liability or damages. This extends generally to benefits from insurance that the plaintiff has purchased, such as reimbursement of hospitalization and doctors' bills, to gifts made to the plaintiff from rich aunts or uncles, or from an employer in the form of payment of wages not earned. It also extends to the benefits of collective bargaining agreements between the union and the company, for such things as sick leave or accident disability payments, as well as to government benefits.

One concern raised by the collateral source rule is that holding the defendant liable for particular items might allow plaintiff to recover twice for these items. In order to know whether the plaintiff will keep a double recovery we must know more than simply whether the defendant is to be given credit for money or services plaintiff has already received. If the defendant is given that credit, then of course the plaintiff will not be paid twice. But if the defendant is not given credit the result will depend on matters explored in the following case.

Frost v. Porter Leasing Corp.

Supreme Judicial Court of Massachusetts, 1982.
386 Mass. 425, 436 N.E.2d 387.

[Frost was injured in a motor vehicle accident. He and his wife sued the other driver for medical expenses incurred, pain and suffering, impaired earning capacity, and future expenses. His wife's claim was for loss of consortium. While this case was pending, Frost received medical expense benefits of $22,700 under a union health plan paid for by his employer. The insurer, Union Labor, intervened in the Frosts' tort action, claiming a right of subrogation as to damages plaintiff might recover for medical expenses. The insurer made no claim directly against the other driver. The Frosts then settled their tort claim for a lump sum of $250,000. In this phase of the case, the trial judge concluded that the insurer had a right of subrogation in the proceeds of the settlement to the extent it had paid Frost, less a share of the costs the Frosts had incurred in obtaining a settlement.]

■ Before HENNESSEY, C.J., and WILKINS, LIACOS, ABRAMS and O'CONNOR, JJ.

■ HENNESSEY, CHIEF JUSTICE.

A Superior Court judge has reported the question "[w]hether a group insurer which provides medical and hospital expenses benefits to an insured has a right of subrogation in a recovery by the insured against a tortfeasor for personal injuries even though the group insurance policy contains no express provision entitling the insurer to subrogation rights." We conclude that the insurer has no right, in the absence of a subrogation clause, to share in the insured's recovery against the tortfeasor.

.   .   .

Subrogation is an equitable adjustment of rights that operates when a creditor or victim of loss is entitled to recover from two sources, one of which bears a primary legal responsibility. If the secondary source (the subrogee) pays the obligation, it succeeds to the rights of the party it has paid (the creditor or loss victim, called the subrogor) against the third, primarily responsible party. [ ] The doctrine of subrogation applies, within limits to be discussed shortly, to payments under policies of insurance. Upon payment, the insurer is entitled to share the benefit of any rights of recovery the insured may have against a tortfeasor for the same loss covered by the insurance. [ ] If the insured recovers from the tortfeasor, the insurer's right becomes a right to the proceeds in the hands of the insured.[3] [ ]

An insurer's right of subrogation may be reserved in an agreement between the insurer and the insured, [ ] or may arise by implication, as a matter of general law [ ].[4] Here, Union Labor admits that Frost's insurance policy contained no provision for subrogation. Union Labor's claim is one of implied subrogation, and we express no opinion on the ability of parties to fix their rights by contract. [ ]

The reason for implied subrogation under contracts of insurance is to prevent an unwarranted windfall to the insured. [ ] If the insured recovers from both the insurer and the tortfeasor, his compensation may exceed his actual loss. Duplicative recovery is "a result which the law has never looked upon with favor." [ ] It is contrary to the indemnity purposes that underlie many insurance contracts, and produces a form of unjust enrichment. [ ] Further, duplicative recoveries by particular accident victims cause an inefficient distribution of the overall resources available for accident compensation. Subrogation returns any excess to the insurer, who can then recycle it in the form of lower insurance costs. See Fleming, The Collateral Source Rule and Loss Allocation in Tort Law, 54 Cal.L.Rev. 1478, 1481–1484 (1966).

Nevertheless, rights of subrogation do not arise automatically upon payment of benefits under any contract of insurance. The availability of subrogation has generally depended on the type of coverage involved. Courts have readily implied rights of subrogation under policies covering property damage. [ ] The insurer's obligation under a policy of property insurance is viewed only as a duty to indemnify the insured for actual loss, and not as an absolute liability to pay a certain sum of money upon the happening of an event. [ ] Moreover, the insured's loss is generally liquidated, and tort recovery is comparable, if not identical, to insurance coverage. [ ] Therefore, the insured's actual loss, and the amount of any excess compensation from the combination of insurance proceeds and tort recovery, can be determined with certainty.

On the other hand, courts have not recognized implied rights of subrogation in the area of "personal insurance," a category that has included medical expense benefits as well as life insurance and other forms of accident insurance. [ ] Personal insurance is said to be less a contract of indemnity than a form of investment, imposing on the insurer an absolute duty to pay if the named condition occurs. [ ] Further the

---

3. If the tortfeasor has settled with the insured, with knowledge of the insurer's claim, some courts have permitted the insurer to proceed against the tortfeasor. [ ]

4. In addition, statutes may provide for subrogation. [ ]

insured's receipt of both tort damages and insurance benefits may not produce a measurably duplicative recovery. The insured is likely to have suffered intangible losses that are insusceptible to precise measurement, and the two sources of his recovery may cover different ranges of loss and be differently affected by considerations such as fault. [   ]

Commentators have objected to the courts' classification of medical expense policies with other forms of personal insurance, and have argued that subrogation rights should be implied upon payment of benefits for medical and hospital expenses. They point out that medical coverage, like property insurance, is designed to indemnify the insured for quantifiable economic losses, and bears little similarity to an investment. [   ]

Although we recognize the indemnity character of medical and hospital expense benefits, we do not feel that the principles that support subrogation under policies of property insurance would be served by extending implied rights of subrogation into the field of insurance for personal injuries. Subrogation rights, as we have said, are implied to prevent unwarranted compensation and to facilitate sound distribution of compensation resources. If medical expenses are isolated from the other consequences of an accident, excess compensation of an insured accident victim may appear definite and quantifiable. However, when subrogation is based on broad principles of equity and efficiency, rather than on the contract of the parties, isolation of medical expenses is artificial, and the accident victim's position should be viewed as a whole. [   ] Subrogation played no part in the bargain between insurer and insured,[5] and in this circumstance, the courts should not intervene to adjust the rights of the parties unless all the adverse consequences of the accident have been offset. [   ]

When the insured's losses are viewed in their entirety, duplicative compensation is both uncertain and unlikely. [   ] The insured may be faced with property damage, pain and suffering, and diminished earning capacity, in addition to medical bills. The costs of litigation, or the decision to settle, may reduce his overall recovery. Yet the insurer's implied right of subrogation must be limited to excessive recovery if it is to conform to the purposes that justify it. Further, when the insured has not agreed to subrogation, doubt should be resolved in his favor. [   ]

Perhaps a formula could be devised by which subrogation could be confined to recapture of duplicative compensation. The insurer might, for example, be permitted to recover if it could demonstrate that the insured's net recovery (insurance proceeds and tort recovery, less costs of collection) exceeded fair compensation for the insured's losses. [   ] However, the costs of implementing the formula could well undercut its justifications, particularly when, as here, the insured had reached a lump-sum settlement with the tortfeasor. [   ] If the inquiry covered the insured's overall loss

---

5. Union Labor points out that the premiums for Frost's policy were paid by Frost's employer rather than by Frost himself. The fact that the benefits do not flow to the party who has paid premiums, however, should not detract from the force of legitimate expectations, both of the beneficiary and of the one who has paid. This is particularly true when, as here, the policy is an employment benefit, bargained for by the insured's union.

from the accident—as in fairness it should—determination of the extent of excess recovery could be equally as complex as the personal injury trial the original parties sought to avoid by settlement. [ ] Thus, litigation over subrogation would impose additional burdens on the insured, and cut into his overall compensation for injury. Moreover, this added step in the adjustment of rights would detract from any generalized benefits that subrogation might bring to the sound use and distribution of resources available to compensate loss. Much of the "windfall" produced by overlapping coverage would be absorbed by the costs of dividing it, rather than recycled to reduce the costs of insurance. [ ]

For these reasons, we conclude that, in the absence of a subrogation agreement between the insurer and the insured, an insurer that has paid medical or hospital expense benefits has no right to share in the proceeds of the insured's recovery against a tortfeasor. Accordingly, we answer the reported question in the negative.

So ordered.

■ WILKINS, JUSTICE (concurring).

I agree with the conclusion of the court that, in the absence of a provision for subrogation in the applicable insurance policy, an insurer providing health insurance is not entitled to subrogation as to amounts paid or payable by a tortfeasor to the insured. I do not reach this result because of the asserted problems of administration of such a system of subrogation to which the court makes reference. The problems are manageable, and most are not substantial. I reach my conclusion on the ground that, in fairness to an insured, a policy should disclose the possibility of subrogation claims. A person or group purchasing coverage for medical costs should know the limitations of such coverage, and, as a realistic matter, a lay person cannot be expected to have knowledge of a common law right of subrogation.

I reject the implications of the opinion that subrogation presents substantial problems with respect to insurance payments made for medical expenses incurred as the result of injuries caused by a third party wrongdoer. The amount of the insured's loss, the insurer's payment, and the tort recovery are known with certainty. The subrogated insurer should acknowledge a proportionate reduction in its claim to reflect the services and expenses of the claimant's attorney in collecting on the tort claim. If the claim is settled, as most are, the subrogated insurer should accept a proportionate and reasonable reduction in its subrogation claim to reflect the discount that the claimant accepted in order to obtain a settlement. Assuming prompt assertion of the subrogation claim, the amount to be paid to the insurer on its subrogation claim can be readily determined in most cases as part of the settlement process.

Subrogation is a reasonable method of assisting in holding down the costs of health insurance. It prevents an undeserved windfall to the insured. It is appropriate to consider the matter of medical expenses apart from other aspects of the injured person's claim. Whatever uncertainty may exist with respect to other elements of damages, the amount paid under the medical insurance policy can be ascertained and dealt with independently. I see no justification for denying subrogation, as the court seems to suggest, because, in settling a case, the claimant may not have been made whole on all elements of his damages. The claimant can be and is made whole on his medical costs, to the extent of his coverage. A health insurer should not be obliged to forbear asserting subrogation rights in order to assist in making the claimant whole on some other aspect of his damages, such as lost wages and pain and suffering, for which the insured has not purchased coverage from the health insurer.

NOTES AND QUESTIONS

1. How does the majority distinguish between "property" insurance and "personal" insurance? What consequences flow from that distinction? Would the same result follow if plaintiff had obtained a judgment instead of having settled?

2. Under the concurrer's view, when would subrogation be allowed? How would legal expenses be allocated?

3. Consider the implications of each of the following independent fact situations.

a. P's mother renders gratuitous medical services for P, who was negligently hurt by D.

b. P's rich relative gives P money to pay his hospital bills for harm caused by D's negligence.

c. P's house is badly burned by a fire caused by P's careless smoking. The fire insurer pays P the agreed value of $90,000 for the damage down.

d. P's house is badly burned by D's negligence. P's insurer pays to P the $90,000 agreed value of the house and proceeds against D. P has no other uncovered losses.

e. When D's negligence badly burns P's house, P is inside and is hurt while escaping. P's fire insurer pays the $90,000; P's medical insurer pays $20,000 in medical bills that P incurred; P also sustained an uninsured loss of $10,000 in earnings; assume also that pain and suffering would total $60,000. If D denies liability and won't settle, how do matters proceed?

4. The concurrer suggests that when subrogation is allowed the amount should be reduced if the underlying tort claim is settled rather than litigated. Why? How would that work if, in part (e) of the last note, the parties settle for $120,000?

5. How much of the $250,000 settlement in *Frost* should be allocated to medical expenses paid by Union Labor? In that connection, consider Smith v. Marzolf, 59 Ill.App.3d 635, 375 N.E.2d 995 (1978), in which P was injured by D's negligence. P was entitled to up to $50,000 of first-party benefits from Aetna for his medical bills and lost income. P sued D, and P's wife sued D for loss of consortium. The parties agreed to settle the case by allocating $10,000 to P's claim and $65,000 to his wife's. Aetna objected that it had already paid P almost $17,000 and future payments up to the $50,000 limit were likely. P and D then rewrote their settlement to give P $17,000 and his wife $58,000. Aetna still objected. The trial judge called the settlement "absolutely ridiculous" and a fraud on Aetna's subrogation rights. His refusal to permit the settlement was upheld on appeal because P had breached his duties to Aetna. Is it clear why Aetna should be involved in these settlement talks?

6. On the costs of subrogation, consider the following excerpt from Conard, The Economic Treatment of Automobile Injuries, 63 Mich.L.Rev. 279, 311 (1964):

> Consider the case of a one thousand dollar hospital bill incurred by a Blue Cross policyholder. When his bill is paid by Blue Cross, the cost to all Blue Cross policyholders combined is about 1,080 dollars. Assume further that Blue Cross obtains reimbursement by virtue of subrogation from Drivers' Liability Company, which has insured the tort-feasor. Blue Cross will presumably pay at least twenty-five per cent in collection expenses and will net about 750 dollars out of the one thousand dollars paid by Drivers' Liability. But the policyholders of Drivers' Liability will have incurred corresponding premium costs of sixteen hundred dollars, since liability insurers work at an expense rate equivalent to about sixty per cent of payouts. The net effect of the subrogation is to make liability insurance policyholders pay sixteen hundred dollars in order to save 750 dollars for health insurance policyholders. Probably a large majority of the health insurance policyholders are also liability insurance policyholders, who have their costs doubled by subrogation without any increase of their benefits. The principal beneficiaries of the shift are insurance companies and lawyers.

Professor Conard derived the cost figures used in his passage from other studies that he summarized as follows at pp. 290–91 of his article:

> The Michigan study also estimated total expenses of the damage system, adding to lawyers' fees the litigation expenses of claimants themselves, the costs of selling and administering insurance, and the costs of keeping courts open for injury cases. This summation indicated that the operating costs of the damage system are about 120 per cent of the net benefits that go to the injury victims themselves; the net amounts that the victims get are less than the total retained by insurance companies, law offices, and courts. Presumably, the cost ratio would be even higher in such states as New York and Illinois, where it appears that the legal expenses are substantially higher than in Michigan.
>
> In contrast, private loss insurance systems (embracing principally life insurance and health insurance) showed average costs of about twenty-two per cent of net benefits. In some Blue Cross systems the operating costs drop to less than five per cent of the net benefits, and in Social Security programs they drop to about two per cent.

Although the percentages have changed some since Conard wrote, the overall pattern persists. See, e.g., Priest, The Current Insurance Crisis and Modern Tort Law, 96 Yale L.J. 1521, 1560 (1987):

The administrative costs of insurance delivered through tort law are vastly greater than the administrative costs of any first-party insurance regime. Blue Cross–Blue Shield first-party health insurance administration costs are 10% of benefits; SSI disability insurance administrative costs are 8% of benefits; Workers' Compensation disability insurance administration costs are (a much-criticized) 21% of benefits. In contrast, tort law administrative costs are estimated to be 53% of net plaintiff benefits.

The last figure is drawn from J.Kakalik & N.Pace, Costs and Compensation Paid in Tort Litigation (RAND 1986) and is broken down further there at p.70:

> The legal fees and expenses paid by plaintiffs as a percent of total compensation were essentially the same for auto tort (31 percent) and other tort cases (30 percent). However, defendants' costs of litigation differ significantly. For auto tort cases, which are often straightforward, defense legal fees and expenses were an estimated 16 percent of total compensation. For other (nonauto) tort cases, which are often more complex, defense legal fees and expenses were much higher—28 percent of total compensation paid.

> The plaintiffs' net compensation as a percentage of the total expenditures was 52 percent for auto torts and 43 percent for all other torts. This difference primarily reflects the higher defendants' litigation costs for nonauto torts.

Why might cost differences exist between first-party and third-party insurance? We return to some possible implications of these cost differences at p. 698, infra.

7. In the Conard excerpt, is it likely that the insured will bring a tort action against the defendant? If so, how does this affect the costs of obtaining subrogation? How might Conard's example work in the case of property damage?

8. In Helfend v. Southern California Rapid Transit District, 2 Cal.3d 1, 465 P.2d 61, 84 Cal.Rptr. 173 (1970), in plaintiff's case the trial judge refused to permit the defendant to show that plaintiff's medical expenses had been met in part by payments from Blue Cross. The court held that public agencies should be subject to the same rules that apply to private defendants. After noting that the Blue Cross contract contained a subrogation provision, the court continued:

> Hence, the plaintiff receives no double recovery; the collateral source rule simply serves as a means of by-passing the antiquated doctrine of non-assignment of tortious actions and permits a proper transfer of risk from the plaintiff's insurer to the tortfeasor by way of the victim's tort recovery. The double shift from the tortfeasor to the victim and then from the victim to his insurance carrier can normally occur with little cost in that the insurance carrier is often intimately involved in the initial litigation and quite automatically receives its part of the tort settlement or verdict.

Even in cases in which the contract or the law precludes subrogation or refund of benefits, or in situations in which the collateral source waives such subrogation or refund, the rule performs entirely necessary functions in the computation of damages. For example, the cost of medical care often provides both attorneys and juries in tort cases with an important measure for assessing the plaintiff's general damages. [ ] To permit the defendant to tell the jury that the plaintiff has been recompensed by a collateral source for his medical costs might irretrievably upset the complex, delicate, and somewhat indefinable calculations which result in the normal jury verdict. [ ]

We also note that generally the jury is not informed that plaintiff's attorney will receive a large portion of the plaintiff's recovery in contingent fees or that personal injury damages are not taxable to the plaintiff and are normally deductible by the defendant. Hence, the plaintiff rarely actually receives full compensation for his injuries as computed by the jury. The collateral source rule partially serves to compensate for the attorney's share and does not actually render "double recovery" for the plaintiff. . . .

Pain and suffering, punitive damages, refusal to tell the jury about income tax aspects of damages, and now the collateral source rule have all been justified as ways to allow for the attorney's fee. Can it sustain all of them? A footnote in *Helfend* recognizes that this justification for the collateral source rule applies only to the plaintiffs who benefit from the rule, and is "only an incomplete and haphazard solution to providing all tort victims with full compensation." Just how "full" should "full compensation" be? We do not now compensate a plaintiff for time away from work to testify in the case, or to consult with a lawyer. Except in death cases, courts usually award interest only from the date of the judgment and not the harm. Do we really mean to achieve "full compensation"? Should we?

9. Is the justification for the collateral source rule dependent on the right of reimbursement or subrogation of insurers? Putting subrogation aside, why can't the "double recovery" of medical benefits or wage loss replacement benefits by an individual who has paid continuing premiums for such benefits be regarded as a return on an investment that has no bearing on the defendant's tort obligation? In response, can it be argued that the possibility of a tortious accident is only a secondary reason for acquiring these forms of insurance?

10. Some implications of widespread first-party insurance are suggested in the following article.

The Collateral Source Rule and Loss Allocation in Tort Law

John Fleming.
54 Calif.L.Rev. 1478, 1546–49 (1966).

Two most perplexing features haunt the present state of American law. One arises directly from the last-mentioned fact that such reimbursement to the other fund cannot in general be technically accomplished without the aid of the collateral source rule, that is, precluding the tortfeasor from arguing that his liability has been reduced by the collateral subvention. Thus, whereas the collateral source rule is often enough invoked by courts wholly indifferent as to whether this will result in double recovery, there are others which at least condone it on the ground that, in the individual case, double recovery will be avoided by subrogation or some other like technique for passing the excess on to the collateral source. Finally, one also occasionally encounters a court purposefully insisting on the collateral source rule precisely in order to accomplish such a shifting of the loss.

Turning from double recovery to a consideration of other alternatives, we note that these differ from the former in posing a decision as to which of two sources of compensation to treat as the primary and which as the secondary. In contrast to cumulation of benefits, they force a confrontation with a basic policy orientation whether accident losses generally, or any particular accident loss, should be absorbed by the tortfeasor or by a collateral source, whether in accordance with the regime of tort law or the regime of private or social insurance. It calls for a fixing of priorities pursuant to relevant contemporary social and economic values as to loss allocation. In particular, the following criteria can be isolated as most important in their bearing on this assignment: (1) the reprehensiveness of the defendant's conduct, (2) the desirability of attributing the cost to the loss-causing enterprise for reasons of accident-prevention, proper cost allocation, etc., and (3) the function and, more important still, the economic base of the particular collateral compensation regime.

Not surprisingly, the predominant response has been to regard the tortfeasor as the primary source of compensation. Imbued with the philosophic values of a culture that has traditionally regarded tort law as the only and proper system for allocating accident losses, it is still widely considered as almost axiomatic that if an injurer's conduct justifies his being compelled to relieve the injured from the loss he has inflicted, it is also sufficient reason for his relieving anybody else who might otherwise have undertaken the job of reparation. This approach, dominated by lingering notions of promoting an individualistic morality against "wrongdoers,"[275] is reinforced by the impression that it would also reduce the cost to the community in general, and the plaintiff in particular, in maintaining the collateral fund. It is strongest in cases of private insurance, where to reduce the tortfeasor's liability would look like diverting the fruit of the plaintiff's own thrift into the pockets of one who least "deserves" it; but it has also found ardent advocates among social security organizations ever watchful to save the public purse.

These primarily moralistic postulates are gradually yielding in their appeal to an economic value system which places in the forefront the high

---

275. Even among tortfeasors, it is familiar doctrine to discriminate between one guilty of fault and another liable for faultless causation. This explains the right of *indem-* *nity* accorded to the latter against the former even in jurisdictions that do not allow so much as contribution between tortfeasors. . . .

collection costs of reshifting the loss from a collateral source to the tortfeasor, the attendant wastefulness of multiple insurance and, most important of all perhaps, an awareness that in these days, when tort liability qualifies as a significant source of compensation only in cases of defendants who can pass on the loss through liability insurance or pricing of their goods or services, the question is not so much whether a wrongdoer deserves to be relieved as which of several competing "risk communities" should bear the loss. Loss-bearing has become collectivized, whether it falls on the defendant or some other regime, like insurance or social security, to fill the role as conduit for distribution. While this focus does not provide ready-made solutions, still less generally valid answers, it stimulates a probe all along the line whether in any particular case there is sufficient justification for going to the trouble and expense of shifting the loss to the tortfeasor from some other regime that has already footed the bill and could as well or even better absorb it. Social security, for example, because of its broad base of contributors, has a strong claim for displacing *pro tanto* any "risk pool" represented by tort defendants. On the other hand, very special hazards presented by certain enterprises (for example, nuclear power stations) may make it advisable, for reasons of proper economic cost allocation as well as in the interest of maximizing accident prevention, to assign the ultimate loss to that enterprise rather than spread it on a broader base where these advantages would be lost. If deterrence in the old crude sense has any continuing appeal as a justification for tort liability, it will be confined to situations where it can realistically perform an admonitory function, namely, only against defendants guilty of serious misconduct. Somewhat paradoxically, tort law would shrink, at least in this respect, to its original starting-point as an adjunct of the criminal law in sanctioning immoral conduct. In several European countries, especially Scandinavia and Britain, vast encroachments on the erstwhile primacy of tort liability have already taken place along these lines. In the United States, this process of emancipation from the paralyzing legacy of largely obsolete folklore is still in its infancy, but is bound to gain increasing momentum as social security and other collateral regimes are assuming a greater role in the business of meeting accident costs.

In the upshot, there is thus emerging a second tier of principles of loss allocation; the first being concerned with the traditional problem of whether the person injured should be compensated at all, and the second with whether the tortfeasor rather than some other available fund should bear the ultimate burden of compensation. As a result, in many instances tort liability will become only an *excess* or a *guarantee* liability, its function being merely to allot responsibility for compensation to a person (labelled "tortfeasor") *to the extent that the cost of compensation has not been met by another source.*

In many ways this development represents a much more dramatic innovation than the sensational trend of recent years towards strict liability in the consumer protection area. It is more important by far because it adds an entirely new element to the grammar of loss allocation. Tort liability has ceased to be the sole point of reference in any inquiry, legislative or judicial, as to how particular accident losses should be absorbed.

NOTES AND QUESTIONS

1. What are the arguments in favor of Fleming's suggestion? Is the point limited to "social security"? What about cases in which the plaintiff has private medical and hospital coverage and private income-protection insurance?

2. Fleming suggests that cases involving "very special hazards" might well be treated differently. Why might this be? Why should this reasoning apply only to "very special hazards"?

3. What are the strongest general arguments against "displacing" tort law?

4. What view of Fleming's approach might be taken by those who emphasize the deterrent value of tort law? Recall the passage from Posner at p. 7, supra.

5. *Legal fees: subrogation v. liens.* Both opinions in *Frost* note that the insurer must share the legal costs incurred by the insured because of the nature of subrogation. Even in the tort cases that Fleming would preserve, there will be questions of legal fees. Recall that in the Conard examples, p. 686, supra, it was assumed that the insurer would incur some legal costs.

The allocation of these fees is gaining importance and involves both subrogation and liens. In re Guardianship of Bloomquist, 246 Neb. 711, 523 N.W.2d 352 (1994), involved an application for court approval of the $100,000 settlement of a minor victim's tort claim. A hospital that provided $16,500 in billed services intervened in the proceedings to satisfy its "lien" for this amount without having to share in the legal expenses incurred in obtaining the settlement—primarily the one-third contingent fee that the victim's guardian had agreed to pay the lawyer.

The relevant statute provided that any physician, nurse or hospital providing medical services was entitled to a lien against the recipient that could be enforced against that person's property. (Similar provisions protect mechanics, contractors and others who provide services to customers.) One provision of the hospital lien statute gave the provider a lien "upon any sum awarded the injured person in judgment or obtained by settlement." The hospital argued that it was a creditor—that the patient was legally obligated to pay the bills whether or not there was any tort recovery. Thus, there was no reason to reduce its lien by amounts this patient might pay someone else to acquire the funds to repay the hospital.

The guardian relied on the "common fund" doctrine—an "equitable concept that an attorney who performs services in creating a fund should in equity and good conscience be allowed compensation out of the whole fund from all those who seek to benefit from it." Applying the doctrine would reduce the hospital's recovery by one third.

Although "most courts" have rejected the common fund theory in lien cases, the Nebraska court concluded that this situation very closely approximated subrogation—stepping into the shoes of the patient—and should be treated similarly. Since the "common fund" applies to subrogation, it should also apply to liens. The reality was that without the lawsuit the lien was worthless. "In both situations, the claim or lien will only be paid if the injured party incurs the cost to effectuate a settlement or judgment."

Under the Nebraska statute, the hospital had to rely entirely on the patient to bring the suit. "If the injured person elects not to prosecute a claim, then the lien itself is worthless. The hospital may not stand in the patient's shoes, but the hospital is entirely dependent upon the patient's attorney."

If the patient has independent means, the hospital can recover its full bill without depending on the tort claim. This might involve asserting the lien on the patient's assets, such as a house or bank account or possibly the patient's wages. Note that each of these steps involves its own expenses.

For a similar analysis applying the common fund doctrine to a lien, and creating a direct conflict with another appellate case, see City and County of San Francisco v. Sweet, 32 Cal.App.4th 1483, 38 Cal.Rptr.2d 620 (1995), review granted. The court asserted that without the patient's efforts, "the county would recover nothing on its lien or would incur litigation expense in proceeding directly against the third party [which is allowed under California law if the victim does not sue within a specified period]. . . . It is a matter of simple fairness to require the county to bear a share of the expense incurred in producing that recovery." We return to the world of liens in Chapter XI in the context of workers' compensation and automobile no-fault statutes.

6. *Statutory change.* In recent years more than a dozen states have either abolished or sharply restricted the role of the collateral source rule. Again, the California was the leader in the mid–1970s as part of its legislation to ease a perceived medical malpractice insurance crisis. Civil Code § 3333.1 provided that in a malpractice action if all or a part of the victim's medical bills had been paid by the victim's own insurance or some other source unrelated to the defendant, the jury should be told this—but not told what, if anything, to do with the information.

More recently, other states have modified the rule. Indeed, New Jersey had enacted a statute before the decision in *Bandel*, p. 645, supra, though it was not applicable to that case:

> In any civil action brought for personal injury or death, [except under the auto no-fault statute], if a plaintiff receives or is entitled to receive benefits for the injuries allegedly incurred from any other source other than a joint tortfeasor, the benefits, other than workers' compensation benefits or the proceeds from a life insurance policy, shall be disclosed to the court and the amount thereof which duplicates any benefit contained in the award shall be deducted from any award recovered by the plaintiff, less any premium paid to an insurer directly

by the plaintiff's family on behalf of the plaintiff for the policy period during which the benefits are payable. Any party to the action shall be permitted to introduce evidence regarding any of the matters described in this act.

Why exclude life insurance payments? Workers' compensation? What would happen if this act had applied to *Bandel*? New York first changed the collateral source rule for malpractice cases and then extended the change to all cases a few years later in N.Y. CPLR § 4545 (c):

> In any action brought to recover damages for personal injury, injury to property or wrongful death, where the plaintiff seeks to recover for the cost of medical care, . . . loss of earnings or other economic loss, evidence shall be admissible for consideration by the court to establish that any such past or future cost or expense was or will, with reasonable certainty, be replaced or indemnified, in whole or in part, from any collateral source such as insurance (except for life insurance), social security (except [Medicare]), workers' compensation or employee benefit programs (except such collateral sources entitled by law to liens against any recovery of the plaintiff). If the court finds that any such cost or expense was or will, with reasonable certainty, be replaced or indemnified from any collateral source, it shall reduce the amount of the award by such finding, minus an amount equal to the premiums paid by the plaintiff for such benefits for the two-year period immediately preceding the accrual of such action and minus an amount equal to the projected future cost to the plaintiff of maintaining such benefits. In order to find that any future cost or expense will, with reasonable certainty, be replaced or indemnified by the collateral source, the court must find that the plaintiff is legally entitled to the continued receipt of such collateral source, pursuant to a contract or otherwise enforceable agreement, subject only to the continued payment of a premium and such other financial obligations as may be required by such agreement.

How would this statute affect the hypotheticals in note 3 after *Frost*? What might "reasonable certainty" cover in this context? Would you have voted for the New York statute?

2. LIABILITY INSURANCE

We now consider the development of liability insurance. Virtually every private defendant who has been sued in every case we have read in this course, has probably been covered by insurance protecting to some extent against liability in that very case. Indeed, these cases were probably defended and litigated by the liability insurer and its attorneys. Some very large companies self-insure and would defend cases themselves with in-house counsel or would retain outside counsel. Large government defendants—states and the federal government—often self-insure as well, relying on the taxing power to make up any remaining uncovered liability losses. Smaller governments, such as towns and cities, often use private liability insurers to protect against crushing losses.

We will emphasize in this section the development of the institution of liability insurance, considering most extensively the development of automobile insurance because it has the longest history of involvement with accident law. (Liability insurance also made possible the development of workers' compensation legislation—a subject we consider in Chapter XI.)

The development of the automobile created an immediate awareness of the dangers of the product along with a concern about financial responsibility for accidents. Although courts continued to rely on substantive law that was developed during the days of the horse and buggy, the new problem was solvency of those who now had the power to do much more harm than previously. At first the courts tried to expand the group of responsible defendants by creating doctrines such as the "family purpose" doctrine (owner of a car held vicariously liable to strangers for torts of anyone using the car to carry out a family purpose) and "joint enterprise" (each member of a group venture vicariously liable for the torts of their driver).

These steps helped but did not assure financial responsibility because some car owners might not have the ability to respond in damages and also because of the gap left when the owner permitted a non-family member to drive the car. Under the traditional law of bailments the owner was not responsible for the negligence of the bailee unless there had been a negligent entrustment in the first instance. Recall *Vince*, p. 152, supra. Many states met this latter concern by adopting legislation making the owner liable for the negligence of any person operating the car with the express or implied permission of the owner—even if the owner used due care in selecting the permittee. Some states limit this liability to a small dollar amount. See, e.g. Calif. Vehicle Code § 17151 (liability under this provision limited to $15,000/$30,000). What rationale might support such a limit?

Liability insurance began to emerge along with the automobile at the start of the twentieth century. Why might a person who bought a car decide to carry liability insurance? Which owners would be most likely to buy such insurance? At the outset, the insurance was known as "indemnity" insurance—the company agreed that if the insured was required to pay a victim for an accident, and actually did pay, the insurer would reimburse (indemnify) the insured for that amount. If the amount of the judgment was beyond the ability of the insured to pay, the victim was left unsatisfied and the insurer had to reimburse the insured only for whatever amount the victim had been able to wring from the insured. Apparently, insurers sometimes colluded with insureds to transfer the insured's assets to others so as to avoid all payments to victims. Soon, the policies were converted to "liability" policies, under which the insurer is obligated to pay the victim up to the policy's limits when the insured's liability was established.

Automobile policies had to take into account judicial impositions of liability that deviated from the paradigm case in which the owner and the driver were the same person. Two contract provisions emerged. One covered liability for the negligence of anyone driving the car with the owner's permission—the so-called "omnibus" clause. The other, the "drive-other-car" clause, provided that the insured was protected when driving not only the insured's own car but also any other car being driven with the permission of its owner. These provisions were necessary because, from the outset, automobile liability insurance was written for particular vehicles rather than for individual drivers.

Initially some thought that liability insurance would make the insured careless of the safety of others—the "moral hazard" problem. This was borne out occasionally in reported cases, as when, in Herschensohn v. Weisman, 80 N.H. 557, 119 A. 705 (1923), plaintiff passenger told defendant that he was driving carelessly and was assured, "Don't worry. I carry insurance for that." Despite such cases and the possibility of a diminished sense of responsibility, the advantages of liability insurance sustained it. What are those advantages? The disadvantages?

During this early period of liability insurance, the decision whether to acquire it was completely voluntary. But as early as the 1920s states became concerned about the insolvency of many negligent motorists. States began a series of legislative efforts to encourage motorists to carry liability insurance. Briefly, the steps were as follows. First, states passed financial responsibility laws requiring that after a judgment of liability in a first accident, a motorist had to give proof of adequate insurance or assets to be able to pay relatively small future judgments. Some states required this showing immediately after involvement in an accident rather than waiting until a first judgment of liability.

The problem with both forms of legislation was that there was no requirement that this level of solvency exist before the first negligently caused accident. The statutes came into play only after a first accident— for which the motorist might be unable to respond. A few states sought to fill this gap by denying driving privileges after a first accident unless the owner could show ability to pay for *that* accident if later found liable for it. The hope was that fear of this outcome would encourage the acquisition of insurance before any accident. Other states began to try to meet insolvency by creating "unsatisfied judgment funds" to which victims would have recourse up to limited maximum amounts, if they could not collect judgments from those liable for the injuries.

In 1927 Massachusetts required that motorists demonstrate a minimum amount of non-cancellable liability coverage before being permitted to register their cars. No state followed that route until New York and North Carolina in the mid–1950s. (As this movement might have been gaining momentum, the "no-fault" movement was getting started and drew attention away from compulsory insurance, as we shall see in Chapter XI.) Among the problems of compulsory insurance, in addition to such gaps as hit-and-run accidents and out-of-state drivers, was what to do with a driver who was unable to obtain the required insurance from any private carrier. The answer has been to place such a person in an "assigned risk" pool—a group made up of the insurers in the state who write liability insurance— which must accept the applicant unless his driving record is badly flawed.

But what premium will the assigned-risk plan be able to charge? The state insurance commissioner is under great pressure to keep the rates down—so that motorists will not be forced off the road or forced to violate the vehicle-registration laws. There is also pressure to keep to a minimum the number of drivers rejected by the assigned risk plan. (These problems existed as well in states that had assigned risk plans without compulsory insurance except that in those states motorists could drive legally without insurance if they could not afford or did not want to pay the premiums.)

To counter the increasing regulation of the insurance field caused by increased legislative concern for uncompensated victims, insurers began offering, as part of their liability coverage, a clause that provided financial protection against being injured by negligent uninsured motorists. In effect, the insurer stood in the shoes of the uninsured motorist in a claim by the insured. (The complications of this situation are explored in the *Lalomia* case, p. 702, infra.) In addition, liability insurers added "med pay" provisions offering medical benefits to all persons injured in an accident without regard to fault.

By this point, the original justification for automobile liability insurance—protecting persons of means against having their funds diminished by their negligent harming of others—had given way to a highly regulated form of virtually compulsory insurance to assure that victims of negligent motorists would be compensated to some extent. (That extent, however, might be as low as $10,000/$20,000. Effective in 1996, New York increased its minimum liability coverage to $25,000/$50,000 for injuries other than death and double those limits in death cases—still far below the harm likely to be incurred in any serious auto accident.) Using the same framework as uninsured motorist coverage, insureds may now acquire "underinsured motorist" coverage. This coverage provides insureds additional protection if the person who negligently hurts them has lower, even if legally adequate, liability limits in his or her policy than those in the insured's policy. These policies are considered at length in Staub v. Hanover Ins. Co., 251 N.J.Super. 66, 596 A.2d 1096 (1991) and Allstate Ins. Co. v. Dejbod, 63 Wash.App. 278, 818 P.2d 608 (1991).

Constitutional limits have restrained the states' efforts in this area. In Bell v. Burson, 402 U.S. 535 (1971), the Court held that where the question of fault was central to the regulatory policy of these statutes, it was a denial of due process of law for the state to suspend a motorist's license without a pre-suspension hearing at which the driver could show a lack of fault. A statute requiring liability insurance or the deposit of a bond as a precondition for all drivers would have avoided this constitutional problem.

In Perez v. Campbell, 402 U.S. 637 (1971), the Court held invalid under the Supremacy Clause a state statute providing that "discharge in bankruptcy following the rendering of [a judgment resulting from an automobile accident] shall not relieve the judgment debtor" from any "state obligations under its safety responsibility act, including payment of past judgments." A requirement that the insolvent motorist had to satisfy judgments arising from his or her negligence before being able to drive again, was held to conflict with the federal bankruptcy law's goal of giving debtors "a new opportunity in life and a clear field for future effort unhampered by the pressure and discouragement of preexisting debt."

Despite the blandishments and compulsion, perhaps 20 percent of all American motorists are uninsured. The figure is surely higher in some states. See, e.g., Uninsured Drivers: New Push for Law, S.F. Examiner, Feb. 19, 1995 at A-1, showing a statewide California figure of 31.5%. An accompanying chart indicates that in at least nine zip codes in the Bay Area, the figure exceeds 50 percent. Is this a sufficient concern to warrant further steps? If so, what might be done?

We have been tracing common-law and legislative efforts to enhance the likelihood that negligent motorists will be able to respond in damages to their victims. Why was there no comparable concern during that period for victims of auto accidents in which fault could not be established?

Non-auto liability insurance. The development of automobile liability insurance has been the subject of more legislation than has the development of liability insurance for medical malpractice, defective products, or liability for defective premises. Unless they self-insure, larger enterprises usually rely upon a standard form of commercial general liability (CGL) coverage to protect against liability for bodily injury. For specific risks, such as pollution or product liability, these companies may acquire in addition a special purpose coverage. Smaller companies often buy combined liability and property coverage called "commercial multi-peril" coverage. Physicians buy professional liability coverage—either from private insurers or, more recently, from "mutual" insurance companies formed by physicians' associations to compete with the commercial carriers.

The volume of non-auto liability insurance has grown dramatically. In the three decades after 1958 the annual premiums written for commercial general liability, product liability, environmental liability, and similar coverage (excluding only auto and medical) rose from $784 million to some $20 billion. The total premiums for medical malpractice rose from $895 million in 1975 to over $4 billion in 1988.

Although there have been alleged "crises" in the pricing of these coverages, they have remained in the private sector with no legislative efforts to coerce the acquisition of coverage. Why, for example, not require some minimum liability coverage as a condition of practicing medicine? From time to time, in response to instability in the pricing and availability of these liability coverages, legislatures have changed substantive tort rules to make liability harder to establish which, in turn, has made the relevant insurance either cheaper or more readily available. Might some of the instability in liability markets be due to the voluntary nature of this insurance with the safer manufacturers (or physicians) opting out and choosing to self-insure, leaving the more dangerous and the untested newer entrants in the liability insurance markets? This thesis, based on the principle of "adverse selection," is developed in Priest, The Current Insurance Crisis in Modern Tort Law, 96 Yale L.J. 1521 (1987). For general discussion of the perceived insurance crisis of the mid–1980s, see Abraham, Making Sense of the Liability Insurance Crisis, 48 Ohio St.L.J. 399 (1987).

3.   THE IMPACT OF INSURANCE ON TORT LITIGATION

a.   THE IMPACT ON SUBSTANTIVE RULINGS

Although judicial opinions in tort cases rarely spoke of loss or liability insurance, their impact was unmistakable.   Courts are now somewhat more explicit, as in *Rowland v. Christian*, p. 172, supra, and *Kelly v. Gwinnell*, p. 157, supra, for example, which refer to the prevalence of liability insurance—but not to whether the particular defendant was insured.

Judge Friendly was particularly explicit about the role of liability insurance in affecting attitudes toward the boundaries of tort liability.   In *Kinsman I,* discussed at p. 378, supra, Judge Friendly observed that "[w]here the [liability] line will be drawn will vary from age to age; as society has come to rely increasingly on insurance and other methods of loss-sharing, the point may lie further off than a century ago."   Also, in an omitted footnote in *Steinhauser,* p. 345, supra, after noting the broad acceptance of the "thin-skull" doctrine, he stated "[t]he seeming severity of this doctrine is mitigated by the prevalence of liability insurance which spreads the risks."

Judge Friendly's observations undoubtedly find support in the greater frequency with which juries are permitted to find negligence and product defect in the great mass of unspectacular cases.   They undoubtedly also go far to explain such judicial developments as the family purpose doctrine, p. 694, supra, and the changes in family liability, p. 195, supra.   Liability insurance also helps explain such cases as *Maloney v. Rath*, p. 8, supra, in which the car owner was held liable for the negligence of her service station mechanic.

We turn now to two fact patterns in which the existence of insurance—either loss or liability—has played an important part in judicial analysis.

Fire/Water Company Cases.   Although we are primarily concerned with personal injuries, we have had occasion to consider cases involving property damage.   For the most part, we have not drawn sharp distinctions between the results in the two types of cases.   But the role of first-party loss insurance in certain situations may explain the outcomes of certain property damage cases.   The 1866 *Ryan* case, p. 378, supra, creating the unique New York fire rule, is an early example.   Although the passage quoted earlier sought to explain the case in terms of proximate cause, another passage indicated that the availability of insurance had weighed heavily with the court:

> To sustain such a claim as the present, and to follow the same to its legitimate consequences, would subject to a liability against which no prudence could guard, and to meet which no private fortune would be adequate.   Nearly all fires are caused by negli-

gence, in its extended sense. In a country where wood, coal, gas and oils are universally used, where men are crowded into cities and villages, where servants are employed, and where children find their home in all houses, it is impossible that the most vigilant prudence should guard against the occurrence of accidental or negligent fires. A man may insure his own house or his own furniture, but he cannot insure his neighbor's building or furniture, for the reason that he has no interest in them. To hold that the owner must not only meet his own loss by fire, but that he must guarantee the security of his neighbors on both sides, and to an unlimited extent, would be to create a liability which would be the destruction of all civilized society. No community could long exist, under the operation of such a principle. In a commercial country, each man, to some extent, runs the hazard of his neighbor's conduct, and each, by insurance against such hazards, is enabled to obtain a reasonable security against loss. To neglect such precaution, and to call upon his neighbor, on whose premises a fire originated, to indemnify him instead, would be to award a punishment quite beyond the offense committed. It is to be considered, also, that if the negligent party is liable to the owner of a remote building thus consumed, he would also be liable to the insurance companies who should pay losses to such remote owners. The principle of subrogation would entitle the companies to the benefit of every claim held by the party to whom a loss should be paid.

A defendant at that time could not obtain insurance against liability. Does that justify the court's analysis? Recall the *Losee* case, p. 437, supra, decided in 1873, involving similar considerations about extended liability.

Even before *Ryan,* legislatures had concerned themselves with the relation between fire insurance and liability, as in Mass.Laws 1840, Ch. 85:

> When any injury is done to a building or other property, of any person or corporation, by fire communicated by a locomotive engine of any rail-road corporation, the said rail-road corporation shall be held responsible, in damages, to the person or corporation so injured; and any rail-road corporation shall have an insurable interest in the property for which it may be so held responsible in damages, along its route, and may procure insurance thereon in its own behalf.

What was the philosophy underlying the statute? What was the purpose of the "insurable interest" language? Must negligence be shown? In 1895 the statute was amended by Ch. 293, to provide that if held liable the railroad "shall be entitled to the benefit of any insurance effected upon such property by the owner thereof, less the cost of premium and expense of recovery." Why the change? How would the 1895 act work if the property is fully insured by the owner?

Although New York's fire rule may have been unique, the *Moch* case, p. 131, supra, which relied to some extent on *Ryan,* is followed in the overwhelming majority of states. Would the prevalence of fire insurance explain the result? By the time of *Moch,* water companies could obtain liability insurance—and they could probably raise their rates without fear of losing customers or their franchise. What is the likely relationship between property owners and water users in a large city? In deciding whether to permit an action in *Moch,* is it helpful to think of this problem in terms of a community in which the largest user of water is a fireproof brewery, and in which local houses are close together and made of wood? In *Moch,* it is difficult to support the catastrophe theory because in those states permitting recovery against negligent water companies in fire cases, there is no showing that the rule adversely affected the economy. Should actual or available insurance play any part in judicial analysis?

In Weinberg v. Dinger, 106 N.J. 469, 524 A.2d 366 (1987), the court overruled earlier decisions that had refused to impose liability on water companies that negligently failed to supply water to fight fires. The water companies here contended that "since property owners are invariably insured against loss from fire damage, a rule imposing liability on water companies would simply create a windfall for property-insurance carriers whose subrogated rights would permit them to recoup from water companies sums paid out pursuant to property insurance policies." The court observed that it was aware that increased water costs were "ultimately borne by the consumer [and that liability insurance] constitutes a less efficient method of insuring against fire loss than is afforded by property insurance." (Why is this true?) The court was also aware of the difficulty of obtaining liability insurance in the late 1980s. Nonetheless, relying on such earlier decisions, as *People Express,* p. 282, supra, and *Kelly v. Gwinnell*, p. 157, supra, the court overruled the earlier cases and imposed a duty of due care on water companies. Next, however, it concluded that the action should not lie for insured property losses:

> [W]e abrogate the water company's immunity for losses caused by the negligent failure to maintain adequate water pressure for fire fighting only to the extent of claims that are uninsured or underinsured [so as to avoid the carrier's subrogation claims against the water company]. This determination is made without prejudice to the right of a subrogation claimant, either in this or other litigation, to offer proof tending to demonstrate that any increase in water rates resulting from liability for subrogation claims would be substantially offset by reductions in fire-insurance premiums. If insurance rates were set on the basis of risk and experience, one would expect a high correlation between the increase in water company liability rates and the decrease in fire-insurance rates occasioned by the abrogation of water company immunity in cases like this. If that correlation were to be proven in subsequent litigation, we would be prepared to reconsider our denial of the carrier's right to subrogation against a water company.

One justice dissented from the decision to retain immunity in subrogation cases. Another dissenter opposed any retreat from the preexisting immunity of water companies.

Is it likely that the demanded showing can be made? If the showing is made, why might that influence the majority to eliminate what remains of the immunity of water companies? Is it relevant that the state's water companies are subject to the jurisdiction of the state's public utility commission?

The majority observed in passing that the argument for immunity did not address cases in which personal injury occurred during the fire. Why is this true? The case before the court involved only property damage— and there is apparently no reported case against a water company involving personal injury or death from fire. What is there about claims against water companies that might effectively limit them to property damage claims?

In a recent episode, fire district workers negligently started a fire that destroyed the home of rock star Grace Slick and her husband. Their insurer, Allstate, paid the pair $1.25 million and sought subrogation from the district. The district settled for $895,000, all but $220,000 of which went to Allstate. The payment "virtually wiped out [the district's] funds for acquiring lands to protect them from development." See Dougan, Slick Settlement Cleans Out Agency, S.F. Examiner, Nov. 24, 1994, at A–21. Are there arguments against subrogating Allstate in this situation?

Harm to property. In Eaves Brooks Costume Co. v. Y.B.H. Realty Corp., 76 N.Y.2d 220, 556 N.E.2d 1093, 557 N.Y.S.2d 286 (1990), a commercial tenant sustained a large loss to its inventory when a water sprinkler system malfunctioned and an alarm system failed to warn of the failure. Plaintiff sued both the company that had contracted with the landlord to inspect sprinklers in the building and the installer of the alarm system that had contracted with the landlord to detect water flowing through the sprinklers and to inform the proper persons. Each contract provided a very small limit on liability unless a larger limit were written into the contract. The sprinkler inspection charge was $120 per year and did not include maintenance. The alarm company charged $660 per year.

The unanimous court concluded that the defendants had not "assumed a duty to exercise reasonable care to prevent foreseeable harm to the plaintiff":

> If [the two defendants] were answerable for property damage sustained by one not in contractual privity with them, they would be forced to insure against a risk the amount of which they may not know and cannot control, and as to which contractual limitations of liability may be ineffective. The result would be higher insurance premiums passed along through higher rates to all those who require sprinkler system and alarm services. In effect, the cost of protection for those whose potential loss is the greatest would be subsidized by those with the least to lose. In this

setting, we see no reason to distribute the risk of loss in such a manner.

> Furthermore, the prices paid for defendants' services, according to specific language in the contracts, were calculated on the understanding that the risk of loss remained with the building's owners.   While plaintiff is not bound by the provisions of a contract to which it is not a party, the limited scope of defendants' undertaking is nonetheless relevant in determining whether a tort duty to others should arise from their performance of the contractual obligations.   Moreover, it suggests the need to contain liability within the limits envisioned in the contract in order to keep these services available at an affordable rate.

The court observed that plaintiff retained other remedies:

> [N]othing in our decision precludes plaintiff from seeking damages from the building's owners, and the owners and plaintiff are both in a position to insure against losses such as those sustained here. The plaintiff and the owners know or are in a position to know the value of the goods stored and can negotiate the cost of the lease and limitations on liability accordingly.

Does this fact pattern resemble that of the water company cases?

b.   THE IMPACT OF INSURANCE ON PROCEDURE AND SETTLEMENT

Lalomia v. Bankers & Shippers Ins. Co.

Supreme Court of New York, Appellate Division, 1970.
35 App.Div.2d 114, 312 N.Y.S.2d 1018.

■ BENJAMIN, J.   This action for a declaratory judgment calls upon us to determine which, if any, policies of insurance provide coverage for the plaintiffs, who were involved in a collision with a motorized bicycle.

The tragic accident out of which this litigation arose claimed the lives of 12–year–old Michael Maddock and of Jean Lalomia, a wife and the mother of four children.   At the time of the collision Michael was operating a motorized bicycle, that is, a bicycle from which various operational parts, such as the pedals, had been removed and to which a 3½ H.P. lawn mower gasoline engine had been added.   The motorized bicycle collided with an automobile being operated by Jean Lalomia.

Defendant Bankers & Shippers Insurance Company (hereinafter called B & S) had issued two policies of automobile insurance to defendant Daniel Maddock, Michael's father, each of which covered a different specific automobile.   Under their terms, these policies would only provide coverage for the motorized bicycle if it were held to be an after-acquired "private passenger automobile".   Defendant Maddock had not been required to notify B & S of the acquisition of the motorized bicycle under the terms of the policies, as it had been acquired within 30 days before the accident.

The motorized bicycle, which is classified as a motor-driven cycle (Vehicle and Traffic Law, § 124), is a motor vehicle within the meaning of the Vehicle and Traffic Law [   ]. However, it is not a private passenger automobile either within the meaning of the B & S policies or of regulation 35–A promulgated by the Superintendent of Insurance (11 NYCRR 60.1). B & S is therefore not required to defend or indemnify defendant Maddock as a result of the accident.

To hold that the motor-driven cycle was not a motor vehicle would allow the indiscriminate use of such dangerous contraptions by youngsters on our public highways. It is only when such vehicles are registered and made to conform to minimum standards of safety (the vehicle involved herein had no brakes and could be made to stop only by "shorting" the sparkplug) that accidents of this type can be avoided.

The extension of coverage in policies insuring specific private passenger automobiles to after-acquired private passenger automobiles was not intended to alter the nature of the risk involved. It would be unfair to compel an insurer to automatically extend coverage to a motor-driven cycle, motorcycle or racing car by a strained construction of the words "private passenger automobile."

Defendant Insurance Company of North America had issued a homeowner's policy to defendant Maddock. The policy obligated the insurer to pay all sums which the insured would become legally obligated to pay as damages because of personal injury or property damage. However, the policy excluded from its coverage "the ownership, maintenance, operation, use, loading or unloading" of automobiles or midget automobiles while away from the insured premises. With certain exceptions, the policy defined "automobile" as a "land motor vehicle". As the accident herein took place some three or four blocks from the insured premises, and as the motor-driven cycle was a motor vehicle, this insurer is not liable to defend or indemnify defendant Maddock, either individually or as administrator of Michael Maddock's estate (Michael was also an insured as defined by the policy), insofar as the ownership, maintenance, operation or use of the motorized bicycle is concerned.

However, the complaint in the plaintiffs' negligence action alleges, in effect, that Daniel Maddock was guilty of negligence in placing a dangerous instrumentality in the possession of and at the disposal of a 12–year–old boy, knowing that it could be used in a dangerous manner likely to cause harm to others. These allegations set forth a valid cause of action grounded in common-law negligence [   ]. This theory of action is not directly related to the "ownership, maintenance, operation, use" of the vehicle and imposes an obligation upon the insurer within the terms of its policy [   ].

Defendant Liberty Mutual Insurance Company is liable under the terms of the uninsured motorist endorsement contained in the policy which it issued to plaintiff Laurence Lalomia, who was Jean Lalomia's husband. Although that endorsement, as it appears in the policy, refers to "uninsured automobiles", it is deemed to cover all uninsured motor vehicles (cf.

Early v. MVAIC, 32 A.D.2d 1042, supra; Insurance Law, § 167, subd. 2–a.). The motor-driven cycle involved herein was an uninsured motor vehicle within the meaning of the endorsement.

The obligation imposed upon the Insurance Company of North America under its homeowner's policy is limited to the theory of negligently permitting the use and operation of a dangerous mechanism. As there is no other policy in force with respect to the use, maintenance or operation of the motor-driven cycle, the uninsured motorist endorsement contained in the Liberty policy is applicable. The judgment should be modified accordingly, on the law and the facts, without costs.

■ HOPKINS, ACTING P.J., MUNDER, MARTUSCELLO and KLEINFELD, JJ., concur.

NOTES AND QUESTIONS

1. *Lalomia* was affirmed on the opinion below. 31 N.Y.2d 830, 291 N.E.2d 724, 339 N.Y.S.2d 680 (1972).

2. Note that this was an action for a declaratory judgment. Several of the cases disputing insurance coverage, p. 678, supra, followed the same route. How else might these disputes be resolved?

3. The duty to indemnify must be separated from the duty to defend. If the claims asserted by the plaintiff include at least one covered by the insurance policy, the insurer must defend. At the same time, the insured should obtain independent counsel because of the conflict of interest inherent in the insurer's willingness to let liability be found on the claim for which it is not responsible.

In Public Service Mut. Ins. Co. v. Goldfarb, 53 N.Y.2d 392, 425 N.E.2d 810, 442 N.Y.S.2d 422 (1981), the insured was sued on a variety of claims. The insurer would be liable if certain claims were established but not if plaintiff prevailed on others. In view of the conflict, the court concluded that the insured was "entitled to defense by an attorney of his own choosing, whose reasonable fee is to be paid by the insurer."

4. The jury is not to be told whether the defendant is insured. Why? In cases in which the defendant has insurance, the plaintiff's attorney would like to ask if prospective jurors have any ties with insurance companies. Should such questions be permitted?

In Roman v. Mitchell, 82 N.J. 336, 413 A.2d 322 (1980), the court split 4–3 over the trial judge's action in excluding voir dire questions asking whether any prospective jurors held stock in, or were employed by, a casualty insurance company. The majority thought that the questions "tend to emphasize unduly the fact of insurance coverage. Absent some indication that a basis for asking them exists, they should ordinarily be rejected by the trial court." The majority feared that asking such questions, even in good faith, "can prejudice a defendant's right to a fair trial." One dissenter argued that modern jurors know about the existence of liability insurance and will not use the information to render excessive verdicts. He noted that insurance companies frequently advertised in national magazines to remind the public of the widespread incidence of liability insurance and to urge that jurors use restraint in awards.

In Rodgers v. Pascagoula Public School District, 611 So.2d 942 (Miss. 1992), the verdict against the school district for a bus crash, in which it admitted liability, awarded nothing for pain and suffering or other noneconomic damages. The court ordered additur. Three concurring justices observed:

> I am compelled to question how a jury composed of taxpayers can be expected to render a fair award of damages when operating under the assumption that they, the taxpayers, would ultimately foot the bill. . . . How can we continue [the policy of excluding mention of insurance] because of the presumed prejudice to an insurer when that same insurer can capitalize upon the gross prejudice that a jury of taxpayers will have toward assessing damages for the plaintiff? . . . [In this type of case] I believe that evidence of liability coverage should be admitted to ensure a fair and adequate award, untainted by any misconceptions that it could lighten the pocketbooks of taxpaying jurors.

What is this "misconception"? How will the concurring opinion's position eliminate it?

See also Myers v. Robertson, 891 P.2d 199 (Alaska 1995), ordering that the jury be informed of the existence of liability insurance in a case in which the administrator of the estate of a dead child is suing the parents for negligently causing the death. What is the jury to make of a case like this?

Perhaps the most common approach to admissibility of evidence of insurance is found in Federal Rule of Evidence 411:

> Evidence that a person was or was not insured against liability is not admissible upon the issue whether he acted negligently or otherwise wrongfully. The rule does not require the exclusion of evidence of insurance against liability when offered for another purpose, such as proof of agency, ownership, or control, or bias or prejudice of a witness.

5. In *Lalomia*, Liberty Mutual was both liability insurer and the carrier for the uninsured motorist coverage. If in a two-car crash, an uninsured motorist sues Lalomia, that involves the liability part of the policy. Lalomia's family may also sue Liberty Mutual on the uninsured motorist coverage. Note the potential conflict if both claims proceed, since it is to the insurer's interest to establish that both drivers were not negligent and try to defeat one or both drivers. Moreover, the liability limits may be different on the two coverages. The uninsured motorist coverage may thus make the insured and the insurer adversaries. How serious is this? How else might it have been handled?

6. Even though Mr. Maddock now has an insurer obligated to defend him in at least one phase of the case, do conflicts remain? For an extensive and critical view of insurers' practices in these areas, see Smith, The

Miscegenetic Union of Liability Insurance and Tort Process in the Personal Injury Claims System, 54 Cornell L.Rev. 645 (1969).

7.   Industry efforts to keep the auto and the homeowner's policy from overlapping are collected in Aetna Cas. & Sur. Co. v. Safeco Ins. Co., 103 Cal.App.3d 694, 163 Cal.Rptr. 219 (1980). See also State Farm Fire & Cas. Co. v. Kohl, 131 Cal.App.3d 1031, 182 Cal.Rptr. 720 (1982).

The reasoning of *Lalomia* was explicitly rejected in Barnstable County Mut. Fire Ins. Co. v. Lally, 374 Mass. 602, 373 N.E.2d 966 (1978), in which the homeowner's policy was held not to apply to a claim of negligent entrustment of a motor vehicle. The negligent entrustment theory "derived from the more general concepts of ownership, operation, and use of a motor vehicle" because it involved showing that the defendant owned or controlled the vehicle and permitted the driver to operate it. Compare Salem Group v. Oliver, 128 N.J. 1, 607 A.2d 138 (1992), requiring a homeowner's insurer to defend a claim brought by the insured's minor nephew who was hurt operating the insured's ATV off the premises after having been served alcohol by the insured.

Most courts have rejected *Lalomia*. See the dissent in Cone v. Nationwide Mut.Fire Ins. Co., 75 N.Y.2d 747, 551 N.E.2d 92, 551 N.Y.S.2d 891 (1989), involving entrustment of an ATV. The court, 4–3, followed *Lalomia* and held that the parent's homeowners' insurer was obligated to defend. In the 18 years since *Lalomia* the language of the policy had not become sufficiently clear to deny coverage. The dissenters sought to distinguish *Lalomia* based on changes in the language brought about by the industry's reaction to *Lalomia*. If the attempted distinction failed, the dissenters wanted to overrule *Lalomia*.

The Settlement Process.   The pervasive impact of liability insurance on tort law, as well as its strong tendency to create disparities between the law in action and the law on the books, is treated in detail in H.L. Ross, Settled Out of Court: The Social Process of Insurance Claims Adjustments (1980 ed.). Consider the following excerpts from pp. 237–40:

> In order to process successfully vast numbers of cases, organizations tend to take on the characteristics of "bureaucracy" in the sociological sense of the term: operation on the basis of rules, government by a clear hierarchy, the maintenance of files, etc. Such an organizational form produces competence and efficiency in applying general rules to particular cases, but it is not well suited to making complex and individualized decisions. One form of response of bureaucracies to such demands involves a type of breakdown. There will be long delays, hewing to complicated and minute procedures, and a confusion of means with ends. A common and perhaps more constructive response is to simplify the task. This was the tack taken by the claims men I studied. Phone calls and letters replaced personal visits; only a few witnesses, rather than all possible, would be interviewed; and the law of negligence was made to lean heavily on the much simpler traffic law.

Traffic laws are simple rules, deliberately so because their purpose is to provide a universal and comprehensible set of guidelines for safe and efficient transportation. Negligence law is complex, its purpose being to decide after the fact whether a driver was unreasonably careless. However, all levels of the insurance company claims department will accept the former rules as generally adequate for the latter purpose. The underlying reason for this is the difficulty if not impossibility of investigating and defending a more complex decision concerning negligence in the context of a mass operation. In the routine case, the stakes are not high enough to warrant the effort, and the effort is not made. The information that a given insured violated a specific traffic law and was subsequently involved in an accident will suffice to allocate fault. No attempt is made to analyze why this took place or how. The legal concepts of negligence and fault in action contain no more substance than the simple and mechanical procedures noted here provide.

The law of damages is also simplified in action. Although the measurement of special damages appears rather straightforward even in formal doctrine, some further simplification occurs in action when, for instance, life table calculations are used to compute future earnings. More important, the measurement of pain, suffering, and inconvenience is thoroughly routinized in the ordinary claim. The adjuster generally pays little attention to the claimant's privately experienced discomforts and agonies; I do not recall ever having read recitals of these matters in the statements, which are the key documents in the settlement process and in which all matters considered relevant to the disposition of a claim are recorded. The calculation of general damages is for the most part a matter of multiplying the medical bills by a tacitly but generally accepted arbitrary constant. This practice is justified by claims men on the theory that pain and suffering are very likely to be a function of the amount of medical treatment experienced. There is of course a grain of truth in this theory, but it also contains several sources of error. Types of injury vary considerably in the degree of pain and suffering, the necessity for treatment, and the fees charged for treatment; and the correlations between these elements are low. I believe that the more important reason for the use of the formula is again that all levels of the claims department find it acceptable in justifying payment over and beyond special damages. The formula provides a conventional measurement for phenomena that are so difficult to evaluate as to be almost unmeasurable. It provides a rule by which a rule-oriented organization can proceed, though the rule is never formalized. This simplification also meets the comparable needs of plaintiffs' attorneys and is acceptable to them as well. Because of the mutual acceptability of the formula, attorneys will try to capitalize on it by adding to the use and cost of medical treatment, a procedure known as "building" the file, and adjusters will argue concerning the reasonableness of many items that purport to be medical expenses and thus part of the base to which the formula is applied.

Is this passages reassuring? Disillusioning?

Agreements not to sue that are made after the harm has occurred—usually at the time of a settlement—will be enforced in the absence of factors such as misrepresentation and duress that would also void any contract. The problem of the plaintiff who turns out to be more seriously hurt than anticipated is well discussed in Mangini v. McClurg, 24 N.Y.2d 556, 249 N.E.2d 386, 301 N.Y.S.2d 508 (1969):

> [There are] many reasons, including doubtful liability, the willingness to take a calculated risk, the desire to obtain an earlier rather than a later settlement, and perhaps others, why releasors may wish to effect a settlement and intend to give the releasee a discharge of liability for any unknown injuries—in short to bargain for general peace. When general peace is the consideration, there can be no mutual mistake as to the extent of the injuries, known or unknown.

Some of these considerations, of course, also explain why some claims are settled for less than the damage sustained from known injuries. Citing authorities for the proposition that unknown injuries are not generally within the contemplation of the parties "despite the generality of standardized language in releases," the court concluded that the plaintiffs were entitled to try to prove, "directly or circumstantially, that there was no intention to release a claim for unknown injuries."

Settlement strategies. The variety of possible settlements is virtually unlimited. In the so-called "high-low" settlement, for example, each party wishes to avoid an extreme result. The most likely case is one in which the plaintiff is seriously injured but liability is seriously in doubt. The parties may agree before trial that if plaintiff recovers nothing or less than $100,000, the parties agree that the plaintiff is to receive $100,000. If the final outcome is an award of over $500,000, the parties agree to settle for $500,000. If the outcome is an award between $100,000 and $500,000 the parties agree to abide by that result or they agree on some other amount.

One controversial settlement technique is the so-called Mary Carter agreement, which first appeared in Booth v. Mary Carter Paint Co., 202 So.2d 8 (Fla.App.1967). In this type of agreement, the defendant remains in the case and guarantees the plaintiff a certain payment. The size of that payment depends on the plaintiff's success against the other defendants. The danger of this agreement becomes obvious when the settling defendant testifies at the trial in a manner that helps the plaintiff and hurts the other defendants, who are now adversaries of the agreeing defendant. Some states require that the jury be informed of the existence of the agreement. Other states bar Mary Carter agreements. E.g., Elbaor v. Smith, 845 S.W.2d 240 (Tex. 1992)(voiding such agreements because of a case in which secretly settling defendants sat at defense table and told jury that plaintiff had suffered "devastating" injuries and "astoundingly high" damages, and used their "cross-examination" of the plaintiff to aid her showing of pain and suffering).

In large cases the "structured settlement" has become important. The defendant makes a payment now to cover past expenses and legal fees. The major part of the payment is used to buy an annuity that will provide, say, $50,000 in annual income for the life of the injured victim. The arrangement can be structured so that the annual income is tax free.

In 1982, the Stanford University Hospital settled with the parents of a child rendered quadriplegic and otherwise disabled at birth due to lack of sufficient oxygen, by paying for a series of three annuities that initially yielded $82,000 per year, rising to $275,000 per year in 2002. The money will be used for the child's medical costs and special treatment. If the child lives her expected 76 more years, the payments will amount to $122 million. The package of annuities cost $2.3 million. An economist stated that the present cash value of the settlement was $8 million. N.Y.Times, Sept. 17, 1982 at 12. The payments are guaranteed for 20 years, with that guaranteed money to go to the child's heirs if she dies within 20 years. Cash payments at the outset included $150,000 to each parent, $650,000 to the plaintiff's lawyer, $41,000 for legal expenses, and $209,000 for current medical expenses. This $1.2 million was shared by the hospital and the physician.

The propriety of a settlement made by the insurer without the consent of the insured depends on the contract. In Feliberty v. Damon, 72 N.Y.2d 112, 527 N.E.2d 261, 531 N.Y.S.2d 778 (1988), a physician was sued for malpractice. After an adverse jury verdict setting plaintiff's liability at $743,000 (within the policy limits), the defendant insurer settled the case for $700,000. The physician claimed that the insurer had settled without the physician's consent—and that he had wished to appeal. He alleged that the publicity following the verdict destroyed his practice.

The court recognized that the physician was undoubtedly troubled about the adverse verdict even though he had not had to pay any money. But the short answer was that the contract specified that the "company may make such investigation and such settlement of any claim or suit as it deems expedient." Unlike "bargained-for, and presumably costlier, policy provisions contemplating the insured's consent to settlement [ ], here the parties' contract unambiguously gave the insurer the unconditional right to settle any claim or suit without plaintiff's consent."

c. SUING THE INSURER

Pavia v. State Farm Mutual Automobile Ins. Co.
Court of Appeals of New York, 1993.
82 N.Y.2d 445, 626 N.E.2d 24, 605 N.Y.S.2d 208.

[One evening in April, 1985, Carmine Rosato, a 16–year-old, picked up the 19–year-old plaintiff and another youth in a car belonging to Rosato's mother. The car was insured by defendant with a $100,000 liability limit.

Rosato, whose learner's permit did not authorize driving at night, turned a corner at apparently excessive speed and encountered a double-parked car. In his efforts to avoid that car he collided with a car driven by Amerosa. Plaintiff was seriously hurt.   Further facts are set out in the opinion.]

■ TITONE, JUDGE.

. . .

In October 1985, Pavia commenced a personal injury action against the Rosatos and Mr. Amerosa.   The record reveals that as early as March 1986 a line unit representative at State Farm responsible for a preliminary investigation of plaintiff's claim, concluded that the Rosatos were 100% liable for the accident.   By August 1986, a State Farm claims representative responsible for handling the case on a daily basis was in receipt of medical reports attesting to the severity of plaintiff's injuries.   A physical examination of plaintiff conducted by State Farm's physicians on April 27, 1987 confirmed those findings.   New developments in the case against the Rosatos surfaced on June 9, 1987—the date that Carmine Rosato was deposed.   Through Rosato's testimony, State Farm was led to believe that the double-parked car may have been backing up, suggesting that Rosato's quick maneuvering may have been justified under an "emergency defense"; that witnesses not previously identified could support this version of the incident; that Pavia failed to wear a seat belt; and that drugs were being used in the car that night, possibly supporting an assumption of the risk defense.   By letter dated June 10, 1987, counsel retained for the Rosatos by State Farm acknowledged that the liability forecast was "extremely unfavorable," but recommended that a further inquiry be conducted in light of these new leads.

On June 26, 1987, admittedly without having read Rosato's deposition, plaintiff's counsel wrote to State Farm demanding the full $100,000 policy limit in settlement of the personal injury action and requiring acceptance of the offer within thirty days.   The offer expired without response from State Farm.   By this time, however, State Farm had embarked on a thorough investigation of the potential defenses illuminated by Rosato's deposition. In fact, State Farm had hired an investigator to locate the supposed witnesses who would corroborate Rosato's version of how the events leading to the accident unfolded.   By November 1987, State Farm's efforts to locate those witnesses were abandoned because the search had proved fruitless.   On December 1, 1987, State Farm's Claims Committee, whose members had the authority to offer payments in excess of $50,000, convened for the first time to discuss the reports generated by the claim representative assigned to the case.   On December 16, 1987, the Committee authorized its counsel to offer plaintiff the full policy limits.   This offer was conveyed to plaintiff's attorney by counsel retained by State Farm on the Rosatos' behalf on January 7, 1988 during a "settle or select" conference, but was rejected as "too late."

The trial of the underlying personal injury action commenced in March 1988.   The jury returned a plaintiff's verdict in the amount of $6,322,000, attributing 85% of the fault to Carmine Rosato and 15% to co-defendant

Amerosa. Supreme Court reduced the verdict upon State Farm's motion to $5,000,000 and the Appellate Division modified that judgment by further reducing the verdict to $3,880,000 upon plaintiff's stipulation.

The Rosatos subsequently assigned all causes of action they might have against State Farm to plaintiff by executing an assignment agreement, which included a covenant by plaintiff that he would not execute the excess portion of the judgment against the Rosatos. The Rosatos and plaintiff then commenced this action, alleging essentially that State Farm acted in bad faith by "failing to accept [plaintiff's] policy limits settlement offer within a reasonable time despite the clear liability and obvious damages exceeding the policy limits."

At the ensuing trial on the bad faith action, the jury was presented solely with the following question: "Did the defendant, State Farm, act in gross disregard of the interests of Carmine Rosato and Joanne Rosato, their insured, in that there was a deliberate or reckless decision to disregard the interest of their insured?" The jury answered affirmatively, and Supreme Court entered an "excess" judgment against State Farm in the amount of $4,688,030—the amount of the jury verdict in the underlying personal injury action as modified by the Appellate Division, less $110,000 already paid by State Farm and Amerosa's insurer, plus interest and costs.

The Appellate Division affirmed, holding that the trial court properly charged the jury that, in order to find bad faith, State Farm must have acted in "gross disregard" of the Rosatos' interests, and properly rejected the standard urged by State Farm—that bad faith required "an extraordinary showing of disingenuous or dishonest failure" to carry out the insurance contract (see Gordon v. Nationwide Mut. Ins. Co. (30 N.Y.2d 427, 437, cert. denied, 410 U.S. 931)). The court also rejected State Farm's contention that the evidence adduced at trial was insufficient as a matter of law to present a jury question on the "bad faith" issue, noting that State Farm "possessed the information necessary to accurately assess both the magnitude of Frank Pavia's injuries and the Rosatos' potential exposure well before the June 26, 1987 settlement offer was received" [ ]. Despite our conclusion that the courts below properly applied the "gross disregard" standard, as a matter of law the finding of bad faith is not supported by this record.

II.

The notion that an insurer may be held liable for the breach of its duty of "good faith" in defending and settling claims over which it exercises exclusive control on behalf of its insured is an enduring principle, well-settled in this State's jurisprudence [ ]. The duty of "good faith" settlement is an implied obligation derived from the insurance contract [ ]. Naturally, whenever an insurer is presented with a settlement offer within policy limits a conflict arises between, on the one hand, the insurer's interest in minimizing its payments and on the other hand, the insured's interest in avoiding liability beyond the policy limits [ ]. By refusing to settle within the policy limits, an insurer risks being charged with bad faith on the premise that it has "advanced its own interest by compromising those of its insured" [   ], or even those of an excess insurance carrier who "alone [may be] placed at further risk due to the defendant's intractable opposition to any settlement of the claim" [   ].

At the root of the "bad faith" doctrine is the fact that insurers typically exercise complete control over the settlement and defense of claims against their insureds, and, thus, under established agency principles may fairly be required to act in the insured's best interests [   ]. On the other hand, a countervailing policy consideration exists in the courts' understandable reluctance to expose insurance carriers to liability far beyond the bargained-for policy limits for conduct amounting to a mere mistake in judgment. Thus, established precedent clearly bars a "bad faith" prosecution for conduct amounting to ordinary negligence [   ]. Indeed, in Gordon v Nationwide Mut. Ins. Co. (supra), this Court held that even where an insurer had withdrawn from its insured's defense on the erroneous belief that the policy of insurance had lapsed, the error in judgment could not form the predicate for a bad faith action [   ].

Beyond that principle, the courts have had some difficulty selecting a standard for actionable "bad faith" because of the need to balance the insured's rightful expectations of "good faith" against the insurer's equally legitimate contract expectations. Consequently, a divergence of authority has arisen concerning whether a bad faith finding may be predicated on a showing of the insurer's recklessness or "gross disregard" for the insured's interests [   ], or whether a heightened showing of intentionally harmful, dishonest or disingenuous motive is required [   ].

Faced squarely with the question for the first time, we reject defendant's proposed requirement of a "sinister motive" on the part of the insurer [   ], and hold instead that, in order to establish a prima facie case of bad faith, the plaintiff must establish that the insurer's conduct constituted a "gross disregard" of the insured's interests—that is, a deliberate or reckless failure to place on equal footing the interests of its insured with its own interests when considering a settlement offer [   ]. In other words, a bad faith plaintiff must establish that the defendant insurer engaged in a pattern of behavior evincing a conscious or knowing indifference to the probability that an insured would be held personally accountable for a large judgment if a settlement offer within the policy limits were not accepted.

The gross disregard standard, which was utilized by the trial court here, strikes a fair balance between two extremes by requiring more than ordinary negligence and less than a showing of dishonest motives. The former would remove the latitude that insurers must be accorded in investigating and resisting unfounded claims, while the latter would be all but impossible to satisfy and would effectively insulate insurance carriers from conduct that, while not motivated by malice, has the potential to severely prejudice the rights of its insured. The intermediate standard accomplishes the two-fold goal of protecting both the insured's and the insurer's financial interests.

III.

Having established the proper legal standard, we necessarily shift to the sufficiency of plaintiff's proof in this case. Naturally, proof that a demand for settlement was made is a prerequisite to a bad faith action for failure to settle [   ]. However, evidence that a settlement offer was made and not accepted is not dispositive of the insurer's bad faith. It is settled that an insurer "cannot be compelled to concede liability and settle a questionable claim" [   ] simply "because an opportunity to do so is presented" [   ]. Rather, the plaintiff in a bad faith action must show that "the insured lost an actual opportunity to settle the claim" [   ] at a time when all serious doubts about the insured's liability were removed.

Bad faith is established only "where the liability is clear and the potential recovery far exceeds the insurance coverage" [   ]. However, it does not follow that whenever an injury is severe and the policy limits are significantly lower than a potential recovery the insurer is obliged to accept a settlement offer. The bad faith equation must include consideration of all of the facts and circumstances relating to whether the insurer's investigatory efforts prevented it from making an informed evaluation of the risks of refusing settlement. In making this determination, courts must assess the plaintiff's likelihood of success on the liability issue in the underlying action, the potential magnitude of damages and the financial burden each party may be exposed to as a result of a refusal to settle. Additional considerations include the insurer's failure to properly investigate the claim and any potential defenses thereto, the information available to the insurer at the time the demand for settlement is made, and any other evidence which tends to establish or negate the insurer's bad faith in refusing to settle. The insured's fault in delaying or ceasing settlement negotiations by misrepresenting the facts also factors into the analysis [   ].

Application of the aforementioned principles here leads us to the conclusion that plaintiffs have failed to establish a prima facie case of bad faith. Plaintiffs' allegations of bad faith stem principally from defendant State Farm's failure to abide by a settlement deadline unilaterally established by plaintiff Pavia's counsel and its delay in ultimately offering the policy limits in settlement.

However, defendant's failure to respond to the letter and overall delay under the circumstances of this case cannot serve as a basis for recovery. Permitting an injured plaintiff's chosen timetable for settlement to govern the bad faith inquiry would promote the customary manufacturing of bad faith claims, especially in cases where an insured of meager means is covered by a policy of insurance which could finance only a fraction of the damages in a serious personal injury case. Indeed, insurers would be bombarded with settlement offers imposing arbitrary deadlines and would be encouraged to prematurely settle their insureds' claims at the earliest possible opportunity in contravention of their contractual right and obligation of thorough investigation.

Here, plaintiff's time-limited settlement offer came at a relatively early point in the litigation. Moreover, at the time the 30-day settlement demand was made, there remained several significant questions about the insured's liability, which defendant was entitled to investigate and explore. That defendant could have acted more expeditiously does not convert inattention into a gross disregard for the insured's rights, particularly where, as here, there is no contention that the insurer failed to carry out an investigation, to evaluate the feasibility of settlement [   ], or to offer the policy limits before trial after the weakness of the insured's litigation position was clearly and fully assessed.

The facts that State Farm's preliminary liability forecasts were unfavorable and that the investigation ultimately proved those forecasts accurate certainly do not establish that the insurer was unjustified in engaging in further investigation and failing to effectuate an early settlement. On the contrary, State Farm's failure to conduct the continuing inquiry could have constituted a breach of its obligation to investigate and defend its insured. Moreover, State Farm should not be penalized for the delay in processing the claim and offering the full policy limits in settlement which resulted from its pursuit of an investigation prompted by its insured's representations which ultimately did not materialize [   ].

By any view of the evidence, State Farm's failure to promptly respond to the time-restricted demand did not amount to more than ordinary negligence—an insufficient predicate for a bad faith action. Evident as it may be with hindsight that State Farm should have responded to the settlement offer by at least requesting an extension, its failure to do so was not evidence of willful neglect of the insured's rights, but instead amounted to mistaken judgment or administrative delay in confirming what it had suspected it would do all along—settle for the policy limits. Thus, this record lacks any pattern or indicia of reckless or conscious disregard for the insured's rights upon which we could uphold a bad faith judgment.

     .   .   .   [The Appellate Division's order was reversed and the complaint dismissed.]

■ KAYE, C.J., and SIMONS, HANCOCK, BELLACOSA, SMITH and LEVINE, JJ., concur.

NOTES AND QUESTIONS

1. Is the court persuasive in arguing that a standard of "ordinary negligence" is inappropriate in this type of case?

2. How might settlements be affected by a system that made insurers strictly liable for any failure to settle within the policy limits if that failure results in a higher award than the one rejected?

3. The history of this action has produced a wide range of results. For the complex and illuminating history in California, see Moradi–Shalal v. Fireman's Fund Ins. Cos., 46 Cal.3d 287, 758 P.2d 58, 250 Cal.Rptr. 116 (1988), overruling Royal Globe Ins. Co. v. Superior Court, 23 Cal.3d 880, 592 P.2d 329, 153 Cal.Rptr. 842 (1979), which had used the insurer's statutory obligation to act in good faith as the basis for implying a tort claim for bad faith refusal to settle a third party liability claim.

4. Should an insurer be liable for not offering the insured the chance to pay something now in order to avoid a possibly greater liability later? In Parich v. State Farm Mut. Auto Ins. Co., 919 F.2d 906 (5th Cir.1990), cert. denied 499 U.S. 976 (1991), the insurer refused a $37,000 settlement offer on a $25,000 policy limit without first asking the insured whether he would come up with the extra $12,000. The case went to trial, resulting in a verdict and judgment against the insured for some $400,000. The insurer was held liable for the entire judgment. What if the insurer in that case had asked the insured to come up with the extra $12,000 and the insured had refused? What if, instead of $12,000, the insurer asked the insured to contribute $17,000 to settle the case?

5. Does it matter in these cases whether the dispute is over liability or over the extent of the damages suffered in a clear liability case?

6. The *Pavia* court refused to extend its analysis to punitive damages. In Soto v. State Farm Ins. Co., 83 N.Y.2d 718, 635 N.E.2d 1222, 613 N.Y.S.2d 352 (1994), defendant's insureds were adjudged liable for $420,-000 in compensatory damages and $450,000 in punitive damages in connection with a fatal automobile accident. The insurer had defended the case on the ground that the driver did not have the insured's permission to drive the car. The jury found that the driver (the insured's live-in boyfriend) had permission—and was drunk at the time of the accident. After the judgment, defendant paid plaintiffs the full amount of the compensatory award (not just the $100,000 policy limits). The insureds assigned to the tort plaintiffs the insureds' claim that their insurer acted in bad faith when it refused a pretrial offer from plaintiffs to settle for the policy limits of $50,000 for each of two deaths. In this suit, plaintiff-assignees sought payment of the punitive award as well.

The court declined even though "for purposes of measuring the amounts recoverable in a bad-faith action against an insurer, [a punitive award] is no different in principle from an award of excess personal injury damages; both are unindemnified liabilities to which the insured would not have been exposed if the insurer had acted in good faith to reach a fair pretrial settlement." Nonetheless, the state's goal of "preserving the condemnatory and retributive character of punitive damage awards . . . cannot be reconciled with a conclusion that would allow the insured wrongdoer to divert the economic punishment to an insurer because of the insurer's unrelated, independent wrongful act in improperly refusing a settlement within policy limits":

> Our system of civil justice may be organized so as to allow a wrongdoer to escape the punitive consequences of his own malfeasance in order that the injured plaintiff may enjoy the advantage of a swift and certain pretrial settlement. However, the benefit that a morally culpable wrongdoer obtains as a result of this system, i.e., being released from exposure to liability for punitive damages, is no more than a necessary incident of the process. It is certainly not a right whose loss need be made subject to compensation when a favorable

pretrial settlement offer has been wasted by a reckless or faithless insurer.

In *Taylor*, p. 651, supra, involving punitive damages for drunk driving, the plaintiff's attorney is reported to have stated that the importance of the availability of punitive damages in such cases was not that plaintiff would be able to recover them, but that their availability would encourage the insurer to settle the compensatory claim: "It will expedite settlement. The carrier has a responsibility to avoid the exposure of his client to punitive damages." S.F.Daily Journal, Aug. 24, 1979, at 1.

7. What are the respective interests of the plaintiff, the insured, and the insurer in the *Pavia-Soto* situation? Has the court reached sound accommodations? If the insureds were independently wealthy would your answer change?

For an extreme and complex case of liability in this situation involving law firms as well as insurers, see West American Ins. Co. v. Freeman, 38 Cal.App.4th 1017B, 44 Cal.Rptr.2d 555 (1995), upholding a judgment of $1.3 million in compensatory and $12 million in punitive damages in favor of a builder against his liability insurer.

For a discussion of the various conflicts that may arise between insurers and insureds during settlement negotiations, and possible ways to resolve them, see Syverud, The Duty to Settle, 76 Va.L.Rev 1113 (1990).

8. *Excess coverage obligations.* "Excess insurance carriers" may face the same risks that insureds face. Since it has become common for persons and companies to purchase tiers of insurance ("primary" for the main coverage and "excess" or "umbrella" coverage for catastrophic losses beyond the limits of the primary policy), it is common for different companies to write each coverage. This creates questions analogous to those addressed earlier about the obligations of the primary insurer or the insured to settle the case so as to avoid exposing the excess carrier to severe losses. In Commercial Union Assurance Cos. v. Safeway Stores, Inc., 26 Cal.3d 912, 610 P.2d 1038, 164 Cal.Rptr. 709 (1980), the court concluded that the insured owed no duty to the excess carrier to settle the underlying case if it could do so before reaching the amount at which the excess coverage began. Although an insured may have a "legitimate right to expect" the primary insurer to explore ways to protect the insured, no such expectation runs in favor of the excess carrier against the primary insurer. See also, Continental Casualty Co. v. Pacific Indemnity Co., 134 Cal.App.3d 389, 184 Cal.Rptr. 583 (1982).

9. *Double coverage.* Since several insurance policies may cover the same liability, it has become important to determine the sequence in which the policies come into play. Sometimes this can be decided from the language of the policies—if one states that it is "primary" and the second states that it is only "excess" after others have been exhausted. Sometimes the policies all call for proration with other applicable policies. But if, for example, all the policies claim to be "excess," the language of the policies cannot control. For an introduction to this problem, see Note,

Toward a More Equitable Method of Prorating Liability Insurance Policies, 51 S.Cal.L.Rev. 943 (1978). See also Carriers Ins. Co. v. American Policyholders' Ins. Co., 404 A.2d 216 (Me.1979).

10. *Contribution and indemnity.* The institution of insurance has also influenced attitudes toward contribution and indemnity. Although, in a world without insurance, these devices for sharing or shifting losses were thought to be just, some now argue that insurance has changed the situation. In James, Contribution Among Joint Tortfeasors: A Pragmatic Criticism, 54 Harv.L.Rev. 1156 (1941), Professor Fleming James argued that contribution was used in only two situations: (1) where an insurer or large self-insurer seeks it against an uninsured individual and (2) where an insurer or self-insurer seeks it against another such company. He would prefer barring contribution "even though it mars a theoretical symmetry in the law of negligence." For disagreement, see Gregory, Contribution Among Joint Tortfeasors: A Defense, 54 Harv.L.Rev. 1170 (1941). Does the introduction of comparative negligence among defendants change the arguments? What about deterrence?

CHAPTER XI

A Survey of Alternatives

In recent years, tort reform activity has been largely concentrated on efforts to adopt incremental changes in the existing system. We begin with a brief discussion of the principal types of initiatives in this category. There is a logical progression reflected in considering these strategies immediately after the chapter on damages and insurance. As will become evident, the dominant incremental reform measures in recent years have, in fact, been addressed to the remedial, or damages/insurance, side of the tort system, rather than aimed at altering substantive tort doctrine. Indeed, a number of these initiatives were noted in Chapter X, as we discussed nonpecuniary loss, punitive damages, collateral source recovery, and contingency fees (and earlier, in Chapter V, when we discussed joint and several liability).

After examining incremental tort reform measures in greater detail, we will consider a wide variety of alternatives to the tort system. Some, such as workers' compensation and auto no-fault plans, are designed to replace all or a substantial part of tort law in major areas of injury activity. Others, such as vaccine and birth defect compensation schemes, focus on narrower areas of accidental harm. At the other extreme from these focused plans, we examine comprehensive no-fault and social insurance proposals that would replace much or all of tort law in injury and accident-related disease cases. The common theme in these diverse plans is that they are intended to serve as tort replacement measures. Their premise is that a better system than tort law can be designed to address the problem of accidental harm.

What are the dimensions of that problem? National Safety Council data indicate that in 1994, in a total U.S. population of about 240 million, there were some 92,200 accidental deaths—the three major categories being 43,000 motor vehicle deaths, 26,700 deaths in the home, and 3,000 workplace deaths not involving motor vehicles. An estimated 18.6 million disabling injuries occurred, principally in the home (7.0 million), on the job (3.5 million), and in motor vehicles (2.1 million). In 1992, accidents were the biggest killer of persons from ages one to thirty-seven, with motor vehicles leading in almost every age category.

The National Safety Council report also estimates the costs associated with accidental death and injury. The total of $441 billion for all accidents includes $227 billion in wage and productivity loss, $77.8 billion in medical expenses, and $70 billion in administrative costs (insurance, police and legal costs). The automobile looms large in these figures, with total cost of automobile accidents pegged at $176.5 billion, including $66.4 billion in wage and productivity losses, and $39.1 billion in property losses. By comparison, worker injuries were estimated at $120.7 billion and home injuries at $94.3 billion. See National Safety Council, Accident Facts 1–12 (1995 ed.).

How do these accident figures translate into tort claims? A Department of Justice study of state courts of general jurisdiction in the 75 largest counties in the U.S. by extrapolation estimated that in 1992 about 378,000 tort claims were filed involving 1.4 million plaintiffs and defendants—a claims figure that had held relatively steady for at least seven years. See Smith, et al., Tort Cases in Large Counties: Civil Justice Survey of State Courts, 1992 (Bureau of Justice Statistics Special Report (April 1995)). Since accidents in the home frequently do not give rise to lawsuits and those on the job are generally outside the tort system, the largest number of claims came from motor vehicle accidents. A sample of the overall claims indicated that 60% were auto cases, 17% involved premises liability (commercial as well as residential), 5% were in the medical malpractice area, and 3% involved products liability.

Only 3% of tort cases go to trial (7% in medical malpractice cases). Within one year, 44% of tort cases reach disposition; the mean processing time for all cases being 19.3 months. Auto cases again stand out—they have the shortest processing time among all categories. The most common type of tort case involved one individual suing another (47% of all tort cases—a large majority of auto cases fall in this category). Individuals sue businesses in 37% of the cases and about 5% involve suits by individuals against government agencies or hospitals.

To put tort cases in context, the 1995 Department of Justice study found that tort claims constituted about 10% of all civil filings—the largest category being domestic relations cases (41%). And from another perspective, recall the data from a 1991 RAND study, p. 1, supra, indicating that tort liability payments comprise only 11% of total compensation for loss from all sources in accidental harm cases. For comprehensive discussion of the interrelationship between tort and other sources of payment in accidental harm cases, see Abraham & Liebman, Private Insurance, Social Insurance, and Tort Reform: Toward a New Vision of Compensation for Illness and Injury, 93 Colum.L.Rev. 75 (1993).

Although it has been estimated that in 1985 injury victims obtained about 46 percent of the premiums paid by defendants in tort suits, that percentage varied from 52 percent of total expenditures received by plaintiffs in auto cases to an average of 43 percent in other accident cases. The study estimated that the legal fees and expenses of injury victims constitute about 30–31 percent of the total compensation paid to plaintiffs, and that defendants' legal fees and expenses average about 16 percent of the total compensation paid to plaintiffs in auto cases and 28 percent in non-auto cases. The study estimated that defendants' legal expenses had been growing annually at a rate of 6 percent in auto cases and 15 percent in non-auto cases during the past five years. Trend data were not available for plaintiffs' legal fees and expenses. See J. Kakalik & N. Pace, Costs and Compensation Paid in Tort Litigation (1986).

A system that pays one dollar in benefits for one dollar of premiums is not likely to be the goal. This point is made in Brandau, Compensating Highway Accident Victims Who Pays the Insurance Cost?, 37 Ins.Counsel J. 598 (1970). Adverting to figures on the relative efficiency of various reparation systems, the author suggested (p. 605) that:

> . . . the concept of efficiency often used in describing systems seems to imply that an absolutely efficient system would pay out $1.00 in benefits for every dollar it collected in payments. This is not the case. Such a system would ultimately prove to be very inefficient. Some expense is necessary to determine whether persons applying for benefits are qualified. Any system needs a control to determine eligibility for payments or else the system will be fraught with fraud. Of course, to the extent that there are extensive eligibility requirements, the expense of administering a program goes up. The justification of this expense is not a matter of efficiency, but rather a matter of judgment whether the eligibility requirements are worth the expense of administering the program.

Can the due care issue in negligence cases be regarded as an "eligibility requirement," in Brandau's terms? What about the causation issues in toxic tort cases? Assess the fault system and the tort system generally in Brandau's terms. Keep these considerations in mind as we consider other techniques for meeting the financial consequences of accidents.

A.   Incremental Tort Reform

Within the last 20 years, we can trace three periods of legislative activity related to aspects of tort reform. The first, in the mid–1970s, was centered on medical malpractice. Physicians complained of high malpractice insurance premiums: some left high-risk specialties; others "went bare"—dropped their liability coverage; some went on strike and marched to demand relief. Virtually all state legislatures responded—though with little uniformity. Among the common changes in malpractice cases were: placing caps on the amount that could be awarded for pain and suffering; regulating fees of plaintiffs' attorneys; shortening statutes of limitation; requiring periodic payments as to future awards; and altering or eliminating the collateral source rule.

One prominent example was California, which enacted the Medical Injury Compensation Reform Act (MICRA). The Act limited recovery for pain and suffering in medical malpractice cases to a maximum of $250,000. (Cal.Civ.Code § 3333.2). Also, in any case in which the award of future damages exceeded $50,000, the judge was required, at the request of either party, to direct that the money be paid periodically. If the victim died before the judgment was satisfied, the defendant might be relieved of paying for future medical expenses. The payments for future lost earnings would not be affected by death. (Cal.Code Civ.Pro. § 667.7). In addition, the Act set maximum percentages for contingent fees (Cal.Bus. & Prof. Code § 6146), and provided that if all or part of the victim's medical bills had been paid by the victim's own insurance or some other source unrelated to the defendant, the jury should be told this—but not told what to do with the information. Subrogation was eliminated. (Cal.Civ. Code § 3333.1).

The second wave of activity occurred in the mid–1980s, as the result of increasingly large damage awards, soaring insurance premiums, and, for a growing number of enterprises, the complete unavailability of liability insurance. The extent of this crisis was questioned by critics of the insurance industry (who blamed the industry's problems on the lowering of interest rates from their highs of the early 1980s). Whatever the truth, between 1985 and 1988, 48 state legislatures responded with some variety of tort reform legislation. These enactments addressed the concerns of tort defendants generally rather than the physician-specific statutes of the mid–1970s.

The principal changes were in the damages and insurance areas. A large number of states enacted limitations in one form or another on recovery for noneconomic loss (pain and suffering and/or punitive damages), on joint and several liability, and on the collateral source rule. In all, during this second wave 30 states changed their joint and several liability rules and 23 placed some type of ceiling on pain and suffering awards. Another 25 placed limits on punitive damage awards—either eliminating them, placing caps on them, requiring that they not exceed some fixed ratio to compensatory awards, or requiring that some percentage of the punitive award be paid to the state. Other areas of change involved limitations on attorneys' fees, adoption of special legislation covering dram shop and social host liability for drunken driving, and requirements of periodic payments in large-award cases. These developments are discussed in Sanders and Joyce, "Off to the Races": The 1980s Tort Crisis and the Law Reform Process, 27 Houst.L.Rev. 207 (1990). For an examination of the dramatic impact of these measures on some injury victims, as well as the perceived benefits to liability bearers, in one state that enacted an array of tort limitations during this period, see Geyelin, Tort Reform Test: Overhaul of Civil Law In Colorado Produces Quite Mixed Results, Wall St.J., March 3, 1992 at 1.

Generalization is difficult because each state took its own distinctive approach to tort reform. Even when states began with the same agenda, legislative compromise often produced quite disparate results. The Washington legislature, for example, limited the amount recoverable for all non-monetary losses in personal injury cases by a formula keyed to the state's average wage and the victim's life expectancy. On the other hand, some states enacted flat caps on noneconomic damages, such as Maryland's $350,000.

New York adopted a comprehensive tort reform package that, among other things, altered the collateral source rule and provided for periodic payments. It also provided that most defendants who were held less than fifty percent at fault were liable to the plaintiff only for that percentage of the award for pain and suffering. California, by voter initiative, abolished all joint and several liability for noneconomic damages, p. 325, supra.

In the same period when these across-the-board limitations were being enacted, several states adopted measures to protect defendants in products liability cases. The most common move was adoption of a statute of repose—a statute that protected sellers whose products caused harm more than a certain number of years after they put the product into the stream of commerce. Some states adopted similar legislation for architects and builders. A typical length of time was ten or twelve years. This made it possible that the statute of repose would have run before the victim was hurt. See, e.g., Arsenault v. Pa–Ted Spring Co., 203 Conn. 156, 523 A.2d 1283 (1987)(claim involving 14–year–old product barred by 10–year statute of repose). A few states adopted "useful life" statutes in which the trier of fact must determine the average expected useful life of a generic product to determine if the injury in the case came from the normal aging of the product in question or from a "defect." See, Note, The Evolution of Useful Life Statutes in the Products Liability Reform Effort, 1989 Duke L.J. 1689. Note also that some states, including New Jersey, p. 549, supra, have legislated to make the "open and obvious" nature of a danger relevant in products cases.

Note that all of these reform efforts have been undertaken in state legislatures. The products area, however, raises unique problems in terms of the utility of seeking reform at the state level, as opposed to the federal level. It may well be that state courts developed and expanded tort liability doctrines in this area in part because they had little control over the common law's development and did not want their citizens to face barriers that citizens in other states did not face. The state focus has never been made clearer than in Blankenship v. General Motors Corp., 185 W.Va. 350, 406 S.E.2d 781 (W.Va.1991). In response to questions certified by a federal district court, the court announced that it would adopt the doctrine of crashworthiness in an appropriate case. Although the court stated its doubts about much of existing products law, it also observed that

> West Virginia is a small rural state with .66 percent of the population of the United States. Although some members of this Court have reservations about the wisdom of many aspects of tort law, as a court we are utterly powerless to make the *overall* tort system for cases arising in interstate commerce more rational: Nothing that we do will have any impact whatsoever on the set of economic trade-offs that occur in the *national* economy. And, ironically, trying unilaterally to make the American tort system more rational through being uniquely responsible in West Virginia will only punish our residents severely without, in any regard, improving the system for anyone else.

. . .

. . . In light of the fact that all of our sister states have adopted a cause of action for lack of crashworthiness, General Motors is *already* collecting a product liability premium every time it sells a car anywhere in the world, including West Virginia. [ ] West Virginians, then, are already paying the product liability insurance premium when they buy a General Motors car, so this Court would be both foolish and irresponsible if we held that while West Virginians must pay the premiums, West Virginians can't collect the insurance after they're injured.

The court announced further that if the federal courts were in doubt in any future crashworthiness case in which there was a real split of authority among the states, West Virginia would adopt the rule most favorable to plaintiffs.

How do you react to this position? Should a legislator in West Virginia react any differently if pressed to adopt legislation that would cut back on product liability rules that now favor plaintiffs?

After a brief hiatus, a third wave of tort reform activity arose in the early 1990s—once again featuring packages of reform targeted at some combinations of caps on non-economic loss and punitive damages, limitations on collateral source recovery, elimination of joint and several liability, and in some instances, restrictions on the contingency fee. In B. Franklin, Learning Curve: Lawyers Must Confront Impact of Changes on Litigation Strategies, 81 A.B.A.J. 62 (Aug. 1995), the author reports the following summary data on the cumulative status of incremental law reform efforts in the mid–1990s:

> While the American Tort Reform Association, a primary lobbying group, counts 18 states that impose caps on noneconomic damages, they do not apply the same ceilings or cover the same types of actions.
>
> Illinois, for example, caps noneconomic damages in all tort cases at $500,000, while adjacent Indiana caps noneconomic damages in medical malpractice cases at $750,000. In California, a $250,000 cap applies only to medical malpractice.
>
> Similar variations appear in caps on punitive damages in 29 states and product liability measures in 32 states, according to ATRA estimates.
>
> And, says ATRA, only Colorado, Florida, Montana, North Dakota and Oregon have acted in all five areas usually targeted by tort reform advocates: joint and several liability, product liability, punitive damages, noneconomic damages and the collateral source rule.
>
> Punitive damages are banned altogether in five states, and 21 have toughened standards for punitive damages, forcing plaintiff to show "clear and convincing" evidence of the defendant's conduct,

according to ATRA. In 41 states, plaintiffs must confront the elimination or modification of joint and several liability.

. . .

According to ATLA [another primary lobbying group, on the plaintiffs' side, the American Trial Lawyers' Association], 17 states regulate attorney fees in medical malpractice or other tort cases, either through sliding scales like those in California or by allowing judges to review for reasonableness.

The series of articles in this ABA Journal issue makes the overall point that for all the recent publicity given to expected federal tort reform action, it is the states—as these data indicate—in which sweeping measures have been adopted. In fact, for many sessions Congress has been pressed, without success, to adopt a products liability bill that would cut back on some benefits now held by plaintiffs in products cases. In 1995, riding on the wave of the campaign promises in the Contract with America, the House of Representatives passed a more comprehensive bill that would have capped punitive damages in all civil cases (and non-economic loss in medical malpractice cases), eliminated joint and several liability, and adopted a modified "loser pays" attorneys' fee rule in diversity cases brought in federal court. The Senate passed a more limited set of reforms targeted at punitive damages in products liability cases. After a year of debate behind the scenes, a conference committee agreed on a bill that was very close to the Senate version. Its future was unclear. Lewis, A Compromise on Restricting Liability Suits, N.Y.Times, March 14, 1996 at A11.

––––––––––

Have the incremental tort reform measures been effective in addressing the tort law "crisis"? Although no clear data exist for the 1980s, Patricia Danzon's research on the impact of the mid–1970s reforms in the medical malpractice area suggests some possible effects. Danzon analyzed data for the 1975–1984 period and concluded that damage caps, limits on the collateral source rule, and arbitration procedures had an appreciable effect on reducing the dollar amounts of tort claims and awards; shorter statutes of limitations, together with limits on the collateral source rule, had the greatest effect on reducing the frequency of tort claims. Danzon, The Frequency and Severity of Medical Malpractice Claims: New Evidence, 49 Law & Contemp.Probs. 57 (1986). See also Sloan, Mergenhagen & Bovbjerg, Effects of Tort Reforms on the Value of Closed Medical Malpractice Claims: A Microanalysis, 14 J. Health Politics, Policy and Law 663 (1989). For a comprehensive analysis of the empirical data on claims, award levels and costs in the tort system, concluding that we know very little about how the system in fact works, see Saks, Do We Really Know Anything about the Behavior of the Tort Litigation System—And Why Not?, 140 U.Pa.L.Rev. 1147 (1992).

Whatever the explanation, there seems to be a growing perception that the number of tort claims has levelled off in the past few years after a period of sustained growth. For statistical evidence, see the Department of Justice study, p. 719, supra. This perception correlates with claims that tort doctrine has become less expansive in the same period. This thesis is explored, with an attempt at explanation, in Schwartz, The Beginning and Possible End of the Rise of Modern American Tort Law, 26 Ga. L.Rev. 601 (1992). See also Henderson & Eisenberg, The Quiet Revolution in Products Liability Law: An Empirical Study of Legal Change, 37 UCLA L.Rev. 479 (1990), locating the onset of stabilization in the products area in the mid–1980s.

Reconsider the discussions throughout the course of pain and suffering, punitive damages, joint and several liability, the collateral source rule and the contingency fee. What kinds of limitations, if any, seem especially warranted? A concise treatment of the pros and cons of adopting limitations in each of these areas, as well as an agenda for incremental reform, can be found in the American Bar Association Report of the Action Commission to Improve the Tort System (1987). Do the various legislative reforms serve the overall goals and objectives of the tort system, such as deterring unsafe behavior and compensating accident victims? Do particular reforms advance certain goals while retarding others? Did the discussion of products liability, medical malpractice and other doctrinal topics earlier in the course suggest the need for reform of these substantive rules of liability? For a discussion of the relationship of the joint and several liability limitations and the noneconomic damages ceilings to the tort system's objectives, see Comment, 1986 Tort Reform Legislation: A Systematic Evaluation of Caps on Damages and Limitations on Joint and Several Liability, 73 Cornell L.Rev. 628 (1988).

An especially thorough discussion of the range of tort and insurance reforms considered by New York in the mid–1980s—most of which were adopted—is found in the two volume report of the Governor's Advisory Commission on Liability Insurance, Insuring Our Future (1986).

The constitutionality of many of these reform efforts, particularly the enactment of caps on damages, has often been challenged—in some cases successfully—on state constitutional grounds, including right to jury trial, right to receive damages, denial of equal protection, and right of access to courts. In Knowles v. United States, 1996 WL 37356 (S.D.1996), the court, answering certified questions from a federal court, held that the state's due process clause was violated by a statute that capped overall recovery in a medical malpractice action at $1 million. See State Reform of Tort Laws Proceeds During Calls for Federal Intervention, U.S.L.W., May 24, 1995, p. 8–9. For discussion of constitutional attacks on state legislative limits on punitive damages, most of which have been unsuccessful, see Hallahan, Social Interests versus Plaintiffs' Rights: The Constitutional Battle over Statutory Limitations on Punitive Damages, 26 Loy.U.Chi.L.J. 405 (1995).

B.   OCCUPATIONAL INJURIES—WORKERS' COMPENSATION

Occupational injuries emerged as a serious problem in this country after the Civil War. The rapid pace of industrialization brought a steadily increasing number of accidental injuries and deaths. Along with other accidental injury claims, workers' claims were handled in the tort system until the early years of the twentieth century. Within a decade, however, beginning in 1910, a majority of states enacted workers' compensation laws, replacing the tort remedy with a no-fault compensation scheme. The following excerpt describes these developments and discusses the basic features of the system.

Workers Compensation: Strengthening the Social Compact

Orin Kramer & Richard Briffault.
13–27, 73–75 (1991).

A.   Basic Terms: No–Fault and Exclusive Remedy

At the heart of workers' compensation is a basic quid pro quo: employers must provide employees who suffer work-related injuries or disease with medical and income benefits regardless of whether the employee or the employer was at fault for the injury; employees, in turn, must treat workers' compensation benefits as their exclusive remedy against the employer and give up any common law tort claims against their employers. This no-fault principle embodies two fundamental concerns.

First, it is argued that fault should not be relevant because, as a matter of social justice, business should bear the financial burden of work-related accidents, much like any other cost of production. As Theodore Roosevelt put it, "Exactly as the working man is entitled to his wages, so should he be entitled to indemnity for the injuries sustained in the natural course of his labor." Moreover, making business bear the costs of industrial accidents maximizes employer interest in occupational safety and health and thus reduces the frequency and severity of injury.

Second, no-fault provides greater efficiency. By eliminating fault and making workers' compensation the employee's exclusive remedy, compensation can be provided on a swift, certain and self-executing basis, at minimal administrative cost and without the expense, delays, uncertainties, and adversarial confrontation of attorney involvement and common law litigation. The recent upsurge in attorney involvement due to external pressures and changes in the system now jeopardizes the goal of a low administrative cost, litigation-free, self-executing mechanism.

B.   Origins: Meeting the Challenge of the Industrial Revolution and Overcoming the Restrictions of the Common Law

The Industrial Revolution was accompanied by an enormous upsurge in work–related accidents. The rapid expansion and development of manufacturing, mining, steel mills, and railroads, the deployment of dangerous heavy machinery and high-speed industrial processes, and the employment of large numbers of new, relatively unskilled workers all resulted in unprecedented levels of workplace injuries.

1. The "Unholy Trinity" of Employer Common Law Defenses

Under common law, the employer had a duty to provide a reasonably safe place in which to work and reasonably safe tools, appliances, and working materials. Therefore, in theory the employee who sustained a work-related injury, or his survivors, could bring a tort action for damages against the employer if the injury reflected a breach of the employer's duty of reasonable care. In practice, however, 19th century employers were largely immunized from liability for industrial accidents by three other common law doctrines.

First, under the "fellow servant" rule, an employee could not recover damages from the employer if another employee had contributed to the injury. Since in the large factories, mines and mills of an industrial economy the employer almost inevitably acts through other employees, the fellow servant rule was a nearly insuperable barrier to recovery.

Employers former defenses

Second, under the principle of "contributory negligence," the injured employee could not recover damages if he had in any way negligently contributed to his own injury.

Third, under the doctrine of "assumption of risk," employees were held to have assumed the risk of injury from the customary and observable dangers attendant upon their jobs.

Reformers, concerned about the plight of injured workers and their families, sought to overcome the harsh effects of this "unholy trinity" of employer common law defenses, and around the turn of the century courts and legislatures in several states modified or abandoned one or more of these three rules. However, this liberalization of the common law was of limited benefit to most injured workers since it still left in place the need to prove fault, and that often proved to be as high a hurdle to vault as the "unholy trinity" of defenses.

2. The Burden of Fault

Under the fault system, an employee, or his survivors, needed to hire a lawyer, persuade fellow workers to testify against their employer, and attempt to survive without wages or money for medical bills until the litigation was resolved. Moreover, for many accidents it was difficult to prove that the employer had violated an established standard of care. As a result, although in some cases employees won generous awards, including damages for pain and suffering, in most cases they received little or nothing. One early 20th century study of workers killed on the job found that in 37% of the cases the families of the victims received no compensation, and that in another 42% of the cases the families received less than $500, or well under the average annual salary of $791.

Fault-based litigation, even without the "unholy trinity," was a costly and uncertain gamble for most workers. Employers, too, were troubled by rising levels of litigation and the prospect of serious damages in the few but increasing number of cases in which workers prevailed.

3.   The Adoption of Workers' Compensation

Workers' compensation was pioneered in Germany in the late 19th century. The first American workers' compensation measure was a federal statute adopted in 1908 that provided a limited program for federal workers and served as a forerunner of the current Federal Employees Compensation Act. In 1910, New York enacted the first state workers' compensation program, but the New York Court of Appeals found that the imposition of liability without fault was unconstitutional and invalidated the statute. The first effective state workers' compensation law was passed in Wisconsin in 1911. To avoid the constitutional issue, the state made workers' compensation elective. As an incentive to employer participation, the legislature provided for the waiver of the "unholy trinity" defenses for employers not participating in the program.

The Wisconsin model of "elective" workers' compensation was sustained in the courts and spread rapidly to other states. By the end of 1911, 10 states had adopted workers' compensation, and by 1917 it was on the books in 37 states. Since the enactment of legislation by Mississippi in 1949, there has been a workers' compensation program in every state.

By eliminating the requirement of proof of fault, workers' compensation laws enormously simplified the process of providing medical and disability compensation for injured workers. Employees no longer need plead and prove through costly litigation a standard of reasonable care for the operations of the workplace or of industrial equipment, or establish by a preponderance of the evidence that their employers had violated such a standard. The elimination of fault also removes the element of opprobrium from the employer as the duty to compensate is not based on misconduct but treated as a cost of production. Finally, the no-fault system was intended to eliminate the adversarial atmosphere that surrounds litigation and thus improve the quality of employer-employee relations.

C.   Evolution: The Expansion of Coverage, the Redefinition of Compensable Injury, and the Enhancement of Benefits

Although most states have had workers' compensation programs for more than 70 years, the system has undergone considerable change, particularly in recent decades. State legislatures have repeatedly amended their laws, modifying programs, and experimenting with new provisions. State courts have also played an important role in interpreting and often liberalizing the effects of state laws.

1.   The Pace and Direction of Change

The general direction of state legislatures and courts has been expansion: the inclusion of more workers and workplaces, the liberalization of the definition of compensable injury, the addition of new benefits, and the enhancement of existing benefits. The pace of change accelerated markedly following the publication of the Report of the National Commission on State Workmen's Compensation Laws in 1972 and the increased attention in the 1970s and early 1980s to the problems of occupational disease. Nor has the rate of change slackened significantly since the 1970s. Between 1982 and 1987, there were approximately 900 amendments to state workers' compensation laws, and an additional 155 changes were made in 1988 alone.

Many of these changes have advanced the societal goal of fair and adequate compensation for injured workers. But these changes have also added markedly to the costs of workers' compensation systems. In most states, the current workers' compensation system is, by design, more generous and thus considerably more costly than workers' compensation was in 1911 or 1972.

The expansion of workers' compensation coverage and the enhancement of benefits must be taken into account in assessing the costs of the system and the proper levels of premium for workers' compensation insurance. Indeed, a significant component of the current problems besetting workers' compensation is the failure of the regulatory system in some jurisdictions to respond to the real costs of an expanded compensation system.

2. Expansion of Coverage of Workers and Employers

Initially, workers' compensation was limited to large firms, firms engaged in "hazardous" or "ultra-hazardous" activities, and to limited categories of workers. Moreover, long after the constitutionality of no-fault had been revisited and sustained by most state courts, many states continued to make workers' compensation elective. In 1950, 77% of American workers were covered by workers' compensation laws. As late as 1968, 24 states had significant size-of-firm restrictions, and 23 states still permitted elective coverage.

Among the "essential recommendations" of the National Commission on State Workmen's Compensation Laws was universal workers' compensation coverage. The Commission called for the elimination of "elective" coverage, of the exemption of small employers, of the exemption of any class of employees, and for the extension of coverage to traditionally non-covered workers such as agricultural workers, household workers and government employees.

Although there has not been total state compliance with the National Commission's recommendations, and many states continue to exempt certain categories of workers and employees, the percentage of the work force covered by workers' compensation has grown to 87%. Only three states continue to make the program elective for covered workers. In only four states are fewer than 75% of employees under workers' compensation. In 23 states, more than 90% of all employees are covered by workers' compensation, and in four states and the District of Columbia coverage is universal.

3. Expansion of the Definition of Compensable Injury

a. The Concept of Work–Relatedness

Workers' compensation did not and does not make the employer absolutely responsible for employee health care and disabilities. (For a description of the structure of workers' compensation benefits, see Appendix.) The employer's duty extends only to work-related injuries: injuries which, according to the language of virtually every state law, "arise out of and in the course of employment." In other words, although workers' compensation eliminates the requirement of employer fault, it continues to require proof of *work-related cause.*

i. The Model of the Traumatic Accident

When workers' compensation was first adopted, it did not seem that proof of work-related causation would entail anything like the complexities and ambiguities implicit in fault-based compensation. The prevalent cause of work-related injury was the traumatic accident: a sudden, unexpected event which resulted in immediate injury. Since the place and physical cause of most injuries are readily apparent, it was assumed that employers and administrators could easily distinguish between work-related and non-work-related accidents, without resort to protracted dispute resolution processes, litigation or attorneys. And for the overwhelming majority of claims, that remains the case.

ii. Traditional Gray Areas

There were, of course, always gray areas in determining the work-relatedness of even simple traumatic accidents. Injuries occurring on the employer's premises but outside the production process, such as during coffee breaks or lunch time; injuries involving employee violation of work rules or willful misconduct; and injuries occurring during commutation or off-premises have been a regular source of dispute. But these are a tiny fraction of compensation claims, and in most states these issues have been resolved by court decision or statutory amendment.

iii. Soft Tissue Injuries and Aggravation of Existing Conditions

More numerically significant and more conceptually difficult than the traditional gray areas are soft tissue injuries that result from repeated activity, such as straining, bending, twisting or lifting, over a period of time. In these instances, it is more difficult to determine when the injury has occurred and whether the injury is the result of on-the-job or off-the-job activity. By one count, in 1988 approximately 48% of workplace injuries were the result of repetitive motion.

In aggravation of existing conditions cases, the injury may have occurred on the job, but its severity in terms of medical bills and time lost from work may be a result of a prior injury, unusual personal susceptibility or environmental factors unrelated to work. In this case the employer may seek to limit its liability to the work-related component of the injury. Today in many states the employer is responsible for the full extent of work-related injury, consistent with the well-established doctrine that the employer "takes the employee as he finds him."

Although soft tissue injuries and aggravation of existing conditions claims have added significant new costs to workers' compensation coverage, the real challenge to the work-relatedness requirement and to the system's ability to resolve the causation question without resort to extensive administrative or litigated proceedings has been occupational disease.

b.   The Challenge of Occupational Disease

i.   Initial Limitations on Coverage

Some occupational diseases do not fit within the national model of traumatic accidents. The onset of illness may not occur at the workplace or during the course of employment. Often illness will not result until years after exposure to the causative agent. The manifestations of occupational disease may not be distinctive and may be difficult to distinguish from those of non-occupational ailments or the aging process. The causation of disease may be complex and may involve the interaction of work, heredity, environment, personal lifestyle and other factors.

Most early workers' compensation laws did not provide compensation for disease or only provided coverage for specified, or "scheduled" diseases, like "black lung," silicosis or byssinosis ("brown lung"). These diseases were uniquely occupation-related in the sense that while many workers in an occupation eventually contracted the illness, few people not employed in that occupation ever suffered from the disease.

Moreover, recovery for occupational disease in some states was limited by procedural requirements. Statutes of limitations that ran from the time of last exposure to the disease-causing agent effectively blocked recovery in cases of long latency illnesses. Minimum exposure rules and recency of exposure requirements which had no scientific basis also restricted the availability of coverage, as did statutory provisions affecting the responsibilities of particular employers where the worker was exposed to the disease-causing hazard during a succession of jobs in an industry.

ii.   The Expansion of Coverage

In recent decades, the situation has changed dramatically. In the wake of liberalizing court decisions and the recommendation of the National Commission on State Workmen's Compensation Laws, all 50 states now provide workers' compensation for any work-caused illness. Moreover, many states have relaxed their procedural restrictions, for example, by starting statute of limitations requirements from the onset of the first manifestation of illness rather than from the last exposure to the causative agent. This makes it far easier for workers suffering from diseases with long latency periods to bring claims.

The workers' compensation system is now caught in a vise. On the one hand, expanding scientific and medical knowledge has suggested associations between certain workplace materials, conditions and processes and an increased risk of contracting many ordinary diseases, such as cancer, heart disease, lung diseases, dermatitis, hypertension, and degenerative diseases such as arthritis. Given the complex causation of these diseases, whether the risk actually results in illness may often turn on non-work-related factors.

On the other hand, state workers' compensation laws, although they have abandoned the "scheduled disease" approach, still continue to require that, to be compensable, a disease must result from factors "peculiar to the trade or occupation" and not be an "ordinary disease of life."

The result has been increased litigation over causation and the existence and scope of coverage in the area of occupational disease. In these cases, both claimants and employers or insurers make complex medical and legal arguments. These cases are marked by the claims of conflicting experts, the so-called "dueling doctors," with considerable litigation costs and uncertainty of outcome for all parties.

The overall trend has been to relax the claimant's burden of proof and permit recovery even where work-related factors are a contributing but not the sole cause of disease. In some cases, liability has been found even where work-related contributing causation was only "reasonably probable" in light of current medical knowledge. This means that the employer will have to pay the full costs of an illness which is at best only partially work-related.

It is critical to recognize that occupational diseases today represent only a modest cost in the workers' compensation system. In most states, only about 2% of claims involve work-related illness, and the majority of those claims involve conditions that can be handled easily by the system. However, these claims have a disproportionate impact on total workers' compensation costs. The special issues with respect to the proof of causation drive up administrative costs, while the average indemnity benefit for occupational disease is five times greater than for traumatic injuries.

Moreover, today's claims may be only the leading edge of future occupational disease filings. Scientific knowledge continues to expand our understanding of the relationship between work conditions and health and to provide new bases for claims for compensation. Most significantly, several observers have noted that "a new type of claim is on the horizon," one that portends steeply increased administrative and compensation burdens for the workers' compensation system in future years: mental stress.

iii. The Special Case of Mental Stress

Over the last decade, the number of mental stress claims has exploded, rising from virtually zero to more than 10% of all occupational disease claims. In California, the number of mental stress claims rose 511% from 1980 to 1987. Mental stress now accounts for approximately 25% of all occupational disease claims in California making it the leading source of occupational disease claims in the nation's largest state.

The earliest workers' compensation claims for mental injury grew out of cases based on some physical event, either a traumatic physical accident which resulted in subsequent psychiatric harm, or acute mental stress which led to a physical injury such as a heart attack. These "physical-mental" and "mental-physical" cases have been largely supplanted in notoriety by the so-called "mental-mental" cases in which a highly subjective mental or emotional injury results from a mental or emotional cause, without any physical accident or impairment.

Mental stress claims incorporate all the causation difficulties of some occupational disease claims, but taken to an extreme degree. Most mental stress claims have no single precipitating cause. A study of mental stress claims in California found that 90% are the result of cumulative events.

Few mental stress claims stem from conditions peculiar or unique to particular workplaces or occupations. Rather, a California study found that most such claims are due to non-specific "job pressures" or "harassment," features "pandemic to workplaces." Many mental stress claims involve the aggravation of pre-existing conditions and the interaction of workplace and non-workplace factors.

Mental stress claims are highly subjective, difficult to diagnose, assess, quantify or disprove. Medical knowledge with respect to the cause and treatment of mental stress is imprecise. Standards for determining when a mental or emotional problem rises to the level of illness are uncertain. And there is no uniform or agreed upon definition of what constitutes a compensable psychiatric injury.

The lack of determinate standards and the absence of physical symptoms make the resolution of mental stress claims particularly contentious. Employers and insurers are often skeptical of mental stress claims: a California Workers Compensation Institute study found that "antagonism and suspicion characterize claims management in mental stress cases." The subjectivity of the asserted injury makes mental stress claims especially litigable. In California 99% of mental stress cases are litigated.

Although nationwide there are still relatively few mental stress claims, this may only be the tip of the iceberg. The potential for claims growth is enormous. Virtually every employee is subject to some level of stress. The National Institute of Mental Health estimates that one person in five suffers from some psychiatric disorder. All told, 75% of corporate medical directors consider stress to be fairly pervasive.

A series of forces has contributed and will continue to contribute to the growth of workplace stress. The pace of work is accelerating and job security declining in a more competitive economic environment. Many employees have unfulfilled expectations about work and the quality of life. There has been an expansion of service sector jobs such as secretarial and office-manager, which some have suggested to be particularly stressful.

Social mores have changed so that acknowledgement of mental and emotional illness has become more acceptable, and the acceptance of psychiatric treatment has lost much of its former stigma. The broad and unlimited medical coverage under most state workers' compensation statutes, compared to the more limited coverage of psychiatric treatment under many private health plans, makes workers' compensation a particularly attractive target for mental stress claims.

Moreover, the rapid growth of mental stress claims has occurred despite the fact that in only eight states have appellate courts adopted an expansive definition of compensable mental stress claims. That broader definition provides coverage for stress that constitutes only a gradual increase over ordinary workplace stress and is not unusual in nature or degree. Courts in 21 other states permit compensation only if the mental stress is attributable to a sudden or frightening event, or if stress levels are in excess of ordinary employment conditions. Seven state appellate courts have ruled that "mental-mental" claims are not compensable, while courts in 14 states and the District of Columbia have yet to establish a legal standard for "mental-mental" claims. If more state courts adopt the expansive approach, the number of mental stress claims could soar.

On the other hand, several states have taken steps recently to adopt more objective standards and require that compensable stress derive from unusual workplace conditions. As of this year, Colorado will limit coverage to stress resulting from traumatic or extraordinary events. California's recent reforms require that mental stress claims be based on actual events and exclude compensability for injuries resulting from personnel actions of the employer. Oregon has required "clear and convincing evidence" to establish mental stress claims. But whether these measures are sufficient to check the potential magnitude of mental stress exposure remains to be seen.

4. The Expansion of Benefits

Workers' compensation provides medical benefits, indemnity benefits that compensate for lost wages during the period of recuperation and for permanent disability, and death benefits to the families of occupational injury victims. In the last two decades the levels of indemnity benefits have been very significantly enhanced. Moreover, a new benefit, mandatory vocational rehabilitation, is now provided in most states. Together, the enhancement in benefit levels and the addition of a new benefit have increased costs and contributed to the strains besetting the system.

a. The Enhancement of Benefit Levels

Indemnity benefits replace some specified percentage of lost wages, subject to a statutory ceiling on amount. Initially, benefits were relatively low, since the purpose of workers' compensation in its early years was, in part, not to make up for lost wages but to "prevent hardship." In 1920, only 20 states replaced as much as 60% of lost wages. By the 1960s, about two-thirds of the states had adopted the goal of replacing two-thirds of the injured worker's lost gross wages, but low statutory ceilings held down the amounts actually paid. In 46 states the benefit levels lagged so far below wage levels that a disabled worker earning the state average weekly wage could not receive a benefit that would produce the legislated wage replacement rate. Inevitably, there was a widespread sense that benefit levels were inadequate and that fair treatment of injured employees required a substantial increase in benefits.

i. The Modernization of Benefit Levels

The 1972 Report of the National Commission on State Workmen's Compensation Laws precipitated a major modernization of benefit levels. The Report called on the states to adopt the goal of replacing two-thirds of pre-injury gross pay (or 80% of net wages) and to raise the statutory maximum to no lower than the state average weekly wage. Workers' compensation benefits are exempt from federal income taxation. Two-thirds of gross, or 80% of net, is designed to replace lost wages while maintaining a proper incentive to return to work. All states responded at least in part to the Report's recommendations. Currently, 48 states and the District of Columbia provide for replacement of two-thirds or more of gross wages, or 80% of net wages. In 31 states the statutory maximum for *temporary* disability is at or above the state average weekly wage, while in 29 states the statute maximum for *permanent* disability is at or above the state average weekly wage.

ii. Continuing Increases

Approximately 40 states fix the statutory maximum in terms of the state average weekly wage itself, rather than as a specified dollar amount, so that benefit levels track inflation-driven wage increases. As a result of automatic adjustments and statutory amendments, benefit levels rose in 43 states and the District of Columbia in 1988 and in 42 states in 1989.

iii. Benefit Levels and Benefit Utilization

Increasing benefit levels has two effects on workers' compensation claim costs. First, benefit increases directly raise costs when injured workers file for compensation. Second, benefit increases create incentives for greater utilization: More claims will be filed, and workers may stay out of work longer, thus extending the duration of the benefits period. Studies have found that a 20% increase in indemnity benefits is associated with a 7% increase in indemnity benefit filings and a 24% increase in the duration of indemnity claims. The impact on benefits utilization is particularly significant for less serious claims. In short, a 10% increase in benefit levels is associated with a 5% increase in utilization on top of the benefit increase, so that a 10% increase in benefits will raise aggregate payments by 15%. Most of that increased utilization is due to increased claim frequency, but some is attributable to increases in the duration of disability.

The enhancement of benefit levels in recent years has had a significant impact on the percentage of payroll devoted to workers' compensation and to mounting concerns among employers regarding the system's cost. For many years, workers' compensation amounted to an average of well under 1% of payroll, and there was little annual growth. In 1946 benefits were 0.54% of payroll, in 1960 they were 0.59% of payroll, and as late as 1972 they were still only 0.68%. But over the next decade and a half the percentage of payroll devoted to workers' compensation benefits doubled, to

1.39% in 1986.   Today total average compensation costs are closer to 2% of payroll.   And there is no sign that benefit growth is abating.

. . .

b.   Vocational Rehabilitation: Growth of a New Benefit

Another area of change in the workers' compensation social contract has been vocational rehabilitation.   Most state workers' compensation programs now make some provision for the costs of vocational rehabilitation services for eligible employees, although there is an enormous variance in the quality, extent and utilization of rehabilitation programs.   Several states, including California and Florida, make vocational rehabilitation mandatory.   In these states, rehabilitation has become a substantial and rising component of claim costs.

Vocational rehabilitation consists of the provision of services which attempt to maximize the ability of an injured worker to compete in the labor market.   Rehabilitation is of great potential benefit to both employees and employers.   It can serve to complete the employee's economic and psychological recovery from a disabling accident and improve employee morale, while mitigating the disability expenses attributable to injury and reducing the costs of hiring and training new workers to replace skilled but injured employees.

But vocational services can be quite expensive.   Indeed, both utilization and claim costs have soared in the states with mandatory vocational rehabilitation, far outpacing increases in indemnity claims and costs generally.   In California, the number of cases involving vocational rehabilitation rose from 5,236 in 1978 to 32,579 in 1987, a 440% increase.   And vocational rehabilitation claims have risen at an even faster pace than utilization, with total claim costs escalating 775% in the same period.   By contrast, over the same period personal disability claims rose only 33%, and personal disability claim costs 180%.   When California first adopted mandatory rehabilitation in 1975, it was estimated that vocational rehabilitation would account for 2.7% of claim costs.   Today vocational rehabilitation accounts for 13% of every benefit dollar.   In Florida, 18% of all lost-time cases involve rehabilitation.

. . .

APPENDIX: WORKERS' COMPENSATION BENEFITS PROVIDED

Medical Benefits

In all U.S. jurisdictions, except for the Virgin Islands, there are no limits on medical coverage for conditions resulting from occupational disease or job-related injury.   Medical coverage includes costs for physicians, hospitals, nursing service, physical therapy, dentists, chiropractors, and prosthetic devices.

Permanent Total Disability

Permanent total disability benefits are provided for those claimants whose job-related injury or occupational disease has rendered them permanently unable to engage in substantially remunerative employment. As in temporary total disability cases, claimants usually receive a wage-substitute benefit of 66 2/3% of their full or average weekly wage up to a statutory maximum rate. Permanent total disability claimants, however, are paid for a lifetime in most states and have higher total dollar amounts than temporary total disability claimants. Permanent total disability benefits continue until the claimant returns to substantially remunerative employment, dies, or exhausts the maximum dollar or time amount set by statute. For some statutorily defined severe injuries, such as total blindness, claimants are entitled to continued benefits in some states even if they successfully attain employment after being declared permanently and totally disabled.

Temporary Total Disability

Temporary inability to return to former employment constitutes a condition of temporary total disability, the most commonly awarded disability compensation. Claimants usually receive a wage-substitute benefit of 66 2/3% of the worker's pre-injury wage up to a statutory maximum rate. Temporary total disability payment often requires a waiting period of a few days to a few weeks before payment begins.

Waiting Period

Statutes provide that a waiting period must elapse during which income benefits are not available. The waiting period affects compensation only, since medical and hospital care are provided immediately. For most states the period is either three or seven days, while the remainder fall somewhere in between. If a worker's disability continues, most states provide for payment retroactive to the date of the injury. The retroactive period varies by state from five days to six weeks, with the norm being two to three weeks.

Temporary and Permanent Partial Disability

Partial disability compensation is payable to claimants who have suffered a negative effect on their earnings, earning capacity, or employability due to a job-related injury but are still able to engage in some remunerative employment. Some states calculate payment for earning capacity loss in the same manner as they calculate actual earnings losses, disregarding considerations of future earning capacity.

Vocational Rehabilitation

Vocational rehabilitation is designed to return injured workers to the labor market as rapidly as possible. All but two states (Indiana and South Carolina) have incorporated rehabilitation into their workers' compensation systems. The rehabilitation benefit usually provides an allowance for maintenance—board, lodging and travel, or as much as weekly compensation equivalent to temporary total disability—and payment for physical and vocational rehabilitation. Time limits of six-months to two years accompany the benefits. In some states continued payment of compensation is contingent upon a claimant attempting rehabilitation, while in others claimants are referred for rehabilitation review to determine whether they would be helped by rehabilitation. Compensation is payable until the claimant can return to remunerative employment or until it is determined that the injured worker failed to cooperate with vocational rehabilitation.

Medical Impairment—Permanent Partial Disability

Permanent partial disability awards are provided to give an injured worker an incentive to return to work, or simply to provide a cash award. Non-scheduled awards, or those not fixed by a statute, can be based strictly on medical impairment or the medical impairment's effect upon that individual's earning capacity.

Scheduled awards compensate injured workers through statutorily designated awards for injury. Schedules typically include payments for loss of arm, hand, leg, foot, eye, hearing in one or both ears, toes, and digits of the hand. Massachusetts only schedules benefits for the first six categories, and Georgia, Minnesota, and Nevada have no schedules at all.

Survivor Benefits

Weekly compensation benefits and burial allowances are paid to surviving dependents of workers killed in the course of employment or through occupational disease. Benefits are usually equivalent to 66⅔% of the deceased worker's average weekly wage. About one-third of the states provide a limit on the total death award, and most states end death benefits to a surviving spouse upon remarriage. Surviving children lose benefits when they reach majority, or, if they are full-time students, at age 21, 23, or 25.

NOTES AND QUESTIONS

1. As the excerpt indicates, the first compulsory coverage plan adopted in the United States, enacted by New York early in this century, succumbed to constitutional attack in Ives v. South Buffalo Ry. Co., 201 N.Y. 271, 94 N.E. 431 (1911). After reviewing the possible reasons for the legislature's enactment of the law, the court concluded that the scheme violated the due process clauses of both the state and federal constitutions. The following excerpt from the opinion reflects its tone:

> If the argument in support of this statute is sound we do not see why it cannot logically be carried much further. Poverty and misfortune from every cause are detrimental to the state. It would probably conduce to the welfare of all concerned if there could be a more equal distribution of wealth. Many persons have much more property than they can use to advantage and many more find it impossible to get the means for a comfortable existence. If the legislature can say to an employer, "you must compensate your employee for an injury not caused by you or by your fault," why can it not go further and say to the man of wealth, "you have more property than you need and your

neighbor is so poor that he can barely subsist; in the interest of natural justice you must divide with your neighbor so that he and his dependents shall not become a charge upon the State?" The argument that the risk to an employee should be borne by the employer because it is inherent in the employment, may be economically sound, but it is at war with the legal principle that no employer can be compelled to assume a risk which is inseparable from the work of the employee, and which may exist in spite of a degree of care by the employer far greater than may be exacted by the most drastic law. If it is competent to impose upon an employer, who has omitted no legal duty and has committed no wrong, a liability based solely upon a legislative fiat that his business is inherently dangerous, it is equally competent to visit upon him a special tax for the support of hospitals and other charitable institutions, upon the theory that they are devoted largely to the alleviation of ills primarily due to his business. In its final and simple analysis that is taking the property of A and giving it to B, and that cannot be done under our Constitutions.

New York promptly amended its state constitution to authorize the legislature to adopt a compensation system, and the Supreme Court held that a compulsory compensation system, at least as applied to "hazardous employment," did not violate the federal constitution. New York Central R. Co. v. White, 243 U.S. 188 (1917). The most common reaction to the threat of judicial invalidation was to avoid the compulsory compensation approach and to allow employers to choose whether to participate in the system, but, as noted in the excerpt, to stack the tort rules against employers who opted against compensation.

2. Insurance arrangements under workers' compensation are summarized in Enterprise Responsibility for Personal Injury, Vol. I, The Institutional Framework, Report to the American Law Institute (1991) at 121:

> Rather than simply establish substantive rights and liabilities regarding workplace injuries, workers' compensation laws always require as well that funds be available to satisfy fully all potential claims that might be brought. Larger firms that can demonstrate the capacity to do so are permitted to self-insure (only about 1 percent of firms do so, but their companies comprise nearly 20 percent of payroll coverage). All other employers must purchase WC insurance through private carriers (about 60 percent of coverage) or state funds (about 29 percent).

3. In 1991, workers' compensation covered about 87% of all wage and salary workers, though the percentage varied widely between industrial and agricultural states. 56 Social Security Bulletin,, Fall 1993 at 68. In 1993, the level of disbursements totaled $42.9 billion. About 59% of the amount was in the form of cash compensation to disabled workers or their survivors. The remainder was the value of medical care provided to workers. The premiums paid to insurers or into self-insurance funds in 1993 totaled almost $57.3 billion. 58 Social Security Bulletin, Summer 1995, at 51–52.

4. The amount levied against each employer varies with the risks involved in the particular employment and is measured in terms of a percentage of the employer's payroll. In hazardous industries the rate may be 25%, but if clerical or office positions make up the bulk of an industry's payroll, the basic rates may be well below 1% of payroll. As the excerpt indicates, the overall national average in recent years has been about two percent. These basic rates may be altered for large employers on the basis of safety inspections or past safety experience. For a study of the injury prevention effects of workers' compensation, see M. Moore & W.K. Viscusi, Compensation Mechanisms for Job Risks: Wages, Workers' Compensation, and Product Liability (1990), concluding that the system has a substantial impact on job safety—reducing workplace fatalities alone by about 25% from the expected level without the system in effect.

5. The problems of "arising out of" and "in the course of" the employment continue to cause occasional difficulty, as this sample of cases suggests.

a. In Capizzi v. Southern Dist. Reporters, Inc., 61 N.Y.2d 50, 459 N.E.2d 847, 471 N.Y.S.2d 554 (1984), plaintiff was on a business trip when she slipped and fell in the bathtub of her motel room. The court held that her injuries were compensable because she "was required to work and stay at a place distant from home, placed in a new environment thereby creating a greater risk of injury, and was engaged in a reasonable activity . . . attendant to, although not directly related to her employment duties . . . ."

b. In Lubrano v. Malinet, 65 N.Y.2d 616, 480 N.E.2d 737, 491 N.Y.S.2d 148 (1985), claimant was a 16–year–old gas station attendant. One day, during an idle period, he tried to repeat a lighted match trick that a co-worker had shown him two days before. When he tossed the lighted match into a bucket containing a residue of oil, gasoline, and grease, the bucket exploded, burning him extensively. The court upheld an award:

> Injuries or deaths arising from employee horseplay are compensable under the Workers' Compensation Law if they result from conduct which "may reasonably be regarded as an incident of the employment" [ ]. These commonly known risks of employment occur when employees momentarily abandon work to play, tease, test one another or satisfy their curiosity [ ]. Here, in light of claimant's youth [ ], and the fact that the injury occurred during an idle period and resulted from curiosity about materials related to his work [ ], the Board was warranted in concluding that the incident which caused claimant's injuries was related to his employment. Furthermore, because there was testimony that at least two other workers at the station had previously engaged in the same conduct, the Board's determination that it was cumulative horseplay, and not an isolated incident is supported by substantial evidence.

c. In Richardson v. Fiedler Roofing, Inc., 67 N.Y.2d 246, 493 N.E.2d 228, 502 N.Y.S.2d 125 (1986), the employee, a roofer, while waiting on a roof with no assigned work to do, moved to another part of the roof and removed some copper downspouts to sell as salvage. In the process, he slipped on a patch of ice and fell seven stories to his death. The court, 5–2, affirmed the Board's decision that his death was compensable even though he was engaged in theft at the time of the accident:

> The Board found from the evidence in this case that it was common practice in the industry for roofers to remove copper downspouts and sell them for scrap. It further found that this employer not only knew of the practice but also frequently had been required to pay for or replace downspouts stolen by its employees. Despite this experience, the employer had never disciplined or discharged an employee for these thefts, and after it learned that decedent and his co-worker had been stealing downspouts on the day of the accident, it did not discipline or discharge the co-employee. Accordingly, the Board found that decedent's activities while waiting for necessary work materials to arrive did not constitute a deviation from, or an abandonment of, his employment and that the death arose out of and in the course of decedent's employment. These findings are supported by substantial evidence and thus are conclusive on the court [   ].

d. In Rosen v. First Manhattan Bank, 84 N.Y.2d 856, 641 N.E.2d 1073, 617 N.Y.S.2d 455 (1994), the court upheld a claim as "rooted in events started at or about the premises of the employer," where the claimant was killed in an assault by a co-worker that began with an argument in the lobby of the building and concluded in the stairwell one floor above the employer's premises.

e. A recurring problem arises where an employee is injured while participating in a lunch-time or after-work sports league with other employees. Is this an injury arising out of the course of employment? As suggested by a series of appellate court decisions in California, the answer turns on the employer's degree of involvement with the team, and whether the employee could reasonably believe that participation was a requirement of her employment.

For example, in Ezzy v. W.C.A.B., 146 Cal.App.3d 252, 194 Cal.Rptr. 90 (1983), a second-year law student was injured while playing on the softball team for the law firm for which she was clerking. The employer's insurer denied coverage, claiming the injury did not arise out of the course of employment. The Board agreed, but the Court of Appeal reversed on grounds that one of the firm's partners, a rabid member of the team, had continually reminded the student about upcoming games and urged that she play so the co-ed team would have the required number of females for the game. In addition, the law firm sponsored the team, bought everyone in the firm team jerseys emblazoned with their billing number, screened movies of recent games in the employee lounge, and held a post-season awards banquet for all employees. The court held that, to qualify for benefits in such a case, the injured employee must subjectively believe that her participation in the sporting event was required by her employer, and there must be an objectively reasonable basis for that belief. "The burden rests upon an employer to insure that no subtle or indirect pressure or coercion is applied to induce involuntary participation by an employee." According to the court, the law student met these tests because, as a summer clerk, she was "more than usually vulnerable to pressure or suggestion that she join the law firm's softball team."

For a good survey and analysis of cases in this field, see Smith v. W.C.A.B., 191 Cal.App.3d 127, 236 Cal.Rptr. 248 (1987), (awarding death benefits to widow of math teacher killed while attempting to use a Windsurfer at a school picnic).

6. *Going and Coming.* Suppose an employee is injured on the way to or from work. When is the injury arising out of and in the course of the employment? Compare the following illustrative cases.

a. In Price v. W.C.A.B., 37 Cal.3d 559, 693 P.2d 254, 209 Cal.Rptr. 674 (1984), a worker's injuries were held within the scope of the statute when he arrived early at his place of employment and was hit by a car while waiting for the premises to be unlocked. The going and coming rule which would have barred compensation did not apply because the worker had finished his local commute at the time of the injury. And even though he was pouring oil into his car when he was injured, this personal act was within the course of employment under the "dual purpose rule." Under that rule, where an employee is mixing his own business with his employer's, " 'no nice inquiry will be made as to which business he was actually engaged in at the time of injury, unless it clearly appears that neither directly nor indirectly could he be serving his employer.' [   ]." Here, the employee was "serving the interests of his employer by waiting near the premises to begin work early."

b. In Santa Rosa Junior College v. W.C.A.B., 40 Cal.3d 345, 708 P.2d 673, 220 Cal.Rptr. 94 (1985), a teacher was taking work home from campus when he was killed in a car accident. If he had been required by his employer to work at home, his home would have been considered a second jobsite and injuries sustained in traveling from one jobsite to the other would have been within the scope of the statute. Here, the decision to work at home was voluntary and the teacher's death was not compensable.

c. In Neacosia v. New York Power Authority, 85 N.Y.2d 471, 649 N.E.2d 1188, 626 N.Y.S.2d 44 (1995), the claimant was involved in an auto accident while heading home after dropping off his work uniforms at a dry cleaning establishment. The court held that the determination of the workers' compensation board that the injuries were compensable was entitled to "wide latitude," and that the worker had been pursuing one of many options for complying with the employer's requirement of clean uniforms.

7. *Smoking-related claims.* In Johannesen v. New York City Dept. of Housing Preservation and Development, 84 N.Y.2d 129, 638 N.E.2d 981, 615 N.Y.S.2d 336 (1994), the employee claimed serious aggravation of her bronchial condition by exposure to heavy smoking by co-workers. The claim was upheld as a form of occupational disease compensable under the act.

8. Closely related to the "scope" question is a series of state defenses excluding workers who are injured while engaging in "willful misconduct." These are usually limited to deliberate exposure to danger and are construed narrowly to exclude instinctive behavior and bad judgment. Some violations of work rules are analyzed under this exclusion. Even if violation of such a rule falls short of being willful misconduct, it may bring disqualification under another statutory defense—unreasonable failure to observe safety rules or to use safety devices. This defense exists in almost half of the states. In some, violation will bar all compensation recovery; in others it will reduce compensation by 10 or 15%. Larson, 1A Law of Workmen's Compensation §§ 32.00–33.40 (1995 ed.).

Over half the states provide a statutory defense if the worker was intoxicated at the time of the injury. In most of these, intoxication can serve as a complete bar to compensation, but in a few it will serve only to reduce the award. The major difference among the statutes is the extent of causal connection required between the intoxication and the injury: this ranges from no requirement of causal connection to a requirement of demonstrating that intoxication was the "sole cause" of the injury. Larson, §§ 34.30–34.39. Is it consistent with the theory of the compensation acts to reduce the worker's benefits for misbehavior?

9. Several states increase the employee's compensation when injury results from the employer's violation of safety rules. In RTE Corp. v. Department of Industry, Labor & Human Relations, 88 Wis.2d 283, 276 N.W.2d 290 (1979), the court affirmed a 15% increase in the compensation award because the worker's death had resulted from the employer's violation of a safety regulation whose purpose was to prevent the kind of injury the worker sustained. Is it consistent with workers' compensation theory to increase an award if the employer has violated a safety order?

California Labor Code § 4553 requires that the compensation award be increased by one-half (together with costs and expenses not to exceed $250) if the worker's injury resulted from "serious and willful misconduct" of the employer. Such misconduct has been defined as "more than negligence, however gross. The type of conduct necessary to invoke the penalty . . . is that of a '*quasi* criminal nature, the intentional doing of something either with the knowledge that it is likely to result in serious injury, or with a wanton and reckless disregard of its possible consequences. . . .'" American Smelting & Ref. Co. v. Workers' Compensation Appeals Board, 79 Cal.App.3d 615, 144 Cal.Rptr. 898 (1978).

10. As discussed in the excerpt, growing concern over the steady increase in costs of the system, fueled by the open-endedness of such claims as mental stress and soft tissue injury has led the states to adopt strategies for tightening eligibility standards, benefit payments, and administrative procedures. See Quint, Crackdown on Job–Injury Costs, N.Y.Times, Mar. 16, 1995 at C1. For detailed discussion of the issues, see Schwartz, Waste, Fraud and Abuse in Workers' Compensation: The Recent California Experience, 52 Md.L.Rev 983 (1993).

11. *Permanent partial disability.* The following statute from New York demonstrates the scheduling approach to permanent partial disability.

New York Workers' Compensation Law

Section 15 (1991).

. . .

3. Permanent partial disability. In case of disability partial in character but permanent in quality the compensation shall be sixty-six and two-thirds per centrum of the average weekly wages and shall be paid to the employee for the period named in this subdivision, as follows:

Member lost	Number of weeks' compensation
a. Arm	312
b. Leg	288
c. Hand	244
d. Foot	205
e. Eye	160
f. Thumb	75
g. First finger	46
h. Great toe	38
i. Second finger	30
j. Third finger	25
k. Toe other than great toe	16
l. Fourth finger	15

m. Loss of hearing. Compensation for the complete loss of the hearing of one ear, for sixty weeks, for the loss of hearing of both ears, for one hundred and fifty weeks.

. . .

r. Total loss of use. Compensation for permanent total loss of use of a member shall be the same as for loss of the member.

s. Partial loss or partial loss of use. Compensation for permanent partial loss or loss of use of a member may be for proportionate loss or loss of use of the member. . . .

t. Disfigurement. 1. The board may award proper and equitable compensation for serious facial or head disfigurement, not to exceed twenty thousand dollars, including a disfigurement continuous in length which is partially in the facial area and also extends into the neck region as described in paragraph two hereof.

2. The board, if in its opinion the earning capacity of an employee has been or may in the future be impaired, may award compensation for any serious disfigurement in the region above the sterno clavicular articulations anterior to and including the region of the sterno cleido mastoid muscles on

either side, but no award under subdivisions one and two shall, in the aggregate, exceed twenty thousand dollars.

3. Notwithstanding any other provision hereof, two or more serious disfigurements, not continuous in length, resulting from the same injury, if partially in the facial area and partially in the neck region as described in paragraph two hereof, shall be deemed to be a facial disfigurement.

u. Total or partial loss or loss of use of more than one member or parts of members. In any case in which there shall be a loss or loss of use of more than one member or parts of more than one member set forth in paragraphs a to t, both inclusive, of this subdivision, but not amounting to permanent total disability, the board shall award compensation for the loss or loss of use of each such member or part thereof, which awards shall run consecutively.

v. Additional compensation for impairment of wage earning capacity in certain permanent partial disabilities. Notwithstanding any other provision of this subdivision, additional compensation shall be payable for impairment of wage earning capacity for any period after the termination of an award under paragraph a, b, c, or d, of this subdivision for the loss or loss of use of fifty per centum or more of a member, provided such impairment of earning capacity shall be due solely thereto. . . .

w. Other cases. In all other cases in this class of disability, the compensation shall be sixty-six and two-thirds per centum of the difference between his average weekly wages and his wage-earning capacity thereafter in the same employment or otherwise, payable during the continuance of such partial disability, but subject to reconsideration of the degree of such impairment by the board on its own motion or upon application of any party in interest.

What are the strengths and weaknesses of this approach? Does it seem appropriate that both a construction worker and a law professor would receive the same benefits for loss of an arm—assuming both are above the average weekly wage ceiling—under the statute? Does it seem proper that the law professor would receive these benefits even if she suffered no loss of earning capacity? What justification might be offered for the scheduling of permanent partial disability benefits?

12. *Lump Sums.* In death cases, most states provide lump sum payments to close out accounts when widows or widowers remarry. This raises the general question of lump sum payments in lieu of the periodic payments in some injury situations, too. In many states the lump sum has become common since it is at least superficially attractive to everyone concerned: the claimant, who gets one very large award; the attorney, who thus finds it easier to collect a fee; the employer, who can dispose of the matter once and for all and probably at a lower cost; and the court or administering agency, which avoids further litigation and supervision of the claim. Lump summing, however, does not meet one of the primary goals of the compensation system, provision of a regular benefit payment to take the place of lost wages. The objection is that the worker will find the lump sum soon spent, leaving him or her with no further recourse and in no better position than if there had been no compensation scheme at all. Are the lump sum problems of compensation systems different from those of the common law?

13. *Opting Out.* Up to this point we have been dealing with cases in which the injured worker has sought coverage under a workers' compensation scheme. Sometimes, however, an injured worker may wish to avoid the rule that if an injury is compensable within the system, there may be no other remedy against the employer or co-workers. Though compensation plans originally provided the injured worker's only practical hope of recovery, the modern worker is much more likely to succeed in a tort action against the employer—if allowed to pursue it. In such a case, coverage may be a detriment to the worker.

a.   In some cases the worker claims to be out of the scope of employment at the time of injury, while the employer argues for coverage. For example, in Scott v. Pacific Coast Borax Co., 140 Cal.App.2d 173, 294 P.2d 1039 (1956), the worker's hours had ended and he claimed that he was simply helping a co-worker and friend move a gas pump—that exploded. The worker wanted to sue in tort but the court relied on the provision that said the compensation act "shall be liberally construed by the courts with the purpose of extending their benefits for the protection of persons injured in the course of their employment." Reasonable doubts were to be resolved in favor of coverage. However, in Peckham v. Peckham Materials Corp., 146 App.Div.2d 893, 536 N.Y.S.2d 873 (1989), the court allowed the widow of a company president killed in the crash of a company helicopter to proceed with a tort suit against the employer. In finding that the death had not arisen out of and in the course of employment, the court noted that the decedent was returning from a golf outing with friends when the helicopter crashed; that there was no evidence that business was transacted or discussed while he was golfing; and that company funds were not used to pay for the outing.

b.   Another way to escape the limits of compensation in many states is to prove that the employer committed an intentional tort. See the extended discussion in Magliulo v. Superior Court, 47 Cal.App.3d 760, 121 Cal.Rptr. 621 (1975), allowing a tort action to a waitress whose employer allegedly hit her in anger and threw her down.

Some states provide by statute that the employer may be held liable for conduct short of intentional injury, but almost all states require that the employer must have acted with an actual intent to injure. Thus, in Bardere v. Zafir, 102 App.Div.2d 422, 477 N.Y.S.2d 131, affirmed on other grounds 63 N.Y.2d 850, 472 N.E.2d 37, 482 N.Y.S.2d 261 (1984), the court held that an employer's conduct in removing safety features from a machine to increase its speed, with knowledge that a worker might come in contact with the dangerous machine, was insufficient to establish an intentional tort and overcome the exclusive liability of workers' compensation.

In Johns–Manville Products Corp. v. Contra Costa Superior Court, 27 Cal.3d 465, 612 P.2d 948, 165 Cal.Rptr. 858 (1980), the court held that there could be no tort recovery for the initial injuries of workers who suffered from exposure to asbestos—a California statute which provided for an increased compensation award when a worker's injury resulted from the employer's willful misconduct was intended to be the workers' exclusive remedy. The workers could, however, bring tort claims for aggravation of their injuries caused by alleged willful concealment from doctors and workers of information that asbestos was the cause of the workers' pulmonary problems. Other courts have refused to follow this approach and barred such suits based on the exclusive remedy provisions of workers' compensation statutes. See Abbott v. Gould, Inc., 232 Neb. 907, 443 N.W.2d 591 (1989), cert. denied 493 U.S. 1073 (1990).

Compare Handley v. Unarco Indus., Inc., 124 Ill.App.3d 56, 463 N.E.2d 1011 (1984), in which the court held that asbestos workers could bring a tort claim for their initial injuries where they alleged that the employer had acted with a conscious purpose that asbestos would be trapped in their lungs and bodies, had intended to kill them, had intended bodily harm to them, and had knowingly made false representations to them that asbestos dust was not harmful—with the intent that they would rely on those representations and the knowledge that they would become ill and die.

See also Cole v. Fair Oaks Fire Protection Dist., 43 Cal.3d 148, 729 P.2d 743, 233 Cal.Rptr. 308 (1987), in which the California Supreme Court refused to extend *Johns–Manville* to allow an employee to sue an employer based on a claim of intentional infliction of emotional distress. As a result of a sustained campaign of harassment and humiliation, including an unjustified demotion by his employer in retaliation for his union activities, the plaintiff suffered a severe stroke that rendered him unable to move, care for himself, or communicate other than by blinking his eyes. The court refused to allow the lawsuit to proceed on the basis that the intent element of the tort could be satisfied by a showing that the defendant proceeded with reckless disregard to the possibility of causing emotional injury to the plaintiff. This, according to the majority opinion, could have the effect of transforming virtually every negative personnel decision into a tort claim. The dissent would have carved out an exception to the rule in cases where the employer acted deliberately with intent to cause emotional injuries to the employee. The majority rejected this approach on grounds that plaintiffs could get around the distinction simply by alleging an ulterior purpose behind the employer's actions. This would have the effect of forcing employers to pay the costs of mounting a legal defense which, even if successful, would not eliminate their responsibility to compensate the employee for the emotional injuries under the worker's compensation statute.

14. Sometimes, even though an injury falls within the scope of the statute, the particular harm suffered by the worker is not covered. "Non-disabling'' injuries are often not compensable. The most obvious example is the refusal of compensation systems to pay anything for conventional pain and suffering. Other examples include injury to sexual organs; loss of taste, smell or sensation; disfigurement; and psychic damage.

The fact that a compensation scheme excludes these types of injury does not mean that tort law is available. Thus, in Fetterhoff v. Western Block Co., 49 App.Div.2d 1001, 373 N.Y.S.2d 920 (1975), a worker who alleged that his work-related injury had left him permanently unable to have sexual intercourse was barred from suing in tort even though his loss of sexual function was not compensable under workers' compensation. In Moss v. Southern Excavation, Inc., 271 Ark. 781, 611 S.W.2d 178 (1981), a worker who lost the non-compensable senses of taste and smell in an accident that was covered by worker's compensation was barred from suing in tort for these lost senses.

15. The exclusiveness of the workers' compensation remedy applies not only to the covered worker but also to plaintiffs who are not covered. Compensation schemes do not provide benefits to spouses or children of workers who are injured, or to the non-dependent relatives of workers who are killed. Generally, these family members are not permitted to bring tort actions for loss of consortium or wrongful death. Tort recovery may be allowed, though, where an independent injury has been inflicted on the family member, or where the worker was injured by the employer's intentional conduct. Recovery for loss of consortium is also allowed in some states that call it an independent rather than a derivative cause of action. Larson, Workmen's Compensation Law, § 66.30.

In Bell v. Macy's California, 212 Cal.App.3d 1442, 261 Cal.Rptr. 447 (1989), the court applied the "derivative injury doctrine," which holds that a third party tort action is barred if it is derived from and is dependent on a compensable injury to an employee, to dismiss a tort suit brought by a child who was born with brain damage due to negligent treatment provided to his pregnant mother by a nurse staffing an employer-funded first-aid clinic. The nurse had negligently delayed calling a doctor when the mother, a department store employee who was then seven months pregnant, complained of abdominal pains. The employee suffered a ruptured uterus, and the evidence suggested that the delay in treatment was directly responsible for the child's injuries. The child died four months after his second birthday. Had the child's injuries occurred outside the employer-employee context, the case clearly would have been allowed to proceed. However, the court held that in this case the action was barred by the exclusive remedy provisions of the workers' compensation statute, because the injury to the fetus was derived directly from the employer's treatment of its mother.

After *Bell* was decided, the U.S. Supreme Court, in International Union v. Johnson Controls, Inc., 499 U.S. 187 (1991), held that federal law forbids employers from discriminating against women based on their capacity to become pregnant, so long as their reproductive capacity does not prevent them from performing their jobs. Does this result undermine the logic of *Bell*?

NOTE ON MESHING COMPENSATION AND TORT

Although the worker must come within one of the foregoing exceptions to sue the employer, workers covered by compensation are generally able to sue anyone else they believe violated tort obligations toward them. In some states, this is limited by barring suits against co-workers. In a few states, suits are barred against any third party who is contributing to the compensation system. But in most states any third party may be sued in tort—as though the compensation system did not exist. Moreover, the worker may accept compensation benefits and pursue the tort actions simultaneously without waiving one or the other. This has undoubtedly occurred in many cases we have considered, especially in the defective products area.

In recent years, there has been a great increase in the number of suits brought by injured workers against third parties and a corresponding number of attempts by the third parties to recoup all or part of their payments from the employer. The question in these cases is whether the exclusivity provision in the applicable compensation statute bars actions by third parties who would have been jointly liable with the employer under traditional tort rules, yet who have been held solely liable for the full extent of the injury. To what extent is the latter action simply an indirect suit by the employee that should be barred by the statute? Consider the following discussion of alternative approaches to this problem.

Enterprise Responsibility for Personal Injury Vol. II, Approaches to Legal and Institutional Change

Report to the American Law Institute (1991).
187–92.

III. The Policy Options

A. The Dominance of WC Policy

At this time the great majority of states still deny the third-party manufacturer any contribution at all from the negligent employer toward the full tort damages awarded to the injured employee.

The policy rationale for this position is that the employer, which has been promised full immunity from fault-based tort liability in return for financing no-fault WC benefits for its employees, should not face any erosion in that legal protection through the device of the employee's suing a third party and the third party's forcing the employer to foot a share of the resulting tort award. But the practical consequence is that even in cases in which the employer *was* negligent, the employer will emerge scot-free from any financial contribution to compensate the injuries if tort liability happens to be fixed on a third party and if part of the proceeds are then used to satisfy the employer's lien for its WC payments.

As we noted, from the point of view of compensation policy this result is neutral because the injured worker ends up with full tort damages and no more. From the point of view of administration this position is the most economical because it avoids any need to resolve an often contentious dispute over whether and to what extent the employer was at fault in the accident, as compared with the responsibility of worker and manufacturer. But the price of such administrative saving is a potentially serious gap and distortion in effective prevention. In these kinds of cases the employer faces no legal-financial impact from its misuse of "defective" products; instead, all such incentives are trained on the manufacturer to build costly safeguards into its products in order to avoid the hazards created by a minority of employers who are prepared to disregard the safety and health of their employees.

B.   The Dominance of Tort Policy

In response to that concern, courts in a few jurisdictions have moved to a legal position which effectively ignores the WC exclusivity principle in this context and simply applies a new tort law approach, apportioning burdens among all negligent actors. In effect, these courts are prepared to bear the additional administrative price of establishing and comparing the employer's responsibility for the injury in order to secure the basic tort function of creating a financial incentive for all parties to avoid the legal risk by taking reasonable steps to prevent the injury from occurring in the first place.

The problem in that approach is its focusing on the apparently sensible tort disposition of the immediate case while overlooking the broader policy trade-off within the WC system as a whole. Under tort law the manufacturer will be liable in full for any injuries (in the workplace or otherwise) caused by its products which are defective. . . . By contrast, under WC the employer has immunity from direct tort suit for full damages even where it has been at fault because the same employer is obligated to pay for guaranteed but limited WC benefits to all employees who are hurt on the job, even when the employer was not at fault—indeed, even in cases where the injury was due to the fault of the employee himself or of a judgment-proof outside party. But now, simply because a particular injured employee may happen to have a valid tort claim against a third party, the employer will be required to shoulder an additional financial burden for injuries in its workplace over and above what the community has decided was appropriate under its WC policy.

C.   Substantive Blend of Tort and WC Policy

Recognition of that problem has led a few states to a solution that appeared to mesh more successfully the principles and policies of the WC and tort regimes. The employer would be required to contribute a share of the injured worker's damage award against the third-party manufacturer, but only up to the amount of the employer's financial exposure to pay WC benefits for the injury. In effect, the limited employer contribution to tort damages would offset what otherwise would be the employer's WC lien against the tort award. The simplest legal mechanism for accomplishing that result is to allow the third party to assert the amount of the employer's WC payment as a setoff against the employee's tort claim and to reduce correspondingly the employer's lien against the employee's tort award.

The positive virtue of this substantive policy blend is that the employer continues to bear its expected WC share of the cost of workplace injuries. As a result, the happenstance of third-party tort litigation will not relieve the employer of the normal financial incentive it faces under WC to adopt feasible precautions to avoid injuries to its employees. However, the negative flip side of this new policy is that an additional and expensive contest over the employer's fault in managing its workplace is introduced into what otherwise would be a more straightforward dispute between the employee and the manufacturer about the safety of a particular product. Moreover, complex and often contentious calculations are necessary in order to work out the appropriate reductions and setoffs whenever there is a compromise settlement (rather than an itemized adjudication) of such a tort claim, often involving only partial tort damages where full WC benefits have already been paid.

D. Administrative Accommodation of WC and Tort

To avoid some of these difficulties we endorse a different tack toward the same objective, an approach contained in the proposed Uniform Product Liability Act.

State WC legislation should be altered by eliminating any subrogation right of the employer against the injured worker's tort award. At the same time, product liability law should be altered by reducing the size of tort damages by the amount of WC benefits payable by the employer to the employee.

Note that there are substantial differences between this resolution of the problem and that embodied in Model C above. Under this proposal the manufacturer's tort liability would be reduced only by the WC benefit actually payable by the employer, rather than by some appropriate measure of the culpable employer's share of the larger tort award. At the same time, all employers, not only culpable employers, would lose their subrogation right against the worker's tort award. The aim is to exclude not simply the contentious issue of the employer's comparative fault, but also the very presence of the employer from the tort contest between injured worker and third-party manufacturer. . . . In contrast with the current offset-lien rule in the vast majority of jurisdictions, we would shift a somewhat greater share of the current burden of compensating workers to the considerably cheaper-to-administer WC insurance regime, away from the increasingly expensive tort litigation/liability insurance system. In the long run such a move would enure to the benefit of employers as well, because the manufacturers' rising expenses for product liability insurance and legal fees are eventually incorporated in the prices firms charge customers for their products; and in the case of workplace products, the customers are those very employers.

———————

Which of the alternatives seems most appealing to you? The Report also considers the possibility of eliminating the third-party product liability suit altogether. What would be the arguments for and against this more drastic approach?

NOTE ON RAILROAD AND MARITIME WORKERS

While the states were grappling with problems of workers' injuries, Congress confronted the special situation of persons employed in interstate commerce as that term was understood at the turn of the century. In 1908 Congress passed the Federal Employers' Liability Act (FELA), 45 U.S.C. §§ 51–60. The Act provided that common carriers by railroad while engaging in interstate commerce were liable to negligently injured employees and that any attempt by the employer to contract out of liability would be void. The original version of the Act barred assumption of risk in some situations; a 1939 amendment was held to have "obliterated" the doctrine. Tiller v. Atlantic Coast Line R. Co., 318 U.S. 54 (1943). Comparative negligence applies in all actions against the employer, unless the employer has violated a safety statute—in which case the worker's fault is not considered.

Several Supreme Court decisions in the 1940s and 1950s made the injured railroad worker's path much easier than that of a plaintiff in a common law negligence action. In addition to the elimination of the three major defenses, the task of establishing negligence has been simplified. See Rogers v. Missouri Pacific R. Co., 352 U.S. 500 (1957):

> Under this statute the test of a jury case is simply whether the proofs justify with reason the conclusion that employer negligence played any part, even the slightest, in producing the injury or death for which damages are sought. It does not matter that, from the evidence, the jury may also with reason, on grounds of probability, attribute the result to other causes, including the employee's contributory negligence. Judicial appraisal of the proofs to determine whether a jury question is presented is narrowly limited to the single inquiry whether, with reason, the conclusion may be drawn that negligence of the employer played any part at all in the injury or death. Judges are to fix their sights primarily to make that appraisal and, if that test is met, are bound to find that a case for the jury is made out whether or not the evidence allows the jury a choice of other probabilities. The statute expressly imposes liability upon the employer to pay damages for injury or death due "in whole or *in part* "to its negligence.

Railroad workers have steadfastly refused to give up FELA in favor of a compensation system.

A complex combination of fault, strict liability and compensation systems comes into play when maritime injuries occur.

Members of the crew. Those who are formal members of a ship's crew may sue under the Jones Act, 46 U.S.C. § 688, which makes the provisions of the FELA applicable to crew members. A second remedy is unseaworthiness, a doctrine that holds the shipowner strictly liable in tort whenever any aspect of the ship is not "reasonably fit." Finally, a crew member who falls ill or is hurt while serving on the ship is entitled to "maintenance and cure" until reaching the point of maximum recovery. There is no requirement that the condition be related to the employment. This item is bargained for in most union agreements. These remedies are discussed in historical perspective in Mitchell v. Trawler Racer, Inc., 362 U.S. 539 (1960).

Non-crew members. Many persons work around ships and piers but are not crewmembers. These workers, including longshoreworkers and carpenters, are entitled to compensation for job-related injuries under the Longshoremen's and Harbor Workers' Compensation Act, 33 U.S.C. §§ 901–950. In return for a substantial increase in compensation levels in 1972, Congress withdrew the right of these workers to sue shipowners for unseaworthiness. They do, however, retain their rights to sue shipowners for injuries resulting from negligence.

C.   MOTOR VEHICLE INJURIES

Not long after the automobile became part of daily life the first doubts were raised about the adequacy of legal treatment of automobile accidents. We have already considered the legal theory underlying the fault system and the impact on it of the institution of insurance. Before considering current no-fault alternatives, we review briefly the history of proposed changes—both because they frame the basic issues and because they helped shape the legislation that did follow.

1.   THE PAST

The earliest thinking about extensions of the no-fault concept began shortly after the passage of the workers' compensation statutes. Writers saw that incongruities would occur: if a trolley car collided with an automobile, the employees on the trolley car would be eligible for compensation, but the trolley passengers and car occupants would have to prove fault. Professor Jeremiah Smith in his article, Sequel to Workmen's Compensation Acts, 27 Harv.L.Rev. 235, 363 (1914), concluded that the fault system and the compensation system could not live together in harmony: "In the end, one or the other of the two conflicting theories is likely to prevail. There is no probability, during the present generation, of a repeal of the Workmen's Compensation Acts." Smith then speculated on the creation of a state insurance law that would protect all, not only workers, against accident and disease. "It may include damage wholly due to a natural cause, such as a stroke of lightning. Whether legislation of the above description *ought* to be enacted is a question upon which no opinion is here intimated. Our immediate point is, that the Workmen's Compensation legislation will inevitably give rise to a plausible agitation for such further legislation."* Reconsider the quote from Holmes, p. 6, *supra.*

Fifteen years after Professor Smith wrote, some lawyers and social scientists undertook an empirical analysis of automobile injuries in 8,849 cases across the United States. Their findings were remarkably similar to those of recent studies: "payments do not increase in proportion to the losses sustained; temporary disability cases with small losses are considerably overpaid, those with larger losses are slightly overpaid, while permanent disability cases of earners—the class with the largest losses and greatest need—receive just about enough to meet the losses incurred up to the time of our investigations and get nothing to apply against the continued medical expense or wage loss resulting from their impaired earning ability." They were concerned about delay and uncompensated victims at a time when first-party insurance for injuries was unusual and tort law was the one available resource; workers' compensation was available only when a person was hurt on the job. The study is presented in Report by the Committee to Study Compensation for Automobile Accidents to the Columbia University Council for Research into the Social Sciences (1932).

The study suggested a workers' compensation model after considering its relevance to the automobile situation (134–36):

> In many respects there is a close analogy between the industrial situation where workmen's compensation has been developed and the motor vehicle situation where the application of a like principle is now being discussed. Accidents are inevitable, whether in industry or in the operation of motor vehicles. It has been accepted as sound policy that the major part of the cost of accidents to employees should be borne by the industry, and it is proposed that the major part of the cost of those caused by the operation of motor vehicles should be cast upon the persons for whose benefit the motor vehicles are being operated. The conditions calling for the application of the compensation plan are similar: The failure of the common law system to measure up to a fair estimate of social necessity.

Compensation was to be paid from compulsory insurance carried by every vehicle owner for the benefit of those harmed by the vehicle. The amount of compensation was to be scheduled much as with workers' compensation payments. The group recognized that the amounts of compensation would present different problems because of the greater diversity of potential automobile victims as compared to workers.

---

* Indeed, within two years plans began to appear. See Ballentine, A Compensation Plan for Railway Accident Claims, 29 Harv. L.Rev. 705 (19165), proposing a plan to cover injuries to passengers on railroads and street railways.

For an extended argument rejecting the analogy between the work accident and the auto accident, see W. Blum and H. Kalven, Jr., Public Law Perspectives on a Private Law Problem—Auto Compensation Plans 25–27 (1965). Their basic point was that the existence of the contractual relationship made the work accident a special case. Why might that be?

The developments between the Columbia Plan and the late 1960s can be summarized fairly readily. In 1946, the Canadian province of Saskatchewan enacted a plan under which all auto accident victims received modest no-fault benefits—and could still sue in tort as before. Part of any tort recovery would have to be used to reimburse the fund that had paid the no-fault benefits. The statute and its operation are discussed in R. Keeton and J. O'Connell, Basic Protection for the Traffic Victim 140–48 (1965).

In 1954, Professor Albert Ehrenzweig, in a book entitled "Full Aid" Insurance to the Traffic Victim, built upon the protection afforded accident victims under the no-fault medical payments provision, p. 673, supra, commonly found in auto liability insurance policies. If this were increased in amount and scope, it would be appropriate to free anyone carrying such protection from the burdens of liability for negligence.

In the early 1960s, Nationwide Insurance Company marketed a policy that embodied several of Ehrenzweig's ideas. Under this plan a person injured by the insured's vehicle could choose whether to proceed in tort as usual, or whether to take advantage of a package of modest no-fault benefits. Not surprisingly, victims with good legal claims tended to opt for tort and others opted for the no-fault package.

How much more than the usual liability insurance coverage would you have been willing to pay for the knowledge that, for example, a child darting into your car would receive some compensation even though you were not at fault? The Nationwide experience is discussed in King, The Insurance Industry and Compensation Plans, 43 N.Y.U.L.Rev. 1137 (1968).

During this period, Professors Blum and Kalven argued that if society wanted to compensate all victims of motoring accidents (something about which they were skeptical), motorists should not bear the burden. Their proposal, found in A Stopgap Plan for Compensating Auto Accident Victims, 1968 Ins.L.J. 661, argued that those hurt in cases not involving driver fault should receive money from "general tax revenues." The "widespread temptation" to put this burden on motorists was unsound. They cited accidents in which the victims are drunk, or in which pedestrians are hurt through nobody's fault. "In these instances, the injury in question is no more associated with motoring than it is with pedestrianism, drinking, or living in our society."

The major breakthrough occurred in 1965, with the publication of Basic Protection for the Traffic Victim, by Professors Robert E. Keeton and Jeffrey O'Connell. Not only did the authors attack the operation of the common law fault system in auto cases, they also proposed a new approach and presented a 37–page draft statute practically ready for introduction into state legislatures. Suddenly, no-fault legislation became a political possibility.

Briefly, they utilized a first-party structure building on the medical payments provision that would cover medical expenses and 85% of wages lost up to a total of $10,000, though lost wage payments would be limited to $750 per month. A deductible of $100 or 10% of the work loss, whichever was larger, was imposed to keep small claims from burdening the system. Those who wanted greater no-fault protection would be able to buy it. In any tort action against another driver, the judgment would exclude the first $10,000 of economic loss and the first $5,000 of pain and suffering. In suits against other defendants, such as railroads or car manufacturers, no deductions or exclusions would be made but the no-fault insurer would be reimbursed to prevent double recovery. For a short summary of the plan, see Keeton and O'Connell, Basic Protection Automobile Insurance, 1967 U.Ill.L.F. 400.

The impetus for change in Massachusetts was the great public outcry about high insurance rates. Its liability premiums were the highest in the country. Also, the state was the home of Professor Robert Keeton, who had co-authored the Keeton–O'Connell plan. In 1970, Massachusetts adopted a plan that was traceable to the Keeton–O'Connell plan.

The statute required compulsory no-fault coverage for all medical expenses and 75% of lost earnings incurred within two years up to a combined sum of $2,000. The act made no general provision for collateral sources but did require a worker to use up (subject to later reimbursement) any wage continuation protection before recovering for lost wages. Another provision correlated workers' compensation benefits with the no-fault benefits.

Tort actions for damages were permitted with an exclusion for the first $2,000 of the award. Pain and suffering was recoverable in a tort action if one of the following existed: medical and hospital expenses over $500, death, loss of body member, permanent disfigurement, loss of sight or hearing, or a "fracture." Compulsory liability insurance was continued at low limits to cover the tort action. Insureds could choose a deductible of up to $2,000 for their own losses. An assigned claims plan protected pedestrians and others who were hurt in the state by cars that didn't carry the no-fault coverage. The statute also regulated policy cancellations and renewals and provided explicitly for merit driving discounts, and surcharges for moving violations and involvement in accidents.

2.   THE NEW YORK EXPERIENCE

a.   BACKGROUND

As soon as Massachusetts acted, the scene shifted to New York. In 1970, the state's Insurance Department had prepared a study of the operation of the tort system in auto cases. Automobile Insurance . . . for Whose Benefit?, A Report to Governor Nelson A. Rockefeller by the

Insurance Department of the State of New York (1970). The study concluded that the system had failed. Among its points (pp. 17-44):

1. One in four persons suffering bodily injury in auto accidents obtained "nothing whatever" from the fault system. Recall that New York did not adopt comparative negligence until 1973.

2. Determinations "are made either by an overburdened judiciary on stale facts or else by insurance adjusters in a bargaining process. Part lottery and part bazaar, the fault insurance system is unreliable and unpredictable."

3. Data showed, as in earlier studies, that benefits were malapportioned, with small claims being overcompensated to get rid of them with payments for pain and suffering far in excess of the economic loss sustained. Large claims, however, were being badly underpaid. "The seriously injured receive a sort of negative 'pain and suffering.' "

4. Benefits were not coordinated with other support systems. Thus, 91 percent of workers in New York in 1970 were covered by health insurance and most were also covered by income continuation plans. The collateral source rule operated to provide double recoveries when these persons were hurt. Workers with good fringe benefits got no reduction in their auto premiums. Instead, they got "a chance at redundant payment" if injured in the future.

5. Physical rehabilitation was delayed under the fault system because of the cost involved and the question of whether the victim would be able to pay for rehabilitation if no tort recovery were obtained.

6. The system was inefficient because 56 cents of each premium dollar went to operating expenses of the system. Of the 44 cents that reached victims 8 cents covered economic losses already covered by another source, 21.5 cents covered pain and suffering and only 14.5 cents was for net economic loss not otherwise covered.

7. Finally the litigation system bred overreaching and dishonesty. Insurers deal "with thousands of claimants who are adversaries the company never expects to see again, and is doing so in situations that afford no clear line between rigorous bargaining and downright dishonesty. . . . Too often, especially where injuries are serious, the insurer can simply wait out the injured victim to obtain a more favorable settlement." The highly abstract standard of "fault" and the indeterminate measure of damages "offer rich rewards to the claimant who will lie, the attorney who will inflame, the adjuster who will chisel and the insurance company which will stall or intimidate."

The study also discussed several problems of insurance administration. How many of the enumerated concerns are likely to be unique to auto accidents?

Consider the following discussion of how to evaluate an existing reparation system, taken from Conard, Morgan, Pratt, Voltz and Bombaugh, Automobile Accident Costs and Payments 106-07 (1964):

No valid evaluation of reparation systems can be made which measures them by a single dimension. Some are better than others for procuring medical treatment, some for maintaining subsistence, some for compensating total loss, some for deterring negligence, some for raising the price of hazardous activities, some for spreading broadly the pain of loss, some for economy of operation. If any of the major elements in the scheme is knocked out, some important function will remain unperformed.

This does not mean that nothing in the picture can be changed. In fact, a great many elements in the picture are quite recent. Workmen's compensation entered about fifty years ago; social security was added about twenty-five years ago for survivors' benefits and within the last ten years for disability benefits; hospital and medical insurance is largely a growth of the last fifteen years. It seems probable that further changes will be made in reparation systems, which might include the shifting of functions from one system to another, and altering the linkage between benefits and burdens. When such changes are made, they should be made with a clear perception of the plurality of functions to be performed, and of the plurality of systems now performing them.

For an extended discussion of the issues underlying the adoption of any no-fault proposal, see Blum & Kalven, Ceilings, Costs, and Compulsion in Auto Compensation Legislation, 1973 Utah L.Rev. 341. See also Epstein, Automobile No–Fault Plans: A Second Look at First Principles, 13 Creighton L.Rev. 769 (1980), comparing auto no-fault with systems of strict liability, negligence and no-liability from perspectives of equity, incentives and administrative costs.

b.   THE NEW YORK STATUTE

The New York statute provides one of the most generous sets of no-fault benefits and one of the most significant limitations on tort actions of any of the 20–odd state statutes adopting some version of auto no-fault. The statute was adopted in 1973, and amended frequently to meet problems that appeared during its first years of operation. The statute that follows is the current version. The cross-references to articles six and eight of the Vehicle and Traffic Law are to provisions for compulsory insurance and other devices relating to financial security arrangements.

In reading the statute, keep in mind some general questions. Among those who would get compensated under the statute who was not compensated before? How does the amount of recovery compare with that currently available under tort? If the act is likely to be more expensive than the current system, where will the money come from? If there are savings, who will benefit? What about collateral sources and subrogation? Does the act internalize the costs of auto accidents so that the motoring activity pays for them? Is internalization important? What are the alternatives to internalizing the costs? Is the act conducive to fraudulent claims? More so than the existing system? What, if anything, remains of the tort action? What conception of justice does the statute reflect? How does that conception line up with your own? Is the act likely to have any effect on driving safety? Should safety be left to other parts of the legal system?

When reading a statute, lawyers and judges are usually looking for answers to specific questions. In reading this statute, assume a client who is asking about her rights under New York's current legislation. V is a 25–year–old commercial artist. Although she owns a car that is properly insured under the statute, she was hurt while walking home from a neighborhood movie house one evening. She was run over by a car owned and operated by D, who was probably negligent, and who possessed the proper insurance under the statute. V sustained a broken left arm (she is left-handed) and also sustained a four-inch-long permanent scar on her left forearm. The fracture healed perfectly. She had medical bills of $4,000, of which $2,500 was covered and paid by the group medical policy that she got as a fringe benefit at her office. She was out of work for a month and a half. Her salary was $3000 per month.

(a) What are V's rights?

(b) What if V owned no car?

(c) What if V had driven to and from the movie and collided with D's car?

(d) Some tests on D's new car have suggested that the crash might have been due to a defective steering column. Does it matter if the crash was due to the defect rather than D's negligence?

New York Insurance Law

Article 51, as amended through 1995.

(excluding amendments specifically addressed to issues of managed care organizations that were enacted in 1993 and will expire in 1998).

§ 5101. Title

This article shall be known and may be cited as the "Comprehensive Motor Vehicle Insurance Reparations Act".

§ 5102. Definitions

In this chapter:

(a) "Basic economic loss" means, up to fifty thousand dollars per person of the following combined items, subject to the limitations of section five thousand one hundred eight of this article:

(1) All necessary expenses incurred for: (i) medical, hospital . . . , surgical, nursing, dental, ambulance, x-ray, prescription drug and prosthetic services; (ii) psychiatric, physical and occupational therapy

and rehabilitation; (iii) any non-medical remedial care and treatment rendered in accordance with a religious method of healing recognized by the laws of this state; and (iv) any other professional health services; all without limitation as to time, provided that within one year after the date of the accident causing the injury it is ascertainable that further expenses may be incurred as a result of the injury. For the purpose of determining basic economic loss, the expenses incurred under this paragraph shall be in accordance with the limitations of section five thousand one hundred eight of this article.

(2) Loss of earnings from work which the person would have performed had he not been injured, and reasonable and necessary expenses incurred by such person in obtaining services in lieu of those that he would have performed for income, up to two thousand dollars per month for not more than three years from the date of the accident causing the injury. An employee who is entitled to receive monetary payments, pursuant to statute or contract with the employer, or who receives voluntary monetary benefits paid for by the employer, by reason of the employee's inability to work because of personal injury arising out of the use or operation of a motor vehicle, is not entitled to receive first party benefits for "loss of earnings from work" to the extent that such monetary payments or benefits from the employer do not result in the employee suffering a reduction in income or a reduction in the employee's level of future benefits arising from a subsequent illness or injury.

(3) All other reasonable and necessary expenses incurred, up to twenty-five dollars per day for not more than one year from the date of the accident causing the injury.

(4) "Basic economic loss" shall not include any loss incurred on account of death; subject, however, to the provisions of paragraph four of subsection (a) of section five thousand one hundred three of this article.

(5) "Basic economic loss" shall also include an additional option to purchase, for an additional premium, an additional twenty-five thousand dollars of coverage, [which may be keyed to economic loss or medical bills as the buyer wishes and which comes into play after the first $50,000 is exhausted.] This optional coverage shall be made available and notice with explanation of such coverage [shall be provided by an insurer at the first policy renewal after the effective date of the statute].

(b) "First party benefits" means payments to reimburse a person for basic economic loss on account of personal injury arising out of the use or operation of a motor vehicle, less:

(1) Twenty percent of lost earnings computed pursuant to paragraph two of subsection (a) of this section.

(2) Amounts recovered or recoverable on account of such injury under state or federal laws providing social security disability benefits, or workers' compensation benefits, or disability benefits under article nine of the workers' compensation law, or medicare benefits, other than lifetime reserve days and provided further that the medicare benefits utilized herein

do not result in a reduction of such person's medicare benefits for a subsequent illness or injury.

(3) Amounts deductible under the applicable insurance policy.

(c) "Non-economic loss" means pain and suffering and similar non-monetary detriment.

(d) "Serious injury" means a personal injury which results in death; dismemberment; significant disfigurement; a fracture; loss of a fetus; permanent loss of use of a body organ, member, function or system; permanent consequential limitation of use of a body organ or member; significant limitation of use of a body function or system; or a medically determined injury or impairment of a non-permanent nature which prevents the injured person from performing substantially all of the material acts which constitute such person's usual and customary daily activities for not less than ninety days during the one hundred eighty days immediately following the occurrence of the injury or impairment.

(e) "Owner" [is defined broadly].

(f) "Motor vehicle" [is very broadly defined by reference to include fire and police vehicles, but not to include motorcycles].

(g) "Insurer" means the insurance company or self-insurer, as the case may be, which provides the financial security required by article six or eight of the vehicle and traffic law.

(h) "Member of his household" means a spouse, child or relative of the named insured who regularly resides in his household.

(i) "Uninsured motor vehicle" means a motor vehicle, the owner of which is (i) a financially irresponsible motorist . . . or (ii) unknown and whose identity is unascertainable.

(j) "Covered person" means any pedestrian injured through the use or operation of, or any owner, operator or occupant of, a motor vehicle which has in effect the financial security required by . . . the vehicle and traffic law . . . or any other person entitled to first party benefits.

(k) "Bus" means both a bus and a school bus as defined in sections one hundred four and one hundred forty-two of the vehicle and traffic law.

(*l*)"Compensation provider" means the state insurance fund, or the person, association, corporation or insurance carrier or statutory fund liable under state or federal laws for the payment of workers' compensation benefits or disability benefits under article nine of the workers' compensation law.

(m) "Motorcycle" [is defined by reference to other statutes].

§ 5103. Entitlement to first party benefits; additional financial security required

(a) Every owner's policy of liability insurance issued on a motor vehicle in satisfaction of the requirements of article six or eight of the vehicle and traffic law shall also provide for . . . the payment of first party benefits to:

(1) Persons, other than occupants of another motor vehicle or a motorcycle, for loss arising out of the use or operation in this state of such motor vehicle. In the case of occupants of a bus other than operators, owners, and employees of the owner or operator of the bus, the coverage for first party benefits shall be afforded under the policy or policies, if any, providing first party benefits to the injured person and members of his household for loss arising out of the use or operation of any motor vehicle of such household. In the event there is no such policy, first party benefits shall be provided by the insurer of such bus.

(2) The named insured and members of his household, other than occupants of a motorcycle, for loss arising out of the use or operation of (i) an uninsured motor vehicle or motorcycle, within the United States, its territories or possessions, or Canada; and (ii) an insured motor vehicle or motorcycle outside of this state and within the United States, its territories or possessions, or Canada.

(3) Any New York resident who is neither the owner of a motor vehicle with respect to which coverage for first party benefits is required by this article nor, as a member of a household, is entitled to first party benefits under paragraph two of this subsection, for loss arising out of the use or operation of the insured or self-insured motor vehicle outside of this state and within the United States, its territories or possessions, or Canada.

(4) The estate of any covered person, other than an occupant of another motor vehicle or a motorcycle, a death benefit in the amount of two thousand dollars for the death of such person arising out of the use or operation of such motor vehicle which is in addition to any first party benefits for basic economic loss.

(b) An insurer may exclude from coverage required by subsection (a) hereof a person who:

(1) Intentionally causes his own injury.

(2) Is injured as a result of operating a motor vehicle while in an intoxicated condition or while his ability to operate such vehicle is impaired by the use of a drug . . ..

(3) Is injured while he is: (i) committing an act which would constitute a felony, or seeking to avoid lawful apprehension or arrest by a law enforcement officer, or (ii) operating a motor vehicle in a race or speed test, or (iii) operating or occupying a motor vehicle known to him to be stolen, or (iv) operating or occupying any motor vehicle owned by such injured person with respect to which the coverage required by subsection (a) hereof is not in effect, or (v) a pedestrian, through being struck by any motor vehicle owned by such injured pedestrian with respect to which the coverage required by subsection (a) hereof is not in effect, or (vi) repairing, servicing or otherwise maintaining a motor vehicle if such conduct is within the course of a business of repairing, servicing or otherwise maintaining a motor vehicle and the injury occurs on the business premises.

(c) Insurance offered by any company to satisfy the requirements of subsection (a) of this section shall be offered (1) without a deductible and (2) with a family deductible of up to two hundred dollars (which deductible shall apply only to the loss of the named insured and members of his household). The superintendent may approve a higher deductible in the case of insurance policies providing additional benefits or pursuant to a plan designed and implemented to coordinate first party benefits with other benefits. . . . [Slightly changed wording to become effective June 30, 1998.]

. . .

(f) Every owner's policy of liability insurance issued on a motorcycle or an all terrain vehicle in satisfaction of the requirements of article six or eight of the vehicle and traffic law shall also provide for . . . the payment of first party benefits to persons, other than the occupants of such motorcycle or all terrain vehicle, another motorcycle or all terrain vehicle, or any motor vehicle, for loss arising out of the use or operation of the motorcycle or all terrain vehicle within this state. Every insurer and self-insurer may exclude from the coverage required by this subsection a person who intentionally causes his own injury or is injured while committing an act which would constitute a felony or while seeking to avoid lawful apprehension or arrest by a law enforcement officer.

(g) [A general health insurer may, with the consent of the superintendent of insurance] upon a showing that the company or corporation is qualified to provide for all of the items of basic economic loss specified in paragraph one of subsection (a) of section five thousand one hundred two of this article, provide coverage for such items of basic economic loss to the extent that an insurer would be required to provide under this article. Where a policyholder elects to be covered under such an arrangement the insurer providing coverage for the automobile shall be furnished with the names of all persons covered by the company or corporation under the arrangement and such persons shall not be entitled to benefits for any of the items of basic economic loss specified in such paragraph. The premium for the automobile insurance policy shall be appropriately reduced to reflect the elimination of coverage for such items of basic economic loss. Coverage by the automobile insurer of such eliminated items shall be effected or restored upon request by the insured and payment of the premium for such coverage. All companies and corporations providing coverage for items of basic economic loss pursuant to the authorization of this subsection shall have only those rights and obligations which are applicable to an insurer subject to this article.

. . .

§ 5104. Causes of action for personal injury

(a) Notwithstanding any other law, in any action by or on behalf of a covered person against another covered person for personal injuries arising out of negligence in the use or operation of a motor vehicle in this state, there shall be no right of recovery for non-economic loss, except in the case of a serious injury, or for basic economic loss. The owner, operator or occupant of a motorcycle which has in effect the financial security required by article six or eight of the vehicle and traffic law . . . shall not be subject to an action by or on behalf of a covered person for recovery for non-economic loss, except in the case of a serious injury, or for basic economic loss.

(b) In any action by or on behalf of a covered person, against a non-covered person, where damages for personal injuries arising out of the use or operation of a motor vehicle or a motorcycle may be recovered, an insurer which paid or is liable for first party benefits on account of such injuries has a lien against any recovery to the extent of benefits paid or payable by it to the covered person. No such action may be compromised by the covered person except with the written consent of the insurer, or with the approval of the court, or where the amount of such settlement exceeds fifty thousand dollars. The failure of such person to commence such action within two years after accrual gives the insurer a cause of action for the amount of first party benefits paid or payable against any person who may be liable to the covered person for his personal injuries. The insurer's cause of action shall be in addition to the cause of action of the covered person except that in any action subsequently commenced by the covered person for such injuries, the amount of his basic economic loss shall not be recoverable.

(c) Where there is no right of recovery for basic economic loss, such loss may nevertheless be pleaded and proved to the extent that it is relevant to the proof of non-economic loss.

§ 5105. Settlement between insurers

(a) Any insurer liable for the payment of first party benefits to or on behalf of a covered person and any compensation provider paying benefits in lieu of first party benefits which another insurer would otherwise be obligated to pay pursuant to subsection (a) of section five thousand one hundred three of this article . . . has the right to recover the amount paid from the insurer of any other covered person to the extent that such other covered person would have been liable, but for the provisions of this article, to pay damages in an action at law. In any case, the right to recover exists only if at least one of the motor vehicles involved is a motor vehicle weighing more than six thousand five hundred pounds unloaded or is a motor vehicle used principally for the transportation of persons or property for hire. However, in the case of occupants of a bus other than operators, owners, and employees of the owner or operator of the bus, an insurer which, pursuant to paragraph one of subsection (a) of section five thousand one hundred three of this article, provides coverage for first party benefits for such occupants under a policy providing first party benefits to the injured person and members of his household for loss arising out of the use or operation of any vehicle of such household, shall have no right to recover the amount of such benefits from the insurer of such bus.

(b) The sole remedy of any insurer or compensation provider to recover on a claim arising pursuant to subsection (a) hereof, shall be the submission of the controversy to mandatory arbitration pursuant to procedures promulgated or approved by the superintendent. Such procedures shall also be utilized to resolve all disputes arising between insurers concerning their responsibility for the payment of first party benefits.

(c) The liability of an insurer imposed by this section shall not affect or diminish its obligations under any policy of bodily injury liability insurance.

§ 5106. Fair claims settlement

(a) Payments of first party benefits and additional first party benefits shall be made as the loss is incurred. Such benefits are overdue if not paid within thirty days after the claimant supplies proof of the fact and amount of loss sustained. If proof is not supplied as to the entire claim, the amount which is supported by proof is overdue if not paid within thirty days after such proof is supplied. All overdue payments shall bear interest at the rate of two percent per month. If a valid claim or portion was overdue, the claimant shall also be entitled to recover his attorney's reasonable fee, for services necessarily performed in connection with securing payment of the overdue claim, subject to limitations promulgated by the superintendent in regulations.

(b) Every insurer shall provide a claimant with the option of submitting any dispute involving the insurer's liability to pay first party benefits, or additional first party benefits, the amount thereof or any other matter which may arise pursuant to subsection (a) hereof to arbitration pursuant to simplified procedures to be promulgated or approved by the superintendent.

(c) An award by an arbitrator shall be binding except where vacated or modified by a master arbitrator in accordance with simplified procedures to be promulgated or approved by the superintendent. The grounds for vacating or modifying an arbitrator's award by a master arbitrator shall not be limited to those grounds for review set forth in article seventy-five of the civil practice law and rules. The award of a master arbitrator shall be binding except for the grounds for review set forth in article seventy-five of the civil practice law and rules, and provided further that where the amount of such master arbitrator's award is five thousand dollars or greater, exclusive of interest and attorney's fees, the insurer or the claimant may institute a court action to adjudicate the dispute de novo.

§ 5107. Coverage for non-resident motorists

(a) Every insurer authorized to transact or transacting business in this state, or controlling or controlled by or under common control by or with such an insurer, which sells a policy providing motor vehicle liability insurance coverage or any similar coverage in any state or Canadian province, shall include in each such policy coverage to satisfy the financial security requirements of article six or eight of the vehicle and traffic law and to provide for the payment of first party benefits pursuant to subsection (a) of section five thousand one hundred three of this article when a motor vehicle covered by such policy is used or operated in this state.

(b) Every policy described in subsection (a) hereof shall be construed as having the coverage required by subsection (a) of section five thousand one hundred three of this article.

§ 5108. Limit on charges by providers of health services

[Charges for health services specified in § 5102(a)(1) are not to exceed charges for those procedures set forth in schedules prepared for workers' compensation injuries. No provider of health services "may demand or request any payment in addition to" the authorized charges. Insurers are to report "any patterns of overcharging" within 30 days after they learn of them.]

NOTES AND QUESTIONS

1. *Is it constitutional?* A unanimous court rejected constitutional challenges to the statute in Montgomery v. Daniels, 38 N.Y.2d 41, 340 N.E.2d 444, 378 N.Y.S.2d 1 (1975). The court observed that all line drawing raises questions of why the line was not drawn somewhere else; the test to be used was whether there is a reasonable connection between the perceived problem and the remedy adopted. Reviewing criticisms of the fault law of automobile accidents, the court found the statute responsive. The court also questioned the existence of a constitutional duty to provide a replacement for a remedy that is being abolished, citing the introduction of the guest statute and the abolition of actions for alienation of affections and for breach of promise to marry. It found it unnecessary, however, to decide that point here because the statute does provide a substitute remedy for victims of auto accidents. As for equal protection, the court found all the classifications to have a "reasonable basis."

Finally, the court held that abrogation of the right to recover entailed the abolition of any attaching right to a jury trial; the statute did not replace the jury with another fact finder but instead changed the substantive right. This point had been a problem in 1911 when the court held the then-new workers' compensation law unconstitutional in Ives v. South Buffalo Ry. Co., p. 738, supra. But the *Montgomery* court observed that "Jurisprudence has marched many strides in the intervening years. Reliance on *Ives* is misplaced."

No-fault legislation has survived constitutional attack in most jurisdictions. See, e.g., Dimond v. District of Columbia, 792 F.2d 179 (D.C.Cir. 1986).

Death cases: The original statute provided that basic economic loss did not cover losses due to death. In 1977, § 5103(a)(4) was added to allow for $2,000 in death benefits in addition to basic economic loss. The drafters were concerned about a possible constitutional problem caused by Article I, § 16 of the New York Constitution: "The right of action now existing to recover damages for injuries resulting in death, shall never be abrogated; and the amount recoverable shall not be subject to any statutory limitation." The drafters of the statute left death claims out of the statute but allowed recovery for economic loss up to the death and, now, for a flat sum for death benefits, for funeral expenses. The wrongful death action is left intact with the first party insurer subrogated to any tort recovery. Note that § 5102(d) includes death within "serious injury."

Arbitration. Other provisions were challenged in Country–Wide Ins. Co. v. Harnett, 426 F.Supp. 1030 (S.D.N.Y.1977). The insurer challenged § 5106(b) permitting the claimant, but not the insurer, to demand binding arbitration of any dispute. A three-judge court rejected the challenge on the ground that the state could conclude rationally that the two parties were on different footings so far as the disputed claim was concerned and could treat them differently. Among the differences were the claimant's desire for speedy resolution of disputes and his lesser ability to bear the costs of litigation.

The court also rejected a challenge to the provisions that required insurers to renew policies existing at the time the act was adopted. The statutory goal was to prevent wholesale dumping of insureds from the voluntary markets, forcing them into the assigned risk plan. The court found that the need to protect the public and provide orderly transition justified the provisions. The Supreme Court affirmed without hearing argument. 431 U.S. 934 (1977). Justice White would have heard argument.

2. *First party benefits—Who is eligible?* Before considering the wisdom of the legislation, we must understand how it works. Review the questions posed just before the statute. Each is now presented in the context of specific situations. (In each assume that the person was hurt in a motor vehicle accident, unless that point is in doubt.)

a. An inattentive driver crashes into a tree.

b. An intoxicated driver crashes into a tree.

c. A passenger is hurt when the driver of his car, who is intoxicated, drives off the road. May the passenger recover first party benefits?

In setting forth rules to be followed by insurers in settling claims for first party benefits, the Insurance Department has promulgated the following provisions (11 NYCRR 65.15(*l*)):

(2) An insurer shall pay benefits to an applicant for losses arising out of an accident in the following situations:

(i) where coverage has been excluded for an applicant operating a vehicle while in an intoxicated condition or while the applicant's ability is impaired by the use of a drug, if such intoxicated or drugged condition was not a contributing cause of the accident causing the injuries;

(ii) where coverage has been excluded for an applicant operating or occupying a motor vehicle known to the applicant to be stolen, and the applicant is an involuntary operator or occupant of said vehicle;

(iii) where there is no physical contact between the applicant and a motor vehicle or motorcycle which is the proximate cause of the injury;

(iv) where the motor vehicle or motorcycle is used without the specific permission of the owner but is not a stolen vehicle; or

(v) where the accident arises out of repairing, servicing or otherwise maintaining a motor vehicle or a motorcycle, other than in the course of a business, and for which no charge or fee is contemplated.

Do these provisions appear consistent with the spirit of the legislation?

3. *When can insurers deny benefits?* Insurers have taken advantage of the opportunity afforded in § 5103(b) to write exclusions into their policies for certain types of behavior.

Claimant, "who was intoxicated at the time, climbed onto the hood of an automobile owned and operated by respondent's insured, and began to smash the car's windshield with his foot. It appears that the insured accelerated the car, causing the claimant to fall from the hood, and sustain injuries." The court upheld the arbitrator's award of no-fault benefits. Claimant came within no permissible exclusion in § 5103(b). Nor was the award "contrary to strong public policy." The result was within "the letter and spirit of the no-fault law, which was designed to provide compensation to victims of motor vehicle accidents, regardless of fault." Bamond v. Nationwide Mut. Ins. Co., 75 App.Div.2d 812, 427 N.Y.S.2d 642 (1980), affirmed 52 N.Y.2d 957, 419 N.E.2d 872, 437 N.Y.S.2d 969 (1981).

Husband and wife were having a quarrel while they were driving home at 30 miles per hour. Husband "abruptly exited from the passenger side of the moving car." When the insurer denied benefits, husband sought arbitration. The arbitrator concluded that although the husband had "intentionally left the vehicle" there was "no evidence whatsoever that he intentionally caused his own personal injury." The master arbitrator vacated the arbitrator's award and concluded that there was "no rational basis upon which the arbitrator could have found" the injury to have been unintentional. The court held that the master arbitrator had not exceeded his powers of review in concluding that this behavior constituted "intentional self-caused injury" within the meaning of the statute and the policy. He had not reweighed evidence or credibility. Matter of Smith (Fireman's Ins. Co.), 55 N.Y.2d 224, 433 N.E.2d 509, 448 N.Y.S.2d 444 (1982).

An insurance company wrote a policy that excluded from coverage injury sustained by "any person as a result of operating a motor vehicle while in an intoxicated condition and while his ability to operate such vehicle is impaired by the use of a drug." Decedent's blood test results demonstrated a blood alcohol content of .21 percent, clearly indicating intoxication. Since there was no evidence that driver's ability was also impaired by the use of a drug, the exclusion could not apply. "The exclusionary language herein is clearly plain and unambiguous and, in the exercise of reason, susceptible to but one interpretation." Maxwell v. State Farm Mut. Auto. Ins. Co., 92 App.Div.2d 1049, 461 N.Y.S.2d 541 (1983).

4. *What constitutes "use or operation"?* Section 5102(b) defines "first party benefit" in terms of "injury arising out of the use or operation of a motor vehicle." "Use or operation," under insurance department regulations "includes the loading or unloading of such vehicle but does not include conduct within the course of a business of repairing, servicing, or otherwise maintaining motor vehicles, unless the conduct occurs off the business premises." Boundaries always cause litigation. In each case consider the consequences of a decision either way.

a. P, a pedestrian, was injured in a collision with a bicyclist. P sued the owner of a parked truck that had obstructed his view. Held: the statute was inapplicable because the injuries did not arise out of the use or operation of a motor vehicle. Rather, the truck was "merely parked on a public street and was not, at that time, being used or otherwise engaged in some ongoing activity." Wooster v. Soriano, 167 App.Div.2d 233, 561 N.Y.S.2d 731 (1990).

b. P was hurt when the gas stove she was using in her "mini-motor home" exploded. At the time the vehicle was parked at a campground. The court denied recovery on the ground that "use or operation" contemplated "use of the motor vehicle qua motor vehicle, not the use of equipment built into the vehicle to serve some other function." Reisinger v. Allstate Ins. Co., 58 App.Div.2d 1028, 397 N.Y.S.2d 52 (1977), affirmed on the opinion below 44 N.Y.2d 881, 379 N.E.2d 221, 407 N.Y.S.2d 695 (1978).

c. A bus driver was "stabbed by a passenger whom he refused to discharge from the bus at a location other than a designated bus stop." The driver's claim for no-fault benefits was denied. The injury, although occurring on a bus, did not arise from "the intrinsic nature of the bus, as such, nor did the bus, itself, produce the injury." Matter of Manhattan & Bronx Surface Transit Operating Authority (Gholson), 71 App.Div.2d 1004, 420 N.Y.S.2d 298 (1979).

P was shot by another driver after an accident involving their two cars. The other driver fled the scene and was never apprehended. The court, relying on *Gholson,* denied first-party benefits because the gunshot wound had not arisen from the use or operation of a vehicle. Locascio v. Atlantic Mutual Insurance Co., 127 App.Div.2d 746, 511 N.Y.S.2d 934 (1987), appeal denied 70 N.Y.2d 616, 521 N.E.2d 443, 526 N.Y.S.2d 436 (1988).

d. Claimant fell three to six feet away from the waiting bus that she was going to board. Her heel caught in broken pavement. The arbitrator held claimant an "incipient passenger" who was hurt through the "use or operation" of the bus. Recognizing that judicial review of compulsory arbitration permitted wider judicial review than when voluntary arbitration was involved, the court concluded that the arbitrator's determination lacked a rational basis. "A pedestrian cannot be converted into a user [of a motor vehicle] by virtue of close proximity" to the vehicle. New York City Transit Authority v. Ambrosio, 102 Misc.2d 846, 428 N.Y.S.2d 131 (1980).

e.   P tripped over a fuel hose that had been extended from an oil delivery truck across the sidewalk to an intake valve to supply a building. The truck was being used to deliver oil and the motor was running to pump the oil. The court held that P was entitled to first party benefits. Yanis v. Texaco, Inc., 85 Misc.2d 94, 378 N.Y.S.2d 570 (1975). See also Celona v. Royal Globe Ins. Co., 85 App.Div.2d 635, 444 N.Y.S.2d 934 (1981).

f.   P was injured while sailing over a frozen lake in a "parakite" that was tethered by a rope to the back of a Chevy pick-up truck. Her injuries occurred when she attempted to land the kite. The court upheld an arbitrator's award of benefits: "The operation of the vehicle caused the parakite to be airborne and, at the time of the landing, the parakite was still attached to the vehicle." Pierce v. Utica Mutual Insurance Co., 110 App.Div.2d 1023, 488 N.Y.S.2d 311 (1985). The court also held that the master arbitrator had abused his discretion in reviewing, de novo, the original arbitrator's decision where a rational basis existed for the original finding of coverage.

5. *First party benefits—What is recoverable?* Once the question of eligibility is resolved, the next question becomes the amount of benefits that an eligible victim may recover.

a.   What is the relationship between "first party benefits" and "basic economic loss"?

b.   Are any major medical or other out-of-pocket expenses excluded from the victim's recovery?

c.   What is the maximum wage loss that a covered person may be paid after losing $4,000 in one month? The gross figure of $4,000 should be reduced by 20 percent. Since that amount exceeds $2,000, it should be reduced to the $2,000 maximum. (The $2,000 maximum in § 5102(a)(2) was raised from $1,000 in 1991.) See Kurcsics v. Merchants Mut. Ins. Co., 49 N.Y.2d 451, 403 N.E.2d 159, 426 N.Y.S.2d 454 (1980), which overturned an insurance department regulation that had limited the benefits to 80% of the statutory maximum.

d.   Claimant, a covered person, had medical expenses of $34,000 and lost earnings of $17,000. The insurer deducted 20 percent under § 5102(b)(1) and for Social Security disability payments under § 5102(b)(2). The result was that the insurer paid P $41,000. When claimant presented current medical bills, the insurer responded that its outer limit of liability of $50,000 had already been reached. The court held, 4–1, for the insurer. The statute spoke of $50,000 as the maximum coverage for "basic economic loss." Since first party benefits are defined as basic economic loss less certain setoffs, the $50,000 figure cannot apply to first party benefits. Normile v. Allstate Ins. Co., 87 App.Div.2d 721, 448 N.Y.S.2d 907 (1982). The Court of Appeals affirmed on the decision below, 60 N.Y.2d 1003, 459 N.E.2d 843, 471 N.Y.S.2d 550 (1983), with one judge dissenting on the grounds that the result "allows insurers to avoid their primary responsibility for compensating for basic economic loss, and leaves innocent persons in a position whereby they may be unable to obtain full compensation for their injuries."

e.   What role do deductibles play in the scheme?   Recall §§ 5103(c) and (g).

6.   *First party benefits—Special case of motorcycles.*   The legislature originally excluded motorcyclists from having to provide coverage for themselves or their riders because of the high cost of such coverage.   In 1977, the legislature added "or a motorcycle" to § 5103(a)(1) and added "other than occupants of a motorcycle" to § 5103(a)(2).   At the same time the legislature added § 5103(f) providing that motorcycle liability policies must provide for payment of first party benefits to persons "other than occupants of such motorcycle, or any motor vehicle" for loss arising from the use of the motorcycle.

In Carbone v. Visco, 115 App.Div.2d 948, 497 N.Y.S.2d 524 (1985), the court ruled that an injured motorcyclist is not entitled to first party benefits under the statute.   Although a motorcyclist is required to maintain liability insurance under the financial security provisions of the Insurance Law, first-party benefits under the policy run only to pedestrians.

7.   *First party benefits—Whose insurer pays?*   This problem is often phrased as whether the insurance "follows the car or follows the family."   Consider which insurer pays if C, who owns a car and has a proper insurance policy:

a.   Drives off the road into a tree.

b.   Is a passenger in a friend's car when it goes into a tree.

c.   Is walking across the street and is run down by Y's car.   Does it matter whether Y has insurance?

d.   Is hurt when his car collides with Y's car.   Is § 5105 relevant?

e.   The original version did not mention separate treatment for buses.   What is the purpose of the provision in § 5103(a)(1)?

Does it matter whether the insurance follows the car or the family?

Viruet was driving his uninsured car when he came upon a car in need. He pulled up in front of it, left his own car and had taken two steps to the rear when he was struck by the insured.   The insurer rejected Viruet's claim for no-fault benefits, claiming that he was an occupant of his own car at the time.   The court disagreed.   Viruet testified that he was going to the disabled car and not to his own trunk.   If that was accepted he was a pedestrian.   But even if he was walking toward his own trunk with the intention of opening it and unloading equipment, "he clearly had not yet begun to do so and cannot be held to have been 'operating or occupying' his vehicle at the time he was struck."   General Accident, Fire & Life Ins.Co. v. Viruet, 169 App.Div.2d 608, 564 N.Y.S.2d 754 (1991).   What if had gone to the disabled car and then back to his own trunk to get a jack—and was hit as he was unlocking the trunk?   Relocking it?

Exclusion from coverage for an occupant of a motorcycle is different than for an occupant of a car. See General Accident Fire & Life Ins. Corp., Ltd. v. Avery, 88 App.Div.2d 739, 452 N.Y.S.2d 125 (1982), where plaintiff, who had his "left leg on the ground, his right knee on the seat, his right hand on the right handle bar with his left arm and hand extending down to check his drive train," was deemed not to be an occupant of his motorcycle and thus was entitled to benefits. Compare the implications of calling P in the motorcycle case not an occupant to calling P in the automobile case not an occupant.

8. *What is the role of arbitration?* As the statute and cases indicate, much of the work is handled by arbitrators. Resort to the courts is to be minimized—though when the decision of the master arbitrator awards at least $5,000, the disgruntled litigant may obtain a trial de novo. Short of that, critical questions emerge concerning the standards to be used by the arbitrator; by the master arbitrator reviewing the determination of the first arbitrator; and by the courts when reviewing the determinations of the master arbitrator. These matters are explored in Matter of Petrofsky v. Allstate Ins. Co., 54 N.Y.2d 207, 429 N.E.2d 755, 445 N.Y.S.2d 77 (1981).

The court concluded that the master arbitrator has no power to engage in extensive review of the first arbitrator's determination of fact or to reweigh the evidence. The question is whether or not the evidence is sufficient to support the first arbitrator's determination. The master arbitrator is to determine that the first decision was reached in a "rational manner, that the decision was not arbitrary and capricious, incorrect as a matter of law, in excess of the policy limits, or in conflict with other designated no-fault arbitration proceedings."

Judicial review of the master arbitrator's decision is generally limited to determining that the decision was not arbitrary and capricious and that it had a rational or plausible basis.

9. *Serious injury—Is a tort action available?* The original version of the law contained a two-part definition of serious injury keyed to the nature of the injuries and the amount of the medical expenses. The monetary part provided that a serious injury would be established if reasonable medical costs exceeded $500. This part was repealed in 1977 because that level was attained too frequently, either because of inflation in medical costs or because victims obtained arguably needless medical treatment simply to exceed the $500 level.

Before a claim for pain and suffering can be pursued, the trial court must determine whether the plaintiff has established a prima facie case of serious injury. Licari v. Elliott, 57 N.Y.2d 230, 441 N.E.2d 1088, 455 N.Y.S.2d 570 (1982). Determining what constitutes a "serious injury" under the statute has not been easy. In Miller v. Miller, 100 App.Div.2d 577, 473 N.Y.S.2d 513 (1984), the "infant plaintiff" had suffered an injury in an automobile accident that resulted in the severing of the muscles circling the lips and the consequential inability to pucker. The court held that a "serious injury" had been established: "[T]he 'significant limitation of use of a body function' does not require *permanence,* but instead requires a fact finding on the issue of whether the dysfunction is important enough to reach the level of *significance*. Similarly, the 'permanent loss of . . . a body . . . function' does not involve in any fashion the element of *significance*, but only that of *permanence*. Indeed, if it did, there would be no need to list 'significant limitation of use of a body function' in a separate category." Although the court found that a permanent loss need not be significant to constitute a serious injury, "[t]he fact that this function may not loom large when compared to other muscles and body functions may be relevant on the issue of damages."

Fractures of a bone are clearly covered: tooth fractures are less clear. Compare Kennedy v. Anthony, 195 App.Div.2d 942, 600 N.Y.S.2d 980 (1993)(jury question whether fractured tooth that required "some repair work" and was sensitive to pressure and cold was serious injury) with Spevak v. Spevak, 213 App.Div.2d 622, 624 N.Y.S.2d 232 (1995)(fracture of structure that held one of victim's baby teeth that was "successfully treated by pushing the tooth back into place" was not serious injury; "a broad construction of the statutory term 'fracture' to include a minor tooth injury of the type involved herein would expand rather than narrow the number of personal injury actions, thereby undermining the intent of the Legislature" in enacting the statute).

The court indicated in *Licari* that whether or not there has been serious injury is not always a jury question. In Scheer v. Koubek, 70 N.Y.2d 678, 512 N.E.2d 309, 518 N.Y.S.2d 788 (1987), the court overturned a jury's finding of serious injury where the victim suffered severe, recurring back pain but had suffered no loss of mobility or any permanent disability. Pain alone could not form the basis for a serious injury under the statute. In Caruso v. Hall, 101 App.Div.2d 967, 477 N.Y.S.2d 722 (1984), affirmed 64 N.Y.2d 843, 476 N.E.2d 648, 487 N.Y.S.2d 322 (1985), the court overturned a jury award of $15,000 because a three-inch scar on the top of the victim's head did not constitute significant disfigurement; his hair grew over it within two weeks after the accident. In Savage v. Delacruz, 100 App.Div.2d 707, 474 N.Y.S.2d 850 (1984), the court ruled that a material fact existed whether a sprained ankle and scars in the area of the knee constitute serious injury. The test for determining serious disfigurement is "whether a reasonable person viewing plaintiff's body in its altered state would regard the condition as unattractive, objectionable, or as the subject of pity or scorn."

What if P suffers a one month wage loss of $1,000 in wages and sues the motorist at fault for the $200 deducted under § 5102(b)(1)? Assume that P did not suffer "serious injury." What if P suffered a one month wage loss of $4,000?

In Duran v. Heller, 203 App.Div.2d 414, 610 N.Y.S.2d 562 (1994), a victim who could not show serious injury was barred from recovering damages for pain and suffering from a drunk driver. Is this shocking?

10. *What are the differences between suing a "covered person" and suing someone else?* Do these differences affect the plaintiff's recovery? Recall the problem your client presented.

When the insured may have a tort action against a non-covered person, the value of that claim depends upon whether the first party insurer is entitled to a lien under § 5104(b) and, if so, how large a lien. It is clear that "the insured and the tortfeasors cannot arbitrarily determine between themselves that any settlement is for pain and suffering rather than for items of basic economic loss." Firemen's Ins. Co. v. Bowley, 110 Misc.2d 168, 441 N.Y.S.2d 947 (1981). In such cases, a hearing may be required to allocate the total award. If the parties agree that their settlement only relieves the tortfeasor of liability for pain and suffering (or if the suit claims only such harm), then the insurer is not prejudiced. Allocation issues also exist if the tort case results in a general jury verdict.

See Hyde v. North River Ins. Co., 92 App.Div.2d 1001, 461 N.Y.S.2d 468 (1983) (since recovery by insured against noncovered party was solely for pain, suffering, and future economic loss—carrier had already paid maximum amount—carrier had no lien against proceeds of judgment against tortfeasor). For a case on the risks of settlement with others without protecting the rights of the first party insurer, see Weinberg v. Transamerica Ins. Co., 62 N.Y.2d 379, 465 N.E.2d 819, 477 N.Y.S.2d 99 (1984)("It is the burden of the insured to establish by virtue of an express limitation in the release or of a necessary implication arising from the circumstances of its execution that the release did not operate to prejudice the subrogation rights of the insurer").

In Biette v. Baxter, 57 N.Y.2d 698, 440 N.E.2d 534, 454 N.Y.S.2d 535 (1982), a tort action was brought against the manufacturer of a defective metal plate put in plaintiff's leg as treatment after the auto accident. The court accorded the first party insurer a lien for the amounts it had paid out because of the defective prosthetic device. "Though not a joint tortfeasor, the manufacturer is a noncovered person whose product aggravated the personal injury for which the insurer was required to pay first-party benefits" and this gave rise to a lien under § 5104(b).

11. *What happens to the uncovered victim?* Several lower court cases have struggled with the question of when, if ever, persons who do not qualify as "covered persons" may bring tort actions. Most commonly, these are uninsured drivers, or members of the family of an uninsured driver, who are hurt in a multi-vehicle collision. In each case, the victim has claimed the right to sue in tort under pre–1973 rules on the ground that the statute should not be read to change the common law more than it specifies—and it is silent on the tort rights of uncovered persons.

Several views are possible, including: tort law remains fully applicable; tort law is totally barred; and uncovered persons may sue in tort only if they sustain "serious injury." In Wilson v. E. & J. Trucking Corp., 94 App.Div.2d 666, 462 N.Y.S.2d 660 (1983), a New York resident who registered his car in Connecticut was uninsured in either state. The court ruled that he did not qualify as a "covered person" and thus was not entitled to no-fault benefits for his basic economic loss. Although the trial court awarded him $23,000 from the third-party tortfeasor, the appellate court reduced the award by $2,000 "as the approximate total of medical expenses, loss of earnings and out-of-pocket expenses attributable to the accident."

What about passengers who are also injured? See Millan v. Yan Yee Lau, 99 Misc.2d 630, 420 N.Y.S.2d 529 (App.T.1979), concluding that the uninsured driver should "at the very least" be limited by the threshold requirement of serious injury of § 5102(d) but the "innocent" passengers in the uninsured vehicle should retain their common law tort action.

In Carbone v. Visco, supra, the court held that the injured motorcyclist, who was not covered by first party benefits, "is entitled to pursue his common law remedies in an action against defendants as owner and operator of a motor vehicle involved in the accident. Under these circumstances, he is not required to comply with the 'serious injury' provision of Insurance Law § 5104."

12. *Meshing auto no–fault, workers' compensation, and tort law.* The massive effort to draft no-fault legislation for the motor vehicle was so absorbing and complex that no one seemed to consider the problem of meshing the various systems as they are removed from the operation of tort law. Although § 5102(b)(2) provided that first party benefits do not include amounts recovered or recoverable under workers' compensation, the statute ignored the work-related motor vehicle accident. The courts were quickly engulfed by this problem.

After some uncertainty, the legislature amended the Workers' Compensation Law to provide that the compensation carrier shall have no lien on the proceeds of any recovery as to benefits it paid "which were in lieu of first party benefits which another insurer would have otherwise been obligated to pay" under the no-fault law. "The sole remedy" of the compensation carrier is the settlement process contained in § 5105, but only if at least one vehicle involved weighs more than 6,500 pounds unloaded or is a motor vehicle used principally for the transportation of persons or property for hire; except that as to occupants of a bus or school bus (other than operator or employee) a compensation carrier has no right to proceed under § 5105.

For an extended discussion of the interplay of these regimes, see Dietrick v. Kemper Insurance Co., 76 N.Y.2d 248, 556 N.E.2d 1108, 557 N.Y.S.2d 301 (1990), in which plaintiff suffered a permanently disfiguring scar on her forehead in an auto accident while at work.

13. *Meshing no–fault benefits and uninsured motorist coverage.* When the covered person is the victim of a hit-and-run driver or an identified but uninsured motorist, the covered person's insurance policy is likely to provide for no-fault benefits and for tort damages, if fault can be established, under the uninsured motorist coverage. What happens when, after the insurer has paid no-fault benefits, the victim seeks recovery under the uninsured motorist coverage? The insurers have insisted on an offset to avoid double recovery for the same items. But the courts have held that to the extent the victim has suffered "serious injury," the tort recovery is for pain and suffering so there is no double recovery. Adams v. Government Employees Ins. Co., 52 App.Div.2d 118, 383 N.Y.S.2d 319 (1976) and Sinicropi v. State Farm Ins. Co., 55 App.Div.2d 957, 391 N.Y.S.2d 444 (1977)("The no-fault benefits are for basic economic loss and the uninsured motorist coverage is for pain and suffering and other expenses incurred which are not compensable by no-fault benefits. Neither the Insurance Law nor the insurance policy allows the insurer to set off those benefits.") Is there likely to be a case in which the entire recovery under the uninsured motorist coverage could not reasonably be allocated to items excluded under the no-fault system?

In Page v. Commercial Union Assurance Co., 64 App.Div.2d 850, 407 N.Y.S.2d 343 (1978), $2,000 of the $6,400 in uninsured motorist payments were stated to be for medical expense already paid, or payable, by the no-fault benefits. The court ordered the payment under uninsured motorist coverage reduced by $2,000.

14. *First party pain and suffering?* Traditionally, we have thought about pain and suffering as an adjunct to a negligence action. Indeed, recall that Professor Jaffe, p. 623, supra, doubted that the award could be justified in the absence of fault. One of the stumbling blocks to the development of automobile no-fault plans has been the future of pain and suffering. In a thoroughgoing no-fault plan that abolished all tort recovery, would there be any place for pain and suffering?

To the extent that mixed no-fault plans have allowed tort actions for pain and suffering, how much of this is explained by the felt need to preserve the opportunity for injured victims to recover this item of damages? Has that need been perceived in terms of the desirability of the plaintiff getting the funds—or because of the sense that, in this civilized form of vengeance, the money must come from the defendant? Some have stressed the role of vengeance in personal injury law—particularly in something as personal as automobile driving. See Ehrenzweig, A Psychoanalysis of Negligence, 47 Nw.U.L.Rev. 855 (1953) and Linden, Faulty No Fault: A Critique of the Ontario Law Reform Commission Report on Motor Vehicle Accident Compensation, 13 Osgoode Hall L.J. 449 (1975): "It should be remembered that the tort suit was invented in order to try to assuage the thirst for vengeance in society by furnishing a peaceful substitute to the blood feud. If the right to sue were eliminated altogether, I would worry about people once again resorting to private vengeance upon those who do them wrong. In my view, it is preferable to pursue a wrongdoer with a writ rather than with a rifle." But see Hasson, Blood–Feuds, Writs and Rifles—A Reply to Professor Linden, 14 Osgoode Hall L.J. 445 (1976).

Despite this, it is not clear how much of the desire to retain access to the tort action for all, or at least serious, injuries has been based on the assumption that such a step is essential to preserve access to pain and suffering. For an extensive discussion of first-party insurance coverage for pain and suffering and of the market for such insurance, see Croley & Hanson, The Nonpecuniary Costs of Accidents: Pain-and-Suffering Damages in Tort Law, 108 Harv.L.Rev. 1785 (1995).

15. *Basic questions about the statute.*

a. Why make the first party benefits compulsory? Why not eliminate the tort action in the smaller cases (or all cases) and allow individuals to decide for themselves whether to obtain insurance?

b. Once the decision is made to compel substantial first party protection, why compel the purchase of liability insurance?

c. Is $50,000 an appropriate limit on first party benefits? Why might a state make the figure $5,000? $500,000? In addition to complaints about the tort system mentioned in the Report, some have objected to the tort system because it is regressive. See Hasson, Blood–Feuds, Writs and Rifles—A Reply to Professor Linden, 14 Osgoode Hall L.J. 445, 449 (1976), suggesting that no-fault systems are less regressive than negligence law: "Under the negligence system both a rich man and a poor man pay the same premium but there is no limit as to how much the rich person can recover under the negligence system." By way of contrast, he noted that as to lost income in no-fault systems, "a rich man would have to pay more than a person with a modest income to obtain adequate protection against future loss of income."

See also Lowenfeld and Mendelsohn, The United States and the Warsaw Convention, 80 Harv.L.Rev. 497, 565 (1967), reporting on debates over an international agreement for airplane crashes. The American delegates were arguing for a system with recovery limits higher than the then-ceiling of $8,300. (This was later achieved.) But other countries "asked why the poorer countries, the poorer airlines, and the poorer travelers should pay for the rich ones. Why, in the words of the Nigerian delegate, should the peasant be required to pay for the comfort of the king?" Is this an important concern? What factors should be most important in calculating premiums under the statute? The Warsaw Convention is discussed at p. 790, infra.

d. Should the first party benefits be primary as against private collateral sources such as hospital and accident insurance? Why not make the statutory benefits primary as against state workers' compensation payments? Is the deductible arrangement sound?

e. Is the statute likely to increase accidents?

f. If some limitation on tort law is desired, is the statute's approach to that limitation sound?

g. Might the goal of eliminating small cases have been achieved by excluding the first $10,000 of pain and suffering from the plaintiff's award?

16. *No-fault in the states.* As noted earlier, the Massachusetts version of no-fault provided minimal no-fault benefits but did bar the bringing of some tort actions. As the states began to adopt no-fault statutes in the 1970s, they tended to follow one of two paths. (No state adopted a "pure" no-fault plan that totally abolished tort—as had been proposed in 1968 by some insurers.) About half of the states that did act, adopted what are called "add-on" statutes because they do not change tort law in any way.

Instead, they provide for low first-party benefits to help meet medical expenses and lost wages. If the plaintiff does pursue an available tort action, the first-party insurer is entitled to have its no-fault payments reimbursed from the tort award.

Although it might seem that the combination of first-party benefits plus unaltered tort law should be more expensive than the existing system, there is some evidence that victims who gain quick and easy first-party benefits in small cases may not pursue the available tort remedy.

The other half of the states that have acted, have adopted what are called "mixed" plans. These plans provide some first-party benefits—in amounts varying from small to large—and also bar some plaintiffs from access to the traditional tort system. The generosity of the first-party benefits is usually commensurate with the difficulty of the tort barrier. Massachusetts, as we have seen, adopted a mixed plan with small benefits and a relatively minor barrier to tort actions. Consider how the Massachusetts plan would be changed if the no-fault benefits were raised from $2,000 to $20,000 and the tort exclusion were raised to $20,000. New York's approach is found only in Michigan, which provides even more generous no-fault benefits than New York and comparable restrictions on the tort action. (If a pedestrian who does not own a car is hit by an uninsured motorist, every no-fault state has some mechanism for providing no-fault benefits to the pedestrian.)

"Pure" No–Fault? In 1995, the Hawaii legislature adopted a pure automobile no-fault scheme—the first in the United States. It was vetoed by the governor and did not become law. In March, 1996, California voters are scheduled to vote on an initiative creating a nearly-pure version of auto no-fault, in which the only lawsuits would be against drunk drivers. A month before the initiative the state assembly adopted a very similar bill—with the exception that the assembly bill would return to the current system unless the no-fault system reduced premiums by 25 percent within a year. Bernstein, No–Fault Auto Plan Clears Assembly, L.A. Daily News, Feb. 1, 1996 at N1.

17. *No–fault and property damage.* Our concern has been primarily with the personal injury aspect of no-fault. If that can be handled to the satisfaction of the public, it is unlikely that property damage will cause an insoluble problem. Many motor vehicles on the road today are being bought on time payments. Financing companies insist that the vehicle be insured against damage and have comprehensive coverage to protect the lender's interest in the car in case the buyer defaults on the payments. Thus, when property damage occurs it is almost entirely covered by insurance and does not present serious dislocations. The amount of possible damage is readily ascertained and is unlikely to be great. It will be correlated with ability to bear the loss: the most expensive cars are usually owned by those who can most easily bear the loss—with or without insurance. But these people are also most likely to have their own insurance even if it is not required.

As matters now stand, property damage is generally excluded from coverage in no-fault states and tort law remains in effect. These cases are much easier to settle out of court than are personal injury actions—particularly since smaller sums are involved and most of the disputes are between insurance companies.

For a discussion of the problems of covering property damage, see Brainard and Lord, No-Fault Property Damage: A Canadian Vehicle-to-Vehicle Damage Insurance Proposal—Would it Work in the U.S.?, 1977 Ins.L.J. 663.

18. *Federal legislation?* Finally, we note that although the first steps in no-fault legislation have occurred at the state level, some would like to see the federal government enter the area. Congressional efforts in recent years have failed by close votes. The most seriously discussed legislation is a two-tier approach. Congress would set minimum requirements for the states to meet. The package would be more substantial than New York's and might include no-fault medical benefits in unlimited amount plus a very generous coverage for wage loss. A tort action would be possible along the lines of the New York statute—but excluding fractures. If a state did not "voluntarily" adopt such a plan by the deadline, the next tier—the direct federal plan—would become operative in that state. This plan would be the same as the first tier plan, plus a ban on limiting payments for economic loss and, perhaps, the abolition of all tort actions for pain and suffering.

Although some have argued that such a federal approach would be unconstitutional, the major attacks have been on the ground that the no-fault subject is a good one for state experimentation because there is little need for uniformity. Some states have no high premiums, court congestion, or dissatisfaction with current law. Also, urban states may find certain features more helpful than would rural states. Some have also opposed the federal plan on the merits—that it displaces an unduly large sector of tort law and that add-on plans are working well.

19. *The Horowitz–O'Connell proposal.* During the 1992 presidential election there was discussion of a plan that would permit motorists to choose either no-fault or tort. If they chose the no-fault option and the other person in the accident had done the same, they would both look to their own insurers for benefits, which would not include pain and suffering; they could sue the other for uncovered economic loss, but no suit could be brought against the other to recover pain and suffering. If both had chosen tort, the case would proceed as it now does under common law—for both economic loss and for pain and suffering.

If one had chosen no-fault and the other had chosen tort, the one who had chosen no-fault would get benefits from his or her insurer, could not sue the other driver for pain and suffering, and would be free of a pain and suffering claim from that other driver. The motorist who had chosen full tort coverage would be able to sue the no-fault motorist's insurer for economic loss only; but could also recover for pain and suffering from his own insurer if the no-fault motorist could be shown to have been negligent.

Note the analogy to the situation in which an insured motorist is injured by an uninsured or underinsured motorist—and winds up suing his or her own insurer for damages.   President Bush, who suggested this approach based on the work of Michael Horowitz and Professor Jeffrey O'Connell, estimated those who bought the no-fault coverage would save 50–60 percent of the bodily injury part of their insurance premium.   Since that part is usually about half the total premium, the saving would be in the range of 25–30 percent.   An economist at the Rand Institute for Civil Justice confirmed this level of savings.   If every motorist bought the coverage, the savings were estimated at $10 billion—one third from lower processing and litigating costs; two-thirds from lower payouts.   Passell, Auto Insurance: A Bush Plan to Cut Cost, N.Y.Times, Oct. 17, 1992, at 23. One critic argued that although under current plans high-risk drivers face sky-high premiums, under the proposal they would not; the plan was said to be "very good for high-risk drivers."   Why?   Are safer cars likely to result from the proposal?   Would you vote for such a plan?   Which coverage would you buy?

In late 1995, the plan resurfaced in Congress, in connection with efforts to address budgetary concerns.   See generally, O'Connell, Carroll, Horowitz, Abrahamse, & Kaiser, The Costs of Consumer Choice for Auto Insurance in States Without No–Fault Insurance, 54 Md.L.Rev. 281 (1995), including, in an appendix, a draft Model Legislation for Creation of a Consumer Choice in Motor Vehicle Insurance Act.   For an earlier discussion by the same group, see O'Connell, et al., Consumer Choice in the Auto Insurance Market, 52 Md.L.Rev. 1016 (1993).

D.   FOCUSED NO-FAULT SCHEMES

Workers' compensation established a pattern for addressing perceived deficiencies in the common law tort system.   Although it has not overridden the legislative impulse to adopt incremental changes such as those discussed at the beginning of this chapter, the workers' compensation approach—blocking out a category of accidental harm for no-fault treatment—has been a much-used strategy for effecting major tort reform.   In this section, we examine the principal areas other than workplace and motor vehicle injuries in which the states, and at times the federal government, have decided either to replace or to supplement the tort system with a no-fault scheme.   At the same time, we will look at some of the major no-fault proposals that have been suggested but not yet adopted.

In analyzing the focused no-fault schemes discussed below, consider the rationale for developing alternatives to the tort system, the efficacy of the schemes presented, the nature of the trade-offs involved, and the wisdom of piecemeal revisions in the tort area.   Are the programs that have been instituted special responses to egregious tort system performance?   Could or should similar schemes be adopted more generally? What are the limits of this approach to reform?   On these questions, see generally Rabin, *Some Reflections on the Process of Tort Reform*, 25 San Diego L. Rev. 13 (1988).

The following excerpt describes some of the major no-fault legislation and proposals in the toxics area as part of a larger effort to evaluate the wisdom of adopting a broad-based toxics mass tort compensation scheme.

Some Thoughts on the Efficacy of a Mass Toxics Administrative Compensation Scheme

Robert L. Rabin.
52 Maryland Law Review 951, 955–62 (1993).

II. Toxics Compensation Schemes: Exploratory Models

A. Tort/No–Fault Hybrid: The Price–Anderson Act

The Price–Anderson Act[15] signaled one of the first legislative responses to perceived deficiencies of the common law tort model in dealing with potential mass tort liability. Congress passed the Act in 1957 with the express intent of encouraging investment in nuclear energy research and operations by a private sector daunted by the prospect of multimillion-dollar claims and a constrained insurance market. Overall the Act imposes a set of statutory constraints on possible catastrophic tort liability in the event of a nuclear accident, and has essentially established a hybrid system that combines components of both tort and no-fault compensation models.

The system is financed through a combination of private insurance and mandatory contributions to a common fund—contributions which, in the aggregate, set the limit on total liability for any nuclear incident. In accordance with recent amendments to the Act, each nuclear licensee is required to purchase $150 million of private liability insurance. In addition, each licensee must contribute $63 million to a common compensation fund in the event of a nuclear accident at any plant. The liability limit of the fund, with over 100 plants in operation, is approximately $7 billion at present.[*]

The Price–Anderson funding scheme closely resembles a no-fault model to the extent that it relies substantially on a pooling mechanism to compensate aggrieved parties, thus de-emphasizing the importance of individual responsibility. This pooling mechanism in conjunction with the lack of an experience or risk-rating provision in the statute, blunts the incentives for optimal safety investment by individual firms under Price–Anderson. But at the same time the non-tort sanctions on suboptimal safety that would result from a serious nuclear accident, including the destruction of the facility itself, are very powerful.

---

15. 42 U.S.C. § 2210 (1988).

[*] In 1995, the required amounts were $200 million of liability insurance and a $75 million maximum contribution in case of a nuclear accident. The liability limit of the fund was correspondingly higher.

The Act provides for the adjudication of claims as follows. In the event of an "extraordinary nuclear occurrence" (defined as a dispersal causing substantial radiation levels and damage to offsite victims), all claims are consolidated in the federal court for the district in which the incident occurred. The Act creates strict liability in tort for licensees involved in nuclear incidents and abrogates the defense of contributory fault. By consolidating all claims into one jurisdiction and applying a single body of law, Price–Anderson incorporates certain features of the public law tort model.[16]

With respect to establishing liability, however, Price–Anderson maintains some of the distinctive flavor of traditional tort law. The claims process retains a two-party character, with each individual claimant bearing the burden of establishing causation and particularizing proof of economic loss and intangible harm. In this sense the Price–Anderson approach, in practice, might prove to be almost as inefficient as the standard common law tort approach.

Allen v. United States,[17] a case filed under the Federal Tort Claims Act by alleged victims of the Nevada atomic bomb tests in the 1950's, provides a recent tort analogue that illustrates how causation and damage issues under Price–Anderson might be resolved in practice. After a three-month trial, the district court judge in *Allen* carefully distinguished among the variety of claims on the basis of medical literature on the etiology of various cancers, observational reports on the Nevada fallout, and testimony about victim exposure. Though the judge appears to have mastered the relevant scientific literature, *Allen* engenders deep pessimism about the efficacy of a Price–Anderson approach. The case took five years to dispose of at the trial court level, and, even if it had been affirmed, would still have left many types of claims open to dispute and further litigation.[18] The underlying problem in *Allen* arose from the court's retention of an individualized approach to damages and causation, which ensured a prolonged and costly process of decision. Similar problems would be virtually certain to arise in adjudication under Price–Anderson.[19]

Optimally, successful plaintiffs would collect from the fund the full extent of their proven economic and non-economic damages. However, Price–Anderson empowers the court to reduce the size of present claims proportionately when it appears that the ceiling on damages will be exceeded. In these situations the court is to establish a delayed injury

16. For an articulation of the public law tort model, see Rosenberg, The Causal Connection in Mass Exposure Cases: A "Public Law" Vision of the Tort System, 97 Harvard Law Review 851 (1984).

17. 588 F.Supp. 247 (D.Utah 1984).

18. The case was, in fact, reversed on other grounds (the discretionary act exemption in the Federal Tort Claims act). See Allen v. United States, 816 F.2d 1417 (10th Cir.1987).

19. In recognition of these difficulties, a recent comprehensive review of Price–Anderson recommends generic determinations of causation and scheduled treatment of nonpecuniary loss as elements in a package of "administrative features designed to speed the resolution of claims." See Report to the Congress from the Presidential Commission on Catastrophic Nuclear Accidents 5–10 (1990).

fund, setting aside part of the pooled contributions and insurance for claims arising within twenty years of the incident.[20]

B. Narrowly–Focused No–Fault: The National Childhood Vaccine Injury Act of 1986

The National Childhood Vaccine Injury Act of 1986[21] is in essence a narrowly focused no-fault compensation package affording relief to a designated class of product users, namely, children injured by exposure to certain government-mandated vaccines. Congress passed the Act in response to concerns of the vaccine manufacturers, who had threatened to withdraw from the market in response to the possibility of crushing liability resulting from the infrequent but unavoidable injuries from exposure to vaccines. Like the Price–Anderson Act, the vaccine statute created an alternative to common law tort liability to induce the private sector to make available products deemed essential to the public interest.

The compensation fund is financed by an excise tax on each dose of vaccine disbursed. Since most vaccine manufacturers enjoy a near monopoly position, a rise in the excise tax to pay an increased number of claims would probably not affect any manufacturer's market share. However, a limited measure of non-tort deterrent pressure is probably assured by the political repercussions that might well accompany any significant rise in the price of vaccines.

The Act establishes a two-tier system: alleged victims first proceed under a no-fault approach but retain the back-up option of pursuing a tort claim. Plaintiffs initially file claims in federal district court, where a special master is appointed to gather evidence and determine the award. The claimant must establish injury from a vaccine listed in the Vaccine

---

20. In the mid–1970's a proposed federal no-fault scheme for commercial aviation accident victims was modeled on Price–Anderson, according to its author. See Kennedy, Accidents in Commercial Air Transportation—A Proposed Reform of the Liability and Compensation System, 41 Journal of Air Law & Commerce 247 (1975). Like Price–Anderson, the aviation scheme would establish activity-related liability, eliminating the fault inquiry (and, indeed, establishing a very expansive definition of causal responsibility, since the carrier would also be liable for damage resulting from sabotage). There would also be a governmental indemnity provision for liability in excess of privately available insurance—a key provision, now superseded, of the Price–Anderson approach. Finally, there would be consolidation of all cases in the federal court of the jurisdiction in which the accident occurred, as there is under the nuclear incident legislation.

Nevertheless, there are some critical differences in the approach. Kennedy would

have federal indemnification financed from a surcharge on airline tickets, instead of the general revenue strategy originally adopted in Price–Anderson. Moreover, there is no provision for pooling of liability among the carriers above the insurance limits; rather, the government fund is an exclusive and unlimited source of indemnification. Also, the aviation plan eliminates pain and suffering liability except in cases of "permanent disfigurement or disability"—which, presumably, would be fairly common among survivors. (On the other hand, survival itself is quite uncommon.)

The proposal was never adopted. One can speculate that the capacity of the tort system to deal in a reasonably effective fashion with these "traditional" mass tort cases explains the relatively limited political appeal of the initiative.

21. 42 U.S.C. §§ 300aa–10 to 300aa–33 (West Supp. 1990).

Injury Table, demonstrate that the malady is on the list provided in the Table, and prove that the adverse reaction resulted within an exposure period designated in the Table. Claimants establishing these relatively straightforward conditions create a strong presumption of liability. By substantially eliminating contentious issues of causation, the Act is designed to settle claims in a more efficient manner than would the Price–Anderson Act.

Similarly, the vaccine statute provides a straightforward means of measuring damages. The statute covers all actual medical expenses as well as costs of rehabilitation. In addition, it provides compensation for lost earning power based on the average earnings of workers in the non-farm sector of the economy, determined annually on a prospective basis. The only indeterminate measure of damages is for pain and suffering, which may be awarded by the special master up to a limit of $250,000. Thus the Act strikes a balance between scheduled and individualized compensation, and, with the exception of retaining a scaled-down discretionary decision on pain and suffering, assesses damages in a simple and administratively efficient manner.

The claimant is entitled to reject the special master's award and seek tort relief instead. However, a number of disincentives are introduced to discourage this option. First, the Act adopts the principle of Restatement (Second) of Torts § 402A, comment *k*, which allows an appropriate warning to serve as an effective defense against [strict] liability. In addition, the Act adopts the "learned intermediary" doctrine, which requires adequate notice by the manufacturer only to the party administering the vaccination. Finally, the manufacturer is protected against punitive damage awards if it complies with the federal Food, Drug and Cosmetic Act and the Public Health Act. At least in its first few years of operation, this program design has had almost total success in inducing vaccine injury victims to accept the compensatory award and forgo their right to sue in tort.

In the final analysis, it must be emphasized that the compensation problem addressed by the vaccine statute is relatively narrow in scope. A determinate number of cases arise annually; litigation most often involves a single plaintiff alleging damages against an identifiable manufacturer after a relatively short latency period. The scientific information linking adverse reactions with a limited number of identified diseases is unusually reliable. So in most cases establishing liability under the Vaccine Injury Table is fairly simple. Consequently, the relevance of the vaccine statute to the most troublesome environmental or drug cases, with their mass tort, long-latency, identification, and causation problems, is far from clear.

C. Expansive No–Fault for Toxic Harms: Superfund 301(e) Study Group Report and Environmental Law Institute Model Statute

The Superfund 301(e) Report[22] and the Environmental Law Institute

---

22. A Report to Congress in Compliance with Section 301(e) of the Comprehensive Environmental Response, Compensation, and Liability Act of 1980, S. Comm. on Env't

(ELI) Model Statute[23] both propose no-fault compensation schemes for victims of toxic-related harms. Like the vaccine statute, both allow claimants the opportunity to pursue tort remedies if they are dissatisfied with the no-fault determinations. Unlike the Price–Anderson Act or the vaccine statute, however, neither proposal has been legislatively adopted. Since the Superfund and ELI proposals are relatively similar in scope, they will be considered together.

The Superfund proposal was developed as a by-product of the Superfund legislation of 1980. As such the scope of the proposal is limited to compensating harm that arises from exposure to a hazardous waste— defined by reference to a Toxic Substance Document prepared by a designated agency—released from a site that qualifies for cleanup under the Act. The ELI proposal is considerably broader, extending coverage to harms arising from exposure to a list of "hazardous chemical substances" that includes toxics presently designated under federal statutory schemes or subsequently listed under a petition process implemented by the Fund administrator. Consequently, the ELI proposal would cover harm resulting from exposure to a far wider array of actual or potential toxic agents, including asbestos, Agent Orange, and drugs.

The Superfund proposal would be financed in a manner analogous to the current Superfund design, relying on a tax levied on the production of toxic chemicals and crude oil and the disposal of hazardous waste. The ELI proposal would impose a tax on petroleum and chemical production as well, but would also phase in an annual hazard fee on such production which would reflect the risk-generating characteristics of the substances produced. To the extent that this variable fee is administratively feasible, the ELI financing scheme is superior to the Superfund scheme from a market deterrence perspective.

The adjudication of claims under the two proposals is very similar. The initial no-fault determination under the Superfund scheme addresses causation by a statutory rebuttable presumption, triggered when the claimant establishes that (1) a source was engaged at the time of exposure in the generation, transportation, or disposal of hazardous waste; (2) the claimant was exposed to the hazardous waste; and (3) the injury suffered by the claimant was of the kind known to result from such exposure. The Fund would use a Toxic Substance Document, analogous to the Vaccine Table, to assess the claimant's right to recovery.

Damages awarded under the Superfund proposal would include all medical expenses and two-thirds of lost income up to a high ceiling. Depending on the earning power of an individual claimant, the Superfund proposal would be either more or less generous than the vaccine statute in

& Pub. Works, Serial No. 97–12, 97th Cong. 2d Sess. (Sept. 1982).

23. Trauberman, Statutory Reform of "Toxic Torts": Reliving Legal, Scientific, and Economic Burdens on the Chemical Victim, 7 Harvard Environmental Law Review 177, 250–96 (1983).

compensating for lost wages. However, the Superfund scheme would not allow any recovery for pain and suffering.

If a claimant were dissatisfied with the no-fault award, he would be allowed to initiate a tort claim. Like the vaccine statute, the Superfund scheme creates disincentives to make this mode of action unattractive. Among other provisions, if the tort award is less than 25 percent greater than the no-fault award, the plaintiff must pay the court costs and expert witness fees of the defendant. In addition, the Fund must be reimbursed for payments disbursed in all cases. The ELI proposal creates a far more substantial disincentive to sue by requiring that a claimant return any benefit payments to the Fund *before* initiating a tort suit.

Creating such disincentives, however, raises an important equity concern. To guarantee fairness to potential claimants, both proposals would need careful scrutiny to ensure that statutory award levels were sufficiently generous to avoid claimants' being coerced into accepting a dubious bargain under the no-fault scheme.

One other aspect of the ELI proposal deserves attention. Even though this proposal establishes wider coverage for addressing environmental and other mass toxic tort cases than does the vaccine statute or the Superfund proposal, it remains problematic. It is unclear whether the ELI version of the Toxic Substance Document would provide both a scientifically sound and an efficient basis for resolving the vexing problems of causation. In addition, the ELI proposal leaves unresolved the issue of how the system would shift claims initiated in the tort system to the no-fault scheme once the hazardous nature of the product was well documented. Finally, there is a threshold question of whether the tort system has been an indispensable institutional mechanism—through pretrial discovery and the litigation process—for identifying toxic health hazards in the first instance.[24]

NOTES AND QUESTIONS

1. Drawing on these models, the author cautiously concludes that a strong case could be made for adopting a mass toxics administrative compensation scheme if "there were a clear prospect of a significant number of discrete mass tort cases occurring in the future on the scale of asbestos or the Dalkon Shield." To place this comment in context, consider that the Dalkon Shield settlement trust eventually had to cover about 240,000 claims, and that by 1990 the number of asbestos claims filed against the Johns Manville Co. alone had risen to 100,000.

The main features of such a scheme were sketched out in Enterprise Responsibility for Personal Injury, Vol. II, Approaches to Legal and Institutional Change, Report to the American Law Institute (1991), at p. 481 and would include:

---

24. See, e.g., P. Brodeur, *Outrageous Misconduct: The Asbestos Industry on Trial* (1985).

. . . a broad definition of "toxic harm"—in other words the compensable event—that would include chemical substances for which an identifiable threshold of exposure has been linked with serious illness or disease by scientific consensus. Claimants would be required to establish exposure to a designated source of the substance in order to create a rebuttable presumption of harm. The requisite exposure/source/substance connection could be established either by reference to a Toxic Substance Document adopted by the administrative compensation board, or by judicial referral to the board following a court determination that filed claims indicated the likelihood of a significant number of related, long-latency toxic harm cases.

Compensation would be for pecuniary loss, on the model of workers' compensation, with a modest allowance for scheduled nonpecuniary loss in serious cases. The tort system might be retained, but a claimant would be required to elect between no-fault benefits and a possible tort award. . . . The tort option would be scaled down by allowing only scheduled damages for nonpecuniary loss and by reversing the collateral source rule. The system would be financed, at least at the outset, by a flat tax on the gross revenues of toxics producers.

From this summary description, does a toxics no-fault scheme seem to have significant advantages over the tort system? Is it likely to have greater advantages in mass tort controversies than in "single incident" cases?

2. In thinking about alternatives to the tort system in mass toxics cases, no-fault is not the only possibility. In the article cited in footnote 16 of the Rabin article, David Rosenberg proposes a "public law tort model" that would significantly restructure the tort process in mass tort cases. The model would feature class action treatment of claims, probabilistic determination of causation, proportional liability among defendants, scheduled damages, and "insurance fund judgments" that would provide for later-arising cases. The Report to the American Law Institute, above, presents a later version of the model. See Report at pp. 412–439. On the deficiencies of the traditional tort system in mass toxics cases, see Rabin, Tort System on Trial: The Burden of Mass Toxics Litigation, 98 Yale L. J. 813 (1989). What would be the key questions in deciding whether the public law tort model or an administrative no-fault scheme, if either, is a more desirable alternative to the traditional system in mass toxics cases?

3. Is the problem of creating well-defined boundaries as to what constitutes a "compensable event"—i.e. regarding scope of coverage under a scheme—likely to be surmountable? Recent experience suggests that even the narrowly focused Vaccine Act may be problematic on this score. In early 1995, the Department of Health and Human Services promulgated new regulations reducing the number of potentially eligible recipients through narrower definitions of compensable events in the vaccine injury table, despite a 5–4 vote against the revisions by the Advisory Commission on Childhood Vaccines and the protests of parents' groups. The new regulations as well as commentary received during the hearing period can be found at 60 FR 7678–95 (1995).

For a case on the exclusivity of the Act (recall the similar discussion of this issue under workers' compensation), see Schafer v. American Cyanamid Co., 20 F.3d 1 (1st Cir.1994), holding that the family of a victim compensated under the Act is not barred from bringing loss of consortium suits in tort. For a comprehensive discussion of the program, see Steel, National Childhood Vaccine Injury Compensation Program: Is this the Best We Can Do for Our Children?, 63 Geo.Wash. L.Rev. 144 (1994).

4. *Swine Flu Act.* In the summer of 1976, fearing the possibility of a Swine Flu epidemic of a proportion not encountered since 1918–19, when the flu claimed the lives of over 500,000 Americans, the federal government planned the largest mass-immunization program in the nation's history. Insurance companies, however, refused to underwrite the government's proposed immunization program in light of the potential liability that vaccine manufacturers might encounter, foreshadowed by Reyes v. Wyeth Laboratories, 498 F.2d 1264 (5th Cir.), cert. denied 419 U.S. 1096 (1974). Nor would the vaccine manufacturers provide the necessary vaccine without insurance. In response to the resulting stalemate, Congress passed the Swine Flu Act, 42 U.S.C. § 247b(j)-(1)(1976), which amended the Federal Tort Claims Act to allow those injured by the vaccine to bring suit against the federal government for their injuries.

Under the Swine Flu Act, the United States replaced the named defendant in any plaintiff's suit against a manufacturer or distributor of the vaccine or any public or private agency or medical or health personnel who provided no-cost inoculation. These suits were tried before judges in the appropriate federal district courts, and plaintiffs could proceed on any theory of liability provided by the law of the state in which the act or omission occurred, including negligence, strict liability in tort, and breach of warranty. See e.g., Unthank v. United States, 732 F.2d 1517 (10th Cir.1984)(interpreting the compensatory nature of the Act broadly and finding the government liable on three separate theories of liability). The Act gave the government an indemnification right against the named party defendants based on negligence or contract.

Within two months of the beginning of the immunization program, after 40 million Americans had been inoculated, the federal government stopped the mass vaccinations. The vaccinations had resulted in serious unexpected complications, including a twelve-fold increase in the incidence of Guillain–Barre syndrome, a sometimes severe generalized paralytic disease. At the same time, the fear of a swine flu epidemic had quieted as no new cases of the flu had come to light.

Although the immunization program was over, the lawsuits stemming from the program had just begun. Over the next sixteen years, 4,181 claims were filed, seeking a total of $3.2 billion. By 1993, the U.S. government had settled 393 claims for a total of almost $38 million. Over 1,500 cases went to court, resulting in the government paying out almost $48 million. The total cost to American taxpayers was nearly $93 million.

Garrett, The Coming Plague: Newly Emerging Diseases in a World Out of Balance, 182 (1994).

5. *Black Lung Compensation.* Congress passed the Federal Coal Mine Health and Safety Act of 1969, Pub.L. No. 91–173, 83 Stat. 792 (1969), to aid those suffering from progressive coal mining-related respiratory disorders who were often prevented from recovering damages under state statutes of limitations and generally unable to recover from state workers' compensation plans because these plans did not compensate workers for occupational diseases. The Act has been amended three times since its original enactment. To receive compensation under the current federal black lung program, a miner (defined broadly to include all workers in mining-related work with a high degree of coal dust exposure) must prove the existence of black lung disease (known technically as pneumoconiosis), total disability from the disease, and that the disease was contracted from coal mining-related employment. Causation is presumed if the claimant can show ten years of coal mining-related work and contraction of black lung disease. Total disability is presumed upon proof of existence of a complicated black lung condition. For the current version, see 30 U.S.C. § 901 et seq.

Under the federal program, miners, or their survivors, file claims at a local Social Security Office, from which the claims are forwarded to the Department of Labor for processing. Compensatory payments are made by the last mine for which the miner worked for at least one year, and administrative expenses are paid by a Black Lung Disability Trust Fund, funded by an excise tax on coal.

The black lung program provides an interesting study of the problems associated with a federally coordinated, focused no-fault scheme because the availability of compensation under the program—determined chiefly by the number and strength of its presumptions—has been widened and narrowed substantially over its short life to respond to the need for compensation and subsequent charges of waste and overcompensation. The plan has been the subject of considerable controversy. In 1993, over 75,000 former miners were receiving black lung benefits at an annual cost of $1.3 billion.

For a comprehensive discussion of the Act and its various permutations over time, see P. Barth, The Tragedy of Black Lung: Federal Compensation for Occupational Disease (1987). Recent case law developments are discussed in Mattingly, Federal Black Lung Update, 96 W.Va. L.Rev. 819 (1994).

6. For a proposed no-fault scheme covering smoking-related harms, see Ausness, Compensation for Smoking–Related Injuries: An Alternative to Strict Liability in Tort, 36 Wayne L. Rev. 1085 (1990). The author states that the primary goal of the compensation scheme "would be to process claims for smoking-related injuries quickly and at minimal administrative cost. Compensation would be limited to economic losses and the program would be financed by an excise tax on cigarette manufacturing." Like many of the other toxic no-fault schemes, a smoking-related plan poses questions regarding causation and coverage limitations. In addition, it raises distinctive issues about no-fault and the "deserving" victim. How serious a consideration should this be?

7. *Note on Liability of International Air Carriers.* The Warsaw Convention, Convention for the Unification of Certain Rules Relating to International Transportation by Air, Oct. 12, 1929, 49 Stat. 3000, T.S. No. 876 (1934), note following 49 U.S.C. § 1502, is a multilateral treaty that regulates the liability of international air carriers. The Convention was drafted in 1929 and the United States became a signatory in 1934. Its terms apply to the international carriage of persons, luggage, or goods, performed by aircraft, either for reward or gratuitously. The Supreme Court has noted that the Convention's principal purpose was to provide uniform liability limitations and foster the growth of commercial aviation. Trans World Airlines, Inc. v. Franklin Mint Corp., 466 U.S. 243, 256 (1984).

The Convention establishes a system of strict liability for personal injuries and cargo losses that occur on international flights and limits the damages that passengers may recover. As originally drafted, the Convention limited recovery for loss of life or injury to $8,300. The maximum recovery amount was subsequently increased to $75,000. The Convention's limitations on damages are not applicable in cases of willful misconduct by an international air carrier or its employees. However, even in cases involving willful misconduct, the Convention has been interpreted to preclude recovery of punitive damages. In re Korean Air Lines Disaster, 932 F.2d 1475 (D.C.Cir.), cert. denied 502 U.S. 994 (1991); In re Air Disaster at Lockerbie, Scotland, 928 F.2d 1267 (2d Cir.), cert. denied 502 U.S. 920 (1991).

In Eastern Airlines, Inc. v. Floyd, 499 U.S. 530 (1991), the Supreme Court determined that the Convention does not permit recovery for mental or psychic injuries unaccompanied by physical injury or physical manifestation of injury. Plaintiffs were passengers on defendant's flight from Miami to the Bahamas. Shortly after takeoff, the plane experienced mechanical difficulties. The flight crew attempted to return to Miami, but the malfunctions worsened; the plane began to lose altitude and the crew informed the passengers of an impending landing in the Atlantic Ocean. Before the plane crashed, the crew managed to restart the malfunctioning engine and safely returned the plane to Miami.

Plaintiffs brought an action against the airline for the mental distress they experienced as a result of the incident. A unanimous Court held that Article 17 of the Convention, which provides that a "carrier is liable for damages sustained in the event of the death or wounding of a passenger or any other bodily injury suffered by a passenger, if the accident which caused the damage so sustained took place on board the aircraft or in the course of any of the operations of embarking or disembarking[,]" is applicable only in cases that involve some form of physical injury. Since the Convention's authoritative text was in French, the Court's duty was to interpret "lesion corporelle" (the French term for "bodily injury") as of the time the Convention was drafted.

The Court held that since recovery for wholly psychic injuries "was unknown in many, if not most, jurisdictions in 1929, the drafters most likely would have felt compelled to make an unequivocal reference to purely mental injury if they had specifically intended to allow such recovery." The Court also determined that excluding recovery for mental and psychic injury was consistent with the contracting parties' overriding purpose of providing strict limits on air carrier liability. Reconsider the common-law approach to this issue in the emotional harm cases discussed at p. 226, supra.

For a comprehensive analysis of the Convention and its subsequent modification by various international agreements, see L.B. Goldhirsch, The Warsaw Convention Annotated: A Legal Handbook (1988). See also Lowenfeld & Mendelsohn, The United States and the Warsaw Convention, 80 Harv.L.Rev. 497 (1967). For a panel discussion of aviation law experts on deficiencies in the Convention and a proposed Japanese initiative to eliminate the cap on damages, see The Japanese Initiative: Absolute Liability in International Air Travel, 60 J.Air L. & Com. 819 (1995).

International carriers may have taken the first steps to eliminate the damages cap. See Blum, Airlines Lift the Warsaw Damage Cap, Nat'l L.J., Dec. 4, 1995 at B1.

8. Since the early 1970s, alternatives to the tort system for medical malpractice-related injuries have also received periodic attention. The following note discusses the issues raised.

NOTE ON HEALTH CARE AND NO-FAULT

In 1973 Professors Havighurst and Tancredi presented a model for applying no-fault insurance to medical malpractice claims. "Medical Adversity Insurance"—A No-Fault Approach to Medical Malpractice and Quality Assurance, 51 Milbank Memorial Fund Q. 125, reprinted in 1974 Ins.L.J. 69. That model was expanded two years later in Havighurst, "Medical Adversity Insurance"—Has its Time Come?, 1975 Duke L.J. 1233. Medical Adversity Insurance (MAI) was designed to reduce the overall administrative cost of malpractice litigation by removing certain injuries from the fault system.

MAI policies would list "adverse outcomes," or "compensable events," for which a patient could recover without proof of fault. The lists would be created by medical experts who, on the basis of their experience, would identify adverse results that were probably avoidable: "An event would be added to the list if medical opinion indicated that the event was usually or frequently—though by no means invariably—avoidable under good-quality medical care and that the frequency of the event could be expected to diminish if providers' attention were directed more strongly to the quality of the outcomes being achieved."

In order to recover under the MAI system a patient would have to show that he or she had suffered a designated compensable event (DCE). Negligence would be irrelevant and, because the listed adverse outcomes would be highly specific, cause would not be a problem. The two most complex malpractice issues would thus be avoided. Case-by-case inquiries would ask only whether an adverse outcome had occurred, and what damages had resulted. The damages allowed under the system would depend on the policies issued, but Professor Havighurst suggested these would include at least all medical expenses, and wage losses subject to weekly limits.

The MAI scheme was not designed to replace the present fault system, but to remove a large number of cases from it. Not all victims of malpractice would suffer compensable events on MAI lists. If an unlisted event occurred, the patient would have to resort to the fault system, with whatever improvements could be brought to it.

Is the causation problem in medical cases manageable? Does a medical no-fault proposal based on the compensable event approach overcome the causation difficulties? Does it raise other problems?

In 1986, Professor Tancredi, conceding that a legislatively enacted DCE system was politically unlikely, turned his attention to the prospects for private adoption of the DCE system by insurance providers:

> . . . What is at stake is nothing less than the definition of the physician/patient relationship. The overriding issue is whether the terms of that intensely personal relationship ought to be prescribed exclusively by government through political and legal processes or whether the relationship should instead be shaped at least in part through private negotiation of mutually satisfying arrangements. No-fault insurance offers an attractive opportunity to strengthen physician/patient bonds and to shore up the values of honesty and trust that are essential to a healthy, happy, and therapeutic relationship. Clinicians and others have observed that the current adversary system, which threatens to pit a patient against a health care professional in an acrimonious dispute, discourages the physician from revealing to the patient his doubts and the full truth about the outcomes of his management because such disclosures may trigger a malpractice suit. A no-fault scheme, by which a provider acknowledges risks and undertakes to protect patients against specific harms, should strengthen and improve both the subjective and the objective quality of care.

Tancredi, Designing a No–Fault Alternative, 49 Law & Contemporary Problems 277, 280 (1986). Is there a reason to prefer a state-initiated remedy or does a system of private ordering have advantages over legislation?*

* Professor Jeffrey O'Connell has been a leading advocate of a wide range of privately negotiated no-fault alternatives to the tort system for many years. See J. O'Connell and C. Kelly, The Blame Game: Injuries, Insurance and Injustice (1986) in which he and a co-author advocate adoption of a universal "neo no-fault" scheme in which tort defen-

For a comprehensive analysis of the pros and cons of medical no-fault, see P. Weiler, Medical Malpractice on Trial 132–58 (1991). Prof. Weiler reviews the case for no-fault from a variety of perspectives—compensation, administration and prevention—and concludes that such a system, if it offered broad coverage of serious harms, has great appeal when compared to the present tort approach. Nonetheless, the problems of coverage/causation are sufficiently troublesome to lead him to propose as "an intermediate step" an O'Connell-type elective no-fault system.

Assuming, however, that the present system is to be retained, Weiler offers another proposal, organizational liability. As he states it:

> The technique I favor is to make the hospital or other health care organization primarily liable for all *accidental* (negligent, not intentional) injuries inflicted on patients due to malpractice committed by anyone affiliated with the institution, whether or not the actor is technically an employee of the hospital. In other words, for purposes of personal injury policy, the relationship of hospital and affiliated physicians should be deemed to be the functional equivalent of the relationship of an HMO to its staff physicians. In the HMO context, individual obstetricians or surgeons are not expected personally to pay the large malpractice premium required for their medical specialties, which are much riskier than those of the pediatrician or internist. Likewise, we do not expect that the pilots or mechanics working for an airline company should personally pay the substantial premiums that would be required for insurance against instances of careless behavior in these jobs, slipups that are far riskier than those which might be committed by a flight attendant or passenger agent working for the same airline. Instead, under this proposal each doctor in every specialty is treated as a member of a single firm engaged in the enterprise of health care, with the organization responsible for collecting revenues from the patients who receive the benefits of its services and for purchasing the insurance required to protect against the risk of serious injuries that occur. The analogy, again, is to pilots or mechanics, who are assumed as a matter of course to be parts of the larger enterprise of air travel, with the firm assuming immediate responsibility for injuries caused by the mistakes of its workers, and paying for those costs through revenues collected from all passengers on its flights.

Id. at 124–25.

dants would have the option within 180 days of offering a claimant periodic payment of the claimant's net economic losses. The claimant would be required to accept such an offer once tendered. For an illustration of one of his tailored schemes, see O'Connell, A Neo No-Fault Contract in Lieu of Tort: Pre-accident Guarantees of Post-accident Settlement Offers, 73 Calif.L.Rev. 898 (1985), describing the widely adopted Scholastic Lifetime Medical and Disability Policy which provides for no-fault settlement offers for economic loss in cases of catastrophic injury to high school athletes. For his approach to the health care area, see O'Connell, Neo No-Fault Remedies for Medical Injuries: Coordinated Statutory and Contractual Alternatives, 49 Law & Contemporary Problems 125 (1986). O'Connell discusses his approach to the products liability area in O'Connell, Balanced Proposals for Product Liability Reform, 48 Ohio St.L.J. 317 (1987).

Is the analogy to airline workers apt? From a deterrence perspective, would you expect organizational liability to be more or less effective than the existing tort system? Does it raise fairness concerns between large and small hospitals? High and low risk practitioners? For a summary version of Weiler's work in the area, which grew out of the Harvard Medical Practice Study, Patients, Doctors and Lawyers: Medical Injury, Malpractice Litigation and Patient Compensation in New York (1990), see Weiler, The Case for No–Fault Medical Liability, 52 Md.L.Rev. 908 (1993).

In a review of Weiler's 1991 volume, Sugarman, Doctor No, 58 U.Chi. L.Rev. 1499, 1500–01 (1991), the author summarizes the following data provided on the operations of the system:

. . . of every 100,000 patients discharged from hospitals, nearly 4,000 suffered an "adverse event" from their medical treatment. About one-fourth of these are the result of medical malpractice. In short, hospital patients on average run about a four percent risk of an adverse event and about a one percent risk of medical malpractice. These 100,000 patient discharges and 1,000 malpractice-caused injuries generate about 125 claims. About sixty of the 125 claimants actually receive compensation. The rest of the claims lose at trial or are dropped. Of those sixty successful claimants, about twenty receive payment before they have filed a lawsuit, about thirty-five after a suit is filed but before (or during) trial, and only about five win at trial.

Sugarman goes on to indicate that Weiler's data also report that of every 125 claims that plaintiffs make, some eighty-five appear to expert evaluators to be cases in which no malpractice occurred—and perhaps 30% of these claimants receive some award. Do these data help evaluate the proposals discussed above?

Another roughly contemporaneous proposal, put forward by the American Medical Association, would retain the existing liability structure of the tort system but transfer the adjudication of medical malpractice cases to a specialized administrative tribunal. The proposal is described and discussed in Johnson, Phillips, Orentlicher, and Hatlie, A Fault–Based Administrative Alternative for Resolving Medical Malpractice Claims, 42 Vand. L.Rev. 1365 (1989).

Birth-related Neurological Injuries Compensation Acts. Fears that rising liability costs would deter insurers from covering necessary medical procedures led the states of Virginia and Florida to pass narrowly focused medical no-fault plans. By 1986, two of Virginia's big three malpractice insurance companies had declared a moratorium on new policies and the third refused to cover any obstetricians in practice groups of 10 or fewer because the burden of tort liability for birth-related neurological injuries was too great. In response, the Virginia state legislature passed the Birth–Related Neurological Injury Compensation Act (Injured Infant Act), Va. Code Ann. §§ 38.2–5000 to 5021 (Supp. 1987) over the heavy objections of the state plaintiffs' bar. Under the plan, there is no tort recovery for any severely brain-damaged infants whose injuries were "caused by the deprivation of oxygen or mechanical injury occurring in the course of labor, delivery, or resuscitation in the immediate post-delivery period in a hospital which renders the infant permanently motorically disabled and (i) developmentally disabled or (ii) for infants sufficiently developed to be cognitively evaluated, cognitively disabled." The disability must cause the infant to be "permanently in need of assistance in all activities of daily living." In addition, the delivery must have been performed by an obstetrician participating in the fund, or must have occurred in a participating hospital.

The compensation plan is funded by contributions of $250 per year from all Virginia doctors, $5,000 annually from all participating obstetricians, and $50 per delivery from all participating hospitals (not to exceed $150,000 a year). The Act also provides that, if necessary, insurance companies can be taxed to maintain the fund. The fund pays for all medical expenses, but it has a collateral source rule that relieves it of any expenses that qualify for other private insurance or government coverage. It will also compensate for lost wages from the ages of 18 to 65 in the form of periodic installments equaling one-half of the average weekly wage in Virginia's private, nonfarm sector. Tort actions are excluded against participating physicians and hospitals except in cases of intentional or willful acts.

The establishment of the fund served its primary purpose, that of convincing one of the state's malpractice insurers to continue issuing policies. However, as of mid–1993 only five claims had been filed under the Act and four awards had been paid out.

Critics contend that the scarcity of claims is due to the act's narrow definition of infants who qualify for compensation. Unlike most no-fault plans, whose goal is to compensate all accident victims within a broad activity category, Virginia's plan only gives compensation to a specific subset of birth-related injuries. The type of severe neurological damage covered by the act is relatively rare as opposed to the uncovered birth tragedies of severe mental retardation or cerebral palsy. See Duff, Compensation for Neurologically Impaired Infants: Medical No–Fault in Virginia, 27 Harv.J.Legis. 391 (1990).

More than twenty claims had been filed under the Florida statute, which has a slightly broader definition of defect, by mid–1993. For comparative discussion of the two acts, see Wadlington & Wood, Two "No–Fault" Compensation Schemes for Birth Defective Infants in the United States, in Professional Negligence, March 1991, p. 40. For a generally skeptical view of the need for birth-related injury compensation schemes, see Mehlman, Bad "Bad Baby" Bills, 20 Am.J.L. & Med. 129 (1994).

E. COMPREHENSIVE NO-FAULT AND BEYOND

As we have seen, the academic and political efforts in this country have been addressed primarily to piecemeal revision of tort law. Conceding that limited reform efforts may be politically expedient, however, it does not necessarily follow that considerations of either logic or fairness favor piecemeal revision over system-wide change. At the outset of the no-fault movement, Jeremiah Smith argued this point in his landmark article, Sequel to Workmen's Compensation, 27 Harv.L.Rev. 235 (1913):

> If the fundamental general principle of the modern common law of torts (that fault is requisite to liability) is intrinsically right or expedient, is there sufficient reason why the legislature should make the workmen's case an exception to this general principle? On the other hand, if this statutory rule as to workmen is intrinsically just or expedient, is there sufficient reason for refusing to make this statutory rule the test of the right of recovery on the part of persons other than workmen when they suffer hurt without the fault of either party?

In this section, we focus on comprehensive systems of compensation. We begin by examining the New Zealand experience. An interesting combination of factors led that country to assume a pioneering role in replacing its tort system with a comprehensive no-fault scheme covering all types of accidental injuries.

The New Zealand Experience. In 1967, a Royal Commission headed by Justice Woodhouse, appointed to consider workers' compensation, concluded that employment injuries could not be separated from other injuries. It proposed abolition of the common law of accidental injuries and replacing it with a unified scheme based on five basic propositions: that all citizens must be protected against income loss and permanent disability; compensation should be related to the nature of the injury and not its cause; the scheme must stress physical and vocational recovery along with compensation; benefits should be paid for the duration of the incapacity; and the plan must be expeditious.

It should be stressed that the proposal of the Royal Commission was not a response to any public outcry against the existing tort system. No group, whether victims, physicians, manufacturers, motorists, or insurers had complained about the insurance premiums they were paying, the way their tort claims were being resolved in the courts, or any similar grievance. Rather, the Royal Commission perceived the common law to be a "lottery" in which some claimants received awards while others had to subsist on social welfare payments. There was also too little conscious attention to safety. The Royal Commission concluded that a new approach was needed. "If the scheme can be said to have a single purpose it is 24–hour insurance for every member of the work force, and for the housewives who sustain them." The emphasis was to be on accident prevention and rehabilitation, with compensation a third consideration.

The final version of the Accident Compensation Act became effective in 1974. Although the Act was amended several times, it remained essentially the same until the passage of the Accident Rehabilitation and Compensation Act of 1992, which substantially altered the original program. It may help in considering the discussion that follows to realize that New Zealand has a population of about three million persons and is about the size of Oregon or Colorado. For a comparison of demographic and accident data, see Franklin, Personal Injury Accidents in New Zealand and the United States: Some Striking Similarities, 27 Stan.L.Rev. 653 (1975).

The original Act abolished virtually all common law tort actions. In their place, the program provided for compensation to individuals who experienced a "personal injury by accident." This phrase was interpreted to include occupational disease and illness but to exclude ordinary sickness. Courts also found it difficult to distinguish between "medical, surgical, dental or first aid misadventure," which was covered by the statute, and "damage to the body or mind caused exclusively by disease, infection, or the aging process," which was excluded by the statute.

Compensation was and still is provided to accident victims out of one of three compensation schemes. Workers are protected against accidental injury under the earners' scheme, receiving 80% of lost earnings for the duration of a disability as well as all reasonable medical and rehabilitation expenses. Similar protection is afforded them under the scheme during off-hours. Those injured in motor vehicle accidents—other than earners who are protected under the earners' scheme—receive compensation for medical costs and lost earning capacity out of a fund supported by flat levies on motor vehicle owners. Non-workers, such as the elderly, homemakers, children and students, who are injured in accidents not involving motor vehicles, are compensated for medical costs out of the general treasury. In addition to payments for lost earnings and medical costs, the Act also used to provide for two different types of lump sum payments. The first provided for payments of up to $17,000 NZ (as of 1991) for loss of bodily part or function and the second provided for a payment of up to $10,000 NZ for pain and suffering, disfigurement and the loss of capacity for enjoying life if the loss was sufficiently serious in nature and duration.

The 1992 revisions significantly changed some of the Act's most important provisions. First, the 1992 revisions limited the types of injuries covered under the Act by restricting the definition of accident and by changing the phrase "personal injury by accident" to "personal injury by an accident" such that the accident must now be a separate cause of the injury in order for the injury to be compensable. Therefore, coverage no longer exists when only the result of an act is accidental, or when an injury cannot be attributed to any identifiable external event. Second, the new Act excludes coverage for mental distress not associated with physical injury to the person seeking compensation. Third, the revisions sharply changed the compensation system for "medical misadventure." Although the original Act provided for compensation for medical misadventures without defining the operative phrase, the new Act includes a comprehensive definition of the phrase which requires the injured party to prove something approaching negligence before he or she can receive compensation. Finally, the 1992 revisions eliminated the lump sum payments and replaced them with a much more modest "independence allowance" of up to $40 NZ per week.

In addition to these changes in the coverage and benefit provisions of the Act, the 1992 revisions significantly changed the Act's funding mechanisms. While employers continue to pay for employee injuries sustained on the job, employee injuries that occur off the job are compensated through insurance paid for by employees themselves. Flat levies on automobile owners continue to make up a large portion of the fund used to compensate motor vehicle injuries, but the 1992 revisions also provide for a $0.02/liter gasoline tax aimed at promoting a greater "user-pays" element within the Act. Finally, the 1992 revisions created a new account called the Medical Misadventure Account, funded through premiums paid by health professionals, for the purpose of compensating victims of medical misadventures. This change marked the first time since the passage of the Act that a risk-creating class has been directly held accountable to persons injured by the class. All of these changes arguably mark a distinct philosophical departure from the purposes of the original Act. Whereas the founders of the original plan viewed the scheme as one based on the notion of community responsibility, the present government has characterized the current plan as a scheme of personal accident insurance.

What are your reactions to the New Zealand approach? Do obvious practical, philosophical, or other problems occur to you? For a highly critical response to the 1992 amendments, arguing that the plan has lost much of the social insurance philosophy that once informed it, see Palmer, The Design of Compensation Systems: Tort Principles Rule, O.K.?, 29 Valp.L.Rev. 1115 (1995). For a detailed description and critique of the 1992 revisions, see Miller, An Analysis and Critique of the 1992 Changes to New Zealand's Accident Compensation Scheme, 52 Md.L.Rev. 1070 (1993).

The most extended discussion of the entire philosophy of the New Zealand development and its passage through the political process, is to be found in G. Palmer, Compensation for Incapacity: A Study of Law and Social Change in New Zealand and Australia (1979). As the title suggests, Australia seriously considered the New Zealand development, but lost interest after a change of national government.

Over the years, there was much discussion about adding sickness coverage to the existing act. An early chairman of the ACC suggested that the different treatment was an "anomaly" caused by the influence of the common law. Removing the anomaly would be "a matter of political philosophy and of economics. Political philosophy will determine the extent to which a country will devote a portion of its resources to the care of the disabled. Economics will dictate how far that philosophy can reasonably be applied." Might there be reasons for compensating disability from accident differently from disability due to sickness? The subject is discussed in P. Cane, Atiyah's Accidents, Compensation and the Law (5th ed. 1993), Chapter 16.

Social Insurance Proposals. For a detailed proposal that would go beyond New Zealand and compensate for all disability, whether accident-related or not, see S. Sugarman, Doing Away with Personal Injury Law (1989). As the title suggests, Sugarman would eliminate personal injury law virtually across-the-board, with the sole exception of a limited punitive damage action for intentional torts. His book surveys the literature on the workings of tort law and concludes that the system is a substantial failure from both the perspectives of compensation and deterrence.

Sugarman's comprehensive strategy would extend employment-based income replacement and health benefits to covered beneficiaries, whatever the source of their disability, in cases involving short-term needs (six months or less). In cases involving longer-term income replacement, as well as most cases of disability experienced by the various categories of non-employed persons, coverage would be provided by an expanded Social Security system. The tort system would be abandoned, along with pain and suffering damages, though in serious cases awards for pain and suffering on the original New Zealand model might be permitted. Accident prevention strategies would be left to the regulatory system. Anticipating the argument that his comprehensive plan is politically infeasible at present, Sugarman also outlines a first-step proposal that would concentrate on replacing the tort system in short-term injury cases and on limiting its applicability in longer-term cases through elimination of the collateral source rule and restrictions on pain and suffering recovery.

Does this outline of Sugarman's proposal suggest that the New Zealand approach may be, in fact, too modest in its coverage? Social insurance schemes presently in operation, including the Social Security Disability program, are discussed in Abraham & Liebman, Private Insurance, Social Insurance, and Tort Reform: Toward a New Vision of Compensation for Illness and Injury, 93 Colum.L.Rev. 75 (1993).

For an earlier effort to combine the benefits of social insurance for accidents and the advantages of internalized costs, see Franklin, Replacing the Negligence Lottery: Compensation and Selective Reimbursement, 53 Va.L.Rev. 774 (1967). This essay views the fault system as a lottery: Persons similarly injured may recover, if anything, very different amounts depending on the defendant's behavior and the origin of the injury, and persons committing the same wrongful act may be subject to very different liabilities depending upon the extent of the injury caused, if any, and to whom. Briefly, the goal was to separate the functions of compensation and deterrence, by having the former achieved through a social insurance fund and the latter through uninsurable fines and enterprise reimbursements of the fund for injury-creating activity. A somewhat similar proposal is offered in Pierce, Encouraging Safety: The Limits of Tort Law and Government Regulation, 33 Vand.L.Rev. 1281 (1980).

Professors Blum and Kalven argue that in large part "corrective justice is concerned not with deterring the wrongdoer, but with satisfying the victim's feeling of indignation. If the victim recovers only from the fund, he will not gain the satisfaction of seeing his wrong righted. Nor will it be much different if, after paying the victim, the fund later recovers from the tortfeasor." Blum and Kalven, The Empty Cabinet of Dr. Calabresi—Auto Accidents and General Deterrence, 34 U.Chi.L.Rev. 239, 268–69 (1967). Do you think most victims care about the source of their benefits? Under the current system does the victim see the wrong righted? The authors also urge that the law "not break sharply with the moral traditions of the society" and that the burden of satisfying indignation not be left solely to criminal law. What are these "moral traditions"?

The social insurance aspects of the Franklin, Pierce, Sugarman and New Zealand proposals may all be traced to the influential Beveridge Report of 1942 on Social Insurance and Allied Services in Great Britain. Cmd. 6404. Speaking of workers' compensation, Beveridge said (38–39):

> The pioneer system of social security in Britain was based on a wrong principle and has been dominated by a wrong outlook. It allows claims to be settled by bargaining between unequal parties, permits payment of socially wasteful lump sums instead of pensions in cases of serious incapacity, places the cost of medical care on the workman or charity or poor relief, and over part of the field, large in the numbers covered, though not in the proportion of the total compensation paid, it relies on expensive private insurance. There should be no hesitation in making provision for the results of industrial accident and disease in the future, not by a continuance of the present system of individual employer's liability, but as one branch of a unified Plan for Social Security. If the matter were now being considered in a clear field, it might well be argued that the general principle of a flat rate of compensation for interruption of earnings adopted for all other forms of interruption, should be applied also without reserve or qualification to the results of industrial accident and disease, leaving those who felt the need for greater security, by voluntary insurance, to provide an addition to the flat subsistence guaranteed by the State. If a workman loses his leg in an accident, his needs are the same whether the accident occurred in a factory or in the street; if he is killed, the needs of his widow and other dependents are the same, however the death occurred. Acceptance of this argument and adoption of a flat rate of compensation for disability, however caused, would avoid the anomaly of treating equal needs differently and the administrative and legal difficulties of defining just what injuries were to be treated as arising out of and in the course of employment. Interpretation of these words has been a fruitful cause of disputes in the past; whatever words are chosen, difficulties and anomalies are bound to arise. A complete solution is to be found only in a completely unified scheme for disability without demarcation by the cause of disability.

Although Beveridge did not ultimately recommend a totally unified scheme, subsequent writers have adopted his theoretical exposition.

As early as 1955, Professor Kalven asserted that if poverty could be abolished, tort law could remain intact. "If the poor were not quite so poor, we could decently ask them to provide their own accident insurance." Book Review, 33 Texas L.Rev. 778, 782 (1955). How much criticism of the operation of tort law has been based on a concern for those at or below the poverty level? If one were to agree that poverty is an important problem, how should that affect one's attitude toward tort law?

CHAPTER XII

INTENTIONAL HARM

This chapter brings together personal injuries alleged to have been caused "intentionally." We focus on what the actor sought to achieve, or knew would occur, rather than on his or her motives for acting. Thus the definition of "intent" in the Restatement (Second) of Torts § 8A, requires "that the actor desires to cause consequences of his act, or that he believes that the consequences are substantially certain to result from it." Note that this definition is the final point on the Restatement's continuum from negligence through recklessness to intent. Negligence is defined as "conduct which falls below the standard established by law for the protection of others against unreasonable risk of harm" (§ 282). Recklessness involves a risk that is "substantially greater than that which is necessary to make his conduct negligent" (§ 500). Finally, in defining intent we no longer speak of risk but rather of "desire" to bring about consequences, or belief that such consequences are "substantially certain" to occur. Is that the same as saying that the consequences *are* "substantially certain" to occur? How can we prove what the actor "desires" or "believes"?

The long history of intentional torts has produced special rules for categories such as assault, battery, and false imprisonment. These rules reflect early procedure and the writ system but still have implications for questions of pleading and proof today, as we shall see. Beginning with false imprisonment and carrying through intentional infliction of emotional harm and government liability, we will also see how the courts have responded to distinctly contemporary injury claims by expanding the boundaries of intentional tort doctrine.

A plaintiff who can frame a case as an intentional tort may reap benefits beyond pleading and proof: contributory negligence and even contributory recklessness are not defenses to intentional misconduct, and punitive damages may be available.* Also, although liability for negligently inflicted harm may be discharged in bankruptcy, this does not apply to "willful and malicious injury." 11 U.S.C. § 523(6).

---

* Recall Campbell v. Van Roekel, p. 657, supra, in which the court applied comparative fault in a case involving a reckless defendant—and reduced the compensatory but not the punitive award. Would that be appropriate for intentional torts? Traditionally, courts have not recognized comparative fault as a defense to intentional wrongdoing. For discussion and a proposed limitation on the general rule, see Dear & Zipperstein, Comparative Fault and Intentional Torts: Doctrinal Barriers and Policy Considerations, 24 Santa Clara L.Rev. 1 (1984).

A.   BASIC DOCTRINE

1.   INTENT

Garratt v. Dailey

Supreme Court of Washington, 1955.
46 Wash.2d 197, 279 P.2d 1091.

■ HILL, J.—The liability of an infant for an alleged battery is presented to this court for the first time. Brian Dailey (age five years, nine months) was visiting with Naomi Garratt, an adult and a sister of the plaintiff, Ruth Garratt, likewise an adult, in the backyard of the plaintiff's home, on July 16, 1951. It is plaintiff's contention that she came out into the backyard to talk with Naomi and that, as she started to sit down in a wood and canvas lawn chair, Brian deliberately pulled it out from under her. The only one of the three persons present so testifying was Naomi Garratt. (Ruth Garratt, the plaintiff, did not testify as to how or why she fell.) The trial court, unwilling to accept this testimony, adopted instead Brian Dailey's version of what happened, and made the following findings:

"III. .   . . that while Naomi Garratt and Brian Dailey were in the back yard the plaintiff, Ruth Garratt, came out of her house into the back yard. Some time subsequent thereto defendant, Brian Dailey, picked up a lightly built wood and canvas lawn chair which was then and there located in the back yard of the above described premises, moved it sideways a few feet and seated himself therein, at which time he discovered the plaintiff, Ruth Garratt, about to sit down at the place where the lawn chair had formerly been, at which time he hurriedly got up from the chair and attempted to move it toward Ruth Garratt to aid her in sitting down in the chair; that due to the defendant's small size and lack of dexterity he was unable to get the lawn chair under the plaintiff in time to prevent her from falling to the ground. That plaintiff fell to the ground and sustained a fracture of her hip, and other injuries and damages as hereinafter set forth.

"IV.   That the preponderance of the evidence in this case establishes that when the defendant, Brian Dailey, moved the chair in question *he did not have any wilful or unlawful purpose* in doing so; that *he did not have any intent to injure the plaintiff, or any intent to bring about any unauthorized or offensive contact with her person* or any objects appurtenant thereto; that the circumstances which immediately preceded the fall of the plaintiff established that the defendant, *Brian Dailey, did not have purpose, intent or design to perform a prank or to effect an assault and battery upon the person of the plaintiff.''* (Italics ours, for a purpose hereinafter indicated.)

It is conceded that Ruth Garratt's fall resulted in a fractured hip and other painful and serious injuries. To obviate the necessity of a retrial in the event this court determines that she was entitled to a judgment against

Brian Dailey, the amount of her damage was found to be eleven thousand dollars. Plaintiff appeals from a judgment dismissing the action and asks for the entry of a judgment in that amount or a new trial.

The authorities generally, but with certain notable exceptions [ ], state that, when a minor has committed a tort with force, he is liable to be proceeded against as any other person would be. [   ].

In our analysis of the applicable law, we start with the basic premise that Brian, whether five or fifty-five, must have committed some wrongful act before he could be liable for appellant's injuries.

. . .

It is urged that Brian's action in moving the chair constituted a battery. A definition (not all-inclusive but sufficient for our purpose) of a battery is the intentional infliction of a harmful bodily contact upon another. . . .

We have in this case no question of consent or privilege. We therefore proceed to an immediate consideration of intent and its place in the law of battery. . . .

. . .

We have here the conceded volitional act of Brian, i.e., the moving of a chair. Had the plaintiff proved to the satisfaction of the trial court that Brian moved the chair while she was in the act of sitting down, Brian's action would patently have been for the purpose or with the intent of causing the plaintiff's bodily contact with the ground, and she would be entitled to a judgment against him for the resulting damages. Vosburg v. Putney (1891), 80 Wis. 523, 50 N.W. 403; [   ].

The plaintiff based her case on that theory, and the trial court held that she failed in her proof and accepted Brian's version of the facts rather than that given by the eyewitness who testified for the plaintiff. After the trial court determined that the plaintiff had not established her theory of a battery (i.e., that Brian had pulled the chair out from under the plaintiff while she was in the act of sitting down), it then became concerned with whether a battery was established under the facts as it found them to be.

. . .

A battery would be established if, in addition to plaintiff's fall, it was proved that, when Brian moved the chair, he knew with substantial certainty that the plaintiff would attempt to sit down where the chair had been. If Brian had any of the intents which the trial court found, in the italicized portions of the findings of fact quoted above, that he did not have, he would of course have had the knowledge to which we have referred. The mere absence of any intent to injure the plaintiff or to play a prank on her or to embarrass her, or to commit an assault and battery on her would not absolve him from liability if in fact he had such knowledge. [   ] Without such knowledge, there would be nothing wrongful about Brian's act in moving the chair, and, there being no wrongful act, there would be no liability.

Intentional if — when Brian moved chair he had knowledge that P would attempt to sit down where the chair had been

While a finding that Brian had no such knowledge can be inferred from the findings made, we believe that before the plaintiff's action in such a case should be dismissed there should be no question but that the trial court had passed upon that issue; hence, the case should be remanded for clarification of the findings to specifically cover the question of Brian's knowledge, because intent could be inferred therefrom. If the court finds that he had such knowledge, the necessary intent will be established and the plaintiff will be entitled to recover, even though there was no purpose to injure or embarrass the plaintiff. [ ] If Brian did not have such knowledge, there was no wrongful act by him, and the basic premise of liability on the theory of a battery was not established.

It will be noted that the law of battery as we have discussed it is the law applicable to adults, and no significance has been attached to the fact that Brian was a child less than six years of age when the alleged battery occurred. The only circumstance where Brian's age is of any consequence is in determining what he knew, and there his experience, capacity, and understanding are of course material.

. . .

Remanded for clarification.

■ SCHWELLENBACH, DONWORTH, and WEAVER, JJ., concur.

NOTES AND QUESTIONS

1. What is it precisely that the court says Brian must "intend" in order to be held liable for a battery? Suppose he wasn't thinking about plaintiff one way or the other—he simply grabbed the nearest chair, despite the fact that she was about to sit in it, because he was eager to sit down. Would he have had the requisite intent?

On remand, the trial court found that Brian did have the necessary intent, and entered judgment for the plaintiff for $11,000. The judgment was affirmed on appeal. 49 Wash.2d 499, 304 P.2d 681 (1956).

2. Suppose Brian did not believe to a "substantial certainty" that plaintiff was about to sit down. Might he still be liable on a negligence theory? Can you construct versions of the facts that clarify the distinctions between intentional, reckless and negligent misconduct? Might Brian's age make it more difficult to establish negligence than intentional wrongdoing here? Reconsider the discussion of the reasonable person standard as applied to minors, p. 46, supra. The issue is discussed at length in Weisbart v. Flohr, 260 Cal.App.2d 281, 67 Cal.Rptr. 114 (1968), an action based on theories of negligence and battery by a five-year-old plaintiff against a seven-year-old defendant who put out her eye with a bow-and-arrow. The court upheld a judgment in favor of the defendant on the negligence count, but reversed a similar judgment on the battery claim.

3. Suppose Brian did know to a "substantial certainty" that plaintiff was about to sit in the chair. Does it make sense to have a separate tort category of "intentional torts" for such cases—distinguishing them from situations in which a manufacturer knows with similar certainty that one soda bottle out of 100,000 produced will explode during use?

4.   Compare the prima facie case for intentional battery with that for intentional nuisance, p. 596, supra.   What justifies the Restatement position, in the latter case, that the conduct be not only intentional but also unreasonable?   For the Second Restatement's sections on intent and battery, which track the views expressed in *Garratt*, see §§ 8A, 13–17.   Section 8A defines "intent" as follows:

> The word "intent" is used throughout the Restatement of this Subject to denote that the actor desires to cause consequences of his act, or that he believes that the consequences are substantially certain to result from it.

D comes up behind a person he is quite certain is his friend, and offers the traditional greeting of a slap on the back.   If the other person turns out to be a stranger, has D intended to hit him?   Or suppose that D, hunting in a proper area, reasonably believes that the animal crossing in front of him some distance ahead is a deer.   D shoots and kills the animal only to find that it is in fact P's slender cow.   Did D intend to shoot the cow?

5.   In the cited case of Vosburg v. Putney, the court held that one schoolboy who kicked another in the leg was liable for a battery despite the lack of any subjective intention to do harm.   Moreover, the defendant was held liable for extraordinary harm that resulted because of the exacerbation of a pre-existing injury, the court tersely stating that "the wrongdoer is liable for all injuries resulting directly from the wrongful act, whether they could or could not have been foreseen by him."   Recall the discussion of the thin-skulled plaintiff rule, p. 345, supra.   Is it appropriate to apply a thin-skulled plaintiff rule to cases in which the defendant intended no actual harm to the plaintiff?

Vosburg has remained a great favorite of torts afficionados over the years.   See its centennial celebration, including a sociolegal history of the case, Zile, *Vosburg v.Putney*: A Centennial Story, 1992 Wis.L.Rev. 877, and commentary by James A. Henderson (at 853), Robert L. Rabin (at 863), and J. Willard Hurst (at 875).

6.   *Cause-in-fact.*   On the relation of cause-in-fact problems to intentional torts, consider the following passage from Malone, Ruminations on Cause–In–Fact, 9 Stan.L.Rev. 60, 72–73 (1956):

> Some rules of law are tremendously exacting and rest upon time-honored moral considerations.   They are safeguards for well-established interests of others, and their mantle of protection embraces a large variety of risks.   He who violates such a rule will be held responsible for any harm that can be causally associated in any plausible way with his wrongdoing.   The court, for instance, will seldom hesitate to allow the jury a free range of speculation on the cause issue at the expense of an intentional wrongdoer who is charged with having physically injured another person.

Malone also suggests that in fire cases "Sound judgment may dictate, for instance, that an arsonist be held responsible for a fire contribution that has a much smaller damaging potential than could be recognized in the case of a householder whose lamp was tipped over by the wind." Can these views be justified?

7. *Proximate Cause.* In Baker v. Shymkiv, 6 Ohio St.3d 151, 451 N.E.2d 811 (1983), the plaintiff and decedent, her husband, came home to find the defendants building a trench across their driveway. An angry confrontation occurred. At this point plaintiff left to call the police. When she returned three minutes later she found her husband lying face down in a mud puddle while the defendants were driving away. He was pronounced dead of a heart attack shortly thereafter. The trial judge charged that although the defendants were trespassers they would not be liable for the death unless that harm could have been foreseen or reasonably anticipated by the wrongdoer. The Court of Appeals reversed a defense judgment and the Ohio Supreme Court unanimously affirmed. Quoting from an earlier case, the court reasoned that when confronted with an innocent victim and an intentional wrongdoer, it is not surprising that the interest of the victim in attaining full compensation "is placed above the interest of the wrongdoer in protecting himself against potentially speculative damage awards." The court applied this reasoning to intentional trespassers on the authority of Restatement § 162, which provides that a trespasser is liable for any acts done or activity on the land that harms the possessor, others or property "irrespective of whether his conduct is such as would subject him to liability were he not a trespasser." Comment *f* provides that this rule applies "no matter how otherwise innocent such conduct may be." Accordingly, the court held that "damages caused by an intentional trespasser need not be foreseeable to be compensable." A new trial was ordered.

Should intentional wrongdoers be held to a higher standard of responsibility for extended consequences than negligent parties? See generally, Note, The Tie That Binds: Liability of Intentional Tort–Feasors for Extended Consequences, 14 Stan.L.Rev. 362 (1962). Compare Halberstam v. Welch, 705 F.2d 472 (D.C.Cir.1983), assigning tort liability to a woman whose live-in-companion killed someone who surprised him during a burglary. The woman had not been involved in the burglary, but was heavily involved in "laundering" activities connected with reaping profits from the burglar's stolen goods. The court discusses at length theories of civil conspiracy and aid-and-abetting in developing the concept of joint tort in the context of intentional harm.

8. *Punitive Damages.* As we discussed earlier, in intentional tort cases defendant sometimes may be responsible not only for compensatory damages but for punitive damages as well. Reconsider the discussion of punitive damages for reckless conduct, p. 651, supra. Intentional tort situations have been considered the paradigm case for award of such damages. Should a distinction be drawn between cases involving intent to injure and cases like *Vosburg* in which defendant intended no serious harm?

Why should a plaintiff ever receive such a windfall? A handful of states wholly reject punitive damages in civil cases, and a few limit them in amount to the plaintiff's litigation expenses including attorneys' fees. See Note, An Economic Analysis of the Plaintiff's Windfall from Punitive Damages, 105 Harv.L.Rev. 1900 (1992), analyzing the justifications for punitive damages and proposing that the portion of a punitive damages award in excess of litigation costs be allocated to the state. Punitive damages are not awarded as a matter of law but are discretionary with the trier of fact.

Is it consistent to argue that punitive damages should be permitted in minor intentional harm cases because criminal prosecutions are unlikely, and also in major tort cases such as raping a very young child? Is there less justification for punitive damages when the compensatory award will be high, as in the rape case, than when the compensatory award is likely to be small? Does a compensatory award "punish" the defendant? For comprehensive analysis of the justifications for punitive damages, see Trebilcock and Chapman, Punitive Damages: Divergence in Search of a Rationale, 40 Ala.L.Rev. 741 (1989).

9. *Insurance Considerations.* What good is a judgment for $11,000 against Brian? Parents are not generally liable for the torts of their children. It is true that they have a duty of due care to prevent their children from causing intentional harm or unreasonable risks to others but this applies only when the parents are on notice of the child's tendencies and know or should know that an occasion has arisen calling for their exercise of control. See Restatement, Second, § 316. Alternatively, the parents may be liable for placing a dangerous instrumentality in the hands of one too young or inexperienced to know how to handle it. Compare *Weisbart v. Flohr*, note 2 supra (parents not liable for injury caused by their seven-year-old son's shooting arrow into girl's eye), with Reida v. Lund, 18 Cal.App.3d 698, 96 Cal.Rptr. 102 (1971)(father liable to victims of 16–year-old sniper for father's failure to use due care to keep Swedish Mauser military rifle out of son's hands). In the absence of proof that the boy was a menace (and the lack of a claim by Ruth Garratt against the parents) parental liability cannot explain the suit.

This is another area in which liability insurance has been of considerable importance. Even if the parent's homeowners' policy covers family members, however, there is still a question whether intentional torts have been excluded. In Baldinger v. Consolidated Mutual Ins. Co., 15 App. Div.2d 526, 222 N.Y.S.2d 736 (1961), affirmed without opinion 11 N.Y.2d 1026, 183 N.E.2d 908, 230 N.Y.S.2d 25 (1962), the policy excluded "bodily injury . . . caused intentionally." A six-year-old boy covered by the policy pushed the plaintiff to get her to move. She fell and broke her elbow. Relying on the maxim that an ambiguous provision should be construed against the insurer the court held that the exclusion did not apply because the "injury" was not "caused intentionally but was rather the unintended result of an intentional act." Recall *Lalomia*, p. 702, supra.

The issue is not limited to coverage of minors, of course. Can an insured who is legally insane commit an intentional act? In Economy Preferred Ins. Co. v. Mass, 242 Neb. 842, 497 N.W.2d 6 (1993), the insured, who had shot and killed his father, claimed that he was entitled to insurance coverage despite an intentional act exclusion clause because the trial court had found that he was legally insane at the time of the incident. The appellate court disagreed, holding that even if a mentally ill insured was unable to form the criminal intent necessary for criminal liability, he may nevertheless have still intended or expected the results of the injuries he caused. Therefore, the intentional act exclusion applied, and the insurance company was not obliged to cover its insured. But see Nationwide Insurance Company v. Estate of Kollstedt, 71 Ohio St.3d 624, 646 N.E.2d 816 (1995), in which the court held that an intentional act exclusion clause does not apply when the insured was mentally incapable of committing an intentional act.

What if the insured is acting in self-defense? In Vermont Mutual Ins. Co. v. Singleton, 446 S.E.2d 417 (S.C.1994), the insured had acted in self-defense and had inflicted severe eye injuries upon his attacker. The court applied a two-prong analysis to determine if the intentional act exclusion clause would relieve the insurance company of having to cover the victim's costs under the insured's homeowner's policy. The court held that the first prong, whether the act causing the loss was intentional, was easily satisfied. However, the court found that the second prong, whether the results of the act were intended, was not satisfied. Since the insured intended only to protect himself and not to inflict a specific injury on the victim, the intentional act exclusion clause did not apply.

Finally, when if ever should public policy concerns persuade a court to hold that reckless conduct on the part of an insured should relieve an insurance company of coverage obligations under an intentional act exclusion clause? In R.W. v. T.F., 528 N.W.2d 869 (Minn.1995), a woman sued the insured for negligently transmitting genital herpes to her. The insurance company refused to defend, claiming that the insured's intentional act exclusion clause relieved it of its coverage obligations. The court held for the insurance company, arguing that the insured's actions were "intentional as a matter of law" because the insured knew the transmission of herpes was "substantially likely to occur." In reaching its decision, the court stated that it would be contrary to public policy to "promote the abdication of personal responsibility by providing insurance coverage when an insured engages in unprotected sexual intercourse despite having knowledge that he is infected with herpes, a highly contagious and serious sexually transmitted disease."

10. *Victim Compensation Statutes.* The vast majority of valid intentional tort cases founder on the insolvency of the perpetrator. Statutes may provide some aid to victims of crimes from the state or local treasury, an idea that originated in Great Britain. See Note, Compensation for

Victims of Crime, 33 U.Chi.L.Rev. 531 (1966); Comment, Compensation for Victims of Violent Crimes, 26 Kan.L.Rev. 227 (1978). For comparison of the British approach and a variety of American statutory strategies, see Greer, A Transatlantic Perspective on the Compensation of Crime Victims in the United States, 85 J.Crim. & Criminology 333 (1994).

California, in 1965, was the first state to enact a comprehensive victim compensation statute. Since then, 35 states have enacted some form of victim compensation program. These programs differ from one another significantly both in scope and in level of reparations. The New York program, begun in 1966, is one of the largest and most generous. McKinney's Exec.Law §§ 620–635. In 1994, the New York State Crime Victims Compensation Board approved 11,448 awards from more than twice that many claims, expending $13.5 million; average payouts ranged from $800 to $1,000 in services and compensation. See DeMare, Crime Victims Unite to Promote an Awareness of Their Own Rights, Albany Times Union, Apr. 13, 1995, at A1. The system has experienced backlogs of up to 17,000 claims in recent years with a waiting period of one year. All expenses of the program are funded through general revenues, in contrast with those systems, such as California's, that are funded purely through criminal fines and penalties.

To qualify for benefits under the New York program, a victim of a violent crime generally must report it to the police within seven days, cooperate with the police and prosecutors handling the case, and file a claim within one year of the crime. Until 1977 a claimant had to show direct physical injury or trauma to qualify for benefits. Now, as the result of a 1977 amendment, the program extends benefits to those with crime-induced emotional difficulty and specifically includes costs of psychological counseling in the category of reimbursable medical expenses. Eligible claimants include victims, "good samaritans" injured while attempting to prevent crimes or apprehend criminals, and former dependents of victims or good samaritans whose deaths resulted from violent crimes. The Board pays eligible claimants unlimited medical expenses, up to $3,000 for job rehabilitation, and a maximum of $400 per week in lost earnings subject to a ceiling of $30,000. Recognizing that some victims may need immediate aid, New York provides that up to $1500 may be forwarded to victims in dire need who are expected to fulfill the relevant eligibility requirements.

A victim who is dissatisfied with the decision of the commissioner who reviewed his or her case may appeal the decision to a panel composed of three other commissioners. A claimant wishing to contest the determinations of this panel may seek judicial review. The State Comptroller can also appeal to contest awards asserted to be unwarranted or overgenerous.

Subject to well-defined statutory exceptions, a claim will be rejected if the assailant and victim were blood relatives or in-laws. Claims will be rejected if the victim was participating in the crime, and will be reduced in proportion to causal responsibility for nonparticipant victims (excluding good samaritans) who are adjudged to have contributed to their own injuries. The most common ground for rejection of claims is a claimant's inability to demonstrate financial need. Although the standard used to measure financial distress was softened by a 1985 amendment that changed the statutory language from "serious financial hardship" to "financial difficulty," this test of claimant need is still the most significant bar to monetary recovery. Determination of financial difficulty is based on many factors, including income, "reasonable living expenses," and net financial resources and is administered in a case-by-case manner by the Board.

One author identifies three main arguments used to support this type of legislation: "(1) that the offender has an obligation to make restitution to the victim, and the state an obligation either to expedite such relief or to offer a substitute; (2) that the state is liable because it has failed to fulfill its duty to protect its citizens; and (3) that the state should assume a general social responsibility to aid unfortunates when, as here, such aid would serve compelling social policies." Note, Compensation for Victims of Crime, 33 U.Chi.L.Rev. 531, 533 (1966).

What does New York's hardship requirement indicate about the philosophical basis for the enactment of the statute? What motivates the few states that impose no hardship requirement whatever?

The developments in New York are summarized in annual reports of the State Board. For a detailed survey of the various state compensation programs, see D. Parent, B. Auerbach, & K. Carlson, Compensating Crime Victims: A Summary of Policies and Practices (National Institute of Justice 1992). The philosophical justifications for victim compensation programs are criticized in Henderson, The Wrongs of Victim's Rights, 37 Stan.L.Rev. 937 (1985).

At the turn of the century, several states enacted so-called mob violence statutes providing that persons whose property was damaged or destroyed in a riot might recover their losses from the city or county. The apparent goal was to encourage government officials to take steps to avert damage before it occurred. Governmental responsibility might be found more easily here than in the failure of government to prevent isolated acts of physical violence. Statutes in New York, Illinois, and California were repealed or suspended in the 1960s before any substantial harm occurred from the urban violence of that decade. See Note, Compensation for Victims of Urban Riots, 68 Colum.L.Rev. 57 (1968); Note, Municipal Liability for Riot Damage, 81 Harv.L.Rev. 653 (1968); and Note, Riot Insurance, 77 Yale L.J. 541 (1968).

11. In *Garratt*, the court offered two foundational observations before launching into its discussion of intent. First, the opinion defines the tort of battery, establishing the prima facie case as "the intentional infliction of a harmful bodily contact upon another." Next, the court observes that the most common defenses are not involved: "We have in this case no question of consent or privilege." The following case discusses the related torts of assault and battery in greater detail. We then give independent consideration to false imprisonment and intentional infliction of emotional distress before returning to an excerpt from Morris on Torts that covers the principal defenses to actions for intentional harm.

2.   ASSAULT AND BATTERY

Picard v. Barry Pontiac–Buick, Inc.

Supreme Court of Rhode Island, 1995.
654 A.2d 690.

[In the course of a brake inspection, plaintiff Picard became upset about the service work and contacted a local television news "troubleshooter" reporter. Shortly thereafter, when she returned for a reinspection, Picard took along a camera and photographed defendant service worker as he was inspecting the brakes. There was a dispute as to what happened next. Plaintiff testified that defendant lunged at her and spun her around; defendant denied touching her and testified that he "pointed at plaintiff and said, 'who gave you permission to take my picture?' then walked around the car to plaintiff, placed his index finger on the camera and again asked, 'who gave you permission to take my picture?'" The defendant denied grabbing plaintiff or threatening her in any way. In further testimony, which was less than entirely consistent, plaintiff and her doctor claimed permanent damage to her back as a consequence of the altercation.

At trial, plaintiff prevailed and was awarded $60,366 in compensatory damages and an additional $6,350 in punitive damages. Defendant appealed, arguing "1) that plaintiff failed to prove an assault and battery; 2) that plaintiff failed to prove that defendant's actions in fact caused the alleged harm to her; and 3) that the damage awards were grossly excessive and inappropriate as a matter of law." The supreme court vacated the award and remanded for a new trial on damages.]

■ LEDERBERG, JUSTICE.

. . .

The defendant contended that plaintiff failed to prove the occurrence of an assault because plaintiff was not placed in reasonable fear of imminent bodily harm. Further, defendant argued that plaintiff failed to prove a battery because the evidence failed to establish that defendant intended to inflict an unconsented touching of plaintiff. We disagree with both contentions.

Assault and battery are separate acts, usually arising from the same transaction, each having independent significance. [ ] "An assault is a physical act of a threatening nature or an offer of corporal injury which puts an individual in reasonable fear of imminent bodily harm." [ ] It is a plaintiff's apprehension of injury which renders a defendant's act compensable. [ ]; see also W. Page Keeton et al., Prosser and Keeton on the Law of Torts s 10, at 43 (5th ed. 1984)("[t]he damages recoverable for [assault] are those for the plaintiff's mental disturbance, including fright, humiliation and the like, as well as any physical illness which may result from them"). This apprehension must be the type of fear normally aroused in the mind of a reasonable person. [   ]

The plaintiff testified that she was frightened by defendant's actions. A review of the attendant circumstances attests that such a reaction was reasonable. The defendant admitted approaching plaintiff, and the photograph taken that day clearly showed defendant pointing his finger at plaintiff as defendant approached her. Because plaintiff's apprehension of imminent bodily harm was reasonable at that point, plaintiff has established a prima facie case of assault.

We have defined battery as an act that was intended to cause, and in fact did cause, "an offensive contact with or unconsented touching of or trauma upon the body of another, thereby generally resulting in the consummation of the assault. * * * An intent to injure plaintiff, however, is unnecessary in a situation in which a defendant willfully sets in motion a force that in its ordinary course causes the injury." [   ]

In the instant case, defendant contended that a battery did not occur because defendant did not intend to touch or injure plaintiff. Rather, defendant argued, the evidence showed that he intended to touch plaintiff's camera, not plaintiff's person, and therefore the contact was insufficient to prove battery. With this contention we must disagree. Even if this court were to accept defendant's characterization of the incident, a battery had nonetheless occurred. The defendant failed to prove that his actions were accidental or involuntary. Therefore, defendant's offensive contact with an (*camera*) object attached to or identified with plaintiff's body was sufficient to constitute a battery. As noted in the comments to the Restatement (Second) Torts § 18, comment *c* at 31 (1965): "Unpermitted and intentional contacts with anything so connected with the body as to be customarily regarded as part of the other's person and therefore as partaking of its inviolability is actionable as an offensive contact with his person. There are some things such as clothing or a cane or, indeed, anything directly grasped by the hand which are so intimately connected with one's body as to be universally regarded as part of the person." The defendant's contact with the camera clutched in plaintiff's hand was thus sufficient to constitute a battery. We conclude, therefore, that plaintiff has proven the elements of assault and battery.

. . .

[The court next determined that the medical evidence in support of the claim for compensatory damages was inadequate and that the amount of damages awarded was excessive. In addition, the punitive damage award could not stand because "there was no proof of malice or bad faith."]

In conclusion, we deny in part and sustain in part the defendant's appeal. We affirm the judgment of the Superior Court in respect to the defendant's commission of assault and battery, but we vacate the awards of compensatory and punitive damages. We remand the case to the Superior Court for a new trial on the damages sustained by the plaintiff.

NOTES AND QUESTIONS

1. The early history of assault and battery is traced in C. Morris and C.R. Morris, Morris on Torts (2d ed. 1980) at 21:

> After the Norman Conquest of England the newly established King's court entertained actions of trespass *vi et armis* [with force and arms] for assault and battery.   The crown wrestled jurisdiction from manorial and baronial courts on the ground that the misconduct charged was a breach "of the King's peace."   In the early cases the courts made no clear distinction between criminal prosecutions and civil suits.   After the distinction between tort and crime developed, assault and battery could be prosecuted by the Crown, and the victim could also sue in tort for damages.

For an interesting early case illustrating an assault claim, see I. de S. v. W. de S., Y.B.Lib. Ass. folio 99, pl. 60 (1348) in which defendant, enraged at being told by plaintiff that the tavern was closed for the night, swung his hatchet at her as she stuck her head out of the window of the establishment.   The court rejected the argument that no harm had been done, concluding that an actionable assault had occurred.   The relationship between trespass claims and the later-developing action of trespass on the case is discussed at p. 22, supra, in the historical introduction to negligence in Chapter II.

2. Suppose defendant in *Picard* had gestured menacingly and threatened to harm plaintiff if she took a picture of him—but before she had actually done so.   Would his actions have constituted an assault?   Morris on Torts points out that future-oriented threats were traditionally not considered assaults, quoting from an early common law case in which the court held that the statement, "if it were not assize time, I would run this sword through you," was held not to amount to an assault because of its conditional nature.   How would the qualification for conditional statements apply here?

3. Note that the *Picard* court echoes *Garratt* in holding that an intent to injure is not required to establish a battery.   What precisely was required to establish not just an assault but a battery as well in *Picard*?

4. Why should less than actual physical contact with plaintiff's body ever be sufficient to establish a battery?   And, on the other hand, why should *any* physical contact suffice?   In the leading case of Alcorn v. Mitchell, 63 Ill. 553 (1872), in which a disappointed litigant spat upon his adversary in the courthouse, the court allowed nominal compensatory and fairly substantial punitive damages in the subsequent action for the trespassory act.   What justifications can be offered for these extensions beyond actual physical harm?   Might a spit in the face warrant substantial compensatory damages?

5. Once tortious conduct amounting to an assault and battery was established in *Picard*, is the court acting consistently when it reverses the punitive damage award because of the failure to establish "malice and bad faith?"

3.   FALSE IMPRISONMENT

Lopez v. Winchell's Donut House

Illinois Appellate Court, 1984.
126 Ill.App.3d 46, 466 N.E.2d 1309.

■ LORENZ, JUSTICE:

Plaintiff appeals from an order of the circuit court granting defendant corporation's motion for summary judgment. Plaintiff contends that the trial court erred in entering summary judgment against her because a genuine issue of material fact existed concerning her charge that she was falsely detained and imprisoned. For the reasons which follow, we affirm the trial court's decision.

Count I of plaintiff's unverified two-count complaint alleged that plaintiff was employed as a clerk in defendant's donut shop in Woodridge, Illinois, for approximately three years; that on or about April 8, 1981, defendant, through its agents and employees, Ralph Bell and James Cesario, accused her of selling donuts without registering sales and thereby pocketing defendant's monies; and that she was falsely detained and imprisoned against her will in a room located on defendant's premises, with force, and without probable and reasonable cause, by defendant's employees. Count I of her complaint also alleged that as a result of defendant's employees' wilful and wanton false imprisonment, she was exposed to public disgrace; greatly injured in her good name and reputation; suffered, and still suffers, great mental anguish, humiliation and shock; wrongfully terminated from her employment; required to seek medical attention; all of which prevented her from attending to her usual affairs.

[Defendant's answer consisted of an affirmative defense that it had reasonable grounds to believe that plaintiff had engaged in retail theft and that its inquiry as to whether she had failed to ring up certain retail sales was conducted "in a reasonable manner and for a reasonable length of time." Defendant then moved for summary judgment.]

The motion included portions of plaintiff's deposition which disclosed the following. James Cesario telephoned plaintiff at her home at 4:30 p.m. on April 9, 1981, and asked her to come down to the donut shop; he did not explain his reasons for wanting her to do so. As a result of this call, plaintiff walked to the store from her home, arriving ten minutes later. Upon her arrival at the store, Cesario asked her to accompany him into the baking room, which was located at the rear of the store; Ralph Bell was also present in the room. After Cesario asked plaintiff to sit down, she indicated that they (Cesario and Bell) closed the door and locked it by putting a "little latch on." She stated that the two men told her that they had proof that spotters going from store to store had purchased two dozen donuts from her, but that her register had not shown the sale. After refusing her request to view the "proof," plaintiff stated that she was "too upset" to respond to their questioning regarding the length of time that her alleged "shorting" of the cash drawer had been going on.

She further stated that defendant's employees never told her that she had to answer their questions or face the loss of her job; never directly threatened to fire her; and made no threats of any kind to her during the interrogation. She further testified that she at no time during the interrogation feared for her safety; that she at no time refused to answer any question put to her; that there was never a point in the interrogation that she said, "I want to leave" and was prevented from doing so; and that she got up, left the room and went home when she first decided to do so.

Plaintiff's written response to defendant's motion for summary judgment did not contradict the statements that she had made in her discovery deposition. In her affidavit filed in support of her response to defendant's motion for summary judgment, plaintiff averred that (1) she left the baking room after she began to shake, and when she felt that she was becoming ill; and (2) she was terminated from her employment by defendant.

The trial court entered summary judgment for defendant. Plaintiff appeals from that order. . . .

. . .

Plaintiff asserts that the trial court erred in granting defendant's motion for summary judgment as there exists a genuine issue of material fact. She posits that she felt compelled to remain in the baking room so that she could protect her reputation by protesting her innocence to the two men, and that she left the room once she began to shake and feel ill. Additionally, she attributes her "serious emotional upset" to her feelings of intimidation that she contends were caused by: James Cesario's sitting directly next to her during questioning, yellow pad and pencil in hand; Ralph Bell's repeated statement that his briefcase contained proof of her guilt; and his raised voice.

The common law tort of false imprisonment is defined as an unlawful restraint of an individual's personal liberty or freedom of locomotion. [ ] Imprisonment has been defined as "any unlawful exercise or show of force by which a person is compelled to remain where he does not wish to remain or to go where he does not wish to go." [ ] In order for a false imprisonment to be present, there must be actual or legal intent to restrain. [ ]

Unlawful restraint may be effected by words alone, by acts alone or both [ ]; actual force is unnecessary to an action in false imprisonment. [ ] The Restatement of Torts specifies ways in which an action may bring about the confinement required as an element of false imprisonment, including (1) actual or apparent physical barriers; (2) overpowering physical force, or by submission to physical force; (3) threats of physical force; (4) other duress; and (5) asserted legal authority. Restatement (Second) of Torts §§ 38–41 (1965).

It is essential, however, that the confinement be against the plaintiff's will and if a person voluntarily consents to the confinement, there can be no false imprisonment. [ ] "Moral pressure, as where the plaintiff remains with the defendant to clear himself of suspicion of theft, * * *, is not enough; nor, as in the case of assault, are threats for the future * * *. Any remedy for such wrongs must lie with the more modern tort of the intentional infliction of mental distress." [ ]

Plaintiff principally relies on the court's decision in Marcus v. Liebman (1978) [ ], for support of her position that summary judgment should not have been granted in the instant case. In Marcus v. Liebman, the court extensively examined the concept that threats of a future action are not enough to constitute confinement. [ ] There, the defendant psychiatrist threatened to have plaintiff committed to the Elgin State Hospital, and the *Marcus* court found that this was a present threat, constituting false imprisonment, as opposed to a threat of future action. The court in *Marcus* concluded that the lower court had incorrectly directed a verdict for the defendant, and reversed and remanded the case for trial on the question of imprisonment. The court noted that plaintiff was already voluntarily committed to the psychiatric wing of a private hospital when the defendant made the threat to commit her to a state mental hospital and reasoned, "[A]t the time the alleged threat was made plaintiff was already confined. It was certainly reasonable for the plaintiff to believe that before her release [from the private hospital], commitment procedures could have been concluded." [ ]

Our analysis of the *Marcus* decision, as well as the other cases cited by plaintiff, does not support plaintiff's position. All of these cases are easily distinguishable from the present case, as in each, either physical restraint or present threats of such were present.

In the case at bar, we are confronted with plaintiff's testimony, given under oath, that she voluntarily accompanied James Cesario to the baking room; that she stayed in the room in order to protect her reputation; that she was never threatened with the loss of her job; that she was never in fear of her safety; and that at no time was she prevented from exiting the baking room. Her affidavit, in which she averred that she left the baking room after she began to shake and when she felt that she was becoming ill, does not place into issue material facts which she had previously removed from contention. [ ] In her discovery deposition, given under oath, she stated that she "got up and left" when Ralph Bell asked her how long the cash register "shorting" had been going on.

In the tort of false imprisonment, it is not enough for the plaintiff to have felt "compelled" to remain in the baking room in order to protect her reputation (see Prosser, Torts, § 11); for the evidence must establish a restraint against the plaintiff's will, as where she yields to force, to the threat of force or the assertion of authority. (See Restatement (Second) of Torts §§ 38–41 (1965).) In the present case, our search of the record reveals no evidence that plaintiff yielded to constraint of a threat, express or implied, or to physical force of any kind. Also, absent evidence that plaintiff accompanied Cesario against her will, we cannot say that she was imprisoned or unlawfully detained by defendant's employees. Finally, we find no merit to plaintiff's argument that defendant's affirmative defense constituted an admission of an unlawful restraint.

For the reasons stated above, we conclude that the trial court properly granted defendant's motion for summary judgment, as there exists no question of material fact in the present case.

AFFIRMED.

■ MEJDA, P.J., and SULLIVAN, J., concur.

NOTES AND QUESTIONS

1. In *Lopez,* what appear to be the elements in the prima facie case of false imprisonment? What was the crux of the defendant's affirmative defense?

2. Would summary judgment have been warranted if Bell and Cesario had told plaintiff that they weren't through questioning her when she decided to leave? What if they said that she was free to leave but if she did so she was fired?

3. Suppose that plaintiff was one of three employees who were called in and subjected to the reported interrogation because defendants didn't know which of them had been stealing from the register. Would plaintiff's case remain as strong as in *Lopez?*

4. The circumstances under which individuals have sought to restrain the freedom of movement of others defy generalization. For a bizarre case, involving the leader of a religious sect who imposed sanctions against the plaintiff straying too far from the yacht where she was domiciled, see Whittaker v. Sandford, 110 Me. 77, 85 A. 399 (1912). On the overambitious efforts of two "high-powered" car repossessors, see National Bond & Investment Co. v. Whithorn, 276 Ky. 204, 123 S.W.2d 263 (1938).

False arrest cases constitute a special category. If the imprisonment resulted from an arrest, the defendant must have been legally entitled to make the arrest. Without a privilege, the defendant would be subject to liability for the particular form of false imprisonment known as false arrest. The rules governing false arrest are discussed, in the context of a survey of the historical development of the false imprisonment tort, in Morris on Torts 399–414 (2d ed. 1980).

5. *Malicious Prosecution.* False arrest cases do not reach claims in which, although the warrant and legal forms were proper, no basis existed for the arrest in the first place. The defendant in the original case claims that the complainant began the prosecution without probable cause and for improper purposes. This claim, called an action for malicious prosecution, permits the original defendant, after exoneration, to bring an action for expenses and humiliation sustained in the first case. For an example of the interplay between false arrest and malicious prosecution in the shoplifting context, see Soares v. Ann & Hope of Rhode Island, Inc., 637 A.2d 339 (R.I.1994), upholding a claim that a store initiated criminal proceedings without probable cause.

A more restricted form of this action lies in many states against persons who wrongfully file civil actions. The history of these actions is traced in Note, Groundless Litigation and the Malicious Prosecution Debate: A Historical Analysis, 88 Yale L.J. 1218 (1979). For an interesting analysis of one state's development of the civil action, see Dupre, Case Comment, Yost v. Torok and Abusive Litigation: A New Tort to Solve an Old Problem, 21 Ga.L.Rev. 429 (1986).

Perhaps not surprisingly, some parties who have historically been disgruntled with the tort system are often plaintiffs in malicious prosecution cases. The medical community's experiences with such actions are discussed in Yardley, Malicious Prosecution: A Physician's Need for Reassessment, 60 Chi.-Kent L.Rev. 317 (1984). In City of Long Beach v. Bozek, 31 Cal.3d 527, 645 P.2d 137, 183 Cal.Rptr. 86 (1982), vacated and remanded 459 U.S. 1095, on remand 33 Cal.3d 727, 661 P.2d 1072, 190 Cal.Rptr. 918 (1983), the court held that the government could not bring a malicious prosecution action against an individual who had brought an unsuccessful action against the government. The court's decision is criticized in Faber, City of Long Beach v. Bozek: An Absolute Right to Sue the Government?, 71 Cal.L.Rev. 1258 (1983).

6. *Special Problems of Shoplifting.* The arrest of a suspected shoplifter presents special legal problems because a private citizen is usually the arrester. The problem is significant economically because an estimated $30 billion worth of merchandise is lost to shoplifters each year and retailers annually spend large sums on efforts to avoid such losses. See N.Y. Times, Dec. 4, 1994, § 3, at 13. The losses are hard to itemize and are uninsurable.

Most shoplifting incidents are petty larcenies. In most states the misdemeanor of petty larceny covers theft of merchandise worth less than $50 or $100. Thus, the shopkeeper's suspicion is usually that someone has committed a misdemeanor. There is no time to get an officer or a warrant. At common law, even a peace officer had no privilege to arrest for a misdemeanor committed in the officer's presence—unless the officer had a warrant—if the misdemeanor involved no breach of the peace.

Even states that have liberalized the common law misdemeanor arrest rules for police officers, may require that the offense have occurred in the officer's presence—an unlikely event in shoplifting cases unless the officer is not in uniform. For a "citizen's arrest," most states require that the misdemeanor have been committed in the citizen's presence and that the person arrested be guilty. In these states, even if a suspected theft occurs in the presence of a store employee, the shopkeeper still arrests at his or her peril: the arrested person must be proven guilty. Even in more lenient states the shopkeeper must establish that a misdemeanor has indeed occurred. Then, if a suspect refuses to open packages or explain suspicious conduct, traditional law presents the shopkeeper with the choice of making a possibly unlawful citizen's arrest or letting the suspect go. A similar dilemma is presented if the shopkeeper seeks only to retrieve goods without making an arrest: if, in fact, the suspect has obtained the goods legally, the shopkeeper's reasonable belief that they were stolen will not protect against liability for battery if force is used to retrieve the goods.

Nor can the shopkeeper solve the problem by seeking the assistance of a police officer. The shopkeeper who detains the suspect against his or her will until a police officer arrives has in effect made an arrest. If, instead, the shopkeeper chases a suspect down the street shouting, "Stop that man; he is a thief!," and a police officer arrests him, the shopkeeper will be deemed to have instigated the arrest and will be subject to the standards of a citizen's arrest—though the police officer may be protected as having made the arrest on reasonable grounds.

In 1960, New York enacted General Business Law § 218:

> In any action for false arrest, false imprisonment, unlawful detention, defamation of character, assault, trespass, or invasion of civil rights, brought by any person by reason of having been detained on or in the immediate vicinity of the premises of a retail mercantile establishment for the purpose of investigation or questioning . . . as to the ownership of any merchandise, it shall be a defense to such action that the person was detained in a reasonable manner and for not more than a reasonable time to permit such investigation or questioning by a peace officer . . . or by the owner of the retail mercantile establishment, his authorized employee or agent, and that such officer, owner, employee or agent had reasonable grounds to believe that the person so detained . . . was committing or attempting to commit larceny on such premises of such merchandise. As used in this section, "reasonable grounds" shall include, but not be limited to, knowledge that a person has concealed possession of unpurchased merchandise of a retail mercantile establishment . . . and a "reasonable time" shall mean the time necessary to permit the person detained to make a statement or to refuse to make a statement, and the time necessary to examine employees and records of the mercantile establishment relative to the ownership of the merchandise. . . .

The statute was amended slightly in 1994 to allow the owner of a movie theatre to detain someone reasonably believed to be using a recording device. Similar statutes exist in other states. See, e.g., Calif.Penal Code § 490.5(f). Is this a sound approach? How does it compare with the common law approach in employee theft cases taken by the *Lopez* court? Are there better alternatives?

The New York statute's philosophy and operation are discussed in Jacques v. Sears, Roebuck & Co., 30 N.Y.2d 466, 285 N.E.2d 871, 334 N.Y.S.2d 632 (1972)(protecting merchant who detained customer who had left store without paying for merchandise, but whose prosecution was dropped for lack of intent). See generally, Note, Merchants' Responses to Shoplifting: An Empirical Study, 28 Stan.L.Rev. 589 (1976).

In 1991, New York adopted legislation allowing merchants to impose civil penalties not exceeding $500 on shoplifters who make restitution of the value of the stolen goods; in return for agreeing to an informal settlement, the shoplifter gets no criminal record. See generally, Woo, Most States Now Have Laws Permitting Stores to Impose Civil Fines on Shoplifters, Wall St.J., Sept. 9, 1992 at B1. Is the statute likely to reduce the prospect of false imprisonment actions?

4. INTENTIONAL INFLICTION OF EMOTIONAL DISTRESS

An intentional tort of recent origin is the intentional infliction of emotional distress. Traditionally, courts were reluctant to recognize such an action both because of the difficulties in assuring that actual harm had occurred, an issue we encountered in our consideration of negligently inflicted emotional distress, p. 226, supra, and also because of the belief that a certain amount of verbal abuse is a part of everyday life. This reluctance was still discernible in a 1948 case in which the defendant loudly and repeatedly on a crowded street called the pregnant plaintiff a "goddamned son of a bitch" and "a dirty crook." Plaintiff alleged general physical harm resulting from the shock. A split court refused relief on the ground that there is "no right to recover for bad manners" in the absence of an assault or defamation because of the "speculative" and "sentimental" nature of the injury and the difficulty of measuring damages. Bartow v. Smith, 149 Ohio St. 301, 78 N.E.2d 735 (1948), overruled by Yeager v. Local Union 20, 6 Ohio St.3d 369, 453 N.E.2d 666 (1983).

But other courts had begun to grant relief not only for intentional inflictions of emotional distress involving some physical injury, but also for emotional distress alone—at least where the actor's behavior was particularly offensive. In State Rubbish Collectors Ass'n v. Siliznoff, 38 Cal.2d 330, 240 P.2d 282 (1952), the plaintiff sued for nonpayment of notes and the defendant's cross-complaint asked that the notes be cancelled because of duress. He also sought damages because plaintiff's members had coerced him to sign the notes to pay for a garbage collection contract he had signed with a customer—even though defendant did not belong to plaintiff association. He testified that the encounter was so distressing that he became ill and vomited several times. A jury award of both compensatory and punitive damages was upheld unanimously. For the court, Justice Traynor first concluded that "a cause of action is established when it is shown that one, in the absence of any privilege, intentionally subjects another to the mental suffering incident to serious threats to his physical well-being, whether or not the threats are made under such circumstances as to constitute a technical assault." Where mental suffering is a major element of the damages it is anomalous to deny recovery on the ground that no physical injury followed:

> There are persuasive arguments and analogies that support the recognition of a right to be free from serious, intentional, and unprivileged invasions of mental and emotional tranquility. If a cause of action is otherwise established, it is settled that damages may be given for mental suffering naturally ensuing from the acts complained of [ ], and in the case of many torts, such as assault, battery, false imprisonment, and defamation, mental suffering will

frequently constitute the principal element of damages. [ ] In cases where mental suffering constitutes a major element of damages it is anomalous to deny recovery because the defendant's intentional misconduct fell short of producing some physical injury.

It may be contended that to allow recovery in the absence of physical injury will open the door to unfounded claims and a flood of litigation, and that the requirement that there be physical injury is necessary to insure that serious mental suffering actually occurred. The jury is ordinarily in a better position, however, to determine whether outrageous conduct results in mental distress than whether that distress in turn results in physical injury. From their own experience jurors are aware of the extent and character of the disagreeable emotions that may result from the defendant's conduct, but a difficult medical question is presented when it must be determined if emotional distress resulted in physical injury. . . .

Does the rationale extend beyond threatening situations that don't quite measure up to assaults? Consider the following case.

Womack v. Eldridge

Supreme Court of Virginia, 1974.
215 Va. 338, 210 S.E.2d 145.

■ I'Anson, Chief Justice.

Plaintiff, Danny Lee Womack, instituted this action against the defendant, Rosalie Eldridge, to recover compensatory and punitive damages for mental shock and distress allegedly caused by the defendant's willful, wanton, malicious, fraudulent and deceitful acts and conduct toward him. The question of punitive damages was stricken by the trial court and the jury returned a verdict for the plaintiff in the amount of $45,000. The trial court set aside the verdict . . . on the ground that there could be no recovery for emotional distress in the absence of "physical damage or other bodily harm." We granted plaintiff a writ of error. . . .

Plaintiff assigned numerous errors, but the controlling question is whether one who by extreme and outrageous conduct intentionally or recklessly causes severe emotional distress to another is subject to liability for such emotional distress absent any bodily injury.

The evidence shows that defendant had been engaged in the business of investigating cases for attorneys for many years. She was employed by Richard E. Seifert and his attorney to obtain a photograph of the plaintiff to be used as evidence in the trial of Seifert, who was charged with sexually molesting two young boys. On May 27, 1970, about 8 a.m., defendant went to plaintiff's home and upon gaining admittance told him that she was a Mrs. Jackson from the newspaper and that she was writing an article on Skateland. Defendant asked plaintiff, who was a coach at Skateland, if she could take a picture of him for publication with the article, and he readily consented.

Shortly thereafter defendant delivered the photograph to Seifert's counsel while he was representing Seifert at his preliminary hearing. Seifert's counsel showed plaintiff's photograph to the two young boys and asked if he was the one who molested them. When they replied that he was not, counsel withdrew the photograph and put it in his briefcase. However, the Commonwealth's Attorney then asked to see the photograph and requested additional information about the person shown in it. Defendant was then called to the stand and she supplied the plaintiff's name and address. Plaintiff's photograph in no way resembled Seifert, and the only excuse given by defendant for taking plaintiff's picture was that he was at Skateland when Seifert was arrested. However, the offenses alleged against Seifert did not occur at Skateland.

The Commonwealth's Attorney then directed a detective to go to plaintiff's home and bring him to court. The detective told plaintiff that his photograph had been presented in court; that the Commonwealth's Attorney wanted him to appear at the proceedings; and that he could either appear voluntarily then or he would be summoned. Plaintiff agreed to go voluntarily. When called as a witness, plaintiff testified as to the circumstances under which defendant had obtained his photograph. He also said that he had not molested any children and that he knew nothing about the charges against Seifert.

A police officer questioned plaintiff several times thereafter. Plaintiff was also summoned to appear as a witness before the grand jury but he was not called. However, he was summoned to appear several times at Seifert's trial in the circuit court because of continuances of the cases.

Plaintiff testified that he suffered great shock, distress and nervousness because of defendant's fraud and deceit and her wanton, willful and malicious conduct in obtaining his photograph and turning it over to Seifert's attorney to be used in court. He suffered great anxiety as to what people would think of him and feared that he would be accused of molesting the boys. He had been unable to sleep while the matter was being investigated. While testifying in the instant case he became emotional and incoherent. Plaintiff's wife also testified that her husband experienced great shock and mental depression from the involvement.

. . .

The precise issue presented on this appeal has not been decided by this court.

Courts from other jurisdictions are not in accord on whether there can be a recovery for emotional distress unaccompanied by physical injury. However, most of the courts which have been presented with the question in recent years have held that there may be a recovery against one who by his extreme and outrageous conduct intentionally or recklessly causes another severe emotional distress. . . .

The Restatement (Second) of Torts, § 46 at 71, provides: "(1) One who by extreme and outrageous conduct intentionally or recklessly causes severe emotional distress to another is subject to liability for such emotional distress, and if bodily harm to the other results from it, for such bodily harm." In comment (i) to the Restatement it is expressly stated that this rule also covers a situation where the actor knows that distress is certain, or substantially certain, to result from his conduct.

. . .

A great majority of cases allowing recovery for such a cause of action do so when the act was intentional and the wrongdoer desired the emotional distress or knew or should have known that it would likely result. [ ]

We adopt the view that a cause of action will lie for emotional distress, unaccompanied by physical injury, provided four elements are shown: One, the wrongdoer's conduct was intentional or reckless. This element is satisfied where the wrongdoer had the specific purpose of inflicting emotional distress or where he intended his specific conduct and knew or should have known that emotional distress would likely result. Two, the conduct was outrageous and intolerable in that it offends against the generally accepted standards of decency and morality. This requirement is aimed at limiting frivolous suits and avoiding litigation in situations where only bad manners and mere hurt feelings are involved. Three, there was a causal connection between the wrongdoer's conduct and the emotional distress. Four, the emotional distress was severe.

4 elements

"It is for the court to determine, in the first instance, whether the defendant's conduct may reasonably be regarded as so extreme and outrageous as to permit recovery, or whether it is necessarily so. Where reasonable men may differ, it is for the jury, subject to the control of the court, to determine whether, in the particular case, the conduct has been sufficiently extreme and outrageous to result in liability." Restatement (Second) of Torts, *supra,* at 77.

In the case at bar, reasonable men may disagree as to whether defendant's conduct was extreme and outrageous and whether plaintiff's emotional distress was severe. Thus, the questions presented were for a jury to determine. A jury could conclude from the evidence presented that defendant willfully, recklessly, intentionally and deceitfully obtained plaintiff's photograph for the purpose of permitting her employers to use it as a defense in a criminal case without considering the effect it would have on the plaintiff. There is nothing in the evidence that even suggests that plaintiff may have been involved in the child molesting cases. The record shows that the only possible excuse for involving the plaintiff was that Seifert was arrested at the place where plaintiff was employed. A reasonable person would or should have recognized the likelihood of the serious mental distress that would be caused in involving an innocent person in child molesting cases. If the two boys had hesitated in answering that the man in the photograph was not the one who had molested them, it is evident that the finger of suspicion would have been pointed at the plaintiff.

Defendant contended in her brief, and in oral argument before us . . . that the action of the Commonwealth's Attorney in causing plaintiff's name to be revealed was an intervening cause which absolved her of any liability.

We will not consider those contentions because defendant did not assign cross-error. [   ]

For the reasons stated, the judgment of the court below is reversed, the jury verdict reinstated, and final judgment hereby entered for the plaintiff.

NOTES AND QUESTIONS

1. Suppose the evidence indicated that defendant had been hired without knowledge of the use to which the photograph would be put. Would the Restatement standard of liability, as interpreted by the court, be satisfied? Suppose, instead, defendant knew that it was to be used for purposes of identification in a criminal case—but nothing more. Would the standard be satisfied? Suppose she knew that the photo was to be used to incriminate plaintiff in a case in which he had no involvement—but she took the picture on the street. Would plaintiff have had a colorable claim?

2. If defendant had properly raised the claim that the Commonwealth Attorney was an "intervening cause which absolved her of any liability," should it have altered the disposition of the case?

3. What result if plaintiff had claimed intentional infliction of emotional distress against Seifert's attorney?

4. In Russo v. White, 241 Va. 23, 400 S.E.2d 160, (1991), the court affirmed dismissal of the plaintiff's claim in a case in which she alleged that the defendant had made 340 "hang-up" phone calls to her in a two month period after she refused to go out with him more than once. The court emphasized that plaintiff had not suffered any physical injury as a result of the stress and that defendant had not spoken during the calls. Asserting that the tort of intentional infliction, although recognized since *Womack,* is "not favored" in Virginia, the court quoted from Givelber, The Right to Minimum Social Decency and the Limits of Evenhandness: Intentional Infliction of Emotional Distress by Outrageous Conduct, 82 Colum.L.Rev. 42, 42–43 (1982), in arguing:

> [Intentional infliction of emotional distress] "differs from traditional intentional torts in an important respect: it provides no clear definition of the prohibited conduct." . . . Assault, battery, and false imprisonment "describe specific forms of behavior," but the term "outrageous" "does not objectively describe an act or series of acts; rather, it represents an evaluation of behavior. The concept thus fails to provide clear guidance either to those whose conduct it purports to regulate, or to those who must evaluate that conduct."

Is the distinction drawn between the intentional infliction tort and other intentional torts persuasive? In any event, how serious is the problem? Is it addressed in the *Womack* opinion? Reconsider Justice Traynor's position in *Siliznoff,* p. 820, supra.

5. In an effort to make the standard of liability more concrete, Restatement (Second), § 46, comment *d* states "the case is one in which the recitation of the facts to an average member of the community would arouse his resentment against the actor, and lead him to exclaim, 'Outrageous!' " Givelber, in response, comments that "[t]o suggest, as the Restatement does, that civil liability should turn on the resentments of the average member of the community appears to turn the passions of the moment into law." He then notes that there would be serious constitutional difficulties in making "outrageous conduct" criminal. Do his concerns undermine the legitimacy of the intentional infliction tort?

6. Is there any room for the unusually sensitive plaintiff in these cases?

7. Courts have permitted intentional infliction of emotional distress claims to lie in cases of racial insults and harassment. See, e.g., Wiggs v. Courshon, 355 F.Supp. 206 (S.D.Fla.1973)(upholding verdict against waitress who hurled racial epithets at plaintiff when he inquired about his dinner order). But see, e.g., Bradshaw v. Swagerty, 1 Kan.App.2d 213, 563 P.2d 511 (1977)(plaintiff alleged that defendant, plaintiff's lawyer, hurled racial epithet during dispute over legal bill; court denied recovery on ground that such epithets are "mere insults of the kind which must be tolerated in our roughened society").

Section 46 claims are sometimes brought for cases of racial harassment in the workplace. See, e.g. Alcorn v. Anbro Eng'g Inc., 2 Cal.3d 493, 468 P.2d 216, 86 Cal.Rptr. 88 (1970)(plaintiff, who was shop steward for the company's labor union, told his supervisor that a nonunion employee was not permitted to drive a truck from a job site; supervisor responded with a string of racial insults and fired plaintiff; court allowed plaintiff to proceed with his claim for intentional infliction of emotional distress). Some courts have denied relief for harassment in the workplace on the ground that the employer's words and actions, while offensive, do not constitute "extreme and outrageous" conduct. See, e.g., Patterson v. McLean Credit Union, 805 F.2d 1143 (4th Cir.1986), affirmed in part, vacated in part, and remanded on different grounds 491 U.S. 164 (1989) (plaintiff's allegations that her supervisor gave her too much work, required her to sweep and dust, and commented that blacks are slower than whites, did not rise to level of "extreme and outrageous" conduct). The tort system's response to verbal harassment in the workplace is discussed and criticized in Austin, Employer Abuse, Worker Resistance, and the Tort of Intentional Infliction of Emotional Distress, 41 Stan.L.Rev. 1 (1988).

The racial harassment issue has produced a good deal of commentary. See Delgado, Words That Wound: A Tort Action for Racial Insults, Epithets, and Name–Calling, 17 Harv. C.R.-C.L. L.Rev. 133 (1982); Love, Discriminatory Speech and the Tort of Intentional Infliction of Emotional Distress, 47 Wash. & Lee L.Rev. 123 (1990). The fine line between outrageous conduct and free expression has given rise to serious First

Amendment concerns. For a constitutional defense of the state's ability to provide relief to victims of racial harassment, see Lawrence, If He Hollers Let Him Go: Regulating Racist Speech on Campus, 1990 Duke L.J. 431. For a contrary view, see Note, Dear Professor Lawrence, You Missed the School Bus; Brown v. Board of Education Supports Free Speech on Campus: A Reply, 72 B.U.L.Rev. 953 (1992).

For an argument that legislative developments have largely negated the need for common law protection, see Duffy, Intentional Infliction of Emotional Distress and Employment at Will: The Case against Tortification of Labor and Employment Law, 74 B.U.L.Rev. 387 (1994).

8. *Racial Harassment—Statutory Claims.* Until recently, claims for workplace racial harassment were not actionable under 42 U.S.C. § 1981, an antidiscrimination statute passed during the Reconstruction era, which gives all persons equal rights "to make and enforce contracts." In *Patterson v. McLean Credit Union*, referred to in the preceding note, the United States Supreme Court held that § 1981's protections were limited to issues of contract formation, and thus provided no relief for harassment directed at a worker during the course of his or her employment. Plaintiffs were left with the option of bringing an action under Title VII of the Civil Rights Act of 1964, 42 U.S.C. § 2000e et seq.; however, Title VII's framework for resolution imposes several procedural obstacles not present in a § 1981 action. Congress overruled the Court's interpretation of § 1981 in the Civil Rights Reform Act of 1991, Pub.L. 102–166, 105 Stat. 1071. Thus, claims for racial harassment on the job are now actionable under § 1981.

In Bolden v. PRC Inc., 43 F.3d 545 (10th Cir.1994), plaintiff brought an action against his employer alleging racial discrimination under Title VII. The court found that plaintiff, an African–American, was "a sensitive and serious person working in a shop filled with boorish churls," and "was met with hostility by many of his co-workers." Nonetheless, though his co-workers made two racial remarks to plaintiff, those comments did not amount to the "steady barrage of opprobrious racial comments" that the court required to find "harassment that was racial or stemmed from racial animus." See Oppenheimer, Negligent Discrimination, 141 U.Pa.L.Rev. 899 (1993), articulating a negligence-based theory of employer liability under Title VII.

9. *Sexual Harassment—Statutory Claims.* The law dealing with sexual harassment in the workplace has been dynamic in recent years. Courts have long held that employers violate Title VII if employment benefits are conditioned on sexual favors—so-called "quid pro quo" cases. In 1986, the Supreme Court broadened the Title VII standard to permit claims if discriminatory conduct created an "abusive working environment." Meritor Sav. Bank v. Vinson, 477 U.S. 57 (1986). Appeals courts then split on what type of conduct was necessary to state a claim. One court required serious injury to plaintiff's psychological well-being, Rabidue v. Osceola Refining Co., 805 F.2d 611 (6th Cir.1986), cert. denied 481 U.S. 1041 (1987). Applying a more expansive standard, another court held that the severity and pervasiveness of sexual harassment should be evaluated from the victim's perspective, Ellison v. Brady, 924 F.2d 872 (9th Cir.1991). Since "a sex-blind reasonable person standard tends to . . . systematically ignore the experiences of women," the court held that plaintiffs could state a prima facie case by alleging conduct that "a reasonable woman would consider sufficiently severe or pervasive" to create a hostile working environment.

The Supreme Court rejected both standards in Harris v. Forklift Sys. Inc., 114 S.Ct. 367 (1993). Defendant had asked plaintiff to remove coins from his pants pocket and repeatedly insulted her with comments such as "you're a dumb woman, what do you know?" and, during plaintiff's negotiation of a deal with a customer, "what did you do, promise the guy . . . [sex] Saturday night?" The Court denied that plaintiff had to show psychological injury to recover under Title VII but also declined to adopt a "reasonable woman" standard. Plaintiff had to show conduct "that is . . . severe or pervasive enough to create an objectively hostile or abusive work environment . . . [which] would reasonably be perceived, and is perceived, as hostile or abusive." The finder of fact was instructed to weigh all of the circumstances, including the frequency and severity of the harassment, whether the harassment involves humiliation or physical intimidation, and whether it interferes with employee's work performance.

The Court's standard was subsequently interpreted to mean that, in proving a hostile work environment, plaintiff can rely only on harassing conduct of which she was aware at the time of employment. Hirase–Doi v. U.S. West Communications, 61 F.3d 777 (10th Cir.1995).

In the wake of *Forklift's* caution that "merely offensive" conduct was not actionable, one court reversed a judgment against a defendant employer whose "sense of humor took final shape in adolescence," but who had not threatened plaintiff nor solicited sex or a date with her. Baskerville v. Culligan International Co., 50 F.3d 428 (7th Cir.1995) (per Posner, Ch.J.).

Plaintiffs may also state a cause of action under Title VII if they complain of sexual harassment and are subjected to retaliation. In Dunning v. Simmons Airlines Inc., 62 F.3d 863 (7th Cir.1995), plaintiff complained of sexual harassment and was subsequently assigned involuntarily to unpaid maternity leave. The court awarded plaintiff attorney fees and back pay for her retaliation claim though it made no finding on her sexual harassment claim.

The subject of sexual harassment has received extensive scholarly treatment. See C. MacKinnon, Sexual Harassment of Working Women (1979); Ehrenreich, Pluralist Myths and Powerless Men: The Ideology of Reasonableness in Sexual Harassment Law, 99 Yale L.J. 1177 (1990); Estrich, Sex at Work, 43 Stan.L.Rev. 813 (1991). For commentary since the Court's *Forklift* decision, see Vorwerk, The Forgotten Interest Group: Reforming Title VII to Address the Concerns of Workers While Eliminating Sexual Harassment, 48 Vand.L.Rev. 1019 (1995). A more direct route for suing for sexual harassment may develop under the 1994 Violence Against Women Act, 108 Stat. 1902. In what is reported to be the first federal civil suit under the Act, a student sued in 1966 seeking damages against two student athletes and her university. Bernstein, Civil Rights Lawsuit in Rape Case Challenges Integrity of a Campus, N.Y. Times, Feb. 11, 1996, § 1, p. 1.

Harassment in Schools. In Franklin v. Gwinnett County Pub. Sch., 503 U.S. 60 (1992), a case alleging sexual harassment of a high school student by one of her teachers, the Court implied a private right of action under Title IX of the Education Amendments of 1972, and concluded—in terms that may have implications for other civil rights laws—that "we presume the availability of all appropriate remedies unless Congress has expressly indicated otherwise."

A more difficult question is posed when a student sues a school system for failing to protect her from harassment by other students. In Doe v. Petaluma City Sch. Dist., 54 F.3d 1447 (9th Cir.1995), a student sued her counselor for failing to take action against the students allegedly harassing her. Though the court rejected Doe's claim, it noted that she might have succeeded if the offending conduct had taken place after the Court decided *Franklin.* Had *Franklin* applied, the court suggested Doe could have likened her counselor's responsibility for peer harassment under Title IX to an employer's responsibility to prevent co-worker harassment under Title VII.

For commentary on the law developing in this area, see Baker, Comment, Proposed Title IX Guidelines on Sex–Based Harassment of Students, 43 Emory L.J. 271 (1994).

10. *Credit Practices.* One type of situation that does recur frequently is the bill collector case. The extent to which a creditor may utilize self-help in attempting to collect a debt is debatable. Surely a creditor may write a letter warning the alleged debtor that unless the amount claimed to be due is paid within a certain number of days, a suit will be filed. Surely a creditor may not beat the alleged debtor to a pulp in efforts to collect money. Where should the line be drawn? Is it clear that some self-help should be encouraged so that not every creditor who wants to collect money need initiate a lawsuit? On the assumption that physical violence is never permissible, we may confine our speculation to the words used and the ways in which they are communicated. Consider the following acts allegedly committed by a collection agency seeking repayment of a loan in Sherman v. Field Clinic, 74 Ill.App.3d 21, 392 N.E.2d 154 (1979):

> . . . [t]elephoning plaintiffs' residence 10–20 times per day 3 days per week and 5–6 times per day 2 other days per week; sending numerous letters to plaintiffs' residence; making numerous telephone calls to Mr. Sherman at his place of business, though only Mrs. Sherman was responsible for any debts due the Clinic; threatening to "embarrass" Mr. Sherman by contacting his employers and co-workers; threatening to garnish half of Mr. Sherman's wages; frequently using profane and obscene language in calls to Mr. Sherman; calling and speaking to Mrs. Sherman's 15 year old daughter, plaintiff Deborah Billy, in connection with the debt, though only Mrs. Sherman was

responsible for any debts due the Clinic; frequently making threats to the daughter that Mr. and Mrs. Sherman would be sent to jail for not paying the bill; and frequently using abusive language in calls to Mrs. Sherman.

In considering the propriety of each of the alleged acts if done alone, consider the following questions: (1) What is the basic purpose of the defendant's conduct? Does it "intend" to cause emotional harm? Physical harm? Should the courts focus on the harm that actually ensues, what the defendant intended to cause, or on what a reasonable defendant should have foreseen from its conduct? (2) Should the identity of the defendant matter? This case involves a finance company attempting to collect a loan it has made. Often a suit involves a retail merchant who has sold items on credit and is attempting to collect the debt himself or, more likely today, with the help of a credit collection agency. Larger retailers usually discount customer notes with a finance company that then becomes the creditor. Should each of these parties have the same self-help privilege? (3) If the alleged debtor denies owing the claimed amount, should that situation be treated differently from one in which the debtor admits the debt but claims financial difficulties and wants to delay repayment? (4) Should it matter if the creditor has had serious difficulties in locating the debtor? (5) Might other distinctions prove useful here?

11. *Interference with the Marital Relationship.* For centuries, courts have recognized two actions for intentional interference with the marital relation. The action for "criminal conversation" involved "sexual intercourse of an outsider with husband or wife," and is the tort action based on adultery. Historically, the action was available only to husbands because of the early property rights approach to the relationship between husband and wife. In recent times some states have extended the action to wives as well. But some 20 states have abolished the action entirely either legislatively or judicially. In Neal v. Neal, 125 Idaho 617, 873 P.2d 871 (1994), the court, after rejecting the historical justification for the tort, explained its decision to abolish it:

> Revenge, which may be a motive for bringing the cause of action, has no place in determining the legal rights between two parties. Further, this type of suit may expose the defendant to the extortionate schemes of the plaintiff, since it could ruin the defendant's reputation. Deterrence is not achieved; the nature of the activities underlying criminal conversation, that is sexual activity, are not such that the risk of damages would likely be a deterrent. Finally, since the injuries suffered are intangible, damage awards are not governed by any true standards, making it more likely that they could result from passion or prejudice.

The second tort, for "alienation of affections," applies to behavior by which outsiders through any means succeed in driving a wedge between family members. For a recent decision upholding an award in an alienation case, see Kirk v. Koch, 607 So.2d 1220 (Miss.1992)(jury could have found that defendant "directly and intentionally interfered" with plaintiff's marriage despite lack of showing of sexual relations or affectionate conduct between defendant and plaintiff's spouse).   Again, many states have abolished this action, through judicial decision or by the enactment of "heart balm" statutes prohibiting suits based on alienation grounds.   For an interesting example of common law abolition, see Hoye v. Hoye, 824 S.W.2d 422 (Ky.1992).   The heart balm statutes that eliminate the action for alienation of affections in many states also preclude actions based upon breach of promise to marry and upon seduction.   In Helena Lab.Corp., v. Snyder, 886 S.W.2d 767 (Tex.1994), plaintiff sought to avoid the state's ban on the alienation action by claiming that defendant employer negligently failed to prevent two already-married employees from forming a liaison at the office.   The court found no duty to prevent such conduct.

Constitutional defense.   In reading the next case it is important to know that in New York Times Co. v. Sullivan, 376 U.S. 254 (1964), the Court held that in libel cases public officials (later expanded to include public figures) who sue for false statements that harm their reputations must prove that the defendant made the statement knowing that it was false or recklessly uttered it without caring whether it was true or false. Proof of either prong constitutes "actual malice."   The case is reprinted at p. 929, infra.

Hustler Magazine, Inc. v. Falwell

Supreme Court of the United States, 1988.
485 U.S. 46, 108 S.Ct. 876, 99 L.Ed.2d 41.

■ CHIEF JUSTICE REHNQUIST delivered the opinion of the Court.

Petitioner Hustler Magazine, Inc., is a magazine of nationwide circulation.   Respondent Jerry Falwell, a nationally known minister who has been active as a commentator on politics and public affairs, sued petitioner and its publisher, petitioner Larry Flynt.   . . .

The inside front cover of the November 1983 issue of Hustler Magazine featured a "parody" of an advertisement for Campari Liqueur that contained the name and picture of respondent and was entitled "Jerry Falwell talks about his first time."   This parody was modeled after actual Campari ads that included interviews with various celebrities about their "first times."   Although it was apparent by the end of each interview that this meant the first time they sampled Campari, the ads clearly played on the sexual double entendre of the general subject of "first times."   Copying the form and layout of these Campari ads, Hustler's editors chose respondent as the featured celebrity and drafted an alleged "interview" with him in which he states that his "first time" was during a drunken incestuous rendezvous with his mother in an outhouse.   The Hustler parody portrays respondent and his mother as drunk and immoral, and suggests that respondent is a hypocrite who preaches only when he is drunk.   In small print at the bottom of the page, the ad contains the disclaimer, "ad parody—not to be taken seriously." The magazine's table of contents also lists the ad as "Fiction; Ad and Personality Parody."

Soon after the November issue of Hustler became available to the public, respondent brought this diversity action in the United States District Court for the Western District of Virginia against Hustler Magazine, Inc., Larry C. Flynt, and Flynt Distributing Co. Respondent stated in his complaint that publication of the ad parody in Hustler entitled him to recover damages for libel, invasion of privacy, and intentional infliction of emotional distress. The case proceeded to trial. At the close of the evidence, the District Court granted a directed verdict for petitioners on the invasion of privacy claim. The jury then found against respondent on the libel claim, specifically finding that the ad parody could not "reasonably be understood as describing actual facts about [respondent] or actual events in which [he] participated." [ ] The jury ruled for respondent on the intentional infliction of emotional distress claim, however, and stated that he should be awarded $100,000 in compensatory damages, as well as $50,000 each in punitive damages from petitioners [Hustler Magazine and Flynt]. Petitioners' motion for judgment notwithstanding the verdict was denied.

On appeal, the [Fourth Circuit] affirmed the judgment against petitioners. . . .[3] . . .

This case presents us with a novel question involving First Amendment limitations upon a State's authority to protect its citizens from the intentional infliction of emotional distress. We must decide whether a public figure may recover damages for emotional harm caused by the publication of an ad parody offensive to him, and doubtless gross and repugnant in the eyes of most. Respondent would have us find that a State's interest in protecting public figures from emotional distress is sufficient to deny First Amendment protection to speech that is patently offensive and is intended to inflict emotional injury, even when that speech could not reasonably have been interpreted as stating actual facts about the public figure involved. This we decline to do.

At the heart of the First Amendment is the recognition of the fundamental importance of the free flow of ideas and opinions on matters of public interest and concern. "[T]he freedom to speak one's mind is not only an aspect of individual liberty—and thus a good unto itself—but also is essential to the common quest for truth and the vitality of society as a whole." [ ] We have therefore been particularly vigilant to ensure that individual expressions of ideas remain free from governmentally imposed sanctions. The First Amendment recognizes no such thing as a "false" idea. [ ] As Justice Holmes wrote, "[W]hen men have realized that time has upset many fighting faiths, they may come to believe even more than they believe the very foundations of their own conduct that the ultimate

---

3. Under Virginia law, in an action for intentional infliction of emotional distress a plaintiff must show that the defendant's conduct (1) is intentional or reckless; (2) offends generally accepted standards of decency or morality; (3) is causally connected with the plaintiff's emotional distress; and (4) caused emotional distress that was severe. [ ]

good desired is better reached by free trade in ideas—that the best test of truth is the power of the thought to get itself accepted in the competition of the market. . . ." [   ]

The sort of robust political debate encouraged by the First Amendment is bound to produce speech that is critical of those who hold public office or those public figures who are "intimately involved in the resolution of important public questions or, by reason of their fame, shape events in areas of concern to society at large." [   ] Justice Frankfurter put it succinctly in Baumgartner v. United States, 322 U.S. 665, 673–674 (1944), when he said that "[o]ne of the prerogatives of American citizenship is the right to criticize public men and measures." Such criticism, inevitably, will not always be reasoned or moderate; public figures as well as public officials will be subject to "vehement, caustic, and sometimes unpleasantly sharp attacks," [New York Times]. "[T]he candidate who vaunts his spotless record and sterling integrity cannot convincingly cry 'Foul!' when an opponent or an industrious reporter attempts to demonstrate the contrary." [   ]

Of course, this does not mean that any speech about a public figure is immune from sanction in the form of damages. Since [New York Times] we have consistently ruled that a public figure may hold a speaker liable for the damage to reputation caused by publication of a defamatory falsehood, but only if the statement was made "with knowledge that it was false or with reckless disregard of whether it was false or not." [   ] False statements of fact are particularly valueless; they interfere with the truth-seeking function of the marketplace of ideas, and they cause damage to an individual's reputation that cannot easily be repaired by counter speech, however persuasive or effective. [   ] But even though falsehoods have little value in and of themselves, they are "nevertheless inevitable in free debate," [   ], and a rule that would impose strict liability on a publisher for false factual assertions would have an undoubted "chilling" effect on speech relating to public figures that does have constitutional value. "Freedoms of expression require 'breathing space.'" [   ] This breathing space is provided by a constitutional rule that allows public figures to recover for libel or defamation only when they can prove both that the statement was false and that the statement was made with the requisite level of culpability.

Respondent argues, however, that a different standard should apply in this case because here the State seeks to prevent not reputational damage, but the severe emotional distress suffered by the person who is the subject of an offensive publication. [   ] In respondent's view, and in the view of the Court of Appeals, so long as the utterance was intended to inflict emotional distress, was outrageous, and did in fact inflict serious emotional distress, it is of no constitutional import whether the statement was a fact or an opinion, or whether it was true or false. It is the intent to cause injury that is the gravamen of the tort, and the State's interest in preventing emotional harm simply outweighs whatever interest a speaker may have in speech of this type.

Generally speaking the law does not regard the intent to inflict emotional distress as one which should receive much solicitude, and it is quite understandable that most if not all jurisdictions have chosen to make it civilly culpable where the conduct in question is sufficiently "outrageous." But in the world of debate about public affairs, many things done with motives that are less than admirable are protected by the First Amendment. In [Garrison v. Louisiana, 379 U.S. 64 (1964)], we held that even when a speaker or writer is motivated by hatred or ill-will his expression was protected by the First Amendment:

> "Debate on public issues will not be uninhibited if the speaker must run the risk that it will be proved in court that he spoke out of hatred; even if he did speak out of hatred, utterances honestly believed contribute to the free interchange of ideas and the ascertainment of truth." [ ]

Thus while such a bad motive may be deemed controlling for purposes of tort liability in other areas of the law, we think the First Amendment prohibits such a result in the area of public debate about public figures.

Were we to hold otherwise, there can be little doubt that political cartoonists and satirists would be subjected to damages awards without any showing that their work falsely defamed its subject. Webster's defines a caricature as "the deliberately distorted picturing or imitating of a person, literary style, etc. by exaggerating features or mannerisms for satirical effect." [ ] The appeal of the political cartoon or caricature is often based on exploration of unfortunate physical traits or politically embarrassing events—an exploration often calculated to injure the feelings of the subject of the portrayal. The art of the cartoonist is often not reasoned or evenhanded, but slashing and one-sided. . . .

. . . .

Despite their sometimes caustic nature, from the early cartoon portraying George Washington as an ass down to the present day, graphic depictions and satirical cartoons have played a prominent role in public and political debate. [Thomas] Nast's castigation of the Tweed Ring, Walt McDougall's characterization of presidential candidate James G. Blaine's banquet with the millionaires at Delmonico's as "The Royal Feast of Belshazzar," and numerous other efforts have undoubtedly had an effect on the course and outcome of contemporaneous debate. Lincoln's tall, gangling posture, Teddy Roosevelt's glasses and teeth, and Franklin D. Roosevelt's jutting jaw and cigarette holder have been memorialized by political cartoons with an effect that could not have been obtained by the photographer or the portrait artist. From the viewpoint of history it is clear that our political discourse would have been considerably poorer without them.

Respondent contends, however, that the caricature in question here was so "outrageous" as to distinguish it from more traditional political cartoons. There is no doubt that the caricature of respondent and his mother published in Hustler is at best a distant cousin of the political cartoons described above, and a rather poor relation at that. If it were possible by laying down a principled standard to separate the one from the other, public discourse would probably suffer little or no harm. But we doubt that there is any such standard, and we are quite sure that the pejorative description "outrageous" does not supply one. "Outrageousness" in the area of political and social discourse has an inherent subjectiveness about it which would allow a jury to impose liability on the basis of the jurors' tastes or views, or perhaps on the basis of their dislike of a particular expression. An "outrageousness" standard thus runs afoul of our longstanding refusal to allow damages to be awarded because the speech in question may have an adverse emotional impact on the audience. . . .

. . .

Admittedly, these oft-repeated First Amendment principles, like other principles, are subject to limitations. We recognized in [FCC v. Pacifica Foundation, 438 U.S. 726 (1978)] that speech that is "'vulgar,' 'offensive,' and 'shocking'" is "not entitled to absolute constitutional protection under all circumstances." [ ] In Chaplinsky v. New Hampshire, 315 U.S. 568 (1942), we held that a state could lawfully punish an individual for the use of insulting " 'fighting' words—those which by their very utterance inflict injury or tend to incite an immediate breach of the peace." [ ] These limitations are but recognition of the observation in [Dun & Bradstreet, Inc. v. Greenmoss Builders, 472 U.S. 749 (1985)] that this Court has "long recognized that not all speech is of equal First Amendment importance." But the sort of expression involved in this case does not seem to us to be governed by any exception to the general First Amendment principles stated above.

We conclude that public figures and public officials may not recover for the tort of intentional infliction of emotional distress by reason of publications such as the one here at issue without showing in addition that the publication contains a false statement of fact which was made with "actual malice," i.e., with knowledge that the statement was false or with reckless disregard as to whether or not it was true. This is not merely a "blind application" of the *New York Times* standard, [ ], it reflects our considered judgment that such a standard is necessary to give adequate "breathing space" to the freedoms protected by the First Amendment.

Here it is clear that respondent Falwell is a "public figure" for purposes of First Amendment law.[5] The jury found against respondent on his libel claim when it decided that the Hustler ad parody could not "reasonably be understood as describing actual facts about [respondent] or actual events in which [he] participated." [ ] The Court of Appeals interpreted the jury's finding to be that the ad parody "was not reasonably believable," [ ], and in accordance with our custom we accept this finding. Respondent is thus relegated to his claim for damages awarded by the jury

5. Neither party disputes this conclusion. Respondent is the host of a nationally syndicated television show and was the founder and president of a political organization formerly known as the Moral Majority. He is also the founder of Liberty University in Lynchburg, Virginia, and is the author of several books and publications. [ ]

for the intentional infliction of emotional distress by "outrageous" conduct. But for reasons heretofore stated this claim cannot, consistently with the First Amendment, form a basis for the award of damages when the conduct in question is the publication of a caricature such as the ad parody involved here. The judgment of the Court of Appeals is accordingly

Reversed.

■ JUSTICE KENNEDY took no part in the consideration or decision of this case.

■ JUSTICE WHITE, concurring in the judgment.

As I see it, the decision in [*New York Times*] has little to do with this case, for here the jury found that the ad contained no assertion of fact. But I agree with the Court that the judgment below, which penalized the publication of the parody, cannot be squared with the First Amendment.

NOTES AND QUESTIONS

1. Why wasn't the *New York Times* standard violated here? Wasn't the ad depiction a false statement of fact made with "actual malice"? If it wasn't a false statement of fact, as Justice White suggests in his concurring opinion, why does *New York Times* have any relevance to the case?

2. What is the strongest reason for protecting this kind of expression? Should it override the plaintiff's interest in recovery?

3. The court mentions a number of situations where expression is sometimes subject to limitation—obscenity, "fighting words", offensive material. Is the depiction here distinguishable?

4. Should the law protect some minimal level of "civility" in public discourse? See generally, R. Smolla, Jerry Falwell v. Larry Flynt: The First Amendment on Trial (1988); LeBel, Emotional Distress, the First Amendment, and "This Kind of Speech": A Heretical Perspective on Hustler Magazine v. Falwell, 60 Colo.L.Rev. 315 (1989); and Post, The Constitutional Concept of Public Discourse: Outrageous Opinion, Democratic Deliberation, and Hustler Magazine v. Falwell, 103 Harv.L.Rev. 601 (1990).

5. Would you expect the Court's holding to be limited to public figures? What if Hustler parodied, in similar fashion, an anonymous bank clerk? The distinction between public and private figures has received extensive treatment in defamation law. We return to it in the next chapter.

5.   DEFENSES AND PRIVILEGES

Morris on Torts

Clarence Morris and C. Robert Morris.
24–39 (2d ed. 1980).

§ 2.   Consent

Volenti non fit injuria [one who consents cannot receive an injury] has been a respected legal maxim for centuries. Consent, it is said, is a defense to all charges of battery. But cases and holdings that seem alike may raise different policy problems.

Strong and Wiry meet in a gymnasium and agree to a wrestling bout. Wiry throws Strong and breaks his arm. Wiry intends, of course, to throw Strong, but has no thought of injuring him seriously, and follows all of the rules of the sport.

Strong has suffered a loss; however, to compensate him at Wiry's expense would be impolitic. Had Wiry done the very act he did without Strong's consent to wrestle, his conduct might be faulty; but many intentional physical contacts that are wrong when done without permission become privileged when authorized.

That Strong did not say that Wiry could break his arm is of no legal consequence. Wiry's reasonable acts done with Strong's consent are and should be privileged. Of course if Wiry used the occasion with intent either to injure Strong or dangerously to depart from the rules of the sport, he would be at fault and sound policy would justify liability for damages.

Weak and Warpt are members of a queer fanatical sect which has promulgated the tenet, "Parts of the human body are capable of sin which can be expiated only by amputation." Weak confesses to Warpt that she stole a watch with her right hand and asks Warpt to cut it off. Warpt obliges.

Warpt is guilty of serious fault; she could be convicted of mayhem and sent to the penitentiary. Though Weak may be hard pressed to pay her medical expenses and suffers great financial loss because of her disability, her participation is also serious fault; actions like hers too should be deterred. Were people like Weak given a cause of action for damages, such misconduct might become commoner. Since Warpt can be punished as a criminal, the civil court need not concern itself with her escape from tort liability.

In both of these hypothetical cases, *volenti non fit injuria* calls for a judgment for the defendant. But the policy reasons for denying the plaintiff's claim lie in the strength of the injurer's position in the wrestling case, and in the weakness of the victim's position in the fanatic case. An understanding of this difference will focus attention on important considerations in other kinds of cases.

The *volenti* rule, like most legal principles, has been interpreted, elaborated and qualified. The discussion that follows tells about some of its judicial adventures.

The courts have recognized that the *volenti* rule means no more than it says affirmatively. It says that consent is a defense; it does not say that all unauthorized physical contacts are batteries. If a defendant is justified in touching, shoving, or carrying a person without permission, the action is not a battery.

Courts have held that consent may be implied from acts, as well as expressed by words. When a plaintiff has given the defendant a reasonable impression that he or she authorizes a certain contact, the plaintiff's implied consent has the force of a spoken consent.

These last two points often bear on the practice of medicine. A patient may impliedly authorize chest thumpings and pulse takings without uttering special words of consent. A surgeon acting in an emergency is privileged without consent to perform a drastic procedure on an unconscious or irrational patient, if the surgeon reasonably believes that the operation is immediately needed to save the patient's life or to ward off serious harm. Only when a delay entailed in getting consent will not seriously endanger the patient need the surgeon either wait until the patient can personally give consent or seek the authorization of relatives. A reasonable surgical rescue is treated in the same way as any other kind of reasonable rescue.

On the other hand, unauthorized medical treatment in the absence of an emergency is a battery. Ordinarily doctors who impose treatment without their patients' informed consent are at fault, and their kind of conduct should be discouraged by liability.

. . .

. . . In the 1956 case of Kennedy v. Parrott[10] the appellate opinion dealt . . . with the realities of unanticipated needs for surgical procedures that become evident after the patient is anesthetized. In the Kennedy case the patient expected an appendectomy. When a proper incision was made, the surgeon discovered ovarian cysts that threatened future serious surgery unless attended to by a simple, prudent puncture. The surgeon, in this situation, would have practiced surgery foolishly if he had not exceeded the patient's consent. The court held that the surgeon was justified in performing the unanticipated, medically correct procedure. The court said, "[O]rdinarily a surgeon is employed to remedy conditions without any express limitation on his authority [and when unanticipated] conditions . . . make consent impractical, it is unreasonable to hold the physician to the exact operation—particularly when it is internal—that his preliminary examination indicated was necessary. . . . Reason is the soul of the law; the reason of the law being changed, the law is also changed." Compare this case to Lloyd v. Kull,[12] in which the surgeon saw a mole on his patient's leg while he was performing an abdominal operation and flicked it off. This bit of precautionary surgery could have been done about as well at a later time and after consultation. The court held this meddlesome therapy constituted an assault and battery.

. . .

Fights by mutual consent have had a special history. A fight in dead earnest is different from the sport of boxing; brawlers break the peace and are wrongdoers. These fight cases seem, at first glance, analogous to the hypothetical fanatic case; but many courts have allowed an injured fighter to recover in an assault and battery action brought against an antagonist.

---

10. 243 N.C. 355, 90 S.E.2d 754 (1956).   **12.** 329 F.2d 168 (7th Cir.1964).

The opinions circumvent the *volenti* doctrine by stating that unlawful consent is no consent. If courts consistently took this view, many other kinds of plaintiffs who are also so seriously at fault could maintain assault and battery actions. In most of the other kinds of cases in which the plaintiff has been a guilty participant in wrongdoing, however, the plaintiff does not succeed and judges do not mention the legalism that unlawful consent is no consent. Fifty years ago a woman who had consented to sexual intercourse could not maintain a battery action against the man who seduced her.[17] Judges avoided saying that her unlawful consent was no consent, and in its place said that courts would not come to the aid of a wrongdoer whose misconduct resulted in injury.[18]

Some courts (probably a minority) apply this party-to-the-crime rule to fight cases and deny recovery to the vanquished. At first blush this result may seem to be the more politic holding—since both parties are at fault, the plaintiff deserves deterrence as much as does the defendant. But in our opinion, a procedural accident makes the majority view the better. If consent does not bar the vanquished from bringing an assault and battery action, then the victor too has an action for the vanquished's threatening conduct or blows. The victor-defendant can assert this legal claim in the same lawsuit by filing a cross-action. Then the jury can be authorized to find a verdict for each litigant against the other, and the vanquished is almost sure to receive a net judgment smaller than full compensation. Such a judgment leaves each party a financial loser; the victor is required to pay something and the vanquished is not fully compensated. This is better than turning the victor scot free. Our analysis may be subtle, and in actuality the majority view may not always work out so neatly. In jurisdictions following the majority view, defense counsel who sees the worth of a cross-action preserves a chance to argue for a reduced net recovery and forestalls the jury's attempt to compensate the plaintiff fully at the defendant's expense.

· · ·

The *volenti* rule privileges not only physical contact with persons; it applies also to entries on land and use of chattels. An invited guest does not commit a trespass by entering the host's house; a lender of a watch has no claim of conversion against the borrower who abides by the conditions of the loan.

· · ·

§ 3. Self–Defense

Early common law courts did not recognize self-defense as a justification for inflicting injury. A slayer who killed in self-defense was sent to

---

17. See Oberlin v. Upson, 84 Ohio St. 111, 95 N.E. 511 (1911). She could, however, in those days get judgment in contract action for "breach of promise" to marry (an action then universally recognized, and seldom mentioned now). In that kind of suit she could prove seduction to enhance damages.

18. Many people now think that sexual intercourse between consenting unmarried adults is a private matter of no concern to the public. Such an attitude is, of course, inconsistent with viewing "seduction" as a tort, or consent as "*particeps criminis*."

death unless the Crown pardoned him. This position was, of course, repudiated centuries ago and in both criminal and civil cases courts have long allowed pleas of self-defense.

The basic legal principle is: Those who reasonably believe that they are unwarrantedly attacked have a privilege to protect themselves, using only the force that a reasonable person would use under the circumstances. This principle is a general rule recognizing that appropriate self-defense does not result in liability. The rule points in the direction of proper decisions; it calls on courts to determine whether or not a defendant who claims the privilege was free from fault. But the rule does not itemize either the facts that justify use of self-defending force or the kinds of force that the self-defender may use. Cases may be submitted to a jury which will then have to decide (1) what, in fact, the defendant did, and (2) whether this conduct was what it should have been.

The courts have, however, developed specialized rules for various recurring types of self-defense cases. These rules supply more definite criteria of the propriety of some self-defenders' acts. Some examples of such rules are: Force calculated to wound or kill can be used only if the self-defender reasonably fears, and is trying to ward off, severe bodily injury or death. Even then, a defender may have to retreat rather than use such force. Defenders may stand their ground in their dwellings and perhaps in other close personal premises, but otherwise they must retreat rather than use deadly or wounding force if an avenue of retreat is known or should have been known to them. (This rule was rejected in many western states by judges who shared the pioneers' views on honor and cowardice. In those states, self-defenders may stand their ground and oppose force with reasonable counterforce.) When an attack is repulsed and the danger past, the self-defender's privilege to use force ends. This last rule is sometimes called "the excessive beating rule."

These more specialized rules can cut down the scope of jury inquiry and, on occasion, preclude jury submission entirely. If, in a court following the eastern rule, the proof clearly established that an obviously safe avenue of retreat was open to a defendant who nevertheless shot the attacker, the trial judge can direct the jury to find the defendant guilty of assault and battery; or, if the proof raises doubt as to whether or not a reasonable person in the defendant's position would have known that he or she could retreat in safety, that issue can be expressly submitted to a jury. This jury's instructions will foreclose the question of whether or not self-defenders may stand their ground; the jury will be told expressly that the defendant was not privileged to do so. Of course jurors sometimes do not understand their instructions and sometimes accidentally or intentionally ignore them.

The workings of the privilege of self-defense are justified from a policy viewpoint when a defendant is exonerated; defendants not guilty of fault are not held liable. The rules of law orient the judicial process to trial of the issue of the defendant's fault.

When the law of self-defense imposes liability on a defendant who has exceeded the privilege of self-defense, a more difficult policy problem is posed. The law of self-defense was developed in criminal courts and taken over as an apt analogy in tort cases. A self-defender who uses force when none was justified or who uses unreasonably drastic force merits criminal punishment. But in a tort case for battery where the defense of self-defense is raised, the plaintiff is not in the position of the state dealing with a breach of the peace; the plaintiff is an aggressor who is clearly at fault. Such a claimant may be an undeserving candidate for compensation. Of course, the defendant may file a cross-action against the plaintiff-attacker and lay the ground-work for cutting down the plaintiff's net recovery. This may leave both parties bearing part of the loss and may tend to deter each kind of fault. But a plaintiff guilty of serious fault, who complains that the defendant made an error in judgment and dealt with the plaintiff too drastically, may be undeserving of even partial compensation. Though we know of no case in which courts have done so, comparative fault reasoning could be used to justify judgment for the self-defender in such a case. Perhaps would-be litigants have sensed that judges and jurors do not deal generously with plaintiffs guilty of serious fault; few of them have enough gall to bring civil actions for damages.

Sometimes courts may have a chance to refuse to classify some cases of resisted aggression as self-defense cases. Suppose Bellicose advances on Quiet, saying, "Quiet, put up your fists; I'm going to knock the living daylights out of you." Quiet meets this threat with a quick blow on the point of Bellicose's chin, and Bellicose goes down. Bellicose then stands and staggers, obviously *hors de combat*. Nevertheless, the aroused Quiet delivers a second blow that breaks Bellicose's nose. Bellicose brings an assault and battery action claiming damages for the broken nose.

Quiet was privileged to deliver the first blow in self-defense; Bellicose is suing for the damage done by the second blow, and claims no damages for harm done by the first. Under the excessive beating rule, Quiet is liable for the damage done by the second blow; Quiet exceeded the privilege of self-defense. A cross-action for Bellicose's original assault may reduce Bellicose's recovery. But is there any way to present Quiet's case within the framework of rules already discussed protecting Quiet from any liability?

The facts of the case are stated against a background of defense law, and engrossment with that context may blind Quiet's lawyer to another possibility. Counsel could argue that Bellicose's invitation to do battle amounted to an implied consent to a fight to the finish. This alternative classification would do Quiet no good in the jurisdictions in which consent to fight is held to be no defense; but in those jurisdictions in which consent to fight bars recovery, the alternative classification will preclude holding Quiet liable. In these jurisdictions the excessive beating rule has not been repudiated. These courts, then, accidentally have a choice of classification. If Quiet's counsel can persuade the trial judge to call the case as a consent case, the judge may direct a verdict for Quiet. If Bellicose's lawyer can persuade the trial judge to call the case as an excessive beating case, a directed verdict for Quiet becomes improper, and Bellicose will get the case to the jury. Of course, in either event the appellate court may reclassify and decide that the trial judge erred.

The lesson to be learned from Bellicose v. Quiet is that the body of the law is not always consistent. Inconsistencies sometimes leave courts with a choice, a choice that may be exercised with crucial effect on the outcome of litigation. A good advocate develops skill in discovering opportunities to cross doctrinal lines and does not assume that the first approved rules he or she finds are the only applicable rules that judges respect.

§ 4. Protection of Property

The formal principle recognizing the privilege to use self-help to thwart intrusion on land or seizure of chattels is much like the principle approving self-defense; "force reasonable under the circumstances" is the phrase often found in judges' opinions generalizing on the privilege. Severe harm inflicted on wrongdoers for the protection of property is, however, often held to be too drastic, and the courts have developed rules limiting privileged self-help in some kinds of property protection cases to the use of force calculated not to wound or kill.

At early common law when an intruder on land injured by forceful removal brought an action of assault and battery against a land occupant, the ejector's defense of privileged self-help was raised by a plea of *molliter manus imposuit* [he laid his hands on gently]. Gentleness is hardly to be expected from a person "bouncing" an obdurate trespasser; it is not in fact required by the courts.

Occupants are privileged to lead, pull, carry, or push intruders off of their outlying premises (as distinguished from their dwellings and close environs). Should occupants push intruders down, kick them out, or drop them hard, occupants may have used unreasonable and therefore unprivileged force. Even when intruders resist simple ejective force, or when occupants lack sufficient strength or courage to use simple effective force, occupants are not privileged to use wounding force to eject. If occupants intentionally wound or kill they clearly overstep their privilege; and they may overstep it even with a less violent ejectment. Should an intruder go on the offensive, the occupant's privilege of self-defense comes into play and may justify steps more drastic than could be used merely to protect property. There are occasions on which the privileged self-help is too mild to do the job of removing the intruder from outlying premises; then the occupant who does not look to the courts or to public officers for help runs a risk of liability to the intruder.

Extreme measures may be reasonable when taken to protect an occupied dwelling from violent intruders who may injure the occupants. A householder can use reasonable force under the circumstances and may be justified in inflicting severe injury or killing. The law, however, puts a high value on human life and limb, and a householder irked by annoying visitors had better not resort to deadly force. An intruder may, of course, be liable in a cross-action for trespass.

. . .

Reasonable force under the circumstances may normally be used to thwart a wrongful appropriation of chattels; but killing or wounding is usually held reasonable only to thwart a heinous crime. The traditional attitude privileged wounding force to prevent theft; there is, however, a growing view that since life is more precious than property, the privilege should be narrower. If a misappropriation is not a crime or is only a misdemeanor, force calculated to kill or wound is not privileged.

Once a chattel has been grabbed, some self-help may be used to retake the property if the owner acts immediately and prudently. This privilege to use self-help cloaks the owner as long as he or she is in "fresh pursuit;" but the owner may not stop and go about other business without losing this privilege. An owner of a chattel who delivers it over without duress or fraud is not privileged to use force to retake it, even though the receiver threatens to damage or destroy it.

If chattels are deposited without the owner's fault on land of an innocent third party, a peaceful entry to retrieve them is not a trespass—the law authorizes such an entry. Such an entry can be made even though the owner is not in fresh pursuit.

Policy factors involved in the protection of property are much like those bearing on self-defense. The law is designed to set limits on proper self-help, and does a good job of it. Those who stay within the scope of the privileges are not at fault, and even when they happen to injure they should not incur liability. Those who exceed these limits are at fault, and their kind of conduct should be discouraged. In these cases, however, an injured plaintiff is usually also guilty of fault. Again, a cross-action can be filed against claimants who have themselves committed torts, and the jury can be given an opportunity to enter verdicts allowing these plaintiffs less than full compensation. Some intruders or expropriators may be guilty of misconduct so gross that no court should be willing to permit any recovery in their favor; in these cases some defendants will be protected by privileges afforded by the rules—for attack on a dwelling or felonious theft of chattels may be repelled by reasonable force even in some cases though severe injury is inflicted.

Mechanical devices are occasionally used to protect property. Such simple artifices as barbed wire, broken glass mounted on walls, and so forth, may be used in customary ways and places without subjecting the occupant to liability for the scratches and cuts they inflict. The electrified fence has not yet been considered by the courts. Its effectiveness in controlling cattle at low cost is impressive; if and when it threatens serious injuries to persons, liability may attach to its use. Spring guns and man traps are unreasonable protective measures under most circumstances; too often they get the wrong person. The courts say, "One may not do indirectly what he could not do directly," and they hold liable spring gun setters whose devices inflict wounds that they would not be privileged to inflict if they were present. But the principle is not properly reversible; spring gun setters will be held liable for some wounds they would have been privileged to inflict in person. An intruder intent on murder may be repulsed from a dwelling with deadly force, either in person or by spring gun. Moreover, an occupant who *erroneously* but reasonably believes that an intruder intends to murder may use deadly force in person. Spring gun setters who wound mere trespassers, however, cannot justify such wounds on the irrelevant ground that they would have made the same reasonable mistake had they been present in person. Even a criminal trespasser may be allowed damages against a spring gun setter who inflicts serious bodily injury on a petty wrongdoer. In a recent Iowa case, the owner of an unoccupied furnished house, remotely situated, became exasperated by petty marauders' break-ins, and set a spring gun. His victim, a hobbyist looking for old bottles, was seriously injured and recovered a $30,000 judgment.[38]

NOTES AND QUESTIONS

1. *Consent.* Do you agree with Morris's analysis of the difference between the Strong–Wiry case and the Weak–Warpt situation?

As Morris suggests, consent may be found in cases in which the defendant reasonably understood consent from plaintiff's behavior, although plaintiff might reasonably not have realized this—nor intended such consent. Does the defendant win because his case is strong or because the plaintiff's case is weak?

2. As a result of undergoing an illegal abortion, plaintiff sustained serious injury. Her suit on intentional tort and malpractice theories was dismissed by the appellate division because plaintiff and defendant were both guilty of criminal acts and plaintiff, "having participated in an illegal act, may not profit therefrom." The court cited a case in which an heir was not allowed to inherit money from a person the heir had killed.

On appeal, the court of appeals affirmed, 6–1, on the opinion below. Reno v. D'Javid, 42 N.Y.2d 1040, 369 N.E.2d 766, 399 N.Y.S.2d 210 (1977). The dissenter argued that the complaint alleged some post-abortion malpractice that should not be barred under the general rule. He also pointed out that on April 11, 1970, New York adopted a statute legalizing abortion in plaintiff's situation. The statute was to become effective July 1, 1970. The abortion in the case occurred June 6, 1970.

In response to the dissent, the majority said only: "The more grievous violation at issue is not that of the statute prohibiting abortions, itself the object of a changing legislative view, but of the paramount policy imperative that the law, whatever its content at a given time or for however limited a period, be obeyed."

38. Katko v. Briney, 183 N.W.2d 657 (Iowa 1971).

3. In a professional football game, plaintiff safety was covering defendant fullback on pass coverage. When the pass was intercepted on the opposite side of the field, plaintiff tried to block defendant, and fell to the ground. "Acting out of anger and frustration, but without specific intent to injure, Charles Clark stepped forward and struck a blow with his right forearm to the back of the kneeling plaintiff's head with sufficient force to cause both players to fall forward to the ground." The statute of limitations barred suit for an intentional tort, but plaintiff asserted claims of recklessness under § 500 of the Second Restatement and negligence. The judge held, after trial, that plaintiff, who had 13 years of experience in professional football, "must have recognized and accepted the risk that he would be injured by such an act" as defendant committed, and the case went off on assumption of risk. On appeal, the court reversed and remanded for an assessment of plaintiff's rights in view of the official players' code and customs of the sport: "The general customs of football do not approve the intentional punching or striking of others." Hackbart v. Cincinnati Bengals, Inc., 601 F.2d 516 (10th Cir.), cert. denied 444 U.S. 931 (1979). See Nielsen, Controlling Sports Violence: Too Late for the Carrots—Bring on the Big Stick, 74 Iowa L.Rev. 681 (1989).

4. *Self Defense.* In Courvoisier v. Raymond, 23 Colo. 113, 47 P. 284 (1896), defendant was threatened by a group of men. During the confrontation, a man appeared to step from the group and move toward defendant. Defendant shot at the man and hit him. Defendant testified that he thought the man was part of the group and a threat to his safety. In fact, the man shot was a policeman who had come to investigate the disruption. The jury found for the plaintiff after being instructed to do so if, at the time defendant fired, the plaintiff was not assaulting defendant. On appeal, the judgment was reversed for error in the charge. The jury should have been told that if it found the defendant's mistake reasonable, it should decide for defendant.

In Crabtree v. Dawson, 119 Ky. 148, 83 S.W. 557 (1904), defendant had just ejected from a party a man who then threatened to come back and attack him. Shortly thereafter, in a poorly lighted area, the plaintiff came running toward the doorway and the defendant, believing that this was the same man returning and that self-defense was called for, struck plaintiff. What if defendant's belief was reasonable though mistaken? What if he honestly but unreasonably believed self-defense was necessary? How would Morris analyze this case? Could this case be subjected to conventional negligence analysis?

Assume instead that bouncer D tells his friend, F, about the incident and his concern that the evicted man will return. While D's back is turned and he is attending to another matter, P comes running toward D. F sees P running and, seeing that P fits the description of the man D had evicted, F uses reasonable force to keep P from reaching D. Should the question of F's liability to P be analyzed differently from that of D's liability in *Crabtree*? The Restatement Second § 76 states that one who defends a third person is entitled to use the same means as though defending himself if he "correctly or reasonably believes that (a) the circumstances are such as to give the third person a privilege of self-defense, and (b) his intervention is necessary for the protection of the third person." What other views might be taken of the problem?

5. *Protecting Property.* The right to protect property has become a center of controversy since *Katko v. Briney*, cited by Morris. Defendant owned an uninhabited farm house with some antiques and old jars inside. The house had been broken into and contents removed several times. Calls to the sheriff and the posting of signs failed to stop the entries. The defendant then set a spring gun aimed at leg level that would be activated by someone who had already entered the house and then sought to enter this inside room. The plaintiff was thereby injured severely. When his leg healed it was deformed and noticeably shorter. Charged with a felony, the victim was allowed to plead guilty to a misdemeanor of larceny in the nighttime of property worth less than $20 and was fined and received a suspended 60–day jail term.

He then sued defendant for an intentional tort. (Defendant filed no counterclaim. Was this a mistake?) The jury awarded compensatory damages of $20,000 and punitive damages of $10,000. The state supreme court upheld the compensatory damages on the ground that the privilege of protecting property did not extend to infliction of serious bodily harm. The court approved a charge that said that the "only time" use of a spring gun "is justified would be when the trespasser was committing a felony of violence or a felony punishable by death, or where the trespasser was endangering human life by his act." The court expressed no opinion on the propriety of punitive damages because the defendant had not properly raised the point.

Is the result sound? Should the result be different if the defendant erected signs, "These premises protected by spring gun"? For sharply divergent comments on this problem, see Palmer, The Iowa Spring Gun Case: A Study in American Gothic, 56 Iowa L.Rev. 1219 (1971); Posner, Wounding or Killing to Protect a Property Interest, 14 J.L. & Econ. 201 (1971); Comment, Use of Mechanical Devices in the Defense of Property, 24 S.Cal.L.Rev. 133 (1972).

Posner states that neither blanket permission nor blanket prohibition of the use of deadly force to protect property is likely to be the optimal rule. He proposes a "reasonableness test" to determine whether the use of deadly force is justified to protect property interests. The following considerations would be relevant:

(1) the value of the property at stake measured against the costs of human life and limb;

(2) the existence of an adequate legal remedy as an alternative to the use of force;

(3) the location of the property in terms of the difficulty of protecting it by other means;

(4) the kind of warning given;

    (5) the deadliness of the device used;

    (6) the character of the conflicting activities;

    (7) the cost of avoiding interference by other means.

Posner believes that "the dominant purpose of rules of liability is to channel people's conduct, and in such a way that the value of interfering activities is maximized." Is this an area in which the legal rule is likely to have a strong impact in shaping behavior? Is Posner's formulation likely to allow more, or less, use of force to protect property than a standard absolutely prohibiting the use of deadly force except to prevent felonies of violence, felonies punishable by death, and acts that threaten human injury? For a wide-ranging economic analysis of intentional torts, see Landes and Posner, An Economic Theory of Intentional Torts, 1 Int'l Rev. of Law & Econ. 127 (1981).

    6. *Insanity.* Another defense, occasionally raised, that Morris does not discuss, is insanity. In Williams v. Kearbey, 13 Kan.App.2d 564, 775 P.2d 670 (1989), defendant, a minor, shot and injured two people at his junior high school. The wounded individuals brought successful battery actions. The jury found that the defendant was insane at the time of the shootings and defendant argued that because of this fact, he should not be held civilly liable for his torts. The court followed the majority rule that a defendant's insanity does not establish a defense to liability. That rule reflected a policy decision "to impose liability on an insane person rather than leaving the loss on the innocent victim." See also Barylski v. Paul, 38 Mich.App. 614, 196 N.W.2d 868 (1972), suggesting that insanity might be a defense in cases in which the tort required a specific intent (such as the malice required in malicious prosecution), but not in an ordinary battery case.

    7. *Private Necessity.* Suppose a private party uses, or in an extreme case, destroys the property of another in order to preserve his or her own person or property of greater value. Is there a privilege to do so?

    In the leading case of Ploof v. Putnam, 81 Vt. 471, 71 A. 188 (1908), plaintiff moored his sloop at a dock on defendant's private island in order to avoid the hazards of a storm. Defendant's servant cut loose the sloop which, as a result, was battered by the storm. The sloop and its contents were destroyed; plaintiff and his family were injured. In plaintiff's suit for damages, defendant argued that he was simply protecting his private property from use by plaintiff. The court awarded damages to plaintiff, recognizing a privilege, born of necessity, to use defendant's property.

    Assuming a privilege exists, there is the further question whether the party exercising the privilege should nonetheless be liable for damages if in fact the "taking" of another's property results in damage. In *Ploof,* that issue would have been whether defendant had a claim for any damage done to the dock. The issue is raised by the famous case that follows. In reading this case, keep in mind, as well, the question that has been fundamental to our inquiry in this section: what are the essential characteristics of harm done to another that constitute an "intentional" tort?

Vincent v. Lake Erie Transportation Co.

Supreme Court of Minnesota, 1910.
109 Minn. 456, 124 N.W. 221.

■ O'BRIEN, J.

The steamship Reynolds, owned by the defendant, was for the purpose of discharging her cargo on November 27, 1905, moored to plaintiffs' dock in Duluth. While the unloading of the boat was taking place a storm from the northeast developed, which at about ten o'clock p.m., when the unloading was completed, had so grown in violence that the wind was then moving at fifty miles per hour and continued to increase during the night. There is some evidence that one, and perhaps two, boats were able to enter the harbor that night, but it is plain that navigation was practically suspended from the hour mentioned until the morning of the twenty ninth, when the storm abated, and during that time no master would have been justified in attempting to navigate his vessel, if he could avoid doing so. After the discharge of the cargo the Reynolds signaled for a tug to tow her from the dock, but none could be obtained because of the severity of the storm. If the lines holding the ship to the dock had been cast off, she would doubtless have drifted away; but, instead, the lines were kept fast, and as soon as one parted or chafed it was replaced, sometimes with a larger one. The vessel lay upon the outside of the dock, her bow to the east, the wind and waves striking her starboard quarter with such force that she was constantly being lifted and thrown against the dock, resulting in its damage, as found by the jury, to the amount of $500.

We are satisfied that the character of the storm was such that it would have been highly imprudent for the master of the Reynolds to have attempted to leave the dock or to have permitted his vessel to drift away from it. . . . Nothing more was demanded of them than ordinary prudence and care, and the record in this case fully sustains the contention of the appellant that, in holding the vessel fast to the dock, those in charge of her exercised good judgment and prudent seamanship.

It is claimed by the respondent that it was negligence to moor the boat at an exposed part of the wharf, and to continue in that position after it became apparent that the storm was to be more than usually severe. We do not agree with this position. The part of the wharf where the vessel was moored appears to have been commonly used for that purpose. It was situated within the harbor at Duluth, and must, we think, be considered a proper and safe place, and would undoubtedly have been such during what would be considered a very severe storm. The storm which made it unsafe was one which surpassed in violence any which might have reasonably been anticipated.

The appellant contends by ample assignments of error that, because its conduct during the storm was rendered necessary by prudence and good seamanship under conditions over which it had no control, it cannot be held liable for any injury resulting to the property of others, and claims that the jury should have been so instructed. An analysis of the charge given by the trial court is not necessary, as in our opinion the only question for the jury was the amount of damages which the plaintiffs were entitled to recover, and no complaint is made upon that score.

The situation was one in which the ordinary rules regulating property rights were suspended by forces beyond human control, and if, without the direct intervention of some act by the one sought to be held liable, the property of another was injured, such injury must be attributed to the act of God, and not to the wrongful act of the person sought to be charged. If during the storm the Reynolds had entered the harbor, and while there had become disabled and been thrown against the plaintiffs' dock, the plaintiffs could not have recovered. Again, if while attempting to hold fast to the dock the lines had parted, without any negligence, and the vessel carried against some other boat or dock in the harbor, there would be no liability upon her owner. But here those in charge of the vessel deliberately and by their direct efforts held her in such a position that the damage to the dock resulted, and, having thus preserved the ship at the expense of the dock, it seems to us that her owners are responsible to the dock owners to the extent of the injury inflicted.

. . .

Theologians hold that a starving man may, without moral guilt, take what is necessary to sustain life; but it could hardly be said that the obligation would not be upon such person to pay the value of the property so taken when he became able to do so. And so public necessity, in times of war or peace, may require the taking of private property for public purposes; but under our system of jurisprudence compensation must be made.

Let us imagine in this case that for the better mooring of the vessel those in charge of her had appropriated a valuable cable lying upon the dock. No matter how justifiable such appropriation might have been, it would not be claimed that, because of the overwhelming necessity of the situation, the owner of the cable could not recover its value.

This is not a case where life or property was menaced by any object or thing belonging to the plaintiffs, the destruction of which became necessary to prevent the threatened disaster. Nor is it a case where, because of the act of God, or unavoidable accident, the infliction of the injury was beyond the control of the defendant, but is one where the defendant prudently and advisedly availed itself of the plaintiffs' property for the purpose of preserving its own more valuable property, and the plaintiffs are entitled to compensation for the injury done.

Order affirmed.

■ Lewis, J. (dissenting).

I dissent. It was assumed on the trial before the lower court that appellant's liability depended on whether the master of the ship might, in the exercise of reasonable care, have sought a place of safety before the storm made it impossible to leave the dock. The majority opinion assumes that the evidence is conclusive that appellant moored its boat at respondents' dock pursuant to contract, and that the vessel was lawfully in position at the time the additional cables were fastened to the dock, and the reasoning of the opinion is that, because appellant made use of the stronger cables to hold the boat in position, it became liable under the rule that it had voluntarily made use of the property of another for the purpose of saving its own.

In my judgment, if the boat was lawfully in position at the time the storm broke, and the master could not, in the exercise of due care have left that position without subjecting his vessel to the hazards of the storm, then the damage to the dock, caused by the pounding of the boat, was the result of an inevitable accident. If the master was in the exercise of due care, he was not at fault. The reasoning of the opinion admits that if the ropes, or cables, first attached to the dock had not parted, or if, in the first instance, the master had used the stronger cables, there would be no liability. If the master could not, in the exercise of reasonable care, have anticipated the severity of the storm and sought a place of safety before it became impossible, why should he be required to anticipate the severity of the storm, and, in the first instance, use the stronger cables?

I am of the opinion that one who constructs a dock to the navigable line of waters, and enters into contractual relations with the owner of a vessel to moor the same, takes the risk of damage to his dock by a boat caught there by a storm, which event could not have been avoided in the exercise of due care, and further, that the legal status of the parties in such a case is not changed by renewal of cables to keep the boat from being cast adrift at the mercy of the tempest.

■ JAGGARD, J.

■ I concur with LEWIS, J.

NOTES AND QUESTIONS

1. Is it important to the majority that defendant continued to replace the fraying lines? Why does the dissent regard this behavior as inconsequential? Is one position more consistent with the act of God defense than the other?

2. Is *Vincent* an intentional tort case? Would the definition of intent utilized in *Garratt* and the Restatement apply here? Why does the majority think that the defendant should be held liable? Does the rationale bear any similarity to the basis for strict liability?

3. Suppose there had been only a one percent chance that securing the vessel would result in damage to the dock. Would the case then be one of unintended harm? If so, would defendant still have been liable—assuming the likelihood of harm to the dock was far less than the expected harm to the (unsecured) boat? Can the liability rules governing these two situations be reconciled? See Seavey, Negligence—Subjective or Objective?, 41 Harv.L.Rev. 1, 8 (1927).

4. Is the pre-existing contractual relationship between the parties in *Vincent* of any relevance to the assignment of liability? On this score, do you agree with the assumed risk argument at the end of the dissenting opinion? Why does the majority make no reference to the contract? In a case like *Ploof*, where the parties had no contractual relationship, should the result be different?

5. Consider the following analysis from Morris on Torts:

A justification for liability may possibly be brought to light by comparing the Vincent case to Cordas v. Peerless Transportation Co. [27 N.Y.S.2d 198 (N.Y.City Ct.1941)]. In the Cordas case, a pursued armed bandit jumped into a taxi-cab and ordered the driver to get going. The driver started the cab, shifted into neutral, suddenly slammed on his brakes to throw the bandit off-balance, and leaped out. The cab veered onto the sidewalk and injured a pedestrian. The court held the driver was not liable to the pedestrian in spite of the great likelihood that the driver's intentional act, done in a congested downtown locale, would cause injury and was done to save his own hide.

The cab case differs from the dock case in several ways. The cab driver's conduct was fraught with only a possibility of injury; the ship captain's conduct was sure to injure the dock. The cab driver had much less time for deliberation than did the mariner. Another distinction may, however, have great significance. If the wharfinger could not hold the mariner responsible, he might have been tempted to cut the ship loose and risk liability for whatever harm might befall the ship or crew. That risk might not materialize; if the ship happened to weather the storm without damage, the dock owner would then incur no liability. He was sure that his dock would be harmed if the ship remained fast. But if he were assured of compensation for damage to the dock, he would have no incentive to cast the ship loose. In the cab case, however, the pedestrian could do nothing to impede the cab driver from executing his plan of escape. No promise of compensation is needed to affect the pedestrian's behavior; he need not be given assurance of compensation to encourage cooperation.

Do these considerations seem critical? In Fletcher, Corrective Justice for Moderns, 106 Harv.L.Rev. 1658, 1670–71 (1993), the author argues that the key to the case is "the inroad made by the emergency situation on the plaintiff's property rights. The plaintiff is forced, under the circumstances, to keep his dock open to someone who finds himself there when the storm comes up. Because his rights are compromised in the interests of another person, tort law makes up for what he loses under the law of property." Is this a convincing rationale? Compare the explanation of the case from a restitutionary perspective in E. Weinrib, The Idea of Private Law (1995) at 196–203.

6. Consider the following example from the Restatement (Second) of Torts § 73:

A, while driving B, a child of three, in a sleigh, is pursued by a pack of wolves which are rapidly closing upon him. To gain time A throws B to the wolves. The time consumed by the wolves in devouring B enables A to reach shelter a few seconds before the pack can reach him. A is subject to liability under a wrongful death statute for the death of B.

Do you agree that A should be held liable? What are the damages in the wolf case if there is liability? Is the situation distinguishable from *Vincent* and *Cordas*? Should the wolf example be decided differently if A's action were taken to save the lives of seven others as well as his own?

7. Is one party a superior risk-bearer to the other in *Vincent*? In what sense? Should that factor be given great weight? See R. Keeton, Conditional Fault in the Law of Torts, 72 Harv.L.Rev. 401 (1959).

8. Is there any substance to the privilege of private necessity if the party exercising the privilege is obligated to pay damages for harm done?

9. *Public Necessity.* Sometimes property is destroyed for the protection of the general public. In Harrison v. Wisdom, 7 Heisk. (55 Tenn.) 99 (1872), the defendants were residents of a town being approached by the Federal army. The defendants destroyed plaintiff's liquor supply to keep it from the troops. The court concluded that in cases of necessity involving protection of the public, "a private mischief is to be endured rather than a public inconvenience." Also, "Necessity, says Lord Coke, makes that lawful which would be otherwise unlawful: 8 Coke, 69." Should it matter whether the troops ever reached the town?

The same approach was adopted in Surocco v. Geary, 3 Cal. 69 (1853), in which the defendant, who was alcalde of San Francisco ordered the destruction of plaintiff's house to prevent the spread of a major fire. The suit was not for the damage to the house, which would clearly have been destroyed anyway, but rather for chattels that the plaintiff could have removed before the house caught fire, but were lost when the house was blown up. The court denied recovery, saying that in such situations "individual rights of property give way to the higher laws of impending necessity." Are these cases consistent with *Vincent*? As far as compensation is concerned, are there reasons to distinguish between private and public necessity?

The court in *Geary* denied that this was a "taking" of private property in the constitutional sense, a view that was sustained in United States v. Caltex (Philippines), Inc., 344 U.S. 149 (1952), in which the armed forces destroyed valuable property belonging to the plaintiff to keep it from falling into enemy hands. The Court, 7–2, held that there was no compensable taking. The majority noted that "The terse language of the Fifth Amendment is no comprehensive promise that the United States will make whole all who suffer from every ravage and burden of war. This Court has long recognized that in wartime many losses must be attributed solely to the fortunes of war, and not to the sovereign." Justices Black and Douglas dissented on the ground that the property was taken as clearly as are food and animals requisitioned for military use: "Whenever the Government determines that one person's property . . . is essential to the war effort and appropriates it for the common good, the public purse, rather than the individual, should bear the loss." There is a vast literature on compensable takings, a subject which is explored in the Property course.

In Muskopf v. Corning Hospital Dist., 55 Cal.2d 211, 359 P.2d 457, 11 Cal.Rptr. 89 (1961), Justice Traynor noted that abolishing governmental immunity "does not mean that the state is liable for all harms that result from its activities. . . . Thus the harm resulting from free competition among individuals is not actionable, nor is the harm resulting from the diversion of business by the state's relocation of a highway." Why must the state pay for property it takes to build a new highway but not for business losses caused to merchants along the old route? Should the state be able to claim reimbursement from those whose property values increase because of the new highway? What about paying dairy farmers when the state legalizes the sale of oleomargarine? In the same vein, should the government compensate those who are hurt by decreased government spending or emphasis in their fields? Those who lose their jobs may receive unemployment benefits but how about those harmed derivatively, like the restaurants and gas stations near a defense plant that is closed down?

B.   GOVERNMENT LIABILITY

In Chapter III, we considered the circumstances in which various governmental entities might retain a common law immunity from tort liability. In this section, we consider claims against government officials that usually involve deliberate interference with claimed legal rights of citizens. Our earlier focus was liability for miscalculation or negligence. Now we address cases that raise the issue of abuse of power by government officials.

1.   THE FEDERAL CIVIL RIGHTS ACTION

In the years following the end of the Civil War, widespread violence and lawlessness raged in the South. Murders, whippings and other atrocities were perpetrated by members of the Ku Klux Klan and other vigilante groups against blacks and Union sympathizers. Although virtually all these acts of terrorism were violations of state and local law, law enforcement officials did little to intervene and in some cases they tacitly condoned the illegal acts and even conspired with the outlaws. In response to this situation, Congress, under its power to enforce the recently ratified Fourteenth Amendment, passed the Ku Klux Klan Act of 1871. Section 1 of the Act, now codified as 42 U.S.C. § 1983, provides:

> Every person who, under color of any statute, ordinance, regulation, custom, or usage, of any State or Territory, subjects, or causes to be subjected, any citizen of the United States or other

person within the jurisdiction thereof to the deprivation of any rights, privileges, or immunities secured by the Constitution and laws, shall be liable to the party injured in an action at law, suit in equity, or other proper proceeding for redress.

The section lay dormant until Monroe v. Pape, 365 U.S. 167 (1961), in which plaintiffs alleged that "13 Chicago police officers broke into [their] home in the early morning, routed them from bed, made them stand naked in the living room, and ransacked every room, emptying drawers and ripping mattress covers." Further, Mr. Monroe was taken to the police station and held for ten hours without being arraigned or allowed to call his family or attorney. He was released without charges being filed. Plaintiffs alleged that the officers had no search or arrest warrants. They sued the officers and the City of Chicago under § 1983, claiming that defendants acted "under color of the statutes, ordinances, regulations, customs and usages" of the city and state.

The Court upheld the complaint. Although the original purposes of the statute were to "override certain kinds of state laws" and to "provide a remedy where state law was inadequate," the "purposes were much broader. The *third* aim was to provide a federal remedy where the state remedy, though adequate in theory, was not available in practice." The federal remedy was held "supplementary to the state remedy, and the latter need not be first sought and refused before the federal one is invoked." Thus, the fact that Illinois law outlawed unreasonable searches and seizures did not bar the present suit.

The Court then concluded that the officers had acted "under color of" state law, relying on an earlier case in which a plurality had concluded that "Misuse of power, possessed by virtue of state law and made possible only because the wrongdoer is clothed with the authority of state law, is action taken 'under color of' state law."

To state a claim under § 1983 a plaintiff must show that a "person" acting under color of state law, custom, or usage deprived him or her of a federally protected constitutional right. Each of the elements of the prima facie case discussed in *Monroe* has led to extensive litigation, but the principles established by *Monroe* have been generally followed. For an overview of the historical development of § 1983 doctrine, see Eisenberg, Section 1983: Doctrinal Foundations and An Empirical Study, 67 Cornell L.Rev. 482 (1982). See also Weinberg, The Monroe Mystery Solved: Beyond the "Unhappy History" Theory of Civil Rights Litigation, 1991 B.Y.U.L.Rev. 737, explaining the development of § 1983 litigation in terms of the Bill of Rights jurisprudence of the Warren Court.

"Every Person." In Monell v. New York City Dept. of Social Services, 436 U.S. 658 (1978), the Court held that "every person" was broad enough to include municipal corporations as potential defendants. The Court went on to say that "a local government may not be sued under § 1983 for an injury inflicted solely by its employees or agents. Instead, it is when execution of a government's policy or custom, whether made by its lawmakers or by those whose edicts or acts may fairly be said to represent official

policy, inflicts the injury that the government as an entity is responsible under § 1983."

Is this limitation likely to insulate governmental entities from liability very often? In Pembaur v. City of Cincinnati, 475 U.S. 469 (1986), the Court held that a single decision by a county prosecutor that deprived an individual of his Fourth and Fourteenth Amendment rights satisfied *Monell*'s "official policy" standard. The prosecutor had given local sheriffs the go-ahead to break down plaintiff's office door and conduct a search. The Supreme Court reinstated plaintiff's § 1983 action for the allegedly unlawful search. Because state law authorized sheriffs to obtain instructions to search from local prosecutors, and because the sheriffs in the case at bar had followed the prosecutor's directive, the prosecutor effectively acted as the county's "final decisionmaker," thereby exposing the county to § 1983 liability.

A recurring issue before the Court has been whether a municipality's failure to provide adequate training to certain employees, most notably its police force, amounts to an official policy. In City of Canton v. Harris, 489 U.S. 378 (1989), plaintiff was arrested and brought to a police station where she twice slumped to the floor. The police left plaintiff on the floor so she wouldn't fall again, but they never summoned medical assistance for her. After the police released plaintiff, she was taken to a hospital and diagnosed as suffering from various emotional ailments. Plaintiff brought a § 1983 action against the city for its deprivation of her right to receive necessary medical care while in custody. She pointed to the city policy that gave station shift commanders the sole discretion to determine when an arrestee required medical care and the city's failure to train specially its officers to recognize when to summon such care. The Court, in remanding for further proceedings, held that "[t]he inadequacy of police training may serve as a basis for § 1983 liability only where the failure to train amounts to deliberate indifference to the rights of persons with whom the police come into contact." Furthermore, the Court required that the asserted training deficiency must actually have caused the officers' indifference to plaintiff's medical needs.

What constitutes "deliberate indifference?" In Farmer v. Brennan, 114 S.Ct. 1970 (1994), a transsexual prison inmate claimed violation of Eighth Amendment rights by prison officials who placed him in the general prison population, allegedly subjecting him to special risks of harm, which came to fruition. In response to plaintiff's claim of deliberate indifference, the court held that its objective standard under *Canton* was not the appropriate test for cruel and unusual punishment under the Eighth Amendment. Rather, a subjective test was called for:

> We hold instead that a prison official cannot be found liable under the Eighth Amendment for denying an inmate humane conditions of confinement unless the official knows of and disregards an excessive risk to inmate health and safety.

The Court has also refined *Canton* by indicating that not every failure to train government employees amounts to a constitutional violation. In

Collins v. City of Harker Heights, 503 U.S. 115 (1992), the Court rejected a claim involving the death of a city sanitation worker who was asphyxiated in a manhole while attempting to unstop a sewer line. The Court held that the city's inadequate training of the employee did not amount to a violation of due process.

"Acting Under Color" of State Law. In *Monroe,* the Court held that conduct under color of state law embraced conduct of a state official contrary to state law. This holding has been reaffirmed, and today the state action requirement under § 1983 is generally assumed to be identical to the threshold required by the Fourteenth Amendment. In Polk County v. Dodson, 454 U.S. 312 (1981) the court interpreted the "under color of state law" concept narrowly by holding that a public defender was performing an essentially independent, private function in deciding how best to represent her client. Is this likely to create a major exception? For general discussion, see Lugar v. Edmondson Oil Co., Inc., 457 U.S. 922 (1982).

Even private action may be considered "state action" if made possible only because of state support or acquiescence, as where a shopkeeper detains a suspected shoplifter pursuant to an agreement with the police. Adickes v. S.H. Kress & Co., 398 U.S. 144 (1970). The Court has also held that private defendants could not claim the qualified immunity from suit accorded to government officials when the claims against the private defendants were based upon wrongful institution of attachment proceedings under state law. Wyatt v. Cole, 504 U.S. 158 (1992).

See generally, Winter, The Meaning of "Under Color of" Law, 91 Mich.L.Rev. 323 (1992).

"Who subjects another or causes another to be subjected to." Section 1983 creates a cause of action only against a person who "subjects" another or "causes" another "to be subjected" to the deprivation of constitutional rights. A threshold issue was raised in DeShaney v. Winnebago County Dept. of Social Services, 489 U.S. 189 (1989), in which a child under the jurisdiction of defendant county department of social services was seriously injured by his father's sustained pattern of physical abuse. The § 1983 claim against defendant was for denial of a liberty interest in due process by failing to intervene and provide protection. In denying any affirmative obligation on the part of the governmental agency, the Court stated:

> . . . it is well to remember once again that the harm was inflicted not by the State of Wisconsin, but by [plaintiff's] father. The most that can be said of the state functionaries in this case is that they stood by and did nothing when suspicious circumstances dictated a more active role for them.

Recall the discussion of Riss v. City of New York and the notes that followed, at p. 198, supra. Are the considerations that were salient there the same as seem central in the § 1983 context?

The "subjects another or causes another to be subjected" language also raises problems when supervisory officials are sued. Occasionally, plaintiffs can show that the supervisory defendant directed, encouraged or participated in the unlawful conduct of the subordinate officials. Often, however, the supervisor may have been unaware of the conduct until after the harm occurred. In the latter situation, suits against supervisory officials under § 1983 are usually brought under a theory of failure to train subordinates adequately, lack of adequate supervision, or some form of vicarious liability.

Most courts construed this language in § 1983 to require some level of individual blameworthiness and held the doctrine of respondeat superior to be inapplicable. Williams v. Vincent, 508 F.2d 541 (2d Cir.1974). In Rizzo v. Goode, 423 U.S. 362 (1976), citizens brought a § 1983 action against superior officers of the Philadelphia Police Department seeking relief because of the officers' failure to correct unconstitutional conduct by subordinates. After finding a "pattern of frequent police violations" of the rights of minorities, the trial court granted injunctive relief. The Supreme Court reversed, finding insufficient evidence that the supervisory officials had implemented, or acquiesced in, an unconstitutional policy.

"Rights . . . Secured by the Constitution and Laws." In 1980, the Court held that, since § 1983 speaks of rights "secured by the Constitution and laws" of the United States, an action lies under that section for purely statutory violations of federal law. Maine v. Thiboutot, 448 U.S. 1 (1980)(claim under § 1983 for deprivation of welfare benefits to which the plaintiffs claimed entitlement under the federal Social Security Act).

However, § 1983 does not provide a cause of action if (1) the statute in question does not create enforceable "rights" within the meaning of § 1983, or (2) Congress has foreclosed a § 1983 action in the enactment of the statute itself. Wright v. Roanoke Redevelopment & Hous. Auth., 479 U.S. 418 (1987).

In Golden State Transit Corp. v. City of Los Angeles, 493 U.S. 103 (1989), the Supreme Court laid out the basic three-part test for determining whether a particular statute or constitutional provision creates an enforceable "right" under § 1983. First, the provision must create obligations binding on the governmental unit; second, the plaintiff's interest must not be so vague and amorphous as to be beyond the judiciary's competence to enforce; and third, the provision at issue must have been intended to benefit the plaintiff. Applying this test, the Court held that the Supremacy Clause, which gives superior force to federal constitutional and statutory provisions whenever they conflict with state law, does not create rights that are enforceable under § 1983. In contrast, the Court has held that suits for alleged Commerce Clause violations may be brought under § 1983. Dennis v. Higgins, 498 U.S. 439 (1991).

With respect to a particular statutory enactment, Congress may foreclose a § 1983 action in one of two ways. First, Congress may include an express provision to that effect in the statute itself. Second, Congress may invest the statute with a remedial scheme that is sufficiently comprehensive to demonstrate an intent to preclude a judicial remedy via a § 1983 action. Wilder v. Virginia Hosp. Ass'n, 496 U.S. 498 (1990). In Middlesex

County Sewerage Authority v. National Sea Clammers Ass'n, 453 U.S. 1 (1981), the Court found that the extensive enforcement mechanisms in several federal environmental statutes demonstrated a congressional intent to bar § 1983 actions for alleged state violations of those statutes. See Sunstein, Section 1983 and the Private Enforcement of Federal Law, 49 U.Chi.L.Rev. 394 (1982).

Two recent actions arising out of state criminal prosecutions raise issues regarding the nature of the "rights" protected under § 1983. In Heck v. Humphrey, 114 S.Ct. 2364 (1994) the Court held that a § 1983 action could not be brought prior to the time that a conviction has either been "reversed on direct appeal, expunged by executive order, declared invalid by a state tribunal authorized to make such determination, or called into question by a federal court's issuance of a writ of habeas corpus." Petitioner had filed his § 1983 action while appeal from his conviction was still pending. In Albright v. Oliver, 114 S.Ct. 807 (1994), an earlier prosecution had been dismissed on the grounds that it failed to state an offense under Illinois law. The § 1983 claim against the state officials was based on denial of due process in groundlessly prosecuting the plaintiff. The Court held that any such claim, if actionable at all, must be based on the Fourth Amendment rather than on substantive due process—and no Fourth Amendment claim was before the court.

Immunity. A major problem confronting the Court has been the nature of defenses available under the statute. In reading the following case, keep in mind the discussion of governmental liability at p. 197, supra. Do any common considerations underlie the issues raised?

Owen v. City of Independence

Supreme Court of the United States, 1980.
445 U.S. 622, 100 S.Ct. 1398, 63 L.Ed.2d 673.

[Plaintiff was the city's police chief during an investigation of certain departmental practices. He requested a specification of charges and a public hearing. Instead, the City Council voted to release the investigative reports to the press and to the prosecutor, and directed that the City Manager "take all direct and appropriate action" against those involved. The next day the City Manager discharged the plaintiff without holding a hearing.

Plaintiff sued the city, the members of the City Council and the City Manager under § 1983 alleging that, in violation of his constitutional rights, he had been discharged without notice of reasons and without a hearing. The district court dismissed the action. The court of appeals recognized that the plaintiff had been subjected to stigma in connection with his discharge and that the procedure violated plaintiff's constitutional rights. It also observed that the discharge was caused by the "official conduct of the City's lawmakers, or by those whose acts may fairly be said to represent official policy." This brought the case within *Monell*, p. 853, supra. Nonetheless, the court of appeals affirmed the dismissals because, at the time plaintiff was discharged, his constitutional right to a hearing had not yet been recognized. Officials of the city "could not have been aware of [petitioner's] right to a name-clearing hearing in connection with the discharge. The City of Independence should not be charged with predicting the future course of constitutional law." The court of appeals extended the immunity of the city officials, who "acted in good faith and without malice" to the city as well. Thus, the action was dismissed against all defendants.]

■ MR. JUSTICE BRENNAN delivered the opinion of the Court.

. . .

III

Because the question of the scope of a municipality's immunity from liability under § 1983 is essentially one of statutory construction, [ ], the starting point in our analysis must be the language of the statute itself. [ ] By its terms, § 1983 "creates a species of tort liability that on its face admits of no immunities." Imbler v. Pachtman, 424 U.S. 409, 417 (1976). Its language is absolute and unqualified; no mention is made of any privileges, immunities, or defenses that may be asserted. Rather, the Act imposes liability upon *"every person"* who, under color of state law or custom, "subjects, or causes to be subjected, any citizen of the United States . . . to the deprivation of any rights, privileges, or immunities secured by the Constitution and laws." And *Monell* held that these words were intended to encompass municipal corporations as well as natural "persons."

Moreover, the congressional debates surrounding the passage of . . . the forerunner of § 1983—confirm the expansive sweep of the statutory language.

However, notwithstanding § 1983's expansive language and the absence of any express incorporation of common-law immunities, we have, on several occasions, found that a tradition of immunity was so firmly rooted in the common law and was supported by such strong policy reasons that "Congress would have specifically so provided had it wished to abolish the doctrine." Pierson v. Ray, 386 U.S. 547, 555 (1967). Thus in Tenney v. Brandhove, 341 U.S. 367 (1951), after tracing the development of an absolute legislative privilege from its source in 16th-century England to its inclusion in the Federal and State Constitutions, we concluded that Congress "would [not] impinge on a tradition so well grounded in history and reason by covert inclusion in the general language" of § 1983. 341 U.S., at 376.

Subsequent cases have required that we consider the personal liability of various other types of government officials. Noting that "[f]ew doctrines were more solidly established at common law than the immunity of judges from liability for damages for acts committed within their judicial jurisdiction," Pierson v. Ray, supra, at 553–554, held that the absolute immunity traditionally accorded judges was preserved under § 1983. In that same case, local police officers were held to enjoy a "good faith and probable cause" defense to § 1983 suits similar to that which existed in false arrest actions at common law. 386 U.S., at 555–557. Several more recent decisions have found immunities of varying scope appropriate for different state and local officials sued under § 1983. See Procunier v. Navarette, 434 U.S. 555 (1978)(qualified immunity for prison officials and officers); Imbler v. Pachtman, supra (absolute immunity for prosecutors in initiating and presenting the State's case); O'Connor v. Donaldson, 422 U.S. 563 (1975)(qualified immunity for superintendent of state hospital); Wood v. Strickland, 420 U.S. 308 (1975)(qualified immunity for local school board members); Scheuer v. Rhodes, 416 U.S. 232 (1974)(qualified "good-faith" immunity for state Governor and other executive officers for discretionary acts performed in the course of official conduct).

In each of these cases, our finding of § 1983 immunity "was predicated upon a considered inquiry into the immunity historically accorded the relevant official at common law and the interests behind it." Imbler v. Pachtman, 424 U.S., at 421. Where the immunity claimed by the defendant was well established at common law at the time § 1983 was enacted, and where its rationale was compatible with the purposes of the Civil Rights Act, we have construed the statute to incorporate that immunity. But there is no tradition of immunity for municipal corporations, and neither history nor policy support a construction of § 1983 that would justify the qualified immunity accorded the city of Independence by the Court of Appeals. We hold, therefore, that the municipality may not assert the good faith of its officers or agents as a defense to liability under § 1983.[18]

A

Since colonial times, a distinct feature of our Nation's system of governance has been the conferral of political power upon public and municipal corporations for the management of matters of local concern. As *Monell* recounted, by 1871, municipalities—like private corporations—were treated as natural persons for virtually all purposes of constitutional and statutory analysis. In particular, they were routinely sued in both federal and state courts. . . .

. . .

Yet in the hundreds of cases from that era awarding damages against municipal governments for wrongs committed by them, one searches in vain for much mention of a qualified immunity based on the good faith of municipal officers. Indeed, where the issue was discussed at all, the courts

---

18. The governmental immunity at issue in the present case differs significantly from the official immunities involved in our previous decisions. In those cases, various government officers had been sued in their individual capacities, and the immunity served to insulate them from personal liability for damages. Here, in contrast, only the liability of the municipality itself is at issue, not that of its officers, and in the absence of an immunity, any recovery would come from public funds.

had rejected the proposition that a municipality should be privileged where it reasonably believed its actions to be lawful.   .   .   .

.   .   .

To be sure, there were two doctrines that afforded municipal corporations some measure of protection from tort liability. The first sought to distinguish between a municipality's "governmental" and "proprietary" functions; as to the former, the city was held immune, whereas in its exercise of the latter, the city was held to the same standards of liability as any private corporation. The second doctrine immunized a municipality for its "discretionary" or "legislative" activities, but not for those which were "ministerial" in nature. A brief examination of the application and the rationale underlying each of these doctrines demonstrates that Congress could not have intended them to limit a municipality's liability under § 1983.

The governmental-proprietary distinction owed its existence to the dual nature of the municipal corporation. On the one hand, the municipality was a corporate body, capable of performing the same "proprietary" functions as any private corporation, and liable for its torts in the same manner and to the same extent, as well. On the other hand, the municipality was an arm of the State, and when acting in that "governmental" or "public" capacity, it shared the immunity traditionally accorded the sovereign. But the principle of sovereign immunity—itself a somewhat arid fountainhead for municipal immunity[28]—is necessarily nullified when the

---

28. Although it has never been understood how the doctrine of sovereign immunity came to be adopted in the American democracy, it apparently stems from the personal immunity of the English Monarch as expressed in the maxim, "The King can do no wrong." It has been suggested, however, that the meaning traditionally ascribed to this phrase is an ironic perversion of its original intent: "The maxim merely meant that the King was not privileged to do wrong. If his acts were against the law, they were *injuriae* (wrongs). Bracton, while ambiguous in his several statements as to the relation between the King and the law, did not intend to convey the idea that he was incapable of committing a legal wrong." Borchard, Government Liability in Tort, 34 Yale L.J. 1, 2, n. 2 (1924). See also Kates & Kouba, Liability of Public Entities Under Section 1983 of the Civil Rights Act, 45 S.Cal.L.Rev. 131, 142 (1972).

In this country, "[t]he sovereign or governmental immunity doctrine, holding that the state, its subdivisions and municipal entities, may not be held liable for tortious acts, was never completely accepted by the courts, its underlying principle being deemed con-

trary to the basic concept of the law of torts that liability follows negligence, as well as foreign to the spirit of the constitutional guarantee that every person is entitled to a legal remedy for injuries he may receive in his person or property. As a result, the trend of judicial decisions was always to restrict, rather than to expand, the doctrine of municipal immunity." 18 McQuillin § 53.02, p. 104 (footnotes omitted). See also Prosser § 131, p. 984 ("For well over a century the immunity of both the state and the local governments for their torts has been subjected to vigorous criticism, which at length has begun to have its effect"). The seminal opinion of the Florida Supreme Court in Hargrove v. Town of Cocoa Beach, 96 So.2d 130 (1957), has spawned "a minor avalanche of decisions repudiating municipal immunity," Prosser § 131, p. 985, which, in conjunction with legislative abrogation of sovereign immunity, has resulted in the consequence that only a handful of States still cling to the old common-law rule of immunity for governmental functions. See K. Davis, Administrative Law of the Seventies § 25.00 (1976 and Supp.1977)(only two States adhere to the tra-

State expressly or impliedly allows itself, or its creation, to be sued. Municipalities were therefore liable not only for their "proprietary" acts, but also for those "governmental" functions as to which the State had withdrawn their immunity.   And, by the end of the 19th century, courts regularly held that in imposing a specific duty on the municipality either in its charter or by statute, the State had impliedly withdrawn the city's immunity from liability for the nonperformance or misperformance of its obligation. . . .

That the municipality's common-law immunity for "governmental" functions derives from the principle of sovereign immunity also explains why that doctrine could not have served as the basis for the qualified privilege respondent city claims under § 1983.   First, because sovereign immunity insulates the municipality from unconsented suits altogether, the presence or absence of good faith is simply irrelevant.   The critical issue is whether injury occurred while the city was exercising governmental, as opposed to proprietary, powers or obligations—not whether its agents reasonably believed they were acting lawfully in so conducting themselves. More fundamentally, however, the municipality's "governmental" immunity is obviously abrogated by the sovereign's enactment of a statute making it amenable to suit.   Section 1983 was just such a statute.   By including municipalities within the class of "persons" subject to liability for violations of the Federal Constitution and laws, Congress—the supreme sovereign on matters of federal law—abolished whatever vestige of the State's sovereign immunity the municipality possessed.

The second common-law distinction between municipal functions—that protecting the city from suits challenging "discretionary" decisions—was grounded not on the principle of sovereign immunity, but on a concern for separation of powers.   A large part of the municipality's responsibilities involved broad discretionary decisions on issues of public policy—decisions that affected large numbers of persons and called for a delicate balancing of competing considerations.   For a court or jury, in the guise of a tort suit, to review the reasonableness of the city's judgment on these matters would be an infringement upon the powers properly vested in a coordinate and coequal branch of government. . . .

Although many, if not all, of a municipality's activities would seem to involve at least some measure of discretion, the influence of this doctrine on the city's liability was not as significant as might be expected.   For just as the courts implied an exception to the municipality's immunity for its "governmental" functions, here, too, a distinction was made that had the effect of subjecting the city to liability for much of its tortious conduct. While the city retained its immunity for decisions as to whether the public interest required acting in one manner or another, once any particular decision was made, the city was fully liable for any injuries incurred in the execution of its judgment. . . .

ditional common-law immunity from torts in the exercise of governmental functions); Harley & Wasinger, Government Immunity: Despotic Mantle or Creature of Necessity, 16 Washburn L.J. 12, 34–53 (1976).

Once again, an understanding of the rationale underlying the common-law immunity for "discretionary" functions explains why that doctrine cannot serve as the foundation for a good-faith immunity under § 1983. That common-law doctrine merely prevented courts from substituting their own judgment on matters within the lawful discretion of the municipality. But a municipality has no "discretion" to violate the Federal Constitution; its dictates are absolute and imperative. And when a court passes judgment on the municipality's conduct in a § 1983 action, it does not seek to second-guess the "reasonableness" of the city's decision nor to interfere with the local government's resolution of competing policy considerations. Rather, it looks only to whether the municipality has conformed to the requirements of the Federal Constitution and statutes.   .   .   .

In sum, we can discern no "tradition so well grounded in history and reason" that would warrant the conclusion that in enacting § 1 of the Civil Rights Act, the 42d Congress *sub silentio* extended to municipalities a qualified immunity based on the good faith of their officers.   .   .   .

B

Our rejection of a construction of § 1983 that would accord municipalities a qualified immunity for their good-faith constitutional violations is compelled both by the legislative purpose in enacting the statute and by considerations of public policy. The central aim of the Civil Rights Act was to provide protection to those persons wronged by the "'[m]isuse of power, possessed by virtue of state law and made possible only because the wrongdoer is clothed with the authority of state law.'" [*Monroe*]   .   .   .

.   .   .

.   .   . A damages remedy against the offending party is a vital component of any scheme for vindicating cherished constitutional guarantees, and the importance of assuring its efficacy is only accentuated when the wrongdoer is the institution that has been established to protect the very rights it has transgressed. Yet owing to the qualified immunity enjoyed by most government officials, see Scheuer v. Rhodes, 416 U.S. 232 (1974), many victims of municipal malfeasance would be left remediless if the city were also allowed to assert a good-faith defense. Unless countervailing considerations counsel otherwise, the injustice of such a result should not be tolerated.

Moreover, § 1983 was intended not only to provide compensation to the victims of past abuses, but to serve as a deterrent against future constitutional deprivations, as well. [   ] The knowledge that a municipality will be liable for all of its injurious conduct, whether committed in good faith or not, should create an incentive for officials who may harbor doubts about the lawfulness of their intended actions to err on the side of protecting citizens' constitutional rights. Furthermore, the threat that damages might be levied against the city may encourage those in a policymaking position to institute internal rules and programs designed to minimize the likelihood of unintentional infringements on constitutional rights. Such procedures are particularly beneficial in preventing those "systemic" injuries that result not so much from the conduct of any single individual, but from the interactive behavior of several government officials, each of whom may be acting in good faith. [   ]

Our previous decisions conferring qualified immunities on various government officials are not to be read as derogating the significance of the societal interest in compensating the innocent victims of governmental misconduct. Rather, in each case we concluded that overriding considerations of public policy nonetheless demanded that the official be given a measure of protection from personal liability. The concerns that justified those decisions, however, are less compelling, if not wholly inapplicable, when the liability of the municipal entity is at issue.

In Scheuer v. Rhodes, supra, at 240, The Chief Justice identified the two "mutually dependent rationales" on which the doctrine of official immunity rested:

> "(1) the injustice, particularly in the absence of bad faith, of subjecting to liability an officer who is required, by the legal obligations of his position, to exercise discretion; (2) the danger that the threat of such liability would deter his willingness to execute his office with the decisiveness and the judgment required by the public good."[38]

The first consideration is simply not implicated when the damages award comes not from the official's pocket, but from the public treasury. It hardly seems unjust to require a municipal defendant which has violated a citizen's constitutional rights to compensate him for the injury suffered thereby. . . . Elemental notions of fairness dictate that one who causes a loss should bear the loss.

It has been argued, however, that revenue raised by taxation for public use should not be diverted to the benefit of a single or discrete group of taxpayers, particularly where the municipality has at all times acted in good faith. On the contrary, the accepted view is that stated in Thayer v. Boston—"that the city, in its corporate capacity, should be liable to make good the damage sustained by an [unlucky] individual, in consequence of the acts thus done." 36 Mass., at 515. After all, it is the public at large which enjoys the benefits of the government's activities, and it is the public at large which is ultimately responsible for its administration. Thus, even where some constitutional development could not have been foreseen by municipal officials, it is fairer to allocate any resulting financial loss to the inevitable costs of government borne by all the taxpayers, than to allow its

---

38. Wood v. Strickland, 420 U.S. 308 (1975), mentioned a third justification for extending a qualified immunity to public officials: the fear that the threat of personal liability might deter citizens from holding public office. See id., at 320 ("the most capable candidates for school board positions might be deterred from seeking office if heavy burdens upon their private resources from monetary liability were a likely prospect during their tenure"). Such fears are totally unwarranted, of course, once the threat of personal liability is eliminated.

impact to be felt solely by those whose rights, albeit newly recognized, have been violated. [ ][39]

The second rationale mentioned in *Scheuer* also loses its force when it is the municipality, in contrast to the official, whose liability is at issue. At the heart of this justification for a qualified immunity for the individual official is the concern that the threat of *personal* monetary liability will introduce an unwarranted and unconscionable consideration into the decisionmaking process, thus paralyzing the governing official's decisiveness and distorting his judgment on matters of public policy.[40] The inhibiting effect is significantly reduced, if not eliminated, however, when the threat of personal liability is removed. First, as an empirical matter, it is questionable whether the hazard of municipal loss will deter a public officer from the conscientious exercise of his duties; city officials routinely make decisions that either require a large expenditure of municipal funds or involve a substantial risk of depleting the public fisc. [ ] More important, though, is the realization that consideration of the *municipality's* liability for constitutional violations is quite properly the concern of its elected or appointed officials. Indeed, a decisionmaker would be derelict in his duties if, at some point, he did not consider whether his decision comports with constitutional mandates and did not weigh the risk that a violation might result in an award of damages from the public treasury. . . .

IV

In sum, our decision holding that municipalities have no immunity from damages liability flowing from their constitutional violations harmonizes well with developments in the common law and our own pronouncements on official immunities under § 1983. Doctrines of tort law have changed significantly over the past century, and our notions of governmental responsibility should properly reflect that evolution. No longer is individual "blameworthiness" the acid test of liability; the principle of equitable loss-spreading has joined fault as a factor in distributing the costs of official misconduct.

39. Monell v. New York City Dept. of Social Services indicated that the principle of loss-spreading was an insufficient justification for holding the municipality liable under § 1983 on a *respondeat superior* theory. 436 U.S., at 693–694. Here, of course, quite a different situation is presented. Petitioner does not seek to hold the city responsible for the unconstitutional actions of an individual official "*solely* because it employs a tortfeasor." Id., at 691. Rather, liability is predicated on a determination that "the action that is alleged to be unconstitutional implements or executes a policy statement, ordinance, regulation, or decision officially adopted and promulgated by that body's officers." Id., at 690. In this circumstance—when it is the local government itself that is responsible for the constitutional deprivation—it is perfectly reasonable to distribute the loss to the public as a cost of the administration of government, rather than to let the entire burden fall on the injured individual.

40. "The imposition of monetary costs for mistakes which were not unreasonable in the light of all the circumstances would undoubtedly deter even the most conscientious school decisionmaker from exercising his judgment independently, forcefully, and in a manner best serving the long-term interest of the school and the students." Wood v. Strickland, supra, at 319–320.

We believe that today's decision, together with prior precedents in this area, properly allocates these costs among the three principals in the scenario of the § 1983 cause of action: the victim of the constitutional deprivation; the officer whose conduct caused the injury; and the public, as represented by the municipal entity. The innocent individual who is harmed by an abuse of governmental authority is assured that he will be compensated for his injury. The offending official, so long as he conducts himself in good faith, may go about his business secure in the knowledge that a qualified immunity will protect him from personal liability for damages that are more appropriately chargeable to the populace as a whole. And the public will be forced to bear only the costs of injury inflicted by the "execution of a government's policy or custom, whether made by its lawmakers or by those whose edicts or acts may fairly be said to represent official policy." [*Monell.*]

Reversed.

◾ MR. JUSTICE POWELL, with whom THE CHIEF JUSTICE, MR. JUSTICE STEWART, and MR. JUSTICE REHNQUIST join, dissenting.

The Court today holds that the city of Independence may be liable in damages for violating a constitutional right that was unknown when the events in this case occurred. It finds a denial of due process in the city's failure to grant petitioner a hearing to clear his name after he was discharged. But his dismissal involved only the proper exercise of discretionary powers according to prevailing constitutional doctrine. The city imposed no stigma on petitioner that would require a "name clearing" hearing under the Due Process Clause.

On the basis of this alleged deprivation of rights, the Court interprets 42 U.S.C. § 1983 to impose strict liability on municipalities for constitutional violations. This strict liability approach inexplicably departs from this Court's prior decisions under § 1983 and runs counter to the concerns of the 42d Congress when it enacted the statute. The Court's ruling also ignores the vast weight of common-law precedent as well as the current state law of municipal immunity. For these reasons, and because this decision will hamper local governments unnecessarily, I dissent.

I

[The dissent first argues that plaintiff suffered no threshold constitutional deprivation because the denial of a hearing did not impose the "stigma" on him required by earlier precedents.]

II

Having constructed a constitutional deprivation from the valid exercise of governmental authority, the Court holds that municipalities are strictly liable for their constitutional torts. Until two years ago, municipal corporations enjoyed absolute immunity from § 1983 claims. . . .

After today's decision, municipalities will have gone in two short years from absolute immunity under § 1983 to strict liability. As a policy matter, I believe that strict municipal liability unreasonably subjects local governments to damages judgments for actions that were reasonable when performed. It converts municipal governance into a hazardous slalom through constitutional obstacles that often are unknown and unknowable.

The Court's decision also impinges seriously on the prerogatives of municipal entities created and regulated primarily by the States. At the very least, this Court should not initiate a federal intrusion of this magnitude in the absence of explicit congressional action. Yet today's decision is supported by nothing in the text of § 1983. Indeed, it conflicts with the apparent intent of the drafters of the statute, with the common law of municipal tort liability, and with the current state law of municipal immunities.

A

1

. . .

The Court today abandons any attempt to harmonize § 1983 with traditional tort law. It points out that municipal immunity may be abrogated by legislation. Thus, according to the Court, Congress "abolished" municipal immunity when it included municipalities "within the class of 'persons' subject to liability" under § 1983.

This reasoning flies in the face of our prior decisions under this statute. We have held repeatedly that "immunities 'well grounded in history and reason' [were not] abrogated 'by covert inclusion in the general language' of § 1983." Imbler v. Pachtman, supra, at 418, quoting Tenney v. Brandhove, supra, at 376. See Scheuer v. Rhodes, supra, at 243–244; Pierson v. Ray, supra, at 554. The peculiar nature of the Court's position emerges when the status of executive officers under § 1983 is compared with that of local governments. State and local executives are personally liable for bad-faith or unreasonable constitutional torts. Although Congress had the power to make those individuals liable for all such torts, this Court has refused to find an abrogation of traditional immunity in a statute that does not mention immunities. Yet the Court now views the enactment of § 1983 as a direct abolition of traditional municipal immunities. Unless the Court is overruling its previous immunity decisions, the silence in § 1983 must mean that the 42d Congress mutely accepted the immunity of executive officers, but silently rejected common-law municipal immunity. I find this interpretation of the statute singularly implausible.

2

Important public policies support the extension of qualified immunity to local governments. First, as recognized by the doctrine of separation of powers, some governmental decisions should be at least presumptively insulated from judicial review. . . . The allocation of public resources and the operational policies of the government itself are activities that lie peculiarly within the competence of executive and legislative bodies. When charting those policies, a local official should not have to gauge his employer's possible liability under § 1983 if he incorrectly—though reasonably and in good faith—forecasts the course of constitutional law. Excessive judicial intrusion into such decisions can only distort municipal decisionmaking and discredit the courts. Qualified immunity would provide presumptive protection for discretionary acts, while still leaving the municipality liable for bad faith or unreasonable constitutional deprivations.

. . .

The Court now argues that local officials might modify their actions unduly if they face personal liability under § 1983, but that they are unlikely to do so when the locality itself will be held liable. This contention denigrates the sense of responsibility of municipal officers, and misunderstands the political process. Responsible local officials will be concerned about potential judgments against their municipalities for alleged constitutional torts. Moreover, they will be accountable within the political system for subjecting the municipality to adverse judgments. If officials must look over their shoulders at strict municipal liability for unknowable constitutional deprivations, the resulting degree of governmental paralysis will be little different from that caused by fear of personal liability. [ ]

In addition, basic fairness requires a qualified immunity for municipalities. . . . Constitutional law is what the courts say it is, and—as demonstrated by today's decision and its precursor, *Monell*—even the most prescient lawyer would hesitate to give a firm opinion on matters not plainly settled. Municipalities, often acting in the utmost good faith, may not know or anticipate when their action or inaction will be deemed a constitutional violation.

The Court nevertheless suggests that, as a matter of social justice, municipal corporations should be strictly liable even if they could not have known that a particular action would violate the Constitution. After all, the Court urges, local governments can "spread" the costs of any judgment across the local population. The Court neglects, however, the fact that many local governments lack the resources to withstand substantial unanticipated liability under § 1983. Even enthusiastic proponents of municipal liability have conceded that ruinous judgments under the statute could imperil local governments. [ ] By simplistically applying the theorems of welfare economics and ignoring the reality of municipal finance, the Court imposes strict liability on the level of government least able to bear it.[12] For some municipalities, the result could be a severe limitation on their ability to serve the public.

B

The Court searches at length—and in vain—for legal authority to buttress its policy judgment. Despite its general statements to the contrary, the court can find no support for its position in the debates on the

---

12. Ironically, the State and Federal Governments cannot be held liable for constitutional deprivations. The Federal Government has not waived its sovereign immunity against such claims, and the States are protected by the Eleventh Amendment.

civil rights legislation that included § 1983. Indeed, the legislative record suggests that the Members of the 42d Congress would have been dismayed by this ruling. Nor, despite its frequent citation of authorities that are only marginally relevant, can the Court rely on the traditional or current law of municipal tort liability. Both in the 19th century and now, courts and legislatures have recognized the importance of limiting the liability of local governments for official torts. Each of these conventional sources of law points to the need for qualified immunity for local governments.

. . .

The lack of support for the court's view of the common law is evident in its reliance on Thayer v. Boston, 36 Mass. 511 (1837), as its principal authority. *Thayer* did hold broadly that a city could be liable for the authorized acts of its officers. 36 Mass., at 516. But *Thayer* was limited severely by later Massachusetts decisions. . . .

Today's decision also conflicts with the current law in 44 States and the District of Columbia. All of those jurisdictions provide municipal immunity at least analogous to a "good faith" defense against liability for constitutional torts. Thus, for municipalities in almost 90% of our jurisdictions, the Court creates broader liability for constitutional deprivations than for state-law torts.

. . .

C

The Court turns a blind eye to this overwhelming evidence that municipalities have enjoyed a qualified immunity and to the policy considerations that for the life of this Republic have justified its retention. This disregard of precedent and policy is especially unfortunate because suits under § 1983 typically implicate evolving constitutional standards. A good-faith defense is much more important for those actions than in those involving ordinary tort liability. The duty not to run over a pedestrian with a municipal bus is far less likely to change than is the rule as to what process, if any, is due the bus driver if he claims the right to a hearing after discharge.

The right of a discharged government employee to a "name clearing" hearing was not recognized until our decision in Board of Regents v. Roth, 408 U.S. 564 (1972). That ruling was handed down 10 weeks after Owen was discharged and 8 weeks after the city denied his request for a hearing. By stripping the city of any immunity, the court punishes it for failing to predict our decision in *Roth*. As a result, local governments and their officials will face the unnerving prospect of crushing damages judgments whenever a policy valid under current law is later found to be unconstitutional. I can see no justice or wisdom in that outcome.

NOTES AND QUESTIONS

1. Are there persuasive reasons for granting immunities to government officials despite the lack of explicit mention in § 1983? Which opinion is more convincing regarding utilization of the rationale for the individual immunities in deciding whether to similarly insulate government entities from liability? See generally, Sowle, Qualified Immunity in Section 1983 Cases: The Unresolved Issues of the Conditions for its Use and the Burden of Persuasion, 55 Tulane L.Rev. 326 (1981).

As the majority opinion suggests, absolute immunities have traditionally been recognized for officials performing judicial and legislative functions. Can an absolute, as distinguished from a qualified, immunity be justified? Consider Mireles v. Waco, 502 U.S. 9 (1991), in which plaintiff attorney alleged that the defendant judge had ordered bailiffs to drag plaintiff from another courtroom in the building because he was late for the defendant's morning calendar call. The Court summarily decided that absolute immunity applied. The alleged act could not be a nonjudicial action because "a judge's direction to court officers to bring a person . . . before him is a function normally performed by a judge." The action was taken in the "very aid of the judge's jurisdiction over a matter before him" and thus could not be said to have been taken in the absence of jurisdiction. Is an absolute immunity warranted here? What are the limits of the judicial function?

2. In Forrester v. White, 484 U.S. 219 (1988), the Court limited the apparent rule of absolute immunity for judicial officers. The defendant, a state judge who was authorized to hire and fire probation officers, hired plaintiff to be an adult and juvenile probation officer. After promoting plaintiff to a supervisory position, defendant fired her. Plaintiff filed suit under § 1983 alleging sex discrimination in violation of the Fourteenth Amendment's equal protection clause. The Supreme Court rejected defendant's claim that as a judicial officer, he was entitled to absolute immunity from a civil damages suit. Applying a "functional" approach, the Court reasoned that immunity for "truly judicial" acts was needed to protect "judicial independence by insulating judges from vexatious actions prosecuted by disgruntled litigants." In the instant case, plaintiff's allegations went to defendant's administrative responsibilities. The threat of vexatious lawsuits brought by fired employees was not sufficiently grave to justify absolute immunity.

In Imbler v. Pachtman, 424 U.S. 409 (1976), the Court determined that state prosecutors enjoy absolute immunity from § 1983 actions relating to their conduct "in initiating a prosecution and in presenting the State's case," insofar as that conduct is "intimately associated with the judicial phase of the criminal process[.]" In Burns v. Reed, 500 U.S. 478 (1991), the Court held that this absolute immunity shielded a state prosecutor from suit under § 1983 for his alleged presentation of misleading evidence at a hearing in support of a search warrant. Absolute immunity was justified because of the prosecutor's role as advocate for the state and the substantial likelihood of vexatious litigation. However, the Court refused to extend absolute immunity to the same prosecutor for allegedly giving the police erroneous legal advice as to whether they had the requisite "probable cause" to arrest plaintiff. Unlike the prosecutor's immunity for statements made before a judicial tribunal, no historical or common law tradition supported a grant of absolute immunity for a prosecutor's provision of legal advice to the police.

In Buckley v. Fitzsimmons, 509 U.S. 259 (1993), the court held that a prosecutor is entitled only to qualified immunity when engaging in investigatory, rather than prosecutorial functions. Thus the prosecutor only could claim qualified immunity when he allegedly engaged in misconduct while attempting to determine if a bootprint at the crime scene had been left by the suspect.

3. In Quern v. Jordan, 440 U.S. 332 (1979), the Court, relying heavily on the Eleventh Amendment, held that states would be immune from liability under § 1983. However, the plaintiff successfully circumvented state immunity in Kentucky v. Graham, 473 U.S. 159 (1985), by seeking prospective injunctive relief against a state officer in her official capacity. The Court has yet to address the entire range of Eleventh Amendment issues involving prospective versus retroactive relief and injunctive relief versus monetary damages.

4. Is the dissent in *Owen* correct in arguing that the majority imposes strict liability on government entities? Is the underlying official misconduct in these cases likely to be "intentional" according to the traditional definition of intended harm? What are the strongest arguments for subjecting government entities to strict liability in these cases?

5. Should it matter that the constitutional right relied on by plaintiff was declared after the contested dismissal occurred?

6. Is there a satisfactory response to the dissent's argument on the likely consequences of the decision?

7. Although the role of negligence in § 1983 actions was unclear for some time, the Court settled the matter, at least with respect to the due process clause of the Fourteenth Amendment, in Daniels v. Williams, 474 U.S. 327 (1986). The plaintiff in *Daniels,* a jail inmate, slipped on a pillow negligently left on a stairway by defendant, a deputy at the jail. Alleging that defendant's negligence deprived him of his "liberty" interest to be free from bodily injury "without due process of law," plaintiff sued under § 1983. The Court rejected plaintiff's claim, holding that the due process clause does not embody a tort law duty of due care concept. See also Parratt v. Taylor, 451 U.S. 527 (1981)(negligent misplacement of a prisoner's hobby set due to failure to follow rules for sorting incoming mail no violation of due process); Farmer v. Brennan, at p. 854, supra.

In Davidson v. Cannon, 474 U.S. 344 (1986), a companion case to *Daniels,* the Court made clear that the availability of a state law remedy does not affect the rule that no action lies under the due process clause for a state official's negligence. The *Davidson* plaintiff alleged that state prison officials negligently failed to protect him from being attacked by a fellow inmate. Under state law, the prison officials enjoyed immunity from liability for injuries caused by one prisoner to another. Plaintiff argued that the state should be required to provide him an effective remedy. The

Court disagreed, stating that "the Fourteenth Amendment does not require a remedy when there has been no 'deprivation' of a protected interest."

8. What is the proper measure of damages for the deprivation of a constitutional right? In *Monroe,* Justice Harlan, concurring, had suggested that in enacting § 1983 Congress may have believed that:

A deprivation of a constitutional right is significantly different from and more serious than a violation of a state right . . . even though the same act may constitute both a state tort and the deprivation of a constitutional right.

In Carey v. Piphus, 435 U.S. 247 (1978), the plaintiffs had been denied procedural due process by being suspended from high school without a hearing. The court of appeals had held (1) that if the deprivation was in fact justified, the plaintiffs could recover no damages for the suspension but that (2) they could recover substantial presumed damages for the violation of the constitutional right itself. The Supreme Court agreed with the first ruling but reversed the second ruling and held that the plaintiffs would have to present proof of actual injury arising from the violation of the right, including mental and emotional distress. The Court drew on its recent decisions in defamation law, particularly the *Gertz* case, discussed at p. 953, infra. Finally, the court held that even if the plaintiffs could not show actual injury they were entitled to nominal damages of one dollar because their constitutional rights had been violated. See Love, Damages: A Remedy for the Violation of Constitutional Rights, 67 Calif.L.Rev. 1242 (1979).

9. In City of Newport v. Fact Concerts, Inc., 453 U.S. 247 (1981), the Court held that a municipality could not be held liable for punitive damages. Nothing in the legislative history suggested that Congress sought such liability. Moreover, public policy would not permit such liability. Punitive damages were likely to be a windfall to the plaintiff and to cause an "increase in taxes or a reduction of public services for the citizens footing the bill." Although a public official who maliciously and knowingly deprives others of their civil rights may become the "appropriate object of the community's vindictive sentiments," a municipality "can have no malice independent of the malice of its officials. Damages awarded for *punitive* purposes, therefore, are not sensibly assessed against the governmental entity itself."

Nor did the deterrence rationale warrant a different result. Even compensatory damages imposed on a municipality may induce the public to vote the wrongdoers out of office. Also, a punitive award against the specific official is a more likely source of deterrence than the indirect deterrent of imposing punitive damages on the municipality.

10. Section 1985(3). Another section of the Ku Klux Klan Act—now 42 U.S.C. § 1985(3)—creates a damage remedy for citizens deprived of constitutional rights by persons acting in a conspiracy. In Griffin v. Breckenridge, 403 U.S. 88 (1971), the Supreme Court held that section 1985(3) could be invoked to redress injuries inflicted by purely private conspiracies though the participants lacked any state nexus. In *Griffin,* the four black Mississippi plaintiffs alleged that they were driving down the highway when the defendants, two white local residents, mistook the driver for a civil rights worker, stopped the car and clubbed the occupants.

The Court held that in order to state a cause of action under this section a plaintiff must allege the existence of a conspiracy for the purpose of depriving someone of equal protection or equal privileges and immunities, acts in furtherance of the conspiracy, and injury to the person or his property or deprivation of his constitutional rights. The Court stressed that a conspiratorial deprivation would not be redressable under § 1985(3) without proof of "invidiously discriminatory animus." This "animus" involved a "racial or otherwise class-based" attempt to discriminate against a certain group. Without proof of such class-based animus, the asserted constitutional deprivation would not rise above the level of an ordinary "tortious injury."

Section 1985(3) seems unlikely to provide many plaintiffs with an effective remedy. Plaintiffs have generally encountered great difficulty in attempting to demonstrate the requisite class-based animus. See Harrison v. Brooks, 519 F.2d 1358 (1st Cir.1975); McNally v. Pulitzer Pub. Co., 532 F.2d 69 (8th Cir.), cert. denied 429 U.S. 855 (1976). A second hurdle is that Congress may lack the power to bypass the "state action" requirement of the Fourteenth Amendment as to most civil rights. See Cohen v. Illinois Institute of Technology, 524 F.2d 818 (7th Cir.1975), cert. denied 425 U.S. 943 (1976). The Court in *Griffin* avoided this problem by finding Congressional authority to reach the defendant's behavior under the Congressional power to protect the right to travel and under the Thirteenth Amendment (relying here on Jones v. Alfred H. Mayer Co., 392 U.S. 409 (1968), which held that the Thirteenth Amendment authorized Congress to provide remedies for "racially discriminatory private action" aimed at depriving blacks "of the basic rights that the law secures to all free men.")

Are the plaintiffs in *Griffin* better off then they would have been had they proceeded under state law?

11. Does the general overruling of government immunity discussed in *Owen,* provide any support for the majority's approach in the case?

2. LIABILITY OF FEDERAL OFFICIALS

In Chapter III, we considered the availability of remedies against the United States under the Federal Tort Claims Act, p. 215, supra. As we have seen, liability for negligence may be available under the statute, though recovery on a strict liability basis is not permitted. Here, we consider the available remedies for citizens who sustain intentional injury at the hands of federal government employees.

The Federal Tort Claims Act addresses the problem of intentional torts in § 2680(h), which provides that the Act shall not apply to

> (h) Any claim arising out of assault, battery, false imprisonment, false arrest, malicious prosecution, abuse of process, libel,

slander, misrepresentation, deceit, or interference with contract rights: *Provided,* That, with regard to acts or omissions of investigative or law enforcement officers of the United States Government, the provisions of this chapter and section 1346(b) of this title shall apply to any claim arising, on or after the date of the enactment of this proviso, out of assault, battery, false imprisonment, false arrest, abuse of process, or malicious prosecution. For the purpose of this subsection, "investigative or law enforcement officer" means any officer of the United States who is empowered by law to execute searches, to seize evidence, or to make arrests for violations of Federal law.

The part before the proviso was in the original Act. The proviso was added in 1974 largely as the result of several "no-knock" raids carried out by federal narcotics agents. An action against the agents themselves became available only after Bivens v. Six Unknown Named Federal Narcotics Agents, 403 U.S. 388 (1971). But Congress observed that the agents were unlikely to be solvent. On the 1974 amendment, see Boger, Gitenstein, and Verkuil, The Federal Tort Claims Act Intentional Torts Amendment: An Interpretative Analysis, 54 N.C.L.Rev. 497 (1976).

In *Bivens,* the plaintiff alleged that federal agents had ransacked his apartment during an illegal warrantless search. Though the only effective remedy was money damages, § 1983 was inapplicable because the wrongdoers were federal agents and therefore not acting under color of *state* law. Nevertheless, the Supreme Court recognized a federal claim for damages against the federal officials based directly upon the Fourth Amendment, despite the lack of a statutory remedy. Writing for the majority, Justice Brennan stated:

> "[I]t is . . . well settled that where legal rights have been invaded, and a federal statute provides for a general right to sue for such invasion, federal courts may use any available remedy to make good the wrong done." Bell v. Hood, 327 U.S. at 684 (footnote omitted). The present case involves no special factors counselling hesitation in the absence of affirmative action by Congress.

The court offered little guidance on when it would be proper to imply the damage remedy to vindicate Constitutional interests. The Government had argued that the Court should create remedies based on the Constitution only when "essential" to the protection of the right, reasoning that Congress may displace or modify a Court-created remedy for statutory violations but is powerless to modify a remedy that the Court has determined is required by the Constitution. Justice Brennan rejected the "essentiality" standard but offered no alternative.

Once it is recognized that the Constitution creates federally protected interests, it seems clear that the *Bivens* rationale should apply to protect other rights guaranteed by the Constitution as well. Not surprisingly, therefore, claims have been recognized against federal officers for alleged deprivations of other Constitutional rights. See cases cited in McNally v.

Pulitzer Publishing Co., 532 F.2d 69, 76 n. 8 (8th Cir.), cert. denied 429 U.S. 855 (1976).

In Carlson v. Green, 446 U.S. 14 (1980), the Court decided that the fact that plaintiff could sue under the Federal Tort Claims Act did not bar a suit under the *Bivens* doctrine. The two actions were not equivalent. Under *Bivens*, deterrence might be stronger when the action is brought against the individual defendants, and punitive damages are available only under *Bivens*. Also, liability under the FTCA depends on whether a private person "would be liable to the claimant in accordance with the law of the place where the act or omission occurred." This creates a local focus in contrast to *Bivens* which creates a unified system of substantive law.

A *Bivens* action is unavailable, however, where Congress has expressly created an alternative remedial scheme. See, e.g., Chappell v. Wallace, 462 U.S. 296 (1983)(redress against racial discrimination by a superior officer was available through the military justice system); Bush v. Lucas, 462 U.S. 367 (1983)(aerospace engineer allegedly fired in retaliation for exercise of his First Amendment rights had effective remedy through Civil Service System); Schweiker v. Chilicky, 487 U.S. 412 (1988)(individuals who alleged that their Social Security benefits were improperly terminated had effective remedy through congressionally-provided administrative appeal system). For a critical discussion of the Court's rationales for barring certain *Bivens* actions, see Nichol, *Bivens, Chilicky,* and Constitutional Damages Claims, 75 Va.L.Rev. 1117 (1989).

In *Bivens* cases, as in cases under § 1983, the critical issues concern the role of defenses. In Butz v. Economou, 438 U.S. 478 (1978), plaintiff sued several officials in the Department of Agriculture after the Department brought an unsuccessful administrative proceeding against him. He sued under *Bivens* claiming that the officials (including the Secretary, Assistant Secretary, the administrative judge, the hearing examiner who recommended the proceeding, and the attorney who presented the case) had violated his constitutional rights in various ways. The Supreme Court, 5–4, held that when a plaintiff claims that officials of an executive department have violated constitutional rights, the defendants generally are entitled only to qualified immunity of the type developed for state officials in *Scheuer, Wood,* and similar cases under § 1983, that were discussed in *Owen.*

These cases "have recognized that it is not unfair to hold liable the official who knows or should know he is acting outside the law, and that insisting on an awareness of clearly established constitutional limits will not unduly interfere with the exercise of official judgment." Federal officials "will not be liable for mere mistakes in judgment, whether the mistake is one of fact or one of law. But we see no substantial basis for holding, as the United States would have us do, that executive officers generally may with impunity discharge their duties in a way that is known to them to violate the United States Constitution or in a manner that they should know transgresses a clearly established constitutional rule." The majority believed that insubstantial suits "can be quickly terminated" at the pleading stage. (On this score, the Court later held that a plaintiff must "allege the violation of a clearly established constitutional right" to get beyond summary judgment on a defendant's qualified immunity claim. Siegert v. Gilley, 500 U.S. 226 (1991).)

The majority did recognize that there were "some officials whose special functions require a full exemption from liability." Specifically, the analogies to the judicial branch were so apt that they had to be followed. The reason for immunities in the judicial branch is not the officials' location within government, but the "special nature of their responsibilities." The case was remanded to determine how these principles should be applied to the various defendants before the court. Reconsider the discussion of judicial immunity under § 1983 at p. 869, supra.

When a former president was sued for improperly arranging to discharge a government employee who "blew the whistle" on military cost overruns, the Court, 5–4, accorded absolute immunity. Nixon v. Fitzgerald, 457 U.S. 731 (1982). The absolute immunity was "a functionally mandated incident of the President's unique office, rooted in the constitutional tradition of the separation of powers and supported by our history." The immunity extended to "damages liability predicated on his official acts."

Although absolute immunity accorded to other executive officials had been limited to the particular functions of the office, that would be inadequate here. The President "has discretionary responsibilities in a broad variety of areas, many of them highly sensitive. In many cases it would be difficult to determine which of the President's innumerable 'functions' encompassed a particular action." The absolute immunity would extend to acts within the "outer perimeter" of his official responsibility. The action alleged here fell within that broad sweep.

Such a result would not leave the country without sufficient protection against misconduct by its chief executive. Impeachment remained available as did "formal and informal checks" on Presidential action, including "constant scrutiny by the press," oversight by Congress, the desire for reelection, the need to maintain prestige as an element of Presidential influence, and the "President's traditional concern for his historical stature."

In Harlow v. Fitzgerald, 457 U.S. 800 (1982), the Court held that senior aides to the President did not automatically share his immunity for the firing of Fitzgerald. They would receive qualified or good faith immunity. If they claimed that absolute immunity was justified because they were entrusted with discretionary authority in a sensitive area like national security or foreign policy, the defendants had to establish the claim.

Empirical data on the frequency and success of both § 1983 and *Bivens* actions are discussed in Eisenberg & Schwab, The Reality of Constitutional Tort Litigation, 72 Cornell L. Rev. 641 (1987), and Schwab & Eisenberg, Explaining Constitutional Tort Litigation: The Influence of the Attorney Fees Statute and the Government as Defendant, 73 Cornell L. Rev. 719 (1988).

CHAPTER XIII

Defamation

A. COMMON LAW BACKGROUND

1. WHAT IS DEFAMATORY?

As with other torts, defamation has evolved through common-law developments as a matter of state law. Unlike the torts we have already considered, however, the law of defamation has been enormously influenced and reshaped by constitutional considerations of freedom of speech and press. Since 1964, the Supreme Court has become involved in continuing efforts to establish the boundaries between freedom of communication and protection of reputation.

In tracing the developments in this complex area, we must begin with the common law regime. The constitutional developments have not created a totally new legal area; rather, they have altered some of the pre-existing state rules and left others in place. As a result, despite the great impact of the Supreme Court, state law retains great significance in suits for defamation. It is often possible, for example, for a case to be decided under the traditional state rules without any invocation of the First Amendment.

Defamation has a venerable and still influential history. Early in the sixteenth century the common law courts began to recognize a claim for defamation that had previously been within the exclusive jurisdiction of the ecclesiastical courts. Since the common law remedy was framed as an action on the case, with its traditional focus on damages rather than ecclesiastical sanctions, the common law action became extremely popular. In another development during the same period, the Star Chamber assumed jurisdiction over all aspects of the press, and printed defamations came to be treated as crimes. Attacks on officials were seditious libels, and libels against private persons contributed to breaches of the peace. After the Restoration both concepts were preserved: the Star Chamber's view of libel as a crime, and the antecedent common law view of slander as a tort.

Although the English defamation law crossed the Atlantic, it seems never to have been enforced as vigorously in the United States as it was in England. This was true long before any constitutional questions were raised explicitly. In Government and Mass Communications 106–07 (1947), Professor Chafee speculated:

> [The difference] is probably due to the fact that English jurymen and judges live in a different intellectual climate from the fluid and migratory society of the United States. The Englishman is

born into a definite status where he tends to stick for life. What he *is* has at least as much importance as what he *does* in an active career. A slur on his reputation, if not challenged, may cause him to drop several rungs down the social ladder. A man moves within a circle of friends and associates and feels bound to preserve his standing in their eyes. Consequently, *not* to sue for libel is taken as an admission of truth.

An able American has too much else to do to waste time on an expensive libel suit. Most strangers will not read the article, most of his friends will not believe it, and his enemies, who will believe it of course, were against him before. Anyway, it is just one more blow in the rough-and-tumble of politics or business. Even if his reputation is lowered for a while, he can make a fresh start at his home or in a new region and accomplish enough to overwhelm old scandals. A libeled American prefers to vindicate himself by steadily pushing forward his career and not by hiring a lawyer to talk in a courtroom.

Even in the United States, however, certain slurs cannot be ignored, and justify legal recourse. Since the notion of reputation is at the core of the defamation action, we will begin our consideration with a look at that concept. In our discussion of the common law, the fact that the defendant is a publisher or broadcaster rather than an individual will not generally be central.

Romaine v. Kallinger

Supreme Court of New Jersey, 1988.
109 N.J. 282, 537 A.2d 284.

[This case arose out of a nonfiction book, "The Shoemaker," written about a man who went on a criminal rampage. One of the episodes involved events at the Romaine house. Part of that description included the following:

A militant women's libber, Maria Fasching was famous among her friends for her battles on behalf of the weak and downtrodden. She would always try to rescue someone a bully had attacked, and she could not tolerate racists.

Maria thought of herself as a "free spirit." She resisted anything that she considered a restriction on her freedom. She cared for cats that had been hit by cars and for birds with broken wings.

Today, Maria Fasching was on the four-to-midnight shift at Hackensack Hospital, and she wore her nurse's uniform under her coat. In the morning Maria's friend Randi Romaine, who lived in the stucco house, had called Maria and asked her to drop over for coffee. The two women had not seen each other for a long time, for between hospital duties and preparations for her wedding, Maria's schedule was full.

At first Maria said that she couldn't visit because she had to go to a wake. This wake, however, was only for an acquaintance. Randi and her twin sister, Retta, had been Maria's friends since they were all in the first grade. Besides, Maria was eager for news from Randi about a junkie they both knew who was doing time in prison. Finally, Maria changed her mind. She didn't go to the wake, but drove her Volkswagen to the two-story tan stucco house at 124 Glenwood Avenue, the house of Mr. and Mrs. Dewitt Romaine.

During the ensuing episode Fasching was killed. Among the variety of claims pressed by several plaintiffs, we concern ourselves with Randi Romaine's libel claim against the publisher and author. The trial court granted defendants' motion for summary judgment and the Appellate Division affirmed.]

■ HANDLER, J.

. . .

According to plaintiffs, one sentence in the passage falsely depicts the reason for Ms. Fasching's visit: "Besides, Maria was eager for news from Randi about a junkie they both knew who was doing time in prison." . . .

Plaintiff Randi Romaine asserts that the particular sentence is defamatory as a matter of law, or alternatively, that the statement's defamatory content was at least a question for the jury. She claims this sentence falsely accuses her of criminality or associations with criminals. Plaintiff also contends that the false accusation was particularly damaging because it injured Ms. Romaine's professional reputation as a drug counsellor and a social worker, interfering with her ability to obtain future employment.

A defamatory statement is one that is false and "injurious to the reputation of another" or exposes another person to "hatred, contempt or ridicule" or subjects another person to "a loss of the good will and confidence" in which he or she is held by others. [ ]; see W. Keeton, D. Dobbs, R. Keeton & D. Owen, Prosser and Keeton on the Law of Torts, § 111 at 773–78 (5th ed. 1984); see also Restatement (Second) of Torts § 559 (1977)(a defamatory communication is one that "tends so to harm the reputation of another so as to lower him in the estimation of the community or to deter third persons from associating or dealing with him.")

The threshold issue in any defamation case is whether the statement at issue is reasonably susceptible of a defamatory meaning. [ ] This question is one to be decided first by the court. [ ] In making this determination, the court must evaluate the language in question "according to the fair and natural meaning which will be given it by reasonable persons of ordinary intelligence." [ ] In assessing the language, the court must view the publication as a whole and consider particularly the context in which the statement appears. [ ]

If a published statement is susceptible of one meaning only, and that meaning is defamatory, the statement is libelous as a matter of law. [ ] Conversely, if the statement is susceptible of only a non-defamatory meaning, it cannot be considered libelous, justifying dismissal of the action. [ ] However, in cases where the statement is capable of being assigned more than one meaning, one of which is defamatory and another not, the question of whether its content is defamatory is one that must be resolved by the trier of fact. [ ]

Certain kinds of statements denote such defamatory meaning that they are considered defamatory as a matter of law. A prime example is the false attribution of criminality. [ ] Lawrence v. Bauer Publishing & Printing Ltd. [89 N.J. 451, 446 A.2d 469, cert. denied 459 U.S. 999 (1982)](statement that plaintiff might be charged with criminal conduct defamatory as a matter of law). Relying essentially on this example of defamation, plaintiff Randi Romaine contends in this case that the published offending statement must be considered libelous per se. According to Ms. Romaine, the sentence has only a defamatory meaning, in that it accuses her of having engaged in criminal conduct or having associated with criminals relating to drugs.

The trial court concluded, and the Appellate Division agreed, that only the most contorted reading of the offending language could lead to the conclusion that it accuses plaintiff of illegal drug use or criminal associations. We concur in the determinations of the courts below. "[A]ccording to the fair and natural meaning which will be given [this statement] by reasonable persons of ordinary intelligence," *Herrmann v. Newark Morning Ledger Co.*, [ ] it does not attribute any kind of criminality to plaintiff. A reasonable and fair understanding of the statement simply does not yield an interpretation that the plaintiff was or had been in illegal possession of drugs or otherwise engaging in any illegal drug-related activity. See *Valentine v. C.B.S., Inc.*, 698 F.2d 430, 432 (11th Cir.1983)("The Plaintiff's interpretation does not construe the words as the common mind would understand them but is tortured and extreme."); *Forsher v. Bugliosi*, 26 Cal.3d 792, 805, 608 P.2d 716, 723, 163 Cal.Rptr. 628, 635 (1980)("the claimed defamatory nature of the book as it relates to appellant is so obscure and attenuated as to be beyond the realm of reasonableness").

At most, the sentence can be read to imply that plaintiff knew a junkie. Even if we assume that a commonly accepted and well-understood meaning of the term "junkie" is "a narcotics peddler or addict," Webster's Third New International Dictionary 1227 (1981), see also Dictionary of American Slang 300 (2d ed. 1975)(defining "junkie" as a "drug addict"), the statement still does not suggest either direct or indirect involvement by plaintiff herself in any criminal drug-related activities. Absent exceptional circumstances, the mere allegation that plaintiff knows a criminal is not defamatory as a matter of law. See, e.g., Gonzales v. Times Herald Printing Company, 513 S.W.2d 124 (Tex.Civ.App.1974)(statement that plaintiff's husband was engaged in the sale and importation of narcotics did not defame her); Rose v. Daily Mirror, Inc., 284 N.Y. 335, 31 N.E.2d 182 (1940) [ ] (plaintiff not defamed by being mistakenly described as the widow of a mobster); cf. Bufalino v. Associated Press, 692 F.2d 266 (2d Cir.1982)(mere imputation of family relationship with Mafia leader not defamatory; characterization of plaintiff as a political contributor with alleged mob ties found to have a potentially defamatory meaning), cert. den., 462 U.S. 1111 (1983).

Beyond the language itself, we are satisfied that the statement in its contextual setting cannot fairly and reasonably be invested with any defamatory meaning. Maria Fasching, we note, is described in the chapter as a person who had compassion for others and who would care for less fortunate persons. The reasonable meaning of the critical sentence that is implied from this context is that Ms. Fasching's interest in the "junkie" stemmed from sympathy and compassion, not from any predilection toward or involvement in criminal drug activity. As extended to Randi Romaine, the only fair inference to be drawn from the larger context is that Ms. Romaine shared her friend's feelings, attitudes and interests, and that her own interest in the junkie was similar to that of Ms. Fasching's.

We note the further contention that this statement had a defamatory meaning because it implied that the only reason for Ms. Fasching's visit to the Romaine home was her "interest" in news about a "junkie." A review of the full text, however, indicates that there were several reasons for the visit, only one of which was Ms. Fasching's interest in the "junkie." The lower courts soundly rejected this contention.

We conclude that the statement is not defamatory as a matter of law and accordingly uphold the ruling of the lower court on this point.

. . .

[Justice O'Hern dissented on this point, contending that the passage was ambiguous and "reasonably susceptible of a defamatory meaning" and thus presented a jury question.]

NOTES AND QUESTIONS

1. *Publication.* Since harm to reputation is at the core of this tort, it is crucial that someone other than the plaintiff receive the statement. This element, called "publication," has nothing to do with mass circulation or with putting a statement into print. It simply means that the message must reach at least one third party who understands a defamatory thrust from the statement. Thus, making a statement over the telephone to someone other than the plaintiff is a "publication" of that statement. But at common law the plaintiff has to show that the publication was either intentional or negligent; no liability exists if a third person unexpectedly overhears a private conversation between plaintiff and defendant.

In Staples v. Bangor Hydro–Electric Co., 629 A.2d 601 (Me.1993), plaintiff's supervisor told superiors within the company that he had reason to believe that plaintiff had "sabotaged" a company computer. Among the defenses was one asserting that there had been no "publication" of the charge. The court recognized that some states hold that when one agent talks to another agent, the corporation "is simply communicating with itself." The court preferred the other view because "damage to one's reputation within the corporate community may be as devastating as that outside; and that the defense of qualified privilege [discussed at p. 905, infra] provides adequate protection." To hold otherwise "would be to ignore the nature of the right protected by the law of defamation."

With the mass media, of course, virtually all statements are intentionally published in the sense that the defendant intended to make public the words that are now giving rise to suit.

In unusual situations it may be possible to establish "publication" by showing that T posted a defamation and that D did not use due care to remove it promptly. See Tacket v. General Motors Corp., 836 F.2d 1042 (7th Cir.1987), finding a jury question of publication where an unknown person stenciled a 12″ x 48″ defamation of plaintiff employee on a wall of defendant's plant—which remained there for some seven months despite plaintiff's complaints.

2. *What is defamatory?* What is the core notion that makes a statement "defamatory"? Unless D says something as patent as "P murdered X," the determination of whether the statement is actionable usually involves two steps. The first is to determine whether the words will bear the "spin" that plaintiff is seeking to put on them. In *Romaine* this question is whether the words defendant actually used could reasonably be understood to accuse her of "criminality or associations with criminals." If the answer to that is negative, there is nothing further to do. If the answer is affirmative, the second question must be addressed: whether it is defamatory of someone to say that she engages in this sort of behavior or associates with criminals. Usually, the plaintiff will try to telescope these two questions into one by arguing that the words used by defendant can reasonably be understood to make a charge that reasonable recipients could consider defamatory.

The court notes that in determining the meaning of the passage in question the court must seek the "fair and natural meaning which will be given it by reasonable persons of ordinary intelligence." Why is that the standard—as opposed, say, to the "most impressionable" readers? Or the "most intelligent" readers?

3. *What do the words mean?* In interpreting statements, courts consider all of the accoutrements of language, such as punctuation and paragraphing. Thus, in Wildstein v. New York Post Corp., 40 Misc.2d 586, 243 N.Y.S.2d 386, affirmed without opinion 24 App.Div.2d 559, 261 N.Y.S.2d 254 (1965), the defendant wrote that the plaintiff was one of "several women described as 'associated' with" a slain executive. The judge observed that if the word "associated" had not been in quotation marks the statement would not have been defamatory; the quotation marks implied a euphemistic use of the word, suggesting an illicit relationship between plaintiff and the deceased.

a. *Internal context.*   The *Romaine* court also observes that it "must view the publication as a whole." Certainly, it would seem wrong to allow a libel to be based on one sentence of an article or book if the surrounding sentences make clear that the pinpointed sentence should be read innocently.

On the other hand, what if the first paragraph of a newspaper article is defamatory, but is totally explained away in the twentieth paragraph of the story? Should the court still view the article "as a whole"? What if a big headline conveys a defamatory meaning that is removed by the text? What if a caption under a photograph conveys a defamatory meaning but the text of the accompanying article removes it? In Gambuzza v. Time, Inc., 18 App.Div.2d 351, 239 N.Y.S.2d 466 (1963), the court (3–2) concluded that a defamatory caption accompanying a photo spread had to be read together with the text that removed the sting. Generally, courts require that headlines must be read in context with the story. On occasion, courts have held that sensational headlines might be read separately from the text because "a person passing a newsstand . . . may be able to catch a glimpse of a headline without the opportunity or desire to read the accompanying article or may skim through the paper jumping from headline to headline." In *Gambuzza,* however, the caption and text were so close to each other that they had to be read together. The dissenters argued that the critical words in the caption were in bold capital letters and thus should be considered separately.

See also Kunst v. New York World Telegram Corp., 28 App.Div.2d 662, 280 N.Y.S.2d 798 (1967), in which the lead paragraph and a photo caption conveyed a defamatory implication. The majority upheld the complaint because the negation of the sting appeared only in a statement that a "persistent and careful reader would discover near the end of the reasonably lengthy article." A writing must be "construed, not with the high degree of precision expected of and used by lawyers and judges, but as it would be read and understood by an ordinary member of the public to whom it is directed." A dissenter responded that although the negating statement appeared near the end of the article, "the article is to be taken as a whole and read in its entirety." For cases on these questions of context, see R. Smolla, Law of Defamation § 4.07 (1987); Annot., Libel by Newspaper Headline, 95 A.L.R.3d 660 (1979).

b. *External context.*   Although the point is not involved in this case, it is sometimes necessary for the plaintiff to allege facts beyond those asserted in the publication in order to show how the plaintiff was defamed by the publication. For example, suppose an article stated only that the plaintiff had often been seen at "123 Hay Road." What if some in the community knew that there was a brothel at that address? Plaintiff need not show that the defamation was contained solely in the published words. If the words alone do not clearly convey the defamatory thrust explicitly or by implication the plaintiff must plead extrinsic facts that would explain how those who knew the unstated facts would take a defamatory meaning. Such an allegation—that 123 Hay Road is known by many neighbors and others to be a brothel—is called the "inducement."

Where, after putting the explicit statement and added extrinsic facts together, the thrust of the defamation is still not obvious, the plaintiff must allege the "meaning" that plaintiff thinks flows from the combination. This is called the "innuendo." The innuendo is not a fact; it is the plaintiff's assertion of how the passage would be understood by those who received the explicit statement and knew the extrinsic facts (inducement). In our example, it would be that those who know about 123 Hay Road understood the newspaper article to imply that plaintiff frequents a brothel. In most cases, when the explicit statements and the extrinsic facts are combined the nature of the claimed defamation becomes clear.

c. *Roles of judge and jury.* The *Romaine* court observes that if the statement in question is clearly defamatory in its only reasonable reading (or in all its reasonable readings), the court will declare it so. On the other hand, if it is clearly not defamatory in any reasonable reading, the court will dismiss the case. But if there are two or more reasonable meanings that might be attached to the statement (on its face or as expanded upon by external context), with at least one being defamatory and at least one not, the trier of fact is to decide which meaning would be taken. How is the trier to make this determination? What evidence should be admissible on this question?

One simple example of the problem of ambiguity is Rovira v. Boget, 240 N.Y. 314, 148 N.E. 534 (1925), in which, while eating at the ship crew's mess, a member of the largely male French-speaking crew called plaintiff, a stewardess on the same ship, a "cocotte." A French interpreter testified at trial that to some men "cocotte" meant "prostitute." "In other associations it may mean a poached egg." How should the case proceed?

In the *Valentine* case, cited in *Romaine,* the claim arose from a song written by Bob Dylan and Jacques Levy questioning the fairness of a murder trial in which the plaintiff had testified as a witness for the prosecution. The theory of the song was that the criminal defendants had been convicted as the result of a conspiracy between Bello, Bradley and the police. Valentine argued that the fourth stanza asserted that Bello and Bradley lied and that the tenth stanza said that Valentine agreed with Bello's and Bradley's identification of the defendants. Plaintiff argued that putting the two together implied that Valentine had "acquiesced in the lie of the other two witnesses." The court concluded that a "review of the entire song makes it clear this interpretation is not reasonably possible."

At one point the *Romaine* court says that a particular allegation "is not defamatory as a matter of law." Is the court declaring as a matter of law that the statement is not defamatory, or indicating that the issue is one of fact rather than of law?

Illinois takes an unusual approach to ambiguous statements, called the "innocent construction rule." This requires the court to dismiss a defamation case if a reasonable nondefamatory meaning can be ascribed to the statement—even if plaintiff could prove that most readers would have taken the defamatory reading. The situation is summarized in Barter v. Wilson, 159 Ill.App.3d 694, 512 N.E.2d 816, appeal denied 117 Ill.2d 541, 517 N.E.2d 1084 (1987), in which the court held that saying "the fix is in" on plaintiff developer's permit application does not defame the developer. The court used a definition of "fix" from a law dictionary: "determine, settle, make permanent." Thus, the statement could have meant no more than that "a decision had already been made."

4. *Is the ascribed meaning defamatory?* Recall that the *Romaine* court quoted two approaches to determining whether a statement is defamatory—that of the Restatement and that of Prosser & Keeton. How do they differ? Some states, including New York, tend to list a series of more specific criteria. Consider, for example, that of Nichols v. Item Publishers, Inc., 309 N.Y. 596, 132 N.E.2d 860 (1956): a statement that "tends to expose a person to hatred, contempt or aversion, or to induce an evil or unsavory opinion of him in the minds of a substantial number in the community." Does this formulation differ significantly from the ones quoted in *Romaine*? Consider the following passage from R. Sack & S. Baron, Libel, Slander and Related Problems 74 (2d ed. 1994):

> These variations among definitions of defamation have little apparent effect on the actual outcome of cases. If what is libelous in Mississippi is not libelous in New York, or vice versa, it is far more likely to reflect different social circumstances than the language adopted by particular courts to define the term "defamatory."

If that notion is correct, then what is the core that each of the differing formulations is trying to get at—if only for its own state? Apply these varying definitions in each of the following cases.

a. A statement that the plaintiff has died. Decker v. Princeton Packet, Inc., 116 N.J. 418, 561 A.2d 1122 (1989)(an obituary "does not impugn reputation.")

b. An assertion that a lieutenant in the Marine Corps asked his father, a United States Senator, to intervene to prevent his being sent into combat in the Korean War. Defendant argued that this could not be defamatory because it was a "perfectly understandable and human reaction" and that the use of influence to achieve such a goal was not disgraceful or odious, but expectable. The court denied summary judgment: "While perhaps some might read [defendant's] statement in such a charitable light, a great many others would find it highly offensive that a Senator's son simply called home and used his father's political influence to escape combat duty at a time when many other Second Lieutenants and other members of the service were being wounded or killed." Robertson v. McCloskey, 666 F.Supp. 241 (D.D.C.1987).

c. A false statement about incumbents' voting records that makes a group of voters less likely to vote to reelect them. In Tatur v. Solsrud, 174 Wis.2d 735, 498 N.W.2d 232 (1993), the court concluded that misrepresentations about votes on taxes and expenditures could not meet the Restatement's definition of defamatory. "None of the issues mentioned in the letter . . . are of the nature that a vote on one side or the other could harm the reputation of the voting official as to lower him in the estimation of the community or to deter third persons from associating or dealing with him." Even if the misstatements deterred voters from voting for the plaintiffs that is not enough by itself to create defamation on these facts, though the court was unwilling to say that this could never be so as to any falsely reported vote.

d. An assertion that plaintiff small town mayor was "manipulating" the press to keep it from reporting negative matters about the mayor. In West v. Thomson Newspapers, 872 P.2d 999 (Utah 1994), the court held that "Although a dictionary may define and give some content to allegedly defamatory words, it cannot be dispositive. A court simply cannot determine whether a statement is capable of sustaining a defamatory meaning by viewing individual words in isolation; rather it must carefully examine the context in which the statement was made, giving the words their most common and accepted meaning." Read this way, the use of "manipulating" was nothing more than a charge that a person in power, without running afoul of ethical or legal norms, was trying use that power to get a favorable press. "While no politician would welcome such criticism—and indeed might find it personally offensive—this does not render it defamatory. 'A publication is not defamatory simply because it is nettlesome or embarrassing. . . .' [ ] West must establish that the statement is more than sharp criticism." The court said that no reasonable person could consider this charge damaging to reputation.

e. A passage in the book "Den of Thieves" stated that plaintiff lawyer had drafted an affidavit for T to sign. T "read it over and had only one problem: the facts weren't true. He angrily refused to sign, and began looking for new lawyers." Armstrong v. Simon & Schuster, 85 N.Y.2d 373, 625 N.Y.S.2d 477, 649 N.E.2d 825 (1995). The court concluded that the passage was "susceptible to a defamatory meaning: that Armstrong deliberately presented a false affidavit for one client (Cogut) to sign in order to exculpate another client (Lowell), resulting in Cogut's angry discharge of Armstrong and the retention of new counsel." The case involved "allegedly false statements of verifiable fact, with inferences flowing from those facts."

f. Can a question be defamatory? During the Gulf War plaintiff began a project to send to soldiers overseas gift packages. Questions arose about the cost of the package compared to how much donors were being asked to pay. In an article about the controversy, defendant paper noted that one difficult question was "Who will benefit more from the project—GIs or [plaintiff]?" In Chapin v. Knight–Ridder, Inc., 993 F.2d 1087 (4th Cir.1993), the court observed that a question "can conceivably be defamatory [if it must] be reasonably read as an *assertion* of a false *fact*; inquiry itself, however embarrassing or unpleasant to its subject, is not accusation." The question here cannot be read to charge "pocket-lining." Rather, "it simply provokes public scrutiny" of plaintiff's activities.

5. *Insults and name-calling.* At a meeting of about 100 condominium owners, plaintiff wife stood up to make comments supporting those just made by her husband. At this point, defendant, sitting nearby, jumped up and shouted: "Don't listen to these people. They don't like [or hate] Jews. She's a bitch." The court held that neither expression was actionable. Ward v. Zelikovsky, 136 N.J. 516, 643 A.2d 972 (1994). The court used the standard of defamation stated in *Romaine*. Turning first to "content," the court relied largely on a passage from comment *e* to § 566 of the Restatement:

> There are some statements that . . . cannot reasonably be understood to be meant literally and seriously and are obviously mere vituperation and abuse. A certain amount of vulgar name-calling is frequently resorted to by angry people without any real intent to make a defamatory assertion, and it is properly understood by reasonable listeners to amount to nothing more. This is true particularly when it is obvious that the speaker has lost his temper and is merely giving vent to insult. Thus when, in the course of an altercation, the defendant loudly and angrily calls the plaintiff a bastard in the presence of others, he is ordinarily not reasonably to be understood as asserting the fact that plaintiff is of illegitimate birth but only to be abusing him to his face.

Can you think of a situation where the use of "bastard" would be actionable? As to "context," the court stressed the face-to-face confrontation distinguishing words uttered in that context from "words written after time for thought or published in a newspaper [that] may be taken to express the defamatory charge and to be intended to be taken seriously." (The court relied to some extent on a third criterion—"verifiability"—that is discussed in detail at p. 1006, infra, but was not central here.)

As to "bitch," as used here, a reasonable listener "would interpret the term to indicate merely that the speaker disliked Mrs. Ward and is otherwise inarticulate."

As to "dislikes [or hates] Jews," the court also found relevant a line of cases concluding that such political charges had become so common in recent years that they had lost content, citing Stevens v. Tillman, 855 F.2d 394 (7th Cir.1988), cert. denied 489 U.S. 1065 (1989)(charge of being a "racist" is not actionable because word has "been watered down by overuse, becoming common coin in political discourse"). A charge of bigotry might be defamatory if it alleged specific acts, such as making racist statements, or denying employment to another because of race or religion, but there was no such charge or implication in these facts.

6. *Libel by implication.* What if each fact reported in an article is true but they are stated in such a way that the ordinary reader reaches a false, and defamatory, conclusion? In Healey v. New England Newspapers, Inc., 555 A.2d 321 (R.I.), cert. denied 493 U.S. 814 (1989), defendant reported that a man who had been involved in a personnel dispute with the local YMCA had had a heart attack and died while he was participating in a rally about 200 yards from a YMCA board meeting. The story continued that the family of the deceased was angry because they felt he "should have been given early attention by either a doctor or a paramedic at the board meeting." The next paragraph began "Dr. Paul J. Healey is Y president and was at the meeting when Lampinski collapsed." How are these two sentences to be read?

The court upheld a jury verdict and judgment for $302,000. Looking at the evidence in the most favorable light to plaintiff, the court thought a reader could understand that "plaintiff was asked and refused to help Lampinski and that there was enough time for plaintiff to render aid to Lampinski."

The drawing of inferences may be essential to the analysis of many, if not most, defamation cases. Although this presented no special problems at common law, some constitutional questions have been raised. We review these at p. 949, infra.

Remember that ambiguity must be distinguished from the situation in which readers may understand a statement differently because of different backgrounds they bring to the material. Is there a difference between bringing expertise to a subject and simply knowing more about the facts than most readers? In Ben–Oliel v. Press Publishing Co., 251 N.Y. 250, 167 N.E. 432 (1929), the plaintiff, an expert on Palestinian art and customs, was falsely stated to have written an article on that subject that appeared in the defendant's Sunday newspaper. The article would have impressed virtually all the newspaper's regular readers. Unfortunately, the article had several errors that would lead fellow experts to think the writer incompetent. The court held that a jury could find that plaintiff had been defamed in the eyes of the very small number of experts even though they were overwhelmed in number by the ordinary readers.

On this subject, the Second Restatement's section 559 comment *e* states that to be actionable the content of a statement must be of the sort that would hurt the plaintiff "in the eyes of a substantial and respectable minority" of the community. Was the minority substantial in the *Ben–Oliel* case? Should it have to be? The question of whether the minority is "respectable," or needs to be, is raised in the following case.

Matherson v. Marchello

New York Appellate Division, Second Department, 1984.
100 App.Div.2d 233, 473 N.Y.S.2d 998.

■ TITONE, J.P.

. . .

On October 28, 1980, radio station WBAB conducted an interview with the members of a singing group called "The Good Rats." Following a commercial which advertised a Halloween party at an establishment known as "OBI", a discussion ensued in which various members of the group explained that they are no longer permitted to play at OBI South because:

"Good Rat # 1:	Well, you know, we had that law suit with Mr. Matherson.
"A Good Rat:	And we used to fool around with his wife.
"Good Rat # 1:	And we won.
"A Good Rat:	One of us used to fool around with his wife. He wasn't into that too much.
"D.J.:	Oh yea.
"Good Rat # 1: (interrupted and joined by another Good Rat)	We used to start off our gigs over there with the National Anthem, and he was very upset about that, now all of a sudden he's very patriotic and he's using it in his commercials.
"A Good Rat:	I don't think it was his wife that he got so upset about, I think it was when somebody started messing around with his boyfriend that he really freaked out. Really. (Laughter) That did it man."

Plaintiffs, who are husband and wife, subsequently commenced this action against "The Good Rats" (as individuals and against their record company), alleging that the words "we used to fool around with his wife" and "I don't think it was his wife that he got upset about, I think it was when somebody started messing around with his boyfriend that he really freaked out" were defamatory. They seek compensatory and punitive damages for humiliation, mental anguish, loss of reputation and injury to their marital relationship as well as for the loss of customers, business opportunities and good will allegedly suffered by Mr. Matherson. [The lower court] granted defendants' motion to dismiss. . . .

. . .

On the question of whether the allegedly defamatory statements are actionable, our scope of review is limited. . . . Unless we can say, as a matter of law, that the statements could not have had a defamatory connotation, it is for the jury to decide whether or not they did [ ].

Taken in the context of a rock and roll station's interview with musicians, and taking note of contemporary usage, we have no difficulty in concluding that the words "fooling around with his wife" could have been interpreted by listeners to mean that Mrs. Matherson was having an affair with one of the defendants. Such charges are clearly libelous. . . .

The second comment—"I don't think it was his wife that he got upset about, I think it was when somebody started messing around with his boyfriend that he really freaked out"—presents a far more subtle and difficult question (see Imputation of Homosexuality as Defamation, Ann., 3 A.L.R.4th 752). It is plaintiffs' contention that this statement constitutes an imputation of homosexuality which should be recognized as defamatory. Defendants, on the other hand, basically do not deny that such reading is plausible. Rather, they claim that many public officials have acknowledged their homosexuality and, therefore, no social stigma may be attached to such an allegation. We are constrained to reject defendants' position at this point in time.

It cannot be said that social opprobrium of homosexuality does not remain with us today. Rightly or wrongly, many individuals still view homosexuality as immoral (see Newsweek Aug. 8, 1983, p. 33, containing the results of a Gallup poll; [   ]). Legal sanctions imposed upon homosexuals in areas ranging from immigration (Matter of Longstaff, 716 F.2d 1439) to military service (Watkins v. United States Army, 721 F.2d 687) have recently been reaffirmed despite the concurring Judge's observation in *Watkins* (p. 691) that it "demonstrates a callous disregard for the progress American law and society have made toward acknowledging that an individual's choice of life style is not the concern of government, but a fundamental aspect of personal liberty" [   ].

which individuals

In short, despite the fact that an increasing number of homosexuals are publicly expressing satisfaction and even pride in their status, the potential and probable harm of a false charge of homosexuality, in terms of social and economic impact, cannot be ignored. Thus, on the facts of this case, where the plaintiffs are husband and wife, we find, given the narrow scope of review, that the imputation of homosexuality is "reasonably susceptible of a defamatory connotation". . . .

[The order of dismissal was reversed.]

■ THOMPSON, BRACKEN, and RUBIN, JJ., concur.

NOTES AND QUESTIONS

1. Applying the principles developed so far, is the first charge ("fooling around") defamatory as a matter of law—or is it a jury question?

2. The implication of homosexuality raises the question of what attributes we must ascribe to the "ordinary reader" or recipient of the message. It is one thing to ascribe certain reading abilities and certain intelligence. Now must we ask about the value systems of those who receive the message? The court looks to a survey that shows that "many" Americans "still view homosexuality as immoral." Is that the right question? What about those within the listening audience of WBAB? Or is it the views of those that plaintiff cares most about—those who learn about the statement who are in his social, business, or religious circle?

3. In Grant v. Reader's Digest Ass'n, 151 F.2d 733 (2d Cir.1945), cert. denied 326 U.S. 797 (1946), defendant published an article calling the plaintiff (a lawyer) "a legislative representative for the Massachusetts Communist Party." Judge L. Hand stated the question to be whether it was defamatory "to write of a lawyer that he has acted as agent of the Communist Party and is a believer in its aims and methods." Defendant argued that under New York law the question was whether "right thinking" persons would find the assertion defamatory. The court responded that a person "may value his reputation even among those who do not

embrace the prevailing moral standards; and it would seem that the jury should be allowed to appraise how far he should be indemnified for the disesteem of such persons." It suffices "if there be some, as there certainly are," who would think ill of the plaintiff as the result of defendant's assertion "even though they would be 'wrong-thinking' people if they did."

4. Consider the following examples in terms of the nature of defamation and the role of minority attitudes:

a. A statement that the plaintiff was seduced by "the mad monk," Rasputin. Youssoupoff v. Metro–Goldwyn–Mayer Pictures, Ltd., 50 T.L.R. 581, 99 A.L.R. 964 (Eng.C.A.1934). A statement that Rasputin raped the plaintiff.

b. A statement that the plaintiff is of illegitimate birth. Shelby v. Sun Printing & Publishing Ass'n, 38 Hun 474 (1886), affirmed on the opinion below 109 N.Y. 611, 15 N.E. 895 (1888). Can it ever be defamatory to say that someone is of legitimate birth? Has the notion of "illegitimacy" lost its power to defame?

c. A letter from a woman with whom plaintiff had previously been "romantically involved" to a woman with whom plaintiff now had a "personal relationship" stating that plaintiff was "not divorced." Vereen v. Clayborne, 623 A.2d 1190 (D.C.App.1993).

d. A statement that a reputable physician illegally terminated life support services on a terminally ill patient who was in great pain and who had stated in writing several times that he wished to die. Might it be defamatory to say that the physician refused the patient's request to do so?

e. A statement that the plaintiff, who owns a service station and truck stop, reports to the Interstate Commerce Commission the names of truckers who violate I.C.C. rules limiting the number of consecutive hours they may work. Connelly v. McKay, 176 Misc. 685, 28 N.Y.S.2d 327 (1941). Might it be defamatory to say that plaintiff did not report such violators?

What about a story erroneously accusing a mobster of missing his target? See Note, The Community Segment in Defamation Actions: A Dissenting Essay, 58 Yale L.J. 1387 (1949).

For an extensive consideration of the nature of the tort and the interests it might vindicate, see Post, The Social Foundations of Defamation Law: Reputation and the Constitution, 74 Calif.L.Rev. 691 (1986).

5. *Parody.* Should a court accept a defendant's argument that a statement presented as fact is so preposterous it could not be taken seriously? A supermarket tabloid made that argument in Mitchell v. Globe International Publishing, Inc., 773 F.Supp. 1235 (W.D.Ark.1991). Under the headline "World's oldest newspaper carrier, 101, quits because she's pregnant!" the Sun published a story saying that a woman who had been delivering papers in Australia for 94 years became pregnant by a man she met on her paper route. The story was accompanied by a photo of plaintiff, a 96–year old newsstand operator in Mountain Home, Arkansas.

The defendant moved for summary judgment on the ground the story could not be understood to describe actual facts about the plaintiff, in part because "every one is well aware that it is physically impossible for a 101– or 96–year–old woman to be pregnant." The court denied the motion, considering "the surrounding circumstances in which the statements were made, the medium by which they were published, and the audience for which they were intended." Even if the facts stated in the headline could not be believed, the implication of sexual promiscuity could, the judge said. "The articles are written in a purportedly factual manner. . . . The Sun apparently intends for the readers to determine which articles are fact and which are fiction or what percentage of a given article is fact or fiction." The case proceeded to trial and a jury returned a general verdict for the newspaper on the libel claim but awarded Mitchell substantial damages on the alternate theory of false light invasion of privacy, discussed in Chapter XIV.

Compare San Francisco Bay Guardian, Inc. v. Superior Court, 17 Cal.App.4th 655, 21 Cal.Rptr.2d 464 (1993), in which the newspaper's April Fool's edition carried a purported letter from plaintiff landlord asserting such things as that his tenants behaved better after electroshock therapy. Plaintiff presented five readers—his accountant, his attorney, a fellow club member, an acquaintance, and a co-owner of several buildings—who did not understand the parody and took the letter seriously.

The trial court's refusal to dismiss the complaint was reversed on appeal. The average reader, considering the entire newspaper, and the parody section, would understand the parody. The table of contents announced that the edition contained a "special parody section." That section appeared at the end of the regular paper and was printed upside down. It began with a picture of the publisher taking a position "at odds with the usual editorial stance of the Bay Guardian. The parody portion continued with mock articles and pictures, some of which are recognizable as jokes at first glance." Although the letters to the editor were not so obvious, the point was clear there too: the paper announced that it welcomed letters and that "Copies of all unsigned letters will be sent to the Federal Bureau of Investigation for cross-checking. In case of accident, we will notify next of kin."

Could this analysis have been applied to support the Sun's arguments in the *Mitchell* case?

2.   "OF AND CONCERNING" PLAINTIFF

Identification. In addition to showing the defamatory nature of the publication, the plaintiff must show that the statement was understood to refer to, though not necessarily aimed at, the plaintiff. This is not difficult if the plaintiff is named or clearly identified in the publication, but sometimes the requirement can raise serious questions. This element is often called "colloquium" and establishes that the plaintiff is the person (or among the persons) defamed.

A fairly common problem arises from the use of generic file photographs to illustrate a story in the print medium. See, e.g., Morrell v. Forbes, Inc., 603 F.Supp. 1305 (D.Mass.1985)(plaintiff fisherman's photo used to illustrate story about organized crime on the Boston waterfront). See also Clark v. American Broadcasting Cos., Inc., 684 F.2d 1208 (6th Cir.1982), cert. denied 460 U.S. 1040 (1983), involving a program about prostitution. The plaintiff, who had been photographed without her knowledge while walking on a city street, was shown on the screen while the narrator was describing the prevalence of prostitution in the neighborhood. (For the special problems of identification of plaintiffs in works of fiction, see Symposium, Defamation in Fiction, 51 Brooklyn L.Rev. 223 (1985)).

Corporations. It is clear that corporations may be defamation plaintiffs. Section 561 of the Second Restatement states that a corporation for profit may sue if "the matter tends to prejudice it in the conduct of its business or to deter others from dealing with it." A corporation that is not for profit may sue if it "depends upon financial support from the public, and the matter tends to interfere with its activities by prejudicing it in public estimation."

A separate question involves the relationship between a corporation and its shareholders. If the corporation is large and its stock widely held, courts generally conclude that stockholders may not sue for the libel of the corporation. But in closely held corporations, courts have held that a libel of the corporation may be understood by the reasonable audience to be addressed as well to the controlling individuals, even if they are not mentioned in the story. This result is even clearer if the individual and the corporation have the same name. See discussion in Schiavone Construction Co. v. Time Inc., 619 F.Supp. 684 (D.N.J.1985).

Group libel. Different problems arise when the statement is about one or more members of a group of individuals. In such cases might one member be able to claim that the statement hurt his or her personal reputation? At the extreme, an attack on all lawyers in the United States or on all clergymen would be held to be such a general broadside that no individual lawyer or clergyman could sue. The same would be true of broadside attacks on racial, religious, or ethnic groups.

At the other extreme, it is generally accepted that a charge made against a small group may defame all members of that group. For example, a newspaper article may assert that "the officers" of a corporation have embezzled funds. There are only four officers of the corporation. Each of them may be found to have been defamed, even though the statement was that "one of the officers of the corporation" had embezzled funds. The group is small enough so that all four officials are put under a shadow, and most states would permit all four to sue.

As the group grows larger the impact of the statement may depend on the inclusiveness of the language as well as the size of the total group. In one case, a defamatory charge was made against one unidentified member of a 21–member police force. All 21 sued. The trial court's dismissal was affirmed. It was feared that allowing the action would permit a suit by an entire baseball team over a report that one member was disciplined for brawling. Such a result "would chill communication to the marrow." The court explained, "By no stretch of imagination can it be thought to suggest that the conduct of the one [described in the article] is typical of all. Noting the individual's membership in the group does not suggest a common determinant of character so much as simply a practical reference point." But suppose the charge had been against "all but one" of the members of that police force? Such a statement may reflect on each member of the force. Arcand v. Evening Call Publishing Co., 567 F.2d 1163 (1st Cir.1977).

One case presented three aspects of this problem. A book about Dallas stated that "some" Neiman–Marcus department store models were "call girls. . . . The salesgirls are good, too—pretty and often much cheaper. . . ." And "most of the [male] sales staff are fairies, too."

Suits were filed by all nine models, 30 of the 382 saleswomen, and 15 of the 25 salesmen. The defendants did not challenge the right of the nine models to sue. The other two groups were challenged as being too large.

The claim of "the salesgirls" was dismissed. The result would be the same even if the authors had explicitly referred to "all"—and even if all 382 had sued. The judge cited cases rejecting suits when the statements attacked all officials of a statewide union or all the taxicab drivers in Washington, D.C.

On the other hand, the salesmen's case was not dismissed. It was close to others involving members of a posse, or the 12 doctors on a hospital's residential staff. Would the result have been the same if the authors had referred to "some" or "a few" of the men? Neiman–Marcus v. Lait, 13 F.R.D. 311 (S.D.N.Y.1952).

Would the legal system find it administratively difficult to handle a damage action brought by 382 plaintiffs, even though they might deserve some compensation? Is the development of class actions relevant here?

One court has rejected the emphasis on the absolute size of the group in favor of the defined nature of the group, its prominence, and the role of the individual in the group. Using these criteria, the court concluded that 53 members of the 71–member police force of Newburgh, N.Y., in 1972 could sue for a statement in 1979 suggesting that, although they were not indicted for misdeeds along with 18 colleagues, the other 53 must have known what was going on. Brady v. Ottaway Newspapers, Inc., 84 App. Div.2d 226, 445 N.Y.S.2d 786 (1981).

Although defamation of large groups—ethnic, religious, professional— does not result in a cause of action in any state, some states have sought to develop criminal sanctions against such attacks. Although these were held constitutional, 5–4, in Beauharnais v. Illinois, 343 U.S. 250 (1952)(upholding statute barring portrayals of "depravity, criminality, unchastity, or lack of virtue of a class of citizens, of any race, color, creed, or religion" that subjected that group to "contempt, derision, or obloquy or which is produc-

894-928

tive of breach of the peace or riots"), they have been put in some doubt by R.A.V. v. City of St. Paul, 505 U.S. 377 (1992)(invalidating city ordinance punishing anyone who places on public or private property any "symbol, object, appellation, characterization or graffiti, including but not limited to, a burning cross or Nazi swastika, which one knows or has reasonable grounds to know arouses anger, alarm or resentment in others on the basis of race, color, creed, religions or gender").

Apart from constitutional questions, some have argued that the statutes often have the effect of making martyrs of racists and other bigots who can claim that their civil liberties are being violated when they are prosecuted. In addition, it gives such speakers a powerful platform from which to repeat their statements. Others have argued in favor of such statutes. See Arkes, Civility and the Restriction of Speech: Rediscovering the Defamation of Groups, 1974 Sup.Ct.Rev. 281; Note, Group Vilification Reconsidered, 89 Yale L.J. 308 (1979)(justifying criminal punishment of group vilifications involving false statements that bypass the conscious faculties of recipients).

3. STRICT LIABILITY

The common law often held a publisher strictly liable for defamatory statements. Thus, the case was established even if the offending statement appeared to be either neutral or positive, but, when supplemented by other facts, unknown to defendant, turned out to be defamatory. For example, a newspaper might, based on reliable information, incorrectly report a baby's birth. If some readers knew that its parents had been married only three months, the newspaper would be held to have committed defamation because in the eyes of those readers who knew the additional fact the newspaper story suggested unchastity. If a magazine carries what it believes to be fiction but readers reasonably think the words refer to an identifiable plaintiff, a defamation may be found. These subjects are discussed at length in Smith, Jones v. Hulton: Three Conflicting Views as to Defamation, 60 U.Pa.L.Rev. 365, 461 (1912); Holdsworth, A Chapter of Accidents in the Law of Libel, 57 L.Q.Rev. 74 (1941).

In fact, the common law did not impose strict liability on what were viewed as disseminators of the finished product—newsstands, bookstores, and libraries. These institutions were held liable only if the plaintiff could establish that the defendant knew or had reason to know of the presence of the defamation in the work being sold or loaned. The common law may well develop a similar treatment for computer bulletin boards. Cubby, Inc. v. CompuServe, Inc., 776 F.Supp. 135 (S.D.N.Y.1991); Becker, The Liability of Computer Bulletin Board Operators for Defamation Posted by Others, 22 Conn.L.Rev. 203 (1989).

Compare Stratton Oakmont, Inc. v. Prodigy Services Co., 23 Med. L.Rptr. 1794 (N.Y.Sup.1995), in which a trial judge held that Prodigy was potentially liable for defamatory statements by a user of one of its bulletin boards because Prodigy "held itself out as an on-line service that exercised editorial control over the content of messages posted on its computer bulletin boards, thereby expressly differentiating itself from its competition and expressly likening itself to a newspaper. . . ." *Cubby* was distinguishable because CompuServe had no opportunity to review the contents of the publication at issue before it was uploaded. The judge said that "the fear that this Court's finding of publisher status for Prodigy will compel all computer networks to abdicate control of their bulletin boards incorrectly presumes that the market will refuse to compensate a network for its increased control and the resulting increased exposure." The case was settled with the publication of a letter from Prodigy stating that it was "sorry if the offensive statements concerning [plaintiffs] which were posted on [the board] by an unauthorized and unidentified individual, in any way caused injury to their reputation." Is this an "apology"? See Sandberg, *Securities Company That Had Sued Prodigy Services for Libel Drops Suit,* Wall St.J., Oct. 25, 1995 at B3.

Although, as we shall see shortly, the common law developed a few privileges that softened the rigors of strict liability on original publishers, strict liability remained a fixture of the tort well into this century. As we shall see, most of the constitutional development is traceable to this feature.

4. DAMAGES: LIBEL AND SLANDER

Generally, in tort law, plaintiffs are entitled to recover damages for harm they can prove they sustained. Defamation generally—but not always—permits successful plaintiffs to recover proven damages. These may include such proven lost wages and similar losses, as well as proven damages for broad reputational loss. The first type, called "special damages," includes specific identifiable pecuniary losses that the plaintiff can prove he or she sustained and can trace to the defendant's defamatory statement.

The second type, "general damages," includes damages to reputation that the plaintiff has suffered in ways that cannot be easily correlated with dollars and cents. This is usually a claim that the plaintiff has suffered general reputational harm in some community—whether it be a geographical community or one based on, say, religious, social, or professional relationships. Sometimes the plaintiff is able to prove that these losses have occurred—as, for example, by an opinion poll that reveals a massive loss of reputation—even though the damages sustained from that loss are not as obvious as a doctor's bill.

Defamation law has two aspects that are unlike tort law generally. One is that plaintiffs sometimes can recover "presumed" general damages—without proving that they have suffered any actual damage, whether special or general. In awarding damages for "presumed" general damages, the trier is to consider the words used, the medium used, and the predicted response of the community. The other unusual feature is that sometimes the plaintiff must prove the existence of special damages before being allowed to recover *any* general damages—even if plaintiff can prove that the general damages occurred.

[handwritten margin note: How defamation is different from ordinary tort law]

The operation of these two unusual damage rules means that some plaintiffs may receive a substantial recovery without proof of any damages, while others may recover nothing at all because they were required, but were unable, to prove special damages and then were barred from recovering any general damages whether provable or presumed, in cases in which most people would recognize that the plaintiffs had been seriously harmed.

The determination of what damages plaintiffs must prove in defamation cases is largely rooted in history, and requires the introduction of the terms "libel" and "slander." When the relevant damage rules evolved, slanders, generally oral defamations, were sued upon in the common law courts. Libels, generally written defamations, had become a major concern of the English government because of the recent development of printing. Libels were addressed in the Court of Star Chamber. After the Star Chamber was abolished, oral and written defamation were both redressed by the common law courts. Those courts, however, preserved some damage distinctions between the two types of defamation that have survived to our day.

The following case explores the role of the libel-slander distinction.

Matherson v. Marchello

New York Appellate Division, Second Department, 1984.
100 App.Div.2d 233, 473 N.Y.S.2d 998.

[This is the same case reported earlier. In that excerpt, the court considered whether the passages were defamatory. Here the further question is whether the plaintiff must prove special damages in order to proceed with the case.]

■ TITONE, J.P.

. . .

Preliminarily, we observe that if special damages are a necessary ingredient of plaintiffs' cause of action, Special Term properly found the allegations of the complaint to be deficient.

Special damages consist of "the loss of something having economic or pecuniary value" (Restatement, Torts 2d, § 575, Comment b) which "must flow directly from the injury to reputation caused by the defamation; not from the [emotional] effects of defamation" [ ] and it is settled law that they must be fully and accurately identified "with sufficient particularity to identify actual losses" [ ]. When loss of business is claimed, the persons who ceased to be customers must be named and the losses itemized [ ]. "Round figures" or a general allegation of a dollar amount as special damages do not suffice [ ]. Consequently, plaintiffs' nonspecific conclusory allegations do not meet the stringent requirements imposed for pleading special damages [ ].

We must, therefore, determine whether an allegation of special damages is necessary. In large measure, this turns on which branch of the law of defamation is involved. As a result of historical accident, which, though not sensibly defensible today, is so well settled as to be beyond our ability to uproot it [ ], there is a schism between the law governing slander and the law governing libel [ ].[1]

A plaintiff suing in slander must plead special damages unless the defamation falls into any one of four per se categories [allegations (1) of commission of a crime; (2) that harm trade or business; (3) of a loathsome disease; (4) of unchastity in a woman—all discussed in the following case]. *Slander*

On the other hand, a plaintiff suing in libel need not plead or prove special damages. . . . Thus, unlike the law of slander, in the law of libel the existence of damage is conclusively presumed from the publication itself and a plaintiff may rely on general damages. . . . *Libel*

. . .

Traditionally, the demarcation between libel and slander rested upon whether the words were written or spoken [ ]. Written defamations were considered far more serious because, at the time the distinction arose, few persons could read or write and, therefore, anything which was written would carry a louder ring of purported truth [ ]. In addition, a written defamation could be disseminated more widely and carried a degree of permanence.

With the advent of mass communication, the differential was blurred. Motion pictures were held to be libel [ ]. No set rule developed with respect to radio and television [ ]. In some cases, distinction was drawn between [extemporaneous] speech, which was classified as slander, and words read from a script, which were classified as libel [ ]. This distinction was the subject of considerable criticism.

We today hold that defamation which is broadcast by means of radio or television should be classified as libel. As we have noted, one of the primary reasons assigned to justify the imposition of broader liability for libel than for slander has been the greater capacity for harm that a writing is assumed to have because of the wide range of dissemination consequent upon its permanence in form. Given the vast and far-flung audiences reached by the broadcasting media today, it is self-evident that the potential harm to a defamed person is far greater than that involved in a single writing (see Hartmann v. Winchell, [296 N.Y. 296, 304, 73 N.E.2d 30 (1947)], Fuld, J. concurring). Section 568A of the Restatement of Torts, Second, and the more recent decisions in sister States [ ] opt for holding such defamation to be libel and we perceive no basis for perpetuating a meaningless, outmoded, distinction. *In NY TV & radio = libel*

[The court concluded that neither charge required special damages, and reversed the lower court's dismissal and reinstated the complaint.]

1. . . . The distinction has . . . not gone unchallenged. As early as 1812, a defendant urged that a libel read by one person should not be treated more harshly than a slander spoken to hundreds in a crowd. While the Judge conceded the merits of the argument, he refused to overturn the firmly rooted contrary precedents. Thorley v. Lord Kerry [4 Taunt. 355, 128 Eng.Rep. 367 (1812)].

NOTES AND QUESTIONS

1. Which of the justifications offered for the differing treatment of written and oral defamation is strongest? In addition to those offered by the court, consider the notion that a writing still may be given more weight because it requires more thought and planning than a spontaneous oral utterance, which might simply be tossed off. (California, by statute, [Civil Code §§ 46 and 48.5(4)], treats defamations by radio and television as slander.)

2. Although most libels and slanders are conveyed by the use of words or writing, other actions may suffice. See, e.g., K–Mart Corp. v. Washington, 109 Nev. 1180, 866 P.2d 274 (1993), concluding that marching the handcuffed plaintiff customer through defendant's store to the security office was an actionable pantomime that imputed shoplifting and thus was slander per se. But see Bolton v. Department of Human Services, 540 N.W.2d 523 (Minn.1995), in which the court refused to find a defamation when defendant's supervisor silently accompanied plaintiff to the exit door of defendant's facility immediately after plaintiff was discharged. The court observed that in this context "where there is no word spoken or conduct other than a simple escorting" there can be no defamation.

3. In some states, including New York, the answer to the special damages question is complete once the publication has been called libel because in those states libel never requires special damages. In a second group of states, however, even if the statement is called libel, special damages must be shown unless the defamatory sting is clear on its face or, if not clear on its face, the sting, when fleshed out with extrinsic facts, fits into one of the four types of slander per se.

The terms "per se" and "per quod" have different meanings in libel and slander. Consider the following excerpt from R. Sack & S. Baron, Libel, Slander, and Related Problems 134–35 (2d ed. 1994):

> As a practical matter, words that, uttered orally, are slanderous per se, are usually also libelous per se when written. But the reason they are slanderous per se normally has little to do with the reason that they are libelous per se. To say of a woman that she is a whore or of a man that he robs his business associates blind is slanderous per se because it falls within one of the four categories. The same words when written are libelous per se, not because they fit within a slander category, but because they tend on their face to disgrace the person about whom they are written.
>
> Extrinsic facts are unnecessary to explain their defamatory meaning. But the converse is not true. Statements which are libelous per se when written often are not slanderous per se when spoken. However degrading a statement, however injurious to reputation, however outrageous, however plain the defamatory meaning on the face of the statement and therefore however clear that the statement when written is libelous per se, unless the defamatory charge falls within one of the four specific slander categories, it is not slanderous per se when

merely spoken, and "special damages" must be pleaded and proved. To call someone a "coward," for example, is libelous per se but probably not slanderous per se.

Here a footnote states: "Unless the plaintiff is a policeman, professional soldier, or in a similar category, so that an imputation of cowardice tends to injure plaintiff in his or her trade, business, or profession."

Even if special damages must be proven, a plaintiff who is able to do so becomes eligible for general damages as well.

Liberman v. Gelstein

Court of Appeals of New York, 1992.
80 N.Y.2d 429, 605 N.E.2d 344, 590 N.Y.S.2d 857.

[Plaintiff landlord sued a member of the tenants' board of governors for slander. This case involves the second and fifth causes of action. In the second, defendant is alleged to have had the following exchange with Kohler, a fellow member of the board of directors:

"Gelstein: Can you find out from your friend at the precinct which cop is on the take from Liberman?

"Kohler: What are you talking about?

"Gelstein: There is a cop on the take from Liberman. That's why none of the building's cars ever get tickets—they can park anywhere because Liberman's paid them off. He gives them a hundred or two hundred a week."

The fifth cause of action alleged that defendant made the following statement in the presence of employees of the building: "Liberman threw a punch at me. He screamed at my wife and daughter. He called my daughter a slut and threatened to kill me and my family."]

■ KAYE, JUDGE.

. . .

. . . After discovery, defendant sought summary judgment dismissing the complaint. On the second cause of action, defendant invoked the "common interest" qualified privilege, characterizing his conversation with Kohler, a colleague on the board of governors, as an inquiry designed to uncover wrongdoing by the landlord affecting tenants. At his deposition, defendant testified that several vehicles operated by the building's management regularly parked in front of the building beyond the legal limit but never received parking summonses. He further testified that he was told by two building employees, whom he identified, that Liberman was bribing the police to avoid parking tickets. Defendant admitted that he did not know whether the allegations were true, but testified that they "sounded truthful" to him. Accordingly, defendant testified that he approached Kohler—whose friend was captain of the local police precinct—in an effort to discover whether the allegations were true.

. . .

[On the fifth cause of action, defendant argued that the statements were either true, not defamatory, or never made. The lower court dismissed the second cause of action on the ground that it was qualifiedly privileged and that plaintiff had failed to raise triable issues of malice. The fifth cause of action was dismissed on the ground that the words could only have been understood by those who were familiar with the parties' history of conflict as rhetorical hyperbole. The Appellate Division affirmed.]

II.

Slander as a rule is not actionable unless the plaintiff suffers special damage. [ ] Special damages contemplate "the loss of something having economic or pecuniary value" (Restatement § 575, comment *b*; [ ]). Plaintiff has not alleged special damages, and thus his slander claims are not sustainable unless they fall within one of the exceptions to the rule.

The four established exceptions (collectively "slander per se") consist of statements (i) charging plaintiff with a serious crime; (ii) that tend to injure another in his or her trade, business or profession; (iii) that plaintiff has a loathsome disease; or (iv) imputing unchastity to a woman [ ]. When statements fall within one of these categories, the law presumes that damages will result, and they need not be alleged or proven.

Plaintiff claims that both sets of statements were slanderous per se inasmuch as they charged him with criminal conduct. Not every imputation of unlawful behavior, however, is slanderous per se. "With the extension of criminal punishment to many minor offenses, it was obviously necessary to make some distinction as to the character of the crime, since a charge of a traffic violation, for example, would not exclude a person from society, and today would do little, if any, harm to his [or her] reputation at all" (Prosser [ ]). Thus, the law distinguishes between serious and relatively minor offenses, and only statements regarding the former are actionable without proof of damage (see, Restatement § 571, comment *g* [list of crimes actionable as per se slander includes murder, burglary, larceny, arson, rape, kidnapping]).

We agree with plaintiff that defendant's alleged statement that "[t]here is a cop on the take from Liberman" charges a serious crime— bribery (see, Penal Law § 200.00; [ ]). Accordingly, the statements constituting the second cause of action are actionable without the need to establish special harm, and absent any privilege would be sufficient to go to a jury.

We disagree, however, with plaintiff's contention that the statement "Liberman * * * threatened to kill me and my family" was slanderous per se. Plaintiff claims these words falsely attributed to him the commission of the crime of harassment (see, Penal Law § 240.25; [ ]). Harassment is a relatively minor offense in the New York Penal Law—not even a misdemeanor—and thus the harm to the reputation of a person falsely accused of committing harassment would be correspondingly insubstantial. Hence, even if we agreed with plaintiff that the statement would not have been construed by the listeners as rhetorical hyperbole, the cause of action must nevertheless be dismissed because it is not slanderous per se to claim that someone committed harassment.

Plaintiff alternatively argues that the statements in the fifth cause of action tended to harm him in his business as a property owner, and thus are actionable under the "trade, business or profession" exception. That exception, however, is "limited to defamation of a kind incompatible with the proper conduct of the business, trade, profession or office itself. The statement must be made with reference to a matter of significance and importance for that purpose, rather than a more general reflection upon the plaintiff's character or qualities" (Prosser [   ]). Thus, "charges against a clergyman of drunkenness and other moral misconduct affect his fitness for the performance of the duties of his profession, although the same charges against a business man or tradesman do not so affect him" (Restatement § 573, comment *c*). The statements at issue are unrelated to plaintiff's status as a landlord, and therefore do not fall into the "trade, business or profession" exception [   ].

In sum, the second cause of action is on its face sustainable without special damages because it involves charges of serious crime, and the fifth cause of action was correctly dismissed.

[The court concluded that the plaintiff had not presented enough to overcome defendant's privilege as to the bribery charge. The dismissal of the second cause of action was affirmed. We return to this issue at p. 905.]

■ SIMONS, ACTING C.J., and TITONE, HANCOCK and BELLACOSA, JJ., concur with KAYE, J. [JUDGE SMITH dissented in part on an issue related to privilege, discussed infra].

NOTES AND QUESTIONS

1. Why does the second cause of action not require special damages? Why does the fifth cause of action require them? What kinds of special damages might a plaintiff in this situation be able to show?

2. What is so special about these four categories of words? In Nazeri v. Missouri Valley College, 860 S.W.2d 303 (Mo.1993), the court extended the fourth category to any "serious sexual misconduct" following the Second Restatement's gender-neutral approach in § 569, comment *f*.

In *Ward v. Zelikovsky*, p. 886, supra, involving the statement a meeting of condominium owners, the lower court had found the charge of bigotry was actionable and then decided that it did not need special damages. The court reached that position by adding a fifth category to the slander per se list for imputations of racial or ethnic bigotry. In reversing on the ground that the statement was not actionable, the supreme court noted its refusal to add new categories to the four existing ones: the "trend of modern tort law is to focus on the injury not the wrong and the slander per se categories are a relic from tort law's previous age." It left for "another day'' the question of whether to abolish the slander per se categories and require special damages for all slanders.   See Anderson, Reputation, Compensation, and Proof, 25 Wm. & Mary L.Rev. 747 (1984).

3.   In addition to general and special damages, two other classifications loom large in defamation law: nominal damages and punitive damages.   Although nominal damages are unimportant in most tort actions, they may be central in defamation cases.   The award of a symbolic amount such as six cents usually shows that the jury found the attack to be false but also found the words not to have hurt, either because the speaker was not credible or the plaintiff's strong reputation blunted the harm (or his reputation was so low nothing could really hurt it).   See Reynolds v. Pegler, 223 F.2d 429 (2d Cir.), cert. denied 350 U.S. 846 (1955)(upholding a jury award of $1 in compensatory damages and $175,000 in punitive damages against the various defendants.)

4.   Several states at common law have rejected the concept of punitive damages in all tort cases; others have sharply limited the amount of such damages.   Recall p. 670, supra.   Some states have decided to bar punitive damages only in defamation cases and other tort cases involving harm through speech.   As we shall see shortly, recent federal and state constitutional developments may also restrict the availability of such damages in libel cases.

5.   DEFENSES

In this section we consider the variety of state common law or statutory defenses to the basic defamation claim.   Although traditional tort defenses such as consent apply, our focus here is on those defenses unique to defamation law.   See Baker v. Bhajan, 117 N.M. 278, 871 P.2d 374 (1994), applying the consent bar to a plaintiff who, when applying for a job with the state police, signed a contract that ''agreed to release from liability those who provided information . . .   under a guarantee of confidentiality'' when responding to inquiries from the police.

a.   TRUTH

The most obvious defense, but one little relied upon in litigation, is to prove the essential truth of the defamatory statement.   During the period when the English government rigorously used the law of criminal libel, truth was not a defense because unfavorable truths about government or officials were more likely to stir up anti-government attitudes and actions than were falsehoods.   But now truth is recognized as a complete defense to civil libel.   Because the action is intended to compensate those whose reputations are damaged falsely, if the defendant has spoken the truth, the reputational harm is deemed to provide no basis for an action.   (A minority of states purport to require the truth to have been spoken with ''good motives'' or for ''justifiable ends'' or both.)

The defendant need not prove literal truth but must establish the ''sting'' of the charge.   Thus, if the defendant has charged the plaintiff with stealing $25,000 from a bank, truth will be established even if the actual amount was only $12,000. In Masson v. New Yorker Magazine, Inc., 501 U.S. 496 (1991), the Court captured the common law's spirit in observing that the common law of libel "overlooks minor inaccuracies and concentrates upon substantial truth." Thus, the test was whether what was published "would have had a different effect upon the mind of the reader from that which the pleaded truth would have produced." See also Haynes v. Alfred A. Knopf, Inc., 8 F.3d 1222 (7th Cir.1993)(the law protects false "details that, while not trivial, would not if corrected have altered the picture that the true facts paint"). Compare Posadas v. City of Reno, 109 Nev. 448, 851 P.2d 438 (1993), holding actionable a claim based on defendant's false charge that plaintiff police officer had "admitted he lied under oath" (the crime of perjury) when in fact he had admitted to lying (not under oath) to two other officers who questioned him about the charges against him—apparently not a crime.

On the other hand, if the defendant cannot prove any theft whatever but can prove that the plaintiff is a bigamist, this information will not support the defense of truth. It may help mitigate damages to show that the plaintiff's reputation was already in low esteem for other reasons and thus the plaintiff has suffered less harm than might otherwise have occurred.

In Rouch v. Enquirer & News of Battle Creek, 440 Mich. 238, 487 N.W.2d 205 (1992), cert. denied 507 U.S. 967 (1993), defendant newspaper asserted that plaintiff had been "arrested and charged" with sexual assault of a babysitter and that he had been identified by his children. In fact, plaintiff had never been arraigned and he had been identified by the children of his ex-wife. The court upheld the defense of truth. "Charge" has become an umbrella term for all the stages of the criminal process and may be used as synonymous with "accused." The second was a minor inaccuracy. If the article had been written as the plaintiff says it should have been, the court could not "agree that the gist or sting of the article is changed by these minor differences." Should the result have been different if the article had appeared in a legal newspaper read overwhelmingly by lawyers?

The role of headlines needs special attention because of the difficulty of capturing the story in a few words. In Gunduz v. New York Post Co., 188 App.Div.2d 294, 590 N.Y.S.2d 494 (1992), the headline was "Public Enemy No.1" with a much smaller but adjacent sub-head "City moves to yank license of Apple's 'worst taxi driver.'" The story, about New York City's efforts to revoke plaintiff's taxi license, reported that he had received more summonses and violations than any other cab driver in the city, and described incidents of overcharging and abusing customers. The court thought the big headline "was a fair index of the truthful matter contained in the related news article."

Expungement. In Bahr v. Statesman Journal Co., 51 Or.App. 177, 624 P.2d 664 (1981), a newspaper reported that plaintiff, a candidate for public office, in an interview had "refused to discuss a 1964 conviction on an embezzlement charge. . . . 'I have no record of convictions. My record is clean. I have never been convicted of embezzlement.' " In fact, the conviction had occurred and had later been expunged under state law. The expungement statute gave plaintiff the right to deny that he had ever been convicted. But it also provided that the expungement itself could not be relied upon in a civil action in which the truth of the conviction was an element of the lawsuit. Thus, the newspaper's defense of truth succeeded. What result if the statute had not provided explicitly for the contingency of a libel suit?

Truth is little used as a defense, though it would enable a decisive confrontation, perhaps because most statements sued upon are false. Even where the defendant still thinks the statement true, it may be very expensive to establish that truth. A defendant relying on truth usually bears the legal costs of a full-dress trial as well as the sometimes major expense of investigating the matter and gathering enough evidence to ensure the outcome. Particularly when the charge involved is vague and does not allege specific events, the defense of truth may be quite expensive. It can also be risky, because a failed attempt to show truth may only impress the jury with the defendant's intransigence.

Recent constitutional developments have sharply altered the role of truth. See particularly p. 969, infra.

b. PRIVILEGES

Not only are there disadvantages to the defense of truth, there are attractive alternatives. Over the centuries the law of defamation has developed several privileges to protect those who utter defamations.

Absolute privileges. Some privileges are "absolute" in the sense that if the occasion gives rise to an absolute privilege, there will be no liability even if the speaker deliberately lied about the plaintiff. The most significant example of this narrow group is the federal and state constitutional privilege afforded legislators, who may not be sued for defamation for any statement made during debate. High executive officials, judges, and participants in judicial proceedings also have an absolute privilege to speak freely on matters relevant to their obligations. No matter how such a speaker abuses the privilege by lying, no tort liability will flow. See Barr v. Matteo, 360 U.S. 564 (1959).

In Carradine v. State of Minnesota, 511 N.W.2d 733 (Minn. 1994), the court considered immunity for an arresting officer's statements. The court noted that high level executive officials—the state's commissioner of the department of public welfare, for example—had absolute privilege. But the test was not the defendant's level in the hierarchy; the rationale for extending such immunity was that "unless the officer in question is absolutely immune from suit, the officer will timorously, instead of fearlessly, perform the function in question and, as a result, government—that is, the public—will be the ultimate loser."

The court thought this standard justified extending such protection to the officer's arrest report. The report is an essential part of the officer's job; the report is also used by prosecutors in deciding whether to file charges and, if so, what charges; it plays a role in any trial in refreshing recollection and providing the basis for impeachment. The absence of immunity

> may well deter the honest officer from fearlessly and vigorously preparing a detailed, accurate report and increase the likelihood that the officer will hesitate to prepare anything more than a bland report that will be less useful within the department and in any subsequent prosecution and trial. To put it another way, instead of preparing a detailed report, the officer will be tempted to leave out certain details, saving those for trial, when any testimony by the officer is absolutely privileged under the judicial privilege.

This would lead to trial by surprise—something the state has been trying to avoid. On the other hand, statements by the arresting officer in response to press inquiries did not deserve such protection. It was not essential to the officer's duties to respond to the press. Such responses were "allowed" by the department but not required.

In another important area the courts are split over whether a litigant has an absolute privilege to announce publicly and to the press that he has just filed a civil complaint. The act of filing the complaint is absolutely privileged in all states—the split is over the public announcement that summarizes the contents of the complaint. See the discussion in Shahvar v. Superior Court, 25 Cal.App.4th 653, 30 Cal.Rptr.2d 597 (1994), noting that the statutory privilege in California speaks of statements made "in" judicial proceedings not statements "about" such proceedings.

The only absolute privilege granted the media occurs when broadcasters are required to grant equal opportunity on the air to all candidates for the same office. If a candidate commits defamation, the broadcaster is not liable. See Farmers Educational & Cooperative Union of America v. WDAY, Inc., 360 U.S. 525 (1959). The *Medico* case, p. 913, infra, provides another privilege that resembles in some important ways an absolute privilege.

Qualified or conditional privilege. The much more common type of privilege is "qualified" or "conditional," and is considered in the following case. (The terms "qualified" and "conditional" are synonymous.)

Liberman v. Gelstein

Court of Appeals of New York, 1992.
80 N.Y.2d 429, 605 N.E.2d 344, 590 N.Y.S.2d 857.

[The facts are reprinted at p. 899, supra. After finding that the charge concerning the parked cars was actionable, the court turned to the next issue.]

■ KAYE J.

We next consider whether the courts below properly concluded that defendant's conversation with Kohler was conditionally privileged and that plaintiff failed to raise an issue of fact on malice.

Courts have long recognized that the public interest is served by shielding certain communications, though possibly defamatory, from litigation, rather than risk stifling them altogether [ ]. When compelling public policy requires that the speaker be immune from suit, the law affords an absolute privilege, while statements fostering a lesser public interest are only conditionally privileged [ ].

One such conditional, or qualified, privilege extends to a "communication made by one person to another upon a subject in which both have an interest" [ ] This "common interest" privilege (see, Restatement § 596) has been applied, for example, to employees of an organization [ ], members of a faculty tenure committee [ ], and constituent physicians of a health insurance plan [ ]. The rationale for applying the privilege in these circumstances is that so long as the privilege is not abused, the flow of information between persons sharing a common interest should not be impeded.

We thus agree . . . that defendant's conversation with Kohler was conditionally privileged (see, Restatement § 596, comment *d* ["Tenants in common * * * are included within the rule stated in this Section as being conditionally privileged to communicate among themselves matter defamatory of others which concerns their common interests"]). Gelstein and Kohler were members of the governing body of an association formed to protect the tenants' interests. If Liberman was in fact bribing the police so that his cars could occupy spaces in front of the building, that would be inimical to those interests. Thus, Gelstein had a qualified right to communicate his suspicions—though defamatory of Liberman—to Kohler.

The shield provided by a qualified privilege may be dissolved if plaintiff can demonstrate that defendant spoke with "malice" [ ]. Under common law, malice meant spite or ill will [ ]. In New York Times Co. v. Sullivan, 376 U.S. 254 (1964), however, the Supreme Court established an "actual malice" standard for certain cases governed by the First Amendment: "knowledge that [the statement] was false or * * * reckless disregard of whether it was false or not" [ ]. Consequently, the term "malice" has become somewhat confused [ ]. Indeed, as the Supreme Court itself recently acknowledged [Masson v. New Yorker Mag., 501 U.S. 496 (1991)]:

Actual malice under the *New York Times* standard should not be confused with the concept of malice as an evil intent or a motive arising from spite or ill will. . . . We have used the term actual malice as a shorthand to describe the First Amendment protections for speech injurious to reputation and we continue to do so here. But the term can confuse as well as enlighten. In this respect, the phrase may be an unfortunate one.

Nevertheless, malice has now assumed a dual meaning, and we have recognized that the constitutional as well as the common-law standard will suffice to defeat a conditional privilege [   ].

Under the *Times* malice standard, the plaintiff must demonstrate that the "statements [were] made with [a] high degree of awareness of their probable falsity" [   ] In other words, there "must be sufficient evidence to permit the conclusion that the defendant in fact entertained serious doubts as to the truth of [the] publication" [   ]; see also, Restatement § 600, comment *b*.

Applying these principles, we conclude that there is no triable malice issue under the *Times* standard. Although the dissenter below suggested that Gelstein's admission that he did not know whether the bribery charge was true raised a triable issue on malice, there is a critical difference between not knowing whether something is true and being highly aware that it is probably false. Only the latter establishes reckless disregard in a defamation action. Moreover, as the motion court correctly observed, plaintiff's mere characterization of Gelstein's informants as "disgruntled" is insufficient to raise a triable issue. Although plaintiff criticizes defendant for not producing affidavits from the informants—arguing that "it has never been factually established that Gelstein had any source"—it was plaintiff's burden to raise a factual issue on malice, and he did not seek to depose the employees either. In sum, this record is insufficient to raise a triable issue of fact under the *Times* standard of malice.

Similarly, there is insufficient evidence of malice under the common-law definition. A jury could undoubtedly find that, at the time Gelstein discussed his bribery suspicions with Kohler, Gelstein harbored ill will toward Liberman. In this context, however, spite or ill will refers not to defendant's general feelings about plaintiff, but to the speaker's motivation for making the defamatory statements, [   ]. If the defendant's statements were made to further the interest protected by the privilege, it matters not that defendant also despised plaintiff. Thus, a triable issue is raised only if a jury could reasonably conclude that "malice was the one and only cause for the publication" [   ].

Plaintiff has not sustained that burden. Significantly, Gelstein did not make a public announcement of his suspicions—from which an inference could be drawn that his motive was to defame Liberman—but relayed them to a colleague who was in a position to investigate. As noted, the conversation was within the common interest of Gelstein and Kohler, and there is nothing in this record from which a reasonable jury could find that Gelstein was not seeking to advance that common interest.

Thus, the courts below properly concluded that defendant's conversation with Kohler was qualifiedly privileged, and plaintiff failed to raise a fact issue on malice.

Accordingly, the order of the Appellate Division should be affirmed, with costs.

■ SIMONS, ACTING C.J., and TITONE, HANCOCK and BELLACOSA, JJ., concur with KAYE, J.

[Judge Smith dissented in part and would have reinstated the second cause of action. He thought the record indicated that plaintiff might be able to prove either kind of malice and thus overcome the privilege.]

NOTES AND QUESTIONS

1. Why does this situation not deserve an absolute privilege? Why does it deserve a qualified privilege? What if defendant had told his suspicions to a tenant who was not on the board? To a social friend in a nearby building who has a friend on the police force?

2. Consider the introductory note to Restatement § 592A, stating that a qualified privilege is based on the view "that it is essential that true information be given whenever it is reasonably necessary for the protection of one's own interests, the interests of third persons or certain interests of the public." Would that formulation apply to the tenant in *Liberman*?

3. *Employer references.* One important area for qualified privilege protects responses from employers or former employers to inquiries from prospective employers about how an employee performed on the job. See Erickson v. Marsh & McLennan Co., Inc., 117 N.J. 539, 569 A.2d 793 (1990), using three criteria to determine that a qualified privilege was appropriate: "the appropriateness of the occasion on which the defamatory information is published, the legitimacy of the interest thereby sought to be protected or promoted, and the pertinence of the receipt of that information by the recipient."

The immediate concern is to encourage this exchange of information without opening the door to dishonest and attacks on the employee. Traditionally, most states have accorded a qualified privilege based on the "common interest" of the inquirer and the responder—a protection that may not apply when the former employer volunteers information. See Coclin v. Lane Press, Inc., 210 App.Div.2d 98, 620 N.Y.S.2d 41 (1994), finding a qualified privilege when an employer sent information on an employee to an outsider. The court quoted an earlier decision of the court of appeals:

> A communication made bona fide upon any subject matter in which the party communicating has an interest, or in reference to which he has a duty, is privileged if made to a person having a corresponding interest or duty, although it contained criminating matter which, without this privilege, would be slanderous and actionable, and this though the duty be not a legal one, but only a moral or social duty of imperfect obligation.

Recently, however, employers have taken increasingly to refusing to respond to such inquiries or to stating only the dates of employment. Initially, one might have thought that this terse reply itself might carry implied defamation. Today, however, it is such a common technique that it does not carry pejorative meaning. Rather, the concern is that the flow of information has been retarded by employer fears of lawsuits or vengeance. See Rovella, Laws May Ease the Risky Business of Job References, Nat'l L.J., Oct. 23, 1995 at B1, reporting that in a recent study by a consulting firm 63 percent of 1,331 managers said that they had refused to provide information for fear of lawsuits and nearly 40 percent said it was a good idea not to provide information. On the other hand, 73 percent said "that reference checking is more important now" than before.

See also Wald, Board Blames Pilot for Commuter Crash, N.Y.Times, Oct. 25, 1995 at A10, reporting that a pilot suspected of causing a crash had been on the verge of being fired by one airline when he applied for work at a commuter line. The prospective employer had not asked prior employers about the pilot's work—but it would not have mattered because the former employer's policy was not to provide such information. The article reports crash investigators as saying that "few airlines will tell another about a former employee's performance, for fear of being sued by the applicant if the information is used to deny the person a job."

Is this a problem? Should it be handled by changing the qualified privilege to an absolute privilege? By creating a duty to respond when asked about a former employee's record? Note that if the former employer writes a dishonest report that praises the worker as a way of easing the worker's departure that may come back to haunt the employer. In one case, since settled, Rovella reports that several co-employees were killed by a violent colleague who had recently been hired after his former employer allegedly "in an effort to eliminate an unpleasant and potentially danger-ous" situation gave the killer "a neutral reference signed by a company vice president, allegedly omitting the real reasons" for the termination. Is there a duty to disclose an observed potential for violence in a former worker? The issue of making a partial disclosure that may be a misleading half-truth, is discussed in the context of deceit in Chapter XV.

Some statutes may prevent employers from informing prospective employers about disciplinary actions taken against the worker—including true statements. See the discussion of the Illinois statute in Delloma v. Consolidation Coal Co., 996 F.2d 168 (7th Cir.1993). What might motivate this type of legislation?

4. Another important issue here is raised by credit reports. Most states agree that a qualified privilege protects reporting services. E.g., Weir v. Equifax Services, Inc., 210 App.Div.2d 944, 620 N.Y.S.2d 675 (1994); Stationers Corp. v. Dun & Bradstreet, Inc. 62 Cal.2d 412, 398 P.2d 785, 42 Cal.Rptr. 449 (1965). The common law in this area has, however, been largely replaced by litigation under the federal Fair Credit Reporting Act, 15 U.S.C.A. § 1681a(f), granting subjects of credit reports certain protections. See, e.g., Guimond v. Trans Union Credit Information Co., 45 F.3d 1329 (9th Cir.1995); Henson v. CSC Credit Services, 29 F.3d 280 (7th Cir.1994).

5. Efforts to invoke a qualified privilege for general news reporting of matters important to the community have generally failed. In California, for example, Civil Code section 47(c) provides a privilege for "a communication, without malice, to a person interested therein, (1) by one who is also interested, or (2) by one who stands in such a relation to the person interested as to afford a reasonable ground for supposing the motive for the communication innocent, or (3) who is requested by the person interested to give the information."

Although some lower courts had applied this section to media reports of events of public interest in the community, that view was rejected in Brown v. Kelly Broadcasting Co., 48 Cal.3d 711, 771 P.2d 406, 257 Cal. Rptr. 708 (1989). A consumer affairs segment of a daily television news show incorrectly attributed poor workmanship to plaintiff contractor. The court concluded that the legislature had not intended this section to apply to such media reports and that to find such coverage would mean that it "would apply to virtually every defamatory communication. Presumably, the news media generally publish and broadcast only matters that the media believe are of public interest, and the media defendant in every defamation action would therefore argue that the communication was a matter of public interest." Such a privilege would swallow the basic rule. (The court also noted that qualified privileges had developed during a period when strict liability was the rule in libel cases. Since, as we soon discuss, that is no longer the case, the court saw less need for extending them today.)

6. *Abuse.* After a situation warranting a qualified privilege is found, the next question is whether the privilege has been "abused." The criteria for abuse under common law was malice—which meant, as the court indicates, spite or ill will toward the plaintiff. This might be shown by evidence about the relationship, and sometimes might be inferred from defendant's behavior in making the statement to those who had no interest in learning it or not believing what was said. Recall the *Liberman* court's statement that defendant "did not make public announcement of his suspicions—from which an inference could be drawn that his motive was to defame Liberman" rather than to accomplish what he was seeking to accomplish.

7. The arrival of constitutional law has confused the question of abuse under common law. As the court notes, "actual malice" has now taken on the meaning of "knowledge that [the statement] was false or . . . reckless disregard of whether it was false or not." Although we will consider this phrase at length, beginning at p. 943, infra, it is already clear that "actual" (or "constitutional" or "Times") malice focuses on the defendant's attitude toward the truth of the statement—not defendant's attitude toward the person attacked in the statement.

In light of the emergence of the constitutional standards, the courts have adopted various stances. Some have adhered to the idea that abuse is shown by the defendant's ill will or spite toward the plaintiff. Others, such as New York in *Liberman*, and Maine, in *Staples*, p. 880, supra, have concluded that a plaintiff can overcome a qualified privilege by showing either type of malice. Still others, including New Jersey in *Erickson*, note

3, supra, have decided that to show abuse the plaintiff must establish "actual malice" in the constitutional sense. Although the intricacies of "actual malice" will be addressed later, it is important to realize here that the focus in "abuse" cases appears to be shifting from the defendant's attitude toward the plaintiff to defendant's attitude toward the truth.

8. *Fair comment.* Although most common law privileges primarily benefit non-media individuals, one is of special use to the media—fair comment.

Apparently this privilege entered English law in 1808 in Carr v. Hood, 1 Camp. 355, 170 Eng.Rep. 983. The defendant was charged with ridiculing the plaintiff author's talent so severely that sales of his book were discouraged and his reputation was destroyed. The plaintiff's attorney conceded that his client had exposed himself to literary criticism by making the book public, but insisted that the criticism should be "fair and liberal" and seek to enlighten the public about the book rather than to injure the author. The judge noted that ridicule may be an appropriate tool of criticism, but that criticism unrelated to the author as such would not be privileged. He urged that any "attempt against free and liberal criticism" should be resisted "at the threshold." The result was a rule that criticism, regardless of its merit, was privileged if it was made honestly, with honesty being measured by the accuracy of the critic's descriptive observations. If a critic describing a literary, musical, or artistic endeavor gave the "facts" accurately and fairly, the critic's honest conclusions would be privileged as "fair comment."

American law recognized this privilege, and as long as it was applied in cases of literary and artistic criticism it caused little confusion. Classic cases discussing the privilege are Triggs v. Sun Printing & Pub. Ass'n, 179 N.Y. 144, 71 N.E. 739 (1904), Adolf Philipp Co. v. New Yorker Staats–Zeitung, 165 App.Div. 377, 150 N.Y.Supp. 1044 (1914), and Cherry v. Des Moines Leader, 114 Iowa 298, 86 N.W. 323 (1901).

But at the end of the nineteenth century, cases arose in which the privilege of fair comment was claimed with regard to other matters of public interest, including the conduct of politicians. The privilege claimed would permit citizens to criticize and argue about the conduct of their officials, and these cases presented the problem of distinguishing between facts and opinion. In literary criticism the application of the privilege could depend upon the accuracy of the "facts" because they were usually readily apparent—in the book, on the stage, or in the restaurant. When dealing with politics, however, the "facts" were often elusive. This new problem created a judicial split.

In Post Publishing Co. v. Hallam, 59 Fed. 530 (6th Cir.1893), Judge Taft ruled that in order for criticism of officials to be privileged, it must be based upon true underlying facts. The newspaper asserted that it should be judged under the accepted rule that a former master responding to a request for information about a former servant would be privileged if the master stated some "facts" about the servant honestly but mistakenly. Judge Taft refused to apply this rule because in the servant case only the prospective master learned of the defamation, while here the entire public would hear of it. He continued:

> The existence and extent of privilege in communications are determined by balancing the needs and good of society against the right of an individual to enjoy a good reputation when he has done nothing which ought to injure it. The privilege should always cease where the sacrifice of the individual right becomes so great that the public good to be derived from it is outweighed. . . . But, if the privilege is to extend to cases like that at bar, then a man who offers himself as a candidate must submit uncomplainingly to the loss of his reputation, not with a single person or a small class of persons, but with every member of the public, whenever an untrue charge of disgraceful conduct is made against him, if only his accuser honestly believes the charge upon reasonable ground. We think that not only is such a sacrifice not required of everyone who consents to become a candidate for office, but that to sanction such a doctrine would do the public more harm than good.
>
> We are aware that public officers and candidates for public office are often corrupt, when it is impossible to make legal proof thereof, and of course it would be well if the public could be given to know, in such a case, what lies hidden by concealment and perjury from judicial investigation. But the danger that honorable and worthy men may be driven from politics and public service by allowing too great latitude in attacks upon their characters outweighs any benefit that might occasionally accrue to the public from charges of corruption that are true in fact, but are incapable of legal proof. The freedom of the press is not in danger from the enforcement of the rule we uphold. No one reading the newspaper of the present day can be impressed with the idea that statements of fact concerning public men, and charges against them, are unduly guarded or restricted; and yet the rule complained of is the law in many of the states of the Union and in England.

The privilege became more narrow as those courts following the *Hallam* view came to treat questions of motive—why the politician or official acted as he did—as "facts" that had to be true in order for subsequent comment to be privileged.

A contrasting position was taken in Coleman v. MacLennan, 78 Kan. 711, 98 P. 281 (1908), in which the court noted that "men of unimpeachable character from all political parties continually present themselves as candidates in sufficient numbers to fill the public offices and manage the public institutions" even though Kansas had long held that facts relating to matters of public interest are themselves privileged if they are honestly believed to be true; and, if the facts are privileged even if wrong, the comments based upon those facts are also privileged if they are honestly believed. *Coleman* adhered to the state's rejection of the *Hallam* distinction between fact and comment or opinion.

The common law majority view is that a statement is privileged as fair comment only if it is based on true or privileged facts about a matter of public interest. Privileged facts will be discussed below, but it is important to keep in mind that the fair comment privilege applies only where the comment expressed is honestly believed.

The fair comment privilege has become intertwined with constitutional developments that we discuss at p. 999, infra.

c. FAIR AND ACCURATE REPORT

Medico v. Time, Inc.

United States Court of Appeals, Third Circuit, 1981.
643 F.2d 134, certiorari denied, 454 U.S. 836 (1981).

■ Before ADAMS, GARTH and SLOVITER, CIRCUIT JUDGES.

■ ADAMS, CIRCUIT JUDGE.

This appeal from a summary judgment in favor of the defendant presents an important question concerning the law of defamation. We must review the district court's determination that a news magazine enjoys a privilege, under the common law of Pennsylvania, to publish a summary of FBI documents identifying the plaintiff as a member of an organized crime "family." We affirm.

I.

In its March 6, 1978 issue, Time magazine published an article describing suspected criminal activities of then-Congressman Daniel J. Flood.
. . .

As an example of suspected misconduct, the Time article listed the following:

> Among the matters under scrutiny: Ties between Flood and Pennsylvania Rackets Boss Russell Bufalino. The suspected link: the Wilkes–Barre firm of Medico Industries, controlled by President Philip Medico and his brothers. The FBI discovered more than a decade ago that Flood steered Government business to the Medicos and traveled often on their company jet. Investigators say Bufalino frequently visited the Medico offices; agents tape-recorded Bufalino's description of Philip as a capo (chief) in his Mafia family. [Testimony by a former Flood aide] has sparked new investigative interest in the Flood–Medico–Bufalino triangle.

. . .

In January 1980, Time again moved for summary judgment based on the substantial truth of its publication. Time resubmitted the two FBI documents it had proffered to support its initial motion, supplemented with affidavits of two FBI agents. . . .

On this occasion the district court granted Time's motion for summary judgment, but not on the basis of the truth defense. . . .

After declining to hold for Time on the truth theory, the district court considered whether the Time article fell within the common law privilege accorded the press to report on official proceedings. The judge seemed troubled because Pennsylvania courts apparently had so far extended the privilege only to reports of proceedings open to the public, whereas Time had summarized reports which the FBI had kept secret and whose release to Time evidently had been unauthorized. But after an exhaustive analysis of Pennsylvania precedents, the court concluded that Pennsylvania courts, if presented with the question, would find summaries of non-public government reports within the privilege. The district judge then ascertained that the Time article represented a fair and accurate account of the FBI documents. Accordingly he held that the publication was privileged, and awarded summary judgment in favor of Time.

On appeal, Medico argues that the district court incorrectly determined that Time's publication was privileged under Pennsylvania law. Time counters that the district judge accurately construed the applicable state law on privilege, and contends further that the defense of truth applies and affords an alternate basis for affirming the district court.   .   .   .

II.

The fair report privilege on which the district court relied developed as an exception to the common law rule that the republisher of a defamation was subject to liability similar to that risked by the original defamer.   .   .   .   The common law regime created special problems for the press. When a newspaper published a newsworthy account of one person's defamation of another, it was, by virtue of the republication rule, charged with publication of the underlying defamation. Thus, although the common law exonerated one who published a defamation as long as the statement was true, a newspaper in these circumstances traditionally could avail itself of the truth defense only if the truth of the underlying defamation were established.

To ameliorate the chilling effect on the reporting of newsworthy events occasioned by the combined effect of the republication rule and the truth defense, the law has long recognized a privilege for the press[9] to publish accounts of official proceedings or reports even when these contain defamatory statements. So long as the account presents a fair and accurate summary of the proceedings, the law abandons the assumption that the reporter adopts the defamatory remarks as his own.[11] The privilege thus permits a newspaper or other press defendant to relieve itself of liability without establishing the truth of the substance of the statement reported.

9. There is some dispute whether the privilege is available to non-press defendants. The *Restatement* [covers] "any person who makes an oral, written or printed report" on an official proceeding should have access to the defense.   .   .   .

11. [ ]. Analytically, the fair report privilege is similar to the truth defense. Both make verity the issue, although requiring that a report be fair and accurate may allow the press a somewhat greater margin of error than requiring that its report be true.   .   .   .

The fair report privilege has a somewhat more limited scope than the truth defense, however. So long as the speaker establishes the truth of his statement, he is shielded from liability, regardless of his motives; the fair report privilege, on the other hand, can be defeated in most jurisdictions by a showing that the publisher acted for the sole purpose of harming the person defamed.

Unlike many states, Pennsylvania has never codified the fair report privilege. . . . We believe it appropriate to accept as the law of Pennsylvania the version of the fair report privilege embodied in the current *Restatement.*

Section 611 of Restatement (Second) provides:

Report of Official Proceeding or Public Meeting

The publication of defamatory matter concerning another in a report of an official action or proceeding or of a meeting open to the public that deals with a matter of public concern is privileged if the report is accurate and complete or a fair abridgement of the occurrence reported.

With respect to the present controversy, the basic inquiry is whether Time's summary of FBI documents concerning Philip Medico is "a report of an official action or proceeding."[17]

The district court examined and rejected the possibility that the FBI reports in question are not "official" because they are not generally available to the public. Medico does not challenge this reasoning on appeal, and we perceive no need to rehearse arguments that the district court has already canvassed. Medico contends before this Court that the FBI documents should not be deemed "official" because they express only tentative and preliminary conclusions that the FBI has never adopted as accurate. He points out that the title page to the FBI report on La Cosa Nostra bears the following legend: "This document contains neither recommendations nor conclusions of the FBI. It is the property of the FBI and is loaned to your agency; it and its contents are not to be distributed outside your agency."

Neither the text of Section 611 nor the accompanying comments dispose of the issue Medico raises. Section 611 itself speaks only of "official" action or proceedings, without elaborating on when a statement is made in an official capacity. [The court notes that two comments to that section point in different ways on whether the report is within the scope of the privilege. Nor did case law resolve it. The closest case protected a news report that summarized a defamatory civil complaint that had formed

---

17. Although the Time article did not explicitly credit the FBI Report on La Cosa Nostra or the FBI personal file card on Medico as the Magazine's sources of information, the statements about Medico, taken in context, may reasonably be understood to inform the reader that the story was based on FBI materials. . . .

the basis for a temporary restraining order. Hanish v. Westinghouse Broadcasting Co., 487 F.Supp. 397 (E.D.Pa.1980)].[21]

Assuming the court in *Hanish* correctly predicted Pennsylvania law, we think that decision supports application of the Section 611 privilege to the present case. FBI files seem at least as "official" as the pleadings in civil cases. Although civil complaints are instituted, for the most part, by private parties, the FBI documents concerning Medico were compiled by government agents acting in their official capacities. Moreover, the danger that a civil litigant will willfully insert defamatory assertions in his complaint generally would appear at least as great as the risk that a criminal investigatory agency will knowingly include false or malicious statements in its files. If Pennsylvania courts would grant the privilege to newspaper accounts of civil complaints on which a court has acted ex parte, we think it likely that they would grant the privilege to republication of defamatory items from the FBI materials on Medico.

III.

Three policies underlie the fair report privilege, and an examination of them provides further guidance for our decision today. Initially, an agency theory was offered to rationalize a privilege of fair report: one who reports what happens in a public, official proceeding acts as an agent for persons who had a right to attend, and informs them of what they might have seen for themselves. The agency rationale, however, cannot explain application of the privilege to proceedings or reports not open to public inspection.

A theory of public supervision also informs the fair report privilege. Justice Holmes, applying the privilege to accounts of courtroom proceedings, gave the classic formulation of this principle:

> [The privilege is justified by] the security which publicity gives for the proper administration of justice. . . . It is desirable that the trial of causes should take place under the public eye, not because the controversies of one citizen with another are of public concern, but because it is of the highest moment that those who administer justice should always act under the sense of public responsibility and that every citizen should be able to satisfy himself with his own eyes as to the mode in which a public duty is performed.

Cowley v. Pulsifer, 137 Mass. 392, 394 (1884). The supervisory rationale has been invoked in the context of executive action as well.

We believe the public supervision rationale applies to the present case. As public inspection of courtroom proceedings may further the just administration of the laws, public scrutiny of the proceedings and records of criminal investigatory agencies may often have the equally salutary effect

---

21. Considerable controversy surrounds republication of defamations contained in pleadings on which no official action has been taken. . . .

of fostering among those who enforce the laws "the sense of public responsibility." For example, exposing the content of agency records may, in some cases, help ensure impartial enforcement of the laws.

[We need not] decide, however, whether the supervisory rationale is relevant to every republication of documents found in FBI files. For any general supervisory concern with respect to the FBI is heightened in the present case by the public's interest in examining the conduct of individuals it elects to positions of civic trust. Elected officials derive their authority from, and are answerable to, the public. If the citizenry is effectively and responsibly to discharge its obligation to monitor the conduct of its government, there can be no penalty for exposing to general view the possible wrongdoing of government officials. Because the alleged defamation of Medico occurred in an article analyzing the conduct of former Congressman Flood, we believe it implicates this aspect of the supervisory rationale. Moreover, even though Time's publication arguably may have tarnished the reputation of Medico, a private individual, as well as that of Representative Flood, the public has a lively interest in considering the relationships formed by elected officials.

A third rationale for the fair report privilege rests, somewhat tautologically, on the public's interest in learning of important matters.[27] While "mere curiosity in the private affairs of others is of insufficient importance to warrant granting the privilege," the present case does not involve such idle probing. The Time article discussed two topics of legitimate public interest. First, for the same reasons that support the supervisory rationale, examination of the affairs of elected officials is obviously a matter of legitimate public concern. In addition, as various federal courts have already recognized, there is significant public importance to reports on investigations of organized criminal activities, whether or not these implicate government officials.

Because the Time article focused on organized crime, we think the informational rationale is especially relevant. The district court in the case at hand commented on the difficulty of gathering information pertaining to organized criminal activity: "Due to the size, sophistication and secrecy of most organized criminal endeavors, only the largest and most sophisticated intelligence-gathering entities can monitor them effectively. In practice this task has been taken up primarily by the Justice Department of the federal government and, in particular, by the FBI." Indeed, the documents that Time summarized had been compiled by a government agency. In light of the difficulty in obtaining independent corroboration of FBI information, the press may often have to rely on materials the government acquires if it is to report on organized crime at all. We believe Time's

27. . . .

Some jurisdictions rely on the informational rationale to extend the privilege to accounts of the proceedings of public meetings of private, nongovernmental organizations, as long as the meeting deals with matters of concern to the public.

publication of FBI materials mentioning Medico served a legitimate public interest in learning about organized crime.

Care must be taken, of course, to ensure that the supervisory and informational rationales not expand into justifications for reporting any defamatory matter maintained in any government file. Personal interests in privacy are not to be taken lightly, and are not to be overborne by mere invocation of a public need to know.[30] But we believe that the public interest is involved when, as here, information compiled by an enforcement agency may help shed light on a Congressman's alleged criminal or unethical behavior.

. . .

V.

Once the libel defendant establishes the existence of a "privileged occasion" for the publication of a defamatory article, the burden returns to the plaintiff to prove that the defendant abused its privilege. [ ] Pennsylvania recognizes two forms of "abuse": the account of an official report may fail to be fair and accurate,[40] as when the publisher overly embellishes the account, [ ] or the defamatory material may be published for the sole purpose of causing harm to the person defamed. [ ]. Inasmuch as Medico does not allege that Time published its article for the purpose of harming him, the sole issue with respect to abuse of privilege is whether the district court erred in concluding that there was no genuine question whether Time's publication fairly and accurately summarized the FBI materials concerning Medico.

We agree with the district court that nothing in the record suggests that the Time article unfairly or inaccurately reported on the FBI materials. . . .

. . . Time has accurately portrayed the FBI records as indicating that Medico has been identified as part of the Bufalino crime family.

VI.

Medico further contends that Time can avail itself of the fair report privilege only if it actually based its article on the FBI materials; if the report reflects the contents of the official materials merely by coincidence, the privilege does not attach. Medico maintains there is a genuine issue of fact whether Time employees worked with the FBI materials in preparing the article.

Pennsylvania law squarely contradicts this argument. . . .

30. The excesses of the McCarthy era, for example, prompted some commentators to point out the reputational injury the republication of official defamation can cause, and to advocate restricting the fair report privilege. [ ]

40. Placement on the plaintiff of the burden of demonstrating that a privileged report was not fair and accurate traditionally distinguished the fair report privilege from the truth defense, in which defendant bore the burden of proving truth. . . .

VII.

The judgment of the district court granting Time's motion for summary judgment will be affirmed.

NOTES AND QUESTIONS

1. The court discusses three theories that have been asserted to support the fair report privilege. Which one appears most persuasive? Will one generally support a broader protective net than the others?

2. *Coverage of the privilege.* The court understands state law not to require actual reliance on the official report or proceeding. Do the three theories differ on this? The Second Circuit disagreed with the *Medico* court on its reading of Pennsylvania law on the ground that the privilege could not be "divorced from its underlying policy of encouraging the broad dissemination of public records." Protecting a defendant who did not actually rely on an official report "does nothing to encourage the initial reporting of public records and proceedings. Certainly, § 611 should not be interpreted to protect unattributed, defamatory statements supported only after-the-fact through a frantic search of official records." Bufalino v. Associated Press, 692 F.2d 266 (2d Cir.1982), cert. denied 462 U.S. 1111 (1983).

3. In a footnote, the *Bufalino* court observed that "even where the reporter has actually relied on official records, the privilege can be lost through failure to make proper attribution." Would the *Medico* court agree? What do the theories have to say on this point?

4. The coverage varies greatly state by state. In some states, for example, as suggested in *Medico,* the privilege extends to the fact of an arrest and the charges but not to details of the alleged crime that an arresting officer provides.

5. In Rouch v. Enquirer & News of Battle Creek, Mich., 427 Mich. 157, 398 N.W.2d 245 (1986), (a later stage of this case is discussed at p. 903, supra), the newspaper reported oral statements made by the police in connection with the plaintiff's arrest for rape. After plaintiff, who was

---

42. The possible interpretations of Time's publication about Medico may be used to illustrate the different approaches to the truth defense. The Time article is subject to at least three constructions:

A. Medico is a Mafia *capo.*

B. Government agents overheard Bufalino describe Medico as a Mafia *capo.*

C. FBI records indicate that government agents overheard Bufalino describe Medico as a Mafia *capo.*

Under the fair report privilege, the accuracy of C relieves Time of liability. If the privilege did not apply, however, we would have to ascertain whether Pennsylvania law would exonerate Time on the basis of the truth defense if Time established the truth of B, or whether Time would have to prove A. In light of our holding that Time's publication comes under the fair report privilege, we need not dispose of this question. In addition, we need not review the district court's determination that Time has failed to demonstrate the truth of either A or B.

never charged, was exonerated, he sued the newspaper. The paper's reliance on the state's privilege for fair and accurate report of "any public and official proceeding" was rejected on the ground that an "arrest that amounts to no more than an apprehension" was not a "proceeding." The statute was not intended to create a "government action," "arrest record," or "public records" privilege.

The legislature reacted by amending the privilege statute, Mich.Comp. Laws § 600.2911, to extend protection to "a fair and true report of matters of public record, a public and official proceeding, or of a governmental notice, announcement, written or recorded report or record generally available to the public, or act or action of a public body." Should such a statute extend to open meetings of a local political party or the state bar association?

6. Should the fair report privilege cover a report of a proceeding that is not open to the public? Dorsey v. National Enquirer, Inc., 973 F.2d 1431 (9th Cir.1992), involved the singer Arnold Dorsey, whose stage name is Engelbert Humperdinck. The National Enquirer ran a story headlined "Mom of Superstar Singer's Love Child Claims in Court . . . Engelbert has AIDS Virus." The story was based on an affidavit filed by the mother in family court in New York seeking to force Dorsey to buy life insurance naming the child as beneficiary. It stated the mother's "information and belief" that Dorsey "has AIDS related syndrome."

The Enquirer conceded the falsity of the allegation but won summary judgment on the basis of the California statute which recognizes a privilege for a fair and true report "of (1) a judicial, (2) a legislative, or (3) other public official proceeding, or (4) anything said in the course thereof. . . ." Dorsey argued that the wording of subsection (3) implied that subsection (1) covered only public judicial proceedings. But the court construed the statute as applicable to closed judicial proceedings, citing previous decisions applying the privilege to an internal agency report, an FBI "rap sheet," and grand jury proceedings. The court then held that in the absence of disputed facts and where all reasonable inferences from the evidence pointed in the same direction, summary judgment should be granted to the defendant. The addition to the article of some out-of-court remarks did not go beyond the gist or sting of the affidavit.

7. On the question of whether the privilege should extend to reports of actions of foreign governments, see Lee v. The Dong–A Ilbo, 849 F.2d 876 (4th Cir.1988), cert. denied 489 U.S. 1067 (1989)(concluding 2–1 that Virginia would not extend its privilege to a newspaper's accurate report of a press release issued by South Korean intelligence agencies that identified plaintiff as a North Korean agent).

8. *Codification.* As noted in *Medico* and in the discussion of several note cases, many states have adopted legislation to codify this privilege. One typical version is New York's Civil Rights Law § 74, which provides:

A civil action cannot be maintained against [any defendant] for the publication of a fair and true report of any judicial proceeding, legislative proceeding or other official proceeding. . . .

This section does not apply to a libel contained in any other matter added by any person concerned in the publication; or in the report of anything said or done at the time and place of such a proceeding which was not a part thereof.

Notice that this does not protect reports of public meetings held by nongovernmental organizations, such as medical associations or publicly held corporations, or remarks made by political, sports, or entertainment figures outside of official proceedings. Should it? Does it protect a report of remarks made by an audience member at a meeting of a city council? Should it?

If a New York court should be confronted with the *Medico* situation and conclude that the statute does not cover the case, could it nonetheless create a common law fair report privilege to cover the situation? Should it? In Wright v. Grove Sun Newspaper Co., 873 P.2d 983 (Okla.1994), the court concluded that the state statute did not extend protection to the report of a press conference held by a district attorney, but that the common law privilege had not been abrogated by the statute, and it could be used to provide that protection. Recall that in *Rouch*, note 5, supra, the court refused to expand the statute.

9. *Losing the privilege.* Although the defendant must establish the conditions showing that the privilege applies to the situation in the first instance, the plaintiff may be able to establish that the privilege has been lost.

Courts have not required precise use of legal language in testing the accuracy of these reports. How accurate must the report be? See Holy Spirit Ass'n for the Unification of World Christianity v. New York Times Co., 49 N.Y.2d 63, 399 N.E.2d 1185, 424 N.Y.S.2d 165 (1979):

[N]ewspaper accounts of legislative or other official proceedings must be accorded some degree of liberality. When determining whether an article constitutes a "fair and true" report, the language used herein should not be dissected and analyzed with a lexicographer's precision. This is so because a newspaper article is, by its very nature, a condensed report of events which must, of necessity, reflect to some degree the subjective view of its author. Nor should a fair report which is not misleading, composed and phrased in good faith under the exigencies of a publication deadline, be thereafter parsed and dissected on the basis of precise denotative meanings which may literally, although not contextually, be ascribed to the words used.

Most courts adopt a view similar to that in the discussion earlier of "substantial truth." Thus, in Koniak v. Heritage Newspapers, Inc., 198 Mich.App. 577, 499 N.W.2d 346 (1993), the defendant reported that plaintiff had been charged with assaulting someone 30 to 55 times when in fact he had been charged with eight assaults. The court observed that "whether plaintiff assaulted his stepdaughter once, eight times or thirty times would have little effect on the reader."

Although specific decisions may depend on the statutory language involved, in general the courts appear to be quite generous in applying this privilege so long as the defendant appeared to be trying to comply with the provisions. Even so, there are limits. In Crane v. The Arizona Republic, 972 F.2d 1511 (9th Cir.1992), the California privilege covered a report of a Congressional investigation into corruption within the Justice Department. But the article as written, by not giving the dates on which the reporter conducted two interviews, gave the impression that one of the two interviewees must have been lying. For this reason, the court refused to rule as a matter of law that the report was fair and accurate. The case was remanded for trial.

Questions of fairness usually arise in connection with the condensation or summary of a report. Comment f to § 611 states that "although it is unnecessary that the report be exhaustive and complete, it is necessary that nothing be omitted or misplaced in such a manner as to convey an erroneous impression to those who hear or read it, as for example a report of the discreditable testimony in a judicial proceeding and a failure to publish the exculpatory evidence." The matter is discussed in Schiavone Construction Co. v. Time, Inc., 735 F.2d 94 (3d Cir.1984), in which the magazine reported that an individual's name appeared several times in FBI reports concerning the disappearance of Jimmy Hoffa, but failed to quote the passage in the report that said that none of the references "suggested any criminality or organized crime associations" on plaintiff's part. This raised a fact question about fairness that barred summary judgment.

If the incriminating evidence in a trial emerged on the first day of the trial and the exculpatory evidence on the second day is the newspaper obligated to report the second day's events in order to be protected for the first day's events? What if a newspaper reports that defendant was convicted yesterday after a trial—but reversal of the conviction a year later is not reported?

Courts disagree over whether the question of fairness and accuracy are for the court in all cases or whether the jury should resolve close questions. The states are split over whether "malice" in the sense of spite or ill will deprives the defendant of the privilege. Why might the defendant's desire to harm the subject of the article be relevant here?

What if the defendant "knows" or "believes" that the report being published is false? In Rosenberg v. Helinski, 328 Md. 664, 616 A.2d 866 (1992), cert. denied 113 S.Ct. 3041 (1993), the court stated:

> Under the modern view, the privilege exists even if the reporter of defamatory statements made in court believes or knows them to be false; the privilege is abused only if the report fails the test of fairness and accuracy.

Is this consistent with the rationale for the privilege?

For extensive discussion of this privilege, see David Elder, The Fair Report Privilege (1988).

d.   RETRACTION AND OTHER DEFENSES

In this section we consider a variety of defenses that do not go directly to the merits of the claim.   Some, if successful, are complete defenses to the libel claim.   Others, even if successful, are at most partial defenses.

Burnett v. National Enquirer, Inc.

Court of Appeal of California, 1983.
144 Cal.App.3d 991, 193 Cal.Rptr. 206.
Appeal dismissed for want of jurisdiction, 465 U.S. 1014 (1984).

■ Before ROTH, P.J., GATES and BEACH, JJ.

■ ROTH, P.J.

On March 2, 1976, appellant caused to appear in its weekly publication, the National Enquirer, a "gossip column" headlined "Carol Burnett and Henry K. in Row," wherein a four-sentence item specified in its entirety that:

> In a Washington restaurant, a boisterous Carol Burnett had a loud argument with another diner, Henry Kissinger.   Then she traipsed around the place offering everyone a bite of her dessert.   But Carol really raised eyebrows when she accidentally knocked a glass of wine over one diner and started giggling instead of apologizing. The guy wasn't amused and "accidentally" spilled a glass of water over Carol's dress.

Maintaining the item was entirely false and libelous, an attorney for Ms. Burnett, by telegram the same day and by letter one week later, demanded its correction or retraction "within the time and in the manner provided for in Section 48(a) of the Civil Code of the State of California," failing which suit would be brought by his client [respondent herein], a well known actress, comedienne and show-business personality.

In response to the demand, appellant on April 6, 1976, published the following retraction, again in the National Enquirer's gossip column:

> An item in this column on March 2 erroneously reported that Carol Burnett had an argument with Henry Kissinger at a Washington restaurant and became boisterous, disturbing other guests. We understand these events did not occur and we are sorry for any embarrassment our report may have caused Miss Burnett.

On April 8, 1976, respondent, dissatisfied with this effort in mitigation, filed her complaint for libel in the Los Angeles Superior Court. [A jury trial resulted in an award of $300,000 compensatory damages and $1.3 million punitive damages.   The trial judge reduced these to $50,000 and $750,000.] This appeal followed.

. . . [T]he principal issues here are whether the National Enquirer is excluded from the protection afforded by Civil Code section 48a, and whether the damage award and penalty specified in the judgment can stand.

[The court quoted the entire section 48a at this point. The major provisions are that in any action for libel against a "newspaper" or slander in a broadcast, the "plaintiff shall recover no more than special damages unless a correction be demanded and be not published or broadcast, as hereinafter provided." The demand must be written, specifying the "statements claimed to be libelous and demanding that the same be corrected. Said notice and demand must be served within 20 days after knowledge of the publication or broadcast of the statements claimed to be libelous." If the correction be demanded and "be not published or broadcast in substantially as conspicuous a manner in said newspaper or on said broadcasting station as were the statements claimed to be libelous, in a regular issue thereof published or broadcast within three weeks after such service, plaintiff . . . may recover general, special, and exemplary damages." The statute defines each type of damages in conventional terms. Exemplary (punitive) damages were recoverable only if plaintiff proved "actual malice" and then only at the discretion of the trier of fact. "Actual malice" was defined as "that state of mind arising from hatred or ill will toward the plaintiff; provided, however, that such a state of mind occasioned by a good faith belief on the part of the defendant in the truth of the libelous publication or broadcast shall not constitute actual malice." The use of "hatred or ill will" is a conventional form of common law or state law malice. As we shall see, the phrase "actual malice" has acquired constitutional significance—but with a totally different meaning.]

. . .

The National Enquirer is a publication whose masthead claims the "Largest Circulation Of Any Paper in America." It is a member of the American Newspaper Publishers Association. It subscribes to the Reuters News Service. Its staff call themselves newspaper reporters. It describes its business as "newspaper" in its filings with the Los Angeles County Assessor and in its applications for insurance. A State Revenue Department has ruled it qualifies as a newspaper and is thus exempt from sales and use tax. The United States Department of Labor describes it as "belonging to establishments primarily engaged in publishing or printing and publishing newspapers."

By the same token the National Enquirer is designated as a magazine or periodical in eight mass media directories and upon the request and written representation of its general manager in 1960 that "In view of the feature content and general appearance [of the publication], which differ markedly from those of a newspaper . . . ," its classification as a newspaper was changed to that of magazine by the Audit Bureau of Circulation. It does not subscribe to the Associated Press or United Press International news services. According to statements by its Senior Editor it is not a newspaper and its content is based on a consistent formula of "how to" stories, celebrity or medical or personal improvement stories, gossip items and TV column items, together with material from certain other subjects. It provides little or no current coverage of subjects such as politics, sports or crime, does not attribute content to wire services, and in general does not make reference to time. Normal "lead time" for its subject matter is one to three weeks. Its owner allowed it did not generate stories "day to day as a daily newspaper does."

[In addressing the issue whether the trial court erred in denying the Enquirer the benefits of section 48a, the court treated the question as one of law. The trial court had concluded that the statute's major rationale was to protect publications that are "not generally in a position adequately to guard against the publication of material which is untrue." This led the trial court to focus on the element of time and to conclude that the Enquirer's mode of operation did not come within the rationale for the protection.]

Appellant . . . maintains that the special classification approved in Werner v. Southern Cal. etc. Newspapers, [35 Cal.2d 121, 216 P.2d 825 (1950)], depended on the public's interest in the "free dissemination of news," without reference to questions of timeliness; [and that several cases constituted an "unbroken line" of authority consistent with that view. The court explored several earlier cases, including a few that applied the statute to magazines without ever addressing the question.]

[The court concluded that the question was still open.] We nevertheless are of the opinion that what emerges as the better view from the authorities discussed is the proposition that the protection afforded by the statute is limited "to those who engage in the immediate dissemination of news on the ground that the Legislature could reasonably conclude that such enterprises . . . cannot always check their sources for accuracy and their stories for inadvertent publication errors. . . . [ ]"

Seen in this light, the essential question is not then whether any publication is properly denominated a magazine or by some other designation, but simply whether it ought to be characterized as a newspaper or not within the contemplation of § 48a, a question which must be answered, as the trial court supposed, in terms which justify an expanded barrier against damages for libel in those instances, and those only, where the constraints of time as a function of the requirements associated with production of the publication dictate the result.

[The trial court, using the proper rationale,] correctly determined the National Enquirer should not be deemed a newspaper for the purposes of the instant litigation.

[The court then upheld liability but reduced the punitive damages to $150,000. A dissenter would have affirmed the full award.]

NOTES AND QUESTIONS

1. Since special damages are hard to show, p. 895, supra, what is the justification behind the retraction statute? Why do retraction statutes focus on damages rather than liability?

2. Under the court's analysis what result where the defamation appears in a regular edition of a weekly news magazine? In the weekly news section of a Sunday "newspaper"? In a special edition of a weekly news magazine that is produced in response to a major news event?

3. If the court had found the Enquirer eligible to invoke the statute, it would then have had to face the question of whether the defendant had in fact published a "correction." Could it be argued that the correction was inadequate? (In the damages part of the opinion, the court found the correction "evasive" and "incomplete," and considered this relevant in the award of punitive damages.)

4. If the correction is adequate there is the further question whether it was published in substantially as conspicuous a manner as the original story. If the story is published in the same place, as apparently occurred in *Burnett,* there is little problem on this score. What if the correction is published in a regular box on page 2 of the publication that is devoted to corrections but whose headline "Day's Corrections" is smaller than the headline that accompanied the original story that appeared on page 5? Page 1?

Some retraction statutes state simply that the retraction may be taken into account in measuring damages. Even in states without retraction statutes it is generally held that an early correction may be relevant at trial to reduce the plaintiff's damages.

5. Some statutes have been interpreted to apply even though the original defamation is found to have been intentional. The California statute was so interpreted and upheld in the *Werner* case (cited in *Burnett*), which was later settled.

Oregon's statute, which applied unless plaintiff could prove that the defendant "actually intended to defame the plaintiff," was upheld in Holden v. Pioneer Broadcasting Co., 228 Or. 405, 365 P.2d 845 (1961), appeal dismissed and cert. denied 370 U.S. 157 (1962).

About half the states have retraction statutes of some sort. A few states have declared such statutes unconstitutional. See Boswell v. Phoenix Newspapers, Inc., 152 Ariz. 9, 730 P.2d 186 (1986), cert. denied 481 U.S. 1029 (1987)(statute violated state constitutional provision that right of action "to recover damages for injuries shall never be abrogated") and Madison v. Yunker, 180 Mont. 54, 589 P.2d 126 (1978)(statute violated state constitutional provision that courts be "open to every person, and speedy remedy afforded for every injury to person, property, or character").

6. Injunctions have never been available to prevent personal defamation. See Pound, Equitable Relief Against Defamation and Injuries to Personality, 29 Harv.L.Rev. 640 (1916); Leflar, Legal Remedies for Defamation, 6 Ark.L.Rev. 423 (1952); Sedler, Injunctive Relief and Personal Integrity, 9 St. Louis L.J. 147 (1964).

7. In 1993, the National Conference of Commissioners on Uniform State Laws proposed a "Uniform Correction or Clarification of Defamation Act" for adoption by the states. In 1994, that effort was endorsed by the

American Bar Association's House of Delegates 176–130. Although the act is to operate at the state level, its full significance can only be appreciated after the constitutional developments have been considered. The Act is reprinted at p. 1023, infra.

8. *The libel–proof plaintiff.* It has been traditional common law that defendant may show that the plaintiff's reputation was already low either because of earlier publications of the charge in question or for other reasons. This might induce the jury to lower its estimate of the compensatory damage that defendant's defamation had caused plaintiff.

In a recent development, a few courts have moved beyond this mitigation defense and have begun to dismiss libel cases on the ground that the plaintiff's reputation is already so bad that there is no chance that plaintiff can obtain and keep any damage award. In Jackson v. Longcope, 394 Mass. 577, 476 N.E.2d 617 (1985), a convicted multiple murderer sued over a statement that he had raped and strangled all of his victims. The court dismissed the case after concluding that plaintiff's reputation was so poor that he could have suffered no harm from any error in defendant's article: "A libel-proof plaintiff is not entitled to burden a defendant with a trial in which the most favorable result the plaintiff could achieve is an award of nominal damages."

Judge (now Justice) Scalia expressed great skepticism about the doctrine in Liberty Lobby v. Anderson, 746 F.2d 1563 (D.C.Cir.1984), vacated on other grounds 477 U.S. 242 (1986). For the majority, he observed that reputation is not monolithic. The law "proceeds upon the optimistic assumption that there is a little good in all of us—or perhaps the pessimistic assumption that no matter how bad someone is, he can always be worse." He offered this analogy: "It is shameful that Benedict Arnold was a traitor; but he was not a shoplifter to boot, and one should not have been able to make that charge while knowing its falsity with impunity."

See also Simmons Ford, Inc. v. Consumers Union, 516 F.Supp. 742 (S.D.N.Y.1981), in which a plaintiff with a previously good reputation was found to have been rendered libel-proof by the unchallenged or true parts of the article: "Given the abysmal performance and safety evaluations [of plaintiff's electrically powered car] detailed in the article, plaintiffs could not expect to gain more than nominal damages based on the addition to the article of the misstatement relating to federal safety standards."

Is there an analytical difference between (a) concluding that a reputable person has not been hurt in this instance because true statements have already badly hurt this aspect of plaintiff's reputation, and (b) denying an action to the plaintiff in *Jackson?* Can the *Simmons Ford* situation, which is often referred to as involving "incremental harm," be justified on the same basis as the "libel-proof plaintiff" doctrine? See Note, Libel–Proof Plaintiffs and the Question of Injury, 71 Texas L.Rev. 401 (1992).

Single publication rule. At common law, the sale of each individual copy of a publication could be considered a separate cause of action. Most states, either by case law or by adoption of the Uniform Single Publication

Act, 13 U.L.A. 517, have developed the rule that the entire edition of a printed work is to be treated as a single publication and that all damages for this publication must be recovered in a single action. At first this was limited to one action in each state, but now it is recognized that all damages for the nationwide single publication may, and in some cases must, be resolved in a single action. If a new edition of the work is published, however, such as a new edition of a book or a soft-cover version of a hardback book, it is considered a new and separate publication for which a separate cause of action arises.

Jurisdiction. The Supreme Court has twice unanimously denied media defendants special jurisdictional protections over and above those available to other defendants who conduct interstate business. Calder v. Jones, 465 U.S. 783 (1984); Keeton v. Hustler Magazine, Inc., 465 U.S. 770 (1984).

B.   PUBLIC PLAINTIFFS AND THE CONSTITUTION

In Near v. Minnesota, 283 U.S. 697 (1931), in the process of invalidating what it saw as a prior restraint, the majority observed,

> But it is recognized that punishment for the abuse of the liberty accorded to the press is essential to the protection of the public, and that the common-law rules that subject the libeler to responsibility for the public offense, as well as for the private injury, are not abolished by the protection extended in our Constitution.

In the late 1930s a syndicated columnist asserted that Congressman Sweeney was blocking the appointment of a federal judge because the prospective appointee was Jewish. Sweeney sued several newspapers, with varying results. Compare Sweeney v. Patterson, 128 F.2d 457 (D.C.App.), cert. denied 317 U.S. 678 (1942), holding the column privileged, with Sweeney v. Schenectady Union Pub. Co., 122 F.2d 288 (2d Cir.1941), affirmed by an equally divided court 316 U.S. 642 (1942), in which the lower court had found no privilege. This Supreme Court split vote suggested the presence of a difficult constitutional question.

In Chaplinsky v. New Hampshire, 315 U.S. 568 (1942), however, libelous words, along with "fighting words" and obscenity, were said to be among the "well-defined and narrowly limited classes of speech, the prevention and punishment of which have never been thought to raise any Constitutional problem." The proposition that libelous utterances were not "within the area of constitutionally protected speech" was relied upon by Justice Frankfurter, writing for a 5–4 majority in *Beauharnais v. Illinois,* p. 893, supra, to sustain a state criminal libel law.

This sequence set the stage for the following case from Alabama, a state that had long followed the narrow *Hallam* view, p. 911, supra, for criticism of public officials.

1.   PUBLIC OFFICIALS

New York Times Co. v. Sullivan (Together With Abernathy v. Sullivan)

Supreme Court of the United States, 1964.
376 U.S. 254, 84 S.Ct. 710, 11 L.Ed.2d 686.

[This action was based on a full-page advertisement in the New York Times on behalf of several individuals and groups protesting a "wave of terror" against blacks involved in non-violent demonstrations in the South. Plaintiff, one of three elected commissioners of Montgomery, the capital of Alabama, was in charge of the police department. When he demanded a retraction, as state law required, the Times instead responded that it failed to see how he was defamed, even though it did subsequently publish a retraction at the request of the Alabama governor, whose complaint was similar to Sullivan's. Plaintiff then filed suit against the Times and four clergymen whose names appeared—although they denied having authorized this—in the ad. Plaintiff alleged that the third and the sixth paragraphs of the advertisement libelled him:

> "In Montgomery, Alabama, after students sang 'My Country', 'Tis of Thee' on the State Capitol steps, their leaders were expelled from school, and truckloads of police armed with shotguns and tear-gas ringed the Alabama State College Campus. When the entire student body protested to state authorities by refusing to re-register, their dining hall was padlocked in an attempt to starve them into submission."

> .   .   .

> "Again and again the Southern violators have answered Dr. King's peaceful protests with intimidation and violence. They have bombed his home almost killing his wife and child. They have assaulted his person. They have arrested him seven times— for 'speeding,' 'loitering' and similar 'offenses.' And now they have charged him with 'perjury'—a *felony* under which they could imprison him for *ten years*.   .   .   ."

Plaintiff claimed that he was libelled in the third paragraph by the reference to the police, since his responsibilities included supervision of the Montgomery police. He asserted that the paragraph could be read as charging the police with ringing the campus and seeking to starve the students by padlocking the dining hall. As to the sixth paragraph, he contended that the word "they" referred to his department since arrests are usually made by the police and the paragraph could be read as accusing him of committing the acts charged. Several witnesses testified that they read the statements as referring to plaintiff in his capacity as commissioner.

The defendants admitted several inaccuracies in these two paragraphs: the students sang The Star Spangled Banner, not My Country, 'Tis of

Thee; nine students were expelled, not for leading the demonstration, but for demanding service at a lunch counter in the county courthouse; the dining hall was never padlocked; police at no time ringed the campus though they were deployed nearby in large numbers; they were not called to the campus in connection with the demonstration; Dr. King had been arrested only four times; and officers disputed his account of the alleged assault. Plaintiff proved that he had not been commissioner when three of the four arrests occurred and that he had nothing to do with procuring the perjury indictment.

The trial judge charged that the statements were libel per se, that the jury should decide whether they were made "of and concerning" the plaintiff and, if so, general damages were to be presumed. Although noting that punitive damages required more than carelessness, he refused to charge that they required a finding of actual intent to harm or "gross negligence and recklessness." He also refused to order the jury to separate its award of general and punitive damages. The jury returned a verdict for $500,000—the full amount demanded. The Alabama Supreme Court affirmed, holding that malice could be found in several aspects of the Times's conduct.]

■ MR. JUSTICE BRENNAN delivered the opinion of the Court.

. . .

I.

We may dispose at the outset of two grounds asserted to insulate the judgment of the Alabama courts from constitutional scrutiny. The first is the proposition relied on by the State Supreme Court—that "The Fourteenth Amendment is directed against State action and not private action." That proposition has no application to this case. Although this is a civil lawsuit between private parties, the Alabama courts have applied a state rule of law which petitioners claim to impose invalid restrictions on their constitutional freedoms of speech and press. It matters not that that law has been applied in a civil action and that it is common law only, though supplemented by statute. [ ] The test is not the form in which state power has been applied but, whatever the form, whether such power has in fact been exercised. [ ]

The second contention is that the constitutional guarantees of freedom of speech and of the press are inapplicable here, at least so far as the Times is concerned, because the allegedly libelous statements were published as part of a paid, "commercial" advertisement. [The argument was rejected.]

II.

Under Alabama law as applied in this case, a publication is "libelous per se" if the words "tend to injure a person . . . in his reputation" or to "bring [him] into public contempt"; the trial court stated that the standard was met if the words are such as to "injure him in his public office, or impute misconduct to him in his office, or want of official integrity, or want of fidelity to a public trust. . . ." The jury must find that the words were published "of and concerning" the plaintiff, but where the plaintiff is a public official his place in the governmental hierarchy is sufficient evidence to support a finding that his reputation has been affected by statements that reflect upon the agency of which he is in charge. Once "libel per se" has been established, the defendant has no defense as to stated facts unless he can persuade the jury that they were true in all their particulars. [   ]   His privilege of "fair comment" for expressions of opinion depends on the truth of the facts upon which the comment is based. [   ]   Unless he can discharge the burden of proving truth, general damages are presumed, and may be awarded without proof of pecuniary injury. A showing of actual malice is apparently a prerequisite to recovery of punitive damages, and the defendant may in any event forestall a punitive award by a retraction meeting the statutory requirements. Good motives and belief in truth do not negate an inference of malice, but are relevant only in mitigation of punitive damages if the jury chooses to accord them weight. [   ]

recap of "libel per se" and defenses + damages

The question before us is whether this rule of liability, as applied to an action brought by a public official against critics of his official conduct, abridges the freedom of speech and of the press that is guaranteed by the First and Fourteenth Amendments.

Respondent relies heavily, as did the Alabama courts, on statements of this Court to the effect that the Constitution does not protect libelous publications. Those statements do not foreclose our inquiry here. None of the cases sustained the use of libel laws to impose sanctions upon expression critical of the official conduct of public officials. . . . In deciding the question now, we are compelled by neither precedent nor policy to give any more weight to the epithet "libel" than we have to other "mere labels" of state law. NAACP v. Button, 371 U.S. 415, 429 (1963). Like insurrection, contempt, advocacy of unlawful acts, breach of the peace, obscenity, solicitation of legal business, and the various other formulae for the repression of expression that have been challenged in this Court, libel can claim no talismanic immunity from constitutional limitations. It must be measured by standards that satisfy the First Amendment.

The general proposition that freedom of expression upon public questions is secured by the First Amendment has long been settled by our decisions. . . . Mr. Justice Brandeis, in his concurring opinion in Whitney v. California, 274 U.S. 357, 375–376 (1927), gave the principle its classic formulation:

"Those who won our independence believed . . . that public discussion is a political duty; and that this should be a fundamental principle of the American government. . . . Believing in the power of reason as applied through public discussion, they eschewed silence coerced by law—the argument of force in its worst form. Recognizing the occasional tyrannies of governing majorities, they amended the Constitution so that free speech and assembly should be guaranteed."

Thus we consider this case against the background of a profound national commitment to the principle that debate on public issues should be uninhibited, robust, and wide-open, and that it may well include vehement, caustic, and sometimes unpleasantly sharp attacks on government and public officials. See Terminiello v. Chicago, 337 U.S. 1, 4 (1949); De Jonge v. Oregon, 299 U.S. 353, 365 (1937). The present advertisement, as an expression of grievance and protest on one of the major public issues of our time, would seem clearly to qualify for the constitutional protection. *Issue:* The question is whether it forfeits that protection by the falsity of some of its factual statements and by its alleged defamation of respondent.

Authoritative interpretations of the First Amendment guarantees have consistently refused to recognize an exception for any test of truth—whether administered by judges, juries, or administrative officials—and especially one that puts the burden of proving truth on the speaker. Cf. Speiser v. Randall, 357 U.S. 513, 525–526 (1958). The constitutional protection does not turn upon "the truth, popularity, or social utility of the ideas and beliefs which are offered." NAACP v. Button, 371 U.S. 415, 445 (1963). As Madison said, "Some degree of abuse is inseparable from the proper use of every thing; and in no instance is this more true than in that of the press." 4 Elliot's Debates on the Federal Constitution (1876), p. 571. In Cantwell v. Connecticut, 310 U.S. 296, 310 (1940), the Court declared:

> "In the realm of religious faith, and in that of political belief, sharp differences arise. In both fields the tenets of one man may seem the rankest error to his neighbor. To persuade others to his own point of view, the pleader, as we know, at times, resorts to exaggeration, to vilification of men who have been, or are, prominent in church or state, and even to false statement. But the people of this nation have ordained in the light of history, that, in spite of the probability of excesses and abuses, these liberties are, in the long view, essential to enlightened opinion and right conduct on the part of the citizens of a democracy."

That erroneous statement is inevitable in free debate, and that it must be protected if the freedoms of expression are to have the "breathing space" that they "need . . . to survive," NAACP v. Button, 371 U.S. 415, 433 (1963), was also recognized by the Court of Appeals for the District of Columbia Circuit in Sweeney v. Patterson, 128 F.2d 457, 458, cert. denied 317 U.S. 678 (1942). Judge Edgerton spoke for a unanimous court which affirmed the dismissal of a Congressman's libel suit based upon a newspaper article charging him with anti-Semitism in opposing a judicial appointment. He said:

> "Cases which impose liability for erroneous reports of the political conduct of officials reflect the obsolete doctrine that the governed must not criticize their governors. . . . The interest of the public here outweighs the interest of appellant or any other individual. The protection of the public requires not merely discussion, but information. Political conduct and views which

some respectable people approve, and others condemn, are constantly imputed to Congressmen. Errors of fact, particularly in regard to a man's mental states and processes, are inevitable. . . . Whatever is added to the field of libel is taken from the field of free debate."[13]

Injury to official reputation affords no more warrant for repressing speech that would otherwise be free than does factual error. Where judicial officers are involved, this Court has held that concern for the dignity and reputation of the courts does not justify the punishment as criminal contempt of criticism of the judge or his decision. Bridges v. California, 314 U.S. 252 (1941). This is true even though the utterance contains "half-truths" and "misinformation." Pennekamp v. Florida, 328 U.S. 331, 342, 343, n. 5, 345 (1946). . . . Criticism of their official conduct does not lose its constitutional protection merely because it is effective criticism and hence diminishes their official reputations.

If neither factual error nor defamatory content suffices to remove the constitutional shield from criticism of official conduct, the combination of the two elements is no less inadequate. This is the lesson to be drawn from the great controversy over the Sedition Act of 1798, 1 Stat. § 596, which first crystallized a national awareness of the central meaning of the First Amendment. . . .

Although the Sedition Act was never tested in this Court,[16] the attack upon its validity has carried the day in the court of history. Fines levied in its prosecution were repaid by Act of Congress on the ground that it was unconstitutional. . . . The invalidity of the Act has also been assumed by Justices of this Court. [ ] These views reflect a broad consensus that the Act, because of the restraint it imposed upon criticism of government and public officials, was inconsistent with the First Amendment.

There is no force in respondent's argument that the constitutional limitations implicit in the history of the Sedition Act apply only to Congress and not to the States. It is true that the First Amendment was originally addressed only to action by the Federal Government, and that Jefferson, for one, while denying the power of Congress "to controul the freedom of the press," recognized such a power in the States. [ ] But this distinction was eliminated with the adoption of the Fourteenth Amendment and the application to the States of the First Amendment's restrictions. [ ]

---

13. See also Mill, On Liberty (Oxford: Blackwell, 1947), at 47:

". . . [T]o argue sophistically, to suppress facts or arguments, to misstate the elements of the case, or misrepresent the opposite opinion . . . all this, even to the most aggravated degree, is so continually done in perfect good faith, by persons who are not considered, and in many other respects may not deserve to be considered, ignorant or incompetent, that it is rarely possible, on adequate grounds, conscientiously to stamp the misrepresentation as morally culpable; and still less could law presume to interfere with this kind of controversial misconduct."

16. The Act expired by its terms in 1801.

What a State may not constitutionally bring about by means of a criminal statute is likewise beyond the reach of its civil law of libel. The fear of damage awards under a rule such as that invoked by the Alabama courts here may be markedly more inhibiting than the fear of prosecution under a criminal statute. [ ] Alabama, for example, has a criminal libel law which subjects to prosecution "any person who speaks, writes, or prints of and concerning another any accusation falsely and maliciously importing the commission by such person of a felony, or any other indictable offense involving moral turpitude," and which allows as punishment upon conviction a fine not exceeding $500 and a prison sentence of six months. [ ] Presumably a person charged with violation of this statute enjoys ordinary criminal-law safeguards such as the requirements of an indictment and of proof beyond a reasonable doubt. These safeguards are not available to the defendant in a civil action. . . . And since there is no double-jeopardy limitation applicable to civil lawsuits, this is not the only judgment that may be awarded against petitioners for the same publication.[18] Whether or not a newspaper can survive a succession of such judgments, the pall of fear and timidity imposed upon those who would give voice to public criticism is an atmosphere in which the First Amendment freedoms cannot survive. Plainly the Alabama law of civil libel is "a form of regulation that creates hazards to protected freedoms markedly greater than those that attend reliance upon the criminal law." Bantam Books, Inc. v. Sullivan, 372 U.S. 58, 70 (1963).

The state rule of law is not saved by its allowance of the defense of truth. . . . Allowance of the defense of truth, with the burden of proving it on the defendant, does not mean that only false speech will be deterred.[19] Even courts accepting this defense as an adequate safeguard have recognized the difficulties of adducing legal proofs that the alleged libel was true in all its factual particulars. See, e.g., Post Publishing Co. v. Hallam, 59 F. 530, 540 (C.A.6th Cir.1893); see also Noel, Defamation of Public Officers and Candidates, 49 Col.L.Rev. 875, 892 (1949). Under such a rule, would-be critics of official conduct may be deterred from voicing their criticism, even though it is believed to be true and even though it is in fact true, because of doubt whether it can be proved in court or fear of the expense of having to do so. They tend to make only statements which "steer far wider of the unlawful zone." Speiser v. Randall, supra, 357 U.S., at 526. The rule thus dampens the vigor and limits the variety of public debate. It is inconsistent with the First and Fourteenth Amendments.

---

18. The Times states that four other libel suits based on the advertisement have been filed against it by others who have served as Montgomery City Commissioners and by the Governor of Alabama; that another $500,000 verdict has been awarded in the only one of these cases that has yet gone to trial; and that the damages sought in the other three total $2,000,000.

19. Even a false statement may be deemed to make a valuable contribution to public debate, since it brings about "the clearer perception and livelier impression of truth, produced by its collision with error." Mill, On Liberty (Oxford: Blackwell, 1947), at 15; see also Milton, Areopagitica, in Prose Works (Yale, 1959), Vol. II, at 561.

The constitutional guarantees require, we think, a federal rule that prohibits a public official from recovering damages for a defamatory falsehood relating to his official conduct unless he proves that the statement was made with "actual malice"—that is, with knowledge that it was false or with reckless disregard of whether it was false or not. An oft-cited statement of a like rule, which has been adopted by a number of state courts, is found in the Kansas case of Coleman v. MacLennan, 78 Kan. 711, 98 P. 281 (1908). . . .

Such a privilege for criticism of official conduct is appropriately analogous to the protection accorded a public official when *he* is sued for libel by a private citizen. In Barr v. Matteo, 360 U.S. 564, 575 (1959), this Court held the utterance of a federal official to be absolutely privileged if made "within the outer perimeter" of his duties. The States accord the same immunity to statements of their highest officers, although some differentiate their lesser officials and qualify the privilege they enjoy. But all hold that all officials are protected unless actual malice can be proved. The reason for the official privilege is said to be that the threat of damage suits would otherwise "inhibit the fearless, vigorous, and effective administration of policies of government" and "dampen the ardor of all but the most resolute, or the most irresponsible, in the unflinching discharge of their duties." Barr v. Matteo, supra, 360 U.S., at 571. Analogous considerations support the privilege for the citizen-critic of government. It is as much his duty to criticize as it is the official's duty to administer. . . . As Madison said, [ ], "the censorial power is in the people over the Government, and not in the Government over the people." It would give public servants an unjustified preference over the public they serve, if critics of official conduct did not have a fair equivalent of the immunity granted to the officials themselves.

We conclude that such a privilege is required by the First and Fourteenth Amendments.

III.

We hold today that the Constitution delimits a State's power to award damages for libel in actions brought by public officials against critics of their official conduct. Since this is such an action, the rule requiring proof of actual malice is applicable. While Alabama law apparently requires proof of actual malice for an award of punitive damages, where general damages are concerned malice is "presumed." Such a presumption is inconsistent with the federal rule. . . . Since the trial judge did not instruct the jury to differentiate between general and punitive damages, it may be that the verdict was wholly an award of one or the other. But it is impossible to know, in view of the general verdict returned. Because of this uncertainty, the judgment must be reversed and the case remanded.

Since respondent may seek a new trial, we deem that considerations of effective judicial administration require us to review the evidence in the present record to determine whether it could constitutionally support a judgment for respondent. . . .

[handwritten margin note: Actual malice must be proved for punitive and general damages — for public officials]

Applying these standards, we consider that the proof presented to show actual malice lacks the convincing clarity which the constitutional standard demands, and hence that it would not constitutionally sustain the judgment for respondent under the proper rule of law. The case of the individual petitioners requires little discussion. Even assuming that they could constitutionally be found to have authorized the use of their names on the advertisement, there was no evidence whatever that they were aware of any erroneous statements or were in any way reckless in that regard. The judgment against them is thus without constitutional support.

As to the Times, we similarly conclude that the facts do not support a finding of actual malice. [The testimony of the Secretary of the Times that he believed the advertisement to be "substantially correct" was "at least a reasonable [belief], and there was no evidence to impeach the witness' good faith in holding it." Nor was the later retraction for the governor evidence of actual malice toward plaintiff. Leaving open the question of whether failure to retract "may ever constitute such evidence," it could not suffice here because the letter showed reasonable doubt whether the ad referred to plaintiff at all, and also because the letter was not a final refusal. As to evidence that the Times published the ad without first checking news stories in its own files, the Court stated that the "mere presence" of such stories "does not, of course, establish that the Times' knew 'the advertisement was false', since the state of mind required for actual malice would have to be brought home to the persons in the Times' organization having responsibility for the publication of the advertisement." Those persons relied on the "good reputation of many of those whose names were listed as sponsors of the advertisement, and upon the letter from A. Philip Randolph, known to them as a responsible individual, certifying that the use of the names was authorized."]

We also think the evidence was constitutionally defective in another respect: it was incapable of supporting the jury's finding that the allegedly libelous statements were made "of and concerning" respondent. Respondent relies on the words of the advertisement and the testimony of six witnesses to establish a connection between it and himself. . . . There was no reference to respondent in the advertisement, either by name or official position. A number of the allegedly libelous statements—the charges that the dining hall was padlocked and that Dr. King's home was bombed, his person assaulted, and a perjury prosecution instituted against him—did not even concern the police; despite the ingenuity of the arguments which would attach this significance to the word "They," it is plain that these statements could not reasonably be read as accusing respondent of personal involvement in the acts in question. The statements upon which respondent principally relies as referring to him are the two allegations that did concern the police or police functions: that "truckloads of police . . . ringed the Alabama State College Campus" after the demonstration on the State Capitol steps, and that Dr. King had been "arrested . . . seven times." These statements were false only in that the police had been "deployed near" the campus but had not actually "ringed" it and had not gone there in connection with the State Capitol demonstration, and in that Dr. King had been arrested only four times. The ruling that these discrepancies between what was true and what was asserted were sufficient to injure respondent's reputation may itself raise constitutional problems, but we need not consider them here. Although the statements may be taken as referring to the police, they did not on their face make even an oblique reference to respondent as an individual. Support for the asserted reference must, therefore, be sought in the testimony of respondent's witnesses. But none of them suggested any basis for the belief that respondent himself was attacked in the advertisement beyond the bare fact that he was in overall charge of the Police Department and thus bore official responsibility for police conduct; to the extent that some of the witnesses thought respondent to have been charged with ordering or approving the conduct or otherwise being personally involved in it, they based this notion not on any statements in the advertisement, and not on any evidence that he had in fact been so involved, but solely on the unsupported assumption that, because of his official position, he must have been. This reliance on the bare fact of respondent's official position was made explicit by the Supreme Court of Alabama. . . .

This proposition has disquieting implications for criticism of governmental conduct. For good reason, "no court of last resort in this country has ever held, or even suggested, that prosecutions for libel on government have any place in the American system of jurisprudence." City of Chicago v. Tribune Co., 307 Ill. 595, 601, 139 N.E. 86, 88 (1923). The present proposition would sidestep this obstacle by transmuting criticism of government, however impersonal it may seem on its face, into personal criticism, and hence potential libel, of the officials of whom the government is composed. There is no legal alchemy by which a State may thus create the cause of action that would otherwise be denied for a publication which, as respondent himself said of the advertisement, "reflects not only on me but on the other Commissioners and the community." Raising as it does the possibility that a good-faith critic of government will be penalized for his criticism, the proposition relied on by the Alabama courts strikes at the very center of the constitutionally protected area of free expression.[30] We hold that such a proposition may not constitutionally be utilized to establish that an otherwise impersonal attack on governmental operations was a libel of an official responsible for those operations. Since it was relied on exclusively here, and there was no other evidence to connect the statements with respondent, the evidence was constitutionally insufficient to support a finding that the statements referred to respondent.

30. Insofar as the proposition means only that the statements about police conduct libeled respondent by implicitly criticizing his ability to run the Police Department, recovery is also precluded in this case by the doctrine of fair comment. See American Law Institute, Restatement of Torts (1938), § 607. Since the Fourteenth Amendment requires recognition of the conditional privilege for honest misstatements of fact, it follows that a defense of fair comment must be afforded for honest expression of opinion based upon privileged, as well as true, statements of fact. Both defenses are of course defeasible if the public official proves actual malice, as was not done here.

The judgment of the Supreme Court of Alabama is reversed and the case is remanded to that court for further proceedings not inconsistent with this opinion.

Reversed and remanded.

■ MR. JUSTICE BLACK, with whom MR. JUSTICE DOUGLAS joins, concurring.

I concur in reversing this half-million-dollar judgment against the New York Times Company and the four individual defendants. In reversing the Court holds that "the Constitution delimits a State's power to award damages for libel in actions brought by public officials against critics of their official conduct." I base my vote to reverse on the belief that the First and Fourteenth Amendments not merely "delimit" a State's power to award damages to "public officials against critics of their official conduct" but completely prohibit a State from exercising such a power. The Court goes on to hold that a State can subject such critics to damages if "actual malice" can be proved against them. "Malice," even as defined by the Court, is an elusive, abstract concept, hard to prove and hard to disprove. The requirement that malice be proved provides at best an evanescent protection for the right critically to discuss public affairs and certainly does not measure up to the sturdy safeguard embodied in the First Amendment. Unlike the Court, therefore, I vote to reverse exclusively on the ground that the Times and the individual defendants had an absolute unconditional constitutional right to publish in the Times advertisement their criticisms of the Montgomery agencies and officials. . . .

The half-million-dollar verdict does give dramatic proof, however, that state libel laws threaten the very existence of an American press virile enough to publish unpopular views on public affairs and bold enough to criticize the conduct of public officials. . . . In fact, briefs before us show that in Alabama there are now pending eleven libel suits by local and state officials against the Times seeking $5,600,000 and five such suits against the Columbia Broadcasting System seeking $1,700,000. Moreover, this technique for harassing and punishing a free press—now that it has been shown to be possible—is by no means limited to cases with racial overtones; it can be used in other fields where public feelings may make local as well as out-of-state newspapers easy prey for libel verdict seekers. . . . This record certainly does not indicate that any different verdict would have been rendered here whatever the Court had charged the jury about "malice," "truth," "good motives," "justifiable ends," or any other legal formulas which in theory would protect the press. Nor does the record indicate that any of these legalistic words would have caused the courts below to set aside or to reduce the half-million-dollar verdict in any amount.

.   .   .

. . . An unconditional right to say what one pleases about public affairs is what I consider to be the minimum guarantee of the First

Amendment.[6]

I regret that the Court has stopped short of this holding indispensable to preserve our free press from destruction.

■ MR. JUSTICE GOLDBERG, with whom MR. JUSTICE DOUGLAS joins, concurring in the result.

. . .

In my view, the First and Fourteenth Amendments to the Constitution afford to the citizen and to the press an absolute, unconditional privilege to criticize official conduct despite the harm which may flow from excesses and abuses. . . .

. . .

. . . It may be urged that deliberately and maliciously false statements have no conceivable value as free speech. That argument, however, is not responsive to the real issue presented by this case, which is whether that freedom of speech which all agree is constitutionally protected can be effectively safeguarded by a rule allowing the imposition of liability upon a jury's evaluation of the speaker's state of mind. If individual citizens may be held liable in damages for strong words, which a jury finds false and maliciously motivated, there can be little doubt that public debate and advocacy will be constrained. And if newspapers, publishing advertisements dealing with public issues, thereby risk liability, there can also be little doubt that the ability of minority groups to secure publication of their views on public affairs and to seek support for their causes will be greatly diminished. . . .

. . .

This is not to say that the Constitution protects defamatory statements directed against the private conduct of a public official or private citizen. Freedom of press and of speech insures that government will respond to the will of the people and that changes may be obtained by peaceful means. Purely private defamation has little to do with the political ends of a self-governing society. The imposition of liability for private defamation does not abridge the freedom of public speech or any other freedom protected by the First Amendment.[4] . . .

. . .

NOTES AND QUESTIONS

1. What is the problem with strict liability? Would a negligence standard raise the same problems? Would absolute privilege be objectiona-

---

6. Cf. Meiklejohn, Free Speech and Its Relation to Self–Government (1948).

4. In most cases, as in the case at bar, there will be little difficulty in distinguishing defamatory speech relating to private conduct from that relating to official conduct. I rec-

ognize, of course, that there will be a gray area. The difficulties of applying a public-private standard are, however, certainly of a different genre from those attending the differentiation between a malicious and nonmalicious state of mind. . . .

ble? How does the "actual malice" standard appear to differ from the *Hallam* standard, p. 911, supra? The *Coleman* standard?

Do you consider either of the concurring opinions preferable to the majority approach?

2.   Justice Brennan's concern lest speakers have to "steer far wider of the unlawful zone" than legally necessary has been articulated by others as the concern that fear of liability has the potential to "chill" speech. In the cited case of *Speiser v. Randall* the Court invalidated a procedure under which veterans seeking a California tax exemption bore the burden of proving that they had not advocated the overthrow of the government. Justice Brennan, writing in that case, noted that where speech is close to the line between lawful and unlawful,

> the possibility of mistaken factfinding—inherent in all litigation—will create the danger that the legitimate utterance will be penalized. The man who knows that he must bring forth proof and persuade another of the lawfulness of his conduct necessarily must steer far wider of the unlawful zone than if the state must bear these burdens.

How is this concern relevant to the problems raised by libel law?

3.   Which single step seems more likely to prevent the "chilling" of speech: shifting the burden of proving falsity to plaintiffs or introducing "actual malice"? Although the Court might have made only one of these changes, lower courts took the Court's definition of the "actual malice" to have subsumed the showing of falsity as well: proof that the statement was made with "knowledge that it was false or with reckless disregard of whether it was false or not." This is discussed further at p. 943, infra.

4.   Toward the end of the opinion the Court discusses whether the libel was of and concerning the plaintiff. Why isn't that a jury question? For a discussion of how the Times's argument that the article was not about the plaintiff expanded during the oral argument, see Miller and Barron, The Supreme Court, The Adversary System, and the Flow of Information to the Justices: A Preliminary Inquiry, 61 Va.L.Rev. 1187 (1975). For a discussion of the opinion drafting process, see B. Schwartz, Super Chief: Earl Warren and his Supreme Court—A Judicial Biography 531–41 (1983). The story of the Supreme Court's deliberation in the *Sullivan* case is told in intriguing detail in A. Lewis, "Make No Law" (1991).

5.   Commenting after the *Times* case, Professor Kalven speculated on the case's future:

> The closing question, of course, is whether the treatment of seditious libel as the key concept for development of appropriate constitutional doctrine will prove germinal. It is not easy to predict what the Court will see in the *Times* opinion as the years roll by. It may regard the opinion as covering simply one pocket of cases, those dealing with libel of public officials, and not destructive of the earlier notions that are inconsistent only with the larger reading of the Court's action. But the invitation to follow a dialectic progression

from public official to government policy to public policy to matters in the public domain, like art, seems to me to be overwhelming. If the Court accepts the invitation, it will slowly work out for itself the theory of free speech that Alexander Meiklejohn has been offering us for some fifteen years now.

Kalven, The *New York Times* Case: A Note on "The Central Meaning of the First Amendment," 1964 Sup.Ct.Rev. 191, 221. Does his prediction seem sound? Keep it in mind as we proceed.

6. The majority in the *New York Times* case did not explicitly condemn the concurring approaches. A few months later, in *Garrison v. Louisiana*, 379 U.S. 64 (1964), the Court, in an opinion by Justice Brennan, extended the *Times* rule to cases of criminal libel and also held that truth must be a defense in cases brought by public officials. The majority explained its refusal to protect deliberate falsity:

> Although honest utterance, even if inaccurate, may further the fruitful exercise of the right of free speech, it does not follow that the lie, knowingly and deliberately published about a public official, should enjoy a like immunity. At the time the First Amendment was adopted, as today, there were those unscrupulous enough and skillful enough to use the deliberate or reckless falsehood as an effective political tool to unseat the public servant or even topple an administration. [ ] That speech is used as a tool for political ends does not automatically bring it under the protective mantle of the Constitution. For the use of the known lie as a tool is at once at odds with the premises of democratic government and with the orderly manner in which economic, social, or political change is to be effected. Calculated falsehood falls into that class of utterances which "are no essential part of any exposition of ideas, and are of such slight social value as a step to truth that any benefit that may be derived from them is clearly outweighed by the social interest in order and morality. . . ." [*Chaplinsky*]. Hence the knowingly false statement and the false statement made with reckless disregard of the truth, do not enjoy constitutional protection.

In an explicit, but not entirely successful, effort to avoid confusion between common-law malice and "actual malice," the Court observed that

> Debate on public issues will not be uninhibited if the speaker must run the risk that it will be proved in court that he spoke out of hatred; even if he did speak out of hatred, utterances honestly believed contribute to the free interchange of ideas and the ascertainment of the truth.

2. PUBLIC FIGURES

Shortly after New York Times, the Court considered two cases together: Curtis Publishing Co. v. Butts, and Associated Press v. Walker, 388 U.S. 130 (1967).

In *Butts* the defendant magazine had accused the plaintiff athletic director of disclosing his game plan to an opposing coach before their game.

Although he was on the staff of a state university, Butts was paid by a private alumni organization. In *Walker,* the defendant news service reported that the plaintiff, a former United States Army general who resigned to engage in political activity, had personally led students in an attack on federal marshals who were enforcing a desegregation order at the University of Mississippi.

In both cases, lower courts affirmed substantial jury awards against the defendants and refused to apply the *Times* doctrine on the ground that public officials were not involved. The Supreme Court divided several ways, affirming *Butts,* 5–4, and reversing *Walker,* 9–0. Chief Justice Warren wrote the pivotal opinion in which he concluded that both men were "public figures" and that the standard developed in *New York Times* should apply to "public figures" as well:

> To me, differentiation between "public figures" and "public officials" and adoption of separate standards of proof for each has no basis in law, logic, or First Amendment policy. Increasingly in this country, the distinctions between governmental and private sectors are blurred. Since the depression of the 1930's and World War II there has been a rapid fusion of economic and political power, a merging of science, industry, and government, and a high degree of interaction between the intellectual, governmental, and business worlds. Depression, war, international tensions, national and international markets, and the surging growth of science and technology have precipitated national and international problems that demand national and international solutions. While these trends and events have occasioned a consolidation of governmental power, power has also become much more organized in what we have commonly considered to be the private sector. In many situations, policy determinations which traditionally were channeled through formal political institutions are now originated and implemented through a complex array of boards, committees, commissions, corporations, and associations, some only loosely connected with the Government. This blending of positions and power has also occurred in the case of individuals so that many who do not hold public office at the moment are nevertheless intimately involved in the resolution of important public questions or, by reason of their fame, shape events in areas of concern to society at large.

> Viewed in this context then, it is plain that although they are not subject to the restraints of the political process, "public figures," like "public officials," often play an influential role in ordering society. And surely as a class these "public figures" have as ready access as "public officials" to mass media of communication, both to influence policy and to counter criticism of their views and activities. Our citizenry has a legitimate and substantial interest in the conduct of such persons, and freedom of the press to engage in uninhibited debate about their involvement in

public issues and events is as crucial as it is in the case of "public officials." The fact that they are not amenable to the restraints of the political process only underscores the legitimate and substantial nature of the interest, since it means that public opinion may be the only instrument by which society can attempt to influence their conduct.

He found that on the merits the standard had not been met in *Walker*. In *Butts* he found that defendant's counsel had deliberately waived the *Times* doctrine and he also found evidence establishing reckless behavior. He thus voted to reverse *Walker* and affirm *Butts*.

Justice Harlan, joined by three others, argued that something less than the *Times* standard should apply to public figures because criticism of government was not involved:

> We consider and would hold that a "public figure" who is not a public official may also recover damages for a defamatory falsehood whose substance makes substantial danger to reputation apparent, on a showing of highly unreasonable conduct constituting an extreme departure from the standards of investigation and reporting ordinarily adhered to by responsible publishers.

[handwritten margin note: One def. of common law "gross negligence"]

Applying that standard, Justice Harlan concluded that Walker had failed to establish a case, but that Butts had shown that the Saturday Evening Post ignored elementary precautions in preparing a potentially damaging story. Together with the Chief Justice's vote, there were five votes to affirm *Butts*.

Justices Brennan and White agreed with the Chief Justice in *Walker* but found no waiver in *Butts* and would have reversed both cases. They agreed with the Chief Justice that Butts had presented enough evidence to come within the *Times* standard but thought that errors in the charge required a new trial.

Justices Black and Douglas adhered to their position, urged that the *Times* rule be abandoned, and voted to reverse both cases.

Although some courts seemed to regard Justice Harlan's opinion as the prevailing opinion, in part because it came first in the reports, it should have been clear that the same "actual malice" standard that applied in "public official" cases also applied in "public figure" cases. Should it? For an extended argument against identical standards for the two categories, see Schauer, Public Figures, 25 Wm. & Mary L.Rev. 905 (1984).

Later in this chapter we will attempt to identify the critical features of the "public figure." For now, however, the important point is to recognize that the identical "actual malice" rules apply to plaintiffs called "public officials" and to those called "public figures"—and to consider how those rules work.

3.   THE "ACTUAL MALICE" STANDARD

The Court's choice of the phrase "actual malice" in 1964 was the source of much confusion that would not have occurred if the Court had created some new term that had no link with the traditions of common law libel. The phrase "actual malice" did not clearly convey the shift in focus from the common law's attention to hatred, ill will, or spite toward the plaintiff to the new notion of looking at the defendant's attitude toward the truth of the defamatory statement. The Court has had several occasions to consider "actual malice" in detail. After considering substantive aspects of the doctrine, we turn to procedural issues.

a. SUBSTANTIVE ISSUES

In St. Amant v. Thompson, 390 U.S. 727 (1968), the defendant repeated false charges against plaintiff without having checked the charges or investigating the source's reputation for veracity. The Supreme Court concluded that "reckless disregard" had not been shown. It recognized that the term could receive no single "infallible definition" and that its outer limits would have to be developed in "case-to-case adjudication." The record must provide "sufficient evidence to permit the conclusion that the defendant in fact entertained serious doubts as to the truth of his publication" in order for recklessness to be found. Anticipating the argument that this position would encourage publishers not to verify their assertions, Justice White, for the Court, stated:

> The defendant in a defamation action brought by a public official cannot, however, automatically insure a favorable verdict by testifying that he published with a belief that the statements were true. The finder of fact must determine whether the publication was indeed made in good faith. Professions of good faith will be unlikely to prove persuasive, for example, where a story is fabricated by the defendant, is a product of his imagination, or is based wholly on an unverified anonymous telephone call. Nor will they be likely to prevail when the publisher's allegations are so inherently improbable that only a reckless man would have put them in circulation. Likewise, recklessness may be found where there are obvious reasons to doubt the veracity of the informant or the accuracy of his reports.

Justice Fortas dissented on the ground that the failure to make "a good-faith check" of the statement was sufficient to establish "reckless disregard." How would the Court's test apply to an extreme partisan who would readily believe anything derogatory about his opponent?

In the second case, Herbert v. Lando, 441 U.S. 153 (1979), the plaintiff, Colonel Anthony Herbert, an admitted public figure, sued the producer and reporter of the television program "60 Minutes" and the CBS network for remarks on the program about his behavior while in military service in Vietnam. During his deposition, Lando, the producer, was generally responsive but he refused to answer some questions about why he made certain investigations and not others; what he concluded about the honesty of certain people he interviewed for the program; and about conversations he had with Mike Wallace, the reporter, in the preparation of the program segment. Lando contended that these thought processes and internal editorial discussions were protected from disclosure by the First Amendment. The Supreme Court disagreed.

Justice White, for the Court, understood the defendants to be arguing that "the defendant's reckless disregard of truth, a critical element, could not be shown by direct evidence through inquiry into the thoughts, opinions and conclusions of the publisher but could be proved only by objective evidence from which the ultimate fact could be inferred." This was a barrier of some substance, "particularly when defendants themselves are prone to assert their good-faith belief in the truth of their publications, and libel plaintiffs are required to prove knowing or reckless falsehood with 'convincing clarity.' "

Although pretrial discovery techniques had led to "mushrooming litigation costs," this was happening in all areas of litigation. Until major changes in pretrial procedures were developed for all cases, the Court would rely on "what in fact and in law are ample powers of the district judge to prevent abuse."

Plaintiff also sued the Atlantic Monthly for a story written by Lando. The magazine "conducted no independent inquiry into the facts because that is not its practice. It maintains no research department." Since Lando, a freelance author, was "an apparently reasonable journalist" and the article was not "inherently implausible," the magazine had no obligation to investigate the facts and was not vicariously liable for Lando's statements. Herbert v. Lando, 596 F.Supp. 1178 (S.D.N.Y.1984), affirmed on other grounds 781 F.2d 298 (2d Cir.), cert. denied 476 U.S. 1182 (1986).

Would it raise First Amendment problems if a state were to conclude that "actual malice" on the part of an employee in the print shop or a dishonest reporter could subject the publisher to damages?

In Harte–Hanks Communications, Inc. v. Connaughton, 491 U.S. 657 (1989), the newspaper accused a judicial candidate of having used "dirty tricks" to smear his opponent, the incumbent. A unanimous Court upheld an award of $5,000 compensatory and $195,000 punitive damages.

The evidence of "dirty tricks" relied heavily on a source whose credibility had been seriously impugned by other witnesses and whose version of the episode was essentially unconfirmed. Reviewing the record extensively, the Court concluded that actual malice could be found from several uncontroverted findings: (1) the newspaper's failure to interview "the one witness that both [the plaintiff and the source] claimed would verify their conflicting accounts of the relevant events" was "utterly bewildering"; (2) the paper's failure to listen to a tape that the paper had been told exonerated plaintiff, which plaintiff had delivered to the paper at the paper's request; (3) an earlier article on the election that "could be taken to indicate that [the editor] had already decided to publish [the source's] allegations, regardless of how the evidence developed and regardless of whether or not [the source's] story was credible upon ultimate reflection"; (4) that a crucial witness was not interviewed—for a variety of arguably inconsistent reasons offered by defendant's employees.

Accepting the jury's implicit determination that the newspaper's explanations for not interviewing the crucial witness and for not listening to the tape "were not credible, it is likely that the newspaper's inaction was a product of a deliberate decision not to acquire knowledge of facts that might confirm the probable falsity of [the source's] charges. Although failure to investigate will not alone support a finding of actual malice [*St. Amant*], the purposeful avoidance of the truth is in a different category."

In a footnote at that point, the Court noted that it was not suggesting that a newspaper must accept or be shaken by vehement "denials". These are "so commonplace in the world of polemical charge and countercharge that, in themselves, they hardly alert the conscientious reporter to the likelihood of error."

In passing, the Court observed that a "newspaper's motive in publishing the story—whether to promote an opponent's candidacy or to increase its circulation—cannot provide a sufficient basis for finding actual malice."

The Masson case. In Masson v. New Yorker Magazine, Inc., 501 U.S. 496 (1991), plaintiff alleged that an article in defendant magazine written by Janet Malcolm had attributed to plaintiff fabricated quotations that hurt his reputation. The lower courts had upheld summary judgment for the defendants. The Supreme Court reversed. First, the Court concluded that readers of non-fiction in a magazine that "at the relevant time seemed to enjoy a reputation for scrupulous factual accuracy," could take the accuracy of quotations "at face value. A defendant may be able to argue to the jury that quotations should be viewed by the reader as nonliteral or reconstructions, but we conclude that a trier of fact in this case could find that the reasonable reader would understand the quotations to be nearly verbatim reports of statements made by the subject."

The plaintiff then argued that "excepting corrections of grammar or syntax, publication of a quotation with knowledge that it does not contain the words the public figure used demonstrates actual malice." The Court was unwilling to go that far. Interviewers often must reconstruct interviews from notes. Use of language that the subject did not use does not amount to actual malice in that situation. Even if an interview is tape recorded, the "full and exact statement will be reported in only rare circumstances":

> We conclude that a deliberate alteration of the words uttered by a plaintiff does not equate with knowledge of falsity for purposes of [*Times*] unless the alteration results in a material change in the meaning conveyed by the statement. The use of quotation to attribute words not in fact spoken bears in a most important way on that inquiry, but it is not dispositive in every case.

In this case readers may have found the article "especially damning because so much of it appeared to be a selfportrait, told by the [plaintiff] in his own words." The Court doubted that "readers will assume that direct quotations are but a rational interpretation of the speaker's words, and we decline to adopt any such presumption in determining the permissible interpretations of the quotations in question here."

Applying these principles to the case, the Court reversed the summary judgment. It concluded that several passages could be read as more damning in the article than what the plaintiff alleges he in fact said and the record contained evidence that would support a jury determination that Malcolm "deliberately or recklessly altered the quotations."

On remand in the *Masson* case, the court concluded that although a publisher who has no "obvious reasons to doubt" the accuracy of a story "is not required to initiate an investigation that might plant such doubt," once "doubt exists, the publisher must act reasonably in dispelling it." Although this approach puts publishers who fact-check stories "at somewhat of a disadvantage compared to other publishers such as newspapers and supermarket tabloids that cannot or will not engage in thorough fact-checking," the different treatment "makes considerable sense":

> Readers of reputable magazines such as the New Yorker are far more likely to trust the verbatim accuracy of the stories they read than are the readers of supermarket tabloids or even daily newspapers, where they understand the inherent limitations in the fact-finding process. The harm inflicted by a misstatement in a publication known for scrupulously investigating the accuracy of its stories can be far more serious than a similar misstatement in a publication known not to do so.

Masson v. New Yorker Magazine, Inc., 960 F.2d 896(9th Cir.1992). The court did, however, dismiss the case against the publisher of the book into which the New Yorker articles were converted. The publisher was entitled to rely on the New Yorker's reputation for accuracy and on its rejection of the plaintiff's complaints about the series. The book publisher had no "obvious reasons to doubt" the story's accuracy and thus no obligation to investigate.

At the ensuing trial, the jury found actual malice as to two of the five remaining quotations but hung on the question of damages. Impasse Over Damages in New Yorker Libel Case, N.Y.Times, June 4, 1993 at A1. The jury did find that Malcolm was an independent contractor and that the New Yorker did not act with "actual malice." This pair of findings led to the New Yorker's dismissal from the case.

On the retrial, the jury found that two of the five passages were false and that one of them defamed Masson. But the jury found no actual malice and returned a defense verdict. Motions for a new trial were denied and an appeal has been announced. The defense attorney is quoted as attributing the different jury verdicts to two factors: (1) his increased emphasis on actual malice at the second trial and (2) that Ms. Malcolm was "much more persuasive, more convincing, more on top of her facts" the second time. For a period of at least six months, Ms. Malcolm had been coached by a speech consultant who said that he had worked with her "to make her body language less defensive and make her language more reflective of the truth she was telling." Margolick, *Psychoanalyst Loses Libel Suit Against a New Yorker Reporter*, N.Y.Times, Nov. 3, 1994 at A1.

Actual malice in the lower courts. Some important questions about actual malice have been addressed by lower courts. A few follow.

1. Can bits of evidence, each insufficient to show malice, be cumulated? In Tavoulareas v. Piro, 817 F.2d 762 (D.C.Cir.) (en banc), cert. denied 484 U.S. 870 (1987), the court answered with a cautious "yes"—but stated that evidence of the reporter's "ill will or bad motives will support a finding of actual malice only when combined with other, more substantial evidence of a defendant's bad faith."

2. Is lack of fairness in the article probative? In Westmoreland v. CBS, Inc., 601 F.Supp. 66 (S.D.N.Y.1984), the court said no:

> The fairness of the broadcast is not at issue in the libel suit. Publishers and reporters do not commit a libel in a public figure case by publishing unfair one-sided attacks. . . . The fact that a commentary is one sided and sets forth categorical accusations has no tendency to prove that the publisher believed it to be false. The libel law does not require the publisher to grant his accused equal time or fair reply. . . . A publisher who honestly believes in the truth of his accusations . . . is under no obligation under the libel law to treat the subject of his accusations fairly or evenhandedly.

In Costello v. Ocean County Observer, 136 N.J. 594, 643 A.2d 1012 (1994), the court held that a "highly unfair" story did not show actual malice. The fact that the reporter was young and had been a reporter for only seven months was relevant in trying to determine whether his work was the result of actual malice or negligence. The defendants "narrowly escape liability, but they do not escape the loss of credibility that results from slipshod journalism."

3. Is haste alone enough to show malice? In Meisler v. Gannett Co., 12 F.3d 1026 (11th Cir.) cert. denied 114 S.Ct. 2712 (1994), the defendant carried an article based on an Associated Press wire service story marked "URGENT" even though AP indicated that "MORE" would be coming on this story. Although the second version arrived before the deadline, the author of the first version never saw it. Since the writer had no serious doubt about the article's accuracy at the time of publication, actual malice was not established.

4. Can a journalist avoid trial by asserting that he honestly thought he saw something that did not in fact exist? The court said no in Currier v. Western Newspapers, Inc., 175 Ariz. 290, 855 P.2d 1351 (1993), in which plaintiff presented evidence that defendant repeated a defamatory statement after plaintiff had informed the newspapers of the falsity—a columnist's claim that he "believed [he] saw" a crucial signature on a document when it was not in fact there. The court denied summary judgment on the actual malice question: the columnist "either did not look at the public records at all or was careless in reading and recording what he saw."

5. Is failure to investigate enough? In Sweeney v. Prisoners' Legal Services of New York, Inc., 84 N.Y.2d 786, 647 N.E.2d 101, 622 N.Y.S.2d 896 (1995), the court reversed the determination of two lower courts that actual malice had been shown. Failure to investigate standing alone was not enough to establish actual malice. Evidence that defendants purposefully avoided the truth may support a finding of actual malice if supported by evidence that the inaction sprang from a desire not to know, citing *Harte-Hanks, Inc.* In the absence of "some direct evidence that defendants in this case were aware that [the quoted source's charge] was probably false, they cannot be found to have harbored an intent to avoid the truth."

Libel by implication. We have already seen that it is possible to publish a series of statements that are each literally true but which, when put together, lead the average reader to draw a conclusion that is both defamatory and false. Recall p. 886, supra.

We also noted that some courts appeared unwilling to permit such an inference to be drawn by the jury. This unwillingness might have been based on the view that average readers in the specific cases did not and could not reasonably draw the implication that the plaintiff is relying upon. In fact, however, it appears that the courts were relying on a legal proposition drawn from their reading of the *New York Times* case.

In Mihalik v. Duprey, 11 Mass.App. 602, 417 N.E.2d 1238 (1981), the defendants sought to convey to the readership the impression that the plaintiff school board member had behaved improperly by taking his materials to the local trade school to have the students make furniture from them. The defendants left unstated the (apparently not widely known) fact that any local resident could do the same.

In Schaefer v. Lynch, 406 So.2d 185 (La.1981), the plaintiff was director of the state retirement system. The defendant reporter wrote a story that permitted readers to draw the conclusion that plaintiff had used his office to influence commercial lenders so as to further a personal investment. The court reasoned that because statements about public officials are privileged in the absence of actual malice, it "surely follows that all truthful statements are also constitutionally protected. Even though a false implication may be drawn by the public, there is no redress for its servant."

Some courts have gone the other way. In Saenz v. Playboy Enterprises, Inc., 841 F.2d 1309 (7th Cir.1988), a public official was written about in a way that permitted the reader to conclude that while in Uruguay on official government business, the official either knew that Uruguayans were torturing prisoners and did nothing about it or that he participated in the torture.

The court noted that a person may be "disadvantaged greatly in responding to the varying inferences that may be gleaned from inexact accusations." To bar liability in such cases "goes too far; it invokes the spectre of heinous abuse by crafty and mischievous authors whose subtle

art of insinuation is honed for destruction.''   It was for the jury to decide
which meaning to take from the piece:

> We are extremely mindful of the importance and value the
> people and laws of this country place on a free and independent
> press. . . . A legal fiction denying the existence of clearly
> discernible, though not explicit, charges exposes public officials to
> baseless accusations and public mistrust while promoting an un-
> disciplined brand of journalism both unproductive to society and,
> as we see it, unprotected by constitutional considerations.

The court required the plaintiff to show with ''clear and convincing
evidence that the defendants intended or knew of the implications that the
plaintiff is attempting to draw from the allegedly defamatory material.''
The case was dismissed for failure to show this element: ''Not only must
the plaintiff establish that the statement is susceptible of a defamatory
meaning which the defendant knew to be false or which the defendants
published with reckless disregard for its potential falsity, but also that the
defendants intended to imply or were reckless toward the implications.
Evidence of defamatory meaning and recklessness regarding potential
falsity does not alone establish the defendant's intent.''

Even if libel actions based on ''impressions'' are not precluded by
federal constitutional law, should they be barred as a matter of state law?
For a general discussion of implied libel, see Dienes and Levine, Implied
Libel, Defamatory Meanings, and State of Mind: The Promise of *New York
Times Co. v. Sullivan*, 78 Iowa L.Rev. 2337 (1992).

b. PROCEDURAL ISSUES

1. *Convincing clarity.* Although the ''actual malice'' rule is the major
substantive protection available to defendants being sued by public plaintiffs, an important procedural protection developed in *New York Times*
requires public plaintiffs to prove their actual malice cases with ''convincing clarity.''

In Long v. Arcell, 618 F.2d 1145 (5th Cir.1980), cert. denied 449 U.S.
1083 (1981), after a jury finding for the public-figure plaintiff, the trial
court granted the defendant newspaper a judgment notwithstanding the
verdict.   The trial court's ruling was affirmed on appeal.   The only
evidence for the jury involved conflicting accounts of conversations:

> If the applicable burden of proof had been a preponderance of the
> evidence, a jury verdict either way would have to stand.   Similarly,
> if liability could be imposed on a clear and convincing showing of
> negligence, we would be hard pressed to disregard the jury's
> verdict.   We repeat, however, that the plaintiff's burden was to
> prove actual malice by clear and convincing evidence.   This record
> simply does not contain clear and convincing evidence that the
> defendants knew that their information was incorrect or had a
> ''high degree of awareness of . . . [its] probable falsity.''
> [*Garrison*].

Although not required to do so, some states have adopted this heightened burden of proof for some aspects of the state libel action. See, e.g., *Erickson,* p. 908, supra, in which the court gave a qualified privilege to an employer responding to an inquiry about an employee's work. The court then demanded that plaintiff show abuse of the privilege by "clear and convincing evidence." But see *Staples,* p. 880, supra, using a preponderance standard to conclude that plaintiff had shown abuse of a qualified privilege for intracompany communication.

2. *Independent appellate review.* The requirement of clear and convincing evidence has been bolstered by a further explicit requirement that appellate courts must exercise "independent review" to assure that the required proof has been presented with the required clarity. In Bose Corp. v. Consumers Union, 466 U.S. 485 (1984), a federal judge sitting as trier found actual malice and entered judgment against defendant magazine. The court of appeals understood its obligation to be to "independently examin[e] the record to ensure that the district court has applied properly the governing constitutional law and that the plaintiff has indeed satisfied its burden of proof." Using that standard the court of appeals reversed.

The Court, 6–3, upheld the court of appeals. It analogized libel cases to those others in which the unprotected character of particular communications depends upon "judicial evaluation of special facts that have been deemed to have constitutional significance":

> The rule of independent appellate review . . . emerged from the exigency of deciding concrete cases; it is law in its purest form under our common law heritage. It reflects a deeply held conviction that judges—and particularly members of this Court—must exercise such review in order to preserve the precious liberties established and ordained by the Constitution. The question whether the evidence in the record in a defamation case is of the convincing clarity required to strip the utterance of First Amendment protection is not merely a question for the trier of fact. Judges, as expositors of the Constitution, must independently decide whether the evidence in the record is sufficient to cross the constitutional threshold that bars the entry of any judgment that is not supported by clear and convincing proof of "actual malice."

For extended discussion, see the Court's discussion in the *Connaughton* case, p. 945, supra, upholding a determination of actual malice.

Bose is criticized in Monaghan, Constitutional Fact Review, 85 Colum.L.Rev. 229 (1985). See also, Bezanson, Fault, Falsity and Reputation in Public Defamation Law: An Essay on Bose Corporation v. Consumers Union, 8 Hamline L.Rev. 105 (1985).

3. *The summary judgment standard.* In Anderson v. Liberty Lobby, Inc., 477 U.S. 242 (1986), the Court held, 6–3, that the standard for considering summary judgment motions under Federal Rule 56 must take into account the burden plaintiff will have to meet at trial. For public plaintiffs, then, on a summary judgment motion the judge must decide

"whether the evidence in the record could support a reasonable jury finding either that the plaintiff has shown actual malice by clear and convincing evidence or that the plaintiff has not." Using a "preponderance" standard was rejected because it "makes no sense to say that a jury could reasonably find for either party without some benchmark as to what standards govern its deliberations and within what boundaries its ultimate decision must fall, and these standards and boundaries are in fact provided by the applicable evidentiary standards."

The Court denied that its holding denigrated the role of the jury. "Credibility determinations, the weighing of the evidence, and the drawing of legitimate inferences from the facts are jury functions, not those of a judge, whether he is ruling on a motion for summary judgment or for a directed verdict."

Several states, noting that the *Liberty Lobby* case was decided on nonconstitutional grounds, have declined to follow it.

4. *Confidential sources and proof of actual malice.* How can the plaintiff prove actual malice if the defendant journalist asserts reliance on a "confidential source" who is not identified? This important question, beyond the scope of this book, is explored in M. Franklin and D. Anderson, Cases and Materials on Mass Media Law 519–21 (5th ed. 1995).

5. *SLAPP suits.* In recent years, much concern has been expressed about defamation suits brought against persons making public statements in an apparent effort to dissuade them from participating in public discourse. Much of this involved suits against tenants' associations, environmental groups, and persons testifying at city council meetings. See Pring, SLAPPs: Strategic Lawsuits Against Public Participation, 7 Pace Envtl. L.Rev. 3 (1989). The concern led to what have been called anti-SLAPP statutes, which do not alter the substantive law applicable to the case. Rather, they offer procedural devices by which to identify and dismiss at an early stage nonmeritorious suits that interfere with free speech rights. Those who believe that they are the victims of such a suit, may prevail on an early "motion to strike, unless the court determines that the plaintiff has established that there is a probability that the plaintiff will prevail on the claim."

For the California version of the statute, see Cal.Code Civ.Proc. § 425.16. For a discussion of the philosophy behind the statute and how it operates, see Wilcox v. Superior Court, 27 Cal.App.4th 809, 33 Cal.Rptr.2d 446 (1994). See also, Dixon v. Superior Court, 30 Cal.App.4th 733, 36 Cal.Rptr.2d 687 (1994)(applying statute to dismiss suit brought against professor who wrote letters critical of work of surveyor during public review period in environmental impact dispute involving university land) and Lafayette Morehouse, Inc. v. Chronicle Pub.Co., 37 Cal.App.4th 855, 44 Cal.Rptr.2d 46 (1995)(holding statute broad enough to protect a newspaper defendant sued by a university that the paper had criticized).

C.   PRIVATE PLAINTIFFS AND THE CONSTITUTION

Soon after deciding its first "public figure" cases, the Court confronted Rosenbloom v. Metromedia, Inc., 403 U.S. 29 (1971), involving a broadcaster's report that a magazine distributor sold obscene material and was arrested in a police raid.   For a plurality, Justice Brennan, joined by Chief Justice Burger and Justice Blackmun, concluded that the *Times* standards should be extended to "all discussion and communication involving matters of public or general concern, without regard to whether the persons involved are famous or anonymous."   The arrest and the distributor's subsequent claims against the police were thought to fit this category and the *Times* standard was applied.   In reaching that position Justice Brennan concluded that the focus on the plaintiff's status begun in the *Times* case bore "little relationship either to the values protected by the First Amendment or to the nature of our society.   .   .   .   Thus, the idea that certain 'public' figures have voluntarily exposed their entire lives to public inspection, while private individuals have kept theirs carefully shrouded from public view is, at best, a legal fiction."   Discussion of a matter of public concern must be protected even when it involves an unknown person.   If the states fear that private citizens will be unable to respond to adverse publicity, "the solution lies in the direction of ensuring their ability to respond, rather than in stifling public discussion of matters of public concern," a reference to possible use of the right of reply.

Justice White concurred on the narrow ground that the press is privileged to report "upon the official actions of public servants in full detail."   Justice Black provided the fifth vote against liability, for the reasons stated in his earlier opinions.   Justice Douglas did not participate in the case.   Justices Harlan, Stewart and Marshall dissented on various grounds but they agreed that the private plaintiff should be required to prove no more than negligence in this case.   The dissenters also agreed that some limitations on damages should exist.   Yet the dissenters disagreed with each other as well as with the plurality on major points.   The area was ripe for rethinking.

Gertz v. Robert Welch, Inc.

Supreme Court of the United States, 1974.
418 U.S. 323, 94 S.Ct. 2997, 41 L.Ed.2d 789.

[Plaintiff, an attorney, was retained to represent the family of a youth killed by Nuccio, a Chicago policeman.   In that capacity, plaintiff attended the coroner's inquest and filed an action for damages but played no part in a criminal proceeding in which Nuccio was convicted of second degree murder.   Respondent published American Opinion, a monthly outlet for the views of the John Birch Society.   As part of its efforts to alert the public to an alleged nationwide conspiracy to discredit local police, the magazine's editor engaged a regular contributor to write about the Nuccio episode. The article that appeared charged a frame-up against Nuccio and portrayed plaintiff as a "major architect" of the plot. It also falsely asserted that he had a long police record, was an official of the Marxist League for Industrial Democracy, and was a "Leninist" and a "Communist-fronter." The editor said he had no reason to doubt the charges and made no effort to verify them.

Gertz filed an action for libel in District Court because of diversity of citizenship. The trial judge first ruled that Gertz was not a public official or public figure and that under Illinois law there was no defense. The jury awarded $50,000. On further reflection, the judge decided that since a matter of public concern was being discussed, the *Times* rule should apply and he granted the defendant judgment notwithstanding the jury's verdict. He thus anticipated the plurality's approach in *Rosenbloom v. Metromedia, Inc.* The court of appeals, relying on the intervening decision in *Rosenbloom,* affirmed because of the absence of clear and convincing evidence of actual malice. According to *St. Amant v. Thompson,* p. 944, supra, failure to investigate, without more, could not establish reckless disregard for truth. Gertz appealed.]

■ MR. JUSTICE POWELL delivered the opinion of the Court.

. . .

III.

We begin with the common ground. Under the First Amendment there is no such thing as a false idea. However pernicious an opinion may seem, we depend for its correction not on the conscience of judges and juries but on the competition of other ideas. But there is no constitutional value in false statements of fact. Neither the intentional lie nor the careless error materially advances society's interest in "uninhibited, robust, and wide-open" debate on public issues. . . .

Although the erroneous statement of fact is not worthy of constitutional protection, it is nevertheless inevitable in free debate. . . . And punishment of error runs the risk of inducing a cautious and restrictive exercise of the constitutionally guaranteed freedoms of speech and press. Our decisions recognize that a rule of strict liability that compels a publisher or broadcaster to guarantee the accuracy of his factual assertions may lead to intolerable self-censorship. Allowing the media to avoid liability only by proving the truth of all injurious statements does not accord adequate protection to First Amendment liberties. . . . The First Amendment requires that we protect some falsehood in order to protect speech that matters.

The need to avoid self-censorship by the news media is, however, not the only societal value at issue. If it were, this Court would have embraced long ago the view that publishers and broadcasters enjoy an unconditional and indefeasible immunity from liability for defamation. . . .

The legitimate state interest underlying the law of libel is the compensation of individuals for the harm inflicted on them by defamatory falsehood. We would not lightly require the State to abandon this purpose, for, as Mr. Justice Stewart has reminded us, the individual's right to the protection of his own good name

> "reflects no more than our basic concept of the essential dignity and worth of every human being—a concept at the root of any decent system of ordered liberty. The protection of private personality, like the protection of life itself, is left primarily to the individual States under the Ninth and Tenth Amendments. But this does not mean that the right is entitled to any less recognition by this Court as a basic of our constitutional system." Rosenblatt v. Baer, 383 U.S. 75, 92 (1966) (concurring opinion).

Some tension necessarily exists between the need for a vigorous and uninhibited press and the legitimate interest in redressing wrongful injury. . . .

The *New York Times* standard defines the level of constitutional protection appropriate to the context of defamation of a public person. Those who, by reason of the notoriety of their achievements or the vigor and success with which they seek the public's attention, are properly classed as public figures and those who hold governmental office may recover for injury to reputation only on clear and convincing proof that the defamatory falsehood was made with knowledge of its falsity or with reckless disregard for the truth. This standard administers an extremely powerful antidote to the inducement to media self-censorship of the common-law rule of strict liability for libel and slander. And it exacts a correspondingly high price from the victims of defamatory falsehood. Plainly many deserving plaintiffs, including some intentionally subjected to injury, will be unable to surmount the barrier of the *New York Times* test. Despite this substantial abridgment of the state law right to compensation for wrongful hurt to one's reputation, the Court has concluded that the protection of the *New York Times* privilege should be available to publishers and broadcasters of defamatory falsehood concerning public officials and public figures. [ ] We think that these decisions are correct, but we do not find their holdings justified solely by reference to the interest of the press and broadcast media in immunity from liability. Rather, we believe that the *New York Times* rule states an accommodation between this concern and the limited state interest present in the context of libel actions brought by public persons. For the reasons stated below, we conclude that the state interest in compensating injury to the reputation of private individuals requires that a different rule should obtain with respect to them.

Theoretically, of course, the balance between the needs of the press and the individual's claim to compensation for wrongful injury might be struck on a case-by-case basis. As Mr. Justice Harlan hypothesized, "it might seem, purely as an abstract matter, that the most utilitarian approach would be to scrutinize carefully every jury verdict in every libel case, in order to ascertain whether the final judgment leaves fully protected whatever First Amendment values transcend the legitimate state interest in protecting the particular plaintiff who prevailed." [*Rosenbloom*]. But this approach would lead to unpredictable results and uncertain expectations, and it could render our duty to supervise the lower courts unmanageable. Because an *ad hoc* resolution of the competing interests at stake in each particular case is not feasible, we must lay down broad rules of general application. Such rules necessarily treat alike various cases involving differences as well as similarities. Thus it is often true that not all of the considerations which justify adoption of a given rule will obtain in each particular case decided under its authority.

With that caveat we have no difficulty in distinguishing among defamation plaintiffs. The first remedy of any victim of defamation is self-help—using available opportunities to contradict the lie or correct the error and thereby to minimize its adverse impact on reputation. Public officials and public figures usually enjoy significantly greater access to the channels of effective communication and hence have a more realistic opportunity to counteract false statements than private individuals normally enjoy.[9] Private individuals are therefore more vulnerable to injury, and the state interest in protecting them is correspondingly greater.

More important than the likelihood that private individuals will lack effective opportunities for rebuttal, there is a compelling normative consideration underlying the distinction between public and private defamation plaintiffs. An individual who decides to seek governmental office must accept certain necessary consequences of that involvement in public affairs. He runs the risk of closer public scrutiny than might otherwise be the case. And society's interest in the officers of government is not strictly limited to the formal discharge of official duties. As the Court pointed out in [*Garrison v. Louisiana*], the public's interest extends to "anything which might touch on an official's fitness for office. . . . Few personal attributes are more germane to fitness for office than dishonesty, malfeasance, or improper motivation, even though these characteristics may also affect the official's private character."

Those classed as public figures stand in a similar position. Hypothetically, it may be possible for someone to become a public figure through no purposeful action of his own, but the instances of truly involuntary public figures must be exceedingly rare. For the most part those who attain this status have assumed roles of especial prominence in the affairs of society. Some occupy positions of such persuasive power and influence that they are deemed public figures for all purposes. More commonly, those classed as public figures have thrust themselves to the forefront of particular public controversies in order to influence the resolution of the issues involved. In either event, they invite attention and comment.

9. Of course, an opportunity for rebuttal seldom suffices to undo harm of defamatory falsehood. Indeed, the law of defamation is rooted in our experience that the truth rarely catches up with a lie. But the fact that the self-help remedy of rebuttal, standing alone, is inadequate to its task does not mean that it is irrelevant to our inquiry.

Even if the foregoing generalities do not obtain in every instance, the communications media are entitled to act on the assumption that public officials and public figures have voluntarily exposed themselves to increased risk of injury from defamatory falsehood concerning them.   No such assumption is justified with respect to a private individual.   He has not accepted public office or assumed an "influential role in ordering society."   Curtis Publishing Co. v. Butts, [   ], (Warren, C.J., concurring in result).   He has relinquished no part of his interest in the protection of his own good name, and consequently he has a more compelling call on the courts for redress of injury inflicted by defamatory falsehood.   Thus, private individuals are not only more vulnerable to injury than public officials and public figures;   they are also more deserving of recovery.

For these reasons we conclude that the States should retain substantial latitude in their efforts to enforce a legal remedy for defamatory falsehood injurious to the reputation of a private individual.   The extension of the *New York Times* test proposed by the *Rosenbloom* plurality would abridge this legitimate state interest to a degree that we find unacceptable.   And it would occasion the additional difficulty of forcing state and federal judges to decide on an *ad hoc* basis which publications address issues of "general or public interest" and which do not—to determine, in the words of Mr. Justice Marshall, "what information is relevant to self-government."   Rosenbloom v. Metromedia, Inc., 403 U.S., at 79.   We doubt the wisdom of committing this task to the conscience of judges.   Nor does the Constitution require us to draw so thin a line between the drastic alternatives of the *New York Times* privilege and the common law of strict liability for defamatory error.   The "public or general interest" test for determining the applicability of the *New York Times* standard to private defamation actions inadequately serves both of the competing values at stake.   On the one hand, a private individual whose reputation is injured by defamatory falsehood that does concern an issue of public or general interest has no recourse unless he can meet the rigorous requirements of *New York Times*. This is true despite the factors that distinguish the state interest in compensating private individuals from the analogous interest involved in the context of public persons.   On the other hand, a publisher or broadcaster of a defamatory error which a court deems unrelated to an issue of public or general interest may be held liable in damages even if it took every reasonable precaution to ensure the accuracy of its assertions.   And liability may far exceed compensation for any actual injury to the plaintiff, for the jury may be permitted to presume damages without proof of loss and even to award punitive damages.

We hold that, so long as they do not impose liability without fault, the States may define for themselves the appropriate standard of liability for a publisher or broadcaster of defamatory falsehood injurious to a private individual.   This approach provides a more equitable boundary between the competing concerns involved here.   It recognizes the strength of the legitimate state interest in compensating private individuals for wrongful injury to reputation, yet shields the press and broadcast media from the rigors of strict liability for defamation.   At least this conclusion obtains where, as here, the substance of the defamatory statement "makes substantial danger to reputation apparent." [*Butts*] This phrase places in perspective the conclusion we announce today. Our inquiry would involve considerations somewhat different from those discussed above if a State purported to condition civil liability on a factual misstatement whose content did not warn a reasonably prudent editor or broadcaster of its defamatory potential. Cf. *Time, Inc. v. Hill*, 385 U.S. 374 (1967). Such a case is not now before us, and we intimate no view as to its proper resolution.

IV.

Our accommodation of the competing values at stake in defamation suits by private individuals allows the States to impose liability on the publisher or broadcaster of defamatory falsehood on a less demanding showing than that required by *New York Times*. This conclusion is not based on a belief that the considerations which prompted the adoption of the *New York Times* privilege for defamation of public officials and its extension to public figures are wholly inapplicable to the context of private individuals. Rather, we endorse this approach in recognition of the strong and legitimate state interest in compensating private individuals for injury to reputation. But this countervailing state interest extends no further than compensation for actual injury. For the reasons stated below, we hold that the States may not permit recovery of presumed or punitive damages, at least when liability is not based on a showing of knowledge of falsity or reckless disregard for the truth.

The common law of defamation is an oddity of tort law, for it allows recovery of purportedly compensatory damages without evidence of actual loss. Under the traditional rules pertaining to actions for libel, the existence of injury is presumed from the fact of publication. Juries may award substantial sums as compensation for supposed damage to reputation without any proof that such harm actually occurred. The largely uncontrolled discretion of juries to award damages where there is no loss unnecessarily compounds the potential of any system of liability for defamatory falsehood to inhibit the vigorous exercise of First Amendment freedoms. Additionally, the doctrine of presumed damages invites juries to punish unpopular opinion rather than to compensate individuals for injury sustained by the publication of a false fact. More to the point, the States have no substantial interest in securing for plaintiffs such as this petitioner gratuitous awards of money damages far in excess of any actual injury.

We would not, of course, invalidate state law simply because we doubt its wisdom, but here we are attempting to reconcile state law with a competing interest grounded in the constitutional command of the First Amendment. It is therefore appropriate to require that state remedies for defamatory falsehood reach no farther than is necessary to protect the legitimate interest involved. It is necessary to restrict defamation plaintiffs who do not prove knowledge of falsity or reckless disregard for the truth to compensation for actual injury. We need not define "actual injury," as trial courts have wide experience in framing appropriate jury instructions in tort actions.   Suffice it to say that actual injury is not limited to out-of-pocket loss.   Indeed, the more customary types of actual harm inflicted by defamatory falsehood include impairment of reputation and standing in the community, personal humiliation, and mental anguish and suffering.   Of course, juries must be limited by appropriate instructions, and all awards must be supported by competent evidence concerning the injury, although there need be no evidence which assigns an actual dollar value to the injury.

We also find no justification for allowing awards of punitive damages against publishers and broadcasters held liable under state-defined standards of liability for defamation.   In most jurisdictions jury discretion over the amounts awarded is limited only by the gentle rule that they not be excessive.   Consequently, juries assess punitive damages in wholly unpredictable amounts bearing no necessary relation to the actual harm caused. And they remain free to use their discretion selectively to punish expressions of unpopular views.   Like the doctrine of presumed damages, jury discretion to award punitive damages unnecessarily exacerbates the danger of media self-censorship, but, unlike the former rule, punitive damages are wholly irrelevant to the state interest that justifies a negligence standard for private defamation actions.   They are not compensation for injury. Instead, they are private fines levied by civil juries to punish reprehensible conduct and to deter its future occurrence.   In short, the private defamation plaintiff who establishes liability under a less demanding standard than that stated by *New York Times* may recover only such damages as are sufficient to compensate him for actual injury.

V.

Notwithstanding our refusal to extend the *New York Times* privilege to defamation of private individuals, respondent contends that we should affirm the judgment below on the ground that petitioner is either a public official or a public figure.   There is little basis for the former assertion. Several years prior to the present incident, petitioner had served briefly on housing committees appointed by the mayor of Chicago, but at the time of publication he had never held any remunerative governmental position. Respondent admits this but argues that petitioner's appearance at the coroner's inquest rendered him a "de facto public official."   Our cases recognize no such concept.   Respondent's suggestion would sweep all lawyers under the *New York Times* rule as officers of the court and distort the plain meaning of the "public official" category beyond all recognition. We decline to follow it.

Respondent's characterization of petitioner as a public figure raises a different question.   That designation may rest on either of two alternative bases.   In some instances an individual may achieve such pervasive fame or notoriety that he becomes a public figure for all purposes and in all contexts.   More commonly, an individual voluntarily injects himself or is drawn into a particular public controversy and thereby becomes a public figure for a limited range of issues. In either case such persons assume special prominence in the resolution of public questions.

Petitioner has long been active in community and professional affairs. He has served as an officer of local civic groups and of various professional organizations, and he has published several books and articles on legal subjects. Although petitioner was consequently well known in some circles, he had achieved no general fame or notoriety in the community. None of the prospective jurors called at the trial had ever heard of petitioner prior to this litigation, and respondent offered no proof that this response was atypical of the local population. We would not lightly assume that a citizen's participation in community and professional affairs rendered him a public figure for all purposes. Absent clear evidence of general fame or notoriety in the community, and pervasive involvement in the affairs of society, an individual should not be deemed a public personality for all aspects of his life. It is preferable to reduce the public-figure question to a more meaningful context by looking to the nature and extent of an individual's participation in the particular controversy giving rise to the defamation.

In this context it is plain that petitioner was not a public figure. He played a minimal role at the coroner's inquest, and his participation related solely to his representation of a private client. He took no part in the criminal prosecution of Officer Nuccio. Moreover, he never discussed either the criminal or civil litigation with the press and was never quoted as having done so. He plainly did not thrust himself into the vortex of this public issue, nor did he engage the public's attention in an attempt to influence its outcome. We are persuaded that the trial court did not err in refusing to characterize petitioner as a public figure for the purpose of this litigation.

We therefore conclude that the *New York Times* standard is inapplicable to this case and that the trial court erred in entering judgment for respondent. Because the jury was allowed to impose liability without fault and was permitted to presume damages without proof of injury, a new trial is necessary. We reverse and remand for further proceedings in accord with this opinion.

It is so ordered.

■ MR. JUSTICE BLACKMUN, concurring.

[Although I joined the *Rosenbloom* plurality opinion,] I am willing to join, and do join, the Court's opinion and its judgment for two reasons:

1. By removing the specters of presumed and punitive damages in the absence of *New York Times* malice, the Court eliminates significant and powerful motives for self-censorship that otherwise are present in the traditional libel action. By so doing, the Court leaves what should prove to be sufficient and adequate breathing space for a vigorous press. What the Court has done, I believe, will have little, if any, practical effect on the functioning of responsible journalism.

2.   The Court was sadly fractionated in *Rosenbloom*.   A result of that kind inevitably leads to uncertainty.   I feel that it is of profound importance for the Court to come to rest in the defamation area and to have a clearly defined majority position that eliminates the unsureness engendered by *Rosenbloom's* diversity.   If my vote were not needed to create a majority, I would adhere to my prior view.   A definitive ruling, however, is paramount.   [   ]

For these reasons, I join the opinion and the judgment of the Court.

■ MR. CHIEF JUSTICE BURGER, dissenting.

.   .   .

Agreement or disagreement with the law as it has evolved to this time does not alter the fact that it has been orderly development with a consistent basic rationale.   .   .   .   I would prefer to allow this area of law to continue to evolve as it has up to now with respect to private citizens rather than embark on a new doctrinal theory which has no jurisprudential ancestry.

The petitioner here was performing a professional representative role as an advocate in the highest tradition of the law, and under that tradition the advocate is not to be invidiously identified with his client.   The important public policy which underlies this tradition—the right to counsel—would be gravely jeopardized if every lawyer who takes an "unpopular" case, civil or criminal, would automatically become fair game for irresponsible reporters and editors who might, for example, describe the lawyer as a "mob mouthpiece" for representing a client with a serious prior criminal record, or as an "ambulance chaser" for representing a claimant in a personal injury action.

I would reverse the judgment of the Court of Appeals and remand for reinstatement of the verdict of the jury and the entry of an appropriate judgment on that verdict.

■ MR. JUSTICE DOUGLAS, dissenting.

.   .   .

.   .   .   The standard announced today leaves the States free to "define for themselves the appropriate standard of liability for a publisher or broadcaster" in the circumstances of this case.   This of course leaves the simple negligence standard as an option with the jury free to impose damages upon a finding that the publisher failed to act as "a reasonable man."   With such continued erosion of First Amendment protection, I fear that it may well be the reasonable man who refrains from speaking.

Since in my view the First and Fourteenth Amendments prohibit the imposition of damages upon respondent for this discussion of public affairs, I would affirm the judgment below.

■ MR. JUSTICE BRENNAN, dissenting.

I agree with the conclusion, expressed in Part V of the Court's opinion, that, at the time of publication of respondent's article, petitioner could not properly have been viewed as either a "public official" or "public figure"; instead, respondent's article, dealing with an alleged conspiracy to discredit local police forces, concerned petitioner's purported involvement in "an event of public or general interest." . . .

. . .

Although acknowledging that First Amendment values are of no less significance when media reports concern private persons' involvement in matters of public concern, the Court refuses to provide, in such cases, the same level of constitutional protection that has been afforded the media in the context of defamation of public persons. The accommodation that this Court has established between free speech and libel laws in cases involving public officials and public figures—that defamatory falsehood be shown by clear and convincing evidence to have been published with knowledge of falsity or with reckless disregard of truth—is not apt, the Court holds, because the private individual does not have the same degree of access to the media to rebut defamatory comments as does the public person and he has not voluntarily exposed himself to public scrutiny.

While these arguments are forcefully and eloquently presented, I cannot accept them, for the reasons I stated in *Rosenbloom:*

"The *New York Times* standard was applied to libel of a public official or public figure to give effect to the [First] Amendment's function to encourage ventilation of public issues, not because the public official has any less interest in protecting his reputation than an individual in private life. While the argument that public figures need less protection because they can command media attention to counter criticism may be true for some very prominent people, even then it is the rare case where the denial overtakes the original charge. Denials, retractions, and corrections are not 'hot' news, and rarely receive the prominence of the original story. When the public official or public figure is a minor functionary, or has left the position that put him in the public eye . . ., the argument loses all of its force. In the vast majority of libels involving public officials or public figures, the ability to respond through the media will depend on the same complex factor on which the ability of a private individual depends: the unpredictable event of the media's continuing interest in the story. Thus the unproved, and highly improbable, generalization that an as yet [not fully defined] class of 'public figures' involved in matters of public concern will be better able to respond through the media than private individuals also involved in such matters seems too insubstantial a reed on which to rest a constitutional distinction." [ ]

. . .

. . . Under a reasonable-care regime, publishers and broadcasters will have to make pre-publication judgments about juror assessment of such diverse considerations as the size, operating procedures, and financial condition of the newsgathering system, as well as the relative costs and benefits of instituting less frequent and more costly reporting at a higher level of accuracy. [ ] Moreover, in contrast to proof by clear and convincing evidence required under the *Times* test, the burden of proof for reasonable care will doubtless be the preponderance of the evidence. . . .

The Court does not discount altogether the danger that jurors will punish for the expression of unpopular opinions. This probability accounts for the Court's limitation that "the States may not permit recovery of presumed or punitive damages, at least when liability is not based on a showing of knowledge of falsity or reckless disregard for the truth." [ ] But plainly a jury's latitude to impose liability for want of due care poses a far greater threat of suppressing unpopular views than does a possible recovery of presumed or punitive damages. Moreover, the Court's broad-ranging examples of "actual injury," including impairment of reputation and standing in the community, as well as personal humiliation, and mental anguish and suffering, inevitably allow a jury bent on punishing expression of unpopular views a formidable weapon for doing so. Finally, even a limitation of recovery to "actual injury"—however much it reduces the size or frequency of recoveries—will not provide the necessary elbow-room for First Amendment expression. . . .

On the other hand, the uncertainties which the media face under today's decision are largely avoided by the *Times* standard. I reject the argument that my *Rosenbloom* view improperly commits to judges the task of determining what is and what is not an issue of "general or public interest." [A footnote here asserted that states might enact statutes under which plaintiffs unable to prove fault could bring action "for retraction or for publication of a court's determination of falsity"—ed.] I noted in *Rosenbloom* that performance of this task would not always be easy. [ ] But surely the courts, the ultimate arbiters of all disputes concerning clashes of constitutional values, would only be performing one of their traditional functions in undertaking this duty. . . .

■ MR. JUSTICE WHITE, dissenting.

. . .

The impact of today's decision on the traditional law of libel is immediately obvious and indisputable. No longer will the plaintiff be able to rest his case with proof of a libel defamatory on its face or proof of a slander historically actionable *per se*. In addition, he must prove some further degree of culpable conduct on the part of the publisher . . . And if he succeeds in this respect, he faces still another obstacle: [denial of recovery for presumed damages]. The Court rejects the judgment of experience that some publications are so inherently capable of injury, and actual injury so difficult to prove, that the risk of falsehood should be borne by the publisher, not the victim. . . .

So too, the requirement of proving special injury to reputation before general damages may be awarded will clearly eliminate the prevailing rule, worked out over a very long period of time, that, in the case of defamations not actionable *per se,* the recovery of general damages for injury to reputation may also be had if some form of material or pecuniary loss is proved. Finally, an inflexible federal standard is imposed for the award of punitive damages. No longer will it be enough to prove ill will and an attempt to injure.

These are radical changes in the law and severe invasions of the prerogatives of the States. . . .

. . .

The Court evinces a deep-seated antipathy to "liability without fault." But this catch-phrase has no talismanic significance and is almost meaningless in this context where the Court appears to be addressing those libels and slanders that are defamatory on their face and where the publisher is no doubt aware from the nature of the material that it would be inherently damaging to reputation. He publishes notwithstanding, knowing that he will inflict injury. With this knowledge, he must intend to inflict that injury, his excuse being that he is privileged to do so—that he has published the truth. But as it turns out, what he has circulated to the public is a very damaging falsehood. Is he nevertheless "faultless"? Perhaps it can be said that the mistake about his defense was made in good faith, but the fact remains that it is he who launched the publication knowing that it could ruin a reputation.

In these circumstances, the law has heretofore put the risk of falsehood on the publisher where the victim is a private citizen and no grounds of special privilege are invoked. The Court would now shift this risk to the victim, even though he has done nothing to invite the calumny, is wholly innocent of fault, and is helpless to avoid his injury. . . . The press today is vigorous and robust. To me, it is quite incredible to suggest that threats of libel suits from private citizens are causing the press to refrain from publishing the truth. I know of no hard facts to support that proposition, and the Court furnishes none.

The communications industry has increasingly become concentrated in a few powerful hands operating very lucrative businesses reaching across the Nation and into almost every home. Neither the industry as a whole nor its individual components are easily intimidated, and we are fortunate that they are not. Requiring them to pay for the occasional damage they do to private reputation will play no substantial part in their future performance or their existence.

In any event, if the Court's principal concern is to protect the communications industry from large libel judgments, it would appear that its new requirements with respect to general and punitive damages would be ample protection. . . .

It is difficult for me to understand why the ordinary citizen should himself carry the risk of damage and suffer the injury in order to vindicate First Amendment values by protecting the press and others from liability for circulating false information. This is particularly true because such statements serve no purpose whatsoever in furthering the public interest or the search for truth but, on the contrary, may frustrate that search and at the same time inflict great injury on the defenseless individual.   The owners of the press and the stockholders of the communications enterprises can much better bear the burden.   And if they cannot, the public at large should somehow pay for what is essentially a public benefit derived at private expense.

. . .

For the foregoing reasons, I would reverse the judgment of the Court of Appeals and reinstate the jury's verdict.

NOTES AND QUESTIONS

1.   Why did the majority adhere to the *Times* rule for public officials? For public figures?

2.   Why does the majority in *Gertz* prefer its approach to the plurality's approach in *Rosenbloom*?

3.   The *Gertz* retrial, which did not occur for several years, produced a jury verdict for plaintiff for $100,000 compensatory damages and $300,000 punitive damages.   On appeal, the court affirmed.   It concluded that the jury could find "actual malice" on the editor of the magazine, who solicited a person with a "known and unreasonable propensity to label persons or organizations as Communist, to write the article; and after the article was submitted, made virtually no effort to check the validity of statements that were defamatory *per se* of Gertz, and in fact added further defamatory material based on [the writer's] 'facts.' "   It also held that, contrary to most cases involving freelance writers, the conduct of the writer could be imputed to the magazine because of the "significant control" exercised by the editor over the content and focus of the article.   An agency relationship had been created.   Gertz v. Robert Welch, Inc., 680 F.2d 527 (7th Cir. 1982), cert. denied 459 U.S. 1226 (1983).

4.   Even if the constitutional law does not bar punitive damages in cases in which actual malice is shown, state law may impose a variety of impediments, such as barring punitive damages in all tort cases, or in cases involving speech.   Many of the state tort reform statutes that limit punitive damages to a maximum or to a multiple of compensatory damages, though written primarily with personal injury in mind, apply also to defamation actions.   Also, some states require a showing of some further element, such as animosity toward plaintiff, in addition to actual malice. Moreover, some states have demanded that the state law requirements for punitive damages be shown with convincing clarity.

5.   Note that even if the plaintiff is private for constitutional purposes, the state might develop a state law privilege on the same facts.   In Dairy Stores, Inc. v. Sentinel Publishing Co., 104 N.J. 125, 516 A.2d 220 (1986), defendant newspapers during a drought reported that the water plaintiff's local store had bottled and was selling was not the pure spring water it purported to be. Although the lower court had denied defendants' motions for summary judgment on the ground that plaintiff was private and did not need to prove actual malice, the state's highest court thought that "the more appropriate principle is the common-law privilege of fair comment."

Although "constitutional considerations have dominated defamation law in recent years, the common law provides an alternative, and potentially more stable, framework for analyzing statements about matters of public interest." The safety of drinking water was a "paradigm of legitimate public concern." To overcome the state privilege, plaintiff would have to prove "actual malice" in the constitutional sense.

6. Before we explore the nature of negligence and related operational aspects of the *Gertz* case, it is important to note how few cases truly present these questions. The vast majority of reported cases against media (and we would expect unreported cases as well) are litigated as "actual malice" cases and not as negligence cases.

First, plaintiffs mentioned in the media are likely to be either admittedly public or found to be public. Second, even a plaintiff called "private" who wants to recover presumed or punitive damages must go the "actual malice" route from the start. If the jury finds that the plaintiff has succeeded in that effort, there is no occasion to focus on the meaning of "actual injury" damages. Similarly, in cases in which the plaintiff cannot establish "actual injury" damages—no matter what they are held to encompass—the litigation will likely go off on an attempt to prove "actual malice." (There is the further limitation that the Court's language in *Gertz* referred to "publishers" and "broadcasters," leaving doubt about what parts of the case might apply to nonmedia defendants.)

7. Justice White is particularly concerned about having private citizens bear the burden of defamation. If the media cannot bear the expense of the harm they do, the public should "somehow pay for what is essentially a public benefit derived at private expense." It has been widely observed that defamation law has been running counter to the trends in other areas of tort law. Thus, personal injury law has been moving toward greater imposition of liability, through techniques that increase chances of recovery in negligence cases and through development of new doctrines that increase the imposition of strict liability, as in aspects of the law of defective products. Meanwhile, defamation law had been moving the other way—from strict liability to denying liability in many cases unless something substantially greater than negligence can be shown. Is this an even more appropriate occasion for strict liability than the defective products area?

For an extensive discussion of the cross currents in strict liability see Weiler, Defamation, Enterprise Liability, and Freedom of Speech, 17 U.Toronto L.J. 278 (1967). See also Kalven, The Reasonable Man and the First Amendment: *Hill, Butts,* and *Walker,* 1967 Sup.Ct.Rev. 267. But see Anderson, Libel and Press Self–Censorship, 53 Texas L.Rev. 422, 432 n. 52 (1975), arguing that the analogy is flawed because the other enterprises "have no choice but to accept the additional risk of liability if they are to continue their profit-making activities, while most broadcasters and publishers can avoid liability, without discontinuing their activities or reducing their profits, by ceasing to carry material that creates the risk of liability— i.e., by increasing their self-censorship." Can a sound argument be made for strict liability in this area? Note the lack of a first-party insurance device for potential libel victims that would operate along the lines of medical and income-protection insurance available to potential personal injury victims.

8. *The role of negligence.* Justice Powell phrased the permissible standard in private citizen cases negatively: states may use whatever standard they wish "so long as they do not impose liability without fault." It may be theoretically possible to develop a standard more protective than strict liability but less rigorous than negligence, but states have not made the attempt. Note that at the end of part IV, Justice Powell himself used "negligence" in a way that suggests that he thinks that it is the next level above strict liability: " . . . punitive damages are wholly irrelevant to the state interest that justifies a negligence standard for private defamation actions."

Almost all the states that have ruled on this question have set the state standard of care at negligence. The California Supreme Court found 33 states clearly adopting the negligence standard, six applying negligence without discussion, and a few more in which federal courts have interpreted the states as having adopted negligence law. The court found only three or four states that had explicitly refused to adopt the negligence standard. Brown v. Kelly Broadcasting Co., p. 910, supra, (aligning California with the negligence group).

A very few states have adopted some version of the *Rosenbloom* plurality's approach. But by the far the most important aberration has been New York, which has developed its own standard for private figure cases: "where the content of the article is arguably within the sphere of legitimate public concern, which is reasonably related to matters warranting public exposition, the party may recover; however, to warrant such recovery he must first establish, by a preponderance of the evidence, that the publisher acted in a grossly irresponsible manner without due consideration for the standards of information gathering and dissemination ordinarily followed by responsible parties." Chapadeau v. Utica Observer– Dispatch, Inc., 38 N.Y.2d 196, 341 N.E.2d 569, 379 N.Y.S.2d 61 (1975). Is this closer to *Gertz* or to *Rosenbloom?*

New York has since strengthened the defendant's position under *Chapadeau.* In Gaeta v. New York News, Inc., 62 N.Y.2d 340, 465 N.E.2d 802, 477 N.Y.S.2d 82 (1984), defendant wrote a story about the impact of a state program transferring patients from mental hospitals to nursing homes. The story used "the familiar journalistic technique of featuring the experience of a single individual as exemplifying in human terms the plight of many." The patient's mother sued on the ground that the article, in explaining how the patient's mental condition developed, libelously described the mother's conduct. The lower courts both concluded that the discussion of the mother was not "arguably within the sphere of legitimate public concern" and that the *Chapadeau* protection did not apply. This led them to rule that ordinary negligence principles would apply.

The court of appeals reversed on the ground that references to the mother did indeed come within *Chapadeau:*

> [*Chapadeau*] recognized the need for judgment and discretion to be exercised by journalists, subject only to review by the courts to protect against clear abuses. Determining what editorial content is of legitimate public interest and concern is a function for editors. . . . The press, acting responsibly, and not the courts must make the *ad hoc* decisions as to what are matters of public concern, and while subject to review, editorial judgments as to news content will not be second-guessed so long as they are sustainable.

What are the merits and demerits of the New York approach?

9. *How negligence operates.* Justice Powell spoke of the "reasonably prudent editor or broadcaster." The phrase "reasonably prudent" makes sense when applied to automobile drivers or airplane pilots or physicians. But how is that phrase to be applied to a field in which the media vary from sedate, if not stodgy, journals at one extreme to racy tabloids and scandal sheets at the other; from those that treat public relations releases as news to those that disbelieve every statement made by government officials and engage in extensive investigative reporting? What about differences between editors at very well financed and profitable publications or broadcast stations and those at marginal media with small, or nonexistent, research staffs and budgets too tight to keep a libel lawyer on retainer?

The Restatement (Second) of Torts § 580B, comment *h*, suggests that the reasonableness of the investigation varies with the following factors: 1. The "time element"—investigations may be shorter for topical news than for a story that has no time pressure. 2. The "nature of the interest promoted by publication"—a story informing the public of matters important in a democracy may warrant quicker publication than a story involving "mere gossip." 3. "Potential damage to plaintiff if the communication proves to be false"—whether the statement is defamatory on its face; how many readers will understand the defamation; how harmful is the charge. Do these factors take into account "social harm" from publication of a false story?

One court has stated two other factors: the nature and reliability of the source of the information and the "reasonableness in checking the veracity of the information, considering its cost in terms of money, time, personnel, urgency of the publication, nature of the news and any other pertinent element." Torres–Silva v. El Mundo, 3 Med.L.Rptr. 1508 (P.R. 1977). See generally Bloom, Proof of Fault in Media Defamation Litigation, 38 Vand.L.Rev. 247 (1985).

Some have questioned the emphasis on time pressure. In Schaefer, Defamation and the First Amendment, 52 Colo.L.Rev. 1 (1980), the former Chief Justice of Illinois said:

It has been suggested that the press, television, and radio all operate under severe time constraints and that this consideration should excuse or justify defamatory statements. It should not be forgotten, however, that these time constraints are entirely self-imposed. Apparently the media people believe that for competitive reasons it is desirable to be first with a particular news story. My own impression is that the public is massively unconcerned about that question. But if my impression is wrong, deadline pressures afford no more justification for harm caused by negligent attacks upon reputation than for harm caused by a reporter's negligent driving in his haste to cover a story. Both negligent acts are and have been insurable.

Do you agree?

10. *The role of experts.* Another question is whether the standard should be stated in terms of professional negligence or ordinary due care. This may be significant both in formulating the standard and in requiring expert testimony to show the standard and the deviation. The few states that have addressed this question have split. In Gobin v. Globe Pub. Co., 216 Kan. 223, 531 P.2d 76 (1975), the court stated the standard to be "the conduct of the reasonably careful publisher or broadcaster in the community or in similar communities under the existing circumstances." Troman v. Wood, 62 Ill.2d 184, 340 N.E.2d 292 (1975), rejected the professional negligence approach because "it would make the prevailing newspaper practices in a community controlling. In a community having only a single newspaper, the approach suggested would permit that paper to establish its own standards. And in any community it might tend, in 'Gresham's law' fashion, toward a progressive depreciation of the standard of care."

The Second Restatement's § 580B, comment *g*, states that a professional disseminator of news "is held to the skill and experience normally possessed by members of that profession. Customs and practices within the profession are relevant in applying the negligence standard, which is, to a substantial degree, set by the profession itself, though a custom is not controlling." How have courts handled medical malpractice cases involving a single physician in a small community?

11. *Plaintiffs must prove falsity—The Hepps case.* Although the Court's focus has been on the fault requirement, the role of falsity has also raised questions. In Philadelphia Newspapers, Inc. v. Hepps, 475 U.S. 767 (1986), the Court, 5–4, held that the plaintiff had the burden of proving falsity in cases brought by private plaintiffs, at least where the speech was of public concern. For the majority, Justice O'Connor concluded that to "ensure that true speech on matters of public concern is not deterred, we hold that the common-law presumption that defamatory speech is false cannot stand when a plaintiff seeks damages against a media defendant for speech of public concern." (Two of the five joining the majority opinion rejected the limitation to "media" defendants.) Even though this burden would "insulate from liability some speech that is false, but unprovably so," that result was essential to avoid the "chilling" effect that would otherwise accompany true speech on matters of public concern.

The majority asserted that its conclusion added "only marginally to the burdens" on libel plaintiffs because a jury is more likely to accept a "contention that the defendant was at fault in publishing the statements at issue if convinced that the relevant statements were false. As a practical matter, then, evidence offered by plaintiffs on the publisher's fault . . . will generally encompass evidence of the falsity of the matters asserted."

Justice Stevens, for the dissenters, thought the majority result "pernicious," positing a situation in which a defendant, knowing that the plaintiff could not prove the statement false, deliberately lied about the plaintiff. This situation might occur due to the passage of time, the loss of critical records, or the absence of an eyewitness. The majority's analysis was an "obvious blueprint for character assassination."

12. *Procedural issues.* Most courts refuse to apply independent appellate review in cases in which the negligence standard controls. See Levine v. CMP Publications, Inc., 738 F.2d 660 (5th Cir.1984) rehearing and rehearing en banc denied, 753 F.2d 1341 (5th Cir.1985). Most courts also refuse to require "clear and convincing" evidence of negligence. The issue is discussed in Lansdowne v. Beacon Journal Publishing Co., 32 Ohio St.3d 176, 512 N.E.2d 979 (1987).

13. *Actual injury.* As we already seen, the subject of damages in defamation cases was complicated enough at common law. Whether a plaintiff needed to show "special" damages and, if so, what constituted "special" damages produced much litigation. The Supreme Court's introduction, in *Gertz*, of "actual injury damages" did not purport to track any pre-existing concept of damages. Indeed, the Court went out of its way to use examples that showed that the new term did not track "special" damages. The problem has fallen to the lower courts to give content to this term drawing solely from the few sentences in *Gertz* that address the problem—and from the *Firestone* case.

In Time Inc. v. Firestone, 424 U.S. 448 (1976), discussed in detail p. 976, infra, plaintiff withdrew her claim for reputational harm on the eve of trial. Defendant argued that this barred her from recovering under *Gertz*. The Court disagreed. If Florida permitted recoveries in defamation actions that did not claim harm to reputation, *Gertz* did not forbid it:

> In [*Gertz*] we made it clear that States could base awards on elements other than injury to reputation, specifically listing "personal humiliation, and mental anguish and suffering" as examples of injuries which might be compensated consistently with the Constitution upon a showing of fault.

In *Firestone*, the plaintiff had presented evidence from her minister, her attorney in the divorce proceedings, and several friends and neighbors. One of the latter was a physician who testified to "having to administer a sedative to respondent in an attempt to reduce discomfort wrought by her worrying about the article." Plaintiff also testified that she feared the effect that the false report of her adultery might have on her young son when he grew older. "The jury decided these injuries should be compensated by an award of $100,000. We have no warrant for re-examining this determination."

In addition to the reasons discussed earlier, fewer cases discuss actual injury than might be expected because (1) the cases in New York and the few other states have higher standards of liability, which produce fewer discussions of any damage issues than would occur under a negligence standard; and (2) the cases that go off on state issues—as when the defendant argues that plaintiff's proof does not satisfy a state rule requiring "special" damages or requiring certain types of proof for compensatory damages, or when defendant asserts that the damages are excessive under state law. The result of all these is that relatively few courts have been forced to decide the content of *Gertz* "actual injury" damages.

Hearst Corporation v. Hughes, 297 Md. 112, 466 A.2d 486 (1983), chose to follow Florida's path in *Firestone* by permitting recovery of proven "personal humiliation and mental anguish" in the absence of reputational harm, though it noted that other state courts had disagreed. E.g., Gobin v. Globe Publishing Co., 232 Kan. 1, 649 P.2d 1239 (1982). The Maryland court asserted that the Kansas view failed to "respect the centuries of human experience which led to a presumption of harm flowing from words actionable per se. One reason for that common law position was the difficulty a defamation plaintiff has in proving harm to reputation." Since victims of defamation "can reasonably become genuinely upset as a result of the publication," the court saw "no social purpose to be served by requiring the plaintiff additionally to prove actual impairment of reputation."

D.   THE PUBLIC-PRIVATE DISTINCTION

—999

Now that we have considered the two categories developed by the Supreme Court, we turn to the crucial issue of deciding how to classify plaintiffs. We begin with the determination of whether plaintiff is a public official. We then turn to the more complex question of classifying non-governmental plaintiffs.

1.   IDENTIFYING A "PUBLIC OFFICIAL"

In Rosenblatt v. Baer, 383 U.S. 75 (1966), plaintiff Baer had been hired by the three elected county commissioners to supervise a public recreation facility owned by the county. When he sued over a newspaper attack on the management of the facility, Justice Brennan's majority opinion held that Baer might be a "public official" under the *Times* rule:

> Criticism of government is at the very center of the constitutionally protected area of free discussion. . . . It is clear . . .
> that the "public official" designation applies at the very least to

those among the hierarchy of government employees who have, or appear to the public to have, substantial responsibility for or control over the conduct of government affairs.

. . . Where a position in government has such apparent importance that the public has an independent interest in the qualifications and performance of the person who holds it, beyond the general public interest in the qualifications and performance of all government employees, both elements we identified in *New York Times* are present and the *New York Times* malice standards apply.[13]

Justice Stewart's separate concurrence in *Rosenblatt* sought to express the affirmative values to be found in a libel action:

The right of a man to the protection of his own reputation from unjustified invasion and wrongful hurt reflects no more than our basic concept of the essential dignity and worth of every human being—a concept at the root of any decent system of ordered liberty.

From the social perspective, he warned of dangers associated with Senator Joseph McCarthy:

Moreover, the preventive effect of liability for defamation serves an important public purpose. For the rights and values of private personality far transcend mere personal interests. Surely if the 1950's taught us anything, they taught us that the poisonous atmosphere of the easy lie can infect and degrade a whole society.

Candidates. In a pair of cases involving false charges made about a candidate for office, the Court unanimously extended the *Times* rationale to candidates because "it can hardly be doubted that the constitutional guarantee has its fullest and most urgent application precisely to the conduct of campaigns for political office." Monitor Patriot Co. v. Roy, 401 U.S. 265 (1971), and Ocala Star–Banner Co. v. Damron, 401 U.S. 295 (1971). In *Roy,* a newspaper column published three days before the election falsely accused a candidate for the United States Senate of criminal activity that allegedly took place many years earlier. The Court decided that the *Times* rule should include "anything which might touch on an official's fitness for office" when a candidate's behavior is being discussed:

A candidate who, for example, seeks to further his cause through the prominent display of his wife and children can hardly argue that his qualities as a husband or father remain of "purely private" concern. And the candidate who vaunts his spotless

---

13. It is suggested that this test might apply to a night watchman accused of stealing state secrets. But a conclusion that the *New York Times* malice standards apply could not be reached merely because a statement defamatory of some person in government employ catches the public's interest: that conclusion would virtually disregard society's interest in protecting reputation. The employee's position must be one which would invite public scrutiny and discussion of the person holding it, entirely apart from the scrutiny and discussion occasioned by the particular charges in controversy.

record and sterling integrity cannot convincingly cry "Foul!" when an opponent or an industrious reporter attempts to demonstrate the contrary. Any test adequate to safeguard First Amendment guarantees in this area must go far beyond the customary meaning of the phrase "official conduct."

Given the realities of our political life, it is by no means easy to see what statements about a candidate might be altogether without relevance to his fitness for the office he seeks. The clash of reputations is the staple of election campaigns, and damage to reputation is, of course, the essence of libel. But whether there remains some exiguous area of defamation against which a candidate may have full recourse is a question we need not decide in this case.

The Court concluded that a "charge of criminal conduct, no matter how remote in time or place, can never be irrelevant to an official's or a candidate's fitness for office" for purposes of applying the *Times* rule.

In *Damron,* a newspaper reported two weeks before a local election that a candidate had been charged with perjury, when in fact his brother was the one charged. Again, the *Times* rule applied.

Since these early cases, the Supreme Court has given lower courts no guidance except for a dictum in Hutchinson v. Proxmire, 443 U.S. 111 (1979)(discussed p. 977, infra), noting that the Court had not "provided precise boundaries for the category of 'public official'; it cannot be thought to include all public employees, however."

The three-legged stool. Perhaps the most extensive effort to grapple with the "public official" category occurred in Kassel v. Gannett Co., Inc., 875 F.2d 935 (1st Cir.1989), in which plaintiff staff psychologist for the Veterans Administration claimed that he was defamed by an article in defendant's newspaper mistakenly attributing to him a statement about the Vietnam war. The district court ruled that plaintiff was not a public official, and the jury found for the plaintiff. The court of appeals affirmed on the issue of plaintiff's status.

The court thought that the test rested on a "tripodal base." The first leg is the recognition that discussion of issues of public importance must be "uninhibited, robust, and wide-open." Thus, "[p]olicymakers, upper-level administrators, and supervisors" are public officials because they "occupy niches of 'apparent importance' sufficient to give the public an independent interest in the qualifications and performances of the persons who hold them." If, as stated in the *Rosenblatt* footnote, "a night watchman accused of stealing state secrets" is not a public official, then the "inherent attributes of the position, not the occurrence of random events, must signify the line of demarcation."

The second leg entails the plaintiff's access to media to counteract the impact of false and injurious statements (building on *Gertz*). The court explained that "government workers who, by virtue of their employment, may easily defuse erroneous or misleading reports without judicial assistance should more likely be ranked as 'public officials' for libel law purposes. Conversely, those who work for the sovereign, but who enjoy little or no sway over, or 'special' access to, the news media are less likely to be trapped within the seine" of public officialdom.

The final leg, again drawing on *Gertz*, involves the degree to which the plaintiff has assumed the risk of exposure to criticism by the media: "[p]ersons who actively seek positions of influence in public life do so with the knowledge that, if successful in attaining their goals, diminished privacy will result." On the other hand, there are public employees who have not assumed an influential role in government and cannot be said to have "exposed themselves to increasing risk of injury from defamatory falsehood concerning them."

The court then applied its analysis to the facts of the case: (1) plaintiff held a lower level position at the VA that did not invite scrutiny independent of the controversy caused by the defendant's story and did not "govern" in any sense of the word. His job was "seeing patients and administering tests." (2) He did not have access to channels of communication that would enable him to counteract false and injurious statements. The plaintiff's position as staff psychologist "commanded no extraordinary media exposure" and his "duties did not involve answering press inquiries." To focus on the attention he attracted *after* the story was "bootstrapping of the most flagrant sort." (3) There was "no evidence that, by accepting employment as a staff psychologist in a VA hospital, Kassel assumed the risk of sensationalist media coverage."

Is *Kassel* consistent with the two alternative approaches suggested in *Rosenblatt*? Do the self-help and assumed-risk analyses make sense in the context of public officials? Consider *Rosenblatt* and *Kassel* in the context of each of the following occupations.

Police officers and firefighters. There is virtual unanimity that police officers are public officials for defamation purposes. See Britton v. Koep, 470 N.W.2d 518 (Minn.1991), asserting that other states "unanimously have held that police officers, undercover agents, and deputy sheriffs are public officials. The rationale appears to be that, even for those who work undercover or anonymously, [ ], those officers possess significant powers granted by the government."

Firefighters have been treated differently. When one sued over a newscast about his termination for inability to pass the EMT examination, the court thought it "strain[ed] credibility to say that [plaintiff], as a low-ranking fire fighter, had substantial responsibility over the conduct of governmental affairs." The plaintiff here "did not have responsibility or influence comparable to that of a captain of a police force [who had been held public in an earlier case]." Jones v. Palmer Communications, Inc., 440 N.W.2d 884 (Iowa 1989).

Public school teachers. The court are split over whether public school teachers are public officials. Kelley v. Bonney, 221 Conn. 549, 606 A.2d 693 (1992) concluded that they are public officials because they hold a position that "if abused, potentially might cause serious psychological or physical injury to school aged children. Unquestionably, members of society are profoundly interested in the qualifications and performance of the teachers who are responsible for educating and caring for the children in their classrooms." The court cited several cases on both sides of the question.

Public school principals. Courts disagree about public school principals. In Palmer v. Bennington School Dist., 159 Vt. 31, 615 A.2d 498 (1992), an elementary school principal with power to supervise and evaluate teachers and nonprofessional staff, who was charged with financial improprieties was a public official even though he was only one of 12 such principals in the district and was not well known in the region. In Ellerbee v. Mills, 262 Ga. 516, 422 S.E.2d 539 (1992), cert. denied 507 U.S. 1025 (1993), a high school principal, criticized as a principal by a former teacher, was held not to be a public official because "under normal circumstances, a principal simply does not have the relationship with government to warrant 'public official' status under [*Times*]. Principals, in general, are removed from the general conduct of government and are not policymakers at the level intended by the *New York Times* designation of public official."

Social workers. In the relatively few cases presenting the issue, social workers have been held to be public officials. In Kahn v. Bower, 232 Cal.App.3d 1599, 284 Cal.Rptr. 244 (1991), a social worker accused of incompetence was held to be public:

> Nothing in the record before us indicates plaintiff had any significant control over government *policy.* The same may be said, however, of a patrolman. Nonetheless, the power exercised by police officers, and their public visibility, naturally subject them to public scrutiny and make them public officials for purposes of defamation law. Plaintiff too possessed considerable power over the lives affected by her work as a child welfare worker. Her assessments and decisions directly and often immediately determined whether the educational, social, medical and economic needs of developmentally disabled children in her care would adequately be met. She exercised far more control over the lives she touched than does a classroom teacher.

For a similar result, see Villarreal v. Harte–Hanks Communications, Inc., 787 S.W.2d 131 (Tex.App.1990), cert. denied 499 U.S. 923 (1991), in which the court observed that a "child protective services specialist . . . certainly had greater control over governmental affairs than a court reporter, school teacher, attorney or justice of the peace."

Former public officials. Former officials remain public officials for purposes of commentary on their past performance. In Milgroom v. News Group Boston, Inc., 412 Mass. 9, 586 N.E.2d 985 (1992), a former judge criticized for conduct during her tenure on the bench was held to remain a public official for commentary on that performance since the "administration of justice" is a "subject of continuing public interest." See also Zerangue v. TSP Newspapers, Inc., 814 F.2d 1066 (5th Cir.1987)(former public officials remained in category at least six years after losing their jobs for purposes of coverage of their activities while in office).

A former head of the Justice Department organized crime strike force was a public official when charged with having "avoided prosecuting certain organized crime figures." But he was a private person as to charges that after leaving office, as an attorney he exploited personal contacts in the department to seek favorable treatment for his clients. Crane v. The Arizona Republic, 972 F.2d 1511 (9th Cir.1992).

For an extended examination of public official case law, see David Elder, Defamation, Public Officialdom, and the *Rosenblatt v. Baer* Criteria—A Proposal for Revivification Two Decades after *New York Times Co. v. Sullivan,* 33 Buffalo L.Rev. 572 (1984), arguing that lower courts have misconstrued Supreme Court public official cases and that courts should restrict the scope of public officialdom through "thoughtful application of [*Rosenblatt's*] two-part alternative test for 'public official,' infused with the *Gertz* substratal 'assumption of risk' [and] 'compelling normative consideration'" points.

2. IDENTIFYING A "PUBLIC FIGURE"

After *Gertz* it became critically important to be able to distinguish between public and private plaintiffs. The Court addressed that topic in a series of cases that we now briefly summarize, and which are discussed again in the principal case that follows.

The Firestone case. In *Time Inc. v. Firestone,* p. 970, supra, a magazine incorrectly reported that a member of "one of America's wealthier industrial families" had received a divorce because of his wife's adultery. A five-member majority held plaintiff to be private: "Respondent did not assume any role of especial prominence in the affairs of society, other than perhaps Palm Beach society, and she did not thrust herself to the forefront of any particular public controversy in order to influence the resolution of the issues involved in it." The fact that the case may have been of great public interest, did not make plaintiff a public figure. Moreover, the Court observed, plaintiff was compelled to go to court to seek relief in a marital dispute and her involvement was not voluntary. The fact that she held "a few" press conferences during the case did not change her otherwise private status. She did not attempt to use them to influence the outcome of the trial or to thrust herself into an unrelated dispute. (Defendant's added argument that reporting of judicial proceedings should never give rise to recovery for negligence, was rejected as an attempt to resurrect the subject matter criterion, which *Gertz* had rejected.)

The Wolston case. In Wolston v. Reader's Digest Ass'n, 443 U.S. 157 (1979), defendant's 1974 book incorrectly listed plaintiff as one of a group "who were convicted of espionage or falsifying information or perjury and/or contempt charges following espionage indictments or who fled to the Soviet bloc to avoid prosecution." In fact, he had been indicted for and convicted of contempt of court for failing to appear before a grand jury.

During the six weeks in 1958 between his failure to appear and his sentencing, plaintiff's case was the subject of 15 stories in Washington and New York newspapers. "This flurry of publicity subsided" following the sentencing, and plaintiff "succeeded for the most part in returning to the private life he had led" prior to the subpoena. A six-member majority held plaintiff private because he had neither "voluntarily thrust" nor "injected" himself into the forefront of the controversy surrounding the investigation of Soviet espionage in the United States. Wolston had not "engaged the attention of the public in an attempt to influence the resolution of the issues involved. . . . He did not in any way seek to arouse public sentiment in his favor and against the investigation. Thus, this is not a case where a defendant invites a citation for contempt in order to use the contempt citation as a fulcrum to create public discussion about the methods being used in connection with an investigation or prosecution."

The Hutchinson case. In Hutchinson v. Proxmire, 443 U.S. 111 (1979), decided the same day as *Wolston,* defendant, a United States Senator, had criticized government grants to certain scientists, including plaintiff, on the grounds that the grants were examples of wasteful government spending on unjustifiable scientific research. (Absolute privilege did not apply because the claimed defamations were in press releases and newsletters.)

The eight-member majority held plaintiff to be private. Neither the fact that plaintiff had successfully applied for federal funds nor that he had access to media to respond to Senator Proxmire's charges, "demonstrates that Hutchinson was a public figure prior to the controversy." Rather, his "activities and public profile are much like those of countless members of his profession. His published writings reach a relatively small category of professionals concerned with research in human behavior." Those charged with defamation "cannot, by their own conduct, create their own defense by making the claimant a public figure. See [*Wolston*]." Nor had plaintiff "assumed any role of public prominence in the broad question of concern about expenditures."

The Court then left the lower courts to work out the distinction. One early case, Waldbaum v. Fairchild Publications, Inc., 627 F.2d 1287 (D.C.Cir.), cert. denied 449 U.S. 898 (1980), was influential in attempting to follow a path that was faithful to *Gertz* while attempting to put some "flesh on the bones." A recent attempt to grapple with the problem follows.

Foretich v. Capital Cities/ABC, Inc.

United States Court of Appeals, Fourth Circuit, 1994.
37 F.3d 1541.

[Vincent and Doris Foretich sued the producers and broadcasters of a 1992 docudrama in which a character is claimed to have referred to them as "abusers" of their granddaughter, Hilary Foretich. The docudrama was based on a "prolonged and highly publicized child-custody dispute" between Hilary's parents, Dr. Elizabeth Morgan and Dr. Eric Foretich. At the time of their divorce in 1983, Dr. Morgan was awarded temporary custody of the infant Hilary subject to scheduled visitations with Dr. Foretich, whose parents, the plaintiffs, were present during these visits. Over the next few years, Dr. Morgan began to assert that Hilary was being abused on these visits. Efforts to suspend the visits were denied. Dr. Morgan was jailed briefly twice for disobeying court orders.

At one point, Dr. Morgan sued Dr. Foretich and his parents for sexual abuse. The complaint charged Vincent with, among other things, manipulating Hilary's genitals; inserting various foreign objects into her vagina; and orally and anally sodomizing her. Doris was accused, among other things, of "inserting objects into her vagina." The jury rejected the charges and also rejected the grandparents' counterclaim for defamation. The case was reversed in part on appeal but was never retried. During this period Dr. Morgan hid Hilary. When she refused to reveal her whereabouts, she was jailed in August 1985 for civil contempt for what turned out to be twenty-five months. The controversy "generated a torrent of publicity." Each parent "hired a public relations agent and commissioned a toll-free '800' number." Dr. Morgan was released after Congress passed legislation limiting contempt sentences in child-custody cases in the District of Columbia to one year. Hilary was found in 1990 in New Zealand.

After the trial court ruled that plaintiffs were private individuals, an interlocutory appeal was granted. In reviewing the ruling, the court of appeals undertook

> to recount the Foretich grandparents' media exposure in some considerable detail. The record does not suggest that either grandparent ever actively sought out press interviews. But over a period of a few years, and most intensively during and immediately after Dr. Morgan's twenty-five months in jail, they did accede to requests for several newspaper and magazine interviews, attend at least three press conferences or rallies organized by or on behalf of their son, and appear on at least two television shows. The grandparents did not simply confine their remarks to denying Dr. Morgan's allegations. They also described the positive environment that they had provided for Hilary, the negative influence that Dr. Morgan had on the girl, their belief that Dr. Morgan was mentally unstable, and the distress that they had suffered as a result of Dr. Morgan's allegations.

The court relied on "verbatim quotes" because it could not tell when a reporter had paraphrased. No quote was challenged as inaccurate.

The court discussed in some detail 11 articles that quoted one or both of the plaintiffs. Although the following summary will not repeat the quotations, the court will refer to most of them in its opinion. The articles in sequence were: (1) an article after Dr. Morgan filed her abuse suit, reporting plaintiffs' denials of the charges and their assertions that they were incapable of such behavior; (2) an article six days later with similar denials that apparently resulted from an interview; (3) a report six months later of plaintiffs' testimony in the federal abuse trial; (4) a magazine article 18 months later, written after "at least thirty minutes" of interviews with plaintiffs; (5) a newspaper account of an exchange of harsh words in a courtroom between plaintiffs and others that a reporter apparently overheard and repeated; (6) a press conference five months later held by their son, at which Mr. Foretich answered one question with one word and Mrs. Foretich "interjected once" to say that a medical exam of Hilary just after Dr. Morgan's charges had shown no evidence of abuse; (7) another newspaper interview; (8) an interview with Dr. Foretich in his home, with a different newspaper, during which his visiting parents were present—(the plaintiffs had maintained an apartment in their son's home and had stayed there during all of Hilary's visitations); (9) reports of a "press conference and rally" called by Dr. Foretich on the steps of the Capitol to celebrate Hilary's seventh birthday and to demonstrate against the legislation pending in Congress to free Dr. Morgan, at which both plaintiffs were introduced with Mr. Foretich uttering one sentence and Mrs. Foretich saying "about a dozen sentences" about the birthday and how much they missed Hilary; (10) a press conference held in Dr. Foretich's home after Dr. Morgan was released from jail, at which neither plaintiff spoke (though they were introduced by Dr. Foretich's attorney, who talked about the violation of their rights as grandparents); (11) a magazine article based on a five-hour interview with Dr. Foretich at his home. Before Dr. Foretich got home, the reporter spoke with the plaintiffs for about an hour. Mrs. Foretich showed photographs of Hilary and gave the reporter a tour of the room in which Hilary had stayed—which had been left exactly as it was when Hilary was last there. The plaintiffs spoke of their grief and asserted that the last time Hilary was there she had not wanted to go home and had said "I love my mommy, but there's something wrong with her." Once the son arrived the plaintiffs stayed in the room and interjected brief remarks during the five-hour interview.

As to television, the plaintiffs sat in the audience at the Phil Donahue Show while their son, the principal guest, sat on the stage. They were familiar with the format and had signed "guest" releases before the show. When Donahue ran a film clip showing Dr. Morgan saying that Dr. Foretich had been an abused child, Dr. Foretich pointed to his parents in the audience: "I was never—my parents are sitting right there. Those two people, do you believe that they could have. . . ." Donahue "thrust his microphone in front of Doris Foretich and said 'That's not the first time you've heard that accusation.'" She replied "It shocks me every time." She then recounted having lost her other two children and said "do you think that any grandmother who has lost two of her own children would ever—participate—I moved to this house, and I took sole care of my grandchildren. Do you think anybody like that would ever allow anyone to abuse her grandchildren?" Later, responding to an audience member's question, she said that she had taught art to young people for 20 years. "I happen to know that children will do anything their mothers tell them to do."

The plaintiffs also appeared on a British-produced television documentary about the custody dispute that was broadcast on Lifetime Cable

Channel's "Frontline" program in 1990. Only Mrs. Foretich spoke as she showed the reporter Hilary's room, uttering about ten sentences emphasizing how happy Hilary was there and showing the quilt that Hilary sat on and the closet that used to be "packed full of all the things that she loved when she was here." Later, she spoke at greater length about her son and Dr. Morgan, including comments about how Dr. Morgan was now "touted by the women's lib NOW women in this country. She has—she's like a new Joan of Arc. I think she's got notoriety to be noticed. . . . She knows none of this ever happened. She knows in her heart it never happened, as I do."

Finally, a full-length book was published that relied in part on interviews with Mrs. Foretich. She stated that she spoke to the author when he visited at her son's home for "at most 30 minutes." There was no evidence that Mr. Foretich ever spoke to the author.]

■ Before MURNAGHAN, CIRCUIT JUDGE, and BUTZNER and PHILLIPS, SENIOR CIRCUIT JUDGES.

■ MURNAGHAN, CIRCUIT JUDGE.

. . .

C

On November 29, 1992, American Broadcasting Companies, Inc. aired, as its "ABC Sunday Night Movie," a 91–minute docudrama entitled "A Mother's Right: The Elizabeth Morgan Story." Being a "docudrama," the made-for-TV movie presented a dramatized and perhaps somewhat fictionalized account, with actors and actresses playing the roles of Dr. Morgan, Dr. Foretich, Hilary, et al.

[In one scene, upon hearing that Hilary had seemed happy in a supervised visit with her father and paternal grandparents,] Dr. Morgan responds: "It's just like the therapist said. . . . Classic response. She's being kind to her abusers so she won't be hurt again" (emphasis added).

D

. . . Plaintiffs' entire case is based on the utterance of a single sound—the "s" in the word "abusers," which allegedly indicated that Hilary was being abused not only by her father but also by one or both of her paternal grandparents. At the present stage of the litigation, it is undisputed that the "s" that converted the singular "abuser" into the plural "abusers" was included unintentionally.

. . .

II

Because the question of whether a defamation plaintiff is a "limited-purpose public figure" is an issue of law, see [ ]; [*Waldbaum*], we review de novo. In conducting our review, we "must look through the eyes of a reasonable person at the facts taken as a whole." [*Waldbaum*]

III

A

[The court reviewed the development of the *Times-Gertz* doctrine and noted that Virginia had adopted the negligence standard for cases involving private plaintiffs. The court also briefly reviewed *Firestone, Wolston,* and *Hutchinson.*]

B

In the course of deciding *Gertz, Firestone, Hutchinson,* and *Wolston,* the Court developed a two-part inquiry for determining whether a defamation plaintiff is a limited-purpose public figure. First, was there a particular "public controversy" that gave rise to the alleged defamation? Second, was the nature and extent of the plaintiff's participation in that particular controversy sufficient to justify "public figure" status? [ ]

. . .

We have proceeded upon the initial presumption that the defamation plaintiff is a private individual, subject to the defendant's burden of proving that the plaintiff is a public figure to whom the *New York Times* standard applies. [ ] [In earlier cases] we set forth five requirements that the defamation defendant must prove before a court can properly hold that the plaintiff is a public figure for the limited purpose of comment on a particular public controversy: (1) the plaintiff had access to channels of effective communication; (2) the plaintiff voluntarily assumed a role of special prominence in the public controversy; (3) the plaintiff sought to influence the resolution or outcome of the controversy; (4) the controversy existed prior to the publication of the defamatory statement; and (5) the plaintiff retained public-figure status at the time of the alleged defamation. [ ] Typically, we have combined the second and third requirements, to ask "whether the plaintiff ha[d] voluntarily assumed a role of special prominence in a public controversy by attempting to influence the outcome of the controversy." [ ][11]

IV

The first question we must address is whether there was a particular public controversy that gave rise to the alleged defamation.

A

Gertz provided no express definition of a "public controversy," but the Court's subsequent decisions on limited-purpose public figure status provide some useful guidance. . . . In holding that Ms. Firestone was not a limited-purpose public figure, the Supreme Court refused "to equate 'public controversy' with all controversies of interest to the public." [ ]

---

11. From the point of view of the defendants, who bear the burden of proof, the [five-part test] is relatively stringent. By comparison, the D.C. Circuit's test requires the defendant to prove only that the plaintiff "played a sufficiently central role in the controversy." [ ]

The Court rejected the notion that news coverage of a "cause celebre" could create a "public controversy," in the constitutional sense: "Dissolution of a marriage through judicial proceedings is not the sort of 'public controversy' referred to in *Gertz*, even though the marital difficulties of extremely wealthy individuals may be of interest to some portion of the reading public." [   ] Thus, the mere facts that a dispute was litigated and that the litigation garnered some news coverage do not, by themselves, render the dispute a "public controversy." [   ][12]

In 1980, after carefully sifting through the Supreme Court cases, [*Waldbaum*] enunciated an express definition of a "public controversy":

> A public controversy is not simply a matter of interest to the public; it must be a real dispute, the outcome of which affects the general public or some segment of it in an appreciable way.
>   .   .   .   [E]ssentially private concerns or disagreements do not become public controversies simply because they attract attention.   .   .   .   Rather, a public controversy is a dispute that in fact has received public attention because its ramifications will be felt by persons who are not direct participants.

[   ]; see id. at 1292 (defining a "public controversy" as "a specific public dispute that has foreseeable and substantial ramifications for persons beyond its immediate participants"); [   ].

We subsequently adopted the D.C. Circuit's definition. [   ]

B

Next we must determine whether the above-quoted definition encompasses the Morgan–Foretich dispute. We are not, however, the first court to address precisely that question. [A district judge in the District of Columbia had found a public controversy in ruling on another defamation case that arose from one of the articles referred to earlier. Judge Gesell held that the dispute] was a "public controversy," within the meaning of *Gertz, Waldbaum*, and their progeny:

> The controversy and the rulings of the presiding [District of Columbia] Superior Court judge engendered discussion on issues of public concern, including child abuse, women's rights, the intrusion of the state into private affairs, and the limits of punishment for contempt of court.
>
>   .   .   .
>
>   [T]he many public policy issues raised by the Morgan–Foretich dispute made it a genuine public controversy, not merely a lurid personal matter that captured only the voyeuristic attention of the public. Compare Time, Inc. v. Firestone, [   ].

Foretich v. Advance Magazine Publishers, Inc., 765 F.Supp. at 1102, 1107–08; see also Foretich v. CBS, Inc., 619 A.2d 48, 52 (D.C.1993)(plaintiff Dr.

---

12. In *Wolston*, the Court also suggested in [dictum] that there can be no "public controversy" unless the issues involved were truly divisive, or subject to debate. [   ] . . . That [dictum] has been roundly criticized by lower courts and commentators alike. [   ]

Foretich and codefendant Dr. Morgan stipulated that they were both limited-purpose public figures and that therefore, implicitly, their dispute was a "public controversy").

.   .   .

There was ample evidence that the Morgan–Foretich dispute "received public attention because" it had "foreseeable and substantial ramifications for persons beyond its immediate participants." See [*Waldbaum*]. A search of Mead Data Central's NEXIS database reveals more than one thousand news reports on the Morgan–Foretich dispute. The custody battle heightened social awareness of child-abuse allegations and their role in custody disputes, and raised several substantial questions for public debate, including how best to determine which parent is more "fit," how courts can best protect a child's interests during a prolonged custody fight, and what should be the proper role of psychiatric and social-work experts.

Furthermore, Dr. Morgan's prolonged contempt incarceration for refusing to divulge Hilary's whereabouts raised a special set of public policy issues. According to one congressional report, the controversy implicated "local and national issue[s] joining together various political, social, and religious organizations,". . . . The public discussion of those issues ultimately prompted Congress and the President to secure Dr. Morgan's release through federal legislation limiting the power of the District of Columbia courts to impose contempt in child-custody cases. Clearly, the impact of the Morgan–Foretich battle—unlike most child-custody disputes—was felt far beyond the confines of the Morgan and Foretich homes. . . .

V

Having concluded that there was indeed a public controversy that gave rise to the alleged defamation, we must next examine "the nature and extent of [Vincent Foretich's and Doris Foretich's] participation in [that] controversy." . . . Because we find that neither Vincent nor Doris Foretich voluntarily assumed a role of special prominence in the Morgan–Foretich controversy in order to influence its outcome, we need not consider the other elements of the [Fourth Circuit] test.[13]

A

The bare words of the legal test—whether the plaintiff "voluntarily assumed a role of special prominence in a public controversy in order to influence its outcome"—can best be illuminated by reference to *Gertz* and subsequent Supreme Court cases, particularly *Firestone* and *Wolston*. [The court relied upon the language in *Gertz* stating that the plaintiff had not taken part in the criminal prosecution and had "never discussed either the

---

13. In *Foretich v. Advance Magazine Publishers, Inc.,,* discussed supra at Part IV-B, the district court applied a different test, previously enunciated by the D.C. Circuit, and held that Doris Foretich was a limited purpose public figure. [ ] On appeal here, ABC has not claimed that the decision . . . has any collateral estoppel effect with regard to the [requirements] that we find dispositive.

criminal or civil litigation with the press and was never quoted as having done so.'']

In *Firestone*, [the plaintiff] . . . was not a public figure for the purposes of comment on her divorce. [   ] Then–Justice Rehnquist, speaking for the Court, explained that Firestone

[did not] freely choose to publicize issues as to the propriety of her married life. She was compelled to go to court by the State in order to obtain legal release from the bonds of matrimony. . . . [I]n such an instance resort to the judicial process . . . is no more voluntary in a realistic sense than that of the defendant called upon to defend his interests in court.

[   ] The Court went on to explain that most participants in litigation resemble Firestone and should not be deemed public figures, even for the limited purpose of comment on the litigation: they are ''drawn into a public forum largely against their will in order to attempt to obtain the only redress available to them or to defend themselves against actions brought by the State or by others.'' [   ]; see also *Wolston* [   ] (To hold that all persons convicted of a crime automatically become public figures ''would create an 'open season' for all who sought to defame [them].'').

Furthermore, the Court was not swayed by the fact that Firestone had held several press conferences ''during the divorce proceedings in an attempt to satisfy inquiring reporters. . . . Such interviews should have had no effect upon the merits of the legal dispute between [Firestone] and her husband or the outcome of that trial, and we . . . [cannot] assume [   ] that any such purpose was intended.'' [   ]

. . .

[The court quoted at length from *Wolston*'s rejection of the claim that Wolston had ''voluntarily thrust'' or ''injected'' himself into the forefront of any public controversy. More accurately, he had been ''dragged unwillingly into the controversy.'' His voluntary conduct in choosing not to appear before the grand jury was not decisive. He ''never discussed this matter with the press and limited his involvement to that necessary to defend himself against the contempt charge. It is clear that [he] played only a minor role in whatever public controversy there may have been concerning the investigation of Soviet espionage.'' He did not engage ''the attention of the public in an attempt to influence the resolution of the issues involved. . . . His failure to respond to the grand jury's subpoena was in no way calculated to draw attention to himself in order to invite public comment or influence the public with respect to any issue. He did not in any way seek to arouse public sentiment in his favor and against the investigation. Thus, this is not a case where a defendant invites a citation for contempt in order to use the contempt citation as a fulcrum to create public discussion about the methods being used in connection with an investigation or prosecution.'']

B

. . . Specifically, ABC has claimed that Dr. Foretich's parents wittingly allowed their son to use them as ''props'' in a strategy of ''high theater'': Dr. Foretich would highlight the heinous charges that Dr. Morgan had leveled against his elderly and dignified-looking parents, and then ask his audiences rhetorically whether such grandparents could have possibly committed those vile acts, or whether, instead, the fact that Dr. Morgan had made such accusations demonstrated her ''bizarre'' and ''unbalanced'' personality. By ABC's account, the Foretiches—not Dr. Morgan—were responsible for the continued publicity surrounding the charges of grandparental abuse. Therefore, ABC has argued, both Vincent and Doris Foretich voluntarily assumed special roles of prominence in the Morgan–Foretich controversy in order to influence its outcome, and they may not now claim the protections of purely ''private'' persons.

We reject ABC's argument because it pays inadequate attention to the context in which the Foretiches made their public comments and appearances, and, as a result, undervalues their interest in defending their own reputations against the extraordinary attacks launched by Dr. Morgan. The complaint that Dr. Morgan filed in federal district court in 1986 accused the Foretich grandparents of performing very specific sex acts with Hilary, then a three-year-old girl. Those accusations were immediately publicized in The Washington Post and [widely republished over several years]. The resultant publicity doubtless had the potential to destroy Vincent Foretich's and Doris Foretich's reputations, and that potential may well have been realized.

The common law of defamation has long recognized that charges such as those leveled against the Foretich grandparents are so obviously and materially harmful to reputational interests that they must be deemed defamatory per se. We, too, recognize the devastation that public accusations of child sexual abuse can wreak, and we are extremely reluctant to attribute public-figure status to otherwise private persons merely because they have responded to such accusations in a reasonable attempt to vindicate their reputations. Therefore, we hold that a person who has been publicly accused of committing an act of serious sexual misconduct that (if committed in the place of publication and proved beyond a reasonable doubt) would be punishable by imprisonment cannot be deemed a ''limited-purpose public figure'' merely because he or she makes reasonable public replies to those accusations.[17]   . . .

C

In determining the reasonableness of a reply, we need not plow entirely new ground: the common law on the conditional (or qualified)

---

17. In so holding, we follow the *Gertz* Court's advice to formulate ''broad rules of general application'' that accommodate the competing interests of press and personal reputation, rather than to assess each defamation plaintiff on a purely ad hoc, case-by-case basis, which ''would lead to unpredict-able results and uncertain expectations.'' [ ]; see also *Waldbaum*, [ ] (explaining why clear rules for applying *New York Times*, *Gertz* and their progeny ultimately will benefit both the press and the public by making the constitutional law of defamation more predictable).

privilege of reply, also known as the privilege to speak in self-defense or to defend one's reputation, can help guide our discussion. Under the common law, the publication of a defamatory attack constitutes an "occasion" triggering the conditional privilege of reply, but the protection of that privilege is lost if it is "abused." . . . One may abuse, and thus lose, his conditional privilege of reply if, inter alia, (1) his reply includes substantial defamatory matter that is "irrelevant" or "non-responsive" to the initial attack; (2) his reply includes substantial defamatory matter that is "disproportionate" to the initial attack; or (3) the publication of his reply is "excessive," i.e., is addressed to too broad an audience. [ ] Our reading of the extensive case law on abuse of the privilege of reply, [ ], demonstrates, however, that a public response to a public attack may be "uninhibited, robust, and wide-open," [*New York Times*], without stepping over the line into abuse.

. . . By borrowing well-established principles regarding the abuse of the privilege of reply, and applying them to the question of whether a defamation plaintiff is a public figure or a private individual, we hope to import decades of accumulated wisdom from the common law into a relatively recent constitutional doctrine.

(1)

As to the first requirement of reasonableness—that the reply be responsive to the initial attacks—we begin with Dean Prosser's admonition that a person attacked must not add "anything irrelevant and unconnected with the charges made against him, as where he attempts to refute an accusation of immorality by saying that [his accuser] has stolen a horse." [ ] A supposed "reply" is not truly a reply if it is "patently unrelated to the subject matter" of the antecedent attack. One may not "publish any and all kinds of charges against the offender, upon the theory that they tend to degrade him, and thereby discredit his [accusations]." . . .

The Foretiches' public comments and appearances were, in large part, relevant and responsive to Dr. Morgan's accusations against them. They made no public statements until after Dr. Morgan's federal complaint was filed and publicized in August 1986. At that time, their first reactions were to deny the allegations in a concise, forthright fashion. Later, they spoke to reporters in more detail about themselves, their son, and Dr. Morgan.

Most of the Foretiches' statements about themselves were relevant to the attacks against them. For example, it was clearly relevant for Doris Foretich to describe how she had taken Hilary to a doctor, who examined her and found absolutely no physical evidence of abuse. The Foretiches' more general self-descriptions—as "God-loving," "law-abiding," "honorable, clean-living people"—may or may not have sounded convincing, but they were certainly relevant to refuting Dr. Morgan's charges of child molestation. The same can be said for Doris Foretich's repeated attempts to explain that her loss of two children made it impossible for her to mistreat her granddaughters. Both Doris and Vincent Foretich described the sacrifices that they had made to assist their son in raising Hilary—moving from Gloucester to Great Falls; sewing quilts on which Hilary could play with her toys; supplying her with nice clothes and dolls and a pleasant room. Those selfless efforts to enhance the quality of their granddaughter's life tend to contradict the image that Dr. Morgan had painted of her former in-laws as depraved child molesters. Furthermore, the grandparents' descriptions of how they missed Hilary, and of their prayers for her, and of wanting to see her again all served to bolster their denials of Dr. Morgan's allegations. On the other hand, their lengthy descriptions of how the charges had damaged their own lives were not particularly relevant or responsive, but our examination of the record suggests that those descriptions were relatively innocuous.

The Foretiches' descriptions of their son Eric also were relevant to the accusations of child abuse. . . . Doris Foretich's statement on the Donahue Show—that Eric had been "very much loved" as a child—was a clear, direct response to the showing of a videotape in which Dr. Morgan alleged that Eric had been abused as an adolescent (presumably either by his parents or with their acquiescence).

The grandparents' remarks about Dr. Morgan also were, in large part, relevant. Doris Foretich stated that Dr. Morgan "knows in her heart that it [the alleged sexual abuse of Hilary] never happened." Doris Foretich impugned Dr. Morgan's motives by describing the offers of book and movie contracts, the fame, and the high status in the women's movement that had accrued to Dr. Morgan, all as a result of her public campaign against Hilary's father and paternal grandparents. Furthermore, Doris Foretich at least implied that Hilary had been mistreated, if not abused, at the hands of her mother. That allegation was highly relevant, for it suggested that Dr. Morgan may have accused the Foretiches in an attempt to camouflage her own misdeeds.

Neither Doris nor Vincent Foretich strayed far beyond those points. For example, neither attacked Dr. Morgan's qualifications or competence as a physician. Nor did they recount any general impressions of Dr. Morgan that they had formed during her brief marriage to their son. Moreover, they never commented directly on Dr. Morgan's contempt citation or imprisonment, on the legislation pending in Congress, or on how the D.C. courts should rule on the ultimate questions of custody and visitation rights. Rather, the Foretiches adhered quite closely to the topics most relevant to rebutting the allegations of child sexual abuse against them.

(2)

Next we must determine whether the Foretiches' public statements were "reasonably proportionate to the magnitude of the . . . first attack." In making that determination, we remain at all times aware that the allegation initially leveled here—concerning mistreatment of a little girl—was as destructive to reputation as virtually any charge imaginable. Thus, a reply would have to be truly outrageous before we would deem it "altogether disproportionate to the occasion." . . .

Turning again to the common law, we observe that a person under attack may properly allege, in Dean Prosser's words, "that his accuser is an unmitigated liar and the truth is not in him." . . . "Honest indignation and strong words," "colorful verbiage," and even hyperbole and "exaggerated statements" of fact all may be uttered in self-defense without stepping over the line into unreasonable behavior. . . .

We do not believe that the Foretiches' public comments came even close to being disproportionate to Dr. Morgan's attacks. They described their former daughter-in-law as "mentally ill," "sick," and "not in her right mind." They labeled her allegations as "heinous lie[s]," "downright filth," and "filthy dirt"—"like from the bottom of a cesspool." Those remarks may have been rather strong, but not when compared to Dr. Morgan's accusations. . . .

(3)

Finally, in considering the reasonableness of the Foretiches' public statements, we must ask to whom those statements were directed. . . . "The reply must reasonably focus on the audience which heard the attack." If an accusation of criminal sexual misconduct had been published only to a very limited audience, it obviously would be an abuse to respond in every newspaper and on every television and radio station in the country. But where the original attack was widespread, the response can be widely disseminated as well. . . .

. . .

(4)

Because the Foretiches' public responses to Dr. Morgan's accusations were responsive, proportionate, and not excessively published, they were "reasonable." We acknowledge that some of their public statements were probably intended (at least in part) to influence the outcome of the custody dispute or of the legislative debate in Congress. But we also recognize that, in the circumstances of this particular case, it is almost impossible to extricate statements made in self-defense from statements intended to influence the outcome of the controversy. A favorable outcome of the ultimate dispute—i.e., granting custody of Hilary, or at least unsupervised visitation rights, to Dr. Foretich—would have done more to vindicate Vincent and Doris Foretiches' reputations than any reply could have ever accomplished. Looking "through the eyes of a reasonable person at the facts taken as a whole," [ ], we conclude that the Foretiches' primary motive was to defend their own good names against Dr. Morgan's accusations and that their public statements can most fairly be characterized as measured defensive replies to her attacks, rather than as efforts to thrust themselves to the forefront of a public controversy in order to influence its outcome. Therefore, we hold that Vincent and Doris Foretich were private individuals, not limited-purpose public figures.

. . . .

VI

. . . We see no good reason "why someone dragged into a controversy should be able to speak publicly only at the expense of forgoing a private person's protection from defamation." [ ] By allowing the Foretiches to defend their good names without succumbing to public-figure status, we protect not only their own interests in reputation, but also society's interest in free speech. Further extending the *New York Times* actual-malice standard here would serve only to muzzle persons who stand falsely accused of heinous acts and to undermine the very freedom of speech in whose name the extension is demanded. By freely permitting the Foretiches to respond to Dr. Morgan's charges against them—charges that have never been proved in any court of law—we foster both the individual interest in self-expression and the social interest in the discovery and dissemination of truth—the very goals that animate our First Amendment jurisprudence.

[The court affirmed and remanded for further proceedings.]

NOTES AND QUESTIONS

1. Why does the court find a "public controversy"? How does this case differ in that regard from *Firestone*?

2. Why does the court find that plaintiffs are private? Who should have the burden of proof on that question? Is the common law self-defense (reply) privilege an apt analogy to use in deciding the constitutional question of whether plaintiffs are public or private?

3. Is the difference in standards between the Fourth Circuit and the District of Columbia Circuit likely to affect many cases? Does this kind of intercircuit dispute raise serious problems for national media?

4. The court says that any irrelevant statements by plaintiffs were "innocuous." How much irrelevant or newly attacking material would the court have had to find to declare the plaintiffs public? Is it a matter of comparing the amounts of protected and unprotected speech? A matter of intent? Does it depend on the substance of the remarks?

5. The court notes that both *Gertz* and *Waldbaum* emphasize how important it is to judge these matters by general standards so that others will know where they stand. What kind of guidance can you draw from this case to advise others?

6. It is clear under federal law that the question of whether plaintiff is public or private is a question for the court. As in *Foretich*, the court in Kassel v. Gannett Co., p. 973, supra, concluded that the issue "must be decided by the trial judge even where disputed fact questions prevent the resolution of the issue on a motion for summary judgment." Most state cases agree.

7. *General public figures.* General public figures have been few and far between since *Gertz*. According to *Waldbaum*,

[A] general public figure is a well-known "celebrity," his name a "household word." The public recognizes him and follows his words and deeds, either because it regards his ideas, conduct, or judgment as worthy of the attention or because he actively pursues that consideration.

Is that consistent with *Gertz*? Is it a useful way to approach the question? See also Buckley v. Littell, 539 F.2d 882 (2d Cir.1976), cert. denied 429 U.S. 1062 (1977)(William F. Buckley, Jr.); Carson v. Allied News Co., 529 F.2d 206 (7th Cir.1976)(Johnny Carson); Chuy v. Philadelphia Eagles Football Club, 595 F.2d 1265 (3d Cir.1979) (en banc) (a professional football player who is alleged to have a career-ending disease is a public figure). All except *Waldbaum* were decided before *Hutchinson* and *Wolston*. Which of the following might meet the *Waldbaum* standard: Hillary Rodham Clinton? The Rev. Jesse Jackson? Michael Jordan? David Letterman? Dan Rather? Robert Redford? John Updike? Oprah Winfrey? Is law-student familiarity with these names or lack thereof probative? Conclusive?

8. *Involuntary public figures.* Involuntary public figures have been very rare. For cases finding such figures, see Meeropol v. Nizer, 560 F.2d 1061 (2d Cir.1977), cert. denied 434 U.S. 1013 (1978)(children of convicted spies Julius and Ethel Rosenberg); Carson v. Allied News Co., 529 F.2d 206 (7th Cir.1976)(Johnny Carson's wife—unless she is "voluntary" because she married a famous person); Street v. National Broadcasting Co., 645 F.2d 1227 (6th Cir.), cert. granted and then dismissed after settlement, 454 U.S. 1095 (1981)(main prosecution witness in famous Scottsboro case of 1931, in which nine black youths in Alabama were accused of raping plaintiff and another white woman; alleged defamation occurred 40 years after trial). Are these cases consistent with *Gertz* and *Wolston?*

In Dameron v. Washington Magazine, Inc., 779 F.2d 736(D.C.Cir.1985), cert. denied 476 U.S. 1141 (1986), plaintiff had been the only air traffic controller on duty in 1974 when a plane approaching Dulles Airport crashed into Mt. Weather. Plaintiff testified in administrative and judicial proceedings that followed. In that case claims based on controller negligence were dismissed. In 1982 a plane crashed into the Potomac River. The story on the 1982 crash in defendant's city magazine included a sidebar on earlier local plane crashes and their causes. In that list the 1974 crash was attributed to "controller" failure. Plaintiff sued for libel. The district judge granted the magazine summary judgment.

The court of appeals held that persons "can become involved in public controversies and affairs without their consent or will. Air-controller Dameron, who had the misfortune to have a tragedy occur on his watch, is such a person" and became an involuntary public figure for the limited purpose of discussions of the Mt. Weather crash:

In *Waldbaum* this court set out a three-part framework for analyzing whether someone has become a limited-purpose public figure. Under this test the court must determine that there is a public controversy; ascertain that the plaintiff played a sufficiently central role in that controversy; and find that the alleged defamation was germane to the plaintiff's involvement in the controversy. [ ] Central to the second prong of the *Waldbaum* analysis is an inquiry into the plaintiff's voluntary actions that have caused him to become embroiled in a public controversy. [ ] This analysis clearly must be modified somewhat to accommodate the possibility of a potentially involuntary limited-purpose public figure that is presented here. We think, however, that the facts here satisfy the Supreme Court's definition of a public figure and an appropriately modified *Waldbaum* inquiry. There was indisputably a public controversy here. Nor can it be doubted that the alleged defamation was germane to the question of controller responsibility for air safety in general and the Mt. Weather crash in particular. There is no question that Dameron played a central, albeit involuntary, role in this controversy.

The case was distinguishable from *Wolston* because Dameron was "a central figure, however involuntarily, in the discrete and specific public controversy with respect to which he was allegedly defamed—the controversy over the cause of the Mt. Weather crash." *Wolston* was "tangential to the investigation of Soviet espionage in general." If Dameron can prove that he was not a cause of the Mt. Weather crash, might he still be a central figure in the "controversy" over the cause of that crash? Would this amount to permitting the defendant to make Dameron a public figure by falsely accusing him?

Involvement with organized crime figures has led some courts to find the plaintiff to be an involuntary public figure. Defendant magazine said of plaintiff, an attorney who represented persons alleged to have criminal connections, that he had "contributed down payments of up to $25,000 on grass transactions. Charges against him were dismissed because he cooperated with further investigations." Although recognizing that "mere newsworthiness" is not sufficient, the court first concluded that the issue of "drug trafficking" was "a real dispute, the outcome of which affects the general public or some segment of it." As to plaintiff's part in it, the court noted that sometimes one can be a public figure without voluntary actions. "For example, sports figures are generally considered public figures because of their positions as athletes or coaches. [ ] If a position itself is so prominent that its occupant unavoidably enters the limelight, then a person who voluntarily assumes such a position may be presumed to have accepted public figure status." Marcone v. Penthouse International, Ltd., 754 F.2d 1072, cert. denied 474 U.S. 864 (1985).

The court said that the so-called "involuntary" public figure is not a separate category, but "merely one way an individual may come to be considered a general or limited purpose public figure. Thus, to the extent a person attains public figure status by position, status, or notorious act he might be considered an involuntary public figure."

A person's job may produce at least limited-purpose public figure status by virtue of the associations it entails. Plaintiff's job brought him into constant contact, socially and officially, with a group of people that included the mayor of the District of Columbia. Several members of the group were involved in drugs. When a woman in the group died of an overdose the media paid much attention to the group and the drug issue. The court observed that plaintiff's behavior "before any controversy arose put him at [the controversy's] center" when it did arise:

> One may hobnob with high officials without becoming a public figure, but one who does so runs the risk that personal tragedies that for less well-connected people would pass unnoticed may place him at the heart of a public controversy. Clyburn engaged in conduct that he knew markedly raised the chances that he would become embroiled in a public controversy.

Clyburn v. News World Communications, Inc., 903 F.2d 29 (D.C.Cir.1990).

9. *Limited purpose public figures.* Consider the following capsule descriptions of recent cases raising the issue.

a. A surgeon who was championing a new technique on local radio and television programming. The court concluded that plaintiff had stepped out of the realm of his practice by seeking access to media. Park v. Capital Cities Communications Inc., 181 App.Div.2d 192, 585 N.Y.S.2d 902 (1992).

Compare Georgia Society of Plastic Surgeons v. Anderson, 257 Ga. 710, 363 S.E.2d 140 (1987), holding that an otolaryngologist who wrote an article in the Journal of the Medical Association of Georgia arguing that ear, nose and throat specialists, rather than plastic surgeons, should do certain surgery, was a private person when he sued over a sharp response in the same journal.

b. A person who had filed over 24 lawsuits in a decade and was accused of "'working a scam' by filing numerous lawsuits to extract monetary settlements on a full-time basis." The court held that plaintiff was not a public figure because he was not pervasively well known and had not voluntarily placed himself in a public controversy. Kumaran v. Brotman, 247 Ill.App.3d 216, 617 N.E.2d 191 (1993).

c. An attorney asserted to have overcharged a client. He was not a public official or a public figure despite serving as an acting municipal judge, being an appointed member of the state Racing Commission, and having been elected by fellow lawyers to be second vice-president of the state bar (which was solely advisory to the state supreme court) because these roles did not relate to this controversy. The court found him to be private. Hinerman v. The Daily Gazette Co., 188 W.Va. 157, 423 S.E.2d 560 (1992), cert. denied 507 U.S. 960 (1993). What if the claim had appeared in the state bar journal?

d. An operator of a jai alai fronton who had been accused by defendant broadcaster of arson and other crimes in connection with the burning of his fronton. Defendant's program discussed the problems of gambling and arson in the jai alai world. In Silvester v. American Broadcasting Companies, Inc., 839 F.2d 1491 (11th Cir.1988), the court relied on *Waldbaum*'s three criteria, to hold plaintiff a limited purpose public figure. First, there was a major public controversy over "corruption in the jai alai industry." Plaintiff's argument that "he had been pushed into the lime-light through a press-created controversy," was rejected in part because ABC had not previously covered jai alai at all. (Might this lack of prior coverage help plaintiff?) Second, the plaintiffs were in a position to "invite attention and comment" with respect to their participation in the controversy. They were prominent in the industry and "because they were the primary or sole focus of certain aspects of the controversy, they were in a position to influence its outcome." Certain public announcements, such as offering a reward for the arsonists, indicated that plaintiff had "voluntarily thrust himself forward in an attempt to influence the public's view on the issue and to arouse their sympathy to his position." Third, the broadcast was germane to the plaintiff's participation in the controversy.

10. *Corporations as public figures.* The overwhelming majority of courts have concluded that the fact of incorporation alone does not make the plaintiff a public figure. See Schiavone Construction Co. v. Time, Inc., 619 F.Supp. 684 (D.N.J.1985); Bank of Oregon v. Independent News, Inc., 298 Or. 434, 693 P.2d 35, cert. denied 474 U.S. 826 (1985). Contra, Jadwin v. Minneapolis Star and Tribune Co., 367 N.W.2d 476 (Minn.1985):

> We hold . . . that corporate plaintiffs in defamation actions must prove actual malice by media defendants when the defendants establish that the defamatory material concerns matters of legitimate public interest in the geographic area in which the defamatory material is published, either because of the nature of the business conducted or because the public has an especially strong interest in the investigation or disclosure of the commercial information at issue. Such a rule will encourage the media to probe the business world to the depth which is necessary to permit the kind of business reporting vital to an informed public.

For other discussions of the issue see Steaks Unlimited, Inc. v. Deaner, 623 F.2d 264 (3d Cir.1980)(seller of inspected but ungraded frozen beef who advertised extensively is limited-purpose public figure for broadcast report questioning the quality of the meat and plaintiff's sales practices); Arctic Co., Ltd. v. Loudoun Times Mirror, 624 F.2d 518 (4th Cir.1980), cert. denied 449 U.S. 1102 (1981)(private firm contracting to provide county with environmental report is not a public figure for article in local paper criticizing quality of plaintiff's work because it is "not generally known in the community" and was performing "narrowly-defined professional service in a highly technical field"); Bruno & Stillman, Inc. v. Globe Newspaper Co., 633 F.2d 583 (1st Cir.1980)(largest regional manufacturer and seller of fishing boats, "the paradigm middle echelon, successful manufacturer-merchant," is private person in suit over newspaper stories listing defects in its boats—success or size alone does not make plaintiff public); Saro Corp. v. Waterman Broadcasting Corp., 595 So.2d 87 (Fla.App.1992)(transmission shop said to have recommended unneeded repair work and charged for work not done is private person because it engaged in no effort to gain attention in controversy and was "dragged into a limelight it least desired"). Would any of these be decided differently if the plaintiff were a private entrepreneur?

Private Plaintiffs and Matters of Public Interest

We have seen that some states have made state law bases for recovery more burdensome than the Supreme Court has required, e.g. the New York rejection of *Gertz*, p. 967, supra. When, if ever, may they award presumed or punitive damages without a showing of "actual malice"? In short, has *Gertz* occupied the entire field of defamation?

As a start, recall that while *Gertz* was categorizing plaintiffs, its rules were said to apply in cases involving "publishers" or "broadcasters." Justice Powell's opinion did not speak of "defendants" but rather used mass media defendants. This has led to questions about whether the *Gertz* requirements apply (1) to all cases involving mass media, and (2) to any cases that do not involve mass media.

Some answers began to appear in Dun & Bradstreet, Inc. v. Greenmoss Builders, Inc., 472 U.S. 749 (1985). D & B, the credit reporting agency, whose business involves providing confidential information to subscribers about the credit ratings of businesses and others, sent a report to five subscribers stating that Greenmoss Builders, Inc. had filed a voluntary petition for bankruptcy. The report, prepared by a high school student employed by the defendant to review state bankruptcy proceedings, had incorrectly attributed to Greenmoss a bankruptcy petition filed by one of its former employees.

The trial judge permitted the jury to award presumed and punitive damages without finding actual malice. The jury awarded $50,000 in compensatory damages and $300,000 in punitive damages. The Vermont Supreme Court upheld the award on the ground that as a "matter of federal constitutional law, the media protections outlined in *Gertz* are inapplicable to nonmedia defamation actions." The Supreme Court affirmed, 5–4, but on grounds that did not involve the distinction between media and non-media defendants.

For a plurality of three, Justice Powell interpreted *Gertz* to apply only to cases in which the expression involved (variously) "a public issue," "public speech," or "an issue of public concern." Although no passages in *Gertz* drew this distinction, the "context of *Gertz*" was such that the opinion could have applied only to "cases involving public speech." Justice Powell asserted that in this case the First Amendment interest differed from that in *Gertz*:

> We have long recognized that not all speech is of equal First Amendment importance. It is speech on "matters of public concern" that is "at the heart of the First Amendment's protec-

tion. . . ." In contrast, speech on matters of purely private concern is of less First Amendment concern. . . .

While such speech is not totally unprotected by the First Amendment, [   ], its protections are less stringent. In *Gertz*, we found that the state interest in awarding presumed and punitive damages was not "substantial" in view of their effect on speech at the core of First Amendment concern. [   ] This interest, however, *is* "substantial" relative to the incidental effect these remedies may have on speech of significantly less constitutional interest. The rationale of the common law rules has been the experience and judgment of history that "proof of actual damage will be impossible in a great many cases where, from the character of the defamatory words and the circumstances of publication, it is all but certain that serious harm has resulted in fact." [   ] As a result, courts for centuries have allowed juries to presume that some damage occurred from many defamatory utterances and publications. [   ] This rule furthers the state interest in providing remedies for defamation by ensuring that those remedies are effective. In light of the reduced constitutional value of speech involving no matters of public concern, we hold that the state interest adequately supports awards of presumed and punitive damages—even absent a showing of "actual malice."

Justice Powell also replied to the dissenters:

If the dissent were the law, a woman of impeccable character who was branded a "whore" by a jealous neighbor would have no effective recourse unless she could prove "actual malice" by clear and convincing evidence. This is not malice in the ordinary sense, but in the more demanding sense of *New York Times*. The dissent, would, in effect, constitutionalize the entire common law of libel.

Finally, Justice Powell briefly explained why the speech in the case did not "involve a matter of public concern":

In a related context, we have held that "[w]hether . . . speech addressed a matter of public concern must be determined by [the expression's] content, form, and context . . . as revealed by the whole record." Connick v. Myers, 461 U.S. at 147–148 [district attorney's power to discipline an assistant depends in part on whether the assistant's speech that provoked the discipline involved a "matter of public interest"—eds.]. These factors indicate that petitioner's credit report concerns no public issue. It was speech solely in the individual interest of the speaker and its specific business audience. [   ] This particular interest warrants no special protection when—as in this case—the speech is wholly false and clearly damaging to the victim's business reputation. [   ] Moreover, since the credit report was made available only to five subscribers, who, under the terms of the subscription agreement, could not disseminate it further, it cannot be said that the report involves any "strong interest in the free flow of commercial information." [ ] There is simply no credible argument that this type of credit reporting requires special protection to ensure that "debate on public issues [will] be uninhibited, robust and wide-open."

In addition, the speech here, like advertising, is hardy and unlikely to be deterred by incidental state regulation. [ ] It is solely motivated by the desire for profit, which, we have noted, is a force less likely to be deterred than others. [ ] Arguably, the reporting here was also more objectively verifiable than speech deserving of greater protection. [ ] In any case, the market provides a powerful incentive to a credit reporting agency to be accurate, since false credit reporting is of no use to creditors. Thus, any incremental "chilling" effect of libel suits would be of decreased significance.

Chief Justice Burger concurred in the judgment only because he felt bound by *Gertz* until it was overruled. He thought *Gertz* was limited to expressions that concern "a matter of general public importance, and that the expression in question here related to a matter of essentially private concern."

Justice White also concurred only in the judgment. He thought both *Times* and *Gertz* had been wrongly decided: He asserted that Justice Powell "declines to follow the *Gertz* approach," which Justice White thought "was intended to reach cases that involve any false statements of fact injurious to reputation, whether the statement is made privately or publicly and whether or not it implicates a matter of public importance."

Justice White agreed with the result in *Greenmoss* because (1) he was still unreconciled to *Gertz* and (2) strict liability should be used for publications that do not deal with matters of public importance. (He also suggested alternative approaches that the Court might take in these cases—alternatives that we consider p. 1021, infra, as part of a more general look at possible "reform".)

There were thus five votes for the recovery of presumed and punitive damages without a showing of actual malice.

Justice Brennan, joined by Justices Marshall, Blackmun and Stevens, dissented. Although protecting the speech in this case is admittedly not the "central meaning of the First Amendment," *Gertz* "makes clear that the First Amendment nonetheless requires restraints on presumed and punitive damages awards for this expression." Apart from unhappiness that the majority justices were "cut[ting] away the protective mantle of *Gertz*," Justice Brennan objected that "[w]ithout explaining what *is* a 'matter of public concern,' the plurality opinion proceeds to serve up a smorgasbord of reasons why the speech at issue here is not, [ ], and on this basis affirms" the award. Any standard that can be gleaned from the opinions is "impoverished" and "irreconcilable with First Amendment principles. The credit reporting at issue here surely involves a subject matter of sufficient public concern to require the comprehensive protections of *Gertz.*"

Speech about "economic matters . . . is an important part of our public discourse." An "announcement of the bankruptcy of a local company is information of potentially great concern to residents of the community where the company is located; like the labor dispute at issue in *Thornhill,* such a bankruptcy 'in a single factory may have economic repercussions for a whole region.'"

Justice Brennan asserted in a footnote that, since the subject matter "would clearly receive the comprehensive protections of *Gertz* were the speech publicly disseminated, [the] factor of confidential circulation to a limited number of subscribers is perhaps properly understood as the linchpin" of Justice Powell's analysis.

NOTES AND QUESTIONS

1. As noted, *Greenmoss* went off on issues other than the nature of the defendant. In fact, a majority of the justices rejected any distinction between media and nonmedia defendants.

Justice White thought that the plurality had "wisely" refrained from relying on the distinction. It "makes no sense to give the most protection to those publishers who reach the most readers and therefore pollute the channels of communication with the most misinformation and do the most damage to private reputation."

The four dissenters also rejected the distinction. First, in light of the growing power of mass media and their growing concentration, "protection for the speech of nonmedia defendants is essential to ensure a diversity of perspectives." In addition, "transformations in the technological and economic structure of the communications industry [have produced] an increasing convergence of what might be labeled 'media' and 'nonmedia.'"

Since this case, nonmedia defendants have not been stripped of *Gertz* protection solely because of their nonmedia status. See, e.g., Underwager v. Salter, 22 F.3d 730 (7th Cir.), cert. denied 115 S.Ct. 351 (1994) (holding that Wisconsin law would require public figure to prove actual malice in suit against nonmedia defendant).

2. Might *Greenmoss* allow recovery without meeting *Gertz*'s requirements in a suit by a private plaintiff defamed in a tabloid's story about plaintiff's social life? No media defendant has been held liable to a private plaintiff in a reported case without at least *Gertz* requirements being met.

3. Is there any basis for reading *Greenmoss* as allowing public plaintiffs to recover without having to show "actual malice"? See, e.g., Dworkin v. Hustler Magazine Inc., 867 F.2d 1188 (9th Cir.), cert. denied 493 U.S. 812 (1989) ("we doubt that it is possible to have speech about a public figure but not of public concern"). Why should that be?

4. If the media-nonmedia distinction is not at work, why did the defendant lose *Greenmoss*? Why was this information not a matter of

public concern? Was it that only five persons received the information?
Was it that the five could not disseminate it further? Most observers have
thought that this limited circulation explained the case because it seems
unlikely that news of a commercial bankruptcy would not qualify as a
matter of public interest. Indeed it seems certain that *Gertz* would have
applied if the erroneous report had appeared in the local newspaper.

5. Notice that the case applies only to the award of presumed and
punitive damages without proof of "actual malice." Does its logic also
suggest that the plaintiff need not prove any fault in this type of case?
Recall that Justice Powell volunteered that even this kind of speech "is not
totally unprotected by the First Amendment." Might this be the protection against strict liability?

6. In Snead v. Redland Aggregates, Ltd., 998 F.2d 1325 (5th Cir.
1993), cert. dismissed 114 S.Ct. 1587 (1994), one party sued over a press
release issued (in connection with a complaint) by the other party after
failed negotiations between the two. The court treated the case as one
involving a private plaintiff and private content so as to come within the
framework of *Greenmoss*. The court, concluding that five justices there
supported the use of "common law standards" for what it called "private
private" cases, held that presumed and punitive damages could be awarded
without a showing of fault.

7. Why did Justice Powell think that the dissent's approach would
deny the "woman of impeccable character . . . effective recourse unless she could prove 'actual malice' "? Does it?

Consider Johnson v. Johnson, 654 A.2d 1212 (R.I.1995), in which, in a
restaurant, defendant ex-husband call his ex-wife a "whore." Although
the trial judge concluded that the statement was true, he upheld a jury
award of $5,000 compensatory and $20,000 punitive damages. Under the
state's constitution, in civil and criminal actions for libel or slander "the
truth, unless published or uttered from malicious motives, shall be sufficient defense to the person charged." The court upheld the finding that
the words had been uttered with ill will sufficient to sustain the compensatory award. But the provocation of the situation was such that punitive
damages were not permissible under state law. Although the court noted
that the defendant had not preserved "federal constitutional issues," it
nonetheless concluded that no federal rule prevented the recovery here.
Greenmoss showed that *Gertz* did not apply since the statement was not of
public concern. Nor did the *Garrison* case, p. 941, supra, which "absolutely prohibits punishment of truthful criticisms of public officials" apply to
Johnson "because we are not dealing with public officials, public figures, or
even matters of public concern."

8. In Nadel v. Regents of the University of California, 28 Cal.App.4th
1251, 34 Cal.Rptr.2d 188 (1994), cert. denied 116 S.Ct. 672 (1995), the
court of appeal held that government officials were entitled to the protection of the *New York Times* doctrine in comments made about public
figures. In a case of first impression the court was sensitive to the need to
add a third consideration to the two ("unfettered interchange of ideas" and

"protection of vulnerable citizens from defamation") already used in the development of the *Times* line. That third was framed as "the overarching constitutional interest in protecting people from abuses of governmental power." The court approved a passage from Shiffrin, Governmental Speech, 27 UCLA L.Rev. 565 (1980):

> Government has legitimate interests in informing, in educating, and in persuading. If government is to secure cooperation in implementing its programs, if it is to be able to maintain a dialogue with its citizens about their needs and the extent to which government can or should meet those needs, government must be able to communicate. An approach that would invalidate all controversial government speech would seriously impair the democratic process.

The court recognized that government had unique power in the war of words with citizens—and that "[e]vents of the past few decades have demonstrated that government is quite capable of misleading the public and defaming its citizens." But the extent of this concern had become "debatable in light of general post-Watergate skepticism about anything government has to say." Moreover, this "claim of plaintiff vulnerability could be made as to any 'big media' defendant." The court concluded that holding government officials to liability under the *New York Times* doctrine would reduce potential abuse of power since officials would know they could be held liable under *Times* or *Gertz*. Common law strict liability was thought inconsistent with the role government had to play in the public debate.

As a separate ground for its result, the court noted that in *New York Times,* the Court had suggested that since government officials were often protected for their speech, giving citizens a comparable protection would balance the power. That view suggested that in this case constitutional protection was needed to put the officials not otherwise protected in balance with the citizens.

9. It is important to keep in mind that even if *Greenmoss* is read to permit easier paths to recovery, state law need not agree.

10. The role of punitive damages is discussed p. 1018, *infra*.

End 2nd semester

E.   THE PRESS AS COMMENTATOR

Dictum in Justice Powell's *Gertz* opinion denying the concept of a "false idea" was once thought to suggest another constitutional defense. Many lower courts understood this to create a means by which defendants were able to win cases on "constitutional" grounds as early as the motion to dismiss the complaint. The Court had already decided a case involving a citizen's charge at a city council meeting that plaintiff was "blackmailing" the city in connection with pending real estate negotiations. Greenbelt Cooperative Publishing Ass'n v. Bresler, 398 U.S. 6 (1970). Although in some contexts a charge of "blackmail" might be understood as charging a specific crime, that was not true in this case. The word was "no more than rhetorical hyperbole, a vigorous epithet used by those who considered Bresler's vigorous negotiating position extremely unreasonable." Since no reasonable reader could have taken the report to charge a crime in context, the words were not actionable.

In Letter Carriers v. Austin, 418 U.S. 264 (1974), decided at the same time as *Gertz,* the Court held that no one could reasonably understand the publication of Jack London's famous definition of a "scab" as a "traitor to his God, his country, his family and his class," to be a charge of the crime of treason. The words were being used "in a loose figurative sense . . . merely rhetorical hyperbole, a lusty and imaginative expression of the contempt felt by union members to those who refuse to join them."

Lower courts extended the analysis to claims based on vague language, such as calling plaintiff a "fellow traveler" of the fascists or describing a magazine as an "openly fascist journal." One court called these "loosely definable, variously interpretable statements of opinion . . . made inextricably in the contest of political, social, or philosophical debate." But the same court declared actionable the following charge:

> Like Westbrook Pegler, who lied day after day in his column about Quentin Reynolds and goaded him into a lawsuit, Buckley could be taken to court by any one of several people who had enough money to hire competent legal counsel and nothing else to do.

Buckley v. Littell, 539 F.2d 882 (2d Cir.1976), cert. denied 429 U.S. 1062 (1977). Why the different treatments?

The "epithet" or "rhetorical hyperbole" analysis had been part of the common law long before the libel area began being constitutionalized. As one court summarized the reasons in rejecting an action by someone referred to as one of "those bastards":

> [I]t is perfectly apparent that [the words] were used as mere epithets, as terms of abuse and opprobrium. As such they had no real meaning except to indicate that the individual who used them was under a strong emotional feeling of dislike toward those about whom he used them. Not being intended or understood as statements of fact they are impossible of proof or disproof. Indeed such words of vituperation and abuse reflect more on the character of the user than they do on that of the individual to whom they are intended to refer.

Curtis Publishing Co. v. Birdsong, 360 F.2d 344 (5th Cir.1966). Do these reasons justify the common law rule? What if the speaker "intended" the words to be understood as statements of fact?

In the 1980s a number of courts recognized a constitutional defense for "opinion." A good example is Ollman v. Evans, 750 F.2d 970 (D.C.Cir. 1984) (en banc), cert. denied 471 U.S. 1127 (1985). Briefly, syndicated columnists Evans and Novak argued against the proposed appointment of a Marxist political science professor to head the Department of Government and Politics at the University of Maryland. Among other statements, the column quoted a political scientist who, refusing to be identified, was said to have asserted that "Ollman has no status within the profession, but is a pure and simple activist." The president of the University of Maryland rejected the appointment.

The trial judge's dismissal was affirmed by a split court that produced seven opinions. The lead opinion emphasized four factors for analysis: (1) "the common usage or meaning of the specific language of the challenged statements itself"; (2) "the statement's verifiability—is the statement capable of being objectively characterized as true or false?"; (3) "the full context of the statement—the entire article or column"; and (4) "the broader context or setting in which the statement appears. Different types of writing have . . . widely varying social conventions which signal to the reader the likelihood of a statement's being either fact or opinion."

After lower courts spent some years arguing over the *Ollman* approach, the Supreme Court addressed the issue.

Milkovich v. Lorain Journal Co.

Supreme Court of the United States, 1990.
497 U.S. 1, 110 S.Ct. 2695, 111 L.Ed.2d 1.

[Milkovich was coach of the Maple Heights High School wrestling team, which was involved in a brawl with a competing team. After a hearing, the Ohio High School Athletic Association (OHSAA) censured Milkovich and placed his team on probation. Parents of some of the team members sued to enjoin OHSAA from enforcing the probation, contending OHSAA's investigation and hearing violated due process. Milkovich and Scott, the superintendent, testifying at a judicial hearing on the suit, both denied that Milkovich had incited the brawl through his behavior toward the crowd and a meet official. The judge granted the restraining order sought by the parents. A sports columnist who had attended the meet, but not the judicial hearing, wrote about the hearing in a column published the next day in the defendant newspaper. The headline was "Maple beat the law with the 'big lie.'" The theme of the column was that at the judicial hearing Milkovich and Scott misrepresented Milkovich's role in the altercation and thereby prevented the team from receiving the punishment it deserved. The concluding paragraphs of the column were as follows:

> "Anyone who attended the meet, whether he be from Maple Heights, Mentor [the opposing school] or impartial observer, knows in his heart that Milkovich and Scott lied at the hearing after each having given his solemn oath to tell the truth."

> "But they got away with it."

> "Is that the kind of lesson we want our young people learning from their high school administrators and coaches?"

> "I think not."

Milkovich and Scott both sued the newspaper, alleging that the column accused them of perjury and thus was libelous per se. After 15 years of litigation and several appeals, the Ohio Court of Appeals held in Milkovich's case that the column was constitutionally protected opinion and granted the newspaper's motion for summary judgment.   The Supreme Court reversed.]

■ CHIEF JUSTICE REHNQUIST delivered the opinion of the Court.

[The opinion reviewed the various constitutional limitations imposed on state libel law in the series of cases beginning with New York Times v. Sullivan.   The Court also mentioned *Hepps,* p. 969, supra, and its holding in Hustler Magazine, Inc. v. Falwell, p. 830, supra, that an ad parody "could not reasonably have been interpreted as stating actual facts about the public figure involved."]

Respondents would have us recognize, in addition to the established safeguards discussed above, still another First Amendment–based protection for defamatory statements which are categorized as "opinion" as opposed to "fact."   For this proposition they rely principally on the following dictum from our opinion in *Gertz:*

> "Under the First Amendment there is no such thing as a false idea.   However pernicious an opinion may seem, we depend for its correction not on the conscience of judges and juries but on the competition of other ideas.   But there is no constitutional value in false statements of fact."   [   ]

Judge Friendly appropriately observed that this passage "has become the opening salvo in all arguments for protection from defamation actions on the ground of opinion, even though the case did not remotely concern the question."   [Cianci v. New Times Publishing Co., 639 F.2d 54 (2d Cir. 1980)].   Read in context, though, the fair meaning of the passage is to equate the word "opinion" in the second sentence with the word "idea" in the first sentence.   Under this view, the language was merely a reiteration of Justice Holmes' classic "marketplace of ideas" concept.   [   ]

Thus we do not think this passage from *Gertz* was intended to create a wholesale defamation exemption for anything that might be labeled "opinion."   Not only would such an interpretation be contrary to the tenor and the context of the passage, but it would also ignore the fact that expressions of "opinion" may often imply an assertion of objective fact.

If a speaker says, "In my opinion John Jones is a liar," he implies a knowledge of facts which lead to the conclusion that Jones told an untruth. Even if the speaker states the facts upon which he bases his opinion, if those facts are either incorrect or incomplete, or if his assessment of them is erroneous, the statement may still imply a false assertion of fact.   Simply couching such statements in terms of opinion does not dispel these implications;   and the statement, "In my opinion Jones is a liar," can cause as much damage to reputation as the statement, "Jones is a liar."   As Judge Friendly aptly stated: "[It] would be destructive of the law of libel if a writer could escape liability for accusations of [defamatory conduct] simply by using, explicitly or implicitly, the words 'I think,' " see *Cianci* [   ].   It is worthy of note that at common law, even the privilege of fair comment did not extend to a "false statement of fact, whether it was expressly stated or implied from an expression of opinion." Restatement (Second) of Torts, supra, § 566 Comment *a*.

Apart from their reliance on the *Gertz* dictum, respondents do not really contend that a statement such as, "In my opinion John Jones is a liar," should be protected by a separate privilege for "opinion" under the First Amendment. But they do contend that in every defamation case the First Amendment mandates an inquiry into whether a statement is "opinion" or "fact," and that only the latter statements may be actionable. They propose that a number of factors developed by the lower courts (in what we hold was a mistaken reliance on the *Gertz* dictum) be considered in deciding which is which. But we think the " 'breathing space' " which " 'freedoms of expression require to survive' " [ ] is adequately secured by existing constitutional doctrine without the creation of an artificial dichotomy between "opinion" and fact.

Foremost, we think *Hepps* stands for the proposition that a statement on matters of public concern must be provable as false before there can be liability under state defamation law, at least in situations, like the present, where a media defendant is involved.[6] Thus, unlike the statement, "In my opinion Mayor Jones is a liar," the statement, "In my opinion Mayor Jones shows his abysmal ignorance by accepting the teachings of Marx and Lenin," would not be actionable. *Hepps* ensures that a statement of opinion relating to matters of public concern which does not contain a provably false factual connotation will receive full constitutional protection.

Next, the *Bresler–Letter Carriers–Falwell* line of cases provide protection for statements that cannot "reasonably [be] interpreted as stating actual facts" about an individual. [ ] This provides assurance that public debate will not suffer for lack of "imaginative expression" or the "rhetorical hyperbole" which has traditionally added much to the discourse of our nation. [ ]

The *New York Times–Butts* and *Gertz* culpability requirements further ensure that debate on public issues remains "uninhibited, robust, and wide-open." [ ] Thus, where a statement of "opinion" on a matter of public concern reasonably implies false and defamatory facts regarding public figures or officials, those individuals must show that such statements were made with knowledge of their false implications or with reckless disregard of their truth. Similarly, where such a statement involves a private figure on a matter of public concern, a plaintiff must show that the false connotations were made with some level of fault as required by *Gertz*. Finally, the enhanced appellate review required by *Bose Corp.*, provides assurance that the foregoing determinations will be made in a manner so as not to "constitute a forbidden intrusion of the field of free expression." [ ]

---

6. In *Hepps* the Court reserved judgment on cases involving nonmedia defendants, [ ] and accordingly we do the same. Prior to *Hepps*, of course, where public-official or public-figure plaintiffs were involved, the *New York Times* rule already required a showing of falsity before liability could result. [ ]

We are not persuaded that, in addition to these protections, an additional separate constitutional privilege for "opinion" is required to ensure the freedom of expression guaranteed by the First Amendment. The dispositive question in the present case then becomes whether or not a reasonable factfinder could conclude that the statements [in the column] imply an assertion that petitioner Milkovich perjured himself in a judicial proceeding. We think this question must be answered in the affirmative. . . . This is not the sort of loose, figurative or hyperbolic language which would negate the impression that the writer was seriously maintaining petitioner committed the crime of perjury. Nor does the general tenor of the article negate this impression.

We also think the connotation that petitioner committed perjury is sufficiently factual to be susceptible of being proved true or false. A determination of whether petitioner lied in this instance can be made on a core of objective evidence by comparing, inter alia, petitioner's testimony before the trial court. As the [Ohio Supreme Court noted in the case of the superintendent] "[w]hether or not H. Don Scott did indeed perjure himself is certainly verifiable by a perjury action with evidence adduced from the transcripts and witnesses present at the hearing. Unlike a subjective assertion the averred defamatory language is an articulation of an objectively verifiable event." [ ] So too with petitioner Milkovich.

The numerous decisions discussed above establishing First Amendment protection for defendants in defamation actions surely demonstrate the Court's recognition of the Amendment's vital guarantee of free and uninhibited discussion of public issues. But there is also another side to the equation; we have regularly acknowledged the "important social values which underlie the law of defamation,". . . .

We believe our decision in the present case holds the balance true. The judgment of the Ohio Court of Appeals is reversed and the case remanded for further proceedings not inconsistent with this opinion.

■ [Justice Brennan, joined by Justice Marshall, dissented. He said the Court addressed the opinion issue "cogently and almost entirely correctly," and agreed that the lower courts had been under a "misimpression that there is a so-called opinion privilege wholly in addition to the protections we have already found to be guaranteed by the First Amendment." But he disagreed with the application of agreed principles to the facts: "I find that the challenged statements cannot reasonably be interpreted as either stating or implying defamatory facts about petitioner. Under the rule articulated in the majority opinion, therefore, the statements are due 'full constitutional protection.' "

He characterized the columnist's assumption that Milkovich lied as "patently conjecture" and asserted that conjecture is as important to the free flow of ideas and opinions as "imaginative expression" and "rhetorical hyperbole," which the majority agreed are protected. He offered several examples:

Did NASA officials ignore sound warnings that the Challenger Space Shuttle would explode? Did Cuban–American leaders arrange for John Fitzgerald Kennedy's assassination? Was Kurt Waldheim a Nazi officer? Such questions are matters of public concern long before all the facts are unearthed, if they ever are. Conjecture is a means of fueling a national discourse on such questions and stimulating public pressure for answers from those who know more.

The dissent argued that the language of the column itself made clear to readers that the columnist was engaging in speculation, personal judgment, emotional rhetoric, and moral outrage. "No reasonable reader could understand [the columnist] to be impliedly asserting—as fact—that Milkovich had perjured himself."]

NOTES AND QUESTIONS

1. Why does the constitution require protection of rhetorical hyperbole but not opinion? Is rhetorical hyperbole less likely to damage reputation? Is it a more valuable form of speech?

2. The majority says "the statement, 'In my opinion Mayor Jones shows his abysmal ignorance by accepting the teachings of Marx and Lenin,' would not be actionable." If the mayor does not accept the teachings of Marx and Lenin, might the statement be actionable? Does the Court mean only that the statement that the mayor is abysmally ignorant is not actionable if the rest of the statement is true?

3. What should the trial judge do if persuaded that the lay readers of a mass-circulation publication took a statement as one of fact but that there is simply no way in which to try the truth or falsity of the statement? For example, what result if a survey showed that virtually all who read that statement concluded that it asserted a "fact." Does that affect the verifiability issue?

4. The procedural history of the *Milkovich* case, described at length in omitted portions of the majority opinion, illustrates the persistence and endurance that libel litigation sometimes demands of its participants. The column was published in 1974. The case settled shortly after this opinion.

5. In Moldea v. New York Times Co., 22 F.3d 310 (D.C.Cir.), cert. denied 115 S.Ct. 202 (1994), a book reviewer asserted that the plaintiff's book on professional football contained "too much sloppy journalism to trust the bulk" of the book. It then cited six examples to support the statement. In plaintiff's suit, the court first held, 2–1, that the analysis of actionability should be no different in a book review than in a hard news story. If anything, a harsh book review in the Times Book Review "is at least as damaging as accusations of incompetence made against an attorney or a surgeon in a legal or medical journal."

On a motion for rehearing, the panel withdrew its first opinion and unanimously held for defendant. Its earlier opinion had understood *Milko-*

vich to "disavow the importance of context." Instead, the panel now concluded that the standard for book reviews should make statements of opinion actionable "only when the interpretations are unsupportable by reference to the written work." Here, the "correct measure of the challenged statements' verifiability as a matter of law is whether no reasonable person could find that the review's characterizations were supportable interpretations of [the book]." That could not be found here. If, on the other hand, defendant had attacked the book "because it asserted that African–Americans make poor football coaches, that reading would be 'unsupportable by reference to the written work,' because nothing in Moldea's book even hints at this notion."

6. In Stevens v. Tillman, 855 F.2d 394, (7th Cir.1988), cert. denied 489 U.S. 1065 (1989), defendant called plaintiff a "racist." The court dismissed the claim on the ground that "racist" has lost its core meaning and is no longer actionable when used by itself. Courts cannot insist that speakers cling to older core meanings of words. "In daily life 'racist' is hurled about so indiscriminately that it is no more than a verbal slap in the face." Is this pre-*Milkovich* analysis still valid? The court in *Ward v. Zelikovsky*, p. 886, supra, relied heavily on Stevens v. Tillman in its discussion of the charge of "disliking" or "hating Jews." Does *Milkovich* require the results in these cases?

7. In Staples v. Bangor Hydro–Electric Co., p. 880, supra, involving a supervisor's statement that plaintiff had "sabotaged" computers, the court held that "the jury could rationally find that [the supervisor's] statement that he had reason to believe that [plaintiff] had sabotaged the computers implied the existence of undisclosed defamatory facts."

The Phantom of the Opera. In Phantom Touring, Inc. v. Affiliated Publications, 953 F.2d 724 (1st Cir.), cert. denied 504 U.S. 974 (1992), two competing stage versions of "Phantom of the Opera," both derived from a public domain novel, were playing in the United States. The earlier version was Kenneth Hill's; the later was the much more popular version by Andrew Lloyd Webber. Just before ticket sales were to begin in Boston for the Hill version the Boston Globe published two articles by its critic Kelly suggesting that readers be wary of Hill's "Fake Phantom" which it said had been "thriving off the confusion created by the two productions." One article quoted a Washington Post critic to the effect that Hill's version "bears as much resemblance to its celebrated counterpart as Jell–O does to Baked Alaska," and described Hill's version as "a rip-off, a fraud, a scandal, a snake-oil job." Other statements are discussed below. The lower court dismissed the libel case.

The court of appeals recognized that since *Milkovich* there was no longer a "wholesale defamation exemption for anything that might be labeled opinion." Nonetheless, *Milkovich* had reaffirmed three major propositions. First, the challenged statements "must be provably false." Thus, " 'That's the worst play I've ever seen' would be protected not because it is labeled an opinion but because it is so subjective that it is not 'susceptible of being proved true or false.' " (What if the plaintiff playwright has proof that the speaker in fact really liked the play but wrote what he did solely because he held a personal grudge against the plaintiff?)

Second, *Milkovich* had protected speech that could not reasonably be interpreted as stating "actual facts" about a person: those involving parody, "loose figurative speech," or "rhetorical hyperbole." Thus, following the *Greenbelt* case, a critic writing that the "producer who decided to charge admission for that show is committing highway robbery," would be protected because no reasonable reader could understand this to be an accusation of robbery. Context was all-important in determining how readers might understand the crucial words.

Third, the court thought it was required to make an independent examination of the whole record on this issue, just as *Bose* required independent review of the actual malice issue.

The court concluded that the rip off-fraud-scandal-snake oil passage was "not only figurative and hyperbolic, but we also can imagine no objective evidence to disprove it." The same applied to assertions that Hill's version was "fake" or "phony."

The most serious issue involved passages that could be read on their face to assert that the confusion was intentional—even though the advertising stated that there was no connection between the two shows. Arguably a charge of "deliberate deception" could be proven false by showing, for example, longstanding plans to tour the Hill show before Webber's version rose to prominence. But the "sum effect of the format, tone and entire content of the articles is to make it unmistakably clear that Kelly was expressing a point of view only." The language appeared in a column generally understood to be more opinionated than a typical news report. (Although this was given no weight in *Milkovich*, the *Phantom* court thought that was only because of the facts of that case—not because context was never relevant.)

Kelly's language was seen as subjective by design. His "snide, exasperated language indicated that his comments represented his personal appraisal of the factual information contained in the article." Of "greatest importance" was the breadth of the articles, "which not only discussed all the facts underlying his views, but also gave information from which readers might draw contrary conclusions. In effect, the articles offered a self-contained give-and-take, a kind of verbal debate between Kelly and those persons responsible for booking and marketing" plaintiff's version. The "assertion of deceit reasonably could be understood only as Kelly's personal conclusion about the information presented, not as a statement of fact." Kelly had noted that others did not share his negative view of the merit of Hill's version, that it had had some lengthy runs, and its producer was quoted to the effect that "critics may not like us, but audiences do." This "full disclosure of the facts underlying his judgment—none of which have been challenged as false—makes this case fundamentally different" from *Milkovich*:

The reporter [in *Milkovich*] had not been at the judicial proceeding. The column noted, however, that he had been the only non-involved person at both the controversial meet and the administrative hearing, a fact that could have suggested to readers that he was uniquely situated to draw the inference of lying. The column contained no response from the targets of the criticism.

Thus, the article in *Milkovich*, unlike Kelly's "Phantom" columns, was not based on facts accessible to everyone. Indeed, a reader reasonably could have understood the reporter in *Milkovich* to be suggesting that he was singularly capable of evaluating the plaintiffs' conduct. In contrast, neither of Kelly's columns indicated that he, or anyone else, had more information about Phantom Touring's marketing practices than was reported in the articles.

Is the court's approach compromised if the plaintiff can present ten witnesses who say they read the column and understood that the author "must have had more facts" than he stated?

State law. Some states have asserted that the state's constitutional law applicable to comments may provide broader protection than *Milkovich* offers.

See Immuno AG. v. Moor–Jankowski, 77 N.Y.2d 235, 567 N.E.2d 1270, 566 N.Y.S.2d 906, cert. denied 500 U.S. 954 (1991), involving a letter to the editor of a scientific journal criticizing plaintiff corporation's plan to use chimpanzees in a hepatitis research project. The corporation claimed it was defamed by the writer's suggestion that chimpanzees released after the corporation's experiments might spread disease among their counterparts in the wild. In a pre-*Milkovich* decision employing the *Ollman* analysis, the court held that the letter was protected opinion under the state and federal constitutions. After deciding *Milkovich*, the Supreme Court remanded *Immuno* for reconsideration in light of *Milkovich.*

The state court adhered to its earlier result. First, the letter was held to be protected under the federal constitution even after *Milkovich*. The court interpreted *Milkovich* as holding that "except for special situations of loose, figurative, hyperbolic language, statements that contain or imply assertions of provably false fact will likely be actionable." But it concluded that *Milkovich* left intact the requirement that the plaintiff prove falsity, and it held that the corporation had not raised triable issues of falsity.

Second, the court held that the state constitution requires that more attention be paid to the context of the defamatory statement than does the federal constitution after *Milkovich,* and that the New York court's pre-*Milkovich* decisions continue to provide the appropriate means of determining whether a statement is actionable under the state constitution. "[W]e believe an analysis that begins by looking at the content of the whole communication, its tone and apparent purpose [ ] better balances the values at stake than an analysis that first examines the challenged statements for express and implied factual assertions, and finds them actionable unless couched in loose, figurative or hyperbolic language in charged circumstances."

In 600 W. 115th St. Corp. v. Von Gutfeld, 80 N.Y.2d 130, 603 N.E.2d 930, 589 N.Y.S.2d 825 (1992), cert. denied 508 U.S. 910 (1993), at an open tenants' meeting defendant tenant said that the plaintiff landlord's proposal to set up a sidewalk cafe was "illegal" and "as fraudulent as you can get." The court held that under both the *Milkovich* view and the state constitutional approach these statements were not reasonably understandable as charges of crime or wrongdoing.

The New York court suggested the limits of its approach in Gross v. New York Times Co., 82 N.Y.2d 146, 623 N.E.2d 1163, 603 N.Y.S.2d 813 (1993), involving a series of investigative articles about plaintiff's conduct when he was New York City's Chief Medical Examiner. One article reported that unnamed sources had accused plaintiff of having "produced a series of misleading or inaccurate autopsy reports on people who died in custody of the police." He was said to have "instituted a policy of special handling for police-custody cases," to have performed some of these autopsies himself, and to have "intervened to alter the findings of other pathologists." He was said to have changed one report to show that death resulted from a surgical procedure rather than from a fractured skull. One pathologist who reviewed the record was quoted as saying that if plaintiff was acting honestly he was "unbelievably incompetent" and if he was acting deliberately "he may well have been looking for a way out for the police."

The court denied a motion to dismiss. Though some of the reports are properly understood as hypotheses based on stated facts, "charges that plaintiff engaged in cover-ups, directed the creation of 'misleading' autopsy reports and was guilty of 'possibly illegal' conduct" would be "understood by the reasonable reader as assertions of fact." The charges of "corrupt" conduct here "cannot be treated as a mere rhetorical flourish" or the speculative accusation of an angry but ill-informed citizen, made during the course of a heated debate [citing *Von Gutfeld*]:

> Rather, the accusation was made in the course of a lengthy, copiously documented newspaper series that was written only after what purported to be a thorough investigation. Having been offered as a special feature series rather than as coverage of a current news story, the disputed articles were calculated to give the impression they were "the product of some deliberation, not of the heat of the moment."

Should it matter if none of the reportorial team knew anything about medicine (and each article in the series said as much) and that all the actionable language comes from quotations or summaries of what was said by plaintiff's colleagues and by pathologists the newspaper asked to review the records? Might this be relevant on the question of "actual malice"?

See also *West v. Thomson Newspapers*, p. 885, supra, in which defendant charged a public official with "trying to manipulate the press." In dismissing the claims, the court held that Utah's constitution was more protective of speech than the First Amendment as interpreted in *Milkovich*. The court relied on the wide open 19th century history of the state's press at the time the state's constitution was adopted.

F.   THE PRESS AS REPEATER

As noted earlier, the common law developed the fair report privilege to protect those who repeated certain kinds of statements. A situation not traditionally covered by that privilege is addressed in the following case.

Edwards v. National Audubon Society, Inc.

United States Court of Appeals, Second Circuit, 1977.
556 F.2d 113.
Certiorari denied 434 U.S. 1002 (1977).

[The National Audubon Society was in the forefront of groups opposing the use of pesticides, such as DDT, because of their effect on the environment. Proponents of pesticides argued that without DDT millions of human beings would die of disease and starvation. The Society conducted an annual count of birds, which showed a steady increase in sightings despite increased use of pesticides. Some scientists cited these counts to show that pesticides were not harming animal life. The Society believed that the increased sightings were due to more watchers using more skill and better observation areas. Upset by what he thought was misuse of the annual counts, Arbib, editor of the Society's publication, *American Birds*, wrote an attack in the foreword to one issue. He concluded that whenever members hear a "scientist" use bird counts to deny that pesticides are harmful, "you are in the presence of someone who is being paid to lie, or is parroting something he knows little about." Arbib apparently had no "factual basis" for the charge.

Devlin, a nature reporter for the New York Times, read the article and called Arbib to find out who he was attacking. After Devlin's "persistent urging that many eminent persons associated with the pesticide industry might be hurt unnecessarily by the Society's indiscriminate attack," Arbib promised to furnish some names. Arbib turned to Clement, a Society vice-president, who told Arbib that he could not call any specific person a paid liar. Clement did, however, identify for Arbib those who Clement thought had most persistently "misused" the bird count.

Arbib then gave Devlin the names of five scientists. Arbib testified that he told Devlin that these five were misusers but not necessarily "paid liars." Devlin "flatly denied" that Arbib had said this. Devlin sought responses from the five. He reached three, who all denied the charges. Devlin then wrote a story saying that although the article in *American Birds* did not identify its objects, "Mr. Arbib said in an interview that they included" the five scientists.

Three of the five scientists sued the Society and the Times for libel. At the trial, the judge charged, among other things, that the jury could find that Devlin had "actual malice" if he had serious doubts about the accuracy of Arbib's statements in the interview—even if he was sure he was accurately reporting Arbib's comments. The jury exonerated Arbib, but held the Times and Clement liable. The trial judge upheld the verdict against the Times on the ground that the jury could have found Devlin reckless in publishing accurate quotes without investigating further after the strong denials. On appeal, the court exonerated Clement because the evidence was "insufficient" to support the jury's verdict that he knew the scientists would be identified as being "paid liars." The court's discussion of the New York Times follows.]

■ Before KAUFMAN, CHIEF JUDGE, CLARK, ASSOCIATE JUSTICE and JAMESON, DISTRICT JUDGE.

■ IRVING R. KAUFMAN, CHIEF JUDGE.

In a society which takes seriously the principle that government rests upon the consent of the governed, freedom of the press must be the most cherished tenet. It is elementary that a democracy cannot long survive unless the people are provided the information needed to form judgments on issues that affect their ability to intelligently govern themselves. . . .

We are invited today to affirm a libel judgment against the *New York Times* for accurately reporting dramatic statements of the National Audubon Society attacking the good faith of prominent scientists supporting continued use of the insecticide DDT. There can be little doubt that the *Times* reasonably considered these accusations of a leading environmentalist organization to be newsworthy. . . . We are convinced that the First Amendment requires us to decline [this invitation]. Accordingly we will reverse and order the complaint dismissed.

I.

[The court recounted the facts.]

II.

Implicit in the jury's verdict against Clement is the finding, which we must accept, that the *Times* accurately reported the five scientists whose names were furnished by Arbib were the "paid liars" referred to in the *American Birds* Foreword. We believe that a libel judgment against the *Times*, in the face of this finding of fact, is constitutionally impermissible.

At stake in this case is a fundamental principle. Succinctly stated, when a responsible, prominent organization like the National Audubon Society makes serious charges against a public figure, the First Amendment protects the accurate and disinterested reporting of those charges, regardless of the reporter's private views regarding their validity. See Time Inc. v. Pape, 401 U.S. 279 (1971); Medina v. Time Inc., 439 F.2d 1129 (1st Cir.1971). What is newsworthy about such accusations is that they were made. We do not believe that the press may be required under the First

Amendment to suppress newsworthy statements merely because it has serious doubts regarding their truth. Nor must the press take up cudgels against dubious charges in order to publish them without fear of liability for defamation. [ ] The public interest in being fully informed about controversies that often rage around sensitive issues demands that the press be afforded the freedom to report such charges without assuming responsibility for them.

The contours of the press's right of neutral reportage are, of course, defined by the principle that gives life to it. Literal accuracy is not a prerequisite: if we are to enjoy the blessings of a robust and unintimidated press, we must provide immunity from defamation suits where the journalist believes, reasonably and in good faith, that his report accurately conveys the charges made. [ ] It is equally clear, however, that a publisher who in fact espouses or concurs in the charges made by others, or who deliberately distorts these statements to launch a personal attack of his own on a public figure, cannot rely on a privilege of neutral reportage. In such instances he assumes responsibility for the underlying accusations. [ ]

It is clear here, that Devlin reported Audubon's charges fairly and accurately. He did not in any way espouse the Society's accusations: indeed, Devlin published the maligned scientists' outraged reactions in the same article that contained the Society's attack. The *Times* article, in short, was the exemplar of fair and dispassionate reporting of an unfortunate but newsworthy contretemps. Accordingly, we hold that it was privileged under the First Amendment.

III.

Even absent the special protection afforded to neutral reportage, see *Time Inc. v. Pape,* supra, the evidence adduced at trial was manifestly insufficient to demonstrate "actual malice" on the part of the *Times*. It is uncontested that Devlin was unaware of the baselessness of the Audubon Society's dramatic allegations. Nor was there a shred of evidence from which the jury might have found that Devlin entertained serious doubts concerning the truth of Arbib's charge that the appellees were "paid liars."

It is conceded that the *Times* might have published the Audubon Society's accusations without fear of liability had Devlin but refrained from eliciting the views of the Society's victims. The appellees would punish the *Times* for its effort to confirm the story, apparently maintaining that a little prudence is a dangerous thing. They assert that once Devlin heard the scientists' denials and received materials explaining their general stand in the DDT controversy, he became charged with the duty to publish absolutely nothing until he conducted a full-scale investigation plumbing to the bottom of the matter.

We do not believe, however, that the scientists' responses to Devlin's inquiries could be found sufficient to warn Devlin of the probable falsity of the Society's charges. Surely liability under the "clear and convincing proof" standard of *New York Times v. Sullivan* cannot be predicated on mere denials, however vehement; such denials are so commonplace in the world of potential charge and countercharge that, in themselves, they hardly alert the conscientious reporter to the likelihood of error. . . .

. . .

V.

We do not underestimate the pain and distress which the publication of the Audubon Society's thoughtless charges has caused the appellees. And we are fully aware that, in Professor Emerson's words,

> A member of a civilized society should have some measure of protection against unwarranted attack upon his honor, his dignity and his standing in the community.

Our holding today does not in any way condone the mischievous and unwarranted assault on the good name of the appellees, who appear from their writings to have entered the lists in favor of DDT in good faith and from humanitarian motives that ought to be beyond reproach.

Nevertheless, we believe that the interest of a public figure in the purity of his reputation cannot be allowed to obstruct that vital pulse of ideas and intelligence on which an informed and self-governing people depend. It is unfortunate that the exercise of liberties so precious as freedom of speech and of the press may sometimes do harm that the state is powerless to recompense; but this is the price that must be paid for the blessings of a democratic way of life.

We believe that the *New York Times* cannot, consistently with the First Amendment, be afflicted with a libel judgment for the accurate reporting of newsworthy accusations made by a responsible and well-noted organization like the National Audubon Society.

[The complaint was dismissed.]

NOTES AND QUESTIONS

1. How does the "neutral report" privilege developed here differ from the common law privilege of fair and accurate report that we explored p. 913, supra? How often are the two likely to overlap?

2. In the court's language, "Succinctly stated, when a responsible, prominent organization . . . makes serious charges against a public figure, the First Amendment protects the accurate and disinterested reporting of those charges, regardless of the reporter's private views of their validity." In the following notes we explore these elements in more detail.

"Responsible, prominent organization." What is there in the nature of this privilege that should require that the charge come from this type of source? For example, consider an even-handed story that reported a youth's charges that plaintiff police officer had coerced the youth to confess to a murder that he had not committed. The article carried the officer's denial and his suggestion that the youth, a "slow-spoken young man who

has a speech impediment" (according to the reporter) with "the mind of a 9–year–old" (according to his mother) confessed to get attention. See Stockton Newspapers, Inc. v. San Joaquin Superior Court, 206 Cal.App.3d 966, 254 Cal.Rptr. 389 (1988).

What if the source of the defamation is a rumor? In Martin v. Wilson Publishing Co., 497 A.2d 322 (R.I.1985), the defendant paper reported on the reactions of a very small community whose residents were concerned that plaintiff was acquiring a vast percentage of the property in the community. Despite his announced good intentions for the community, plaintiff's actions made many residents apprehensive:

> Some residents stretch available facts when they imagine Mr. Martin is connected with the 1974 rash of fires in the village (the abandoned depot, the back of the Shannock Spa, and even that old barn he loved). Local fire officials feel that certain local kids did it for kicks. The same imaginations note that the fire at the old Shannock mill before he bought it made it cheaper (but less valuable), or that the fire there since he bought it might have been profitable (though derelict buildings, such as it was, are customarily uninsurable).

Defendant's effort to analogize the situation to the common law fair report privilege was rejected because at governmental proceedings identifiable persons participate. In public proceedings those who are attacked may attend and defend themselves. But the "spreading of rumors does not give the person defamed by them the opportunity to rebut the underlying allegation of the rumor. To attempt to defend against a rumor is not unlike attempting to joust with a cloud. Publication of a rumor further fuels the continued repetition and does so in an especially egregious way by enshrining it in print." Even if the court were inclined to adopt *Edwards*, it would not do so here because no "prominent responsible organization" had made the charges.

What if time is of the essence? Assume that there is a rumor in the community that a candidate in a forthcoming election participated in a massive fraud that is under investigation. The local paper runs an article before the election truthfully announcing that the rumor—which it repeats—is being widely discussed and then reporting that despite extensive efforts the paper found nothing to support the rumor. Might the candidate have an action? What if, in the above example, the newspaper in the course of normal election coverage truthfully reports the existence and content of the rumor but makes no effort to check its accuracy? See Frederick Schauer, Slightly Guilty, 1993 U.Chi.L.Forum 83.

Outside the election context, consider the example from R. Sack & S. Baron, Libel, Slander and Related Problems 409–10 (2d ed. 1994): "Suppose a rumor surfaces that the chairman of a large publicly held brokerage firm is about to be indicted for securities fraud and, as a result, the stock of the company falls precipitously." Can a story explaining why the stock fell be reported without running the risk of liability for libel? Is this a stronger, or weaker, case for legal protection than the election situation? In a footnote to their example, Sack and Baron state: "The republisher may, of course, be expected to report that a rumor is no more than that and to state that the rumor is false if it is known to be." What does "known" mean here? Was the falsity "known" in *Martin*? Is this requirement consistent with the rationale of the privilege?

"Makes serious charges." Why must the charges be serious? Why is it not enough that charges are flying between two persons or groups? Beyond that, must the charges be "made" in public before the newspaper writes its story? *Edwards* arose in large part because the Audubon Society had its own media outlets and had published its own charges in the first instance.

Suppose there is no accusation in circulation until the reporter elicits it? In McManus v. Doubleday & Co., Inc., 513 F.Supp. 1383 (S.D.N.Y. 1981), defendant's book asserted about the plaintiff priest, who was national coordinator for some Irish–American groups, that his "Irish Embassy file bears the mention 'homicidal tendencies.'" The information was said to have come from an interview with an Embassy official that the author initiated. The court rejected the neutral report defense. The judge first quoted *Edwards* for the view that the privilege was to keep the public "fully informed about controversies that often rage around sensitive issues." Unlike the reporter in *Edwards*, "who simply reported an autonomous news event, albeit with certain factual embellishments, [the author here] was engaged in purely investigative reporting. Unlike *Edwards*, no controversy raged around the libelous statements before the reporter entered the scene. . . . Since there is no indication in the *Edwards* opinion that the neutral reportage privilege was meant to cover investigative reporting, and since including reports of such journalist-induced charges within the protection of the privilege is unnecessary for promoting the purposes of *Edwards*, the freer reporting of raging controversies," the court denied the privilege. Would the analysis differ if the official had come to the author and volunteered the information?

"Against a public figure." Why must the plaintiff be a public figure (or official)? In Dixson v. Newsweek, Inc., 562 F.2d 626 (10th Cir.1977), plaintiff was vice-president of a regional air carrier that had suffered severe financial losses for several years. In a story about new management taking over the carrier, one source was quoted as saying that Dixson had been a cause of the problems. The court rejected *Edwards* on the ground that Dixson was a private figure.

Dixson, in turn, was rejected in April v. Reflector–Herald, Inc., 46 Ohio App.3d 95, 546 N.E.2d 466 (1988). The story involved conflicting views of why the plaintiff, "a former part-time cook at the Huron County Sheriff's Office," was discharged and why public money was paid to settle her claim. The court agreed that she was a private plaintiff. (Is that wrong?) Relying upon *Edwards*, the court said it saw "no legitimate difference between the press's accurate reporting of accusations made against a private figure and those made against a public figure, when the accusations themselves are newsworthy and concern a matter of public interest."

"Accurate and disinterested reporting of those charges." It seems agreed (except possibly in the rumor situation) that the publication must take no position on where the truth lies in the dispute. For an extended analysis of a case rejecting the privilege on the ground that the publication in fact took sides, see *Cianci*, p. 1002, supra.

What if one side attacks publicly and the other side refuses to comment? How, if at all, is the local newspaper to report this situation? Can the newspaper preserve the privilege by including in the story the accurate statement that "repeated phone calls to [the plaintiff or an attorney] were not returned"?

What if the article is indeed written with scrupulous fairness by a writer who does not honestly believe one side? In the *Stockton Newspapers* case, for example, the reporter admitted having doubts about the truth of the youth's story. Some have argued that a neutral report is of little use to the public because in most situations readers cannot judge the credibility of the sources being quoted. "Where the reporter has knowledge of falsity or serious doubts about the truth of a charge, meeting the 'actual malice' test, the reporter should be under a duty to report that information. Where there is reason to know the falsity of a statement, the reporter must do more than merely print a refutation." Note, The Privilege of Neutral Reportage, 1978 Utah L.Rev. 347.

Consider K.D. Sowle, Defamation and the First Amendment: The Case for a Constitutional Privilege of Fair Report, 54 N.Y.U.L.Rev. 469, 520 (1979), proposing a constitutional privilege to protect a publisher from liability for defamation for

(a)(1) reports of public proceedings of all branches and all levels of government, including reports concerning pleadings filed with a court and available for public inspection, whether or not they have been the object of official actions, and including reports of public, official pronouncements about non-public government activities; *and*

(2) reports of public nongovernmental statements and proceedings dealing with matters of legitimate public concern;

(b) if the reports are fair and accurate, or published with due care to ensure fairness and accuracy;

(c) whether or not defamatory statements reported are republished with knowledge of their falsity or reckless disregard of their truth, or with any other form of common law malice;

(d) provided that the publication purports to be an account of a public statement or proceeding encompassed within the privilege.

As noted, virtually every element of *Edwards* has been interpreted narrowly by some courts. These disagreements may induce courts to expand the common law privilege to avoid entering the *Edwards* controversy. In Chapin v. Knight–Ridder, Inc., 993 F.2d 1087 (4th Cir.1993), for example, the court concluded that the state's fair report privilege would cover a report of the unofficial remarks of a congressman, and noted that until "we face a case with a 'prominent, responsible' but nongovernmental speaker, we need not cast our lot one way or the other on the full *Edwards* fair reportage privilege."

Finally, some courts have flatly rejected *Edwards*. See, e.g., Hogan v. Herald Co., 58 N.Y.2d 630, 444 N.E.2d 1002, 458 N.Y.S.2d 538 (1982).

Broadcasting. In print journalism, the editor is able to make a considered judgment about what outside submissions warrant publication, as with letters to the editor or syndicated material. See Franklin, Libel and Letters to the Editor: Toward an Open Forum, 57 Colo.L.Rev. 651 (1986). In broadcasting, with live call-in shows, that element of reflection and the ability to identify the persons submitting views are missing. So far as defamation is concerned it will be difficult to establish actual malice or negligence if the broadcaster has no opportunity to review the material for libel or falsity before it is broadcast. Could a court properly conclude that using a live call-in format was itself actionable because it gave irresponsible callers the opportunity to defame others over the airwaves? (The much-publicized delay buttons are much more suited to preventing vulgarity than to allowing the person in charge to prevent subtle defamations.) See, e.g., Pacella v. Milford Radio Corp., 18 Mass.App. 6, 462 N.E.2d 355 (1984), affirmed by an equally divided court 394 Mass. 1051, 476 N.E.2d 595, cert. denied 474 U.S. 844 (1985).

G.   REFORM PROPOSALS

1.   NEED FOR REFORM?

The current state of libel law has been deplored by almost everyone affected by it.

Plaintiffs. As the sections on doctrine suggest, plaintiffs have had a most difficult time winning cases under the "actual malice" rule. Their success rate, leaving aside a relatively small number of settlements, runs under 10 percent. Plaintiffs whose primary interest was in showing the falsity of the story rather than in obtaining dollars, might have been satisfied if the system had offered them a chance to prove that falsity. But with over 75 percent of the cases resulting in summary judgments for the defendant, the issue of truth or falsity is rarely decided. A case that produces a jury verdict of falsity but without actual malice, is a rarity.

Plaintiffs who can get past summary judgment succeed with juries well over 50 percent of the time. But defendants appeal virtually all jury losses and obtain reversals or partial relief in some 70 percent of the cases. Most of these lead to dismissals; a few lead to new trials or reduced awards.

Private plaintiffs who seek to recover only for actual injury fare somewhat better because they get to juries more often, win before juries at least as often, and are not likely to lose their awards on appeal for failure to prove negligence.

Defendants. As a group, defendants obviously cannot complain about their overall success rate in these cases. But they do contend that the constitutional protections should operate earlier in the litigation process; that pretrial discovery is expensive; and that appeals are necessary to obtain reversals of so many plaintiffs' trial judgments.

Larger media stress the high costs of successful defense and suggest that they are being diverted from the investigative reporting that they should be doing by the demands of litigation. They are not yet worried about damage awards because, although claims have been filed for hundreds of millions of dollars, the largest judgment against media finally upheld on appeal has not exceeded $3 million, though at least two judgments of $15 million have withstood intermediate appeal. See Prozeralik v. Capital Cities Communications, Inc., 188 App.Div.2d 178, 593 N.Y.S.2d 662 (upholding award of $1.4 million for financial loss, $4 million for humiliation, loss of reputation, and embarrassment, and $10 million in punitive damages) reversed and remanded on liability questions, 82 N.Y.2d 466, 626 N.E.2d 34, 605 N.Y.S.2d 218 (1993). A retrial resulted in a judgment of $6 million for loss of reputation, $3.5 million for emotional and related harm, and $500,000 in punitive damages. On appeal, the court, 3–2, modified by striking the punitive damages. 635 N.Y.S.2d 913 (App.Div. 1995). The dissenters would have reduced the compensatory awards to $500,000 and $250,000 respectively. A further appeal is being sought.

In Sprague v. Walter, 441 Pa.Super. 1, 656 A.2d 890 (1995), the court upheld awards against Philadelphia Newspapers, Inc. of $2.5 million in compensatory damages but reduced a punitive award from $31.5 million to $21.5 million. Further appeal was denied and the case was settled. N.Y. Times, Apr. 2, 1996 at A8. The cases arose out of articles written in 1973 about events in 1963. In an earlier trial the plaintiff had been awarded $1.5 million in compensatory damages and $3 million in punitive damages. That judgment had been overturned on defendant's appeal and a new trial ordered. Sprague v. Walter, 518 Pa. 425, 543 A.2d 1078 (1988).

Smaller media claim concern about the very fact of being sued and having to spend money for legal defense. They assert that a judgment of tens of thousands of dollars, much less millions, might bankrupt them—and that insurance is expensive because of the large defense costs (but that may account for the low payouts). Smaller media claim that insurance is not much protection for several reasons. First, libel insurance is frequently written with a "deductible" or retained exposure under which the insured bears the first several thousand dollars of expenses in the case. This amount is intended to cause the management to consider carefully the material it is about to run and whether it wants to engage in investigative reporting at all. Second, one of the few major libel insurers has begun requiring that in addition to the "deductible," insureds bear 20 percent of the legal expenses throughout the case, whatever the outcome. Smaller media claim the problem with both these limits on coverage is that the publication may suffer uncovered losses whenever it is sued, even if it ultimately wins the case. Thus, smaller media may be more likely to stop doing investigative reporting or to avoid running stories that may antagonize litigious persons or groups in the community. One counter pressure is the increased willingness of courts to award attorneys fees to defendants who win baseless suits.

Public. If the defendants are likely to perceive the situation as "chilling" and to respond by reducing their coverage of important activities, the public may lose by learning less true information about how our government and society are functioning. Although occasional stories purport to document the "chilling effect," it is something that major media figures do not like to talk about and often deny. Smaller media, on the other hand, do assert that this is affecting their coverage.

But note that, to the extent the public now benefits from the constitutional protections we have been considering, these benefits are being financed by the victims of the defamations who cannot recover for the harm they have suffered. Should the public be paying in some way for the harms individual victims are suffering so that the public can get its "uninhibited, robust, and wide-open" debate? Recall Justice White's comments, p. 964, supra. For a discussion of this line of thought with explorations of various funding mechanisms, see Schauer, Uncoupling Free Speech, 92 Colum.L.Rev. 1321 (1992).

Data. A look at some data may provide insight into the operation of the system. In the decade of the 1980s, 213 libel cases were tried by jury to a verdict. Another 22 jury trials were ended by directed verdicts. As noted above, data suggest that about 3 in 4 cases that are started do not get to the trial stage because motions to dismiss (generally state law privileges) or summary judgments (constitutional privileges) derail them. This would suggest that some 1,000 cases were commenced against media during the decade based on 254 trials begun (including here 19 bench trials that will be discussed separately).

Of the 213 jury trials that reached verdict, plaintiff got verdicts in 158 or 74 percent of the cases, with defendants winning 55 (26%). The compensatory damages awarded in the 158 cases totalled some $88 million, averaging $557,000 per case—far above the jury average for medical malpractice and product liability cases. In 90 (57%) of the 158 cases, the juries awarded punitive damages as well. These totalled $144 million, averaging $1.6 million over the 90 cases (or $911,000 if averaged over the 158 cases). The total jury awards in the 158 cases thus ran $232 million, with punitive damages accounting for 62 percent of the total (even though they were awarded in only 90 cases). The average plaintiff's verdict in the 158 cases was $1,468,000; the median was $200,000.

The plaintiffs were public in 144 cases and private in 97 of the cases in which that information was available. Note that this is probably not the ratio in which suits are brought. Far more suits brought by public plaintiffs are dismissed in pre-trial stages than are suits brought by private plaintiffs—at least if the private plaintiffs are not seeking presumed or punitive damages. Plaintiffs prevailed at trial in 64 percent of the actual malice cases and 73 percent of the negligence cases.

Note that not all plaintiffs who prove actual malice recover punitive damages. Some states bar punitive damages in all cases; a few bar them in cases involving communications. In others, including the important state of New York, plaintiffs seeking punitive damages must prove, in addition to actual malice, some further element, such as spite or ill will—something difficult to show in most media cases.

In post-trial motions, the plaintiff's verdict was changed in 45 of the 158 cases: 16 judgments n.o.v.; 26 remittiturs; and 3 new trials. Of a total of 147 appeals, 78 (53%) were reversed (and either dismissed or remanded for new trials) and 25 (17%) had damages reduced. This 70 percent reversal rate is substantially higher than for civil litigation generally.

Plaintiffs either obtained outright affirmance or had a reduced award affirmed in approximately 60 jury cases yielding total damages of slightly over $17 million, an average total award of $261,000.

Of the 19 bench trials, 9 plaintiffs got damage awards totalling $3.26 million compensatory (average $362,000) plus $5.9 million punitive (awarded in 3 cases) for a total of $9.16 million. The average award was just over $1 million; the median was $165,000. On appeal, 2 were affirmed for a total of $444,000 (average $222,000). Adding the trial results yields 167 jury and bench awards of $241.2 million that were reduced to some 60 winners of $17.7 million after appeals.

Although these figures, which come from the Libel Defense Resource Bulletin No.1, Jan. 31, 1994, are reported also for 1990–93, these numbers are too small to be reliable and most of the appeals in these cases have not yet been decided. It appears preliminarily that for the years 1990–93 the number of trials has dropped from some 25 per year to 14 per year. (It is unclear whether this might be due to fewer cases being filed or to more cases being dismissed before trial.) During the four years, plaintiffs won 34 (63%) of 54 jury trials and 2 of 3 bench trials. The 34 jury awards, including 5 of $10 million or more (compared to 4 during all of the 1980s) totalled $202 million. The average award was almost $6 million; the median about $590,000.

What is one to make of all these numbers? Taking the broad picture, it seems clear that if the defendant cannot prevail before trial, one or more appeals lie ahead for the vast majority. It is also clear that the awards of jury (and judge as well) are very unlikely to survive that appeal. Much expensive legal effort has been exerted by all concerned to reach a result that often produces no award or requires a retrial. The vast bulk of libel insurance is not paid to plaintiffs but is absorbed in defense and legal expenses.

From the standpoint of the individual newspaper or broadcaster, one might focus on the variance in the awards: an average near $1.5 million but a median of $200,000. The award need bear no relationship to any obvious anchors, such as the medical bills and lost earnings found in physical injury cases. It is thus no surprise that once a case is begun, little expense is spared in defending it. It is little solace that "most" awards are reduced or overturned on appeal. In an individual case an award may be affirmed on appeal that may seriously impede the defendant's continued viability.

2. PROPOSED REFORMS

By and large, the proposals for change have focused on two main avenues: constitutional change at the doctrinal level and statutory or common law changes that seek to work within the existing constitutional framework. (A third approach is already in existence with some courts trying interstitial changes such as channeling discovery to a single issue that might be dispositive or assessing legal fees against parties who are not proceeding in good faith.)

Changes in case law. In the first category are the suggestions of either overruling *New York Times* and/or *Gertz* or cutting back on their scope or level of protection. This is usually tied to some proposed change in damage rules. In the *Greenmoss* case, p. 994, supra, Justice White observed that the law had evolved in an unsatisfactory way:

> The *New York Times* rule thus countenances two evils: first, the stream of information about public officials and public affairs is polluted and often remains polluted by false information; and second, the reputation and professional life of the defeated plaintiff may be destroyed by falsehoods that might have been avoided with a reasonable effort to investigate the facts. In terms of the First Amendment and reputational interest at stake, these seem grossly perverse results.

He noted that there was "much talk" about "liability without fault and the unfairness of presuming damages." But if the goal was to protect the press "from intimidating damages liability that might lead to excessive timidity, . . . it is evident that the Court engaged in severe overkill" in both *New York Times* and *Gertz.*

Justice White then suggested that the Court might better have (1) barred or limited punitive damages; or (2) barred or limited presumed damages. In such a situation strict liability could have been retained and the defamed public official "upon proving falsity, could at least have had a judgment to that effect. . . . He might have also recovered a modest amount, enough perhaps to pay his litigation expenses."

He doubted that defendants would be "unduly chilled by having to pay for the actual damages caused to those they defame." Other "commercial enterprises in this country not in the business of disseminating information must pay for the damage they cause as a cost of doing business, and it is difficult to argue that the United States did not have a free and vigorous press before the rule in *New York Times* was announced. In any event, the *New York Times* standard was formulated to protect the press from the chilling danger of numerous large damage awards. Nothing in the central rationale behind *New York Times* demands an absolute immunity from suits to establish the falsity of a defamatory misstatement about a public figure where the plaintiff cannot make out a jury case of actual malice."

As for *Gertz,* he thought the common law should control libel suits by private persons. He doubted that the case had saved the press a great deal of money or made "any measurable contribution to First Amendment or reputational values since its announcement. . . . I suspect the press would be no worse off financially if the common-law rules were to apply and if the judiciary were careful to insist that damages awards be kept within bounds. A legislative solution to the damages problem would also be appropriate. Moreover, since libel plaintiffs are very likely more interested in clearing their names than in damages, I doubt that limiting recoveries would deter or be unfair to them. In any event, I cannot assume that the press, as successful and powerful as it is, will be intimidated into withholding news that by decent journalistic standards it believes to be true." Is there any reason why judicial control over damages should be more difficult here than in tort law generally?

For other suggestions that the focus be on control of damages rather than changing the rules of liability, see, e.g., Epstein, Was *New York Times v. Sullivan* Wrong? 53 U.Chi.L.Rev. 782 (1986); Anderson, Reputation, Compensation and Proof, 25 Wm. & Mary L.Rev. 747 (1984).

Proposals within existing law. The second type of change is the statutory approach within existing constitutional lines. Aside from damage limitation plans, these have tended to fall into one of two groups. One centers on a type of declaratory judgment action that permits an adjudication of the truth or falsity of the defamatory charge without addressing questions of fault. In this first group, critics have disagreed over whether the shift from a damage action to a declaratory judgment action should occur at the plaintiff's behest or whether the defendant should control the choice. Compare Franklin, A Declaratory Judgment Alternative to Current Libel Law, 74 Calif.L.Rev. 809 (1986) (proposing that plaintiff control that decision) with Barrett, Declaratory Judgment for Libel: A Better Alternative, 74 Calif.L.Rev. 847 (1986) (proposing that the choice be given to defendants).

Judge Pierre Leval, who presided over the famous libel case brought by General William Westmoreland against CBS, argued afterwards that a plaintiff could get around the constitutional strictures of the *New York Times* case by bringing an action for declaratory judgment and explicitly stating that no damages were being sought. Of course, that alone would not suffice unless state law permitted such an action. Leval, The No–Money, No–Fault Libel Suit: Keeping *Sullivan* in its Proper Place, 101 Harv.L.Rev. 1287 (1988). The article also discusses negotiated agreements in which the parties might agree to dispense with the actual malice rule but litigate falsity.

The second approach centers on retraction and reply as ways to reduce or eliminate the harm done, working with the common law remedies discussed at 923, supra.

Needless to say, these proposals have been quite controversial. A drafting committee of the National Conference of Commissioners on Uniform State Laws worked for three years on a proposed Uniform Defamation Act. Initially the drafters proposed to standardize and codify existing defamation law and add an option that would allow plaintiffs to seek a judicial finding of falsity in lieu of damages. Opposition from the media forced the committee to abandon those goals. The chairman said the media "are stridently opposed to our provisions relating to a vindication action and are unalterably opposed to broad defamation legislation of any kind." He recommended that the proposed uniform act be withdrawn, but said it might still be possible draft a more modest uniform "correction and clarification" act. See News Notes, 21 Med.L.Rptr. No. 14, June 8, 1993.

In fact, such a "more modest" proposal did emerge from the commissioners in 1993.

UNIFORM CORRECTION OR CLARIFICATION OF DEFAMATION ACT (1993)

§ 1. Definitions.

In this [Act]:

(1) "Defamatory" means tending to harm reputation.

(2) "Economic loss" means special, pecuniary loss caused by a false and defamatory publication.

(3) "Person" means an individual, corporation, business trust, estate, trust, partnership, association, joint venture, or other legal or commercial entity. The term does not include a government or governmental subdivision, agency, or instrumentality.

§ 2. Scope.

(a) This [Act] applies to any [claim for relief], however characterized, for damages arising out of harm to personal reputation caused by the false content of a publication that is published on or after the effective date of this [Act].

(b) This [Act] applies to all publications, including writings, broadcasts, oral communications, electronic transmissions, or other forms of transmitting information.

§ 3. Request for Correction or Clarification.

(a) A person may maintain an action for defamation only if:

(1) the person has made a timely and adequate request for correction or clarification from the defendant; or

(2) the defendant has made a correction or clarification.

(b) A request for correction or clarification is timely if made within the period of limitation for commencement of an action for defamation. However, a person who, within 90 days after knowledge of the publication, fails to make a good-faith attempt to request a correction or clarification may recover only provable economic loss.

(c) A request for correction or clarification is adequate if it:

(1) is made in writing and reasonably identifies the person making the request;

(2) specifies with particularity the statement alleged to be false and defamatory and, to the extent known, the time and place of publication;

(3) alleges the defamatory meaning of the statement;

(4) specifies the circumstances giving rise to any defamatory meaning of the statement which arises from other than the express language of the publication; and

(5) states that the alleged defamatory meaning of the statement is false.

(d) In the absence of a previous adequate request, service of a [summons and complaint] stating a [claim for relief] for defamation and containing the information required in subsection (c) constitutes an adequate request for correction or clarification.

(e) The period of limitation for commencement of a defamation action is tolled during the period allowed in Section 6(a) for responding to a request for correction or clarification.

§ 4.   Disclosure of Evidence of Falsity.

(a) A person who has been requested to make a correction or clarification may ask the requester to disclose reasonably available information material to the falsity of the allegedly defamatory statement.

(b) If a correction or clarification is not made, a person who unreasonably fails to disclose the information after a request to do so may recover only provable economic loss.

(c) A correction or clarification is timely if published within 25 days after receipt of information disclosed pursuant to subsection (a) or 45 days after receipt of a request for correction or clarification, whichever is later.

§ 5.   Effect of Correction or Clarification.

If a timely and sufficient correction or clarification is made, a person may recover only provable economic loss, as mitigated by the correction or clarification.

§ 6.   Timely and Sufficient Correction or Clarification.

(a) A correction or clarification is timely if it is published before, or within 45 days after, receipt of a request for correction or clarification, unless the period is extended under Section 4(c).

(b) A correction or clarification is sufficient if it:

(1) is published with a prominence and in a manner and medium reasonably likely to reach substantially the same audience as the publication complained of;

(2) refers to the statement being corrected or clarified and:

(i) corrects the statement;

(ii) in the case of defamatory meaning arising from other than the express language of the publication, disclaims an intent to communicate that meaning or to assert its truth; or

(iii) in the case of a statement attributed to another person, identifies the person and disclaims an intent to assert the truth of the statement; and

(3) is communicated to the person who has made a request for correction or clarification.

.   .   .

§ 8.   Offer to Correct or Clarify.

(a) If a timely correction or clarification is no longer possible, the publisher of an alleged defamatory statement may offer, at any time before trial, to make a correction or clarification.   The offer must be made in writing to the person allegedly defamed by the publication and:

(1) contain the publisher's offer to:

(i) publish, at the person's request, a sufficient correction or clarification; and

(ii) pay the person's reasonable expenses of litigation, including attorney's fees, incurred before publication of the correction or clarification; and

(2) be accompanied by a copy of the proposed correction or clarification and the plan for its publication.

(b) If the person accepts in writing an offer to correct or clarify made pursuant to subsection (a):

(1) the person is barred from commencing an action against the publisher based on the statement; or

(2) if an action has been commenced, the court shall dismiss the action against the defendant with prejudice after the defendant complies with the terms of the offer.

(c) A person who does not accept an offer made in conformance with subsection (a) may recover in an action based on the statement only:

(1) damages for provable economic loss; and

(2) reasonable expenses of litigation, including attorney's fees, incurred before the offer, unless the person failed to make a good-faith attempt to request a correction or clarification in accordance

with Section 3(b) or failed to disclose information in accordance
with Section 4.

.   .   .

NOTES AND QUESTIONS

1. What are the strengths of this approach? The weaknesses? In
Miami Herald Pub.Co. v. Tornillo, 418 U.S. 241 (1974), the Court invalidated a state statute that required newspapers that had attacked a person in
their columns to permit that person to respond in the paper. Does this
proposal raise similar problems?

2. The House of Delegates of the American Bar Association approved
this proposal of the Uniform Commissioners at its February 1994 meeting
by the unusually close vote of 174–130. For an extended discussion of the
development and text of the Uniform Act, see Ackerman, Bringing Coher-
ence to Defamation Law Through Uniform Legislation: The Search for an
Elegant Solution, 72 N.C.L.Rev. 291 (1994).

3. For an elaborate empirical study of libel litigation and a proposal
that libel cases be removed from the damage context and placed in the
setting of some alternative mode of dispute resolution, see R. Bezanson, G.
Cranberg, and J. Soloski, Libel Law and the Press: Myth and Reality
(1987). Professor, later Dean, Bezanson was the reporter and drafter of
the proposals developed by the Uniform Commissioners.

4. Proposals introduced in several state legislatures to implement
libel reform have rarely gotten out of committee. See generally, Bezanson,
The Libel Tort Today, 45 Wash. & Lee L.Rev. 535 (1988) and LeBel,
Reforming the Tort of Defamation: An Accommodation of the Competing
Interests Within the Current Constitutional Framework, 66 Nebr.L.Rev.
249 (1987).

5. Most commentators and critics have concluded that reform must
come from the legislative branch. For a differing view, see Anderson, Is
Libel Law Worth Reforming?, 140 U.Pa.L.Rev. 487 (1991), agreeing that
the "present law of libel is a failure," and then suggesting that the
Supreme Court itself should be "the principal reformer of libel law":

> The Court would prescribe new accommodations of speech and reputa-
> tional interests as a matter of constitutional law. It might decree, for
> example, that the Constitution requires no showing of fault if the
> remedy sought is only a declaration of falsity. It might announce new
> limitations of damages, with corresponding reductions in plaintiff's
> burdens. The Court might devise a more sophisticated accommoda-
> tion, one that addresses the dynamics and costs of libel litigation as
> well as questions of fault and remedies. It might explicitly authorize
> trial judges to decide at the outset whether the challenged statement
> was sufficiently factual, harmful, and remote from truth to be justifi-
> ably burdened by further litigation. Acknowledging that effective
> protection of speech requires a diminished role for juries, it might

authorize even more aggressive use of summary judgment and judicial review. The Court might even take the assessment of damages out of the jury's hands.

Comprehensive law reform is not a familiar task for the Supreme Court. It is not accustomed to reviewing systems of law rather than specific rules. Case-by-case adjudication of specific constitutional issues does not invite advocacy on the redesign of an entire branch of tort law. Those are weighty objections, but they come too late. Over the past quarter century, case by case and bit by bit, the Court has thoroughly revised the common law of libel. It has created not merely a few constitutional limitations on state tort rules, but a matrix of substantive principles, evidentiary rules, and de facto innovations in judge-jury roles and other procedural matters. These are all constitutionally based and can only be changed by those who have the power to change constitutional rules. Having created the system that is the source of so much dissatisfaction, the Court cannot now demur on the ground that law reform is not its business.

How should the Supreme Court respond?

CHAPTER XIV

PROTECTING PRIVACY

Privacy is a relatively new legal concept with many facets. We focus first on disclosure by the press of true statements that an individual would rather not have publicly disseminated. This is sometimes called the tort of "public disclosure of private facts." We then turn to statements that present the plaintiff in a "false light," a tort that recalls defamation. We turn next to the "intrusion" aspect of privacy to ask how far others may go either to obtain information from unwilling sources or to impart information to unwilling recipients. We conclude with a section in which, although the word "privacy" is used, it appears that the plaintiffs are relying more upon a notion of "publicity" than of privacy.

A. PUBLIC DISCLOSURE OF TRUTH

1. STATE TORT ANALYSIS

The idea that this interest should be legally protected can be traced to a law review article by Louis D. Brandeis and his law partner, Samuel D. Warren. The Right to Privacy, 4 Harv.L.Rev. 193 (1890). The authors, reacting to the editorial practices of Boston newspapers, particularly a report about a family gathering the Warrens had thought was private, made clear their concerns:

> The press is overstepping in every direction the obvious bounds of propriety and of decency. Gossip is no longer the resource of the idle and of the vicious, but has become a trade, which is pursued with industry as well as effrontery. To satisfy a prurient taste the details of sexual relations are spread broadcast in the columns of the daily papers. To occupy the indolent, column upon column is filled with idle gossip, which can only be procured by intrusion upon the domestic circle. . . . When personal gossip attains the dignity of print, and crowds the space available for matters of real interest to the community, what wonder that the ignorant and thoughtless mistake its relative importance. Easy of comprehension, appealing to that weak side of human nature which is never wholly cast down by the misfortunes and frailties of our neighbors, no one can be surprised that it usurps the place of interest in brains capable of other things. Triviality destroys at once robustness of thought and delicacy of feelings. No enthusiasm can flourish, no generous impulse can survive under its blighting influence.

Working with a variety of rather remote precedents from other areas of law, the authors developed an argument that courts should recognize an action for invasion of privacy by media publication.

The theory was rejected in the first major case to consider it. In Roberson v. Rochester Folding Box Co., 171 N.Y. 538, 64 N.E. 442 (1902), the defendants, a flour company and a box company, obtained a good likeness of the plaintiff, a very pretty girl, and reproduced it on their advertising posters. Plaintiff said she was humiliated and suffered great distress. The court, 4–3, rejected a common law privacy action on grounds that suggested concern about innovating after so many centuries; an inability to see how the doctrine, once accepted, could be judicially limited to appropriate situations; and skepticism about finding liability for an action that might actually please some potential "victims." The Warren and Brandeis article was discussed at length, but the court concluded that the precedents relied upon were too remote to sustain the proposed right.

The outcry was immediate. At its next session, the New York legislature created a statutory right of privacy (New York Civil Rights Law, §§ 50 and 51). The basic provision was that "a person, firm or corporation that uses for advertising purposes, or the purposes of trade, the name, portrait or picture of any living person without having first obtained the written consent of such person, or if a minor of his or her parent or guardian, is guilty of a misdemeanor." The other section provided for an injunction and created an action for compensatory and punitive damages.

Other states, perhaps learning from the New York experience, slowly began to develop a common law right to privacy that was not influenced by statutory language and not limited to advertising invasions. In addition to an action for commercial use of one's name, the courts also developed an action for truthful use of plaintiff's name in situations that were thought to be outside the areas of legitimate public concern. The action for invasion of privacy by publication of true editorial material began to take hold during the 1920s and early 1930s.

Courts in the late 1930s became more attentive to the Supreme Court's expanding protection of expression. Operating on a common law level, they tended to broaden protection for the media by taking a narrow view of what were legitimately private areas.

The newsworthiness defense expanded because courts were reluctant to impose normative standards of what should be newsworthy. Instead, they leaned toward a descriptive definition that protected whatever an editor had decided would interest his or her readers. See, Comment, The Right of Privacy: Normative–Descriptive Confusion in the Defense of Newsworthiness, 30 U.Chi.L.Rev. 722 (1963). By the 1960s, it was unclear whether the action for invasion of privacy had any remaining vitality. See, Kalven, Privacy in Tort Law—Were Warren and Brandeis Wrong? 31 Law and Contemporary Problems 326 (1966); Bloustein, Privacy, Tort Law, and the Constitution: Is Warren and Brandeis' Tort Petty and Unconstitutional As Well?, 46 Texas L.Rev. 611 (1968).

It was precisely during the last part of the 1960s and the beginning of the 1970s, however, that society began sensing that privacy as a general social value was threatened in different ways by the encroachment of computers, data banks, and electronic devices, as well as the media. The concept of privacy was also expanded in Supreme Court cases dealing with birth control, abortion, and other personal issues.

The new thinking broadened the area of privacy protection and reduced the area once covered by common law notions of newsworthiness. At the same time, however, the defamation cases, beginning with *New York Times Co. v. Sullivan*, were signalling a counter trend of press protection.

Since we are dealing, in the first instance at least, with a state tort action, it is appropriate to begin our consideration with a sampling of recent state cases to see what types of situations give rise to "public disclosure" cases.

The New York Situation. As noted, the New York experience has been substantially different from that of the vast majority of states, which developed a common law jurisprudence. New York's highest court still adheres to the rule that actions for truthful revelations must be based on the statute. For example, in Freihofer v. Hearst Corp., 65 N.Y.2d 135, 480 N.E.2d 349, 490 N.Y.S.2d 735 (1985), plaintiff husband in a divorce action sued defendant newspaper for stories relating to the action. The stories were based upon the reporter's having read some court documents that, by statute, were to be kept confidential by court officials. Since the reporter did not violate the confidentiality statute, the court held that the only basis for liability would be the privacy statute. The articles were not published for "advertising purposes" and were not for "purposes of trade" even though they were published to help the paper make a profit. The critical factor under the statute "is the content of the published article in terms of whether it is newsworthy, which is a question of law, and not the defendant's motive to increase circulation."

See also Stephano v. News Group Publications, Inc., 64 N.Y.2d 174, 474 N.E.2d 580, 485 N.Y.S.2d 220 (1984), declaring that the newsworthiness exception in the statute "applies not only to reports of political happenings and social trends [ ], but also to news stories and articles of consumer interest including developments in the fashion world." In that case, the court rejected an action by a male model whose photograph in a "bomber jacket" was used in a magazine's "Best Bets" column. The text included the approximate price of the jacket, the name of the designer, and the names of three stores where the jacket could be bought. The court concluded that the use was not for advertising purposes nor was it an advertisement in disguise. Similar information was used in reviews or in news announcements of new products or new books or movies. "In short, the plaintiff has not presented any facts which would set this particular article apart from the numerous other legitimate news items concerning new products."

To avoid the complications of the New York statute, we will focus on common law cases.

Haynes v. Alfred A. Knopf, Inc.

United States Court of Appeals, Seventh Circuit, 1993.
8 F.3d 1222.

[The book, "The Promised Land: The Great Black Migration and How It Changed America," by Nicholas Lemann, used the life of Ruby Lee Daniels to illustrate its themes about the social, political, and economic effects of the movement of blacks from the rural South to the cities of the North between 1940 and 1970. The author switched back and forth between discussion of that migration in general, and its personal dimensions as reflected in Daniels's descriptions of her life and experiences, beginning when she was a sharecropper in Mississippi and progressing through her move to Chicago and her life there over the next 40 years. Among the things she discussed was her relationship with her ex-husband, Luther Haynes. She depicted him as a man who drank heavily, who neglected his children, could not keep a job, was unfaithful, and eventually left her for another woman. The court quoted one excerpt:

> It got to the point where [Luther] would go out on Friday evenings after picking up his paycheck and Ruby would hope he wouldn't come home, because she knew he would be drunk. On the Friday evenings when he did come home—over the years Ruby developed a devastating imitation of Luther, and could re-create the scene quite vividly—he would walk into the apartment, put on a record and turn up the volume, and saunter into their bedroom, a bottle in one hand and a cigarette in the other, in the mood for love. On one such night, Ruby's last child, Kevin, was conceived. Kevin always had something wrong with him—he was very moody, he was scrawny, and he had a severe speech impediment. Ruby was never able to find out exactly what the problem was, but she blamed it on Luther; all that alcohol must have gotten into his sperm, she said.

Haynes admitted many of the incidents in the book, but alleged that they had all occurred 25 years earlier, and that since then he had reformed, remarried, and lived an exemplary life. He and his present wife, Dorothy, sued the author and publisher for libel and invasion of privacy. The trial court granted summary judgment for the defendants. The court first held that the plaintiffs had no libel claim because the defamatory statements about them were substantially true. It then turned to the privacy claim.]

■ Before POSNER, CHIEF JUDGE, and MANION and WOOD, CIRCUIT JUDGES.

■ POSNER, CHIEF JUDGE:

. . .

The major claim in the complaint, and the focus of the appeal, is . . . invasion of the right of privacy. In tort law the term "right of privacy" covers several distinct wrongs. Using a celebrity's (or other person's) name or picture in advertising without his consent. [ ] Tapping someone's phone, or otherwise invading a person's private space. [ ] Harassing a celebrity by following her too closely, albeit on a public street.

[ ] Casting a person in a false light by publicizing details of the person's life that while true are so selected or highlighted as to convey a misleading impression of the person's character. [ ] Publicizing personal facts that while true and not misleading are so intimate that their disclosure to the public is deeply embarrassing to the person thus exposed and is perceived as gratuitous by the community. [ ] The last, the publicizing of personal facts, is the aspect of the invasion of privacy charged by the Hayneses.

Even people who have nothing rationally to be ashamed of can be mortified by the publication of intimate details of their life. Most people in no way deformed or disfigured would nevertheless be deeply upset if nude photographs of themselves were published in a newspaper or a book. They feel the same way about photographs of their sexual activities, however "normal," or about a narrative of those activities, or about having their medical records publicized. Although it is well known that every human being defecates, no adult human being in our society wants a newspaper to show a picture of him defecating. The desire for privacy illustrated by these examples is a mysterious but deep fact about human personality. It deserves and in our society receives legal protection. The nature of the injury shows, by the way, that the defendants are wrong to argue that this branch of the right of privacy requires proof of special damages. [ ]

But this is not the character of the depictions of the Hayneses in *The Promised Land*. Although the plaintiffs claim that the book depicts their "sex life" and "ridicules" Luther Haynes's lovemaking (the reference is to the passage we quoted in which the author refers to Ruby's "devastating imitation" of Luther's manner when he would come home Friday nights in an amorous mood), these characterizations are misleading. No sexual act is described in the book. No intimate details are revealed. Entering one's bedroom with a bottle in one hand and a cigarette in the other is not foreplay. Ruby's speculation that Kevin's problems may have been due to Luther's having been a heavy drinker is not the narration of a sexual act.

.   .   .

[The branch of privacy law in this case] is concerned with the propriety of stripping away the veil of privacy with which we cover the embarrassing, the shameful, the tabooed, truths about us. [ ] The revelations in the book are not about the intimate details of the Hayneses' life. They are about misconduct, in particular Luther's. (There is very little about Dorothy in the book, apart from the fact that she had an affair with Luther while he was still married to Ruby and that they eventually became and have remained lawfully married.) The revelations are about his heavy drinking, his unstable employment, his adultery, his irresponsible and neglectful behavior toward his wife and children. So we must consider cases in which the right of privacy has been invoked as a shield against the revelation of previous misconduct.

Two early cases illustrate the range of judicial thinking. In *Melvin v. Reid*, 297 Pac. 91 (Cal.App.1931), the plaintiff was a former prostitute, who had been prosecuted but acquitted of murder. She later had married and (she alleged) for seven years had lived a blameless respectable life in a community in which her lurid past was unknown—when all was revealed in a movie about the murder case which used her maiden name. The court held that these allegations stated a claim for invasion of privacy. The Hayneses' claim is similar although less dramatic. They have been a respectable married couple for two decades. Luther's alcohol problem is behind him. He has steady employment as a doorman. His wife is a nurse, and in 1990 he told Lemann that the couple's combined income was $60,000 a year. He is not in trouble with the domestic relations court. He is a deacon of his church. He has come a long way from sharecropping in Mississippi and public housing in Chicago and he and his wife want to bury their past just as Mrs. Melvin wanted to do and in *Melvin v. Reid* was held entitled to do. [   ] In Luther Haynes's own words, from his deposition, "I know I haven't been no angel, but since almost 30 years ago I have turned my life completely around. I stopped the drinking and all this bad habits and stuff like that, which I deny, some of [it] I didn't deny, because I have changed my life. It take me almost 30 years to change it and I am deeply in my church. I look good in the eyes of my church members and my community. Now, what is going to happen now when this public reads this garbage which I didn't tell Mr. Lemann to write? Then all this is going to go down the drain. And I worked like a son of a gun to build myself up in a good reputation and he has torn it down."

But with *Melvin v. Reid* compare *Sidis v. F–R Publishing Corp.*, 113 F.2d 806 (2d Cir.1940), another old case but one more consonant with modern thinking about the proper balance between the right of privacy and the freedom of the press. A child prodigy had flamed out; he was now an eccentric recluse. The New Yorker ran a "where is he now" article about him. The article, entitled "April Fool," did not reveal any misconduct by Sidis but it depicted him in mocking tones as a comical failure, in much the same way that the report of Ruby's "devastating imitation" of the amorous Luther Haynes could be thought to have depicted him as a comical failure, albeit with sinister consequences absent from Sidis's case. The invasion of Sidis's privacy was palpable. But the publisher won. No intimate physical details of Sidis's life had been revealed; and on the other side was the undoubted newsworthiness of a child prodigy, as of a woman prosecuted for murder. Sidis, unlike Mrs. Melvin, was not permitted to bury his past.

. . . .

. . . People who do not desire the limelight and do not deliberately choose a way of life or course of conduct calculated to thrust them into it nevertheless have no legal right to extinguish it if the experiences that have befallen them are newsworthy, even if they would prefer that those experiences be kept private. The possibility of an involuntary loss of privacy is recognized in the modern formulations of this branch of the privacy tort, which require not only that the private facts publicized be such as would make a reasonable person deeply offended by such publicity but also that they be facts in which the public has no legitimate interest. [   ]

The two criteria, offensiveness and newsworthiness, are related. An individual, and more pertinently perhaps the community, is most offended by the publication of intimate personal facts when the community has no interest in them beyond the voyeuristic thrill of penetrating the wall of privacy that surrounds a stranger. The reader of a book about the black migration to the North would have no legitimate interest in the details of Luther Haynes's sex life; but no such details are disclosed. Such a reader does have a legitimate interest in the aspects of Luther's conduct that the book reveals. For one of Lemann's major themes is the transposition virtually intact of a sharecropper morality characterized by a family structure "matriarchal and elastic" and by an "extremely unstable" marriage bond to the slums of the northern cities, and the interaction, largely random and sometimes perverse, of that morality with governmental programs to alleviate poverty. Public aid policies discouraged Ruby and Luther from living together, public housing policies precipitated a marriage doomed to fail. No detail in the book claimed to invade the Hayneses' privacy is not germane to the story that the author wanted to tell, a story not only of legitimate but of transcendent public interest.

The Hayneses question whether the linkage between the author's theme and their private life really is organic. They point out that many social histories do not mention individuals at all, let alone by name. That is true. Much of social science, including social history, proceeds by abstraction, aggregation, and quantification rather than by case studies. . . . But it would be absurd to suggest that cliometric or other aggregative, impersonal methods of doing social history are the only proper way to go about it and presumptuous to claim even that they are the best way. Lemann's book has been praised to the skies by distinguished scholars, among them black scholars covering a large portion of the ideological spectrum—Henry Louis Gates, Jr., William Junius Wilson, and Patricia Williams. Lemann's methodology places the individual case history at center stage. If he cannot tell the story of Ruby Daniels without waivers from every person who she thinks did her wrong, he cannot write this book.

Well, argue the Hayneses, at least Lemann could have changed their names. But the use of pseudonyms would not have gotten Lemann and Knopf off the legal hook. The details of the Hayneses' lives recounted in the book would identify them unmistakably to anyone who has known the Hayneses well for a long time (members of their families, for example), or who knew them before they got married; and no more is required. . . . Lemann would have had to change some, perhaps many, of the details. But then he would no longer have been writing history. He would have been writing fiction. The nonquantitative study of living persons would be abolished as a category of scholarship, to be replaced by the sociological novel. That is a genre with a distinguished history punctuated by famous names, such as Dickens, Zola, Stowe, Dreiser, Sinclair, Steinbeck, and Wolfe, but we do not think that the law of privacy makes it (or that the First Amendment would permit the law of privacy to make it) the exclusive format for a social history of living persons that tells their story rather than treating them as data points in a statistical study. Reporting the true facts about real people is necessary to "obviate any impression that the problems raised in the [book] are remote or hypothetical." [ ] And surely a composite portrait of ghetto residents would be attacked as racial stereotyping.

The Promised Land does not afford the reader a titillating glimpse of tabooed activities. The tone is decorous and restrained. Painful though it is for the Hayneses to see a past they would rather forget brought into the public view, the public needs the information conveyed by the book, including the information about Luther and Dorothy Haynes, in order to evaluate the profound social and political questions that the book raises. Given the *Cox* decision [discussed below], moreover, all the discreditable facts about the Hayneses that are contained in judicial records are beyond the power of tort law to conceal; and the disclosure of those facts alone would strip away the Hayneses' privacy as effectively as *The Promised Land* has done. (This case, it could be argued, has stripped them of their privacy, since their story is now part of a judicial record—the record of this case.) We do not think it is an answer that Lemann got his facts from Ruby Daniels rather than from judicial records. The courts got the facts from Ruby. We cannot see what difference it makes that Lemann went to the source.

Ordinarily the evaluation and comparison of offensiveness and news-worthiness would be, like other questions of the application of a legal standard to the facts of a particular case, matters for a jury, not for a judge on a motion for summary judgment. But summary judgment is properly granted to a defendant when on the basis of the evidence obtained in pretrial discovery no reasonable jury could render a verdict for the plaintiff, [ ], and that is the situation here. . . .

Illinois has been a follower rather than a leader in recognizing claims of invasion of privacy. [ ]. The plaintiffs are asking us to innovate boldly in the name of the Illinois courts, and such a request is better addressed to those courts than to a federal court. . . .

Does it follow, as the Hayneses' lawyer asked us rhetorically at oral argument, that a journalist who wanted to write a book about contemporary sexual practices could include the intimate details of named living persons' sexual acts without the persons' consent? Not necessarily, although the revelation of such details in the memoirs of former spouses and lovers is common enough and rarely provokes a lawsuit even when the former spouse or lover is still alive. The core of the branch of privacy law with which we deal in this case is the protection of those intimate physical details the publicizing of which would be not merely embarrassing and painful but deeply shocking to the average person subjected to such exposure. The public has a legitimate interest in sexuality, but that interest may be outweighed in such a case by the injury to the sensibilities of the person made use of by the author in such a way. [ ]At least the balance would be sufficiently close to preclude summary judgment for the author and publisher. [ ]

The judgment for the defendants is affirmed.

NOTES AND QUESTIONS

1. Compare *Melvin v. Reid* and *Sidis*. Are the cases distinguishable or are they in conflict?

2. Does the plaintiff in *Haynes* lose because the material was not sufficiently offensive? Because although it was offensive it was nonetheless "newsworthy" or "of legitimate concern to the public"? Are the two factors related? Compare the approach of the Second Restatement in § 652D:

> One who gives publicity to a matter concerning the private life of another is subject to liability to the other for invasion of his privacy, if the matter publicized is of a kind that
>
> (a) would be highly offensive to a reasonable person, and
>
> (b) is not of legitimate concern to the public.

Does this formulation suggest any interaction among the elements?

3. It should not be surprising that those who seek the public limelight should be thought to have a lesser claim to privacy protection than those brought into the glare of publicity simply because they are either the unfortunate victims of an accident or crime or are otherwise swept up in an event. But involuntary subjects may not be that much different. As comment *f* to § 652D puts it:

> These persons are regarded as properly subject to the public interest, and publishers are permitted to satisfy the curiosity of the public as to its heroes, leaders, villains and victims, and those who are closely associated with them. As in the case of the voluntary public figure, the authorized publicity is not limited to the event that itself arouses the public interest, and to some extent includes publicity given to facts about the individual that would otherwise be purely private.

As comment *h* adds:

> Permissible publicity to information concerning either voluntary or involuntary public figures is not limited to the particular events that arouse the interest of the public. That interest, once aroused by the event, may legitimately extend, to some reasonable degree, to further information concerning the individual and to facts about him, which are not public and which, in the case of one who had not become a public figure, would be regarded as an invasion of his purely private life. Thus the life history of one accused of murder, together with such heretofore private facts as may throw some light upon what kind of person he is, his possible guilt or innocence, or his reasons for committing the crime, are a matter of legitimate public interest. . . . On the same basis the home life and daily habits of a motion picture actress may be of legitimate and reasonable interest to the public that sees her on the screen.

The extent of the authority to make public private facts is not, however, unlimited. There may be some intimate details of her life, such as sexual relations, which even the actress is entitled to keep to herself. In determining what is a matter of legitimate public interest, account must be taken of the customs and conventions of the community; and in the last analysis what is proper becomes a matter of the community mores. The line is to be drawn when the publicity ceases to be the giving of information to which the public is entitled, and becomes a morbid and sensational prying into private lives for its own sake, with which a reasonable member of the public, with decent standards, would say that he had no concern.

4. What is the justification for using plaintiff's name? In some privacy cases the event is important and the question is whether to name some participant in the event who happened to have something embarrassing happen to him or her. For example, there is the question whether to identify a rape victim who is not independently newsworthy, or whether to name a local resident on whom a load of manure was accidentally dumped.

On the other hand, some stories are newsworthy because they involve already newsworthy people. Of all the people each day who get parking citations, the newspapers are likely to be interested in very few—but probably would be interested to learn that the mayor's spouse picked up ten parking violations in three days. Or the paper might find irony if a recently released felon assaulted the daughter of a parent who has been active in urging early release for violent felons.

How different are these two types of situations? What fact pattern is involved in *Knopf?*

5. Ross v. Midwest Communications, Inc., 870 F.2d 271 (5th Cir.), cert. denied 493 U.S. 935 (1989), involved the identification of a rape victim. Defendant's investigative reporting team came to the conclusion that a man convicted in two rape cases had been wrongly convicted. In its program to that effect it presented facts about the two rapes, including the identities of the victims and a photograph of the house in which plaintiff had lived at the time.

The court of appeals affirmed a summary judgment for the defendant. Although plaintiff claimed that all the facts about the rape were private, her major claim was that defendant should not have identified her as the victim. The court relying on an earlier case stated that the name and the photograph "strengthen the impact and credibility of the article. They obviate any impression that the problems raised in the article are remote or hypothetical." The court noted that the "infamous Janet Cooke controversy (about the fabricated, Pulitzer–Prize winning Washington Post series on the child-addict, Jimmy) suggests the legitimate ground for doubts that may arise about the accuracy of a documentary that uses only pseudonyms." Since the program sought to persuade the public and the authorities that an innocent man had been convicted, it was especially important to use real names.

The court did leave open the possibility of recovery where "the details of the rape victim's experience are not so uniquely crucial to the story as they are in this case, or when the publisher's 'public concern' goes to a general, sociological issue."

6. In Gilbert v. Medical Economics Co., 665 F.2d 305 (10th Cir.1981), an article about malpractice identified plaintiff anesthesiologist as one who had negligently caused two serious injuries. To establish its thesis that this type of situation resulted from a "collapse" of self-policing and hospital disciplinary action, the article reported plaintiff's "history of psychiatric and related personal problems." Plaintiff conceded that the topic was newsworthy but asserted that her name and accompanying private facts about her personal and marital life added nothing to the article. Any relationship was "purely speculative."

The court disagreed. The name and photograph obviated any impression that the article lacked solid foundation. The facts were connected to the article by "the rational inference that plaintiff's personal problems were the underlying cause of the acts of alleged malpractice." Editors must be permitted leeway in drawing inferences that one event is connected with another. The connection was "not so purely conjectural that no reasonable editor could draw them other than through guesswork and speculation."

7. In Virgil v. Time Inc. 527 F.2d 1122 (9th Cir.1975), cert. denied, 425 U.S. 998 (1976), a prominent surfer sued over a story that reported, among other things, his diving head first down a flight of stairs and eating "spiders and other insects," as well as that he had never learned to read and that other surfers thought him "abnormal." All these were thought to have some bearing on plaintiff's "reckless disregard for his own safety" in body surfing. Nonetheless, summary judgment was inappropriate. The court thought an issue remained as to whether the revelations were of "legitimate public concern" and the trial court was to consider whether the article might be found to be "morbid and sensational prying."

On remand, the trial judge granted the magazine summary judgment. Although the facts were "generally unflattering and perhaps embarrassing," they did not approach being highly offensive. "Even if" offensiveness were found, the magazine was entitled to summary judgment because the parties "agree that body surfing at the Wedge is a matter of legitimate public interest, and it cannot be doubted that Mike Virgil's unique prowess at the same is also of legitimate public interest. Any reasonable person . . . would have to conclude that the personal facts concerning Mike Virgil were included as a legitimate journalistic attempt to explain Virgil's extremely daring and dangerous style of body surfing at the Wedge. There is no possibility that a juror could conclude that the personal facts were included for any inherent morbid, sensational, or curiosity appeal they might have." Virgil v. Sports Illustrated, 424 F.Supp. 1286 (S.D.Cal.1976).

8. Must the editor's judgment concerning the relationship of the plaintiff's name or photograph to a story be reasonable as well as honest? What does "reasonable" mean in this context? What if the court thinks that the editor honestly saw a connection between two events but that most people would not see it the same way? Most editors?

9. Might the nature of the publication be relevant? Could a daily newspaper in plaintiff's hometown identify a rape victim—while a distant paper could not? Vice versa?

What if the disclosure in *Haynes* had been made in a tabloid newspaper or on a television talk show? What missing element might that supply?

10. In defamation the source of the statement was relevant and often crucial to the decision. Here, the court says that the source is not important. What is the difference?

11. Consider a news article reporting that a young woman concealed her pregnancy from her friends and family, gave birth alone, and then had her brother deliver the baby to a nearby hospital. The article named the woman. Plaintiff argued that even if the story was newsworthy, her identity was not. The court ordered summary judgment against plaintiff. Although articles on sensitive topics "sometimes avoid divulging the names of individuals involved, no principle of tort law requires this journalistic approach." Plaintiff's act was newsworthy and she was not "merely the involuntary victim of an event of public interest; her own voluntary and extraordinary actions created the newsworthy event." Finally, the court noted in a footnote, "We do not suggest that a modicum of journalistic self-restraint would not have been salutary. Indeed, we have ourselves omitted plaintiff's name from this opinion." Pasadena Star–News v. Superior Court, 203 Cal.App.3d 131, 249 Cal.Rptr. 729 (1988).

Rejecting the Privacy Action. A few states have rejected the "true-facts" privacy action. In Anderson v. Fisher Broadcasting Companies, Inc., 300 Or. 452, 712 P.2d 803 (1986), the court on state law grounds rejected the privacy action brought by an accident victim against a television station that used film of him, bleeding and in pain, in promotional spots for a forthcoming special news report on emergency medical treatment. In so doing, the court observed

> What is "private" so as to make its publication offensive likely differs among communities, between generations, and among ethnic, religious, or other social groups, as well as among individuals. Likewise, one reader's or viewer's "news" is another's tedium or trivia. The editorial judgment of what is "newsworthy" is not so readily submitted to the ad hoc review of a jury as [the lower court] believed. It is not properly a community standard. Even when some editors themselves vie to tailor "news" to satisfy popular tastes, others may believe that the community should see or hear facts or ideas that the majority finds uninteresting or offensive.

See also Hall v. Post, 323 N.C. 259, 372 S.E.2d 711 (1988), rejecting the action largely because it will generally duplicate the action for intentional infliction of emotional distress.

Before becoming a judge, Professor Richard Posner suggested that a person who seeks to withhold some part of his or her past was trying to present a misrepresentation to the public. Although the individual was free to try to hide this information, Posner argued that the law should not impose sanctions on those who tell the public the truth about such a person. Posner, The Right of Privacy, 12 Ga.L.Rev. 393 (1978). Five comments on the article immediately follow it.

Is it relevant to the question of creating this type of action that, even when the law permits publication, the press often decides against publication because of ethical concerns? These issues are frequently discussed among journalists.

With the three basic elements of the action in mind, consider the following array of privacy cases.

Some Illustrations

Sexual Matters

1. During an assassination attempt on President Ford in San Francisco, Oliver Sipple knocked the arm of the assailant, Sara Jane Moore, as she sought to aim a second shot at the President. Sipple was the object of extensive media attention, including stories that disclosed his homosexuality. Sipple, asserting that relatives who lived in the Midwest did not know of his sexual preference, sued the San Francisco Chronicle. The newspaper defended in part on the argument that privacy was not involved because Sipple had marched in gay parades and had acknowledged that at least 100 to 500 people in San Francisco knew he was a homosexual.

Summary judgment was affirmed on appeal. First, the facts were not private. Second, they were newsworthy. The article was prompted by "legitimate political considerations, i.e., to dispel the false public opinion that gays were timid, weak and unheroic figures and to raise the equally important political question whether the President of the United States entertained a discriminatory attitude or bias against a minority group such as homosexuals." Sipple v. Chronicle Publishing Co., 154 Cal.App.3d 1040, 201 Cal.Rptr. 665 (1984).

2. Plaintiff was kidnapped by her estranged husband and taken to an apartment. He forced her to disrobe and then beat her. Police came. After the husband committed suicide, police hurried plaintiff from the apartment nude "save for a mere towel." Defendant's photographer's picture of the partially covered woman appeared in the paper.

On appeal, plaintiff's judgment for $1,000 compensatory and $9,000 punitive damages was reversed and the case was dismissed. Cape Publications, Inc. v. Bridges, 423 So.2d 426 (Fla.App.1982), cert. denied 464 U.S. 893 (1983).

3. A group of Pittsburgh Steelers fans urged a photographer from Sports Illustrated to take pictures of them. The photographer did so. From among many photographs available for use, the editors chose one

that showed the plaintiff with his fly open. Neff v. Time, Inc., 406 F.Supp. 858 (W.D.Pa.1976)(case dismissed).

Criminal Behavior

4. A magazine article, to prove that truck hijacking was a chancy venture, reported that 11 years earlier the plaintiff and another had hijacked a truck in Kentucky, only to find that it contained four bowling pin spotting machines. The article was published in 1967, by which time plaintiff alleged that he had served his time, had become rehabilitated, and was living in California with family and friends who did not know about his past. Briscoe v. Reader's Digest Ass'n, 4 Cal.3d 529, 483 P.2d 34, 93 Cal.Rptr. 866 (1971)(case remanded to determine whether the defendant published with "reckless disregard" for the article's offensiveness).

5. Plaintiff was arrested for drunk driving. At the police station, he was "hitting and banging on his cell door, hollering and cursing from the time of his arrest" until five hours later. A local broadcaster taped some of the noise and played excerpts on the radio. Holman v. Central Arkansas Broadcasting Co., 610 F.2d 542 (8th Cir.1979)(case dismissed).

Embarrassment or Ridicule

6. Regardie's, a monthly magazine, ran an article in September 1986, that purported to be a list with short biographies of Washington's 100 wealthiest individuals. It also carried a list of those included in previous years but omitted this year because the minimum net worth had risen from $20 million to $30 million. In this "Gone But Not Forgotten" group was plaintiff, a lawyer, who was said to have made his fortune in real estate. Plaintiff explained his failure to sue the prior year on the ground that it seemed best to refrain from pursuing the matter to avoid further publicity. The data had been collected from court files, tax ledgers, and federal and city agency records. The case was dismissed for lack of any private facts. Wolf v. Regardie, 553 A.2d 1213 (D.C.App.1989).

7. A newspaper article reported that the basketball team at the state university was in trouble because four named players, of the eight who were returning, "are on academic probation and in danger of flunking." Bilney v. Evening Star Newspaper Co., 43 Md.App. 560, 406 A.2d 652 (1979)(case dismissed).

8. Plaintiff was a janitor who found $240,000 that had fallen from an armored car. He returned it (and received a reward of $10,000) to the scorn of his neighbors and his children's friends. When their hostile reaction was reported, he received many congratulatory letters and messages, including one from President Kennedy. The full story was reported in a periodical and reprinted in a college English textbook. Johnson v. Harcourt, Brace, Jovanovich, Inc., 43 Cal.App.3d 880, 118 Cal.Rptr. 370 (1974)(case dismissed.)

9. Defendants searched the trash bin at an abortion clinic and obtained the names of two women who were scheduled to have abortions the following day. When the women arrived defendants raised "large signs"

listing the plaintiffs' real names that implored them, among other things, not to "kill their babies." Doe v. Mills, 212 Mich.App. 73, 536 N.W.2d 824 (1995)(summary judgment reversed; the court also upheld an action for intentional infliction of emotional distress).

Private Information. Which of the foregoing cases seemed strongest in this regard? Which weakest? Courts have uniformly rejected the claim that information about one person can invade another's privacy. E.g., Hendrickson v. California Newspapers, Inc., 48 Cal.App.3d 59, 121 Cal. Rptr. 429 (1975)(obituary of deceased reported that he had a criminal record and also named his survivors); Fry v. Ionia Sentinel–Standard, 101 Mich.App. 725, 300 N.W.2d 687 (1980)(news story reported that plaintiff's husband and a woman had been killed in accidental fire, and identified dead man's wife and children as his survivors).

Highly Offensive to a Reasonable Person. Which of the foregoing cases seemed strongest in this regard? Which seemed weakest? Although the article in the *Sidis* case was "merciless in its dissection of intimate details," that did not mean that it would be highly offensive to reasonable persons. That some people may wish to keep private some of their quirks does not mean that reasonable people would find the revelation of that information highly offensive.

"Newsworthiness" or "Legitimate Concern." Which of the cases presented the weakest claim to being newsworthy? The strongest?

In the *Haynes* excerpt, Judge Posner observed that facts contained in "judicial records are beyond the power of tort law to conceal." He also mentioned that in certain situations the First Amendment would not permit privacy law to recognize a tort. We turn now to cases that explore the range of constitutional limits on the privacy tort.

2. CONSTITUTIONAL PRIVILEGE

In 1975, the Supreme Court decided its first "true-facts" privacy case. In Cox Broadcasting Corp. v. Cohn, 420 U.S. 469 (1975), a 17–year–old had been raped in Georgia and did not survive. A Georgia criminal statute made it a misdemeanor for "any news media or any other person to print and publish, broadcast, televise or disseminate through any other medium of public discussion . . . the name or identity of any female who may have been raped." During a recess in a criminal hearing in the case, a television reporter was allowed to inspect the indictment, which named the victim. Cox Broadcasting used the victim's name in reporting on the case that night.

The victim's father brought a tort action for revelation of his daughter's name. The state supreme court held that the complaint stated a common law action for damages. A First Amendment defense was rejected on the ground that the statute was an authoritative declaration that Georgia considered a rape victim's name not to be a matter of public concern. The court could discern "no public interest or general concern about the identity of the victim of such a crime as will make the right to disclose the identity of the victim rise to the level of First Amendment protection."

The Supreme Court reversed. Cox Broadcasting argued for a "broad holding that the press may not be made criminally or civilly liable for publishing information that is neither false nor misleading but absolutely accurate, however damaging it may be to reputation or individual sensibilities." Justice White's majority opinion avoided the broad ground by addressing the narrower question of "whether the State may impose sanctions on the accurate publication of the name of a rape victim obtained from public records—more specifically, from judicial records which are maintained in connection with a public prosecution and which themselves are open to public inspection. We are convinced that the State may not do so."

Justice White noted that the public relies on the press to provide in convenient form the facts about the operation of government. Without such information "most of us and many of our representatives would be unable to vote intelligently or to register opinions on the administration of government generally." The "commission of crime, prosecutions resulting from it, and judicial proceedings arising from the prosecutions . . . are without question events of legitimate concern to the public and consequently fall within the responsibility of the press to report the operations of government."

Justice White noted that the developing law of privacy afforded the press a privilege to report the events of judicial proceedings. "By placing the information in the public domain on official court records, the State must be presumed to have concluded that the public interest was thereby being served. Public records by their very nature are of interest to those concerned with the administration of government, and a public benefit is performed by the reporting of the true contents of the records by the media." Freedom to publish material released by government is of "critical importance to our type of government in which the citizenry is the final judge of the proper conduct of public business." In such situations, "the States may not impose sanctions on the publication of truthful information contained in official court records open to public inspection."

The Court was "reluctant to embark on a course that would make public records generally available to the media but forbid their publication if offensive to the sensibilities of the supposed reasonable man. Such a rule would make it very difficult for the media to inform citizens about the public business and yet stay within the law. The rule would invite timidity and self-censorship and very likely lead to the suppression of many items that would otherwise be published and that should be made available to the public.''

To appreciate fully the significance of the following case it is necessary to be familiar with the major features of a few Supreme Court cases in which the press disclosed information despite a judge's order or a statute to the contrary.   Oklahoma Publishing Co. v. District Court, 430 U.S. 308 (1977), struck down a judge's order barring the identification of juveniles when the judge in fact had held an open proceeding that allowed those present to learn the identity by observation.   Landmark Communications, Inc. v. Virginia, 435 U.S. 829 (1978), struck down a state bar against the publication of truthful news reports that a sitting judge was under investigation by a state commission.   Smith v. Daily Mail Publishing Co., 443 U.S. 97 (1979), barred criminal prosecution against a newspaper that, in violation of a statute against such conduct, had identified a juvenile suspect based on interviews with eyewitnesses to the event.

These three cases, decided after *Cox Broadcasting,* came into play as the Court decided another case involving the identification of rape victims. At the time, Florida was one of a handful of states that sought to prevent such publications by criminal statute.

The Florida Star v. B.J.F.

Supreme Court of the United States, 1989.
491 U.S. 524, 109 S.Ct. 2603, 105 L.Ed.2d 443.

■ JUSTICE MARSHALL delivered the opinion of the Court.

Florida Stat. section 794.03 (1987) makes it unlawful to ''print, publish, or broadcast . . .   in any instrument of mass communication'' the name of the victim of a sexual offense.   Pursuant to this statute, appellant The Florida Star was found civilly liable for publishing the name of a rape victim which it had obtained from a publicly released police report.   The issue presented here is whether this result comports with the First Amendment.   We hold that it does not.

I

The Florida Star is a weekly newspaper which serves the community of Jacksonville, Florida, and which has an average circulation of approximately 18,000 copies.   A regular feature of the newspaper is its ''Police Reports'' section.   The section, typically two to three pages in length, contains brief articles describing local criminal incidents under police investigation. On October 20, 1983, appellee B.J.F. reported to the Duval County, Florida, Sheriff's Department (the Department) that she had been robbed and sexually assaulted by an unknown assailant.   The Department prepared a report on the incident which identified B.J.F., by her full name.   The Department then placed the report in its press room.   The Department does not restrict access either to the press room or to the reports made available therein.

A Florida Star reporter-trainee sent to the press room copied the police report verbatim, including B.J.F.'s full name, on a blank duplicate of the Department's forms. A Florida Star reporter then prepared a one-paragraph article about the crime, derived entirely from the trainee's copy of the police report. The article included B.J.F.'s full name. It appeared in the "Robberies" subsection of the "Police Reports" section on October 29, 1983, one of fifty-four police blotter stories in that day's edition. The article read: "[B.J.F.] reported on Thursday, October 20, she was crossing Brentwood Park, which is in the 500 block of Golfair Boulevard, enroute to her bus stop, when an unknown black man ran up behind the lady and placed a knife to her neck and told her not to yell. The suspect then undressed the lady and had sexual intercourse with her before fleeing the scene with her 60 cents, Timex watch and gold necklace. Patrol efforts have been suspended concerning this incident because of lack of evidence."

In printing B.J.F.'s full name, The Florida Star violated its internal policy of not publishing the names of sexual offense victims.

[B.J.F. sued both the newspaper and the Sheriff's Department. The latter settled for $2,500. The Star's motion to dismiss was denied.]

At the ensuing day-long trial, B.J.F. testified that she had suffered emotional distress from the publication of her name. She stated that she had heard about the article from fellow workers and acquaintances; that her mother had received several threatening phone calls from a man who stated that he would rape B.J.F. again; and that these events had forced B.J.F. to change her phone number and residence, to seek police protection, and to obtain mental health counseling. In defense, The Florida Star put forth evidence indicating that the newspaper had learned B.J.F.'s name from the incident report released by the Department, and that the newspaper's violation of its internal rule against publishing the names of sexual offense victims was inadvertent.

At the close of B.J.F.'s case, and again at the close of its defense, The Florida Star moved for a directed verdict. On both occasions, the trial judge denied these motions. He ruled from the bench that section 794.03 was constitutional because it reflected a proper balance between the First Amendment and privacy rights, as it applied only to a narrow set of "rather sensitive . . . criminal offenses." [ ] At the close of the newspaper's defense, the judge granted B.J.F.'s motion for a directed verdict on the issue of negligence, finding the newspaper per se negligent based upon its violation of section 794.03. [ ] This ruling left the jury to consider only the questions of causation and damages. The judge instructed the jury that it could award B.J.F. punitive damages if it found that the newspaper had "acted with reckless indifference to the rights of others." [ ] The jury awarded B.J.F. $75,000 in compensatory damages and $25,000 in punitive damages. Against the actual damage award, the judge set off B.J.F.'s settlement with the Department.

The First District Court of Appeal affirmed in a three-paragraph per curiam opinion. . . . The Supreme Court of Florida denied discretionary review.

The Florida Star appealed to this Court. We noted probable jurisdiction, [ ], and now reverse.

II

The tension between the right which the First Amendment accords to a free press, on the one hand, and the protections which various statutes and common-law doctrines accord to personal privacy against the publication of truthful information, on the other, is a subject we have addressed several times in recent years. Our decisions in cases involving government attempts to sanction the accurate dissemination of information as invasive of privacy, have not, however, exhaustively considered this conflict. On the contrary, although our decisions have without exception upheld the press' right to publish, we have emphasized each time that we were resolving this conflict only as it arose in a discrete factual context.

The parties to this case frame their contentions in light of a trilogy of cases which have presented, in different contexts, the conflict between truthful reporting and state-protected privacy interests. [The Court briefly reviewed *Cox Broadcasting, Oklahoma Publishing,* and *Daily Mail.*]

Appellant takes the position that this case is indistinguishable from *Cox Broadcasting.* [ ] Alternatively, it urges that our decisions in the above trilogy, and in other cases in which we have held that the right of the press to publish truth overcame asserted interests other than personal privacy, can be distilled to yield a broader First Amendment principle that the press may never be punished, civilly or criminally, for publishing the truth. [ ] Appellee counters that the privacy trilogy is inapposite, because in each case the private information already appeared on a "public record," [ ] and because the privacy interests at stake were far less profound than in the present case. [ ] In the alternative, appellee urges that *Cox Broadcasting* be overruled and replaced with a categorical rule that publication of the name of a rape victim never enjoys constitutional protection. [ ]

We conclude that imposing damages on appellant for publishing B.J.F.'s name violates the First Amendment, although not for either of the reasons appellant urges. Despite the strong resemblance this case bears to *Cox Broadcasting,* that case cannot fairly be read as controlling here. The name of the rape victim in that case was obtained from courthouse records that were open to public inspection, a fact which Justice White's opinion for the Court repeatedly noted, [ ] (noting "special protected nature of accurate reports of *judicial* proceedings")(emphasis added); [ ]. Significantly, one of the reasons we gave in *Cox Broadcasting* for invalidating the challenged damages award was the important role the press plays in subjecting trials to public scrutiny and thereby helping guarantee their fairness. [ ] That role is not directly compromised where, as here, the information in question comes from a police report prepared and disseminated at a time at which not only had no adversarial criminal proceedings begun, but no suspect had been identified.

Nor need we accept appellant's invitation to hold broadly that truthful publication may never be punished consistent with the First Amendment. Our cases have carefully eschewed reaching this ultimate question, mindful that the future may bring scenarios which prudence counsels our not resolving anticipatorily. See, e.g., Near v. Minnesota [ ] (hypothesizing "publication of the sailing dates of transports or the number and location of troops"); see also Garrison v. Louisiana, [ ] (endorsing absolute defense of truth "where discussion of public affairs is concerned," but leaving unsettled the constitutional implications of truthfulness "in the discrete area of purely private libels"); Landmark Communications, Inc. v. Virginia, 435 U.S. 829, 838 (1978); Time, Inc. v. Hill, 385 U.S. 374, 383, n. 7 (1967). Indeed, in *Cox Broadcasting,* we pointedly refused to answer even the less sweeping question "whether truthful publications may ever be subjected to civil or criminal liability" for invading "an area of privacy" defined by the State. [ ] Respecting the fact that press freedom and privacy rights are both "plainly rooted in the traditions and significant concerns of our society," we instead focused on the less sweeping issue of "whether the State may impose sanctions on the accurate publication of the name of a rape victim obtained from public records—more specifically, from judicial records which are maintained in connection with a public prosecution and which themselves are open to public inspection." [ ] We continue to believe that the sensitivity and significance of the interests presented in clashes between First Amendment and privacy rights counsel relying on limited principles that sweep no more broadly than the appropriate context of the instant case.

In our view, this case is appropriately analyzed with reference to such a limited First Amendment principle. It is the one, in fact, which we articulated in *Daily Mail* in our synthesis of prior cases involving attempts to punish truthful publication: "[I]f a newspaper lawfully obtains truthful information about a matter of public significance then state officials may not constitutionally punish publication of the information, absent a need to further a state interest of the highest order." [ ] According the press the ample protection provided by that principle is supported by at least three separate considerations, in addition to, of course, the overarching "public interest, secured by the Constitution, in the dissemination of truth." [ ] The cases on which the *Daily Mail* synthesis relied demonstrate these considerations.

First, because the *Daily Mail* formulation only protects the publication of information which a newspaper has "lawfully obtain[ed]," [ ], the government retains ample means of safeguarding significant interests upon which publication may impinge, including protecting a rape victim's anonymity. To the extent sensitive information rests in private hands, the government may under some circumstances forbid its nonconsensual acquisition, thereby bringing outside of the *Daily Mail* principle the publication of any information so acquired. To the extent sensitive information is in the government's custody, it has even greater power to forestall or mitigate the injury caused by its release. The government may classify certain information, establish and enforce procedures ensuring its redacted release, and extend a damages remedy against the government or its officials where the government's mishandling of sensitive information leads to its dissemination. Where information is entrusted to the government, a less drastic means than punishing truthful publication almost always exists for guarding against the dissemination of private facts. See, e.g., [*Landmark Communications*] ("much of the risk [from disclosure of sensitive information regarding judicial disciplinary proceedings] can be eliminated through careful internal procedures to protect the confidentiality of Commission proceedings"); [*Oklahoma Publishing*] (noting trial judge's failure to avail himself of the opportunity, provided by a state statute, to close juvenile hearing to the public, including members of the press, who later broadcast juvenile defendant's name); [*Cox Broadcasting*] ("If there are privacy interests to be protected in judicial proceedings, the States must respond by means which avoid public documentation or other exposure of private information").[8]

A second consideration undergirding the *Daily Mail* principle is the fact that punishing the press for its dissemination of information which is already publicly available is relatively unlikely to advance the interests in the service of which the State seeks to act. It is not, of course, always the case that information lawfully acquired by the press is known, or accessible, to others. But where the government has made certain information publicly available, it is highly anomalous to sanction persons other than the source of its release. We noted this anomaly in *Cox Broadcasting*: "By placing the information in the public domain on official court records, the State must be presumed to have concluded that the public interest was thereby being served." [   ] The *Daily Mail* formulation reflects the fact that it is a limited set of cases indeed where, despite the accessibility of the public to certain information, a meaningful public interest is served by restricting its further release by other entities, like the press. As *Daily Mail* observed in its summary of *Oklahoma Publishing,* "once the truthful information was 'publicly revealed' or 'in the public domain' the court could not constitutionally restrain its dissemination." [   ]

A third and final consideration is the "timidity and self-censorship" which may result from allowing the media to be punished for publishing certain truthful information. [   ] *Cox Broadcasting* noted this concern with overdeterrence in the context of information made public through official court records, but the fear of excessive media self-suppression is applicable as well to other information released without qualification, by the government. A contrary rule, [denying] protection to those who rely

---

8. The *Daily Mail* principle does not settle the issue of whether, in cases where information has been acquired *unlawfully* by a newspaper or by a source, government may ever punish not only the unlawful acquisition, but the ensuing publication as well. This issue was raised but not definitively resolved in New York Times Co. v. United States, 403 U.S. 713 (1971), and reserved in [*Landmark Communications*]. We have no occasion to address it here.

on the government's implied representations of the lawfulness of dissemination, would force upon the media the onerous obligation of sifting through government press releases, reports, and pronouncements to prune out material arguably unlawful for publication. This situation could inhere even where the newspaper's sole object was to reproduce, with no substantial change, the government's rendition of the event in question.

Applied to the instant case, the *Daily Mail* principle clearly commands reversal. The first inquiry is whether the newspaper "lawfully obtain[ed] truthful information about a matter of public significance." [ ] It is undisputed that the news article describing the assault on B.J.F. was accurate. In addition, appellant lawfully obtained B.J.F.'s name. Appellee's argument to the contrary is based on the fact that under Florida law, police reports which reveal the identity of the victim of a sexual offense are not among the matters of "public record" which the public, by law, is entitled to inspect. [ ] But the fact that the state officials are not required to disclose such reports does not make it unlawful for a newspaper to receive them when furnished by the government. Nor does the fact that the. Department apparently failed to fulfill its obligation under section 794.03 not to "cause or allow to be . . . published" the name of a sexual offense victim make the newspaper's ensuing receipt of this information unlawful. Even assuming the Constitution permitted a State to proscribe *receipt* of information, Florida has not taken this step. It is clear, furthermore, that the news article concerned "a matter of public significance," [ ] in the sense in which the *Daily Mail* synthesis of prior cases used that term. That is, the article generally, as opposed to the specific identity contained within it, involved a matter of paramount public import: the commission, and investigation, of a violent crime which had been reported to authorities. See *Cox Broadcasting* (article identifying victim of rape-murder); [*Oklahoma Publishing*] (article identifying juvenile alleged to have committed murder); [*Daily Mail*] (same); cf. [*Landmark Communications*] (article identifying judges whose conduct was being investigated).

The second inquiry is whether imposing liability on appellant pursuant to section 794.03 serves "a need to further a state interest of the highest order." [*Daily Mail*] Appellee argues that a rule punishing publication furthers three closely related interests: the privacy of victims of sexual offenses; the physical safety of such victims, who may be targeted for retaliation if their names become known to their assailants; and the goal of encouraging victims of such crimes to report these offenses without fear of exposure. [ ]

At a time in which we are daily reminded of the tragic reality of rape, it is undeniable that these are highly significant interests, a fact underscored by the Florida Legislature's explicit attempt to protect these interests by enacting a criminal statute prohibiting much dissemination of victim identities. We accordingly do not rule out the possibility that, in a proper case, imposing civil sanctions for publication of the name of a rape victim might be so overwhelmingly necessary to advance these interests as to satisfy the *Daily Mail* standard. For three independent reasons, however, imposing liability for publication under the circumstances of this case is too precipitous a means of advancing these interests to convince us that there is a "need" within the meaning of the *Daily Mail* formulation for Florida to take this extreme step. Cf. *Landmark Communications* (invalidating penalty on publication despite State's expressed interest in nondissemination, reflected in statute prohibiting unauthorized divulging of names of judges under investigation).

First is the manner in which appellant obtained the identifying information in question. As we have noted, where the government itself provides information to the media, it is most appropriate to assume that the government had, but failed to utilize, far more limited means of guarding against dissemination than the extreme step of punishing truthful speech. That assumption is richly borne out in this case. B.J.F.'s identity would never have come to light were it not for the erroneous, if inadvertent, inclusion by the Department of her full name in an accident report made available in a press room open to the public. Florida's policy against disclosure of rape victims' identities, reflected in section 794.03, was undercut by the Department's failure to abide by this policy. Where, as here, the government has failed to police itself in disseminating information, it is clear under *Cox Broadcasting, Oklahoma Publishing,* and *Landmark Communications* that the imposition of damages against the press for its subsequent publication can hardly be said to be a narrowly tailored means of safeguarding anonymity. [   ] Once the government has placed such information in the public domain, "reliance must rest upon the judgment of those who decide what to publish or broadcast," [*Cox Broadcasting*] and hopes for restitution must rest upon the willingness of the government to compensate victims for their loss of privacy, and to protect them from the other consequences of its mishandling of the information which these victims provided in confidence.

That appellant gained access to the information in question through a government news release makes it especially likely that, if liability were to be imposed, self-censorship would result. Reliance on a news release is a paradigmatically "routine newspaper reporting techniqu[e]." [*Daily Mail*] The government's issuance of such a release, without qualification, can only convey to recipients that the government considered dissemination lawful, and indeed expected the recipients to disseminate the information further. Had appellant merely reproduced the news release prepared and released by the Department, imposing civil damages would surely violate the First Amendment. The fact that appellant converted the police report into a news story by adding the linguistic connecting tissue necessary to transform the report's facts into full sentences cannot change this result.

A second problem with Florida's imposition of liability for publication is the broad sweep of the negligence per se standard applied under the civil cause of action implied from section 794.03. Unlike claims based on the common law tort of invasion of privacy, [   ], civil actions based on section 794.03 require no case-by-case findings that the disclosure of a fact about a person's private life was one that a reasonable person would find highly offensive. On the contrary, under the per se theory of negligence adopted by the courts below, liability follows automatically from publication. This is so regardless of whether the identity of the victim is already known throughout the community; whether the victim has voluntarily called public attention to the offense; or whether the identity of the victim has otherwise become a reasonable subject of public concern—because, perhaps, questions have arisen whether the victim fabricated an assault by a particular person. Nor is there a scienter requirement of any kind under section 794.03, engendering the perverse result that truthful publications challenged pursuant to this cause of action are less protected by the First Amendment than even the least protected defamatory falsehoods: those involving purely private figures, where liability is evaluated under a standard, usually applied by a jury, of ordinary negligence. See Gertz v. Robert Welch, Inc., [ ]. We have previously noted the impermissibility of categorical prohibitions upon media access where important First Amendment interests are at stake. See Globe Newspaper Co. v. Superior Court, 457 U.S. 596, 608 (1982)(invalidating state statute providing for the categorical exclusion of the public from trials of sexual offenses involving juvenile victims.) More individualized adjudication is no less indispensable where the State, seeking to safeguard the anonymity of crime victims, sets its face against publication of their names.

Third, and finally, the facial under-inclusiveness of section 794.03 raises serious doubts about whether Florida is, in fact, serving, with this statute, the significant interests which appellee invokes in support of affirmance. Section 794.03 prohibits the publication of identifying information only if this information appears in an "instrument of mass communication," a term the statute does not define. Section 794.03 does not prohibit the spread by other means of the identities of victims of sexual offenses. An individual who maliciously spreads word of the identity of a rape victim is thus not covered, despite the fact that the communication of such information to persons who live near, or work with, the victim may have consequences equally devastating as the exposure of her name to large numbers of strangers. [ ]

When a State attempts the extraordinary measure of punishing truthful publication in the name of privacy, it must demonstrate its commitment to advancing this interest by applying its prohibition evenhandedly, to the small time disseminator as well as the media giant. Where important First Amendment interests are at stake, the mass scope of disclosure is not an acceptable surrogate for injury. A ban on disclosures effected by "instrument[s] of mass communication" simply cannot be defended on the ground that partial prohibitions may effect partial relief. See [*Daily Mail*] (statute is insufficiently tailored to interest in protecting anonymity where it restricted only newspapers, not the electronic media or other forms of publication, from identifying juvenile defendants); *id.*, at 110 (Rehnquist, J., concurring in judgment)(same); cf. Arkansas Writers' Project, Inc. v. Ragland, 481 U.S. 221, 229 (1987); Minneapolis Star & Tribune Co. v. Minnesota Comm'r of Revenue, 460 U.S. 575, 585 (1983). Without more careful and inclusive precautions against alternative forms of dissemination, we cannot conclude that Florida's selective ban on publication by the mass media satisfactorily accomplishes its stated purpose.

III

Our holding today is limited. We do not hold that truthful publication is automatically constitutionally protected, or that there is no zone of personal privacy within which the State may protect the individual from intrusion by the press, or even that a State may never punish publication of the name of a victim of a sexual offense. We hold only that where a newspaper publishes truthful information which it has lawfully obtained, punishment may lawfully be imposed, if at all, only when narrowly tailored to a state interest of the highest order, and that no such interest is satisfactorily served by imposing liability . . . under the facts of this case. The decision below is therefore reversed.

■ JUSTICE SCALIA, concurring in part and concurring in the judgment.

I think it sufficient to decide this case to rely upon the third ground set forth in the Court's opinion [ ]: that a law cannot be regarded as protecting an interest "of the highest order" [ ], and thus as justifying a restriction upon truthful speech, when it leaves appreciable damage to that supposedly vital interest unprohibited. I would anticipate that the rape victim's discomfort at the dissemination of news of her misfortune among friends and acquaintances would be at least as great as her discomfort at its publication by the media to people to whom she is only a name. Yet the law in question does not prohibit the former in either oral or written form. Nor is it clear, as I think it must be to validate this statute, that Florida's general privacy law would prohibit such gossip. Nor, finally, is it credible that the interest meant to be served by the statute is the protection of the victim against a rapist still at large—an interest that arguably would extend only to mass publication. There would be little reason to limit a statute with that objective to rape alone; or to extend it to all rapes, whether or not the felon has been apprehended and confined. In any case, the instructions here did not require the jury to find that the rapist was at large.

This law has every appearance of a prohibition that society is prepared to impose upon the press but not upon itself. Such a prohibition does not protect an interest "of the highest order." For that reason, I agree that the judgment of the court below must be reversed.

■ [JUSTICE WHITE, joined by CHIEF JUSTICE REHNQUIST and JUSTICE O'CONNOR, dissented. He distinguished the three cases on which the Court relied (but noted that *Oklahoma Publishing* was much less relied upon than the other two). The "State-law scheme [in *Cox Broadcasting*] made public disclosure of the victim's name almost inevitable; here, Florida law forbids such disclosure." "By amending its public records statute to exempt rape victims' names from disclosure [ ], and forbidding its officials from releasing such information, [ ], the State has taken virtually every step imaginable to prevent what happened here." *Cox Broadcasting* bars the state only from making the press "its first line of defense in withholding private information from the public—it cannot ask the press to secrete private facts that the State makes no effort to safeguard in the first place."

Justice White distinguished *Daily Mail* on the ground that it involved revelation of the name of the perpetrator of a murder and this case involved a victim: "whatever rights alleged criminals have to maintain their anonymity pending an adjudication of guilt—the rights of crime victims must be infinitely more substantial." Also, *Daily Mail* noted that the case involved "no issue of privacy." "But in this case, there is an issue of privacy—indeed, this is the principal issue—and therefore, this case falls outside of [*Daily Mail*]."

Justice White then turned to the Court's "independent" reasons for deciding *Florida Star*. First, the government's release of the information was "inadvertent." When the state makes a mistake in its efforts to protect privacy "it is not too much to ask the press, in instances such as this, to respect simple standards of decency and refrain from publishing a victim's name, address, and/or phone number." In a footnote at this point, Justice White noted that the Court's proper concern for a free press should "be balanced against rival interests in a civilized and humane society. An absolutist view of the former leads to insensitivity as to the latter."

Second, the Court's concern about strict liability was unavailable on this record because the jury found the Star reckless. In any event, it was permissible for the standard of care to be set by the legislature rather than the courts.

As to the third point—under-inclusiveness—Justice White was willing to accept the apparent legislative conclusion that "neighborhood gossips do not pose the danger and intrusion to rape victims that 'instrument[s] of mass communication' do. Simply put: Florida wanted to prevent the widespread distribution of rape victims' names, and therefore enacted a statute tailored almost as precisely as possible to achieving that end." Moreover, it was entirely possible that Florida's common law of privacy might apply against neighborhood gossips in an appropriate case.

Justice White then turned to "more general principles at issue here to see if they recommend the Court's result." He feared that the result would "obliterate one of the most noteworthy legal inventions of the 20th-century: the tort of the publication of private facts." If the plaintiff here could not prevail it was hard to imagine who could win such a case. There was no public interest in identifying the plaintiff here and "no public interest in immunizing the press from liability in the rare cases where a State's efforts to protect a victim's privacy have failed."]

NOTES AND QUESTIONS

1. Why is the Star's case not precisely covered by *Cox Broadcasting?*

2. Why is the Star's case not precisely covered by *Daily Mail?*

3. How might the Star's case have been analyzed in a state in which there was no statute?

4. How might the Star's case have been analyzed if the Star had learned about the name from an eyewitness rather than as the result of a mistake in the sheriff's office?

5. What might change if it turned out that the Star got the name from a sheriff's deputy who violated a statute in revealing the name?

6. In *Briscoe v. Reader's Digest Ass'n,* p. 1041, supra, involving the allegedly rehabilitated hijacker, the court stated that "Ideally, his neighbors should recognize his present worth and forget his past life of shame. But men are not so divine as to forgive the past trespasses of others, and plaintiff therefore endeavored to reveal as little as possible of his past life." The court concluded that it was for the trier of fact to decide whether plaintiff had been rehabilitated, whether "identifying him as a former criminal would be highly offensive and injurious to the reasonable man," whether defendant published the information "with a reckless disregard for its offensiveness," and whether any independent justification existed for printing plaintiff's identity. How is each determination to be made? How much of *Briscoe* remains after *Cox* and *Florida Star*?

7. In *Romaine v. Kallinger,* reprinted at p. 877, supra, for its discussion of defamation, the court also addressed a claim that the book had invaded the plaintiff's privacy. The court concluded that the claim failed because "the facts revealed are not private, and even if they were private, they are of legitimate concern to the public and so privileged under the 'newsworthiness' exception to the 'unreasonable publication of private facts' claim." The facts were not private because they were contained in nonconfidential official court records of the trial. Plaintiff argued that *Cox Broadcasting* did not apply because eight years had passed between the crime and the book. The court refused to read *Cox Broadcasting* to limit the protection accorded to reports of official records "if the events are not contemporaneous or recent." It also cited courts that had applied the *Cox Broadcasting* rationale to cases in which 19 and 23 years had passed.

Even if the facts were private, their revelation was privileged because they were newsworthy. The "[e]xtensive contemporaneous publicity [given to murder cases of this sort] is a strong indication that the subject is one that is clearly newsworthy. [ ] Moreover, the facts surrounding the commission of a crime are subjects of legitimate public concern. [ ] This concern extends to victims and other individuals who unwillingly become involved in the commission of a crime or its prosecution."

Plaintiff argued that the staleness detracted from the newsworthy quality of the report. The court disagreed: "The news value and public interest in criminal events are not abated by the passage of time. [ ] Most courts that have addressed the effect of the passage of time on the public interest have concluded that a lapse of time does not dilute newsworthiness or lessen the legitimacy of the public's concern." The court was "not persuaded" by *Briscoe* because that case was bottomed on the rehabilitative process and could be applied only in that area. The court agreed with other cases that had seen *Briscoe* as an exception to the "more general rule that 'once a man has become a public figure, or news, he remains a matter of legitimate recall to the public mind to the end of his days.' '' Finally, the *Romaine* court thought *Briscoe* 's viability had been ended by *Cox Broadcasting*'s holding on public records.

Is the privilege in *Cox Broadcasting* and *Florida Star* so broad that it bars exceptions such as one that would facilitate the rehabilitation of criminals? Do these cases affect expungement practices?

8. In *Haynes*, p. 1031, supra, although basing his decision on state law grounds, Judge Posner also discussed the implications of constitutional developments for his analysis. Noting that states had divided along the *Melvin-Sidis* line until *Cox Broadcasting*, he observed that *Cox* "may have consigned the entire *Melvin* line to the outer darkness." He noted that *Cox* protected the publication of information contained in public records "even if publication would offend the sensibilities of a reasonable person." In both *Cox* and in *Florida Star* the Court had been "careful not to hold that states can never provide a tort remedy to a person about whom truthful, but intensely private, information of some interest to the public is published":

> We do not think the Court was being coy in *Cox* or *Florida Star* in declining to declare the tort of publicizing intensely personal facts totally defunct. (Indeed, the author of *Cox* dissented in *Florida Star*.) The publication of facts in a public record or other official document, such as the police report in the *Florida Star*, is not to be equated to publishing a photo of a couple making love or of a person undergoing some intimate medical procedure; we even doubt that it would make a difference in such a case if the photograph had been printed in a government document (say the patient's file in a Veterans Administration hospital).

> Yet despite the limited scope of the holdings of *Cox* and *Florida Star*, the implications of those decisions for the branch of the right of privacy that limits the publication of private facts are profound, even for a case such as this in which, unlike *Melvin v. Reid*, the primary source of the allegedly humiliating personal facts is not a public record. (The primary source is Ruby Daniels.) The Court must believe that the First Amendment greatly circumscribes the right even of a private figure to obtain damages for the publication of newsworthy facts about him, even when they are facts of a kind that people want very much to conceal. To be identified in the newspaper as a rape victim is intensely embarrassing. And it is not invited embarrassment. . . .

> . . .

> . . . No modern cases decided after *Cox*, and precious few before, go as far as the plaintiffs would have us go in this case. Almost all the recent cases on which they rely, [ ], involve the vindication of paramount social interests, such as the protection of children, patients, and witnesses—interests not involved in this case. The plaintiffs' best post-*Cox* cases are Vassiliades v. Garfinckel's, [492 A.2d 580 (D.C.App. 1985)] and Huskey v. National Broadcasting Co., 632 F.Supp. 1282,

1290–92 (N.D.Ill.1986), the former involving before-and-after photos of a face lift, the latter involving television pictures of a prisoner dressed only in gym shorts. Photographic invasions of privacy usually are more painful than narrative ones, and even partial nudity is a considerable aggravating factor. *Vassiliades* also involved the special issue of patient rights, though it was not emphasized by the court.

The court decided that Illinois would not follow these two cases. Does Judge Posner suggest a distinction between names and photographs? What kind of privacy action might pass Supreme Court muster?

9. In State v. Globe Communications Corp., 648 So.2d 110 (Fla.1994), the Globe was prosecuted for violating the Florida statute involved in *Florida Star* by identifying the complainant in the rape trial of William Kennedy Smith. The state eventually conceded that the statute could not be constitutionally applied against the Globe, but argued that it was not facially invalid. The court, relying heavily on *Florida Star*, disagreed. Nonetheless it observed that "Although we decline to rewrite section 794.03 to correct the defects outlined in *Florida Star*, we do not rule out the possibility that the legislature could fashion a statute that would pass constitutional muster." Is it likely to be easier to frame a constitutional statute in this area or to find a fact situation that will give rise to a permissible common law tort action?

———

The Problem for Editors. In *Virgil*, p. 1038, supra, the publisher argued that the First Amendment protected all true statements from liability. The court disagreed:

> To hold that privilege extends to all true statements would seem to deny the existence of "private" facts, for if facts be facts— that is, if they be true—they would not (at least to the press) be private, and the press would be free to publicize them to the extent it sees fit. The extent to which areas of privacy continue to exist, then, would appear to be based not on rights bestowed by law but on the taste and discretion of the press. We cannot accept this result.

Defendant then made a different argument:

> A press which must depend upon a governmental determination as to what facts are of "public interest" in order to avoid liability for their truthful publication is not free at all. . . . A constitutional rule can be fashioned which protects all the interests involved. This goal is achieved by providing a privilege for truthful publications which is defeasible only when the court concludes as a matter of law that the truthful publication complained of constitutes a clear abuse of the editor's constitutional discretion to publish and discuss subjects and facts which in his judgment are matters of public interest.

Again the court disagreed. In libel and obscenity cases juries utilize community standards, and the court thought they should do so here, too, "subject to close judicial scrutiny to ensure that the jury resolutions comport with First Amendment principles." What is the difference between Time's position and that adopted by the court?

The courts have tended to take this area case by case, and editors complain that such an approach breeds intolerable uncertainty. An editor must decide today what might happen in court in several years—and the standards are said to be vague. Who can predict what will be found "highly offensive to a reasonable person" or to violate "community standards and mores"? Juries given these questions may punish unpopular publishers or broadcasters.

Compare this situation with that confronting an editor in the defamation area. There the editor, with advice from lawyers, must decide whether the *Times* or *Gertz* rule applies and then decide whether the publication's conduct meets that standard. And truth is always a defense. Do you see a sharp difference between the editor's position in defamation and in privacy? See Ingber, Rethinking Intangible Injuries: A Focus on Remedy, 73 Calif.L.Rev. 772, 849–56 (1985).

Successful Plaintiffs. During the 1960s and 1970s it began to look as though the public disclosure tort was interesting academically but was not working in the courts. The 1980s began to show signs of change.

In Diaz v. Oakland Tribune, Inc., 139 Cal.App.3d 118, 188 Cal.Rptr. 762 (1983), a columnist wrote of plaintiff:

> More education stuff: The students at the College of Alameda will be surprised to learn that their student body president, Toni Diaz, is no lady, but is in fact a man whose real name is Antonio.

> Now I realize that in these times, such a matter is no big deal, but I suspect his female classmates in P.E. 97 may wish to make other showering arrangements.

The plaintiff had had transsexual surgery. A judgment for $775,000 (of which $250,000 was compensatory) was reversed on appeal for trial errors but the court went out of its way to say that recovery was permitted on these facts and that the size of the recovery might not be a problem. The author knew the result would be "devastating" but never sought to contact plaintiff beforehand. His attempt to be "flip" and what the jury could find to be his "callous and conscious disregard for Diaz's privacy interests" justified the punitive award. The case was then settled.

A plaintiff won—and kept—a privacy award of $1,500 actual and $25,000 punitive damages in Hawkins v. Multimedia, Inc., 288 S.C. 569, 344 S.E.2d 145, cert. denied 479 U.S. 1012 (1986)(Brennan, J., dissenting). In a sidebar article to a story on teenage pregnancies, defendant's newspaper identified plaintiff as the teenage father of an illegitimate child. Most of the article focused on the teenage mother. After the mother identified plaintiff as the father, the reporter called plaintiff twice to obtain comments. The reporter first spoke with plaintiff's mother. The second time she spoke with the reluctant plaintiff for three or four minutes. "In neither call did the reporter request permission to identify or quote [plaintiff]."

Over defendant's objection, the trial judge charged that a minor cannot consent to an invasion of privacy. The appellate court did not reach the issue because it found that defendant had failed to establish consent in the first place. Although plaintiff did not hang up immediately, he was "very shy." He never agreed to the use of his name.

The court rejected defense arguments that the article was of "general interest" because that defense requires "legitimate" public interest. "Public or general interest does not mean mere curiosity, and newsworthiness is not necessarily the test." This issue was properly submitted to the jury.

Finally, the trial judge refused the defendant's charge that "malice must be shown by clear and convincing evidence." The appellate court concluded that malice "need not be shown to recover for invasion of privacy." It is relevant only for punitive damages. The proper burden for punitive damages was not argued at trial and could not be raised on appeal.

Enjoining Invasions of Privacy. As *Haynes* noted, even successful plaintiffs sacrifice, rather than protect, the sought privacy. This has led plaintiffs who obtain advance notice of an impending invasion to seek injunctive relief. Although injunctions in defamation cases have long been impermissible for nonconstitutional reasons, the situation in privacy is not so clear.

Twice the Supreme Court has been prepared to address the issue. The first case involved an unauthorized biography of a sports star. The Supreme Court asked the parties specifically to address the propriety of injunctive relief. Julian Messner, Inc. v. Spahn, 393 U.S. 818 (1968). Then the parties settled the case. 393 U.S. 1046 (1969). The second time the Court heard argument in a case in which a patient was trying to prevent her analyst from publishing a book about the therapy. Plaintiff claimed that the disguises used in the book were too thin to protect her privacy and that an implied covenant barred such a book. The state courts had enjoined publication of the book pending the outcome of the litigation. The Supreme Court granted certiorari, Roe v. Doe, 417 U.S. 907 (1974), heard arguments and then dismissed the writ as having been "improvidently granted." 420 U.S. 307 (1975). On remand, the state court found liability and ordered all of the books, except for 220 that had been distributed early, destroyed. Doe v. Roe, 93 Misc.2d 201, 400 N.Y.S.2d 668 (1977).

In a case involving the movie "Titticut Follies" the state courts had enjoined the general distribution of the movie because it invaded the privacy of inmates of a state institution for the criminally insane. The Supreme Court denied certiorari over a long dissent by Justice Harlan, joined by Justice Brennan. Justice Douglas also dissented. Wiseman v. Massachusetts, 398 U.S. 960 (1970). A petition for rehearing was denied over the dissents of Justices Harlan, Brennan, and Blackmun. "Mr. Justice Douglas took no part in the consideration or decision of this motion and petition." 400 U.S. 954 (1970). In the summer of 1991, a judge lifted the injunction and the film was shown publicly.

B. FALSE-LIGHT PRIVACY

The conventional idea of invasion of privacy as conceived by Warren and Brandeis involved true statements about aspects of plaintiff's life that others had no business knowing. But along the way, a few cases involved false charges that placed the plaintiff in a false light but did not harm his "reputation" so as to permit an action for defamation. As one example, a group used the plaintiff's name without authorization on a petition to the governor to veto a bill. Although falsely stating that plaintiff had signed the petition would not have been defamatory, the court found the situation actionable because it cast plaintiff in a false light. Hinish v. Meier & Frank Co., 166 Or. 482, 113 P.2d 438 (1941).

The line between defamation and privacy was obviously being tested by this type of case. But the line between this and the "true" privacy case also became blurred after Time, Inc. v. Hill, 385 U.S. 374 (1967). In 1952, James Hill and his family were held hostage in their home for 19 hours by three escaped convicts who apparently treated them decently. The incident received extensive nationwide coverage. Thereafter the Hills moved to another state, sought seclusion and refused to make public appearances. A novel modeled in general on the event was published the following year. In 1955, Life magazine in a very short article announced that a play and a motion picture were being made from the novel, which they said was "inspired" by the Hill episode. The play, "a heart-stopping account of how a family rose to heroism in a crisis," would enable the public to see the Hill story "re-enacted." Photographs in the magazine showed actors performing scenes from the play at the house at which the original events had occurred. The Hills claimed that the story was inaccurate because the novel and the play showed the convicts committing violence on the father and uttering a "verbal sexual insult" at the daughter.

Suit was brought under the New York statute that required plaintiff to show that the article was being used for advertising purposes or for purposes of trade. A truthful article, no matter how unpleasant for the Hills, would not have been actionable. The state courts had previously indicated that falsity would show that the article was really for purposes of trade and not for public enlightenment. The state courts allowed recovery after lengthy litigation.

The Supreme Court by a very fragile majority decided that the privilege to comment on matters of public interest had constitutional protection and could not be lost by the introduction of falsity unless the falsity was either deliberate or reckless. The Court used the defamation analogy that was then being developed in the wake of *New York Times* and applied it to this privacy case that involved falsity, ignoring the fact that the falsity was relatively trivial. Was the false report any more harmful than an absolutely true one would have been? If not, why does the falsity matter? The Court had not yet considered defamation actions by private citizens. (The preliminary vote of the Court in *Time, Inc. v. Hill* favored the Hills. For the story and the opinions in that first stage, see B. Schwartz, The Unpublished Opinions of the Warren Court 240–303 (1985). For an account of the case from the vantage point of the Hills' attorney, Richard M. Nixon, see L. Garment, Annals of Law: The Hill Case, The New Yorker, Apr. 17, 1989 at 90.)

For contemporaneous comment, see Kalven, The Reasonable Man and the First Amendment: *Hill, Butts,* and *Walker,* 1967 Sup.Ct.Rev. 267.

Cantrell v. Forest City Publishing Co.

Supreme Court of the United States, 1974.
419 U.S. 245, 95 S.Ct. 465, 42 L.Ed.2d 419.

■ MR. JUSTICE STEWART delivered the opinion of the Court.

Margaret Cantrell and four of her minor children brought this diversity action in a Federal District Court for invasion of privacy against the Forest City Publishing Co., publisher of a Cleveland newspaper, the Plain Dealer, and against Joseph Eszterhas, a reporter formerly employed by the Plain Dealer, and Richard Conway, a Plain Dealer photographer. The Cantrells alleged that an article published in the Plain Dealer Sunday Magazine unreasonably placed their family in a false light before the public through its many inaccuracies and untruths. The District Judge struck the claims relating to punitive damages as to all the plaintiffs and dismissed the actions of three of the Cantrell children in their entirety, but allowed the case to go to the jury as to Mrs. Cantrell and her oldest son, William. The jury returned a verdict* against all three of the respondents for compensatory money damages in favor of these two plaintiffs.

The Court of Appeals for the Sixth Circuit reversed, holding that, in the light of the First and Fourteenth Amendments, the District Judge should have granted the respondents' motion for a directed verdict as to all the Cantrells' claims.   .   .   .

I.

On December 1967, Margaret Cantrell's husband Melvin was killed along with 43 other people when the Silver Bridge across the Ohio River at Point Pleasant, West Virginia, collapsed. The respondent Eszterhas was assigned by the Plain Dealer to cover the story of the disaster. He wrote a "news feature" story focusing on the funeral of Melvin Cantrell and the impact of his death on the Cantrell family.

* The verdict was for $60,000—ed.

Five months later, after conferring with the Sunday Magazine editor of the Plain Dealer, Eszterhas and photographer Conway returned to the Point Pleasant area to write a follow-up feature. The two men went to the Cantrell residence, where Eszterhas talked with the children and Conway took 50 pictures. Mrs. Cantrell was not at home at any time during the 60 to 90 minutes that the men were at the Cantrell residence.

Eszterhas' story appeared as the lead feature in the August 4, 1968, edition of the Plain Dealer Sunday Magazine. The article stressed the family's abject poverty; the children's old, ill-fitting clothes and the deteriorating condition of their home were detailed in both the text and accompanying photographs. As he had done in his original, prize-winning article on the Silver Bridge disaster, Eszterhas used the Cantrell family to illustrate the impact of the bridge collapse on the lives of the people in the Point Pleasant area.

It is conceded that the story contained a number of inaccuracies and false statements. Most conspicuously, although Mrs. Cantrell was not present at any time during the reporter's visit to her home, Eszterhas wrote, "Margaret Cantrell will talk neither about what happened nor about how they are doing. She wears the same mask of non-expression she wore at the funeral. She is a proud woman. Her world has changed. She says that after it happened, the people in town offered to help them out with money and they refused to take it." Other significant misrepresentations were contained in details of Eszterhas' descriptions of the poverty in which the Cantrells were living and the dirty and dilapidated conditions of the Cantrell home.

The case went to the jury on a so-called "false light" theory of invasion of privacy. In essence, the theory of the case was that by publishing the false feature story about the Cantrells and thereby making them the objects of pity and ridicule, the respondents damaged Mrs. Cantrell and her son William by causing them to suffer outrage, mental distress, shame, and humiliation.[2]

II.

In [Hill], the Court considered a similar false-light, invasion-of-privacy action. The New York Court of Appeals had interpreted New York Civil Rights Law §§ 50–51 to give a "newsworthy person" a right of action when his or her name, picture or portrait was the subject of a "fictitious" report or article. Material and substantial falsification was the test for recovery. [ ]. Under this doctrine the New York courts awarded the plaintiff James Hill compensatory damages based on his complaint that Life Magazine had falsely reported that a new Broadway play portrayed the Hill family's

---

2. Although this is a diversity action based on state tort law, there is remarkably little discussion of the relevant Ohio or West Virginia law by the District Court, the Court of Appeals, and counsel for the parties. It is clear, however, that both Ohio and West Vir- ginia recognize a legally protected interest in privacy. [ ] Publicity that places the plaintiff in a false light in the public eye is generally recognized as one of the several distinct kinds of invasions actionable under the privacy rubric. [ ]

experience in being held hostage by three escaped convicts. This Court, guided by its decision in *New York Times Co. v. Sullivan*, [ ], which recognized constitutional limits on a State's power to award damages for libel in actions brought by public officials, held that the constitutional protections for speech and press precluded the application of the New York statute to allow recovery for "false reports of matters of public interest in the absence of proof that the defendant published the report with knowledge of its falsity or in reckless disregard of the truth." [ ] Although the jury could have reasonably concluded from the evidence in the *Hill* case that Life had engaged in knowing falsehood or had recklessly disregarded the truth in stating in the article that "the story re-enacted" the Hill family's experience, the Court concluded that the trial judge's instructions had not confined the jury to such a finding as a predicate for liability as required by the Constitution. [ ].

The District Judge in the case before us, in contrast to the trial judge in *Time Inc. v. Hill*, did instruct the jury that liability could be imposed only if it concluded that the false statements in the Sunday Magazine feature article on the Cantrells had been made with knowledge of their falsity or in reckless disregard of the truth. No objection was made by any of the parties to this knowing-or-reckless-falsehood instruction. Consequently, this case presents no occasion to consider whether a State may constitutionally apply a more relaxed standard of liability for a publisher or broadcaster of false statements injurious to a private individual under a false-light theory of invasion of privacy, or whether the constitutional standard announced in *Time Inc. v. Hill* applies to all false-light cases. Cf. [*Gertz*]. Rather, the sole question that we need decide is whether the Court of Appeals erred in setting aside the jury's verdict.

III.

At the close of the petitioners' case-in-chief, the District Judge struck the demand for punitive damages. He found that Mrs. Cantrell had failed to present any evidence to support the charges that the invasion of privacy "was done maliciously within the legal definition of that term." The Court of Appeals interpreted this finding to be a determination by the District Judge that there was no evidence of knowing falsity or reckless disregard of the truth introduced at the trial. Having made such a determination, the Court of Appeals held that the District Judge should have granted the motion for a directed verdict for respondents as to all the Cantrells' claims. [ ]

. . .

Although the verbal record of the District Court proceedings is not entirely unambiguous, the conclusion is inescapable that the District Judge was referring to the common-law standard of malice rather than to the *New York Times* "actual malice" standard when he dismissed the punitive damages claims. . . .

Moreover, the District Judge was clearly correct in believing that the evidence introduced at trial was sufficient to support a jury finding that the respondents Joseph Eszterhas and Forest City Publishing Co. had publish- ed knowing or reckless falsehoods about the Cantrells.[5] There was no dispute during the trial that Eszterhas, who did not testify, must have known that a number of the statements in the feature story were untrue. In particular, his article plainly implied that Mrs. Cantrell had been present during his visit to her home and that Eszterhas had observed her "wear[ing] the same mask of non-expression she wore [at her husband's] funeral." These were "calculated falsehoods," and the jury was plainly justified in finding that Eszterhas had portrayed the Cantrells in a false light through knowing or reckless untruth.

The Court of Appeals concluded that there was no evidence that Forest City Publishing Co. had knowledge of any of the inaccuracies contained in Eszterhas' article. However, there was sufficient evidence for the jury to find that Eszterhas' writing of the feature was within the scope of his employment at the Plain Dealer and that Forest City Publishing Co. was therefore liable under traditional doctrines of *respondeat superior*. . . .

For the foregoing reasons, the judgment of the Court of Appeals is reversed and the case is remanded to that court with directions to enter a judgment affirming the judgment of the District Court as to the respon- dents Forest City Publishing Co. and Joseph Eszterhas.

It is so ordered.

■ MR. JUSTICE DOUGLAS, dissenting.

. . .

A bridge accident catapulted the Cantrells into the public eye and their disaster became newsworthy. To make the First Amendment freedom to report the news turn on subtle differences between common-law malice and actual malice is to stand the Amendment on its head. Those who write the current news seldom have the objective, dispassionate point of view—or the time—of scientific analysts. They deal in fast-moving events and the need for "spot" reporting. The jury under today's formula sits as a censor with broad powers—not to impose a prior restraint, but to lay heavy damages on the press. The press is "free" only if the jury is sufficiently disenchanted with the Cantrells to let the press be free of this damages claim. That regime is thought by some to be a way of supervising the press which is better than not supervising it at all. But the installation of the Court's regime would require a constitutional amendment. Whatever might be the ultimate reach of the doctrine Mr. Justice Black and I have embraced, it seems clear that in matters of public import such as the present news reporting, there must be freedom from damages lest the press be frightened into playing a more ignoble role than the Framers visualized.

I would affirm the judgment of the Court of Appeals.

5. Although we conclude that the jury verdicts should have been sustained as to Eszterhas and Forest City Publishing Co., we agree with the Court of Appeals' conclusion that there was insufficient evidence to sup- port the jury's verdict against the photogra- pher Conway. . . .

NOTES AND QUESTIONS

1. How would you analyze a defamation action brought by the Cantrells? How would you analyze a public disclosure privacy action brought by the Cantrells?

2. Justice Stewart readily analyzes this case as involving the "false light" category of privacy. Might it also be analyzed as a public disclosure privacy case in which the media claimed the defense of newsworthiness but lost because the defense is not available when the material reported is deliberately or recklessly false? What are the differences between the two analyses?

A few years after *Cantrell,* in *Zacchini v. Scripps–Howard Broadcasting Co.,* p. 1093, infra, the Court approvingly quoted Dean Prosser's statement that the interest protected in false light actions "is clearly that of reputation, with the same overtones of mental distress as in defamation." Under this view, why might a state permit liability for errors that do not harm reputation?

3. What is this tort getting at? A few states have doubted its utility and have rejected it. See, e.g., Renwick v. The News and Observer Publishing Co., 310 N.C. 312, 312 S.E.2d 405, cert. denied 469 U.S. 858 (1984), in which the court noted that in states that recognize the action "the false light need not necessarily be a defamatory light. [ ] In many if not most cases, however, the false light is defamatory and an action for libel or slander will also lie." The court relied on language from *Hill* to explain that it would "create a grave risk of serious impairment of the indispensable service of a free press in a free society if we saddle the press with the impossible burden of verifying to a certainty the facts associated in news articles with a person's name, picture or portrait, particularly as related to nondefamatory matter." The court thought the action "constitutionally suspect" and thought it "would not differ significantly" from the existing defamation action. See also Cain v. Hearst Corp., 878 S.W.2d 577 (Tex.1994)(rejecting false light action because it "substantially duplicates the tort of defamation while lacking many of its procedural limitations.")

4. States that have adopted the action must determine the relation between false light and defamation, including whether the array of common-law and statutory limitations on defamation, such as retraction statutes, special damage requirements, and statutes of limitations, apply as well to false light privacy.

In Fellows v. National Enquirer, Inc., 42 Cal.3d 234, 721 P.2d 97, 228 Cal.Rptr. 215 (1986), defendant's article asserted that "Gorgeous Angie Dickinson's all smiles about the new man in her life—TV producer Arthur Fellows. Angie's steady-dating Fellows all over TinselTown, and happily posed for photographers with him as they exited the swanky Spago restaurant in Beverly Hills." Accompanying the article was a photograph of Dickinson and Fellows over the caption stating that Dickinson was "Dating a Producer."

Fellows demanded a retraction under Calif.Civil Code § 48a, asserting that plaintiff "has never dated Miss Dickinson, is not 'the new man in her life,' and has been married to Phyllis Fellows for the last 18 years." Defendant refused retraction and plaintiff sued for libel and false light privacy. Plaintiff withdrew his libel claim and proceeded solely on a false light claim with no allegation of special damages.

Under California law, libel that relied on extrinsic facts had to be supported by special damages. Civil Code § 45a. Plaintiff's privacy claim asserted that he had been falsely portrayed as the "new man" in Dickinson's life and as "steady-dating" her. The trial judge dismissed the privacy claim for lack of special damages and was affirmed on appeal.

The clear purpose of section 45a was to provide additional protection to libel defendants. Since "virtually every published defamation would support an action for false light invasion of privacy, exempting such actions from the requirement of proving special damages would render the statute a nullity." Under this rationale is there any state requirement that protects libel defendants that would not also be applied to plaintiffs who sue on a false light theory? What should happen if a false light claim is based on language that does not rise to the level of being defamatory? The court went out of its way to announce that its ruling did not apply to false light claims "that would be actionable as a public disclosure of private facts had the representation made in the publication been true."

5. In Peoples Bank & Trust Co. v. Globe International Pub., Inc., 978 F.2d 1065 (8th Cir.1992), defendant's supermarket tabloid (Sun) ran a story about a 101–year-old Australian newspaper carrier who became pregnant by one of her customers. The story included a photo of plaintiff, a 96–year-old woman. The jury rejected her libel claim but awarded damages on her false-light claim. Is this consistent? The court rejected defendant's argument that the entire tabloid was fiction and could only be understood that way on the ground that the magazine combined true stories and fiction so thoroughly that even its writers could not tell which were which. The readers could reasonably have believed that this story portrayed actual facts and that the defendant had "recklessly failed to anticipate that result." After remand, plaintiff was awarded $150,000 compensatory damages and $850,000 in punitive damages. See 817 F.Supp. 72 (W.D.Ark.), appeal dismissed 14 F.3d 607 (8th Cir.), cert. denied 114 S.Ct. 343 (1993).

6. What is the nature of the *respondeat superior* problem in *Cantrell*? Might this point be significant in future defamation cases in determining whose behavior to evaluate in considering liability? Recall the second appeal in *Gertz,* p. 953, supra.

7. How are compensatory damages to be measured in this case? Is the falsity relevant in that calculation?

8. In Machleder v. Diaz, 618 F.Supp. 1367 (S.D.N.Y.1985), the jury found a television station and its reporter liable for presenting the plaintiff in a false light as the result of an "ambush" interview. The crew caught the 71–year–old plaintiff off guard and began questioning him on camera. He was shown saying such things as "get that damn camera out of here" and generally not responding effectively to claims that his small company had polluted a nearby area.

> P: I don't want to be involved with you people . . .
>
> D: Just tell me why—why are those chemicals dumped in the back . . .
>
> P: I don't want . . . I don't need . . . I don't need any publicity . . .
>
> D: Why are those chemicals dumped in the back?
>
> P: We don't . . . we didn't dump 'em.

In fact, plaintiff had reported the presence of the chemicals to the authorities two years earlier, as the program noted.

The jury rejected plaintiff's claims for libel, slander, trespass, and assault, but awarded plaintiff $250,000 in compensatory damages and $1,000,000 in punitive damages on the false light claim that the program made him appear "intemperate and evasive." The court of appeals reversed. Machleder v. Diaz, 801 F.2d 46 (2d Cir.1986), cert. denied 479 U.S. 1088 (1987). "Any portrayal of plaintiff as intemperate and evasive could not be false since it was based on his own conduct which was accurately captured by the cameras." Even if falsity had been found, the case should still have been dismissed because as a matter of law the portrayal was not "highly offensive."

9. In Dempsey v. National Enquirer, 702 F.Supp. 934 (D.Me.1989), plaintiff, an experienced pilot, had fallen out of a small airplane in flight but clung to the open boarding ladder on the side and survived his co-pilot's emergency landing with only a few scratches. Defendant Star magazine carried a story about the episode. The article was prefaced by a short third person narrative that concluded: "Here, Dempsey . . . tells in his own words how he found himself suddenly thrust into the ultimate daredevil stunt." The by-line said "by Henry Dempsey" and the article was a dramatic first person narrative that included quoted statements purporting to be Dempsey's reactions. Plaintiff alleged that he had never been interviewed by Star, had not given them information, and had not written the article in question. Defendant moved to dismiss plaintiff's false light claim.

The court denied the motion. Although the article was essentially a true account of what had happened to plaintiff, this article "unequivocally attributed authorship to the plaintiff." This falsity could be found by a jury to portray plaintiff as "otherwise than as he is," and to be highly offensive to a reasonable person.

Recall the *Masson* case, p. 946, supra, involving the claim of fabricated quotations. Might plaintiff have relied also on a false light theory?

10. *False Light by Association?* A few cases have permitted a false light recovery to persons whose photographs have appeared in certain magazines without their consent. One involved a model whose nude photographs appeared in Hustler magazine. Douglass v. Hustler Magazine, Inc., 769 F.2d 1128 (7th Cir.1985), cert. denied 475 U.S. 1094 (1986). After the court described the magazine's contents, it concluded that a jury could reasonably find that the magazine was offensive and that "to be depicted as voluntarily associated with [Hustler] . . . is unquestionably degrading to a normal person, especially if the depiction is erotic." For other reasons, plaintiff's judgment was reversed and a new trial ordered.

In Braun v. Flynt, 726 F.2d 245 (5th Cir.), cert. denied 469 U.S. 883 (1984), plaintiff was employed at an amusement park. Part of her job included working in a novelty act with "Ralph, the Diving Pig." "Treading water in a pool, plaintiff would hold out a bottle of milk with a nipple on it. Ralph would dive into the pool and feed from the bottle." Publicity photographs of the act were used without authorization in Chic Magazine in a section entitled "Chic Thrills," a collection of vignettes, most of which "either concerned sex overtly or were accompanied by a photograph or cartoon of an overtly sexual nature." According to the court, the "particular issue of the magazine with which the case is involved contained numerous explicit photographs of female genitalia. Suffice it to say that *Chic* is a glossy, oversized, hard-core men's magazine."

From that base, the court concluded that the jury had implicitly found that "the ordinary reader automatically will form an unfavorable opinion about the character of a woman whose picture appears in *Chic* magazine." Even if no reader thought plaintiff unchaste, the jury "might have found that the publication implied Mrs. Braun's approval of the opinions expressed in *Chic* or that it implied Mrs. Braun had consented to having her picture in *Chic*. Either of these findings would support the jury verdict that the publication placed Mrs. Braun in a false light highly offensive to a reasonable person." A reduced judgment was upheld.

In Faloona v. Hustler Magazine, Inc., 799 F.2d 1000 (5th Cir.1986), cert. denied 479 U.S. 1088 (1987), plaintiffs had consented to be photographed nude for two books on human sexuality. Hustler published an excerpt from one book and a review of the other. Both were accompanied by photographs of plaintiffs. Their false light theory was rejected on the ground that "no reasonable person could consider the photographs as indicating plaintiffs' approval of *Hustler,* or that they were willing to pose nude for *Hustler*. It is obvious that the photographs were reproductions from the books being reviewed or excerpted. No tie to *Hustler* is claimed or suggested. It is this sharp definition of context which distinguishes this case from" *Douglass* and *Braun*.

In the absence of the clear context in *Faloona,* why might readers in the *Douglass* and *Braun* cases think that persons whose names and photographs appear in a publication have had any control over that use?

In a second case involving the pilot who fell from his plane, Dempsey v. National Enquirer, 702 F.Supp. 927 (D.Me.1988), the court refused to apply the *Douglass* and *Braun* cases to an article that appeared in the Enquirer. The text of the Enquirer article about the episode quoted statements given to the magazine by "friends" or by "an airport official" or a "neighbor." These negated the idea that plaintiff had cooperated or associated with the magazine itself. Moreover, "even if the article could imply that the plaintiff consented to the publication," the complaint failed to show that "association per se with the [National Enquirer] would be highly objectionable to a reasonable person." *Douglass* and *Braun* did not apply because there was no allegation here that the Enquirer was a magazine like the ones involved in those cases.

11. *Actual Malice or Negligence?* In a footnote to his concurring opinion in *Cox Broadcasting,* p. 1042, supra, Justice Powell observed:

> . . . The Court's abandonment of the "matter of general or public interest" standard as the determinative factor for deciding whether to apply the *New York Times* malice standard to defamation litigation brought by private individuals, [ ], calls into question the conceptual basis of *Time, Inc. v. Hill.* In neither *Gertz* nor our more recent decision in [*Cantrell*], however, have we been called upon to determine whether a State may constitutionally apply a more relaxed standard of liability under a false-light theory of invasion of privacy. [ ]

How might *Hill* have been compromised?

The question of actual malice or negligence in false light cases has persisted. The situation is summarized in Lovgren v. Citizens First National Bank of Princeton, 126 Ill.2d 411, 534 N.E.2d 987 (1989), in which the court upheld such a claim in favor of a plaintiff whose property was advertised without his consent as being up for sale at a forthcoming public auction. After summarizing the *Hill–Cantrell* sequence, the court concluded that it would, as a matter of state law, insist on "actual malice." It quoted from the Prosser & Keeton treatise:

> It is suggested that virtually all actionable invasions of privacy have been intentional invasions or invasions of a kind that defendant knew or had reason to know would not only be offensive but rightly so and are therefore examples of outrageous conduct that was committed with knowledge or with reason to know that it would cause severe mental stress. Recovery for an invasion of privacy on the ground that the plaintiff was depicted in a false light makes sense only when the account, if true, would not have been actionable as an invasion of privacy. In other words, the outrageous character of the publicity comes about in part by virtue of the fact that some part of the matter reported was false and deliberately so.

Is it that most cases fit this pattern or is it that this should be the minimum for this type of tort for some other reason? If the falsity is the key notion then why shouldn't the state use the same standards that it has developed for libel? Is there something "weaker" or "less important" about the false light action than about libel? (In the *Lovgren* case the "highly offensive" element was satisfied by "the allegation that the unauthorized advertisement made it practically impossible for plaintiff to obtain refinancing of his mortgage loan. A trier of fact could conclude that the defendants knew that the publication of this false fact would prove highly offensive to the plaintiff.")

In discussing the requirement that the publication be "highly offensive to a reasonable person" the *Lovgren* court cautioned that "minor mistakes in reporting, even if made deliberately, or false facts that offend a hyper-sensitive individual will not satisfy this element." What might motivate the court to protect deliberately false reporting?

The same point was made in one of the *Dempsey* cases involving the pilot who fell out of his plane. In his suit for an article that he alleged was replete with quotations falsely ascribed to him, the court held that, even if the alleged falsehoods existed, the publication was "not so offensive as to be 'highly objectionable to a reasonable person.'" Even if they were deliberate?

Do these cases suggest that the combination of serious fault and highly offensive falsity is essential to persuade states to adopt this tort? Even if states would adopt the tort on lesser grounds does the combination meet the constitutional minimum? For a critical review of the tort, see Zimmerman, False Light Invasion of Privacy: The Light That Failed, 64 N.Y.U.L.Rev. 364 (1989).

When prominent plaintiffs complain about false assertions that they endorse a particular publication or other enterprise, courts have developed an analysis that we consider at p. 1092, infra.

C. INTRUSION

In this section we consider efforts to gather information about or from an unwilling source. Intrusion may also involve efforts to impart information or "noise" to an unwilling recipient. We begin with cases that do not involve consent. We then turn to cases in which the defendant argues consent.

Nader v. General Motors Corp.

Court of Appeals of New York, 1970.
25 N.Y.2d 560, 255 N.E.2d 765, 307 N.Y.S.2d 647.

[Plaintiff Ralph Nader, a famous author and lecturer on consumer safety, had been a severe critic of defendant for several years. Nader alleged that the defendant, learning that he was about to publish a book, "Unsafe At Any Speed," initiated a series of efforts to intimidate him and suppress his criticism. These included inquiries into his political, social, racial, and religious views, his integrity, and his sexual behavior; casting aspersions on his character; keeping him under lengthy surveillance in public places; having "girls" accost him to entrap him into illicit relationships; making threatening, harassing and obnoxious telephone calls to him;

tapping his telephone and eavesdropping mechanically and electronically on his private conversations; conducting a continuing and harassing investigation of him. The parties agreed that the law of the District of Columbia controlled the litigation. The trial court denied defendant's motion to dismiss the privacy claims in the case and the appellate division affirmed.]

■ CHIEF JUDGE FULD.

. . .

Turning, then, to the law of the District of Columbia, it appears that its courts have not only recognized a common-law action for invasion of privacy but have broadened the scope of that tort beyond its traditional limits. (See Pearson v. Dodd, 410 F.2d 701; Afro–American Pub. Co. v. Jaffe, 366 F.2d 649; [ ].) Thus, in the most recent of its cases on the subject, [*Pearson*], the Federal Court of Appeals for the District of Columbia declared:

> "We approve the extension of the tort of invasion of privacy to instances of *intrusion,* whether by physical trespass or not, into spheres from which an ordinary man in a plaintiff's position could reasonably expect that the particular defendant should be excluded." (Italics supplied.)

It is this form of invasion of privacy—initially termed "intrusion" by Dean Prosser in 1960 (Privacy, 48 Cal.L.Rev. 383, 389 et seq.; Torts, § 112)—on which the two challenged causes of action are predicated.

Quite obviously, some intrusions into one's private sphere are inevitable concomitants of life in an industrial and densely populated society, which the law does not seek to proscribe even if it were possible to do so. "The law does not provide a remedy for every annoyance that occurs in everyday life." [ ] However, the District of Columbia courts have held that the law should and does protect against certain types of intrusive conduct, and we must, therefore, determine whether the plaintiff's allegations are actionable as violations of the right to privacy under the law of that jurisdiction. To do so, we must, in effect, predict what the judges of that jurisdiction's highest court would hold if this case were presented to them. [ ] In other words, what would the Court of Appeals for the District of Columbia hold is the character of the "privacy" sought to be protected? More specifically, would that court accord an individual a right, as the plaintiff before us insists, to be protected against any interference whatsoever with his personal seclusion and solitude? Or would it adopt a more restrictive view of the right as the appellant urges, merely protecting the individual from intrusion into "something secret," from snooping and prying into his private affairs?

The classic article by Warren and Brandeis [ ]—to which [*Pearson*] referred as the source of the District's common-law action for invasion of privacy [ ]—was premised, to a large extent, on principles originally developed in the field of copyright law. The authors thus based their thesis on a right granted by the common law to "each individual . . . of determining, ordinarily, to what extent his thoughts, sentiments and emotions shall be communicated to others" [ ]. Their principal concern appeared to be not with a broad "right to be let alone" (Cooley, Torts [2d ed.], p. 29) but, rather, with the right to protect oneself from having one's private affairs known to others and to keep secret or intimate facts about oneself from the prying eyes or ears of others.

In recognizing the existence of a common-law cause of action for invasion of privacy in the District of Columbia, the Court of Appeals has expressly adopted this latter formulation of the nature of the right. [ ] Quoting from the Restatement, Torts (§ 867), the court in the *Jaffe* case [ ] has declared that "[l]iability attaches to a person who 'unreasonably and seriously interferes with another's interest in *not having his affairs known to others.*' " (Emphasis supplied.) And, in *Pearson,* where the court extended the tort of invasion of privacy to instances of "intrusion," it again indicated, contrary to the plaintiff's submission, that the interest protected was one's right to keep knowledge about oneself from exposure to others, the right to prevent "*the obtaining of the information* by improperly intrusive means" ([ ]; emphasis supplied). In other jurisdictions, too, the cases which have recognized a remedy for invasion of privacy founded upon intrusive conduct have generally involved the gathering of private facts or information through improper means. [ ]

It should be emphasized that the mere gathering of information about a particular individual does not give rise to a cause of action under this theory. Privacy is invaded only if the information sought is of a confidential nature and the defendant's conduct was unreasonably intrusive. Just as a common-law copyright is lost when material is published, so, too, there can be no invasion of privacy where the information sought is open to public view or has been voluntarily revealed to others. [ ] In order to sustain a cause of action for invasion of privacy, therefore, the plaintiff must show that the appellant's conduct was truly "intrusive" and that it was designed to elicit information which would not be available through normal inquiry or observation.

The majority of the Appellate Division in the present case stated that *all of "[t]he activities complained of"* in the first two counts constituted actionable invasions of privacy under the law of the District of Columbia [ ]. We do not agree with that sweeping determination. At most, only two of the activities charged to the appellant are, in our view, actionable as invasions of privacy under the law of the District of Columbia. However, since the first two counts include allegations which are sufficient to state a cause of action, we could—as the concurring opinion notes—merely affirm the order before us without further elaboration. To do so, though, would be a disservice both to the judge who will be called upon to try this case and to the litigants themselves. In other words, we deem it desirable, nay essential, that we go further and, for the guidance of the trial court and counsel, indicate the extent to which the plaintiff is entitled to rely on the various allegations in support of his privacy claim.

. . . .

Turning, then, to the particular acts charged in the complaint, we cannot find any basis for a claim of invasion of privacy, under District of Columbia law, in the allegations that the appellant, through its agents or employees, interviewed many persons who knew the plaintiff, asking questions about him and casting aspersions on his character. Although those inquiries may have uncovered information of a personal nature, it is difficult to see how they may be said to have invaded the plaintiff's privacy. Information about the plaintiff which was already known to others could hardly be regarded as private to the plaintiff. Presumably, the plaintiff had previously revealed the information to such other persons, and he would necessarily assume the risk that a friend or acquaintance in whom he had confided might breach the confidence. If, as alleged, the question tended to disparage the plaintiff's character, his remedy would seem to be by way of an action for defamation not for breach of his right to privacy. [ ]

Nor can we find any actionable invasion of privacy in the allegations that the appellant caused the plaintiff to be accosted by girls with illicit proposals, or that it was responsible for the making of a large number of threatening and harassing telephone calls to the plaintiff's home at odd hours. Neither of these activities, howsoever offensive and disturbing, involved intrusion for the purpose of gathering information of a private and confidential nature.

As already indicated, it is manifestly neither practical nor desirable for the law to provide a remedy against any and all activity which an individual might find annoying. On the other hand, where severe mental pain or anguish is inflicted through a deliberate and malicious campaign of harassment or intimidation, a remedy is available in the form of an action for the intentional infliction of emotional distress—the theory underlying the plaintiff's third cause of action. But the elements of such an action are decidedly different from those governing the tort of invasion of privacy, and just as we have carefully guarded against the use of the prima facie tort doctrine to circumvent the limitations relating to other established tort remedies [ ], we should be wary of any attempt to rely on the tort of invasion of privacy as a means of avoiding the more stringent pleading and proof requirements for an action for infliction of emotional distress. (See, e.g., Clark v. Associated Retail Credit Men, 105 F.2d 62, 65 [Ct.App.D.C.].)

Apart, however, from the foregoing allegations which we find inadequate to spell out a cause of action for invasion of privacy under District of Columbia law, the complaint contains allegations concerning other activities by the appellant or its agents which do satisfy the requirements for such a cause of action. The one which most clearly meets those requirements is the charge that the appellant and its codefendants engaged in unauthorized wiretapping and eavesdropping by mechanical and electronic means. [*Pearson*] expressly recognized that such conduct constitutes a tortious intrusion [ ], and other jurisdictions have reached a similar conclusion. [ ] In point of fact, the appellant does not dispute this, acknowledging that, to the extent the two challenged counts charge it with wiretapping and eavesdropping, an actionable invasion of privacy has been stated.

There are additional allegations that the appellant hired people to shadow the plaintiff and keep him under surveillance. In particular, he claims that, on one occasion, one of its agents followed him into a bank, getting sufficiently close to him to see the denomination of the bills he was withdrawing from his account. From what we have already said, it is manifest that the mere observation of the plaintiff in a public place does not amount to an invasion of his privacy. But, under certain circumstances, surveillance may be so "overzealous" as to render it actionable. (See [*Pearson*]; Pinkerton Nat. Detective Agency v. Stevens, 108 Ga.App. 159.) Whether or not the surveillance in the present case falls into this latter category will depend on the nature of the proof. A person does not automatically make public everything he does merely by being in a public place, and the mere fact that Nader was in a bank did not give anyone the right to try to discover the amount of money he was withdrawing. On the other hand, if the plaintiff acted in such a way as to reveal that fact to any casual observer, then, it may not be said that the appellant intruded into his private sphere. In any event, though, it is enough for present purposes to say that the surveillance allegation is not insufficient as a matter of law.

Since, then, the first two causes of action do contain allegations which are adequate to state a cause of action for invasion of privacy under District of Columbia law, the courts below properly denied the appellant's motion to dismiss those causes of action. It is settled that, so long as a pleading sets forth allegations which suffice to spell out a claim for relief, it is not subject to dismissal by reason of the inclusion therein of additional nonactionable allegations. [   ]

We would but add that the allegations concerning the interviewing of third persons, the accosting by girls and the annoying and threatening telephone calls, though insufficient to support a cause of action for invasion of privacy, are pertinent to the plaintiff's third cause of action—in which those allegations are reiterated—charging the intentional infliction of emotional distress. However, as already noted, it will be necessary for the plaintiff to meet the additional requirements prescribed by the law of the District of Columbia for the maintenance of a cause of action under that theory.

The order appealed from should be affirmed, with costs.   .   .   .

■ BREITEL, J. (concurring in result). There is no doubt that the first and second causes of action are sufficient in alleging an invasion of privacy under what appears to be the applicable law in the District of Columbia [   ]. This should be the end of this court's proper concern with the pleadings, the only matter before the court being a motion to dismiss specified causes of action for insufficiency.

Thus it is not proper, it is submitted, for the court directly or indirectly to analyze particular allegations in the pleadings, once the causes of action are found sufficient, in order to determine whether they would alternatively sustain one cause of action or another, or whether evidence offered in support of the allegations is relevant only as to one rather than to another cause of action. Particularly, it is inappropriate to decide that several of the allegations as they now appear are referable only to the more restricted tort of intentional infliction of mental distress rather than to the common-law right of privacy upon which the first and second causes of action depend. The third cause of action is quite restricted. Thus many of the quite offensive acts charged will not be actionable unless plaintiff succeeds in the very difficult, if not impossible, task of showing that defendants' activities were designed, actually or virtually, to make plaintiff unhappy and not to uncover disgraceful information about him. The real issue in the volatile and developing law of privacy is whether a private person is entitled to be free of certain grave offensive intrusions unsupported by palpable social or economic excuse or justification.

True, scholars, in trying to define the elusive concept of the right of privacy, have, as of the present, subdivided the common law right into separate classifications, most significantly distinguishing between unreasonable intrusion and unreasonable publicity. [ ] This does not mean, however, that the classifications are either frozen or exhausted or that several of the classifications may not overlap.

Concretely applied to this case, it is suggested, for example, that it is premature to hold that the attempted entrapment of plaintiff in a public place by seemingly promiscuous ladies is no invasion of any of the categories of the right to privacy and is restricted to a much more limited cause of action for intentional infliction of mental distress. Moreover, it does not strain credulity or imagination to conceive of the systematic "public" surveillance of another as being the implementation of a plan to intrude on the privacy of another. Although acts performed in "public," especially if taken singly or in small numbers, may not be confidential, at least arguably a right to privacy may nevertheless be invaded through extensive or exhaustive monitoring and cataloguing of acts normally disconnected and anonymous.

These are but illustrations of the problems raised in attempting to determine issues of relevancy and allocability of evidence in advance of a trial record. The other allegations so treated involve harassing telephone calls, and investigatory interviews. It is just as important that while allegations treated singly may not constitute a cause of action, they may do so in combination, or serve to enhance other violations of the right to privacy.

It is not unimportant that plaintiff contends that a giant corporation had allegedly sought by surreptitious and unusual methods to silence an unusually effective critic. If there was such a plan, and only a trial would show that, it is unduly restrictive of the future trial to allocate the evidence beforehand based only on a pleader's specification of overt acts on the bold assumption that they are not connected causally or do not bear on intent and motive.

It should be observed, too, that the right to privacy, even as thus far developed, does not always refer to that which is not known to the public or is confidential. Indeed, the statutory right of privacy in this State and perhaps the most traditional right of privacy in the "common law sense" relates to the commercialized publicity of one's face or name, perhaps the two most public aspects of an individual. [ ].

There is still further difficulty. In this State thus far there has been no recognition of a common law right of privacy, but only that which derives from a statute of rather limited scope (Civil Rights Law, §§ 50, 51; Flores v. Mosler Safe Co., 7 N.Y.2d 276, 280; Roberson v. Rochester Folding Box Co., 171 N.Y. 538, 556–557). Consequently, this court must undertake the hazardous task of applying what is at present the quite different law of the District of Columbia. True, this may be the court's burden eventually, if the case were to return to it for review after trial, especially if the plaintiff were to prevail upon such a trial. However, there is no occasion to advance, now, into a complicated, subtle and still-changing field of law of another jurisdiction, solely to determine before trial the relevancy and allocability among pleaded causes of action of projected but not yet offered items of evidence. It is not overstatement to say that in the District of Columbia the law of the right of privacy is still inchoate in its development, perhaps more so than in many other jurisdictions that accept this newly coined common-law cause of action, despite unequivocal acceptance as a doctrine and extension by dictum to cases of intrusion [*Pearson*]. In the absence of a trial record, the court should avoid any unnecessary extrapolation of what the District of Columbia Court of Appeals has characterized as "an untried and developing area of tort law" [*Pearson*].

. . .

The broad statements in the opinion of the Appellate Division can be met, as this court has done so often, by declaring that they are not necessarily adopted in concluding that a cause or causes of action have been stated.

Accordingly, because of the prematurity of ruling on any other question but the sufficiency of the causes of action, I concur in result only.

▪ JUDGES SCILEPPI, BERGAN and GIBSON concur with CHIEF JUDGE FULD; JUDGE BREITEL concurs in result in an opinion in which JUDGES BURKE and JASEN concur.

NOTES AND QUESTIONS

1. As a matter of judicial strategy, who has the better of the argument about how far the appellate opinion should go at this time? Is your view affected by the fact that a few months later General Motors, denying any wrongdoing, paid Nader $425,000 to settle his claims for $2,000,000 in compensatory damages and $7,000,000 in punitive damages? Actions against two detective agencies were also dropped as part of the settlement. N.Y. Times, Aug. 14, 1970, at 1.

2. This case, in addition to presenting a range of asserted invasions by means of intrusion into plaintiff's privacy, also indicates the close relationship between the tort aspects of privacy law and other tort areas. The alleged surveillance provides a good example. Can you suggest facts that would make surveillance an invasion of privacy? An intentional infliction of emotional distress? A defamation? Are these categories mutually exclusive or might the same surveillance situation be actionable under two or more categories?

3. Is there a given degree of surveillance that must be shown before there can be any action at all? Under any theory what is the minimum that Nader must show about the bank episode? Might you be liable for looking over the shoulder of the person in line ahead of you at the bank?

4. Even if such surveillance is shown, what justifications might be available to the defense? Perhaps the most common instances are insurance companies' efforts to ascertain whether claimants are hurt as seriously as they allege. Should this behavior be permitted at all? If so, what limits should be placed upon it? In Pinkerton National Detective Agency, Inc., v. Stevens, 108 Ga.App. 159, 132 S.E.2d 119 (1963), cited in *Nader,* plaintiff alleged that detectives spied on her home intermittently for five months; that they followed her when she left the house; cut a hole in her hedge to peek through and came up to the windows to peep and to eavesdrop day and night. The plaintiff became upset, developed nervous spasms, sleeplessness, nightmares and a bad rash, and needed medical and psychiatric aid. The court said that "[b]y making a claim for personal injury appellant must expect reasonable inquiry and investigation to be made of her claim and to this extent her interest in privacy is circumscribed. . . . This petition does not limit the defendant's acts to that reasonable and unobtrusive observation which would ordinarily be used to catch one in normal activities unaware, but sets out a course of conduct which would disturb an ordinary person without hypersensitive reactions," and then held that the petition stated a cause of action for invasion of privacy.

Similarly, creditors are given leeway to attempt to reach the debtor and to recover what is claimed to be owing. See Montgomery Ward v. Shope, 286 N.W.2d 806 (S.D.1979).

5. In *Pearson v. Dodd,* discussed in *Nader,* two employees of Senator Thomas Dodd and two former employees secretly removed papers from the Senator's file overnight, photocopied them, replaced the originals, and gave the copies to defendant newspaper columnists who knew the manner in which they had been obtained. The court refused to hold the defendants liable for the actions of those who actually invaded the files:

> If we were to hold appellants liable for invasion of privacy on these facts, we would establish the proposition that one who receives information from an intruder, knowing it has been obtained by improper intrusion, is guilty of a tort. In an untried and developing area of tort law, we are not prepared to go so far. A person approached by an eavesdropper with an offer to share in the information gathered

through the eavesdropping would perhaps play the nobler part should he spurn the offer and shut his ears. However, it seems to us that at this point it would place too great a strain on human weakness to hold one liable in damages who merely succumbs to temptation and listens.

What is the significance of the court's conclusion that this is a developing area of law? Is the same analysis applicable to those who look over shoulders at the bank?

6. *Conversion.* In *Pearson v. Dodd*, the plaintiff also alleged that his papers had been converted. The court rejected the contention in an extended passage that set out the nature of conversion and related actions:

Conversion is the substantive tort theory which underlay the ancient common law form of action for trover. A plaintiff in trover alleged that he had lost a chattel which he rightfully possessed, and that the defendant had found it and converted it to his own use. With time, the allegations of losing and finding became fictional, leaving the question of whether the defendant had "converted" the property the only operative one.

The most distinctive feature of conversion is its measure of damages, which is the value of the goods converted. The theory is that the "converting" defendant has in some way treated the goods as if they were his own, so that the plaintiff can properly ask the court to decree a forced sale of the property from the rightful possessor to the converter.

Because of this stringent measure of damages, it has long been recognized that not every wrongful interference with the personal property of another is a conversion. Where the intermeddling falls short of the complete or very substantial deprivation of possessory rights in the property, the tort committed is not conversion, but the lesser wrong of trespass to chattels.

The Restatement, Second, Torts has marked the distinction by defining conversion as:

". . . [A]n intentional exercise of dominion or control over a chattel which so seriously interferes with the right of another to control it that the actor may justly be required to pay the other the full value of the chattel."

Less serious interferences fall under the Restatement's definition of trespass.

The difference is more than a semantic one. The measure of damages in trespass is not the whole value of the property interfered with, but rather the actual diminution in its value caused by the interference. More important for this case, a judgment for conversion can be obtained with only nominal damages whereas liability for trespass to chattels exists only on a showing of actual damage to the property interfered with. . . .

It is clear that on the agreed facts appellants committed no conversion of the physical documents taken from appellee's files. Those documents were removed from the files at night, photocopied, and returned to the files undamaged before office operations resumed in the morning. Insofar as the documents' value to appellee resided in their usefulness as records of the business of his office, appellee was clearly not substantially deprived of his use of them.

The court then considered whether the documents had some derivative value beyond physical possession, and concluded:

> The question here is not whether appellee had a right to keep his files from prying eyes, but whether the information taken from those files falls under the protection of the law of property, enforceable by a suit for conversion. In our view, it does not. The information included the contents of letters to appellee from supplicants, and office records of other kinds, the nature of which is not fully revealed by the record. Insofar as we can tell, none of it amounts to literary property, to scientific invention, or to secret plans formulated by appellee for the conduct of commerce. Nor does it appear to be information held in any way for sale by appellee, analogous to the fresh news copy produced by a wire service.

> Appellee complains, not of the misappropriation of property bought or created by him, but of the exposure of information either (1) injurious to his reputation or (2) revelatory of matters which he believes he has a right to keep to himself. Injuries of this type are redressed at law by suit for libel and invasion of privacy respectively, where defendants' liability for those torts can be established under the limitations created by common law and by the Constitution.

A concurring judge observed that "Conduct for which a law enforcement officer would be soundly castigated is, by the phraseology of the majority opinion, found tolerable; conduct which, if engaged in by government agents would lead to the suppression of evidence obtained by these means, is approved when used for the profit of the press." Since the court's review was confined to the amended complaint as restricted by certain stipulations, he also concluded that Dodd would hardly be without legal remedy "if the entire factual situation herein were before us on pleadings encompassing all possible legal aspects suggested by the facts."

7. The *Nader* majority emphasizes that not every annoyance in life has a legal remedy. How might the majority react to Vernars v. Young, 539 F.2d 966 (3d Cir.1976) in which the court upheld a complaint alleging that defendant, principal officer of a small corporation, opened and read without consent mail addressed to plaintiff, another officer of the corporation, even though the mail was "addressed to her and marked personal." The court relied on the Restatement (Second) § 652B, providing that "One who intentionally intrudes . . . upon the solitude or seclusion of another, or his private affairs or concerns, is subject to liability . . . if the intrusion would be highly offensive to a reasonable person." Is it relevant that plaintiff might have avoided this situation by having personal mail sent to her home or a postal box rather than her office?

8. Should it be an invasion of privacy to ask neighbors about Nader's views, interests, and sexual habits? Can you add facts that might convert this inquiry into an intentional infliction of emotional distress? A defamation? If you find an action under any of these theories, would you permit the defendant the same justifications allowed for surveillance?

9. Nader alleged that the invasions were all intentional. Should that be a necessary element in this type of invasion of privacy?

10. For another example of intrusion by photography, see Estate of Berthiaume v. Pratt, M.D., 365 A.2d 792 (Me.1976) in which the deceased, a patient of a physician other than the defendant, objected to defendant physician's efforts to photograph him as he lay dying in a hospital bed. A jury could have found that the patient had objected as strongly as he could by raising a clenched fist and moving his head. The court held that even in the absence of publication of the photographs, a jury could find that an actionable intrusion had occurred. The court rejected defendant's argument that these photographs would allow better evaluation of the progress of malignancy of the face in other patients. No matter how valuable the photographs would be to medical science, the plaintiff still had control over whether his "facial characteristics should be recorded for another's benefit."

Would that analysis hold even if the photographs might save the lives of 50 patients now in the hospital with the same condition? Is this like sacrificing one victim to save the lives of 50 other members of the community from the wrath of an approaching army? Recall, p. 851, supra.

11. In Melvin v. Burling, 141 Ill.App.3d 786, 490 N.E.2d 1011 (1986), plaintiffs brought an action for invasion of privacy based on the intentional ordering of merchandise in their name, without their consent. The court first determined that a cause of action based on intrusion does exist in Illinois. To support the action, the court indicated that the following facts must be shown: (1) an unauthorized intrusion or prying into plaintiff's seclusion; (2) the intrusion must be offensive or objectionable to a reasonable person; (3) the matter upon which the intrusion occurs must be private; and (4) the intrusion must cause anguish and suffering. The court held that sufficient facts to sustain all elements were present, and reversed the lower court's dismissal of the case.

12. In Harkey v. Abate, 131 Mich.App. 177, 346 N.W.2d 74 (1983), the court reinstated plaintiff's claim for invasion of privacy against the owner of a skating rink who had installed see-through panels in the roof of a public restroom. The court held that even though plaintiff may not have been able to prove that she had been watched through the panels, "the installation of the hidden viewing devices alone constitutes an interference" with an individual's privacy, "which a reasonable person would find highly offensive." Whether plaintiff was actually watched through the panels, the court noted, should go to the issue of damages.

Galella v. Onassis

United States Court of Appeals, Second Circuit, 1973.
487 F.2d 986.

[Photographer Ron Galella sued Jacqueline Kennedy Onassis for false arrest and malicious prosecution after he was arrested by Secret Service agents protecting Mrs. Onassis's children, John and Caroline. Mrs. Onassis denied the charges and counterclaimed for injunctive relief against Galella's continuous efforts to photograph her and her children. The court of appeals affirmed the dismissal of Galella's claim. The portion of the opinion that follows deals with the propriety of the District Court's grant of injunctive relief to Mrs. Onassis and to the government, which had intervened in its capacity as protector of the children's safety.]

■ Before SMITH, HAYS and TIMBERS, CIRCUIT JUDGES.

■ J. JOSEPH SMITH, CIRCUIT JUDGE:

. . .

Galella fancies himself as a "paparazzo" (literally a kind of annoying insect, perhaps roughly equivalent to the English "gadfly.") Paparazzi make themselves as visible to the public and obnoxious to their photographic subjects as possible to aid in the advertisement and wide sale of their works.

Some examples of Galella's conduct brought out at trial are illustrative. Galella took pictures of John Kennedy riding his bicycle in Central Park across the way from his home. He jumped out into the boy's path, causing the agents concern for John's safety. The agents' reaction and interrogation of Galella led to Galella's arrest and his action against the agents; Galella on other occasions interrupted Caroline at tennis, and invaded the children's private schools. At one time he came uncomfortably close in a power boat to Mrs. Onassis swimming. He often jumped and postured around while taking pictures of her party notably at a theater opening but also on numerous other occasions. He followed a practice of bribing apartment house, restaurant and nightclub doormen as well as romancing a family servant to keep him advised of the movements of the family.

. . .

After a six-week trial the court dismissed Galella's claim and granted relief to both the defendant and the intervenor. Galella was enjoined from (1) keeping the defendant and her children under surveillance or following any of them; (2) approaching within 100 yards of the home of defendant or her children, or within 100 yards of either child's school or within 75 yards of either child or 50 yards of defendant; (3) using the name, portrait or picture of defendant or her children for advertising; (4) attempting to communicate with defendant or her children except through her attorney.

. . .

Discrediting all of Galella's testimony[10] the court found the photographer guilty of harassment, intentional infliction of emotional distress, assault and battery, commercial exploitation of defendant's personality, and invasion of privacy. Fully crediting defendant's testimony, the court found no liability on Galella's claim. Evidence offered by the defense showed that Galella had on occasion intentionally physically touched Mrs. Onassis and her daughter, caused fear of physical contact in his frenzied attempts to get their pictures, followed defendant and her children too closely in an automobile, endangered the safety of the children while they were swimming, water skiing and horseback riding. Galella cannot successfully challenge the court's finding of tortious conduct.[11]

Finding that Galella had "insinuated himself into the very fabric of Mrs. Onassis' life . . . " the court framed its relief in part on the need to prevent further invasion of the defendant's privacy. Whether or not this accords with present New York law, there is no doubt that it is sustainable under New York's proscription of harassment.

Of course legitimate countervailing social needs may warrant some intrusion despite an individual's reasonable expectation of privacy and freedom from harassment. However the interference allowed may be no greater than that necessary to protect the overriding public interest. Mrs. Onassis was properly found to be a public figure and thus subject to news coverage. [ ] Nonetheless, Galella's action went far beyond the reasonable bounds of news gathering. When weighed against the *de minimis* public importance of the daily activities of the defendant, Galella's constant surveillance, his obtrusive and intruding presence, was unwarranted and unreasonable. If there were any doubt in our minds, Galella's inexcusable conduct toward defendant's minor children would resolve it.

Galella does not seriously dispute the court's finding of tortious conduct. Rather, he sets up the First Amendment as a wall of immunity protecting newsmen from any liability for their conduct while gathering news. There is no such scope to the First Amendment right. Crimes and torts committed in news gathering are not protected. [ ] There is no threat to a free press in requiring its agents to act within the law.

. . .

Injunctive relief is appropriate. Galella has stated his intention to continue his coverage of defendant so long as she is newsworthy, and his continued harassment even while the temporary restraining orders were in effect indicate that no voluntary change in this technique can be expected.

---

10. The court's findings on credibility are indeed broad, but they are supported in the record. Galella demonstrated a galling lack of respect for the truth and gave no indication of any consciousness of the meaning of the oath he had taken. Not only did he admit blatantly lying in his testimony, he admitted attempting to have other witnesses lie for him.

11. Harassment is a criminal offense [in New York] when with intent to harass a person follows another in a public place, inflicts physical contact or engages in any annoying conduct without legitimate cause. Galella was found to have engaged in this proscribed conduct. Conduct sufficient to invoke criminal liability for harassment may be the basis for private action. [ ]

New York courts have found similar conduct sufficient to support a claim for injunctive relief. [   ]

The injunction, however, is broader than is required to protect the defendant.   Relief must be tailored to protect Mrs. Onassis from the "paparazzo" attack which distinguishes Galella's behavior from that of other photographers; it should not unnecessarily infringe on reasonable efforts to "cover" defendant.   Therefore, we modify the court's order to prohibit only (1) any approach within twenty-five (25) feet of defendant or any touching of the person of the defendant Jacqueline Onassis; (2) any blocking of her movement in public places and thoroughfares; (3) any act foreseeably or reasonably calculated to place the life and safety of defendant in jeopardy; and (4) any conduct which would reasonably be foreseen to harass, alarm, or frighten the defendant.

Any further restriction on Galella's taking and selling pictures of defendant for news coverage is, however, improper and unwarranted by the evidence. [   ]

Likewise, we affirm the grant of injunctive relief to the government modified to prohibit any action interfering with Secret Service agents' protective duties.   Galella thus may be enjoined from (a) entering the children's schools or play areas; (b) engaging in action calculated or reasonably foreseen to place the children's safety or well being in jeopardy, or which would threaten or create physical injury; (c) taking any action which could reasonably be foreseen to harass, alarm, or frighten the children; and (d) from approaching within thirty (30) feet of the children.

As modified, the relief granted fully allows Galella the opportunity to photograph and report on Mrs. Onassis' public activities.   Any prior restraint on news gathering is minuscule and fully supported by the findings.

.   .   .

■ TIMBERS, CIRCUIT JUDGE [dissented from the reduction of the distance limits imposed by the trial judge].

.   .   .

NOTES AND QUESTIONS

1. In 1982, Galella was found guilty of 12 violations of the earlier order for taking photographs within 25 feet of Mrs. Onassis.   The judge suspended a fine of $120,000 when Galella agreed to pay the $10,000 in legal fees incurred by Onassis and agreed never again to photograph her. Galella was told that if he should renege, the judge would revive the $10,000 fine or impose a six-month jail sentence for each violation. N.Y.L.J., Mar. 25, 1982 at 1. See Galella v. Onassis, 533 F.Supp. 1076.

2. The court's analysis was affected by the fact that New York law controlled and the New York statute made it difficult to press a direct privacy claim.   But the court in an omitted footnote suggested that the New York courts would not read the statute to preclude the judicial development of an action that treated unjustified intrusion into one's solitude as an actionable tort. The court thought the statute was directed only to liability for publishing as opposed to gathering activities. Nonetheless, the court did not need to reach the question since it found liability on clearer grounds.

3. Might § 652B of the Second Restatement, p. 1078, supra, apply to Galella's actions?

4. The court observes that the plaintiff is a "public figure." What is the significance of that in this type of case? What if the plaintiff was an ordinary citizen whose pretty face attracted Galella—and the publications that purchased his photographs?

5. In 1975, it was disclosed that a reporter had been sifting through the contents of garbage cans outside the home of Secretary of State Henry Kissinger. If the cans were on the public sidewalk waiting to be emptied by the garbage collectors, has the reporter committed any tort? In a very short editorial, Editor & Publisher, July 19, 1975, at 6, attacked the practice: "Pawing through someone else's garbage is a revolting exercise and doing it in the name of journalism makes it none the less so."

In California v. Greenwood, 486 U.S. 35 (1988), the Court rejected a claim that criminal defendants had a reasonable expectation of privacy with respect to trash that was searched by police after the defendants had placed it on the street for collection. Writing for a six-member majority, Justice White said, "It is common knowledge that plastic garbage bags left on or at the side of a public street are readily accessible to animals, children, scavengers, snoops, and other members of the public. . . . Accordingly, having deposited their garbage in an area particularly suited for public inspection and . . . for the express purpose of having strangers take it, [ ] respondents could have had no reasonable expectation of privacy in the inculpatory items that they discarded."

6. *Stalking.* Recently, courts and legislatures have begun developing sanctions against "stalking." In addition to criminal sanctions, some states have developed civil remedies. Calif.Civ.Code § 1708.7 requires the plaintiff to show that the defendant (1) engaged in a "pattern of conduct the intent of which was to follow, alarm, or harass" the plaintiff, (2) as a result of which the plaintiff "reasonably feared for his or her safety, or the safety of an immediate family member," and (3) that the defendant either violated a restraining order, or made a "credible threat with the intent to place the plaintiff in reasonable fear for his or her safety, or the safety of an immediate family member and, on at least one occasion, the plaintiff clearly and definitively demanded that the defendant cease and abate the pattern of conduct and that the defendant persisted in his or pattern of conduct." Damages and an injunction are available. Would this have been useful to the plaintiff in *Galella v. Onassis*? For common law liability for stalking, see Summers v. Bailey, 55 F.3d 1564 (11th Cir.1995)(seller of store liable under Florida law for stalking buyer in an attempt to regain the store).

Desnick v. American Broadcasting Companies, Inc.

United States Court of Appeals, Seventh Circuit, 1995.
44 F.3d 1345.

[The plaintiffs, two doctors and the ophthalmic clinic known as the "Desnick Eye Center" at which they worked, appeal from the dismissal of their suit against the ABC television network, a producer of the ABC program PrimeTime Live named Entine, and the program's main reporter, Donaldson. The complaint alleged that Entine told Dr. Desnick, the clinic's owner—who is not a plaintiff in this case—that he wanted to do a segment on cataract practice; that it would not involve "ambush" interviews or "undercover" surveillance, and that it would be "fair and balanced." Plaintiff permitted an ABC crew to film an operation "live" and to interview personnel in the Chicago office. Plaintiff Clinic alleged that unbeknownst to it, Entine dispatched persons who posed as patients with concealed cameras to other Desnick eye centers in Indiana and Wisconsin where the individual doctors worked.]

■ Before POSNER, CHIEF JUDGE, and COFFEY and MANION, CIRCUIT JUDGES.

■ POSNER, CHIEF JUDGE.

. . .

The program aired on June 10. Donaldson introduces the segment by saying, "We begin tonight with the story of a so called 'big cutter,' Dr. James Desnick. . . . [I]n our undercover investigation of the big cutter you'll meet tonight, we turned up evidence that he may also be a big charger, doing unnecessary cataract surgery for the money." . . . Donaldson tells the viewer that PrimeTime Live has hired a professor of ophthalmology to examine the test patients who had been told they needed cataract surgery, and the professor tells the viewer that they didn't need it. With regard to one he says, "I think it would be near malpractice to do surgery on him." Later in the segment he denies that this could just be an honest difference of opinion between professionals.

[The court detailed other parts of the program including interviews with former staff members; interviews with some patients who reported bad results; reports that records were changed and that machines were tampered with so that patients would think that they had cataracts; and a report of an administrative proceeding charging Dr. Desnick with malpractice and deception. Also, in an "ambush" interview, Donaldson is shown accosting Desnick at O'Hare Airport: "Is it true, Doctor, that you changed medical records to show less vision than your patients actually have? We've been told, Doctor, that you've changed the glare machine so we have a different reading. Is that correct? Doctor, why won't you respond to the questions?" The court refused to dismiss the defamation claim.]

The second class of claims in this case concerns, as we said, the methods that the defendants used to create the broadcast segment. There are four such claims: that the defendants committed a trespass in insinuating the test patients into the Wisconsin and Indiana offices of the Desnick Eye Center, that they invaded the right of privacy of the Center and its doctors at those offices (specifically Glazer and Simon), that they violated federal and state statutes regulating electronic surveillance, and that they committed fraud by gaining access to the Chicago office by means of a false promise that they would present a "fair and balanced" picture of the Center's operations and would not use "ambush" interviews or undercover surveillance.

To enter upon another's land without consent is a trespass. The force of this rule has, it is true, been diluted somewhat by concepts of privilege and of implied consent. But there is no journalists' privilege to trespass. [ ]; Le Mistral, Inc. v. Columbia Broadcasting System, 61 A.D.2d 491, 402 N.Y.S.2d 815 (1978). And there can be no implied consent in any nonfictitious sense of the term when express consent is procured by a misrepresentation or a misleading omission. The Desnick Eye Center would not have agreed to the entry of the test patients into its offices had it known they wanted eye examinations only in order to gather material for a television expose of the Center and that they were going to make secret videotapes of the examinations. Yet some cases, illustrated by Martin v. Fidelity & Casualty Co., 421 So.2d 109, 111 (Ala.1982), deem consent effective even though it was procured by fraud. There must be something to this surprising result. Without it a restaurant critic could not conceal his identity when he ordered a meal, or a browser pretend to be interested in merchandise that he could not afford to buy. Dinner guests would be trespassers if they were false friends who never would have been invited had the host known their true character, and a consumer who in an effort to bargain down an automobile dealer falsely claimed to be able to buy the same car elsewhere at a lower price would be a trespasser in the dealer's showroom. Some of these might be classified as privileged trespasses, designed to promote competition. Others might be thought justified by some kind of implied consent—the restaurant critic for example might point by way of analogy to the use of the "fair use" defense by book reviewers charged with copyright infringement and argue that the restaurant industry as a whole would be injured if restaurants could exclude critics. But most such efforts at rationalization would be little better than evasions. The fact is that consent to an entry is often given legal effect even though the entrant has intentions that if known to the owner of the property would cause him for perfectly understandable and generally ethical or at least lawful reasons to revoke his consent.

The law's willingness to give effect to consent procured by fraud is not limited to the tort of trespass. The Restatement gives the example of a man who obtains consent to sexual intercourse by promising a woman $100, yet (unbeknownst to her, of course) he pays her with a counterfeit bill and intended to do so from the start. The man is not guilty of battery, even though unconsented to sexual intercourse is a battery. Restatement (Second) of Torts sec. 892B, illustration 9, pp. 373–74 (1979). Yet we know that to conceal the fact that one has a venereal disease transforms "consensual" intercourse into battery. [ ] Seduction, standardly effected by false promises of love, is not rape, [ ]; intercourse under the pretense of rendering medical or psychiatric treatment is, at least in most states. [ ]

It certainly is battery. [ ] Trespass presents close parallels. If a homeowner opens his door to a purported meter reader who is in fact nothing of the sort—just a busybody curious about the interior of the home—the homeowner's consent to his entry is not a defense to a suit for trespass. [ ] And likewise if a competitor gained entry to a business firm's premises posing as a customer but in fact hoping to steal the firm's trade secrets. [ ]

How to distinguish the two classes of case—the seducer from the medical impersonator, the restaurant critic from the meter reader impersonator? The answer can have nothing to do with fraud; there is fraud in all the cases. It has to do with the interest that the torts in question, battery and trespass, protect. The one protects the inviolability of the person, the other the inviolability of the person's property. The woman who is seduced wants to have sex with her seducer, and the restaurant owner wants to have customers. The woman who is victimized by the medical impersonator has no desire to have sex with her doctor; she wants medical treatment. And the homeowner victimized by the phony meter reader does not want strangers in his house unless they have authorized service functions. The dealer's objection to the customer who claims falsely to have a lower price from a competing dealer is not to the physical presence of the customer, but to the fraud that he is trying to perpetuate. The lines are not bright—they are not even inevitable. They are the traces of the old forms of action, which have resulted in a multitude of artificial distinctions in modern law. But that is nothing new.

There was no invasion in the present case of any of the specific interests that the tort of trespass seeks to protect. The test patients entered offices that were open to anyone expressing a desire for ophthalmic services and videotaped physicians engaged in professional, not personal, communications with strangers (the testers themselves). The activities of the offices were not disrupted, as in [ ], another case of gaining entry by false pretenses. See also Le Mistral, Inc. v. Columbia Broadcasting System, [ ]. Nor was there any "inva[sion of] a person's private space," [ ], as in our hypothetical meter reader case, as in the famous case of De May v. Roberts, 46 Mich. 160, 9 N.W. 146 (1881)(where a doctor, called to the plaintiff's home to deliver her baby, brought along with him a friend who was curious to see a birth but was not a medical doctor, and represented the friend to be his medical assistant), as in one of its numerous modern counterparts, Miller v. National Broadcasting Co., 232 Cal.Rptr. 668, 679 (Ct.App.1986), and as in Dietemann v. Time, Inc., 449 F.2d 245 (9th Cir.1971), on which the plaintiffs in our case rely. *Dietemann* involved a home. True, the portion invaded was an office, where the plaintiff performed quack healing of nonexistent ailments. The parallel to this case is plain enough, but there is a difference. Dietemann was not in business, and did not advertise his services or charge for them. His quackery was private.

No embarrassingly intimate details of anybody's life were publicized in the present case. There was no eavesdropping on a private conversation;

the testers recorded their own conversations with the Desnick Eye Center's physicians. There was no violation of the doctor patient privilege. There was no theft, or intent to steal, trade secrets; no disruption of decorum, of peace and quiet; no noisy or distracting demonstrations. Had the testers been undercover FBI agents, there would have been no violation of the Fourth Amendment, because there would have been no invasion of a legally protected interest in property or privacy. [   ] "Testers" who pose as prospective home buyers in order to gather evidence of housing discrimination are not trespassers even if they are private persons not acting under color of law. [   ] The situation of the defendants' "testers" is analogous. Like testers seeking evidence of violation of antidiscrimination laws, the defendants' test patients gained entry into the plaintiffs' premises by misrepresenting their purposes (more precisely by a misleading omission to disclose those purposes). But the entry was not invasive in the sense of infringing the kind of interest of the plaintiffs that the law of trespass protects; it was not an interference with the ownership or possession of land. We need not consider what if any difference it would make if the plaintiffs had festooned the premises with signs forbidding the entry of testers or other snoops. Perhaps none, [   ], but that is an issue for another day.

What we have said largely disposes of two other claims: infringement of the right of privacy, and illegal wiretapping. The right of privacy embraces several distinct interests, but the only ones conceivably involved here are the closely related interests in concealing intimate personal facts and in preventing intrusion into legitimately private activities, such as phone conversations. [   ] As we have said already, no intimate personal facts concerning the two individual plaintiffs (remember that Dr. Desnick himself is not a plaintiff) were revealed; and the only conversations that were recorded were conversations with the testers themselves. [   ]

The federal and state wiretapping statutes that the plaintiffs invoke allow one party to a conversation to record the conversation unless his purpose in doing so is to commit a crime or a tort or (in the case of the state, but not the federal, law) to do "other injurious acts." 18 U.S.C. § 2511(2)(d); [   ]. The defendants did not order the camera armed testers into the Desnick Eye Center's premises in order to commit a crime or tort. Maybe the program as it was eventually broadcast was tortious, for we have said that the defamation count was dismissed prematurely. But there is no suggestion that the defendants sent the testers into the Wisconsin and Indiana offices for the purpose of defaming the plaintiffs by charging tampering with the glare machine. The purpose, by the plaintiffs' own account, was to see whether the Center's physicians would recommend cataract surgery on the testers. By the same token it was not to injure the Desnick Eye Center, unless the public exposure of misconduct is an "injurious act" within the meaning of the Wisconsin statute. Telling the world the truth about a Medicare fraud is hardly what the framers of the statute could have had in mind in forbidding a person to record his own conversations if he was trying to commit an "injurious act." [   ]

Last is the charge of fraud in the defendants' gaining entry to the Chicago office and being permitted while there to interview staff and film a cataract operation, and in their obtaining the Desnick Eye Center's informational videotape. [The court held that under the unusual law of Illinois, promissory fraud was not actionable unless it was part of a scheme to defraud. Since that did not exist here there was no basis for liability. Nor did harm flow from the alleged fraud.]

One further point about the claims concerning the making of the program segment, as distinct from the content of the segment itself, needs to be made. The Supreme Court in the name of the First Amendment has hedged about defamation suits, even when not brought by public figures, with many safeguards designed to protect a vigorous market in ideas and opinions. Today's "tabloid" style investigative television reportage, conducted by networks desperate for viewers in an increasingly competitive television market [ ], constitutes—although it is often shrill, one sided, and offensive, and sometimes defamatory—an important part of that market. It is entitled to all the safeguards with which the Supreme Court has surrounded liability for defamation. And it is entitled to them regardless of the name of the tort, see, e.g., Hustler Magazine, Inc. v. Falwell, 485 U.S. 46 (1988), and, we add, regardless of whether the tort suit is aimed at the content of the broadcast or the production of the broadcast. If the broadcast itself does not contain actionable defamation, and no established rights are invaded in the process of creating it (for the media have no general immunity from tort or contract liability, [.]), then the target has no legal remedy even if the investigatory tactics used by the network are surreptitious, confrontational, unscrupulous, and ungentlemanly. In this case, there may have been—it is too early to tell—an actionable defamation, and if so the plaintiffs have a remedy. But none of their established rights under either state law or the federal wiretapping law was infringed by the making, as opposed to the dissemination, of the broadcast segment of which they complain, with the possible and possibly abandoned exception of contract law.

Affirmed in Part, Reversed in Part, and Remanded.

NOTES AND QUESTIONS

1. *Trespass.* We have explored the notion of trespass twice already. In the first instance, p. 165, supra, we considered actions for personal injury brought by entrants on land. In the second instance, p. 588, supra, we considered actions brought by land owners for invasions of their possessory interests. How does the trespass action in this case differ?

2. In the cited *Le Mistral* case, employees of WCBS–TV were ordered to take a camera crew to visit restaurants that had been cited for health code violations. Defendants entered plaintiff's restaurant at lunch time "with cameras rolling" and used bright lights that were necessary to get the pictures. The jury could find that the crew entered "in a noisy and obtrusive fashion and following the loud commands of the reporter, Rich, to photograph the patrons dining." Some patrons left without paying their bills. Others "hid their faces behind napkins or table cloths or hid themselves beneath tables." This was held an actionable trespass. When Rich claimed that the restaurant was a place of public accommodation, the court responded that defendants admitted that the crew "did not seek to avail themselves of the plaintiff's 'accommodation'; they had no intention of purchasing food or drink."

How does this case fit into the *Desnick* court's analysis?

3. In the cited *Dietemann* case, a reporter and photographer went to the entrance of plaintiff's home and falsely stated that one of them needed advice and that they had been referred by someone. After being admitted to plaintiff's home and taken into his den, the defendants secretly taped and photographed as the plaintiff waved a wand over the "patient" and advised her that she had a lump in her breast because she had eaten rancid butter 11 years, 9 months and 7 days earlier. Photos and a story appeared in defendant's magazine.

The court stated that the initial entry was not actionable because "one who invites another to his home or office takes a risk that the visitor may not be what he seems, and that the visitor may repeat all he hears and observes when he leaves." (Why is that?) But the surreptitious use of tape recorders and cameras was actionable. One "does not and should not be required to take the risk that what is heard and seen will be transmitted by photograph or recording, or in our modern world, in full living color and hi-fi to the public at large or to any segment of it that the visitor may select. A different rule could have a most pernicious effect upon the dignity of man and it would surely lead to guarded conversations and conduct where candor is most valued, e.g., in the case of doctors and lawyers."

How does this case fit into the *Desnick* court's analysis? Is there a difference between a tape recorder, which preserves the words actually spoken, and a camera, which creates and preserves visual images that the reporters could have described afterward only verbally and only from memory?

4. Should it be relevant that *Le Mistral* was brought on a trespass theory and that *Dietemann* was brought on a privacy theory?

5. In *Desnick* why did the court's disposition of the trespass claim also dispose of the privacy claim?

6. Restatement (Second) of Torts § 892B provides that consent to the conduct of another is effective "for all consequences of the conduct and for the invasion of any interests resulting from it" unless within the limitation of subsection (2):

> If the person consenting to the conduct of another is induced to consent by a substantial mistake concerning the nature of the invasion of his interests or the extent of the harm to be expected from it and the mistake is known to the other or is induced by the other's misrepresen-

tation, the consent is not effective for the unexpected invasion or harm.

Is this relevant in *Desnick*? To Dietemann's misunderstanding about who sent the visitors and why they were there?

7. *Wiretapping.* Why does the wiretapping claim fail in *Desnick*? The federal statute is less protective than some state provisions because it exempts from the ban any conversation in which one party records the contents or in which one party authorizes a third party to record it.

Florida made it criminal for any "person not acting under color of law" to intercept a wire or oral communication unless all parties to the communication had given prior consent. Reporters and others challenged the statute, claiming that the use of concealed recording equipment was essential to investigative reporting for three reasons: it aided accuracy of reporting; persons being interviewed would not be candid if they knew they were being recorded; and the recording provided corroboration in case of suit for defamation.

The Florida Supreme Court upheld the statute's constitutionality. The statute allows "each party to a conversation to have an expectation of privacy from interception by another party to the conversation. It does not exclude any source from the press, intrude upon the activities of the news media in contacting sources, prevent the parties to the communication from consenting to the recording, or restrict the publication of any information gained from the communication. First Amendment rights do not include a constitutional right to corroborate news gathering activities when the legislature has statutorily recognized the private rights of individuals."

The court quoted *Dietemann's* concern about the effect on the "dignity of man." In response to the argument that secret recording may be the only way to get credible information about crime, the court stated that protection against intrusion might extend even to a person "reasonably suspected of committing a crime." Shevin v. Sunbeam Television Corp., 351 So.2d 723 (Fla.1977).

The Supreme Court dismissed the appeal by the press for want of a substantial federal question, 435 U.S. 920 (1978). Justices Brennan, White and Blackmun would have noted probable jurisdiction and set the case for oral argument.

8. In Ribas v. Clark, 38 Cal.3d 355, 696 P.2d 637, 212 Cal.Rptr. 143 (1985), a wife asked the defendant to listen in on an extension phone as she talked to her estranged husband. The husband learned about the episode when the defendant testified in an arbitration hearing about matters she overheard. He then sued for violation of Calif.Penal Code § 631(a), which provides in relevant part for punishment of any person "who . . . intentionally taps, or makes any unauthorized connection . . . with any . . . telephone wire, line, cable or instrument, . . . or who willfully and without the consent of all parties to the communication, or in any unauthorized manner, reads, or attempts to read, or to learn the contents or meaning of any message . . . while the same is in transit . . . , or is being sent from, or received at any place within this state. . . ."

Section 637.2 provided a civil action against violators for the greater of $3,000 or trebled actual damages. The court upheld the complaint. The statute was read broadly to bar "far more than illicit wiretapping," including the recording of a conversation without the other's consent:

> While one who imparts private information risks the betrayal of his confidence by the other party, a substantial distinction has been recognized between the secondhand repetition of the contents of a conversation and its simultaneous dissemination to an unannounced second auditor, whether that auditor be a person or mechanical device. [ ]
>
> As one commentator has noted, such secret monitoring denies the speaker an important aspect of privacy of communication—the right to control the nature and extent of the firsthand dissemination of his statement. [ ] Partly because of this factor, the Privacy Act has been read to require the assent of all parties to a communication before another may listen.

9. In Cassidy v. American Broadcasting Cos., 60 Ill.App.3d 831, 377 N.E.2d 126 (1978), plaintiff, an undercover policeman, was sent to a massage parlor. After paying $30 he was escorted to a room by a model to see " 'de-luxe' lingerie modeling." Upon entering he noticed camera lights and remarked that the lights made the room quite warm. He asked, "What are we on, TV?" The model replied "Yes, we're making a movie." As plaintiff reclined on the bed watching the model change her lingerie several times, he made suggestive remarks and advances. He then arrested the model for solicitation. The entire scene was in fact being photographed from an adjacent room by a local television station through a two-way mirror, because the manager of the parlor had complained that police were harassing him.

Plaintiff sued the station for damages. One claim was based on a tort duty derived from an eavesdropping statute similar to Florida's. The court held the statute inapplicable because only pictures but no sounds were picked up from the room. In any event, the plaintiff apparently did not intend his remarks to be private because he knew that someone might be making a movie of his conduct. He testified his actions were in the line of duty as an officer and that if the model wished to sell him a completed film he would use it as evidence in his investigation. Plaintiff had no expectation of privacy.

The court rejected an intrusion claim on the ground that plaintiff was a "public official performing a laudable public service and discharging a public duty." In such cases, no privacy interest exists.

10. *Measuring Damages.* Several cases have involved the question whether the liability imposed for tortious conduct while gathering news extends to damages for the article that is subsequently published. Notice that it is one thing to say that the truth of the resulting publication or its social utility is not a defense to the initial tortious behavior. It is quite different to argue that the plaintiff may use the subsequent article to establish recoverable harm proximately flowing from the initial tort. *Dietemann* suggests that harm from the improperly obtained publication may be included as part of the damages. *Dodd* disagrees.

See King and Muto, Compensatory Damages for Newsgatherer Torts: Toward a Workable Standard, 14 U.C.D.L.Rev. 919 (1981).

D.   APPROPRIATION

"Appropriation" claims involve the attempts of celebrities to control the exploitation of their names, likenesses, and fame and any pecuniary value resulting therefrom. The claim was explicitly recognized for the first time in Haelan Laboratories v. Topps Chewing Gum, Inc., 202 F.2d 866 (2d Cir.), cert. denied 346 U.S. 816 (1953), in which the court spoke of the need to protect the proprietary interest of celebrities in their names and likenesses. *Haelan* involved a famous baseball player who had assigned the right to the use of his name and likeness to a bubblegum manufacturer for the promotion of its products. A competing manufacturer subsequently induced the ballplayer to enter into a similar contract with full knowledge of the preexisting agreement. The court recognized the ballplayer's right to control commercial use of his name and likeness as a method through which such misappropriation could be prevented.

Since *Haelan,* similar claims have been recognized by most states. Although some states have adopted the action as a separate common law remedy, most have developed it as an offshoot of either the common law right of privacy or of a privacy statute.

Is the claim a type of privacy, or should it properly be conceptualized as a distinct tort? One inherent difference between it and the more traditional privacy rights is that privacy protects against undesired public intrusion into one's personal life, while the right of publicity is usually invoked to protect against persons who would profit by taking, without compensation, something the celebrity would prefer to sell. For example, a famous person may not generally object to commercial exploitation of his or her name or other feature but may want to be compensated for it. But some cases appear to go beyond the desire for compensation. See, e.g., Martin Luther King, Jr., Center for Social Change, Inc. v. American Heritage Products, Inc., 250 Ga. 135, 296 S.E.2d 697 (1982), in which plaintiff successfully stopped defendant from making plastic busts of the late Dr. King. Could plaintiff have stopped a "recognized" painter from painting a portrait of Dr. King?

Whether or not the claim for appropriation is considered as a subset of privacy rights has important implications for its judicial development. For example, it is unclear whether it survives the death of the celebrity in whom the right is based; that is, whether a celebrity's heirs or assigns can profit from any such right after the famous person has died. Courts that have found the right to be descendible have analogized it to an ordinary property right or a copyright, both of which are inheritable. Courts that have found no descendible right have emphasized the personal nature of the claim, the analogy to rights of privacy, which are not inheritable, and the line-drawing difficulties inherent in any development of a right that survives the death of the celebrity.

Zacchini v. Scripps–Howard Broadcasting Co.

Supreme Court of the United States, 1977.
433 U.S. 562, 97 S.Ct. 2849, 53 L.Ed.2d 965.

■ MR. JUSTICE WHITE delivered the opinion of the Court.

Petitioner, Hugo Zacchini, is an entertainer. He performs a "human cannonball" act in which he is shot from a cannon into a net some 200 feet away. Each performance occupies some 15 seconds. In August and September 1972, petitioner was engaged to perform his act on a regular basis at the Geauga County Fair in Burton, Ohio. He performed in a fenced area, surrounded by grandstands, at the fair grounds. Members of the public attending the fair were not charged a separate admission fee to observe his act.

On August 30, a freelance reporter for Scripps–Howard Broadcasting Co., the operator of a television broadcasting station and respondent in this case, attended the fair. He carried a small movie camera. Petitioner noticed the reporter and asked him not to film the performance. The reporter did not do so on that day; but on the instructions of the producer of respondent's daily newscast, he returned the following day and video-taped the entire act. This film clip, approximately 15 seconds in length, was shown on the 11 o'clock news program that night, together with favorable commentary.[1]

Petitioner then brought this action for damages, alleging that he is "engaged in the entertainment business," that the act he performs is one "invented by his father and . . . performed only by his family for the last fifty years," that respondent "showed and commercialized the film of his act without his consent," and that such conduct was an "unlawful appropriation of plaintiff's professional property." App. 4–5. Respondent answered and moved for summary judgment, which was granted by the trial court.

. . .

1. The script of the commentary accompanying the film clip read as follows:

"This . . . now . . . is the story of a *true spectator* sport . . . the sport of human cannonballing . . . in fact, the great *Zacchini* is about the only human cannonball around, these days . . . just hap-pens that, *where* he is, is the Great Geauga County Fair, in Burton . . . and believe me, although it's not a *long* act, it's a thriller . . . and you real-ly need to see it *in person* . . . to appreciate it. . . ." (Emphasis in original.)

.   .   .   Insofar as the Ohio Supreme Court held that the First and Fourteenth Amendments of the United States Constitution required judgment for respondent, we reverse the judgment of that court.

.   .   .

Even if the judgment in favor of respondent must nevertheless be understood as ultimately resting on Ohio law, it appears that at the very least the Ohio court felt compelled by what it understood to be federal constitutional considerations to construe and apply its own law in the manner it did.   In this event, we have jurisdiction and should decide the federal issue; for if the state court erred in its understanding of our cases and of the First and Fourteenth Amendments we should so declare, leaving the state court free to decide the privilege issue solely as a matter of Ohio law.   [   ]   If the Supreme Court of Ohio "held as it did because it felt under compulsion of federal law as enunciated by this Court so to hold, it should be relieved of that compulsion.   It should be freed to decide   .   .   . these suits according to its own local law."   [   ]

The Ohio Supreme Court relied heavily on Time, Inc. v. Hill, [   ], but that case does not mandate a media privilege to televise a performer's entire act without his consent.   Involved in Time, Inc. v. Hill was a claim under the New York "Right of Privacy" statute that Life Magazine, in the course of reviewing a new play, had connected the play with a long-past incident involving petitioner and his family and had falsely described their experience and conduct at that time.   The complaint sought damages for humiliation and suffering flowing from these nondefamatory falsehoods that allegedly invaded Hill's privacy.   The Court held, however, that the opening of a new play linked to an actual incident was a matter of public interest and that Hill could not recover without showing that the Life report was knowingly false or was published with reckless disregard for the truth—the same rigorous standard that had been applied in New York Times Co. v. Sullivan [   ].

Time, Inc. v. Hill, which was hotly contested and decided by a divided Court, involved an entirely different tort from the "right of publicity" recognized by the Ohio Supreme Court.   .   .   .

The differences between these two torts are important.   First, the State's interests in providing a cause of action in each instance are different.   "The interest protected" in permitting recovery for placing the plaintiff in a false light "is clearly that of reputation, with the same overtones of mental distress as in defamation."   Prosser, [Privacy, 48 Calif.L.Rev. 383, 400 (1960)].   By contrast, the State's interest in permitting a "right of publicity" is in protecting the proprietary interest of the individual in his act in part to encourage such entertainment.   As we later note, the State's interest is closely analogous to the goals of patent and copyright law, focusing on the right of the individual to reap the reward of his endeavors and having little to do with protecting feelings or reputation.   Second, the two torts differ in the degree to which they intrude on dissemination of information to the public.   In "false light" cases the only way to protect the interests involved is to attempt to minimize publication of the damaging matter, while in "right of publicity" cases the only question is who gets to do the publishing. An entertainer such as petitioner usually has no objection to the widespread publication of his act as long as he gets the commercial benefit of such publication. Indeed, in the present case petitioner did not seek to enjoin the broadcast of his act; he simply sought compensation for the broadcast in the form of damages.

Nor does it appear that our later cases such as [*Rosenbloom; Gertz;* and *Firestone*] require or furnish substantial support for the Ohio court's privilege ruling. These cases, like *New York Times,* emphasize the protection extended to the press by the First Amendment in defamation cases, particularly when suit is brought by a public official or a public figure. None of them involve an alleged appropriation by the press of a right of publicity existing under state law.

Moreover, Time, Inc. v. Hill, New York Times, [*Rosenbloom*], *Gertz,* and *Firestone* all involved the reporting of events; in none of them was there an attempt to broadcast or publish an entire act for which the performer ordinarily gets paid. It is evident, and there is no claim here to the contrary, that petitioner's state-law right of publicity would not serve to prevent respondent from reporting the newsworthy facts about petitioner's act. Wherever the line in particular situations is to be drawn between media reports that are protected and those that are not, we are quite sure that the First and Fourteenth Amendments do not immunize the media when they broadcast a performer's entire act without his consent. The Constitution no more prevents a State from requiring respondent to compensate petitioner for broadcasting his act on television than it would privilege respondent to film and broadcast a copyrighted dramatic work without liability to the copyright owner, [ ], or to film and broadcast a prize fight, [ ], or a baseball game, [ ], where the promoters or the participants had other plans for publicizing the event. There are ample reasons for reaching this conclusion.

The broadcast of a film of petitioner's entire act poses a substantial threat to the economic value of that performance. As the Ohio court recognized, this act is the product of petitioner's own talents and energy, the end result of much time, effort, and expense. Much of its economic value lies in the "right of exclusive control over the publicity given to his performance"; if the public can see the act free on television, it will be less willing to pay to see it at the fair.[12] The effect of a public broadcast of the performance is similar to preventing petitioner from charging an admission fee. . . . Moreover, the broadcast of petitioner's entire performance, unlike the unauthorized use of another's name for purposes of trade or the incidental use of a name or picture by the press, goes to the heart of

---

12. It is possible, of course, that respondent's news broadcast increased the value of petitioner's performance by stimulating the public's interest in seeing the act live. In these circumstances, petitioner would not be able to prove damages and thus would not recover. But petitioner has alleged that the broadcast injured him to the extent of $25,000. App. 5, and we think the State should be allowed to authorize compensation of this injury if proved.

petitioner's ability to earn a living as an entertainer. Thus, in this case, Ohio has recognized what may be the strongest case for a "right of publicity"—involving, not the appropriation of an entertainer's reputation to enhance the attractiveness of a commercial product, but the appropriation of the very activity by which the entertainer acquired his reputation in the first place.

Of course, Ohio's decision to protect petitioner's right of publicity here rests on more than a desire to compensate the performer for the time and effort invested in his act; the protection provides an economic incentive for him to make the investment required to produce a performance of interest to the public. This same consideration underlies the patent and copyright laws long enforced by this Court. . . .

There is no doubt that entertainment, as well as news, enjoys First Amendment protection. It is also true that entertainment itself can be important news. Time, Inc., v. Hill. But it is important to note that neither the public nor respondent will be deprived of the benefit of petitioner's performance as long as his commercial stake in his act is appropriately recognized. Petitioner does not seek to enjoin the broadcast of his performance; he simply wants to be paid for it. Nor do we think that a state-law damages remedy against respondent would represent a species of liability without fault contrary to the letter or spirit of Gertz v. Robert Welch, Inc., [   ]. Respondent knew exactly that petitioner objected to televising his act but nevertheless displayed the entire film.

We conclude that although the State of Ohio may as a matter of its own law privilege the press in the circumstances of this case, the First and Fourteenth Amendments do not require it to do so.

Reversed.

■ Mr. Justice Powell, with whom Mr. Justice Brennan and Mr. Justice Marshall join, dissenting.

Disclaiming any attempt to do more than decide the narrow case before us, the Court reverses the decision of the Supreme Court of Ohio based on repeated incantation of a single formula: "a performer's entire act." The holding today is summed up in one sentence:

> "Wherever the line in particular situations is to be drawn between media reports that are protected and those that are not, we are quite sure that the First and Fourteenth Amendments do not immunize the media when they broadcast a performer's entire act without his consent."

I doubt that this formula provides a standard clear enough even for resolution of this case.[1] In any event, I am not persuaded that the Court's

---

1. Although the record is not explicit, it is unlikely that the "act" commenced abruptly with the explosion that launched petitioner on his way, ending with the landing in the net a few seconds later. One may assume that the actual firing was preceded by some fanfare, possibly stretching over several minutes, to heighten the audience's anticipation: introduction of the performer, description of the uniqueness and danger, last-minute

opinion is appropriately sensitive to the First Amendment values at stake, and I therefore dissent.

Although the Court would draw no distinction, [ ] I do not view respondent's action as comparable to unauthorized commercial broadcasts of sporting events, theatrical performances, and the like where the broadcaster keeps the profits. There is no suggestion here that respondent made any such use of the film. Instead, it simply reported on what petitioner concedes to be a newsworthy event, in a way hardly surprising for a television station—by means of film coverage. The report was part of an ordinary daily news program, consuming a total of 15 seconds. It is a routine example of the press fulfilling the informing function so vital to our system.

The Court's holding that the station's ordinary news report may give rise to substantial liability has disturbing implications, for the decision could lead to a degree of media self-censorship. [ ] Hereafter whenever a television news editor is unsure whether certain film footage received from a camera crew might be held to portray an "entire act," he may decline coverage—even of clearly newsworthy events—or confine the broadcast to watered-down verbal reporting, perhaps with an occasional still picture. The public is then the loser. This is hardly the kind of news reportage that the First Amendment is meant to foster. [ ]

In my view the First Amendment commands a different analytical starting point from the one selected by the Court. Rather than begin with a quantitative analysis of the performer's behavior—is this or is this not his entire act?—we should direct initial attention to the actions of the news media: what use did the station make of the film footage? When a film is used, as here, for a routine portion of a regular news program, I would hold that the First Amendment protects the station from a "right of publicity" or "appropriation" suit, absent a strong showing by the plaintiff that the news broadcast was a subterfuge or cover for private or commercial exploitation.[4]

. . . In a suit like the one before us, however, the plaintiff does not complain about the fact of exposure to the public, but rather about its timing or manner. He welcomes some publicity, but seeks to retain control over means and manner as a way to maximize for himself the monetary benefits that flow from such publication. But having made the matter

---

checking of the apparatus, and entry into the cannon, all accompanied by suitably ominous commentary from the master of ceremonies. If this is found to be the case on remand, then respondent could not be said to have appropriated the "entire act" in its 15-second news-clip—and the Court's opinion then would afford no guidance for resolution of the case. Moreover, in future cases involving different performances, similar difficulties in determining just what constitutes the "entire act" are inevitable.

4. This case requires no detailed specification of the standards for identifying a subterfuge, since there is no claim here that respondent's news use was anything but bona fide. [ ] I would point out, however, that selling time during a news broadcast to advertisers in the customary fashion does not make for "commercial exploitation" in the sense intended here. [ ]

public—having chosen, in essence, to make it newsworthy—he cannot, consistent with the First Amendment, complain of routine news reportage. Cf. Gertz v. Robert Welch, Inc., [   ] (clarifying the different liability standards appropriate in defamation suits, depending on whether or not the plaintiff is a public figure).

Since the film clip here was undeniably treated as news and since there is no claim that the use was subterfuge, respondent's actions were constitutionally privileged. I would affirm.

[Mr. Justice Stevens dissented on the ground that he could not tell whether the Ohio Supreme Court had relied on federal constitutional issues in deciding the case. He would have remanded the case to that court "for clarification of its holding before deciding the federal constitutional issue."]

On remand, the Ohio Supreme Court took advantage of the opportunity afforded by the majority opinion and decided that nothing in the Ohio Constitution protected the behavior of the media defendant. The case was remanded for trial and for assessment of damages if liability was established. Zacchini v. Scripps–Howard Broadcasting Co., 54 Ohio St.2d 286, 376 N.E.2d 582 (1978).

NOTES AND QUESTIONS

1.   How important is it that the majority treats the 15 seconds as the "entire act"? In a case involving the televising of a figure skating championship, a telecaster argued that a short newscast drawn from hours of film would not be an "entire" act under *Zacchini*. The judge, however, said it was "conceivable that a two-minute broadcast, focused solely on the top performer of the day, would embody the essence of the commercially valuable performance, and thus could possibly be a broadcast of the entire act." The case went off on other issues. Post Newsweek Stations–Connecticut, Inc. v. Travelers Insurance Co., 510 F.Supp. 81 (D.Conn. 1981).

2.   Does *Zacchini* involve an aspect of "privacy"? Of "publicity"? Why did the defendant in *Cox Broadcasting* not have to pay for using the name of the rape victim while the defendant in *Zacchini* may have to pay for what it did?

3.   After *Zacchini*, what would happen in a case in which a street artist who survives on contributions from passersby—a mime, an accordionist, a dancer—is photographed by the local television station and shown in a story about summer diversions on the streets of the city? Is the street artist's claim as strong as Zacchini's?

4.   Promoters of entertainment and sports events normally protect their rights by controlling access to the event. Terms of admission often prohibit use of cameras or tape recorders. Broadcasting rights are protect-

ed by allowing only those who have contracted with the promoters to set up their broadcasting equipment. Performers, in turn, protect their interests through their contracts with the promoters; whether the promoter has a right to authorize a live broadcast of a concert, for example, is usually determined by the terms of the contract between the performer and the promoter.

If Zacchini did not protect his rights contractually, why should the courts provide him a remedy through tort law? The television station was permitted—probably even encouraged—by the fair officials to broadcast film of various events at the fair. Should the station be entitled to rely on that invitation without inquiring into the officials' authority to extend it?

5. Plaintiffs generally have been unsuccessful when they have tried to invoke *Zacchini* to create a cause of action not otherwise provided by the law of copyright or the tort of commercial exploitation of name or likeness. Actress Ginger Rogers relied on *Zacchini* in an attempt to prevent Federico Fellini from using the title "Ginger and Fred" for his 1986 movie about an Italian dancing couple. The district court characterized *Zacchini* as a "narrowly drawn opinion effectively limited to its facts," and distinguished it on the ground that "Ginger and Fred" did not threaten Rogers's economic viability. Rogers v. Grimaldi, 695 F.Supp. 112 (S.D.N.Y.1988), affirmed 875 F.2d 994 (2d Cir.1989).

6. Another important question is to what extent a news organization can make unauthorized use of the research and labor of a competitor either by directly copying its work or by "appropriating" the facts contained in its news release. Although the substance of news cannot be protected by common law or statutory copyright, the doctrine of unfair competition has been used to protect the gatherer of news from the direct, unauthorized reproduction of its material for commercial use. In International News Service v. Associated Press, 248 U.S. 215 (1918), I.N.S. was enjoined from copying news from A.P. bulletin boards and early editions of A.P. member newspapers until "the commercial value" of the news to the complainant and all of its members had passed. The Court found unfair competition in the taking of material acquired through the expenditure of skill, labor, and money by A.P., for the purpose of diverting "a material portion of the profit" to I.N.S. Although the Court condemned the "habitual failure" of I.N.S. to give credit to A.P. as the source of its news, the misrepresentation was not considered essential to a finding of unfair competition: "It is something more than the advantage of celebrity of which complainant is being deprived." We return to this case at p. 1157, infra.

In 1964, in two cases dealing with product imitations, the Supreme Court held that an action for unfair competition based upon the copying of an unpatentable article could not be maintained unless the copier misrepresented its goods to be originals. Sears Roebuck & Co. v. Stiffel Co., 376 U.S. 225 (1964); Compco Corp. v. Day–Brite Lighting, Inc., 376 U.S. 234 (1964). In a broad dictum, Justice Black stated that "when an article is unprotected by a patent or a copyright, state law may not forbid others to copy that article."

State courts, however, have been reluctant to abandon the misappropriation doctrine. Two years after *Sears* and *Compco*, a New York publisher of a financial newsletter was enjoined from using information about government and municipal bonds gathered by a competitor. Bond Buyer v. Dealers Digest Publishing Co., 25 App.Div.2d 158, 267 N.Y.S.2d 944 (1966). Federal courts have also been reluctant to apply the *Sears* and *Compco* decisions to the media. In a suit seeking to prohibit defendant from reproducing plaintiff's edition of an uncopyrightable book through the use of less expensive photographic processes, Grove Press, Inc. v. Collectors Publication, Inc., 264 F.Supp. 603 (C.D.Cal.1967), the court, in granting the preliminary injunction, said that "unfair appropriation of the property of a competitor is unfair competition and redressable in a situation of this kind despite the holdings in *Sears* . . . and *Compco*." These lower courts correctly anticipated that the Court would retreat from the *Sears* dictum. See Goldstein v. California, 412 U.S. 546 (1973)(states may forbid unauthorized re-recordings) and Kewanee Oil Co. v. Bicron Corp., 416 U.S. 470 (1974)(federal patent laws do not preempt state trade secret law).

White v. Samsung Electronics America, Inc.

United States Court of Appeals, Ninth Circuit, 1992.
971 F.2d 1395.
On Petition for Rehearing and Rehearing en banc 989 F.2d 1512 (9th Cir. en banc 1993).
Certiorari denied, 113 S.Ct. 2443 (1993).

■ Before: GOODWIN, PREGERSON, and ALARCON, CIRCUIT JUDGES.

■ GOODWIN, SENIOR CIRCUIT JUDGE:

This case involves a promotional "fame and fortune" dispute. In running a particular advertisement without Vanna White's permission, defendants Samsung Electronics America, Inc. (Samsung) and David Deutsch Associates, Inc. (Deutsch) attempted to capitalize on White's fame to enhance their fortune. White sued, alleging infringement of various intellectual property rights, but the district court granted summary judgment in favor of the defendants. We affirm in part, reverse in part, and remand.

Plaintiff Vanna White is the hostess of "Wheel of Fortune," one of the most popular game shows in television history. An estimated forty million people watch the program daily. Capitalizing on the fame which her participation in the show has bestowed on her, White markets her identity to various advertisers.

The dispute in this case arose out of a series of advertisements prepared for Samsung by Deutsch. The series ran in at least half a dozen publications with widespread, and in some cases national, circulation. Each of the advertisements in the series followed the same theme. Each depicted a current item from popular culture and a Samsung electronic product. Each was set in the twenty-first century and conveyed the message that the Samsung product would still be in use by that time. By hypothesizing outrageous future outcomes for the cultural items, the ads created humorous effects. For example, one lampooned current popular notions of an unhealthy diet by depicting a raw steak with the caption: "Revealed to be health food. 2010 A.D." Another depicted irreverent "news"-show host Morton Downey Jr. in front of an American flag with the caption: "Presidential candidate. 2008 A.D."

The advertisement which prompted the current dispute was for Samsung video-cassette recorders (VCRs). The ad depicted a robot, dressed in a wig, gown, and jewelry which Deutsch consciously selected to resemble White's hair and dress. The robot was posed next to a game board which is instantly recognizable as the Wheel of Fortune game show set, in a stance for which White is famous. The caption of the ad read: "Longest-running game show. 2012 A.D." Defendants referred to the ad as the "Vanna White" ad. Unlike the other celebrities used in the campaign, White neither consented to the ads nor was she paid.

Following the circulation of the robot ad, White sued Samsung and Deutsch in federal district court under: (1) California Civil Code § 3344; (2) the California common law right of publicity; and (3) § 43(a) of the Lanham Act, 15 U.S.C. § 1125(a). The district court granted summary judgment against White on each of her claims. White now appeals.

I. Section 3344

White first argues that the district court erred in rejecting her claim under section 3344. Section 3344(a) provides, in pertinent part, that "[a]ny person who knowingly uses another's name, voice, signature, photograph, or likeness, in any manner, . . . for purposes of advertising or selling, . . . without such person's prior consent . . . shall be liable for any damages sustained by the person or persons injured as a result thereof."

White argues that the Samsung advertisement used her "likeness" in contravention of section 3344. In Midler v. Ford Motor Co., 849 F.2d 460 (9th Cir.1988), this court rejected Bette Midler's section 3344 claim concerning a Ford television commercial in which a Midler "sound-alike" sang a song which Midler had made famous. In rejecting Midler's claim, this court noted that "[t]he defendants did not use Midler's name or anything else whose use is prohibited by the statute. The voice they used was [another person's], not hers. The term 'likeness' refers to a visual image not a vocal imitation." Id. at 463.

In this case, Samsung and Deutsch used a robot with mechanical features, and not, for example, a manikin molded to White's precise features. Without deciding for all purposes when a caricature or impressionistic resemblance might become a "likeness," we agree with the district court that the robot at issue here was not White's "likeness" within the meaning of section 3344. Accordingly, we affirm the court's dismissal of White's section 3344 claim.

II. Right of Publicity

White next argues that the district court erred in granting summary judgment to defendants on White's common law right of publicity claim.

In Eastwood v. Superior Court, 149 Cal.App. 409, 198 Cal.Rptr. 342 (1983), the California court of appeal stated that the common law right of publicity cause of action "may be pleaded by alleging (1) the defendant's use of the plaintiff's identity; (2) the appropriation of plaintiff's name or likeness to defendant's advantage, commercially or otherwise; (3) lack of consent; and (4) resulting injury." [ ] The district court dismissed White's claim for failure to satisfy Eastwood's second prong, reasoning that defendants had not appropriated White's "name or likeness" with their robot ad. We agree that the robot ad did not make use of White's name or likeness. However, the common law right of publicity is not so confined.

The *Eastwood* court did not hold that the right of publicity cause of action could be pleaded only by alleging an appropriation of name or likeness. Eastwood involved an unauthorized use of photographs of Clint Eastwood and of his name. Accordingly, the Eastwood court had no occasion to consider the extent beyond the use of name or likeness to which the right of publicity reaches. That court held only that the right of publicity cause of action "may be" pleaded by alleging, inter alia, appropriation of name or likeness, not that the action may be pleaded only in those terms.

The "name or likeness" formulation referred to in *Eastwood* originated not as an element of the right of publicity cause of action, but as a description of the types of cases in which the cause of action had been recognized. The source of this formulation is Prosser, Privacy, 48 Cal. L.Rev. 383, 401–07 (1960), one of the earliest and most enduring articulations of the common law right of publicity cause of action. In looking at the case law to that point, Prosser recognized that right of publicity cases involved one of two basic factual scenarios: name appropriation, and picture or other likeness appropriation. [ ]

. . .

Since Prosser's early formulation, the case law has borne out his insight that the right of publicity is not limited to the appropriation of name or likeness. In Motschenbacher v. R.J. Reynolds Tobacco Co., 498 F.2d 821 (9th Cir.1974), the defendant had used a photograph of the plaintiff's race car in a television commercial. Although the plaintiff appeared driving the car in the photograph, his features were not visible. Even though the defendant had not appropriated the plaintiff's name or likeness, this court held that plaintiff's California right of publicity claim should reach the jury.

In *Midler*, this court held that, even though the defendants had not used Midler's name or likeness, Midler had stated a claim for violation of her California common law right of publicity because "the defendants . . . for their own profit in selling their product did appropriate part of her identity" by using a Midler sound-alike. [ ]

In Carson v. Here's Johnny Portable Toilets, Inc., 698 F.2d 831 (6th Cir.1983), the defendant had marketed portable toilets under the brand name "Here's Johnny"—Johnny Carson's signature "Tonight Show" introduction—without Carson's permission. The district court had dismissed Carson's Michigan common law right of publicity claim because the defendants had not used Carson's "name or likeness." [ ] In reversing the district court, the sixth circuit found "the district court's conception of the right of publicity . . . too narrow" and held that the right was implicated because the defendant had appropriated Carson's identity by using, inter alia, the phrase "Here's Johnny." [ ].

These cases teach not only that the common law right of publicity reaches means of appropriation other than name or likeness, but that the specific means of appropriation are relevant only for determining whether the defendant has in fact appropriated the plaintiff's identity. The right of publicity does not require that appropriations of identity be accomplished through particular means to be actionable. It is noteworthy that the Midler and Carson defendants not only avoided using the plaintiff's name or likeness, but they also avoided appropriating the celebrity's voice, signature, and photograph. The photograph in *Motschenbacher* did include the plaintiff, but because the plaintiff was not visible the driver could have been an actor or dummy and the analysis in the case would have been the same.

Although the defendants in these cases avoided the most obvious means of appropriating the plaintiffs' identities, each of their actions directly implicated the commercial interests which the right of publicity is designed to protect. . . .

It is not important how the defendant has appropriated the plaintiff's identity, but whether the defendant has done so. *Motschenbacher, Midler,* and *Carson* teach the impossibility of treating the right of publicity as guarding only against a laundry list of specific means of appropriating identity. A rule which says that the right of publicity can be infringed only through the use of nine different methods of appropriating identity merely challenges the clever advertising strategist to come up with the tenth.

Indeed, if we treated the means of appropriation as dispositive in our analysis of the right of publicity, we would not only weaken the right but effectively eviscerate it. The right would fail to protect those plaintiffs most in need of its protection. Advertisers use celebrities to promote their products. The more popular the celebrity, the greater the number of people who recognize her, and the greater the visibility for the product. The identities of the most popular celebrities are not only the most attractive for advertisers, but also the easiest to evoke without resorting to obvious means such as name, likeness, or voice.

. . .

Viewed separately, the individual aspects of the advertisement in the present case say little. Viewed together, they leave little doubt about the celebrity the ad is meant to depict. The female-shaped robot is wearing a long gown, blond wig, and large jewelry. Vanna White dresses exactly like this at times, but so do many other women. The robot is in the process of turning a block letter on a game-board. Vanna White dresses like this while turning letters on a game-board but perhaps similarly attired Scrabble-playing women do this as well. The robot is standing on what looks to be the Wheel of Fortune game show set. Vanna White dresses like this, turns letters, and does this on the Wheel of Fortune game show. She is the only one. Indeed, defendants themselves referred to their ad as the "Vanna White" ad. We are not surprised.

Television and other media create marketable celebrity identity value. Considerable energy and ingenuity are expended by those who have achieved celebrity value to exploit it for profit. The law protects the celebrity's sole right to exploit this value whether the celebrity has achieved her fame out of rare ability, dumb luck, or a combination thereof. We decline Samsung and Deutch's invitation to permit the evisceration of the common law right of publicity through means as facile as those in this case. Because White has alleged facts showing that Samsung and Deutsch had appropriated her identity, the district court erred by rejecting, on summary judgment, White's common law right of publicity claim.

[The dismissal of the Lanham Act claim was reversed.]

IV. The Parody Defense

In defense, defendants cite a number of cases for the proposition that their robot ad constituted protected speech. The only cases they cite which are even remotely relevant to this case are Hustler Magazine v. Falwell, 485 U.S. 46 (1988) and L.L. Bean, Inc. v. Drake Publishers, Inc., 811 F.2d 26 (1st Cir.1987). Those cases involved parodies of advertisements run for the purpose of poking fun at Jerry Falwell and L.L. Bean, respectively. This case involves a true advertisement run for the purpose of selling Samsung VCRs. The ad's spoof of Vanna White and Wheel of Fortune is subservient and only tangentially related to the ad's primary message: "buy Samsung VCRs." Defendants' parody arguments are better addressed to non-commercial parodies. The difference between a "parody" and a "knock-off" is the difference between fun and profit.

V. Conclusion

In remanding this case, we hold only that White has pleaded claims which can go to the jury for its decision.

Affirmed in Part, Reversed in Part, and Remanded.

■ ALARCON, CIRCUIT JUDGE, concurring in part, dissenting in part:

Vanna White seeks recovery from Samsung based on three theories: the right to privacy, the right to publicity, and the Lanham Act. I concur in the majority's conclusions on the right to privacy. I respectfully dissent from its holdings on the right to publicity and the Lanham Act claims. . . .

.   .   .

CONCLUSION

The protection of intellectual property presents the courts with the necessity of balancing competing interests. On the one hand, we wish to protect and reward the work and investment of those who create intellectual property. In so doing, however, we must prevent the creation of a monopoly that would inhibit the creative expressions of others. We have traditionally balanced those interests by allowing the copying of an idea, but protecting a unique expression of it. Samsung clearly used the idea of a glamorous female game show hostess. Just as clearly, it avoided appropriating Vanna White's expression of that role. Samsung did not use a likeness of her. The performer depicted in the commercial advertisement is unmistakably a lifeless robot. Vanna White has presented no evidence that any consumer confused the robot with her identity. Indeed, no reasonable consumer could confuse the robot with Vanna White or believe that, because the robot appeared in the advertisement, Vanna White endorsed Samsung's product.

I would affirm the district court's judgment in all respects.

[The panel voted unanimously to deny a petition for rehearing. A majority of the circuit's active judges voted to deny a rehearing en banc. Three judged dissented.]

■ KOZINSKI, CIRCUIT JUDGE, with whom CIRCUIT JUDGES O'SCANNLAIN and KLEINFELD join, dissenting from the order rejecting the suggestion for rehearing en banc.

I

Saddam Hussein wants to keep advertisers from using his picture in unflattering contexts. Clint Eastwood doesn't want tabloids to write about him. Rudolf Valentino's heirs want to control his film biography. The Girl Scouts don't want their image soiled by association with certain activities. George Lucas wants to keep Strategic Defense Initiative fans from calling it "Star Wars." Pepsico doesn't want singers to use the word "Pepsi" in their songs. Guy Lombardo wants an exclusive property right to ads that show big bands playing on New Year's Eve. Uri Geller thinks he should be paid for ads showing psychics bending metal through telekinesis. Paul Prudhomme, that household name, thinks the same about ads featuring corpulent bearded chefs. And scads of copyright holders see purple when their creations are made fun of. [The opinion cites references for each example.]

Something very dangerous is going on here. Private property, including intellectual property, is essential to our way of life. It provides an incentive for investment and innovation; it stimulates the flourishing of our culture; it protects the moral entitlements of people to the fruits of their labors. But reducing too much to private property can be bad medicine. Private land, for instance, is far more useful if separated from other private land by public streets, roads and highways. Public parks, utility rights-of-way and sewers reduce the amount of land in private hands, but vastly enhance the value of the property that remains.

So too it is with intellectual property. Overprotecting intellectual property is as harmful as underprotecting it. Creativity is impossible without a rich public domain. Nothing today, likely nothing since we tamed fire, is genuinely new: Culture, like science and technology, grows by accretion, each new creator building on the works of those who came before. Overprotection stifles the very creative forces it's supposed to nurture.

The panel's opinion is a classic case of overprotection. Concerned about what it sees as a wrong done to Vanna White, the panel majority erects a property right of remarkable and dangerous breadth: Under the majority's opinion, it's now a tort for advertisers to remind the public of a celebrity. Not to use a celebrity's name, voice, signature or likeness; not to imply the celebrity endorses a product; but simply to evoke the celebrity's image in the public's mind. This Orwellian notion withdraws far more from the public domain than prudence and common sense allow. It conflicts with the Copyright Act and the Copyright Clause. It raises serious First Amendment problems. It's bad law, and it deserves a long, hard second look.

II

. . .

The ad that spawned this litigation starred a robot dressed in a wig, gown and jewelry reminiscent of Vanna White's hair and dress; the robot was posed next to a Wheel-of-Fortune-like game board. The caption read "Longest-running game show. 2012 A.D." The gag here, I take it, was that Samsung would still be around when White had been replaced by a robot.

Perhaps failing to see the humor, White sued, alleging Samsung infringed her right of publicity by "appropriating" her "identity." Under California law, White has the exclusive right to use her name, likeness, signature and voice for commercial purposes. [ ] But Samsung didn't use her name, voice or signature, and it certainly didn't use her likeness. The ad just wouldn't have been funny had it depicted White or someone who resembled her—the whole joke was that the game show host(ess) was a robot, not a real person. No one seeing the ad could have thought this was supposed to be White in 2012.

The district judge quite reasonably held that, because Samsung didn't use White's name, likeness, voice or signature, it didn't violate her right of publicity. [ ] Not so, says the panel majority: The California right of publicity can't possibly be limited to name and likeness. If it were, the majority reasons, a "clever advertising strategist" could avoid using White's name or likeness but nevertheless remind people of her with impunity, "effectively eviscerat[ing]" her rights. To prevent this "evisceration," the panel majority holds that the right of publicity must extend beyond name and likeness, to any "appropriation" of White's "identity"—anything that "evoke[s]" her personality. [   ]

III

But what does "evisceration" mean in intellectual property law? Intellectual property rights aren't like some constitutional rights, absolute guarantees protected against all kinds of interference, subtle as well as blatant. They cast no penumbras, emit no emanations: The very point of intellectual property laws is that they protect only against certain specific kinds of appropriation. I can't publish unauthorized copies of, say, Presumed Innocent; I can't make a movie out of it. But I'm perfectly free to write a book about an idealistic young prosecutor on trial for a crime he didn't commit. So what if I got the idea from Presumed Innocent? So what if it reminds readers of the original? Have I "eviscerated" Scott Turow's intellectual property rights? Certainly not. All creators draw in part on the work of those who came before, referring to it, building on it, poking fun at it; we call this creativity, not piracy.

The majority isn't, in fact, preventing the "evisceration" of Vanna White's existing rights; it's creating a new and much broader property right, a right unknown in California law.[16] It's replacing the existing balance between the interests of the celebrity and those of the public by a different balance, one substantially more favorable to the celebrity. Instead of having an exclusive right in her name, likeness, signature or voice, every famous person now has an exclusive right to anything that reminds the viewer of her. After all, that's all Samsung did: It used an inanimate object to remind people of White, to "evoke [her identity]."

Consider how sweeping this new right is. What is it about the ad that makes people think of White? It's not the robot's wig, clothes or jewelry; there must be ten million blond women (many of them quasi-famous) who wear dresses and jewelry like White's. It's that the robot is posed near the "Wheel of Fortune" game board. Remove the game board from the ad, and no one would think of Vanna White. But once you include the game board, anybody standing beside it—a brunette woman, a man wearing women's clothes, a monkey in a wig and gown—would evoke White's image, precisely the way the robot did. It's the "Wheel of Fortune" set, not the robot's face or dress or jewelry that evokes White's image. The panel is giving White an exclusive right not in what she looks like or who she is, but in what she does for a living.[18]

16. . . .

Neither have we previously interpreted California law to cover pure "identity." [Midler], and Waits v. Frito–Lay, Inc., 978 F.2d 1093 (9th Cir.1992), dealt with appropriation of a celebrity's voice. [   ]. [Motschenbacher] stressed that, though the plaintiff's likeness wasn't directly recognizable by itself, the surrounding circumstances would have made viewers think the likeness was the plaintiff's. [   ]

18. Once the right of publicity is extended beyond specific physical characteristics, this will become a recurring problem: Outside name, likeness and voice, the things that most reliably remind the public of celebrities are the actions or roles they're famous for. A commercial with an astronaut setting

This is entirely the wrong place to strike the balance. Intellectual property rights aren't free: They're imposed at the expense of future creators and of the public at large. Where would we be if Charles Lindbergh had an exclusive right in the concept of a heroic solo aviator? If Arthur Conan Doyle had gotten a copyright in the idea of the detective story, or Albert Einstein had patented the theory of relativity? If every author and celebrity had been given the right to keep people from mocking them or their work? Surely this would have made the world poorer, not richer, culturally as well as economically.

This is why intellectual property law is full of careful balances between what's set aside for the owner and what's left in the public domain for the rest of us: The relatively short life of patents; the longer, but finite, life of copyrights; copyright's idea-expression dichotomy; the fair use doctrine; the prohibition on copyrighting facts; the compulsory license of television broadcasts and musical compositions; federal preemption of overbroad state intellectual property laws; the nominative use doctrine in trademark law; the right to make soundalike recordings. All of these diminish an intellectual property owner's rights. All let the public use something created by someone else. But all are necessary to maintain a free environment in which creative genius can flourish.

The intellectual property right created by the panel here has none of these essential limitations: No fair use exception; no right to parody; no idea-expression dichotomy. It impoverishes the public domain, to the detriment of future creators and the public at large. Instead of well-defined, limited characteristics such as name, likeness or voice, advertisers will now have to cope with vague claims of "appropriation of identity," claims often made by people with a wholly exaggerated sense of their own fame and significance. [ ] Future Vanna Whites might not get the chance to create their personae, because their employers may fear some celebrity will claim the persona is too similar to her own. The public will be robbed of parodies of celebrities, and our culture will be deprived of the valuable safety valve that parody and mockery create.

Moreover, consider the moral dimension, about which the panel majority seems to have gotten so exercised. Saying Samsung "appropriated" something of White's begs the question: Should White have the exclusive right to something as broad and amorphous as her "identity"? Samsung's ad didn't simply copy White's schtick—like all parody, it created something new. True, Samsung did it to make money, but White does whatever she does to make money, too; the majority talks of "the difference between fun and profit," [ ], but in the entertainment industry fun is profit. Why is

foot on the moon would evoke the image of Neil Armstrong. Any masked man on horseback would remind people (over a certain age) of Clayton Moore. And any number of songs—"My Way," "Yellow Submarine," "Like a Virgin," "Beat It," "Michael, Row the Boat Ashore," to name only a few— instantly evoke an image of the person or group who made them famous, regardless of who is singing. [ ] Cf. *Motschenbacher*, where the claim was that viewers would think plaintiff was actually in the commercial, and not merely that the commercial reminded people of him.

Vanna White's right to exclusive for-profit use of her persona—a persona that might not even be her own creation, but that of a writer, director or producer—superior to Samsung's right to profit by creating its own inventions? Why should she have such absolute rights to control the conduct of others, unlimited by the idea-expression dichotomy or by the fair use doctrine?

To paraphrase only slightly Feist Publications, Inc. v. Rural Telephone Service Co., 499 U.S. 340 (1991), it may seem unfair that much of the fruit of a creator's labor may be used by others without compensation. But this is not some unforeseen byproduct of our intellectual property system; it is the system's very essence. Intellectual property law assures authors the right to their original expression, but encourages others to build freely on the ideas that underlie it. This result is neither unfair nor unfortunate: It is the means by which intellectual property law advances the progress of science and art. We give authors certain exclusive rights, but in exchange we get a richer public domain. The majority ignores this wise teaching, and all of us are the poorer for it.

IV

The panel, however, does more than misinterpret California law: By refusing to recognize a parody exception to the right of publicity, the panel directly contradicts the federal Copyright Act. Samsung didn't merely parody Vanna White. It parodied Vanna White appearing in "Wheel of Fortune," a copyrighted television show, and parodies of copyrighted works are governed by federal copyright law.

Copyright law specifically gives the world at large the right to make "fair use" parodies, parodies that don't borrow too much of the original. . . .

The majority's decision decimates this federal scheme. It's impossible to parody a movie or a TV show without at the same time "evok[ing]" the "identit[ies]" of the actors. . . . The public's right to make a fair use parody and the copyright owner's right to license a derivative work are useless if the parodist is held hostage by every actor whose "identity" he might need to "appropriate."

Our court is in a unique position here. State courts are unlikely to be particularly sensitive to federal preemption, which, after all, is a matter of first concern to the federal courts. The Supreme Court is unlikely to consider the issue because the right of publicity seems so much a matter of state law. That leaves us. . . . In a case where the copyright owner isn't even a party—where no one has the interests of copyright owners at heart—the majority creates a rule that greatly diminishes the rights of copyright holders in this circuit.

V

The majority's decision also conflicts with the federal copyright system in another, more insidious way. Under the dormant Copyright Clause, state intellectual property laws can stand only so long as they don't "prejudice the interests of other States." [ ] A state law criminalizing record piracy, for instance, is permissible because citizens of other states would "remain free to copy within their borders those works which may be protected elsewhere." [ ] But the right of publicity isn't geographically limited. A right of publicity created by one state applies to conduct everywhere, so long as it involves a celebrity domiciled in that state. If a Wyoming resident creates an ad that features a California domiciliary's name or likeness, he'll be subject to California right of publicity law even if he's careful to keep the ad from being shown in California. [ ]

. . .

VI

Finally, I can't see how giving White the power to keep others from evoking her image in the public's mind can be squared with the First Amendment. Where does White get this right to control our thoughts? The majority's creation goes way beyond the protection given a trademark or a copyrighted work, or a person's name or likeness. All those things control one particular way of expressing an idea, one way of referring to an object or a person. But not allowing any means of reminding people of someone? That's a speech restriction unparalleled in First Amendment law.

What's more, I doubt even a name-and-likeness-only right of publicity can stand without a parody exception. The First Amendment isn't just about religion or politics—it's also about protecting the free development of our national culture. Parody, humor, irreverence are all vital components of the marketplace of ideas. The last thing we need, the last thing the First Amendment will tolerate, is a law that lets public figures keep people from mocking them, or from "evok[ing]" their images in the mind of the public. [ ] [29]

The majority dismisses the First Amendment issue out of hand because Samsung's ad was commercial speech. [ ] So what? Commercial speech may be less protected by the First Amendment than noncommercial speech, but less protected means protected nonetheless. . . .

In our pop culture, where salesmanship must be entertaining and entertainment must sell, the line between the commercial and noncommercial has not merely blurred; it has disappeared. Is the Samsung parody any different from a parody on Saturday Night Live or in Spy Magazine? Both are equally profit-motivated. Both use a celebrity's identity to sell things—one to sell VCRs, the other to sell advertising. Both mock their subjects. Both try to make people laugh. Both add something, perhaps something worthwhile and memorable, perhaps not, to our culture. Both

---

29. The majority's failure to recognize a parody exception to the right of publicity would apply equally to parodies of politicians as of actresses. . . . (Samsung planned another ad that would show a dollar bill with Richard Nixon's face on it and the caption "Dollar bill, 2025 A.D. . . .," but Nixon refused permission to use his likeness); [ ].

are things that the people being portrayed might dearly want to suppress.
[ ]

. . .

VII

For better or worse, we are the Court of Appeals for the Hollywood Circuit. Millions of people toil in the shadow of the law we make, and much of their livelihood is made possible by the existence of intellectual property rights. But much of their livelihood—and much of the vibrancy of our culture—also depends on the existence of other intangible rights: The right to draw ideas from a rich and varied public domain, and the right to mock, for profit as well as fun, the cultural icons of our time.

In the name of avoiding the "evisceration" of a celebrity's rights in her image, the majority diminishes the rights of copyright holders and the public at large. In the name of fostering creativity, the majority suppresses it. Vanna White and those like her have been given something they never had before, and they've been given it at our expense. I cannot agree.

[An appendix to the dissent consisting of two photographs appears on pages 1112 and 1113.]

NOTES AND QUESTIONS

1. Note that two different issues inhere in this type of case: (1) is the plaintiff sufficiently identified and (2) if so, what may defendant do or say without incurring liability. Are both questions involved in *Samsung*?

2. Why does the panel majority uphold the publicity action but reject the action under § 3344? If the California legislature approves the result in this case, how might it redraft § 3344 to reach this case?

3. Could a jury reasonably conclude that plaintiff is endorsing Samsung products? Does the publicity action depend on that showing?

4. What analysis if the robot is dressed to resemble the witch from *Snow White*?

5. Who has the better of the argument over the parody defense? Should it matter whether the parody occurs in an article in Spy magazine or in an advertisement?

6. *The Eastwood Case.* In the *Eastwood* case, discussed in *Samsung*, Clint Eastwood sued the National Enquirer for the unauthorized use of his likeness on the cover and in related television advertisements about a false nondefamatory story inside the issue. The story involved allegations that Eastwood was romantically involved with two female celebrities. The court concluded that the use was commercial exploitation and was not privileged under state or federal law. The trial court had improperly sustained a demurrer to the complaint. The court of appeal saw no reason why Eastwood should have to show that he was being falsely said to be endorsing the National Enquirer. This was one way to impose liability but it was not essential. The court also concluded that the article was not necessarily protected as a news account because of an allegation that the story was a calculated falsehood. The court discussed at length the emerging right of publicity.

APPENDIX

Vanna White

In a more recent episode a federal jury has awarded Eastwood $150,-000 against the National Enquirer for a "bogus interview with him published in December 1993." The theory was that although the alleged interview was not necessarily defamatory, "Clint didn't want to be associated with the National Enquirer." The defendant asserted that it was unaware that the interview that it had purchased from a freelancer was bogus. See Nat'l L.J., Nov. 13, 1995 at A22.

Might each of these claims have been analyzed as false-light cases?

Ms. C3PO?

7. *Cher's Case.* In Cher v. Forum International, Ltd., 7 Med.L.Rptr. 2593 (C.D.Cal.1982), the judge, after a nonjury trial, awarded the plaintiff entertainer $763,000 for loss of her right of publicity. Cher had agreed to give an interview to Us Magazine, reserving the right to bar publication if she did not like the results. She exercised that right. The interviewer, however, then sold the interview to the two defendant magazines, each of which published excerpts. One defendant's cover asserted that it was an exclusive interview. Cher alleged that she would not have given either of the defendants an interview because she did not approve of them.

On the appeal in Cher's case, the court reversed as to one magazine but affirmed as to the other. Cher v. Forum International, Ltd., 692 F.2d 634 (9th Cir.1982), cert. denied 462 U.S. 1120 (1983). Star had put on its cover "Exclusive Series" followed by "Cher: My life, my husbands and my many, many men." The court concluded that Star "was entitled to inform its readers that the issue contained an article about Cher, that the article was based on an interview with Cher herself, and that the article had not previously appeared elsewhere." The words used to convey that information "cannot support a finding of the knowing or reckless falsity required under *Time, Inc. v. Hill.*" Nor did the words convey the false claim that Cher endorsed the magazine. The then-existing version of the California "right of publicity" statute had an express exception for news accounts that was held to cover this case.

Forum magazine changed the text to make it appear that Forum was posing the questions to Cher in an interview—"apparently a common practice in the industry." The cover said "Exclusive: Cher Talks Straight." Forum also used Cher's name on a subscription pullout card that asserted that things Cher would not tell Us Magazine she was telling Forum. The card also stated "So join Cher and Forum's hundreds of thousands of other adventurous readers today." The claim that Cher was telling Forum readers things she would not tell Us was "patently false. This kind of mendacity is not prosected by the First Amendment. . . ." The falsity was particularly clear here because Us was a magazine to which Cher *was* willing to give an interview.

The trial court had also found liability for the "join Cher" language on the card. Although the court of appeals thought the language somewhat ambiguous, it was willing to accept the trial court's reading that this was an implied endorsement of Forum and its conclusion that the falsity of that reading showed a reckless disregard for the truth. The court of appeals concluded that "no matter how carefully the editorial staff of Forum may have trod the border between the actionable and the protected, the advertising staff engaged in the kind of knowing falsity that strips away the protection of the First Amendment."

9. *Advertising prior work.* New York has decided that a medium's use of an earlier story to advertise its own product does not come within "advertising purposes" under the statute. In Booth v. Curtis Publishing Co., 15 App.Div.2d 343, 223 N.Y.S.2d 737, affirmed without opinion 11 N.Y.2d 907, 182 N.E.2d 812, 228 N.Y.S.2d 468 (1962), Holiday magazine published a photograph of actress Shirley Booth in a story about a prominent resort. The color photograph was "a very striking one, show[ing] Miss Booth in the water up to her neck, but wearing a brimmed, high-crowned street hat of straw." Several months after the story appeared, Holiday took out full-page advertisements in the New Yorker and Advertising Age magazines. Both reprinted the Booth photograph as a sample of the content of Holiday magazine. "Because of the photograph's striking qualities it would be quite effective in drawing attention to the advertisements; but it was also a sample of magazine content."

The court found the use of the photograph to be an "incidental" mentioning of plaintiff in the course of advertising itself. "It stands to reason that a publication can best prove its worth and illustrate its content by submission of complete copies of or extraction from past editions. . . . And, of course, it is true that the publisher must advertise in other public media, just as it must by poster, circular, cover, or soliciting letter. This is a practical necessity which the law may not ignore in giving effect to the purposes of the statute."

Although the court recognized that "realistically" the use of the photograph attracted the attention of the reader, that use was outweighed by the magazine's need to demonstrate its content. Finally, nothing in the advertisement suggested that plaintiff endorsed defendant's magazine.

This was followed in Namath v. Sports Illustrated, 48 App.Div.2d 487, 371 N.Y.S.2d 10 (1975), affirmed 39 N.Y.2d 897, 352 N.E.2d 584, 386 N.Y.S.2d 397 (1976). See also Montana v. San Jose Mercury News, Inc., 34 Cal.App.4th 790, 40 Cal.Rptr.2d 639 (1995)(denying claim by former football star for defendant newspaper's sale of poster reproductions of its newspaper pages that showed plaintiff's photograph).

10. Consider this series of hypotheticals from Shiffrin, The First Amendment and Economic Regulation: Away from a General Theory of the First Amendment, 78 Nw.U.L.Rev. 1212, 1257 n. 275 (1983):

A magazine may have a profit motive in taking a particular position on a particular subject, but the courts will ordinarily not count that motivation as significant. In thinking about profit motive and the dissemination of truth consider these examples: (1) Without his consent, Mercedes Benz *truthfully* advertises that Frank Sinatra drives a Mercedes. Sinatra sues for misappropriation. Does it make a difference if Mercedes in its ad says, "We didn't ask Sinatra's permission to tell you this" or "Sinatra doesn't want us to tell you this but . . . "? (2) Suppose *Time* magazine writes a story on Mercedes Benz and puts Sinatra on the cover with a picture of his Mercedes. Suppose they put Sinatra on the cover purely for reasons of profit. (3) Suppose Time Inc. advertises: "Get the recent issue of *Time* with Frank Sinatra on the cover with his Mercedes." (4) Suppose *Time* truthfully advertises: "Sinatra doesn't want us to tell you this, but he is one of our regular readers."

What if an author writes "An Unauthorized Biography of Vanna White"? Can any photograph of her be used on the front cover?

11. *The Riggins case.* In Town & Country Properties, Inc. v. Riggins, 249 Va. 387, 457 S.E.2d 356 (1995), defendant realtor distributed some 1600 one-page flyers inviting real estate brokers to an open house to view "John Riggins' Former Home." Riggins was "formerly a prominent professional football player" who still made his living in the area by working as a part-time commentator on a radio sports program and by making appearances for which he charged between $5,000 and $90,000— unless it was for a charitable cause. When he learned of the flyer he claimed to have been " 'angry,' 'humiliated,' and felt a loss of 'integrity and dignity.' Plaintiff said he felt 'violated and that his livelihood had been 'threatened by this flyer.' " His suit was under a statute almost identical to New York's, for having had his "name" used without his consent "for advertising purposes or for purposes of trade."

A judgment for $25,000 compensatory and similar amount for punitive damages was upheld on appeal. That the flyer was truthful was no defense because it was used for both of the barred purposes. The name was not relevant to information about the house such as its physical condition, architectural features or quality. "Simply, this is not the type of commercial speech accorded constitutional protection." The amount of the award was supported by expert testimony and fell within the range of his prior fees. Punitive damages were justified under the statute where the name is "knowingly used."

How might this case be analyzed in a state without legislation in this area? How does this fit into Shiffrin's four examples?

12. What if the product "admits" to being a fictional account of a celebrity's life? In Hicks v. Casablanca Records, 464 F.Supp. 426 (S.D.N.Y. 1978), defendants based a novel on a fictionalized explanation of Agatha Christie's mysterious 11–day disappearance in 1926.

The court engrafted upon the right of publicity a protection for "matters of news, history, biography, and other factual subjects of public interest, despite the necessary references to" the names of living persons. That protection did not apply here, however, because the 11–day episode discussed in the book was fictional and did not purport to be biographical.

The book was accorded constitutional protection. Although fiction, it did not contain deliberate falsehood and did not falsely purport to be biographical. The reader would know by the word "novel" that the work was fictitious. The "protection usually accorded novels and movies outweighs whatever publicity rights plaintiffs may possess."

Docudramas. How should one analyze the relatively new technique of the "docudrama," in which the program mixes truth and fiction? When ABC announced in 1982 that it was planning a docudrama on the life of Elizabeth Taylor, the actress responded by seeking an injunction. Her first theory was that "I am my own commodity. I am my own industry." Someday "I will write my autobiography, and perhaps film it, but that will be my choice. By doing this, ABC is taking away from my income." What if she had tried to block an unauthorized biography?

Taylor's second theory was false light invasion of privacy. "They plan to use my name throughout the show, to hire an actress who supposedly resembles me and to have her speak lines which they want the public to believe I used in numerous personal and private conversations."

Taylor's lawyer contended: "The docudrama is a fairly new form of expression. It's not biography, it's not a documentary and its not her story. It's a drama. We're talking about a live actress who is entitled not to have lies told about her. When you mix fact and fiction and say this is a life story, no matter how flattering you are, you're showing the subject in a false light, and creating a wrong image.''

Later, ABC announced that it had dropped its plans, for "creative reasons." This account of the dispute is taken mainly from Lewin, Whose Life Is It Anyway? Legally, It's Hard to Tell, N.Y.Times, Nov. 21, 1982, § II, at 1. See Manson, The Television Docudrama and the Right of Publicity, Comm. & the Law, Feb. 1985, at 41, concluding that since the docudrama is "neither fiction nor straight documentary" it does not fall within the protection accorded "biographies and documentaries; it does not provide a dissemination of information. Furthermore, the docudrama does not come under the first amendment protection of drama; it is not evident to the public that the events depicted in the docudrama are fictitious." By its "very nature, the docudrama tends to confuse the viewer, making it difficult to discern when true events in the life of the public figure portrayed merge and blend with purely fanciful fabrications. To confuse the viewer is a disservice to the public—to society. Further, confusion also diminishes and thereby damages the value of the public figure's 'name, likeness and persona.' ''

Which is the easier case for the plaintiff—complaining about a work that is called fiction or a docudrama?

See generally, Bloom, Preventing the Misappropriation of Identity: Beyond the "Right of Publicity," 13 Hastings Comm/Ent L.J. 489 (1991).

Nonfamous Plaintiffs. A teenager was filmed at an accident site by a TV news crew. She had gone to the site of a car accident in the mistaken belief that her boyfriend's sister might have been killed. The news photographer sold the footage to a film producer. That footage later found its way into a movie called *Faces of Death,* which has been banned in 46 countries because of its grisly content. In the movie, the footage of the teenager was edited to make it appear that she was reacting to seeing the bloody body of a bicyclist killed by a semitrailer truck. What harm, if any, has the teenager suffered? Should she have an action for false light privacy? For commercial appropriation of her face? The teenager sued the photographer, the film's producer, and its distributor, seeking royalties, damages, and an injunction barring exhibition until her scene is deleted. Editor & Publisher, Jan. 28, 1989, at 26. How would you measure her damages on each claim?

In Staruski v. Continental Tel.Co., 154 Vt. 568, 581 A.2d 266 (Vt.1990), plaintiff's employer, without consent, ran her name, photo and a purported statement about what work she did and how she enjoyed her work. Although plaintiff was not a famous person she was entitled to sue for the appropriation of her name and likeness for commercial purposes. Although there may be "incidental" uses, as in crowd scenes in commercials, there was "nothing incidental about plaintiff's appearance in the ad."

Recall that the *Roberson* case itself involved a nonfamous person whose face was used for an advertisement.

CHAPTER XV

INTENTIONAL ECONOMIC HARM

We turn now to a group of economic torts. These subjects are not being raised for the first time. Recall, for example, that we have already considered questions of the duty owed by attorneys and accountants to nonclients, p. 268, supra. The question there was one of the scope of liability for negligence. Here we consider the scope of liability for intentional misrepresentation. We continue with an examination of intentional efforts to interfere with the contract rights or expected economic advantage of others. Again, recall that we considered the scope of liability for negligent interferences with these interests in Chapter IV.

A. MISREPRESENTATION

1. INTRODUCTION

Although we have been concerned primarily with physical acts that have caused harm, we have also had occasion to consider situations in which words caused harm. Recall the problems of product labels and instructions, p. 522, supra, and the incorrect accounting reports and legal advice that caused harm to others, p. 268, supra. In this section we explore the problem of misrepresentation, emphasizing the cases in which the parties are dealing directly with one another. The fear of unlimited liability, which played such a large role earlier, recedes—to be replaced by problems of determining the boundary between contract and tort. Although we addressed this problem earlier in connection with the line between the Uniform Commercial Code and tort law, p. 578, supra, our focus here is on the use of words that mislead and cause economic harm to the relying party.

Sometimes it is clear that only one form of remedy, if any, is available. Thus, when the only problem is a failure to fulfill a contractual obligation, usually no tort remedy is available. But consider Channel Master Corp. v. Aluminum Ltd. Sales, Inc., 4 N.Y.2d 403, 151 N.E.2d 833, 176 N.Y.S.2d 259 (1958), in which defendant orally expressed willingness to supply 400,000 pounds of aluminum ingot per month to plaintiff for five months. When the defendant failed to supply the ingots, the statute of frauds barred any contractual action. But the court held that a tort action might still lie:

> The present action is in tort, not contract, depending not upon agreement between the parties, but rather upon deliberate misrepresentation of fact, relied on by the plaintiff to his detriment. . . . If the proof of a promise or contract, void under

the statute of frauds, is essential to maintain the action, there may be no recovery, but, on the other hand, one who fraudulently misrepresents himself as intending to perform an agreement is subject to liability *in tort* whether the agreement is enforcible or not. [ ] The policy of the statute of frauds is "not directed at cases of dishonesty in making" a promise [ ]; never intended as an instrument to immunize fraudulent conduct, the statute may not be so employed.

In The Common Law Tradition—Deciding Appeals 473 (1960), Professor Karl Llewellyn attacks the statute of frauds holding in *Channel Master:*

> The situation is one in which the torts theorists (Restatement, Harper and James, Prosser, all gathered and cited) have launched as unconsidered a jamboree as ever has been suggested in the books: in the instant "application" of the idea, word-of-mouth negotiations for a contract which have led to no acceptance, which need not have led even to an offer, and which would in an action on an actually completed contract be incapable of submission to the jury for lack of a signed writing—these become admissible in the teeth of the statute against frauds and perjuries, admissible moreover, in such fashion as to allow damages of a range and extent which would be dubious of procurement in any action based on an agreement fully closed, formally authenticated, and unambiguously relied on. All of this by virtue of merely adjusting the pleadings and the evidence to run down an alley which is rather easier to travel with persuasiveness than is the alley of contract-closing. . . .

Questions about allowing tort remedies where contract actions are barred may arise when consideration fails, when the statute of limitations differs, or when the contract itself asserts that neither party is relying on oral statements that are not reflected in the written contract—with states disagreeing about each one.

If both tort and contract actions are available, the plaintiff's preference will depend upon the specific facts of the case. The measure of compensatory damages may differ. Punitive damages may be available in tort but not in contract actions. Statutes of limitation may exclude one or the other. Of course, the plaintiff may have to prove some fault in the tort action but need not prove such fault in the contract action.

Although the remedy of rescission does not require a showing of fault, Seneca Wire and Mfg. Co. v. A. B. Leach & Co., 247 N.Y. 1, 159 N.E. 700 (1928), the plaintiff may not be in a position to undo the transaction after learning about the misrepresentation. The parties may have engaged in further deals or actions that make it impossible to rescind. See, e.g., Mertens v. Wolfeboro National Bank, 119 N.H. 453, 402 A.2d 1335 (1979).

2. DECEIT

The tort actions arising from misrepresentations first became clearly identified in cases involving deliberate misstatements. Actions for this type of misrepresentation became known as actions for "deceit" or "fraud."

Scienter. In the leading English case, Derry v. Peek, 14 A.C. 337 (H.L.1889), Lord Herschell stated that:

> [F]raud is proved when it is shown that a false representation has been made (1) knowingly, or (2) without belief in its truth, or (3) recklessly, careless whether it be true or false. Although I have treated the second and third as distinct cases, I think the third is but an instance of the second, for one who makes a statement under such circumstances can have no real belief in the truth of what he states. To prevent a false statement being fraudulent, there must, I think, always be an honest belief in its truth.

As a corollary he noted that "making a false statement through want of care falls far short of, and is a very different thing from fraud, and the same may be said of a false representation honestly believed though on insufficient grounds." On the matter of belief he stated:

> I quite admit that the statements of witnesses as to their belief are by no means to be accepted blindfolded. The probabilities must be considered. Whenever it is necessary to arrive at a conclusion as to the state of mind of another person, and to determine whether his belief under given circumstances was such as he alleges, we can only do so by applying the standard of conduct which our own experience of the ways of men has enabled us to form; by asking ourselves whether a reasonable man situated as the defendants were, with their knowledge and means of knowledge, might well believe what they state they did believe, and consider that the representations made were substantially true.

How does this compare with the notion of "actual malice" developed in libel cases? What is the apparent role of honest, but unreasonable, belief?

In Chatham Furnace Co. v. Moffatt, 147 Mass. 403, 18 N.E. 168 (1888), the court stated:

> The charge of fraudulent intent, in an action for deceit, may be maintained by proof of a statement made, as of the party's own knowledge, which is false, provided the thing stated is not merely matter of opinion, estimate or judgment, but is susceptible of actual knowledge, and in such case it is not necessary to make any further proof of an actual intent to deceive. The fraud consists in stating that the party knows the thing to exist, when he does not know it to exist, and if he does not know it to exist he must ordinarily be deemed to know that he does not. Forgetfulness of its existence after a former knowledge, or a mere belief of its existence, will not warrant or excuse a statement of actual knowledge.

The types of conduct discussed in *Derry v. Peek* come to be grouped under the Latin term "scienter." The elements of the action for deceit were stated by the court in *Channel Master* to be "misrepresentation of a material existing fact, falsity, *scienter,* deception and injury."

In *Greycas, Inc. v. Proud*, p. 281, supra, involving the attorney who incorrectly asserted that no liens existed on a client's property, Judge Posner noted that although the plaintiff was suing for negligent misrepresentation, the case appeared to be one of fraud:

> No doubt Proud was negligent in failing to conduct a search, but we are not clear why the misrepresentation is alleged to be negligent rather than deliberate and hence fraudulent. . . . Proud did not merely say, "There are no liens"; he said, "I have conducted a U.C.C., tax, and judgment search"; and not only is this statement, too, a false one, but its falsehood cannot have been inadvertent, for Proud knew he had not conducted such a search.

The court then speculated about the plaintiff's choice of theory:

> It may have feared that Proud's insurance policy for professional malpractice excluded deliberate wrongdoing from its coverage, or may not have wanted to bear the higher burden of proving fraud, or may have feared that an accusation of fraud would make it harder to settle the case—for most cases, of course, are settled, though this one has not been.

The passage about the "the higher burden of proving fraud" refers to the fact that in civil fraud cases, most state courts have stated that plaintiffs must prove their cases with "clear and convincing evidence." The explanation has generally been based on the close relationship between civil and criminal fraud or on the ease with which plaintiff may claim that the defendant has made a specific statement at a time when no one else was present. This position has been rejected in a few states on the ground that there is no reason to reject the usual "preponderance of the evidence" standard in civil cases involving fraud. See the discussion in Liodas v. Sahadi, 19 Cal.3d 278, 562 P.2d 316, 137 Cal.Rptr. 635 (1977).

Ambit. Even when courts found the requisite scienter to justify a deceit action, they generally restricted the persons eligible to recover damages by permitting recovery only by those to whom the misrepresentations were made. If a prospective victim declined to go ahead but told a friend about the opportunity, early courts denied the friend an action.

The ambit has been expanding. See, e.g., Geernaert v. Mitchell, 31 Cal.App.4th 601, 37 Cal.Rptr.2d 483 (1995), extending a fraudulent seller's liability to a buyer several steps down the chain where each successive seller (perhaps innocently) repeated the misrepresentation. Nonetheless, it still appears that the ambits of liability for misrepresentation are narrower for both intentional and negligent tortfeasors than they are for those who commit intentional or negligent acts resulting in physical injury or damage to property. This, of course, recalls the reservations courts expressed about extending liability for economic harm caused by negligence, in Chapter IV.

Material Existing Fact. Problems of scienter aside, the greatest difficulty has surrounded the efforts to identify a "material existing fact." Why should a fact have to be "material" if it is deliberately false and achieves its purpose of deceiving the plaintiff to his detriment? Does the requirement help in determining whether the defendant should have foreseen or did foresee the plaintiff's reliance on the misrepresentation? Restatement (Second) of Torts § 538(2) provides that a fact is material if "(a) to its existence or nonexistence a reasonable man would attach importance in determining his choice of action in the transaction in question, or (b) the maker of the representation knows or has reason to know that its recipient regards or is likely to regard the matter as important although a reasonable man would not so regard it." What kinds of situations are excluded? Should they be?

The term "existing fact" has a broad sweep. Courts generally consider a statement of intention to be a statement of "existing fact" because a "person's intent, his state of mind . . . is capable of ascertainment." Moreover, according to the Second Restatement's § 525, comment *f*, a statement in the form of a "prediction or promise as to the future course of events may justifiably be interpreted as a statement that the maker knows of nothing which will make the fulfillment of his prediction or promise impossible or improbable."

In California Conserving Co. v. D'Avanzo, 62 F.2d 528 (2d Cir.1933), defendant, when he was in dire financial straits, bought goods from the plaintiff on credit. He went bankrupt and the plaintiff sought to reclaim the goods for fraud. If successful, he need not have shared pro rata with other creditors. In discussing the alleged fraud Judge Learned Hand observed:

> He may mean to pay if he survives, though he knows that he is extremely unlikely to do so. If his promise declares only that he intends to pay it would be hard in such a case to say that he has deceived the seller; and the doctrine presupposes some deceit. But promises, like other utterances, must be read with their usual implications. True, they are predictions and no one can foretell the future; the seller knows this as well as the buyer. However, a man's affairs may reach such a pass that ordinarily honest persons would no longer buy, if they had no greater chance to pay; and the seller is entitled to rely upon that implication. He may assume that the buyer would not promise if the odds were so heavy against him. He may read the promise as more than the declaration of a conditional intent, as affirming that that intent had reasonable hope of fruition. In that event, if the buyer knows that it has no such hope, he deceives the seller, as much as though he intended not to pay at all. This duty does not indeed depend upon what reasonable persons would think of his chances.

Another aspect of defining "fact" involves the distinction between "fact" and "opinion." Consider the statement of Judge Learned Hand in Vulcan Metals Co. v. Simmons Mfg. Co., 248 Fed. 853 (2d Cir.1918), involving claims made concerning a vacuum cleaner. To induce the buyer to take over Simmons's vacuum cleaner manufacturing business, the company made a number of representations about the product:

> They include commendations of the cleanliness, economy, and efficiency of the machine; that it was absolutely perfect in even the smallest detail; that water power, by which it worked, marked the most economical means of operating a vacuum cleaner with the greatest efficiency; that the cleaning was more thoroughly done than by beating or brushing; that, having been perfected, it was a necessity which every one could afford; that it was so simple that a child of six could use it; that it worked completely and thoroughly; that it was simple, long-lived, easily operated, and effective; that it was the only sanitary portable cleaner on the market; that perfect satisfaction would result from its use; that it would last a lifetime; that it was the only practical jet machine on the market; and that perfect satisfaction would result from its use, if properly adjusted.

Speaking of these general claims, Judge Hand observed:

> An opinion is a fact, and it may be a very relevant fact; the expression of an opinion is the assertion of a belief, and any rule which condones the expression of a consciously false opinion condones a consciously false statement of fact. When the parties are so situated that the buyer may reasonably rely upon the expression of the seller's opinion, it is no excuse to give a false one. [ ] And so it makes much difference whether the parties stand "on an equality." For example, we should treat very differently the expressed opinion of a chemist to a layman about the properties of a composition from the same opinion between chemist and chemist, when the buyer had full opportunity to examine. The reason of the rule lies, we think, in this: There are some kinds of talk which no sensible man takes seriously, and if he does he suffers from his credulity. If we were all scrupulously honest, it would not be so; but, as it is, neither party usually believes what the seller says about his own opinions, and each knows it. Such statements, like the claims of campaign managers before election, are rather designed to allay the suspicion which would attend their absence than to be understood as having any relation to objective truth. It is quite true that they induce a compliant temper in the buyer, but it is by a much more subtle process than through the acceptance of his claims for his wares.
>
> .   .   .
>
> In the case at bar, since the buyer was allowed full opportunity to examine the cleaner and to test it out, we put the parties upon an equality. It seems to us that general statements as to what the cleaner would do, even though consciously false, were not of a kind to be taken literally by the buyer. As between manufacturer and customer, it may not be so; but this was the case of

taking over a business, after ample chance to investigate. Such a buyer, who the seller rightly expects will undertake an independent and adequate inquiry into the actual merits of what he gets, has no right to treat as material in his determination statements like these. The standard of honesty permitted by the rule may not be the best; but, as Holmes, J., says in Deming v. Darling, 148 Mass. 504, 20 N.E. 107, 2 L.R.A. 743, the chance that the higgling preparatory to a bargain may be afterwards translated into assurances of quality may perhaps be a set-off to the actual wrong allowed by the rule as it stands. We therefore think that the District Court was right in disregarding all these misrepresentations.

Why should "consciously false" statements ever be protected? What element of the misrepresentation action is missing?

Compare Powell v. Flechter, 45 N.Y.St.Rep. 294, 18 N.Y.S. 451 (1892), in which defendant vendor knowingly misrepresented to plaintiff purchaser, "a woman utterly ignorant of violins and their value," that a violin was made by Gaspard di Dniffoprugear and was worth at least $1,000. The trial record showed that plaintiff did not rely on the representation of make but did rely on the representation of value. On defendant's appeal from a judgment for plaintiff, the court stated that an intentionally false statement as to value is actionable "where one in purchasing goods, the value of which can only be known to experts, relies upon the vendor, who is a dealer in such goods, to give him accurate information concerning them."

Do consumers generally expect honesty in all types of transactions? Do merchants expect honesty from each other? Should the law here be trying to tailor the rules to what typical parties actually expect, or should it attempt to mold expectations?

In Banner v. Lyon & Healy, Inc., 249 App.Div. 569, 293 N.Y.S. 236 (1937), affirmed without opinion 277 N.Y. 570, 13 N.E.2d 774 (1938), defendant sold plaintiff a violin represented as having been made by Stradivarius. There was evidence that it was made by another violin maker. The court considered the statement to be one of opinion:

> When the sale took place in 1919, Stradivarius had been dead for some 200 years, a fact known to the whole world and to the parties concerned. Plaintiff himself was a noted violinist, generally familiar with violins and those made by Stradivarius. In these circumstances, he must have understood that the defendant Freeman, in any representations made, was but expressing his opinion and honest belief that the instrument was in all respects genuine.

Would a different result follow if the purchaser were the plaintiff in *Powell*?

Although "fact" is usually contrasted with "opinion," it is also contrasted with "law." In National Conversion Corp. v. Cedar Bldg. Corp., 23 N.Y.2d 621, 246 N.E.2d 351, 298 N.Y.S.2d 499 (1969), the defendant lessor stated that the land plaintiff proposed to lease had no zoning restraints, and could be used for garbage conversion. The land was in fact zoned for light manufacturing, which permitted garbage conversion only if odors were not readily detectable at the lot lines. On appeal from a plaintiff's judgment the defendant argued that the representation was not actionable. The unanimous court disagreed:

> Landlords also contend that only a misrepresentation of law rather than of fact is involved and, therefore, that fraud will not lie. There is no longer any doubt that the law has recognized, even in this State, a sharp distinction between a pure opinion of law which may not, except in unusual circumstances, base an action in tort, and a mixed statement of fact as to what the law is or whether it is applicable. . . .

> Most important it is that the law has outgrown the oversimple dichotomy between law and fact in the resolution of issues in deceit. It has been said that "a statement as to the law, like a statement as to anything else, may be intended and understood either as one of fact or one of opinion only, according to the circumstances of the case" [   ] The statements in this case, both before the execution of the lease, and in the body of the lease, exemplify ideally an instance in which the statements are not intended or understood merely as an expression of opinion. Landlords said they knew the premises were in an unrestricted district. This meant that they knew as a fact, that the zoning resolution did not restrict the use of the particular premises, and tenant so understood it. . . .

A curious case of misrepresentation of law was raised by the Watergate break-in, when a burglar sought to recover from his superiors for having told him that the break-in would be legal. The court held that even if the representation were actionable, the burglar's reliance was unreasonable. Democratic National Committee v. McCord, 416 F.Supp. 505 (D.D.C.1976).

Not all misrepresentations are made with words. One important cluster of cases involves acts of active concealment—cases in which defendants paint over leaking surfaces to hide them from a prospective buyer. These cases have presented no problems for the courts and have been analyzed as though the defendant had made a deliberate misrepresentation. See Herzog v. Capital Co., 27 Cal.2d 349, 164 P.2d 8 (1945). A situation that still presented serious problems is that of nondisclosure, discussed in the following case.

Ollerman v. O'Rourke Co., Inc.

Supreme Court of Wisconsin, 1980.
94 Wis.2d 17, 288 N.W.2d 95.

■ ABRAHAMSON, JUSTICE.

This appeal is from an order overruling the motion of O'Rourke Co., Inc., the seller, . . . to dismiss Roy Ollerman's, the buyer's, amended complaint for failing to state a claim upon which relief can be granted. We conclude that the complaint states a claim, and we affirm the order of the circuit court.

[The buyer alleged that he bought a vacant lot in order to build a house; and that while excavating for the house a well was uncapped and water was released.]

The complaint further alleges that the seller is a corporation engaged in the business of developing and selling real estate; that it is experienced in matters of real estate; that it had owned and subdivided the area of real estate in which the subject lot is located; that it was offering the subject lot and other lots in the same area for public sale; that it is familiar with the particular area of real estate in which the lot is located; that the area is zoned residential and that the seller knew it was zoned residential.

The complaint further states that the buyer "was a stranger to the area"; that he was inexperienced in matters of real estate transactions; that he purchased the lot to construct a house; that he did not know of the existence of a well under the land surface hidden from view; that if he had known of the well, he either would not have purchased the property or would have purchased it at a lower price; that the well constituted a defective condition of the lot; that the well made the property worth less for residential purposes than he had been led to believe; that the well made the property unsuitable for building without added expense; and that the seller's failure to disclose the existence of the well was relied upon by the buyer and he was thereby induced to buy this lot in ignorance of the well.

. . .

Additional allegations applicable to what is labeled in the complaint as the "first cause of action" are that the seller, through its agents, knew of the existence of the underground well and, in order to induce buyer to buy the land, "falsely and with intent to defraud," failed to disclose this fact which it had a duty to disclose and which would have had a material bearing on the construction of a residence on the property.

[A "second cause of action" alleged that defendant knew or should have known about the well, and had a duty to ascertain and disclose such information.]

. . .

This court has recognized that misrepresentation is a generic concept separable into the three familiar tort classifications: intent (sometimes called fraudulent misrepresentation, deceit or intentional deceit), negligence and strict responsibility.

. . .

II.

We discuss first whether the complaint states a claim for intentional misrepresentation. Initially we observe, as did the seller, that the complaint does not allege the first two elements of the tort of intentional misrepresentation, namely that the seller made a representation of fact and that the representation was untrue. The gravamen of the wrong is the nature of the false words used and the reliance which they may reasonably induce. In lieu of these allegations of false words, the complaint recites that the seller failed to disclose a fact, the existence of the well. The general rule is that silence, a failure to disclose a fact, is not an intentional misrepresentation unless the seller has a duty to disclose.[7] If there is a duty to disclose a fact, failure to disclose that fact is treated in the law as equivalent to a representation of the non existence of the fact. . . .

The question thus presented in the case at bar is whether the seller had a duty to disclose to the buyer the existence of the well. If there is a duty to disclose, the seller incurs tort liability for intentional misrepresentation (i.e. the representation of the non-existence of the fact), if the elements of the tort of intentional misrepresentation are proved. [ ]

The question of legal duty presents an issue of law. . . .

We recognize that the traditional rule in Wisconsin is that in an action for intentional misrepresentation the seller of real estate, dealing at arm's length with the buyer, has no duty to disclose information to the buyer and therefore has no liability in an action for intentional misrepresentation for failure to disclose.

The traditional legal rule that there is no duty to disclose in an arm's-length transaction is part of the common law doctrine of caveat emptor which is traced to the attitude of rugged individualism reflected in the business economy and the law of the 19th century. The law of misrepresentation has traditionally been closely aligned with mores of the commercial world because the type of interest protected by the law of misrepresentation in business transactions is the interest in formulating business judgments without being misled by others that is, an interest in not being cheated.

Under the doctrine of caveat emptor no person was required to tell all that he or she knew in a business transaction, for in a free market the diligent should not be deprived of the fruits of superior skill and knowledge lawfully acquired. The business world, and the law reflecting business mores and morals, required the parties to a transaction to use their faculties and exercise ordinary business sense, and not to call on the law to stand in loco parentis to protect them in their ordinary dealings with other business people.

> "The picture in sales and in land deals is, in the beginning, that of a community whose trade is simple and face to face and whose traders are neighbors. The goods and the land were there to be seen during the negotiation and particularly in the case of land, everybody knew everybody's land; if not, trade was an arm's

---

7. 3 Restatement (Second) of Torts, sec. 551, Comment *b* (1977) states: " . . . In the absence of a duty of disclosure . . . one who is negotiating a business transaction is not liable in deceit because of his failure to disclose a fact that he knows his adversary would regard as material. . . ." [ ]

length proposition with wits matched against skill. Of course caveat emptor would be the rule in such a society. But caveat emptor was more than a rule of no liability; it was a philosophy that left each individual to his own devices with a minimum of public imposition of standards of fair practice. In the beginning the common law did grant relief from fraud and did recognize that if the seller made an express promise as to his product at the time of the sale he remained liable after the sale on this 'collateral' promise. Indeed covenants for title in the deed were such collateral promises which survived the sale." Dunham, Vendor's Obligation as to Fitness of Land for a Particular Purpose, 37 Minn.L.R. 108, 110 (1953).

Over the years society's attitudes toward good faith and fair dealing in business transactions have undergone significant change, and this change has been reflected in the law. Courts have departed from or relaxed the "no duty to disclose" rule by carving out exceptions to the rule and by refusing to adhere to the rule when it works an injustice. Thus courts have held that the rule does not apply where the seller actively conceals a defect or where he prevents investigation; [13] where the seller has told a half-truth or has made an ambiguous statement if the seller's intent is to create a false impression and he does so; where there is a fiduciary relationship between the parties; or where the facts are peculiarly and exclusively within the knowledge of one party to the transaction and the other party is not in a position to discover the facts for himself.

On the basis of the complaint, the case at bar does not appear to fall into one of these well-recognized exceptions to the "no duty to disclose" rule. However, Dean Prosser has found a "rather amorphous tendency on the part of most courts toward finding a duty of disclosure in cases where the defendant has special knowledge or means of knowledge not open to the plaintiff and is aware that the plaintiff is acting under a misapprehension as to facts which could be of importance to him, and would probably affect his decision."

Dean Keeton described these cases abandoning the "no duty to disclose" rule as follows:

"In the present stage of the law, the decisions show a drawing away from this idea (that nondisclosure is not actionable), and there can be seen an attempt by many courts to reach a just result in so far as possible, but yet maintaining the degree of certainty which the law must have. The statement may often be found that if either party to a contract of sale conceals or suppresses a material fact which he is in good faith bound to disclose then his silence is fraudulent.

13. 3 Restatement (Second) of Torts, sec. 550 (1977) states: "One party to a transaction who by concealment or other action intentionally prevents the other from acquiring material information is subject to the same liability to the other, for pecuniary loss as though he had stated the nonexistence of the matter that the other was thus prevented from discovering." [   ]

"The attitude of the courts toward nondisclosure is undergoing a change and . . . it would seem that the object of the law in these cases should be to impose on parties to the transaction a duty to speak whenever justice, equity, and fair dealing demand it. This statement is made only with reference to instances where the party to be charged is an actor in the transaction. This duty to speak does not result from an implied representation by silence, but exists because a refusal to speak constitutes unfair conduct." Fraud Concealment and Nondisclosure, 15 Tex.L.Rev. 1, 31 (1936).

The test Dean Keeton derives from the cases to determine when the rule of nondisclosure should be abandoned—that is "whenever justice, equity and fair dealing demand it"—presents, as one writer states, "a somewhat nebulous standard, praiseworthy as looking toward more stringent business ethics, but possibly difficult of practical application." [ ]

. . .

The draftsmen of the most recent Restatement of Torts (Second)(1977) have attempted to formulate a rule embodying this trend in the cases toward a more frequent recognition of a duty to disclose. Sec. 551(1) of the Restatement sets forth the traditional rule that one who fails to disclose a fact that he knows may induce reliance in a business transaction is subject to the same liability as if he had represented the nonexistence of the matter that he failed to disclose if, and only if, he is under a duty to exercise reasonable care to disclose the matter in question.[17] Subsection (2) of sec. 551 then sets forth the conditions under which the seller has a duty to use reasonable care to disclose certain information.[18] Sec. 551(2)(e) is the "catch-all" provision setting forth conditions under which a duty to disclose exists; it states that a party to a transaction is under a duty to exercise reasonable care to disclose to the other "facts basic to the transaction, if he knows that the other is about to enter into it under a mistake as to them, and that the other, because of the relationship between them, the customs of the trade or other objective circumstances, would reasonably expect a

---

17. Sec. 551 Liability for Nondisclosure "(1) One who fails to disclose to another a fact that he knows may justifiably induce the other to act or refrain from acting in a business transaction is subject to the same liability to the other as though he had represented the nonexistence of the matter that he has failed to disclose, if, but only if, he is under a duty to the other to exercise reasonable care to disclose the matter in question."

18. Sec. 551 "(2) One party to a business transaction is under a duty to exercise reasonable care to disclose to the other before the transaction is consummated (a) matters known to him that the other is entitled to know because of a fiduciary or other similar relation of trust and confidence between them; and (b) matters known to him that he

knows to be necessary to prevent his partial or ambiguous statement of the facts from being misleading; and (c) subsequently acquired information that he knows will make untrue or misleading a previous representation that when made was true or believed to be so; and (d) the falsity of a representation not made with the expectation that it would be acted upon, if he subsequently learns that the other is about to act in reliance upon it in a transaction with him; and (e) facts basic to the transaction, if he knows that the other is about to enter into it under a mistake as to them, and that the other, because of the relationship between them, the customs of the trade or other objective circumstances, would reasonably expect a disclosure of those facts."

disclosure of those facts." Comment *l* to sec. 551 recognizes the difficulty of specifying the factors that give rise to a reasonable expectation of disclosure:

"*l*. The continuing development of modern business ethics has, however, limited to some extent this privilege to take advantage of ignorance. There are situations in which the defendant not only knows that his bargaining adversary is acting under a mistake basic to the transaction, but also knows that the adversary, by reason of the relation between them, the customs of the trade or other objective circumstances, is reasonably relying upon a disclosure of the unrevealed fact if it exists. In this type of case good faith and fair dealing may require a disclosure.

"It is extremely difficult to be specific as to the factors that give rise to this known, and reasonable, expectation of disclosure. In general, the cases in which the rule stated in Clause (e) has been applied have been those in which the advantage taken of the plaintiff's ignorance is so shocking to the ethical sense of the community, and is so extreme and unfair, as to amount to a form of swindling, in which the plaintiff is led by appearances into a bargain that is a trap, of whose essence and substance he is unaware. In such a case, even in a tort action for deceit, the plaintiff is entitled to be compensated for the loss that he has sustained."

Section 551(2)(e) of the Restatement (Second) of Torts limits the duty to disclose to disclosure of those "facts basic" to the transaction. Comment *j* to sec. 551 differentiates between basic facts and material facts as follows: "A basic fact is a fact that is assumed by the parties as a basis for the transaction itself. It is a fact that goes to the basis, or essence, of the transaction, and is an important part of the substance of what is bargained for or dealt with. Other facts may serve as important and persuasive inducements to enter into the transaction, but not go to its essence. These facts may be material, but they are not basic."

However, the draftsmen of the Restatement recognized that the law was developing to expand the duty to disclosure beyond the duty described in sec. 551.

"There are indications, also, that with changing ethical attitudes in many fields of modern business, the concept of facts basic to the transaction may be expanding and the duty to use reasonable care to disclose the facts may be increasing somewhat. This Subsection is not intended to impede that development." Comment L, Sec. 551, 3 Restatement (Second) of Torts (1977).

This court has moved away from the rule of caveat emptor in real estate transactions, as have courts in other states.

. . .

An analysis of the cases of this jurisdiction and others indicates that the presence of the following elements is significant to persuade a court of the fairness and equity of imposing a duty on a vendor of real estate to disclose known facts: the condition is "latent" and not readily observable by the purchaser; the purchaser acts upon the reasonable assumption that the condition does (or does not) exist; the vendor has special knowledge or means of knowledge not available to the purchaser; and the existence of the condition is material to the transaction, that is, it influences whether the transaction is concluded at all or at the same price.

The seller argues that public policy demands that we not abandon the traditional rule that no action lies against the seller of real estate for failure to disclose in an arm's-length transaction. The seller contends, in its brief, that if this court affirms the circuit court's order overruling the motion to dismiss and allows the buyer to proceed to trial, the court is adopting "what really amounts to a strict policy of 'let the seller beware.'" The seller goes on to state, "Woe indeed to anyone who sells a home, a vacant lot or other piece of real estate and fails to itemize with particularity or give written notice to each prospective buyer of every conceivable condition in and around the property, regardless of whether such a condition is dangerous, defective or could become so by the negligence or recklessness of others. A seller of real estate is not and should not be made an insurer or guarantor of the competence of those with whom the purchaser may later contract."

The seller's position is that imposing a duty to disclose on a vendor of real estate dealing at arm's length with a purchaser would result in an element of uncertainty pervading real estate transactions; that there would be chaos if a vendor were subject to liability after parting with ownership and control of the property; that a rash of litigation would ensue; and that a purchaser could protect himself or herself by inspection and inquiry and by demanding warranties.

The seller's arguments are not persuasive in light of the facts alleged in the complaint and our narrow holding in this case.

Where the vendor is in the real estate business and is skilled and knowledgeable and the purchaser is not, the purchaser is in a poor position to discover a condition which is not readily discernible, and the purchaser may justifiably rely on the knowledge and skill of the vendor. Thus, in this instant case a strong argument for imposing a duty on the seller to disclose material facts is this "reliance factor." The buyer portrayed in this complaint had a reasonable expectation of honesty in the marketplace, that is, that the vendor would disclose material facts which it knew and which were not readily discernible. Under these circumstances the law should impose a duty of honesty on the seller.

In order to determine whether the complaint states a claim for intentional misrepresentation we hold that a subdivider-vendor of a residential lot has a duty to a "non-commercial" purchaser to disclose facts which are known to the vendor, which are material to the transaction, and which are not readily discernible to the purchaser. A fact is known to the vendor if the vendor has actual knowledge of the fact or if the vendor acted in reckless disregard as to the existence of the fact. This usage of the word "know" is the same as in an action for intentional misrepresentation based on a false statement. [ ] A fact is material if a reasonable purchaser would attach importance to its existence or nonexistence in determining the choice of action in the transaction in question; or if the vendor knows or has reason to know that the purchaser regards or is likely to regard the matter as important in determining the choice of action, although a reasonable purchaser would not so regard it. See 3 Restatement (Second) of Torts, sec. 538 (1977). Whether the fact is or is not readily discernible will depend on the nature of the fact, the relation of the vendor and purchaser and the nature of the transaction.

The seller's brief asserts that the well is not a material fact because it does not constitute a defective condition; that the existence of the well was well known in the community; and that the buyer should have made inquiry about the lot. These are matters to be raised at trial, not on a motion to dismiss. The buyer must prove at trial that the existence of the well was a material fact and that his reliance was justifiable.[26]

III.

We turn now to the second cause of action, an action in negligence based on misrepresentation. [The court observed that this was a more

---

26. We previously discussed the purchaser's reliance on the seller in determining whether to impose a duty on the seller to disclose material facts which are not readily discernible. "Reliance" is thus an important factor in determining the existence of the duty to disclose, but it is also an element of the tort of intentional misrepresentation. The buyer in the case at bar has to prove the elements of intentional misrepresentation which this court has frequently set forth: " 'To be actionable the false representation must consist, first, of a statement of fact which is untrue; second, that it was made with intent to defraud and for the purpose of inducing the other party to act upon it; third, that he did in fact rely on it and was induced thereby to act, to his injury or damage.' " [ ] As we noted previously, the failure to disclose (silence), if there is a duty to speak, is typically treated as the equivalent of a representation of the nonexistence of the fact. [ ] Goldfarb, in his article entitled Fraud & Nondisclosure in the Vendor–Purchaser Relation, 8 Western R.L.Rev. 5, 6–9 (1956), points up some of the difficulties of treating a "nondisclosure" as if it were fraudulent misrepresentation especially as to the element of reliance:

"The courts and commentators treat actionable silence or, as it is more often

denominated, 'actionable nondisclosure' as a variety of misrepresentation. It is one of the implied theses of the present inquiry that it is not logical, or even helpful, to do so. True, under some circumstances, a failure to speak may amount to the equivalent of an actual, verbal representation of fact. Silence is, after all, a type of conduct, or at least of forbearance. If the representation thus implied is, in fact, false, and if the other elements of fraud are present, the plaintiff ought to be entitled to a remedy. But, under many circumstances, silence is merely silence. It says nothing. The silent party may fail to deny or assert a given fact. But it may be unfair and unreasonable to label his behavior as a representation, much less a misrepresentation. And yet, even under such circumstances, the silence may be tortious." "The courts' insistence on relating such nondisclosure to misrepresentation seems to stem from a tradition of labeling and categorizing. It will avail us little to fight this tendency. It is enough to be aware of it. This awareness alone can help prevent us from falling prey to that most treacherous of semantic traps: the tyranny of labels." . . .

difficult duty to establish and deferred a ruling on its validity until the case had been tried.]

We have enumerated several public policy reasons for not imposing liability despite a finding of negligence as a causal factor producing injury:

"(1) The injury is too remote from the negligence; or (2) the injury is too wholly out of proportion to the culpability of the negligent tortfeasor; or (3) in retrospect it appears too highly extraordinary that the negligence should have brought about the harm; or (4) because allowance of recovery would place too unreasonable a burden on the negligent tortfeasor; or (5) because allowance of recovery would be too likely to open the way for fraudulent claims; or (6) allowance of recovery would enter a field that has no sensible or just stopping point." [   ]

Courts have imposed liability in negligence actions for personal injury or property damage caused by false statements or caused by nondisclosure. However, courts have been more reluctant to impose liability in negligence actions for misrepresentations causing pecuniary loss (not resulting from bodily harm or physical damage to property). . . .

. . .

Similarly, the draftsmen of the Restatement of Torts (Second), in discussing liability for information negligently supplied for the guidance of others in their business transactions, caution that the scope of liability for failing to exercise reasonable care in supplying correct information is not determined by the rules that govern liability for the negligent supplying of chattels that imperil the security of persons or property or other negligent misrepresentation that results in physical harm. When there is no intent to deceive, but only negligence, the fault of the maker of the misrepresentation is sufficiently less to justify a narrower responsibility for its consequences.

The reason a narrower scope of liability is fixed for negligent misrepresentation than for deceit is to be found in the difference between the obligations of honesty and of care, and in the significance of this difference to the reasonable expectations of the users of information that is supplied in connection with commercial transactions. Honesty requires only that the maker of a representation speak in good faith and without consciousness of a lack of any basis for belief in the truth or accuracy of what he says. The standard of honesty is unequivocal and ascertainable without regard to the character of the transaction in which the information will ultimately be relied upon or the situation of the party relying upon it. Any user of commercial information may reasonably expect the observance of this standard by a supplier of information to whom his use is reasonably foreseeable.

On the other hand, it does not follow that every user of commercial information may hold every maker to a duty of care.

By limiting the liability for negligence of a supplier of information to be used in commercial transactions to cases in which he manifests an intent to supply the information for the sort of use in which the plaintiff's loss occurs, the law promotes the important social policy of encouraging the flow of commercial information upon which the operation of the economy rests. The limitation applies, however, only in the case of information supplied in good faith, for no interest of society is served by promoting the flow of information not genuinely believed by its maker to be true. Restatement (Second) of Torts, sec. 552, Comment *a* (1977). [ ]

. . .

We conclude that at the complaint and motion-to-dismiss stage in the case at bar we cannot resolve the public policy issues involved; a full trial must precede the trial court's and appellate court's determination of the issue as to what liability, if any, attaches to the seller for its failure to exercise ordinary care in ascertaining or disclosing the existence of the well. A trial court or jury finding as to negligence, damage and the causal relation between them would be material and helpful in evaluating the public policy considerations. [ ]

. . .

For the reasons set forth, we hold that the allegations of the complaint state a claim upon which relief can be granted and that the motion to dismiss the complaint was properly overruled.

[Three concurring justices agreed that the complaint set forth a claim on which relief could be granted. They disagreed with the majority's extended discussion of the law when only an amended complaint was before it. "There is no necessity for expounding on various legal principles relating to the theories of recovery advanced by the plaintiff at the pleading stage. In most instances, attempting to decide the law of the case when the case has not been tried and the facts are not before the court is an appellate practice to be avoided."]

NOTES AND QUESTIONS

1. The complaint asserts that the seller "falsely and with intent to defraud" failed to disclose the well's existence. How can silence ever be "false"? How might it be found false in this case?

2. The court lists several categories of cases in which courts had already decided that silence was actionable, but notes that plaintiff's case "does not appear to fall into" any of them. Why not? What is the basis on which this complaint is upheld?

3. When the court lists the elements that it finds working toward a duty to disclose in this case one of them is that "the vendor has special knowledge or means of knowledge not available to the purchaser." Can the purchaser ever have such knowledge?

4. What is the role of "reliance" in this case? Reliance is considered extensively after these notes.

5. Why does the court defer decision on a duty to use due care to ascertain and reveal important information?

6. The trend away from caveat emptor continues. In Strawn v. Canuso, 140 N.J. 43, 657 A.2d 420 (1995), the court held that the developer and broker had a duty to disclose to home buyers the existence of a nearby off-site closed landfill, where the conditions are known to the developer or broker and "unknown and not readily observable by the buyer if the existence of those conditions is of sufficient materiality to affect the habitability, use, or enjoyment of the property and, therefore, render the property substantially less desirable or valuable to the objectively reasonable buyer." See also Stambovsky v. Ackley, 169 App.Div.2d 254, 572 N.Y.S.2d 672 (1991)(duty to disclose that house had been "haunted"—the so-called "poltergeist case"); Reed v. King, 145 Cal.App.3d 261, 193 Cal. Rptr. 130 (1983)(duty on brokers to disclose that multiple murders had occurred in the house); Silva v. Stevens, 156 Vt. 94, 589 A.2d 852 (1991)(duty to disclose may arise in arm's-length transaction from the "relations of the parties, such as that of trust or confidence, or superior knowledge or means of knowledge"—here historical facts that were not readily accessible to the buyer).

7. *Duty of due care.* So far as the duty of due care is concerned, a few cases reject any such duty in arm's length cases. E.g., South County, Inc. v. First Western Loan Co., 315 Ark. 722, 871 S.W.2d 325 (1994)(no action where developer claimed that a lender had negligently misrepresented intent to make a loan thus inducing the developer to continue spending on the proposed development; deceit action was adequate protection). Recall also, *Onita Pacific*, p. 276, supra and the disagreement among the courts on this question discussed at that point.

8. *Partial disclosure.* In Junius Constr. Corp. v. Cohen, 257 N.Y. 393, 178 N.E. 672 (1931), plaintiff was to buy some land from defendant, who informed plaintiff that the final maps of the local governing body showed two roads that, if opened, would modify the plot's boundaries to minor extents. Defendant did not tell plaintiff about a third street which, if opened, would cut the plot in half. Judge Cardozo stated:

> Misrepresentation, if there was any, as to a risk so vital was something that went to the very essence of the bargain. We do not say that the seller was under a duty to mention the projected streets at all. That question is not here. What we say is merely this, that having undertaken or professed to mention them, he could not fairly stop half way, listing those that were unimportant and keeping silent as to the other. The enumeration of two streets, described as unopened but projected,

was a tacit representation that the land to be conveyed was subject to no others, and certainly subject to no others materially affecting the value of the purchase.

Does the rationale apply only to other roads or would it extend to sewer lines? How about a forthcoming tax increase? Are there any limits?

In *Silva v. Stevens,* supra, the court also imposed an independent duty to speak where the defendant engages in a partial disclosure—that noted leaks had been present but had been fixed—actionable fraud could be found as to other leaks even if there had been no duty to say anything in the first place. To the same effect, see Gibb v. Citicorp Mortgage, Inc., 246 Neb. 355, 518 N.W.2d 910 (1994), in which buyer was shown visible termite damage that had been fixed and assured that this was the only such damage in the house—although defendants knew that there was extensive more unfixed termite damage that was not visible.

Falsity. The element of "falsity" has presented little legal difficulty although, of course, it produces many questions of fact. The courts earlier concluded that although statements might literally be accurate, they might be found to be false if they would mislead recipients. In Remeikis v. Boss & Phelps, Inc., 419 A.2d 986 (D.C.App.1980), a termite report stated that there was "no visible evidence of present termite activity." Although literally true, it might be actionable if "made to create a false impression" as with extensive "invisible" damage or visible evidence of "past" activity. The court relied on an earlier case in which the seller of a rooming house was held liable for a statement that accurately told the level of present rentals but that left the incorrect impression that those rental charges were legally permissible.

Reliance. The element of reliance is really a composite of several different ideas. The first is "actual" reliance, which corresponds to the actual causation requirement in other torts. If the plaintiff has not relied on the defendant's misrepresentation, then the critical connection between misconduct and damages is missing. In Nader v. Allegheny Airlines, Inc., 626 F.2d 1031 (D.C.Cir.1980), the plaintiff was "bumped" from a plane because by the time he arrived other confirmed passengers on the over-booked flight had already been seated. As a result he missed a rally at which he was to deliver a speech. He asserted that the airline had misrepresented its policy concerning "confirmed" reservations by not informing passengers that it engaged in overbooking. Among the reasons for dismissing the case, the court noted that Nader "was an extraordinarily knowledgeable passenger, an able lawyer and a famous and distinguished advocate of consumer rights, including the rights of airline passengers." In fact, he had been bumped twice before in similar situations, the second time only two days before he reserved his seat for the Allegheny flight. It "cannot be said that Nader relied on his confirmed reservation with Allegheny as a guarantee of passage."

A proximate cause aspect of reliance requires that plaintiff's harm must come from reliance on the misrepresented fact. Thus, if D misrepresents several facts about a company's financial health in order to induce P to buy that company's stock, D is not liable if the stock suddenly falls in value because of the unexpected death of the company's chief operating officer—even though P would not have bought the stock had D not misrepresented. See Restatement (Second) § 548A.

The reliance must also be "justifiable." Restatement (Second) § 545A, comment *b*, addresses the matter as follows:

> Although the plaintiff's reliance on the misrepresentation must be justifiable, . . . this does not mean that his conduct must conform to the standard of the reasonable man. Justification is a matter of the qualities and characteristics of the particular plaintiff, and the circumstances of the particular case, rather than of the application of a community standard of conduct to all cases. Negligent reliance and action sometimes will not be justifiable, and the recovery will be barred accordingly; but this is not always the case. There will be cases in which a plaintiff may be justified in relying upon the representation, even though his conduct in doing so does not conform to the community standard of knowledge, intelligence, judgment or care. Thus, under the rule stated in § 540, the recipient of a fraudulent misrepresentation is not required to investigate its truth, even when a reasonable man of ordinary caution would do so before taking action; and it is only when he knows of the falsity or it is obvious to him that his reliance is not justified. (See § 541). . . .

> Cases frequently arise in which negligent reliance is justified, when the defendant knows of the plaintiff's incapacity to conform to the standard of conduct of a reasonable man, or of his credulity, gullibility or other tendency to depart from it, and deliberately practices upon the deficiencies of the plaintiff in order to deceive him. . . . Thus one who presents a document to an illiterate man, misrepresenting its contents, and invites him to sign it, knowing that he cannot read it, cannot be heard to say that he is negligent in doing so. The same may be true when there is a relation of trust and confidence between the parties or the defendant has made successful efforts to win the confidence of the plaintiff and then takes advantage of it to deceive him.

Does this discussion of reliance clarify its role on remand in *Ollerman?*

Defenses. The courts generally agree that contributory negligence is no defense whatever to intentional misrepresentation. See Florenzano v. Olson, 387 N.W.2d 168 (Minn.1986). There is some disagreement, though, over whether comparative negligence should be used when the defendant has negligently misrepresented. The court in *Florenzano* concluded that the reasons that warranted using comparative negligence in personal injury cases applied as well to cases of economic harm. See also, *Greycas, Inc. v. Proud,* p. 281, supra, asserting that plaintiff's negligence "is as much a defense to negligent misrepresentation as to any other tort of negligence." The leading case contra is Carroll v. Gava, 98 Cal.App.3d 892, 159 Cal.Rptr. 778 (1979), in which the court said that in business deals it is important for the information to be accurate. Denying the defense of comparative negligence will encourage those who provide information to make it accurate. Is the element of justifiable reliance adequately distinguished from a defense of contributory negligence?

Merger and "as is" clauses. Courts increasingly conclude that the existence of an "as is" provision in the contract or a statement that the buyer is relying only on a personal inspection will not prevent the plaintiff from showing that fraud had occurred. See, e.g., Ron Greenspan Volkswagen, Inc. v. Ford Motor Land Devel.Corp., 32 Cal.App.4th 985, 38 Cal.Rptr.2d 783 (1995)("when the agreement itself is procured by fraud, none of its provisions have any legal or binding effect"). The *Gibb* and *Silva* cases, supra, involving partial disclosures, both involved clauses that unsuccessfully attempted to negate any claim of reliance. Whether reliance is justifiable when the contract contains such a disclaimer is generally a question of fact. Beyond that, however, courts do require plaintiffs, even in claims of fraudulent concealment, show that they exercised "diligent attention, observation and judgment," though they may rely upon a representation in all cases if it is a positive statement of fact and if an investigation would be required to discover the truth.

Damages. A plaintiff who surmounts these difficulties is entitled to damages. There is confusion over the proper way to measure the compensatory award. The tort standard would appear to be the cost of the property plaintiff bought less the actual value of that property. This is the usual out-of-pocket rule. But some states use the difference between what the value would have been if the representations had been true and the actual value—the usual contract measure, often called the benefit-of-the-bargain rule. Some states follow one or the other exclusively. Others use one or the other depending on the specific facts. See, e.g., American Family Service Corp. v. Michelfelder, 968 F.2d 667 (8th Cir.1992)(prospective buyer entitled to benefit-of-the-bargain damages where seller misrepresented intent to sell).

The choice of the compensatory rule may affect the state's attitude toward punitive damages in deceit cases. In Walker v. Sheldon, 10 N.Y.2d 401, 179 N.E.2d 497, 223 N.Y.S.2d 488 (1961), plaintiff alleged that defendants' misrepresentations were made "in the regular course of" their business "and as the basis of their business knowing that plaintiff would, as others similarly situated had in the past, act upon said representations." The complaint asked compensatory damages of $1,380 and punitive damages of $75,000. Defendants moved to strike the request for punitive damages as irrelevant and prejudicial. The court of appeals, 4–3, affirmed denial of the motion. The majority recognized that in "ordinary" fraud and deceit cases it did not allow punitive damages, but held that where defendant's conduct "evinced a high degree of moral turpitude and demonstrated such wanton dishonesty as to imply a criminal indifference to civil obligations" punitive damages might lie. It noted that punitive damages often induce the victim to take action against a wrongdoer that he might not otherwise take:

Exemplary damages are more likely to serve their desired purpose of deterring similar conduct in a fraud case, such as that before us, than in any other area of tort. One who acts out of anger or hate, for instance, in committing assault or libel, is not likely to be deterred by the fear of punitive damages. On the other hand, those who deliberately and coolly engage in a far-flung fraudulent scheme, systematically conducted for profit, are very much more likely to pause and consider the consequences if they have to pay more than the actual loss suffered by an individual plaintiff. An occasional award of compensatory damages against such parties would have little deterrent effect. A judgment simply for compensatory damages would require the offender to do no more than return the money which he had taken from the plaintiff.

The dissent condemned the use of tort law for deterrence, and urged that the criminal law be reserved for deterrence and tort law used for compensation only. It viewed the recovery of punitive damages by the plaintiff as an unjust windfall. If hesitant plaintiffs had to be encouraged to sue, the dissent preferred that they be permitted to recover court costs or some other finite amount, rather than having access to the broad discretion of a jury. Does this debate add anything to the battle over the general propriety of punitive damages in tort law? Recall the discussion at p. 650, supra.

Might the majority in *Walker* have been influenced by the fact that New York follows the out-of-pocket rule? Note also that some of the legislative changes in the law of punitive damages, discussed p. 670, supra, may well limit such recoveries even for fraud.

3.   STRICT LIABILITY

Because the law allows rescission of contracts on grounds of innocent, negligent, or fraudulent misrepresentations, there has been a recent movement away from the scienter requirement. The focal point of the debate has been Restatement (Second) of Torts § 552C, which provides in part that "One who, in a sale, rental or exchange transaction with another, makes a misrepresentation . . . is subject to the other for pecuniary loss caused to him . . . even though it is not made fraudulently or negligently." Subsection (2) provides that the amount recoverable is "limited to the difference between the value of what the other has parted with and the value of what he has received in the transaction." A caveat expresses no opinion whether strict liability might apply to other types of business transactions.

Comment *b* observes that "it is difficult to say with certainty whether this rule should be regarded as one of strict liability in the law of torts, eliminating the requirement of intent or negligence in making the representation, or one of the law of restitution, eliminating the requirement of rescinding and restoring the status quo."

Although the Restatement expresses no view on extensions to other types of transactions, a few courts have imposed strict liability on agents selling for their principals. Imposing such liability in a case involving the condition of a well on the property, the court in Bevins v. Ballard, 655 P.2d 757 (Alaska 1982), explained that purchasers are entitled to rely on real estate brokers' representations because brokers "are licensed professionals, possessing superior knowledge of the realty they sell and the real estate market generally." Brokers can guard against liability by "investigating the owner's statements, or by disclaiming knowledge, by requiring the seller to sign at the time of listing a statement setting forth representations which will be made, certifying that they are true and providing for indemnification if they are not." The court noted that this approach might be particularly appropriate in land cases because the seller frequently moves from the jurisdiction after the sale.

Liability is rejected in Hoffman v. Connall, 108 Wash.2d 69, 736 P.2d 242 (1987), involving a misrepresentation of boundary lines. Brokers had no duty to verify a seller's representations unless they had reason to doubt them. A negligence standard adequately protected innocent buyers in these cases. Moreover, buyers could protect themselves by purchasing title insurance.

Section 552C is discussed extensively in Hill, Damages for Innocent Misrepresentation, 73 Colum.L.Rev. 679 (1973). The development of a strict liability action is discussed in United States Fidelity and Guaranty Co. v. Black, 412 Mich. 99, 313 N.W.2d 77 (1981).

B. INTERFERENCE WITH CONTRACT

Earlier we had occasion to consider questions arising when the defendant's negligence interfered with the contractual relations of others. Recall the case of the negligence that forced an airline to close down for a day, p. 282, supra. Those defendants had no desire to interfere with anyone's contracts and the cases tested how far courts thought it appropriate to extend liability for this type of harm.

Now we consider cases in which defendants, knowing of the existence of a contract between the plaintiff and a third party, deliberately undertake to interfere with that contractual relationship.

Imperial Ice Co. v. Rossier

Supreme Court of California, 1941.
18 Cal.2d 33, 112 P.2d 631.

■ TRAYNOR, J. The California Consumers Company purchased from S.L. Coker an ice distributing business, inclusive of good will, located in territory comprising the city of Santa Monica and the former city of Sawtelle. In the purchase agreement Coker contracted as follows: "I do further agree in consideration of said purchase and in connection therewith, that I will not engage in the business of selling and or distributing ice, either directly or indirectly, in the above described territory so long as the purchasers, or anyone deriving title to the good will of said business from said purchasers, shall be engaged in a like business therein." Plaintiff, the Imperial Ice Company, acquired from the successor in interest of the California Consumers Company full title to this ice distributing business, including the right to enforce the covenant not to compete. Coker subsequently began selling in the same territory, in violation of the contract, ice supplied to him by a company owned by W. Rossier, J.A. Matheson, and Fred Matheson. Plaintiff thereupon brought this action in the superior court for an injunction to restrain Coker from violating the contract and to restrain Rossier and the Mathesons from inducing Coker to violate the contract. The complaint alleges that Rossier and the Mathesons induced Coker to violate his contract so that they might sell ice to him at a profit. The trial court sustained without leave to amend a demurrer to the complaint of the defendants Rossier and the Mathesons and gave judgment for those defendants. Plaintiff has appealed from the judgment on the sole ground that the complaint stated a cause of action against the defendants Rossier and the Mathesons for inducing the breach of contract.

The question thus presented to this court is under what circumstances may an action be maintained against a defendant who has induced a third party to violate a contract with the plaintiff.

It is universally recognized that an action will lie for inducing breach of contract by a resort to means in themselves unlawful such as libel, slander, fraud, physical violence, or threats of such action. [ ] Most jurisdictions also hold that an action will lie for inducing a breach of contract by the use of moral, social, or economic pressures, in themselves lawful, unless there is sufficient justification for such inducement. [ ]

Such justification exists when a person induces a breach of contract to protect an interest that has greater social value than insuring the stability of the contract. (Rest., Torts, sec. 767.) Thus, a person is justified in inducing the breach of a contract the enforcement of which would be injurious to health, safety, or good morals. (Brimelow v. Casson, (1924) 1 Ch. 302; [ ].) The interest of labor in improving working conditions is of sufficient social importance to justify peaceful labor tactics otherwise lawful, though they have the effect of inducing breaches of contracts between employer and employee or employer and customer. [ ] In numerous other situations justification exists (see Rest., Torts, secs. 766 to 774) depending upon the importance of the interest protected. The presence or absence of ill-will, sometimes referred to as "malice," is immaterial, except as it indicates whether or not an interest is actually being protected. (Boyson v. Thorn, 98 Cal. 578, [ ].)

It is well established, however, that a person is not justified in inducing a breach of contract simply because he is in competition with one of the parties to the contract and seeks to further his own economic advantage at the expense of the other. [ ] Whatever interest society has in encouraging free and open competition by means not in themselves unlawful, contractual stability is generally accepted as of greater importance than competitive freedom. Competitive freedom, however, is of sufficient importance to justify one competitor in inducing a third party to forsake another competitor if no contractual relationship exists between the latter two. [ ] A person is likewise free to carry on his business, including reduction of prices, advertising, and solicitation in the usual lawful manner although some third party may be induced thereby to breach his contract with a competitor in favor of dealing with the advertiser. [ ] Again, if two parties have separate contracts with a third, each may resort to any legitimate means at his disposal to secure performance of his contract even though the necessary result will be to cause a breach of the other contract. [ ] A party may not, however, under the guise of competition actively and affirmatively induce the breach of a competitor's contract in order to secure an economic advantage over that competitor. The act of inducing the breach must be an intentional one. If the actor had no knowledge of the existence of the contract or his actions were not intended to induce a breach, he cannot be held liable though an actual breach results from his lawful and proper acts. [ ]

In California the case of Boyson v. Thorn, supra, has been considered by many as establishing the proposition that no action will lie in this state for inducing breach of contract by means which are not otherwise unlawful. In that case the manager of a hotel induced the owner of the hotel to evict plaintiffs in violation of a contract. The complaint expressly alleged the existence of malicious motives on the part of the manager. This court affirmed a judgment entered on an order which sustained a demurrer without leave to amend, stating that an act otherwise lawful was not rendered unlawful by the existence of "malice." It is clear that the confidential relationship that existed between the manager of the hotel and the owner justified the manager in advising the owner to violate his contract with plaintiffs. His conduct thus being justified, it was lawful despite the existence of ill-will or malice on his part. The statements to the effect that no interference with contractual relations is actionable if the means employed are otherwise lawful were not necessary to the decision and should be disregarded. . . .

The complaint in the present case alleges that defendants actively induced Coker to violate his contract with plaintiffs so that they might sell ice to him. The contract gave to plaintiff the right to sell ice in the stated territory free from the competition of Coker. The defendants, by virtue of their interest in the sale of ice in that territory, were in effect competing with plaintiff. By inducing Coker to violate his contract, as alleged in the complaint, they sought to further their own economic advantage at plaintiff's expense. Such conduct is not justified. Had defendants merely sold ice to Coker without actively inducing him to violate his contract, his distribution of the ice in the forbidden territory in violation of his contract would not then have rendered defendants liable. They may carry on their business of selling ice as usual without incurring liability for breaches of contract by their customers. It is necessary to prove that they intentionally and actively induced the breach. Since the complaint alleges that they did so and asks for an injunction on the grounds that damages would be inadequate, it states a cause of action, and the demurrer should therefore have been overruled.

The judgment is reversed.

■ EDMONDS, J., SHENK, J., and GIBSON, C.J., concurred. CURTIS, J., concurred in the judgment.

NOTES AND QUESTIONS

1. This action originated in Lumley v. Gye, 2 El. & Bl. 216, 118 Eng.Rep. 749 (1853), involving Lumley, who was lessee and manager of Queen's Theatre, Johanna Wagner, a world-famous singer, and Gye, who was Lumley's competitor. Gye, by offering more money, apparently induced Wagner to breach her contract to perform for a stated period in Lumley's theatre. Lumley then brought an action to enforce a negative covenant in his contract with Wagner that prohibited her from performing for anyone else during the term of her contract without Lumley's consent. That injunction was granted in Lumley v. Wagner, 1 DeG., M. & G. 604, 42 Eng.Rep. 687 (1852), but apparently Wagner decided to sing for no one and did not return to the plaintiff's theatre. (Why didn't Lumley ask specific performance of his contract? Isn't enforcement of the negative covenant uncomfortably close to ordering performance?) When the first action did not bring Wagner back, Lumley brought his second action—against Gye for inducing breach of contract. Although a statute had been passed in 1349, in the wake of the Black Death, designed to deter scarce workers from changing their jobs, it had been limited to master-servant relations. In Lumley v. Gye, such meddling was barred in personal service contracts as well. The doctrine has since been extended to protect contracts generally from intentional interference. Do Lumley and Imperial Ice Co. need tort actions in addition to their contract actions?

2. Assuming that the elements of the tort action have been satisfied, what should determine whether the plaintiff receives damages, an injunction, or both? How do these remedies against inducing breach of contract relate to the plaintiff's possible action against the party who has been induced to breach?

3. For a recent discussion of whether plaintiff must prove "improper" motives or the defendant has the burden of justifying the behavior, see United Truck Leasing Corp. v. Geltman, 406 Mass. 811, 551 N.E.2d 20 (1990). For a recent adoption of the action, see Kenty v. Transamerica Premium Ins.Co., 72 Ohio St.3d 415, 650 N.E.2d 863 (1995).

4. *Mixed Motive.* Generally, if the defendant has a legitimate economic justification for interfering with the plaintiff's contract, additional improper motives will not defeat the privilege. E.g., Trepanier v. Getting Organized, Inc., 155 Vt. 259, 583 A.2d 583 (1990). Some courts, however, when confronted with both proper and improper motives, have sought the "dominant" one. In such cases the defendant has the burden of proving that the predominant motive justified the interference. See also Crandall

Corp. v. Navistar Int'l Trans. Corp., 302 S.C. 265, 395 S.E.2d 179 (1990). Since evidence in cases involving multiple motives is usually conflicting, virtually all of these cases go to a jury. See Hatten v. Union Oil Co., 778 P.2d 1150 (Alaska 1989)(reversing defendant's summary judgment where the question was whether defendant had interfered with plaintiff's employment contract with a third party because defendant had been concerned about safety on its premises or because it was angry with plaintiff for another reason).

5. Why does *Imperial Ice* say that contractual stability is "generally accepted as of greater importance than competitive freedom"? In Perlman, Interference with Contract and Other Economic Expectancies: A Clash of Tort and Contract Theory, 49 U.Chi.L.Rev. 61 (1982), the author suggests that the notion of "efficient breach" in contract law should lead to the encouragement of breaches that serve the social interest in putting limited resources to higher-valued uses unless the means are unlawful: "In the case of other lawful acts, tort liability works at cross-purposes with contract policies. Contract remedies seem to promote efficiency, whereas the addition of inducer liability inhibits efficient outcomes." See generally A. Kronman and R. Posner, The Economics of Contract Law (1979).

6. As *Imperial Ice* indicates, a defendant may justify an otherwise unpermitted interference with the contract relations of others. It is clear that one cannot interfere with a contract for a finite term on the ground of economic self-interest. Bank of New York v. Berisford, Int'l, 190 App. Div.2d 622, 594 N.Y.S.2d 152 (1993). Beyond that, deciding whether the interest that defendant is seeking to protect "has greater social value than insuring the stability of contract" is a difficult and often unpredictable task.

In the cited Brimelow v. Casson, the producer of a touring company of dancers sued an actors' association for inducing theatre owners to breach their contracts that permitted plaintiff to perform in their theaters. The defendants had told the owners that since the plaintiff refused to pay his dancers a living wage, several of them had to resort to immorality to support themselves. The owners responded by cancelling the leases. The court held that the association was privileged to tell this to the owners and to ask them to breach the contract. Apparently the charges were true. What if the defendants had honestly believed the charges but had been misled by some of the dancers? What result if the defendants had been unable to persuade the owners by their true stories but did succeed by threatening physical violence unless the owners agreed to cancel plaintiff's troupe? As Perlman indicates, some acceptable justifications have become crystallized, such as giving advice in family relationships and seeking to enforce conflicting claims against the same promisor.

It is permissible to interfere in order to protect your own contract rights. In Personal Preference Video, Inc. v. Home Box Office, Inc., 986 F.2d 110 (5th Cir.1993), plaintiff understood that it had certain exclusive telecast rights to a boxing match. When it appeared that the contracting party had subsequently given a second party conflicting rights, plaintiff took steps that interfered with that second contract. The privilege was held to apply "if (1) the interference was done in a bona fide exercise of the defendant's own rights or (2) the defendant had an equal or superior right in the subject matter to that of the plaintiff. [   ] This privilege extends to good faith assertions of colorable legal rights."

It is generally permissible to talk with plaintiff's dissatisfied customers but not to attempt to enlist satisfied customers who are under contract with the plaintiff. See Kendall/Hunt Publishing Co. v. Rowe, 424 N.W.2d 235 (Iowa 1988).

One of the most important justifications has been the claim of labor organizations referred to in *Imperial Ice*. So long as violent and other tortious means are not involved, the states' power to impose liability for such action has been preempted by federal legislation regulating labor-management relations. United Auto., Aircraft and Agr. Implement Workers v. Russell, 356 U.S. 634 (1958). To the extent traditional torts are involved, state law is still applicable. Concerted refusals to deal that seek to gain competitive advantage are now regulated extensively by antitrust legislation at both the federal and state levels. This is explored in courses on Antitrust Law, Labor Law and Unfair Competition.

7. There is some confusion over how far these doctrines extend to contracts that are voidable or terminable at will. See Guard–Life Corp. v. S. Parker Hardware Manufacturing Corp., 50 N.Y.2d 183, 406 N.E.2d 445, 428 N.Y.S.2d 628 (1980), concluding that liability may flow from interference with a contract that was voidable for lack of mutuality. See also Sterner v. Marathon Oil Co., 767 S.W.2d 686 (Tex.1989), permitting the interference action when the contract was terminable at will. On the other hand, the fact that either party can void the contract or terminate at will may well affect the measure of damages or the scope of privilege to interfere.

8. On occasion, the defendant's interference does not take the form of inducing the promisor to breach, but rather involves efforts to make it more difficult for the promisor to perform. For example, in McNary v. Chamberlain, 34 Conn. 384 (1867), plaintiff alleged that the defendant, knowing that the town was paying plaintiff a flat rate to keep a particular road in good repair, dumped stones and rubbish on the road and clogged a drain to flood the road. The court held that a claim had been stated because defendant "knew that the plaintiff had made such a contract, and took advantage of its existence to injure him in the manner described. He made use of the contract as an instrument to accomplish his purpose. As well may it be claimed that where one beats another with a bludgeon, the injury is too remote because the damage was done by the bludgeon."

By analogy, a party whose act renders the performance of a contract of less or no value to the person entitled to its benefits, may be liable in tort for interfering with the contract. In DEP Corp. v. Interstate Cigar Co., 622 F.2d 621 (2d Cir.1980), a British corporation, which had the world-wide distribution rights to Pears Soap, entered into a contract that gave plaintiff the exclusive right to distribute the product in the United States and

Puerto Rico. Defendants bought Pears Soap through European middlemen and sold the soap in the United States, despite plaintiff's exclusive distribution rights. The district court's dismissal was reversed. Defendants had knowingly interfered with plaintiff's exclusive distribution contract.

9. *Consultants.* Consultants hired by a business to advise it cannot be liable when they suggest that the business breach its contract with the plaintiff so long as the consultant was asked for advice and gave it honestly and in good faith. See Trepanier v. Getting Organized, Inc., 155 Vt. 259, 583 A.2d 583 (1990). See also Pacific Gas & Elec. Co. v. Bear Stearns & Co., 50 Cal.3d 1118, 791 P.2d 587, 270 Cal.Rptr. 1 (1990), protecting a consultant that advised its client to sue to terminate its contract with plaintiff. To allow an action against the consultant "when the only interference alleged is that defendant induced the bringing of potentially meritorious litigation would be an unwarranted expansion of the scope of these torts and a pernicious barrier to free access to the courts."

10. Courts have not extended this action beyond intentional interferences. See Union Camp Corp. v. Southern Bulk Indus., Inc., 259 Ga. 828, 388 S.E.2d 524 (1990). Non-intentional harm may be actionable as negligent infliction of economic harm, discussed in Chapter IV.

11. *The Pennzoil–Texaco Case.* The biggest civil judgment in American history involved a suit for interference with contract. In 1983, Pennzoil entered into negotiations with major shareholders of Getty Oil Co., that would have given Pennzoil 43 percent of Getty's shares with the understanding that Pennzoil would acquire control of Getty if it could work out a restructuring agreement acceptable to Getty's board. A month later, Pennzoil and Getty began drafting a definitive merger agreement. As this agreement was being reached, Getty representatives entered into negotiations to sell Getty shares to Texaco. When the share sale was announced Pennzoil informed the Getty board that it expected Getty to honor its arrangement with Pennzoil. Nonetheless, Texaco and Getty eventually signed a formal merger agreement that gave Texaco control over Getty.

Pennzoil's suit against Texaco in Texas alleged interference with Pennzoil's contractual relations with Getty. The jury returned a verdict for $10.53 billion, including $7.53 in compensatory damages and $3 billion in punitive damages. On appeal, liability was affirmed but the punitive award was reduced to $1 billion. Texaco, Inc. v. Pennzoil, Co., 729 S.W.2d 768 (Tex.App.1987), cert. dismissed 485 U.S. 994 (1988). Efforts to set the judgment aside failed and the parties ultimately settled for $3 billion. The episode is noted in 33 N.Y.L.Sch.L.Rev. 111 (1988).

C. Interference With Prospective Economic Advantage

We have just examined instances in which defendants were found liable for damages resulting from intentional interference with existing contractual relationships. The question of how far that action might extend beyond contracts has been the subject of much discussion and confusion. The following case addresses the issue—and at the same time reappraises *Imperial Ice v. Rossier*.

Della Penna v. Toyota Motor Sales, U.S.A., Inc.,

Supreme Court of California, 1995.
11 Cal.4th 376, 902 P.2d 740, 45 Cal.Rptr.2d 436.

■ ARABIAN, J.

We granted review to reexamine, in light of divergent rulings from the Court of Appeal and a doctrinal evolution among other state high courts, the elements of the tort variously known as interference with "prospective economic advantage," "prospective contractual relations," or "prospective economic relations," and the allocation of the burdens of proof between the parties to such an action. . . .

[Toyota was trying to prevent imported Lexus autos from being re-exported to Japan and took several steps to prevent that from happening. When it became apparent that this was in fact happening, defendant compiled a list of "offenders" and warned its dealers that those who did business with such offenders faced possible sanctions. Plaintiff did a profitable business as a wholesaler buying Lexus cars from retailers at near retail prices and exporting them to Japan for resale. As a result of defendant's efforts, plaintiff's supply of cars dried up.

When its tort claim for interference with prospective economic advantage was tried to a jury, the judge decided, over objection, to charge that the plaintiff had the burden of showing that the defendant's interference was "wrongful." After losing that objection, plaintiff framed a definition of "wrongful" that the judge read to the jury that included conduct "outside the realm of legitimate business transactions. . . . Wrongfulness may lie in the method used or by virtue of an improper motive." The jury returned a defense verdict. The court of appeal reversed on the ground that the judge erred by putting the burden of proof on the plaintiff.]

II

A

[The court began by noting that Lumley v. Gye, p. 1143, supra was generally thought to be the origin of the "two torts—interference with contract and its sibling, interference with prospective economic relations—in the form in which they have come down to us."]

The opinion in *Lumley* dealt, of course, with conduct intended to induce the breach of an existing contract, not conduct intended to prevent or persuade others not to contract with the plaintiff. That such an interference with prospective economic relations might itself be tortious was confirmed by the Queen's Bench over the next 40 years. [The court discussed Temperton v. Russell (1893) 1 Q.B. 714, in which a labor union in a dispute with builders demanded that the builders' suppliers cease furnishing materials to the builder. If a supplier failed to comply the union would bring pressure on those who supplied that supplier to cease doing so. In a suit by one supplier against the union, the court recognized a tort action on the ground that "in the words of Lord Esher, the Master of the Rolls, 'the distinction . . . between the claim for inducing persons to break contracts already entered into . . . and . . . inducing persons not to enter into contracts . . . can [not] prevail.' "]

"There was the same wrongful intent in both cases, wrongful because malicious," Lord Esher wrote. "There was the same kind of injury to the plaintiff. It seems rather a fine distinction to say that, where a defendant maliciously induces a person not to carry out a contract already made with the plaintiff and so injures the plaintiff, it is actionable, but where he injures the plaintiff by maliciously preventing a person from entering into a contract with the plaintiff, which he otherwise would have entered into, it is not actionable." [*Temperton*].

As a number of courts and commentators have observed, the keystone of the liability imposed in [*Lumley* and *Temperton*] to judge from the opinions of the justices, appears to have been the "malicious" intent of a defendant in enticing an employee to breach her contract with the plaintiff, and damaging the business of one who refused to cooperate with the union in achieving its bargaining aims. While some have doubted whether the use of the word "malicious" amounted to anything more than an intent to commit an act, knowing it would harm the plaintiff (see, e.g., Dobbs, Tortious Interference with Contractual Relationships (1980) 34 Ark. L.Rev. 335, 347, fn. 37), Dean Keeton, assessing the state of the tort as late as 1984, remarked that "[w]ith intent to interfere as the usual basis of the action, the cases have turned almost entirely upon the defendant's motive or purpose and the means by which he has sought to accomplish it. As in the cases of interference with contract, any manner of intentional invasion of the plaintiff's interests may be sufficient if the purpose is not a proper one." [ ]

[Historically] the plaintiff need only allege a "prima facie tort" by showing the defendant's awareness of the economic relation, a deliberate interference with it, and the plaintiff's resulting injury. [ ] By this account of the matter—the traditional view of the torts and the one adopted by the first Restatement of Torts—the burden then passed to the defendant to demonstrate that its conduct was privileged, that is, "justified" by a recognized defense such as the protection of others or, more likely in this context, the defendant's own competitive business interests. [ ]

These and related features of the economic relations tort and the requirements surrounding its proof and defense led, however, to calls for a reexamination and reform as early as the 1920's. . . . The nature of the wrong itself seemed to many unduly vague, inviting suit and hampering the presentation of coherent defenses. More critically in the view of others, the procedural effects of applying the prima facie tort principle to what is essentially a business context led to even more untoward consequences.

. . .

Calls for a reformulation of both the elements and the means of establishing the economic relations tort reached a height around the time the Restatement Second of Torts was being prepared for publication and are reflected in its departures from its predecessor's version. Acknowledging criticism, the American Law Institute discarded the prima facie tort requirement of the first Restatement. A new provision, section 766B, required that the defendant's conduct be "improper," and adopted a multifactor "balancing" approach, identifying seven factors for the trier of fact to weigh in determining a defendant's liability. The Restatement Second of Torts, however, declined to take a position on the issue of which of the parties bore the burden of proof, relying on the "considerable disagreement on who has the burden of pleading and proving certain matters" and the observation that "the law in this area has not fully congealed but is still in a formative stage" [   ]. In addition, the Restatement Second provided that a defendant might escape liability by showing that his conduct was justifiable and did not include the use of "wrongful means." [   ]

B

In the meantime, however, an increasing number of state high courts had traveled well beyond the Second Restatement's reforms by redefining and otherwise recasting the elements of the economic relations tort and the burdens surrounding its proof and defenses. In Top Service Body Shop, Inc. v. Allstate Ins. Co. (Ore.1978) 582 P.2d 1365 (1978) (*Top Service*), the Oregon Supreme Court, assessing this "most fluid and rapidly growing tort," noted that "efforts to consolidate both recognized and unsettled lines of development into a general theory of 'tortious interference' have brought to the surface the difficulties of defining the elements of so general a tort without sweeping within its terms a wide variety of socially very different conduct." [   ]

Recognizing the force of these criticisms, the court went on to hold in *Top Service* [   ], that a claim of interference with economic relations "is made out when interference resulting in injury to another *is wrongful by some measure beyond the fact of the interference itself.* Defendant's liability may arise from improper motives or from the use of improper means. They may be wrongful by reason of a statute or other regulation, or a recognized rule of common law, or perhaps an established standard of a trade or profession. No question of privilege arises unless the interference would be wrongful but for the privilege; it becomes an issue only if the acts charged would be tortious on the part of an unprivileged defendant." [   ]; (italics added).

[The court then traced similar developments in other courts, concluding that "over the past decade or so, close to a majority of the high courts of American jurisdictions have imported into the economic relations tort variations on the *Top Service* line of reasoning, explicitly approving a rule that requires the plaintiff in such a suit to plead and prove the alleged interference was either 'wrongful,' 'improper,' 'illegal,' 'independently tortious' or some variant on these formulations."]

III

In California, the development of the economic relations tort has paralleled its evolution in other jurisdictions. For many years this court declined to adopt the holding of [*Lumley*] on the ground that, as we reasoned in Boyson v. Thorn (1893) 98 Cal. 578, "[i]t is a truism of the law that an act which does not amount to a legal injury cannot be actionable because it is done with a bad intent. . . . If it is right, and the means used to procure the breach are right, the motive cannot make it a wrong. . . ." [ ]. In Imperial Ice Co. v. Rossier [ ], however, a unanimous court, speaking through Justice Traynor, pronounced these statements in *Boyson* "not necessary to the decision" and directed that they be "disregarded." [ ] California thus joined the majority of jurisdictions in adopting the view of the first Restatement of Torts by stating that "an action will lie for *unjustifiably* inducing a breach of contract." ([ ]; italics added.)

[The court then traced its own thinking in this area at length. It then noted that developments in the court of appeal had "if anything, outdistanced our own formulations of the elements of the tort and the allocation of the burden of proof in at least two respects." The first was that plaintiff was being given the burden of proving "wrongful" conduct. The second was that defendant could "defeat liability by showing that its conduct was not independently 'wrongful.' "]

IV

In searching for a means to recast the elements of the economic relations tort and allocate the associated burdens of proof, we are guided by an overmastering concern articulated by high courts of other jurisdictions and legal commentators: The need to draw and enforce a sharpened distinction between claims for the tortious disruption of an existing contract and claims that a prospective contractual or economic relationship has been interfered with by the defendant. Many of the cases do in fact acknowledge a greater array of justificatory defenses against claims of interference with prospective relations. Still, in our view and that of several other courts and commentators, the notion that the two torts are analytically unitary and derive from a common principle sacrifices practical wisdom to theoretical insight, promoting the idea that the interests invaded are of nearly equal dignity. They are not.

The courts provide a damage remedy against third party conduct intended to disrupt an existing contract precisely because the exchange of promises resulting in such a formally cemented economic relationship is deemed worthy of protection from interference by a stranger to the agreement. Economic relationships short of contractual, however, should stand on a different legal footing as far as the potential for tort liability is reckoned. Because ours is a culture firmly wedded to the social rewards of commercial contests, the law usually takes care to draw lines of legal liability in a way that maximizes areas of competition free of legal penalties.

. . . Our courts should, in short, firmly distinguish the two kinds of business contexts, bringing a greater solicitude to those relationships that have ripened into agreements, while recognizing that relationships short of that subsist in a zone where the rewards and risks of competition are dominant.

Beyond that, we need not tread today. It is sufficient to dispose of the issue before us in this case by holding that a plaintiff seeking to recover for alleged interference with prospective economic relations has the burden of pleading and proving that the defendant's interference was wrongful "by some measure beyond the fact of the interference itself." [ ]It follows that the trial court did not commit error when it [required] the jury to find that defendant's interference was "wrongful." And because the instruction defining "wrongful conduct" given the jury by the trial court was offered by plaintiff himself, we have no occasion to review its sufficiency in this case. The question of whether additional refinements to the plaintiff's pleading and proof burdens merit adoption by California courts—questions embracing the precise scope of "wrongfulness," or whether a "disinterested malevolence," in Justice Holmes's words (American Bank & Trust Co. v. Federal Reserve Bank (1921) 256 U.S. 350, 358) is an actionable interference in itself, or whether the underlying policy justification for the tort, the efficient allocation of social resources, justifies including as actionable conduct that is recognized as anticompetitive under established state and federal positive law [ ]—are matters that can await another day and a more appropriate case.

. . . The judgment of the Court of Appeal is reversed and the cause is remanded with directions to affirm the judgment of the trial court.

■ LUCAS, C.J., and KENNARD, BAXTER, GEORGE and WERDEGAR, JJ., concur.

■ Concurring opinion by MOSK, J.

. . .

Like the majority, I would reverse the Court of Appeal's judgment in this regard. As I shall explain, I believe that any instructional error was not prejudicial.

I

With the dissonance caused by such terms as "malice," "justification," and "privilege" [ ], the common law on the tort of intentional interference with prospective economic advantage, both in American jurisdictions generally and in California specifically, is fast approaching incoherence. [ ]

. . .

A

One reason for the common law's near-incoherence on the~~ce of~~ dis- intentional interference with prospective economic advantage r covered in its doctrinal basis.

During the second half of the 19th century and the first half of the 20th, as the times pressed hard on both law and society, common law courts, first in England and then in the United States, developed what has become known as the "prima facie tort doctrine." [   ] The traditional source was the old action on the case. [   ] The analytical object was a framework "capable of assisting comprehension and guiding an internal systematic development of the subject matter" [   ] to the end that "principle rather than precedent" might govern [   ].

In Mogul Steamship Company v. McGregor, Gow, & Co. (1889) 23 Q.B.D. 598, 613, affirmed [1892] A.C. 25, Lord Justice Bowen in the Court of Appeal made the famous statement of the prima facie tort doctrine: "[I]ntentionally to do that which is calculated in the ordinary course of events to damage, and which does, in fact, damage another in that person's property or trade, is actionable if done without just cause or excuse."

In Aikens v. Wisconsin (1904) 195 U.S. 194, 204, Justice Holmes, who "was in large measure responsible for the introduction of the [prima facie tort] doctrine in this country" [   ], made the equally famous statement: "It has been considered that, prima facie, the intentional infliction of temporal damage is a cause of action, which, as a matter of substantive law, whatever may be the form of pleading, requires a justification if the defendant is to escape."

In the middle of this century, Dean Pound made the following restatement: "One who intentionally does anything which on its face is injurious to another is liable to repair the resulting damage unless he can establish a liberty or privilege by identifying his claim to act as he did with some recognized public or social interest." (3 Pound, Jurisprudence (1959) p. 9.)

. . .

The prima facie tort doctrine exhibits a general deficiency. Perhaps it has resulted in a kind of "internal systematic development of the subject matter." [   ] But if it has, it has done so by sacrificing an external connection to society. "The idea is that 'intentional infliction of harm' is, prima facie, a tort. The problem is that almost any legitimate act can cause 'intentional' harm. . . ." [Dobbs] Therefore, "[i]t must be understood that intentional infliction of harm . . . covers a multitude of desirable acts as well as a multitude of sins". [   ] "The prima facie tort rule, then, is not a rule about wrongdoing at all. It seems to be a philosophical effort to state all"—or at least much—of "tort law in a single sentence rather than an effort to state a meaningful principle." [Dobbs] "[P]rinciple rather than precedent" may indeed govern. [   ] But it is a principle that is peculiarly empty.

. . .

B

intent second reason for the common law's near-incoherence on the tort of covered interference with prospective economic advantage may be dis- in the law itself.

To borrow words from Brennan v. United Hatters (1906) 73 N.J.L. (44 Vroom) 729, 742 [65 A. 165, 171], the premise of the tort seems to be that, "[i]n a civilized community which recognizes the right of private property among its institutions, the notion is intolerable that a man should be protected by the law in the enjoyment of property once it is acquired, but left unprotected by the law in his efforts to acquire it."

The tort's "protectionist" premise, however, is at war with itself. For the person who deserves protection in the acquisition of property is not only the interfered-with party but also the interfering party. . . .

Further, liability under the tort may threaten values of greater breadth and higher dignity than those of the tort itself.

One is the common law's policy of freedom of competition. "'The policy of the common law has always been in favor of free competition, which proverbially is the life of trade. So long as the plaintiff's contractual relations are merely contemplated or potential, it is considered to be in the interest of the public that any competitor should be free to divert them to himself by all fair and reasonable means. . . . In short, it is no tort to beat a business rival to prospective customers. Thus, in the absence of prohibition by statute, illegitimate means, or some other unlawful element, a defendant seeking to increase his own business may cut rates or prices, allow discounts or rebates, enter into secret negotiations behind the plaintiff's back, refuse to deal with him or threaten to discharge employees who do, or even refuse to deal with third parties unless they cease dealing with the plaintiff, all without incurring liability.' " [   ]

. . .

C

A third reason for the common law's near-incoherence on the tort of intentional interference with prospective economic advantage may be discovered in its focus on the interfering party's motive, that is, why he seeks whatever it is that he seeks through his interference, and on his moral character as revealed thereby.

[In an extended discussion of *Boyson v. Thorn*, supra, Justice Mosk approvingly quoted its language that "the existence of a bad motive, in the case of an act which is not in itself illegal, will not convert that act into a civil wrong for which reparation is due." He concluded that *Imperial Ice v. Rossier* had erred when it rejected *Boyson*'s assertion that motive was irrelevant.]

The untoward results of the focus on the interfering party's motive may present themselves in individual cases in the form of arbitrary and capricious outcomes. [   ] In matters in which the trier of fact believes it has discerned good motive or at least persuades itself it has, an interfering party who has both engaged in objectively bad conduct and produced objectively bad consequences may evade liability for injury. By contrast, in matters in which it adopts a contrary view, an interfering party who has neither engaged in such conduct nor produced such consequences may be made to pay for what is simply damnum absque injuria. In a word, much may depend on mere appearances and perceptions and on nothing more.

.   .   .

II

With all this said, we are put to the question: What are we to do about the tort of intentional interference with prospective economic advantage?

It would be unreasonable to choose to do nothing. As stated, in this regard the common law is approaching incoherence. It is not about to turn to consistency of its own accord.

It would also be unreasonable to choose abolition. Such a course commands little support among courts or commentators. That is unsurprising. Most agree that the interfering party should not be granted general immunity, but should be exposed to liability under at least some circumstances. [ ] For just as "[i]t cannot be . . . a theorem of justice that liability is always just" [ ], neither can it be a principle of law that immunity is invariably proper.

In view of the foregoing, the only reasonable choice is reformulation. .   .   .

It follows that the tort may be satisfied by intentional interference with prospective economic advantage by independently tortious means. [ ]

[In an extended discussion, Justice Mosk develops bases for recovery in this situation. Although the harm is generally directed at the plaintiff, that is not required—as in cases in which the defendant makes misrepresentations to third parties to persuade them not to deal with plaintiff. The tort also may be satisfied by a showing of "restraint of trade, including monopolization." The common "independently tortious means" including "assault and battery, defamation, and fraud and deceit, are well defined and long settled." Such an approach would remove the tort's "protectionist" premise, leaving plaintiffs subject only to defendant's use of "independently tortious means or restraints of trade." He then turned to the case at bar.]

Under the tort as reformulated, it is plain that the Court of Appeal erred. To be sure, the instructions appear erroneous. They did not expressly require objective, and unlawful, conduct or consequences. Neither, it seems, did they do so impliedly. Any error, however, was not prejudicial. The reason is manifest. To the extent that they were satisfied by mere "wrongfulness"—which, at Della Penna's request, was defined under a kind of " 'business ethics' standard" as behavior "outside the realm of legitimate business transactions" because of "method" or "motive"—they were satisfied by far too little. For to that extent they did not demand the use of independently tortious means or restraints of trade. It is true that their focus on motive—"[w]rongfulness may lie . . . by virtue of an improper motive"—might threaten an arbitrary and capricious outcome in a given case. The same is true of their use of the term "wrongful" and its cognates, which are inherently ambiguous [ ]. But, in spite of the foregoing, there is simply no basis to conclude that the outcome here was either arbitrary or capricious.

IV

It is evident in the analysis presented above that, on many points, I agree with the majority's discussion of the tort of intentional interference with prospective economic advantage and Della Penna's claim against Toyota asserting such a cause of action.

On two major points, however, I am compelled to state my disagreement.

First, I would not adopt the "standard" of "wrongfulness." As I have noted, the term and its cognates are inherently ambiguous. They should probably be avoided. They should surely not be embraced. . . .

Second, if I were to adopt such a "standard," I would not allow it to remain undefined. Otherwise, our effort . . . to rationalize the governing principles would be undermined. Formerly, the interfering party as defendant was left "knowing he was entitled to some defense, but not knowing what defenses would be accounted sufficient." . . . Any definition of the "standard," of course, should avoid suggesting that the interfering party's motive might be material for present purposes. As I have explained, the focus on this issue is inappropriate. [ ] A position of this sort, one must acknowledge, would result in the imposition of no liability on a person who is purely, but merely, "malicious"—who acts, to quote Justice Holmes, with "disinterested malevolence" (Amer. Bank & Trust Co. v. Federal Bank (1921) 256 U.S. 350, 358). Although such a person might be held responsible in conscience, he should not be made answerable in tort. To reiterate: "The law has no roving commission to root out bad people or people whose minds may harbor bad thoughts." . . .

. . .

NOTES AND QUESTIONS

1. What was the error that the court of appeal found in the trial judge's conduct in this case? Why did the supreme court reject that determination?

2. What are the consequences of the majority's decision? Should plaintiff's case ever have gone to trial?

3. How did the first and second Restatements differ? Did the court adopt the approach of either one? Section 767 lists the seven factors referred to by the court that are to be considered in determining whether or not an intentional interference with either a contractual or prospective contractual relation is improper:

(a) the nature of the actor's conduct,

(b) the actor's motive,

(c) the interests of the other with which the actor's conduct interferes,

(d) the interests sought to be advanced by the actor,

(e) the social interests in protecting the freedom of action of the actor and the contractual interests of the other,

(f) the proximity or remoteness of the actor's conduct to the interference, and

(g) the relations between the parties.

How might these factors have affected *Imperial Ice*? *Della Penna*? How might the majority react to these factors? How might Justice Mosk?

4. Does the majority reject the result of *Imperial Ice*? The analysis? What is the concurring opinion's stance concerning that case? What differences between interference with contract and interference with prospective economic advantage can be justified?

5. *Unlawful means.* Justice Mosk identifies several independently tortious means of inflicting harm. In the business context, other types of conduct have also been important. We briefly review a few of these, which are covered more extensively in courses on Unfair Competition and Copyright.

a. False Statements About a Competitor's Product. The action of "slander of title" or "trade libel" or "disparagement" has evolved to cover false statements concerning ownership of goods and was further extended to untrue statements dealing with the quality of goods as well as the title to them. See, e.g., System Operations, Inc. v. Scientific Games Development Corp., 555 F.2d 1131 (3d Cir.1977) listing the elements of disparagement as the "(1) publication (2) with malice (3) of false allegations concerning plaintiff's property or product (4) causing special damages, i.e. pecuniary harm." As might be expected, "malice" is a subject of confusion. Some attacks on product quality may impugn management and be actionable as defamations. See Harwood Pharmacal Co. v. National Broadcasting Co., 9 N.Y.2d 460, 174 N.E.2d 602, 214 N.Y.S.2d 725 (1961).

State law has flatly barred injunctions in defamation cases. Since disparagement occurs in the context of competition, some courts have been willing to view the disparagement as the basis of a tort for unfair competition or intentional interference with economic advantage and have permitted injunctive relief on those bases. Now that the Supreme Court has accorded "commercial speech" at least some First Amendment protection (Virginia State Bd. of Pharmacy v. Virginia Citizens Consumer Council, Inc., 425 U.S. 748 (1976)), courts may become increasingly reluctant to enjoin speech in commercial contexts.

b. False Statements About a Firm's Own Product. Tort actions may be harder to ground where the falsity is in the puffing of the speaker's own product rather than the disparagement of a competitor's product. It has been harder to show that plaintiff suffered from the statement—and how much.

In Mosler Safe Co. v. Ely–Norris Safe Company, 273 U.S. 132 (1927), Mosler falsely advertised that its safes had explosion-proof chambers. The Supreme Court refused to allow a suit by a company whose safes did have such a device. What if Ely–Norris Safe Company were the only manufacturer of explosion-proof safes? What about a class action? The inaccessibility of a tort action led to the creation of statutory remedies to deter false advertising.

c. Conscious Imitation of a Product's Appearance. A statutory or common law action for trademark infringement or an action for unfair competition will lie when a competitor "passes off" its own product as that of another competitor by the use of intentionally similar and potentially confusing trademarks or trade dress. See Harold F. Ritchie, Inc. v. Chesebrough–Pond's, Inc., 281 F.2d 755 (2d Cir.1960), in which defendant was found liable for infringement of plaintiff's registered trademark "Brylcreem" by the marketing of its hair care product, "Valcream."

In Harlequin Enterprises Ltd. v. Gulf & Western Corp., 644 F.2d 946 (2d Cir.1981), the court held that defendant's deliberate imitation of the cover format of Harlequin Romances for its own series titled "Silhouette Romances" was properly enjoined since the covers were so "startlingly" similar that "[a]n ordinary lover of romance fiction would not recognize the disparities without setting out to find them [and a] buyer who did notice the difference between the names and colophons would be reasonably justified in believing that the products came from the same publisher."

d. Misappropriation of Patents, Copyrights and Trade Secrets. Patents and copyrights provide specific protection for products and writings that meet certain statutory requirements. Infringement of a patent or copyright gives rise to an action for damages and injunction under federal statutes.

Trade secrets do not enjoy the same type or level of protection accorded to patents. Whereas an inventor has a monopoly on a patented invention for a statutory period of time, competitors can make use of a company's trade secret so long as the information was obtained in a legitimate manner—reverse engineering, independent research, or disclosure by the firm itself, for example. But improper methods used by a competitor to acquire another's trade secrets will lead to a common law tort action.

The tortious methods may be unlawful in themselves, such as fraud, theft, wiretapping or other acts of industrial espionage. Liability may also be based on inducing others to divulge secret business information told them in confidence. Kewanee Oil v. Bicron Corp., 416 U.S. 470 (1974). See also Note, A Balanced Approach to Employer–Employee Trade Secrets Disputes in California, 31 Hastings L.J. 671 (1980).

e. Misappropriation of Other Commercial "Quasi–Property." In International News Service v. Associated Press, 248 U.S. 215 (1918), the Supreme Court went beyond the traditional protections of copyright, patent, trademark and trade secret, and extended protection to material that was not copyrightable. INS and AP were rivals in gathering news and

supplying newspapers with that information. When INS was found to have
been copying the facts from AP, the Court permitted INS to be enjoined
from such behavior. Justice Brandeis, in a famous dissent, attacked the
majority's finding of a new private right and considered the problem one
best left to the legislature:

> Plaintiff further contended that defendant's practice constitutes unfair
> competition, because there is "appropriation without cost to itself of
> values created by" the plaintiff; and it is upon this ground that the
> decision of this court appears to be based. To appropriate and use for
> profit, knowledge and ideas produced by other men, without making
> compensation or even acknowledgment, may be inconsistent with a
> finer sense of propriety; but, with the exceptions indicated above
> [copyright and patent], the law has heretofore sanctioned the practice.
>
>   .   .   .
>
> Courts are ill-equipped to make the investigations which should
> precede a determination of the limitations which should be set upon
> any property right in news or of the circumstances under which news
> gathered by a private agency should be deemed affected with a public
> interest.

See Baird, Common Law Intellectual Property and the Legacy of
International News Service v. Associated Press, 50 U.Chi.L.Rev. 411 (1983).

The issue has been further clouded by the Supreme Court's decisions
in Sears, Roebuck & Co. v. Stiffel, 376 U.S. 225 (1964) and Compco Corp. v.
Day–Brite Lighting, Inc., 376 U.S. 234 (1964), in which the Court overturned lower courts' findings of liability for unfair competition for copying
the designs of unpatented lighting fixtures. In discussing the federal preemption of certain state unfair competition laws, Justice Black observed in
Sears:

> To allow a State by use of its law of unfair competition to prevent
> the copying of an article which represents too slight an advance to be
> patented would be to permit the State to block off from the public
> something which federal law has said belongs to the public. The result
> would be that while federal law grants only 14 to 17 years' protection
> to genuine inventions, see 35 U.S.C. §§ 154, 173, States could allow
> perpetual protection to articles too lacking in novelty to merit any
> patent at all under federal constitutional standards. This would be too
> great an encroachment on the federal patent system to be tolerated.

Sears and *Compco* did not refer to the INS decision.

6. *Non–Competitive Situations.* Actions for tortious interference
with prospective economic advantage also occur in situations not involving
competition.

a. A party who unjustifiably interferes with another's prospect of
obtaining employment can be found liable for those acts. See Ledwith v.
International Paper Co., 64 N.Y.S.2d 810, affirmed 271 App.Div. 864, 66
N.Y.S.2d 625 (1946)(defendant, after firing plaintiff, wrote 128 letters to

companies that had customarily dealt with plaintiff in the course of business to state that the parties were no longer connected); Centeno v. Roseville Community Hospital, 107 Cal.App.3d 62, 167 Cal.Rptr. 183 (1979)(holding that defendant hospital would be liable for intentional interference with plaintiff doctor's right to pursue a calling by refusing to allow him to use its facilities, unless the hospital could justify its actions).

b. An employee terminable at will does not have a property right in future employment, as does a worker with a contract for a specified period of time. But the employee's prospective economic advantage arising from the expected continuation of his present employment is protected from a third party's unprivileged interference. Defendant will be held liable if plaintiff's discharge was procured by the use of improper means, such as slander or defamation. If lawful means are used, there is again disagreement over the role of "improper" motives.

In Smith v. Ford Motor Co., 289 N.C. 71, 221 S.E.2d 282 (1976), the court ruled that defendant automobile manufacturer's application of economic pressure causing plaintiff to be discharged from his employment would lead to liability for tortious interference unless Ford could show a legitimate business interest on which to base a privilege.

On the other hand, an at-will employee cannot indirectly avoid the risk of being discharged by suing in tort for such claims as wrongful discharge, or intentional infliction of emotional distress. Murphy v. American Home Products, Corp., 58 N.Y.2d 293, 448 N.E.2d 86, 461 N.Y.S.2d 232 (1983).

c. Disparagement. In Auvil v. CBS "60 Minutes", 67 F.3d 816 (9th Cir.1995), defendant in 1989 reported that "the most potent cancer-causing agent in our food supply is a substance sprayed on apples to keep them on the trees longer and make them look better" and that those most at risk were children. Following the broadcast, "consumer demand for apples and apple products decreased dramatically." A disparagement action was allowed to proceed and then dismissed for failure to prove falsity. As a result of the broadcast, several states adopted statutes creating civil actions in behalf of producers of perishable products against anyone who "wilfully or maliciously" disseminates "false information" that a food product is not safe for human consumption. "False information" is defined as "not based on reliable, scientific facts and reliable scientific data which the disseminator knows or should have known to be false." See Fla.Stat.Ann. § 865.065 (1994).

d. Perjury. Those who claim that they have been harmed by perjured testimony given in judicial proceedings have tried to recover their damages from the alleged perjurer. These have failed in all but one state. Cooper v. Parker–Hughey, 894 P.2d 1096 (Okla.1995)(following general rule that grants witnesses absolute immunity from civil liability and recognizing that Maine, by statute, is the only state contra). What is the policy behind protecting alleged perjurers?

7. When boycotts or other concerted actions do not involve labor disputes or economic conflicts, they tend to have political, social, or religious ramifications.

a. In Watch Tower Bible & Tract Society v. Dougherty, 337 Pa. 286, 11 A.2d 147 (1940), the defendants Roman Catholic Archbishop of Philadelphia and a priest were sued by the plaintiff religious society. For ten years the plaintiff had conducted a series of radio programs on a Philadelphia station owned indirectly by a department store. The priest objected that the plaintiff "attacks the Catholic Church, misrepresents her teachings and foments religious hatred and bigotry," and threatened to cancel his charge account at the store if it renewed the plaintiff's contract to broadcast. The plaintiff also alleged that the defendants urged their parishioners to inundate the store with similar messages. The store refused to renew plaintiff's contract. The trial court's dismissal of the complaint was affirmed in one paragraph:

> The order of the court below was proper. No valid cause of action was pleaded. The defendants are leaders of their church. They cannot be mulcted in damages for protesting against the utterances of one who they believe attacks their church and misrepresents its teachings nor for inducing their adherents to make similar protests. A right of action does not arise merely because a group withdraws its patronage or threatens to do so and induces others to do likewise where the objects sought to be obtained are legitimate.

What if defendants' threat to withdraw patronage had been made during the term of plaintiff's contract?

b. In Missouri v. National Organization of Women, 620 F.2d 1301 (8th Cir.), cert. denied 449 U.S. 842 (1980), the State of Missouri brought a suit to enjoin NOW's campaign discouraging groups from scheduling conventions in states that had not ratified the proposed Equal Rights Amendment. The district court's denial of relief was affirmed. Because NOW's concerted action was an effort to exercise its First Amendment right to petition the government and to seek to influence the legislature's actions, the Sherman Antitrust Act did not apply and liability for tortious interference with an advantageous relationship did not lie. "[T]he right to petition is of such importance that it is not an improper interference even when exercised by way of a boycott."

Would the case be different if NOW sought to persuade groups that had already signed agreements to hold their conventions in Missouri to cancel those plans?

c. In National Ass'n for the Advancement of Colored People v. Claiborne Hardware Co., 458 U.S. 886 (1982), the NAACP organized a boycott of white merchants in Claiborne County, Mississippi, to gain acceptance of "a lengthy list of demands for equality and racial justice." Some violence occurred during the boycott. Merchants who had suffered economic losses during the extended boycott sued the NAACP for damages for the concerted conduct. The state courts found that violence and the fear of reprisal had been influential in causing some blacks to withhold patronage from the white merchants. This led to the conclusion that the NAACP was liable for all the damages resulting from the boycott, a total of more than one million dollars.

The Supreme Court unanimously reversed. The boycott "clearly involved constitutionally protected activity":

. . . Through speech, assembly, and petition—rather than through riot or revolution—petitioners sought to change a social order that had consistently treated them as second-class citizens.

The presence of protected activity, however, does not end the relevant constitutional inquiry. Governmental regulation that has an incidental effect on First Amendment freedoms may be justified in certain narrowly defined instances. [ ] A nonviolent and totally voluntary boycott may have a disruptive effect on local economic conditions. This Court has recognized the strong governmental interest in certain forms of economic regulation, even though such regulation may have an incidental effect on rights of speech and association. [ ] The right of business entities to "associate" to suppress competition may be curtailed. [ ] Unfair trade practices may be restricted. Secondary boycotts and picketing by labor unions may be prohibited, as part of "Congress' striking of the delicate balance between union freedom of expression and the ability of neutral employers, employees, and consumers to remain free from coerced participation in industrial strife." [ ]

While states have broad power to regulate economic activity, we do not find a comparable right to prohibit peaceful political activity such as that found in the boycott in this case. . . .

. . .

The First Amendment does not protect violence. "Certainly violence has no sanctuary in the First Amendment, and the use of weapons, gunpowder, and gasoline may not constitutionally masquerade under the guise of 'advocacy.'" [ ] Although the extent and significance of the violence in this case is vigorously disputed by the parties, there is no question that acts of violence occurred. No federal rule of law restricts a State from imposing tort liability for business losses that are caused by violence and by threats of violence. When such conduct occurs in the context of constitutionally protected activity, however, "precision of regulation" is demanded. [ ] Specifically, the presence of activity protected by the First Amendment imposes restraints on the grounds that may give rise to damage liability and on the persons who may be held accountable for those damages. . . .

. . . While the State legitimately may impose damages for the consequences of violent conduct, it may not award compensation for the consequences of nonviolent, protected activity. Only those losses proximately caused by unlawful conduct may be recovered.

. . .

The taint of violence colored the conduct of some of the petitioners. They, of course, may be held liable for the consequences of their violent deeds. The burden of demonstrating that it colored the entire collective effort, however, is not satisfied by evidence that violence occurred or even that violence contributed to the success of the boycott. A massive and prolonged effort to change the social, political, and economic structure of a local environment cannot be characterized as a violent conspiracy simply by reference to the ephemeral consequences of relatively few violent acts.

Questions about the legality of various "means" have not been common.

8. *Breach of Contract as a Tort.* The common law has traditionally attempted to treat contract and tort as two distinct and almost wholly separate areas of law. Thus, breach of contract has traditionally been actionable only in contract despite the fact that the breach was being used to harm the other party. The critical differences between the contract and tort treatments are the nature of the remedies and the characterization of the precipitating action. Although tort remedies are bounded by relatively loose constraints of causation and foreseeability, contract law generally permits recovery only for readily foreseeable damages to tangible interests. As explained in the introductory note to Chapter 16 of the Restatement, Second, Contracts (1975):

> [t]he traditional goal of the law of contract remedies has not been compulsion of the promisor to perform his promise but compensation of the promisee for the loss resulting from breach. "Willful" breaches have not been distinguished from other breaches, punitive damages have not been awarded for breach of contract, and specific performance has not been granted where compensation in damages is an adequate substitute for the injured party.

These differences in remedial schemes are driven by the notion that the breaching party in a contract action is not regarded as a wrongdoer. Under the common law a promisor is not under an unequivocal duty to perform. Rather the duty is to perform or to breach and pay damages. The promisor is not only privileged to breach and pay damages, but is positively expected to do so whenever the gains to be had from breaching exceed the costs of paying damages. The underlying theoretical claim is one of allocative efficiency: when a promisor has an opportunity, through breach, to improve his or her condition while making good any losses suffered by the promisee, the breach will result in an improved allocation of resources.

Because the notion of harm in contract law has remained relatively stable while tort law has greatly expanded its classes of compensable harm, some now see the allocative efficiency argument that supports the tort/contract separation as an artificial barrier that denies contract plaintiffs reasonable compensation. Until recently, however, the wall between contract and tort has been a relatively solid one. The only area in which the courts have generally been willing to blur the distinction has been in insurance disputes, as described above in Chapter X. Although many states have embraced the third party insurance tort of breach of the implied covenant of good faith and fair dealing, and others have extended the use of the bad faith action to first party insurance disputes, few states have recognized the validity of this tort outside of the insurance context. A minority of states have, however, cautiously begun to extend its boundaries.

a. The Commercial Contract. The leading case on the tort of bad faith breach was Seaman's Direct Buying Service, Inc. v. Standard Oil Co., 36 Cal.3d 752, 686 P.2d 1158, 206 Cal.Rptr. 354 (1984), in which the court suggested that the tort action ought to be available when the contractual relationship in question was analogous to that between insurer and insured—and the defendant in bad faith denied the existing of the contract. After a period of confusion and criticism, the court overruled *Seaman's* but announced that "nothing in this opinion should be read as affecting the existing precedent governing enforcement of the implied covenant in insurance cases." Freeman & Mills, Inc. v. Belcher Oil Co., 11 Cal.4th 85, 900 P.2d 669, 44 Cal.Rptr.2d 420 (1995)("it seems anomalous to characterize as 'tortious' the bad faith denial of the existence of a contract, while treating as 'contractual' the denial of liability or responsibility under an acknowledged contract").

In K.M.C. Co., Inc. v. Irving Trust Co., 757 F.2d 752 (6th Cir.1985), the court, applying New York law, upheld a magistrate's decision imposing $7.5 million in compensatory damages on the Irving Trust Company for refusing to honor plaintiff's request to draw funds on its line of credit. Although recognizing that the contract between the parties did not require the lender to extend the loan in question, the court held that a lender violates the implied duty of good faith and fair dealing when, in the context of an ongoing business relationship, its refusal to extend a requested loan is objectively unreasonable. Liability for such a refusal is not conditioned upon proof of any actual bad faith.

Contrast, however, Flagship Nat. Bank v. Gray Distribution Systems, Inc., 485 So.2d 1336 (Fla.App.1986), in which the court reversed a decision awarding borrowers $3.2 million in compensatory and punitive damages for a lender's refusal to extend its loan beyond an explicit contractual limit. The court held that, absent an explicit contractual agreement, a lender is under no duty to supply an existing customer with a line of credit. The state's statutory good faith requirement could not be imposed to override the express terms in a contract. The court criticized the *K.M.C.* approach.

b. The Employment Context. A few courts have applied the tort of breach of the implied covenant of good faith and fair dealing in the employment context. At the outset, it is crucial to distinguish the tort of bad faith breach from the tort of wrongful discharge. The latter is an action that an employee may bring if he or she has been dismissed for refusing to participate in an immoral or illegal act or for asserting constitutional or statutory rights, as in Nees v. Hocks, 272 Or. 210, 536 P.2d 512 (1975)(firing an employee who refused to seek exemption from jury duty was actionable); Tameny v. Atlantic Richfield Co., 27 Cal.3d 167, 610 P.2d 1330, 164 Cal.Rptr. 839 (1980)(firing an employee who refused to commit illegal price fixing was actionable); Kraus v. New Rochelle Hosp.Med.Center, 628 N.Y.S.2d 360 (App.Div.1995)(recognizing action under statute for retaliatory firing where plaintiff reported on unsafe medical practice of hospital personnel); Phillips v. Butterball Farms Co., 448 Mich. 239, 531 N.W.2d 144 (1995)(action for discharge in retaliation for filing workers' compensation claim); McArn v. Allied Bruce–Terminix Co., 626 So.2d 603 (Miss.1993)(action for discharge for refusal to participate in illegal act or for reporting such an act); compare Hennessey v. Coastal Eagle Point Oil Co., 129 N.J. 81, 609 A.2d 11 (1992)(upholding firing of at-will employee in safety-sensitive position who failed random urine test because firing did not "violate clear mandate of public policy").

c. **Refusal to Contract.** In Schimmel v. Norcal Mut. Ins. Co., 39 Cal.App.4th 1282, 46 Cal.Rptr.2d 401 (1995), the plaintiff physician alleged that when his malpractice policy expired, defendant insurer refused to renew it for reasons, including the ethnicity of his patients, that allegedly violated public policy. The court held that there was no tort duty to renew a fixed term policy whatever the reason or for no reason whatever. The only exception in the state is automobile insurance which, as the result of a ballot initiative, must be renewed. Employment cases were inapposite; even if apposite, there was the crucial difference that the employment cases involved firing employees who were under at-will arrangements—not term contracts.

9. *"Disinterested malevolence."* How does Justice Mosk's position differ from that of the majority on the question of "disinterested malevolence"? Consider some of the classic cases that raise this issue.

a. In Tuttle v. Buck, 107 Minn. 145, 119 N.W. 946 (1909), plaintiff, a village barber, alleged that the local banker was trying to destroy plaintiff's business by, among other things, employing a series of barbers to operate a competing shop rent-free when he could not find a barber to rent it. Although plaintiff also alleged that the defendant's sole purpose was to destroy the plaintiff's business and not to serve "any legitimate interest of his own," there was apparently no explicit allegation that the defendant was planning to close his own shop after he succeeded in eliminating plaintiff. The trial judge denied a motion to dismiss the complaint and the supreme court affirmed. On appeal, the court in *Tuttle* stated:

> To divert to one's self the customers of a business rival by the offer of goods at lower prices is in general a legitimate mode of serving one's own interest, and justifiable as fair competition. But when a man starts an opposition place of business, not for the sake of profit to himself, but regardless of loss to himself, and for the sole purpose of driving his competitor out of business, and with the intention of himself retiring upon the accomplishment of his malevolent purpose, he is guilty of a wanton wrong and an actionable tort. In such a case he would not be exercising his legal right, or doing an act which can be judged separately from the motive which actuated him. To call such conduct competition is a perversion of terms. It is simply the application of force without legal justification, which in its moral quality may be no better than highway robbery.

Why is it a "perversion" to speak of this behavior as competition? What if the defendant can establish that after driving plaintiff out of business he plans to continue his barbershop, which will then become profitable, at least until another competitor appears?

b. In Beardsley v. Kilmer, 236 N.Y. 80, 140 N.E. 203 (1923), defendants manufactured a patent medicine called "Swamp Root" in the city of Binghamton. The plaintiff was managing editor and a major stockholder of the Binghamton Herald, which, under his direction, frequently ridiculed the defendants' product. The defendants, provoked by plaintiff's attacks, threatened to drive the newspaper out of business. By 1910 the plaintiff's paper had been forced out of business. The evidence at trial showed that the defendants had mixed motives in starting their paper: to force the plaintiff's paper out of business, to defend themselves against what the defendants thought were unfair charges, and to "give Binghamton the best paper in the state." There was no evidence that the defendants' paper was "not an enterprising, creditable and reputable paper, or that it was unsuccessful or unprofitable." The lower court had dismissed the complaint. On appeal, the court said:

> [I]f our interpretation of the evidence is correct we have a case where the plaintiff is complaining of and seeking redress for injuries caused by an act which is the product of mixed motives some of which are perfectly legitimate. The question is whether his cause of action can successfully rest upon such a foundation. We feel sure it cannot. . . .
>
> [This view finds] recent support in one of Mr. Justice Holmes' epigrammatic phrases which, in a discussion of this general subject, speaks of "disinterested malevolence" and which is supposed to mean that the genesis which will make a lawful act unlawful must be a malicious one unmixed with any other and exclusively directed to injury and damage of another. (American Bank & Trust Co. v. Fed. Reserve Bank of Atlanta, 256 U.S. 350.)
>
> . . . We cannot afford to move the law to a stage where any person who, for his own advantage, starts a new business will be compelled to submit to the decision of a jury the question whether also there was not a malicious purpose to injure some person who is thus brought under a new and disadvantageous competition.

Would it be useful to try to weigh each motive? What would happen in *Beardsley* if the court concluded that the defendants were mainly eager to destroy the plaintiff but also that they thought it might be fun to run a newspaper and that the city would benefit from their doing so?

Compare section 870 of the Restatement (Second) of Torts (1977):

> One who intentionally causes injury to another is subject to liability to the other for that injury, if his conduct is generally culpable and not justifiable under the circumstances. This liability may be imposed although the actor's conduct does not come within a traditional category of tort liability.

Does section 870 appear to require "disinterested malevolence"? Should it?

INDEX

References are to Pages

†